# LEE'S LIEUTENANTS

*A Study in Command*

DOUGLAS SOUTHALL FREEMAN

VOLUME III
*Gettysburg to Appomattox*

SCRIBNER CLASSICS

SCRIBNER
1230 Avenue of the Americas
New York, NY 10020

First Scribner Edition
SCRIBNER and design are trademarks of Simon & Schuster Inc.
Manufactured in the United States of America

3   5   7   9   10   8   6   4   2

The Library of Congress has cataloged the
Charles Scribner's Sons edition as follows:

Freeman, Douglas Southall, 1886–1953.
Lee's lieutenants, a study in command, by Douglas Southall Freeman.
New York, C. Scribner's sons, 1942–44.
3 v. illus. (ports.) maps (part fold.) 24 cm.
"Short-title index": v.3, p. 781–784. "Select critical bibliography":
v.3, p. [797]–825.
Contents: v.1. Manassas to Malvern hill.—v.2. Cedar mountain to
Chancellorsville.—v.3. Gettysburg to Appomattox.
1. United States—History—Civil War, 1861–1865—Campaigns.
2. Confederate States of America—Biography. 3. United States—
History—Civil War, 1861–1865—Biography. 4. United States—History—
Civil War, 1861–1865—Regimental histories. 5. Confederate States of
America. Army of Northern Virginia. I. Title.
E470.2.F7   973.73   42-24582
MARC

ISBN 0-684-83785-4

# CONTENTS

## APPENDICES

# ILLUSTRATIONS

INTRODUCTION

# INTRODUCTION

WHEN THIS NARRATIVE opens in June, 1863, the Army of Northern Virginia had been reorganized into three Corps. Gen. R. E. Lee was conscious of the immense loss the Southern Confederacy had sustained in the death of "Stonewall" Jackson, and he doubtless was aware of the weight of his words when he said of his fallen lieutenant, "I know not how to replace him." Hopeful that God would "raise up someone" in Jackson's place, Lee had to rely during a critical summer on the experience of the troops to offset the change in officers. He believed his troops invincible; he had to test newly promoted lieutenants and a veteran corps commander who had been leading a semi-independent army. To a certain point the events of June are presented, for these reasons, as a study of the state of mind of three men, "Jeb" Stuart, Ewell and Longstreet.

Unless it was the tone of Longstreet's correspondence during the operations in front of Suffolk in the spring of 1863, nothing in the previous conduct of these officers could have prepared their commander or their subordinates for what happened in Pennsylvania. Stuart almost certainly was prompted to undertake a long raid in order to restore the reputation he felt had been impaired in the Battle of Brandy Station. "Dick" Ewell made an advance that equalled in dash and decision almost any achievement of his predecessor Jackson, and then, in a single hour, Ewell appeared to be a changed man. He was irresolute and unable to exercise the discretion Lee's system of command allowed him. Longstreet, in turn, sought to procure an advantage of ground similar to that which he had enjoyed at Fredericksburg. He mistakenly believed that he had gained the commanding General's approval of a tactical defensive if there had to be a strategic offensive.

These three states of mind were disclosed during the preliminaries of a campaign which brought the Army of Northern Virginia into fateful collision with its adversary at Gettysburg. The absence of Stuart, the indecision of Ewell and the sulking of Longstreet complicated adverse conditions of combat; but the traditional easy explanation of defeat at Gettysburg as the direct and exclusive result of the shortcomings of these three men cannot be sustained. On the contrary, as respects Longstreet, who often was presented as "the villain of the piece," a review of all the material evidence rehabilitates him to this extent: Although he did not realize how far and how fast the Federal left had been extended southward on Cemetery Ridge during the night of July 1 and the early morning of July 2, he was correct in maintaining that the position could not be taken by assault. As Appendix II shows, the Union left from early morning was stronger than the Confederates assumed. The record definitely qualifies the familiar assertion that on the whole of the Federal left, South of the "little clump of trees," more and more Federal troops arrived while Longstreet delayed his deployment. The Confederates probably were unable to see much of the lower end of the Federal position on Cemetery Ridge for the reason given in Appendix I; but the Union troops, whether visible or not, were there in strength. Almost certainly they could have repulsed any attack that could have been made on them at the earliest hour at which Longstreet could have put McLaws and Hood into action.

The papers of Col. S. R. Johnston dissolve most of the mystery concerning reconnaissance on the Confederate right that same fateful 2nd of July. It would appear that Johnston visited Little Round Top an hour or thereabouts after the withdrawal of Candy's Brigade of Getty's Division, which had bivouacked on that eminence the night of July 1-2. Had Colonel Johnston reached Little Round Top an hour earlier he might have seen Candy's men. An hour later he might have observed Sickles's line. Johnston's experience perhaps has a place among the "might-have-beens" of American history. In that category belongs, also, the singular error in the deployment of Scales's and Lane's Brigades of Trimble's Division before the charge of July 3. Both incidents add to the high drama of Gettysburg, but they scarcely could have affected the result had they been shaped otherwise.

For the purposes of this study, Gettysburg represents a wane in Confederate command at a time when the Federals under Meade were more experienced and, with a few exceptions, better led and more efficiently co-ordinated than ever they had been. The demands of the field were beyond the capacity and resources of a

Confederate Army which, it must never be forgotten, had taken the offensive immediately after a most extensive reorganization. On July 2–3, the South lost Dorsey Pender, other capable Generals, many field officers and veteran troops by the thousand; but lack proved as serious as loss. Lee had in Pennsylvania no executive officer of the first class of military ability to cry "Press on, press on" and to galvanize the offensive. Lacking Jackson, Lee could not win. The price of victory at Chancellorsville was defeat at Gettysburg.

Even when Chancellorsville was to some minds a remote scene in the swift action of the war, the death of the irreplaceable Jackson remained one of the two principal reasons why army command was weakened progressively after May, 1863. The other reason was the excessive attrition of the period between the launching of Grant's attack on the Rapidan, May 4, 1864, and the crossing of the James six weeks later. As summarized in Chapter XXII, this rapid attrition involved the serious wounding of the commander of the First Corps, the incapacitation of the leader of the Second, and the illness, during a critical week, of the chief of the Third Corps. The initial month of Grant's relentless assault witnessed the loss of 37 per cent of the Confederate general officers who opposed him.

These ruinous casualties raise one of the most delicate questions of command. Much of the combat of May, 1864, was in thick woods where fighting was at close quarters. The Army of the Potomac held the initiative most of the time and attacked furiously. Even veteran Confederate troops sometimes wavered and, occasionally, as on the morning of May 6, yielded to panic. General officers rushed into the fighting to rally their men and to set an example. In so doing, they were killed. This happened later, also, in the Valley campaign, where Rodes, Dodson Ramseur and "Sandie" Pendleton were slain. At desperate hours, when soldiers most needed intelligent direction, many of their officers took chances more desperate and, falling, made disaster complete. The question is whether the gain to troops' morale from the presence of their general officers at the front was compensation for the fatal exposure of leaders whose death hastened the doom of the Confederacy.

To this question there may be two answers; but whatever the

individual may conclude in reading the story, the army command was weakened beyond recovery. Wade Hampton, John B. Gordon and William Mahone developed rapidly during the summer of 1864. One or another of them was responsible for most of the fine feats of the last nine months of the Army's life; but three excellent soldiers could not take the place of a score who had fallen and had found no successors. Insofar as effective army command was beyond the control of the one man Lee, the war was over when Grant reached James River. After that time, Lee did not have a sufficient number of qualified subordinates to maintain the discipline and to direct the operations of any Army which contained fewer and fewer veteran volunteers and more and more sullen, disaffected conscripts. The competent Generals who escaped bullets and disease were hampered in almost every action by some man who, like Keitt at Cold Harbor or Joel Griffin on the Vaughn Road, was unable to meet the exactions of the field. The darkening autumn of command was upon the Army long before the summer of 1864 ended. A student who has become acquainted with the general officers of the Army of 1863 will have the sense of being in the company of strangers after the Battle of the Crater.

Before these new actors came on the stage for the final, overwhelming climax of the tragedy, two of the principals had been engaged in what their enemies had styled bitter farces. One of these was Longstreet's operation in East Tennessee, which was the largest activity that fell to the lot of any of Lee's lieutenants in the unhappy interlude between Gettysburg and the Wilderness. The story is a strange one in itself and has added interest because of the analogy between Longstreet's difficulties and those of Jackson in dealing with problems of personnel.

Jackson's sense of duty doubtless was responsible for his frequent arrest of subordinates and for his long vendetta with A. P. Hill. If it be proper to credit Jackson's motives, it cannot be unjust to repeat the opinion that his inability to keep peace with his officers would have disqualified him for army command which normally involves more of administration than of combat. Longstreet is subject to the same balance of entries for his controversies with McLaws, Jerome Robertson and E. M. Law. Doubtless he would have denied all that was alleged against him by McLaws in the letter to Miss Lizzie Ewell. With certainty it may be said that McLaws would not have made those charges had he not believed them valid. The equities of the other cases are not sufficiently clear to justify discussion. What puzzles a reader is not a conflict of military opinion or of personality but the contrast between Longstreet with the Army of Northern Virginia and Longstreet in Tennessee. His Corps had been conspicuously free of disputes while he was with Lee. No sooner was Longstreet in semi-independent command in Tennessee than trouble began. The conclusion in Longstreet's case probably has to be the same as with his more renowned comrade, Jackson. As an army commander Longstreet scarcely would have been able to make his proud, ambitious subordinates pull together as a team.

The other semi-independent campaign by one of Lee's lieutenants was that of Jubal A. Early in the Shenandoah Valley. This operation deserves more attention than it has received at the hands of soldiers or of military historians. As an effective diversion by a small force it must command respect, though one reasonably may ask whether its results prior to the Third Battle of Winchester were due to Early's bold maneuvering or to Sheridan's delay under orders from Grant.

The initial success of Early is, in either event, less instructive than the reasons for his subsequent failure. Lee was correct in saying that Early was too much disposed to fight a battle by Divisions, instead of throwing the full strength of his Army into action. Early's other principal fault as an autonomous commander was his singular ineptitude in handling his cavalry. This began, apparently, when Early was on detached service in the winter of 1863-'64 and was displeased with the behavior of "Imboden's men." Early then developed a prejudice against "irregular" cavalry, a term applied to troopers who did not belong to partisan rangers but insisted that they had enlisted for service in a limited area near their home. By the summer of 1864, Early seems to have concluded that the greater part of his mounted troops were undependable. He devoted more energy to criticizing than to disciplining them. A military student who reviews Early's limited correspondence on the subject is left in doubt whether the faults the General attributed to most of his cavalry were or were not alleged to cover Early's own lack of skill in handling mounted troops.

The instance is a classic one of the disaster that may flow from neglect by a competent soldier of an arm of the service that must be co-ordinated with those he understands and directs.

By the time Early was defeated and no longer was able to detain Sheridan in the Shenandoah Valley, Sherman's advance in the Carolinas and the shortage of horses in Virginia had led to the detachment from Lee's Army of Hampton and of Butler's Division of cavalry. On April 1, 1865, the exposed Confederate flank was the more readily turned because of the humiliating absence of Pickett and of Fitz Lee at the moment of G. K. Warren's attack. Thereafter, the débâcle was as swift as it was inevitable.

The contagion of disorder that attended the retreat from Petersburg was communicated to the service of supply. Hunger and cumulative fatigue resulted from the collapse of the commissary as surely as from long marches and swift, admirably conducted pursuit. Military history presents many examples of seasoned troops who often have marched and have fought when they had convinced themselves that they already had reached the limit of their endurance. Other cases there have been of Generals who have exacted more than the minds of the men could endure even though legs did not fail altogether. In this particular, among others, the later stages of the retreat to Appomattox will repay most careful study. The paucity and confusion of personal narratives, the gaps and the contradictions, are themselves clinical exhibits of fatigue. Good soldiers kept the road, but their mental reactions were slow and mechanical.

This was the state of mind of what was left of the Army on the day it had to meet the Federal assaults at Sayler's Creek. Exhaustion increased every difficulty of terrain and deployment and multiplied the adverse odds of superior Federal force. In all but formal surrender, the end came that 6th of April, which was for most of the men the fifth day of fighting and marching and starving.

Three days later, only the ghost of the Army remained. In presentation, the dénouement of Appomattox does not permit an epilogue in which the tragedy is reviewed. After the men have received parole and have said farewell to their officers, the final curtain must fall immediately. To state historical conclusions while the survivors stand in the red mud of the road to the Courthouse would be to spoil the drama and to detain spectators who are leaving their seats. It consequently has seemed necessary to put last things first and to set down here the principal lessons in command the story of the Army of Northern Virginia holds for those who must fight the battles of their nation now and in wars to come.

1. Professional training in arms for men who were to exercise command was vindicated throughout the history of the Army of Northern Virginia. Precisely as training in medicine saves lives, so does careful instruction in the art of war. This elementary truth was not admitted in 1861. The onset of the contest disclosed a bitter difference in military theory that was not expressed in its entirety by any leader, though it was inherent in many fiery appeals and in much of the legislation of the time. One theory might be termed the inherited tradition of the American Revolution. Robert Toombs and men of like mind believed that individual bravery and massed, furious assault would defeat an enemy whom they absurdly underrated. Toombs felt in March, 1861, what he said a year later: "If I had my way, I would fight them on every inch of ground they invaded, and never cease to fight them as long as I could rally men to defend their homes." Many political leaders, sharing this view, had a contempt for professional training in arms. It entailed, they thought, needless preparation and it bred overcaution. Their argument was in part Danton's exhortation, *Il nous faut de l'audace, encore de l'audace et toujours de l'audace.* In part their cry echoed Patrick Henry's confident assertion that a people "armed in the holy cause of liberty . . ." were "invincible by any force which our enemy can send against us."

The other view was that of men of professional military training, who had studied Napoleon, had fought in Mexico or on the frontier and had observed at a distance the events of the Crimean War. These soldiers saw the deep foreshadow of a contest in which, for the first time, the telegraph and the railroad would be employed. They knew that valor was not enough to win battles, that organization was slow, that preparation was imperative and that the might of the Union could be despised only by those who were ignorant of it. While fire-eating politicians were declaiming, Lee was warning, "The war may last ten years" and "it is important that conflict be not provoked before we are ready."

This difference of theory was never composed. To the end, many officers from civilian life had bitter sarcasms for the "West

Pointers." Insistently, sometimes angrily, the critics asked if there were not thousands of men in the South mentally equal to the graduates of the Military Academy. Overlooked altogether was the fact that admission to West Point was in a measure selective and that discipline and instruction there included a constant winnowing of those who possessed no discoverable aptitude for a military career. Graduates of the Academy often angered civilian officers by an alleged show of superiority and caste feeling, but the balance of credit was overwhelmingly on the side of professional military training. The Army of Northern Virginia could not have been organized or commanded successfully without West Point.

2. While West Point men were the backbone of the Army command, they would not of themselves have sufficed in number for the training, discipline and direction even of the first wave of volunteers. As is explained in Appendix II of Volume I, the Confederate resources of trained command were critically limited. Of West Point graduates, officers of the regular establishment who had not attended the Academy, and former non-professional officers of the Mexican War, Virginia at the time of secession could not count more than 200. Other Southern States listed 184 living graduates of the Academy and 36 non-graduate officers of the United States Army.

This hopelessly small body of approximately 420 officers of military experience and technical knowledge was supplemented, to the salvation of the South, by the graduates of two State military schools which had given excellent instruction for two decades. The Virginia Military Institute had about 425 such men, the South Carolina Military Academy trained half that number. Nearly all these, if physically able, entered the Confederate Army, and had on it an influence second only to that of West Point. This scarcely was realized at the time. Had they known the facts, Northern politicians and journals that denounced the resignation of regular army officers as treason might have drawn the same indictment, in the abstract, against South Carolina and Virginia. The men who had attended their military schools furnished, in the main, the most useful Confederate field officers.

Together, these two classes of officers did not give the Confederacy a corps numerically adequate. In large measure the story of the command of the Army of Northern Virginia, as traced in these

volumes, is that of an effort to assure leadership by professional and semi-professional soldiers and to utilize, in addition, those civilians who showed aptitude. There was no organized instruction of these officers drawn from the bar, from public office, from private business and from the farm. What they learned, they acquired by reading, by observation in camp, and by experience in the stern school of combat.

3. Possession of professional training proved to be no guarantee of success as a combat officer. None could tell, before the actual test of battle, which of the professional soldiers would be most apt to excel. Several of those who had the highest reputation before the war proved incapable of effective leadership under battle conditions. Further, no arm of the service and no particular branch of the staff excelled in the number of outstanding soldiers it gave the Confederacy. In none did the percentage of failure vary perceptibly from the average. Command was essentially a gamble, and a gamble in human nature as surely as in military aptitude.

4. If an officer of average intelligence did not engage in combat, approximately a year with troops appears to have been necessary to determine even roughly his full capabilities in general administration and in the maintenance of discipline and of morale. Outstanding men learned far more quickly. A dolt might disclose his stupidity within two months but, if cunning, he might conceal it for twelve. Where a Brigadier was not on field duty, surprisingly little of his development seems to have depended on the character of direction he had at the hands of his division commander. The best of the Major Generals never lacked Brigadiers who were slothful administrators; some excellent brigade commanders were to be found in Divisions indolently directed. The instructional function of divisional command often was ignored or was left to the inspectors.

5. When officers endured battle test, they demonstrated quickly whether they would or would not progress. In one battle there might be a deceptive element of good luck or of bad; in a campaign, these factors usually were balanced. Some of the men most applauded for their conduct in the First Battle of Manassas disappointed the South later. Scarcely any officers who earned a good name during the Peninsula Campaign failed to sustain it.

After the Seven Days there might be a question how far such men as Robert Rodes, Dorsey Pender and John Gordon would develop but there remained no doubt that they had the essential qualities of command. The amazing development of the Army of Northern Virginia between July 1 and September 1, 1862, was due in large measure to the promptness with which incompetent or temperamentally weak division commanders were relieved of command. These men had maintained their reputation as qualified professional soldiers prior to the time active campaigning began, but they soon demonstrated the immense mischief they could do in battle. Victory at Second Manassas doubtless would have been impossible under the organization that existed at Malvern Hill.

6. Comparatively few officers who had no professional training in arms displayed special aptitude for high command. Numbers of them made excellent Colonels. Of the many politicians and lawyers who succeeded in procuring commission as Brigadier General, less than half a dozen could have been regarded at the time of the first invasion of Maryland, September, 1862, as prob- ably apt to fulfil every essential requirement at that rank and perhaps to rise to divisional command. The later success of such men as Wade Hampton and John B. Gordon was interesting, but these two and perhaps J. B. Kershaw were the exceptions. They were the more conspicuous because they were few in number. It would have been "good politics" and a "recognition" of States and "acquiescence in public demand" to have promoted some of the earnest Brigadiers of civilian background, but records justify the policy Lee formulated and Davis supported: A division commander had to be a professional soldier. Prior to the time when attrition compelled contrary action, the Army of Northern Virginia never had a Major General of infantry who had not received professional training. This fact had high significance. Martial as were the traditions of the South, endless as were the assertions that bravery not training decided battles, the experience of his Army did not indicate to Lee that he safely could entrust Divisions to men who had learned after the spring of 1861 all they knew of war. At least three Brigadiers from civil life, men of large influence, left the Army of Northern Virginia because Lee would not promote them.

7. Until Sharpsburg exacted heavy toll of general officers there was no indication that the school of combat would fail to produce

a sufficient number of new Brigadiers to take the place of casualties and of incompetent "political Generals" who, providentially, might be relieved, transferred or induced to resign. Statute law and strict construction of its terms hampered Lee in 1862 and continued to embarrass him until the approval, May 31, 1864, of the measure for the appointment of temporary general officers. Because of legal restrictions and seniority, a few of the appointments made in the reorganization of October-November, 1862, were of doubtful wisdom. Most of the promotions seemed safe. Some raised expectations. The next major reorganization, that of May, 1863, found competent men definitely more difficult to procure. After Gettysburg some Brigades had to be left for months without Generals because men who were entitled to advancement by seniority could not be trusted with more than one regiment. As stated in an earlier paragraph, by the time the Wilderness had taken its toll, in May, 1864, the old command had, in effect, been destroyed. Perhaps some of those named Brigadier Generals subsequent to June, 1864, owed their commission to the tragic fact that Brigades were no larger than regiments had been. A Colonel might not be out of his depth in directing a force that would not count, perhaps, 1000 rifles.

These things apart, the monitory fact should be reiterated because it needs to be remembered in every war: Although the Army of Northern Virginia had numerous intelligent, well-educated field officers, who were accustomed to lead in civil life, experience in combat did not qualify many of these men for promotion to the rank of general officer. Many a Colonel fought with measurable success for two or even three years and never received consideration as a Brigadier. While the restrictions of law may have been responsible for this in some instances, the truth remained: battle experience was no substitute for lack of aptitude and seldom a substitute for professional training in youth. Throughout the war, the average age of Confederate general officers was lowered steadily, but this involved the promotion of some young professional soldier far more frequently than it represented the advancement of a former civilian. Nearly all the conspicuous young Generals were graduates of West Point or of State military schools.

8. Those commanders who shone most in prolonged field operations were, in general, those who had displayed the greatest dili-

gence in keeping their troops disciplined and physically fit while in camp. This should have been accepted as a truism, but it was not. Some officers, especially in the first year of war, scorned all comfort for their troops and almost all camp discipline. The men's sole task, they said, was to whip the enemy. Everything else was casual and temporary. The result often was needless sickness and a ghastly death rate from measles, pneumonia and typhoid. Set against this negligence, the history of a consistently distinguished Brigade, such as that, say, of John R. Cooke, shows daily effort on the part of a commander who "looked after his men." That was the language in which, years after the war, the veterans recorded their highest praise of their ablest leaders. In retrospect, from General Lee to the youngest Colonel, the standard test of excellence was the same. If he was a good officer, "he looked after his men." That inclusive term covered renewal of clothing and regard for the commissary as surely as the phrase implied knowledge of the art of war and ability to achieve necessary results with minimum losses. A commander who did these things could take demoralized, ill-disciplined troops and bring them to furious fighting pitch. Laziness and lack of vigilance sometimes ruined troops who had good records.

This decline would have been more frequent late in the war if veteran soldiers had not learned on their own account what to do and what to avoid. More than once, corps commanders, Longstreet in particular, relied upon experienced Brigades to instruct a new commander and to protect him, as well as themselves, from the consequences of blunder. Like American soldiers of every war, the men of the Army of Northern Virginia always were willing to fight. Uniformly, they were as good as the average of their officers; frequently they were better. They seldom failed in open fighting to repay their General and their Colonels for all the time spent in maintaining a clean, orderly camp and in enforcing just, wholesome discipline. During the last despairing months of universal suffering, those Divisions suffered most who had the least industrious officers. With allowance for special circumstance, such as the advantage enjoyed by Field and Mahone in the retreat to Appomattox, the units that stood firmly in the final hours were those whose officers never relaxed effort or discipline.

9. The greatness of the Army was in its supreme command and

in its infantry, "that body of incomparable infantry," as Swinton
styled it. Always the artillery had inferior guns, unless these were
captured or imported. Usually their ammunition was poor. The
cavalry in the campaigns of 1864-'65 were hampered and then were
half-immobilized by the shortage of horses. Simultaneously, the
Federal mounted troops were improving fast under bold and vigorous leaders. In spite of these differences, the average performance of the field officers of the cavalry and of the artillery was
above that of infantry officers of like rank. The cavalry never complained of any lack of men competent to lead Brigades. Battery
commanders, ranking as Captains, were the Army's best at that
grade, with the exception of the engineers. The same thing could
be said with even more assurance of the Majors, Lieutenant Colonels and Colonels of the battalions of artillery. These conditions
were due to the fact that in 1861 many men of superior education
and social station, reading emulously of Napoleon and of Murat,
organized batteries or troops of cavalry. Because casualties in these
arms of the service were relatively lower than in the infantry, men
remained in command who were capable of gaining, at their
modest rank, from the experience of combat.

10. The product of selection, training, combat and survival was
not a composite or a "typical" officer. It is not possible to lay
three-score sketches on one another, as if they were photographic
negatives, and to say: "*This* is Lee's lieutenant." The men named
in these pages interest by reason of their differences, not of their
similarities. As the tragedy deepens, the struggle of the impersonal
Army to save itself from ruin dims personalities. The drama of
1864-'65 becomes almost exclusively a study in command and
ceases to be a succession of scenes in which an individual officer
holds the stage. Few of the lieutenants retain their personality in
the snows of the Petersburg trenches and in the night of the retreat. When one is able, after a season, to forget the poignancy of
the 9th of April and to look back over the four years, the throng
and the clash of personality, in an age of individualism, puts talk
of "type" out of place. Had Shakespeare himself lived three centuries later, he would have found on the roster of Lee's Army men
as diverse as those in the pages of Holinshed's *Chronicles* or
North's translation of Plutarch's *Lives*.

Were ever men more consistently themselves? Beauregard, with

a Napoleonic complex and a reputation to maintain; "Joe" Johnston, who had a grievance, a scorn of detail and an amazing ability to make men believe in him; Magruder, the ever-galloping giant; Gustavus Smith, possessed of a sensitive pomposity that offset his administrative ability and colored curiously his unwillingness to assume responsibility; Harvey Hill, whom combat stimulated and routine paralyzed; Benjamin Huger, of high impulses, balked by a slowness that must have been due to disease; the political Generals, similar only in their self-confidence and in their flow of fiery eloquence; Powell Hill, who was full of contradictions, able and negligent, co-operative with his subordinates and both punctilious and contentious in his dealings with his corps chief; "Old Pete" Longstreet, brusque, but self-contained, always at his best in battle, a reliable lieutenant but beyond his depth in autonomous command; "Jeb" Stuart, a praise-loving exhibitionist, as colorful as his uniform, a superb intelligence officer and an instructor who always trained a sufficient number of capable men to make good his losses; "Dick" Anderson, too much of a gentleman to assert himself; Wade Hampton, the Grand Seigneur and huntsman who developed with each new responsibility but never, like Stuart, looked on war as sport; the ramrod John B. Gordon, whose attack was sharp though his sentences might be florid; diminutive "Billy" Mahone, growing up as soon as he got a Division; John B. Hood, with capacities as a combat officer that were matched by the valor of his troops; William N. Pendleton, able as an organizer and always explaining something at great length and in labyrinthine sentences; Fitz Lee, the laughing cavalier, and Tom Rosser, the daring Lochinvar; Pelham and Pegram, seldom together but always in spirit the Castor and Pollux of the guns; Heth the ill-fortuned and Wilcox the observant; Pender the diligent and Ramseur the hard-hitting; the caustic Early and the Nordic Rodes —the list lengthens but all stand out as individuals. Devotion and that same quality of individualism are all they have in common. Besides this score, a hundred in memory ride past, to be recognized. greeted and perhaps forgotten again. When the rear file passes, one is regretful that more of them could not be sketched, but one is grateful for the privilege of hearing so many of them talk and of watching them fight.

Two of them, if only two, Lee, the captain of the host, and his

right arm, Jackson, are to be added to those of one's acquaintances, living or dead, real persons or the creation of literature, by whom one's personal philosophy of life is shaped beyond understanding. "Stonewall" Jackson on daily association may or may not appear lovable, but he undeniably is a personality distinguishable in the largest American company. His strong, stern character may be lacking in beauty; it has unextinguishable vitality. Lee was more nearly rounded, more harmonious in all his parts, more capable of dealing considerately with men of diverse and stubborn nature. His virtue awed; it did not irritate. Men might hate him, but they could not ridicule him. He mingled patience with prayer and seldom lost temper in searching for truth. Men found him reserved and never free in praise, but had they seen the letters he slowly, gravely wrote his sensitive chief they would have known what they could not perceive—that the supreme commander of an Army, to be successful in a democracy, must needs be a diplomatist as well as a strategist. In the Army itself, the soldiers who cheered Jackson were reverently silent in the presence of Lee. His spirit pervaded and dominated every rank, grade and arm of the service. The strategy always was his. When corps command was weak, his had likewise to be the tactics. In the evils he prevented, as surely as in his positive military achievements; when seen through the eyes of his subordinates as certainly as when one looks at him across the table in his tent, he is a great soldier and a great man. Twenty years study of him confirms and deepens every conviction of that.

After so long an association with Lee's lieutenants, one is tempted to follow them from Appomattox and to see how their military experience helped or hampered them after a long war, a question destined again to be of immense interest to Americans. Inquiry soon showed that after 1865 the field of adventure of Confederate leaders ranged far in a pattern of much diversity. A recountal would have to be, in large measure, a history of the Reconstruction. It has seemed best, for that reason, to compress into a few pages (Appendix V) a summary statement of the careers followed by the general officers of the Army of Northern Virginia. It scarcely need be added that except for the work of a few of the senior engineers, the economic rebuilding of the South was a task that fell to the younger men, those who had not lost hope in the death of an old order, those who had led the companies or had carried the rifles. The former Generals and occasionally the Colonels held the high political offices and the college presidencies, though some of these men were brought low by adversity. Privates and lieutenants and captains and majors developed the coalfields, rebuilt the shipyards, made Birmingham great, and extended the market for Southern cotton. Their lives in peace were worthy of their record in war. They need no other epitaph.

Westbourne,                         Douglas Southall Freeman
Richmond, Va.
May 30, 1944.

# "Dramatis Personæ"

The eight officers whose photographs appear on the following pages are younger than most of their predecessors, and they are presented in virtually the order of their rise to fame in 1863-'64; but the sequence of the other leaders is not that of relative military eminence. Death is destroying many soldiers of promise. Costly battles are depriving old leaders of their troops. New Generals occasionally direct Brigades larger than veteran Divisions now are. There is confusion of command, and democracy in disaster.

## JOHN BELL HOOD

With a wound received in a great hour at Gettysburg he passes from the scene to return no more, but his old comrades of the Army of Northern Virginia read with pride of his feats at Chickamauga and, after months, of his appointment to command the Army of Tennessee. His new responsibility is beyond the resources of a crippled General. He has a winter of catastrophe and has to ask that which breaks a soldier's heart—that he be relieved. Perhaps he never should have been assigned an army. At heart he is an executive officer, not a strategist.

## LAFAYETTE McLAWS

The square and solid Georgian—he now is 42—has no lustre in the red glare of Gettysburg, though the fault is scarcely his. He goes with Longstreet to Tennessee and there, he avers, he comes under the wrath of his chief because he will not share in an attempt to oust Braxton Bragg. An unhappy story of bitterness and court martial is shaped with difficulty to Longstreet's purpose in this particular: McLaws never commands a First Corps Division again. After the war, happily, there is to be reconciliation and goodwill between the two.

## ROBERT FREDERICK HOKE

The wound received at Salem Church keeps this promising North Carolinian of 26 from sharing the honors and the anguish of Gettysburg. His chance comes the next year in his native State and it brings him promotion and acclaim. The rest may have been circumstance; it may have been a desire to preserve his new reputation. It is unpleasant but it is the fact: subsequent to that success at Plymouth, if he is fighting beside another Division, there nearly always is a failure of co-operation. Neither his State nor his command loses faith in him.

*The three corps commanders continue under Gen. R. E. Lee until*
*May, 1864, when two of them leave the Army.*

## JAMES LONGSTREET

"Stonewall" Jackson's death has left him first in reputation among Lee's lieutenants. He is beguiled by circumstances into thinking himself a strategist as well as an executive officer. His failure at Gettysburg is one result of his mistake concerning his aptitudes. Sent to the Army of Tennessee, he is disillusioned and embittered. Slowly he loses faith in victory, but he unflinchingly returns to his Corps after a wound received in his great hour. At the end he stands by his Chief and says, "General, unless he offers us honorable terms, come back and let us fight it out!"

## RICHARD STODDERT EWELL

"Old Bald Head" dazzles and then dismays the Army during an advance into Pennsylvania. After exploits that would have added to the fame of "Stonewall" himself, Ewell loses the power of decision. Close to his commanding General, he cannot exercise the discretion allotted him, though he often has displayed initiative and sound judgment when operating alone or under "Old Jack" who always said "Do this." "Dick" Ewell's decline is of the body and of the intellect. His spirit is as firm as ever.

## AMBROSE POWELL HILL

The commander of the new Third Corps holds the affection of his staff and the admiration of his men. He is magnetic and attractive. Now that Jackson is dead, Hill engages in no more controversies, but he is not the same man who impetuously led the fighting "Light Division." He does not fail beyond excuse or explanation; he does not succeed. Although few say it in plain words, he is not fulfilling the hopes of the Army. It may be because of ill health or a sense of larger, overburdening responsibility.

## WILLIAM DORSEY PENDER

As the Army enters Pennsylvania, the new Major General, who is 29, writes eagerly of his Division. He knows that his young wife in North Carolina does not favor the invasion of the North, because she thinks the Lord will not bless the Southern cause if the Confederacy does more than defend its own territory. He half agrees but he knows, as a trained soldier, that a whole-hearted offensive often is the most prudent defensive. The campaign must be fought. If it is won and victory is achieved, he will go back to North Carolina, live with his family and quit army life forever. So run his letters. Then, abruptly, they stop. He fights successfully another battle with all his stubborn energy, and he is awaiting action at Gettysburg when he is wounded once again. This time he cannot laugh it off. They miss him on the 3rd of July, 1863, when part of his Division is deployed wrongly.

## JUBAL ANDERSON EARLY

The fires of ambition burn, as always, behind those black eyes of "Old Jube" Early. He finds it easy to impress on generous "Dick" Ewell the views he never even thought of suggesting to the austere "Stonewall." Perhaps, as Early talks and observes how Ewell is failing, he dreams of corps command of his own. He has one bitter humiliation at Rappahannock Bridge in the autumn of 1863, but the next summer he receives the Second Corps and leads it in the very country where Jackson fought in '62. Much that is bold and soldierly is credited to "Jube," but he has a prejudice against the cavalry, whom he does not understand, and in a campaign against a Union cavalryman who has overwhelming superiority of force, "Jube" suffers defeat worse than his worst enemies could have wished for him. His sharp tongue is so critical of others that men refuse to see his excellences as a soldier.

WILLIAM DORSEY PENDER

## WADE HAMPTON

The Grand Seigneur of South Carolina receives some ugly wounds at Gettysburg, where the rivalry between himself and Fitz Lee almost leads to an open quarrel. Wade Hampton's defiant physique and his unconquerable spirit bring him back to field duty with a Major General's commission and a new responsibility when his senior falls. There is hesitation at Headquarters about assigning Hampton to command of the cavalry corps, because he is not a professional soldier; but in an emergency he directs a battle and wins so shining a victory that the old troopers are proud to call him "Jeb" Stuart's successor. His men say he is a "born soldier." They do not know that he thinks more often of the fallen, one of his own sons among them, than of command and power and glory. This much his troopers realize—that he believes in superior force and that he does not ask the impossible of hungry men on feeble horses.

## JAMES EWELL BROWN STUART

"Jeb," the noisy, irrepressible chief of the cavalry corps, the exhibitionist "Jeb," who loves praise and never will admit that he has been beaten, "Jeb," the superb intelligence officer, has a new distinction. He may not realize it but he is becoming a remarkable instructor of cavalrymen. The infantry command is so weakened that some Brigades admittedly are not in the hands of competent Generals. In the cavalry there always are more men capable of leading Brigades than there are Brigades to lead. It is fortunately so, because "Jeb's" days of shining success are over. The blue cavalry knows how to fight now. It counts too many sabres. One humiliation leads Stuart to a reckless adventure and then to a long verbal defense. He continues to be an unexcelled reconnaissance officer, with vast aptitude for analyzing intelligence reports, but he is absent on the day of all days when he could reconnoitre the Federal position. His end is hard, though it is curiously like that of his friend Jackson.

WADE HAMPTON

## JOHN BROWN GORDON

As thin as Mahone but tall enough to make almost two of him, Gordon duplicates the rise of the Virginian and, like him, stirs something of the jealous venom of "Jube" Early. Between Early and Mahone, in 1871, there is to be a raucous quarrel; Gordon's treatment at Early's hands is stiff silence when the Georgian merits praise. A Brigadier at the beginning of May, 1864, Gordon has a Division before the month is out. By the late winter, he is commanding Early's corps, and is next to Longstreet in confidential discussions with the commanding General. A certain freshness, a boldness, a freedom, an originality in sound military design are Gordon's. He differs from most orators in that his actions outdo his exhortations. Character makes chivalry an instinct with John Gordon. No wonder an admiring soldier says of him: "He's most the prettiest thing you ever did see on a field of fight. It'ud put fight into a whipped chicken just to look at him!"

## HENRY HETH

This high-blooded Virginian of 37, mentally capable and socially captivating, has earned at Chancellorsville the rank of Major General. As a professional soldier he now should cancel the ill-fortune that had been his in West Virginia. For a time it looks as if he has. A few folds of paper inside his hat save him from a fatal wound. In his first battle, his direction of his troops is sound. Two days later, though he is not in field command, he sees his weakened Division wrecked. On the retreat, he has to pay the price often exacted of the rearguard. Still again, in the autumn of 1863, his troops are the victims of his corps commander's impetuosity. Another time, when he wants to withdraw his men from an exposed position, Hill says, "The men shall not be disturbed." Rout follows. Heth's seems to be the fate of living to exemplify the maxim that a soldier, to be good, must have good luck.

JOHN BROWN GORDON

## GEORGE EDWARD PICKETT

When Longstreet tells his favorite division commander that the Virginia Division is to share in the final charge on the Union position at Gettysburg, George Pickett looks and acts as if great military fortune has come to him. By midafternoon that 3rd of July, 1863, when the charge has been repulsed, George Pickett's tale is told. Neither he nor his Division ever is the same again. For more than a year and a half, Pickett is a garrison General. Under the strain of a sudden responsibility, his health fails him. At Five Forks, where the enemy rolls up his flank force, whispers spread that he is attending a "shad bake" when he should have been with his men. In the death-spasm of the Army, he is relieved of command, but he is with his troops to the last hour. Fortune does not mock him without honor. "As valiant as Pickett's charge" has become a supreme martial metaphor.

## CADMUS MARCELLUS WILCOX

Promotion comes at length to the man who has helped to win a battle by observing that the hostile pickets at Banks's Ford have their haversacks over their shoulders. Advancement and the leadership of a stalwart Division bring no such praise as has been his at Salem Church. His brother, a Texas Congressman, dies in Richmond; Cadmus, a bachelor, is harassed because he is so far from the orphans. He wants to be transferred to another front. Denied that, he meets hard duty with courage, though never with inspiration. More than once, his Division loses heavily, but negligence never is linked with defeat. If he gains no new prestige, he forfeits no good opinion for character and steadiness. Through the last black winter of the war, his men give an honorable account of themselves. By army standards, Wilcox is mature, almost old—39 at Gettysburg.

GEORGE   EDWARD   PICKETT

## WILLIAM MAHONE

"Billy" Mahone's is as strange a rise to fame as the Army witnesses in devastating 1864. After the war, when his ambitions soar, his henchmen will say he has been a great soldier from the first. The reports do not show it. As a Brigadier he is not lacking in diligence but he is without special distinction. A dozen of his rank might be named before him. Promotion transforms him. Dispute and caution give place to fierce action. His men become the most renowned shock troops of the Army. In the last phase of the war, when he boasts the age of 38, he is the most conspicuous division commander. Small, and as lean as a starvation year, he lives in unconcealed comfort and does not hesitate to question even the commanding General. Men do not always like him or take him at his own estimate but they have to admit that he knows how to fight.

## RICHARD HERON ANDERSON

"Dick" Anderson does not thrive in the Third Corps to which he is assigned in the reorganization after Chancellorsville. Perhaps he misses the guiding hand of "Peter" Longstreet. It may be that Powell Hill does not know how to deal with the South Carolinian at Gettysburg. Ten sterile months follow. Then, by a simple decision, promptly executed, Anderson thrills the Army and probably saves it from a defeat. He has his reward in promotion and in the continuing command of the First Corps until the return of the wounded Longstreet in the autumn of 1864. Then the considerate Lee sees to it that he retains his temporary rank of Lieutenant General; but the Corps assigned is little more than a Division. Part of it loses heart. So does Anderson. Among the hills that run down to a little creek, most of his men are captured. That last scene would be blackest tragedy if the memory of Chancellorsville and Spotsylvania did not linger.

WILLIAM  MAHONE

## STEPHEN DODSON RAMSEUR

He was 25 and less than two years out of West Point when they made him Colonel. Seven months later he was a Brigadier General. Perhaps it was because this fine face was so boyish that he hid it behind a bristling beard that made him look fiercely 40. He has all the ambitions and all the sensitiveness of a boy, but at 27 he handles a Brigade as easily as he would have drilled a squad. In a desperate hour, when the front is almost severed by a shrewd thrust, he counterattacks with wild daring. A Division is his reward, a veteran Division, the day after he is 27. With these troops he shares in a spectacular campaign under "Jube" Early and he wins new honors, though he suffers one reverse that almost breaks his heart. Ramseur has the promise of something dearer than military distinction. One day, when a battle is in prospect, he hears that the crisis is past and that the baby is born. More than that he never learns.

## THOMAS LAFAYETTE ROSSER

This giant young trooper is half a year older than Ramseur and was in the class below him at West Point. Rosser had not waited for graduation in '61. He had resigned, has fought hard and has risen fast and now, at the time of Gettysburg, he has the prospect of a general's commission. It is given him in September, 1863. After it come heartbreaks and hard battles. He almost loses the good opinion of "Jube" Early because he wants his young wife to be near the front. A valorous exploit restores him in his commander's eyes, but, for the attainment of larger fame, it is getting late in the life of the Confederacy. Cedar Creek and Tom's Brook cancel Trevilian and New Creek. It is bitter; it is bewildering; it does not break his spirit. Nothing, apparently, could do that to Rosser.

STEPHEN  DODSON  RAMSEUR

## FITZHUGH LEE

If there were a Confederate Frans Hals, he would paint Fitz Lee, but he would ask this laughing cavalier of the South to trim that patriarchal beard. Fitz would laugh more boisterously than ever, but would say "No." That beard protects his youth precisely as Stuart's conceals a receding chin. A man who is a Major General before he is 28 needs to look old to be the companion of "Jeb" and the rival of Wade Hampton, the only two men who out-rank him. Fitz's laughter is before and after the fight. Combat is no jest. Although arthritis hampers him, he fights hard, finds feed for his horses and learns much of the art of command. Lack of mounts weakens the cavalry during the last winter of the war, but circumstance places him honorably at the head of the Corps. From the final scene he rides off in the hope of fighting in North Carolina or, if need be, in Texas.

## WILLIAM HENRY FITZHUGH LEE

Sometimes the careless confuse Fitz Lee and his cousin of the longer, kindred name. On occasion, the unadvanced Colonels and the stranded Captains of cavalry ask how many more Lees must be promoted before other men have a chance. William Henry Fitzhugh, "Rooney" for short, is not of a nature to seek promotion because of his name. Nor is he so unmindful of his name and obligation as the commanding General's son that he fails to earn promotion. He does not scintillate in conversation or in planning. At 27, when he becomes a Major General, he is bulky and perhaps appears slow; but if he possessed what he wholly lacks, the stomach for self-advertisement, he could say in truth that he has distinguished himself in every battle he has fought. Perhaps his deepest, most secret pride is that he has not failed his father in any of a score of battles. "Marse Robert" is secretly proud, too, that he never calls in vain on his son.

FITZHUGH LEE

## WILLIAM JOHNSON PEGRAM

The shy, nearsighted young student continues in these last chapters to be one of those rare men who expand in battle. He finds his sport in battle. Combat is to him what strong drink would have been to many a similar retiring nature. Because the Third Corps fights few battles, he is not conspicuous for ten months after Gettysburg. Later, the stench and the stagnation of the Petersburg trenches are repulsive to him. When the caissons begin to roll and the nervous teams tug at the traces, he is himself again. There is talk of making him a Brigadier General of infantry. Some of the ablest men in the Army think he should be promoted. Lee is unwilling to have Pegram leave the artillery though he esteems the battalion commander as among the best of his soldiers. Pegram would have preferred that his end should be similar to that of his brother John, in the roar of action; but, as it befell, he dies like a boy he is—23 and a Colonel of artillery.

## ROBERT EMMETT RODES

The young professor of engineering at the Virginia Military Institute continues to look like a Norse god in Confederate gray, but he does not retain as division commander the consistent distinction that has been his as a Brigadier. Perhaps on July 1 at Gettysburg—the first day he ever has led his own Division in battle—he tries too hard with feeble instruments. The next day, he halts his advance before it attempts to scale Cemetery Hill. Doubtless he is right, but it is not like the Rodes of Chancellorsville. When he gets back to the Wilderness in 1864, he has the furious, oldtime dash, and at the Bloody Angle he rivals his comrades Gordon and Ramseur. With them, under "Jube" Early, he goes to the Shenandoah Valley, and there, at a moment when he did not know the battle is lost, he leaves unanswered the question whether he would have realized fully his promise as a soldier.

WILLIAM JOHNSON PEGRAM

## EDWARD JOHNSON

The fashionable ladies may laugh at Edward Johnson's social oddities and may say that his head is in three tiers, like the papal tiara, but after he receives a Division and leads it in battle, no soldier ever laughs at "Old Allegheny." Johnson does well in nearly all his fights, hits hard and wins the confidence of his men. A great career might have been his if certain guns had not been withdrawn that rainy night of the 11th of May, 1864. The result is honorable even if Johnson is captured along with most of his famous command.

## CHARLES WILLIAM FIELD

"Old Pete" Longstreet does not relish the assignment of this convalescent officer to the command of Hood's Division, which the Lieutenant General desired for Micah Jenkins. Consequently, Charles Field, 36 years of age, has no warmth of welcome when he reports to the First Corps. In his first battle after that, he does well, and by the time Longstreet recovers from a wound, Field is a fixture. He sometimes fails, but he possesses unmistakable, if indefinable, military sense. When the final muster roll is made, Field's is the strongest, stoutest Division of them all.

## JOSEPH BREVARD KERSHAW

This South Carolina lawyer, 41 in 1863, continues to display aptitude in command and, at a time when the First Corps is strife-riven, he keeps his poise and the good opinion of his comrades. The fatal spring of 1864, which finds him a Major General, brings him many hours of high hazard. Kershaw passes through them all as if they were the unvexing incidents of a quiet life. Even in the hour when his troops are surrounded, he loses none of his dignity. Behind that dignity is character, in the moulding of which religion has first place.

# LEE'S LIEUTENANTS

## VOLUME THREE

### Part One of

### Gettysburg to Appomattox

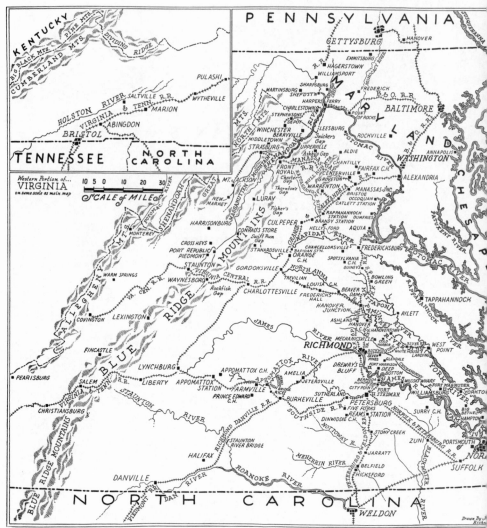

BATTLEGROUNDS OF THE ARMY OF NORTHERN VIRGINIA

# CHAPTER I

## Much Pomp Ends in Humiliation

"Jeb" Stuart was to blame. All his enemies said that. The advance of the Army of Northern Virginia toward the Potomac in June, 1863, would not have met that humiliating, initial check if the chief of the cavalry had not been so intent on displaying his increased force. He now had five cavalry Brigades of 9536 officers and men—more than ever he had commanded.[1] Lee must see them, Lee and all the young ladies of the Piedmont region of Virginia.

After May 20, when Stuart moved his headquarters from Orange to Culpeper,[2] he set his staff to work on plans for such a pageant as the continent never had witnessed. The stage for it fairly thrust itself upon him: It was a long wide field in the vicinity of Brandy Station, between Culpeper and the Rappahannock. At the ideal site on this field was a hillock no craftsman could have excelled in the design of a reviewing stand. To complete perfection, the field was so close to the Orange and Alexandria Railroad that a halted train would offer seats for spectators.[3] Stuart pitched his tents on nearby Fleetwood Hill, overlooking Brandy Station, to supervise everything, and he set June 5 as the date. Each staff officer must provide himself a new uniform and must see to it that mounts were flawless. A ball must be arranged in Culpeper the night before the review and, perhaps, another after the cavalry had shown its magnificence.[4]

[1] O. R., 25, pt. 2, p. 825; H. B. McClellan, 293.
[2] W. W. Blackford's MS Memoirs, 307.
[3] Maj. Daniel A. Grimsley in his Battles in Culpeper County, Virginia . . ., p. 8, stated that the review took place on the Auburn estate. "A furrow was made with a plow, beginning at a point not far from the dividing line between the Auburn estate and the Hall estate and about 300 yards West of the railroad, on the land now [1900] owned by Mr. Schlosser, and extending in a line parallel with the railroad, along by the broad-spreading elm tree that stood in the flat in rear of the grave yard, on the Ross estate, quite to the run . . . The horse artillery . . . was formed in batteries along the ridge in rear of, and on the west side of the branch . . . General Lee occupied a little hillock, immediately on the west side of the railroad, some 300 or 400 yards North of the station at Inlet." This is almost at the junction of U. S. Route 15 and Virginia Route 665.
[4] 2 von Borcke, 264–65.

Preparation was repaid. From Charlottesville and from the nearer towns on the O. & A. came streams of guests. With Heros von Borcke as his aide, Ex-Secretary George W. Randolph of the War Department arrived to be Stuart's particular guest. Wagons and ambulances distributed beauty at every hospitable gate. All preliminaries were auspicious, though, to be sure, the ball on the evening of the 4th at the Court House was somewhat overpraised by a newspaper reporter as a "gay and dazzling scene, illuminated by floods of light from numerous chandeliers." Von Borcke, who never depreciated anything he planned or shared, reluctantly had to admit that "a few tallow candles" were all that challenged the darkness of the Court House.[5]

By 8 o'clock [6] on the bright morning of June 5, Stuart and his staff, in their new uniforms,[7] started for Brandy Station. Heralded by buglers and welcomed by throngs, the cavalcade rode triumphantly upon the field. One disappointment there was, one only, but it was serious: the commanding General of the Army was concerned with some difficult matters of logistics and could not be present.[8] For General Lee, of course, there was no substitute. Stuart made the best of this. With his staff he started down the front of a line of horses that extended for a mile and a half. On its flank were twenty-four of Beckham's guns, the famous rifles and Napoleons that had been Pelham's. As the reviewing party reached each Brigadier, he and his staff fell in behind. The cavalcade swept to the left flank [9] and then, in regulation manner, rode the length of the line in rear.

It was 10 o'clock or after when Stuart wheeled from the right flank and took his position on the knoll, beneath a gallantly flying Confederate flag. Again the bugles sounded. The troopers farthest on Stuart's right moved out in columns of squadrons and passed at a walk. Then, when the cavalry had ridden the whole length of the front and had doubled back, the second "march past" began at the trot. A hundred yards from the reviewing stand, the men spurred to a gallop, drew sabres, raised the "rebel yell" and dashed by the admiring "Jeb" at a furious gait. On the ridge west of the

[5] 2 von Borcke, 264–65. The German's memory failed him or his imagination ran away with him in his reference to moon rise and continued dancing on the "spacious verandah." The moon, just at the first quarter, set at 11:56 P.M.
[6] 2 von Borcke, 265.
[7] Ibid. and W. W. Blackford's MS Memoirs, 310.
    H. B. McClellan, 261.                              [9] Grimsley, op. cit., 8

branch, Beckham opened with blank charges as if to repel attack.

It was thrilling even to those who had seen those same squadrons yell and thunder past when shells were emptying saddles and the smell and smoke of battle were in the air. For the ladies, the gallop, the excitement, the foxhunters' call from nearly 10,000 throats were overwhelming. Those feminine spectators who had handsome male companions put their handkerchiefs to their eyes and swayed and gracefully swooned. It was observed, strangely enough, that those girls who had come with parents and those who were attended by awkward swains, did not faint.[10] Every one went home to praise the cavalry and its commander. At night, there was another ball; but it was danced more comfortably, if less deftly, under the sparkling heavens, on the greensward, and to the crackling and pungency of great fires.[11]

To the men in the ranks, unbidden to dances, the whole review was a bother. It was a bore even, except for that high moment when each soldier was approaching the stand furiously as if he were going to seize the fairest girl on the hill and bear her off across the pommel of his saddle. Officers, though more favored, had to admit that a long review and all the prologue and aftermath were enough of display. It was not, therefore, with responsive ears that officers heard these orders on the 7th: Prepare for review tomorrow by the commanding General on the same field at Brandy Station. Lee had arrived and wished to see in what condition were officers and men for the next hard adventure across the Potomac.[12]

Had there been zest, there was not time for many invitations.[13] The only one of record served the purpose of thousands. "Come and see the review," said Fitz Lee to John Hood and added politely, "and bring any of your people." On the 8th, perhaps before the commanding General appeared, Hood arrived—with

<hr/>

[10] 2 von Borcke, 266; W. W. Blackford's MS Memoirs, 310; G. W. Beale, 83.
[11] Von Borcke, loc. cit.                    [12] H. B. McClellan, 261.
[13] G. W. Beale, op. cit., 83, said that a train of spectators from Orange and Culpeper witnessed the review of the 8th and in this he may have recorded fact, but in most narratives there is natural confusion of some incidents of two affairs similar in many ways. Neese, op. cit., 168, said a special train from Richmond came up for the review of the 5th. As Neese wrongly reported that Hood's Division was present that day, the cannoneer may have been mistaken in this also. His diary contains so many post bellum additions that one finds difficulty in separating the original from the elaborated items. In general, the briefer the item the closer its conformity to the notes Neese made at the time.

his entire Division. The Texan rode out and joined some of the cavalry officers. "You invited me and my 'people'," said Hood, with a laugh, "and you see I have brought them!"

Fitz Lee knew how jealous the infantry were of every man who had a mount of any description. In particular, at the moment, the jest-loving Fitz wished to make reservation concerning a favorite jibe by the foot soldiers at all evidence of poor horsemanship on the part of the cavalry. So, instantly, young Lee, in cheerful banter, answered Hood: "Well, don't let them halloo, 'Here's your mule!' at the review."

"If they do," laughed Wade Hampton, "we will charge you!" [14]

Stuart now had the satisfaction of welcoming formally the notables he had missed at the first review. General Lee rode magnificently on the field. After him came Longstreet and the other leading figures of the First and Second Corps. Soon all were ready for the ride down the long, long line. A lively clip was set by the commanding General. It was not too brisk for "Jeb," of course, but it was unpleasant for General Pendleton and, no doubt, for all the awkward riders. When the cavalcade had gone down the front and back to the hillock, Stuart prepared to have his Brigades pass in review, but as he looked to his flank, he noticed that "Grumble" Jones's men were out of place. They were loitering as if they had been given "at ease." Quickly Stuart sent Lieut. Frank Robertson to ask why Jones was not in the saddle and on the alert for the movement of the Brigade next him. When Robertson arrived, he found "Grumble" lying comfortably on the ground as if a review was last and least of the concerns of the Laurel Brigade. Anger and reviling greeted the inquiry from Stuart, but as young Robertson rode off in silent wrath, he observed that "Boots and Saddles" was sounded promptly for Jones's men. [15]

The review went well enough as far as it went. That is to say, Stuart could see that Lee observed keenly and proudly the marching squadrons, but there was no gallop, no yelling and no service of the guns. Lee forbade that. The horses needed their flesh, the gunners their powder. Let the march past be at a walk.

It was a vast show of strength to those who remembered the few

[14] *Wearing of the Gray*, 317. Hood had been ordered on the 3rd of May from the Rapidan to Culpeper. *O. R.*, 27, pt. 2, p. 293.
[15] *In the Saddle with Stuart*, MS, 16–17.

mounted battalions that had fought at First Manassas; but in comparison with the display of the 5th, it was tame and, in at least one particular, it might have produced riotous laughter. Preston Chew of the horse artillery must have known the Texans were prepared to yell "Here's your mule" but he permitted George Neese, acting First Sergeant, to ride at the head of the battery astride a mule with ears about a foot long. Fortunately, Stuart saw the mule before it reached that part of the field where Hood's men were waiting. An aide dashed up to Chew and had him hustle Neese off before the infantry observed him; but if they had started that cry about the mule. . . . Neese was nonchalant. He protested afterwards that personally he cared little about the matter; but he had in honesty to add: "the mule looked a little bit surprised, and, I think, felt ashamed of himself and his waving ears, which cost him his prominent position in the grand cavalcade." [16]

The review over, the men walked their horses to the camps, which soon were bivouacs. All the equipage was packed for an early move on the morning of June 9. Lee was about to start Ewell and Longstreet for the Potomac: the cavalry were to cross the Rappahannock River and to cover the march. From the preparations, the men could tell that a large operation was about to be started but they were less interested than usual. The explanation by one of "Lige" White's Captains was that the troopers were "worried out by the military foppery and display (which was Stuart's greatest weakness)." [17]

Stuart himself fared scarcely better than did his men. On Fleetwood Hill everything except two tent-flies was in headquarters wagons.[18] He had a simple bed, but from the grassy eminence he could enjoy a prospect of rural beauty. For several miles, the land, here open and there wooded, had just enough of curve and grade to escape monotony. Where the clover had not yet been cut, it spread its perfume. On ground newly plowed, brown or red, the corn was a foot high and ready for thinning. Wheat, already golden, waited the scythe.[19] Toward the Northeast, on the Fleet-

---

16 *Neese*, 169–70.  17 *F. M. Myers*, 181.
18 *H. B. McClellan*, 263.
19 Dr. Thomas E. Hughes of Richmond, who operates the ancestral farm about fifteen miles from Brandy, kindly examined his records to establish for the writer the average condition of crops in this region as of June 9.

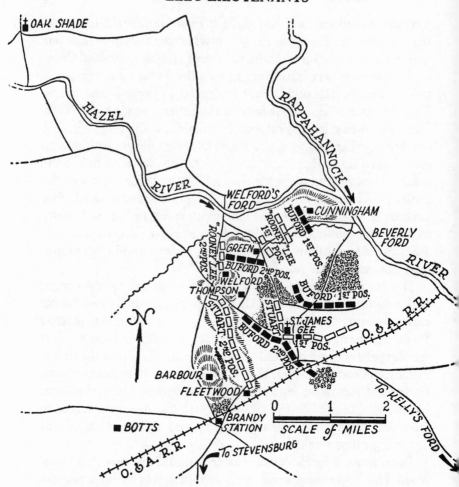

The Battlefield of Brandy Station—after *H. B. McClellan,* with correction of the location of Welford's Ford according to Meade's map in *O. R. Atlas,* Plate XLIV–3.

wood side of the straight Orange and Alexandria Railroad, woods cut off a view of the declivity of the Rappahannock. Farther eastward were hills where lived the Paynes and the Jamesons. Downstream, beyond green fields and greener forests was Kelly's Ford, forever mournful in cavalrymen's memory because Pelham had fallen there.

After darkness, across the Rappahannock, not a campfire was visible to suggest that the enemy's cavalry under Alfred Pleasanton had sensed the movement of Lee's Army and had begun reconnaissance.[20] Dispositions for the night, in anticipation of the morning march, placed Fitz Lee's Brigade North of the Hazel River and in the vicinity of Oak Shade Church, about seven and a half miles Northwest of Fleetwood. Fitz was near at hand but was sick and unable to exercise command.[21] Acting in his place was Col. Tom Munford of the Second Virginia. Down the Hazel, "Rooney" Lee's Brigade was at Welford's plantation, close to Welford's Ford, which was about two miles West of the point where the Hazel joins the Rappahannock.[22] At Beverly Ford, a major crossing of the Rappahannock, about a mile and a half above the railroad bridge, "Grumble" Jones had placed good pickets. Two miles back from the ford his men were bivouacked along the Brandy road. In front of Jones's Brigade were four batteries of horse artillery, the careless exposure of which was in due time to bring peril. At Norman's Ford, below the railroad, a guard was placed but the ford at the time scarcely could have been in condition for use.[23] Kelly's Ford, four miles down the Rappahannock from the railroad crossing, was in the care of Robertson's pickets. His Brigade and Wade Hampton's were spread where pasturage was good between the Barbour Farm and Stevensburg, a distance of about five miles.[24] All these dispositions were made in the belief that the front was safe and the enemy remote.

The pickets did their duty through the pleasant June night. After the moon set about 2 o'clock, a haze spread over the river in the vicinity of Beverly Ford.[25] On the narrow road that ran southward through woods for a mile and more, the darkness was unrelieved by the starlight.[26] Although war had swept away most of the man-made obstacles—fences and gates and draw-bars—and

---

20 Col. F. C. Newhall in *Annals*, 137. On May 22, 1863, Brig. Gen. Alfred Pleasanton had assumed command of the Cavalry Corps of the Army of the Potomac "during the absence of Major General Stoneman" (*O. R.*, 25, pt. 2, p. 513), who, on July 28, was announced as Chief of the Cavalry Bureau (*O. R.*, 27, pt. 3, p. 11).

21 This probably was because of the "inflammatory rheumatism" from which he then was suffering at intervals.

22 Many wartime maps show Welford's Ford as if it were on the Rappahannock, just above Beverly Ford. Welford's—all the maps spell it with one "l" in contrast to the "ll" of the Wilderness—is correctly figured in *O. R. Atlas*, Plates XLIV–3 and LXXXVII–2, 3.

23 None of the dispositions indicated that any crossing was planned there or that it was regarded as a point requiring a heavy guard.

24 Part of Robertson's men were as far westward as the farm of John Minor Botts, an "Old Whig" politician of some distinction. See *H. B. McClellan*, 262; *O. R.*, 27, pt. 2, p. 680, *Annals*, 395, *Beale*, 67.

25 *Annals*, 138.            26 *McClellan*, 264.

had created as fair a field as knights could have asked for a tour-
ney,[27] there were treacherous ditches across some of the fields near
the river.[28] A horseman had to trust his mount and, if he were
nervous, he did well to proceed at a walk and with caution. Sound
carried far and loudly.

Just at the cool, hazy dawn [29] of June 9, Stuart on Fleetwood
Hill heard the sound of firing from the direction of Beverly Ford.
He could not misunderstand the character or the import of the
pop-pop-pop and the defiant, echoing answer. The enemy must
be crossing. There could be no other explanation. Soon a dashing
courier on a panting horse brought the news from "Grumble"
Jones: The Federals were on the south side of the Rappahannock
at Beverly Ford and were advancing in strength.[30] "Jeb" immediately directed that the wagon trains be started for Culpeper and
he prepared to reinforce "Grumble."

The engagement opened in this manner was full of military
sensation.[31] Narrowly and by persistent fighting, the exposed
guns of the horse artillery were withdrawn to the vicinity of a
little brick church, "a modest sanctuary," [32] St. James' by name.[33]
In woods to the North of this building, beyond an open field, the
Federals soon began to deploy, but before they opened an attack,
Stuart received two messages that the enemy was crossing at Kelly's
Ford, four miles downstream. "Jeb" sent reinforcements in that
direction [34] and summoned all his other troopers to the front and
up-stream flank of the Federals who had moved toward Brandy
by way of Beverly Ford.[35]

In confidence that these dispositions would protect his front,
Stuart watched some clever woods fighting by Wade Hampton. It
was difficult, but it progressed.[36] The situation seemed entirely in
hand when "Grumble" Jones sent word of a threatened attack on
the right flank by troops that had crossed below Beverly Ford.
Stuart's pride and his dislike of "Grumble" probably shaped his

27 W. W. Blackford's MS Memoirs, 315.
28 McClellan, 264.                    29 Ibid., 284; Memoir of Ulric Dahlgren, 146.
30 O. R., 27, pt. 2, p. 680.
31 The Battle of Brandy Station is not described in full detail here because, from the
Confederate side, nothing of importance is to be added to the clear, trustworthy account
in H. B. McClellan. Virtually all subsequent narratives appear to be based on that book.
32 Col. F. C. Newhall in Annals, 140.
33 For the removal of the guns, see O. R., 27, pt. 2, pp. 748, 749, 757, 772; H. B.
McClellan, 264 ff.
34 O. R., 27, pt. 2, pp. 680, 727          35 Ibid., 681, 721.
36 Cf. O. R., 27, pt. 2, p. 721.

answer. "Tell General Jones," he said, "to attend to the Yankees in his front, and I'll watch the flanks."

Jones's reply was: "So he thinks they ain't coming, does he? Well, let him alone; he'll damn soon see for himself." [37]

About noon [38] a courier spurred to Stuart from Major McClellan, who had been left at Fleetwood: Hostile cavalry in strength, [39] the staff officer reported, was almost at Brandy!

Stuart had confidence in Henry McClellan, but he was incredulous. "Ride back there," Stuart said to Capt. James F. Hart of the horse artillery, "and see what this foolishness is about!" [40] Obediently Captain Hart started for Fleetwood but he did not have to send back a report. Before he had gone far, Frank Deane, an intelligent, confidential headquarters clerk, galloped up to Stuart. "General," cried Deane, before he reached Stuart, "the Yankees are at Brandy!"

In mocking confirmation, there rolled down at that instant from the hill the sound of rapid fire. Stuart immediately ordered two regiments of Jones's Brigade back to Fleetwood. [41] With equal decision, when Stuart's aide arrived, "Grumble" directed Asher Harman to take his Twelfth Virginia and "Lige" White's battalion and to hurry to the high ground above Brandy. Stuart himself started after them. As soon as he got out of the woods South of the church, his mood must have become grim. Instead of two regiments, a long column was in sight and was mounting Fleetwood Hill boldly. Stuart snapped out orders for one and then for a second of Wade Hampton's regiments to ride at a gallop for the heights—a superfluous order, as it proved, because the South Carolinian had seen the Union troopers and already was withdrawing to meet them. [42]

A fine situation, surely, this was for the day after a review. The most distinguished regiments of the Cavalry Division caught in

37 F. M. Myers, 183.  38 Cf. O. R., 27, pt. 2, pp. 732, 768.
39 McClellan did not give the estimated strength of the enemy in his account of the incident (op. cit., 270–71), but Stuart wrote: "The force moving on Fleetwood was at first reported to be two regiments" (O. R., 27, pt. 2, p. 681). It is possible, of course, that Stuart here was referring to the report from Kelly's Ford and not to the report from Fleetwood.
40 Hart in Philadelphia Weekly Times, June 26, 1880.
41 In his MS memoir, Robertson wrote, p. 18, that Stuart said, "Go, go fast to General Hampton and tell him to send a regiment at a gallop," but Stuart's contemporary report (O. R., 27, pt. 2, p. 681)stated that the first call was for two regiments from Jones. It is quite possible that Robertson carried both messages, and in writing of them many years later, confused the incidents.
42 O. R., 27, pt. 2, pp. 681, 721–22; H. B. McClellan, 271.

the rear while engaged heavily in front! Nothing but hard, stand-
up combat could win the field now. In the first clash, the Confederate advance to Fleetwood was repulsed.[43] The next charge
carried the hill and drove the Federals eastward across the railroad,[44] but for a few minutes only did the Southerners remain
in possession of the long hill.[45] The counter-attack of the bluecoats was swift and effective. Part of Fleetwood was theirs again.
Stuart saw that all his cavalry and all his artillery must be massed
on Fleetwood if he was to hold it against an adversary who, most
incredibly, had assumed the offensive. Repulse of a sharp attack
by Flournoy's Sixth Virginia demonstrated that the Federals were
in strength and, prisoners said, were of the Division of David
Gregg, who had crossed at Kelly's Ford.[46]

These Federals surged forward again and sought to get to the
top of the hill three guns they had advanced to its foot. As the
bluecoats pushed up the eminence, those Confederates who looked
from Fleetwood in the direction of St. James' Church saw a sight
that made veterans catch their breath and stare and lift their hats
in admiration. Hampton's regiments were coming up in magnificent order. On the right, in advance [47] was Cobb's Legion under
Pierce Young; in support, and almost *en échelon*, was Black's
First South Carolina; on the left, slightly to the rear and moving
less rapidly, were the First North Carolina and the Jeff Davis
Legion. Sweeping in splendor across the field abreast of Hampton's column was Hart's horse artillery.

Young and Black pressed straight on; [48] Hampton diverged to
the East in order to get under the side of the hill and to trap the
enemy his right regiments drove from the high ground.[49] Soon
the Federals around Fleetwood House saw Young's object and,
with a gallantry that matched his, they threw themselves at him.
Young changed his column to the left,[50] met them, made them
wheel, and then, in close columns of squadrons, he swept over the
hill.[51] The enemy withdrew this time toward the East, in the
direction of Hampton's advance. Almost immediately there was a
rolling mêlée, confused by smoke and dust; but when this cleared,

---

[43] H. B. McClellan, 272 n.                    [44] O. R., 27, pt. 2, p. 769.
[45] H. B. McClellan, 273–74.                   [46] O. R., 27, pt. 2, p. 755.
[47] Left and North of Confederate observers around Fleetwood House.
[48] H. B. McClellan, 277; O. R., 27, pt. 2, p. 732.
[49] O. R., 27, pt. 2, p. 732.                  [50] Ibid., 728
[51] O. R., 27, pt. 2, p. 732.

Hampton still was advancing. The enemy was falling back toward Brandy Station and the woods to the South of it. Said Hampton later: "The capture of the whole force which had been driven from the hill would have been almost certain but that our own artillery, which had again been posted on the hill . . . opened a heavy and well-directed fire at the head of my column. The delay rendered necessary to make this fire cease enabled the enemy to reach the woods in his rear." [52]

While Young had been sweeping over the ridge, Harman and White had been pressing along Fleetwood Hill and had cut off part of the 1st New Jersey Cavalry in the direction of the Barbour House.[53] The Confederate cavalrymen apparently did not know these blue cavalrymen were separated and without support. Nor did the Southern artillerists realize that Federals were West of them. Suddenly, the Unionists dashed among the guns—not in the hope of carrying off so handsome a prize but because the batteries blocked the only apparent avenue of escape. A brief, furious fight followed. Pistols answered sabres. With no better weapon than a sponge-staff, one Confederate knocked a bluecoat from a horse.[54] The Federals, beaten off, made their way to Brandy Station.[55] To clear the ground adjoining the station became the next task of Stuart. This was undertaken by Lunsford Lomax and his Eleventh Virginia of Jones's Brigade. In a charge down both sides of the road from Fleetwood to Brandy, Lomax easily drove the enemy back toward Stevensburg.[56]

This charge would have removed Stuart's last concern, had not a new development come. All day Stuart had been on the lookout for Federal infantry. To Capt. W. W. Blackford he had assigned the special duty of watching for any evidence of their presence. "It was not long," said Blackford, "before I found them with my powerful field glasses deployed as skirmishers and though they kept low in the grass I could see the color of their trimmings and

[52] O. R., 27, pt. 2, p. 722.

[53] This property, Belleville, is separated from Fleetwood by a deep ravine, but many of the Federal reports confused the two estates.

[54] O. R., 27, pt. 2, pp. 772–73. Subsequently, the Confederates learned that the 1st New Jersey at the time was under the command of their old antagonist of the Valley, Sir Percy Wyndham, who had been Jackson's prisoner the evening Ashby was killed. See Vol. I, p. 432. Wyndham, commanding a Brigade at Brandy, did not permit any of the gallantry of this charge to be lost in his narration of it. O. R., 27, pt. 1, p. 966.

[55] Ibid.

[56] O. R., 27, pt. 2, pp. 749–50, 763.

their bayonet scabbards." [57] On Stuart's order, Blackford rode six miles to Longstreet's headquarters, whence the intelligence was communicated to Lee. In anticipation of a summons, Rodes already had advanced his Division to the Botts Farm and now on orders from Ewell, he started for Brandy.[58]

While Rodes was marching, Stuart's position on Fleetwood was being consolidated. Hampton, Jones and all the horse artillery were deploying on the ridge. The three Federal guns, which the enemy had sought repeatedly to carry to the crest, were silent prizes of war. "Rooney" Lee had held his original position on the left of Jones long enough to discourage the Federals North of St. James' Church from rapid pursuit of Hampton and Jones when those two officers moved for Fleetwood. Then, repelling attacks, young Lee had moved southward to another strong flank position.[59]

Against the front of these three Brigades, increased to four by the late arrival of Munford on "Rooney" Lee's left, the Federals under Gregg were wise enough not to shatter their weary squadrons. Further attack by the column from Beverly Ford was feeble and was confined to the left. Before Rodes got his infantry from Botts's Farm to Brandy, the enemy was withdrawing toward Beverly Ford.[60]

The Battle of Brandy Station [61] was over. A mellow glow after sunset, a "burnished and glowing horizon," a soft haze over wood and river ended in splendor an ugly day.[62] Stuart had been mortified by his failure to win a dazzling victory and he was resolved now to reestablish his headquarters on Fleetwood Hill so that he could say he held his ground. Wrote Blackford: ". . . when we reached the place it was covered so thickly with the dead horses and men, and the blue bottle flies were swarming so thick over the

[57] W. W. Blackford's MS Memoirs, 317.

[58] O. R., 27, pt. 2, pp. 439–40, 546, 564. Major Grimsley, op. cit., 12, stated that Gen. R. E. Lee observed part of the action from the cupola of the Barbour House. Hotchkiss' MS Diary, 205, confirmed this and recorded that at one time it appeared that Lee, Ewell and their staffs might be compelled to beat off an attack.

[59] On the high ground West of the Green and Thompson Houses. This part of the action is of some interest as an example of the tactical value of a flank element, even though it is not engaged; but because of his wound, "Rooney" Lee filed no report. A few accounts of his fight were collected by McClellan and were summarized op. cit., 280 ff, but they and the fragmentary reports are so vague that any attempt to reconstruct from them the details of W. H. F. Lee's action would be mere guesswork.

[60] O. R., 27, pt. 2, p. 546.

[61] As frequently styled Fleetwood Hill and in Federal reports often called Beverly Ford.

[62] Annals, 144.

blood stains on the ground that there was not room enough to pitch the tents among them. So the General reluctantly consented to camping at another place." [63] His casualties had been 523. Those of the Federals subsequently were ascertained to be 936, of whom 486 were prisoners of war.[64]

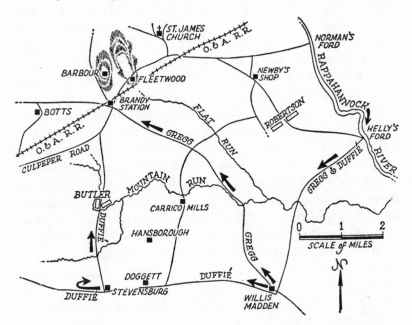

Approaches to Brandy Station from Kelly's Ford—after *H. B. McClellan.*

By his campfire, before he received these figures, Stuart had to ask how Gregg had eluded Beverley Robertson, who had been sent toward Kelly's Ford for the very purpose of blocking an advance from that direction. Robertson did not have a single casualty to report [65] and he admitted that his command, although opposed to the enemy during the entire day, was not at any time actively engaged.[66] It took a preliminary report by Robertson, a more detailed account, which Stuart declared unsatisfactory,[67] and a revised narrative, which Stuart had to elaborate, to make plain the facts without disclosing the reason.[68] Robertson had moved from his bivouac down the road which runs from Brandy toward Kelly's

63 *W. W. Blackford's MS Memoirs*, 318.  64 *H. B. McClellan*, 293.
65 *O. R.*, 27, pt. 2, p. 737.  66 *Ibid.*, 734.
67 *Annals*, 401.  68 *O. R.*, 27, pt. 2, pp. 733–36.

Ford by way of Fleetwood and Newby's Shop.[69] Opposite Brown's Farm,[70] Robertson had met the commanding officer of his pickets who were retiring from Kelly's in the face of overwhelming enemy forces. This officer, Capt. William White, reported Federal infantry and field guns directly in Robertson's front. Robertson dismounted the greater part of his force, reconnoitered and soon learned that the enemy were moving toward Brandy and the Orange and Alexandria Railroad by two of the roads to the South of him. It was then that Robertson made what Stuart subsequently pronounced the wrong decision. Had Robertson sent part of his force southward with promptness, he might have caught Gregg on the flank. Instead, Robertson reasoned that he could not divide his small Brigade or abandon the road he was covering. He remained where he was, reported the situation to Stuart and at length suggested that he swing southward and westward and get in rear of the Federals who already had passed toward Brandy and Stevensburg beyond his right.[71] Stuart's answer was that Robertson should hold his front. Said "Jeb" a few days later, in explanation, "it was too late . . . and it would have been extremely hazardous for him to have interposed his command between the enemy's infantry and artillery and the column of cavalry that had already passed on the right flank." [72] Robertson obeyed orders. When he was free, at length, to return to Brandy, the engagement was in its final stage.[73]

A report more distressing than Robertson's was made by the Second South Carolina and the Fourth Virginia, which had been sent to Stevensburg, five and a half miles South of Brandy. In a confused, far-spreading fight,[74] their 500 men [75] had held off a column under Col. Alfred N. Duffié, but they had paid with the

[69] Robertson nowhere in his reports stated that this was his route but he could not have reached his known position by any other road unless he had gone by the one from Brandy toward Willis Madden's and, when opposite Carrico's Mill, had taken a farm road across Flat Run to Brown's. In the event he used this road he probably would have had a collision with Gregg.
[70] Almost on the second Confederate position in the Battle of Kelly's Ford. See Vol. II, p. 461.
[71] O. R., 27, pt. 2, p. 734.                    [72] Ibid., 735.
[73] Ibid., 736.
[74] The details are so fully covered in H. B. McClellan, 286 ff, that they need not be reviewed here.
[75] Maj. N. T. Lipscomb reported that the Second South Carolina went into action with 220 men (O. R., 27, pt. 2, p. 729). Because the troopers of the Fourth Virginia more readily could replace their horses (cf. H. B. McClellan, 259), it is probable that this regiment was somewhat larger than the other, but 280 would be a liberal figure.

loss of valuable officers. Lt. Col. Frank Hampton of the Second South Carolina, Wade Hampton's brother, was mortally wounded.[76] Later in the action, near the crossing of Mountain Run,[77] Calbraith Butler, Colonel of that regiment, and Will Farley, Stuart's chief scout, were sitting on their horses, almost side by side in the road, though their mounts were headed in opposite directions. As the officers were deploying the troopers for a stand, a Federal fieldpiece on the flank was fired at them. The first projectile took off Colonel Butler's foot, passed through his horse and Farley's and severed the Captain's leg.[78] Staff officers rushed to Butler and the couriers to Farley; but as soon as Butler had been placed in a blanket for removal to the rear he said to the officers in the stately speech which did not fail some of the Southern leaders even in the midst of pain: "I wish that you two gentlemen, as you have placed me in the hands of my own men, would go and take charge of Captain Farley."

They found the scout lying on a blanket and in flawless composure of mind. As there chanced to be at hand an old flat trough, which could be used as a stretcher, they lifted Farley into it and told the men of the medical detachment to take him out of danger. What followed is one of the classic incidents of the entire war and is told best in the words of John T. Rhett:

"Just as we were about to send [Farley] away, he called me to him, and pointing to the leg that had been cut off by the ball . . . he asked me to bring it to him. I did so. He took it, pressed it to his bosom as one would a child, and said, smiling—

" 'It is an old friend, gentlemen, and I do not wish to part from it.'

"Captain Chesnut [79] and myself shook hands with him, bidding him good-bye, and expressed the hope that we should soon again see him. He said—

" 'Good-bye, gentlemen, and forever. I know my condition, and we will not meet again. I thank you for your kindness. It is a pleasure to me that I have fallen into the hands of good Carolinians at my last moment.'

---

[76] O. R., 27, pt. 2, pp. 684, 729; *Annals*, 400; *Mrs. Chesnut*, 237.
[77] About a mile North of Stevensburg on the road to Brandy.
[78] 2 *von Borcke*, 280; H. B. *McClellan*, 291; O. R., 27, pt. 2, p. 730.
[79] Most probably John Chesnut who, according to Mrs. Chesnut's *Diary*, was with Stuart's command.

"Courteously, even smilingly, he nodded his head to us as the men bore him away. He died within a few hours. I have never seen a man whose demeanor, in the face of certain, painful, and quick death, was so superb. I have never encountered anything so brave from first to last." [80]

Stuart's own tribute was to the same effect: "[Captain Farley] displayed even in death the same loftiness of bearing and fortitude which have characterized him through life. He had served without emolument, long, faithfully, and always with distinction. No nobler champion has fallen." [81] Other reliable scouts Stuart had and still others he developed. Ahead of Franklin Stringfellow were adventures as amazing as any that Farley had met with cold, calculating valor; but there never was in the cavalry Division another scout who in every quality was the peer of Farley.[82] Defense that took a man so nearly irreplaceable was not defense but defeat. Another serious loss, though not fatal, was that of "Rooney" Lee, who received an ugly leg wound.[83]

If Robertson's report and Butler's stubborn fight explained why Gregg had and Duffié had not reached the rear of Stuart's forces at St. James' Church, Stuart felt that he had reason to be disappointed over the failure of Tom Munford to bring Fitz Lee's men into action before mid-afternoon, but in this the equities were divided.[84]

[80] Narrative addressed to Gen. M. C. Butler in *H. B. McClellan*, 291–92.

[81] *O. R.*, 27, pt. 2, p. 685. In a letter to Farley's mother, Aug. 10, 1863, Stuart said: ". . . I cannot longer postpone a tribute due to one of Carolina's noblest sons, universally admired and beloved. It is needless to tell his Mother what were his noble traits of character, but I thought it might be gratifying to her broken spirit to know from me how much he was appreciated and how sorely his loss is felt. His bravery amounted to heroism of the highest order, and there are letters on file in the War Department attesting his merit, which I felt it my duty, unsolicited by him, to write."—*Farley MSS.*

[82] In *Wearing of the Gray*, Cooke's excellent sketch of Farley, quoted *supra*, Vol. I, p. 280, included the pathetic item that Farley had entrusted to a lady of Culpeper his new uniform coat—doubtless the one purchased by Stuart's order for the cavalry review —and had said to her, "If anything befalls me, wrap me in this and send me to my Mother" (*loc. cit.*, 146). It is believed that some materials for a sketch of Farley are in existence. The writer is indebted to E. D. Smith, Jr., for a copy of Stuart's letter, quoted in note 81 *supra*, and also for a copy of an interesting letter from Farley to his mother, May 9, 1862. This deals with events of the preceding week.

[83] *O. R.*, 27, pt. 2, pp. 683, 771.

[84] *O. R.*, 27, pt. 2, pp. 683, 737–39. It should be added that so far as the writer has examined the vast *Munford MSS* he has found little in them concerning Brandy Station. General Munford manifestly was not ashamed of his conduct at Brandy, but neither was he proud of it. Perhaps some of the post bellum criticism of Munford's part in this battle originated in an error unwittingly made by Maj. H. B. McClellan on his map of the "Vicinity of Brandy Station." The Major neglected to mark Welford's Ford, and he located it, unmarked, about two and a half, instead of two miles, West by air from Beverly Ford. This shifts the orientation, of course, and puts the ford in wrong relationship to the flank of "Rooney" Lee. More material was an error in placing the route of Munford

Although Stuart did not know it at the time, he had a compensating gift of Fortune in a delay of the Federal crossing at Kelly's Ford. Buford had been on the south bank of Beverly Ford by early dawn, but Duffié, despite Gregg's imperative orders, started late and had some unexplained and unexpected difficulty in getting to Kelly's Ford.[85] For this reason, Gregg did not begin his passage of the stream till after 5 o'clock.[86] Had he moved from Kelly's Ford when Buford advanced from Beverly Ford, the two forces, attacking almost simultaneously from North and from East, could have given "Jeb" his unhappiest day.

Most fortunate of all was Stuart in a dramatic occurrence at Fleetwood in the moment of Gregg's onslaught. Either by Stuart's order or because its ammunition was reduced to a few almost worthless shells, one gun of Hart's Battery was at the foot of Fleetwood Hill in the early morning.[87] This little howitzer had been observed by Maj. Henry McClellan, whom Stuart, it will be remembered, had left at Fleetwood when he galloped to St. James' Church. As soon as McClellan confirmed excited reports that the Federals were at Brandy Station, he hurried Carter and the gun to the crest of Fleetwood. Search of the limber chest showed a few round shots along with the defective shells. Carter boldly opened a slow fire. Although there were no Confederates on Fleetwood Hill at that time, except McClellan, Carter and the men serving the piece, they held off the Federals long enough for Harman and White to reach the hill before Gregg's men had occupied it completely.[88] This piece of good luck—more than a man should have asked—Stuart acknowledged in his report to the extent only that he deplored the fact that "the artillery sent to [Fleetwood] Hill had little ammunition."[89] There was a fine compliment for McClellan in the report but it was second to praise of von Borcke

along the road South of Hazel River and West of the road from Welford's crossing. Von Borcke and Scheibert in *Die grosse Reiterschlacht bei Brandy Station*, 104, Skizze D, located the ford approximately but erred in fixing the position of Munford at 2 P.M. Some of their other sketches of Munford's position also are inaccurate.

[85] *O. R.*, 27, pt. 1, p. 950.

[86] Gregg said, *ibid.*, "until between 5 and 6 o'clock," which usually would have meant much nearer 6 than 5.

[87] Stuart (*O. R.*, 27, pt. 2, p. 681) stated that he ordered to Fleetwood "a section of artillery in reserve"; Beckham (*ibid.*, 772) reported that two guns had been placed by Stuart's order on "Pettis' Hill" which is the name he used for Fleetwood. McClellan (*op. cit.*, 269) said: "A six-pounder howitzer, from Chew's battery, under charge of Lieut. John W. Carter, which had been retired from the fight near the river because its ammunition was exhausted, was halted at the bottom of the hill . . ." This beyond doubt was the gun Beckham mentioned. though he insisted two were there.

[88] H. B. *McClellan*, 269–70.          [89] *O. R.*, 27, pt. 2, p. 681.

among the staff officers, and it was without a suggestion that McClellan's promptness had prevented the seizure by the enemy of the strongest position on the field of battle.[90]

Truth was, "Jeb" Stuart was humiliated more deeply than ever he had been in his campaigning, humiliated and, if not disillusioned, disconcerted. The Federal cavalry never had battled so hard and never had stood up so stubbornly. Most of the day, they had held the offensive and had given as good as they had taken.[91] Outwardly, Stuart would not admit it. He wrote, in fact, a flamboyant and congratulatory order in which he proclaimed a victory and assured his men that "nothing but the enemy's infantry, strongly posted in the woods, saved his cavalry from capture or annihilation." [92] Other participants were not so sure. The Federals boasted then and often thereafter that they had struck in time to prevent a raid that Stuart had planned to launch on June 10.[93] While this was not true, it hurt Stuart to think that the bluecoats at any time could hold him. He had fought his heaviest battle after thunderous, demonstrative reviews of more troops than ever had been under his command. Instead of a thrilling victory that every man in the Army would have to acclaim, there was sarcastic talk of an exposed rear and of a surprise!

The commanding General understood. Stuart was sure of that. On receipt of Stuart's report, which his enemies would have said was not entirely candid, Lee wrote: "The dispositions made by you to meet the strong attack of the enemy appear to have been judicious and well planned. The troops were well and skillfully managed, and with few exceptions conducted themselves with marked gallantry." [94] That was reassuring if not quite so laudatory as might be desired. Fair minded men took into account the final victory though they did not ignore the surprise. Stuart never saw what his West Point classmate, Dorsey Pender wrote, but he must have heard echoes of similar comment. Said Pender: "I suppose it is all right that Stuart should get all the blame, for when anything handsome is done he gets all the credit. A bad rule

90 *Ibid.*, 685.

91 "One result of incalculable importance certainly did follow this battle—it *made* the Federal cavalry. Up to that time confessedly inferior to the Southern horsemen, they gained on this day that confidence in themselves and in their commanders which enabled them to contest so fiercely the subsequent battlefields of June, July and October." H. B. McClellan, 294.

92 *O. R.*, 27, pt. 2, pp. 719-20.    93 *O. R.*, 27. pt. 1, pp. 903-04.

94 *O. R.*, 27, pt. 2, p. 687.

either way. He however retrieved the surprise by whipping them in the end." [95]

Surprise—that was the word on which that infernal *Examiner* harped in Richmond. The paper did not call Stuart by name, but it might as well have done so. Its words stuck in the mind:

The more the circumstances of the late affair at Brandy Station are considered, the less pleasant do they appear. If this was an isolated case, it might be excused under the convenient head of accident or chance. But this puffed up cavalry of the Army of Northern Virginia has been twice, if not three times, surprised since the battles of December, and such repeated accidents can be regarded as nothing but the necessary consequences of negligence and bad management. If the war was a tournament, invented and supported for the pleasure of a few vain and weak-headed officers, these disasters might be dismissed with compassion. But the country pays dearly for the blunders which encourage the enemy to overrun and devastate the land, with a cavalry which is daily learning to despise the mounted troops of the Confederacy. The surprise on this occasion was the most complete that has occurred. The Confederate cavalry was carelessly strewn over the country, with the Rappahannock only between it and an enemy who has already proven his enterprise to our cost. . . . In the end the enemy retired, or was driven, it is not yet clearly known which, across the river. Nor is it certainly known whether the fortunate result was achieved by the cavalry alone or with the assistance of Confederate infantry in the neighborhood. . . . Events of this description have been lately too frequent to admit of the supposition that they are the results of hazard. They are the effects of causes which will produce like effects while they are permitted to operate, and they require the earnest attention both of the chiefs of the Government and the heads of the Army. The enemy is evidently determined to employ his cavalry extensively, and has spared no pains or cost to perfect that arm. The only effective means of preventing the mischief it may do is to reorganize our own forces, enforce a stricter discipline among the men and insist on more earnestness among the officers in the discharge of their very important duty.[96]

That rankled . . . "tournament . . . vain and weak-headed officers . . . surprise . . . reorganization . . . more earnestness on the part of officers."

"Jeb" would show whether the criticism was justified! [97]

95 To Mrs. Pender, MS, June 12, 1863—*Pender MSS.*
96 *Richmond Examiner*, June 12, 1863, p. 2, col. 1.
97 The sketch of Stuart is continued, *infra*, p. 51.

# CHAPTER II

## As if a Second Jackson Had Come

Stuart's humiliation in the Battle of Brandy Station did not delay the advance of the Army of Northern Virginia toward the Potomac. On the 10th of June Ewell's Second Corps set the pace at a brisk staccato. By way of Gaines' Cross Roads, Chester Gap and Front Royal, the Divisions of Edward Johnson and Early reached the vicinity of Winchester on the 13th.[1] Their prey was a Federal force of an estimated 6000 to 8000 men under Maj. Gen. Robert H. Milroy. The Division of Rodes was directed to Berryville, where it was hoped he could capture an outpost of 1800. With Rodes moved the 1500 cavalry of Brig. Gen. Albert G. Jenkins. These troopers from Western Virginia were newcomers to the Valley and were unfamiliar with the discipline and the tactics of Stuart.[2]

Reconnaissance by Ewell on the hot, cloudy morning of June 14[3] showed no Federal troops anywhere near at hand except West of Winchester. There they held ground from which Ewell had planned to launch his attack[4] against the known fortified positions of the enemy to the North and Northwest. "Old Bald Head" did not swear at this discovery. He had broken that bad habit, which Mrs. Ewell had disapproved. Oaths did not become a professed Christian, successor to the sainted Jackson. So, instead of oaths, the crippled Ewell drove to Early's position South of the town.

When the corps commander found him, "Old Jube" had fight in his black eyes. He had seen the Federals, damn 'em, on that high ground he had coveted. They had a fort—call it the west fort[5]— on which they were throwing up dirt. East of it and nearer Winchester, at a distance of about 900 yards, they had another and a

---

[1] For the details of the advance, see *O. R.*, 27, pt. 2, pp. 440, 460, 547, 556; *Hotchkiss' MS Diary*, 207, 209; E. A. Moore, 179.
[2] They joined after the infantry had passed Crooked Run. *O. R.*, 27, pt. 2, p. 440; *Hotchkiss' MS Diary*, 207.
[3] *Hotchkiss' MS Diary*, 209.          [4] *O. R.*, 27, pt. 2, p. 440.
[5] This name does not appear on any of the maps or in any of the records. It is used here and is entered on the map simply to facilitate reference and to avoid confusion with the "Main" or "Flag Fort" and the "Star Fort," which were so styled at that time.

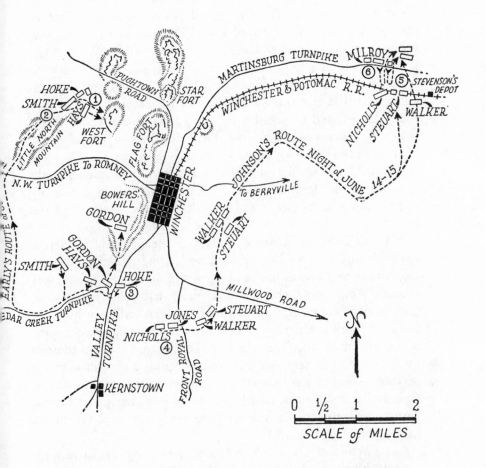

Battlefield of "Second Winchester," June 14–15, 1863, and of Stephenson's Depot, June 15, 1863—after Jed. Hotchkiss in *O. R. Atlas,* Plate XLIII–3. (1) and (2) artillery positions of Jones and Brown in Early's attack of June 14; (3) on the right of Hoke on June 13, and co-operating with Gordon on the 14th, was the small Maryland command, not here figured, of Lt. Col. J. R. Herbert; (4) Nicholls's and Jones's troops did not participate in the first advance of the Brigades of Steuart and of Walker on June 14 to the East of the town; (5) Dement's (Contee's) Battery was on either side of the bridge over the Winchester and Potomac Railroad; (6) Milroy's troops, turning South and attacking on June 15, fell back North of the railroad, where most of them were captured by Walker's Brigade. The Harpers Ferry turnout from the Martinsburg Turnpike was beyond the northeastern corner of this sketch. Harpers Ferry could be reached, also, by way of the Berryville Turnpike.

larger, which evidently was their main defense. North of this, across the Pughtown Road, they had other earthworks. One of them was a fort in the form of a star. This chain of fortifications was strong, *but*, Early explained, it was vulnerable! West of the position in the enemy's hands, the position Ewell had hoped to seize, was Little North Mountain. Although it was not a mountain and it did not run North, it afforded cover. From it, said Early, he believed he could silence the guns in the west fort, on which the enemy was laboring. That west fort commanded the main defense, the Flag Fort, as the Confederates already were styling it.[6] Early would move the greater part of his men secretly to Little North Mountain, would run out guns, would silence the west fort, would capture it and then drive the Federals out of the Flag Fort.[7]

"Old Bald Head" listened, surveyed the ground, pondered, assented promptly. In his report, Ewell wrote of Early, "I coincided with his views as to the best point of attack . . ." That was enough. Action followed decision. Early left John B. Gordon, the Maryland troops, and some guns on Bowers' Hill Southwest of the town. On the East, Ewell saw to it that Ed. Johnson occupied the enemy while "Jube" marched by a concealed, circuitous route to Little North Mountain. All was done as briskly and with as much decision as if Jackson himself were directing the movement.[8] It took until 4 P.M., but by that hour, unobserved, Early had Hays's, Smith's and part of Hoke's Brigade ready for deployment on Little North Mountain.[9]

At six o'clock or a little later—"about an hour by sun," according to "Old Jube's" reckoning [10]—"Dick" Ewell was awaiting the attack and jumping about more impatiently than ever on the eastern side of the town. Early's artillerists stood by the gun wheels in the edge of the wood. The infantry fought flies and speculated on what was going to happen, and cursed a country in which there was so little water.[11] From Hays, now, came word that he was deployed. Early snapped a command. The artillerists bent their backs to the wheels. Out into the open rolled twenty pieces—twelve to a

[6] *O. R.*, 27, pt. 2, p. 447.
[7] *O. R.*, 27, pt. 2, pp. 440, 460; *Early*, 244.
[8] For the details of Early's march and Johnson's demonstration, see *O. R.*, 27, pt. 2, pp. 440, 461, 462, 494, 516; *Early*, 244–45; *Hotchkiss' MS Diary*, 211.
[9] *O. R.*, 27, pt. 2, pp. 441, 461, 462, 477, 500.
[10] *O. R.*, 27, pt. 2, pp. 441, 462.          [11] Cf. *ibid.*, 462.

convenient orchard, eight to a cornfield that offered a clear field of fire. Almost in the same instant, all twenty guns roared, to the amazement of the startled Federals in the west fort. Back to the work ran bluecoats who had been watching Gordon's demonstration Southwest of the town. Then scarcely a head was to be seen in the fort,[12] but there was scant delay in meeting the challenge of Early's guns. Sixteen shells to the minute the Federals soon were sending.[13]

It was a gallant but not too long a duel. In forty-five minutes the Federal fire died away.[14] Now, Hays! He was off at the word and got within the anticipated distance of the west fort before the Unionists gave any evidence that he had been seen. In a few minutes he was through the abatis, his cheering men were leaping over the parapet, they had the guns, they were turning them; now they were firing on the bluecoats who were trying to re-form and to recapture the works. The fort was Hays's! Federal troops were running from two defenses on the left and were taking refuge in the Flag Fort.[15]

At his quarters on the Millwood Road, "Dick" Ewell had his field glasses glued to his eyes and, as he watched, he thought he saw "Jube" among the first to mount the parapet. In another instant, tears of excitement obscured Ewell's vision. "Hurrah for the Louisiana boys! There's Early! I hope the old fellow won't be hurt!" As he spoke, he felt a thud, a shock, and a momentary loss of balance. He had been hit squarely in the chest, but by a spent ball, which inflicted no worse hurt than a bruise.[16]

"Old Bald Head" got a scolding from his doctor, the faithful Hunter McGuire. It troubled Ewell not at all. His mind was on the probable effect of the capture of the west fort. That loss might induce Milroy to retreat under protecting darkness. If the Federals did not wait for another fight, then by the bones of the mighty "Stonewall," the enemy must be pursued. The decision was prompt; the choice of means and route was not long delayed. Milroy would have to leave Winchester via the Turnpike that ran northward. At Stephenson's Depot, about four miles from the town, he could turn northeastward toward Harpers Ferry or he could continue straight on to Martinsburg. Ed. Johnson, then,

12 *Ibid.*, 450, 462, 477.          13 *McKim*, 146.
14 *O. R.*, 27, pt. 2, p. 462.          15 *Ibid.*, 441, 462–63, 478.
16 *Gilmor*, 87.

must march in the night with the greater part of his Division and abundant artillery, and, at the nearest convenient place, must get across Milroy's line of withdrawal. If Milroy did not retreat, Johnson must be sufficiently close to Winchester to have a heavy hand at dawn in supporting Early.[17]

Put Johnson on the road; tell him to halt at a point about two miles and a half from Winchester.[18] As for Early, he was making dirt fly as he "turned the works from which the enemy had fled. He was putting his artillery into the forts, also, so that if Milroy still held the Flag Fort on the morning of the 15th, the attack could be renewed.[19]

Long before a night of baffling darkness[20] began to gray, "Allegheny" Johnson found his byway too rough. He consequently turned by a better road, toward Stephenson's Depot on the Winchester and Potomac Railroad. There, he was told, the Turnpike paralleled the railway and offered a strong position at which to meet an enemy who might be retreating either to Martinsburg or to Harpers Ferry. By 3:30 A.M., the head of Johnson's column reached a bridge over the railroad half a mile East of the station. Johnson halted the troops and, with his staff, pushed on to reconnoitre. In a moment, he heard the neighing of horses and the mumble of voices. Randolph McKim, riding ahead, had the welcome of pistol shots from a dim file he encountered in the road.[21]

Milroy it must be—and he must be bagged! Johnson did not hesitate. "Maryland" Steuart should go to the right; part of Nicholls's Louisianians should extend to the left, Walker with Jackson's old Brigade must . . . but Walker was not there. Nobody had seen him. Do without him, then. Twelve hundred men, the number at hand, were few for the task, but they could take shelter behind a stone wall now visible, and they could use the railroad cut as a parapet. Two guns of Dement's Battery could guard the bridge; the remaining artillery could take position on the edge of the woods on the left of the road.[22] Snowden Andrews was in command of this artillery: he needed no instructions.

[17] O. R., 27, pt. 2, pp. 441, 500.     [18] Ibid.
[19] O. R., 27, pt. 2, pp. 441, 463, 494. Ewell's headquarters for the night of June 14–15 were near Bowles' House on the Front Royal road, a few hundred yards from the Millwood Turnpike. O. R. Atlas, Plate XLIII–3; Hotchkiss' MS Diary, 211.
[20] O. R., 27, pt. 2, p. 501.     [21] McKim, 148; O. R., 27, pt. 2, pp. 441, 501.
[22] O. R., 27, pt. 2, pp. 441, 501, 502, 541.

Quick the deployment was, but none too quick, because now, with a cheer [23] and heavy volleys,[24] the Federals were attacking as if they were determined to cut their way through the Confederate line on the road to Harpers Ferry.[25] Such an attack was gore and glory for "Old Allegheny." He waved his long walking stick and he shouted encouragement to his troops,[26] over whose heads, fortunately, most of the Federal fire was passing.[27] Soon the Federals were repulsed, but they were able to keep within rifle range of the bridge and to shoot down one after another of the men of Dement's Battery. These soldiers were Marylanders. Their pride was at stake in a battle close to their own soil. They fought the more furiously as their numbers thinned. When the Federals tried to carry the bridge, the blast of the Southern guns was redoubled.[28] Manifestly, the enemy had no artillery.[29] Otherwise he would have opened on these defiant fieldpieces.

Milroy now was thought to be changing his tactics. If he neither could break the line nor carry the bridge, he must try to envelop the flanks. He made the effort at a time when some of the Confederates were down to their last cartridge,[30] but if he had a chance it vanished when Walker came up on the right. The commander of the Stonewall Brigade had not received notice of the Division's march, and had not started from Winchester till midnight.[31] On the outbreak of the firing, he still was a mile to the rear. Hastening forward, he formed on Steuart's flank. Two regiments of Nicholls's Brigade, who constituted the final reserve, were brought almost simultaneously to the front. The timing and the placing of these reinforcements were as perfect as a textbook example. Walker scarcely waited to let his men catch breath. Then he plunged forward. In the absence of Johnson from that part of the line, Steuart as senior officer directed the reserve regiments of Nicholls to advance with Walker.[32] Boldly, Snowden Andrews prepared to charge the enemy with a section of artillery, in the belief that he could dash through the ragged line and open from the rear of the Federals.[33] It was not necessary. "Colonel," cried

23 Ibid., 501.
25 O. R., 27, pt. 2, p. 441.
27 Ibid.
29 Ibid., 441.
31 O. R., 27, pt. 2, pp. 501–02, 517.
32 O. R., 27, pt. 2, pp. 441, 508, 512, 513.
33 O. R., 27, pt. 2, p. 542.

24 McKim, 149.
26 McKim, 149–50.
28 O. R., 27, pt. 2, pp. 501, 508, 512.
30 O. R., 27, pt. 2, pp. 501, 508.

Lieut. C. S. Contee, who had been shot in both legs while firing from the bridge, "I have a sergeant and two men, and the enemy is retreating."[34]

Milroy with 200 or 300 cavalry got away. The other Federal troops, confused by the swirling mêlée, began to surrender. Soon the prisoners numbered more than 2300.[35] "If we had been one hour sooner," grumbled Casler of the Stonewall Brigade, "we would have had our line formed across the road and captured the whole 'outfit.' "[36] Late as they considered themselves, some of the Southerners unhitched the teams from the wagons and galloped off down the Pike. Ostensibly, they were fired by zeal to catch the Federals who had scattered. Actually, confessed Casler, "they were after the wagon train ahead of the infantry, and made a fine capture."[37] Johnson himself could not refrain from the pursuit, and although he fell off his horse when the animal stumbled in Opequon Creek,[38] he asserted afterward that he had taken 30 prisoners "with his opera glass."[39]

Back in Winchester, Ewell had received word that the Federals had evacuated their works during the night. From that time, he had hoped that Johnson would waylay the retreating column. Now that "Old Bald Head" had the good news, he sent a message to Rodes to intercept the Federals if possible.[40] For his own part, Ewell made ready to resume on the 16th the advance to the Potomac. Almost in the words of Jackson, he called on the troops to "unite . . . in returning thanks to our Heavenly Father for the signal success which has crowned the valor of this command." Chaplains were directed to hold religious services "in acknowledgment of Divine favor," but as the day was Monday, Ewell thriftily enjoined that thanks be returned "at such times as may be most convenient."[41]

He lingered long enough in Winchester to attend a celebration on the afternoon of the 16th, when rejoicing soldiers ran up at the main fort, proudly renamed Fort Jackson, a flag made from captured Stars and Stripes. When ladies called on him for a speech, Ewell piped: "I can't make a speech to ladies. I never made a

34 Tunstall Smith, *R. Snowden Andrews*, 96.
35 *O. R.*, 27, pt. 2, p. 441.
36 *Casler*, 240.
37 *Ibid.*, 243.
38 *Douglas*, 242.
39 *Hotchkiss' MS Diary*, 213.
40 *O. R.*, 27, pt. 2, p. 442.
41 *O. R.*, 27, pt. 3, p. 894.

speech to but one lady in my life. My friend General Early"—and
he pointed to that warrior—"can speak. He will address you,
ladies." Early was not to be outdone: "I never have been able to
make a speech to one lady," the bachelor shot back, "much less to
so many." [42]

The two could afford to jest. Their Provost Marshals had cor-
raled by that hour a total of 3358 prisoners.[43] Ordnance officers had
the whole of Milroy's artillery—four 20-pounder Parrotts, seventeen 3-inch rifles and two 24-pounder howitzers.[44] More than that
scarcely could have been asked in compensation for Confederate
losses that did not exceed 269.[45] "This," said Jed. Hotchkiss, "has
been one of the most complete successes of the war; our men behaved splendidly." [46] Honors were equally divided. The general
plan had been that of Ewell, who knew the ground thoroughly;
the execution had been Early's and Johnson's. In recognition of
what had been accomplished on the 14th, Ewell put "Old Jube"
temporarily in command of Winchester,[47] and in his report he
wrote explicitly of the attack on the west fort, "This result established the correctness of Early's views as to the point of attack, and
rendered the main fort untenable." [48]

Enough of flag raising and yelling and felicitation! The mission
of the Second Corps was not in Winchester but across the Potomac.
Rodes already was there with his Division. On the 13th, he had
started for Berryville in the hope of capturing that post, but he
was inexperienced in the employment of cavalry. His cavalry
commander, Brig. Gen. Albert G. Jenkins, was unaccustomed to
operating with infantry that marched as fast as Rodes's men did.
Through poor co-operation, the Federals escaped from Berryville.
Much the same thing happened in front of Martinsburg, which was
entered on the 14th. The next day, Jenkins pushed boldly across
the Potomac and headed for Pennsylvania. Rodes followed on the
16th as far as Williamsport on the Maryland side of the river, but
there he was to remain till the other Divisions overtook him and
his men found some relief for their bruised feet.[49]

Ewell did not keep Rodes waiting long. On the evening of the

[42] *Old Bald Head,* 140, with Early's retort from *Hotchkiss' MS Diary,* 213.
[43] *O. R.,* 27, pt. 2, p. 464.               [44] *Ibid.,* 456.
[45] *Ibid.,* 442.
[46] Letter to his wife, June 15, 1863—*Hotchkiss Papers.*
[47] *O. R.,* 27, pt. 2, p. 464.               [48] *Ibid.,* 441.
[49] Rodes's report, abundant in all needful detail, is in *O. R.,* 27, pt. 2, pp. 547-50.

16th, corps headquarters were at Boyd's near Bunker Hill.[50] The 17th—a hot day with a high wind and much dust [51] witnessed "a most oppressive march." [52] By the evening of the 18th, Johnson was encamped on the old battlefield of Sharpsburg.[53] Early, having started his prisoners southward, was en route to Shepherdstown.[54] In accordance with new orders from Lee,[55] sunset of the 19th found the van of the Second Corps near Hagerstown and the rear on the southern shore of the Potomac.[56] Jackson himself would not have been ashamed of that advance in June weather.

Through all of this, Ewell was brisk and diligent. On the afternoon of the 21st, he notified Lee that he was ready to move the entire Corps northward. Permission came promptly [57] and with it a suggestion that, if food could be found, the Army might follow into the enemy's country. Said Lee: "Your progress and direction will, of course, depend upon the development of circumstances. If Harrisburg comes within your means, capture it." [58] The strategy behind these orders was Lee's, not Ewell's, but the aim of the proposed operations was plain: Lee was hoping to lure the Army of the Potomac out of Virginia and to subsist his own forces during the summer on the rich abundance of Pennsylvania. He also sought an opportunity of striking a blow and even of compelling the Federal administration to retain in the East, or to recall, troops designated for operations elsewhere. By a vigorous campaign of maneuver, the enemy's plans for the hot months might be disarranged. Virginia might be free of an enemy who destroyed what he did not consume.[59]

Ewell's part in this was understood, from the outset, to be essentially that of collecting horses and cattle and flour. As it concerned him, the enterprise was primarily an offensive for the bene-

---

[50] *Hotchkiss' MS Diary*, 213.
[52] *McKim*, 155.
[54] *Ibid.*, 464.
[56] *Ibid.*, 442–43, 464, 551.

[51] *Ibid.*, 215.
[53] *O. R.*, 27, pt. 2, pp. 442, 464, 503.
[55] *O. R.*, 27, pt. 3, pp. 900–01.

[57] Ewell in his report, *O. R.*, 27, pt. 2, p. 443, wrote that on the afternoon of the 21st, he received orders "to take Harrisburg," but Lee's letter of the 22nd (*O. R.*, 27, pt. 3, p. 914) reads as if it were the first in which Lee formally authorized the advance of the entire Second Corps. Until the 19th (cf. *ibid.*, 905), and possibly until the 20th, Lee had not felt that he had supports near enough to permit the rear Division of Ewell to abandon the line of the Potomac. In 3 *R. E. Lee*, 40, an error was made as respects the position of Early. He was not in Maryland, but had reached Shepherdstown on the 19th and remained there until the 22nd, when he crossed (*O. R.*, 27, pt. 2, p. 464).

[58] *O. R.*, 27, pt. 3, p. 914.

[59] Lee's plan is sketched with some reticence in his report (*O. R.*, 27, pt. 2, p. 305). Details and attendant circumstances are set forth in 3 *R. E. Lee*, 18 ff.

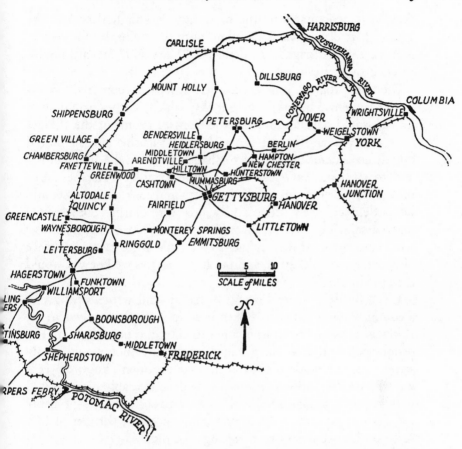

Routes from the Potomac to Carlisle, Harrisburg, Gettysburg and York—after Jed. Hotchkiss in *O. R. Atlas*, Plate CXVI-1.

fit of the commissary; "Old Bald Head" was to be a glorified Major Hawkes and Major Harman combined. That was not quite all. Latest instructions were more soldierly. The suggestion that he might be able to capture Harrisburg became in Ewell's eager mind orders to do so.

Even before he received Lee's instructions on the 22nd,[60] Ewell had started Johnson and Rodes for Greencastle, Pennsylvania; but that evening he recalled Rodes to headquarters between Boonsborough and Hagerstown,[61] and discussed with him the choice of lines of advance. Lee had suggested three.[62] In complying, Ewell

[60] *O. R.*, 27, pt. 3, p. 910.     [61] At Beaver Creek. *O. R.*, 27, pt. 2, p. 551.
[62] *O. R.*, 27, pt. 3, p. 914.

decided to send Early by the most easterly and Rodes's and the greater part of Johnson's Division, with the trains, by the central highways. One Brigade only, that of "Maryland" Steuart, he dispatched by westerly roads.[63]

On these routes, June 23–24, the troops encountered no organized enemy, but they met looks, which, if they could have killed, would have annihilated the Corps. In some of the villages near the border, the residents showed surprise but submitted quietly to orders [64] which were shaped to spare the unoffending and to curb the vandal in the Southern ranks.[65] As the Corps moved deeper into the enemy's country and took sleek horses and fat cattle, faces grew sullen and words were sharp.[66] Some of the natives, said John Casler, "would look very sour at us, when we would ask them for their names so we could write them on a piece of paper, so we told them, and put it in water as we knew it would turn to vinegar." [67]

Ewell himself noted the acid in the air and wrote teasingly to a cousin whose mother had been born in York, Pennsylvania: "It is like a renewal of Mexican times to enter a captured town. The people look as sour as vinegar and, I have no doubt, would gladly send us all to Kingdom come if they could. I don't know as yet if we will get to York—anyhow, we will be tolerably close to it. I will let your relations off tolerably easy on your account—probably not taking more than a few forks and spoons and trifles of that sort—no houseburning or anything like that." [68]

The fatness of the land amazed the Confederates, precisely as it had Stuart's troopers in the raid of October, 1862. "It's like a hole full of blubber to a Greenlander," Ewell chirped.[69] Said Jed. Hotchkiss: "The land is full of everything and we have an abundance." [70] General needs were met by forced purchase or by formal requisition on the towns.[71] This system applied even to a matter of some twenty-five barrels of sauerkraut, concerning which the worthies of Chambersburg showed sensitiveness.[72] Far more

---

[63] O. R., 27, pt. 2, p. 443.
[64] Hotchkiss' MS Diary, 217.
[65] O. R., 27, pt. 2, p. 551; pt. 3, p. 914.
[66] Hotchkiss' MS Diary, 219.
[67] Casler, 247.
[68] Hamlin's Ewell, 121.
[69] Jed. Hotchkiss to his wife, June 25, 1863—Hotchkiss Papers.
[70] Hotchkiss' MS Diary, 219.
[71] O. R., 27, pt. 2, p. 443.
[72] Old Bald Head, 141–42, with quotation from Hoke, The Great Invasion of Pennsylvania.

popular were the abundant ripe cherries.[73] "It is wonderful," Ewell wrote, "how well our hungry, foot-sore, ragged men behave in this land of plenty—better than at home." [74]

Daily as the columns advanced, "Old Bald Head" called fcr maps, maps and more maps,[75] and he studied how to scour the country for the supplies Lee expected him to collect. On such a mission the Corps could not move rapidly, but Ewell continued to regard as an order Lee's permission to take Harrisburg if he could. On the 25th, probably, Ewell received instructions to keep one Division East of the mountains. This was to be done to deter the Federal Army, if it crossed the Potomac, from moving westward before Lee could concentrate. In addition, Lee suggested or Ewell himself decided that the troops placed East of the dividing mountains could undertake to destroy the bridge across the Susquehanna at Wrightsville, which was a short distance Northeast of York.[76]

While this mission was in process of execution, "Old Bald Head" moved without resistance toward Carlisle, which he reached on the 27th of June.[77] "Jube" Early had a more diverting adventure. At the outset, on leaving Greenwood, he directed that the nearby ironworks of Thaddeus Stevens be burned. In the venom this act aroused in Stevens's heart, it was an expensive fire for the South and it entailed a long account of woe during reconstruction. At the time, it seemed to Early a fitting reprisal for like destruction wrought in the Confederacy by Northern troops. "This I did on my own responsibility," Early was careful to record, "as neither General Lee nor General Ewell knew I would encounter these works." [78]

From Greenwood, via Cashtown, Early proceeded to Gettysburg, where he stampeded a regiment of raw Pennsylvania militia

---

[73] Hotchkiss' MS Diary, 219; 2 N. C. Regts., 234.

[74] To Miss Lizzie Ewell, Hamlin's Ewell, 121.

[75] Hotchkiss' MS Diary, 219.

[76] It seems almost impossible, on the basis of known evidence, to be explicit concerning the time Ewell was ordered to send a Division East of the mountains, or when the plan for the destruction of the Columbia (Wrightsville) Bridge was formulated. In Early, 255, the language would suggest that the whole plan originated with Lee, but this is not clearly to be inferred from Lee's report (O. R., 27, pt. 2, p. 307) or from Ewell's (ibid., 443). It is entirely possible that the advance as far as York was Ewell's own addition to the plan of the commanding General.

[77] O. R., 27, pt. 2, p. 443.

[78] Early, 256. Stevens's ironworks were at Caledonia, fifteen miles West of Gettysburg and about three miles East of the present Black's Gap, which was Greenwood on Lee's map.

and camped for the night. He undertook to levy contribution of supplies or of money on the town but got only a few boxes of freight that had not been removed from the railway station.[79] The next morning, June 27, he advanced toward York. If that day were typical of others in Pennsylvania, one farmer after another came out to the road and made mysterious gestures to the passing troops. What this mummery implied, Early was curious to know. Upon inquiry, he found that the Army had been preceded by sundry imaginative gentry who, for a consideration, had disclosed to natives certain "signs" the employment of which would protect a family and its belongings from molestation by the terrible, oncoming "rebels." [80]

A different price the people of York were prepared to pay. After Gordon encamped at nightfall of the 27th four miles from the town, a committee of citizens arrived and made formal surrender of the place. On the 28th, while Early moved to cut off any retreating enemy, Gordon entered York. As his men hurried through the town en route to Columbia Bridge, they were so dust-covered and wild in appearance that they scared the women,[81] but "Extra Billy" Smith, who commanded the leading Brigade of Early's own column, atoned in his own fashion. When he saw that the people were thronging the way, Smith sent back for "those tooting fellows," as he called his bandsmen. On their arrival, blaring "Dixie," he had them change to "Yankee Doodle." Then he rode out in front of his staff and proceeded in his triumph through the streets. He bowed, he smiled, he displayed so genial and courteous a mien that by the time he reached the centre of the town, he had elicited some cheers. These he accepted immediately as an invitation to make a speech. Oblivious of the rear Brigades, he stopped the column and directed the men to stack arms. Next he loosed a bantering, half-joking flow of eloquence to the effect that warm weather in Virginia had led his men to "take an outing" in Pennsylvania. He was in the flood of this, to his own manifest satisfaction and to the amusement of his auditors, when a volley of oaths roared down the street as "Jube" Early sought wrathfully to make his way through the ranks that Smith's deliverance had

[79] Much detail of these incidents will be found in *Early*, 256, and in M. Jacobs *Notes on the Invasion of Maryland and Pennsylvania and the Battle of Gettysburg* (cited hereafter as *Jacobs*), 20.
[80] *Early*, 265.                         [81] *Gordon*, 143.

halted. At last, with many weird explosions of unpremeditated profanity, "Old Jube" reached the still declaiming Smith.

"General Smith," Early demanded, "what the devil are you about, stopping the head of the column in this cursed town?"

Smith's answer was naïve and unruffled: "Having a little fun, General, which is good for all of us, and at the same time teaching these people something that will be good for them and won't do us any harm." [82]

There was no quarreling with a man who talked in that manner. Early got the column moving, made requisition of cash in the sum of $28,000 [83] and, before night, rode on to Wrightsville. [84] Gordon, as always, had marched fast, and had received from some secret Southern sympathizer an accurate report of where he might expect to meet the Federal militia and how he best could approach the Susquehanna. [85] All this information Gordon had found accurate and relevant; but, before he could seize both ends of the long bridge, the enemy set it afire. [86] Early was disappointed. He had been planning ambitiously to cross the river via Columbia Bridge, to cut the Pennsylvania Central Railroad, and to assail Harrisburg in rear while Ewell attacked from the South. "In the worst contingency that might arise," said Early later, he would rely "upon being able to mount my Division from the immense number of horses that had been run across the river, and then move to the West, destroying the railroads and canals, and returning back again to a place of safety." [87]

Now all such grandiose plans were frustrated. Ewell's adventure, too, was approaching a climax far different from that which "Old Bald Head" had planned or wished. As he approached Carlisle from Chambersburg, Ewell had continued to collect cattle. The number sent back for the subsistence of the two Corps that were following him had totaled 3000. Ewell was pleased but, naturally, was more interested in reaching the State capital. The day he entered Carlisle, he proceeded immediately to send Jenkins and the corps engineer to reconnoitre the defenses of Harrisburg.

[82] *Stiles*, 203–05.          [83] *Jacobs*, 20–21.
[84] *O. R.*, 27, pt. 2, p. 466.          [85] *Gordon*, 143, 147.
[86] *O. R.*, 27, pt. 2, p. 466. Although the Confederates, with much exertion, were able to save the greater part of Wrightsville from the spread of the fire, they were accused subsequently of trying to destroy the town. Cf. *O. R.*, 27, pt. 2, p. 492; *Gordon*, 148–49; *Early*, 260.
[87] *O. R.*, 27, pt. 2, p. 467.

Busy as he was that Saturday, he found time to receive a number
of ministers who had a question of conscience to ask: Would he
object if they prayed on the Sabbath, as rubric required, for the
President of the United States?

"Certainly not," chirped Ewell. "Pray for him. I'm sure he needs
it!" [88]

While the good townsfolk prayed, Ewell on the Sabbath had
his own halting devotions and, in the afternoon, was a central
figure in the raising of the Confederate flag over the famous old
Carlisle Barracks, where so many cavalrymen had served. A great
event that flag-raising was. Gen. Isaac R. Trimble, who knew
Pennsylvania better than did any of the other Confederates, had
arrived at Carlisle full of fight. As there was no command for him,
he offered his services as voluntary aide to Ewell.[89] He of course
had observations to make to Pennsylvanians on an occasion so
historic as the hoisting of the Stars and Bars at Carlisle. Rodes,
also, and the newly arrived Brigadier Junius Daniel made what
Hotchkiss termed "remarks," a word that usually suggests the
hope of a brief speech and the fear of a long.[90] Ewell himself
spoke a few words—he was no orator—but his mind remained on
Harrisburg, not on Carlisle. If Jenkins's reconnaissance was favorable, Ewell was resolved to start his infantry the next day for the
Susquehanna. The new month must yield a new prize, the handsomest the Confederacy yet had won.

Jenkins's report on the 29th was encouraging.[91] Orders accordingly were given Rodes to start for Harrisburg during the afternoon, which proved somewhat rainy.[92] Expectation in Carlisle
was mounting to excitement when, from the South, there arrived
a headquarters courier. He brought a letter written in haste at
Lee's order: The Federal Army, said the commanding General,
was reported to have crossed the Potomac and to have reached
Frederick, Maryland. Ewell must move southward and rejoin the

[88] *Douglas*, 246. An over-elaborate version of the incident is in *Stiles*, 205–06.
[89] *Old Bald Head*, 143. Trimble had not been willing to remain in charge of the
quiet Valley District while battle was predicted in Maryland and in Pennsylvania. On the
22nd, he reported himself fit for field duty. When Lee could offer him nothing more
than Jenkins's Brigade and the Maryland Line as a command, Trimble decided, apparently,
to join the invading forces and to perform whatever duty he could. See *O. R.*, 27, pt. 3,
p. 923.
[90] *Hotchkiss' MS Diary*, 221.
[91] *O. R.*, 27, pt. 2, p. 551.
[92] *Hotchkiss' MS Diary*, 221.

other Corps. Early, too, must conform.[93] For the first recorded time during the expedition, the married and converted Ewell of the summer of 1863 reverted to the bachelor, unregenerate Ewell of Jackson's Valley campaign. He did not swear, but he did not pretend to conceal his displeasure at being compelled to forgo an advance on Harrisburg. As soon as practicable, he started Johnson's Division for Chambersburg and he prepared for Rodes to follow.[94] Orders were dispatched immediately for Early to leave the vicinity of York and to rejoin the Corps West of the mountains.[95]

After Johnson had gone some miles, there came new orders from Lee: Instead of reconcentrating at Chambersburg, the Army should assemble around Gettysburg.[96] There, East of the mountains, it seemed preferable to challenge the enemy. This change of unpleasant orders upset Ewell still further. He had now to advance through an unfamiliar country at the same time that he had to abandon the advance on Harrisburg. Besides, Lee put on him a responsibility of choice concerning a matter regarding which he was ignorant. Lee said: "When you come to Heidlersburg, you can either move directly on Gettysburg or turn down to Cash-

[93] On the night of the 27th, Lee sent one courier with orders for Ewell to countermarch to Chambersburg. A second letter was written at 7:30 on the morning of the 28th and was dispatched so hastily from Lee's headquarters at Chambersburg that no copy was made. This letter directed that Ewell move toward Gettysburg, rather than Chambersburg, because Lee thought "it preferable to keep on the east side of the mountains" (*O. R.*, 27, pt. 3, pp. 943–44). From the somewhat limited references available, it would appear that the first of these letters prompted the movement of Johnson and the second of them shaped the itinerary of Rodes. During the revived "Gettysburg controversy" (D. S. Freeman, *The South to Posterity*, 169), Col. John S. Mosby based part of his argument on the dating of these two dispatches (*Stuart's Cavalry in the Gettysburg Campaign*, 117 ff), and he maintained that Ewell must have received on the 28th Lee's order of the 27th (*ibid.*, 122). All the existing evidence is that the letter of the 27th, written at night, did not reach Ewell until the 29th. If it had arrived on the 28th, Ewell would not have had a fruitless reconnaissance of Harrisburg made on the morning of the 29th. Nor is it in any degree probable that if he had received on the 28th orders to return to Chambersburg, he would have delayed execution until the 29th. *Hotchkiss' MS Diary*, 221, and Rodes's report (*O. R.*, 27, pt. 2, pp. 551–52) virtually preclude even the possibility that orders to turn southward arrived at Ewell's headquarters on the 28th. Ewell's report (*ibid.*, 443) is phrased as if the only orders received by him were those that reached Carlisle on the 29th and directed the march on Cashtown. Dispatch of Johnson to Chambersburg, as set forth in the text, shows that the orders of the night of June 27 were received prior to those of June 28, otherwise Johnson would not have been started for the objective which was mentioned in the letter of the 27th but was changed by the letter of the 28th.

[94] *Hotchkiss' MS Diary*, 221.

[95] Early's brief description of these orders, and of an enclosed "copy of a note from General Lee," is confirmatory evidence that Ewell's first orders of the 29th were based on Lee's instructions of the night of June 27 for a return of the Second Corps to Chambersburg, which is West of the mountains. See *O. R.*, 27, pt. 2, p. 467.

[96] *O. R.*, 27, pt. 3. p. 943.

town." [97] Ewell was disturbed that Lee should have made that discretionary. Hotchkiss had to write in his diary: "The General was quite testy and hard to please, because disappointed, and had everyone flying around. I got up in the night to answer questions and make him a map." [98]

Ewell decided that Johnson should continue toward Chambersburg to protect the trains [99] and, having done that, should turn at Green Village. This arranged, Ewell, on the morning of the 30th of June, obediently if unhappily ordered Rodes to start toward Gettysburg. During the days at Carlisle, Ewell had not damaged the town and had countenanced no violence on private individuals. The worst that had been done, to his knowledge, was what Edward Johnson might have termed a work of necessity. Many of "Old Allegheny's" men had been barefooted; most of them were road-worn; [100] the prisoners had been well shod. This had suggested an exchange. En route to Carlisle, Johnson had lined up his captured Pennsylvania militiamen in their new Federal uniforms and had relieved them of their shoes and socks for the benefit of his soldiers. John Casler recalled: "Some of our men thought it was cruel, but Johnson said they were going home and could get other shoes quicker than he could, as he had work for his men to do." [101] Ed. Moore was amused, rather than shocked. Said he of the prisoners: ". . . they were greatly crestfallen . . . After losing their footgear all spirit seemed to have gone out of them. They lingered, it may be, in anticipation of the greeting when met by wives and little ones at home, after having sallied forth so valiantly in their defense. How embarrassing bare feet would be instead of the expected trophies of war." [102] On this episode, so far as is known, Ewell had no comment, but he added to it no indignity, no hardship to the townspeople. "Agreeably to the views of the General commanding," he reported later, "I did not burn Carlisle Barracks." [103]

To Heidlersburg, on the road to Gettysburg, "Dick" Ewell made his way before sundown on June 30.[104] This easy march had a disconcerting end. In a note which another headquarters courier delivered, Ewell was told again by Lee to move to Cashtown or

[97] Ibid.
[99] O. R., 27, pt. 2, p. 450.
[101] Casler, 253.
[103] O. R., 27, pt. 2, p. 443.

[98] Op. cit., 221.
[100] McKim, 166.
[102] E. A. Moore, 185.
[104] 26 S.H.S.P., 122.

to Gettysburg as circumstances might dictate.[105] Ewell received also
a message from A. P. Hill who said that he was at Cashtown and
that the enemy's cavalry and probably other troops in undetermined strength had been observed that day at Gettysburg.[106] In
this state of affairs, Ewell was perplexed. As Ewell puzzled over his
discretionary orders, he was relieved to see Early ride over from a
point three miles distant where "Jube's" Division had camped for
the night. Rodes and Trimble, as well as Early, were called to informal council. Lee's orders were read again and again. On them
Ewell commented sharply. He was as outspoken and caustic as
he had been in the Spring of 1862 in his criticism of Jackson's
mysterious orders. The more Ewell talked, the more did he confuse the issue. Trimble alone had a suggestion based on the
realities. He had seen Lee on the 27th and had discussed with the
commanding General the geography of that part of Pennsylvania.
Lee intended, said Trimble, to assail the advance of the enemy.
If Federals were in Gettysburg, Lee would want Ewell there.[107]
Ewell fumed and protested, but decided nothing that night.

If Ewell was disturbed, his chief was not. Nor were "Old Bald
Head's" division commanders. They were more than satisfied
with their new leader. After three weeks of high distinction and
of well-nigh flawless performance, his first period of semi-independent service as head of the Second Corps was about to end.
Ewell had started June 10 from the upper Rappahannock; he had
been recalled June 29 when Jenkins was shelling Federal works on
the Susquehanna. Twenty-eight guns [108] and close to 4000 prisoners had been captured. Besides all the food, mounts and quartermasters' supplies seized and issued in Pennsylvania to Ewell's own
men, some 5000 barrels of flour, in addition to the 3000 cattle,
had been located for the Chief Commissary of the Army. A train-
load of ordnance and medical stores had been dispatched from
Chambersburg.[109] All this had been achieved with losses that
scarcely exceeded 300 and with straggling so limited in scale that

---

105 *O. R.*, 27, pt. 2, p. 444.
106 Trimble, *loc. cit.*, wrote that Ewell had information the XI Corps was at Gettysburg, but A. P. Hill's report, *O. R.*, 27, pt. 2, p. 607, stated correctly the intelligence Hill
sent Ewell, who had from no other source any news of the enemy's movements.
107 Trimble in 26 *S.H.S.P.*, 122.
108 In addition to the twenty-three captured at Winchester by Ewell, five had been
taken by Rodes at Martinsburg. *O. R.*, 27, pt. 2, p. 549.
109 *O. R.*, 27, pt. 2, p. 443.

it found no mention in reports. Of the logistics, one young soldier testified: "Our march had been admirably conducted. We were always on the road at an early hour and, without hurry or the usual halts caused by troops crowding on one another, we made good distances each day and were in camp by sunset. I never before or afterward saw the men so buoyant . . . The horses, too, invigorated by abundant food, carried higher heads and pulled with firmer tread." [110] Ewell's was the first credit for his men's morale. Without storming or scolding he had directed wisely and had executed promptly. His first operations as a corps commander seemed to duplicate, if not to outdo, the cherished accomplishments of the dead "Stonewall." As Ewell approached Gettysburg, almost every Confederate soldier would have asserted that a fitting successor to Jackson had been found. Except for his grumbling over discretionary orders, Ewell at no time during the campaign had given the least evidence of any lack of decision. On the contrary, his "Yes" and his "No," his "Do" and his "Do not" had been clear and instant.[111]

[110] *E. A. Moore,* 184–85.
[111] The sketches of Ewell and of his subordinates are resumed *infra*, Chapter V.

# CHAPTER III

## LONGSTREET DEVELOPS A THEORY

THE SECOND of Lee's lieutenants whose state of mind was to influence the operations in Pennsylvania had shared two victories and one drawn battle after the Army in August, 1862, had left Richmond. In all three of those contests, Second Manassas, Sharpsburg and Fredericksburg, James Longstreet had been most fortunate. He had been able to take a defensive position and to receive the enemy's assaults. At Second Manassas, the attack had been on Jackson, but Longstreet's counterstroke of August 30 had been demolishing. Narrowly the following month, on the heights above the Antietam, "Peter" Longstreet had beaten back with discouraging Union losses the onslaught of the enemy and, outnumbered, he had recrossed the Potomac with all his guns and most of his wounded. Fredericksburg, from his position, had been a triumph of the defensive.

On this foundation of experience, Longstreet reared a tactical theory that if the Confederates could be maneuvered to commanding ground, close to their adversaries, the Federals always could be induced to attack. Longstreet built up, also, a conviction that a small Southern force, comparatively, could repulse any charge the Union Army could deliver. Most fully he subscribed to Jackson's observation: "We sometimes fail to drive the enemy from a position; they always fail to drive us." [1]

While he was developing this theory of a superior tactical defensive, Longstreet watched intently the operations in Tennessee and the Gulf States. He followed in newspapers the reports of Braxton Bragg's withdrawal to Tullahoma after the battle of Stone's River; with regretful eye, Longstreet already had read of Hindman's defeat at Prairie Grove, and he doubtless wondered where the Confederacy could find the reinforcements for Pemberton at Vicksburg.

In speculating on the future employment of the divided forces

[1] *Annals,* 417.

39

of Pemberton and of Bragg, who were under Joseph E. Johnston's titular command, Longstreet made his first known venture in grand strategy. There was nothing sensational about the plan he evolved. It simply was to rely boldly upon the defensive power of the Army of Northern Virginia and to utilize the inner lines of the Confederacy. He concluded that half of Lee's forces could remain defiantly on the line of the Rappahannock, and that the other half could reinforce Bragg and help in destroying Rosecrans. Then all the strength the Confederacy commanded in a wide region could be turned against the Federal Divisions that were mustering to capture the strategic town of Vicksburg.

A part, at least, of this plan, which manifestly was more readily drafted than executed, its author communicated to Lee on the 23rd of January. Longstreet must have regarded the date and the proposal as important because, more than two months later, he recalled precisely when he had put his plan before the commanding General.[2] One implication of this theory in March had been that Lee could afford to dispatch the two remaining Divisions of the First Corps to the line of the Blackwater in Southside Virginia where, it will be recalled, Longstreet had been operating with Pickett and Hood. "I think it utterly impossible," Longstreet told his chief then, "for the enemy to move against your position until the roads are sufficiently dry for him to move around you and turn your position."[3] For these, as for other suggestions from his general officers, Lee expressed his thanks, but he could not agree to march additional troops to the vicinity of Suffolk and to leave no more than one Corps of infantry, with some cavalry, between Richmond and the enemy. Longstreet was not offended by Lee's unwillingness to send the other units of the First Corps to him. Nor was Longstreet shaken in his conviction that he had a sound plan.

When the summons came on April 29 for Longstreet to evacuate the Suffolk front and to return to the Rappahannock, he explained promptly that his wagons were at a distance from him and that he could not start his infantry until the trains were assembled and

[2] The proposal of January 23 must have been verbal. No record of it has been found, but the substance of it he must have epitomized when he said in April: "I have thought since about January 23 last (when I made the same suggestion to you) that one Army Corps could hold the line of the Rappahannock while the other was operating elsewhere." O. R., 18, 959.

[3] O. R., 18, 950. Cf. Longstreet to D. H. Hill, ibid., 1047.

sent to the rear. Subsequently he wrote: "The calls became so frequent and so urgent . . . that I inquired if we should abandon our trains. To this no answer came: and I was left to the exercise of my own judgment." [4] This statement would indicate that he did not receive or else had forgotten, when he wrote, the telegram the Adjutant General dispatched him on the 30th: "The order sent you was to secure all possible dispatch without incurring loss of train or unnecessary hazard of troops." [5] General French, who scarcely could have been accounted an impartial witness, insisted that Longstreet was slow in returning to Lee,[6] but neither Hood [7] nor the commanding General thought that Longstreet had delayed beyond the necessities of the situation.[8] Whether or not the start could fairly be considered dilatory, the march was satisfactory. Longstreet noted that some of his troops covered thirty-four miles in a single night.[9]

The arrival of Longstreet in Petersburg, on his withdrawal from the Blackwater, was in circumstances that emphasized his importance in the eyes of the administration. Gen. George Stoneman, who had left General Hooker's front immediately before the opening of the Battle of Chancellorsville, was raiding widely to the North and Northwest of Richmond. It was any man's guess where the Union cavalry, whose numbers were reported large, would strike.[10] To meet an attack on Richmond itself, Arnold Elzey was doing all his physical condition permitted; but after the raiders were reported within eight miles of the capital,[11] there was comfort to the War Department in the knowledge that a soldier of Longstreet's experienced ability was at hand. He himself was alarmed, for a moment, that Petersburg might be assailed,[12] but he never lost his reassuring composure, and he swiftly ordered the necessary disposition of troops and obstruction of roads.[13] As it happened, Stoneman halted his advance and was preparing to withdraw by the time Longstreet reached Petersburg.[14]

Unaware that the raid was ending, Longstreet went to Richmond on the evening of May 5 [15] and the next day conferred with

4 *Longstreet*, 326.
5 *O. R.*, 18, 1035.
6 *French*, 170.
7 *Hood*, 52.
8 *O. R.*, 18, 1049.
9 *O. R.*, 25, pt. 2, pp. 777–78.
10 *Cf.* Longstreet, *O. R.*, 18, 1046.
11 Hungary Station, now Laurel, *O. R.*, 25, pt. 2, p. 775.
12 *O. R.*, 25, pt. 2, p. 778.
13 *O. R.*, 18, 1046 ff.
14 *O. R.*, 25, pt. 1, pp. 1061–62.
15 *O. R.*, 25, pt. 2, p. 1045.

the President. On a review of all that was known of the position of the Federals, Davis thought Longstreet should proceed at once to rejoin the Army on the Rappahannock. Longstreet did not take that view. He believed that the restoration of Lee's railway communications, which Stoneman had cut, was the most important task to be performed at the moment. "[I] fear," he said, "that this may not be accomplished if I leave it unfinished." [16] Nor was he satisfied that the threat to the city was past. Accordingly, he asked and received permission to remain for a day or two in Richmond.

That brief halt at the Confederate capital set another stone of conviction on the path of James Longstreet The Secretary of War, James A. Seddon, was a man who had great art in making his guests feel that their opinions were desired on public questions. Sometimes, perhaps, he flattered by consulting. When Longstreet called, the Secretary welcomed him and, among other things, spoke of the difficulty of collecting troops and supplies in Mississippi for the relief of Vicksburg. At some stage of the conversation, the possibility of sending the whole or a part of Longstreet's Corps to reinforce Johnston was mentioned.[17]

The suggestion led Longstreet to present the theory he had been cherishing since January: To attempting the direct relief of Vicksburg, said Longstreet, the Confederacy had a simpler and an easier alternative. Johnston might take his force at Jackson, Mississippi, and advance to Tullahoma, where Bragg's Army was awaiting a move by Rosecrans. Simultaneously, Longstreet could take his Corps [18] or the two Divisions of it then returning to Lee [19] and could proceed by rail to Tullahoma.[20] These two converging columns, said Longstreet, would make Johnston strong enough to crush Rosecrans and then would permit a march for Ohio. As soon as the North faced the prospect of invasion, Longstreet continued, Grant would be recalled from Vicksburg to defend Ohio. The whole operation, Longstreet concluded, simply meant the

[16] *O. R.*, 18, 1050.

[17] This statement unfortunately has to be vague because of differences between Longstreet's narrative in *Annals*, 415–16, and that in *Longstreet*, 327–28, though the difference did not concern the major proposal by Longstreet for the reinforcement of Bragg.

[18] *Annals*, 416.

[19] *Longstreet*, 327. It is not known why, in his second account of this interview, Longstreet referred to two Divisions, though in the earlier narrative he mentioned the entire First Corps.

[20] The route, via the Virginia and Tennessee Railroad and thence by Knoxville and Chattanooga, was almost a straight line to the Southwest. as far as Stevenson, Alabama, which is approximately 35 miles SSE of Tullahoma

employment of inner lines, which were the sole means by which the South could "equalize the contest." [21]

Seddon mildly suggested that the objection to the plan was the manifest one that it weakened too heavily the Army defending Richmond.[22] Perhaps, also, the Secretary of War stated that "Grant was such an obstinate fellow that he could only be induced to quit Vicksburg by terribly hard knocks." [23] Longstreet could not admit the validity of either of these contentions. Said he afterwards, "I was very thoroughly impressed with the practicability of the plan."

Gratifying it was, in any event, to have been given the full confidence of the Secretary and to have been asked for counsel on what was the most fateful question of strategy the government had to face in the summer of 1863. Still another distinction came to Longstreet before he left Richmond for the Rappahannock. On the 8th of May he received from the commanding General a letter in which Lee politely, almost deferentially, explained that Longstreet had not been expected to return in time to participate in the campaign of Chancellorsville. With the consideration he always showed for faithful subordinates, Lee wrote: "My letter of the 1st . . . was to apprise you of my intended movement and to express the wish rather than the expectation that one of your Divisions could cooperate in it. I did not intend to express the opinion that you could reach me in time, as I did not think it practicable." The commanding General went on to suggest that Longstreet should not distress the men of the First Corps by forced marches or "sacrifice for that purpose any public interest that your sudden departure might make it necessary to abandon." Lee added: "The only immediate service that your troops could render would be to protect our communications from the enemy's cavalry and assist in punishing them for the damage they have done." It had been precisely for this reason that Longstreet had post-

21 *Longstreet*, 327; *Annals*, 416.

22 In Longstreet's own words, "the difficulty of withdrawing the force suggested from Lee's Army" (*Annals*, 416).

23 *Longstreet*, 327–28. Here, again, in his second narrative, Longstreet modified somewhat the statement made in *Annals*. As the account in *Annals* was written about 1879, or approximately fifteen years before that in *Longstreet*, the natural critique would be to accept the earlier version; but two considerations have shaped the text: First, the argument concerning the "obstinacy" of Grant has verisimilitude; second, by the time Longstreet wrote his longer military memoir, he had been the object of so much controversy that he may have thought it wise to adduce arguments he had not included in the article republished in *Annals*.

poned his departure from Richmond even when the President had suggested haste. Thus by the words of his chief was Longstreet vindicated.[24] Promptly he forwarded to the Secretary of War the letter of Lee and a dispatch that announced Stoneman's return to the Federal lines. Longstreet could not forbear telling Seddon in a postscript "I received a dispatch from General Lee asking the arrangements that I have ordered in reference to his communication with this city." [25]

On the 9th of May, Longstreet came back in satisfaction of spirit to Fredericksburg heights. His mind was full of his plan for a defensive in the East and an offensive from Tennessee with "Joe" Johnston, whom he regarded as the greatest soldier of the Confederacy.[26] Longstreet believed in this strategy but he had no immediate opportunity of presenting it. He found his chief in acutest distress because of the gloomy turn in the illness of Jackson.[27] The next afternoon, it will be recalled, Jackson died. Longstreet by that tragedy became the most conspicuous of Lee's surviving lieutenants. None of the others had comparable reputation; none so surely could present all his views to the commanding General.

While Lee mourned over Jackson, weighed the merits of possible successors, and considered the reorganization of the Army into three Corps, Longstreet had time for an examination of the tactics and strategy of Chancellorsville. Because it had been the Army's one major battle in which he had no part, he felt that he could approach it in detachment. To the contest he applied the theory he had advocated in dispatches to Lee—"to stand behind our intrenched lines and await the return of my troops from Suffolk." [28] So considered, Longstreet did not approve Lee's operation. The battle itself, Longstreet conceded, "was certainly grand," [29] but he argued that if Lee had held to a strict defensive, the result would have been better.[30] Longstreet never explained how he reached the conclusion that Lee, by defensive tactics, could have kept Hooker from outflanking the Confederate left and cutting communications via the R. F. & P. Railroad.

[24] O. R., 18, 1049.                    [25] Ibid., 1052.
[26] Philadelphia Weekly Times, July 27, 1879, p. 8.
[27] 3 B. & L., 244–45. This article by Longstreet, styled "Lee's Invasion of Pennsylvania," stands chronologically nearer the account in Annals than that in Longstreet, but, as will appear in Chapter VII, it is, in some particulars, at variance with both of them.
[28] Longstreet, 329.                    [29] Ibid.
[30] An elaboration of Longstreet's views will be found in ibid., 329–30.

The point to be stressed is not that Longstreet was correct or incorrect in his appraisal but that in making it, he showed himself an unqualified advocate of a tactical defensive by the Army of Northern Virginia. Its strategy might be offensive, but not its tactics. Longstreet's military creed, at this period of the war, was avowedly that of the counsel Napoleon gave Marmont at the beginning of an invasion—"Select your ground and make the enemy attack you."[31]

In this state of mind, when he found Lee free to hear him, Longstreet submitted his plan for the reinforcement of Bragg, an offensive against Rosecrans and the attempted invasion of Ohio as a means of forcing the recall of Grant from Vicksburg. In Longstreet's first account of this conference, he wrote: "The idea seemed to be a new one to [Lee], but he was evidently seriously impressed with it."[32] Longstreet's final version was: "[Lee] recognized the suggestion as of good combination, and giving strong assurance of success . . ."[33] Encouraged by this, and by Lee's attentive hearing, Longstreet reviewed all his arguments in favor of detaching part of the Confederate troops on the Rappahannock for an offensive against Rosecrans.

The proposal was given unbiased consideration by Lee. In the end, it was rejected. Face to face with Hooker's army, which numerically was much superior, Lee did not feel that he safely could divide his forces.[34] The alternative, so far as it concerned Vicksburg, was for Johnston to reinforce Pemberton, instead of sending help to Bragg for an advance against Rosecrans.[35] As for the Army of Northern Virginia, Lee asked, in effect, what better service could it render the other Confederate armies and their common cause than to invade the North and threaten Washington?[36]

Longstreet frankly opposed such an offensive. It would involve

31 *Annals*, 417.                    32 *Annals*, 416.
33 *Longstreet*, 331.
34 *Annals*, 416; 3 *B. & L.*, 246; *Longstreet*, 331.
35 See 3 *R. E. Lee*, 19.
36 In *Annals*, 416, Longstreet stated that Lee asked if "I did not think an invasion of Maryland and Pennsylvania . . . would accomplish the same result." The language in *Longstreet*, 331, is: "[Lee] reflected upon the matter one or two days, and then fell upon the plan of invading the Northern soil, and so threatening Washington as to bring about the same result." The preponderance of evidence is that Lee did not believe there was large prospect that the invasion of Pennsylvania would lead the Washington government to recall troops from the West. In his report, *O. R.*, 27, pt. 2, p. 305, Lee included this only as a possibility. There is no way of ascertaining whether Lee mentioned the plan for the invasion of Pennsylvania to Longstreet before or after the decision in favor of an offensive North of the Potomac had been reached during Lee's visit to Richmond, May 14–17. See 3 *R. E. Lee*, 19.

too many hazards, he said, and would call for longer and more extensive preparation than a drive through Tennessee and Kentucky would entail.[37] He argued; he restated the case for his own plan; he pointed out the difficulties of an advance in the enemy's country. When Longstreet saw that Lee had reached a final decision on the larger question of strategy, the argument was turned to tactics. In detail, Longstreet reviewed the theory he had formulated. He recorded later: "I suggested that, after piercing Pennsylvania and menacing Washington, we should choose a strong position, and force the Federals to attack us, observing that the popular clamor throughout the North would speedily force the Federal general to attempt to drive us out. I recalled to [Lee] the battle of Fredericksburg as an instance of a defensive battle, when, with a few thousand men, we hurled the whole Federal army back, crippling and demoralizing it, with trifling loss to our own troops . . ."[38]

To this argument, as he subsequently admitted, Longstreet held with "great persistency." He did not find his chief in opposition. Lee agreed with the principle, though he never had any thought of committing himself to a tactical policy that was to be applied regardless of circumstance. To Lee's mind, any such commitment would have been a negation of strategy.[39] Longstreet mistook courtesy for consent and believed that Lee had pledged himself to defensive tactics though the strategy might be offensive. Said Longstreet subsequently: "I suggested that we should have all the details and purposes so well arranged and so impressed upon our minds that when the critical moment should come, we could refer to our calmer moments and know we were carrying out our original plans." He even went so far as to assure Lee that the function of the commanding General could be limited to the protection of the flanks: "I stated to General Lee that if he would allow me to handle my Corps so as to receive the attack of the Federal army, I would beat it off without calling on him for help except to guard my right and left." The Battle of Fredericksburg, Longstreet kept saying, was an example of what he hoped to achieve in Pennsylvania.[40]

[37] *Annals*, 416.  [38] *Annals*, 417.
[39] For Lee's later observations on this point, see *infra*, p. 107. Longstreet's three statements of the acquiescence of Lee in his plan will be found in *Annals*, 417; 3 *B. & L.* 247; *Longstreet*, 331.
[40] 3 *B. & L.*, 247.

As opportunity offered, Longstreet tried to indoctrinate other commanders with his theory of offensive strategy and defensive tactics. In particular, when the Army was about to start for Pennsylvania, Lee called Ewell to headquarters for final instructions. Longstreet, sitting by, heard Lee explain everything to Ewell, and then he added on his own account that if the Confederates in Virginia "were ever going to make an offensive battle it should be done South of the Potomac—adding that we might have an opportunity to cross the Rappahannock and make a battle there." Longstreet said this deliberately because he wanted to open a discussion which, he explained later, "would give Ewell a better idea of the plan of operations." [41]

After the advance of the Army began, Longstreet had in mind the possibility that Lee might attack the enemy should an opening appear. Stuart's battle at Brandy Station made Longstreet especially apprehensive, as he put it, that Lee might follow up the advantage by "pouring the heavy force concentrated at Culpeper Court House upon this detachment of the Federals." When Lee refrained from pursuing Pleasanton's cavalry, Longstreet told himself that Lee "had determined to make a defensive battle, and would not allow any casual advantage to precipitate a general engagement." [42]

Cheerfully, then, on a flawlessly arranged march behind the Second Corps, Longstreet moved his troops toward the Potomac. As the First Corps approached that river, Longstreet had the responsibility of giving to "Jeb" Stuart some fateful orders presently to be described. These apart, the advance was without sensation, but the crossing of the Potomac at Williamsport was not without humor. As the long, long columns approached the stream, the men halted, took off their trousers and shoes, and made these into bundles which, with their cartridge boxes, they carried on their shoulders. The hour of their wading of the river happened to be that which various Maryland ladies, "mostly young and guileless," had selected for a pilgrimage to Virginia soil. Carriages and columns of half-naked men, going in opposite directions, met in the stream from which the abashed ladies could not retreat. There were embarrassed and averted looks, but, as Adjutant Owen of the Washington Artillery wrote, with as much of philosophy as of exaggeration, "50,000 men without their trousers on can't be passed in review every day of the week." [43]

Clothed again, the men of the First Corps pushed confidently northward and, on the 27th, reached Chambersburg, Pennsylvania.[44] The Third Corps was with the First; Ewell was at Carlisle; the movements of Early were not known at Army Headquarters. Stuart, too, was detached, but as nothing had been heard from him, it was supposed that the Federal Army still was in Virginia and that the Confederate cavalry were watching Hooker.[45] The troopers of Imboden had operated on the left of Ewell as he had advanced toward the Susquehanna, and they had destroyed many bridges; [46] but they, too, had disappeared. They were, in reality, resting idly at Hancock, Maryland, more than fifty miles Southwest of Chambersburg. When this became known it was to provoke the wrath of Lee as did few events of the war.[47] On the 27th–28th, it was assumed that the mounted forces were doing their full duty and that all was well; but there was uneasiness, almost exasperation, over the failure of the cavalry to send in any information of the enemy's movements.

In this disagreeable state, when the Army was in the dark, Longstreet put the Confederacy in his debt. While "Old Pete" had been at Suffolk, Secretary Seddon had dispatched to corps headquarters a Mississippian of adventurous spirit who offered to serve as a spy. This man, known only as Harrison, was about 30 years of age.[48] He was 5 feet, 8 inches tall, was bearded and slightly stooped and had penetrating hazel eyes.[49] All spies were suspected of being double traitors and of giving the enemy as much information as they got from him; but Longstreet employed Harrison and found the man both active and trustworthy.

Before the Army left Culpeper, Longstreet directed Harrison to go to Washington and to glean intelligence. When Harrison asked where he should report on his return, Longstreet remarked evasively that headquarters of the First Corps were large enough for any intelligent man to find.[50] A staff officer noted subse-

[43] *Owen*, 240.                                [44] *O. R.*, 27, pt. 2, p. 358.
[45] *O. R.*, 27, pt. 2, p. 316.
[46] *O. R.*, 27, pt. 2, pp. 296–97; pt. 3, p. 924.
[47] *Longstreet*, 359, 546.                    [48] *Sorrel*, 153.
[49] Longstreet in 3 *B. & L.*, 244.
[50] *Longstreet*, 333. Sorrel, *op. cit.*, 158, quoted Longstreet as replying: "With the Army; I shall be sure to be with it."

quently: Longstreet "was very far from giving even to his trusted scout information as to his movement. But Harrison knew all the same; he knew pretty much everything that was going on." [51]

Harrison disappeared; the Army moved northward; on the night of June 28, travel-worn and dirty, the spy appeared at the Confederate outposts. He was arrested and was taken to headquarters where, of course, he was recognized and was escorted to Longstreet's tent.[52] Harrison had news of first importance: The Federal Army had left Virginia and had moved North of the Potomac; at least two Corps were close to Frederick; once more, the command had been transferred. This time, the new leader of the Army of the Potomac was Maj. Gen. George Meade.[53]

In the absence of Stuart's cavalry, none of this information had reached Army Headquarters. Even if the cavalry had been at hand, some of the facts unearthed by Harrison might not have been discovered. Credit, then, was due Harrison and, indirectly, Longstreet. Corps commanders usually employed spies, but Longstreet, with his usual care for detail, saw to it that his spies were well-chosen and diligent.

Harrison's report produced an immediate change in the dispositions of the Army. In order to keep the enemy at maximum distance from the lines of supply, A. P. Hill was directed to move his Corps East of the mountains. Longstreet was to follow. Pickett's Division should be left on guard at Chambersburg. On the 30th, Hood and McLaws, with their own and the reserve artillery, moved to Greenwood, which they reached about 2 P.M. There they halted and there they remained for the night.[54] Lee established his headquarters near Longstreet's.[55] An English military observer who was with the two men that day wrote in his diary, before he blew out his candle that 30th of June: "The relations between Lee and Longstreet are quite touching—they are almost always together . . . It is impossible to please Longstreet more than by praising

[51] *Sorrel,* 158.
[52] In the *Fairfax MSS* is a letter in which Col. John W. Fairfax described to Gen. Custis Lee, Sept. 21, 1896, some of the circumstances of Harrison's arrival and examination. When Fairfax told Gen. R. E. Lee of Harrison's report, the General asked: "What do you think of Harrison?" The reply of Fairfax was: "General Lee, I do not think much of any scout, but General Longstreet thinks a good deal of Harrison." In a moment Lee said: "I do not know what to do. I cannot hear from General Stuart, the eye of the Army. You can take Harrison back."
[53] *Longstreet,* 346–47; *O. R.,* 27, pt. 2, p. 358; *Marshall,* 218; *Sorrel,* 160, 161; *Annals,* 419, 632. Most of the relevant circumstances are described in 3 *R. E. Lee,* 60–61.
[54] *O. R.,* 27, pt. 2, p. 358.          [55] *Annals,* 420.

Lee. I believe these two Generals to be as little ambitious and as thoroughly unselfish as any men in the world." [56] There was no difference between them as they approached the crisis of their cause. No difference there was, but—to repeat a fact soon to make history—each misunderstood the other's view of the course they were to follow: In Longstreet's mind, Lee was committed morally to a tactical defensive, which was Longstreet's own conception and, to his way of thinking, an essential of Confederate success. Lee never had intended to commit himself to that tactical policy and he did not know that Longstreet considered him so pledged. [57]

[56] Arthur Lyon-Fremantle, *Three Months in the Southern States* (cited hereafter as *Fremantle*), 243.

[57] For the next detailed references to Longstreet's part in the Gettysburg campaign, see *infra*, p. 106.

# CHAPTER IV

## The Price of 125 Wagons

Different far from Longstreet's state of mind and different no less from Ewell's was that in which "Jeb" Stuart looked forward to a second invasion of the North. Ewell entered Pennsylvania with reputation much heightened, Stuart with fame impaired. Longstreet was resolved to justify a tactical theory, Stuart to vindicate his name as a leader. That slur on him in the *Richmond Examiner* was not the only one.[1] The *Richmond Dispatch,* too, had said that he had been surprised at Brandy.[2] In Charleston, the *Mercury* had made similar allegation.[3] The alert *Richmond Sentinel,* which spoke with some authority on military affairs, had cried: "Vigilance, vigilance, more vigilance, is the lesson taught us by the Brandy surprise, and which must not be forgotten by the victory which was wrested from defeat. Let all learn it, from the Major General down to the picket."[4] As an administration organ, the *Richmond Enquirer* had been forbearant; the *Whig* had been laudatory in reference to "our brilliant young cavalry chieftain,"[5] but rumor had undone this and had outrun the most hostile reports. It was said openly in the city that "Stuart's headquarters had been fired into before the enemy's presence was known,"[6] and that Stuart had been outgeneralled.[7] The indignant whisper was that the surprise had occurred because Stuart and his officers were "rollicking, frolicking and running after girls." The simple ball held the night before the battle was debauched by innuendo. Many persons believed in Richmond that both President Davis and General Lee had reprimanded Stuart with much severity.

These rumors at last were mentioned in print in order that they might be denied by Stuart's admirers.[8] Denial gave them wider currency. A Culpeper lady wrote Mr. Davis, anonymously but

1 See *supra*, p. 19.    2 Issue of June 12, 1863.
3 June 13, 1863.    4 June 12, 1863.
5 June 11, 1863.    6 *Richmond Dispatch*, June 12, 1863.
7 *Ibid.*
8 *Richmond Whig*, June 17: *Richmond Dispatch*, June 18, 1863.

fervently: "President, allow a true Southern lady to say, General S's conduct since in Culpeper is perfectly ridiculous, having repeated reviews for the benefit of his lady friends, he riding up and down the line thronged with those ladies, he decorated with flowers, apparently a monkey show on hand and he the monkey. In fact General Stuart is nothing more or less than one of those fops, devoting his whole time to his lady friends' company." "Jeb's" friends on the President's staff thought this letter amusing and they forwarded it to Stuart with their compliments and with the "suggestion that he cease his attentions to the ladies or make them more general." [9] This advice, with the anonymous letter, did not reach the cavalry commander before he entered Pennsyl-- vania, but it represented an opinion unhappily prevalent, an opinion that hurt and goaded a praise-loving man. Even Federal staff officers learned of the criticism of Stuart from Southern journals that were smuggled through the lines. The papers, Gen. Daniel Butterfield telegraphed General Halleck, "call upon [Stuart] to do something to retrieve his reputation." [10] If that scarcely was a sound interpretation of comment, there could be no mistaking the meaning of a prediction with which the *Richmond Whig* concluded an editorial defense of the Beau Sabreur: "We shall be surprised, if the gallant Stuart does not, before many days, make the enemy repent sorely the temerity that led them to under- take as bold and insulting a feat [as the advance on Brandy]." [11]

Stuart read, raged, and doubtless resolved that the *Whig's* pre- diction should be fulfilled. Vindication of the confidence of friends would be, at the same time, refutation of the calumny of foes, but first must come opportunity. His immediate duty, though difficult, was the unspectacular one of screening Hill and Longstreet while they were moving toward the Potomac. As Hampton had re- mained temporarily on the Rappahannock and Jones's Brigade was detached,[12] Stuart did not wish at the outset to risk a general en- gagement. At the same time, he had to keep the enemy East of the Blue Ridge, so that the northward march of the Confederate infantry down the Shenandoah Valley would not be interrupted. This mission called for shrewd maneuver. From June 17 through June 21, on the roads that divide at Aldie and run to Ashby's and

---

[9] *H. B. McClellan MSS.* The endorsement was by Custis Lee, June 23, 1863.
[10] *O. R.*, 27, pt. 1, p. 41.                    [11] *Richmond Whig,* June 16, 1863.
[12] *O. R.*, 37, pt. 2, p. 689.

Snicker's Gaps, Stuart had to direct much fighting. Clashes were frequent and furious though they usually were on a small scale. Nearly all the Confederate Brigadiers had the honor of advances and the humiliation of hasty withdrawals before the Union cavalry of Alfred Pleasanton, David Gregg and John Buford. These bluecoated troopers demonstrated that the vigor of the attack at Brandy Station was not accidental. They now were an experienced, confident and well-led corps and they scarcely resembled in anything but uniform the clumsy horsemen through whom or over whom Stuart's men had ridden in 1862. The day of easy Confederate cavalry triumphs was gone. All that the "butternut" Southerners possessed of courage, resourcefulness and endurance, they needed in those fights around Aldie, Middleburg and Upperville.

Perhaps the finest feat of the operations was credited to Wade Hampton. On the road to Ashby's Gap, June 21, one of Robertson's regiments broke while passing through Upperville. Hampton immediately charged the enemy and repulsed the Federals. They were Gregg's stubborn men, and they came back vigorously. Hampton turned to the nearest troops, drew his sabre, lifted himself in his stirrups and shouted, "First North Carolina, follow me!" Five squadrons only of that regiment were at hand, but they spurred after Hampton. By the time they had delivered their attack and had ridden back, the other squadrons of the same command were ready to advance. Hampton proudly wrote afterwards: ". . . this series of charges went on until all my regiments named had charged three times, and I had gained ground to the right and front of more than half a mile. At this moment the Second South Carolina was brought up in good order from the rear, and under its protection I reformed my command, and retired in column of regiments, at a walk and without molestation."[13] Said Maj. Henry McClellan in comment: "This success was mainly due to that personal influence which . . . has marked Hampton as a leader of men."[14] Stuart, reporting officially, chose "brilliant" as the fitting word to describe Hampton's fighting that day.[15]

Stuart surprised his companions during these vexing operations

13 *Philadelphia Weekly Times,* July 20, 1878, quoted in *H. B. McClellan,* 311-12.
14 *H. B. McClellan,* 313. The next detailed reference to Hampton is *infra,* p. 195.
15 *O. R.,* 27, pt. 2, p. 691. The *Rosser MSS* contain a letter of June 18 in which Rosser described in some detail the action of the preceding day.

in Loudoun and Fauquier. He watched the ebb and flow of the final action and he watched the gauge of his reserves, but, until the situation grew tense at Upperville, he had little part in the fighting. Henry McClellan recorded: "I asked the reason of this unusual proceeding, and he replied that he had given all necessary instructions to his brigade commanders, and he wished them to feel the responsibility resting upon them, and to gain whatever honor the field might bring." [16] The only other occasion in which Stuart had not shared actively the hardest of the fighting was in that difficult hour at White's Ford, on the return from Maryland in October, 1862. Then, it will be remembered, he sent word to "Rooney" Lee that he was "fully occupied where he was, and that the ford must be gained at all hazards." [17]

The losses in these engagements were not excessive, though they included a crippling neck wound for Heros von Borcke.[18] Stuart mourned him and, while fighting defensively, planned offensively. Now that all the infantry were West of the Blue Ridge, he reasoned that it would be possible to leave one or two Brigades of cavalry to defend the gaps, and with the remaining three to descend on the enemy and harass Hooker in any advance the Federals might make to parallel Lee's own. If Hooker crossed the Potomac, Stuart could do the same thing or could rejoin the Army on its advance into Pennsylvania.[19] This expedition could be started as soon as the Union cavalry withdrew from their inquisitive and persistent daily attacks.

"Jeb" suggested such an operation to Lee and gained approval of the general idea. Longstreet, also, was favorable. The one basic stipulation made by Lee was that as soon as Stuart found that the Federals were moving into Maryland, the Confederate cavalry, too, must pass the Potomac and must cover the flank of the advancing Southern infantry.[20] By the night of the 21st, this much of the plan

---

[16] H. B. McClellan, 314.

[17] Ibid., 157.

[18] W. W. Blackford's MS Memoirs, 321–22; 2 von Borcke, 296.

[19] Stuart wrote in his report, O. R., 27, pt. 2, p. 692, as if from the inception of his plan, he had intended to make his raid between Washington and the enemy, and to cross into Maryland. The recollection of Colonel Marshall (op. cit., 201), was that the initial plan did not contemplate the passage of the Potomac. As between the two statements, that of Stuart was much nearer the event and, as will appear later, was challenged and then accepted after the campaign ended. If Stuart did not at the outset propose that he go into Maryland, he almost certainly hoped from the first to do so.

[20] This virtually is a paraphrase of Marshall, 201. The date of Stuart's first discussion with General Lee of this plan has to be left in doubt. See 3 R. E. Lee, 41, n. 58.

was accepted. On the 22nd of June, the Federals did not return to contest the roads to the mountain gaps. As soon as the mist cleared away, it was manifest that the enemy was retiring toward the Bull Run mountains.[21] Stuart sent Tom Rosser and others in pursuit, and himself, at 7:45, wrote Longstreet, his nearest superior officer, of the enemy's withdrawal.[22] Lines were re-established to the eastward.[23] The country between Aldie and the Blue Ridge was secure; the task of screening the infantry was nearing completion.

Late in the evening of the 22nd, one of the couriers of the First Corps brought Stuart a note from Longstreet, who enclosed a letter from the commanding General. Lee expressed concern lest the retirement of the Federal cavalry might mean that Hooker was stealing a march on the Confederate Army and might get into Maryland before it did. Then Stuart read: "If you find that [Hooker] is moving northward, and that two Brigades can guard the Blue Ridge and take care of your rear, you can move with the other three into Maryland, and take position on General Ewell's right, place yourself in communication with him, guard his flank, keep him informed of the enemy's movements, and collect all the supplies you can for the use of the army." There followed information of Ewell's line of advance and explicit orders against plundering in the enemy's country.[24]

Longstreet's covering note explained that Lee had forwarded the letter to be transmitted in the event Stuart could be spared the front of the First Corps and could be sent across the Potomac without disclosing the march of the infantry. "Old Pete" approved, if Stuart thought the cavalry could make the move successfully. The prospect, Longstreet went on, was that Stuart would be less apt to disclose the Confederate plan to the enemy if the cavalry crossed the Potomac in rear of the Federals. It would be well, the commander of the First Corps concluded, if Stuart delayed the start until certain he could move northward into Maryland in rear of the Unionists.[25]

A gracious Providence scarcely could have shapea opportunity more to Stuart's wishes! Eagerly on the morning of the 23rd "Jeb" had his outposts and his scouts search for the enemy. Reports were

21 *O. R.*, 27, pt. 2, p. 691.  22 Cf. *O. R.*, 27, pt. 3, p. 913
23 *O. R.*, 27, pt. 2, p. 691.  24 *O. R.*, 27, pt. 3, p. 913.
25 *Ibid.*, 915.

encouraging. There were some indications that Federal cavalry might be moving toward Warrenton, but Maj. John S. Mosby, the boldest and most responsible of partisan rangers, wrote that the enemy was inactive East of Blue Ridge Mountain and was encamped over so wide an area that Stuart easily could push his way between two of the corps.[26] All this information Stuart promptly forwarded to Lee. Together, the intelligence developed a possible contingency not covered by orders: Major Mosby thought the Federal infantry had been stationary for almost a week.[27] If they did not start an advance, new instructions were necessary. Stuart doubtless asked for them.

Evening of the 23rd brought one of those searching, persistent summer rains that usually outlast the night. Stuart, at Rector's Cross Roads,[28] had shelter, but at bedtime he insisted that his oil-cloth and blankets be spread under a tree. Henry McClellan remonstrated in vain. "No," Stuart answered, with a tone of finality, "my men are exposed to this rain, and I will not fare any better than they." [29] He went to sleep soundly, despite the downpour, but late in the night, he awakened instantly, and in his full wit, when McClellan called his name.

The Major had a dispatch from Army Headquarters. It had been brought through the wet, black night by a courier and it had been sealed and marked "Confidential." Stuart observed immediately that the seal, contrary to army usage, had been broken. In explanation, McClellan said that he had opened the letter in order to see if the contents justified him in awakening the General. Stuart reprimanded McClellan mildly and read the communication. It was from Lee and was written at 5 P.M. in answer to Stuart's messages of the morning. Lee gave his decision on some trivial question that had been raised regarding purchases, and then he spoke of the enemy's uncertain movements. Said the commander, in two brief paragraphs that were to weigh in the balance of a nation's destiny:

If General Hooker's army remains inactive, you can leave two brigades to watch him, and withdraw with the three others, but should

[26] J. S. Mosby, *Stuart's Cavalry in the Gettysburg Campaign* (cited hereafter as *Mosby, Stuart's Cavalry*), 76.
[27] *Op. cit.*, 76.
[28] About 2.7 miles west of Middleburg on the road to Upperville.
[29] *H. B. McClellan*, 316.

he not appear to be moving northward, I think you had better withdraw this side of the mountains tomorrow night, cross at Shepherdstown next day, and move over to Frederickstown.

You will, however, be able to judge whether you can pass around their army without hindrance, doing them all the damage you can, and cross the river east of the mountains. In either case, after crossing the river, you must move on and feel the right of Ewell's troops, collecting information, provisions, &c.

Other paragraphs gave general instructions for the cavalry to be left behind. Lee added: ". . . I think the sooner you cross into Maryland after tomorrow, [June 24] the better." [30]

That was language to chew and to digest. "If General Hooker's army" remained "inactive," then three Brigades of Stuart's cavalry and presumably "Jeb" himself must return to the main army. The proviso was firm, but discretion was left. Stuart was free to determine whether he could "pass around" the Federal Army "without hindrance." If he could do that, he could cross the river "East of the mountains."

Taken together, then, the instructions of June 22 and of June 23 coupled two conditions for a crossing West of the mountains: If Hooker remained inactive *and* Stuart could not pass around Hooker's sprawling force unhindered, then three Confederate cavalry Brigades must rejoin the main Army and cross via Shepherdstown. That was displeasing to Stuart not only because it robbed him of independent adventure but also because it would throw his columns on congested roads.[31] Stuart reasoned that he had authority to cross East of the Blue Ridge [32] even in the rear of the enemy, if this could be done without hindrance. "Jeb" knew that this term was not intended to exclude contact with the enemy.

[30] *O. R.*, 27, pt. 3, p. 923. For the circumstances in which this letter was written, see 3 *R. E. Lee*, 44 ff. In *H. B. McClellan*, 317, is a statement of Major McClellan's recollection of the contents of the letter Stuart received during the night. While his digest varies perceptibly from the actual document, there can be no doubt the Major was referring to the letter quoted above.

[31] *W. W. Blackford's MS Memoirs*, 326.

[32] Subsequently, in the "Gettysburg controversy," some of Stuart's critics insisted that his orders carried the implication that he was to cross immediately to the East of the mountains. There was nothing in the orders or in the military situation to justify this contention. In Longstreet's note of the 22nd to Stuart, the commander of the First Corps quoted a lost letter in which Lee said that Stuart might pass through Hopewell Gap and pass "by the rear of the enemy" (*O. R.*, 27, pt. 3, p. 915). Lee in his report wrote that Stuart was left to exercise his judgment to cross the Potomac "East or West" of the Blue Ridge. Had there been any order more specific than that, Lee doubtless would have stated it.

LEE'S LIEUTENANTS

Lee had been told that Stuart could delay the Federals by getting in their rear.[33] Besides, Lee's letter of June 23 enjoined Stuart to do the Federals "all the damage you can."

What was possible was permissible. That, as Stuart saw it, was the substance of his orders. So far as the records show, he did not define "hindrance" rigidly in terms of days and hours. He did not realize that he would be hindered most seriously were he delayed in crossing the Potomac to "feel the right of Ewell" and to collect information and provisions. Stuart summed up his interpretation of his orders when he said later: "In the exercise of the discretion vested in me by the commanding general, it was deemed practicable to move entirely in the enemy's rear, intercepting his communications with his base (Washington), and, inflicting damage upon his rear, to rejoin the army in Pennsylvania in time to participate in its actual conflicts." [34]

In the conviction that he could shape his route as opportunity required, Stuart on the 24th made his preparations. His hope was that after he crossed Bull Run Mountain, he would find the Federal troops so disposed that he could use the roads West of Centreville.[35] Major Mosby accordingly was directed to proceed to the Potomac in the vicinity of Dranesville and to select a suitable crossing for the Brigades that would follow.[36] The men were to cook three days' rations to be carried on their persons. Horses, like men, must live off the land. No thought was given, apparently, to the possibility of delay if forage were unprocurable. All the wagons and half the guns were to remain South of the Potomac. Six field-pieces, their caissons and the ambulances were to be the only wheeled vehicles. The rendezvous was to be at Salem.[37] Everything must be ready to move soon after midnight of the 24th–25th. Lee had said, "The sooner you cross into Maryland, after tomorrow, the better." [38] "Jeb" would not lose a minute.

Orders were to take three Brigades and to leave two. Jenkins's

[33] O. R., 27, pt. 2, p. 316.
[34] O. R., 27, pt. 2, p. 707.
[35] O. R., 27, pt. 2, p. 693. Some of Stuart's critics entirely disregarded this statement of Stuart's route as first projected.
[36] O. R., 27, pt. 2, p. 693. In his Stuart's Cavalry, 91–92, Mosby by some lapse of memory failed to mention that this was his specific mission. As he stated it, he and his rangers were to meet Stuart at an assigned place on the Little River Turnpike.
[37] H. B. McClellan, 318. Salem was on the Manassas Gap Railroad, eight miles West of Thoroughfare Gap.
[38] O. R., 27, pt. 3, p. 923.

troops need not be taken into account at the moment, because they already were in Pennsylvania. The five Brigades among which choice had to be made by Stuart were Hampton's, Fitz Lee's, "Rooney" Lee's, "Grumble" Jones's and Beverly Robertson's. It was Longstreet's expectation that Hampton would be left in the mountains[39] but "Jeb" had other plans. The harder duty should be assigned the strongest units. Lee's orders had been: "Give instructions to the commander of the brigades left behind to watch the flank and rear of the army, and (in event of the enemy leaving their front) retire from the mountains West of the Shenandoah, leaving sufficient pickets to guard the passes, and bringing everything clean along the Valley, closing upon the rear of the army." [40] That, surely, was duty less exacting than a long raid in the enemy's country would be. To watch the mountain passes and to clear the Valley was, moreover, the type of duty in which "Grumble" Jones was proficient. He was rated the best outpost officer in the cavalry Division; he had commanded for months in the Shenandoah region. Besides, he was the one officer of distinction, among all his subordinates, with whom Stuart could not operate on friendly terms. Often Stuart had praised Jones. At least as frequently he had protested against having Jones under him. Let Jones and his large Brigade remain to guard the gaps and the Great Valley. With him, Beverly Robertson could maneuver or wait. Robertson's men were less experienced than any of the others. Everyone knew, also, that Robertson was entirely unpredictable in battle. He would not be suited for the work that might be awaiting the Confederates North of the Potomac.

The sole difficulty about leaving "Grumble" and Bev. Robertson in the mountains, while the others made a smashing raid into Maryland and Pennsylvania, was the old one of seniority: Although "Grumble" Jones was much the more efficient officer of the two and had stood often the test of combat, Robertson was of prior commission. Well . . . the arrangement might not be ideal, but the one alternative was impossible: Nothing should be done to break up the combination of Hampton and the Lees. They had shared numerous raids; they were a team that knew how to fight together. That was the positive, the essential consideration. Rob-

[39] O. R., 27, pt. 3, p. 915.
[40] O. R., 27, pt. 3, p. 923.

ertson must be guided, as far as practicable, by carefully drawn orders.[41]

These instructions for Robertson were in detail and were as explicit as a situation of probable change permitted. The tone was detached, somewhat superior perhaps, and wholly lacking in any suggestion that if Robertson could get on with "Grumble" Jones he could learn something from that officer. Instead of hinting this tactfully or stating it bluntly, Stuart said: "You will instruct General Jones from time to time as the movement progresses or events may require, and report anything of importance to General Longstreet . . ."[42] Orders for Jones's guidance were prepared also and were transmitted through Robertson.[43]

By nightfall of the 24th all instructions had been given. Thousands of troopers clattered into Salem. The man whom Stuart most joyfully welcomed was Fitz Lee. That laughing cavalier had been groaning with inflammatory rheumatism for a month and now returned eagerly to duty.[44] His cousin, "Rooney" Lee, was the most lamented of absentees, but there was comfort in the assurance that he was rallying from the leg wound he had received at Brandy Station. In his absence, the Third Cavalry Brigade was under its senior Colonel, John R. Chambliss. Temporarily, in reports, the Brigade was styled Chambliss' and without discredit to men or commander. Chambliss, 30, was a West Pointer, a retired Lieutenant of the "Old Army" and a competent man who was learning rapidly.[45]

With these brigadiers, old and new, Stuart got the column underway about 1 A.M. of the 25th. The early start not only was in soldierly accord with instructions but also was necessary for

[41] Subsequently, Stuart was blamed for leaving Robertson in charge of the rearguard. Maj. Henry McClellan, op. cit., 318, did not "profess to give authoritatively" the reasons that guided Stuart, but explained that the adopted arrangement (1) gave Stuart the men on whom he knew he personally could rely, (2) divided the cavalry with substantial equality, (3) assured the service of Jones on the type of duty "Grumble" best could perform, and (4) rid Stuart, during the expedition, of the man most unacceptable to him. The further guess was hazarded by McClellan that Stuart hoped the numerical superiority of Jones's Brigade would cause Robertson to "give full weight" to Jones's "suggestions and counsels." This may or may not have been in Stuart's mind, but, as noted in the text, his instructions to Robertson did not contain a hint that the senior of the two Brigadiers might profit by counsel with the junior. See O. R., 27, pt. 3, pp. 927–28. For a critique of Stuart's conduct in this selection of officers, see infra, pp. 207, 213.
[42] O. R., 27, pt. 3, p. 927.      [43] Unfortunately they have not been found.
[44] O. R., 27, pt. 2, p. 692. Col. Thomas Munford resumed his regimental command. The march of Fitz Lee's Brigade was from Snicker's Gap.
[45] Cullum No. 1609, a classmate of James B. McPherson, Phil. Sheridan and John B Hood. For a sketch of Chambliss, see 3 C. M. H., 582.

concealment from Federal outposts on Bull Run Mountain. Stuart's plan was to advance through Glasscock's Gap, to march to Hay Market, and then to turn northward.[46] This route, if clear, offered the shortest road to the flank of Ewell in Pennsylvania.

Passage through Bull Run Mountain was easy and unobserved,[47] but after Stuart was East of the gaps on the familiar Warrenton-Centreville Turnpike, he soon encountered Hancock's II Corps. Past Hay Market, this mass of Federal infantry was moving North toward Gum Spring[48]—almost the line of march that Stuart intended to follow. Mosby was not at hand to explain this Federal activity, but such information as Stuart could collect from natives indicated that the Union forces still were at Centreville, Union Mills[49] and at Wolf Run Shoals.[50]

In the light of this intelligence, after a brief bombardment of the nearest moving troops, Stuart withdrew a few miles and camped somewhat unhappily at Buckland in a heavy rain.[51] A report of the movement of Hancock's Corps was sent to Lee,[52] but if Stuart that night debated whether he should turn back and cross the Potomac West of the Blue Ridge, he dropped no hint of it and asked no advice.[53] Probabilities are that he gave no thought to withdrawal. "Hindrance" was not substantial. He would go on. The quickest, surest route would be southeastward and then northward. If the march were rapid enough, it would put the cavalry between the Federals and Washington . . . Washington! The very name itself was an argument for the downstream crossing![54]

Hopefully, on the morning of June 26, the three Brigades moved

[46] O. R., 27, pt. 2, p. 693.
[47] O. R., 27, pt. 2, p. 692. Glasscock's Gap is opposite New Baltimore, about seven miles N by E of Warrenton.
[48] Close to the Little River Turnpike and eleven miles North of Groveton. Stuart called the place Gum Springs. Most of the maps use the singular. Hancock was on the march from Thoroughfare Gap to Edwards' Ferry. See Francis A. Walker's History of the Second Army Corps, 259-60.
[49] On Bull Run at the crossing of the Orange and Alexandria Railroad.
[50] On the Occoquan, four miles downstream from Union Mills.
[51] O. R., 27, pt. 2, p. 693. Buckland, otherwise Buckland Mills, is about five miles East of New Baltimore.
[52] Ibid.     [53] Cf. H. B. McClellan, 321.
[54] Although much argument has been indulged concerning what Stuart should or should not have done after he found his road blocked, the language of his report, O. R., 27, pt. 2, p. 693, scarcely permits a doubt that he hesitated over any question except that of route East of the mountains. The question of disregard of orders, from the standpoint of Army Headquarters, is discussed in 3 R. E. Lee, Appendix III-1, pp. 547 ff. A review appears infra. p. 207 ff.

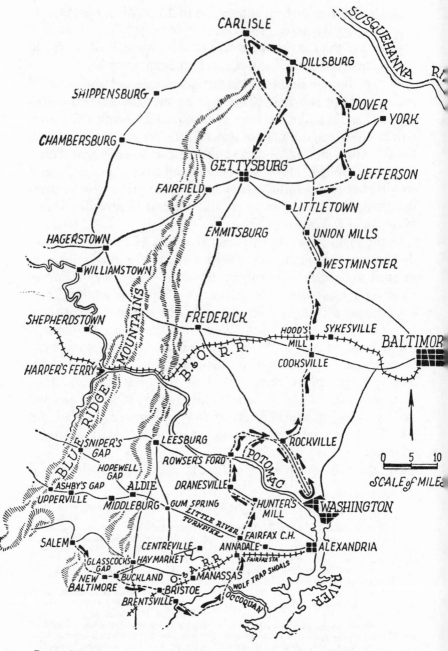

**Route of Stuart's Raid** from Salem, Va., June 25, to Gettysburg, Penna., July 2, **1863**
—after *H. B. McClellan*

from Buckland East to Bristoe Station, which was wistfully remembered for the proximity of Manassas Junction, scene of joyful
plundering. From Bristoe, the march was past Brentsville [55] and
then on a long northerly arc to a bivouac a few miles South of
Wolf Run Shoals on the Occoquan. Nowhere on these twenty-two
or twenty-three miles of road were any Federals encountered,[56]
but nowhere was any forage found. The country had been swept
bare.[57] Horses that had endured hard service in the fighting
around Aldie and Middleburg now gave signs of approaching
exhaustion. Halts had to be called to graze the weakened animals.[58]

Had "Jeb" Stuart possessed the mathematical mind of his dead
friend "Stonewall" Jackson, the cavalry commander in the dawn
of June 27 would have made some humiliating calculations. He
had left Salem more than fifty hours previously, but he had not
covered more than thirty-four miles. Orders had been to cross
the Potomac as soon as practicable after the 24th. He still was two
score miles, perhaps farther, from the nearest ford. The fast
moving cavalry had covered less ground in two days than the most
laggard infantry would have accounted respectable.

Stuart was too experienced and realistic a soldier to have
ignored this; but none of his companions recorded subsequently
that he spoke on the 27th of any tardiness. He was interested far
more in the news sent by his outposts that the Federals had disappeared from Wolf Run Shoals. That opened the way.

To Wolf Run Shoals, then, the march must be directed and
thence toward the Potomac. Major Mosby had not arrived to
report where the cavalry best could cross that wide stream, but a
ford must be found.[59] In quest of it, Hampton must be the
advance. Fitz Lee could swing to the right, after reaching the railway North of the Occoquan, and could ascertain whether the
enemy was on the Little River Turnpike in the vicinity of Annandale.[60]

Onward the other troopers toiled to the Orange and Alexandria

[55] Four miles Southeast of Bristoe.  [56] O. R., 27, pt. 2, p. 693.
[57] H. B. McClellan, 323.  [58] O. R., 27, pt. 2, p. 693.
[59] O. R., 27. pt 2, p. 693. Mosby had discovered the Federals between him and
Stuart on the 24th and had concluded that Stuart had returned to the West of Bull Run
Mountain. Accordingly Mosby himself rode back to his haunts (Mosby, Stuart's Cavalry,
170, 178).
[60] O. R., 27, pt. 2, p. 693. Annandale is five and a half miles Southeast of Fairfax
Court House on the Little River Turnpike.

Railroad at Fairfax Station. About 8:30 the enemy was sighted—
a cavalry detachment, which Hampton's leading regiment pursued and scattered.[61] Without further incident, the Confederate
van reached Fairfax Court House, where, to the infinite cheer of
hungry boys, several sutlers' shacks were found.[62] Asking no by-
your-leave other than that of the Almighty, the "ravenous rebs"
fell upon the establishments and emptied them.[63] Perhaps it was as
much for the pleasure of the men as for the grazing of the horses
that Stuart allowed a halt of several hours at the Court House.[64]

While "Jeb" was there, word came from Fitz Lee that no force
of the enemy was at Annandale. Fitz's information, confirmed
by Hampton's reconnaissance, was that the Army of the Potomac
was converging on Leesburg and that the local defense troops
were retiring to Washington.[65] In this situation, the best approach
to the Potomac from Fairfax Court House would be via the road
between Leesburg and Alexandria. This road, paralleling the
river, led down to the fords which, on that stretch of the Potomac,
were few and deep.

The march proceeded heavily, because of the condition of the
horses. Once the Leesburg and Alexandria Turnpike was reached,
Stuart directed the head of the column Northwest to Dranesville,[66]
scene of his unprosperous clash of Dec. 20, 1861.[67] There the trail
of the enemy was fresh. Directly West of the village, Federal
campfires still were smouldering: Sedgwick's VI Corps, said the
villagers, had marched off that morning in the direction of Leesburg.[68]

If the enemy was that close, the Confederates did not have a
wide choice of the few fords nearby. The best of them, Edwards'
Ferry, of course was within the Federal lines. All the others were
bad, but, after reconnaissance and delay, the troopers and the guns
crossed without loss at Rowser's Ford.[69] Stuart then had been on
the road seventy-two hours and still was on the southern edge of
Maryland soil. He did not know where Lee was. All the informa-

---

[61] This force consisted of Cos. B and C of Scott's Nine Hundred, 11th New York
cavalry. Of 100 men, about eighteen escaped (O. R., 27, pt. 1, pp. 1037–38).
[62] Beale, 78.                              [63] G. W. Beale, 112.
[64] O. R., 27, pt. 2, p. 693.               [65] Ibid.
[66] Fifteen miles Southeast of Leesburg.    [67] See supra, Vol. I, p. 276.
[68] O. R., 27, pt. 2, p. 693. This information was correct. Cf. ibid., pt. 1, p. 666.
[69] Many of the reports style this the "crossing at Seneca Fords." For the interesting
details of the search and examination of the various fords, see H. B. McClellan, 323–24;
Beale, 78; W. W. Blackford's MS Memoirs, 328; O. R., 27, pt. 2, p. 693.

tion the cavalryman got from sympathetic Marylanders—all they

tion the cavalryman got from sympathetic Marylanders—all they knew—was that Hooker had been at Poolesville on the 27th and that the Army of the Potomac was en route to Frederick.[70] In this state of affairs, Lee's instructions of June 22 and of June 23 applied: ". . . take position on General Ewell's right, place yourself in communication with him," and, again, ". . . after crossing the river you must move on and feel the right of Ewell's troops, collecting information, provisions, &c." Said Stuart afterwards, when his adherence to these orders had been brought into question: "I realized the importance of joining our Army in Pennsylvania, and resumed the journey northward early on the 28th." [71]

The intention was undeniable. So were three obstacles. The first was lack of information of Ewell's position. Of this, Lee had said on the 22nd: "One column of General Ewell's army will probably move toward the Susquehanna by the Emmitsburg route; another by Chambersburg." [72] Directly from Emmitsburg northward, a good road led to Gettysburg and thence on to Dillsburg and Harrisburg; but if the Federals were at Frederick, the road to Emmitsburg, as Stuart knew from his experience in the October raid,[73] was one to be avoided. The alternative route to the Susquehanna was via Hanover, whence Stuart might move either North to Carlisle or Northeast to York. All that Stuart could decide on the 28th, then, was to proceed in the direction of Hanover.

In making that movement, a second manifest obstacle to a swift march was the condition of men and mounts. They were worn and hungry by the time they entered the enemy's country and they must be subsisted on what could be collected. Some delay was certain to result from this.

The third obstacle to a prompt junction with Ewell began to develop almost in the hour the cavalry reached Maryland. It was the familiar one, the delight of the men in the most destructive foe of discipline—booty. On the canal, at first arrival, the cavalry had captured several passing boats. Two of these had been laden with whiskey, but this was destroyed before it could do any harm.[74] After that, no prizes were found on the way to Rockville, which was reached shortly after noon.[75] The people of the village

[70] O. R., 27, pt. 2, p. 694.     [71] Ibid.
[72] O. R., 27, pt. 3, p. 913.     [73] See Vol. II, pp. 290–91.
[74] F. S. Robertson, In the Saddle with Stuart, MS, 22.
[75] H. B. McClellan, 324.

were dressed in their Sunday best and were full of curiosity.[76] Pupils of a girls' school were smiling and Southern in sympathy.[77] After an exchange of amenities and the destruction of the telegraph, Stuart might have ordered the march resumed promptly, had not the cavalrymen suddenly had the most lamentable good fortune that ever had fallen to their lot.

Rockville, as it chanced, was on the direct supply line between Washington and Hooker's Army. Up this road, toward Rockville, Stuart was informed, a Federal wagon train was moving. All the Confederates had to do was to wait. Before long, the mounted guards approached. They were almost at the town before they realized it was in hostile hands. Once the "butternuts" were seen, the Union guards wheeled their horses and galloped back to spread the alarm. When they reached the wagons, the drivers became excited, frantically turned their teams in the road and started at a fast trot for Washington. In the mad chase that followed, the Confederates reached the trains, destroyed many vehicles and brought back to Rockville 125 of them. Said Col. R. L. T. Beale:[78] "The wagons were brand new, the mules fat and sleek and the harness in use for the first time. Such a train we had never seen before and did not see again." [79] Eagerly the men examined the contents of the vehicles. Most of the loads were oats and corn, welcome enough to the hungry cavalry horses. In other wagons were bread, crackers, bacon, sugar, hams and a considerable volume of bottled whiskey.[80] Singularly little of this ever reached the quartermasters. This wagon train was "Jeb's" stumbling-block. The length of the road and the weariness of his men might be surmounted by cheer and resolution; but a captured train of "125 best United States model wagons and splendid teams with gay caparisons" [81]—this must be brought back to Virginia, no matter where, meantime, it had to be carried.

Stuart professed subsequently in his report that he considered an advance on Washington and abstained solely because of the time required for such a move.[82] He must have written this for hostile consumption, but at the time he determined, as a minimum

---

[76] Beale, 79.          [77] W. W. Blackford's MS Memoirs, 330.
[78] Later Brigadier General; then Colonel of the Ninth Virginia. His brief account of the chase, op. cit., 79–80, contained some unfamiliar detail.
[79] Beale, 80; cf. G. W. Beale, 112.          [80] Beale, 80.
[81] O. R., 27, pt. 2, p. 694.          [82] O. R., 27, pt. 2, p. 694.

next exploit, to cut the enemy's second line of supply, that of the Baltimore and Ohio Railroad. With good luck, this would not be difficult. From Rockville the distance northward to the railroad, which ran on a wide arc, was about twenty-five miles [83] and in the direction of Stuart's advance toward Hanover.

Unhappily if inevitably, Chambliss' men had become scattered in their pursuit of the wagon train. They and the other Brigades had accumulated about 400 prisoners. Much time was lost in starting the captured wagons on the road, in collecting the far-spread detachments, and in deciding what to do with the prisoners. Most of them were paroled at Rockville, but it was tedious business to write paroles for so many and to procure the signatures.[84] Even when the prisoners were reduced in number, they encumbered the advance.

Early on the morning of the 29th, after a night march of about twenty miles, the van encountered at Cooksville, three miles South of the railroad, a small Federal command. To scatter this was easy, but additional prisoners proved a nuisance. Although the guards and teamsters brought from Rockville were released, the new captives slowed movement. When the railroad was reached at Hood's Mill, more delay occurred. Fitz Lee went off, under orders, to burn a bridge at Sykesville, two and a half miles East of the crossing. The main force halted to tear up the track where they struck it. For tired men, with few tools, this was time-devouring work.[85] Nor did it yield the excitement of fine, smashing wrecks of the sort that had been enjoyed the previous August at Bristoe Station.[86] Several trains approached encouragingly, but in every instance, when the engineer sighted the broken track, he applied his brakes and then backed away. The only reward Stuart got was the doubtful one of possessing for some hours a railroad that otherwise might have been employed in the service of the enemy.[87]

While "Jeb's" men were tearing rails from the track and were damning the alert engineers of the B. & O., he and some of his officers were getting such information as they could of the enemy and of Lee's advance. Friendly Marylanders knew only that the

[83] *Ibid.*
[84] *H. B. McClellan,* 326.
[85] *H. B. McClellan,* 326; *O. R.,* 27, pt. 2, p. 695.
[86] See *supra,* Vol. II, p. 91 ff.
[87] *O. R.,* 27, pt. 2, p. 695.

Army of the Union was around Frederick and was moving north-ward. Newspapers told of the presence of Ewell in Pennsylvania and of his march toward Harrisburg. Of Early's movement to York, the papers received by Stuart probably contained no report.[88]

Still uncertain where he would reach Ewell's right column, Stuart continued the destruction of the B. & O. until about noon of the 29th. Then he started for Westminster, fifteen miles to the North, and on the main road from Gettysburg to Baltimore. The march was without incident until, about 5 P.M., the van reached the outskirts of Westminster and, to its surprise, had to receive immediately the charge of Union cavalry. In a few minutes, the "Johnny Rebs" saw that the Federals were few in number and their supports weak. Superior force soon captured or drove off the whole contingent, which proved to be the First Delaware, but the courage of the attack was not forgotten.[89]

In Westminster, Stuart's men found forage enough for the horses of the entire command. Distribution and feeding kept some of the troopers up nearly all night.[90] At the railroad station, rations in abundance were uncovered. Those of the cavalrymen who were free to eat heartily, to feed their horses, and then to go beyond the town for a good night's sleep felt that the weary day had not been in vain.[91] For his own part, Stuart would have been hurt and ashamed had he known how anxiously Lee was inquiring for news of him and how faltering was the movement of the Army in the absence of the cavalry. Ignorant of his chief's distress, Stuart was not concerned that day, apparently, because of his wagon train. It lengthened his column and placed his rearguard danger-ously far from his van, but the long halt at Hood's Mill had al-

---

[88] This has to be left in doubt because Stuart nowhere stated in his report what newspapers he procured, or when. He wrote only, and without reference to date (*O. R.,* 27, pt. 2, p. 707): "The newspapers of the enemy, my only source of information, chronicled [Early's arrival at York] and at Wrightsville with great particularity." Early entered York on the 28th. Reports of the surrender of the town were sent the United States War Department that day, but no available newspapers that could have fallen into Stuart's hands during the forenoon of the 29th carried any report of Early's arrival at York. The *National Intelligencer* (Washington) of June 29, p. 3, col. 4, stated that Early had reached the railroad between York and Hanover. That afternoon, the *Evening Bulletin* (Philadelphia) p. 2, col. 1, announced that Early was at Gettysburg. On the morning of the 30th, the *Philadelphia Inquirer*, p. 1, col. 3, and the *National Republican* (Washington) p. 1, col. 4, placed Early in York.

[89] Cf. H. B. *McClellan,* 326. The report of the commanding officer, Maj. N. B. Knight, is in *O. R.,* 27, pt. 2, pp. 201–03.

[90] *O. R.,* 27, pt. 2, p. 695.

[91] *Beale,* 81. The advance brigade bivouacked at Union Mills, about six miles North of Westminster on the road to Gettysburg. *O. R.,* 27, pt. 2, p. 69.

lowed ample time for the wagons to reach Westminster. During the night, scouts brought word that the enemy's cavalry was at Littletown, six miles to the Northwest of Union Mills and across the line in Pennsylvania.[92] If this intelligence caused Stuart to ask whether he should not burn his captured wagons, now that the enemy was at hand, the records give no hint. Said Major McClellan afterwards, "it was not in Stuart's nature to abandon an attempt until it had been proven to be beyond his powers . . ."[93]

The march of June 30, Stuart directed toward Hanover, twelve miles North of Union Mills. At Hanover, it will be remembered, he would be on the Baltimore and Carlisle Turnpike, along which he might push Northwest and rejoin Lee or Ewell on the Susquehanna. If the Confederate infantry were farther down the river, Hanover was the point from which to move to York.[94] En route to Hanover, Chambliss' Brigade was the advance; Hampton was in rear of the wagon train; Fitz Lee covered the left. "Jeb" rode with the van.

When the troopers of the leading regiment, the Thirteenth Virginia, descended about 9:45 from the high ground that overlooks Hanover, they saw on the road ahead of them an advancing squadron of blue cavalry. By a swift charge these Federals were pursued into the streets of the town. Stuart watched, approved, and took his station in a meadow at a point where the road from the South made a right angle turn toward Hanover. The meadow was in high timothy and, on the side nearest the road, was enclosed by a tall, ill-kept hedge,[95] but to these details, scant attention was paid. All eyes were on the town. From it, soon, came Confederates with prisoners and captured ambulances, but they did not have much time in which to enjoy their prizes. A courageous Federal Brigadier[96] had stopped and turned his command and in a few minutes attacked savagely. Before Stuart's own eyes, and past the

92 O. R., 27, pt. 2, p. 695.  93 H. B. McClellan, 327.
94 In his report, Stuart never stated what he considered his ultimate objective prior to the night march of June 30. He may have thought circumstance so completely would shape his advance that he could have no predetermined objective. The hint that shapes the statement in the text is Stuart's remark that when he reached Hanover, he found "a large column of cavalry passing through, going toward the gap of the mountains which I intended using" (O. R., 27, pt. 2, p. 695). Had Stuart been referring to the pass West of Cashtown, he scarcely would have gone toward Hanover. On the other hand, if Carlisle was a possible objective, Hanover was the proper approach.
95 W. W. Blackford's MS Memoirs, 332.
96 Brig. Gen. Elon J. Farnsworth, promoted June 29 and killed July 3. Cf. O. R., 27, pt. 1, pp. 992, 993.

hedge, his men ran to the rear in a manner to make their commander blush. He and his staff officers spurred out to the road and sought to halt the fugitives, but shouts and pleas and orders were unheard or unheeded.

"Rally them, Blackford," cried Stuart, in a laughing confession of his own failure. With that, he pulled up the rein and jumped his mare over a low strip of the hedge. Blackford followed. For a few minutes the General and his staff fired at the blue column that was sweeping along the road in pursuit of the Confederates who had entered the town. Suddenly Stuart became aware that a flanking party of Federals had entered the meadow and was dashing straight toward him. Inglorious flight was the alternative to surrender. Stuart turned, touched his mount with the spur and galloped away. The other officers scattered. So tall was the timothy that Stuart saw nothing of what was ahead of him until, in a flash, he found himself almost on the edge of a gully that seemed fifteen feet across and four or five feet deep. It was a desperate jump even for a fine thoroughbred mare,[97] but it was not beyond her strength and skill. Said Blackford afterwards, "I shall never forget the glimpse I then saw of this beautiful animal away up in midair over the chasm and Stuart's fine figure sitting erect and firm in the saddle." [98] The mare landed on her feet and, in an instant, was off. Several of the staff were less successful but, incredibly, all of them escaped.[99]

When Stuart smilingly rode up to Chambliss' men, they received him with a stare and then with a yell of delight. Word had passed that "Jeb" had been captured. Every man had felt himself shaken by the news and now was stronger for seeing the General unhurt and calm.[100] On the hill, where he soon brought some of his field guns into play Stuart knew that his command was safe. He easily discouraged any farther advance by the enemy, but his men were so scattered and his column so extended that he could not strike a counter-blow immediately.[101] Had it not been for those captured wagons, all three of the Brigades would have been together and

---

[97] This was Virginia, Stuart's favorite mount.
[98] W. W. Blackford's MS Memoirs, 332–33.
[99] Blackford, loc. cit.; H. B. McClellan, 328. There are some differences between Colonel Blackford's and Major McClellan's narratives of this incident, but they are reconcilable.
[100] Cf. Beale, 83.
[101] O. R., 27, pt. 2, pp. 695–96.

could have ended the action quickly. A lesser encumbrance were the prisoners who, surprisingly, now numbered 400—as many as had been paroled at Rockville and Cooksville. Hampered as he was by his train, Stuart could not bring himself to abandon it. He believed he was not far from the protection of the Confederate infantry, and, he later explained, he reasoned that if he parked the wagons temporarily and then made a detour during the night, he might bring the vehicles to his chief for use in collecting provisions from rich Pennsylvania.[102]

Once again, the crux of a military solution was the choice of a line of march. Stuart studied his map and reviewed all he could ascertain of his adversary's movements. Apparently the Federal commander, who the prisoners said was Brig. Gen. Judson Kilpatrick, was operating to the westward. To escape him, the wagons should go eastward before turning North again. Such a detour could be made by way of Jefferson, eight miles East of Hanover. After Jefferson was reached, the column could strike North again and could go either to York, by turning to the right, or straight to Dover and then, paralleling the Susquehanna, could get to Carlisle. Either while Stuart was debating this, or else later in the day, he was handed newspapers that told of Early's arrival on the 28th—two days previously—in York.[103] That indicated for the cavalry an advance to unite with "Jube." After the enemy was dislodged from the streets of Hanover and was driven westward, the Confederate column began another of its deadly night marches. Said Stuart afterwards: "Whole regiments slept in the saddle, their faithful animals keeping the road unguided." Now and again some boy, nodding to one side, fell from his saddle with a thud[104] but his comrades were too benumbed to laugh.

Such was the night of June 30 for "Jeb" Stuart, third of the men whose state of mind was making history for America while the Confederate Army converged on Gettysburg. He had gone on and on in the exercise of the discretion Lee had given. Almost six days Stuart had been on his raid. Not a single time had he heard from any of the infantry commanders with whom he was directed to co-operate. One dispatch only had he sent, and that on the 25th.

102 *Ibid.*, 696; H. B. McClellan, 329.
103 *Cf.* note *supra* 88 and O. R., 27, pt. 2, p. 707.
104 O. R., 27, pt. 2, p. 696.

Other adventure was to be his,[105] but nothing he had achieved and nothing he could hope to accomplish with his exhausted men could offset the harm which the events of coming days were to show he already had done his chief and his cause.

[105] For Stuart's next experiences, see *infra*, p. 136.

# CHAPTER V

## Promise of Another Triumph

That night of June 30, while Stuart's sleepy boys were falling off their horses, "Dick" Ewell was fuming over discretionary orders. Longstreet confidently was expecting his plan of a tactical defensive to be accepted by his chief. A. P. Hill was preparing for the advance of part of his troops from Cashtown to Gettysburg at the end of a long advance from the Rappahannock. During the early days of June, his had been the most interesting of all assignments. When Lee made ready to move toward Pennsylvania, he planned to leave Hill and the whole of the Third Corps to watch Hooker's Army and to occupy it while the First and Second Corps slipped away. Hill's orders were to hold the enemy, to retreat southward if overwhelmed, and to pursue if Hooker evacuated Stafford Heights. "You are desired," Lee wrote, "to open any official communications sent to me, and, if necessary, act upon them, according to the dictates of your good judgment." [1] That was the most responsible assignment, the most shining proof of Lee's confidence, that the new corps commander could have asked or received.

Hill's instructions were written on the morning of June 5, when Lee was about to strike his tent and to follow the First and Second Corps up the river. Before the commanding General could start, the Federals began to stir on Stafford Heights.[2] Hill observed this activity and concluded that, once again, the Unionists were about to cross the river and challenge the works on the ridge. Accordingly, he ordered Heth to move nearer the town, and he sent to the rear his lovely young wife who, in the judgment of at least one of Hill's subordinates, had lingered imprudently long at the front.[3] That afternoon, protected by artillery, the enemy laid a pontoon bridge opposite the mouth of Deep Run.[4] Over this bridge moved

[1] O. R., 27 pt. 3, pp. 859–60.      [2] O. R., 27 pt. 2, p. 293.
[3] W. Dorsey Pender to his wife, MS, June 7, 1863. Pender added prudentially: "I know you are too good a wife to have given me as much anxiety and trouble as she gave the General"—*Pender MSS.*
[4] O. R., 27, pt. 2, p. 305.

a strong column that took shelter under the bank of the river.[5] Lee watched this crossing and decided that Ewell, then marching to Culpeper, should be halted until the extent of the Federal movement was ascertained.[6] The next afternoon, Hill was told by the commanding General that the force on the right bank of the river did not appear too strong for the Third Corps to handle.[7] With good wishes to his lieutenant, Lee rode to overtake the troops who were to invade the Northern States. Hill was left to watch and to worst the enemy.

That was easy. The Federals brought over a few guns and they dug a line of rifle pits;[8] but Hooker believed the Southerners on the ridge had been reinforced[9] and he did not change his original plan, which was that of reconnaissance and demonstration.[10] The Confederates soon read their adversary's intention.[11] In the nonchalant words of an officer of McGowan's Brigade, the enemy did not indulge "in anything more hostile than music and cheering, or, on one or two occasions, such a bold display of pickets as to require a few shells at our hands. . . ."[12]

By the morning of June 14, the Federals had left the right bank of the Rappahannock. Gradually during the day, the thousands of vehicles and tents that had stood for months on Stafford Heights vanished. Hill dispatched scouts across the stream,[13] but he did not probe the Federal positions. Correctly he assumed that Hooker was abandoning the line of the Rappahannock to interpose between Lee and Washington. The duty of the Third Corps now was to follow the main army. "Dick" Anderson was started the same 14th of June for Culpeper.[14] Harry Heth followed with his Division on the 15th. Dorsey Pender was left to make quite certain the Unionists were not employing a ruse. When satisfied on that score, Pender was to move. From his last camp at Hamilton's Crossing the North Carolinian wrote his young wife: "Thus far, General Lee's plans have worked admirably; so says General Hill,

[5] The first unit to cross was the 2nd Brigade of the 2nd Division, VI Corps. O. R., 27, pt. 1, p. 676.
[6] O. R., 27, pt. 2, p. 293. In Lee's final report on Gettysburg, ibid., 305, the crossing wrongly is dated June 6.
[7] O. R., 27, pt. 2, p. 293.    [8] O. R., 27, pt. 2, p. 294.
[9] O. R., 2', pt. 1, p. 36.    [10] O. R., 27, pt. 1, pp. 32-33.
[11] Pendleton in O. R., 27, pt. 2, p. 347; Dorsey Pender to his wife, MS, June 9, 10, 12, 1863—Pender MSS.
[12] Caldwell, 91.
[13] O. R., 57, pt. 2, pp. 723-24.    [14] O. R., 27, pt. 2, p. 613.

who I suppose knows them . . . May God in his goodness be more gracious than in our last trial [the invasion of Maryland]. We certainly may be allowed to hope as our mission is one of peace altho through blood. The enemy seem to think we have 90,000 men, which will scare them so badly they will be half whipt before they commence the fight. I do not anticipate any fight this side of the Potomac." [15]

Swiftly Pender marched toward the other Divisions, which proceeded via Culpeper, Front Royal, Berryville, Charlestown, Shepherdstown, and Boonsborough to Hagerstown. Thence the line of advance was Greencastle, Chambersburg and Fayetteville.[16] Frequently, at the end of a long day on a dusty road, Dorsey Pender wrote down his reflections on religion, on the Southern revolution and on the responsibilities of a new commander. All his sympathies were with the younger officers. Before he left the Rappahannock he had applauded his wife's portrayal of a senior from the "old army," who had made a failure in the field. Said Pender: "What a blessing it was that so few of those old fellows came over from the old service. They would have all claimed high positions and been able to do nothing to help the cause." [17] Equally, upon promotion to divisional command, Pender had insisted on the advancement of men from his own State. Said he to one officer: "You know I have a first rate Commissary with my Brigade, and no doubt you supposed I would take him with me, but he is not a North Carolinian and you are, and I think our state has not had a fair share of Staff Officers, and it has been my ambition to make her troops equal to any in the Army. For that reason I want them officered by North Carolinians as far as practicable." [18] With or without men of his own State, he had to admit: "Responsibility is a load that is anything but pleasant." [19]

The advance prospered. "We have a grand race on hand between Lee and Hooker," said Pender, who explained: "We have the inside track, Hooker going to Washington and we by Winchester." [20] Again from Berryville: "Everything thus far has worked

15 To his wife, MS, June 15, 1863—*Pender MSS.*
16 The itinerary is given in Anderson's report, *O. R.,* 27 pt. 2, p. 613.
17 To his wife, MS, June 9, 1863—*Pender MSS.*
18 Letter of D. T. Carraway, September, 1893—*Pender MSS.*
19 To his wife, MS, June 17, 1863—*Pender MSS.*
20 *Ibid.,* June 17, 1863.

admirably . . . Keep in good spirits, honey, and hope that this summer's work will tend to shorten the war." [21]

Pender's views were far exceeded by those the newspapers were expressing. Now that the editors surmised Lee was preparing for invasion, they predicted great results.[22] With discernment, one Richmond paper observed: "General Lee intends something much more serious than a mere incursion into Pennsylvania . . . The South is, for a time relieved, and the North is bearing the whole burden of the war." [23] Other journals, led by the *Charleston Mercury,* clamored for reprisal and destruction.[24] Pender, in contrast, wrote: "Tomorrow I do what I know will cause you grief and that is to cross the Potomac . . . may the Lord prosper this crossing and bring us early peace out of it." [25] After he was in Pennsylvania he wrote: "I am tired of invasion for altho they have made us suffer all that people can suffer, I cannot get my resentment to that point to make me indifferent to what goes on here." [26]

During the marches that stirred these thoughts, Hill, Pender and the other commanders of the Third Corps had for a time the company of Lee. Pender wrote: "Lee was in fine spirits but said he was going to shoot us if we did not keep our men from straggling. They marched finely coming up here. I told him if he gave us authority to shoot those under us he might take the same privilege with us." [27] Of detailed plans Lee said little, but he raised many hopes when he told Pender that if the Army of Northern Virginia met and crushed Hooker, and Vicksburg and Port Hudson did their part, "our prospects of peace are very fine." [28]

Contact bred new confidence. Said Pender after the Third Corps had reached Fayetteville, Pennsylvania: "Everything seems to be going finely. We might get to Philadelphia without a fight, I believe, if we should desire to go. General Lee intimates to no one what he is up to, and we can only surmise. I hope we may be

[21] *Ibid.,* June 21, 1863.
[22] *Richmond Examiner,* June 23; *Richmond Dispatch,* June 27, July 2; *Richmond Enquirer,* July 2, 1863.
[23] *Richmond Dispatch,* July 2, 1863.
[24] *Richmond Whig,* June 22; *Charleston Mercury,* June 23, June 24, 1863.
[25] To his wife, MS, June 24, 1863—*Pender MSS.*    [26] *Ibid.,* June 28, 1863.
[27] To his wife, MS, June 23, 1863—*Pender MSS.*
[28] *Ibid.* Pender's exact words are one evidence that Longstreet was mistaken in assuming Lee committed to a tactical defensive: "The General says he wants to meet [Hooker] as soon as possible and crush him . . ."

in Harrisburg in three days . . . Our men seem to be in the spirit and feel confident. I never saw troops march as ours do. They will go 15 or 20 miles a day without having a straggler, and whoop and yell on all occasions. I wish we could meet Hooker and have the matter settled at once." [29]

Part of that wish was realized. On the 29th, it will be remembered,[30] Lee directed that all the Corps move East of the mountains in order to hold the enemy there and to prevent interruption of his lines of communication with Virginia when he desired to reopen them.[31] Hill was to advance in the direction of Cashtown. Longstreet was to follow. Ewell was to march from Carlisle.

The movement was undertaken smoothly by Hill and with the readiness that already had prompted Pender to say that Hill as Lieutenant General was "managing the march" and would give as much satisfaction as he had in divisional command.[32] Under Hill's direction, Heth proceeded to Cashtown that same day, June 29. While Pender advanced to Cashtown on the 30th, Johnston Pettigrew, of Heth's Division, proceeded toward Gettysburg, where he had heard he would find some shoes for his barefooted men. Heth remained at Cashtown and, after the practice of Confederates in Northern States, undertook to do a bit of shopping. His particular need was a hat. In his quest, his Quartermaster had anticipated him and had requisitioned all the headgear of the stores. From the hats available, he invited Heth to take his pick. The one that appealed most to Heth was too large for him. Not to be balked by this, a clerk at divisional headquarters put several folds of paper between the hat and sweat band and pronounced it a fit. Heth thanked his officer and, as the event proved, had the best of reason for doing so.[33]

Although Heth got his hat at Cashtown, Pettigrew missed the shoes at Gettysburg. Late in the afternoon of June 30, the magnificent Carolinian returned to Cashtown and reported that as his troops neared Gettysburg, which is eight miles Southeast of Cashtown, they encountered cavalry outposts. Some of the officers thought they heard, as if on the other side of the town, the roll of infantry drums. Pettigrew wisely had concluded that as he had

29 *Ibid.*, June 28, 1863.                    30 See *supra*, p. 35.
31 *O. R.*, 27, pt. 2, p. 317.
32 Pender to his wife, MS, June 28, 1863—*Pender MSS.*
33 *Heth's MS Memoirs*, 146–47.

no cavalry to ascertain the strength of the force in Gettysburg, he should return and report.

Hill arrived from Fayetteville after Pettigrew came back to Cashtown from Gettysburg. At Heth's instance, Pettigrew repeated to Hill the story of his day's experiences. Said Hill confidently: "The only force at Gettysburg is cavalry, probably a detachment of observation. I am just from General Lee, and the information he has from his scouts corroborates that I have received from mine—that is, the enemy are still at Middleburg, and have not struck their tents." [34]

"If there is no objection," Heth answered immediately, "I will take my Division tomorrow and go to Gettysburg and get those shoes."

"None in the world." [35]

On those four words fate hung. At 5 o'clock the next morning, July 1, Heth started for Gettysburg. No special attention was given to the place the different units had in the advancing column. In front was the veteran Brigade of Archer, which at Chancellorsville had captured Hazel Grove.[36] "Joe" Davis's Brigade followed in strength under its inexperienced, pleasant and unpretending Brigadier.[37] Pettigrew's North Carolinians and Field's Virginians, led by Col. J. M. Brockenbrough, were behind Davis. The artillery was the excellent battalion of Maj. William J. Pegram. Prudently, Hill decided to have Pender's Division follow Heth immediately.[38] Anderson's Division, which was at Fayetteville, was to move that morning to Cashtown and was to start early, in order to clear the road from Shippensburg to Greenwood for the advance of Edward Johnson with Ewell's reserve artillery and trains.[39]

The day was warm. Water was scarce. Otherwise the march was not unpleasant. Nothing of any importance occurred until, about three miles West of Gettysburg, blue videttes were en-

---

[34] Needless to say, Hill's reference was to Middleburg, Maryland, sixteen miles South of Gettysburg.

[35] Heth in 4 S.H.S.P., 157. The language in his MS Memoirs is slightly different.

[36] See supra, Vol II, p. 586.

[37] "General Davis is a very pleasant and unpretending gentleman . . ." L. M. Blackford to his mother, MS, March 11, 1863—Blackford Papers.

[38] The wisdom of sending so strong a column on what was in effect a reconnaissance has been much disputed. Cf. D. G. McIntosh, "Review of the Gettysburg Campaign," 37 S.H.S.P., 74 ff. See also infra, p. 170.

[39] Lee to Anderson, MS, June 30, 1863—Anderson MSS.

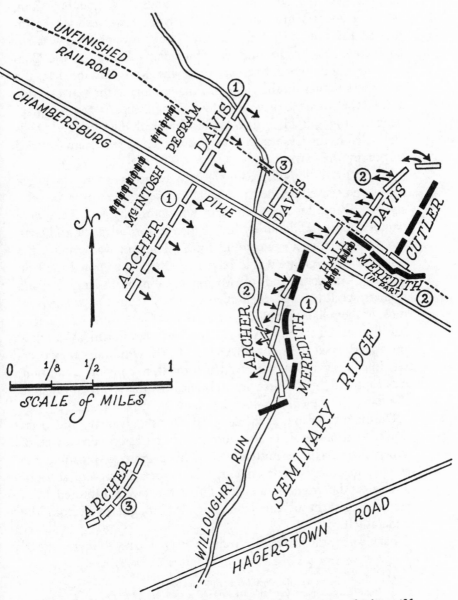

UNFINISHED RAILROAD

CHAMBERSBURG

PEGRAM

DAVIS

①

McINTOSH

ARCHER

①

PIKE

③

DAVIS

②

DAVIS

CUTLER

HALL

MEREDITH (IN PART)

②

②

ARCHER

MEREDITH

①

SEMINARY RIDGE

WILLOUGHBY RUN

ARCHER

③

HAGERSTOWN ROAD

0    ⅛    ½    1

SCALE of MILES

Sketch of Heth's "Feeling-out" Advance toward Gettysburg, Morning of July 1, 1863. The encircled numerals indicate the successive positions. After John B. Bachelder.

countered. They withdrew promptly [40] and did not delay the advance. As the column descended toward Willoughby Run, which is about a mile and a half from the town, everything indicated the presence of the enemy,[41] but no opposition was encountered. No hostile line was observed.[42] Ahead, on the Confederate right, woods were close to the Run. On the left, the cover was higher up the ridge. Heth, employing the usual tactics, shelled the woods to drive out any lurking troops.[43] Nothing happened. At length, Heth had Archer deploy on the right and Davis on the left of the Cashtown Road,[44] and then he sent them forward to occupy the town.

Down to Willoughby Run the two Brigades went. Davis got across and started up the hill. Archer moved his left over the little stream. Before his right regiment was across the run, there were pauses, shouts and desultory fire. Federals were advancing! Davis, too, quickly met an oncoming force. The fire was instant, the clash furious. As fate would have it, Archer encountered the Iron Brigade,[45] a command of Michigan, Wisconsin and Indiana soldiers who deserved their name.[46] They fought as savagely as most of them had that bloody afternoon at Groveton when "Dick" Ewell attacked them.[47] At any time they were formidable. Now they overlapped the right of Archer. In a few minutes they overwhelmed his thin Brigade. Archer himself, in pathetic exhaustion, was captured [48]—the first general officer of the Army to fall into the hands of the enemy since Lee had taken command.

On the other flank, as it happened, Davis's advancing line overlapped that of the Federals, who quickly retreated. From lack of experience, Davis permitted two of his regiments, pursuing the enemy, to enter a railroad cut, where their files were at right angles to the front of attack. There they were captured by a reserve regiment of the Iron Brigade, brought over from the Federal left.

Back, then, the wreck of Archer's Brigade and the remnant of

[40] O. R., 27, pt. 2, p. 317.  [41] Heth in O. R., 27, pt. 2, p. 637.
[42] Heth in 4 S.H.S.P., 158.  [43] 4 S.H.S.P., 158.
[44] Its proper name was the Chambersburg Turnpike.
[45] Brig. Gen. Solomon Meredith's 1st Brigade, 1st Division, I Corps.
[46] Cf. O. R., 27, pt. 1, pp. 155, 245.
[47] See supra, Vol. II, pp. 108–09. The Brigade then had been John Gibbon's, and had been the 4th Brigade, 1st Division, III Corps. The sole difference in the composition of the Brigade was the addition of the 24th Michigan, Col. Henry A. Morrow.
[48] O. R., 27, pt. 2, p. 646; 8 C. V., 535–37, 19 ibid., 420.

Davis's surged. Their reconnaissance had been costly.[49] With unconscious humor, Heth subsequently wrote: "The enemy had now been felt, and found to be in heavy force in and around Gettysburg.[50] Heth might have said, the enemy had been felt and had been found to bristle. No choice remained except to renew the fight or to quit the field. At the moment, Heth was senior Confederate officer in contact with the enemy. Neither Lee nor Hill had arrived. Heth consequently had to make his own decisions. He concluded that the safe and soldierly thing to do was to put his infantry in line of battle, to cover his front with his artillery and to prepare for a new advance. All this he did, but he left Davis's Brigade out of the line because he believed the regiments had been too badly shattered to fight again that day. Pegram's artillerymen found the best positions and occupied them. David McIntosh brought up his battalion and added its fire. Where sharpshooters or advanced units were close enough to the enemy, they plied their rifles and kept up the semblance of contest. Heth waited an hour, two hours. He scarcely hoped the enemy would attack him but he desired to delay his own assault if he could, until Hill arrived or Pender was in support.[51]

At length Lee rode over from Cashtown. Heth reported and learned, if he did not know already, that Lee did not wish a major battle joined before the converging Southern columns were all in position. Soon, too, word came that Pender was arriving with his Division. Desultory action continued. The enemy appeared to be strong. His artillery returned shell for shell, though the Confederates believed they had the better of the duel. Whenever

49 *O. R.*, 27, pt. 2, pp. 317, 638, 646 ff, 649. This phase of the action was reported by all the Confederate commanders, except General Lee, with much reticence. The best of all the accounts is that of Maj. Gen. Abner Doubleday, commanding 3rd Division, I Corps, and, after the death of Maj. Gen. John F. Reynolds, acting chief on July 1 of the I Corps (*O. R.*, 27 pt. 1, p. 243 ff). Reports do not show the number of prisoners lost by the Confederates. In Heth's account (*O. R.*, 27, pt. 2, p. 638), the total for Archer was given as "some 60 or 70." The report of the temporary head of the Brigade, Lt. Col. S. G. Shepard (*ibid.*, 646), put the number at "some 75." In the tabular return of casualties for the entire campaign, Archer's Brigade was charged with 517 captured or missing. That figure included those lost or left behind in the charge of July 3 (*O. R.*, 27, pt. 2, p. 344). Davis's report (*ibid.*, 648 ff) gave no statement of losses. The tabular return (*ibid.*, 344) charged him with total casualties of 897, or 220 in excess of all those, prisoners included, that were lost from Archer's Brigade. In the two regiments of Davis's that suffered most from capture on July 1, the killed and wounded July 1–3 were 497.

50 *O. R.*, 27, pt. 2, p. 638.

51 Heth did not say this in his report, but the length of his delay is evidence that he was waiting for reinforcements.

Federal infantry showed themselves in any number, Pegram and McIntosh opened on them.[52]

Between 2:30 and 3:00 o'clock, the Confederates observed that Union troops on the ridge in front of them were shifting to the northward. Soon, from that quarter, came the welcome sound of Southern guns. In obedience to Lee's orders,[53] Ewell's Second Corps was approaching Gettysburg. Tom Carter's Battalion of artillery had opened. Rodes's Division was forming almost at right angle to Heth and was preparing to attack.[54] Early that morning of the 1st of July, Rodes had left Heidlersburg and had headed for Cashtown, but a message from Hill to Ewell had caused "Old Bald Head" to make Gettysburg the objective of the march. On the road, Ewell received from Army Headquarters the same information that by this time had been given Heth: If the Confederates encountered the enemy in large force, they were to avoid a general engagement, if practicable, until the entire army was at hand.[55] Four miles from Gettysburg, Rodes had heard the sound of firing and had prepared for action. As he had drawn nearer and had ascertained where Hill was fighting, Rodes had seen that if he continued along the ridge to the East of Willoughby Run, he could assail in flank the Federals who were opposing Hill. With only one Brigade deployed, Rodes had moved down the high ground called Seminary Ridge; but after he had flushed Federal cavalry, he had deployed on a front of three Brigades. Advancing in this manner about one mile, Rodes had reached an eminence.[56]

There, with kindling eye, Rodes had seen at a distance of about 800 yards what he had assumed to be the full force of the Federals who were facing Hill. "To get at these troops properly"—the words are his own [57]—Rodes had to move by his right flank and to change direction somewhat to the West. In preparation, two

[52] O. R., 27, pt. 2, p. 674.                     [53] See supra, p. 35.
[54] O. R., 27, pt. 2, pp. 317, 552. Immense and detailed as is the literature on Gettysburg, much confusion exists regarding the state of the battle when Rodes reached the scene. Federal reports suggest more action at the time than do the Confederate accounts. Cf. Carl Schurz's report, O. R., 27, pt. 1, p. 552.
[55] O. R., 27, pt. 2, p. 444.
[56] The knoll Northeast of the Mummasburg Road, opposite the Forney House. All positions described in the text, unless otherwise credited, are taken from the maps of John B. Bachelder. These maps are not free of mistakes but, detail considered, they remain the best in existence.
[57] O. R., 27, pt. 2, p. 552. Rodes's report is the only satisfactory Confederate account of this part of the action of July 1.

batteries of Carter's Battalion were ordered to an elevation immediately West of the knoll where Rodes had his field headquarters.[58] Quickly the gunners opened fire to enfilade the Federal line that faced Hill. As Rodes watched the startled action of the Union forces, he thought for a moment that they were caught by surprise and might be routed. Soon he observed troops pouring out of Gettysburg as if to deploy against him. Directly southward, also, the blue regiments began to change front and to draw a line across the ridge. Although Rodes did not and, in the circumstances, could not know it, the whole of the I Corps now was being arrayed against him and Hill. Toward Rodes's left, two Divisions of Howard's XI Corps—adversaries of Chancellorsville —were moving.[59]

Rodes had been assured that Early's Division of the Second Corps would arrive in a short time and would take position nearer Gettysburg. Consequently, Rodes determined to hold with his left and to attack with his right. George Doles, wholly capable, was directed to place his veteran troops on the left and to stop any movement to turn that flank. This arrangement made O'Neal's Brigade, formerly Rodes's own, a major element of the column of attack. Iverson, who was West of O'Neal, would share the advance. Junius Daniel's Brigade, which had never fought in Virginia, was supporting Iverson. In reserve was one of the Brigades that had earned greatest fame at Chancellorsville, Ramseur's North Carolinians. Within the time available, this deployment probably was unavoidable, but it was far from ideal. It left the well-tested Brigadiers, Ramseur and Doles, out of the first attack and put the direction of the assault on O'Neal and on Iverson, who had not distinguished themselves in the battles of May.

It chanced, also, from the nature of the ground and the line of attack, that a gap existed between Doles's right and O'Neal's left. In order to cover this gap, Rodes directed the Fifth Alabama, O'Neal's left regiment, not to participate in the advance of the Brigade, but to stay where it was and to await Rodes's personal orders.[60] Further, as O'Neal's right regiment was somewhat ex-

---

58 Colonel Carter, in his report (*O. R.*, 27, pt. 2, p. 602), mistook the Mummasburg for the Chambersburg or Cashtown Road.
59 Schurz's and Barlow's Divisions. Steinwehr's Division was on Cemetery Hill (*O. R.*, 27, pt. 1, pp. 721, 727).
60 *O. R.*, 27, pt. 2, p. 553.

posed, Rodes recalled it to position in line with Daniel's Brigade. These arrangements either angered or confused O'Neal.

Soon it was apparent that the Federals did not intend to await Rodes's attack in the wood they occupied. They moved boldly out to attack Rodes, whose fighting spirit rose at the sight of them. He would strike at once! In person, he pointed out to O'Neal the line of advance of the left regiment of the four that were to drive straight for the advancing enemy. Iverson was to move simultaneously and on the right of O'Neal. The Brigade of Daniel was to support Iverson. If not needed for that purpose, it was to attack on the right.[61]

All this was arranged while O'Neal, on foot, was at Rodes's field headquarters. When Rodes at length was ready to order the advance against the approaching Federals, O'Neal remarked that neither he nor his staff officers had any horses at hand or any mounted couriers with them. He did not know how he could get his orders to Col. Cullen A. Battle, commander of the regiment [62] that had been recalled from an exposed position and had been placed on a line with Daniel's Brigade. Rodes answered that one of his officers would carry O'Neal's order, and, with no more delay, Rodes started for the front.[63]

The advance was launched. In a few minutes it went awry. O'Neal's front seemed narrow. He had three regiments only in line, though his Brigade included five. By some misunderstanding, he had authorized the Third Alabama to remain on Daniel's flank and not to move forward.[64] Units were mingled. Direction was faulty. Between O'Neal and Doles, the gap widened. Another gap appeared between O'Neal and Iverson. In a short time, it was apparent that Iverson's line of advance was exposing the whole of Daniel's supporting Brigade.[65]

Promptly now the fine Alabama regiments of O'Neal opened their fire but, in their confusion, they could not drive the enemy, who had halted and engaged. Observing this, Rodes turned back to get the Fifth Alabama, the reserve regiment he had intended to use in filling the gap between O'Neal and Doles.[66] To Rodes's surprise, he found that O'Neal had remained with the Fifth instead of going forward to direct the advancing regiments. "The

61 Ibid.
63 O. R., 27, pt. 2, pp. 553–54
65 O. R., 27, pt. 2, p. 444.

62 The Third Alabama.
64 O. R., 27, pt. 2, p. 553.
66 O. R., 27, pt. 2, p. 553.

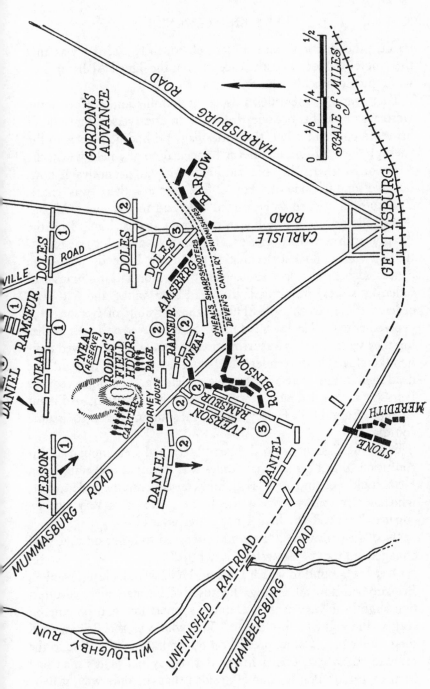

Sketch of attack of Rodes's Division, near Gettysburg, Afternoon of July 1, 1863. The encircled numerals indicate the successive positions. O'Neal's Third Alabama operated with Daniel's Brigade. In the final position of Daniel, that regiment is the unit immediately under the numeral 3. After John B. Bachelder.

result," the division commander subsequently stated, "was that the whole Brigade, with the exception of the Third Alabama . . . was repulsed quickly, and with loss." [67]

That was not the full measure of humiliation. Before long, word was brought to Rodes from the frantic Iverson that one of his regiments had raised the white flag and had gone over to the enemy! Such a thing had never happened on any field where the Army of Northern Virginia had fought; it was inconceivable now, but Iverson affirmed it. For a few minutes there was chaos. Rodes's plan seemed to be ruined. He had to fight with his left destroyed and, for all he knew, employed against him. Soon the ghastly truth was discovered: In Iverson's advance, his line of battle had come under a decimating fire from Federals who were concealed behind a low stone wall. The North Carolinians had fallen by scores, almost as if they had been halted and had been ordered to lie down. Still fighting, the left units of Iverson were exposed when O'Neal was repulsed. Some of Iverson's men, realizing they were about to be surrounded and slaughtered, waved their handkerchiefs in surrender. Iverson saw this and thought the dead men in line were alive and were yielding.[68] So unnerved was Iverson, as his Brigade scattered, that his Assistant Adjutant General, Capt. D. P. Halsey, had to rally the men and to assume command.[69]

From the Cashtown Road, Harry Heth had seen enough of this confusion to feel certain that Rodes was having a desperate fight. Heth could not find A. P. Hill, and consequently he rode to Lee, who silently was watching the battle. "Rodes is very heavily engaged," said Heth, "had I not better attack?"

"No," Lee answered, "I am not prepared to bring on a general engagement today—Longstreet is not up." [70]

Over the ground to which Lee and Heth were looking, Daniel's Brigade was now advancing. Because Iverson had changed direction slightly in his advance, Daniel's support line had become, in reality, the right flank element. The whole of the Brigade was soon under fire. Daniel pressed on but found himself close to the railroad cut where, earlier in the day, many of Davis's men had been captured. Boldly, Daniel decided that the only way of driv-

[67] O. R., 27, pt. 2, p. 553.        [68] O. R., 27. pt. 2, pp. 444, 554, 579–8ᴄ.
[69] Ibid., 445.        [70] 4 S.H.S.P.. 158.

ing the enemy from that shelter was to get astride it and to sweep it with his fire. To the West, at a distance of a few hundred yards, Daniel saw some troops of the Third Corps, and he hurried an officer to them to ask help in driving the Federals from the cut. The Confederates on the right made no move to co-operate.[71] Daniel accordingly had to take one of his regiments and move it southward by its right flank, so that it could face eastward, perpendicular to the cut, while the remainder of the regiments, in line from West to East, continued to face southward.[72] This was undertaken approximately at the time the left of Iverson was being turned and some of his men were surrendering.[73]

Daniel got his regiment astride the cut and began to advance, but he could not throw all his troops immediately into the assault he was determined to deliver against the enemy to the South of him. Ramseur, with the reserve Brigade, was being advanced to support the centre, where O'Neal and Iverson had been repulsed. George Doles, on the left, was fully occupied with Federals who evidently knew there was a gap between him and the shattered flank of O'Neal.[74]

The prospect was grim. All of Rodes's troops now were engaged or soon were to be. The young divisional commander who had won plaudits at Chancellorsville was not sweeping the field. He was, on the contrary, in undeniable difficulty. His men were fighting gallantly enough, but clumsy mistakes and nervous failures of leadership had almost wrecked the Division in front of an enemy who was strong, vigorous, confident. Robert Rodes might be headed for a humiliating defeat.

Then, once again, as so often had happened to Lee's Army, the most desperate moment proved the most fortunate. On the left of Rodes, where Doles was hard pressed, Gordon's Brigade of "Jube" Early's men arrived from the North and rushed into action. About the same time, with Lee's consent, Hill sent Heth forward.

---

[71] O. R., 27, pt. 2, p. 567. These troops must have been the Forty-second Mississippi and the Fifty-fifth North Carolina of Davis's Brigade. Many of the officers of these regiments had been wounded earlier in the day. Among them were Col. J. K. Connally and Maj. A. H. Belo of the Fifty-fifth North Carolina (O. R., 27, pt. 2, p. 649), who had been involved in the double duel during the Suffolk campaign. See supra, Vol. II, pp. 487–89.
[72] O. R., 27, pt. 2, p. 567.      [73] Ibid.
[74] Doles narrowly escaped death or capture by the Federals when his horse dashed for the Union lines. Fortunately, he fell off in a wheatfield before the animal reached the enemy (5 C. V., 614.)

When the Division grew weary and Heth himself fell with a head wound, Hill sent Pender's Division through the ranks of Heth to clear Seminary Ridge. It was done with the fierce might that always made Pender's charges terrifying. The enemy stood for a time and poured a destructive fire into the advancing graycoats, but the spirit of the entire Division was that of the color-bearer of the Thirteenth North Carolina. A projectile almost tore this boy's right arm from the socket. Scarcely pausing, he shifted the flagstaff to his left hand and continued to press on with the cry, "Forward, forward!" [75] Such men were not to be repulsed.[76]

From lines where dead were thickly strewn, Rodes was able, meantime, to advance Daniel and Ramseur and parts of O'Neal's and Iverson's Brigades. Doles, relieved by Gordon's intervention, attacked as if he wished to be avenged for having to maintain an earlier defensive.[77] Seminary Ridge was cleared, though some blue units fought valiantly to cover the retreat.[78] Beyond that high ground, General Hill did not think it prudent to advance his exhausted and now disordered troops.[79] Rodes's right Brigades —or what was left of them—also rested on the captured ridge. Ramseur and Doles, of the same Division, pursued the enemy into Gettysburg.[80] Gordon, on a superb black stallion, pressed magnificently forward. "General," asked a young officer, "where are your dead men?"

The shouted answer was: "I haven't got any, sir; the Almighty has covered my men with His shield and buckler." [81]

---

[75] His name was W. F. Faucette, Big Falls, North Carolina (Gordon, 114).
[76] One of the fullest accounts of the advance of Pender's Division is in a letter of Abner Perrin to Gov. M. L. Bonham, July 29, 1863; Miss. Valley Hist. Review, March, 1938, p. 520 ff.
[77] O. R., 27, pt. 2, pp. 317, 445, 468, 554, 638–39. It is almost impossible to determine from the reports the exact status of Rodes's fight when Early attacked and Hill sent Heth forward again. The movements of Daniel's Brigade appear to be the basis of any timing of the other operations, but Daniel (O. R., 27, pt. 2, p. 567) is not explicit. The final assault by the Confederates was about 4 P.M. (O. R., 27, pt. 1, p. 250); the order to retire to Cemetery Hill was given by Gen. O. O. Howard at 4:10 (ibid., 704). General Howard reported that "the columns reached Cemetery Hill" at 4:30 (ibid.). The first Confederate troops from the North came within sight of Cemetery Hill prior to 4:00.
[78] Cf. O. R., 27, pt. 1, pp. 250–51, where Gen. Abner Doubleday listed several of the units that were conspicuous for brave rearguard action.
[79] O. R., 27, pt. 2, p. 607.      [80] Ibid., 555.
[81] Stiles, 211. Gordon's inspiring presence in battle was the pride and amazement of his men. Stiles remembered (ibid., 211–12) that when he asked what was the command of a wounded man he was lifting from a box-car, the man replied: "I belong to Gordon's old brigade, Cap'n. Did you ever see the Gin'ral in battle? He's most the prettiest thing you ever did see on a field of fight. It'ud put fight into a whipped chicken just to look at him!"

Hays's Brigade of Early's Division, losing few,[82] also fought its way into town,[83] where Union soldiers of the I and of the XI Corps were crowded in confusion and bewilderment.[84] About 4000 prisoners were captured in the town; an additional 1000 were taken on the ridge and elsewhere.[85] Flags had been seized, too. One of them came out of Gettysburg in the hands of a wounded North Carolinian, whose dying request was that it should be delivered to President Davis.[86] Everywhere among the Confederates the same exultant spirit prevailed. Rodes's discomfiture and the earlier repulse of Davis and of Archer were forgotten. Gettysburg, the soldiers felt, was Chancellorsville all over again: the enemy was being routed. Officers of the high command were no less pleased, but they had no time for rejoicing. A new decision had to be made.

[82] O. R., 27, pt. 2, p. 480.
[83] Ibid., 555.
[84] O. R., 27, pt. 1, pp. 251, 704.
[85] O. R., 27, pt. 2, pp. 317, 445.
[86] N. C. Regts., 276–77.

# CHAPTER VI

## EWELL CANNOT REACH A DECISION

IN THE DIRECTION of Rodes's battle and of Early's advance, "Dick" Ewell had small part. The fight of Rodes had been too swift, too full of change and too confused for the corps commander to have any useful role. Ewell had the sound, soldierly sense not to interfere where he could not aid. As for Early, his dispositions had been prompt and confident. They had called for no correction. Ewell's only important decision had been reached while Carter's Battalion had been firing at the Federals who had been advancing before Rodes's infantry had gone into action. At that time, a courier from Lee had arrived with acknowledgment of Ewell's report of his movement toward Gettysburg. The courier brought, also, the message Heth and Hill already had received, namely, that if the officers found the enemy "too large," Lee did not want an engagement brought on till the remaining Divisions arrived. Ewell had pondered these instructions but his blood was up. He had concluded that he could not break off the fight without disaster, and he had pressed it vigorously.[1]

Now that the enemy was being driven out of Gettysburg, Ewell rode toward the town and had a nearer view of the high ground to the South of it. A mile away, almost directly opposite the main street, was Cemetery Hill, which was about eighty feet above the level of the centre of Gettysburg.[2] Somewhat closer to the town and on the opposite side of the road that climbed the ridge was a second eminence, East Cemetery Hill, almost as high. Still farther eastward, around the head of a ravine, the ground rose nearly another 100 feet to a rocky, ragged and wood covered eminence which the natives called Culp's Hill. From the crest of Cemetery Hill to the top of Culp's Hill, as Ewell looked at them, the distance was slightly more than half a mile.[3] These elevations dominated the town. It was manifest, also, that Cemetery Hill and an eleva-

---

[1] O. R., 27, pt. 2, p. 444.
[2] Five hundred feet compared with 412 according to Bachelder's map.
[3] To be exact, 3100 feet.

tion South of it constituted a natural defense against attack from
Seminary Ridge, the high ground where Hill's weary men were
awaiting orders.

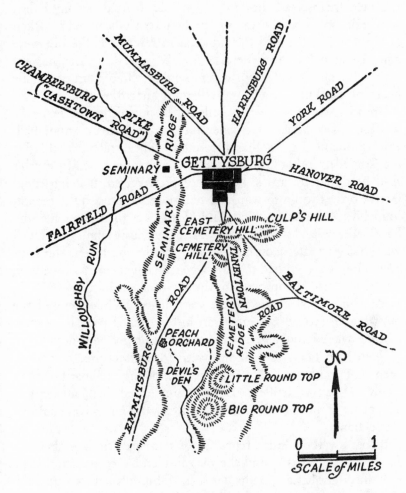

Gettysburg and Vicinity.

On Cemetery and East Cemetery Hills, Federal infantry were
visible, but in what numbers it was difficult to ascertain quickly
at a time of excited confusion. The bluecoats were facing North
and West and evidently were to defend the hill. Nothing in their
action, or lack of it, indicated that they had been in battle. Toward
them—a thrilling sight for Southern eyes—were moving the Union

troops who had been driven from Seminary Ridge.[4] Some were without formation. Others, dogged and better controlled, moved slowly in column. If these troops reached the eminence and entrenched themselves, they might be able to hold out until they were reinforced; but many of the Southern officers who looked at Cemetery Hill stated the situation in reverse: If the hill were attacked at once, the Federals could be routed. It was not yet 4 o'clock. The summer sun was more than three hours above the horizon. Darkness would not fall until after 8 o'clock.

Gordon, who had been halted in full pursuit of the Federals, was for instant attack. He believed that a swift thrust at one Federal command after another, before they concentrated, would give the Confederates the hill and the victory.[5] He hurried to Ewell's field headquarters in the hope, perhaps unvoiced, that he would receive orders to go forward. Ewell he found on a quiet mount, immobile. Outwardly, "Old Bald Head" was the same man who had made swift decision three weeks previously, the same Ewell who that very afternoon had decided that he must press the fight even though Lee wished to avoid a general engagement. Inwardly, something had happened to the will of Richard Ewell. In place of his usual chatter, there was silence. While some of the most fateful seconds in American history ticked past, he waited. Gordon waited, too, tensely expectant, but he got no orders.

Then Kyd Douglas rode up from Edward Johnson, who had been sent southward, West of the mountains, to guard Ewell's trains and reserve artillery. Douglas announced that Johnson was advancing along the Chambersburg Road and on arrival could go into action.[6]

Before Ewell made any reply, Gordon broke disciplinary bounds. In the ardor of battle and the magnitude of the opportunity, he disdained etiquette. He could join Johnson's attack, he said. Cemetery Hill could be taken before dark.

The old-time "Dick" Ewell would have piped "Yes, attack!"

[4] 4 *S.H.S.P.*, 254, 256–57.    [5] *Gordon*, 155–56.
[6] Douglas's language, *op. cit.*, 247, was: "General Johnson directed me . . . to say that he was marching on Gettysburg rapidly, with his Division in prime condition and was ready to put it in as soon as he got there." General Johnson's own statement of the obstacles encountered on the march, and of the condition of his men on arrival (*O. R.*, 27, pt. 2, p. 504), makes it certain that in his late narrative of the incident, Major Douglas unintentionally exaggerated the readiness of Johnson to go into action.

before the words were off Gordon's lips. This new, changed Lieutenant General paid no heed to Gordon. Deliberately Ewell turned
to Douglas with this answer to the message the staff officer had
brought: Johnson should continue his advance until well to the
front. Then he should halt and await orders.[7]

There was nothing more for Gordon to say; but some auditors
who had been on the staff of "Stonewall" Jackson scarcely could
believe their own ears, or credit the eyes which told them the man
before them was the once-decisive "Dick" Ewell. As Douglas
saluted and turned away, "Sandie" Pendleton said in a low voice,
with intense feeling: "Oh, for the presence and inspiration of 'Old
Jack' for just one hour!" [8]

Ewell did not hear this. In a few minutes, with Gordon still by
his side, he started into Gettysburg. He found, quickly enough,
that some Federals still remained in the town. From behind
buildings and fences there came a fusillade. Several men fell.
Gordon heard the ugly, familiar thud of a minié ball close by.
Ewell had been struck.

"Are you hurt, sir?" cried Gordon.

Ewell was calm. "No, no, I'm not hurt. But suppose that ball
had struck you: we would have had the trouble of carrying you
off the field, sir. You see how much better fixed for a fight I am
than you are. It don't hurt a bit to be shot in a wooden leg." [9]
That sounded like the old Ewell . . . but still, though thousands
of Federal refugees were climbing Cemetery Hill, there was no
decision.

The Lieutenant General and the excited, resolute young Brigadier rode on to the town square, which was filled with Confederate
soldiers and their prisoners. Ewell seemed in no hurry. Presently
he drew rein under a tree and chatted cheerfully with those who,
as always, gathered around mounted men. When a young officer
brought him a bottle of wine that had been pilfered from some
cellar, Ewell declined it with thanks and continued his pleasant-
ries. It began to look as if he did not intend to make a decision on

---

[7] In op. cit., 247, Douglas quoted Ewell as saying: "General Lee told me to come to
Gettysburg and gave me no orders to go any further. I do not feel like advancing and
making an attack without orders from him, and he is back at Cashtown." This explicit
language has to be rejected because Ewell's own report (O. R., 27, pt. 2, p. 444) made
it plain that prior to this he had received later instructions from Lee.
[8] Douglas. 247.                         [9] Gordon, 157.

his own account. Other officers echoed "Sandie" Pendleton's amazed comment over the inaction of Ewell. Said one of the company long afterwards: "It was a moment of most critical importance, more evidently critical to us now, than it would seem to any one then. But even then, some of us w.. had served on Jackson's staff, sat in a group in our saddles, and one said sadly, 'Jackson is not here.' Our corps commander . . . was simply waiting for orders, when every moment of the time could not be balanced with gold." [10]

As troublesome firing persisted in the town, Ewell was prevailed upon to leave the square and to go to a house in the outskirts, not far from the County Almshouse. [11] Gradually then his composure began to weaken. While more and more Federals made their way to Cemetery Hill, he grew restless and excited. Presently up rode General Trimble, who, having no command as yet, continued as a volunteer aide. "Well, General," Trimble began in the candor of long association, "we have had a grand success; are you not going to follow it up and push our advantage?"

Ewell answered, in effect, "General Lee has instructed me not to bring on a general engagement without orders, and I will wait for them."

Trimble replied instantly that Lee's orders could not apply, that a hard battle already had been fought, and that the advantage should be developed. Ewell visibly was disturbed by this, but he made no reply. Trimble persisted. Still Ewell asserted that he should not act further without orders. In wrath, which he probably did not conceal, Trimble mounted and rode off to see for himself what opportunity offered. [12]

A decision concerning the position to be taken by Edward Johnson could not be delayed, but Early must share in making it.

10 Capt. James Power Smith in 33 S.H.S.P., 144. In Mil. An. La., 186, is a statement that Ewell laughed when Harry Hays appeared anxious to attack. The Lieutenant General is said to have wanted to know if the Louisianians would never have their bellyful of fighting—if they could not wait a day. Hays is alleged to have replied that he wanted to attack then to prevent the slaughter of his men later. As no authority is given for this incident, it has to be omitted as unconfirmed, though there is nothing in Hays's report (O. R., 27, pt. 2, p. 479) that renders it improbable.

11 Mrs. Elsie Singmaster Lewars states that Ewell was in this Blocher House off the Biglerville road for a short time only. He was also in the Lady barn on Benner's Hill for a brief time. His real headquarters, now marked by an upturned cannon, were on the Hanover Road, about 150 yards West of Rock Creek (Letter of Dec. 27, 1942).

12 Trimble in 26 S.H.S.P., 123.

"Jube" had been in Gettysburg the previous week, when no Federal troops were there. Perhaps Early might know where Johnson best could be placed. Col. Abner Smead, corps inspector, was directed to find Early and to ask the General's opinion.[13]

Probably while Smead was on this mission, General Trimble came back. He was more than ever convinced from what he had observed that no time should be lost in occupying the high ground Southeast of Gettysburg. "General," said Trimble in his emphatic manner, pointing to Culp's Hill, "*there* is an eminence of commanding position, and not now occupied, as it ought to be by us or by the enemy soon." He went on: "I advise you to send a Brigade and hold it if we are to remain h~re."

"Are you sure it commands the town?" asked Ewell.

"Certainly it does, as you can see, and it ought to be held by us at once."

Ewell resented this persistence and he made some impatient answer.[14]

The next exchange is based on tradition, because neither man ever wrote directly of it, but the probability is that Trimble cried: "Give me a Brigade and I will engage to take that hill."

Ewell had no answer.

"Give me a good regiment and I will do it!"

When Ewell shook his head, Trimble stalked off. He would not serve, even as volunteer aide, under such an officer![15]

At such an insubordinate display of temper, Ewell a year previously would have stormed and sworn and would have put Trimble under arrest. As it was, Ewell made no answer that anyone remembered. Soon he was listening to Colonel Smead, who

[13] 4 *S.H.S.P.*, 255. This incident has to be reconstructed on the basis of Early's account of Colonel Smead's arrival.

[14] 26 *S.H.S.P.*, 123–24.

[15] General Trimble, in his account of Gettysburg, narrated no part of the conversation beyond the statement that "General Ewell made some impatient reply, and the conversation dropped" (26 *S.H.S.P.*, 124). Dr. R. H. McKim (40 *ibid.*, 273), quoted the remainder of the conversation. In McKim's version, Trimble began by saying, "Give me a Division, and I will engage to take that hill." That is eliminated because reference to a request for a Brigade fits in flawlessly with Trimble's own statement that he previously had urged the dispatch of a Brigade to Culp's Hill. Throughout his narrative of Gettysburg, Trimble wrote with much restraint concerning Ewell, because of their long and affectionate association; but there is every reason to assume that after the war, in Baltimore, where Dr. McKim as well as Trimble lived, the old soldier related the details he did not print. Dr. McKim, a careful student of history, described the incident with no suggestion that the exchange was disputable. He set it down as accepted fact.

had seen Early.[16] The General, said Smead, advised that Johnson, on arrival, move at once against Culp's Hill because it commanded the enemy's position—precisely the counsel Trimble had
given.

Smead must have added that Early was irritated because "Extra
Billy" Smith had sent a wild report that the enemy was advancing
down the York Road against the Confederate left and rear. Such
a move Early thought wholly improbable, but he had felt compelled to send Gordon in that direction with orders to assume
direction of Smith's as well as of his own Brigade.[17] This report
somewhat alarmed Ewell. He wanted more details of the situation
on his left and he wished Early's counsel at first hand. A messenger was sent at once to bring Early to field headquarters. Until
the General arrived, nothing was to be done.

As soon as Early could be found and conducted to Ewell's
post of command, "Jube" repeated the counsel he had sent by
Smead: Culp's Hill, which apparently was unoccupied by the
enemy, should be taken by Johnson. Further, Early went on, he
had been watching the disordered retreat of the Federals to
Cemetery Hill, and he felt sure that eminence could be taken
readily if Ewell would advance from the North and Hill would
attack from the West. Early added that he had sent, by one of
Pender's officers, a verbal suggestion to Hill that the Third Corps
make the assault.[18] The high ground could and should be taken
at once by storm. That was imperative.

Part of this counsel seemed to Ewell to be practicable. He sent
orders to Johnson to move through Gettysburg by using the tracks
of the Gettysburg and Hanover Railroad,[19] and he accepted,
though with no enthusiasm, the suggestion that he get help from
his right in an attack on Cemetery Hill. Lieut. J. P. Smith must
ride to General Lee, if the commanding General had arrived on
the field, and must tell him that Ewell could attack and take the
hill if given support from the West.[20]

[16] To establish the chronological order of all the incidents of the afternoon, as they
relate to Ewell, is to put together a historical jig-saw puzzle; but this appears to be the
time at which the return of Smead fits most accurately into the pattern. While warning
has to be entered against acceptance of all the details in precisely the order here given,
the exact chronology is not so important as the cumulative effect of the various incidents
on the mind of Ewell.
[17] 4 S.H.S.P., 255; O. R., 27, pt. 2, p. 469.
[18] O. R., 27, pt. 2, p. 469; 4 S.H.S.P., 255–56; Early, 270.
[19] See note 32 infra.                          [20] Smith in 33 S.H.S.P., 144–45.

Probably while Smith was on his way to Lee with Ewell's message, Maj. Walter Taylor of the headquarters staff visited Ewell. From Seminary Ridge, said Taylor, the commanding General could see the Federals retreating over the hills without organization and in great confusion. It would only be necessary to press "those people," Lee went on, to secure possession of the heights. If possible, Lee wished Ewell to do this.[21] Before Ewell could consider this, Smith return with a supplementary message: Lee "regretted that his people were not up to support [Ewell] on the right, but he wished [Ewell] to take the Cemetery Hill if it were possible. He would ride over very soon to see the chief of the Second Corps." [22]

All this meant that if Cemetery Hill was to be taken, Ewell must do it with his own men. More than that, whether the staff officers made the fact plain or not, Lee meant that his earlier orders for the avoidance of a general engagement still applied. To quote Lee's own words: "General Ewell was . . . instructed to carry the hill occupied by the enemy, if he found it practicable, but to avoid a general engagement until the arrival of the others corps of the army, which were ordered to hasten forward." [23]

Ewell now determined to reconnoitre, and he invited Early to ride with him. They had not proceeded far when they came, once again, under the fire of the enemy's sharpshooters in the southern edge of town. That did not trouble Ewell, but he showed some concern over the activity of the Union batteries. While Colonel Smead had been with Early, the Federal guns had been confident, defiant even.[24] Besides . . . there might be truth to that report of Federals marching down from York. It was known that Stuart had been in a fight the previous day at Hanover. The Union troops who were said to be on the York road might be those who had been engaged with "Jeb." Still again, the force with which Ewell could attack immediately was small. Early had detached two Brigades under Gordon to operate on the left. Rodes was known to have suffered heavily during the afternoon. The Southern troops were encumbered with close to 4000 prisoners. Two Brigades of Early, then,

---

21 These are almost Taylor's own words in his *Four Years with General Lee* (cited hereafter as *Taylor's Four Years*), 95. Substantially the same language was used in Taylor's other accounts of this incident in 4 *S.H.S.P.*, 83, 127, and in his *General Lee*, 190.
22 33 *S.H.S.P.*, 145.
23 *O. R.*, 27, pt. 2, p. 318.                    24 4 *S.H.S.P.*, 255-56.

and the tired survivors of Rodes's confused charges—these were all Ewell had for the attack till Johnson arrived. Nor would this force of Early and of Rodes have any support from the right. Lee himself said that.

As for the artillery, the Confederate battalions that had not been engaged that afternoon had not found positions from which to assail those noisy batteries on Cemetery Hill. Johnson would arrive shortly with his strong Division, which had not been in action since it had fought at Stephenson's Depot. If Johnson was near at hand, he soon could seize Culp's Hill and from it could dominate Cemetery Hill.

So Ewell reasoned.[25] Although Ewell did not communicate his thoughts to Early, who still continued to urge an attack on Cemetery Hill, "Old Jube" saw that his corps commander now was disinclined to make any move before the arrival of Johnson.

Together, after Ewell and Early encountered the sharpshooters' fire, they turned back toward field headquarters. Soon Rodes joined them. After driving the enemy from Seminary Ridge he had refrained from ordering his tired men to press on to Cemetery Hill. His reasons had been two: he had received late notice from Ewell that Lee did not wish a general engagement precipitated, and he had not felt that his weakened Division, without support, could overcome the Federals who, he thought, were organizing a "formidable line of infantry and artillery immediately in [his] front." [26] No further orders had reached Rodes. After drawing his lines and throwing out his skirmishers, he now came to report.

"Old Bald Head" had no instructions for either of the divisional commanders. He was waiting for Johnson's arrival and also for the promised visit from Lee. Nor could Ewell dismiss his concern regarding the situation on the left. Early continued to insist that the trouble was not a hostile advance but panic on the part of "Extra Billy" Smith; but in the face of these confident assertions, new rumors came from cavalrymen of an approaching Federal column. Early discredited these rumors. The troopers, he argued,

<hr/>

[25] His appraisal of the situation, given briefly in *O. R.*, 27 pt. 2, p. 445, is supplemented by the reflections of Early in 4 *S.H.S.P.*, 256–57.
[26] *O. R.*, 27, pt. 2, p. 555. J. P. Smith (33 *S.H.S.P.*, 144) asserted that Rodes shared Early's belief in the wisdom of an immediate general attack on Cemetery Hill. No other positive evidence to that effect has come under the writer's eye.

were waifs from Stuart's fight at Hanover on the 30th. They knew nothing of the real situation.

Ewell remained skeptical and presently chose to see for himself if the left actually was in danger of being turned. With Early and Rodes, he went to high ground overlooking Rock Creek, East of Gettysburg, from which a long stretch of the highway to York was visible. After sweeping the field with his glasses, Rodes was inclined to believe the Unionists were moving on the road or were spread through the nearby fields. Ewell remained in doubt. Early held to his theory that the enemy was not on that flank.

As the three Generals discussed the probability, skirmishers appeared at a distance on the right and to the South of the York Road. They were too far off for their uniforms to be distinguished at the moment, but they appeared to be moving toward the hill.

"There they come now!" cried Rodes, who believed them to be Federals.

Early doubtless swore.[27] Gordon, he explained, was in the direction of the skirmishers' advance. Besides, if the skirmishers were hostile, they would have opened fire. Ewell still did not profess to know whether he was looking at friend or foe, but he directed one of his staff to ascertain. Early sent an officer of his own to accompany Ewell's Lieutenant.[28]

It was close to sunset. Not a blow had been struck against the enemy on the hills South of Gettysburg. Early, despairing of action, felt that he must return to his command and assign Hays and Avery[29] their positions for the night.[30] Ewell, for his part, soon went back with Rodes to the temporary headquarters he had established North of the town.[31] There he received a message that Johnson's Division was arriving on the western outskirts, via the Cashtown Road.[32] The corps commander probably learned also

[27] His own admission was that he "replied in somewhat emphatic language" (4 S.H.S.P., 256).
[28] 4 S.H.S.P., 256.
[29] Col. Isaac E. Avery, Sixth North Carolina, senior Colonel commanding Hoke's Brigade while Hoke was recovering from the wound received at Salem Church. See supra, Vol. II, p. 634. Avery was mortally wounded July 2 (O. R., 27, pt. 2, p. 471).
[30] 4 S.H.S.P., 257.        [31] Ibid.
[32] The time of Johnson's arrival was disputed needlessly during the Gettysburg controversy because some of the participants in the argument did not realize that the Division was strung out a long way on the road and that the lapse between the appearance of the leading and the rear units must have been several hours. Col. J. M. Williams, commanding Nicholls's Brigade, wrote that while on the Cashtown Road, before reaching Gettysburg, he received orders to move to the East of the town along the railroad. Apparently he did not stop for any length of time on the western outskirts. See O. R., 27, pt. 2, p

that the two staff officers who had not yet returned from reconnaissance on the York Road had sent back word that the skirmishers seen from the hill were Confederate—Smith's men whom
Gordon was placing where he thought they should have been in
the first instance.[33]

Now, while distant objects still were dimly descernible through
gathering dusk, there was a stir outside Ewell's quarters: The
commanding General was dismounting. Cordially Ewell met him
and escorted him to a little arbor in rear of the house, the coolest
available place that warm night. Ewell had not seen Lee since the
Second Corps had marched from Brandy Station on the 10th of
June. All communication had been by letter or by messenger. In
fact, except for the advance from Culpeper to Brandy, while Stuart
had been fighting on June 9 this was the first time Ewell ever had
been directly under Lee in combat. Always previously, during
Lee's command, Ewell had received his orders from Jackson.
Chance decided that at a time when everything forecast a great
battle, the Second Corps commander was to have his introduction,
as an immediate subordinate, to the mind of Lee. Immediately
Ewell sent in haste for Early. No effort was made to reach Johnson and to have him share the council. Rodes was asked to remain.

Conversation had not proceeded far when Early answered the
summons. As Ewell sat silently in the arbor, Lee asked for details
of the situation on the front of the Second Corps. No reference
was made to the possibility of attack that evening on Cemetery
Hill. Without discussion, all four of the officers realized that the
time for this was past. The question to be considered was that of
action the next day.

After the first few minutes of conference, Ewell saw that Lee
intended to attack as soon as possible,[34] and he gave the commanding General all the information he had. His divisional leaders

513; and also 526, 531. Probably because of slow marching of advanced regiments along
the railroad, rear units, including the Stonewall Brigade, were much delayed after they
reached the town (*ibid.*, 518, 530). No serious error can be made if it is assumed that
the centre of the Division reached Gettysburg about 7 P.M. Randolph H. McKim, who was
with "Maryland" Steuart's men, wrote (*op. cit.*, 194), "They entered the town . . . a little
before dark, (The time . . . I fix by the fact that I easily read a letter handed me . . .)."
The reports in *O. R.*, which had not appeared at the time of the Gettysburg controversy,
invalidated Early's contention (4 *S.H.S.P.*, 257), that Johnson, waiting near the college,
was in rear of Rodes's and Early's lines and had the town between him and the enemy.
Early made that assertion to answer those who said that Johnson could have seized
Culp's Hill during the late afternoon of July 1.
[33] 4 *S.H.S.P.*, 256; *O. R.*, 27, pt. 2, p. 445.          [34] 4 *S.H.S.P.*, 271.

supplemented it with details—how Rodes had lost perhaps 2500 men, how he and Early between them had collected so many prisoners that the assignment of guards had weakened regiments, how the confusion about the situation on the York Road had arisen, and how Johnson, after a long march, was awaiting orders to move to the left and to occupy Culp's Hill. When all this had been explained, Ewell heard Lee ask: "Can't you, with your Corps, attack on this flank at daylight tomorrow?" [35]

Ewell had no immediate answer, but Early did. Although neither the senior nor the junior of those present, "Jube" felt that his partial reconnaissance that afternoon and his casual examination of the ground the previous week, en route to York, gave him a better understanding of the terrain than any of the other officers possessed. He said flatly that he did not believe an attack should be made southward from Gettysburg against Cemetery Hill the next day. Deployment and ascent would be difficult in the face of any enemy who evidently was concentrating and fortifying. Success in attack was doubtful. Loss inevitably would be large. Early subsequently reported the remainder of his argument to this effect: "I then called General Lee's attention to the Round Tops, the outline of which we could see,[36] though dusk was approaching, and suggested that those heights must evidently command the enemy's position and render it untenable; and I also called his attention to the more practicable nature of the ascents on that side of the town, adding the suggestion that the attack could be made on that side, and from our right flank, with better chances of success." [37]

Ewell listened and concurred. Rodes, too, believed no attack could prudently be made against the hill from the front of the Second Corps. At length, as if convinced, the commanding General said questioningly: "Then perhaps I had better draw you around towards my right, as the line will be very long and thin if you remain here, and the enemy may come down and break through it?" [38]

[35] 4 S.H.S.P., 271.
[36] This statement creates concern for the accuracy of memory that Early often asserted. The Blocher House is in a depression, from which the Round Tops are not visible.
[37] O. R., 27, pt. 2, p. 272.
[38] Early remarked (4 S.H.S.P., 272), "This was very nearly the language [Lee] used," and he felt justified in employing quotation marks.

Again it was Early who, without a by-your-leave, spoke up before Ewell attempted to answer. Lee need have no concern, said "Jube"; the enemy could not break the line the Second Corps would draw. Later, in explaining this, Early stated that he was led to make this remark because he knew his men would be much depressed to give up the ground and the muskets they had captured. A move to the right, moreover, would compel Early to leave in the hands of the enemy his badly wounded men. The terrain, in Early's opinion, was a guarantee that the front of the Second Corps could be held. Said Early: "On that part of the line it was more difficult for the enemy to come down from the heights to attack us than for us to ascend them to attack him, difficult as the latter would have been." [39]

Ewell found that Early's opinion and his own once more were in accord. He said so. Rodes was on the same side.[40] Unanimous as were these views, it must have been manifest to Ewell that his counsel was not altogether to Lee's liking. The commanding General, in fact, was perplexed, almost stunned, at finding a defensive state of mind among his lieutenants. In the end, before Lee rode off, this understanding was reached: Lee was to attack the next morning on the right, as early as practicable; Ewell was to make a demonstration on the left, was to convert this into an attack if opportunity offered, and was to pursue the Federals if the attack on the right drove the blue army from its position.[41]

Rodes and Early returned to their troops. Ewell, left alone, received soon the staff officers who had been reconnoitering on the York Road. They reported that they had been on Culp's Hill. So far as they could ascertain, it was unoccupied.[42] As part of John-

---

[39] Ibid., 473. Early noted (10 S.H.S.P., 548 n.) that if Lee had planned a defensive battle the arrangement of the Confederate line would have been faulty, because of its length and form. For offensive action, Early thought "the arrangement was the best that could have been made." He explained: "Had we concentrated our whole force at one point, the enemy could have concentrated correspondingly, and we would not have been in as favorable a position for taking advantage of success."

[40] 10 S.H.S.P., 548 n.

[41] O. R., 27, pt. 2, pp. 318–19; 446; 4 S.H.S.P., 274–75. For other references to the conference, see 3 R. E. Lee, 80, n. 41. It must be added that the account published in 20 C. V., 465, and that quoted in Old Bald Head, 148–49, are marred by the failing memory of the authors.

[42] The return of these men, Lieut. T. T. Turner and Robert D. Early, volunteer civilian aide to Early, must have been subsequent to Lee's departure. Otherwise there would have been no point in Ewell's reference to it in the incident that follows in the text. Cf. O. R., 27 pt. 2, p. 446.

son's Division was then moving into position, it was reasonable to assume those veterans could seize Culp's Hill. If so, delay during the afternoon would have cost nothing.

By the time this prospect developed, Ewell received a note from Lee. The commanding General considerately stated that he had examined anew the situation on the right and had concluded that an attack there had a good prospect of success.[43] Unless Ewell was satisfied that the Second Corps could be used to advantage where it was, said Lee, it should be moved to the right. The plan that had been discarded at the council in the arbor was to be adopted.

This stirred Ewell. Now that reconnaissance showed Culp's Hill unoccupied, he felt there was good prospect of striking a heavy blow there. He would not throw away that opportunity without presenting to Lee the report of the reconnaissance. The only way to do this would be to ride over to Army Headquarters.

As loyally as when Ewell had gone to Jackson on the 18th of May, 1862, to see if there were not some way of disregarding orders that he considered unwise,[44] "Old Bald Head" rode through the night to Lee's headquarters. He found the commanding General attentive, as always, and ready to consider alternatives. Lee's one reason for deciding to shift Ewell to the right had been doubt of the ability of Ewell to make up his mind to do anything.[45] Now that Ewell had determined to attack Culp's Hill, Lee with few words agreed that the Second Corps should remain on the left. The plan that had been formulated at Ewell's headquarters was reaffirmed: In the morning the attack would begin on the right; a demonstration was to be made on the left and, if promising, was to be turned into an assault.

Back Ewell rode to his own front. When he got there, after midnight, he hurried one of his aides to Johnson, of whose movements during the preceding three or four hours Ewell knew little. The aide was to tell Johnson to occupy Culp's Hill if this had not already been done. No time must be lost in taking the ground that was, in Ewell's opinion, the key to the Federal citadel.

After the staff officer left, Ewell probably attempted to sleep,

43 For the considerations that influenced Lee, see 3 R. E. Lee, 80–82.
44 See supra, Vol. I, pp. 361–62.
45 For further reference to Ewell's state of mind, see infra, pp. 171–72.

but the news he received on the officer's return was enough to drive slumber from startled eyes. Johnson sent word that he had formed line of battle and had sent up Culp's Hill a reconnaissance party to see if the enemy had stolen across from Cemetery Hill. This party had encountered the Federals in superior numbers. The enemy undoubtedly was on the eminence Johnson was ordered to take.

While Johnson was relating this to him, said the staff officer, a paper taken from a captured Federal courier had been handed Johnson. The division commander had read it, had commented on it, and had forwarded it to Ewell. There it was. Ewell opened it and scrutinized it.

Headquarters Fifth Corps,<br>Bonaughtown, July 2, 1863

Major-General Slocum:

General: On the receipt of General Meade's note to you, of the 1st instant, I left Hanover at 7 p. m., and marched 9 miles to Bonaughtown, en route to Gettysburg. I shall resume my march at 4 a. m. Crawford's division had not reached Hanover at the hour I left there.

Very respectfully, your obedient servant,<br>GEORGE SYKES,<br>Major-General, Commanding[46]

Bonaughtown . . . the map showed it four miles East of Gettysburg. Ugh! Sykes was there, George Sykes with whom Ewell had been two years at West Point; George Sykes who had those ten regiments of old army regulars in one of his Divisions. He was almost in rear of the position Johnson was to occupy. The commander of the V Corp was writing, also, to Henry Slocum, chief of the XII Corps. Slocum must be close to Gettysburg and perhaps near the place in which the courier had been taken. Prisoners had said earlier in the evening that the Federals had two corps around the town, the I and the XI. A third corps might have arrived;[47] a fourth was to reach Gettysburg early the next morning.

[46] O. R., 27, pt. 3, p. 483. The message printed there is addressed to Maj. Gen. Daniel Butterfield, but the notation is "(Similar dispatch to General Slocum)."

[47] The XII Corps of two Divisions had moved on the morning of July 1 to Two Taverns, four miles Southeast of Gettysburg, and, after receipt of news of the action at Gettysburg, had advanced to the town. One Division was East of Rock Creek; the other had been moved to the extreme left of the Federal position (O. R., 27, pt. 1, p. 758).

Ewell's staff officer continued his report: General Johnson, in sending the captured dispatch, had said that he would not attack until Ewell was apprised of the fact that the Federals occupied Culp's Hill. Further orders would be awaited by Johnson.

"Day was now breaking," Ewell wrote afterwards, "and it was too late for any change of place." [48]

[48] *O. R.*, 27, pt. 2, p. 446. It is probable that "place" is a misreading of "plan."

# CHAPTER VII

## The Army Slips Back a Year

James Longstreet's 1st of July was as unsatisfactory as Ewell's. From camp near an abandoned sawmill close to Greenwood, Longstreet rode toward Gettysburg in the company of the commanding General until the sound of Hill's battle prompted Lee to hurry forward. Longstreet followed. With him moved McLaws's and Hood's Division. Pickett was left at Chambersburg; Law's Brigade was held on guard at New Guilford about two miles south of Fayetteville.[1] Because of the crowding of the road, Longstreet's advance was slow but without important incident.[2] About 5 P.M. Longstreet joined Lee on Seminary Ridge whence there was a wide sweep of vision—the town ahead, a long, trough-like meadow to the right front and, East of that, stone-littered Cemetery Ridge, which swept southward and gave place to the two eminences that bulked almost as if they were mountains—Round Top and Little Round Top.

Longstreet had a few minutes in which to examine the terrain because he saw that Lee was engaged with messages and orders. These being dispatched, Lee walked over and pointed out to Longstreet that part of the ridge to which the enemy had retreated after the battle of the afternoon.[3] Slowly and carefully, Longstreet studied through his glasses the position of the enemy, studied it with an eye to the defensive tactics he thought the Confederates should employ. He saw movement on the right, along a road that ran up the meadow to Gettysburg. This, he learned, was called the Emmitsburg Road. It passed, on the extreme right, the two Round Tops. There, and nearer Gettysburg, nearly all the way to the hill just South of the town, Longstreet observed that the sides of the ridge were rough and were an obstacle to a swift descent by the Federals for an attack on Seminary Ridge. A certain satis-

[1] O. R., 27, pt. 2, p. 538.
[2] For the details, see Longstreet in *Annals*, 420; 3 *R. E. Lee*, 66; O. R., 27, pt. 2, pp 358, 504.
[3] *Annals*, 420; 3 *B. & L.*, 339.

faction there was for Longstreet in the strength of the Federal position: it discouraged a Confederate attack and invited the defensive on which his heart was set. Fortune was smiling on him! It had given him the ideal theatre for another Fredericksburg, an easy repulse of a foolish assault and rich fruits of victory from the Longstreet plan!

For five or ten minutes Longstreet studied the field. At length he lowered his glasses and turned to Lee. Then commenced a long conference that was broken by the arrival and report of officers, but renewed earnestly.[4] Lee began with some observation to the effect that he felt he should attack the enemy. Longstreet immediately objected that this was not desirable. He may have added that an attack was contrary to the plan discussed before the Army left Virginia. If that was part of Longstreet's remark, Lee ignored it then and did not remember it afterwards, because he never had intended to commit himself to any such plan, and he may not even have understood to what Longstreet referred. Five years later, when Lee was discussing some phases of Gettysburg with Col. William Allan, Lee mentioned a "reported correspondence of Longstreet," in which Longstreet was alleged to have said that Lee was under promise not to fight a general battle in Pennsylvania. Lee said he did not believe Longstreet ever made the statement, "that the idea was absurd, that he never made any such promise, and never thought of doing any such thing."[5] In

4 Of what was said, there is unfortunately no detailed report. Lee never described to any known person his recollection of it. All he ever said of the exchange was that he did not believe Longstreet held an opinion credited to the Lieutenant General. Longstreet, for his part, published three versions of the conference. The first was in the *Philadelphia Weekly Times* of Nov. 3, 1877, and was reprinted in *Annals,* 414 ff, under the heading "Lee in Pennsylvania." Longstreet's second account appeared in the *Century Magazine* and later in 3 *B. & L.,* 244 ff, as "Lee's Invasion of Pennsylvania." Chapter XXVI of *Manassas to Appomattox* contained the final narrative. In many details, some of which are important, the three accounts are irreconcilable. It was said of the first of these papers that Longstreet used the services of a "professional writer" (Early in 4 *S.H.S.P.,* 282), though Longstreet insisted this was because of his semi-paralyzed arm. (Second article from the *Philadelphia Weekly Times,* reprinted in 5 *S.H.S.P.,* 257. The specific admissions concerning the services of the writer, "generously tendered me by the editor of the *Times,*" appear in *ibid.,* 259. They are omitted in the version of the article that appears in *Annals.*) Employment of another such writer in the preparation of Longstreet's final memoirs also was known (Jed. Hotchkiss in a letter of Jan. 25, 1897, to Henry A. White credited the *Atlanta Commercial* of Jan. 18, 1897, with the statement that *From Manassas to Appomattox* had been edited by P. J. Moran of Atlanta, who was described as a former Lieutenant in a Negro regiment). For these reasons it is impossible to determine what occurred between Lee and Longstreet, or even whether Longstreet's recollection of his own words is, in the nuances, accurately reported in his narratives.

5 Col. William Allan, memorandum of Apr. 15, 1868, after a conversation with General Lee, published in *Marshall,* 248–52.

his own report, Lee said candidly that he had not intended to "deliver a general battle so far from our base unless attacked," [6] but he had never contemplated a campaign without the possibility of a battle, and he certainly had made no pledge concerning that or the strategy or the tactics to be employed. Intention to avoid battle and a pledge to do so were entirely different, though easily confused.[7]

Whatever the language of Longstreet's objection that afternoon on Seminary Ridge, Lee answered, in effect, If the enemy is there tomorrow, we must attack him.[8]

If he is there tomorrow, Longstreet answered substantially, it is because he is anxious that we should attack him—a good reason, in my judgment, for not doing so.[9]

This remark opened a frank exchange of views. Longstreet contended that the ground in their front meant nothing. The sound general strategy, he said, was to get between Meade and Washington, to threaten the flank and rear of the Federals and to force them to attack on good defensible terrain, of which the country offered abundance. If operations became necessary in the district where the Army then was, the Confederate troops should be shifted toward Round Top. Meade then could be threatened, if maneuver was the aim, or attacked to better advantage if battle was to be delivered.[10]

In what manner Lee answered this, Longstreet apparently did not recall or, if he remembered, did not relate. Longstreet got the

[6] O. R. 27, pt. 2, p. 318.

[7] Lee's remark to Pender, *supra*, Chap. V, p. 76, may be cited again as proof that Lee did not intend, regardless of circumstance, to adhere to the defensive.

[8] In *Annals*, 420, Longstreet used in direct quotation the words in the text. By the time he came to write his article for 3 *B. & L.*, Longstreet remembered the language of Lee as: "No, the enemy is there and I am going to attack him there" (*ibid.*, 339). In Longstreet, 358, the quotation is: "If he is there tomorrow, I will attack him." In this confusion of evidence, it has seemed prudent to accept the earliest version as the most probable but not to regard it as an explicit quotation.

[9] *Annals*, 421. In 3 *B. & L.*, 339, Longstreet did not employ direct quotation. The language in Longstreet, 385, is: "If he is there tomorrow, it will be because he wants you to attack. If that height has become the objective, why not take it at once?"

[10] This is the substance of Longstreet's argument in *Annals*, 420. When he wrote the article in 3 *B. & L.*, 339, Longstreet reversed the previous order of the dialogue. Instead of starting with Lee's remark that he might attack, Longstreet represented himself, in direct quotation, as arguing succinctly: "If we could have chosen a point to meet our plan of operation, I do not think we could have found a better one than that upon which they are now concentrating." He then recited the main arguments he had given in *Annals*. The account in Longstreet, 358, gave none of the argument in detail. It represented Longstreet simply as saying, after his examination of the ground: "We could not call the enemy to position better suited to our plans. All that we have to do is to file around his left and secure good ground between him and his capital."

impression that Lee believed the enemy could be beaten in detail and, further, that the commanding General was off balance. Subsequently Longstreet wrote: "[Lee] seemed under a subdued excitement, which occasionally took possession of him when 'the hunt was up,' and threatened his superb equipoise. The sharp battle fought by Hill and Ewell on that day had given him a taste of victory." [11] Actually, Lee was reasoning the larger alternatives. He could withdraw; he could remain where he was and await the next Federal move; or he could attack without delay. To retreat with the trains over the mountains in the face of a strong, pursuing adversary was to take heavy risks. As for waiting, it would not be possible to remain on the defensive for any length of time. Supplies were low; the Army was living on the land; the Federals easily could block the passes of the mountain and could limit the area in which the Southern Army could forage. Hunger, perhaps starvation, might be the cost of a prolonged defensive.[12]

If, by elimination, an offensive was indicated, the Army either could maneuver to the right, as Longstreet urged, or it could attack the Federals before they could concentrate. The objections to maneuvering between the enemy and Washington were manifest: In the absence of the cavalry, the position of the enemy could not be determined readily. Nor could a safe advance be assured. Even if the trains could be protected, a southward shift of position might involve days of delay during which the Army would suffer for food precisely as it would if it remained on the defensive. So little possibility did Lee see of successful maneuver that he scarcely could have regarded it as a separate alternative. Immediate attack was, in Lee's eyes, the wisest course. He was the more disposed to it because of the spirit of the Army and the initial victory of Hill and Ewell.[13] Besides, there was good reason to assume that Cemetery Ridge was not held, as yet, in strength. Lee's own succinct appraisal was: "A battle had, therefore, become in a measure unavoidable, and the success already gained gave hope of a favorable issue." [14]

11 *Annals*, 421.  12 *O. R.*, 27, pt. 2, p. 318.
13 The Second and Third Corps had captured more than 9600 prisoners after they had left the Rappahannock.
14 *O. R.*, 27, pt. 2, p. 318. The best summary of Lee's military reasoning at this stage of the battle is that of Gen. Frederick Maurice, *Robert E. Lee, the Soldier*, 206–07.

It is not known how much of this Lee explained to Longstreet. The commanding General was convinced in his own mind. As he was unaware of the extent to which the heart of his senior lieutenant was fixed upon a defensive, he probably wasted few words and employed no diplomacy. Longstreet said little more, but when Lee asked him where the First Corps was, a young observer noticed that Longstreet gave the position of McLaws's Division "and then was indefinite and non-commital."[15] Doubtless Longstreet heard, as he waited, that a partial reconnaissance had been made about three-quarters of a mile south of the Chambersburg Road to find artillery positions to cover the flank. Later "Old Pete" may have been informed that a second and more extensive reconnaissance had been made to the right by S. R. Johnston and Proctor Smith and that nothing of importance had been ascertained.[16] No Federal forces had been observed in motion or in position down the ridge.

Still later, after Lee returned from his conference with Ewell,[17] he must have told his corps commanders that he intended to take the offensive the next day. Armistead Long testified years afterward: "[General Lee] turned to Longstreet and Hill . . . and said: 'Gentlemen, we will attack the enemy in the morning as early as practicable.' "[18] When Longstreet left Army field headquarters late in the evening,[19] he was sure of Lee's intention to attack, but he was not sure Lee had decided where the attack would be delivered or with what force.[20] For his own part, Longstreet was determined to prevent, if he could, an attack he believed

[15] 33 S.H.S.P., 145.
[16] S. R. Johnston to Lafayette McLaws, MS, June 27, 1892; Johnston to Fitz Lee, MS, Feb. 16, 1878—S. R. Johnston MSS.
[17] See supra, p. 102.
[18] Long, 277. This remark was made, according to Long's timing, before Lee went to see Ewell, but all the circumstantial evidence is to the contrary.
[19] Here Longstreet's account in Annals, 422, is followed: "I left General Lee quite late on the night of the 1st." In his old age General Longstreet wrote: "When I left General Lee, about 7 o'clock in the evening . . ." (op. cit., 361).
[20] Annals, 422. In the Gettysburg controversy of 1877–78, some of General Lee's defenders asserted that Lee on the night of July 1 gave General Longstreet specific orders to attack early the next morning. Longstreet denied this as "totally false." In the article here quoted, he said: ". . . General Lee never, in his life, gave me orders to attack at a specific hour. He was perfectly satisfied that, when I had my troops in position, and was ordered to attack, no time was ever lost. On the night of the 1st I left him without any orders at all" (ibid.). This phase of the controversy might have been avoided if it had been conceded on both sides that Longstreet received no direct orders, but that Lee decided, probably after Longstreet left, to make the attack on the right and with Longstreet's troops. This solution accords with all the probabilities and runs counter to none of the known evidence.

to be unwise.[21] He was as gloomy as he was determined. When his Medical Director, Dr. J. S. Dorsey Cullen, spoke on the road back to camp of the victory won that day, "Old Pete" shook his head. It would have been better not to have fought, he said, than to have left the Federals in control of a position from which the whole Army would be needed, and then at great sacrifice, to drive the enemy.[22]

After a few hours' sleep, Longstreet arose about 3 A.M. and soon started back toward Gettysburg from the camp of his Corps on Marsh Creek.[23] He found Lee already on Seminary Ridge anxious to ascertain how heavily the Federals had been reinforced during the night on the opposing high ground. Capt. S. R. Johnston, of the headquarters engineers, and Maj. J. J. Clarke, of Longstreet's engineers, already had been sent to reconnoitre as far as possible to the right.[24] Without waiting for a report of this reconnaissance, Longstreet renewed his argument for the defensive tactics of a maneuver around the left of the Union Army. His appeal made no impression on the commanding General. Lee still believed that the one practicable course was to attack the Federals on Cemetery Ridge at once and to rout them before they could complete their concentration. As Longstreet could not shake the judgment of his chief, he shifted the discussion to a canvass of the results that might be anticipated from the battle Lee proposed to wage.[25]

When A. P. Hill arrived, he joined the conference. Briefly, it was decided that Longstreet should deliver the attack from the ex-

[21] 3 B. & L., 340. Longstreet did not mention in Annals any purpose on his part to defer consideration of his plan until the 2nd because he thought Lee would be more amenable the next day. Statement to this effect was published first in 3 B. & L. and was repeated, substantially, in Longstreet, 359. These later statements created much resentment among General Lee's supporters, who interpreted Longstreet's remarks as an insinuation that Lee had lost both judgment and temper during the afternoon of the 1st.

[22] Cullen in Longstreet, 383–84 n.

[23] Ibid., though Dr. Cullen slightly underestimated the distance from Gettysburg.

[24] S. R. Johnston to Lafayette McLaws, MS, June 27, 1892—S. R. Johnston MSS. The initials of Clarke were given by Johnston as J. C., but there is no doubt concerning the identification.

[25] This is the account Longstreet gave originally in Annals, 422. In 3 B. & L., 340, he merely stated that he "again proposed to move to Meade's left and rear," and he proceeded to describe Lee's actions in an effort to show that the commanding General had left him and had proceeded to the left to consider an attack there. In Longstreet, 362, he asserted that "the stars were shining brightly on the morning of the 2nd, when I reported at General Lee's headquarters and asked for orders." In this, General Longstreet put the time of arrival probably an hour and a half ahead of that at which he actually met his commander. See 3 R. E. Lee, 552–53, for the evidence. The quoted language of Longstreet, asking for orders, would indicate, also, that he did not know Lee had decided to attack on the right.

treme Confederate right. Troops for the assault soon would be at hand. Hood's Division, the van of that Corps, now, about 7 or 7:30, was approaching. Behind Hood was McLaws. Both Divisions were in loose order and were extended far back on the Cashtown road.[26] Hood had left the bivouac about 3 A.M., after no more than two hours' rest.[27] McLaws first had been ordered to march at 4 A.M., but had been directed by Longstreet during the night not to move the Division until sunrise.[28]

As Hood came forward to report his presence, Longstreet heard Lee say to the Texan, in a brief exchange of greetings, "The enemy is here, and if we do not whip him, he will whip us.[29] By the time McLaws arrived, Lee had matured the tactical plan of attack, and he summoned the Georgian in order to explain what McLaws's Division had to do. Longstreet was walking nearby at the moment, but he could hear Lee's instructions. Soon Lee had explained a plan for an oblique attack on Cemetery Ridge and the Emmitsburg Road, which ran between Seminary and Cemetery Ridge. Longstreet listened.

"Can you do it?" asked Lee of McLaws.

"I know of nothing to prevent me," said McLaws substantially, "but I will take a party of skirmishers and go in advance and reconnoitre."

"Captain Johnston of my staff," Lee answered, "has been ordered to reconnoitre the ground, and I expect he is about ready."

"I will go with him," McLaws began, but he got no further. Longstreet strode up and broke in: "No, sir, I do not wish you to leave your Division." Then Longstreet leaned over and drew his finger across the map. "I wish your Division placed so."

"No, General," Lee replied quietly, "I wish it placed just opposite."

[26] For the disputed time of their arrival, see 3 R. E. Lee, 553-54. In Longstreet's report (O. R., 27, pt. 2, p. 358) the statement is made that McLaws's Division reached Marsh Creek, four miles from Gettysburg, "a little after dark." McLaws filed no report, but in 7 S.H.S.P., 68, he stated that he arrived on the creek after midnight.

[27] This is based on Longstreet's statement (O. R., 27, pt. 2, p. 358) that Hood reached Marsh Creek after midnight. Hood is authority (Advance and Retreat, 56) for the fact that his troops "were allowed to halt and rest only about two hours."

[28] McLaws in 7 S.H.S.P., 68. No reason was given then, or thereafter, for the change of hour, but the reasonable assumption is that Longstreet considered Hood the better marcher and gave him the road.

[29] Hood, 57.

McLaws observed that he would like, in either event, to go over the ground with Johnston. Bluntly, Longstreet forbade. He manifestly was irritated.[30]

Lee said nothing and gave no indication that he knew Longstreet was angry. With "Old Pete" on one side and Hill on the other, he sat on a fallen tree, map on knee, and talked of the arrangements for the action. While the three were discussing, Johnston and Clarke returned from their reconnaissance. At Lee's direction, Johnston reported. What he said of his ride was interesting enough, but there was nothing in his report or in his manner to indicate that a decisive moment of the campaign had been reached. Half way to Little Round Top, said Johnston, he had ridden behind a Confederate picket line and had not attempted to mount Cemetery Ridge. When he reached Little Round Top he had gone forward and had climbed to a shoulder of that eminence. He had found no enemy there, and he had seen no organized force anywhere. Although Johnston may not have reported to the commanding General the time of this incident, it had been about 5:30 o'clock. Johnston and Clarke then had ridden southward to a point opposite the southern end of Round Top. There they had turned back. While they were returning they had seen three or four Federal cavalrymen moving toward Gettysburg, but they did not think the troopers had observed them.[31]

Lee was visibly interested in Johnston's report. When the engineer mentioned his reconnaissance of Little Round Top, Lee asked, "Did you get there?" Johnston assured the General that he had.

Lee then turned to Longstreet and said, "I think you had better move on." [32]

Johnston stepped back; Longstreet remained attentive as Lee resumed study of the map. At that time, if there was any evidence of Federal activity immediately opposite Lee's field headquarters, the enemy was not seen in strength. Johnston's report indicated that the Union forces were not on the dominating ground farther southward. The decision of Lee to attack the enemy was con-

---

30 McLaws in 7 S.H.S.P., 68. McLaws, needless to say, confused Johnston's movements. The General thought the reconnaissance officer was "ready" to start. Actually Johnston was almost "ready" to report.

31 Johnston MSS, loc. cit. For the importance of this incident and for the circumstances in which Johnston failed to observe the Federals, see infra, p. 174.

32 Johnston to G. W. Peterkin, MS, n.d.—S. R. Johnston MSS.

firmed. If the Confederates could launch an oblique assault North of the two Round Tops, could get astride Cemetery Ridge at its lowest point there [33] and could sweep up the ridge, the Federals could be driven from it! [34] That was Lee's conclu-- sion.

Soon the commanding General rode off to the left for another conference with Ewell over the employment of the left in co-operation with the attack by the First Corps. Longstreet, of course, was expected to make his preparations during Lee's absence, but the Lieutenant General was less disposed than ever to deliver his attack. He had no reason to believe that Johnston's report of the reconnaissance was incorrect. Longstreet, on the contrary, assumed that the lower end of the ridge was unoccupied by the enemy, but he felt that the attack should not be made. If he must assault, he would delay until the entire First Corps was at hand. He said to Hood, after Lee had left: "The General is a little nervous this morning; he wishes me to attack; I do not wish to do so without Pickett. I never like to go into battle with one boot off." [35]

At 11 o'clock, or a little later, Longstreet saw Lee ride up again to the hill where field headquarters of the First Corps had been established. [36] To all who had seen Lee on the left, it had been apparent that he had been expecting Longstreet to attack and that he was disappointed because he had not heard the guns of the First Corps. The previous evening, in discussing the desirability of an attack on the right, Lee had confessed, with less than his usual caution, that he hesitated to attack on that flank because Longstreet would have to deliver the blow. "Longstreet is a very good fighter when he gets into position and gets everything ready," Lee had said, "but he is so slow." [37] Now Lee probably could not con-

---

[33] For this feature of the terrain, see Meade in *O. R.*, 27, pt. 1, p. 116.

[34] There is some conflict of testimony between Johnston and McLaws concerning the time of Johnston's return. Johnston thought it was about 7; McLaws set it an hour later. As Johnston carried no watch that day (*cf.* Johnston to Fitz Lee, MS, Feb. 16, 1878), McLaws's account is accepted. As set forth in a letter to Johnston, MS June 8, 1892, and in 7 *S.H.S.P.*, McLaws's statement conforms to the known facts.

[35] *Hood*, 57.

[36] In *Annals*, 442, Longstreet said Lee returned at 9 o'clock, which was the hour at which Longstreet subsequently wrote that Lee started to ride to Ewell's headquarters. In *Longstreet*, 363, the statement is that Lee came back at 10 o'clock. Because of the numerous incidents known to have occurred while Lee was on the left, it seems likely that the hour was past 11 when Lee rejoined Longstreet. See 3 *R. E. Lee*, 93, n. 23.

[37] Early in 4 *S.H.S.P.*, 274.

ceal altogether from Longstreet his disappointment that nothing had been accomplished, but his first remark was that it would not do to have Ewell open the attack.[38] If Longstreet made any reply to this, it was perfunctory.

The morning was almost past. Opposite Lee's post of command, a ridge that had appeared to be almost unoccupied at sunrise [39] now was bristling with men and guns. Despite the increase of Federal strength, Lee believed that he had no alternative to attacking as speedily as possible and, further, that his tactical plan would obviate the necessity of a frontal assault. Quietly, then, and in violation of a long practice of merely "suggesting" movements to lieutenants, Lee gave the explicit order: with that part of his command available, Longstreet was to attack along the Emmitsburg Road in the manner explained earlier that morning to McLaws.[40]

As a soldier, Longstreet did not think of disobeying, but he asked permission to wait until Law's Brigade arrived from New Guilford. As that fine command would come up in a short time, Lee consented that the advance be delayed till Law was at hand. Then the General rode off to investigate a report that Federals were in a small wood on the front of Hill's Corps.[41] No relief of mind came to Longstreet now that he was alone. He said nothing to expose his thoughts, but his every important act for the next few hours showed that he had resolved to put on Lee the entire responsibility for what happened. In plain, ugly words, he sulked. His depression was so manifest that it was observed and remembered by a junior officer who seldom saw him.[42] The dissent of Longstreet's mind was a brake on his energies. About noon, he had word that Law had joined Hood after a long, swift march,[43]

38 *Annals,* 442. Longstreet quoted this observation as proof that Lee, even then, had not made up his mind to attack on the right. Another interpretation manifestly is that Lee made the remark to reinforce his conclusion that the First Corps must deliver the assault.

39 For the failure of the Confederates to realize the strength of the Federal force on Cemetery Ridge from early morning, see *infra* p. 118 and the detailed critique in Chapter IX, p. 174.

40 *Annals,* 442; *O. R.,* 27, pt. 2, p. 318.

41 3 *R. E. Lee,* 93; *Annals,* 422; *O. R.,* 27 pt. 2, p. 358. Law filed no report on Gettysburg, but he stated in 3 *B. & L.,* 319, that he left New Guilford at 3 A.M. on the 2nd and reached Gettysburg "shortly before noon."

42 *Dickert,* 235.

43 Law computed at twenty-four miles the distance covered in nine hours. 3 *B. & L.,* 319.

and he ordered the advance begun, but he left the direction of the van entirely to Capt. S. R. Johnston, of the engineers, the reconnaissance officer whom Lee had put at his disposal. Longstreet himself remained near the middle of the column. For a time, the commanding General rode with him, but of what passed between them, no record survives. When Lee turned back, Longstreet was in authority as complete as he cared to have it. He had the large discretion that Lee's system of command allowed the senior lieutenants. Longstreet could act or refer to G.H.Q. as he desired.

Doubt surrounds the events that immediately followed. Captain Johnston [44] stated that he rode with Longstreet at the head of the column and that, when they came to a point where the road was visible from the Federal position, he so informed Longstreet. At the same time, said Johnston, he showed Longstreet a route across a field concealed from observation by the enemy. Longstreet preferred the road and, when the column reached the exposed point, halted it and let Hood's Division take the lead. McLaws's version is that he rode with Johnston, came to the hill visible to the enemy, halted there, told Longstreet that the column could be seen by the enemy, and suggested that the two Divisions countermarch and follow a route he had reconnoitered during the forenoon. This was done, said McLaws, though it put Hood's Division, not his, in advance.[45] As this account by McLaws is confirmed by the only contemporary report,[46] it must be adjudged substantially correct. Longstreet wrote [47] that Johnston led the head of the column to high ground where it would be visible to the enemy. When word of this was sent back after some delay, said Longstreet, he saw Round Top from the road where he was waiting. He knew that the advance was discovered and he decided he might as well continue his march.[48] Because of his determination to obey the letter of his instructions, he refused to withdraw McLaws's Division from the guidance of Johnston. Over Hood's Division he consid-

[44] Quoted by Fitz Lee in 5 S.H.S.P., 183–84.
[45] 7 S.H.S.P., 69.
[46] This is by Gen. J. B. Kershaw, who said (O. R., 27, pt. 2, pp. 366–67), that McLaws countermarched and went forward again under cover of the woods.
[47] Annals, 423.
[48] Actually, if the fragmentary dispatches of the signal station on Round Top indicate what was seen of Longstreet's trips, the first observed movement may have been the countermarch of McLaws (cf. O. R., 27 pt. 3, p. 448). According to Capt. L. B. Norton, chief signal officer, it was 3:30 P.M. when Longstreet's men were seen to be concentrating on the Federal left, opposite Sickles's III Corps.

ered that he had authority, and he directed that command to take the lead. McLaws brought up the rear.[49]

Where the Federal left flank rested, Longstreet did not know, though he had seen nothing to indicate that it extended far down the Ridge toward Round Top. "How are you going in?" he asked McLaws.

"That," answered McLaws, "will be determined when I can see what is in my front."

"There is nothing in your front; you will be entirely on the flank of the enemy."

"Then," said the division commander, "I will continue my march in columns of companies, and after arriving on the flank as far as is necessary, will face to the left and march on the enemy."

"That suits me," replied Longstreet, and rode off.[50]

About that time, Longstreet met Joseph B. Kershaw, who was moving forward with his Brigade of McLaws's Division. Longstreet stopped Kershaw and told the South Carolinian to turn to the left at a schoolhouse near Willoughby Run, and to proceed by a lane that would carry him East of the Emmitsburg Road. Then Kershaw was to face North and was to attack along the ridge. Kershaw's advance would be towards Gettysburg. His left, as he swept along the ridge, was to be East of the Emmitsburg Road.[51]

This accorded with plans. Lee had been told of two good artillery positions in that vicinity. One was opposite Round Top; the other was in a peach orchard directly East of rising ground on the Emmitsburg Road, about 1600 yards Northwest of Little Round Top. Lee had concluded that good artillery preparation would make possible the oblique attack that would clear the Peach Orchard and put the Confederate right on the lowest part of Cemetery Ridge and on the flank of the Federals. As the Confederate attack advanced, A. P. Hill's right Division, which chanced to be "Dick" Anderson's, was to co-operate. The remainder of Hill's Corps was to demonstrate in order to prevent the detachment to right or to left of the Federal forces that faced

49 *Annals*, 423. To complete the story of this strange incident, it might be noted that Captain (later Colonel) Johnston served as General Longstreet's engineer during the winter of 1864–65, when Longstreet was in command North of James River (cf. *O. R.*, 46, pt. 3, pp. 1360, 1365, 1369). Relations were so cordial that Johnston subsequently declined to be party to the controversy over Longstreet's movements on the 2nd. *Cf.* Johnston to Lafayette McLaws, MS, June 27, 1892—*S. R. Johnston MSS.*
50 7 *S.H.S.P.*, 69–70.            51 *O. R.*, 27, pt. 2, pp. 366–67.

Hill's left. Ewell was to feint, also, as soon as he heard the sound of Longstreet's guns, and, as already arranged, he was to convert this into a real attack if opportunity offered.[52]

The major assumption of this plan was that the Federal line on Cemetery Ridge was short. As the morning passed, bluecoats had been sent in large and apparently in rising numbers on the northern end of the ridge and on Cemetery Hill, but southward, the roll of the field was such that from army headquarters on Seminary Ridge, the lower end of the opposite high ground could not be seen. On no other evidence than that of Johnston's and Clarke's reconnaissance, the Confederates had assumed that the Federal left did not extend far and that it could be turned easily when the men of the First Corps were astride the ridge.[53] As his earlier remarks to McLaws proved, Longstreet was of this opinion, which was Lee's also. Consequently when the Lieutenant General presently heard firing from the front McLaws was to occupy, he did not ride back to see what resistance the Division was encountering. He told himself that McLaws must have engaged an outpost only, but he reasoned that he should extend his right farther to the South in order to be certain that he outflanked the Federal left.[54] Hood accordingly was instructed to form on McLaws's right, and to throw the extended right across the Emmitsburg Road.

After giving his order, Longstreet waited. Nothing happened. Fire was desultory. The afternoon air brought no sound of the "rebel yell." Puzzled and provoked, Longstreet sent to inquire why McLaws had not opened the attack.[55] In front, said Long-

---

[52] *O. R.*, 27, pt. 2, pp. 318–19. The instructions given Hill are not set forth at length in any of the reports. Lee's preliminary account of the battle (*O. R.*, 27, pt. 2, p. 308) stated that Hill was to threaten the enemy and was "to avail himself of any opportunity that might present itself to attack." The final report (*ibid.*, 318) corrected this language and stated that Hill was "to cooperate with his right division in Longstreet's attack." As Hill recalled his orders when he wrote his report in November, 1863, he was to co-operate with "such of my brigades as could join in with [Longstreet's] troops in the attack" (*ibid.*, 608). Anderson's report (*ibid.*, 614) made plain the fact that his orders to attack were explicit and that he expected Longstreet's advance to be almost at right angles to his own.

[53] For observations on this subject by Supt. J. Walter Coleman and Dr. Frederick Tilberg of the Gettysburg National Military Park, see Appendix I.

[54] *Cf.* McLaws in 7 *S.H.S.P.*, 70.

[55] Reservation has to be made concerning the sequence of events at this stage of the opening action. Longstreet's report (*O. R.*, 27, pt. 2, pp. 358–59) lacked detail. Neither Hood nor McLaws filed any report. McLaws's account (7 *S.H.S.P.*, 64) contained some manifest errors. In *Hood*, 55 ff, is a narrative which is accurate but is of little use regarding incidents not on Hood's own front. None of Longstreet's three versions of the

street, was nothing more than a regiment and a battery. McLaws's answer was prompt: He would charge as soon as the Division was formed, but the Federals were in great strength in his front. They held the Peach Orchard and they spread far to McLaws's right. Abundant artillery was with them.[56] McLaws probably did not state then what Captain Johnston subsequently told friends—that the sight of those strong units in the orchard was the first evidence he had received that day of a force in position to oppose the Confederates on that flank.[57] Whatever the scope of the report from McLaws's front, Longstreet thought it exaggerated, or else he reasoned that Hood, going speedily into action, would get beyond the Federal flank. McLaws's instructions were renewed. He must attack at once.

This time McLaws replied that the Federals guns were so numerous the Confederate batteries must be used against them. The divisional leader explained that careful preparation for the attack was necessary to prevent failure. He would go forward, McLaws said, as soon as the artillery had opened and his men had deployed, but he wished Longstreet would ride to the front and see for himself. Longstreet gave no heed to this: McLaws was in the position assigned by Lee for the attack Lee had ordered; McLaws must go forward. Let him understand that the order was peremptory.[58]

Scarcely had the staff officer touched his horse and started with these instructions to McLaws than a messenger arrived from Hood. The Texan had worse news than yet had been forwarded: the Federal line extended almost to Round Top! From the Peach Orchard southward, the Union front was concave. Batteries were in position. An attack across the Emmitsburg Road, in the manner contemplated by Lee's orders, was impossible. It would expose flank and rear to the enemy's fire. Besides, Hood reported, some

events of the afternoon was specific in timing. Of necessity, McLaws's order of happenings has to be followed, though not in confidence that his memory was accurate. The chief point in doubt is at what stage of the exchange of messages with McLaws, over the beginning of the attack, Longstreet heard from Hood. Some of the evidence would indicate that Longstreet ordered McLaws to go into action before Hood was deployed, but the stronger probability is that both Hood and McLaws took longer to get into position than Longstreet had anticipated.

56 McLaws, *loc cit.*, 72, did not state that he informed Longstreet the enemy was in the Peach Orchard, but, of course, the division commander must have informed Long-street of that fact at this or another early stage of their exchanges.

57 S. R. Johnston to Lafayette McLaws, MS June 27, 1892—*S. R. Johnston MSS.*

58 McLaws, *loc. cit.*

of his Texas scouts had reconnoitered the southern end of Round Top and had found no troops there. The scouts believed it would be easy to turn Round Top, to get in rear of the enemy and to reach the Union wagon trains. Hood asked that the attack-order be suspended and that he be allowed to move around the Federal left.[59]

Longstreet shook his head. No, "General Lee's orders are to attack up the Emmitsburg Road." Tell Hood that.

The messenger did not stop to argue. None of Longstreet's staff officers suggested that in a situation that had been misunderstood from the first or had been changed decisively by the discovery of so large a Union force on the flank, Lee should be informed. Longstreet apparently did not feel that he should delay the assault still further for a report to the commanding General, but he did conclude that if Hood was not yet deployed, McLaws must wait until the Texan was ready to go forward.[60]

Almost before the courier could spur away with this message to McLaws, another officer arrived from Hood. The divisional chief presented his compliments and repeated his request: he feared that nothing could be accomplished under his orders. Would not Longstreet permit him to undertake to turn Round Top? Again the answer from Longstreet: "General Lee's orders are to attack up the Emmitsburg Road."[61]

About this time, the Confederate artillery opened in front of Hood and of McLaws.[62] Porter Alexander had chosen his positions well and he soon was delivering a heavy fire on the infantry and artillery in the Peach Orchard.[63] As the salvoes shook the countryside, there arrived still another of Hood's staff officers with the same plea: The enemy's position was one of great strength; Hood thought the Confederate attack could be repelled easily, and he asked permission to try the turning movement. For a third time Longstreet's answer was, "General Lee's orders are to attack up the Emmitsburg Road."

[59] *Hood*, 57–58.                    [60] 7 *S.H.S.P.*, 72.
[61] *Hood*, 58.

[62] Alexander in his official reports gave the time at which the fire was opened as "about 4 o'clock" (*O. R.*, 27, pt. 2, p. 429), which hour accords with what is known of other events during the afternoon. In *Longstreet*, 369, the hour was given at 3 P.M. The inclination of General Longstreet in his last book was to shorten the time between the issuance of the attack-order and the actual advance of the lines.

[63] *O. R.*, 27, pt. 2, pp. 375, 428, 429.

To reinforce this as a final, imperative order, Longstreet sent Maj. John W. Fairfax to Hood and himself soon rode over to the high ground on the extreme right,[64] where Hood's veterans were waiting. Earnestly but briefly, Hood expressed his regret that Longstreet would not permit him to advance under the southern flank of Round Top. Longstreet varied his answer to the extent only of saying, "We must obey the orders of General Lee." [65]

Hood argued no further. He had made his request. Longstreet had seen the ground. Orders stood. The Texan gave the word for the advance. Longstreet watched the start and then, in bitter mood, rode North to McLaws's position.[66] A sharp question was the greeting to McLaws: "Why is not a battery placed here?"

"General," answered McLaws, "if a battery is placed there it will draw the enemy's artillery right among my lines formed for the charge, and will of itself be in the way of my charge and tend to demoralize my men."

The order came on the instant. Put a battery there! McLaws called for guns. They were brought forward and were opened quickly. The Federals spotted the fieldpieces and turned on them some of their own abundant artillery. Limbs of the trees began to fall among the waiting men. Fragments of exploding shells killed or wounded. McLaws mounted and rode along the line with orders for the men to lie down, but he could not allay their uneasiness. In the Peach Orchard, which was distant less than 600 yards,[67] Union troops were moving as if they intended to attack. This was more than could be endured by Gen. William Barksdale, he of the battle of the pontoons at Fredericksburg.[68] Those Federals must be driven, those batteries taken.

"General," he kept pleading with McLaws, "let me go; General, let me charge."

McLaws, in the presence of the corps commander, was of course subject to Longstreet's orders, but he tried to assuage Barksdale by saying he would let the bluecoats come half way and then would

[64] The Bushman and Kern properties.

[65] Hood, 59. Alexander, op. cit., 394, wrote: "It is not likely that the movement proposed by Hood would have accomplished much. Already our lines were dangerously extended, and to have pushed one or two divisions past the III Corps and around the mountain would have invited their destruction. Had our army been more united and able to follow up the move in force, it might have proved a successful one." That, too, may be doubtful.

[66] Hood, 59; McLaws in 7 S.H.S.P., 72.

[67] At the nearest point, opposite the Warfield House.          [68] See Vol. II, p. 332 ff.

meet them on even terms.[69] A few minutes later, as Longstreet passed, Barksdale impetuously came up to him: "I wish you would let me go in, General. I will take that battery in five minutes."

"Wait a little," answered Longstreet, "we are all going in presently." [70]

Hood's attack by this time already was becoming confused. Two of his Brigades divided and then advanced in three parts.[71] One of the Colonels failed to go forward with his troops;[72] within twenty minutes Hood fell with a bad arm wound;[73] Evander Law, assuming command of the Division, pushed his own Brigade over Round Top, grappled with the enemy on Little Round Top, and, after a sharp fight, scampered down the west side of the lower eminence and piled up there a breastwork of stones.[74] Awkwardly but gallantly, and with heavy losses, the rest of the Division fought its way as far as it could without support on its left. Law halted it on the best defensive line he could find and hurriedly sought McLaws, whose troops, by Longstreet's orders, had remained inactive while Law had been fighting.

"Joe" Kershaw, commanding on the right of McLaws's front, received the appeal for help and forwarded it to his chief.[75] Mc-Laws had been awaiting word from Longstreet to launch his attack,[76] and he almost certainly inquired of Longstreet whether he should advance, but of this the records say nothing.[77] Longstreet was not to be hurried. He had Kershaw wait until the signal gun was fired. Then "Old Pete" went forward on foot with Kershaw as far as the Emmitsburg Road,[78] whence the South Carolinians advanced in an effort to seize the Peach Orchard and to

[69] 7 S.H.S.P., 73.
[70] Fitzgerald Ross, Cities and Camps of the Confederate States (cited hereafter as Ross), 55.
[71] Alexander, 395–96. This is the least clouded account of a neglected part of the battle.
[72] O. R., 27, pt. 2, p. 395; Oates, 217.          [73] Hood, 59.
[74] Law in 3 B. & L., 324; 8 C. V., 344–49. For the Federal account of the resistance offered by Vincent's 3rd Brigade of William Barnes's 1st Division of George Sykes's V Corps, see O. R., 27, pt. 1, pp. 601 ff, 617.
[75] See Law in 3 B. & L., 325.
[76] Cf. McLaws in describing events about an hour previously: "But, as I was waiting General Longstreet's will, I told General Barksdale . . ." etc. 7 S.H.S.P., 73.
[77] McLaws wrote: "Hood . . . being pressed on his left, sent to me for assistance, and the charge of my division was ordered." Ibid. Kershaw wrote of the various orders given him: "These directions I received in various messages from the lieutenant general and the major general commanding, and in part by personal communication with them." O. R., 27, pt. 2, p. 367.
[78] 3 B. & L., 334.

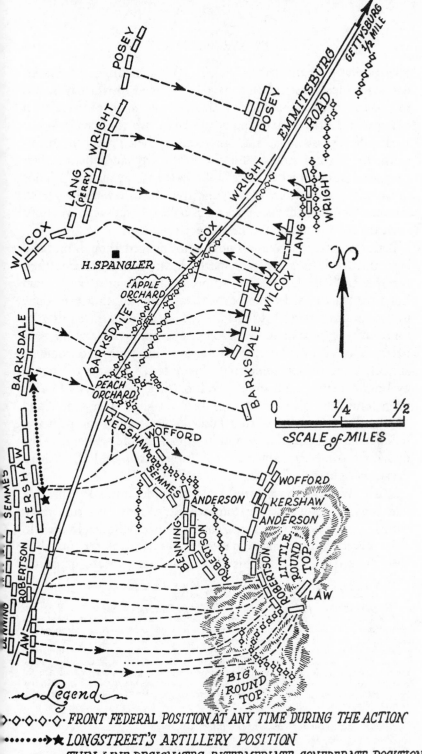

POSEY
POSEY
WRIGHT
LANG (PERRY)
WILCOX
WRIGHT
WILCOX
WRIGHT
LANG
WILCOX
H. SPANGLER
APPLE ORCHARD
BARKSDALE
BARKSDALE
BARKSDALE
PEACH ORCHARD
KERSHAW
WOFFORD
WOFFORD
KERSHAW
SEMMES
ANDERSON
ANDERSON
KERSHAW
SEMMES
BENNING
ROBERTSON
ROBERTSON
ROBERTSON
LITTLE ROUND TOP
LAW
BENNING
LAW
BIG ROUND TOP

EMMITSBURG ROAD
GETTYSBURG ½ MILE

N

0    ¼    ½
SCALE of MILES

~ Legend ~

⟩·◇·◇·◇·◇· FRONT FEDERAL POSITION AT ANY TIME DURING THE ACTION

······▶★ LONGSTREET'S ARTILLERY POSITION

———— THIN LINE DESIGNATES INTERMEDIATE CONFDERATE POSITIONS

Sketch of the Attack of the Confederate Right South of Gettysburg, July 2, 1863—
after John B. Bachelder.

take position on the left of Hood. By some mischance, Barksdale's advance, which should have been timed to Kershaw's, was
so delayed that Kershaw had to change front to cover his left. In
doing so, his Brigade split and advanced in two columns.[79] When
Barksdale's Mississippians at last received their orders to go forward, they swept straight for the Peach Orchard. Before their
advance a strong picket fence disappeared in an instant.[80] They
drove the enemy from among the trees but they could get no
farther. Semmes then came to Kershaw's support; Wofford
pushed forward to aid Semmes and Kershaw.

Both Longstreet's Divisions now were engaged, though they had
been thrown into action piecemeal. As always, they made their
fire count. "I do not hesitate to pronounce [their action]," said
Longstreet afterward, "the best three hours' fighting ever done
by any troops on any battlefield." [81] They met the Federals with
fury, but they began to feel soon a menacing enfilade on their
left.[82] That flank was next Anderson: his time had come to
attack. As Anderson understood his orders,[83] he was to engage
by Brigades from right to left—Wilcox first, then Perry's Florida
Brigade under Col. David Lang, then Wright's Georgians,[84] and
finally, the Brigade of Carnot Posey.[85] Apparently the plan was
for Mahone to be in reserve and in support of the artillery.[86] The
divisional front consequently was, from right to left, Wilcox,
Perry, Wright and Posey.

When Wilcox, about 6:20,[87] saw that McLaws's left Brigade
had begun its advance, he commenced to move his stout Alabamians, but he discovered that Barksdale had obliqued to the left.
Wilcox accordingly decided to move by his left flank for enough to
clear Barksdale's left.[88] This took time and perhaps explained

[79] O. R., 27, pt. 2, pp. 367, 368.          [80] 7 S.H.S.P., 74.
[81] Annals, 424.                             [82] Ibid., 425.
[83] O. R., 27, pt. 2, p. 614.                [84] O. R., 27, pt. 2, pp. 618, 622, 631.
[85] O. R., 27, pt. 2, p. 633. This is of some importance because Wright subsequently
insisted that Posey did not advance (ibid., 623). Alexander years afterward mentioned an
assertion that the day's battle was lost because Posey and Mahone did not participate. Anderson is said by Alexander to have admitted that the two did not share in the action
because the division commander had been ordered by A. P. Hill to hold those Brigades in
reserve (Alexander, 401). Not a line in any of the reports gives color to this. On the
contrary, Anderson wrote as if his orders were to throw in the whole of his Division.
Posey stated specifically: "In the afternoon, I received an order to advance after Brigadier
General Wright . . ." (loc. cit.).
[86] O. R., 27, pt. 2, p. 621.
[87] Ibid., 620. Anderson (ibid., 614) put the hour at 5:30.
[88] O. R., 27, pt. 2, p. 618.

why Longstreet felt that he was receiving no help on that flank.[89] At last Wilcox got his line in motion. On his left Perry's small Florida Brigade, and on Perry's left Wright's Georgians quickly followed.[90] Then it developed that Posey's troops were badly placed and were unable to advance as a unit. Three of the regiments had been thrown forward as skirmishers [91] and were not under the ready control of their General.

Wilcox's advance was over rising ground to the Emmitsburg Road, and then down grade to a shallow ravine above which towered the ridge. The Alabamians who had made military history at Salem Church reached the road and endured a heavy artillery fire as they went on to the ravine. There they were met by Federals who boldly descended from the right.[92] Perry's Florida troops under Col. David Lang advanced as far as Wilcox did and for a time, together, they drove the enemy.

Wright's advance was superb. The commander is himself the best historian of the attack. He described it fully in a letter to his wife, five days later, while the heat of the charge still was on him: "As soon as we emerged from the woods and came into the open fields, the enemy poured a most terrific fire of shells into our ranks. We rushed down the hillside and reaching the valley, we found it was broken by a series of small ridges and hollows, running parallel with the enemy's line on the mountain, and in the first of these depressions or hollows, our line paused for breath. Then we rushed over the next ridge into the succeeding hollow, and thus we worked our way across that terrible field for more than a mile, under the most furious fire of artillery I had ever seen. When we reached the base of the range upon which the enemy was posted, they opened upon us with their infantry, and raked our whole line with grape and canister from more than twenty guns.

"We were now within a few hundred yards of the enemy's guns, and had up to this time suffered but little loss, the small ridge I

---

[89] *Annals,* 425.
[90] Cf. *Alexander,* 400: "These two charges followed with the least delay of any during the affair."
[91] Two had been sent out on orders from Anderson; the third was moved forward by Posey himself (*O. R.,* 27, pt. 2, p. 633).
[92] *O. R.,* 27, pt. 2, p. 618. These Federals belonged to the Division of Andrew A. Humphreys, III Corps, a gentleman with whom the Army of Northern Virginia was to have many unhappy conflicts. Cf. *ibid.,* pt. 1, p. 532 ff.

have spoken of protecting our men from the enemy's fire, except as we would pass on their tops which we always did in a run, thus exposing ourselves very little to the enemy's fire. But we were in a hot place, and looking to my left through the smoke, I perceived that neither Posey nor Mahone had advanced, and that my left was wholly unprotected. I immediately dispatched a courier to General Anderson informing him of the fact, who answered that both Posey and Mahone had been ordered in and that he would reiterate the order. That I must go on. Before my courier returned, Perry's Brigade on my right gave way, and shamefully ran to the rear.

"My Brigade had now climbed up the side of the mountain nearly to the enemy's guns, and being left without support either on the right or left, enabled the enemy to concentrate a heavy fire upon my small command, but my brave men passed rapidly and steadily on, until we approached within fifty or sixty yards of the enemy's batteries, when we encountered a heavy body of infantry posted behind a stone wall. The side of the mountain was so precipitous here that my men could with difficulty *climb* it, but we strove on, and reaching the stone fence, *drove the Yankee infantry from behind it,* and then taking cover from the fence we soon *shot all the gunners of the enemy's artillery,* and rushing over the fence seized their guns. We had now accomplished our task. We had stormed the enemy's strong position, had driven off his infantry, had captured all his guns in our front, except a few which he succeeded in carrying off, and had up to this minute suffered but comparatively little loss.

"Just after taking the enemy's batteries we perceived a heavy column of Yankee Infantry on our right flank. They had taken advantage of the gap left in our line by the falling back of Perry's Brigade, and had filed around a piece of timber on our right, and had gotten into the gap left by Perry's Brigade and were rapidly getting into our rear. Posey *had not advanced on our left,* and a strong body of the enemy was advancing down the sides of the mountain to gain our left flank and rear. Thus we were perfectly isolated from any portion of our Army a *mile* in its advance. And although we had gained the enemy's works and captured his guns, we were about to be sacrificed to the bad management and cowardly conduct of others. For a moment I thought all was lost, and that my gallant little band would all be inevitably killed or captured. Colonel Hall of the Twenty-second had been killed, Colonel Gibson of the Forty-eighth seriously wounded, and while at the enemy's guns with his hands on the horses, Major Ross of the Second Georgia Battalion had just been shot down. Nearly all my company officers had been killed or wounded. Everything looked gloomy in the extreme, but the men remained *firm and cool to the last.* The enemy had now gotten completely in our rear, *and were advancing upon us over the very ground we had passed in attacking them.* A large force concentrated in our front and artillery [was] brought into position and opened upon us. Then was a prayer said.

"We must face about and cut our way out of the net-work of bristling bayonets, which stretched around us on every side. With cheers and good order we turned our faces to the enemy in our rear, and abandoning our captured guns we rushed upon the flanking column of the enemy and *literally cut our way out,* and fell back about one-half the distance we had gone over, and then reformed our line. But alas, very few of the brave spirits who so recently had passed over that line buoyant in spirit and confident of success, now answered to the order that calmly sang out upon the air, 'Fall in, Wright's Brigade, and here we'll stand again'." [93]

Wright had not been alone in sending to Anderson for help. When Cadmus Wilcox had seen the odds he faced, he had asked for reinforcement. His A.A.G. returned and reported that Anderson had sent word, "Tell General Wilcox to hold his own, that things will change." In addition, Anderson had dispatched Wilcox's staff officer to Mahone with an order for the Virginian to advance, but Mahone was reported to have said that he had instructions to hold his position and that he would not leave it. "But," the aide was alleged to have answered, "I am just from General Anderson and he orders you to advance." Mahone is said to have

[93] A. R. Wright to Mrs. Wright, MS, July 7, 1863, courteously placed at the disposal of the writer by A. R. Wright of Atlanta, Georgia, grandson of the General. Wright's official account of this charge (*O. R.,* 27, pt. 2, pp. 623–24) contained the statement that Perry's Brigade did not advance beyond the Emmitsburg Road. Wright probably was misled by seeing the Florida troops halt at the road before they advanced approximately a quarter of a mile beyond it. Lang's report is explicit concerning his advance (*O. R.,* 27, pt. 2, p. 631). The troops who met Wright were Gibbon's 2nd Division of Hancock's II Corps, reinforced by Williams's (Ruger's) 1st Division of Slocum's XII Corps (cf. *O. R.,* 27, pt. 1, p. 417).

replied, "No, I have my orders from General Anderson himself to remain here." [94]

The attack, in a word, had been uncoordinated on the right. Wright fell back because Posey had not covered his left flank or Perry his right. Posey never got his skirmishers into a compact body to act with the one regiment that attempted to charge.[95] Perry's men withdrew in the belief that Wilcox had done so and had exposed their right.[96] Wilcox abandoned his assault in the face of invincible resistance when he felt he had support neither on the right nor on the left.[97] In the failure of these Brigades of Anderson's Division to break the enemy's front, the experience of Mc-Laws and of Hood was duplicated. Each Division had fought its battle almost alone and in no case with its full strength exerted. That was not like "Dick" Anderson and not like James Longstreet.

For the opening of Longstreet's battle, "Dick" Ewell had been waiting all day. Along his own front, he had nothing more violent than intermittent skirmishing to the left [98] and some galling artillery fire on his right, where Daniel was sent by Rodes to establish contact with the left of Pender.[99] To assure action in accordance with the plan for the day's battle,[100] Lee, it will be remembered, had been to visit Ewell during the morning. While there, Lee several times had said with manifest point, "We did not or could not pursue our advantage of yesterday, and now the enemy are in good position." [101] For a time Lee impatiently had waited on the left for the sound of Longstreet's guns and then had ridden off to see why the battle was delayed.[102] Ewell had been left to guard the left and to strike if he could. In Early's company, Ewell rode to the ridge in rear of Edward Johnson's position and located batteries to play on Cemetery Hill and Culp's Hill.[103] More than that Ewell did not attempt to do. He gave no explicit instruction to Rodes and Early and Johnson regarding their co-operation.[104] Nor did he visit the various Divisions or send staff officers to ascer-

[94] C. M. Wilcox to R. E. Lee, n. d. approximately 1866, Lee MSS, printed in 3 R. E. Lee, 555.
[95] O. R., 27, pt. 2, pp. 633–35.  [96] Ibid., 632.
[97] Ibid., 618.  [98] O. R., 27, pt. 2, pp. 504, 518.
[99] Ibid., 555.  [100] O. R., 27, pt. 2, p. 446.
[101] 26 S.H.S.P., 125. See also 4 ibid., 289; Venable in Longstreet, 380 n.
[102] Long, 281.  [103] O. R., 27, pt. 2, p. 470; Early, 272.
[104] Cf. Rodes, O. R., 27, pt. 2, p. 556.

tain if the troops of the Corps were posted for the demonstration. All these details he left to Early, to Rodes and to Johnson.

On the basis of guess or of word from the right, report circulated among Ewell's subordinates that the attack of Longstreet would be delivered at 4 o'clock. Early made ready by posting John B. Gordon's Brigade in rear of Hoke's,[105] and Hays's,[106] so that he would give weight to his demonstration. The Brigade of "Extra Billy" Smith was left to guard the York Road, from which the previous afternoon had come the unfounded stories of Federal advance. This new disposition of Smith and of Gordon was the sole change on Ewell's front before Longstreet's artillery began to roar.

As soon as the direction of the sound made it certain that the guns were those of the First Corps, Ewell ordered Edward Johnson's batteries to open on Cemetery Hill. The artillery with Johnson was Snowden Andrews's Maryland Battalion, to which the Rockbridge Artillery was added from the reserve.[107] As Andrews still was incapacitated by wounds, young Maj. Joseph W. Latimer directed the guns, the same able, daring boy who had won many plaudits for his conduct at Winchester and for his handling of Ewell's batteries at Cedar Mountain.[108] No sooner did he begin now to fire than the Union batteries answered him wrathfully with heavier metal.

While the firing was in progress, Ewell decided to turn the demonstration into an assault. What he saw in the bombardment to think it held promise of a successful infantry attack, neither he nor anyone else ever explained; but he sent word to Early to attack when Johnson did.[109] Rodes was instructed, in his own words, "to cooperate with the attacking force as soon as any opportunity of doing so with good effect was offered." [110] A staff officer was dispatched beyond Rodes's flank to the nearest Division of the Third Corps—Ewell did not know which Division it was—to ask what it was going to do.

Some time was required to bring back this answer: The Division

---

[105] Some of the reports consistently referred to the Brigade as Avery's. See *supra*, p. 99.
[106] *O. R.*, 27, pt. 2, p. 470.                    [107] *O. R.*, 27, pt. 2, p. 446.
[108] Latimer's guns, according to Bachelder's map of the Second Day at Gettysburg, were on Benner's Hill, East of the town and between Rock Creek and the Hanover Road.
[109] *O. R.*, 27, pt. 2, p. 470.                    [110] *Ibid.*, 556.

was that of Dorsey Pender, but he had been wounded in mid-afternoon and had been succeeded in command by his senior Brigadier, James H. Lane. That officer said the only orders given him by Pender were to attack if an opportunity was presented.[111] Ewell sat down immediately and wrote Lane that he was advancing with his Corps and that he requested Lane's co-operation. This note Ewell sent to Lane directly. Ewell did not attempt to communicate with A. P. Hill because there was not sufficient time before the assault was to be delivered.[112]

When this note was dispatched, Latimer's Battalion was being overwhelmed by the fire directed against it. The Major was compelled to send word to Johnson that his position was untenable. Such an admission by so stubborn a fighter did not have to be verified. Without hesitation, Johnson directed Latimer to cease firing and to withdraw all the guns except four, which should be left to cover the advance of the infantry.[113] As quickly as the messages could be passed, Latimer sent away his guns, but with crippled gun-crews this was a work of long minutes. Ewell heard the slackening of the fire and then its conclusion. He had received no answer to the appeal sent Lane for assistance on the right, but he determined to make the attack even though he had no assurance of help on that flank. Orders were dispatched to Johnson to begin the assault by taking Culp's Hill.[114] Early and then Rodes were to follow on their front.

The sun had been near its setting when the artillery duel ended.[115] On the rough and wooded hillside, whatever was done by Johnson's men must be done within an hour; but the start of the attack was slow for a reason that was vexatious though not sufficient to preclude an assault. Skirmishing had been active before the order reached Johnson.[116] The Stonewall Brigade had

---

[111] O. R., 27, pt. 2, p. 447.

[112] Ibid. Lane stated (ibid., 666) that he first was informed by Rodes's A.A.G., Maj. H. A. Whiting, that Rodes would "advance at dark" and wished Lane to protect his flank. "I did not give him a definite answer," Lane reported later, "as I had sent [Maj. Jos. A. Engelhard] to notify General Hill of General Pender's fall, and to receive instructions." Later, said Lane, he was notified by Ewell that the Second Corps would move on the enemy's position that night. "I told Major Whiting that I would act without awaiting instructions from General Hill" (Ibid., 666).

[113] O. R., 27, pt. 2, p. 504. Ewell (ibid., 446) stated that the four guns were left to repel infantry attack.

[114] Ewell (O. R., 27, pt. 2, p. 447) wrote merely that "Johnson ordered forward his Division" etc. Johnson (ibid., 504) said: "In obedience to an order from the lieutenant-general commanding, I then advanced . . ."

[115] Ibid., 447.          [116] Ibid., 518.

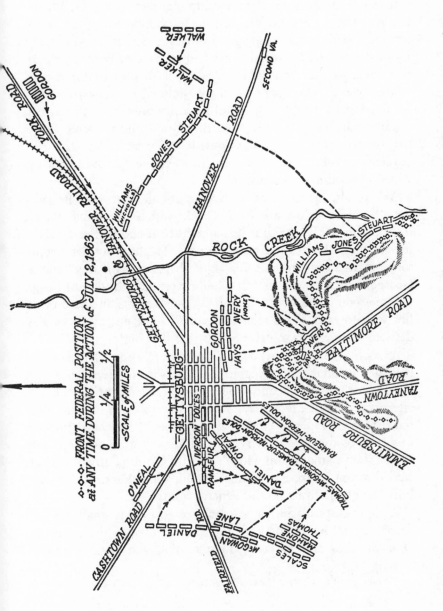

Sketch of the Attack of the Confederate Left on Culp's Hill, East Cemetery Hill and Cemetery Hill, Gettysburg, July 2, 1863 —after John B. Bachelder.

suffered so much from sharpshooting that Gen. James A. Walker had sent out the Second Virginia to clear a field and wood on the left. This regiment was engaged and was under artillery fire when Johnson was told to advance. He had to leave to Walker's discretion the part the Stonewall Brigade was to play in the assault. Walker was a V.M.I. man and a good soldier. He reasoned that as his movement would be made of necessity in sight of the enemy, his advance along with the other Brigades would be public notice that the flank and rear of the Confederates were uncovered. Consequently, Walker decided to remain where he was until darkness would conceal his withdrawal.[117]

As a result, Johnson had to start his assault with three Brigades only.[118] In his front was Rock Creek, which was impassable at some points.[119] By the time he had crossed it and had reached the foot of the hill, darkness had fallen.[120] This did not deter Johnson, but in their groping, his right Brigades soon met repulse. George Steuart on the left got a footing on the hillside. Although his line soon could be traced only by the fact that the flash of his fire was upward,[121] his men hung on.[122] The enemy by 11 P.M. desisted from efforts to drive Steuart out that night.

As soon as "Jube" Early ascertained that Johnson's Division had launched its attack, he prepared to go forward in accordance with an understanding he and Rodes had reached during the late afternoon to attack together.[123] Early, like Johnson, had no more than three Brigades to employ in the fight,[124] and he decided to keep one of these as a reserve. In his assault he would use only Hays's Louisianians and Hoke's North Carolina troops. These were directed to take East Cemetery Hill, which lies next Cemetery Hill, the key position on the Federal front.

With fine spirit, Early's veterans passed over a small knoll,[125] descended into a ravine and then pushed toward the eminence. One line they crashed easily, in spite of Union artillery and in-

---

[117] Ibid., 504, 518–19.
[118] From right to left, J. M. Jones, Francis Nicholls (Col. J. M. Williams) and G. H. Steuart.
[119] Ibid., 447.                    [120] Johnson in ibid., 504.
[121] McKim, 196.
[122] O. R., 27, pt. 2, pp. 504, 510; McKim, loc. cit.      [123] O. R., 27, pt. 2, p. 556.
[124] Smith's Virginia Brigade, it will be recalled, had been detached to guard the York Road. O. R., 27, pt. 2, pp. 470, 489.
[125] The one at an elevation of 424 feet, about 500 yards Southwest of William Culp's House.

fantry who were pouring down a frantic fire. Fortunately for the Southerners, as the lead from thousands of small arms and the countless fragments of shell broke among the rocks, the smoke and the merciful darkness covered the human targets.[126] Casualties were not heavy. Near the foot of East Cemetery Hill, the shouting Confederates climbed a stone wall behind which Federal riflemen had been contesting their advance. Prisoners were taken and were told to make their own way to the rear. An abatis was passed, rifle pits were overrun, the climb was continued. Then, at last, the crest was reached. Hays straightened his line and threw it forward in a bold rush. Guns were seized. Flags were captured. Prisoners held up powder-smoked hands. "At that moment," said Hays, "every piece of artillery which had been fired upon us was silenced." [127]

For a few minutes there was quiet, but for a few minutes only. Through the shadows, now, the Confederates could see heavy masses of infantry South of them on the crest of the ridge. The rumble of many voices was audible. A line was advancing. Hays did not know whether it was Union or Confederate. He had been cautioned to watch for friends on either flank and in front, because Longstreet or Johnson or Rodes might mount the ridge before he got there. That powerful advancing line might belong to one of them. As Hays questioned, a wave of fire swept along the front of the approaching troops. Hays did not reply. The fire might have come from Confederates who mistook his troops for Federals. Another volley—shouts, oaths, and the cry of wounded men. Still Hays would not shout an order. A third volley! This time it was so close that the flash of the muskets lighted the uniforms of the men: they were blue.

Hays gave them every bullet he had in the rifles of his two Brigades. For a time, firing fast, he held them off. Soon he saw behind the first line a second. In the rear of the second line still another force was gathering. To these odds he could oppose no troops except those of his own and Hoke's Brigade. Gordon, whom Early had placed in support, had not mounted the hill, because Early had seen nothing to indicate that Rodes was advancing on the right. Further resistance on the crest would be a

[126] *O. R.*, 27, pt. 2, pp. 470, 480.
[127] *O. R.*, 27, pt. 2, p. 480. Hays's account of this advance is the best.

waste of life. Hays must give up that prize of guns and of commanding ground. Like Wright an hour previously, Hays had to retreat for lack of help at the decisive moment. As befitted men who so boldly had challenged Fortune, Hays's two Brigades were able to withdraw to the foot of the hill with little additional loss.[128]

Support of Hays by Rodes had failed for reasons that were explicable in themselves, but they were seen that July evening as a part of a perversity of Fate that strengthened the fine Federal defense. Rodes had sent word to Lane that he would attack at dark.[129] From Lane, he had received no immediate, positive assurance of help, but a little later, Maj. Henry A. Whiting, A.A.G. to Rodes, must have delivered to Rodes the message from Lane that Pender's Division would co-operate in Ewell's attack. Needless to say, a mistake was made in not sending this message to corps headquarters also, in answer to Ewell's note that had solicited assistance on the right.[130] After receipt of assurance from Pender's Division, Rodes could advance in some confidence that his right would be covered by Lane.[131]

When Early started forward, Rodes did so, but most of Rodes's men at that time were in line on one of the main east-and-west streets of Gettysburg. To move the troops westward and southwestward through the town consumed long, expensive minutes. Line of battle, after exasperating delay, was drawn beyond the city streets, but Rodes had to drive in the Federal skirmishers and to advance his extreme right approximately 1200 yards before he could open fire. Early had scarcely more than half that distance to go,[132] and did not have any elaborate maneuver to execute. When Early attacked, Rodes still was advancing. At the moment Hays was hoping vainly for the arrival of reinforcements, Dodson

---

[128] O. R., 27, pt. 2, pp. 447, 470, 480–81.　　　[129] O. R., 27, pt. 2, p. 556.
[130] O. R., 27, pt. 2, p. 666.

[131] It is to be noted that Ewell, in his report, complained of the lack of support by Hill's Corps (O. R., 27, pt. 2, p. 447), but that Rodes (ibid., 556) made no such complaint.

[132] Rodes stated in his report (O. R., 27, pt. 1, p. 556) that he had to cover 1200 to 1400 yards. Actually, if it be assumed that contact would have been established upon crossing the Emmitsburg Road, the distance to be covered by Ramseur's right regiment, after forming line of battle West of the town, would have been about 1200 yards. The Brigades of the centre and left had less ground to traverse, but their deployment and advance had, of course, to be timed by that of the right, which had a long "wheel" to make.

Ramseur and George Doles were halting their column and were debating whether they should attempt to storm the frowning position ahead of them. Ramseur wrote afterwards: ". . . batteries were discovered in position to pour upon our lines direct, cross and enfilade fires. Two lines of infantry behind stone walls and breastworks were supporting those batteries." The young Confederate Brigadiers had shown at Chancellorsville and on many a lesser field that they did not fear adverse odds, but this time they did not think they should attack what they considered a field fortress until they had asked Rodes.[133]

By the time their messenger reached Rodes, their question had answered itself. Rodes had been notified that Early was withdrawing from East Cemetery Hill. To Rodes it appeared a useless sacrifice of life to deliver an isolated attack with his Division and such support as Lane could give him on his right.[134] Accordingly, the Division quietly withdrew about 200 yards to the bed of an old abandoned road, from which Rodes hoped he could spring forward with advantage the next morning.[135]

The battle of July 2 now was ending. On the extreme right, along the western slope of Little Round Top, some of Hood's men were building with boulders a fortification to protect the barren ground they had won. Peach Orchard remained in Confederate hands. Far to the left, in the darkness, "Maryland" Steuart's men still were holding a section of the front trenches of the enemy.[136] These three strips of Pennsylvania soil might be, as Lee hoped, the points of departure for a decisive attack the next day but if any one in the exhausted Confederate Army remembered a corresponding night two months before, when Jackson

133 O. R., 27, pt. 2, p. 588. Ramseur stated that he was within 200 yards of the enemy's position when he halted. He must have been referring to the ground occupied by the 8th Ohio, which was on picket duty. See Bachelder's map of the Second Day's Battle and O. R., 27, pt. 1, p. 461. The main line of the enemy, at the nearest point, was at least 500 yards from the ground where Ramseur halted.

134 O. R., 27, pt. 2, p. 556. A critique of Rodes's conduct will be found infra, p. 177, but it may be noted here that approximately thirty of the fifty-two guns assigned the XI Corps (O. R., 27, pt. 1, p. 749) could have been brought to bear on Rodes. An indeterminable number on the right of the I Corps also could have been employed. The infantry in front of Rodes were Schurz's and Steinwehr's Divisions of the XI Corps. On the left, within supporting distance and unengaged, was the greater part of the I Corps. Apparently in neither Federal Corps did any of the officers who filed a published report observe Rodes's advance. All attention was fixed on Early's attack.

135 O. R., 27, pt. 2, p. 556.
136 O. R., 27, pt. 2, p. 510; cf. ibid., pt. 1, p. 759.

# 136 LEE'S LIEUTENANTS

was wounded near Chancellorsville, the contrast must have been worse than a humiliation. In the Wilderness, May 2, all the troops working together to strike a joint blow; at Gettysburg—a battle of Divisions, of Brigades even! In tactical effort, this was not the Army of Chancellorsville, but the Army of Malvern Hill. It had unlearned the lessons of a year. Said Walter Taylor afterward: "The whole affair was disjointed. There was an utter absence of accord in the movements of the several commands . . ." [137]

Every Division on the field had been engaged either the first day or the second. The two Brigades that had escaped most lightly were "Extra Billy" Smith's of Early's command and William Mahone's of the forces under Anderson. Both these had been exposed to artillery but neither had infantry action. Mahone's skirmishers had exchanged fire with the enemy. [138] The sole infantry reinforcement was Pickett's Division of Longstreet's Corps. These troops, numbering less than 5000, [139] had reached the stone bridge on the Cashtown Road during the early afternoon [140] and could go into battle the next morning. [141] No other reinforcement of any sort would be available except Stuart's cavalry.

"Jeb" at last had rejoined the Army. [142] After his night march from Hanover [143] he had reached Dover on the morning of July 1 but had not found any Confederates there. The natives would tell him nothing. Such information as he could get from the newspapers led him to conclude that Early had moved in the direction of Shippensburg, which was indicated as Lee's point of concentra-

[137] *Taylor's Four Years*, 99.  [138] *O. R.*, 27, pt. 2, pp. 489, 621.

[139] Longstreet, 3 *B. & L.*, 345, stated that Pickett had 4900. Walter Harrison, *Pickett's Men* (cited hereafter as *Walter Harrison*), 90, credited the Division with 4481 muskets and effective strength, rank and file, of 4700. Pickett, on June 21, had written Lee that he had "not more than 4795 men," and he had urged that if his absent Brigades were not returned to him in time for the campaign, another Brigade might be assigned him. Said Pickett: "I ask this in no spirit of complaint, but merely as an act of justice to my division and myself, for it is well known that a small division will be expected to do the same amount of hard service as a large one, and, as the army is now divided, my division will be, I think, decidedly the weakest" (*O. R.*, 27, pt. 3, p. 910. For Lee's answer, see *ibid.*, 994). At the time of this correspondence, Jenkins's Brigade, as well as Corse's, was regarded as part of Pickett's Division. Details of Pickett's return to the Army of Northern Virginia will be found in *O. R.*, 18, 1062, 1091; *ibid.*, 25, pt. 2, pp. 802, 827; *ibid.*, 51, pt. 2, p. 710; 1 *R.W.C.D.*, 326.

[140] *Walter Harrison*, 88, 90.

[141] Pickett's artillery, Dearing's Battalion, was brought up during the night and placed in rear of the First Corps (*O. R.*, 27, pt. 2, p. 388).

[142] For the last detailed references to him, see *supra*, p. 72.

[143] See *supra*, p. 72.

tion.[144] Stuart rested his men and horses for a few hours and sent out a few daring riders in the hope that one or another of them would locate the Confederate Army.[145] Then "Jeb" started the entire column for Carlisle, via Dillsburg. He chose this objective because he reasoned that if the Southern infantry had advanced to the Susquehanna and were not in the vicinity of York, they must be around Carlisle or Harrisburg.

In the late afternoon of July 1, when the thin van of Fitz Lee's Brigade reached Carlisle, it found the pleasant little town garrisoned. The weary troopers scarcely were in condition to clear the place. As one young soldier wrote his mother: "From our great exertion, constant mental excitement, want of sleep and food, the men were overcome and so tired and stupid as almost to be ignorant of what was taking place around them. Couriers in attempting to deliver orders to officers would be compelled to give them a shake and call before they could make them understand . . . Thoughts of saving wagons were now gone from many of us, and we began to consider only how we ourselves might escape."[146] Blackest of all the discouragements was the grim admission by officers that all rations had been consumed. Until more were requisitioned after capturing Carlisle, the men must go hungry.[147]

Stuart was undisturbed. "He seemed," George W. Beale wrote, "neither to suppose that his train was in danger nor that his men were not in a condition to fight"[148]—a combination of negatives Stuart's admiring troopers seldom would have employed against him.

Reports were that militia, not regular troops, held the town. With some artillery in addition to infantry, they were said to be preparing to fight from the houses.[149] Stuart had with him few men at the time, because the column was spread out for miles on the road from Dover, but briskly, with an officer and bugler,[150] he had Fitz Lee send in a flag of truce to demand the surrender of

144 O. R., 27, pt. 2, p. 696.
145 W. W. Blackford's MS Memoirs, 334–335.
146 G. W. Beale to his mother, July 13, 1863, in G. W. Beale, 114.
147 O. R., 27, pt. 2, p. 696.      148 G. W. Beale, 114.
149 The defenders numbered 2000 militia, who had one battery. O. R., 27, pt. 3, p. 493.
150 Frank Robertson, op. cit.

Carlisle or the evacuation of the women and children. Had he
known then that the place was in the keeping of Brig. Gen. W. F.
("Baldy") Smith,[151] he might have saved himself the trouble of
making the demand. Smith was quite willing to fight and sent
back word that he had told non-combatants to leave the town.
Stuart renewed the demand and gave warning that if the town
were not surrendered, he would burn it. When this threat proved
futile, Stuart began a slow shelling with a battery. His men moved
as if they were in a dream. Afterward, some of them scarcely knew
whether they actually had bombarded the town or merely threatened to do so. Truth was, Stuart made a great noise and sought to
drive the militia in panic from the town, but he did little damage.[152]

Happily, Stuart was saved both waste of his shells and the
destruction of civilian property. Up the road from the South came
one of the messengers Stuart had dispatched while at Dover. The
rider had found the Army! It had been engaged that 1st of July
with the enemy's advance; General Lee directed that Stuart move
to Gettysburg.[153] "Jeb" did not delay compliance. He reasoned
that Wade Hampton, en route from Dover, had not yet passed
Dillsburg, whence the main road led to Gettysburg. A courier
accordingly was dispatched to Hampton with instructions to turn
southward at Dillsburg and to march ten miles on the road to
Gettysburg that night. The other Brigades were given orders to
move in the same direction. At Stuart's instance the cavalry barracks were burned,[154] but no other buildings were set afire.

Wearily, the gunners limbered up. The exhausted troopers
mounted their staggering horses. Carlisle was left behind. Col.
R. L. T. Beale of the Ninth Virginia Cavalry was entrusted with
the wagon train which all men now were damning as warmly as
they had praised it when they captured it.[155] In some manner,
Colonel Beale found a guide who showed him the short-cuts
across the fields toward Papertown,[156] where a brief halt was

[151] Smith had been promoted Major General, but the nomination having been rejected
by the Senate, he had been returned to his rank of Brigadier General.
[152] See W. F. Smith's report, O. R., 27, pt. 2, p. 221. Cf. Stuart, ibid., p. 697.
[153] O. R., 27, pt. 2, p. 697; H. B. McClellan, 330.
[154] O. R., 27, pt. 2, p. 697; ibid., pt. 3, p. 493; H. B. McClellan, 330.
[155] See supra p. 66.
[156] Beale had attended Dickinson College and knew the country. Papertown was six
miles South of Carlisle on the Baltimore and Carlisle Turnpike.

called. "Here some of our men," wrote Colonel Beale, "were busy in a search for rations, but most of them, suffering an agony for sleep, lay on the road with bridles in hand, some on rocks, and others on the wet earth, slumbering soundly." [157] Rest was brief. The men were shaken or aroused by shouts and were marched onward till flesh could stand no more.

It was afternoon on the 2nd when Stuart, riding ahead, reached his anxious chief on Seminary Ridge. No record of the exchange between them is known to exist. The tradition is that Lee said, "Well, General Stuart, you are here at last" [158]—that and little besides. Need of the presence of the cavalry was shown immediately by a clash at Hunterstown, five miles Northeast of Gettysburg, between Hampton and a Union cavalry force which the Confederates believed to be moving against the rear of the Army.[159] Because the Federals were driven off, Stuart reported that he had arrived "just in time to thwart" a bold dash,[160] and he believed from what he saw of the field that Pennsylvania the next day would be opened to the Confederates through the defeat of the enemy.[161]

To be prepared for whatever opportunities might come, Stuart sent word to the Ninth Virginia Cavalry, and perhaps to other regiments also, that he wished the men to remain in the saddle all night. Colonel Beale answered that he would comply cheerfully, of course, but that the limit of endurance of the men had been reached. Unless the troopers got rest, Beale tactfully intimated, neither they nor their horses would be fit for any service on the 3rd.[162] This statement awakened Stuart to the fact that others lacked his defiant endurance. The courier was instructed to say that Beale was correct. Men had been seen, said Stuart, who had fallen asleep while their horses were trying to get over a fence. Tomorrow they might renew the battle. For the short summer night, they should have repose and renewal of strength! [163]

---

[157] Beale, 84.   [158] Thomason, 440.
[159] Actually, this was Kilpatrick's 3rd Division of the Cavalry Corps, which was proceeding under orders to the "road from Gettysburg to Abbottstown," i.e., the York Road, to "see that the [Confederates] did not turn our flank" (O. R., 27, pt. 1, p. 992).
[160] O. R., 27, pt. 2, p. 697. Hampton's account is in ibid., 724. Kilpatrick insisted that he was attacked by "Stuart, Hampton and Lee," who were driven "with great loss" (O. R., 27, pt. 1, p. 992). General Pleasanton accepted this as an authentic account of what happened (Ibid., 914).
[161] Beale, 86.
[162] Ibid.   [163] C. W. Beale, 115.

Stuart may have been disappointed that no applause greeted his return from his longest raid, which he was to persuade himself was his greatest; but of his thoughts he said nothing to any of his lieutenants who left memoirs. Much the same silence covers the reflections of the two other men whose state of mind added to the dangers of the invasion. To the limited extent that Ewell's subsequent report [164] may be assumed to reflect his feelings at the time of the battle, he was chagrined that Rodes had not been able to advance because of assumed lack of support on the right. Said Ewell afterward: "The want of co-operation on the right made it more difficult for Rodes's division to attack, though, had it been otherwise, I have every reason to believe, from the eminent success attending the assault of Hays and Avery, that the enemy's lines would have been carried." [165]

Longstreet, the last of the trio, had lost something of his sullenness, though not of his depression. Outwardly he seemed almost philosophical. "We have not been so successful as we wished," he told the Austrian military observer, and attributed this chiefly to the fact that Barksdale had been killed and Hood wounded.[166] Inwardly, Longstreet still was determined to argue that Meade's position could be turned and the tactical defensive recovered. After darkness offered concealment, he sent out his scouts toward the southern end of Round Top, and he did not go to Army Headquarters to report or to ask for orders.

[164] It is undated.
[165] O. R., 27, pt. 2, p. 447. Rodes s comment (*ibid.*, 556) showed him intent on the possibilities of the next day.
[166] Ross, 59.

# CHAPTER VIII

## LONGSTREET'S BITTEREST DAY

AT DAWN, July 3, "Dick" Ewell proceeded to execute his orders for a renewal of his attack against the Federal right.[1] He had directed during the night that Johnson's Division be strengthened by Smith's Brigade of Early's Division and he had instructed Rodes to send Johnson all the troops that could be spared without risking the loss of Rodes's position. Rodes was disheartened by this order because he hoped to storm Cemetery Hill, but he sent "Old Allegheny" the Brigades of Daniel and O'Neal.[2]

Johnson on his own account had recalled the Stonewall Brigade from its flank position and had placed it in support of his other Brigades, which, it will be recalled, were those of John M. Jones, Nicholls and Steuart. With six Brigades at his disposal, Johnson unhesitatingly prepared to assault Culp's Hill, but he knew little of the enemy's dispositions. Steuart's Brigade alone had gained strategic ground in the twilight attack of the previous evening. Even Steuart was not aware of the importance of the position he had taken. His left was within 330 yards of the Baltimore Turnpike. Less than a mile directly West of him was a "little clump of trees" that was destined to be the objective that day of the decisive charge of the battle. "The ground was rough," Gen. O. O. Howard afterward wrote, "and the woods so thick that the Confederate generals did not realize till morning what they had gained."[3]

During the night, Steuart's men had heard the familiar rumble of moving guns, and they had concluded that the Federals were evacuating Culp's Hill. Disillusionment was swift. With the dawn there swept over the hill a furious Federal bombardment. Directed at Steuart's position, it come from the South at close

---

[1] O. R., 27, pt. 1, p. 477.
[2] With the exception of the Fifth Alabama of O'Neal. O. R., 27, pt. 2, pp. 556, 558, 593.
[3] Quoted in McKim, 199.

range and from the ridge to the West at a range still shorter.[4] For fifteen minutes these guns, twenty in number, continued to blast Steuart's trenches from front and from left flank. Then came a brief pause. At 5:30, strengthened by six other fieldpieces, the Federals resumed their fire.[5] To it, the Confederates could not oppose anything heavier than a rifle. The hillside was so steep and the approaches so difficult that it was impossible to drag guns to Steuart's position or to bring them to bear from the east side of Rock Creek.[6] Despite this inequality of fire power, Confederate losses were light. Steuart had his men well in hand and he instructed them to keep under cover. When his ammunition ran low, one of his staff took three men from the ranks, walked more than a mile to the ordnance train and brought back two large boxes of cartridges to the foot of the hill. There they dumped the cartridges into a blanket, slung the blanket on a sapling and mounted the hill with the sapling over their shoulders.[7]

To the right and North of Steuart,[8] Johnson's other troops traded blows with the enemy to no purpose. At length Johnson moved Daniel's Brigade close to that of Steuart and directed the two to deliver another attack with the support of the units on the right.[9] Neither Steuart nor Daniel believed that the attack could succeed,[10] but they made ready to advance. Soon "Maryland" Steuart told his soldiers to leap over their breastworks and to form line of battle at a wide angle to the works, in order to get the correct position for their advance. By the time the men could form this line, the enemy was pouring a brisk fire into their ranks. Steuart drew his sabre, yelled "Charge bayonets!" and started forward with

[4] Joseph M. Knap's Pennsylvania Battery and Charles E. Winegar's New York gunners were South of the Baltimore Turnpike at the eminence known as Slocum's Headquarters. Edward Muhlenberg's Regulars (Battery F., 4th Arty.) and David Kinzie's Regulars (Battery K, 5th Arty.) were West of the turnpike and about 600 yards East of General Meade's Headquarters. *O. R.*, 27, pt. 1, p. 237.

[5] The additional battery was James Rigby's Maryland Battery of six 3-inch rifles. *O. R.*, 27, pt. 1, p. 237.

[6] *McKim*, 200; *O. R.*, 27, pt. 2, p. 544.

[7] Although McKim, *op. cit.*, 201, did not so state, he must have been the staff officer who made the journey.

[8] At one time the Forty-Ninth and Fiftieth Virginia were almost in his rear.

[9] Daniel (*O. R.*, 27, pt. 2, p. 568) stated that the charge was made by him "in conjunction with General Steuart," but if he meant to say that his men and Steuart's men were the sole participants in the charge, there is nothing in superior reports to confirm him. James A. Walker's report (*ibid.*, 519) would indicate, though it does not affirm positively, that the Stonewall Brigade participated in the third assault of the day.

[10] *McKim*, 203; *cf.* Daniel in *O. R.*, 27, pt. 2, p. 846.

his men. Some of them fell away soon. The left was checked; the right became exposed; the centre pressed on until the fire was overwhelming.[11] Said one chivalrous Northern officer who had a gallant hand in the repulse, "[they] left most of their dead in line with our own."[12] Daniel had to halt when Steuart did, but one of the North Carolina regiments found itself where it had a perfect field of fire on Federals moving from one line to another. Before the regiment retired it had created on the Union side another line of dead.[13] With the failure of this attack, the Confederates yielded the initiative [14] to the Federals, who, by 10:30 A.M., had recovered most of the ground occupied by the Confederates on the 2nd.[15] The heavy losses of those wasteful assaults were the more lamentable by reason of the fact that half an hour after Johnson attacked in accordance with orders, a courier brought to Second Corps headquarters a message in which Lee told Ewell that Longstreet would not advance till 10 o'clock. Ewell was directed to delay his forward movement until he could deliver it simultaneously with Longstreet. The message came too late to assure any co-ordination of attack, but the fault was neither Lee's nor Ewell's.

During the night of July 2–3, Longstreet had not reconciled himself to a continuance of the offensive. Although Lee wrote later that he gave Longstreet on the 2nd orders "to attack the next morning," [16] Longstreet either was slow or else he was resolved to oppose to the last a plan he believed dangerous. He said afterward that he never was "so depressed as upon that day," [17] but he found grim encouragement in the report his scouts made on their return from the southern end of Round Top. They had not gone far enough, or else had not stayed sufficiently late, to encounter two Brigades of the VI Corps that had been sent to the

11 McKim, 204; corrected by *O. R.*, 27, pt. 2, p. 511.
12 Brig. Gen. Thomas L. Kane, commanding the 2nd Brigade of Geary's 2nd Division, Slocum's XII Corps. General Kane wrote that the men who fell while at grips with his Pennsylvanians were the First Maryland Battalion. It may be remembered that General Kane had been organizer and first Colonel of the "Pennsylvania Bucktails."
13 *O. R.*, 27, pt. 2, pp. 569, 575.        14 *Ibid.*, 504, 511.
15 *O. R.*, 27, pt. 1, pp. 761, 775. Students of the operation on the Federal right, July 3, may find it worth while to take into account the contradictions between Meade's report and Slocum's set forth in *ibid.*, 763 ff. It might be noted, also, that the report of Brig. Gen. Thomas H. Ruger, commanding the 1st Division of the XII Corps, is the most comprehensive and the clearest of those by Federal officers. Unfortunately, the sketch he gave (*ibid.*, 779) of the Confederate position is deceptively inaccurate.
16 *O. R.*, 27, pt. 2, p. 320.        17 *Annals*, 430.

very ground against which Longstreet wished to operate.[18] When, consequently, the scouts insisted that no enemy was beyond Round Top, Longstreet determined to start his troops immediately in that direction and to take the eminence in reverse.[19] Quickly he began to draft orders[20] and he probably was working on the details when Lee rode up to field headquarters of the First Corps.

Longstreet, it will be remembered, had not seen Lee since the commanding General had turned back after riding with him toward the right the previous afternoon. With scant ceremony, Longstreet began: "General, I have had my scouts out all night, and I find that you still have an excellent opportunity to move around to the right of Meade's army, and maneuver him into attacking us."

He probably elaborated, but he could not shake Lee's conviction that the only practicable course left the Confederates was to break the Union centre. Lee did not feel that his troops had been defeated. He considered that failure on the 2nd had been due to lack of co-ordination, and he still believed that, if the Army could throw its full strength against the enemy from the positions already gained for the artillery, he could win the battle.[21] In this belief, Lee reaffirmed his intention of attacking Cemetery Ridge.[22] The whole of the First Corps, he said, must make the assault.

The forces thus assigned for the attack, about 15,000 men, did not seem adequate to Longstreet. He later quoted himself as replying to Lee: "General, I have been a soldier all my life. I have been with soldiers engaged in fights by couples, by squads, companies, regiments and armies, and should know, as well as any-

---

[18] These were Brig. Gen. David A. Russell's 3rd Brigade of Brig Gen. J. J. Bartlett's 1st Division of Maj. Gen. John Sedgwick's VI Corps and Col. L. A. Grant's 2nd Brigade of Brig. Gen. Albion W. Howe's 2nd Division of the same Corps (*O. R.*, 27, pt. 1, p. 674 ff). From Sedgwick's report (*ibid.*, 663), it is difficult to ascertain whether the disposition of these Brigades was made by Sedgwick or, more probably, by Meade.

[19] *O. R.*, 27, pt. 2, p. 359.

[20] In the absence of reports by any of his division commanders, the details of these orders, if issued, cannot be determined.

[21] *O. R.*, 27, pt. 2, p. 320.

[22] In *Annals*, 429, Longstreet said that Lee raised a fist toward the opposite ridge and answered: "The enemy is there and I am going to strike him." Longstreet's next narrative (3 *B. & L.*, 342) quoted Lee as saying: "No, I am going to take them where they are on Cemetery Hill. I want you to take Pickett's Division and make the attack. I will reinforce you by two Divisions of the Third Corps." Finally, in *Longstreet*, 386–87, there is no direct quoted conversation but a long argumentative statement of reasons for not attacking with the whole of the First Corps. The reader must judge for himself whether those arguments are based on information Longstreet could have possessed in its entirety at that time.

one, what soldiers can do. It is my opinion that no 15,000 men ever arrayed for battle can take that position."[23]

Lee reiterated his purpose to attack. Longstreet turned away to give the requisite orders.[24] Soon he was back with a new objection. The whole First Corps, said he, could not be employed in the attack. Hood's Division and McLaws's were exposed to attack from the Round Tops and were weakened by the battle of July 2. If they were withdrawn, the enemy would turn the Confederate right.[25] On this point, Longstreet prevailed. Probably in the hope of placating Longstreet and of giving him faith in the movement, Lee agreed to leave McLaws and Hood where they were. Their place would be taken by Heth's Division and by half of Pender's.[26] This decision to use Heth appears to have been made quickly and without ascertaining the condition of the troops. The omission was to prove itself one of the worst of the many mistakes of Gettysburg.

Longstreet next argued that the distance was too great for a successful assault. When told that it was about 1400 yards, covered in large part by the Confederate artillery, he insisted that the column of attack would be enfiladed from Round Top. To this Col. Armistead Long of Lee's staff, an artillerist of high reputation, answered that the guns on the eminence could be silenced.[27] Tactically this assurance almost certainly was unjustified,[28] but the state of mind of the two Generals was such that neither of them disputed Long's assertion.

Longstreet now had exhausted his arguments. Bitterly he wrote afterward of Lee: "He knew that I did not believe that success was possible; that care and time should be taken to give the troops the benefit of positions and the grounds; and he should have put an officer in charge who had more confidence in his plan. Two thirds of the troops were of other commands, and there was no

---

23 *Annals*, 429. The language in 3 *B. & L.*, 343, is altogether different but the argument is the same.

24 This seems the order of events, but the records are vague. Lee noted (*O. R.*, 27, pt. 2, p. 320) that Longstreet was "delayed" by the force occupying Round Top. That would indicate an interval between Longstreet's first protest and his insistence that McLaws and Hood be not employed.

25 Longstreet denied in *Annals*, 431–32 n, that Lee ordered him, as Col. Walter Taylor affirmed, to attack with the entire Corps; but in *Longstreet*, 386, he stated that this was Lee's intention and he cited Taylor as authority. The argument against using Hood and McLaws in the assault is given in *Annals* and in *Longstreet*, loc. cit.

26 *Longstreet*, 386.

27 *O. R.*, 27, pt. 2, p. 359; *Longstreet*, 386; *Long*, 288.            28 *Alexander*, 416.

reason for putting the assaulting forces under my charge." [29]  To this, of course, the answer was that Lee, with Jackson dead, had no other subordinate of the same experience or military grasp as Longstreet.

The troops designated for the assault were at hand. Pickett's Division had arrived from the Cashtown Road between 7 and 9 A.M. and had moved southward on the western side of Seminary Ridge.[30] When Pickett rode up to report, Longstreet explained the plan of operation and entrusted to him the posting of the various Brigades. The plan was of the simplest: When all preparations had been made, the artillery was to bombard the Federal front and weaken or silence the Federal batteries. This fire was to centre on a "little clump of trees" opposite Pender's position.[31] To that grove, after the bombardment, the infantry were to advance. The design was that none of the troops should be brought to the crest of Seminary Ridge and exposed to the enemy's artillery fire until the time for the charge arrived. Then the line of battle, previously established by Pickett, was to come over the ridge, go forward and converge on the objective. Pickett, who had three Brigades only, decided to put Garnett and Kemper in the first line and Armistead in the second. In rear and to the right of Pickett's line, Longstreet determined to employ Wilcox as a flank guard. On Pickett's left, Johnston Pettigrew was to advance the Division of the wounded Harry Heth. In support of Pettigrew were to be Scales's and Lane's Brigades of Dorsey Pender's Division. To the command of this Division, Trimble belatedly was appointed. Over Trimble and Pettigrew, Longstreet was to have control for the day,[32] and if he needed additional troops, he was to be free to call on A. P. Hill for them.[33]

As Longstreet explained these dispositions to Pickett, he observed that his junior was hopeful of success though conscious that the contest would be severe.[34] A little later, Colonel Alexander talked with the division commander and found that Pickett was

[29] Longstreet, 388.
[30] Walter Harrison, op. cit., 91, gave the hour of arrival as 7. Maj. Charles S. Peyton in his report (O. R., 27, pt. 2, p. 385) stated that Garnett's Brigade arrived "about 9 A.M."
[31] In early printings of 3 R. E. Lee, 111 ff, this "clump of trees" erroneously was styled Ziegler's Grove. The correct location of Ziegler's Grove is 400 yards farther North on Cemetery Ridge.
[32] O. R., 27, pt. 2, pp. 320, 359.
[33] Ibid., 320.                    [34] 3 B. & L. 343.

"entirely sanguine of success in the charge, and was only congratulating himself on the opportunity."[35] Alexander had the responsible duty of posting the batteries to deliver the preparatory bombardment. He was instructed, also, to station himself where he best could observe the fire and could determine when Pickett should charge.[36]

Besides directing these arrangements with manifest depression of spirits, Longstreet had twice to ride the length of the corps front with Lee, who was resolved that for the success of the decisive attack on the Federal centre, no preparation should be neglected. Longstreet was not pleased with this supervision. He told Lee, to quote his later words, "that we had been more particular in giving the orders than ever before; that the commanders had been sent for, and the point of attack had been carefully designated, and that the commanders had been directed to communicate to their subordinates, and through them to every soldier in the command, the work that was before them, so that they should nerve themselves for the attack, and fully understand it."[37]

Powell Hill was assumed to understand equally well the part his Corps was to have in the unfolding drama. The two Lieutenant Generals were on speaking terms and had in some measure abandoned the antagonism that led to the transfer of Hill from Longstreet after the Seven Days[38] but they were not cordial and may not even have been genuinely co-operative in spirit. Their commander must have taken for granted that they would arrange between themselves the preparation of the troops of the Third Corps for the assault. Actually, each of the lieutenants seems to have left this to the other. The sensitive Hill, always mindful of military etiquette, may have concluded that he must not interfere in the least after his troops temporarily had been transferred. Longstreet may have considered that the troops were under Hill, and were supervised by that officer, until they were ordered to advance. No inquiry appears to have been made to ascertain whether the regimental command of Pettigrew's Division was adequate after the losses of July 1. As the Division then was extended along Seminary Ridge, Brockenbrough's weak Brigade

[35] Alexander in 4 S.H.S.P., 105.     [36] Alexander, 418.
[37] Annals, 432.
[38] See Vol. I, p. 664 ff. Cf. Sorrel, 89: "Later on"—he attempted to give no date after the quarrel—"Longstreet and Hill became fairly good friends."

under Col. Robert M. Mayo [39] and "Joe" Davis's shattered, inex, perienced troops, almost without field officers,[40] were to be on the extreme left. If anyone questioned the prudence of this arrangement, no hint of it has survived.

This was not the full measure of unrealized absence of effective liaison between the two Corps. Lee intended that Pender's two Brigades should be *en échelon* on the left of Pettigrew,[41] as a second line; but, here again, the records do not show that either of the two corps commanders gave instruction to effect this. When Lane came to Longstreet to report for orders, Longstreet told him to form in rear of Pettigrew. Nowhere did Lane indicate in his report that he was told of any plan for *échelon*.[42]

Military remissness always is clearer in retrospect than in prospect. The man who now became the central figure for two bloody hours at Gettysburg was so depressed by his conviction of the unwisdom of an attack that he was not conscious of any failure in preparation. Longstreet was not and could not be reconciled to delivering the assault, but he and the cause he represented now were being dragged by the very ticking of his watch to the inevitable hour. During the early morning, there scarcely had been a cannon shot on the Confederate right. As the warming sun rose higher, the skirmishers quieted. Over the Confederate centre and right, there hung a sinister silence not unlike that which had prevailed that 30th day of August, 1862, near Groveton, when Longstreet had awaited the Federal attack in full confidence that he could repel it.

Now, an hour before noon, blue skirmishers undertook to wrest from Hill's men a barn and a dwelling in front of Pettigrew's right.[43] Part of a supporting Union regiment came out of the works to seize this nest of sharpshooters.[44] Third Corps batteries opened to defend the marksmen's shelter; the Unionists returned the challenge in kind. Soon, Porter Alexander remarked, "the whole of Hill's artillery in position, which I think was 63 guns,

---

[39] For the unexplained transfer of command, see *infra*, p. 185.
[40] For the condition of this command see *infra*, Chap. IX, p. 186, and Chap. X, p. 195.
[41] See *infra*, p. 182 ff.          [42] Cf. *O. R.*, 27, pt. 2, p. 666.
[43] This property, which bears no name on Bachelder's map, was about 530 yards West and slightly South of Emanuel Trostle's.
[44] It was the 14th Connecticut, Maj. Theodore G. Ellis, of Col. Thomas A. Smyth's 2nd Brigade, 3rd Division, II Corps. See *O. R.*, 27, pt. 1, pp. 465, 467.

were heavily engaged with about an equal number of the enemy's guns for over a half hour . . ." [45] At the time, neither Hill nor his chief of artillery seems to have asked whether so much of the artillery ammunition of the Corps should have been wasted in any unnecessary cannonade. To the right, Porter Alexander forbade his seventy-five guns to have any part in this exchange, because he knew he would need every round of his short supply of ammunition if he was to clear the way for Pickett and for Pettigrew.[46] Nobody else concerned himself in any special degree to ascertain what ammunition was available, or where it was. Guns, like ammunition, were assumed to be ample, though Alexander gratefully accepted the offer by General Pendleton of seven 12-pounder howitzers which belonged to the Third Corps. They were useless on the front of that Corps, General Pendleton explained, because of their short range.[47] These guns were placed in rear of the First Corps, whence they could be summoned to follow the charging infantry.

While Longstreet was not acquainted with this, he was attentive to Alexander's preparations. About noon he sent word to the artillerist that he would himself give the signal for the opening of the bombardment.[48] All the batteries were to be notified that the signal was to be two guns fired in succession by Miller's Third company of the Washington Artillery. With Pickett, on Seminary Ridge, Longstreet waited. When Adjutant W. M. Owen of the Washington Artillery came to report that the batteries had been informed of the signal, Longstreet answered quietly, "All right, tell Colonel Walton I will send him word when to begin." [49] If, in this remark, "Old Pete" seemed altogether himself, his grip on his temper was as uncertain as his depression was deep. During the morning, when the Adjutant of Pickett's Division was asking instructions, Longstreet "seemed to be in anything but a pleasant humor at the prospect 'over the hill,' for he snorted out" an implied rebuke of the young officer. Then, conscious that he "had unnecessarily snubbed a poor sub," he spoke more kindly.[50]

[45] 4 *S.H.S.P.*, 103.                          [46] *Ibid.*
[47] Alexander in 4 *S.H.S.P.*, 103. In *Alexander*, 418, the number is given as nine. It is impossible to say which figure is correct, though naturally Alexander's earlier statement is followed. The Third Corps had fifteen guns of this type. See *O. R.*, 27, pt. 2, p. 356.
[48] 4 *S.H.S.P.*, 104.
[49] *Owen*, 248.                          [50] *Walter Harrison*, 92.

The last of Pickett's infantry had been put in position about the time [51] Longstreet notified Alexander that he personally would give the order to fire the signal guns. "Dick" Garnett was there with officers who had won their stars and wreath while he vainly had been seeking to correct the injustice he felt Jackson had done him after Kernstown. Lewis Armistead was in place, Armistead of Malvern Hill. James L. Kemper had his Brigade on the ridge. Wilcox was close by. To the left, one only of Heth's Brigades was going into the charge under its regular commander. That one was the newest and least experienced of them all, Joseph R. Davis's. The Brigade of Pettigrew would be under Col. J. K. Marshall; Archer's would be led by Col. B. D. Fry. Both Archer's and Davis's Brigades, to repeat, were almost without field officers because of the tragic losses of July 1. In the most difficult charge the Army of Northern Virginia ever had made, many of these regiments would be directed by company officers.

One of the supporting Brigades of Pender's Division, James H. Lane's, the old command of L. O'B. Branch, was headed by its regular commander. The other Brigade was Alfred Scales's, formerly Pender's, which had lost fifty-five of its officers on the 1st of July.[52] This command now was to be taken into action by Col. William Lowrance of the Thirty-fourth North Carolina, an officer who never previously had exercised brigade command in the field. In a word, of six Brigades to the left of Pickett, that of Lane alone was in the keeping of a Brigadier of tested combat experience.

The dangerous deployment of the second line was not relieved as the hour for the attack approached. Scales and Lane were in rear of Heth's Division, where Longstreet had told them to take station, but their front was by no means as long as that of Heth. The two Brigades were centered, moreover, on Pettigrew's line. The result would be that the left of the broad column of attack would consist of one line only.[53] None of the officers on that part of the front inquired whether this was as Longstreet desired. If Lane felt any responsibility for the exposure of the left by centering the

[51] That is to say, about noon. *Cf.* Alexander in 4 *S.H.S.P.*, 104, and Peyton in *O. R.*, 27, pt. 2, p. 385.
[52] *O. R.*, 27, pt. 2, p. 670. Cf. *infra*, Chap. XII, p. 196.
[53] Lane in *O. R.*, 27, pt. 2, p. 666.

Brigades in support, he had been relieved of that responsibility. Isaac Trimble had arrived to take command of Pender's men aftei Jim Lane had put them in position. Of the disposition of the troops, Trimble knew scarcely anything. A part of the little time he might have given to an examination of the front, he devoted to making a speech to his men. No question was raised, apparently, concerning any shift of the second line to the extreme left. Trimble was not told, if in fact Lane knew, that two Brigades in support of Pettigrew were expected to advance *en échelon* to cover the left of Pettigrew.[54] The overconfidence of Lee, the depression of Longstreet and the probable misapprehension of A. P. Hill caused many things to be overlooked that July day.

Afternoon it now was. The bombardment must begin. Longstreet realized this but he said later he was unwilling at the moment to entrust himself with the entire responsibility of ordering the guns to open.[55] With dragging hand, he wrote Alexander this note:

Colonel: If the artillery fire does not have the effect to drive off the enemy or greatly demoralize him so as to make our efforts pretty certain, I would prefer that you should not advise General Pickett to make the charge. I shall rely a great deal on your good judgment to determine the matter, and shall expect you to let General Pickett know when the moment offers.

Respectfully,
J. Longstreet,
Lieut.-General

To Colonel E. P. Alexander, Artillery.[56]

After this, came one of the strangest incidents of a bewildering day: Longstreet went off into the woods and lay down. This was done, he explained in his old age, "to study for some new thought that might aid the assaulting column." [57] If study did not lapse into unconsciousness, at least one witness was mistaken. Colonel Fremantle, the British observer who was with Longstreet at the

[54] See *infra*, p. 182.
[55] This wording is substantially Longstreet's own. *Annals*, 430.
[56] 4 *S.H.S.P.*, 104. This and succeeding messages are reprinted in *Alexander*, 421 ff.
[57] *Longstreet*, 391.

time, recorded that "The General then dismounted and went to sleep for a short time." [58]

Sleeping or reflecting, the General was aroused when a courier brought back from Alexander a note which showed that the young artillerist thought Longstreet had in mind some alternative to an assault. The note made it clear, also, in a manner entirely disciplined, that the Colonel did not think he should be asked to assume the responsibility of the corps commander. Alexander wrote substantially as follows:

General: I will only be able to judge of the effect of our fire on the enemy by his return fire, for his infantry is but little exposed to view and the smoke will obscure the whole field. If, as I infer from your note, there is any alternative to this attack, it should be carefully considered before opening our fire, for it will take all the artillery ammunition we have left to test this one thoroughly, and if the result is unfavorable, we will have none left for another effort. And even if this is entirely successful it can only be so at a very bloody cost.

Very respectfully, &c.,
E. P. Alexander, Colonel Artillery [59]

That was honest warning but confused writing. Longstreet might have read it over twice and not have been quite sure of the meaning of any part of it except the first sentence. The depressed General evidently did not grasp the full meaning of what Alexander said about the supply of ammunition. Nor did Longstreet reflect that Alexander, like himself, was doubtful of the success of the charge now that responsibility for it was being placed on him. [60] The point that stuck in Longstreet's mind was that Alexander apparently wanted to know how to determine when the charge should be made. Accordingly Longstreet wrote:

Hd. Qrs., July 3rd, 1863.
Colonel: The intention is to advance the infantry if the artillery has the desired effect of driving the enemy's off, or having other effect such as to

[58] *Fremantle*, 263.
[59] 4 *S.H.S.P.*, 104. Alexander explained that he kept no copy of this communication but that he "retained a vivid recollection" of the contents. "It was expressed very nearly" as here quoted
[60] Cf. *Alexander*, 421: "Until that moment, though I fully recognized the strength of the enemy's position, I had not doubted that we would carry it, in my confidence that Lee was ordering it. But here was a proposition that *I* should decide the question. Overwhelming reasons against the assault at once seemed to stare me in the face."

warrant us in making the attack. When that moment arrives advise General P., and of course advance such artillery as you use in aiding the attack.

Respectfully,

J. Longstreet, Lieut.-General, Commanding.

To Colonel Alexander.[61]

Subsequently Longstreet explained: "I still desired to save my men, and felt that if the artillery did not produce the desired effect, I would be justified in holding Pickett off." [62] The young Colonel's acknowledgment read simply:

General: When our artillery fire is doing its best I shall advise General Pickett to advance.[63]

It was now 1 P.M. From the fields the heat was rising, but a west wind was blowing.[64] The cannonade on Hill's front had died away. Federal pickets had captured the house and barn between the lines and had set them afire.[65] The artillery along the entire line was silent. Skirmishing was light.[66] Longstreet knew that all the orders had been issued and that all the troops were in position. He swept the field with his glasses to see if the guns were well placed and, at last, he wrote this note to his corps chief of artillery:

Hdqrs., July 3rd, 1863.

Colonel: Let the batteries open; order great care and precision in firing. If the batteries in the peach-orchard cannot be used against the point we intend attacking, let them open on the rocky hill.

Most respectfully,

J. Longstreet, Lieut.-General Commanding

To Col. Walton, Chief of Artillery.[67]

---

[61] 4 *S.H.S.P.*, 105. Pathetically, after many years, though he must have known that Alexander had printed the original of this message, Longstreet summarized it thus: "[Alexander] was informed that there was no alternative; that I had found no way out of it; that General Lee had considered and would listen to nothing else; that orders had gone for the guns to give signal for the batteries; that he should call the troops at the first opportunity or lull in the enemy's fire." (*Longstreet*, 391.) It scarcely need be added that in Longstreet's final narrative of Gettysburg it is futile to look for correct chronology. The General's memory was tragically confused.

[62] *Annals*, 430.

[63] 4 *S.H.S.P.*, 106. In *Alexander*, 422, appeared a later and slightly different text. General Alexander explained that the original had not been preserved.

[64] *Gordon*, 165.          [65] *O. R.*, 27, pt. 1, p. 465.

[66] 4 *S.H.S.P.*, 106.

[67] *Owen*, 248. Slight variations in heading and signature have been conformed to the style of the existing notes addressed to Alexander.

In no more time than was required for a messenger to reach Walton and for another to run from the Colonel to the nearest guns, Longstreet heard one cannon shot in the vicinity of the Apple Orchard,[68] and then another. It was 1:07 P.M.[69] In a few seconds, battery after battery, firing salvoes, acknowledged the signal. At first the answer of the Federals was slow,[70] as if they doubted whether the Confederates were in earnest. Then from Cemetery Ridge came the swelling bass of guns in chorus. Smoke clouds rose opposite the Peach Orchard, to the right and to the left till the whole ridge was screened.

It was on! For success or failure, for the refutation of Longstreet's fears or for the vindication of his belief that the enemy's position was impregnable, the testing bombardment had begun. Longstreet looked, listened, and after a time rode toward the Emmitsburg Road, near the Apple Orchard, where Maj. James Dearing's guns were flaming.[71] Although the smoke concealed the explosion of the shells, it was manifest that the Confederate fire was shaking the enemy. For once, the Southerners appeared to have more guns in action than the enemy was employing on the front of attack,[72] though the deliberate Union fire was effective. Far off to the left the guns of the Second Corps opened; nearer, the batteries of the Third Corps went into action; between Ewell's and Hill's artillerists, there was no co-ordination of attack.[73] After Longstreet had watched the exchange for some minutes, he concluded that Union batteries were being withdrawn and were being replaced.[74] From this he reasoned that the attack must be

[68] The Apple Orchard, opposite the house of H. Spangler, was immediately East of the Emmitsburg Road, about 650 yards North of the Peach Orchard. The two orchards frequently were confused in reports.

[69] *Jacobs,* 44. The time of this intelligent Gettysburg observer has been accepted as probably correct.

[70] *Alexander,* 422.

[71] Dearing's Battalion was posted between the Codori and the Rogers houses, with the centre of the battalion about 530 yards North of the Apple Orchard.

[72] Cf. *O. R.,* 27, pt. 1, p. 239. Gen. Henry J. Hunt there estimated that he brought eighty guns to bear. Alexander had seventy-five in action. Third Corps artillery, on the left of the First, included eighty guns, but probably not more than forty of these were in position to deliver direct fire of the sort Hunt had in mind when he spoke of his eighty guns. In the entire action of July 3, Alexander computed that the Federals used 220 guns and the Confederates 172. (*Alexander,* 419).

[73] *O. R.,* 27, pt. 2, pp. 456, 610. For a critique of the Confederate artillery tactics at Gettysburg, see *infra,* p. 178 ff.

[74] *O. R.,* 27, pt. 2, p. 360. He must have seen arriving and departing caissons, because Hunt's report (*loc. cit.*) and that of Capt. John G. Hazzard, commanding the artillery of the II Corps (*ibid.,* 480), indicated that no Federal batteries were withdrawn until the Confederate infantry were close to Cemetery Ridge.

delivered soon. Otherwise there would not be time for a successful infantry action before nightfall.[75] He accordingly told Dearing
to refill the ammunition chests and to prepare to follow the
advance.[76]

Then Longstreet spurred his horse back through the roar of
the artillery duel and entered the edge of the woods in front of
Pickett's anxious men. Pickett himself was nearby. Slowly dismounting, Longstreet waited. The ridges were shaking with the
violence of the cannonade. Every battery was surrounded by
smoke. The stench of battle was in the air. Shells struck and
shattered limbs of trees, or ploughed up the stony earth of
Seminary Ridge or shrieked in disappointed wrath overhead.
Westward, still high in heaven, the sun was half veiled as if
unwilling to witness the murder of the sons of light. Fury ruled
the field. The loudest shout of men was drowned by the ceaseless, pulsing roar of the guns.

A courier rode up to General Pickett, dismounted, saluted and
handed him a folded paper. Pickett read it and strode toward
Longstreet. The moment had come. That note must be from
Alexander. Now it was in Longstreet's hands, open:

General: If you are coming at all you must come immediately or I cannot give you proper support; but the enemy's fire has not slackened
materially, and at least 18 guns are still firing from the cemetery itself.[77]

As Longstreet read, Pickett waited. Longstreet said nothing.
"General," asked Pickett, "shall I advance?"

There was no reply.[78] Pickett did not move. His eyes were on
his chief. Slowly Longstreet dropped his chin on his uniform
collar. That was his answer. Pickett wished only to be sure: "I
shall lead my Division forward, sir." Not a word was there from
Longstreet. He turned from Pickett and prepared to mount. By
the time he was on his horse, Pickett had walked away.

In the saddle of command again, the stir of action possessed

[75] O. R., 27, pt. 2, p. 360.                    [76] O. R., 27, pt. 2, p. 360.
[77] 4 S.H.S.P., 107. The artillerist thought the "little clump of trees" marked a cemetery. A later version of this lost dispatch is in Alexander, 423. The time of dispatch,
said the author, was 1:25. Details of Pickett's brief exchange with Longstreet are
variously given. Longstreet's first account in Annals, 430, seems to be entitled to priority.
[78] "My feelings had so overcome me," Longstreet wrote, "that I would not speak,
for fear of betraying my want of confidence to him" (Annals, 430-31). A few minutes
later Longstreet did not hesitate to express to Porter Alexander his "want of confidence"
in the success of the charge.

Longstreet. He quickly guided his mount to Alexander's post near the flaming Peach Orchard. There the General found the young artillerist blazing away with his guns and watching excitedly the little clump of trees. Alexander, like Longstreet, had thought he had seen fieldpieces hauled away from the ground the Confederates were to storm, but he had not been sure what this meant. Union fire had slackened. No fresh guns had appeared; if any batteries had moved, they had not opened from new positions. It was now or never for the infantry! If Pickett did not start at once, Alexander repeated, the artillery could not give adequate support.[79] Ammunition was very low. The seven howitzers loaned by Pendleton to follow the charge had disappeared.[80]

Longstreet had been told in Alexander's first, confused note that ammunition would not suffice for more than one heavy bombardment, but the fact had not impressed itself on the General's mind. Now he was startled: "Go and stop Pickett right where he is," Longstreet cried, "and replenish your ammunition."

"We can't do that, sir! The train has but little. It would take an hour to distribute it, and meanwhile the enemy would improve the time." [81]

Longstreet stood irresolute for a moment. Then, in unwonted emotion, he said: "I don't want to make this charge; I don't believe it can succeed. I would stop Pickett now, but that General Lee has ordered it and expects it." He paused as if inviting Alexander to say again that the ammunition chests were almost empty and that the howitzers could not be brought into play.

The pause was prolonged. Longstreet would not ask explicitly whether the artillerist agreed with him; Alexander did not think he should express an opinion on so large a subject unless directed to do so.[82] At length, as if the fates themselves gave the answer,

[79] After Alexander had written Pickett the message that had been shown to Longstreet on the ridge, Alexander had dispatched Pickett separately two copies of a note that read: "For God's sake, come quickly; the 18 guns are gone." An expanded, later version of this paper is given in *Alexander*, 423.

[80] 4 *S.H.S.P.*, 108. For the circumstances of the withdrawal of these guns, some of which were in the line of Federal fire, see *Alexander*, 420.

[81] So *Alexander*, 424. In his earlier account (4 *S.H.S.P.*, 108) Alexander did not quote himself directly. He said: "I answered that the ammunition wagons had been nearly emptied, replacing expenditures of the day before, that not over 20 rounds to the gun were left—too little to accomplish much—and that while this was being done the enemy would recover from the effect of the fire we were now giving him."

[82] Alexander explained, in his memoirs, 424: "I felt that he was inviting a word of acquiescence on my part and that if given he would again order, 'Stop Pickett where he is.' But I was too conscious of my own youth and inexperience to express an opinion not

down Seminary Ridge came Garnett's Brigade. On his right, Kemper was emerging. Heth's men had much farther to go because of the wider angle between Seminary Ridge and the Emmitsburg Road,[83] but at length they advanced into the open. Soon there was a halt. Lagging units caught up. At a shouted word of command, the long line was dressed.[84] The west wind lifted the smoke. Nineteen battle flags began to flap.

When every regiment had taken its place, the advance was resumed. "Sergeant," cried Armistead to a man of the Fifty-third Virginia, "are you going to put those colors on the enemy's works today?"

"I will try, sir, and if mortal man can do it, it shall be done!" [85]

As Kemper had started, he had cried: "Armistead, hurry up; I am going to charge those heights and carry them, and I wanted you to support me."

Armistead's answer was: "I'll do it! Look at my line; it never looked better on dress parade." [86]

Every soldier within hearing had been stirred by Pickett's appeal, "Up, men, and to your posts! Don't forget today that you are from Old Virginia." [87]

Farther up the line, Pettigrew was calling to one of his officers, "Now, Colonel, for the honor of the good Old North State, forward!" [88]

Soon the line was passing Longstreet, whose pride rose with his concern. Salutes were exchanged. In old affection for the chief of the Division, Longstreet observed how jauntily Pickett went on.[89] Garnett, too sick to walk, was wrapped in a blue overcoat, but he sat his great black horse in soldierly composure.[90] Longstreet looked and admired as men of his old Brigade stepped

directly asked. So I remained silent while Longstreet fought his battle out alone and obeyed his orders."
[83] *Cf.* Lane in 5 *S.H.S.P.,* 39, and Trimble in 9 *ibid.,* 30–31.
[84] 32 *S.H.S.P.,* 34.
[85] 32 *S.H.S.P.,* 186.
[86] 37 *S.H.S.P.,* 148.
[87] D. E. Johnston, *The Story of a Confederate Boy,* 205–06.
[88] 2 *N. C. Regts.,* 365.
[89] *O. R.,* 27, pt. 2, p. 360; 3 *B. & L.,* 345. The advance of Pickett past Longstreet and his subsequent report to Longstreet from a point still nearer the front are a sufficient answer to the old slander that Pickett and his staff remained at or near the Spangler barn which, in reality, was burned on the 2nd of July.
[90] Alexander in 4 *S.H.S.P.,* 108.

forward,[91] but he saw already that the right of his onmarching troops would be exposed to artillery fire from the vicinity of Round Top. Batteries were ordered to engage the Federals in that quarter.

By the time the troops came within range of the Federal artillery, Longstreet had conquered the emotion he had displayed in talking with Alexander. Quietly, Longstreet got down from his horse, perched his bulky form on a rail fence,[92] and watched with sharp, professional eye as much as he could see of the attack. "The advance was made in very handsome style," he said afterward, "all the troops keeping their lines accurately, and taking the fire of the batteries with great coolness and deliberation."[93] Below him, at increasing distance, he probably identified Armistead with hat on the point of an uplifted sabre as a guide to the men. Garnett was visible, too, on horseback, and Kemper and Colonel Hunton and Col. Lewis Williams. All of them, like Garnett, were too sick to go on foot.[94] Soon their flawless line halted briefly in a little depression[95] and then it went steadfastly into the full fury of the enemy's fire. Most of the Confederate guns were silent by this time. If they were served any longer, no ammunition would be left for them when they followed the infantry.

As Longstreet gazed in all his stubbornness of battle, a panting messenger spoke: General Pickett sent word that the enemy's lines would be taken; reinforcements would be needed. Immediately Longstreet directed a member of his staff to tell Wilcox to go forward at once; let him support the assault.[96] Dispatch a second officer with the same order in event the first were killed.[97]

Again, now—eyes on the attack. Pickett's troops were charging gloriously. They even might reach the blue line without losing their formation. They were within canister range; they defied it; they kept straight on. So did the right Brigades of Heth's Division. On the left of Pettigrew's Division, Mayo's men and Davis's Brigade began to hesitate. At the first report of this, Longstreet notified Pettigrew.[98] Another officer went to "Dick" Anderson

[91] The First and Eleventh Virginia of Kemper's Brigade.
[92] 3 B. & L., 346.                    [93] O. R., 27, pt. 2, p. 360.
[94] Cf. R. E. Lee, 122.                [95] O. R., 27, pt. 2, p. 360.
[96] The position of Wilcox's Brigade then was about 200 yards West of the Emmitsburg Road.
[97] Anderson also sent orders for Wilcox to advance (O. R., 27, pt. 2, p. 620).
[98] Ross, 63.

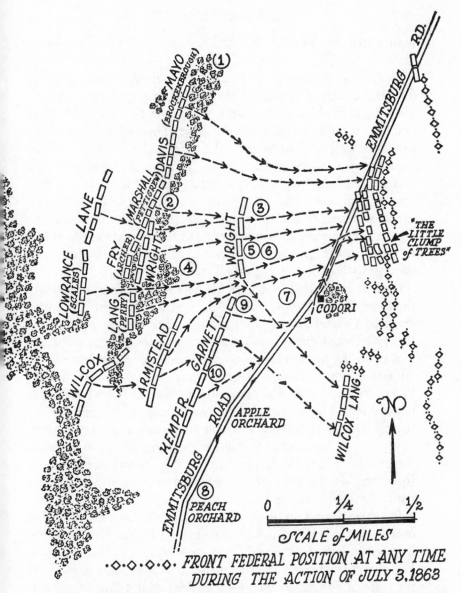

MAYO

(BROCKENBROUGH)

(1)

DAVIS
(PETTIGREW)

MARSHALL

FRY
(ARCHER)

WRIGHT

LANE

LOWRANCE
(SCALES)

LANG
(PERRY)

WILCOX

ARMISTEAD

GARNETT

KEMPER

EMMITSBURG ROAD

(8)
PEACH
ORCHARD

(2)

(4)

(10)

(9)

WRIGHT

(3)

(5) (6)

(7)

CODORI

EMMITSBURG RD.

"THE
LITTLE
CLUMP
of TREES"

WILCOX LANG

APPLE
ORCHARD

N

0          ¼          ½

*SCALE of MILES*

**·◇·◇·◇·◇·  FRONT FEDERAL POSITION AT ANY TIME
DURING THE ACTION OF JULY 3,1863**

etch of the lines of advance of Pickett, Pettigrew and Trimble, at Gettysburg, afternoon of July 3, 1863.
e encircled numerals indicate: 1–2, position of the massed artillery of the Third Corps; 3, the advance
sition of Poague's Artillery Battalion, Third Corps; 4, position of Woolfolk's Battery, First Corps; 5, posi-
n of Wright's Brigade which did not participate in the charge but went out to rally the broken assault-
ops; 6, position of Cabell's Artillery Battalion, First Corps; 7–8, position of the massed artillery of the
rst Corps from the vicinity of the Codori House to the Peach Orchard; 9–10, intermediate position of
lcox, directly in front of the position occupied by Garnett before the final stage of the assault—
after John B. Bachelder

with instruction to move forward in support of Heth and Petti-grew.[99]

Pickett and Pettigrew's right Brigades soon were converging on the little clump of trees. All the battleflags appeared to be running together. Under that band of red, the line was moving at double time and was climbing the ridge. Smoke lifted or shifted; sunlit Federal standards could be glimpsed. A Southern flag would cease to wave, would fall, would rise, would drop again. It disappeared from sight till brave hands lifted it and carried it forward. Shells cut gaps. Men spread the ranks to fill them. The flanks withered under the flame. Amazingly on the right and centre, the formation was retained. On the left, where Mayo had no support, the ground was littered. Discouraged soldiers were turning back or were lying down among the dead.

Garnett has halted to deliver his first volley. Kemper is doing the same thing. Faintly audible through the wrathful roar of a hundred Federal guns is the high quaver of the rebel yell. This time, where the smoke is swept away for a moment, the colors are higher on the hill but they are less numerous. A few batteries of Alexander's have limbered up and are following the infantry. Pickett keeps on. Fry and Marshall do. More of Mayo's men have halted; scores have started to retreat; some are running to the rear.[100] Davis's regiments, with untested leaders, are wavering on their left. A few officers are attempting to rally them. Beyond the extreme left of the front of attack, the Federals are emerging from their works as if they intend to sweep down and destroy the entire flank of Pettigrew.

In support—and not in échelon—Scales and Lane are marching over Pettigrew's fallen and are close behind his survivors, but they have kept their line separate.[101] In the few minutes that they hold Longstreet's gaze, the left has melted away or has merged with the right of Pettigrew. Now—the entire line has disappeared into the dust and smoke that overhang the ridge. The gaunt, desperate men in the thin Southern ranks are grappling unseen with the Federals beyond the stone wall. All the might of the enemy is

[99] *O. R.*, 27, pt. 2, p. 360.
[100] *Cf.* A. R. Wright to Mrs. Wright, MS, July 7, 1863. "On the left, Pettigrew's line wavers—it pauses—all is lost—it falls back—it runs. Some of the officers attempt to rally their men . . . But one thought seems to actuate them all, and that is to gain a safe place far in the rear."—*Wright MSS.*
[101] See Trimble in 9 *S.H.S.P.*, 33.

now thrown against them. They struggle, they stab, they use the butt end of muskets they cannot load. It is hell, it is death for the bravest of them. A mat of fallen red flags lies under the trees. Longstreet strains eyes and ears and knows who the victor in that unequal struggle will be. Sternly he orders an officer to halt the advance of Anderson [102] and then, half hypnotized, he turns again to watch the ridge. For a few moments there is the blank of utter suspense, then a perceptible decline in the infantry fire and then a slow trickle backward of men who do not appear to be wounded.[103]

"I wouldn't have missed this for anything," cried Colonel Fremantle who had that moment joined Longstreet and mistook the advance of a support column on the right for the beginning of a charge.

Longstreet on the top of the worm fence laughed grimly as he replied: "The devil you wouldn't! I would like to have missed it very much; we've attacked and been repulsed: look there!"

Fremantle turned and saw the field between the two ridges "covered," as he said, "with Confederates slowly and sulkily returning toward us in small broken parties, under a heavy fire of artillery." [104] In words that must have burned his lips, the General told the Britisher what had happened. "No person," Fremantle attested, "could have been more calm or self-possessed than General Longstreet under these trying circumstances, aggravated as they now were by the movements of the enemy, who began to show a strong disposition to advance. . . . Difficulties seem to make no other impression on him than to make him a little more savage." [105]

Longstreet ordered General Wright to move out and to collect and rally the fugitives; nearly all the staff of First Corps Headquarters were dispatched for the same purpose;[106] but, strangely, Longstreet did nothing to halt the advance of Wilcox or of the little Florida Brigade that was to follow Wilcox.[107] The Alabama Brigade rushed forward to no purpose whatsoever. "Not a man of the Division that I was ordered to support could I see," Wilcox later wrote in unconcealed disgust.[108]

102 O. R., 27, pt. 2, p. 360.    103 Alexander, 424–25.
104 Fremantle, 265–66.            105 Ibid., 266.
106 O. R., 27, pt. 2, p. 360.
107 Alexander, 425; O. R., 27, pt. 2, pp. 620, 632.
108 O. R., 27, pt. 2, p. 620. Wilcox and Col. David Lang, commanding Perry's Brigade, withdrew as soon as they saw they could accomplish nothing except the slaughter of their men.

Longstreet perhaps observed scarcely at all the advance of Wilcox,[109] because he now expected a counter-attack and busied himself in preparations to meet it. He sent Sorrel to recall McLaws's and Hood's Divisions to the positions from which they had advanced on the 2nd.[110] Then "Peter" rode out among the advanced batteries to reconnoitre and to direct their fire.[111] In the steadiness of his gunners, he found reassurance. They had little ammunition but they had even less thought of withdrawing.[112] If the enemy advanced, they would meet him.

By this time, the survivors of the charge were coming up the slope from the meadow and were passing the artillery. The men were in every mood of repulse. Some raged, some swore, some blasphemed, some scarcely could believe they had been repulsed. They shook their fists and dared the enemy to charge *their* heights. Dazed and exhausted, some looked blankly ahead, or kept their eyes on the ground. In the face of others was the uncertainty of escape from pursuing furies. Many of the veterans groaned and tried to stanch ugly, streaming wounds. A few called out for comrades who were dead or for companies that existed no more. Every emotion there was of vain and costly assault, every one except a consciousness that more than a battle had been lost: The enemy had beaten them back; they could do no more. The rest of it—war's decision, America's destiny, the doom of the Confederacy—all this was read afterward into the story of their return.

Longstreet was heartened by the fact that the troops passed him at a walk. They would rally, he felt, as soon as they reached the shelter of the ridge.[113] The terse words he spoke he tried to fit to the individual. One General who said he could not rally his men was met with sarcasm: "Very well; never mind, then, General, just let them remain where they are: the enemy's going to advance and will spare you the trouble." [114]

As Longstreet waited the advance of the Federals, all the while steadying the troops, he felt a craving for a stimulant. He turned to Fremantle and asked if the British Colonel had on his person anything to drink. Some rum, Fremantle answered, and drew

[109] In his official report (*O. R.*, 27, pt. 2, p. 360) Longstreet did not mention Wilcox's advance.
[110] 7 *S.H.S.P.*, 88.
[111] *O. R.*, 27, pt. 2, p. 360.                    [112] *Longstreet*, 395.
[113] *Ibid*                                          [114] *Fremantle*, 267.

out a silver flask. Longstreet drank gratefully and returned the flask, but the Britisher asked him to keep it and its contents. With a smile and thanks Longstreet put the flask in his pocket and went on with his preparations for meeting the counter-attack which might be delivered at any moment. Perhaps he was conscious of Lee's presence in the field on the same mission as his own, but if he saw his chief both he and the General were too busy for conversation.[115]

Tense moments passed. The confusion scarcely was reduced as yet. Men moved purposelessly as if they had lost direction. Some of the more seriously wounded dragged themselves up the ridge. The enemy continued an uncertain fire. Nobody knew what to expect next. Longstreet himself forgot some of his dispositions and sent Sorrel spurring back to McLaws to inquire why that officer had left the position from which, a few minutes previously, he had ordered McLaws to withdraw.[116] Soon, Federal skirmishers advanced from Cemetery Ridge, with every indication that a line would follow, but in the face of artillery fire, they withdrew.[117] Empty threats were made. If the Confederates were disorganized, the enemy was irresolute. While "Dick" Anderson's Division stood ready to repel assault, where Longstreet had halted the line, no enemy came within range.

When it was no longer probable that the enemy would attack, Longstreet rode off to the right,[118] probably to examine the situation there and to ascertain the truth of a rumor that Federal cavalry had penetrated to the Confederate rear. Soon Longstreet must have learned that a bold charge by two regiments of Federal horse under Brig. Gen. Elon S. Farnsworth had confused temporarily the flank elements of Hood's Division, but had ended in the repulse of the Union troopers and the death of their leader.[119] Longstreet had no responsibility for, and perhaps no knowledge of, a more expensive but no less futile action waged that afternoon by the Confederate cavalry beyond Ewell's left flank.[120]

---

[115] Cf. 3 B. & L., 347; Fremantle, 267.
[116] 7 S.H.S.P., 88.                        [117] 3 B. & L., 347; O. R., 27, pt. 2, p. 360.
[118] Fremantle, 267.
[119] The attacking regiments were the 1st West Virginia and the 1st Vermont. Total Federal casualties were approximately 287 (O. R., 27, pt. 1, pp. 992–93). Official reports of this attack are meagre, though it was the theme of much descriptive and of no little imaginative writing. Perhaps the best unofficial narrative is that of Capt. H. C. Parsons in 3 B. & L., 393 ff.
[120] For the details of this action, see infra, p. 210.

After the fire of the opposing forces died in darkness, there was no further argument over the course the Army must follow. One thing only could be done. With food supplies low and artillery ammunition almost exhausted, retreat was imperative. That was as plain to the average intelligent soldier as it was to Lee and his lieutenants. Before instructions came from G. H. Q., Longstreet directed that his artillery be withdrawn gradually to Seminary Ridge[121] and he went out, after a time, to see how the skirmish line was faring.

Near the Peach Orchard, in a position boldly advanced, Longstreet found a battery. "Whose are these guns?" he demanded. Out of the shadows stepped a tall man with a pipe in his mouth. "I am the Captain," said he. Immediately Longstreet recognized him as his friend "Buck" Miller of the Washington Artillery, who had been one of his favorites since Sharpsburg.[122] In answer to the General's question why he was so far in front of the infantry, Miller answered cheerily, "I am out here to have a little skirmishing on my own account, if the Yanks come out of their holes." The prospect of a skirmish with 12-pounder howitzers amused Longstreet. Through the darkness, across the field of death, his laugh rang out.[123]

Back at his headquarters, Longstreet received orders to prepare for the retreat. The wagons and the wounded were, of course, to be started before the infantry moved. Withdrawal was to be by way of the Fairfield or Hagerstown Road and across the mountains which Lee had considered so dangerous an obstacle to orderly retirement.[124] Hill was to lead, Longstreet to follow, Ewell to bring up the rear.

To arranging his part of the details of this retreat, Longstreet devoted part of the evening. On the morning of the 4th of July he was afield early to ascertain what was the prospect of the development the Army had most to fear—a heavy attack by Meade. Soon, across the field, came a flag of truce, which was accepted. When the officer in charge had stated his other business he announced: "General Longstreet is wounded and a prisoner, but will be taken care of." That delighted Longstreet. He sent back word

121 O. R., 27, pt. 2, p. 430; Alexander, 426.
122 See Vol. II, pp. 213–14.
123 Owen, 255, with the conversation changed from the third person to the first.
124 Cf. supra, p. 109.

that he was extremely grateful but that as he was neither wounded nor a prisoner, he could take care of himself. His humor was better because of his answer.[125]

As the forenoon passed without a single thrust from Cemetery Ridge and nothing more formidable than Federal reconnaissance,[126] Longstreet and the other Confederate commanders permitted themselves to hope that Meade had been too heavily injured to strike.[127] From a central position where he could survey the long sweep of the Federal line, Longstreet watched while the skies darkened over the silent battleground. "He is looking well," one observer remarked, "and seems evidently determined to put on the best face possible." Presently Longstreet asked of a young artillerist, "What o'clock is it?"

"Eleven fifty-five," answered William Miller Owen of the Washington Artillery, who went on: "General, this is the 'Glorious Fourth'; we should have a salute from the other side at noon."

Longstreet waited. Noon came and passed. Not a gun was fired. Said Longstreet with satisfaction: "Their artillery was too much crippled yesterday to think of salutes. Meade is not in good spirits this morning." [128]

In another hour, rain began to fall. With difficulty the ambulances and the wagons were started toward the mountains through a downpour. After darkness the infantry began to move from Seminary Ridge along the Fairfield Road. A grim but not a despairing march it was. In most hearts there was bitterness and humiliation that the columns were headed for the Potomac, instead of Baltimore or Philadelphia. None realized, to repeat, that Gettysburg was more than a battle in which the Army, winning two days, had been unable on the third to drive the enemy from a position of great strength. Mercifully or tragically, none could see that the afternoon of the Confederacy had come.

If, in ignorance of this, any shadow of resentment still lay on

125 *Fremantle*, 272–73. The officer mistaken for Longstreet was Col. R. M. Powell of the Fifth Texas (3 *B. & L.*, 320).

126 *Cf.* Meade in *O. R.*, 27, pt. 1, p. 117.

127 Meade took this view of his situation and determined not to follow "the bad example [Lee] had set me in ruining himself attacking a strong position." *O. R.*, 27, pt. 3, p. 539. Cf. *ibid.*, 533, 535, 537, 554, 558, and *ibid.*, pt. 1, p. 80. This last reference, July 6, announced Meade's intention to give battle. He would do so, he said, "trusting, should misfortune overtake me, that a sufficient number of my force, in connection with that you have in Washington, could reach that place so as to render it secure."

128 *Owen*, 255.

the soul of James Longstreet, it was lightened by the fire of his own bivouac. There, while the rain poured down, Lee came and spoke briefly of the struggle. "It's all my fault," he said, "I thought my men were invincible." [129] Longstreet's only recorded observations that day or the next were tactical. Colonel Fremantle remembered that Longstreet said the mistake of the Confederates was "in not concentrating the Army more, and making the attack . . . with 30,000 men instead of 15,000." The troops who gave way, Longstreet explained, "were young soldiers who had never been under fire before." [130] Not one word did Fremantle report of any contention by Longstreet that the basic tactics of battle had been defective.

From that bivouac on the Fairfield Road, Longstreet and his companions resumed on the 5th of July a retreat that seemed half nightmare, half mercy. Unvoiced, unadmitted, was the fear of many a leader that Meade by some miracle of a march might catch the Confederate column while it was strung out on the road. The Federal cavalry did not strike the wagon train once as it crossed the mountains.[131] With slight loss only, the vehicles on the 6th reached Williamsport. There Providence seemed to interpose between the wagons and safety, because the Potomac was past fording. Fortunately, Imboden held off a vigorous Federal attack until Stuart came up and drove back the enemy.[132] It was a narrow escape.

The infantry and artillery reached Hagerstown on the afternoon of the 6th and during the morning of the 7th and there they took up a line to cover the crossings of the Potomac between Williamsport and Falling Waters.[133] Little by little, as uninjured men rested, their old defiant spirit, if not their full confidence, returned. If Meade came, they would meet him! Until the 12th of July, nothing occurred except cavalry clashes and occasional skirmishes.[134] That day, the Federal infantry approached. Lee's ragged veterans steeled themselves for another Antietam, but to

[129] *Owen,* 256.

[130] *Fremantle,* 275. This remark could mean only that Longstreet thought the break began in Davis's Brigade, because that was the one Brigade in the charge that could have been said to consist of young, inexperienced troops. For a discussion of this point, see *infra,* pp. 181, 186.

[131] *O. R.,* 27, pt. 2, pp. 322, 700–01.

[132] *Ibid.*

[133] *Ibid.,* 323.                               [134] *Ibid.,* 323, 703.

Southern eyes the enemy appeared more anxious to cover himself with entrenchments of Maryland earth than to prepare for attack. All the while, Confederate detachments under the eyes of Jackson's former Quartermaster, Maj. J. A. Harman, were building pontoons to take the place of those that had been swept away by high water or damaged by the enemy. The 13th of July found the Potomac still high at Williamsport but passable. At Falling Waters a satisfactory pontoon bridge was ready. During the later hours of the night of July 13–14, and the forenoon of the 14th, the Army passed back to Virginia. Harry Heth was left under vexing conditions to cover the rear. He did so with the loss of two guns and of approximately 500 stragglers from many Brigades. Difficulties considered, Heth's performance was wholy creditable, but the Federals would not have it so. Because some of their leaders sensed public disappointment that Lee had escaped, they exaggerated Heth's withdrawal of the rearguard as a serious Confederate disaster.[135] In spite of Lee's report, which vindicated Heth,[136] the enemy's view was accepted uncritically by many Southerners. The belief wrongly persisted that Heth had been derelict and that Falling Waters was a Roncesvalles.[137]

[135] Cf. *O. R.*, 27, pt. 2, p. 303.          [136] *O. R.*, 27, pt. 2, p. 323.

[137] 10 *S.H.S.P.*, 553 n; *O. R.*, 27, pt. 2, pp. 323, 353, 361, 705. Heth's report (*ibid.*, 640–41) is a characteristically candid account of what happened. In his *MS Memoirs*, Heth added nothing to facts already known about the affair.

# CHAPTER IX

## "Jackson Is Not Here"

BACK ON Virginia soil, one young officer wrote grimly: "... The campaign is a failure and the worst failure that the South has ever made. Gettysburg sets off Fredericksburg. Lee seems to have become as weak as Burnside. And no blow since the fall of New Orleans has been so telling against us." [1] Few in the Army of Northern Virginia would say that or would admit any defeat at Gettysburg. First reports in Southern newspapers were jubilant. "A brilliant and crushing victory [had] been achieved"; [2] 14,000 or 40,000 prisoners had been captured; [3] Lee was marching on Baltimore. [4] When it was manifest, instead, that Lee had withdrawn to the Potomac, the public was assured that "there is nothing bad in this news beyond a disappointment." [5] Lee had fallen back to secure his "vast train of materials," fifteen miles long, [6] or else he had withdrawn because of lack of provisions. [7] He was "perfectly master of the situation" [8] and if he had commanded 20,000 more troops, "he could have followed up Meade's army and taken Baltimore and Washington." [9]

A few days later the result was declared "favorable to the South," [10] but the success "had not been decisive" [11] because of "the semblance of a retreat." [12] The "retrograde movement" had been "dictated by strategy and prudence." [13] Results of the campaign were a mixture of good and evil with a predominance of good. [14] Not until July 25 could even the anti-administration *Richmond Examiner* bring itself to speak of the "repulse at Gettysburg." By July 30, 1863, having blown hot, the *Charleston Mercury* blew cold and asserted: "It is impossible for an invasion to have been more foolish and disastrous." That was an extremist's view.

[1] James Pleasants to Mrs. D. H. Gordon, MS, July 17, 1863—*Gordon MSS.*
[2] *Charleston Mercury*, July 8, 1863.
[3] *Richmond Enquirer*, July 7; *Richmond Examiner*, July 10, 1863.
[4] *Richmond Dispatch*, July 6, 1863.
[5] *Richmond Examiner*, July 9, 1863.      [6] *Ibid.*, July 14, 1863.
[7] *Richmond Dispatch*, July 10, 1863.      [8] *Ibid.*
[9] *Richmond Enquirer*, July 11, 1863.      [10] *Richmond Whig*, July 14, 1863.
[11] *Richmond Enquirer*, July 15, 1863.      [12] *Richmond Whig*, July 14, 1863.
[13] *Charleston Mercury*, July 16, 1863.      [14] *Richmond Dispatch*, July 18, 1863.

Two days previously the *Richmond Dispatch* had scolded those "fools" who "cried out that the scheme" for the invasion of the North "was impracticable."

In the state of mind that prevailed immediately after the battle, critical discussion was considered unpatriotic. The present-day student, on the other hand, finds Gettysburg the most interesting of all the battles of the Army of Northern Virginia. It is the campaign that provokes the warmest, longest debate because it is in bewildering contrast to the operations that preceded it. While this makes almost any intelligent review of the operations intriguing, every reader must be cautioned at the outset that there is no "secret" of Gettysburg, no single failure which, if ascertained and appraised justly, "explains" the outcome. A score of circumstances, working together, rather than any one, wrought a major Confederate defeat.

Many reasons for the non-success of the invasion sprang from the reorganization necessitated by the death of Jackson. That is why this critique of the battle carries the caption, "Jackson Is Not Here." In detail, the reasons for failure that inhered in the new organization have been reviewed elsewhere.[15] They were the absence of the more efficient cavalry units, the awkward leadership of men in new and more responsible positions, the state of mind of Stuart, of Longstreet and of Ewell, the overconfidence of Lee, the poor handling of the artillery, and the lack of co-ordination in attack.

Of exterior factors, the first, which deserves more emphasis than it has received, was the limitation imposed on Lee's action by the factor of time. The campaign was fought while the Army was living off the country and was without supply lines to Virginia. Much of the collection of supplies had to be undertaken with little cavalry. Lee stated this succinctly: ". . . we were unable to await an attack, as the country was unfavorable for collecting supplies in the presence of the enemy, who could restrain our foraging parties by holding the mountain passes . . ."[16] A second exterior factor was the extent and thinness of the line. Five miles and more in length and shaped like a great fish-hook, it made communication and concentration difficult.

Always to be considered were the skill, persistence and might

15 See 3 *R. E. Lee*, 147 ff.      16 *O. R.*, 27, pt. 2, p. 318.

with which the Army of the Potomac defended on the 2nd and 3rd of July a position of natural strength. In Southern studies of Gettysburg, this third factor is more often assumed than stated, but it was in July, 1863, a disillusioning reality and a gloomy warning of what the Confederacy might expect of Northern veterans under competent leadership. The Army of the Potomac fought well in every battle where the blunders of rash or incompetent commanders did not paralyze or counteract the effort of the men. At Gettysburg, the magnificent Federal Divisions had strong ground, interior lines, the sense of fighting for home, knowledge of combat, and the intelligent, courageous leadership of George Gordon Meade, of Winfield Scott Hancock, and of other wholly capable captains. Vigorous and experienced as was Lee's Army, it could not prevail over that adversary.

These were the larger reasons for the Confederate defeat as seen from the standpoint of the high command. As this review proceeds now to examine the principal moves in their chronological order, it will be observed that all the Confederate errors of overconfidence, bad organization and inept leadership were aggravated by the factors of chance and circumstance which the Federals, for the first time in the long contest of the two Armies, were in position to capitalize fully.

At the beginning, the approach of the Confederates to the battlefield was incautious. From the time the Army entered Pennsylvania, it was blinded by the absence of Stuart. Nothing was comparable to this in preparing the way for a tragedy.[17] On the 1st of July, having no information beyond that collected the previous day by Pettigrew, the van of the Third Corps advanced without cavalry. Contact by the front Division was with a strong Federal Corps. Another Union Corps was immediately at hand. Before the Confederates were aware of it, their leading Divisions were engaged beyond easy conclusion. Lee must have been speaking of this when he said in his report: "It had not been intended to deliver a general battle so far from our base unless attacked, but coming unexpectedly upon the whole Federal Army, to withdraw through the mountains with our extensive trains would have been difficult and dangerous."[18] For this, the greater part of the

[17] Stuart's part in the campaign is considered more in detail, *infra*, p. 206 ff.
[18] *O R.*, 27, pt. 2, p. 318.

blame rested on Stuart, who should have been present to reconnoitre. Obvious blame, also, would be charged against Powell
Hill, if he had not been sick on the 1st.[19] Never before had he
been ill on a day of battle, though it will be remembered that he
had been incapacitated at Chancellorsville. As sickness was frequent after his promotion to corps command, it is in order to ask
whether he may not have become more subject to psychosomatic
ills after new responsibility was placed on him.

As the Second Corps advanced to the aid of the Third, that first
afternoon of the battle, Rodes's line of battle was formed in a
manner that put the best Brigadiers where the fighting was lightest
and the feeblest men in the most difficult fray. Ramseur and Doles
should have formed, if possible, the column of attack. Instead, the
burden of the assault fell on Iverson and O'Neal, both of whom
were inexperienced. Junius Daniel, co-operating on their right,
won golden opinions.[20] When the fighting was over, Lee, who
had seen part of it, told Rodes, "I am proud of your Division"; [21]
but after all the facts were known, the employment of Rodes's
Division must have been judged distinctly below expectations.

The final debate of the first day concerns Ewell's conduct and,
particularly, the question whether he should have assaulted Cemetery Hill as soon as he reached Gettysburg. The circumstances
were almost unique in the history of the Army of Northern Virginia. Nothing that had happened from the time the Army had
left the Rappahannock had indicated, even to the slightest, that
Ewell was lacking in power of decision as a corps commander.
Everything on the march, at Winchester and en route to Carlisle,
had been marked by so much promptitude, positiveness and unhesitating action that no superior would have hesitated to allow
discretion to Ewell or would have imagined for a moment that
the commander of the Second Corps would hesitate to exercise
that discretion.

In the drama of July 1, Ewell performed his part flawlessly
until the action on Seminary Ridge was won. It is difficult to
criticize him for anything he did until he entered the town and
as difficult to praise him for anything he did thereafter. In detail,

[19] *Fremantle*, 254.
[20] *O. R.*, 27, pt. 2, pp. 553–54; 1 *N. C. Regts.*, 637; 2 *ibid.*, 235; *Lee's Dispatches*,
95, 146 ff, 225 ff. These references cover all three of the men and not Daniel only.
[21] *O. R.*, 27, pt. 2, p. 559.

all stages of his hesitation can be defended and perhaps justified. Together they present the picture of a man who could not come to a decision within the time swift action might have brought victory. Years after the battle, when leaders on both sides were free to speculate, Gen. W. S. Hancock said: ". . . in my opinion, if the Confederates had continued the pursuit of General Howard on the afternoon of the 1st July at Gettysburg, they would have driven him over and beyond Cemetery Hill. After I had arrived upon the field, assumed the command, and made my dispositions for defending that point (say 4 P.M.) I do not think the Confederate force then present could have carried it." [22] John B. Bachelder, the most thorough of all the early students of the battle, was of opinion that a Confederate attack, delivered within an hour after the defeat of the I and XI Corps, would have been successful. At any subsequent hour, Mr. Bachelder thought, an assault would have been repulsed.[23] Among Confederate critics, though General Early urged the attack when the Federals were driven through Gettysburg, he said, in later argument, that he thought Ewell's decision was correct.[24]

Those admittedly are opinions. The one possible, though unsatisfactory, basis for a conclusion is the strength of the Federal force on Cemetery Hill at the time Ewell might have reconnoitred and then have pressed through the town on the heels of the defeated Brigades. Adolph Steinwehr's 2nd Division of the XI Corps, which had marched from Emmitsburg that morning, had reached the field at 2 P.M. and had received instructions to defend Cemetery Hill. One of its two Brigades later had been dispatched North of the town to reinforce Maj. Gen. Carl Schurz's 3rd Division.[25] The Brigade left upon the hill [26] probably numbered about 1500 effectives.[27] Its artillery was Capt. Michael Wiedrich's Battery of six 3-inch rifles.[28] Together, this was an exceedingly small force, but its size, of course, was not apparent to Ewell at the time. Manifestly, in the confusion of a strange field, he cannot be blamed too

[22] 5 S.H.S.P., 168.
[23] Ibid., 172.
[24] 4 S.H.S.P., 260.
[25] O. R., 27, pt. 1, p. 721.
[26] That of Col. Orland Smith.
[27] The Division on July 4, 1863 had 2109 officers and men present for duty (O. R., 27, pt. 1, p. 153). Smith's losses during the three days' fighting were 348 (ibid., 183). Those of the Brigade of Col. Charles R. Coster were 597. Thus the strength of the Division on the morning of July 1 was about 3054. The Brigades apparently were of approximately the same size.
[28] O. R., 27, pt. 1, pp. 747, 751

heavily for ignorance of the extreme weakness of his adversary. The impression persists that he did not display the initiative, resolution and boldness to be expected of a good soldier.

On the 2nd of July, co-ordination among the Corps was lacking, with the result that the battle opened late. Reconnaissance was inadequate. The Confederate high command was deceived concerning the strength of the Federal left. When action was begun, it was poorly directed on both flanks. The engagement on the right of Lee's line probably should not have been fought at all under the vague and misfounded plan of the commanding General. Errors of subordinates deprived it of whatever chance of success it might have had. This is a broad indictment, but historically, count by count, it is a "true bill." The Second Corps was ready in the early morning to make its demonstration but was delayed because Longstreet did not open the fight. All reasons for Longstreet's failure to attack during the forenoon [29] are, needless to say, the subject of one of the most familiar controversies of Gettysburg. Much may be asserted and sustained with show of logic, but there can be no escaping the conclusion that Longstreet's behavior on the 2nd was that of a man who sulked because his plan was rejected by his chief. This conclusion is not inferential. It need not be framed from the testimony of those who hated Longstreet after the war as a political renegade. Longstreet's own Assistant Adjutant General is the only witness who need be called. With all the evidence before him, Moxley Sorrel wrote: "The story has been in part told by Longstreet. We can discover that he did not want to fight on the ground or on the plan adopted by the General-in-Chief. As Longstreet was not to be made willing and Lee refused to change or could not change, the former failed to conceal some anger. There was apparent apathy in his movements. They lacked the fire and the point of his usual bearing on the battlefield." [30] Sorrel might have added that Longstreet took approximately seven hours to move McLaws and Hood two miles and a half and to put them into action, though they were not exposed to fire till they began their advance against the Federal positions.

Beyond this it is not just to go in criticizing Longstreet's conduct on the 2nd, prior to the time his march to the right was begun.

[29] See *supra*, p. 111 ff. and 3 *R. E. Lee*, 86 ff.   [30] *Sorrel*, 163-64.

His attitude was wrong but his instinct was correct. He should have obeyed orders, but the orders should not have been given. Information concerning the enemy's left was scant and inaccurate. At 4 A.M., it will be remembered, Capt. S. R. Johnston [31] had started with Maj. J. J. Clarke of Longstreet's engineers to reconnoitre the extreme right. As noted already, the two climbed the slope of Little Round Top. From that point they saw no enemy. Descending, they rode southward till they reached approximately the ground of Farnsworth's charge on the 3rd. Nowhere did they encounter any Federals until they turned back toward Lee's post of command, and then they saw only three or four Union troopers moving up the Emmitsburg Road toward Gettysburg. All this was between 4 and approximately 7 A.M.[32] Johnston stated subsequently that he was convinced this was the first reconnaissance on the Federal left. He believed that the reconnaissance said by General Pendleton to have been made on the morning of the 2nd actually had been undertaken on the afternoon of the 1st and had been limited. Johnston was certain that he had not participated on the 2nd, as Pendleton had stated, with that officer and two others in an examination of the ground.[33]

The reconnaissance of Johnston was accurate, so far as he went. No Federals were on Little Round Top if he arrived there as late as 5:30, but he had missed them on that eminence [34] by a margin of minutes. Two Federal regiments, the 5th Ohio and the 147th Pennsylvania, a total of about 600 men of Col. Charles Candy's Brigade of Geary's Division of the XII Corps, had occupied the Round Tops during the night of July 1–2. They evacuated the

[31] Subsequently Lieutenant Colonel.
[32] S. R. Johnston to Lafayette McLaws, MS copy, June 27, 1892; to Bishop G. W. Peterkin, MS draft, n.d.; to Fitz Lee, MS copies, Feb. 11, 16, 1878—S. R. Johnston MSS.
[33] Pendleton wrote (O. R., 27, pt. 2, p. 350) that "from the farthest occupied point on the right and front," with Col. A. L. Long, Col. R. L. Walker and Captain Johnston, he "surveyed the enemy's position toward some estimate of the ground and the best mode of attack." He added "so far as judgment could be formed from such a view," assault might succeed. This language usually has been regarded as a statement of a formal reconnaissance, but the passage may mean only that Pendleton, who never minimized his exploits, simply "surveyed" the ground from a distance. Pendleton's first reference to a reconnaissance, as such, on the morning of the 2nd, was made in an address of January, 1873 (Pendleton, 286). It was to this address that Johnston referred. In Walker's brief report of the Gettysburg campaign, there was no reference to any reconnaissance by him on the morning of July 2 (O. R., 27, pt. 2, p. 610). Long in his Memoirs of Robert E. Lee said (pp. 280–81) that "at an early hour on the morning of the 2nd" he was directed to examine the position of the Confederate artillery. He wrote that he "examined the whole line from right to left," but this manifestly was with reference to the artillery and not for reconnaissance. Long mentioned no companions.
[34] For participants' confusion of the Round Tops, see Appendix II.

two eminences and started for the Union right about 5 A.M. The two Brigades of the Division were moving northward when Johnston was on the ridge of Round Top. He did not see them. If he had . . .

That is not the end of the curious factor of chance that fateful morning. Johnston stated that along the Confederate front for approximately half the distance to Round Top, he found Confederate pickets extended.[35] The engineer did not attempt to pass this picket line and to climb the southern stretches of Cemetery Ridge. Had he done so, he might have been captured; but if he had escaped, he might have been able to bring back information the Confederate critics of Longstreet never possessed during the Gettysburg campaign or during the controversy of 1877–78. It was this: By 9 A.M., July 2, the Federals had between Ziegler's Grove and the Round Tops at least 18,200 men ready to fight.[36] The ridge, in short, was adequately protected against Confederate frontal attack by the time Longstreet had his two Divisions in the first position they occupied after they reached Seminary Ridge.[37] Most of the troops who were thought to be moving into position on the ridge, while Longstreet loitered, actually had been there since early morning and merely had been advanced to positions where many of them were visible to the Confederates.

All question of the effect of Longstreet's delay must, therefore, be limited to a discussion of what might have been accomplished early in the day on the extreme Federal left, at the Round Tops or directly North of them. The tradition must be discarded that the whole of Cemetery Ridge, South of the flank of the XI Corps, was unoccupied on the morning of the 2nd. By the time McLaws and Hood arrived from their bivouac, that part of the ridge was held by strong, well-placed troops. In that fact, which is historically verifiable, much of the criticism of Longstreet evaporates. There remains the consideration, not so easily determined, whether a thorough reconnaissance could have been made, and whether, in the absence of it, battle should have been joined. A small part only of the responsibility for this rests on Longstreet. The chief blame is that of Stuart, absent when most needed for reconnaissance.

It is difficult to describe Lee's plan of battle for the First Corps,

35 Johnston to Fitz Lee, MS copy, Feb. 16, 1878—*S. R. Johnston MSS.*
36 For Buford's cavalry, see *O. R.*, 27, pt. 1, pp. 927–28.
37 For the detailed evidence on this point, see Appendix II.

July 2, in terms of practicable maneuver on the ground in front of Longstreet. Obviously, when the commander of the column of attack found the plan contrary to the hard actualities of the field, he should have notified Lee. Had Longstreet been himself in temper, he would have done this. When the belated attack reluctantly was delivered by Longstreet, it lacked even an approach to unity. The plan was for a progressive attack from right to center, but progression never contemplated destruction, unit by unit. Hood's Division was allowed to wear dull its fighting edge before McLaws went into action. McLaws's advance was not followed immediately by that of Anderson, who apparently knew little of what was planned. The assault on the right could not even be termed a clumsy battle by unsupported Divisions. Scarcely at any time during the afternoon was the full strength of any Division hurled against the enemy. As the attacks of Semmes, Wofford, Barksdale, Wilcox and Posey show, there was little support from Third Corps artillery, except that given by two or three batteries of Lane's Battalion, which employed not more than sixteen guns at the maximum.[38] For that matter, the participation of Hill in the operation was so slight that his name scarcely appears in reports of the day's operations.[39]

The mismanagement of the action during the afternoon of July 2 on the front of Ewell's Corps was principally in loose direction or in no direction at all. Apparently Ewell knew little of the condition of his units. Both he and Johnson seemed unaware of the fact that James A. Walker's Stonewall Brigade already was somewhat heavily committed when the order was issued for Johnson's

[38] The doubt concerning the number of guns is due to the language of Maj. John Lane's report. He stated (O. R., 27, pt. 2, pp. 635–36) that one of his batteries "went into action early on the second day's battle," but it is not clear whether he meant the battle of July 2 or the battle of the second day on which the battalion was engaged, namely, July 3. Lane's Battalion of artillery had been detached on the morning of the 2nd from Anderson's Division. The reason was not explained, but it probably was to give Walker a larger force to be concentrated at any point along the front. For Walker's somewhat curious observations on the use of his artillery on the 2nd, see O. R., 27, pt. 2, p. 610.

[39] His own report devoted twenty-eight printed lines to the day's action. Anderson's account of the day contained two indirect references to Hill but it did not mention him by name. The Brigadiers did not speak of the corps commander in their account of the attack. In Lee's official narrative of the events of the 2nd, there are a few words on Hill's position but the only other allusion is in connection with orders given Hill (O. R., 27, pt. 2, p. 318). The Federals did not see evidence of any marked activity on the part of Hill's left. Maj. Gen. W. S. Hancock's report (O. R., 27, pt. 1, pp. 369–72) was concerned chiefly with occurrences farther southward on Cemetery Ridge, after Maj. Gen. D. E. Sickles had been wounded and his III Corps placed under Hancock. The report of Maj. Gen. John Newton, commanding the I Corps (ibid., 261), ignored Hill's left.

assault on Culp's Hill. Early's attack was prompt and vigorous but was delivered with only two of his Brigades. Smith's regiments that day were treated as if their leader could not be trusted in action. Such frail liaison as existed between Early and Rodes was effected by those two officers and not by Ewell. The Lieutenant General does not seem to have taken into account the greater distance that Rodes had to cover before he could join in the attack on Cemetery Hill.[40] If, further, the records tell the whole story Ewell did not know what Division was on the right of his Corps and did not take any step to elicit its aid till the attack was about to be launched.

Ewell's semi-passive role did not destroy the initiative of all his subordinates. Early's conduct on the 2nd was soldierly. He does not seem to have been as much disposed as he had been on the 1st to seek to impose his will. His attack on East Cemetery Hill followed quickly that of Johnson on Culp's Hill. Early was wise also —if indeed the decision was his and not Hays's—in abandoning the assault when he did. Whether Early could have achieved more if he had used Gordon [41] as well as Hays and Avery is, needless to say, a matter of opinion. On Early's left, Edward Johnson may be charged with failure to make proper reconnaissance of Rock Creek. In other respects his performance on the 2nd, though not brilliant, was vigorous.[42]

Rodes manifestly should not have neglected, as he did, to calculate precisely the time required for him and for Early to deliver their attacks simultaneously. Negligent in that, Rodes made an awkward deployment on his right, but, apparently, he did not fail to establish contact with the left flank of Pender's Division, then under command of General Lane. To the allegation that Rodes should have assaulted Cemetery Hill, an answer is given, in part, by the character of the men who shared Rodes's decision against delivering the attack. If Dodson Ramseur and George Doles had been timid men, or men partial to the defensive, their agreement to halt the advance might be disputable; but they were, in reality, among the most daring, hardest fighters of the Army. If they agreed with their militant commander that the hill could not be

40 Strictly speaking, Rodes was to attack Cemetery Hill and Early was to assail East Cemetery Hill.
41 The next references of any consequence to Gordon will be found on p. 350 ff.
42 For the next important employment of Rodes, Johnson and Early, see Chapter XV.

carried, few who knew them in the Army would maintain the contrary. The fact remains that the enemy seems to have expected no attack by Rodes on Cemetery Hill—a situation that usually spells opportunity. A student who examines the details and then puts them together as the day's record of a divisional commander scarcely can escape the conclusion that Rodes's 2nd of July was in disappointing contrast to his 2nd of May. Dash was lacking.

The employment of Ewell's artillery on July 2 was as inefficient as that of Hill's guns. In an exposed position, Latimer's Battalion had no supporting batteries, no relief. While the "Boy Major" was being driven from his position at the price of a wound that proved fatal, four batteries and no more were preparing for the advance of Early and of Rodes.[43] Two battalions of artillery, one of them Colonel Tom Carter's command, were left idle all the while North of Gettysburg.[44] Some of the inaction of the gunners of the Second Corps had to be attributed, no doubt, to the absence of the wounded corps chief of artillery, Stapleton Crutchfield, but that circumstance should have made Ewell more diligent. It did not.

On the 3rd of July, the lack of co-ordination in attack was scarcely less than on the 2nd. A rereading of the details [45] will make this clear. More specifically, the first of three familiar questions raised by the final Confederate attack is whether an attempt should have been made to break the centre of the Federal position. On this, little more is to be said. Lee felt at the time that the assault was in a measure unavoidable and that, if the full strength of the Army could be brought to bear, the attack would be successful.[46] The responsibility was that of the commanding General. He accepted it and he meant precisely what he said when he told Longstreet: "It's all my fault; I thought my men were invincible." [47]

The second criticism of the Confederate operations of the third day is that the artillery preparation for the charge of Pickett and of Pettigrew was inadequate and that where the bombardment was well handled, it had to be halted because ammunition was exhausted. This criticism is justified. Gettysburg demonstrated that the reorganization of the artillery gave flexibility within a

[43] O. R., 27, pt. 2, p. 456.
[44] Ibid., 603, 605. The other battalion was Nelson's.
[45] See supra, p. 146 ff.
[46] For the details, see 3 R. E. Lee, 107 ff.          [47] Owen, 257; see supra, p. 166.

Corps, but among the Corps there was little co-operation. Pendle ton had neither the prestige nor the authority to assure the employment of all the guns as one weapon under one leader. He appears in the campaign more as a consultant than as a commander. Porter Alexander subsequently argued convincingly that if sufficient guns had been massed on the Confederate centre to silence the batteries on Cemetery Hill, the column that attacked Cemetery Ridge would not have been exposed to so heavy a flank fire.[48] All the reports of the fire directed against the hill attest the effectiveness of that fire and the surprising vulnerability of the position.[49] In addition to this loss of opportunity, there was scant liaison. The powerful artillery of the Third Corps was not used heavily at the time it would have been most useful.[50] To the extent that the artillery of the Second Corps was employed on the day of the charge, Col. Tom Carter's was the one battalion that was effective.[51] In Hill's and Ewell's Corps, Alexander computed that fifty-six guns were not used, and that of the eighty-four employed, eighty were parallel to the line of the enemy, though an enfilade of part of the Union position would have been possible.[52]

In the judgment of Lee, the slackening of the artillery fire had so positive an influence on the failure of the assault that he felt constrained to express in his report his ignorance of the low state of ammunition when the attack was delivered. Each battery had carried into Pennsylvania from 130 to 150 rounds. This supply, which included the canister for close action, was in the caissons. The ordnance train certainly did not have more than 100 rounds per gun and, in Porter Alexander's opinion, subsequently expressed, may not have had more than sixty rounds.

So far as the records show, no check was made on the morning

48 *Alexander*, 419, 427. For the next references to Pendleton. see *infra*, pp. 280, 339.
49 See *O. R.*, 27, pt. 2, pp. 351, 603–04, 635–36, 647; *Alexander*, 427.
50 See *O. R.*, 27, pt. 2, pp. 635–36, 647, 652–53. Capt. E. B. Brunson's report (*ibid.*, 677–79) reads as if that officer, senior captain, headed Pegram's battalion throughout the campaign, but Col. R. Lindsay Walker noted (*ibid.*, 610) that Pegram resumed command June 30, at Cashtown. Pegram did admirably at Gettysburg. He had developed fever while at home after the Battle of Chancellorsville, but as soon as he heard that the Army was bound for the enemy's country, he started northward. Fever was still upon him when he overtook the Army. General Lee saw him before the young cannoneer reported to Hill and the commander said cheerfully to the Lieutenant General: "I have good news for you; Major Pegram is up." Hill answered, "Yes, that *is* good news." On the 1st, in the midst of action, Hill paused to shake hands with the young artillerist (14 *S.H.S.P.*, 6, 15–16). The next detailed references to Pegram will be found *infra*, Chapter XXXIII.
51 *O. R.*, 27, pt. 2, pp. 427–95, 544.
52 *Alexander*, 419.      53 4 *S.H.S.P.*, 103.

of the 3rd of July to ascertain how heavily the firing of the previous days had depleted the supply. Those batteries that had emptied their caissons drove them to the ordnance wagons and replenished. The wagons themselves were not refilled from the reserve trains, which were farther from the Confederate right than from any other part of the line.[54] Alexander thought later that the caissons of the Third Corps must have been drawn upon heavily during the useless morning cannonade, while the pickets were contending for the house and barn between the lines.[55] He husbanded carefully the supply of the First Corps batteries until the time to open the main bombardment; but before Pickett began his advance, some of Dearing's caissons[56] were empty. An hour and a half previously Dearing had sent for more ammunition, but he had not received it.[57]

When other battalion commanders sent their caissons to the point designated by Pendleton as the advanced position of the ordnance train, they found that the wagons had disappeared. Some person, not identified in any of the reports, had moved the wagons to the rear because shells had been exploding near by. The drivers of the caissons had to go farther and, when they reached the wagons, found little there. They had accordingly to proceed to the more distant reserve trains.[58] As a result, many of the guns of the Third Corps[59] and a number of those in the First[60] stood idle for lack of ammunition at a time when the Federals were shattering the flank of the advancing line. Technically, the blame may have rested on the Ordnance Officer of the First Corps for not supervising properly the flow of ammunition to the guns, but Col. Lindsay Walker must bear his share of blame, also, for permitting so much of the ammunition of the Third Corps to be wasted during the forenoon to no good purpose. More fundamentally, the lack of effective general supervision of the artillery and of the ordnance supplies was responsible.

The column that delivered the attack, like the cannonade that preceded it, was inadequate for the task assigned it and tactically, in at least three respects, it was not well employed. First of all,

---

[54] O. R., 27, pt. 2, p. 352.                [55] See *supra*, p. 148; *Alexander*, 431.
[56] Maj. James Dearing, it will be remembered, was in command of the artillery battalion that served with Pickett's Division.
[57] O. R., 27, pt. 2, p. 389.               [58] *Ibid.*, 352.
[59] Cf. *Alexander*, 431.                   [60] O. R., 27, pt. 2, p. 389.

a wrong choice was made when Heth's Division was chosen to join Pickett's in the final assault. Heth's Division probably was selected because it was conveniently at hand and had been in reserve on the 2nd;[61] but Army Headquarters were guilty of a most serious omission in not ascertaining the condition of the command before it was designated for further action. Said Col. C. S. Venable: "They were terribly mistaken about Heth's Division in the planning. It had not recovered, having suffered more than was reported on the first day."[62] The loss had been worse on July 1 among officers than in the ranks. As noted already,[63] Davis's Brigade on the left flank was almost without field officers.[64] In Pettigrew's Division, not one of the men who led a Brigade during the charge possessed long experience in handling so many men. Command was not equal to the occasion. Heth himself, it will be remembered, had not resumed his duties because of the head wound received on the 1st. His luck then had been extraordinary. A minié ball had struck his hat band squarely, had broken the outer coating of the skull and had cracked the inner coating, but had not penetrated the brain. Heth thought this was because of the thicknesses of paper placed under the sweat band by a head-quarters clerk when the hat had been fitted at Cashtown.[65] The division commander was able to move about on the 3rd, but the troops were under the direction of Johnston Pettigrew, the senior Brigadier. Pettigrew was a man of large intellectual capacity but of limited field service. He never had led a Division in action.

In these circumstances, it seems reasonable to suppose that Pender's Division would have done better than Heth's if for no other reason than that it had suffered less in the first day's battle. Anderson might have used Mahone and Wilcox, or Mahone and Wright, to support Pender in the manner Lane and Scales supported Heth.[66] Change of these troops could have been made within the time taken to deploy Pickett.

61 *O. R.*, 27, pt. 2, p. 608.
62 Quoted in *Taylor's Four Years*, 103 n. Longstreet wrote Heth: "That your Division, with bloody noses after its severe fight of the 1st, was put in to do a great part in the assault of the 3rd was a serious error, and events doubly show that your Division should not have been ordered as a part of the column to march a mile under concentrated fires and carry positions held by veterans of four times our numbers, very strongly posted."
—*Heth's MS Memoirs*, 149.
63 See *supra*, p. 148.                    64 See *infra*, p. 196.
65 See *supra*, p. 77 and *Heth's MS Memoirs*, 146–47.
66 The next phases of Anderson's military career are described *infra*, pp. 243, 374 ff.

Besides being unwisely selected, the column of attack, in the second place, had its supporting troops improperly placed. Lane's and Scales's Brigades were moved into position by Lane, who acted as division commander after Pender had been wounded about sunset on the 2nd. It evidently was not the intention of Lee to permit Lane to carry the Division into action; but the delay in making another assignment was overlong. Sixteen hours elapsed [67] after the fall of Pender, and the two Brigades were deployed for the charge when Trimble rode up and, by Lee's orders, superseded Lane. Later, General Pettigrew told Col. C. S. Venable that he had understood Trimble was to be in échelon on the left of Heth's Division.[68] While this fact is not mentioned specifically in any of the reports, it was the formation used, perhaps unwisely,[69] in the attack on the 2nd and it was substantially the order of advance proposed for Wilcox on the 3rd. Apparently, when Lane placed his Brigade and Scales's behind the right of Pettigrew's Division, Lane knew nothing of any orders to advance *en échelon*. Lane was aware that, as he stood, he could give no protection to Pettigrew's left, because his position would be:

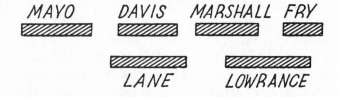

As Lane explained it in his report: "Heth's Division was much larger than Lowrance [Scales's] Brigade and my own, which were its only support, and there was consequently no second line in rear of its left." [70] Had the lines been drawn as Pettigrew understood they were to be, the advance manifestly would have been:

---

[67] The timing is by Lane's report (*O. R.*, 27, pt. 2, p. 666). Hill's report (*O. R.*, 27, pt. 2, p. 608) stated that Trimble reported to him while Heth's and Pender's men were "filing off to their positions" for the assault. Lane (*ibid.*, 666) and Maj. Jos. A. Engelhard, who reported for Pender's Division (*ibid.*, 659), said that the line had been formed when Trimble assumed command. Col. W. L. J. Lowrance, commanding Scales's Brigade, reported (*ibid.*, 671) that the line remained in position "at least one hour" under heavy artillery fire before moving forward. As the artillery bombardment preceding the charge began at 1 o'clock, Trimble may not have reached his new command until 12:30 or perhaps a few minutes later.

[68] 41 *S.H.S.P.*, 44.                    [69] Cf. *Alexander*, 400, 403-04.
[70] *O. R.*, 27, pt. 2, p. 666.

MAYO      DAVIS    MARSHALL  FRY

LOWRANCE

SCALES

If échelon was not contemplated, the flank might have been given better protection by centring Lowrance and Scales in rear of Pettigrew, or even by placing them on the left, rather than on the right, in rear of Pettigrew. On the opposite flank, where Longstreet had one Brigade only in his second line, he did not place that Brigade in a position corresponding to that of Scales and Lane, next the centre of the front line of six Brigades.[71] While it is not possible to say precisely where the flank of the second line rested on the right, the probability is that the flank was extended in such a manner as to give this order of battle:

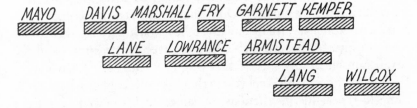

MAYO    DAVIS  MARSHALL  FRY   GARNETT  KEMPER

LANE    LOWRANCE   ARMISTEAD

LANG    WILCOX

Most soldiers and students probably will agree that the misplacement of Lowrance and of Scales was a serious defect in the operation and conceivably, though not certainly, was one reason for the repulse of the assault. Consequently, it is of importance to know who was to blame for a deployment that gave Pettigrew one line only on his exposed left. Prima facie, to judge from Lane's report, the responsibility was Longstreet's. In reporting on the battle, Lane said: ". . . I was ordered by General Hill . . . to move in person to the right, with the two brigades forming my second line, and to report to General Longstreet as a support to Pettigrew.

71 Longstreet (O. R., 27, pt. 2, p. 359) described the order of battle on the right in this manner: "Pickett's division was arranged, two brigades in the front line, supported by his third brigade, and Wilcox's brigade was ordered to move in rear of his right flank, to protect it from any force the enemy might attempt to move against it." Bachelder, on somewhat doubtful authority, centred Armistead in the second line.

General Longstreet ordered me to form in rear of the right of Heth's division, commanded by General Pettigrew." [72] If those orders were wrong, as they certainly appear to be, then part of the blame should be placed at Longstreet's door; but when Lane found that his line did not extend to the left of Pettigrew, he manifestly should have notified Longstreet. Again, as chance had it, when Lane was relieved between the time the line was formed and the assault was begun, Trimble, his successor, should, in theory, have acquainted Longstreet with the situation. Trimble's two accounts of his assumption of command and of the subsequent charge [73] contain no reference to the fact that his line was not so long as Heth's. It is doubtful if Trimble knew enough about the situation, on short notice, to see how dangerous his deployment was. He certainly did not report it to Longstreet. [74] If it is fair to say that Longstreet should have been acquainted with his own order of battle, it may be answered that the officers on that flank should have seen that he was better informed.

This would seem to apply to officers from Hill downward. Hill had been with Longstreet when Lee had given them their instructions during the forenoon. [75] Directions to both corps commanders had been explicit: While Longstreet was attacking, Hill was to be ready to give further assistance to Longstreet, if necessary, and to "avail himself of any success that might be gained." [76] That was Lee's language in his report. Perhaps by oversight, when Hill came to repeat his instructions, he stated in his official narrative only that he was "directed to hold [his] line" and to send troops to support Longstreet. [77]

Although, by these instructions, Hill technically was relieved of responsibility when Pettigrew's Division and half of Pender's were placed under Longstreet, it would have been the part of good comradeship to send an officer to Longstreet and to say that the lines were formed and that the left of Lane's Brigade extended to such and such a point in rear of Pettigrew. This may have been expecting too much of a man who had disliked Longstreet, but it is by lack of co-operation in matters seemingly as small as this that battles sometimes are lost.

A perplexing question arising here is that of the relative respon-

[72] O. R., 27, pt. 2, p. 666.  [73] 9 S.H.S.P., 32–33; 26 ibid., 126.
[74] 9 S.H.S.P., 33.  [75] Cf. 3 R. E. Lee, 114.
[76] O. R., 27, pt. 2, p. 320.  [77] Ibid., 608.

sibility of Longstreet and of Hill for the handling of those units of the Third Corps placed under Longstreet's command. Unfortunately the question cannot be answered. Longstreet certainly exercised command over Heth and Trimble after the attack began, but it is impossible to say whether the order that gave him temporary control of the greater part of the Third Corps was accepted by him as imposing any responsibility for the preliminary arrangement and the final deployment of the troops of Hill's command. Hill, for his part, may have felt that he had no right to exercise any control over those troops after they had been placed at Longstreet's disposal.[78] This unanswered question has its sharpest point in the tragic and cruel wastage of Wilcox's Brigade in a futile advance after Pickett had gone forward. Wilcox apparently was under everybody's order and nobody's.[79]

The third tactical defect in the employment of an inadequate column of attack was that two weak units were put on the left flank. Brockenbrough's Brigade, on the unsupported left of Pettigrew's line, had been C. W. Field's. In 1862, it ranked as one of the finest members of Hill's "Light Division," but it had been without its regular commander for ten months.[80] Under Harry Heth it had recovered somewhat. At Chancellorsville on the 3rd of May, when the Brigade was led by Col. J. M. Brockenbrough, it had been reduced greatly in numbers,[81] though it had been credited with good performance.[82] The troops suffered further in the action of July 1. On the 3rd, for reasons that do not appear in the records, the Brigade was commanded by Col. Robert M. Mayo of the Forty-seventh Virginia.[83] Successive change of leaders doubtless weakened the discipline of the Brigade.

[78] The next phase of Hill's career is described *infra*, p. 238 ff.
[79] See his report (*O. R.*, 27, pt. 2, p. 617 ff; *Alexander*, 425).
[80] Field had not yet recovered from the wound received at Second Manassas. See Vol. II, p. 118.
[81] *Casualties*, 279; *O. R.*, 25, pt. 1, p. 807.
[82] *Cf.* Heth's commendation (*ibid.*, p. 892).
[83] This is not set forth explicitly in *O. R.*, though Heth (*ibid.*, 27, pt. 2, p. 638) mentioned anonymously "the officer who made the report of the part taken by Brockenbrough's brigade" in the action of July 1. This report nowhere appears in the records. The sketch of Colonel Brockenbrough in 3 *C.M.H.*, 757, said of him: "At Gettysburg he . . . had a hand in the first day's victorious battle, which drove the enemy through Gettysburg to the heights beyond. After the Gettysburg campaign Colonel Brockenbrough was placed on detached duty and served the Confederacy in other fields of duty." His name is not among those of wounded Colonels at Gettysburg. The Fortieth Virginia is listed as under his command as late as the published return of Oct. 31, 1863. For Colonel Brockenbrough's previous military record, see *O. R.*, 5, 1066; *ibid.*, 11, pt. 2, p. 842; *ibid.*, 12, pt. 2, pp. 549, 558, 671; pt. 3, p. 833; *ibid.*, 19, pt. 1, p. 147; *ibid.*, pp. 21, 650; *ibid.*, 25, pt. 1, pp. 889 ff, 894 ff.

Next Brockenbrough's Brigade, to the right, was that of Joseph R. Davis—brave, inexperienced troops under an officer who matched his men. In the battle of July 1, as noted already,[84] the Brigade had lost all except two of its field officers and many of its company officers and men. Neither Davis's Brigade nor Brockenbrough's should have been placed on the exposed left, which was without help from Trimble's short line. Pettigrew had given Brockenbrough and Davis their place in the order of battle on the 2nd, when it did not matter greatly who was on the left of the Division and who on the right. Next day, the line simply was moved to the left about a quarter of a mile.[85] To say that the relative strength of the various Brigades of this Division should have been known to Longstreet would be overcritical, but to say that the weakness of the left should have been disregarded by all the responsible officers would be to set an exceedingly low standard of command. Wherever the judgment of the individual student may place the responsibility for presenting so weak a flank to a powerful adversary, this will be agreed: Through negligence or overconfidence, the organization failed to provide the strongest order of battle its numbers made possible.

All the contemporary accounts agree that the first wavering and then the first abandonment of the culminating charge were in these Brigades on the left. Men from nearly all the regiments pressed on and reached the ridge, but they could not hold their ground. Most of the troops under Mayo and Davis started back to their own lines before they reached the ridge. The evidence on this score is overwhelming[86] and never was disputed until mistaken State pride led some Southerners to maintain that the whole line pushed to Cemetery Ridge, where it encountered a defense no troops could have overcome. Heth was so conscious of the criticism of his Division that his life was saddened. Those who knew the facts never blamed him. Longstreet went further. Years after-

---

[84] See *supra*, p. 181.                    [85] Davis in *O. R.*, 27, pt. 2, p. 650.
[86] *Cf.* Longstreet's report, *O. R.*, 27, pt. 2, p. 360; the report of Maj. J. Jones, surviving commander of Pettigrew's Division, *ibid.*, 642 ff; *Ross*, 63; *Fremantle*, 266, 274; 2 *N. C. Regts.*, 43–44; 5 *ibid.*, 125, 130, 134; G. W. *Beale*, 119–20; *Hotchkiss' MS Diary*. It is traditional, also, that the severity of Pickett's strictures on the Brigades on the extreme left was the reason General Lee requested him (*O. R.*, 27, pt. 3, p. 1075) to destroy his report. In a letter from L. M. Blackford to his mother, Aug. 16, 1863, Osmun Latrobe is quoted as saying that the break of Heth's men caused the loss of the ridge. Heth's men, said Blackford, denied that they were intended to be Pickett's support, but Latrobe insisted they had been so designated.—*Blackford MSS.*

ward, Heth asked him if it were true that he had asserted Cemetery Ridge would have been held if Heth's Division had done as
well as Pickett's. The answer of Longstreet was, "No, and I never
said it and never thought it." [87] This could mean only that Longstreet, at the unspecified date of his reply, still was of opinion that
the charge could not have succeeded by any effort two Divisions
could have made.

With the reasons for the failure of the assault against the Federal centre, on the third day of the battle, detailed criticism ends.
Two facts should be stressed. The first is that Stuart refused, as
always, to admit any shortcoming on his part in the Pennsylvania
campaign, but that the other three men who were responsible for
the chief failures at Gettysburg accepted the blame without hesitation. Next to that of Malvern Hill, the Battle of Gettysburg was
the worst fought of all the engagements of General Lee. When he
said "It's all my fault," he meant that his own responsibility was
greater than that of any and all the other officers. Ewell was no
less frank. Months later he told General Hunton that "it took a
dozen blunders to lose Gettysburg and he had committed a good
many of them." [88] Longstreet was criticized specifically in Lee's
final report for one thing only. Said Lee: "General Longstreet's
dispositions were not completed as early as was expected, but before notice could be sent to General Ewell, General Johnson had
already become engaged, and it was too late to recall him." [89] The
other criticism of Longstreet, inferential rather than direct, was
that Army Headquarters should have been notified of the shortage of ammunition.[90] Lee must have felt that the advance should
have been halted when it was found that the artillery no longer
could support the advancing infantry. Longstreet's own contemporary statement, in a letter to his uncle, is that he thought "the
campaign would have been successful" had "we drawn the enemy
into attack upon our carefully-chosen position in its rear"—whatever that might mean. Longstreet proceeded to say: "General Lee
chose the plans adopted; and he is the person appointed to choose
and to order. I consider it a part of my duty to express my views
to the commanding General. If he approves and adopts them, it

[87] Heth's MS Memoirs, 149. For Heth after Gettysburg, see infra, p. 242 ff.
[88] Hunton, 98. For the next extended references to Ewell, see infra, pp. 269, 329.
[89] O. R., 27, pt. 2, p. 320. This reference, needless to say, is to events of July 3.
[90] Ibid., 221.

is well; if he does not, it is my duty to adopt his views, and to execute his orders as faithfully as if they were my own. I cannot help but think that great results would have obtained had my views been thought better of; yet I am much inclined to accept the present condition as for the best. I hope and trust that it is so . . . I fancy that no good ideas upon that campaign will be mentioned at any time, that did not receive their share of consideration by General Lee. The few things that he might have overlooked himself were, I believe, suggested by myself. As we failed, I must take my share of the responsibility. In fact, I would prefer that all the blame should rest upon me. As General Lee is our commander, he should have the support and influence we can give him. If the blame, if there is any, can be shifted from him to me, I shall help him and our cause by taking it. I desire, therefore, that all the responsibility that can be put upon me shall go there, and shall remain there. The truth will be known in time, and I shall leave that to show how much of the responsibility of Gettysburg rests on my shoulders . . ." [91]

Some parts of this letter manifestly are obscure, perhaps contradictory, but the final clarification lies where it may not be pursued—in the mind of the man who wrote. Lee never gave any intimation that he considered Longstreet's failure at Gettysburg more than the error of a good soldier. To the oft-repeated statement that this was proof of excessive good nature on the part of a commander who should have dismissed Longstreet, the all-sufficient answer is that Lee had no one with whom he could have supplanted Longstreet. It was not until years afterward, when Gettysburg was seen as the turning point of the war, that criticism of Longstreet became, in effect, blame for the loss of the battle that lost the war. The sum of just accusation against Longstreet is that he held too tenaciously to his favorite theory of defensive tactics, that he sulked and delayed on the 2nd when his tactics were rejected, that he did not use his forces in their full strength on the 2nd, and that he did not exercise the same care in the direction of Third Corps units that he gave to his own dispositions on the final day of the battle. To Longstreet's credit was the belief that Cemetery Ridge, on July 2-3, was too strong to be stormed successfully. If, when the balance of Longstreet's account is struck, it still is

[91] *Annals*, 414–15.

adverse to him, it does not warrant the traditional accusation that he was the villain of the piece. The mistakes of Lee and of Ewell and the long absence of Stuart were personal factors of failure as serious as Longstreet's.[92]

The second observation in summarizing Gettysburg is the familiar one, so often repeated in these pages that it may be monotonous, but so much an essential part of the record that it must never be omitted: Wherever the blame might be placed, it did not rest on the men in the ranks. Lee said in his preliminary report: "The conduct of the troops was all that I could desire or expect, and they deserve success so far as it can be deserved by heroic valor and fortitude. More may have been required of them than they were able to perform, but my admiration of their noble qualities and confidence in their ability to cope successfully with the enemy has suffered no abatement from the issue of this protracted and sanguinary conflict." [93] The final report of Lee was written in January, 1864, when some of the results of the battle were plainer than they had been immediately after the return to Virginia. Lee's language in that document was the fairest of epitaphs of those who fought and fell: "The privations and hardships of the march and camp were cheerfully encountered, and borne with a fortitude unsurpassed by our ancestors in their struggle for independence, while their courage in battle entitles them to rank with the soldiers of any army and of any time." [94]

[92] The sketch of Longstreet is resumed *infra*, p. 220.
[93] *O. R.*, 27, pt. 2, p. 309.       [94] *Ibid.*, 325.

# CHAPTER X

## THE PRICE OF GETTYSBURG

THE CASUALTIES of the Gettysburg campaign made the hardest veteran shudder. Of rank and file, the killed were computed at 2592, the wounded at 12,709 and the missing at 5150, a total of 20,451. If this figure was materially in error, it was below the actual loss [1] and, as estimated, was a bare 2598 under the Federal aggregate of 23,049.[2] Not even at Sharpsburg had bullets claimed so many general officers. Six had been killed or mortally wounded, three had been captured, and eight had been wounded. As the Army had entered Pennsylvania with fifty-two officers above the rank of Colonel,[3] almost exactly a third of them had become casualties. Several of these, notably Harry Heth, A. G. Jenkins, and Jerome Robertson, were so lightly wounded that they returned to duty within a few days; but in addition to the six who had been slain, at least five had been made prisoners or had been wounded so severely that their ability to take up their duties again was in doubt. By the most optimistic estimate, then, 20 per cent of the general officers would have to be replaced. Several others, as will appear in a later paragraph, should not again be entrusted with troops.

Among the lost officers were several of established place or developing promise. The killed or mortally wounded were Lewis A. Armistead, William Barksdale, Richard B. Garnett, Dorsey Pender, Johnston Pettigrew and Paul Semmes. The captured were Isaac R. Trimble and James L. Kemper, both badly hurt, and James J. Archer, unwounded but much enfeebled. The most seriously injured of those carried back to Virginia were John B. Hood and Wade Hampton.[4]

[1] O. R., 27, pt. 2, p. 345. The editors of O. R. noted, for example, that the nominal list of prisoners taken "at and about Gettysburg, July 1 to 5, inclusive," wounded and unwounded, reached a total of 12,227.
[2] O. R., 27, pt. 1, p. 187: killed 3155, wounded 14,529, missing 5365.
[3] All absentees, whether sick, wounded or detached, are excluded.
[4] The other wounded, besides Heth, A. G. Jenkins and Jerome B. Robertson, already mentioned, were G. T. Anderson, John M. Jones and Alfred M. Scales. It should be remembered, also, that Semmes and Pender survived until they were South of the Potomac, though they are numbered here with the killed.

These eleven men would have been an excessive price to pay for a victory. As the toll of leadership in a lost battle, the casualties probably were appraised correctly by a Britisher who had accompanied A. P. Hill's Division in the operations from Fredericksburg through Gettysburg. In warmest terms he lauded the offensive prowess of the Confederate troops, "but," said he, "they will never do it again." He named the officers of his acquaintance who had fallen during the months he had been with the Second Corps—Gregg, Paxton, Jackson and Pender—and he asked: "Don't you see your system feeds upon itself? You cannot fill the places of these men. Your men do wonders, but every time at a cost you cannot afford." [5]

The excellence of the fallen leaders was the subject of many a letter to their kin, many an article in the newspapers. Until the day of the great charge at Gettysburg, Lewis Armistead never had such an hour as came to him at Malvern Hill, but he had been consistently a good officer. When the time came on July 3 for his Brigade to go forward, he cried, "Rise, men!" Then in a voice heard far down the line, he said: "Men, remember what you are fighting for—your homes, your firesides, and your sweethearts. Follow me!" [6] Always their leader, he kept 50 yards in front of them as they went forward.[7] At the stone wall he was among the first to leap over.[8] Beyond it he fell.[9]

William Barksdale, though not professionally trained to arms, had proved his mettle at Fredericksburg in the battle of the pontoons, and he died where he would have chosen—in battle at the head of his men.[10] "Dick" Garnett had won the affection of all his officers during the months he had commanded a Brigade in Pickett's Division. He had been sick and was almost incapacitated for duty on the 3rd of July, but he insisted on leading the charge of his Brigade, though he had to ride and to offer a target to every marksman.[11] "This is a desperate thing to attempt," he

---

[5] 14 S.H.S.P., 211, with the statement changed to direct quotation.
[6] 2 C. V., 271.                             [7] O. R., 27, pt. 2, p. 1000.
[8] 20 C. V., 379.
[9] Supra, p. 157 ff. An absurd story long circulated that Armistead, while dying, lamented his action in joining the Confederacy. For the facts of the kindness he received at the hands of Gen. W. S. Hancock, while dying, see D. X. Junkin, Life of Hancock, 117–18. See also 10 S.H.S.P., 428; 11 S.H.S.P., 285. Lee's tribute to Armistead appears in O. R., 27, pt. 2, p. 325.
[10] O. R., 27, pt. 2, pp. 310, 325, 359; Miss Brock, 238.
[11] 4 S.H.S.P., 108.

told Armistead, before the advance began, but he acquiesced courageously, if silently, in Armistead's answer: "It is, but the issue is
with the Almighty, and we must leave it in his hands." [12] Of like
spirit was Paul Semmes, whose brother Raphael had made the
name *Alabama* dreaded on every sea-lane of the Atlantic. Semmes
was seriously wounded in the advance of McLaws's Division on
the afternoon of the 2nd [13] and was transported to Virginia in
one of the first ambulances to cross the angry Potomac. He came
to his end on July 10 with the proud assurance, "I consider it a
privilege to die for my country." [14]

Johnston Pettigrew was among the most deplored of the casualties. After Heth was wounded on the 1st of July, Pettigrew had
shown great energy the second day in trying to make good the
losses of the initial onslaught. The North Carolinian ordered all
lightly wounded men, all the cooks and all those on extra duty
to enter the ranks.[15] It was through his efforts that the Division
presented in the charge of the 3rd so many men with bandaged
heads and arms that they were conspicuous from Lee's post of
command.[16] Pettigrew himself received a wound in the hand
during that assault, but he was one of the last to leave the field
after the repulse.[17] When Heth was able to resume command of
his Division, Pettigrew returned to the head of his Brigade and
was directing it on the evening of July 13–14. Shortly before midnight,[18] while Heth was endeavoring to get the rearguard across
the Potomac, a small contingent of Federal cavalry made a mad
attack through some epaulements. In the brief mêlée that ensued,
nearly all the blue troopers were killed or captured, but one of
them inflicted a grievous abdominal wound on Pettigrew.[19]

Medical officers saw immediately that the General's meagre
chance of recovery hung on quiet and care. They proposed to
place him in a nearby barn and to trust him to the Federal surgeons who certainly would use the structure as a hospital. Pettigrew would not consent to this. He would rather die, he said,
than again be taken prisoner. Devoted men accordingly put him
on a litter, carried him across the river and, in steady relays, transported him twenty-two miles to Bunker Hill. On the long, agoniz-

---

[12] 3 *R. E. Lee*, 120. For Garnett's handling of his men and the circumstances of his
death, see *O. R.*, 27, pt. 2, pp. 310, 325, 386, 387; 14 *C. V.*, 81.
[13] *O. R.*, 27, pt. 2, p. 359.          [14] 6 *C. M. H.*, 436.
[15] 2 *N. C. Regts.*, 362.               [16] 5 *N. C. Regts.*, 104.
[17] 2 *N. C. Regts.*, 365, 366.          [18] *O. R.*, 27, pt. 2, p. 640.
[19] *Ibid.*, 640–41; 1 *N. C. Regts.*, 591; 2 *ibid.*, 376–77; 3 *ibid.*, 110; 4 *ibid.*, 559 ff.

ing journey he was the inspiration of his soldiers. "Boys," he said, as he observed their sympathetic distress, "don't be disheartened; maybe I will fool the doctors yet." General Lee bore him company part of the way. Thousands prayed for him. He found shelter in the Boyd home near Bunker Hill and there, July 17, he expired.[20] "The Army," said Lee, "has lost a brave soldier and the Confederacy an accomplished officer."[21] J. C. Haskell, who knew the Carolinian long and well, characterized him more fully: "Pettigrew seemed to have every attribute of a great soldier, uniting with the brightest mind and an active body a disposition which made him the idol of his men, and a courage which nothing could daunt. He was so full of theoretical knowledge that I think it really impaired his usefulness, but experience, which he was getting fast, would have soon corrected that and I believe that few would have had a brighter career."[22] For none who fought so briefly in the Army of Northern Virginia was there more praise while living or more laments when dead.[23]

Curiously similar to Johnston Pettigrew's was the fate of Dorsey Pender. He passed unscathed through the hard fighting of July 1 and, on the afternoon of the 2nd, while Hood and McLaws were attacking on the right, he was sitting with two friends on a granite boulder near the left of his line on Seminary Ridge. His well-knit body was alert, his gray eyes were kindled. Everything about him bespoke courage, agility and endurance.[24] As he talked with his comrades, the Federal fire spread furiously along the front. "Major," said Pender to Joseph Engelhard, "this indicates an assault, and we will ride down our line."[25] The two went off together. Near the right of the divisional front, not long before sunset,[26] Pender was struck on the leg by a fragment of shell, about two inches square.[27] The wound manifestly was serious,

20 2 N. C. Regts., 376–77.

21 O. R., 27, pt. 3, p. 1016. For Longstreet's tribute, see ibid., pt. 2, p. 362; for Heth's, ibid., 638–39, 641. Lieut. Col. S. G. Shepard, who headed the remnant of Archer's Brigade while it was under Pettigrew's direction, praised him in ibid., 648.

22 J. C. Haskell's MS Rems., 72.

23 Because of Pettigrew's short connection with the Army, he has not been sketched in detail. The following references will supplement those in O. R., and D. A. B.: Richmond Whig (from Charleston Courier) June 7, Aug. 23, 1862; Richmond Dispatch, Apr. 24, 26, May 2, 3, July 2, Aug. 8, 1861; June 19, Aug. 7, 1862; Mrs. Chesnut, 145, 173. Interesting notes on some of his early associates appear in 4 N. C. Regts., 562 n and Grimes, 127. A fine letter, readily overlooked, will be found in O. R., 51, pt. 2, p. 712.

24 1 N. C. Regts., 764–65.

25 W. A. Montgomery, Life and Character of Maj. Gen. W. D. Pender, 20–21; W. C. Lee to Donald Gilliam, MS, Oct. 21, 1893—Pender MSS.; O. R., 27, pt. 2, p. 658.

26 Cf. O. R., 27, pt. 2, p. 665.

27 Letter of L. G. Lewis, MS, Oct. 21, 1893—Pender MSS.

but Pender had been hit so often that he could not believe this injury mortal.[28] Regretfully he turned over the command to James H. Lane and undertook in an ambulance the long and miserable journey across the Potomac. At length he reached Staunton, Virginia, but by that time infection had spread. Amputation became necessary on July 18. Although he never rallied from the operation,[29] he looked squarely at his last enemy: "Tell my wife I do not fear to die. I can confidently resign my soul to God, trusting in the atonement of our Lord Jesus Christ. My only regret is to leave her and our children. I have always tried to do my duty in every sphere of life in which Providence has placed me." [30]

Pender's death deepened the disappointments of Gettysburg. Said Lee: "He served with this Army from the beginning of the war, and took a distinguished part in all its engagements. Wounded on several occasions, he never left his command in action until he received the injury that resulted in his death. His promise and usefulness as an officer were only equaled by the purity and excellence of his private life." [31] Privately, the commanding General was quoted as saying that Pender was the most promising of the younger officers of the Army.[32] An even higher tribute Lee paid Pender the next autumn when the death of John B. Hood in the Battle of Chickamauga erroneously was reported. Lee wrote the President: "I am gradually losing my best men—Jackson, Pender, Hood." [33]

Hood himself had been hit in the arm by a shrapnel shot while he was mounted and in the act of turning to give a command. The bullet must have struck a nerve because Hood fell from his horse "utterly prostrated and almost fainting." Although the wound did not appear to be serious, Hood realized that he could not keep the field and he called immediately for his senior Brigadier, E. M. Law, and for his surgeon.[34] He was so dazed that when he reached the field hospital in a school, he scarcely observed the bursting of

[28] Letter of J. G. Field, n. d.—Pender MSS.
[29] Lewis letter, loc. cit.                    [30] Montgomery, op. cit., 22.
[31] O. R., 27, pt. 2, p. 325.
[32] Letter of Gen. G. C. Wharton, MS, Sept. 5, 1893—Pender MSS.
[33] O. R., 29, pt. 2, p. 743. For Hill's tribute to Pender, see O. R., 27, pt. 2, p. 608. In addition, Hill is said to have declared Pender the best officer of like rank he ever had known. Gen. A. M. Scales, successor in command of Pender's Brigade, remarked of his chief: "The higher [Pender's] promotion, the better fitted he seemed for his position." (40 S.H.S.P., 214).
[34] J. C. Haskell's MS Rems., 63; O. R., 27, pt. 2, pp. 320. 359.

a shell almost in his face.[35] At first there was fear he would lose the arm,[36] but by July 15, when he was in Virginia, safe in a Charlottesville hospital, his comrade Wade Hampton was able to write: "He is doing well, and his arm will be saved. All he needs now is good nursing, together with cheerful company and generous living. . . ."[37] Although Hood's wounded arm was never again to have its full strength,[38] he was not to be counted with the dead or with the invalided.[39]

Nor was Hampton, though his wounds, too, were severe. He had to admit that much: ". . . I have been handled pretty roughly, having received two sabre cuts on the head—one of which cut through the table of my skull—and a shrapnel shot in my body, which is there yet. But I am doing well and hope in a few days to be able to go home."[40] In the background was an unpleasant clash with Fitz Lee, who impetuously ordered a charge in the absence of Hampton during the afternoon of July 3. Hampton's report[41] was a disavowal of responsibility for an action fought contrary to the plans he had made.[42]

If Hampton and Hood could be regarded as temporarily absent while nursing their wounds, the fate of Isaac Trimble was uncertain. In the charge on the afternoon of the 3rd, he fell with another leg wound, one so severe that amputation was necessary. As his condition did not permit his removal with the Army, he had to be left in the hands of enemies, some of whom had for him a vindictive hate as an alleged "bridge burner" of 1861 and a "dangerous man."[43] None could say when, if ever, he would resume his command. The same was true of J. J. Archer, though he had fewer personal enemies than Trimble delighted to count. James L. Kemper, a badly wounded Virginian, might hope for early exchange if he survived his injury. The remaining six general officers who had been struck during the battle would be back on duty before many weeks.[44]

Field officers had been slaughtered. Seven of the nine Colonels,

[35] 5 C. V., 552.                         [36] Southern Generals, 387.
[37] Mrs. Wright, 142. Cf. Mrs. Chestnut, 229–30.
[38] Southern Generals, loc. cit.
[39] The sketch of Hood is resumed infra, p. 225.
[40] To Senator Louis T. Wigfall, July 15, 1863; Mrs. Wright, 143. Cf. ibid., 148 and O. R., 27, pt. 2, p. 322.
[41] O. R., 27, pt. 2, p. 725.                  [42] For the details, see infra, p. 210.
[43] O. R., 27, pt. 2, pp. 321, 362, 608, 659; ibid., pt. 3, p. 646.
[44] They were, to repeat, Harry Heth, who was hors de combat for a few days only, A. M. Scales, A. G. Jenkins, J. B. Robertson, G. T. Anderson and John M. Jones.

Lieutenant Colonels and Majors of Davis's Brigade were killed or wounded in the first day's battle;[45] every field officer of Scales's Brigade, save one, had fallen in that action along with their General.[46] Four of Cadmus Wilcox's Colonels were wounded on the 2nd.[47] When the charge of July 3 ended, Archer's Brigade had only two unwounded field officers with the troops, Pettigrew had one, Davis had none.[48] Regimental command of Pickett's Division virtually was destroyed. Five of the Colonels were killed,[49] two were mortally wounded, and five received injuries from which they recovered. Among the slain Colonels of the Division were three—Lewis Williams, Robert C. Allen and W. Tazewell Patton —who had been room-mates at V. M. I., had been graduated the same day, had been lawyers before the war and had all been chosen to command Virginia regiments.[50] In the same Division three Lieutenant Colonels were killed; four others, commanding regiments, were wounded. Of all the field officers in the fifteen regiments of Pickett's men, one only, Lieut. Col. Jos. C. Cabell, escaped unhurt.[51]

In the aggregate, eleven, at least, of the Army's Colonels were killed or mortally wounded. In addition, seven Colonels fell into the hands of the enemy. Most of them were wounded. The number may have been even higher.[52] Several of these were men almost mature enough for the permanent command of Brigades.[53] Losses among the Lieutenant Colonels and Majors were equally high. Many regiments marched back to Virginia under Captains.

45 O. R., 27, pt. 2, pp. 649–50.          46 Ibid., 658, 660.
47 Ibid., 619.                            48 O. R., 27, pt. 2, p. 651.
49 The number usually is given as six, but John C. Owens of the Ninth Virginia, counted as a Colonel, actually was a Major, though the senior regimental officer present (O. R., 27, pt. 2,· p. 284).
50 20 S.H.S.P., 308; Memorial V. M. I., 26, 425, 535.
51 37 S.H.S.P., 193.
52 Doubt has to be admitted because the reports of many Brigades never were filed. Colonels known to have been killed or mortally wounded were: R. C. Allen, Twenty-eighth Virginia; I. E. Avery, Sixth North Carolina; D. H. Christie, Twenty-third North Carolina; W. D. DeSaussure, Fifteenth South Carolina; E. C. Edmonds, Thirty-eighth Virginia; James G. Hodges, Fourteenth Virginia; John Bowie Magruder, Fifty-seventh Virginia; W. T. Patton, Seventh Virginia; W. D. Stuart, Fifty-sixth Virginia; Joseph Wasden, Twenty-second Georgia; Lewis B. Williams, First Virginia. The captured Colonels suffering from wounds were: P. S. Evans, Sixty-third North Carolina; B. D. Fry, Thirteenth Alabama; W. H. Forney, Tenth Alabama; William Gibson, Forty-eighth Georgia; J. K. Marshall, Fifty-second North Carolina, and R. M. Powell, Fifth Texas. The well-known Colonel of the Twelfth Virginia Cavalry, A. W. Harman, had not been at Gettysburg, because of a wound sustained at Brandy (O. R., 27, pt. 2, p. 767), but he was captured on July 14 near Bolivar Heights, while the Army was returning to Virginia (O. R., 27, pt. 2, pp. 705–06).
53 For a sketch of John Bowie Magruder, see 27 S.H.S.P., 205 ff and (by the same author) W. H. Stewart, A Pair of Blankets, 102 ff. A sketch of Col. James G. Hodges will be found in 37 S.H.S.P., 184 ff.

Garnett's Brigade was commanded by a Major,[54] "Tige" Anderson's[55] and James Archer's[56] were in the care of Lieutenant Colonels.[57] Some of these losses never were made good. As late as the autumn of 1864, regiments of the First Corps were suffering in discipline because so many field officers had been wounded and left on the field at Gettysburg.[58]

Among the junior officers who fell, Joseph W. Latimer was much mourned. He was in his second year at V. M. I. when hostilities began, but he went with the corps to Richmond, soon received commission as Lieutenant of Artillery and, during the First Battle of Winchester, won the admiration of "Dick" Ewell for intrepidity. It pleased "Old Bald Head" to style Latimer his "Young Napoleon" and to give the boy all opportunity. At Gettysburg, though not 21, Major Latimer handled Snowden Andrews's guns with daring and persistence. His wound, which was received while one of the last rounds was being fired in the unequal duel,[59] did not prove fatal till he returned to Virginia. Praise for him ran through the reports of the Second Corps.[60] Those who knew the younger artillerists ranked Latimer with Pegram and with Pelham.[61]

The task of replacing some of these dead officers was past performance. In the first few days after the battle, Lee did not even attempt it. The instant work was that of holding together the commands that had been decimated or had been disorganized by the loss of senior officers. Orders came promptly for Pickett's Division to serve as Provost Guard and to take charge of the prisoners bound for Virginia; but the threat of an attack by Federals necessitated the speedy return of the survivors to the line. When Pickett expressed the disappointment of officers at this resumption of field duty, Lee had to say: "I need not tell you how essential it is not to diminish this army by a single man . . ."[62] Pickett himself had been considered as temporary commander of Hood's Division but, at his own request, he was allowed to remain with his own shattered regiments.[63] Pender's men were united for

[54] C. S. Peyton, Nineteenth Virginia. See O. R., 27, pt. 2, pp. 284, 385.
[55] Ibid., 285.      [56] Ibid., 289.
[57] William Luffman and S. G. Shepard.      [58] Sorrel, 270.
[59] See supra, p. 130 ff.      [60] O. R., 27, pt. 2, pp. 446, 505, 544.
[61] See J. C. Wise, The Long Arm of Lee (cited hereafter as Wise), v. 2, p. 653; Memorial V. M. I., 328 ff.
[62] O. R., 27, pt. 3, p. 986. Cf. ibid., 983, 987; Walter Harrison, 105 ff.
[63] Walter Harrison, loc. cit.

the time with Heth's Division, though in a few days the return of stragglers and convalescents so swelled the ranks that the two commands were separated.[64] Iverson conveniently was made temporary Provost Marshal. His Brigade was "attached"—a humiliating word!—to that of Ramseur. The few files that had been Archer's regiments were "attached" similarly to Pettigrew's until the death of the North Carolinian. Then they were joined tentatively with Field's Brigade, which Colonel Brockenbrough and then Colonel Mayo had led.[65] It was apparent, also, that Joseph Davis's remnant should be consolidated with some other Brigade, especially as Davis had contracted fever and might face long absence from his command; but in this case Lee had to step lightly lest he offend the President, Davis's uncle.[66]

After the Army rested a few days in Virginia, and the uncertainty regarding the fate of some of the missing officers was removed, a Major General had to be named in succession to Dorsey Pender. It was not necessary to select another officer of like rank to take the place of Isaac Trimble because he might be exchanged, when recovered, and was without a Division anyway. New Brigadiers had to be found, if possible, to take the place of Paul Semmes, of William Barksdale, of Lewis Armistead, of "Dick" Garnett and of Johnston Pettigrew. Decision might wait, for a time, as respected James Archer and James Kemper, both of them prisoners of war. In "Extra Billy" Smith's place a competent man was imperative. Otherwise a once-splendid Brigade would be ruined. That made six Brigadiers. As it was manifest that O'Neal could not succeed to Rodes's old Brigade, a seventh Brigadier was needed there. If an eighth could be found, Alfred Iverson might be given some other permanent duty. One Division commander, then, and at least eight new Brigadiers were needed.

An appraisal of the Colonels who had marched to Gettysburg might have shown that some who had not been ready for promotion in May had been developed by responsibility; but several of the ablest and bravest of those Colonels were dead. Scrutiny of the record of those who had passed through the red fury of the battles of July showed four infantrymen only who could be promoted confidently and at once. One of these was Eppa Hunton, Colonel of the Eighth Virginia, Garnett's Brigade, Pickett's Divi-

[64] O. R., 27, pt. 2, p. 667; ibid., pt. 3, pp. 1048–49.
[65] O. R., 27, pt. 2, pp. 993–94, 1048–49.   [66] Cf. O. R., 27, pt. 3, pp. 1030, 1049.

sion. Hunton, in his fortieth year and by profession a lawyer, had been in the service since the outbreak of hostilities and, after Sharpsburg, had been recommended by the other Colonels of the Brigade as a successor to Pickett, in preference to Garnett, when Pickett was promoted.[67] Now the advancement earned by Hunton could be given him without conflict or embarrassment. As of August 3, he was appointed and was assigned promptly to Garnett's Brigade.[68]

Another automatic promotion, so to say, was that of Benjamin G. Humphreys, Colonel of the Twenty-first Mississippi, Barksdale's Brigade, McLaws's Division. Humphreys had been Barksdale's mainstay and had been well tested. He was 54 and therefore among the older Colonels, but he had spent more than a year at West Point before he and other cadets had been dismissed for pranks on Christmas Eve, 1826. As a planter and lawmaker he had shown capacity. His army record was clean. Promotion, which was as logical as it had been long delayed, was awarded him August 14.[69]

In Rodes's old Brigade, once O'Neal was passed by, the man qualified for promotion by his fine conduct at Gettysburg was Col. Cullen A. Battle of the Third Alabama. He and his regiment had been detached from O'Neal's Brigade before the advance on the afternoon of July 1, for reasons differently explained by Rodes and by O'Neal.[70] At the crisis of the fighting, Battle had joined Ramseur and had fought fiercely. Rodes did not commend Battle in his report, presumably because he thought the Colonel had played a lone hand; but Ramseur said: "Colonel Battle . . . rendered brilliant and invaluable service. Attaching his regiment to my command on his own responsibility, he came in at the right place, at the right time, and in the right way." [71] Battle's previous record being on parity with his furious advance on Seminary Ridge, he was promoted Brigadier General on August 25 [72]—a vigorous, hard-hitting man of 38, a lawyer and a politician but able and self-taught in the school of war.[73]

[67] See Vol. II, p. 267.
[68] Wright, 109. Hunton's privately printed Autobiography is cited several times in these pages. An acceptable sketch of him will be found in 3 C. M. H., 603 ff.
[69] Wright, 103. Humphreys, who had a post bellum career of distinction, is sketched in D. A. B. and also in 7 C. M. H., Miss., 259.
[70] See supra, pp. 83-84.
[71] O. R., 27, pt. 2, p. 587.
[72] To rank from August 20, 1863. Wright, 110.
[73] He is sketched in D. A. B. and in 7 C. M. H., Ala., 388 ff.

The only other senior Colonel who could be advanced to fill an existing vacancy was Goode Bryan of the Sixteenth Georgia. In his case the vacancy was not in his own Brigade, Wofford's, but in that of another Georgia Brigade, Paul Semmes's of the same Division, McLaws's. A year before, there might have been a bitter protest that the commanding General "went outside" the Brigade to name a successor to a Brigadier; but if there was any complaint over the advancement of Bryan, it does not appear in the records. The reason undoubtedly was the fact that Bryan was a graduate of West Point, and was accounted a regular, though his service in the "old army" had been brief.[74] As far as Lee could, he applied the rule that professional soldiers could be appointed to command without consideration of the State of their birth and without regard to seniority except as among themselves. This rule never was formulated legally but it often was invoked. In Bryan's case there was the additional, though not the compelling, consideration that he was a veteran of the war with Mexico.[75]

When these four—Hunton, Humphreys, Battle and Bryan—were named, the list of eligibles was exhausted. Several Colonels of late commission were abler soldiers than the ranking field officers of their Brigades, perhaps, but law and regulations forbade their promotion over their seniors. Again, it might be assumed, optimistically, that future battles of the Army would show merit that had not previously been displayed. Some captured officers might be exchanged. Wounded veterans might be returned. Decision undoubtedly would be reached in some instances where promotion was delayed. Until one or another of these things happened, the grim truth was written on the army roster in the list of vacancies at the head of Brigades. As of August 31, two of Pickett's Brigades, two of Hood's,[76] one of Rodes's, one of "Dick" Anderson's, and two of Heth's,[77] a total of eight infantry Brigades, were without permanent commanders of appropriate rank.[78]

The measure of the Army's need of commanders, exhibited by

[74] No. 25 in the class of 1834, resigned Apr. 30, 1835. *Cullum* No. 774.
[75] Major of the First Alabama Volunteers. *Cullum*, loc. cit.
[76] One of these vacancies existed because Brig. Gen. E. M. Law was acting divisional commander.
[77] Of these, one was in Archer's Brigade which temporarily was consolidated with Brockenbrough's or Field's.
[78] *O. R.*, 29, pt. 2, p. 682 ff. Not counted are those Brigades listed under Colonels who had received promotion but, for one reason or another, had not assumed their new rank. Omitted, also, are those instances in which Colonels were commanding Brigades during the absence on leave or during the sickness of the regular Brigadiers.

these figures, was illustrated by the swift advancement of Henry Harrison Walker, a West Pointer of the class of 1853, who was known to his comrades as "Mud." [79] He had been a First Lieutenant of the Sixth Infantry when he had resigned to join the Confederacy. At Gaines' Mill, while serving as Lieutenant Colonel of the Fortieth Virginia, he had been twice wounded. His brigade commander, Charles W. Field, had described him as a "most gallant and meritorious officer" [80] but he was not well known in the Army. After a long illness he had assumed direction of a convalescents' camp. From this, he was called while the Army was in Pennsylvania, and, on July 1, he was commissioned Brigadier General. Sent immediately to Lee, he was given charge temporarily of two Brigades, Archer's and Field's. Then he was assigned permanently to the command of Field's, the Brigade with which he was serving when wounded. [81]

The case of Alfred Iverson was handled in the most considerate manner. There must have been clamor against him in his North Carolina Brigade and a demand for the appointment of a native of the State. When Iverson had discharged his duties as Provost Marshal at Williamsport, he was transferred for a time to Nicholls's Brigade, Johnson's Division. [82] Later in the year, Iverson quietly was ordered to Georgia to organize the cavalry there. [83] The choice of his successor and the problem of morale among the North Carolina troops are part of another chapter in the history of the army command. So is the story of various interesting promotions in the cavalry.

If some of the brigade vacancies had to be left because no qualified senior Colonels were available to fill them, there could be no temporizing with the command of Pender's Division. None of the Brigadiers of the Division was available. McGowan was absent, wounded; James H. Lane and Alfred Scales were recent appointees; Edward L. Thomas was a capable officer, but as he commanded the Georgia unit in a Division that included two North Carolina Brigades and one South Carolina Brigade, his advancement, said Lee, might "create dissatisfaction." [84] Trimble,

[79] No. 41 in his class; Cullum No. 1620.
[80] O. R., 11, pt. 2, p. 842.
[81] O. R., 27, pt. 3, pp. 998, 1061; 3 C. M. H., 675; Wright, 107.
[82] O. R., 27, pt. 3, pp. 993, 1016, 1025; O. R., 29, pt. 2, pp. 706, 723–24.
[83] O. R., 29, pt. 2, pp. 771–72, 775; O. R., 51, pt. 2, p. 772.
[84] Lee's Dispatches, 115–16.

who would have served admirably, was wounded and a prisoner. One or another of the excellent young cavalrymen or artillerists might have been almost as vigorous as Pender, but the line between the infantry and the other arms was so sharply drawn that promotion from one to the other was rare and provocative of discontent.

In the eyes of Lee, the best man available for the vacancy was Cadmus Wilcox, who was recommended on August 1, a fortnight after Pender died of his wound. Lee wrote: "General Wilcox is one of the oldest brigadiers in the service, a highly capable officer, has served from the commencement of the war and deserves promotion. Being an officer of the regular army he is properly assignable anywhere." [85] Davis's acceptance of the recommendation was prompt and unqualified. On August 13, Wilcox was appointed Major General.[86] Among his associates the choice was a popular one. Every officer of rank knew of Wilcox's fight at Salem Church.[87] Some doubtless felt that he should have been promoted immediately after that battle. If there was any grumbling among the Carolinians and the Georgians of Pender's Division, the records captured no echo of it.

Wilcox, it will be remembered, now was 39 years of age and had been in the military service for twenty-one years as cadet and as officer in the United States and the Confederate armies. There scarcely had been a break in the routine of duty from the time he was 18. The result was the imposition, so to speak, on a kindly, generous, friendly nature of a military exactness of speech, of manner and of action. When Colonel Fremantle's *Three Months in the Southern States* appeared, Wilcox was represented as coming to Lee after Pickett's charge to "explain, almost crying, the state of his brigade." [88] This did not suit Wilcox. He or some friend took care to see, in one of the earliest collection of Confederate biographical sketches, that his proper statement to the commanding General was given. It was "that he did not like to make a disagreeable report, but that there was no protection to the great number of batteries on the Emmitsburg Road, but his single Brigade, which was very much reduced in numbers." [89]

That was Wilcox—off duty, genial and informal, on duty

[85] *Lee's Dispatches*, 116.
[86] *Wright*, 35; to rank from Aug. 3, 1863.
[87] See Vol. II, p. 619 ff.     [88] *Op. cit.*, 269.
[89] *Companions in Arms*, 504.

precise and insistent on precision. When he was outdone in his regard for the professional amenities, he had the grace to laugh at the incident and at himself. En route to Gettysburg, Wilcox directed that none of his men leave camp to forage for fruit or even for a pair of chickens that patriotically wished to give themselves to the Confederate cause. These instructions were prompted both by Lee's own order to respect private property and by Wilcox's belief that if any of his men wandered off they would fall into the hands of lurking militia. In plain violation of all warnings and orders, Wilcox caught Private Pat Martin near headquarters with a handsome string of chickens. Pat was small and young and had been assigned to drive the headquarters wagon because of his tender years and immaturity. If, now, Pat was old enough to go foraging, he was old enough to take his place in the line of battle. So reasoning, Wilcox reprimanded the boy and sent him back to his regiment. The next sight the General had of the forager was at the most furious stage of the battle of July 2. Wilcox was under heavy fire. One courier had been killed, another had a bloody wound. The General's bridle rein had been cut by a bullet; his horse was rearing. In this confusion, with shells bursting everywhere, Pat appeared with a file of men whom he promptly ordered into line to face Wilcox. Smartly the boy saluted. "Here are your chickens, sir," he said. They were sixteen Federal prisoners he was conducting to the rear.[90]

If Wilcox did not laugh then, he did afterward and, as always, in a manner to make friends. He might not rise above the rank of Major General; he might not be brilliant as a divisional chief; but he had earned that promotion at Salem Church. In all the Army's battles he had been dependable and by every campfire he had been the gentleman.[91]

Such was the reorganization of the infantry. The words that most nearly describe it, incomplete reorganization, partial reorganization, were the grimmest of all proofs that attrition of command now exceeded renewal through the school of experience. Circumstance emphasized this. By one of the curious tricks of ironic time, the Army of Northern Virginia recrossed the Potomac one year to the very day from the date of Jackson's movement toward Gordonsville after the battles around Richmond. On July

[90] *Ibid.*, 505.                    [91] His sketch is continued *infra*, p. 351 ff.

13-14, 1862, the great offensive in the direction of the enemy's country was beginning; now it was ending. How many leaders had fallen, how many changes had come since Lee, at the close of the Seven Days, had cast off the incompetents and had chosen the promising men for promotion! Run the eye down the roster of the Army as it marched toward Second Manassas and as it came wearily back from Gettysburg to a lean and hungry land:

Of Longstreet's former "Right Wing," the commander now was Lieutenant General and next in rank to Lee.

Anderson's Division: Armistead, dead; Mahone and Wright on duty with the Army.

McLaws's Division:[92] Its commander still on duty; Kershaw, present; Howell Cobb, transferred; Semmes, dead; Barksdale, dead.

David Jones's Division: The Division no longer in existence; Jones, dead; Toombs, resigned; Drayton, sent elsewhere; "Tige" Anderson, wounded.

Longstreet's own Division: Wilcox, promoted; Pryor, deprived of troops; Featherston, transferred; Kemper, wounded and a prisoner; Micah Jenkins, detached; Pickett, promoted.

Whiting's Division: Its commander on coast defense duty at Wilmington; Hood, promoted but wounded; Law, with his Brigade; "Shanks" Evans, back in the Carolinas.

Of Jackson's "Left Wing," the great commander dead.

Jackson's own Division: Winder, dead; Taliaferro, on other duty; Col. W. S. H. Baylor, dead; Starke, dead.

Powell Hill's Division: Its leader a Lieutenant General. His Brigadiers: Branch, dead; Pender, dead; Gregg, dead; Archer, captured; Field, still incapacitated; Thomas, with the troops.

Harvey Hill's Division:[93] Its commander transferred to North Carolina; Ripley, returned to South Carolina; Rodes, promoted; Garland, dead; George B. Anderson, dead; Colquitt, sent elsewhere.

Ewell's Division: Maimed "Dick" Ewell, corps commander; Lawton, transferred; his senior Colonel and virtual successor Marcellus Douglass, dead; Trimble, twice wounded and now a

---

[92] McLaws, it will be remembered, did not rejoin the Army until the Second Manassas had been fought.

[93] Strictly speaking, not with the forces that moved to Second Manassas in August, 1862.

prisoner, though promoted; Jube Early, a Major General; Harry Hays, at his usual post.

In short, of the general officers of infantry, serving with the Army July 15, 1862, or thereabouts, one had died of disease and ten of wounds. In addition, Tom Cobb and Franklin Paxton had been promoted after the beginning of the offensive in July, 1862, and had been killed before the advance into Pennsylvania. "Dick" Garnett had been returned to command and had been numbered among the dead. More surprising, because effected quietly, were the ten transfers and two resignations.[94] Of these twelve changes, nine and possibly ten had been welcome to the commanding General because the men had been found incompetent or mediocre or troublesome. Two other general officers, promoted or assigned after the campaign of Second Manassas, had been tried and found wanting.[95] One had left the Army under charges. Still another, Francis Nicholls, probably had been incapacitated permanently for duty in the field.

For the Army that stubbornly took up, July 14, 1863, the task of defending Virginia with thinned ranks, the result of twelve months' battles was this organization: Six of the nine infantry Divisions were under officers who had not commanded them, or the corresponding forces, in July, 1862.[96] Five—five only—of the thirty-eight infantry Brigades were led by men who had held the rank of Brigadier General twelve months previously.[97] The surviving commanders of Gettysburg were, by comparison with those of July, 1862, a new Army without a Jackson. Lee's words of May, after the death of "Stonewall," had grayer, sombre meaning: "We must all do more than formerly."

[94] Besides Toombs, it is here considered that William Smith resigned though his final resignation was of his commission as Major General, which he held without assignment of troops from Aug. 13 to Dec. 31, 1863. General Early noted (*O. R.*, 27, pt. 2, p. 472) that Smith tendered on July 10 his resignation as Brigadier General and received leave of absence.

[95] Iverson and Colston.

[96] Hood is counted with McLaws and Anderson because he was in actual command of a demi-Division late in July, 1862, though not then a Major General.

[97] Namely, J. B. Kershaw, Geo. H. Steuart, C. M. Wilcox, A. R. Wright, William Mahone. In this list Wilcox is included because, on July 14, 1863, he had not been appointed a Major General. Harry Hays narrowly missed inclusion. His appointment was dated July 25, 1862 (*Wright*, 86).

# CHAPTER XI

## The Cavalry Are Reshuffled

THE REORGANIZATION made necessary by the losses at Gettysburg was accomplished, in part, during a series of interesting but not particularly instructive maneuvers. By the 3rd of August, all the Confederate infantry were South of the Rapidan on either side of the Orange and Alexandria Railroad.[1] This withdrawal, as always, was covered by the cavalry. Their absence during the Pennsylvania campaign had been much discussed. Among those officers who realized how the Army had groped in the dark while Stuart was riding to the Susequehanna, there was disappointment over his conduct "and a disposition to hold him strictly to account." [2] Stuart himself did not indicate, either by word or by bearing, that he thought his role discreditable or his service inconsiderable. "My cavalry," he wrote his wife, "has nobly sustained its reputation, and done better and harder fighting than it ever has since the war." [3] He was slow to write his report. Several times he had to be prodded before he filed the lengthy paper with Col. Charles Marshall, who usually prepared the first draft of General Lee's official accounts of operations.[4]

Stuart's narrative was detailed but was less flamboyant than usual.[5] Near the close of the document its author sought to vindicate on five grounds the entire course of his operations in Pennsylvania: He had put Washington on the defensive; the "overweening" Federal cavalry he had drawn "from its aggressive attitude toward our flank near Williamsport and Hagerstown"; he had occupied the VI Corps and had prevented its earlier arrival at Gettysburg; the march of Meade had been delayed; Confederate trains had been more readily secured than if they had been de-

[1] This operation can be followed conveniently in Meade's frequent reports, *O. R.*, 27, pt. 1, p. 95 ff, in 2 *Meade*, 136, and in Lee's report, *O. R.*, 27, pt. 2, p. 324. Day-by-day Confederate correspondence, which explains the minor phases of the withdrawal, is in *ibid.*, pt. 3, p. 1024 ff. Some facts of interest will be found in *Early*, 284–85.
[2] Col. D. G. McIntosh in 37 *S.H.S.P.*, 94.
[3] July 10, 1863. He added: "Pray, without ceasing, that God will grant us the victory." (8 *S.H.S.P.*, 455).
[4] *Marshall*, 214–15.
[5] It is dated Aug. 20, 1863, and is to be found in *O. R.*, 27, pt. 2, p. 687.

fended directly by Stuart's force, which would not have sufficed to guard all the mountain passes.

To the charge that he should have been in front of the Army on July 1, Stuart replied in his report that Jenkins's men had been selected as the advance guard of the Army and numerically were adequate for the mission. If, said Stuart, "the peculiar functions of the cavalry with the army were not satisfactorily performed in the absence of my command, it should rather be attributed to the fact that Jenkins' brigade was not as efficient as it ought to have been, and as its numbers (3800) on leaving Virginia warranted us in expecting."[6] Against the criticism that he should not have gone to York, Stuart defended himself with the argument that he had expected Early to be there. The route the cavalry followed to York, he said, was quite as direct as the alternative line of advance and was more expeditious. Besides, Early should have left word of his movements when he marched from York.[7]

When Stuart deposited this report at Army Headquarters, he tried to get Marshall to say that the conduct of the cavalry had been justified. Marshall, who had his draft of Stuart's orders to defend, at once replied that it would have been better if Stuart had "obeyed orders" and had been at hand to give information of the movements of the enemy. In an argument that followed, Marshall thought that he scored in prevailing upon Stuart to admit that the movement of the cavalry had not been under Lee's orders but at the discretion of its commander.[8]

Marshall proceeded to use Stuart's report in preparing that of Lee. In the draft of the general report submitted for Lee's approval, Marshall wrote that Stuart had disobeyed orders in crossing the Potomac where he did. Much of the responsibility for the failure in Pennsylvania was placed by Marshall on Stuart's shoulders. Lee would not accept this part of Marshall's draft. The commanding General did not question the record as Marshall presented it, but he said he could not adopt Marshall's conclusions, or charge Stuart with the facts as Marshall stated them, unless the full truth were disclosed by a court martial.[9]

In the final text of Lee's report, the statement was made that

[6] Stuart much exaggerated the strength of Jenkins.
[7] *O. R.*, 27, pt. 2, p. 708.                [8] *Marshall*, 215–16.
[9] This is Col. D. G. McIntosh's recollection (37 *S.H.S.P.*, 94–95) of a statement made to him and others after the war by Colonel Marshall. There is no reason to doubt its substantial accuracy. Marshall apparently did not challenge Stuart's overstatement of the size of Jenkins's Brigade.

Stuart's crossing of the Potomac between the Federal Army and Washington was "in the exercise of the discretion given him." [10] With equal candor, Lee recorded that Stuart was "instructed to lose no time in placing his command on the right of our column as soon as he should perceive the enemy moving northward." [11] Lee wrote further: "The movements of the army preceding the battle of Gettysburg had been much embarrassed by the absence of the cavalry." [12] This was the measure of official criticism visited on Stuart.[13] The full measure of historical criticism did not come in time to hurt his pride, though it impaired his fame.[14] "Stuart was innocent of most of the charges made against him, but he disregarded his principal mission of moving to the right flank of Ewell." Orders were violated by Stuart when he encountered material "hindrance" and did not turn back. Lee had cherished the hope that "Jeb" could attack Hooker's trains and hamper the Federal operations, but the commanding General did not authorize or expect any such long raid as Stuart made.[16] "Jeb's" worst shortcoming, ignored at the time, was his absence on the morning of July 2 when adoption of a sound battle-plan depended on careful reconnaissance of the Federal left.

If Stuart felt himself aggrieved because he could not win acceptance of his view of the Gettysburg campaign, he did not pour his complaint into the ear of anyone except Marshall, who recorded his observations. Outwardly, Stuart was busy with a reorganization of his forces. The task was different this time. Imboden had angered Lee greatly by remaining at Hancock.[16] Jenkins's men had shown their inexperience in fighting of the sort familiar to the veteran troopers of "Jeb's" command. Beverley Robertson had been slow in moving from the positions he had been left to defend in the Blue Ridge of Virginia. Not until July 3 did he join Lee.[17] During the retreat from Pennsylvania, Robertson had aroused Stuart's wrath by not holding a pass entrusted to him.[18] In con-

[10] O. R., 27, pt. 2, p. 321.
[11] Ibid., 316.                              [12] Ibid., 321.
[13] For evidence of Lee's continuing confidence in him, immediately after Gettysburg, see the instructions for recrossing the Potomac: ". . . I rely upon your good judgment, energy, and boldness . . . and trust you may be as successful as you have been on former occasions" (O. R., 27, pt. 3, p. 1001).
[14] The fullest defense of Stuart, a defense carried beyond sound argument, is that of John S. Mosby, Stuart's Cavalry in the Gettysburg Campaign.
[15] This is the conclusion reached in 3 R. E. Lee, 547 ff after a review of the evidence.
[16] See supra, p. 48.                        [17] O. R., 27, pt. 2, p. 322.
[18] Ibid., 700.

trast, all the Brigadiers who had accompanied Stuart had done admirably. The embarrassment of the cavalry command was not lack of ability but the abundance of it. Calbraith Butler, Williams Wickham, Tom Rosser, Pierce Young, Lawrence Baker—all these Colonels deserved promotion. Lunsford L. Lomax, a West Pointer of the class of 1856 and a former officer in East Tennessee, had been brought back to Virginia, probably at the instance of Fitz Lee, and had been assigned to the Eleventh Virginia as Colonel.[19] He evidently was of the material of higher command.

When "Jeb" decided to get men promoted he usually found a way. It may have been at his instance that General Lee had discussed with the President in the spring of 1863 a new organization of the cavalry. Now Stuart convinced the commanding General that the existing Brigades were too large. Fitz Lee had five regiments and one battalion, "Rooney" Lee's substitute five regiments, Hampton three regiments and three "legions"; Jones commanded four regiments and a battalion. Jenkins had three regiments and two battalions; but these men from Western Virginia insisted they were raised for special or local service and were entitled to remain together. Lee thought it unwise to raise an issue with them. He wrote of all this to the President on the 1st of August and expressed the belief that three full regiments or four, if weak, were as large a cavalry command as one man could direct.[20]

On this basis, Lee explained, the cavalry would include seven Brigades. These should be divided into two Divisions, at the head of which should be Major Generals. For the command of one of these newly organized Divisions, Lee recommended Wade Hampton, who "deserves [promotion] both from his service and his gallantry." Fitz Lee was recommended for the other Division. Of him, said the uncle and commanding General: "I do not wish to speak so positively, but I do not know of any other officer in the cavalry who has done better service. I should admire both more if they were more rigid in their discipline, but I know how difficult

19 *Cullum* No. 1731, graduated 21st in his class. The best sketch of Lomax is that by Dr. James E. Walmsley in *D. A. B.* For Lomax's assignments and rank in the United States Army, see *Cullum* and *Army Register*, 1860. His appointment to a Virginia commission is noted in *O. R.*, 51, pt. 2, p. 40. See also 21 *C. V.*, 450. Ashby's old troopers opposed Lomax at first because they hoped for the promotion of Lt. Col. O. R. Funsten. Tradition is that Gen. R. E. Lee recommended Funsten but that the War Department named Lomax. See *Laurel Brigade*, 115–16. For Stuart's tribute to Funsten, on the promotion of Rosser, see *O. R.*, 29, pt. 2, pp. 802–03.
20 *O. R.*, 27, pt. 3, p. 1068.

it is to establish discipline in our armies and therefore make allowances." [21]

If Fitz Lee and Hampton were made Major Generals, two vacancies would be created. By relieving Bev. Robertson, a third man could be advanced.[22] Reduction of the size of the Brigades would make possible the selection of a fourth Brigadier. Doubtless on Stuart's recommendation, Lee proposed that Calbraith Butler succeed Hampton, that Williams Wickham take Fitz Lee's diminished command, that Lawrence Baker have a Brigade built on Robertson's command, and that another of the reorganized Brigades be given Lunsford Lomax.[23] It developed that Lomax had been appointed by Davis before Lee's letter of August 1 was received. Lawrence Baker had received the same honor.[24] The others were appointed as Lee had recommended—Butler and Wickham to be Brigadiers,[25] Hampton and Fitz Lee to be Major Generals.[26] The average age of all these men was 33. Two of the Brigadiers and one of the Major Generals were 27.

The real triumph of this reshuffle was that the promotion of Hampton and of Fitz Lee had been arranged in a manner that did not aggravate the rivalry that always was suspected but never was avowed. Between them at Gettysburg, bad feeling probably had developed. Stuart on the 3rd of July had moved to the East of Ewell's position and had encountered the Federal horse in strength. Without telling either Hampton or Fitz Lee what he planned to do, he had gone to the left while the Brigades were being deployed. When Stuart had reached a position from which he had believed he could strike the enemy's rear, he had seen that the enemy had observed the debouchment of Hampton and Lee. Stuart had been compelled then to change plan. In order to show them the ground where he intended to operate, he had been prompted to send for his two senior Brigadiers.[27] Hampton had

[21] O. R., 27, pt. 3, p. 1069.
[22] O. R., 27, pt. 3, pp. 1006, 1007, 1075. Robertson was assigned in October to command of the Second District of South Carolina (O. R., 28, pt. 2, p. 421) where he remained in service till the district had to be evacuated on the approach of Sherman (3 C. M. H., 658). Robertson's case was one in which Stuart's judgment was correct from the first contacts in Southern service. On Oct. 21, 1861, "Jeb" had told his wife: "I find Bev. Robertson by far the most troublesome man I have to deal with . . ." Bingham Duncan, ed., Letters of General J. E. B. Stuart to His Wife, 1861, p. 16.
[23] O. R., 27, pt. 3, p. 1069.
[24] July 30, to rank from July 23, 1863. Wright, 108.
[25] September 2, to rank from Sept. 1, 1863. Wright, 110, 111.
[26] September 3, to rank from Aug. 3, 1863. Wright, 35.
[27] O. R., 27, pt. 2, p. 697.

decided, on receipt of Stuart's message, that he and Fitz Lee should not leave their position at the same time. By arrangement with Fitz, he had started out to find Stuart and had told Lee that when he returned, the younger man should go to "Jeb."

Hampton had searched in vain for Stuart. Returning, he had been surprised to find that his Brigade was beginning a charge by orders of Fitz Lee. Immediately Hampton had countermanded what he considered an injudicious movement and had moved his men back to their former position. A little later, when Chambliss had sent to Fitz Lee for help, Fitz had referred the request to Hampton, who was nearer Chambliss's flank. Hampton had decided that Chambliss needed assistance and had sent two regiments to aid that officer. These troops had advanced too far. In trying to extricate them, Hampton had been wounded.[28] He had felt that Fitz Lee had been rash, and in his report, which had not been forwarded when the promotions were being considered by Lee, he was to state the facts as he had seen them. Stuart knew the fine qualities of both men and sought by praising them in his report to avoid offense to either. When that document was written, Hampton was to be described as that "brave and distinguished officer."[29] Fitz Lee "was always in the right place and contributed his usual conspicuous share to the success of the day."[30] Where it had counted most, both men had been linked together in Lee's letter that had urged their promotion. The commanding General had put their names in the same sentence: "I further propose to your consideration the promotion of Generals Hampton and Fitzhugh Lee to the rank of major-general."[31]

All this care had been repaid. Both men were satisfied. When they headed Divisions, the cavalry force became in organization a Corps. Confederate law provided that "each army corps shall be commanded by a lieutenant general,"[32] but the establishment of a Corps of cavalry was not announced by Army Headquarters. Nor was Stuart's advancement suggested to the President by Lee. Nowhere in the records is there a line of any date to show that Lee ever considered Stuart's promotion above the rank to which "Jeb" was appointed after the Seven Days. This could not have been for any reason personal to Stuart. For him Lee always had affectionate

28 O. R., 27, pt. 2, pp. 724–25.        29 Ibid., 698.
30 Ibid.        31 O. R., 27, pt. 3, p. 1069.
32 Act of Sept. 18, 1862.

regard. Consequently, the most probable explanation is that Lee did not believe the command of the cavalry carried with it a responsibility equal to that borne by the men who led the infantry Corps. It never was Lee's inclination to confer honorific titles or to assign rank beyond that necessary to accomplish results.[33]

If Stuart was not dissatisfied and Hampton and Fitz Lee were pleased, the reorganization could be judged a success; but in accordance with the history of promotion from the days of Trojan wars, almost as many officers were offended as were pleased. Tom Rosser of the Fifth might have maintained that his title to advancement was as good as that of any of those who were made general officers. Similarly, Col. Tom Munford of the Second Virginia was aggrieved. He was one of the senior colonels of cavalry in the Army of Northern Virginia[34] and had shared in almost every campaign after that of First Manassas.

Stuart was embarrassed over the unhappiness of these two officers. In January, 1863, he had recommended the creation of an additional Brigade of cavalry and in warm eulogium had urged that Rosser be appointed to it. Said Stuart: ". . . Rosser in daily engagement with the enemy vindicated his claims as an admirable outpost commander, vigilant, active and accurate in conclusions about enemy's designs, in battle a bold and dashing leader, on the march and in bivouac a rigid disciplinarian, but at the same time exacting the confidence of his entire command." In forwarding this letter through Army Headquarters, Stuart said: ". . . no officer that I have met with in the Confederacy combines in a more eminent degree the characteristics of the cavalry commander . . . He is an officer of superior ability[,] possesses in an extraordinary degree the talent to command and the skill to lead with coolness and decision of character."[35]

From this recommendation, Stuart had not withdrawn, so far as the records show, but Rosser had fallen into disfavor with the War Department. His regiment had declined in efficiency; his own morale was low. Then in May, 1863, he married a girl of great charm. For a time he suffered intensely because of separation from her. Probably, too, he was not so diligent in the camp

---

[33] "I think rank of but trivial importance, so that it is sufficient for the individual to exercise command." Lee to Stuart, May 23, 1863 (O. R., 25, pt. 2, p. 820).
[34] 3 C. M. H., 639.
[35] Stuart to S. Cooper, Jan. 13, 1863—Rosser MSS.

as he was on the field of battle. Occasionally his conscience re-
buked him for drinking, but his bride's letters rallied him. Before
Gettysburg, she wrote him and suggested that every day at a given
hour they pray for each other. Rosser acquiesced earnestly. During the hard fight around Aldie he wrote her: "Yesterday, whilst
your prayers were going up to heaven for the safety of your husband, I was riding with sabre in hand—midst bullets and shells in
the defense of my country—and not until I had got into camp did
I return thanks to a Wise and Merciful God, the Savior of Man-
kind, for the preservation of my life . . . I feel that I am growing
a better man, and I know it is the influence which you exercise
over me that induces me to change my moral condition—and Betty
at the time specified I will bow myself in the presence of my God
and raise my voice with yours to a throne of Grace in reverent sup-
plication. I can't help feeling, my darling Betty, that I was created
for some good. I have a good Heart and I feel that God placed me
on Earth to abide a fixed date and to fulfill a special destiny." [36]
In this spirit Rosser had overcome whatever objection there was
to his promotion, but there was no Brigade for him until the long,
ugly feud between Stuart and "Grumble" Jones reached a climax.

Stuart's decision to leave Jones to guard the Virginia mountain
passes, under the direction of Beverley Robertson during the preliminaries of the Gettysburg campaign, had fired anew the animosities that previously had led Jones to tender his resignation.[37]
All the tact and diplomacy of Lee failed to soften the feeling of
either man. At length, early in September,[38] a direct verbal clash
occurred. Concerning the details, tight-lipped reticence was observed by the participants. All that is known of the affair is that
Stuart arrested Jones for disrespect to his superior officer and subsequently brought him before a court martial.[39] Jones swore that
even if he were acquitted he never would serve again under Stuart,
who was equally anxious to be rid of him. "Grumble" might have
saved his oath because the court found him guilty.

The patient commanding General had respect for Jones's abilities and more than once had defended the troublesome officer, but
he now reluctantly concluded that Jones must be sent elsewhere.[40]

36 T. L. Rosser to Mrs. Rosser, MS, June 18, 1863—*Rosser MSS.*
37 See *supra*, p. 60.                          38 *Laurel Brigade,* 168.
39 *Ibid.,* and *O. R.,* 29, pt. 2, pp. 771–72.
40 *O. R.* loc. cit. and 779, 788; *ibid.,* 51. pt. 2. p. 772.

When the court's sentence was approved, Jones was deprived of his command but was ordered to Southwest Virginia to take charge of the cavalry there.[41] For a time the resentment on the part of Jones's men was furious, because they thought "Grumble" had been sacrificed to the animosity of Stuart,[42] but they were reconciled by Stuart's friendliness to them and by the wisdom of his choice of a new brigade commander. Promptly and confidently, Stuart recommended and Lee endorsed the promotion of Rosser of the Fifth Virginia,[43] who on October 10 was commissioned Brigadier General.[44]

Munford's case took a different turn. When he was told that Rosser would be recommended ahead of him,[45] he took it manfully, but his friends appealed to General Lee. In answer to one of these admirers of Munford's, the commanding General wrote that he would recommend the promotion of the Colonel "whenever I can do so consistently with those principles by which I am guided in these matters." Lee went on: "I necessarily consult the opinions of those whose opportunities of knowing what will best promote the interests of the service are better than my own. Many things in addition to services and capacity have to be considered in the appointment of a brigade commander, though these of course are the chief." [46]

In much the same spirit, Lee answered a letter from the beloved George Wythe Munford, Secretary of the Commonwealth of Virginia and father of the disappointed Colonel. After repeating substantially the same considerations, Lee wrote: "I beg leave to express my approval of the patriotic sentiments of your letter which I think should be entertained by every man at this time. All personal feelings and aspirations should be subordinated to the great end of rendering all the service in every man's power to the common cause. The man who is actuated by this principle will I think find in the end, ample compensation for any disappointment of his personal wishes and aspirations, in the consciousness of duty faithfully performed, and it will generally happen that it is the most certain road to honorable advancement. That such will be

[41] O. R., 29, pt. 2, p. 779.              [42] Laurel Brigade, 168–69.
[43] Stuart to Rosser, MS, Sept. 30, 1863—Rosser MSS.
[44] Wright, 114; O. R., 29, pt. 2, p. 788. The next detailed references to Rosser are infra, p. 251 ff.
[45] Stuart to Rosser, MS, Sept. 30, 1863—Rosser MSS.
[46] Lee to Beverley Tucker, MS, Oct. 28, 1863—Munford MSS.

the action of your son, his previous conduct leads me to expect, and that the result will meet his expectations and those of his friends, I have no doubt." [47]

Even where incidents as distressing as this did not arise, reorganization was endless. On August 1, before the name of Lawrence Baker was presented formally for promotion, he was wounded so seriously that he might be invalided. To act for Baker, during his incapacity, the choice of Lee and of Stuart was James B. Gordon, former Lieutenant Colonel of the First North Carolina and then Colonel in succession to Baker.[48] Before the war, Gordon had been a merchant and politician of Wilkes County, North Carolina. He was 41 years old and without professional military training, but he had been distinguished for bravery and intelligent leadership in all the battles of his Brigade.[49] It was a departure from hampering bad precedent to name a Colonel to the next grade while there was a prospect that his senior would return to the field. The necessity of maintaining discipline was the reason for abandonment of a rule Lee often had reason to deplore.

Calbraith Butler was recovering slowly from the wound received at Brandy. For the temporary direction of his Brigade, Stuart and Lee recommended and the President nominated [50] Pierce Manning Butler Young, Colonel of Cobb's Legion, South Carolinian by birth and Georgian in uprearing. Young had been a cadet at West Point but had resigned on the secession of Georgia prior to his graduation. He now was in his twenty-seventh year, of splendid manners and great magnetism, though considered somewhat spoilt. His record had been of the highest.[51]

With the appointment of Rosser and of Young, the reorganization of the Cavalry Corps was complete. Hampton's Division consisted of the Brigades of James B. Gordon (Baker's), Pierce M. B. Young (Butler's), and Thomas L. Rosser, formerly Jones's. In Fitz Lee's Division were Col. J. R. Chambliss's (W. H. F. Lee's), Lomax's,[52] and Wickham's.[53] In command, this was a force en-

---

[47] Munford MSS.
[48] Appointed Sept. 28, 1863; Wright, 113.
[49] For a sketch, see 4 C.M.H., 312–14.
[50] October 10, to rank from Sept. 28, 1863; Wright, 114; O. R., 29, pt. 2, p. 788.
[51] Sketch in D. A. B. by Fletcher M. Green; cf. 6 C. M. H., 458, where the date of Young's birth is incorrectly given. For an amusing account of his attempt to get Lawrence Baker to fight a duel with him, see 25 S.H.S.P., 147.
[52] Formerly part of Fitz Lee's and Jones's, with the Fifteenth Virginia added.
[53] The core of Fitz Lee's former Brigade.

tirely different from that which Stuart had carried into Pennsylvania, as recently as the last week in June,[54] except for one significant fact: The two most renowned of the former Brigadiers were now divisional commanders. Before them was fame.[55]

[54] *Cf.* the organization table in *O. R.*, 29, pt. 2, p. 902, with that in *ibid.*, 27, pt. 2, pp. 290–91.

[55] The sketches of Stuart and of Hampton are resumed *infra*, p. 248 ff.

# CHAPTER XII

## THE DETACHMENT OF LONGSTREET

WHILE THE CAVALRY were being reorganized under new Brigadiers, the infantry command was confronted with a new problem, mass desertion. This began, in all except name, as soon as Gettysburg was lost. On the afternoon of the 4th of July, when the wagon train was started for the Potomac, about 5000 unwounded men slipped away from their posts and went with the vehicles. Many of these men were captured by the enemy,[1] many were returned to their commands, others were listed A.W.O.L. Of the wounded or sick men who went to hospital, some quietly disappeared. Regimental officers never knew whether these men deserted after discharge from the hospitals or died without report by the surgeons.[2] The calamity threatened by these conditions was to be read from the rolls of the Army at the end of July. Present for duty were 41,135 infantry and artillerists. The aggregate present, cavalry excluded, were 53,286,[3] a decline of more than 20,000, in all probability, from the figures of June 30.[4]

To rally the negligent and to shame the cowardly, a general order for the return of absentees was issued July 26 by Army Headquarters. Lee's language was firm: "To remain at home in this, the hour of your country's need, is unworthy the manhood of a Southern soldier. While you proudly boast that you belong to the Army of Northern Virginia, let it not be said that you deserted your comrades in a contest in which everything you hold dear is at stake . . ."[5] Doubt of the success of Lee's appeal to absentees was expressed by its author. "I do not know whether it will have much effect," Lee wrote the President, "unless accompanied by the declaration of an amnesty."

The words of Lee were emphasized by events. Fifty men of Scales's shattered Brigade deserted on the night of July 29. Of

[1] O. R., 27, pt. 3, p. 1048.    [2] O. R., 27, pt. 2, p. 328.
[3] O. R., 27, pt. 3, p. 1065.
[4] The "return" for June 30 is not believed to be in existence.
[5] O. R., 27, pt. 2, p. 1040.

217

these soldiers, forty-two belonged to the Twenty-second North Carolina, a regiment that had an honorable name. Several of the companies of this regiment had come from the western, mountainous counties where slaves were few and Union sentiment had been strong.[6] It was assumed immediately that these men were conscripts who had been prompted to desert by seditious articles in the Raleigh *Standard*. The editor of that paper, William Woods Holden, changed his political coat every time the wind veered.[7] He now was proclaiming that conscription was unconstitutional. His arguments could not always be answered within the command to which the conscripts belonged, because, it will be remembered, on July 1 the Brigade had lost fifty-five of its officers and had concluded the day's action with only one field officer uninjured.[8] Pender, who had held the Division in his grasp, was dead of his wound. Approximately 100 men of the Twenty-second had fallen at Gettysburg.[9] General Scales might have exploded the absurdities of Holden and might have stiffened discipline, but he was absent on account of his injuries.

These conditions, which were typical of those in many regiments, explained though they did not excuse the behavior of the North Carolina soldiers. The Army command was startled and humiliated; but President Davis followed the advice Lee had given him and on the 11th of August offered a general pardon to deserters who would return to their commands. All soldiers who were under trial or were serving sentence for desertion were released. The only exception was in the case of men twice convicted of desertion.[10] Amnesty was supplemented for a brief time in the Army of Northern Virginia by a system of furloughs to soldiers of meritorious conduct, though the number of men rewarded in this manner could represent a bare 2 per cent of the enlisted strength.[11] "Extra Billy" Smith, newly commissioned Major General, was sent on a speaking tour to supplement amnesty and furloughs and to stir the people by his eloquence.[12] Assemblies were held by many of the North Carolina regiments to reaffirm their

[6] For the origin of the regiment, see 2 *N. C. Regts.*, 161–62.
[7] *O. R.*, 27, pt. 3, p. 1052.          [8] *O. R.*, 27, pt. 2, p. 670.
[9] *Ibid.*, 349. Dead and wounded were 89. Captured and missing were not listed, but in a Brigade of five regiments numbered 110.
[10] *O. R.*, 29, pt. 2, pp. 641–42.
[11] *O. R.*, 51, pt. 2, p. 755; *ibid.*, 29, pt. 2, p. 647.
[12] *O. R.*, 27, pt. 2, pp. 645–46.

loyalty and to denounce the "factious and treasonable course" of the *Standard*.[13]

The effect of all of this was nil. Some men even presumed upon the amnesty to go home without leave, in the expectation that if they returned before the twenty days of mercy expired, no punishment could be inflicted. Numbers of Virginians who had wearied of the hard infantry service deserted to join one or another of the companies of partisan rangers, who were supposed to combine good living and high adventure. Faithful soldiers were gnawed by discontent as they observed the tenderness shown deserters.[14]

Few commanders seem to have asked themselves whether their own shortcoming as army administrators, rather than the innate baseness of deserters, was responsible for the steady disappearance of men who previously had fought well. Lee realized some of the causes of discontent,[15] but when amnesty and furloughs had been tried, he abandoned hope of stopping desertion otherwise than by the imposition of death sentences on men who were captured after leaving the ranks. Troops were sent to the river crossings, at one of which more than 1000 deserters had been counted in a fortnight.[16] A band of runaways, caught on James River, put up a fight and killed several of the men sent to arrest them. Brought back to the Army, members of this gang were tried and convicted. Ten ringleaders were sentenced to be shot. Their appeals were denied. On a given day, their Division, which happened to be that of Edward Johnson, was marched into a field and placed in line on three sides of a hollow square. On the fourth side were the ten doomed men, tied to small wooden crosses. At the word of command, firing squads killed all of them. The Division then was marched past so that every soldier could see for himself the twisted corpses and the still-wet blood.[17] The good soldier, who was the average soldier, did not need this lesson. He already had shown his loyalty, and if he belonged to the First Corps he soon demonstrated his devotion anew in operations that had their unhappy origin in events of the summer in the Far South.

The fall of Vicksburg on July 4 had been followed by a retreat

---

[13] L. M. Blackford to his mother, MS, Aug. 12, 1863—*Blackford MSS.*
[14] *O. R.*, 29, pt. 2, pp. 649–50.          [15] Cf. *O. R.*, 29, pt. 2, p. 723.
[16] 2 *R.W.C.D.*, 4; *O. R.*, 29, pt. 2, pp. 650, 651, 672, 692, 768; *Lee's Dispatches*, 122–24.
[17] *McHenry Howard*, 226–27; *Sorrel*, 217–18.

on the part of Gen. Joseph E. Johnston to Jackson, Mississippi. Pursued and besieged there, he withdrew to Morton. Said Davis in disgust on July 21, "General Johnston, after evacuating Jackson, retreated to the east, to the pine woods of Mississippi, and if he has any other plan than that of watching the enemy it has not been communicated." [18] Fortunately, General Grant, after overwhelming Pemberton, most recklessly dispersed his forces and did not threaten Johnston.

Remote as these maneuvers appeared from Virginia, the government knew how closely they were related to battles on the Rapidan. If Johnston's army in Mississippi were considered the Confederate left, on the long front from the "Father of Waters" to the Rapidan, the centre was Braxton Bragg's Army of Tennessee. This force was idle in front of Chattanooga, Tennessee. A Federal army under Gen. W. S. Rosecrans and another under Gen. A. E. Burnside seemed as reluctant to attack Bragg as he was to assail them. Unattached to Bragg but affecting nearly all his movements was the Confederate right, the Army of Northern Virginia, which, despite Gettysburg, still had faith in itself and in its commander. [19]

Almost all the Southern leaders agreed that they could not maintain a strict defensive. To win, Confederate armies had to strike. The difference of opinion concerned the place—left, centre or right. If Johnston had an answer, he did not communicate it. [20] Bragg proposed on July 17 that he reinforce Johnston for an attack on Grant, but Johnston dismissed this with four gloomy words: "It is too late." [21] Lee believed that if his army could recover sufficient strength, the best hope of the Confederacy lay in the renewal of the offensive against the Federals in Northern Virginia. [22] General Samuel Cooper thought that perhaps the wisest course would be to strengthen Bragg from Johnston's army and to attack Rosecrans. [23] Leonidas Polk believed that a concentration against Rosecrans was the soundest strategy. [24] Longstreet was aggressively convinced that this was the imperative strategy

---

[18] 5 *Rowland's Davis*, 579, quoted in Stanley F. Horn, *The Army of Tennessee*, 220.
[19] For the conception of a single Confederate front East of the Mississippi, see R. S. Henry, *The Story of the Confederacy*, 307.
[20] He mentioned no plan in his *Narrative*, 252 ff. Nor did his correspondence in *O. R.*, 24, pt. 3, or *O. R.*, 30, pt. 4, contain any suggestion of action prior to Chickamauga.
[21] Horn, *op. cit.*, 239.
[22] See 3 *R. E. Lee*, 162 ff.
[23] *Cf.* Horn, *op. cit.*, 239–40.
[24] *O. R.*, 23, pt. 2. pp. 932–33.

but that the troops to give Bragg offensive power should come from Virginia, not from Mississippi. With unwonted eagerness, Longstreet renewed the argument he had advanced while in Richmond during May at the conclusion of the Suffolk campaign. Lee's army might be reduced temporarily; one Corps, at least, might be sent to Tennessee. Bragg then should be able to crush the Federal forces under Gen. Rosecrans before they could be reinforced. Unless this were done, Longstreet wrote subsequently, he feared at the time that the Federals would follow their triumph at Vicksburg with a march through Georgia. That would wreck the Confederacy.

In this conviction, Longstreet about the middle of August wrote the Secretary of War a general outline of a proposed transfer of troops from Lee's Army to Bragg's. This letter was dispatched, Longstreet later explained, in accordance with Seddon's invitation to address him personally when circumstances made that course desirable. Longstreet told Seddon that he had not discussed the subject with Lee, who, like many other commanders, said Longstreet, was loath to approve detachments that would place troops beyond immediate control.[25] This secrecy did not persist. In conversation with Lee soon afterward, Longstreet argued that Bragg should be reinforced from the Army of Northern Virginia for an attack on Rosecrans.

This alternative to his own plan had, of course, been in Lee's mind. If the decision were to strengthen Bragg at the expense of the Army of Northern Virginia, would Longstreet care to have the command of the forces sent to the West? When Lee made the inquiry, Longstreet showed that he already had been considering the possibility. He would accept, said Longstreet, on two conditions which he had framed carefully: First, he must have opportunity of winning the confidence of the forces before leading them into action; second, he must be given assurance that any success would be exploited.[26]

By this time, it seems likely that Longstreet had abandoned the theory of a strategic offensive and a tactical defensive. He now favored a full offensive in Tennessee or, probably, even in the East. Late in August, Lee went to Richmond and discussed with Presi-

---

[25] *Longstreet,* 433–34. The text of Longstreet's letter to Seddon has not been found
[26] *Longstreet,* 434.

dent Davis the general strategic situation. As a result, on the 31st,
Lee wrote Longstreet, who had been left in command on the
Rapidan, "to prepare the army for offensive operations." [27]
Promptly Longstreet replied that he did not see how the Army of
Northern Virginia could attack effectively unless it was "strong
enough to cross the Potomac." One tenable implication was that
if an advance in the enemy's country was possible, he favored for
September the strategy he had opposed in June. He added that
from limited knowledge of the situation, he thought the best
opportunity for great results was in Tennessee.[28]

In some fashion, word was spread during the next few days that
Longstreet was going to Tennessee and, what was more, was
going as Bragg's successor, not as one of Bragg's corps commanders. Years afterward, an officer of Longstreet's staff insisted
that broad hints had been dropped that Lee's senior lieutenant was
to head the Army of Tennessee.[29] This was not in the mind of the
President at the moment but Longstreet did not hesitate to suggest
it to Lee. The Army of Northern Virginia, he said on September
5, could maintain a safe defensive with a reduced force and, if
need be, could retire to the Richmond defenses. In the event the
First Corps could not be spared from the Army of Northern
Virginia, he thought the Confederacy "might accomplish something" by giving him three specified Brigades from the Richmond
front, putting him "in Bragg's place" and transferring the commander of the Army of Tennessee to the head of the First Corps
under Lee. If the Corps went to Tennessee, a good battalion of
artillery should be sent also. Longstreet continued: "We would
surely make [30] no great risk in such a change and we might gain
a great deal. I feel that I am influenced by no personal motive in
this suggestion, and will most cheerfully give up, when we have a
fair prospect of holding our western country. I doubt if General
Bragg has confidence in his troops or himself either. He is not
likely to do a great deal for us." [31] In this bid for command, Longstreet was entirely confident. Nothing he wrote on the subject
disclosed any doubt on his part that he could administer and
lead successfully the contentious Army of Tennessee.

[27] O. R., 51, pt. 2, p. 761; Longstreet, 435.      [28] O. R., 29, pt. 2, pp. 693–94.
[29] Col. John W. Fairfax to General Longstreet, Apr. 16, 1898—Fairfax MSS.
[30] This is almost certainly a lapsus pennae. "Take" must have been meant.
[31] O. R., 29, pt. 2, p. 699.

The President wished Lee to assume general command in the region where Johnston and Bragg were operating, but when Lee expressed belief that officers already on the ground could do better, Davis acquiesced, though perhaps reluctantly.[32] With Lee's acquiescence, the swift, final decision was to send the greater part of Longstreet's Corps to reinforce Bragg, who was to continue at the head of the Army. On the night of September 6, Lee in person gave orders to the Quartermaster General to prepare the transportation.[33] By the 8th, troops were moving toward Richmond from the camps on the Rapidan.[34]

Longstreet made no complaint that he was not to supplant Bragg, but he busied himself in exchanging some of the Brigades that were to go with him. This was made possible by the fact that simultaneously with the troop movement to Tennessee, detachment had to be made from the troops in Virginia to reinforce Charleston, South Carolina, which for almost two months had been under violent attack.[35] The first arrangement was that Longstreet should supply two Brigades from his Corps for the garrison of Charleston and should carry all the others to Tennessee. Longstreet concluded that if this had to be done, he should leave in South Carolina two weakened Georgia Brigades, Bryan's and "Tige" Anderson's, and thereby reduce the prospect of desertion from these commands when they were on the Georgia-Tennessee boundary, close to home.[36]

Not content with this, Longstreet opened negotiations to substitute other troops for Pickett's Division in the movement to Tennessee. The President was desirous of having some of the famous Virginia regiments sent to Bragg's Army,[37] but Longstreet knew that Pickett's men were few in number and were dangerously lacking in officers.[38] "Old Pete" reasoned that it might be better to leave Pickett in the Richmond defenses and to take in his place the Brigades of Micah Jenkins and Henry A. Wise, who then were stationed close to the capital. In urging this, Longstreet undoubtedly was angling to have Micah Jenkins rejoin him. The young South Carolinian was a splendid fighter, was eating out

[32] Ibid., 700–01, 702.    [33] O. R., 29, pt. 2, p. 720.
[34] Ibid., 706.
[35] O. R., 28, pt. 2, pp. 339, 342. The day of the decision to send Longstreet to Tennessee, September 6, was the fifty-eighth day of the attack. Cf. ibid., 342.
[36] Cf. O. R., 29, pt. 2, p. 683.    [37] Ibid., 706.
[38] O. R., 29, pt. 2, pp. 706, 773.

his heart in enforced idleness, and was anxious to reunite his excellent troops with their old comrades.[39] Longstreet had success in asking for Jenkins's men, but he changed his mind about Wise's Brigade when he found that those Virginia troops, though of splendid personnel and morale, had not been engaged in a major battle since that of Seven Pines. In the end, Pickett was left on the quiet Richmond sector, "Tige" Anderson's [40] and Wise's Brigades were sent to South Carolina,[41] Jenkins was taken from Richmond, and Bryan's Brigade was retained with its Division.

Before these details had been completed the time came for Longstreet to leave the Rapidan. He had his baggage packed, his headquarters' records placed in chests and his tents struck. Then he rode over to Lee's headquarters to say farewell. The commanding General was reconciled to the temporary detachment of the First Corps, but was apprehensive that he would be held to a strict defensive and perhaps would be forced to retreat to the Richmond area during the absence of so large a part of his Army. It was manifest to Longstreet that Lee hoped the First Corps would help in destroying Rosecrans and then would return quickly to Virginia.[42]

After the friendliest of farewells, Longstreet left Lee's tent and started for his horse. Lee followed him, but in silence. With no more of ceremony, Longstreet put his foot into the stirrup and was about to mount when Lee spoke again: "Now, General, you must beat those people out in the West."

Immediately Longstreet withdrew his foot from the stirrup, stood squarely on the ground and answered: "If I live; but I would not give a single man of my command for a fruitless victory." Lee replied that it should be so. Plans to pursue a success already were being made.[43]

[39] For Jenkins's pleas to be sent back to the Army of Northern Virginia while he was on detached service, see *O. R.*, 27, pt. 3, pp. 908, 1005; *ibid.*, 51, pt. 2, p. 745. For the movements and condition of Jenkins's Brigade during the summer of 1863, see *O. R.*, 18, 993, 1088; *ibid.*, 25, pt. 2, pp. 791, 811, 827, 843; *ibid.*, 27, pt. 2, p. 293; *ibid.*, 29, pt. 2, p. 694; *ibid.*, 51, pt. 2, p. 734.

[40] *O. R.*, 29, pt. 2, p. 713. For Anderson's arrival in Charleston, see *O. R.*, 28, pt. 1, pp. 128, 129, 404. The Brigade remained at Charleston until October 7 and then joined Bragg. *Ibid.*, 142.

[41] *O. R.*, 29, pt. 2, p. 713. The last of Wise's men reached Charleston September 19. *O. R.*, 28, pt. 1, p. 131.

[42] Cf. *O. R.*, 29, pt. 2, p. 712.

[43] *Longstreet*, 437. It will not be forgotten, of course, that Longstreet wrote this more than thirty years after the event. The quotations probably are not the exact words used at the time. Longstreet's departure from the Rapidan was on September 9 or 10.

In the Confederate capital, Longstreet had disappointment, satisfaction and a measure of amusement. His chief regret was a vexatious change of route. All the logistics of the operation had been based on the dispatch of the troops directly to Chattanooga by way of the Virginia and Tennessee Railroad, past Bristol and Knoxville. The Federals prevented this. Burnside's advance in East Tennessee led Maj. Gen. Simon B. Buckner to evacuate Knoxville, which on the 2nd of September the Federals occupied.[44] Chattanooga fell to the Unionists on the 9th.[45] That same day witnessed the surrender of the 2000 Confederates who had been defending Cumberland Gap between Virginia and Tennessee.[46] Federal cavalry were almost certain to proceed from the Gap to the railroad.[47] All Confederate reinforcements had now to be routed by the overloaded railway that led South from Richmond. Delay would be inevitable at the very time speed was essential to success. That irked Longstreet but did not discourage him.[48] More alarming by far than the change of route was the manifest familiarity of hundreds with what was to have been a secret troop movement. The *New York Herald* of September 9 printed a full account of Longstreet's detachment, even to the discussion whether Wise and Jenkins would accompany the First Corps.[49]

As partial compensation for this, Longstreet must have had deep satisfaction with the welcome accorded him in the capital. Gettysburg had not impaired his fame. He was as distinguished a figure, the object of as much deference, as when he had been in Richmond during May. Nor was he the only hero. Perhaps the most heartmoving demonstration of the Corps' appearance near the city was staged by Hood's men when they greeted their wounded chief. Although Hood had not recovered the use of his arm, some of the

---

44 *O. R.*, 30, pt. 2, p. 21; pt. 3, p. 333. Bragg's report of this, dated Sept. 4, 1863, carried the President's endorsement of September 12, as if it had that day been read for the first time; but the *Richmond Dispatch* of September 3 announced the loss of Knoxville. The *Richmond Examiner* of the 4th disputed the accuracy of this report, but on the 8th the *Examiner* acknowledged that the Federals occupied Knoxville. The next day Jones recorded in his diary Longstreet's change of route, which had become necessary because the "enemy possesses the Knoxville Road" (2 *R.W.C.D.*, 37).

45 *O. R.*, 30, pt. 2, p. 549.

46 The report of the defending officer, Brig. Gen. John W. Frazer, appears in *O. R.*, 30, pt. 2, p. 607 ff. At the time, General Frazer was accused of cowardice or worse, but in 2 *Davis*, 427 n, the Confederate President expressed the belief that great injustice had been done the Southern commander at the Gap.

47 Actually, Bristol, Va.-Tenn., was not occupied until September 18 (*O. R.*, 30, pt. 2, p. 592).

48 Cf. *Longstreet*, 436.       49 *O. R.*, 29, pt. 2, pp. 719–20.

brigade and regimental officers appealed to him to resume his command. Hood courageously assented,[50] and thereby deferred a clash between Micah Jenkins and Evander Law, who were bitter rivals. Law had handled Hood's Division during the time its regular commander was wounded, and he had directed it well; but Law was junior in commission to Jenkins by two months and a half and, of course, would have been compelled to yield the command if Hood had not returned.[51]

Relieved by this return of Hood to duty, Longstreet had a laugh in Richmond over the performance of Harrison, the spy who had brought the news of the Federal crossing of the Potomac after Lee had entered Pennsylvania in June. While the Army was on the Rapidan, Harrison was idle and, on his own application, was given permission to visit Richmond. Before he left Corps headquarters he remarked to Moxley Sorrel, "Colonel, if by any chance you should be in Richmond next week, I hope you will take in the theatre one evening."

"What is the attraction?" Sorrel innocently inquired.

"Myself," said Harrison, who continued: "I have made a bet of $50 greenbacks that I play Cassio and play him successfully."

"Are you an actor?"

"No, but I can play."

At the time of this odd conversation, Sorrel did not know the Corps was to move, but he went to Richmond and to the theatre precisely as Harrison had hoped he would. As predicted, the play was *Othello*. In the second scene, the Moor protested to Iago in the street—

" . . . for know, Iago,
But that I love the gentle Desdemona,
I would not my unhous'd free condition
Put into circumscription and confine
For the sea's worth. But, look! what lights come yond?"

With somewhat discouraged torches, a few men walked on the stage. One of them had a familiar look. Presently he spoke:

"The Duke does greet you, general;
And he requires your haste-post-haste appearance
Even on the instant."

[50] *Hood,* 55.
[51] *Wright,* 86, 89; *Sorrel,* 182–83. In this, General Sorrel erred in saying that Jenkins succeeded Hood at Gettysburg. Jenkins was not in that campaign.

The voice and the manner were unmistakable. Cassio was Harrison, but not a professional spy turned amateur actor. Evidently Harrison was a professional actor as well as spy, though his stage presence might not have on it the stamp of Drury Lane. That was not quite all. As the drama proceeded, it was manifest that the gentleman playing Othello had drawn part of his inspiration from some other source than Shakespeare. Later Sorrel had to confess: " 'Othello' was in drink, 'Cassio' was really quite far gone, and even 'Desdemona' was under more than one suspicion that evening." It was diverting and ludicrous but, as concerned Harrison, it was disconcerting. Sorrel thought it well to investigate the habits of the actor-spy. He found that Harrison was both drinking and gambling and, all in all, might not be a safe agent of espionage. The man was dismissed from Longstreet's service and was returned to the Secretary of War, who originally had commended him to the General. A time was to come in Tennessee when "Old Pete" needed just such a man as Harrison. Then Sorrel searched in vain for the spy.[52]

On the day that Cassio Harrison was strutting as the lieutenant of Othello, the men of McLaws's and Hood's Division were moving slowly southward. Alexander's Battalion of Artillery was to follow them.[53] The journey was full of excitement for troops who seemed almost to have forgotten Round Top and the Emmitsburg Road. "Never before," said Sorrel,[54] "were so many troops moved over such worn-out railways, none first-class from the beginning." He elaborated: "Never before were such crazy cars —passenger, baggage, mail, coal, box, platform, all and every sort wabbling on the jumping strap iron—used for hauling good soldiers."

The box cars were loaded with as many men on top as inside and soon were stripped in a manner amusingly described by Augustus Dickert. Said that historian of Kershaw's Brigade: "The cars on all railroads in which troops were transported were little more than skeleton cars; the weather being warm, the troops cut all but the frame work loose with knives and axes. They further-

---

[52] *Sorrel*, 181–82. After the war Harrison was occasionally seen in reduced circumstances in Baltimore. His career, if it could be traced, might be full of interest. Nothing is known of his espionage except during approximately six months of 1863.
[53] Alexander, *op. cit.*, 449, gave the schedule of his journey. His men covered the 843 miles from Richmond to Ringgold Station, 12 miles from Chickamauga, in seven days and ten hours.
[54] *Op. cit.*, 185.

more wished to see outside and witness the fine country and delightful scenery that lay along the route; nor could those inside bear the idea of being shut up in a box car while their comrades on top were cheering and yelling themselves hoarse at the waving of handkerchiefs and flags in the hands of the pretty women and the hats thrown in the air by the old men and boys along the roadside as the trains sped through the . . . Carolinas and Georgia." [55] En route, when their trains stopped in Raleigh, some of the troops tried to wreck the plant of the offensive *Standard*, but the episode scarcely deserved the excitement it aroused in the mind of Governor Zebulon Vance.[56] It in no way involved Longstreet or his discipline.

The detached Lieutenant General was planning intently his advance and was volunteering advice to Lee on the strategy that might be used in the event the departure of the First Corps made necessary the abandonment of Richmond temporarily. By September 12, Longstreet had advanced the troop movement to the stage where he could prepare for his own departure southward on the 14th. Accordingly he wrote his old commander a letter in which, after advising that certain positions below Richmond be held, he gave this assurance: "If I can do anything [in the West], it shall be done promptly. If I cannot, I shall advise you to recall me. If I did not think our move a necessary one, my regrets at leaving you would be distressing to me, as it seems to be with the officers and men of my command. Believing it to be necessary, I hope to accept it and my other personal inconveniences cheerfully and hopefully. All that we have to be proud of has been accomplished under your eye and under your orders. Our affections for you are stronger, if it be possible for them to be stronger, than our admiration for you." [57]

It was bravely said, was honestly felt and, as concerned Longstreet himself, it was hopefully written in strange and unhappy contrast to the experiences that awaited him in Tennessee.

[55] *Dickert*, 264.
[56] *O. R.*, 51, pt. 2, pp. 763, 764, 765, 767, 768, 770–71, 777–78.
[57] *O. R.*, 29, pt. 2, pp. 713–14.

# CHAPTER XIII

## LONGSTREET AND HILL IN DISTRESS

ON THE LONG journey southward to reinforce Bragg in an attack on Rosecrans, three Brigades of Hood were moved ahead of any of McLaws's men. "Rock" Benning of Hood's command was the first to reach Atlanta; but on his arrival, September 12, he had to delay his advance until he procured shoes for his men. Jerome Robertson with Hood's old Texas Brigade consequently preceded Benning on the 14th from Atlanta, but Benning and Law followed the next day to the vicinity of Resaca, whence they marched to join their comrades.[1] Hood himself was on their heels. He reached Ringgold Station, seven miles from West Chickamauga Creek, on the early afternoon of September 18. Although he still was wearing his arm in a sling as a result of the wound received at Gettysburg, he had his horse leap from the train door, mounted the animal and rode to the sound of the firing along Chickamauga Creek, where Rosecrans and Bragg already were engaged.[2]

That afternoon and evening, Kershaw's and Humphrey's Brigades of McLaws's Division arrived near Catoosa Station,[3] about 2 miles Southeast of Ringgold, detrained there and marched to Ringgold but they did not begin their advance from that point until the night of September 19, after the close of the first day's battle.[4] They then were ordered forward by their old commander, "Peter" Longstreet. With two of his staff, Longstreet reached Catoosa on the afternoon of the 19th.[5] No arrangement had been made to meet him. In trying to find Bragg, he found the enemy instead, but escaped by riding swiftly away.

At last, about 11 P.M., Longstreet reached Bragg's headquarters, only to learn that his new commander was asleep. When Bragg

---

[1] O. R., 30, pt. 4, pp. 643, 649, 652.
[2] Hood, 61. For the developments preceding Chickamauga, which are not considered an essential part of a sketch of Longstreet or of a history of the Army of Northern Virginia, see Horn, 239 ff.
[3] Longstreet styled it (O. R., 30, pt. 2, p. 287) Catoosa Platform.
[4] O. R., 30, pt. 2, p. 503.      [5] O. R., 30, pt. 2, p. 287.

was aroused, "Old Pete" had an hour's conference with him.[6] Already Bragg had assigned Hood to command McLaws's troops and Bushrod R. Johnson's Division of the Army of Tennessee in addition to his own three Brigades.[7] To Longstreet now, without hesitation, though in the face of the enemy, Bragg committed the whole left wing of the Army, which consisted of five Divisions of infantry, three battalions of artillery and some batteries attached to Brigades.[8] With few of the officers of these troops did Longstreet have any acquaintance whatsoever; but in the right wing of Bragg's Army, under command of Lieut. Gen. Leonidas Polk, was a Corps with whose chief Longstreet knew he would be on terms of old intimacy. This corps commander was no other than Harvey Hill, who, in July, had been promoted Lieutenant General for service with "Joe" Johnston and then had been sent to Bragg to take the Corps vacated by the transfer of W. J. Hardee to Mississippi.[9] It was pleasant to know that so close a friend was at hand, but no time was afforded during the exciting night of September 19–20 for exchanges between Longstreet and Hill.

The next day's battle, with much fumbling, was opened on the right. Then it was taken up progressively on the left. When Longstreet's veterans and their new comrades at length could go forward, they did so magnificently. Hood headed the column of attack in the critical operation of the day and equaled any of his exploits in Virginia, but at the supreme moment of the day fell with his thigh fractured by a rifle bullet.[10] Priceless minutes were lost after Hood was wounded. For a time the troops of the left wing delivered disjointed attacks, but Longstreet re-established his usual grip on his men and soon had all his troops violently engaged with the exception of one Division. To maintain a

---

[6] *Sorrel*, 188–89.                    [7] *Hood*, 62.

[8] Longstreet had none of his artillery with him. Alexander's Battalion had not yet arrived (Cf. *Alexander*, 449).

[9] *O. R.*, 23, pt. 2, pp. 908–09. For Hill's actions during the Federal threat against Richmond while the Gettysburg campaign was in progress, see 5 *Rowland*, 522; *O. R.*, 27, pt. 3, pp. 898, 936, 939, 945 ff, 949, 950, 956 ff, 962, 984, 1001; *ibid.*, 51, pt. 2, p. 728. Hill was promoted Lieutenant General July 11, 1863 (*Wright*, 16), and was announced as corps commander, Army of Tennessee, July 19, 1863 (*O. R.*, 23, pt. 2, p. 918). When Hill wrote in 3 *B. & L.*, 638–39 of his appointment, his memory was at fault. He was not assigned by Davis to command in succession to Hardee but to serve under Joseph E. Johnston in Mississippi. The decision to send Hill to Bragg and Hardee to Johnston was reached the day after Hill had been ordered to Johnston. See *O. R.*, 23, pt. 2, pp. 908–09. For this reason, Hill's account of his interview with President Davis is not quoted in the text. It will be found in 3 *B. & L.*, loc. cit.

[10] *O. R.*, 30, pt. 2, p. 288.

reserve, he asked then for assistance from Polk's right wing. When told it could not be given him, he husbanded his forces and, with excellent judgment, threw in his last Division at precisely the correct moment. At nightfall, the enemy had been swept from the field.[11]

All the early news of the Battle of Chickamauga that reached Richmond presented it as an overwhelming triumph for the Confederacy. To the Army of Northern Virginia, the outcome was announced in a general order of September 24, which was written in the style of Lee's congratulations to his own troops after one of their victories.[12] The next day, to Longstreet, went a cordial letter from Lee. "If," said the General, "it gives you as much pleasure to receive my warmest congratulations as it does me to convey them, this letter will not be written in vain." Lee continued: "My whole heart and soul have been with you and your brave corps in your late battle. It was natural to hear of Longstreet and Hill charging side by side, and pleasing to find the armies of the east and west vying with each other in valor and devotion to their country." [13]

The distressful part of the first reports was that of heavy casualties. Among the killed, Hood was mentioned. W. T. Wofford, one of McLaws's Brigadiers, was listed as one of those probably slain.[14] Later information was more encouraging. Wofford, as it happened, did not reach the field with his Brigade until after the battle was over.[15] Hood's wound was such that his leg had to be amputated on the field. For a few days his recovery was in doubt, but he rallied. By the end of the first week in October, he was confident he would recover and was said to be asking how long a time would elapse before he could take the field again.[16] The men of his old Brigade, though reduced in number to the proportions of a single regiment, quickly contributed nearly $5000

[11] *O. R.*, 30, pt. 2, p. 289; *Horn,* 269.
[12] *O. R.*, 29, pt. 2, p. 746.
[13] *O. R.*, 29, pt. 2, p. 749.
[14] *O. R.*, 29, pt. 2, p. 743. In this battle fell, also, Sergt. Richard R. Kirkland, aged 20, Co. G., Second South Carolina Infantry, whose conduct at Fredericksburg was one of the glories of that field. See Vol. II, pp. 378–80. Mortally wounded in a charge, he said simply: "Tell Pa goodbye. I did my duty. I died at my post." (16 *C. V.*, 105.)
[15] On September 23, though he gave no details, Bragg stated that half of McLaws's Division had not reached him (*O. R.*, 30, pt. 2, p. 23). Wofford was reported to have left Atlanta on the morning of the 19th (*ibid.*, pt. 4, p. 672), but was not mentioned in existing reports until the 22nd (*ibid.*, pt. 2, p. 505).
[16] *Mrs. Wright*, 149; *Mrs. Chesnut*, 282.

and presented it to him for the purchase of an artificial limb.[17] Their solicitude would have been the deeper had they known that they never were to have him again as their commander. The reputation of the Brigade was to increase. In deep tragedy the fame of Hood was to wane. When he was crippled and defeated and no longer had the bright blue flame of battle in his eye, his old comrades in Virginia were to remember his boldness, his bravery, his chivalry, his magnanimity. He was at his typical finest, W. W. Blackford always thought, in the advance up the Rappahannock in June, 1863. At the sight of Federals who were spread out negligently around a badly located fort, Hood laughed and then said to Blackford: "Major, send a shell first over their heads and let them get in their holes before you open with all your guns." [18]

"Stonewall" Jackson would not have approved that, but Lee would have understood. At the first report of Hood's probable recovery, Lee expressed relief.[19] To personal reasons for rejoicing at the escape of so able a man was added the knowledge that the First Corps and all its officers and men would be needed speedily in Virginia. The letter that carried congratulations to Longstreet on the victory at Chickamauga expressed warmly the conscious-ness of Lee's need of his "Old War Horse." Lee wrote: "Finish the work before you, my dear general, and return to me. I want you badly and you cannot get back too soon." [20]

The situation justified the language. On the 13th of September, Federal cavalry crossed the Rappahannock and forced Stuart to the south side of the Rapidan.[21] For the next fortnight, all the scouts' information and all the other intelligence reports indicated an early advance by the Army of the Potomac.[22] Then, overnight, the outlook in Virginia changed. Confederate lookouts reported on the 24th the disappearance of a large Federal encampment East of Culpeper Court House. Three days later, scouts in the Shenan-doah Valley sent word that Meade's XI and XII Corps, under Gen.

---

[17] James Pleasants to Mrs. D. H. Gordon, MS, Oct. 27, 1863—*Gordon MSS.* For other comments on the wounding of Hood, see *Sorrel,* 191; *Gordon,* 129. His con-valescence in Richmond is described in *Mrs. Chesnut,* 263, 266, 269, 271, 284, 290; *Mrs. Wright,* 162; 2 *R.W.C.D.,* 173. See also *O. R.,* 29, pt. 2, p. 869.
[18] *W. W. Blackford's MS Memoirs,* 309.
[19] *O. R.,* 29, pt. 2, p. 753.
[20] *O. R.,* 29, pt. 2, p. 749.
[21] *O. R.,* 29, pt. 1, p. 134; pt. 2, pp. 720, 727.
[22] *O. R.,* 29, pt. 2, pp. 731, 748, 750, 753.

Joseph Hooker, were to be dispatched to Rosecrans and had been under orders to commence on the night of the 25th their westward movement over the Baltimore and Ohio Railroad.[23] Cumulative proof of the accuracy of this information reached Army Headquarters almost daily.[24] By October 1, Lee was convinced that the two Corps had left Meade.[25]

New plans were made immediately. Instead of awaiting attack, the Army of Northern Virginia once more was to deliver it; but while Lee for the first time believed he could give battle in the absence of Longstreet, that officer was beginning to regret, for the best of reasons, his change from Virginia to Tennessee. During the night of September 20–21, after the enemy had been driven from the field of Chickamauga, Lieut. Gen. Leonidas Polk went to Bragg's headquarters, reported the Army's success and urged that the Confederates immediately pursue. Bragg could not believe the enemy was beaten and he issued no order.[26] Longstreet deliberately forwarded no report that night. "I thought," he said afterward, "that the loud huzzas that spread over the field at dark were a sufficient assurance and notice to anyone within five miles of us."[27]

On the morning of the 21st, when asked for his opinion, Longstreet urged Bragg to take the offensive.[28] The commanding General hesitated, reflected and did not send his columns after the defeated Federals until that afternoon. Then he moved to Missionary Ridge instead of directly against Chattanooga.[29] The explanation given by Bragg in his official report was that "some time in daylight was absolutely necessary" for his exhausted troops to get food and water and to replenish their ammunition.[30] In the judgment of Polk, Longstreet and Harvey Hill, their commander thus yielded to the enemy, by indecision and delay, all the fruits of the victory at Chickamauga.

23 O. R., 29, pt. 2, pp. 753–54. This was excellent intelligence work. Orders for the movement of Howard's XI and Slocum's XII Corps were issued early on the morning of September 24. The movement from Washington began on the night of the 25th. Lee had word of it within less than forty-eight hours. For the Federal correspondence, see O. R., 29, pt. 1, p. 146 ff.
24 Ibid., pt. 2, pp. 756, 757, 759, 766, 769, 772–73.
25 Ibid., 766.
26 Col. W. D. Gale, aide to General Polk in William M. Polk, Leonidas Polk . . ., vol. 2, p. 267.
27 Longstreet to D. H. Hill, July n.d., 1884, quoted in 3 B. & L., 659 n.
28 O. R., 30, pt. 4, p. 705.      29 Polk, op. cit., 2, 269.
30 O. R., 30, pt. 2, p. 34.

Disillusionment came quickly to "Old Pete." By the 25th of September, after he had been with his new chief approximately five days, he felt so outraged that he wrote directly to the Secretary of War in galled criticism of Bragg. With sharp words, Longstreet described the slow beginning of the pursuit and the consequent gain by the enemy of two and a half days in which to strengthen at Chattanooga the defenses the Confederates previously had prepared. Then Longstreet proceeded: "To express my convictions in a few words, our chief has done but one thing that he ought to have done since I joined this army. That was to order the attack upon the 20th. All other things that he has done he ought not to have done. I am convinced that nothing but the hand of God can save us or help us as long as we have our ₁resent commander. . . . Can't you send us General Lee? The army in Virginia can operate defensively, while our operations here should be offensive—until we have recovered Tennessee at all events. We need some such great mind as General Lee's (nothing more) to accomplish this." [31]

There was much more of this unhappy episode—a lost letter from Longstreet to Lee,[32] a plea by Polk for Lee to come to Tennessee,[33] the suspension of Polk from command[34] and a round-robin by Polk, Harvey Hill and others, who urged the President to relieve Bragg of command.[35] This document prompted a visit by Davis to Bragg's headquarters. On the 9th of October the grievances of all the senior officers were heard by the Chief Executive in the presence of Bragg. This procedure did not appeal to Longstreet. He thought it "rather a stretch of authority," he wrote afterward, "even with a President" to ask officers to state their opinion of their commanding officer. Longstreet continued: "I gave an evasive reply [to Davis] and made an effort to turn the channel of thought, but he would not be satisfied, and got back to his question. The condition of the army was briefly referred to, and the failure to make an effort to get the fruits of our success, when the opinion was given, in substance, that our commander

[31] O. R., 30, pt. 4, pp. 705–06.   [32] Polk, op cit., 2, 275.
[33] Ibid., 275–76.
[34] As of September 29; O. R., 30, pt. 2, p. 56.
[35] O. R., 30, pt. 2, pp. 65–66. In Longstreet, 464–65, the statement is made that the round-robin was prepared "about the same time" as Longstreet's letters to the Secretary of War and to General Lee. Actually, Longstreet wrote Seddon September 25, and Lee September 26. The round-robin was dated October 4.

could be of greater service elsewhere than at the head of the Army of Tennessee." Other officers were of the same mind.[30]

The next day, Longstreet received a summons to a private conference with Mr. Davis. It lasted nearly all day. Longstreet could see from the President's manner that a change in the army command was in contemplation, and he conjectured that Mr. Davis was considering him as a possible successor to Bragg.[37] A month previously, it will be remembered, Longstreet had suggested confidently that he take Bragg's army and Bragg assume command of his Corps. Now the outlook was less hopeful. "In my judgment," Longstreet explained later, "our last opportunity was lost when we failed to follow the success at Chickamauga, and capture or disperse the Union army, and it could not be just to the service or myself to call me to a position of such responsibility." In his effort to escape an undesirable assignment, Longstreet forthrightly, perhaps tactlessly, remarked to the President that Bragg's forces were in the military department of Joseph E. Johnston. In no other way could they be used effectively than in combined operations by all of Johnston's troops. Under Johnston, said Longstreet, he gladly would serve in any capacity.

That name, according to Longstreet's later narrative, provoked Davis and led to "severe rebuke," though on what grounds Longstreet did not specify.[38] The temper of both men must have flared. Longstreet verbally tendered his resignation, which Davis rejected. The men of the First Corps, said Davis, would be displeased to lose their commander. The General replied that he could arrange that by taking leave. During his absence, the troops would be accustomed to some other leader.

After the President rejected this proposal, the conversation shifted to the divisional command. Longstreet urged the promotion of Micah Jenkins to lead Hood's Division. Davis inclined to Evander Law, the avowed rival of Jenkins. In Longstreet's proposal, seniority was respected because Jenkins was Law's senior as Brigadier by more than two months.[39] Law, on the other hand, had been with the Division during the time Jenkins had been

36 *Longstreet*, 465.
37 Longstreet, *op. cit.*, 466, did not state that Davis formally offered him Bragg's place. His language was: "[The President] thought to assign me to command."
38 Longstreet's words were: "The suggestion of that name [Johnston's] only served to increase his displeasure, and his severe rebuke" (*op. cit.*, 466).
39 Jenkins, July 22; Law, Oct. 3, 1862; *Wright*, 86, 89. See *supra*, p. 226.

on detached duty in Southern Virginia. After a discussion that probably was stubborn on both sides, Longstreet agreed to the promotion of Law as a means of ending the rivalry. Jenkins's heart, said Longstreet, was in the service: he could submit to anything that seemed best for the Army. To this Davis made no reply. Nor did he formally assign a commander to the Division.[40]

When the President and the Lieutenant General had disagreed thoroughly and had ended their conference, Davis walked to the gate, shook hands cordially and smiled graciously. Longstreet recorded: ". . . a bitter look lurking about [the smile's] margin, and the ground-swell, admonished me that clouds were gathering about headquarters of the First Corps even faster than those that told the doom of the Southern cause."[41] Longstreet evidently thought that he had put himself on Davis's black books by proclaiming his faith in Johnston. The President, in turn, perhaps concluded, with his usual sensitiveness, that Longstreet had joined the forces arrayed against the administration.

After a further conference with officers, the decision of the President, maturely reached, was to retain Bragg in command and to relieve D. H. Hill, who was suspected of writing the round-robin.[42] Longstreet outwardly acquiesced but, in the judgment of Bragg's retiring chief of staff, Longstreet did Bragg more injury than did any of the others. "You may understand how much influence with his troops," this officer wrote Joseph E. Johnston, "a remark from a man of [Longstreet's] standing would have to the effect that B[ragg] was not on the field [of Chickamauga] and Lee would have been."[43] If word of this criticism reached Bragg, he did nothing.

In the controversy, Longstreet's former commander in Virginia was careful not to interfere or, for that matter, ever to admit that differences existed between Bragg and that officer's subordinate

[40] *Longstreet,* 468.

[41] *Ibid.* It should be noted that this rhetorical style was not characteristic of Longstreet during the war. In part, his post bellum critics based on the difference in style their contention that some of the writings attributed to the General were from a different pen. The charge is of present importance only where verbiage obscured Longstreet's meaning.

[42] October 13–15; *O. R.,* 30, pt. 2, pp. 148–49. *Cf.* L. T. Wigfall: "I got a letter from Seddon . . . saying that the President was determined to keep Bragg in command, not that he thought him a great General, but that he was better than any with whom he could replace him. That is, better than Johnston or Longstreet" (*Mrs. Wright,* 160). For Hill's later adventures, see *infra,* p. 317 ff.

[43] *O. R.,* 30, pt. 4, p. 742.

commanders. The letter in which Polk asked Lee to come to Tennessee remained long unanswered because the Army of Northern Virginia, during the second week in October, undertook its projected offensive against Meade's weakened forces. When the operation was over and Lee was free to write Polk, he spoke of "infirmities," some of them physical, that would keep him from service in the West. "I hope," said Lee, "the President has been able to rectify all difficulties in your army, and that Rosecrans will at last be obliged to abandon his position." [44] Longstreet received a somewhat similar and assuaging answer to the letter in which he urged Lee to accept command in the Mississippi Valley. Lee explained the recent operations of the Army of Northern Virginia and concluded: ". . . I missed you dreadfully, and your brave corps. Your cheerful face and strong arms would have been invaluable. I hope you will soon return to me. I trust we may soon be together again. May God preserve you and all with you." [45]

In the brief campaign that delayed Lee's replies to Longstreet and Polk, several new general officers participated. Col. Robert M. Johnston of the Twenty-third North Carolina was promoted to take Iverson's, previously Garland's Brigade. [46] To Pettigrew's Brigade, at appropriate rank, W. W. Kirkland, former Colonel of the Twenty-first North Carolina, was assigned. [47] Col. Leroy A. Stafford, a man of conspicuous courage, was given a wreath around his three stars and was placed in charge of Nicholls's Brigade. In Stafford's case, as in that of Kirkland, promotion was from the same Division but a different Brigade. This was saved from being blasphemy against States' rights because the elevated officers came from the same State as the troops they were to lead. [48] Still again, as it now was manifest that Samuel McGowan would not return at an early date to lead his Brigade, Col. Abner Perrin of the Fourteenth South Carolina was promoted to direct that famous command—to the dire offense of Col. D. H. Hamilton, who thought he should have been advanced. [49]

Seth M. Barton, a Virginian and a West Pointer of the class of

44 Polk, *op. cit.*, 2, 276–77.          45 *Longstreet*, 469–70 n.
46 *Wright*, 111; 4 *C. M. H.*, 320–21.
47 For Kirkland see Vol. I, pp. 355, 488; *Wright*, 110; *O. R.*, 29, pt. 2, p. 701; 4 *C. M. H.*, 321–23.
48 *Wright*, 114–15; 10 *C. M. H.*, La., 317.
49 *Wright*, 111–12; *O. R.*, 29, pt. 2, pp. 739–40; 5 *C. M. H.*, 415; *Caldwell*, 113. Colonel Hamilton resigned in November.

1849,[50] formerly a Brigadier in Stevenson's Division,[51] was exchanged after the surrender of Pemberton's army and was assigned to the command of Lewis Armistead's old Brigade, Pickett's Division.[52] Another general officer to join Lee's army and to take command of a worn Brigade was John Pegram, who last was seen in these pages as the leader of a captured column at Rich Mountain.[53] Pegram had been exchanged and, like Barton, had been given a post in the Western army. There he had won his brigadier's commission [54] and at Chickamauga he had led a Division of cavalry,[55] but for reasons of the heart he had decided to come back to Virginia.[56] On October 11, 1863, he was given "Extra Billy" Smith's Brigade in Early's Division [57]—a promising appointment. No man could have a better introduction to the Army of Northern Virginia than to be presented as the older brother of Maj. William J. Pegram.

It probably did not escape attention that of these six new appointments, two only were by promotion within the Brigades. Johnston and Perrin had been Colonels among the men whom now they were to lead as general officers. Stafford and Kirkland, to repeat, had belonged to the Division of which their new Brigades were a part, but the two men had no previous direct connection with those Brigades. Barton and Pegram, though Virginians, were strangers to their troops. New and grim confirmation there was in all this of the ill-omened truth that the material of command was close to exhaustion.

In the next scene of the drama, where these men were to make their first appearance as general officers, the central figure was to be A. P. Hill. He had not shone at Gettysburg, it will be remembered, and after that defeat, he bore an industrious though not a conspicuous part in restoring the Third Corps to fighting competence. In so far as references to him in extant correspondence and memoirs reflect the figure he displayed in the Army, he continued

[50] *Cullum* No. 1434, twenty-eighth in his class.
[51] *Wright*, 75; appointed Mch. 18, 1862.
[52] *O. R.*, 51, pt. 2, p. 771; assigned as of Oct. 4, 1863. For a sketch of Barton, see 3 *C. M. H.*, 579–81.
[53] See Vol. I, p. 28 ff.                    [54] *Wright*, 98, appointed Nov. 10, 1862.
[55] *O. R.*, 30, pt. 2, p. 528.
[56] Robert S. Henry, an authority on the Army of Tennessee, wrote under date of Apr. 5, 1943: "I do not know why Pegram went back to Virginia, but I am sure that it was not by reason of any dissatisfaction with his services on the part of Forrest."
[57] *O. R.*, 29, pt. 2, p. 783.

less notable as a corps commander in June-September, 1863, than he had been as head of his famous Division. Now Hill had a new opportunity.

Meade early in October was encamped North of Culpeper Court House. Two of his Corps were extended to the Rapidan. The sole inexpensive way of attacking him was to turn his position, to force him to retreat and then to assail him in motion or where the ground was less readily defensible. On the 9th of October the Confederate columns began to move. Fitz Lee was left with his cavalry Division to cover the rear. Stuart, with Hampton's Division,[58] went ahead to protect the Confederate right, which would be the flank nearer the enemy. Ewell and Hill proceeded with their Corps to Madison Court House and on to Culpeper. Hill was a native of Culpeper County with which his family had many ties. The older of the once-prosperous residents could recall when Powell Hill had left in 1842 to enter West Point. Long though his absences had been, he possessed the admiring affection of the people. They scarcely saw him in this advance. His Corps on the 11th of October approached the town from the Southwest but presumably skirted Culpeper and went northward to the district of Stone House Mountain,[59] where rations were issued.

The next morning, October 12, on orders of the commanding General, who was trying to intercept the enemy's retreat, the Third Corps started on a wide circuitous advance toward the Orange and Alexandria Railroad. Ewell had the shorter road via Jeffersonton and Sulphur Springs in the direction of Warrenton. Hill moved by Woodville, Sperryville, Gaines' Cross Roads and Waterloo Bridge.[60] This march over familiar ground was easy in the cool, bracing weather. From the East, as Hill's men swung along, they occasionally heard the sound of artillery. Their own advance was not challenged.[61] On the 13th, the steady march carried the Corps to a halt near Warrenton, which Ewell also had

[58] Hampton was still absent on account of the wound received at Gettysburg. See *supra*, p. 195.

[59] *Early*, 303; Lee in *O. R.*, 29, pt. 1, p. 410. "Presumably" has to be inserted in the text because, curiously enough, there is no direct statement that the Army did or did not enter the town. Lee's reference, *loc. cit.*, to arrival "near" Culpeper on the 11th, and his account of revictualing suggest that the Army was close to the railroad but not in the town. For Lee's own brief visit to the Court House, see 3 *R. E. Lee*, 172–73.

[60] For the references by which Hill's route can be traced, and for a sketch of the two lines of march, see 3 *R. E. Lee*, 174 n, and 175.

[61] *Caldwell*, 114.

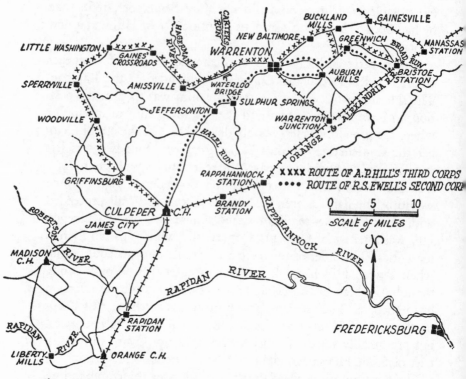

Sketch of the Lines of Advance of the Second and Third Army Corps, Army of Northern
Virginia, from Culpeper Court House to Bristoe Station, Oct. 12–14, 1863. The exact
lines of advance from Orange Court House, via Madison Court House, are not known—
after *William Allan*

reached.[62] Besides the boon of a bivouac in a pleasant country,
some of the men received in their ration white cabbage of a fine-
ness they never had seen. "I confess," wrote one brigade historian,
"to sitting up three-fourths of the night, waiting for a pot of them
to boil." [63]

With full stomach and high heart, the Third Corps resumed
its march on the morning of October 14. The young officer who
kept his vigil by the side of his pot of cabbage recorded the satisfaction of his comrades: "We all entered now fully into the spirit
of the movement. We were convinced that Meade was unwilling
to face us, and we, therefore, anticipated a pleasant affair, if we
should succeed in catching him." [64] In a larger knowledge of the

[62] *O. R.*, 29, pt. 1, p. 410.               [63] *Caldwell*, 115.
[64] *Caldwell*, 115.

situation, Hill himself must have realized that the odds now were against the Confederates in the northward race between the armies. The Federals had started early and they were following the direct roads up the Orange and Alexandria railway. Hill and Ewell had to use roads more remote.[65] Ewell's route for the 14th was to be past Auburn to Greenwich, whence his column would share the road over which the Third Corps would advance. Hill was to reach Greenwich via New Baltimore. All the indications were that the Army of the Potomac was moving toward the Washington defenses.

At Broad Run Church, in the vicinity of New Baltimore, five miles North of Warrenton, Hill received word that a Federal column was moving northward, almost parallel to him. It was supposed to be advancing past Greenwich to the Warrenton Turnpike, which it would reach about one mile East of Buckland. To cope with this Federal force, Hill decided to advance his leading Division along the turnpike toward Buckland. If this Division, which was "Dick" Anderson's, failed to encounter the enemy, it was to proceed southward and rejoin the Corps at Greenwich. To that point on the road to Bristoe Station, Hill directed the march of Heth's and of Wilcox's troops.[66]

Greenwich was reached by the Third Corps about 10 A.M. There, for the first time, Hill's troops definitely were on the trail of the Federals. Fires were still burning. The road toward Bristoe was strewn with the articles retreating soldiers throw away, knapsacks, blankets, guns even. The eyes of the Southerners lighted. It was 1862 again! Their line of advance was distant a few miles only from the Gainesville Road, down which on the 26th of August, nearly fourteen months previously, many of the same regiments had moved to the same objective.[67] Ahead of them, at that time, had been all the delights of plundering the sutlers' establishments and the great base at Manassas. Memory spurred lagging feet. Like speed to Bristoe might yield like prizes. The march became rapid. "It was," said one North Carolinian, "almost like boys chasing a hare."[68]

[65] O. R., 29, pt. 1, p. 411.                [66] O. R., 29, pt. 1, p. 426.
[67] See Vol. II, p. 89 ff.
[68] 2 N. C. Regts., 440. As the Confederates soon ascertained, they were following Maj. Gen. William H. French's III Corps, which had moved northeastward, via Auburn Mills, from Three Mile Station on the Warrenton Railroad. See the report of Brig. Gen. Henry Prince, O. R., 29, pt. 2, p. 314.

Hill rode near the head of his column and, as he approached Bristoe Station, he spurred ahead to see whether the enemy had cleared Broad Run, which flows almost South to a point about half a mile above the station. Hill doubtless knew that the railroad bridge across the Run could be used by infantry and that easy fords existed on either side of the bridge. It was not a crossing where an army need be delayed long, but, of course, there always was a chance that a swift pursuit might surprise an adversary who thought himself safe.

When Hill came to high, open ground in sight of Bristoe Station, he saw thousands of Union soldiers on both banks of Broad Run near the fords. To the northward, beyond the Run, Federal units were moving up the railroad toward Manassas. Nearer at hand, many bluecoats were resting till their turn came to cross the fords and to take up the march.[69] These troops, Hill told himself, were men of the III Corps, whom he had been following from Greenwich. They offered such a mark as no Confederates had been given in Virginia since that May afternoon when Hill and Rodes and Colston had been deployed by Jackson in the woods West of Chancellorsville. Instant action was imperative. Otherwise, Hill reasoned, the enemy would escape. Heth with the leading Division must speed his advance. As soon as Heth was in striking distance he must form line of battle with three Brigades and must keep the other in column as a reserve.[70] Let Poague bring up his artillery battalion immediately! Not a moment must be lost. Such an opportunity might not come again.

Hill's eyes were on the enemy near the fords, and on them only. So eager was he to assail them that he thought Heth's advance and deployment interminable. Soon a staff officer was sent to tell Heth to hurry forward with the troops already in line of battle. If Heth waited to put all his men in position, the Federals would get away.[71] The staff officer spurred on his way with this message, but to Hill it may have seemed a long, long time before Heth's line of battle came in sight. It was a short line, at that. John R.

[69] Hill, in his report, mentioned only the troops on the north bank of the Run, but units which he mistook for part of the III Corps were in the act of crossing at the time of his arrival. See O. R., 29, pt. 1, p. 277.
[70] O. R., 29, pt. 1, pp. 426, 430.
[71] O. R., 29, pt. 1, p. 430. Heth reported that he was a mile and a half from Bristoe when he received Hill's first order to deploy. His narrative and Hill's are reconcilable only on the theory that Hill had ridden ahead of the infantry.

Cooke's Brigade was on the right;[72] Kirkland, with Iverson's old command, was on the left. In rear of them were Henry Walker's Virginians. Walker had not reached the line when the order came for Heth to push forward. Now Walker was trying vainly to catch up with Kirkland and to form on his left.[73]

As these Brigades advanced toward Broad Run, Poague's gunners dashed into position and, at Hill's order, opened fire. A few shots sufficed to send to the north bank of the Run those Federals who had been resting on the nearer shore. Their flight sharpened Hill's combativeness. He would throw Heth's men against the fugitives and would overwhelm them. Heth must move by the left flank, cross the Run and attack.[74]

To Hill's satisfaction, Heth promptly made the shift and began his advance toward the stream. Hill turned to examine the ground between the fords and the advancing line of gray. In doing so, he saw something he had not observed before: Federal skirmishers were visible on the Confederate side of the stream. They were spread southward near the railroad and parallel to it. When Heth's line moved eastward, they would get on its right flank and in its rear.

This indicated that a Federal force still was occupying the ground from which Hill thought all the enemy had retreated across the run, but Hill could not be sure at the moment. He sent back for McIntosh's Battalion of artillery and hurried a messenger, also, to "Dick" Anderson, who was in rear of Heth: Two of Anderson's Brigades must be advanced immediately to cover Heth's right flank. Still another messenger hurried to the advancing line to warn John R. Cooke, commanding Heth's right Brigade, to watch his flank.[75]

Cooke promptly changed the front of one of his regiments and,

[72] John R. Cooke's Brigade, after its commander had been wounded at Fredericksburg, was transferred to North Carolina with Robert Ransom's other troops and was in the field there by Jan. 21, 1863 (O. R., 18, 855). Subsequently the Brigade was sent from Wilmington to Charleston, S. C. It then was assigned to the Third Military District (O. R., 14, 824). The return of the Brigade to Virginia was the subject of long negotiation (O. R., 25, pt. 2, pp. 799–80, 831 ff, 840). Although Cooke's Brigade was made a part of Heth's Division on May 30, 1863 (ibid., 840), and was detached immediately from the Department of North Carolina (ibid., 843), the Brigade did not rejoin Lee immediately. Because of a succession of alarms, Cooke was held around Richmond or on the line of the Annas until about September 25, when he was advanced to Gordonsville (O. R., 29, pt. 2, p. 753).

[73] O. R., 29, pt. 1, pp. 430, 433.        [74] Ibid., 430.
[75] O. R., 29, pt. 1, p. 426.

so far as Hill could see from his command post, drove back the skirmishers.[76] Heth sent a report, moreover, that showed he was alive to the situation: On his right, said Heth, a heavy column of the enemy had appeared. Hill had to halt the Division quickly or order it immediately across the stream in pursuit of the Federals.

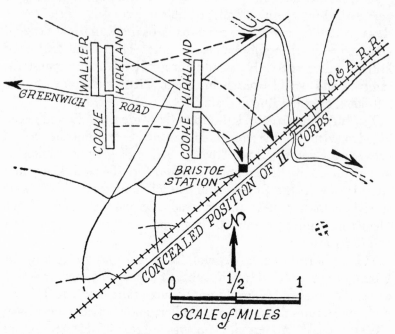

Sketch of the Attack of Cooke and Kirkland at Bristoe Station, Oct. 14, 1863—after *O. R. Atlas*. Plate XLV–7

He reflected for a moment and decided that the movement should be suspended,[77] but he soon changed his mind. Looking to his right, Hill saw the head of Anderson's column. In a short time, Anderson would be on Heth's right and could deal with any Federal force that remained on the right side of the Run. If Heth waited, the enemy might slip away. Impetuously a courier was sent to order Heth to the fords and in pursuit.[78] To save minutes, a second courier was hurried directly to Cooke with instructions to advance at once to the stream and to cross.[79] In order to cover both Anderson's movement and that of Heth, the corps com-

[76] *Ibid.*
[78] *O. R.* 29. pt. 1. p. 426.
[77] *O. R.*, 29, pt. 1, p. 430.
[79] 2 *N. C. Regts.* 441.

mander selected for McIntosh's guns, which now were arriving, a
position in rear of Cooke. Better ground for Poague also was
indicated by Hill.[80]

Soon a rider dashed up to Hill with another message: Heth
sent word that Cooke was certain that as he moved forward, the
Federals near the railroad would take him in flank. Heth wished
to know whether, in this contingency, Cooke should advance.
Hill was positive in his answer: Anderson was coming up; Cooke
would be safe.[81] That was enough for the subordinates. Orders
were orders. In a short time Hill saw Cooke's line come over the
crest of a hill and start forward. Kirkland was on Cooke's left.
Inasmuch as Broad Run coursed almost South toward the railroad,
which itself ran from Northeast to Southwest, Cooke and Kirkland were marching into an obtuse angle. They would continue
that line of advance until they could move by the left flank across
the stream.

Thus Hill hastily had planned the attack, but a furious burst of
fire soon showed how mistaken he had been. Anxious messages
explained what smoke quickly concealed from the eyes. Federals
still were on the Confederate side of the stream in great numbers.
They had not been observed earlier because they had been concealed all the while behind the railroad embankment, which Hill
had not thought to reconnoiter. When Cooke and Kirkland advanced toward the stream, their entire right was exposed to Union
fire from the embankment and from good Union artillery positions in rear of it. Instead of making a flank movement across the
Run, the two Brigades became heavily engaged in front of the
embankment and, to save themselves, had to try to drive the Union
force from its cover.[82]

In the attempt, Cooke's Brigade was slaughtered. Not less than
700 of its men were killed, wounded or captured. The magnificent Twenty-seventh North Carolina, which had earned immortal-
ity at Sharpsburg, sacrificed thirty-three of its officers and 290 of
its 416 men.[83] Kirkland lost 602, of whom nearly half surrendered
after they reached the railroad cut and saw that they could not
escape otherwise than by fighting their way back under fire. Total

[80] O. R., 29, pt. 1, p. 427.
[81] O. R., 29, pt. 1, p. 431.
[82] O. R., 29, pt. 1, pp. 427, 431, 435; 2 N. C. Regts.. 440–41.
[83] 2 N. C. Regts., 443.

casualties in Heth's Division were 1361 and for the Army during the entire operation, 1381 killed and wounded.[84]

Both Cooke and Kirkland were badly wounded [85] to the dire impairment of their shattered commands. In both instances the leaders realized the danger in which the two Brigades were put by Hill's instructions, but they charged boldly. Said Cooke, upon receipt of peremptory orders to go forward when he knew his flank would be exposed: "Well, I will advance, and if they flank me, I will face my men about and cut my way out." [86] Besides Cooke and Kirkland, a third general officer was wounded. In a futile attempt by "Dick" Anderson to cover Heth's flank, Carnot Posey was badly wounded in the left thigh by a ball from a spherical case shot.[87] He was brought off the field and was carried to Charlottesville, Virginia, where on November 13, he was to succumb to his injuries.[88]

For these casualties, no blame was placed on Harry Heth. He had acted in precise accord with his orders from Hill, and he had taken pains to see that the full measure of the danger to the flank of the attacking column was made known to the corps commander. The battle was another instance of the singular ill fortune that pursued Heth, but the responsibility was Hill's, not his.[89] The Army realized this. Criticism of Hill was on every angry lip.[90] In his report, which he filed promptly, Hill admitted that he did not know of the presence behind the railroad embankment of the Federals who, after repulsing the Confederates with light losses on their own part, calmly marched on.[91] The only palliation that Hill could offer was covered by these words: "I am convinced that I made the attack too hastily, and at the same time

---

[84] To this figure of 1381 should be added the 445 missing from Heth's Division (*O. R.*, 29, pt. 1, p. 433). Other units had few. The gross loss, killed, wounded and prisoners, probably was about 1900.

[85] *O. R.*, 29, pt. 1, p. 432.                    [86] 2 *N. C. Regts.*, 441.

[87] *O. R.*, 29, pt. 1, p. 429; W. M. Harris, compiler: *Movements of the Confederate Army . . . from the Diary of Gen. Nat. H. Harris* (cited hereafter as *N. H. Harris*), 23.
[88] 7 *C. M. H.*, Miss., 266.

[89] *Cf.* Hill to Heth, Jan. 13, 1864: ". . . the attack was ordered by me, and most gallantly made by your division" (*O. R.*, 51, pt. 2, p. 811). The next major references to Heth are *infra*, p. 351 ff.

[90] See the references in 3 *R. E. Lee*, 183.

[91] The troops there were Maj. Gen. G. K. Warren's II Corps. Units of that command most heavily engaged at Bristoe Station were the 1st and 3rd Brigades of Brig. Gen. Alexander S. Webb's 2nd Division and the 3rd Brigade of Brig. Gen. Alexander Hays's 3rd Division (*O. R.*, 29, pt. 1, p. 242). These were splendid veterans who had repulsed Pickett at Gettysburg. Warren's casualties were 548 (*ibid.*, 226).

that a delay of half an hour, and there would have been no enemy to attack. In that event I believe I should equally have blamed myself for not attacking at once." [92]

In forwarding to the War Department Hill's confession, the commanding General said in his endorsement: "General Hill explains how, in his haste to attack the Third Army Corps of the enemy, he overlooked the presence of the Second, which was the cause of the disaster that ensued." Secretary Seddon endorsed: "The disaster at Bristoe Station seems due to a gallant but over-hasty pressing of the enemy." President Davis was more realistic: "There was a want of vigilance," he wrote.[93] More painful far to the proud, sensitive Hill must have been Lee's rebuke. The day after the battle, Hill conducted the commanding General over the field and explained what had happened. Lee had little to say and showed plainly in his face that he was disappointed. At last he spoke: "Well, well, General, bury these poor men and let us say no more about it." [94]

[92] O. R., 29, pt. 1, p. 427.      [93] O. R., 29, pt. 1, pp. 427–28.
[94] For the references, see 3 R. E. Lee, 183. The next extended reference to A. P. Hill is infra, p. 351.

# CHAPTER XIV

## "Jeb" Stuart's New Adventures

THE CAVALRY's part in the Bristoe campaign tested "Jeb" Stuart's new divisional organization but not all of his new general officers. Hampton was absent still because of his wounds; Fitz Lee had a vigorous hand in the fighting. Of all the Brigadiers, only Lunsford Lomax and James Gordon were at their posts. The other Brigades, without exception, were led by Colonels. Pierce Young, who had been wounded again on August 1, headed Butler's Brigade as the senior officer present, and he probably did not know, till the campaign was over, that he had been promoted.[1] Rosser, too, participated as a Colonel. "Grumble" Jones's Brigade still was under Colonel Funsten. The troopers of Wickham were in the care of Col. Thomas H. Owen of the Third Virginia.[2] Col. John R. Chambliss Jr., of the Thirteenth Virginia, again directed "Rooney" Lee's Brigade, but he had done this so often that he was to be counted now as a seasoned brigade leader. Exercise of higher command by the other Colonels involved, of course, the care of regiments by Lieutenant Colonels or by Majors. In short, since the Seven Days there scarcely had been a time when so large a part of Stuart's force was under men who had not been tested at the posts they now filled. To the limited extent of its importance, the campaign thus tested the efficiency of the system under which cavalry officers were trained. Stuart himself was tried anew, this time primarily as instructor.

Orders from Army Headquarters, it will be recalled,[3] were that

---

[1] O. R., 27, pt. 2, p. 312; 25 S.H.S.P., 149. DeLeon, in B. B. B., 104, denied, in order that he might repeat, the story that after the lovely Mattie Ould of Richmond was seen with her head on Pierce Young's shoulder, she dismissed the gossip with the bon mot: "There's nothing odd about it; it is only an old head on young shoulders." The difference in the ages of General Young and Miss Ould, daughter of Judge Robert Ould, Commissioner for the Exchange of Prisoners, makes the story improbable for the period of the war. Born Mch. 23, 1850, she knew General Young after the war, when she probably was engaged to him for a time. Her marriage to Oliver Schoolcraft was solemnized in 1876. She died the next year.

[2] O. R., 29, pt. 1, p. 452.

[3] Supra, p. 239.

one Division of cavalry should be left temporarily on the Rapidan and that the other should be employed on the right of the Army during the attempted turning movement. As Stuart of course rode with the van, this arrangement left Fitz Lee on the Rapidan. "Jeb" himself assumed command of the three Brigades of Hampton's men. One of these Brigades was detached on October 10 to cover the advance of the infantry. Stuart consequently advanced against the enemy with the forces of Gordon and of Young, the North and South Carolina troopers.[4] It was the first time "Jeb" had led a large cavalry column in which there were no Virginians.

The start was in the spirit of '62 when the bluecoats could not face the butternut cavalry. By way of Madison Court House, Stuart moved on the 10th toward the enemy in order to make a demonstration and thereby to divert attention from the advance of the infantry. In the first clash a Federal detachment was thrown back upon the main force. The remainder of the 10th, Stuart spent in galloping along the roads and in using his batteries ostentatiously to create the impression that he intended to attack. He finally coaxed the Unionists into charging his guns and then he beat off the assault easily. Meanwhile some of his men had driven the Federals from their signal station on Thoroughfare Mountain,[5] but not until the officer responsible for the station had observed and reported the Confederate advance.[6]

The next morning, October 11, the Federals having disappeared from his front, Stuart proceeded toward Culpeper,[7] which he found the enemy had abandoned. Union cavalry stood in manifest strength between the retiring infantry and Stuart's regiments. Although the return of some of Funsten's squadrons gave Stuart more men,[8] "Jeb" decided against a direct attack on an adversary who was well placed and supplied with ample artillery. The sensible thing to do, "Jeb" reasoned, was to turn the Federal position and get in the enemy's rear on the old battleground of Brandy Station. This appeared to be a course as safe as profitable, and for

[4] Plus Cobb's Georgia Legion and the Jeff Davis Mississippi Legion. Funsten's, i.e. Jones's, Brigade was with Ewell and Hill.

[5] This eminence, about midway between Culpeper and Madison Court Houses, and near the settlement then known as James City, must not be confused with Thoroughfare Gap in Bull Run Mountains. Stuart's account of the day's operations is in O. R., 29, pt. 1, pp. 439–40.

[6] See report of Capt. P. A. Taylor, Signal Corps, U. S. A., in O. R., 29, pt. 1, p. 230.

[7] For a map of this district, see supra, p. 240.

[8] The Eleventh Virginia had been sent to Rixeyville (O. R., 29, pt. 1, p. 455).

this cheering reason: From the East, there rolled the echo of artillery, which Stuart took to be that of Fitz Lee in pursuit of Federals from the line of the Rapidan. To judge from the sound of the firing, Fitz was coming nearer. He would be available with his three Brigades when Stuart struck the enemy.

As Stuart approached Brandy Station via the Rixeyville Road, his pride sank: He saw that the Federals had fathomed his plan and were moving toward Fleetwood Hill in heavy columns from the South. Instinctively, he determined to push on and to charge them before they could reach the high ground he had defended on the humiliating 9th of June. At a faster pace the cavalry of Gordon and of Funsten [9] approached the farm of the old Whig politician, John Minor Botts. From the hill where the mansion stood, Stuart looked eastward across the Orange and Alexandria Railroad toward Stevensburg and there he could see the rising smoke of Fitz Lee's guns.[10]

Fortune seemed to favor the bold. The retreating enemy, moving up the railroad, was squarely between Fitz Lee, closing on Brandy from the East, and Stuart, who was pushing from the West! It was a glorious opportunity to redeem the Brandy of four months previously . . . but just when "Jeb" was about to apply the vise, shells began to fall most unpleasantly close. Fitz Lee had seen the column of Stuart and, mistaking it for arriving Federal reinforcements, was firing on it!

The advance of Gordon and Funsten had been so rapid that the horse artillery was far behind them. The gunners could not open against the Federals to show young Lee that he had friends, not foes, to the West of the railroad.[11] The sole means of informing Fitz of his mistake was to attack the Federals, who already suspected they were in a trap. "Regiment after regiment," as it seemed to Stuart, "broke and dispersed." [12] The reliable Twelfth Virginia was at the head of the column: let it charge the scattering enemy!

Without a second of hesitation, the Twelfth, which had fought previously at Brandy, dashed at the enemy. As Stuart looked, his blue eyes aflame, the regiment swung like a scythe in a harvester's

9 Young had been left on the flank.          10 O. R., 29, pt. 1, p. 443.
11 Cf. O. R., 29, pt. 1, p. 443; H. B. McClellan, 381. For a sketch of the terrain, see supra, p. 6.
12 O. R., 29, pt. 1, p. 443.

hand and cut off many hundreds of the enemy. The Virginians sensed their opportunity and began to yell. If only Fitz Lee would come up now and throw his column against the opposing flank, what a harvest of prisoners there would be! Fitz did not gallop forward. The sound of his firing did not advance.[13] It would be impossible to corral the bluecoats and their madly plunging horses unless Stuart could bring quickly to the front the Fifth and the Sixth North Carolina, whose advancing troopers were spread for hundreds of yards back on the narrow road.

At that moment, a battalion of Federal cavalry, moving in column of squadrons, bore down on the flank of the approaching Carolina regiments. Every one who watched the approach of the battalion observed that the force was small and without support. The Confederates in the road either did not see or did not comprehend. They stopped, they wheeled, and then they made off in utter panic. Stuart himself dashed back to halt them. Gordon pleaded and shouted. Nothing availed. The cavalrymen ran till they were confronted with the drawn pistols of officers who barred the road.

In the place of the fleeing regiments, the Seventh Virginia came up promptly to support the Twelfth, but it was too late to capture the Federals who had been scattered in the first charge.[14] Nor could Fitz Lee, after discovering his error, reach his chief before the Federals had climbed Fleetwood Hill and had planted their artillery on it. Furious Confederate attacks failed to dislodge them. Another attempt to get in their rear simply led the Unionists to begin a defiant withdrawal toward the Rappahannock.

With most of his force, Stuart followed the next morning, October 12, in order to shield the movement of the infantry in the direction of Bristoe. His adventures that day were not instructive,[15] but Tom Rosser and Pierce Young had new experiences in their training for brigade command. Rosser had been left near Fleetwood, with one fieldpiece, to picket against a possible attempt

---

[13] He heard the shouts of the men of the Twelfth, but he thought they were cries of encouragement from newly arrived Federal regiments and he pulled rein instead of applying spur (O. R., 29, pt. 1, p. 443).
[14] O. R., 29, pt. 1, p. 443; H. B. McClellan, 380. The charge on the Carolina regiments was delivered by the 5th New York. Apparently Brig. Gen. H. E. Davies, Jr., commanding the 1st Cavalry Brigade, did not realize the magnitude of the panic the Federal charge created. Cf. O. R., 29, pt. 1, p. 386.
[15] The details are given in O. R., 29, pt. 1, pp. 445-46.

by the enemy to move on Culpeper, which now was being used as Lee's advance depot. Young had been ordered to move to Culpeper with his Brigade and to protect the supplies and the trains.[16] All was quiet at Brandy until about 2 P.M. Then a large Federal force, infantry and cavalry,[17] appeared from the North and advanced as if it intended to reoccupy Culpeper. Rosser at once sent word to Young that he would need support; but with the men at hand, in fortunate ignorance of impossible odds, he began a rearguard action. Early in the fight he received a slight wound and started to the rear to have it dressed, but at that moment he saw his men waver. His wound was forgotten on the instant. He rushed to the hesitating troopers, rallied them, and continued to fight as he gave ground. Soon Young came up, quickly got his five guns in position, drew a long line of dismounted men and waited for Rosser to fall back through it. When Rosser was safe, Young opened with his artillery and discouraged a Federal attack.[18]

Neither side made any further move before nightfall. After darkness Young did not know what to expect, but he reasoned that a show of force might make the enemy cautious. He tried the familiar devices. Fires were lighted in numbers sufficient to keep a Division warm on the coldest night. The Brigade's band was ordered to blow its loudest at one bivouac and then was hurried to another ring of campfires, as if it were a company of rival musicians.[19] The bandsmen might have saved their breath, because next morning the enemy was gone. Meade had ascertained during the night that the Confederate infantry were moving around the Federal flank, and he started northward to protect his rear.[20]

"Jeb" Stuart had anticipated this[21] and he hoped now that he might assail shrewdly a retreating foe. About 10 o'clock on the morning of the 13th, while Hampton's Division was East of Warrenton, Stuart received orders to make a reconnaissance in force toward Catlett's Station, the scene of one of his great adventures

---

[16] O. R., 29, pt. 1, pp. 444, 458.
[17] The infantry were the II, V and VI Corps, which were being countermarched to Culpepper in the belief that Lee was there. Buford's Division were the cavalry (O. R., 29, pt. 1, p. 10).
[18] O. R., 29, pt. 1, pp. 458–59. The sketch of Rosser is resumed *infra*, pp. 274, 278.
[19] H. B. McClellan, 384.          [20] O. R., 29, pt. 1, pp. 10, 459.
[21] O. R., 29, pt. 1, p. 446.

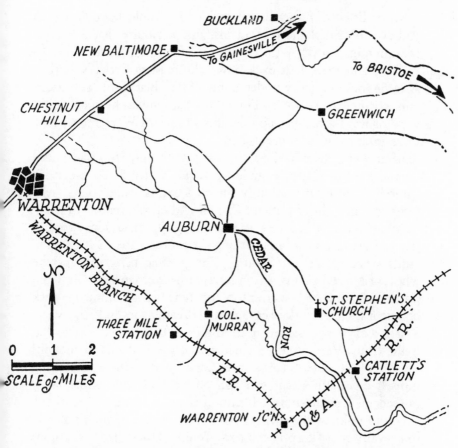

Vicinity of Auburn, where Stuart thought his force surrounded on the night of Oct. 13–14, 1863. The sketch shows, also, the scene of the "Buckland Races," Oct. 19, 1863. There is reason to suspect that the original of this map is inaccurate as respects the course of Cedar Run and the direction of the road from Three Mile Station to Auburn. It is because of this doubt that the location of Stuart's bivouac cannot be determined. See note 28, p. 256. After *O. R. Atlas,* Plate XL–6

the preceding August.[22] Joyfully Stuart sent Lomax ahead and himself started for Auburn.[23] When he arrived at the village he found Lomax there. The Brigadier had learned of the presence of Federals at Warrenton Junction, a bare six miles to the Southeast, and at Three Mile Station, on the little railroad from the Junction to Warrenton. Lomax had waited at Auburn to give this information and to get further orders.

[22] See Vol. II, p. 69 ff.
[23] In reports and correspondence the names Auburn and Auburn Mills are used interchangeably.

Stuart listened, reflected and decided he would leave Lomax at Auburn to protect the rear against the possibility that a Federal column might move up the road from Warrenton Junction toward Auburn and then dash back down the road to Catlett's Station. A reconnoitering party under Capt. W. W. Blackford must ascertain whether the enemy at Three Mile Station was heading northward or was proceeding up the railroad toward Warrenton where Lee's infantry were concentrated.

After doing these obvious but essential things, Stuart advanced on the road to Catlett's Station and got as far as St. Stephen's Church.[24] Pushing cautiously forward beyond that point, "Jeb" came within sight of Catlett's Station and of Warrenton Junction simultaneously. What he saw was enough to make him drop his jaw and grip his sword hilt. Along the railroad, the enemy's thousands were spread northward. The greater part, perhaps the whole of Meade's Army was in retreat toward Manassas! Between Catlett's Station and Warrenton Junction was an immense park of wagons, such a park as cavalrymen dream about in happy sleep. Stuart looked and sensed a triumph: If Lee moved down that night from Warrenton, he could strike the Federals in motion! Maj. Reid Venable, Stuart's Inspector General, who was proving himself especially useful as a staff officer, must ride immediately to General Lee and must tell him of the opportunity.

Until Lee knew the enemy's position and could begin his march, the cavalry must keep in the background. Stuart had seven guns and two Brigades and he believed he might strike a hard blow if he could arrange a surprise; but the gain would be unreckonably greater if Lee could employ the two Corps of infantry against the sprawling, exposed files that were plodding northward. So reasoned "Jeb," and unconsciously gave evidence that he was maturing as a soldier. Fifteen months previously, at Evelington Heights, he had flushed the enemy with a single gun and a few rounds of ammunition.[25]

---

[24] Stuart called this St. Andrews' Church, but the Federal map of the campaign, *O. R. Atlas,* Plate XLV, No. 6, marked it St. Stephen's. Rev. G. MacLaren Brydon, D.D., Historiographer of the Diocese of Virginia, wrote May 17, 1943: "I have no record whatever to show that any Episcopal church in that, or any other section of Fauquier is named St. Andrew. St. Stephen's Church was built about 1837, 'despoiled, desecrated and later burnt' by Federal soldiers during the war and rebuilt on the old site about 1878. It is now a sort of Chapel of Ease in Cedar Run Parish, the present parish church being Grace Church, Casanova."

[25] See Vol. I, p. 640.

The next development was as unexpected as the first sight of that incredible pack of wagons: A courier rode up and reported that when Venable had reached Auburn, en route to Warrenton, he had found the village in the hands of the Federals. Venable sent word that he was making a detour and had every confidence he could get through to Warrenton, but he wished Stuart to know that the enemy was between the Confederate cavalry and Lee.

Nothing was heard from Lomax. All the additional information Stuart received during the afternoon came from Blackford. The engineer, returning from his reconnaissance, confirmed the message from Venable. Beyond all question, the Federals were moving past Auburn. Stuart was cut off. To rejoin the Army, his butternut troopers must ride through or around the enemy. Instead of a night march to descend on the Federals, there might be a hard ride to evade them.

When Stuart approached Auburn, he ran into Federal videttes. Skirmishing began. In the confusion and the gathering twilight, little was learned of the Federals' movements, but the presumption was that the Federals were retreating along the highway to Greenwich and to Bristoe. If this were true, then Stuart was almost surrounded. The one road back to the main Army appeared to be blocked. For a considerable distance, Cedar Run was not fordable except at Auburn.[26] To the East of Stuart were the Federal columns proceeding up the Orange and Alexandria Railroad. South and West and North were the Union troops who evidently had diverged from the main line of retreat at Warrenton Junction and, apparently, intended to come back to that line at Bristoe.[27] To be sure, the two lines of Federal advance in the half ellipse of roads were not dangerously close together. From North to South, Stuart might have as many as five open miles. His range East and West was approximately that, but scarcely more.

Manifestly there was no quick way of slipping from this pen. Troopers, horses, seven guns, the ambulances and ordnance wagons must be hidden until the enemy was gone or a line of escape was found. Search for a concealed refuge began. To the East of Auburn, and almost in sight of it, Stuart observed that the mouth of a little valley came down to the road. The entrance was covered by woods but, at a little distance, the valley was wider. On its

<hr>

[26] O. R., 29, pt. 1, p. 447.     [27] Cf. Stuart in ibid., 447–48.

western side, next the road up which the Federals were thought to be moving, was a cleared, grassy field. Beyond this was a low eminence. The place was ideal! Even the entrance to his hiding place was protected against any except a large force. At two con-venient points on the road, pickets could be concealed in thick bushes twenty yards apart. If a small patrol or a courier came along the road, the first pickets could close behind while those in front barred the way.[28]

With little noise the men moved into the valley. The ambu-lances and guns were brought to safety without stalling. Soon the valley was almost as quiet as it had been before the Confederates arrived; but from the road came the groan of wagon wheels and the sound of marching men's talk. The Federal column was not more than 150 yards from the low ridge on the western side of the valley. As scores of the marching Federals had lanterns, the scene was picturesque even if the outlook was dangerous.[29]

The Confederates, observing all this, agreed that it would be possible to wreck their wagons, to spike and dismount their guns and then to cut their way out. Stuart would not consider such a course. Never would he abandon his guns! The next proposal was his own and was more to his taste: In the darkness, he might go out into the road and turn westward the head of the next divi-sion of the Federal wagon train, and then he might have his men fall silently into the place made vacant by the wagon train and move northward with the main column until a crossroad was reached. This would be easy with a small contingent, but Stuart had to admit that two Brigades of cavalry, occupying a long stretch of road, scarcely could hope to deceive the enemy. Besides, if Major Venable had reached Army Headquarters, Lee might attack from the West at dawn. If the cavalry remained within striking distance of the enemy, they might do great damage.

It was best, then, for Stuart to stay where he was for the night and to look to the main Army to succor him by attacking the enemy. In that conviction, "Jeb" sent off six messengers, one after another, to slip through the Federal column, to ride to Warrenton

<hr/>

28 *W. W. Blackford's MS Memoirs*, 351–52. M. S. Bennett, a life-long resident of Warrenton, kindly wrote under date of June 3, 1943, that the terrain and local tradition were that Stuart's camp was located South of Cedar Run and East of the Double Poplars; but on a further review of the contemporary evidence, Mr. Bennett felt that the site could not be determined with certainty.

29 *W. W. Blackford's MS Memoirs*, 352.

and to inform Lee of the plight of the cavalry. This done, Stuart and his men prepared to "outwatch the stars." [30] The General himself stretched out and, with Captain Blackford's body as a pillow, slept in calm comfort for some time. [31] Confederate officers near the road, directing the pickets, had as pleasant a night as if they had been 'possum hunting. Now and again a dispatch rider would pass the first picket and, a minute later, would run into the second, which would block the road. When he wheeled and started back, he would pull up abruptly in front of a pistol barrel. Each of these captured riders had written messages. None of these papers showed that the Federal officers who wrote them had any knowledge of the proximity of the Confederate mounted troops. [32]

Much the worst vexation of the night was the traditional servant and secret traitor of the fighting man, the army mule. That luckless but stubborn animal, last to be fed and first to be lashed, was left in the traces because he might be needed quickly. Hungry and uncomprehending, knowing that one master was as bad as another, the mule began a plaintive hee-haw. A fellow sufferer took it up. Another and another brayed until the Confederates were sure the passing Federals would hear and investigate. Word was passed for the assignment to each mule of a soldier whose duty it would be to stifle every bray. The men reluctantly went on this odd duty and discharged it with indifferent success. A trooper's intentions might be good, but his alertness would lag. The moment selected for a nod might be that chosen by the animal for its vocal protest against the darkness of the night, the dryness of its throat and the emptiness of its stomach. "Never," remembered Henry McClellan, "was the voice of a mule so harsh." [33] The defiance of that bray, in the presence of the enemy, doubtless was one of ten thousand incidents that added to American metaphor the familiar assertion that a man of superlative effrontery has "the nerve of a government mule."

Although mules brayed as if they, and not the cock, were heralding the day, the October dawn mercifully cloaked the Run, the road and the wood in thick fog. [34] When it was light enough to see through the trees, or over the crest of the ridge, the Confederates saw dimly on the same side of the stream with themselves a

[30] O. R., 29, pt. 1, p. 453; H. B. McClellan, 390–91.
[31] W. W. Blackford's MS Memoirs, 352.      [32] O. R., 29, pt. 1, p. 448.
[33] Op. cit., 390.      [34] O. R., 29, pt. 1, pp. 238, 448.

Federal command that had halted to cook breakfast. Fires were lighted. Coffee pots were produced. The ground dark bean, so rare among Confederates, was dumped prodigally in. If the Confederates did not actually smell the brewing beverage, it made them so envious they could conjure up the odor. Not content to tantalize the hidden butternut troopers, bluecoats began to wander about in search of a spring. It was certain that some of these men would stumble into the Confederates, and then . . . well, load the seven cannon and wheel them quietly to a point just under the crest of the ridge. Loosen swords in the scabbard and take a look at the priming of pistols. Unless Lee had started troops from Warrenton to fall on the flank of the Federals, there might be a more desperate fight than that of Brandy or of Aldie.

Soon, from across the road and from the direction of Warrenton, there came the crack-crack of rifles, as if pickets were engaged. Stuart wanted no further signal of the expected relief. At a shouted word of command the cannon were pushed to the crest and were directed at those campfires. Coffee pots, blasted high, were rained upon the scarlet autumn undergrowth. In the Confederate vernacular, the Federals "skedaddled"—but not far. With surprising, soldierly speed, the nearest Federals formed a line of battle and started straight for the Confederate artillery.

Almost at the same instant, as it seemed to "Jeb," the Confederate fire ceased on the other side of the road. If the horse artillerists and their support observed this, they were too busy on their own front to inquire the reason. They gave their hottest, shell and canister, to the oncoming Federals. The dismounted men fired as fast as if they had been veteran infantry. It was too much for the bluecoats. Quickly their formation was broken. All the while, the Southern officers had been deploying their mounted men on the flank of the guns. Soon a line was in position diagonally across the road to Catlett's Station.

So long as it was probable that the Federals would seek to rush the gun position again, Stuart knew he must remove the pieces or lose them. To cover the withdrawal of the artillery, Gordon ordered the First Carolina to charge. That finely disciplined command dashed forward and confused the Federals but itself became so entangled in the close line of battle that it wheeled and came back to re-form for another charge. Before this could be delivered,

Stuart concluded that a swift movement on a wide arc around the Federal flank might carry the two Brigades out of danger. "Jeb" determined to make the effort. The ambulances and ordnance wagons were ready to move. All the guns were prepared to leave the field. Every man, except the sharpshooters, was in the saddle. Quickly on word of command, the guns were limbered up, the sharpshooters were mounted, and the column was off. Down to the mill-race, which was quickly bridged, and around the flank of the Federals the graycoats dashed—and encountered scarcely a challenging shot.[35] After that, rejoining Lee was merely a matter of keeping awake in the saddle long enough to reach field headquarters.

Many explanations were in order. Lomax, who had disappeared from Auburn after he had been posted there, told how he had undertaken to communicate with Stuart and, failing that, had resisted the advancing Federals and then had joined Fitz Lee, who came up and ordered him to withdraw.[36] Stuart was critical when he ascertained that part of Ewell's command had advanced to his rescue and, as he thought, had quit fighting as soon as he opened fire. Said he: "A vigorous attack with our main body at the time that I expected it would have assured the annihilation of that army corps."[37] In reality, the reports of the Federals show that some of their Brigades were more disturbed by Ewell's fire than by that of the cavalry.[38]

Stuart himself was mistaken concerning the movements of the enemy during his vigil. He thought that the Federals had marched northward through the night, in the direction of Bristoe Station.[39] Truth was, the III Corps had marched from Three Mile Station to Auburn and there had entered the road to Greenwich;[40] but the rear Division of the Corps reached Greenwich at 3 A.M.[41] As Greenwich was five miles from Auburn, the last of the Federals

---

[35] O. R., 29, pt. 1, p. 448; H. B. McClellan, 392, in an account that differs slightly from Stuart's narrative. It is not easy, from the vague and conflicting reports, to determine the exact position of the Confederate front or the line of retreat. Stuart's reference to crossing the mill-race and Major McClellan's emphasis upon the importance of maintaining the left flank, "which extended across the road to Catlett's," would seem to indicate that the withdrawal was South of Auburn and around the rear of the Federals.
[36] O. R., 29, pt. 1, pp. 447, 449, 466.
[37] O. R., 29, pt. 1, p. 448.
[38] Cf. O. R., 29, pt. 1, pp. 239, 254, 256, 271.
[39] O. R., 29, pt. 1, pp. 447–48.     [40] Ibid., 311–12.
[41] Ibid., 314.

had passed Auburn by the time the van reached Greenwich.[42] The head of the II Corps of G. K. Warren, advancing by farm roads on the flank of the III Corps, reached Auburn after dark and bivouacked. As the other Divisions came up, they stopped along-side the road for three miles. At 2 A.M., Warren received orders to proceed from Auburn to Catlett's Station and then to move northward along the railroad. Obediently, Warren placed Brig. Gen. John C. Caldwell's Division facing Warrenton to cover the rear. Before daylight, Warren directed the men to cook breakfast and to prepare to march to Catlett's.[43] Apparently, Stuart did not know when the III Corps stopped passing toward Greenwich. Nor did he realize that the II Corps was headed for Catlett's. For once, his reconnaissance was poor.

The same thing had to be said of his advance later on the 14th, the date of Hill's unhappy experience at Bristoe with that same II Corps of Warren's. By some blunder, Stuart followed the march of a battalion of sharpshooters who were moving toward Catlett's Station. Misled, he did not reach Bristoe till Hill's battle had been fought.[44] On October 15–17, Stuart harassed the still-retiring Federals. In his report he insisted that he procured much information of value and compelled the Unionists to retreat farther than they intended.[45] Lee did not seem to put so high a valuation on the performances of the cavalry those three days. His official account barely mentioned the mounted arm.[46]

Better luck came on the withdrawal. Stuart fell back to Gaines-ville and Hay Market;[47] Fitz Lee retired via Manassas Junction and Bristoe Station.[48] The two Divisions were to meet, if desirable, in the vicinity of Warrenton. On the evening of the 18th of October, Stuart's outposts were attacked with a vigor that led him to think the whole weight of the enemy's cavalry might fall on the Division he commanded in person.[49] Stuart consequently re-treated to the south bank of Broad Run at Buckland, where he believed he could repulse attacks till Fitz Lee arrived. The enemy pursued and, on the morning of the 19th, approached Broad Run,

[42] The III Corps, three Divisions, had on October 10 an aggregate present of 16,915 (O. R., 29, pt. 1, p. 226), which would make the average of a Division about 5600 men.
[43] O. R., 29, pt. 1, pp. 237–38.
[44] O. R., 29, pt. 1, p. 449.
[45] O. R., 29, pt. 1, p. 450.
[46] Cf. ibid., 408, 411.
[47] O. R., 29, pt. 1, p. 452.
[48] Ibid., 463–64.
[49] Ibid., 451, 998.

Across the stream was a bridge Stuart had left intact, but except for this, there was no ford closer than one mile.[50]

Without difficulty, Stuart beat off feeble demonstrations against the bridge until he began to suspect that the enemy was preparing to turn his flank.[51] While "Jeb" was wondering what he should do to meet this threat, a courier arrived from Fitz Lee, who had heard the firing and had appraised the situation. His Division, said Fitz, was approaching from Auburn and would reach the eastern side of the road from Buckland to Warrenton. If Stuart would retire from Broad Run and lure the Federals on, Fitz could come up on their left flank. Then, when Fitz was at hand, he could give a signal by firing a cannon. Stuart thereupon could attack and drive the enemy northward while Fitz struck their flank.[52]

Jubilantly on the instant, Stuart accepted the plan. Details were arranged. Hampton's Division, by Stuart's order, fell back to Chestnut Hill, which is about two and a half miles Northeast of Warrenton.[53] The position was a low range of hills into which ran the wide, straight turnpike. Quietly the Confederate troopers were placed in columns behind depressions in the ridge. Before them was firm ground in the direction of the enemy's advance. Hidden and confident, the Southern cavalry waited and watched the approach of the Federals. A gallant display the enemy made. His equipment, which the Southerners always admired, shone in the dazzling autumn sunshine. Weapons glittered. Flags flapped proudly.[54]

It was magnificent; it soon was to shape itself into an exhilarating Confederate charge; but if the Federals reached the ridge before Fitz Lee's guns were heard . . . "Jeb's" blue eyes shone. He watched as the Federals unsuspectingly came within a quarter of a mile of the low ridge. Confidently they began to mount it. They were scarcely 200 yards from the head of the Confederate column when across the pleasant fields there rolled the sound of Fitz Lee's signal gun.[55] The "bang-bang" of the salvo that followed the signal was as clear a command as ever bugle sounded. Out from the ridge dashed the Southerners. The startled Federals drew rein, looked and then, sensing an ambush, turned and fled in confusion.

---

50 *Ibid.*, 382.
51 *Ibid.*, 451.
52 *O. R.*, 29, pt. 1, pp. 451, 464.
53 *Ibid.*
54 *W. W. Blackford's MS Memoirs* 155.
55 *Ibid.*

Always afterward, Stuart's men called their pursuit "the Buckland Races." Colonel Blackford thought of it as a fox chase of five miles rather than as a race, and he lamented the fact that good horses and open country gave the Federals an advantage Stuart's men could not overcome. "We got only 250 prisoners and eight or ten ambulances," he complained.[56]

Stuart was immensely pleased. His sole regret was that the enemy's loss was light and that Federal artillery was not near enough the front to be overtaken. As always, when he filed his report, Stuart did not permit his exploit to lose any of its lustre, real or imagined. He went a bit beyond most previous assertions of credit, perhaps, when he said: "It is remarkable that Kilpatrick's division seemed to disappear from the field of operations for more than a month, that time being necessary, no doubt, to collect the panic-stricken fugitives."[57] Actually, Kilpatrick's operations were not impaired by the affair. His troopers were afield at the next alarm, which was a minor clash on October 24.[58] Lee made the generous estimate and wrote Stuart: "I congratulate you and your officers and men on this handsome success. The plan was well conceived and skillfully executed."[59]

A proud, commemorative review of the Cavalry Corps on November 5[60] was the official termination of a campaign which a man of a temperament less sanguine than that of Stuart would have regarded with as much concern as satisfaction. The new divisional organization probably had justified itself in spite of the contretemps when Fitz Lee fired into Stuart's lines at Brandy. During the remainder of the campaign Fitz was successful, but that was no surprise, because he had both aptitude and experience. The new Brigadiers had been competent, though none had performed any feat of special brilliance. The men in the ranks, after more than two years of fighting and of loss, were as good as ever they had been. In the art of war they were better. The varied fighting from the Rapidan to Chantilly and back again to the Rappahannock had witnessed the employment of new tactics of sharpshoot-

[56] *Ibid.* Stuart used the same figures in his report (*O. R.*, 29, pt. 1, p. 452). Brig. Gen. Judson Kilpatrick, part of whose Division staged the race, admitted a loss of only 150 men, but he could not deny that his men recrossed Broad Run and, in fact, continued their retreat until they reached infantry support on the Haymarket-Gainesville line (*Ibid.*, 383).

[57] *O. R.*, 29, pt. 1, p. 452.      [58] *O. R.*, 29, pt. 2, p 380.

[59] *Ibid.*, 794; Oct. 19, 1863.

[60] For the details and source references, see 3 *R. E. Lee*, 189, and F. M. Myers, 234.

ing. Selected men of courage and good marksmanship in all the regiments were learning how to advance as skirmishers, how to cope better, mounted or dismounted, with the enemy, and how to operate, if need be, as a separate unit. "They charged with alacrity on every occasion," Stuart wrote, "and pressed forward with so much eagerness that more than once they were surrounded by the enemy and had to fight their way out with their revolvers." [61]

The ominous condition was thus described by Stuart in a paragraph near the close of his report: "The matter of greatest concern to me during this short and eventful campaign was the subject of forage for the horses. Operating in a country worn out in peace, but now more desolate in war, it is remarkable how the horses were able to keep up. But our brave men, actuated by a spirit which prompted them to divide the last crust with their favorite steeds, have not been wanting in the noble attributes of patient endurance as well as heroic daring." [62] Stripped of rhetoric, this meant that subsistence for the animals was failing. So was the supply of horses. Always it had been easy to recruit the cavalry from the infantry, even though every trooper had to provide his own mount. Now the man who lost his horse might find the purchase of another almost impossible. A rising percentage of the cavalry slowly were to revert to the status of infantry. Stuart did not know it, but his organization had been expanded at a time when his mobility was beginning to decline and his ranks to thin. He might not be able to repeat the "Buckland Races." [63]

[61] *O. R.*, 29, pt. 1, p. 444.          [62] *Ibid.*, 452.
[63] The sketch of Stuart is continued, *infra*, p. 278.

# CHAPTER XV

## "Jube" Early's Bad Days and Good

THE INFANTRY command had no "Buckland Races" and no other consolation for the disappointments of the futile march to Bristoe Station. On the contrary, as soon as the Army was back on the line of the Rappahannock, it sustained a disaster unlike any experienced by the troops in all their marching and fighting. Every rank and grade from headquarters to guardhouse was humiliated.

The scene was Rappahannock Bridge, the crossing of the Orange and Alexandria Railroad. Farther down the Rappahannock, in the vicinity of Kelly's Ford, the ground on the north bank so fully commanded the southern side that Confederates on the right or southern bank could not prevent the passage of the river by a strong Federal force at any time.[1] The best that could be done at Kelly's was to hold off the enemy long enough for troops to take position in rear of the ford. Because this situation subjected the Confederate Army to the danger of surprise whenever it was on the Rappahannock, the high command had retained on the north bank of the river at Rappahannock Bridge a tête-de-pont where, if necessary, it could hold part of Meade's Army while it concentrated against the Unionists who attacked at Kelly's. So long as this bridgehead was retained, a crossing farther down the Rappahannock was hazardous for the Federals.[2]

Opinion subsequently differed concerning the strength of the two redoubts and the line of rifle-pits on the left bank at Rappahannock Bridge. The works, originally Federal, had been turned by the Confederates so that they faced North instead of South. Lee considered them "slight";[3] Ewell noted that much labor had been expended;[4] Jubal Early, who described them fully,[5] was most critical of the fortifications.[6] Federal commanders, for reasons that will appear in a moment, pronounced the works formidable.[7]

[1] O. R., 29, pt. 1, pp. 611, 631.
[3] Ibid., 611.
[5] Ibid., 619.
[7] O. R., 29, pt. 1, pp. 575, 587, 588.

[2] Cf. O. R., 29, pt. 1, p. 612.
[4] Ibid., 618.
[6] Ibid., and Early, 316.

Strong or weak, the position was held on November 7 by Harry Hays's Brigade of Early's Division, a trustworthy command of Louisiana veterans. They had access to the right bank of the river by a pontoon bridge that stretched in rear of the main redoubt on the north bank, about 800 yards above the ruins of the railroad crossing.[8] This pontoon bridge, which took the place of the destroyed railroad structure, was beyond the range of any of the Federal batteries and was covered by batteries on the south side of the river.[9] On the Confederate side of the river, the Army extended for several miles opposite the crossing. Hill was to the westward, Ewell to the eastward. Rodes had command of the sector that included Kelly's. The bridgehead and the position opposite it were in Jubal Early's care.

About noon on the 7th of November, the Federals began a demonstration at Kelly's Ford and soon pushed a considerable force of infantry to the southern side. Rodes had poor luck in trying to reinforce the regiment in the rifle-pits with another,[10] but he manned his main position and notified corps and army headquarters. Ewell hurried to the scene.[11] Upstream, Early received word that the enemy in force was approaching the Confederate position North of the river. He put his troops in motion for the site of the old bridge, to which he hastened. En route he met and conferred briefly with Lee, and then he crossed to the exposed redoubts and rifle-pits.

Brief reconnaissance showed "Old Jubilee" that the enemy in strength gradually was drawing nearer the bridgehead. Hays was absent but was said to be returning. He manifestly would need reinforcements. To aid him, Early returned to the south bank and sent the first units that arrived, the greater part of Hoke's Brigade.[12] Hoke himself was detached, but his men, under their hard-fighting senior Colonel, Archibald C. Godwin, marched confidently over the pontoon bridge and into the works. The dispatch of any further reinforcements seemed to Lee to be unnecessary. Early agreed [13] at the bridgehead itself. The Colonel commanding one of the Brigades gave assurance he could hold the position against the whole Federal Army.[14]

---

8 Ibid., 589.
9 Ibid., 613.
10 O. R., 29, pt. 1, pp. 632, 633.
11 Ibid., 618.
12 One regiment was in North Carolina (O. R., 29, pt. 1, p. 612).
13 Ibid., 621.
14 4 B. & L., 87.

A strong south wind was blowing and was carrying the sound of action away from Early. In spite of this, he could tell that the Federals had put more guns into action and had crossed their fire on part of the Confederate line. In some concern, Early sent a staff officer, Maj. Samuel Hale, Jr., across the river to ascertain what this meant. While Hale was on his way, the insistent dark-ness of autumn began to descend.[15] Early could see the flashes of musketry across the river, close to the rifle trenches, but he could make out nothing decisive. Presently, he and General Lee agreed that the fire was slackening. This they took to mean that the enemy had given up the attack. If so, it would not be renewed that evening. The Federals never delivered night attacks against the Army of Northern Virginia. In that belief, Lee started for his headquarters. Early lingered for the return of Major Hale. When that officer reached his chief, it was to report that he had seen both Hays and Godwin. They had faced heavy attacks but they had captured most of the men in the first line thrown against them,[16] and they thought their lines secure. That was the sub-stance of their messages. Sam Hale, powerful and full of courage, added that as he was coming back over the bridge he had over-taken a few of Hays's men who had asserted that their line had been broken. That, said Hale, must be a lie. The men were skulkers.[17]

Early was of the same mind, but he bade another staff officer, Maj. John Daniel, go to the pontoon bridge and get any news that fugitives brought. As a precaution, also, Early directed that a Brigade be sent to the southern end of the pontoons to prevent a Federal dash across them. Almost before he could give the order, the handsome young Daniel was back. Near the bridge, he said, he had met Hays. The General had told him the line was broken, the Louisiana Brigade overwhelmed, and the Federals closing in on Godwin.

Early was appalled. He could not believe Hays's veterans beaten so quickly, or Hoke's in a foredoomed fight. It was an impossible situation, but it was impossible to do anything for them! "I had the mortification," said Early, "of seeing the flashes of their rifles . . . without being able to render them the slightest assistance, as

[15] Sunset was at 5:08.                      [16] O. R.. 29, pt. 1, p. 628.
[17] Early, 313–14.

it would have been folly to attempt to cross the bridge and I could not open with the guns on the south side, as it was so very dark that nothing was visible, and we would have been as apt to fire into our own men as into the enemy." [18] Soon the fire died away. Cheers rose above the wind. Godwin's men were prisoners. From the two Brigades, not more than 600 escaped.[19] Early waited for them to get to safety by way of the pontoon bridge and then he undertook to destroy the crossing.[20] Firing the bridge was considered a most hazardous act because the enemy was expected to open fire the moment a light was struck, but William Effinger of Harrisonburg, Virginia, volunteered for this dangerous duty and discharged it without receiving a single shot from the enemy.[21]

With the enemy already on the south side of the Rappahannock at Kelly's Ford and the bridgehead lost, the Southern Army had to retreat. It moved that night to a line between Culpeper and Brandy and, finding that untenable,[22] recrossed the Rapidan [23] the next night. There, still smarting, the command could appraise the disaster at Rappahannock. Early had 1674 killed, wounded and captured. At Kelly's Ford, the Thirtieth North Carolina had advanced in confusion to support the Second, which was defending the ford. Subsequently, when the Thirtieth refused to leave the shelter of some buildings, nearly all the men were captured along with the other regiment.[24] The total loss among Rodes's men was 349. For the two Divisions that made 2023,[25] a figure that outraged the Second Corps and shocked the entire Army. Said Sandie Pendleton: "It is absolutely sickening, and I feel personally disgraced by the issue of the late campaign, as does every one in the command. Oh, how every day is proving the value of General Jackson to us!" [26]

No blame could be put on the soldiers. As Lee said in his report: "The courage and good conduct of the troops engaged [had] been too often tried to admit of question." [27] Hays's absence at the opening of the action was due to the fact that he was conducting a court of inquiry.[28] He arrived as quickly as his horse could carry

[18] Early, 314.        [19] O. R., 29, pt. 1, p. 610.
[20] Ibid., 613.        [21] E. A. Moore, 207–08.
[22] A sketch of this position appears in O. R., 29, pt. 1, p. 614. In Grimsley, 23, the locations were described in terms of later ownership.
[23] O. R., 29, pt. 1, pp. 611, 616.        [24] O. R., 29, pt. 1, pp. 632, 633.
[25] Ibid., 616.        [26] Pendleton, 305.
[27] O. R., 29, pt. 1, p. 613.        [28] Ibid., 626.

him and, as always, handled well the 800 or 900 men who remained of his Brigade.[29] After Hays was surrounded and a prisoner, his horse took fright and ran. When the enemy began to fire at him, Hays decided he might as well try to reach the bridge, because he could not be in greater danger there than in the midst of shouting enemies. He escaped unhurt.[30] Colonel Godwin, resisting with a remnant of sixty or seventy of his men, heard some one cry that he had ordered a surrender. Instantly Godwin demanded to know who had made that statement and threatened, if he found the coward, to blow the man's brains out. In the end, with his weapons in his hands, Godwin was overcome.[31]

Early felt that he was in no way responsible for the disaster and, in making his report, did not fail to remark that Lee had concluded the enemy would not make a night attack. Said Early: "I am conscious of having done all in my power to defend the position, but I must candidly confess that I did concur in the opinion of the commanding General that the enemy did not have enterprise enough to attempt any serious attack after dark, as such attacks are so foreign to his usual policy, and I therefore was inclined to believe that the position would be safe until morning, though I felt there would be very great danger in a night attack if vigorously made. A different estimate, however, of the enemy's enterprise would have had no effect, as I had no discretion about withdrawing the troops, and, in fact, they could not have been withdrawn with safety after the enemy had gained their immediate front." [32] Almost pathetically, "Old Jube" proceeded to point out what his Division had achieved in the Gettysburg campaign, and how he had captured twenty-seven guns and more than twice as many prisoners as he had lost at Rappahannock Bridge. Three of the four guns lost by Hays, the division commander said, had been won by Hays's men at Winchester. The other captured gun had been hauled off the field of Sharpsburg where it had been abandoned by the enemy.[33]

Lee accepted substantially the explanation given by Early. The one aspect of the fighting on the north bank of the river that provoked mild criticism at Army headquarters was that sharpshooters had not been posted in advance to delay the enemy whose ap-

29 *Ibid.*, 628.                         30 *Ibid.*, 623.
31 *Ibid.*, 623-24.                       32 *O. R.*, 29, pt. 1, pp. 625-26.
33 *Ibid.*, 626.

proach the wind might silence.[34] Rodes was blamed, in kindly
and tactful terms, for advancing a second regiment to the defense
of Kelly's Ford. "It was not intended," Lee reported, "to attack
the enemy until he should have advanced from the river . . ."[35]

The real explanation of the reverse was one which, even after
their experience at Gettysburg, the Confederates were unwilling
to admit: A sound Federal plan of attack had been executed admirably by courageous men. Maj. Gen. John Sedgwick, commanding the right wing of the Army of the Potomac, had employed the
V and VI Corps against Rappahannock Bridge. His artillery,
which included four 20-pounder Parrotts,[36] had been well placed.
The final assault had been delivered by Col. Emory Upton's and
Col. Peter C. Ellmaker's Brigades of Brig. Gen. David A. Russell's
1st Division of the VI Corps. So well handled were these troops,
numbering only 2100,[37] that Upton had been able to occupy the
first line of rifle-pits without firing a shot.[38] French's III Corps at
Kelly's Ford had moved in overwhelming strength and had encountered little resistance.[39]

About three weeks after the Federals had advanced from the
Rappahannock, they threatened a blow on the line of the Rapidan.
On the 26th of November, just as the Confederates were established in huts which they expected to be their winter quarters,
cavalry scouts reported the enemy in movement for the lower
fords of the Rapidan. The possibility of such a move had been
considered at headquarters. Lines of defense had been chosen.
Officers were on the alert. "Dick" Ewell was absent on account of
sickness,[40] but his Corps was in "Jube" Early's care. At the moment, it was impossible to ascertain whether the Federal commander intended to move on Richmond or whether he merely
was preparing to turn the right wing of the Southern Army.[41] An
advance toward the enemy was dictated by either contingency.
Early was to take the lead because the Second Corps was on the
right and nearer the Federals. Hill was to follow Early.[42]

The three roads used by Early gave his own Division and Rodes's

[34] O. R., 29, pt. 1, p. 613.
[36] Ibid., 588.
[38] Ibid., 592.
[40] O. R., 29, pt. 1, p. 827.
[41] Ibid. Actually (ibid., 13) Meade's plan was to turn the Confederate position and
to force Lee to give battle on ground not previously selected. Cf. 2 Meade, 156–57.
[42] O. R., 29, pt. 1, p. 895.

[35] Ibid., 612.
[37] Ibid., 589.
[39] Ibid., 555.

a shorter march than Edward Johnson had. Consequently, in the early afternoon of the 27th, Rodes's men and Early's, under Hays, were the first to establish contact with the enemy in the vicinity of Locust Grove.[43] This settlement was about seven miles Southwest of Wilderness Church and could not be counted directly a part of the region in which "Stonewall" had fallen. Nor did the district of Locust Grove possess the open fields and the agricultural abundance of Orange Court House. Forests were not so nearly all-embracing as in the Wilderness, but the streams were more treacherous. The landscape itself seemed a grumbling protest that it was denied what had been bestowed richly up the Valley of the Rapidan.

In a country reminiscent of the scene of their loftiest triumph, the veterans of the Second Corps were ready for a fight; but as the position of neither Division was good, the decision of General Lee was to await the arrival of Edward Johnson's Division before engaging the Federals.[44] Rodes and Hays accordingly formed line of battle which looked to the Northeast. When Johnson came up, the head of his column formed on Rodes's left and rear. The center and rear of the column extended back on the road toward Bartlett's Mill and constituted virtually a refused flank for the Second Corps.[45]

Johnson had marched with his ambulances and his battalion of artillery between his third and rear Brigades, in order to guard against a surprise attack from the rear.[46] Covering the rear was "Maryland" Steuart's Brigade, which contained some splendid troops that had not always been well led.[47] Shortly after noon,[48] Johnson received from Steuart a report that the divisional ambulances had come under fire from the left and North of the road.[49]

With soldierly care, Johnson immediately sent notice of this to Early, who was close at hand, and himself started at once for Steuart's position. Soon he had assurance from Early that the

[43] Ibid., 831.                                        [44] Ibid., 828.
[45] Cf., Early 319.
[46] The ordnance and the baggage trains had gone by a shorter route (O. R., 29, pt. 1, p. 846).
[47] Three Virginia regiments of the Brigade had been Fulkerson's in Jackson's old Division. The two North Carolina units had been in Roswell Ripley's Brigade. Lt. Col. J. R. Herbert's First Maryland Battalion was a famous command. Steuart, it will be remembered, had succeeded Raleigh Colston in the direction of this Brigade. See Vol. II, p. 703.
[48] O. R., 29, pt. 1, p. 862.
[49] O. R., 29, pt. 1, pp. 832, 846; Early, 320.

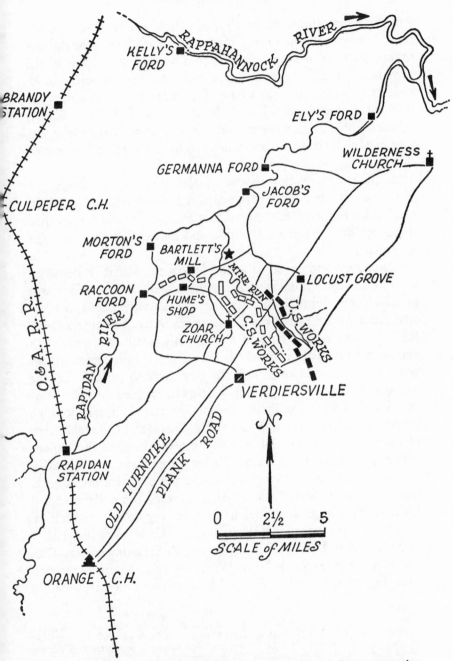

KELLY'S FORD

RAPPAHANNOCK RIVER

BRANDY STATION

ELY'S FORD

GERMANNA FORD

WILDERNESS CHURCH

JACOB'S FORD

CULPEPER C.H.

MORTON'S FORD

BARTLETT'S MILL

RACCOON FORD

HUME'S SHOP

MINE RUN

LOCUST GROVE

U.S. WORKS

C.S. WORKS

O. & A. R. R.

RAPIDAN RIVER

ZOAR CHURCH

C.S. WORKS

VERDIERSVILLE

N

RAPIDAN STATION

OLD TURNPIKE

PLANK ROAD

0   2½   5

SCALE of MILES

ORANGE C.H.

Scene of the Mine Run Operations, Nov. 26–Dec. 2, 1863. Many small streams entering the Rapidan near Mine Run are omitted. The approximate scene of Edward Johnson's engagement of November 27 is indicated by the star—after *O. R. Atlas,* Plate XLV-3

attacking force must be cavalry, of whose presence on the left corps headquarters had been informed.[50] Early's message did not induce Johnson to draw rein. He followed the sound rule of the vigilant commander, when in any doubt, see for yourself; and he rode briskly back to a point East of the intersection with the road that came down from Jacob's Ford on the Rapidan. Nearby, Johnson found Steuart skirmishing heavily with a force which was assumed by the brigade commander, as by Early, to be dismounted cavalry.[51]

In quick appreciation of danger, Johnson ordered Steuart to draw back the left of the Brigade and to form line of battle perpendicular to the road.[52] As quickly as possible, Johnson recalled the other Brigades of his Division and placed them on the right of Steuart.[53]

A stubborn and confused action followed. At first it consisted of heavy skirmishing, in which the Confederates repulsed two attacks. Then Johnson directed that the Division take the offensive and drive the enemy out of the woods in front of the Southern line. Because of the tangled terrain, this involved a somewhat complicated maneuver, in which Brigades and even regiments became separated. At one point the fight was so furious that the Fiftieth Virginia, John M. Jones's Brigade, recoiled near the brow of a low hill and took shelter behind the crest. Captain John C. Johnson, a heavy, large man, became so outraged by the reluctance of his men to face the enemy that he walked out to the highest ground, stretched himself out full length and announced that if any of his men were afraid, they could use him as a breastwork. One witness attested: "Several of them very promptly accepted his challenge, lying down behind him, resting their guns on him. . . . I am happy to say that the gallant captain was not injured." [54] General James A. Walker of the Stonewall Brigade was conspicuous for valor that equalled this. When one of his regiments started back, he seized the colors, jumped his horse over a fence, rode out

[50] Early, 320–21.                          [51] O. R., 29, pt. 1, p. 846.

[52] O. R., 29, pt. 1, p. 846. Most of the historical mistakes regarding this deployment probably have been due to the assumption that Steuart was on an east-and-west stretch of the road. Actually he was on a part of the road that run from Southwest to Northeast. Deployment there put Steuart parallel to the enemy's lines.

[53] Ibid.

[54] Worsham, 188. Captain Johnson's initials are supplied from muster rolls of the regiment in the Virginia State Library.

into an open field and waved the standard to rally the men. Although the Federals were within eighty yards of him and could pour a converging fire upon him, he was not touched. Leroy Stafford, a new Brigadier in charge of Louisiana troops, with like daring rallied his men.[55]

The battle line swung like a pendulum. Regiments advanced, drifted apart and fell back. Officers became uncertain of the position of the Brigades on their flanks. "Jube" Early had to confess afterward that he "could not see any portion of the troops engaged." [56] Some of the regiments exhausted every round of their ammunition, sought vainly to procure more and, in some instances, had to stand their ground with empty guns in their hands. At length, more from bewilderment than from punishment, most of the Confederates fell back a few hundred yards to a fence-line. There they repulsed all attacks till darkness put an end to the fight.

This affair of Payne's Farm was costly. "Maryland" Steuart was wounded lightly in the arm and John M. Jones in the head.[57] Total casualties for the Division were 545, though the wounded were six times more numerous than the killed.[58] Heavy as was this loss for a meeting engagement, with only one Division engaged on the Confederate side, "Jube" Early believed the issue worth the cost. He wrote: "By the check thus given the enemy . . . [Johnson] saved the whole Corps from a very serious disaster, for if the enemy had got possession of the road, he would have been able to come up in rear of the other division[s], while they were confronting the large force at Locust Grove." [59] Johnson was pleased to receive Early's commendation [60] and subsequently, Lee's,[61] but "Old Allegheny's" chief satisfaction, as expressed in his report, was that he had repulsed, as he thought, the whole of French's III and part of Sedgwick's VI Corps. He had done this so thoroughly that he believed the repulse was responsible for the subsequent removal of French from command.[62]

55 O. R., 29, pt. 1, p. 848.                    56 O. R., 29, pt. 1, p. 833.
57 O. R., 29, pt. 1, pp. 848, 856.             58 Ibid., 847.
59 Early, 321.
60 For Early's praise of Johnson at the time, see O. R., 29, pt. 1, p. 833.
61 See infra, p. 277.
62 O. R.. 29, pt. 1, p. 848. It is somewhat difficult to determine the extent to which the fighting of November 27 contributed to the discredit which, on Mch. 23, 1864, led to the removal of Maj. Gen. W. H. French from temporary command of the III Corps and the transfer of his troops to other officers. Maj. Gen. George Sykes and Maj. Gen. John

Troops that followed Johnson's men on the 26th–27th found the road strewn with playing-cards. As usual, this was regarded as evidence that the men of the advanced units thought they were going into action.[63] All the other indications were of a wintry battle, a Fredericksburg fought in the forest. Tom Rosser, whose Brigade had been sent ahead to guard the roads leading toward Fredericksburg,[64] reported that the Federal Army had turned up the Rapidan, after crossing at the fords, and was proceeding to meet the Confederates.[65] Still another proof of the seriousness of the advance was found in the size of the ordnance train of the I and V Army Corps, which Rosser located and attacked. He destroyed thirty-five or forty wagons and brought off eight, together with seven ambulances, 230 animals and ninety-five prisoners.[66]

Skirmishing was in progress all the while on the front of the Second Confederate Corps, East of Mine Run. "Jube" Early previously had examined the vicinity with an eye to its defense,[67] and he knew that the west bank of Mine Run offered better positions than could be found at Locust Grove. He accordingly moved back the Second Corps and "Dick" Anderson's supporting Division on the night of the 27th.[68] As this ground was disadvantageous at some points, Lee directed Early on the 28th to retire a short distance farther to a line[69] that had been selected previously as the strongest available in that district.[70]

Rain fell all day on the 28th.[71] When the downpour ceased, temperature dropped to extreme chill.[72] The wind rose. Any extensive movement by the infantry would involve extreme hard-

Newton simultaneously were deprived of their commands. G. K. Warren received Sykes's V Corps. Newton's I Corps was merged (O. R., 33, 717). All this was done, ostensibly, to reduce the number of Corps. Meade held French responsible for fatal delay in crossing the Rapidan at the opening of the Mine Run campaign, and he blamed the commander of the III Corps for slow movements on the 27th of November (O. R., 29, pt. 1, pp. 13, 14); but he does not appear to have sought French's removal. Shortly after the three officers had been relieved, Meade wrote his wife: "I tried very hard to retain Sykes, Newton, and even French, as division commanders, but without avail" (2 Meade, 185. Cf. O. R., 33, 638). Needless to say, this language makes it plain that Meade esteemed French below Newton and Sykes. During the course of hostilities, French was not again assigned to field duty.

[63] Cf. E. A. Moore, 212: "I never saw or heard of a Bible or prayer-book being cast aside at such a time, but cards were always thrown away by soldiers going into battle."
[64] O. R., 29, pt. 1, p. 828.
[65] Ibid.                              [66] Ibid., 904.
[67] Early, 317.                        [68] O. R., 29, pt. 1, p. 832.
[69] Hume's Old Shop—Zoar Church—Verdiersville.
[70] Part of the line was retired farther to the westward, later in the day (O. R., 29, pt. 1, p. 834).
[71] Ibid., 824.                        [72] Ibid., 826.

ship. In spite of the weather, Stuart was dispatched that evening
to test the enemy's flank and rear, but he was recalled the next
day because the Federals manifestly were concentrating heavily
for an attack on the Confederate right. Shivering graycoats steeled
themselves and piled higher and higher the parapets behind which
they intended, come what might, to hold against their attacking
adversary. Curiously, as it seemed to the Southerners, the Federal
Army also, instead of assaulting, began to intrench.[73]

Except for a cannonade of about an hour on the 29th, the Union
troops made no move. The 30th passed without incident. Blue
columns appeared to march now to the left and now to the right,
but the forest was so thick that nothing could be seen clearly.[74]
On the 1st of December a manifest reduction in the strength of
the artillery opposite Early was explained on the ground that the
batteries in front of Hill's Third Corps had been increased.[75]
When the day passed without a Federal attack, Lee decided to
assume the initiative.[76] Wilcox's and Anderson's Divisions were
shifted to the extreme right, whence it was thought they could
turn the Federal left.[77]

An anxious night of preparation ended in a dawn of disappointment. The Federals had retreated. Nor in that tangled country
could they be overtaken in their withdrawal across the Rapidan.[78]
The reasons given by Meade for the retirement were varied.
Throughout the operation he had suffered disappointments and
failure of logistics. Maj. Gen. W. H. French, commanding the III
Corps, had been unjustifiably slow in crossing at Jacob's Ford and
thereby had been responsible for delaying the general advance.[79]
Again on the 27th, French was alleged to have been tardy.[80]
Meade had intended to attack on the 28th, but he had to delay because of Early's withdrawal beyond Mine Run.[81] The next day,
after reconnaissance, Maj. Gen. G. K. Warren told Meade that
he could turn the Confederate right easily. Without personal examination of the ground, Meade accepted the assurances of Warren
and concentrated heavily on his left in a movement that was seen
and correctly interpreted on the other side of Mine Run.

[73] Early, 323; O. R., 29, pt. 1, p. 834.      [74] O. R., 29, pt. 1, pp. 834–35.
[75] Ibid., 835.                                 [76] Ibid., 829.
[77] Ibid., 896.                                 [78] O. R., 29, pt. 1, pp. 829, 835, 896.
[79] Ibid., 14.                                  [80] Ibid.
[81] Ibid., 16.

To support Warren, preparations were taken in hand for a heavy Federal bombardment on the morning of the 30th and for a subsidiary attack by Sedgwick's VI Corps. Batteries had opened and Sedgwick was ready to advance when a message was handed Meade from Warren. "[The] position and strength of the enemy seem so formidable in my present front," Warren wrote, "that I advise against making the attack here." He explained: "The full light of the sun shows me that I cannot succeed." [82] Meade was astounded.[83] "It was too late," he reported, "to move the troops back and make an attack on the center that day, and General Warren was already so far separated from the right that his movement to turn the enemy's right could not be continued without moving up the rest of the army in support, and abandoning the turnpike road, our main line of communications." [84] By the time Meade could bring back to their former position the troops that had been dispatched to reinforce the II Corps, he believed that Lee had received warning from the bombardment and had made the Confederate position more nearly impregnable.[85] Attack, Meade reasoned, would be slaughter. He confided manfully to his wife: "It was my deliberate judgment that I ought not to attack; I acted on that judgment, and I am willing to stand or fall by it at all hazards." [86] A little later, when he had returned to the north bank of the Rapidan after having been immune from pursuit even by cavalry in the wooded country,[87] Meade with relief wrote the same understanding correspondent: "Of one thing I am sure, that my course has met the full approbation of the army and increased the confidence they before had in me." [88]

The Confederate commanders were disappointed at Meade's unpunished escape,[89] but they were gratified to observe the spirit in which the men had faced wintry rain and chilling wind. "Their steadiness and cheerful resolution in anticipation of an attack," said Lee, "could not have been excelled." [90] This zeal was not abated even by the receipt of news, during Meade's retreat, that Bragg incredibly had lost Missionary Ridge.[91] In Ewell's absence, "Jube" Early had handled the Second Corps with apparent ease

[82] O. R., 29, pt. 1, p. 17. The full text of the dispatch appears in ibid., pt. 2, p. 517.
[83] 2 Meade, 157.                                   [84] O. R., 29, pt. 1, p. 17.
[85] O. R., 29, pt. 1, p. 17.                       [86] 2 Meade, 158.
[87] O. R., 29, pt. 1, p. 829.                      [88] 2 Meade, 159.
[89] Cf. R. E. Lee, Jr., 116.                        [90] O. R., 29, pt. 1, p. 829.
[91] Caldwell, 120.

and with moderate efficiency. A critic might have asked whether Early should not have used either Rodes's Division or his own to aid "Allegheny" Johnson on the 27th of November, but the terrain was so confused and the situation around Locust Grove so uncertain that Early's caution in leaving Johnson to fight his own battle was explicable and probably was justified. There was at the time no suggestion that Early, acting as corps commander, was too much inclined to fight a battle by Divisions. His admission that he "could not see any portion of the troops engaged" in Johnson's fight,[92] was ignored at the time, but if it had been observed, it would have been found to suggest one of the few defects that Early as a soldier thus far had disclosed. He had a poor sense of direction. At Malvern Hill he scarcely could have been blamed for floundering through the forest and the swamp. Many others had been as bewildered as he. More than once thereafter, it is possible that what appeared to have been tardiness was due to his inability to grasp quickly the guiding features of the ground over which he was to operate. At Bristoe Station, Early had become confused by the ground and virtually had lost his way.[93]

Of other officers, three only had opportunity of distinguishing themselves in the Mine Run operations. "Maryland" Steuart fought vigorously when he was assailed on the 27th. He could not be charged with negligence in failing to protect his Brigade against surprise attack. As commander of the rear Brigade, with the divisional ambulances between him and the nearest Brigade, Steuart had his flank guard out.[94] The nature of the ground was such that surprise by the enemy's skirmishers was easy.[95]

As Steuart's superior, Johnson was prompt in grasping the situation and vigorous in correcting it. His troop movements were intelligent. Lee, who never was reckless in praise, probably stated the minimum when he wrote in his report: "The promptness with which this unexpected attack was met and repulsed reflects great credit upon General Johnson and the officers and men of his division."[96] As already noted, Early reported that failure by Johnson would have threatened the rear of the Second Corps.[97]

[92] See *supra*, p. 272, and *O. R.*, 29, pt. 1, p. 833.
[93] Cf. *Early*, 305.
[94] At least, this seems the safe inference from Lee's careful statement (*O. R.*, 29, pt. 1, p. 828) that "the usual precaution had been taken by General Johnson to guard against a flank attack . . ."
[95] *Ibid.*          [96] *Ibid.*          [97] See *supra*. p. 273.

The other officer who added to his soldierly reputation during the fighting on Mine Run was Tom Rosser. His presence close to the ordnance train of Newton's and Sykes's troops was in obedience to orders, but the vigilance of his patrol and the vigor of his onslaught were his own. For some reason, Stuart overlooked in the body of his report all reference to Rosser's exploit, but in a postscript the commander of the Cavalry Corps praised the young Brigadier.[98] When Wade Hampton, who had returned to duty, wrote a laudatory endorsement on Rosser's report, Stuart seconded it. Doubtless the commendation most appreciated by the new Brigadier, now at the mature age of 27, was in the words of Lee, who forwarded Rosser's report to the War Department with this endorsement: "General Rosser in this as in other cases has well performed his duty."[99] The only thing to mar this praise was a petty wrangle over the measure of credit due Rosser's and the other Brigades for their part in a lively affair at Parker's Store, where a cavalry camp of the Federals was surprised.[100]

On the adverse account, the entry concerned a possible defect in the new organization of the Confederate cavalry into Divisions. When the Army started down the Rapidan to meet the Federals, Fitz Lee's Brigades were moved from their winter camps to the upper fords of the river in order to take the place of the Second Corps.[101] This employment of Fitz Lee left only Hampton's Division to serve with the infantry who were to confront Meade. Had a situation of this nature developed before the creation of separate cavalry Divisions, Stuart would have exercised immediate command of the force that proceeded with the foot soldiers. Now that Divisions had been created, Rosser and Young and Gordon were under Hampton. The function of Stuart, in strict military usage, would be to supervise the whole of the cavalry operations but to leave the handling of the three Brigades to Hampton.

That did not accord with "Jeb's" fighting impulses or with his sense of duty. Stuart pushed to the front and took over the direction of the first cavalry Brigade he met. This he did, as he later explained, because he thought Hampton was late. On the arrival of Hampton's second Brigade, Stuart still exercised direct command.[102] Becoming impatient again on the 29th, waiting for

98 O. R., 29, pt. 1, p. 901.   99 Ibid., 905.
100 Ibid., 899, 905–06.   101 O. R., 29, pt. 1, p. 907. See infra, p. 328.
102 O. R., 29, pt. 1, pp. 898–99.

Hampton's advance, "Jeb" started off with Rosser's Brigade which he intended to keep on one flank of the Army while the other two Brigades operated elsewhere. No orders were left for Hampton, except to follow. Hampton did not find Stuart at the point designated for a rendezvous and had no intimation of Stuart's route or intentions, other than that the enemy was to be attacked. No word had been left for the dispatch of any part of the Division by a different route.[103] Hampton accordingly followed Stuart. Near Parker's Store, Hampton found Rosser's Brigade battling defensively with a superior force. The two Brigades with Hampton were thrown into action immediately and were strong enough to drive the enemy from the field.[104] No damage resulted from Stuart's disregard of Hampton, but the methods followed by Stuart were apt to create friction. "Jeb" Stuart evidently was determined to be commander of all the cavalry and to direct any part of it with which he happened to be, organization or no organization.

More serious than this adverse entry in the Mine Run campaign was the general failure of the Army to achieve any military result. That had been true of Bristoe and, most lamentably, of Rappahannock Bridge. For the five months since the return from Pennsylvania, the record had been negative, though more than 4200 casualties had been sustained.[105] In every operation there had been creditable performance. Each failure could be explained logically. The great difference was that before Gettysburg there had been few failures to be explained. From headquarters, where his discerning eyes saw everything, Walter Taylor wrote an ominous sentence, such a sentence as he would not have thought of penning in the spring of 1863: "I only wish the general had good lieutenants; we miss Jackson and Longstreet terribly."[106]

103 O. R., 29, pt. 1, p. 902.
104 Stuart's account, which is followed here, is in O. R., 29, pt. 1, pp. 898–900.
105 For the detailed figures, see 3 R. E. Lee, 203, n. 110.
106 3 R. E. Lee, 204, with reference to the Taylor MSS. For the next references to Ewell, see p. 329 ff; for Early, see pp. 325 ff, 350 ff; for Johnson, see p. 349; for Stuart, see p. 346 ff.

# CHAPTER XVI

## Longstreet is Weighed

AFTER MINE RUN, the infantry of the Army of Northern Virginia fought no battle for five months. Promotions were few during that period because fatalities were negligible. In January, 1864, John R. Chambliss, Jr., who had acted for months as commander of "Rooney" Lee's troopers, was made Brigadier General.[1] The next month, Col. Nathaniel H. Harris of the Nineteenth Mississippi, an officer of proven parts, was advanced in rank[2] to succeed Carnot Posey, who died in November of the wound received at Bristoe Station.[3]

The only other promotions were in the artillery, which had not shown at Gettysburg in the Second and Third Corps a leadership equal to that of the First. In September, 1863, Armistead L. Long of Lee's staff had been advanced from Colonel to Brigadier General and had been placed in charge of the guns of the Second Corps, which had not been handled acceptably by the corps chief after the wounding of Stapleton Crutchfield. Before the war, Long had been an artillerist of some reputation and in 1862–63 had been used often by Lee in reconnaissance and in posting batteries. Long was returned regretfully from staff to line, because he was most useful at Army Headquarters; but Lee did not feel that a man of Long's experience should be withheld from a field service in which men of professional training were few.[4]

Concerning other artillerists, Pendleton, at Lee's instance, reported in detail. Some were recommended for higher rank. Transfer was proposed for several who, in Pendleton's opinion, were incompetent or physically incapacitated. The principal promotion suggested by Pendleton was that of E. Porter Alexander to the rank of Brigadier General and to command the artillery of the

---

[1] Under the Act of Oct. 13, 1862, for the appointment of twenty general officers. See Vol. II, p. 256. For Chambliss' promotion, see *Wright*, 136; 3 *C. M. H.*, 582 ff.
[2] *O. R.*, 33, 1207.
[3] *O. R.*, 29, pt. 1, p. 429; *Wright*, 135; 7 *C. M. H.*, Miss., 265.
[4] For Long, see *Wright*, 131; 3 *C. M. H.*, 630.

First Corps. Like advancement was not advocated for R. Lindsay Walker, chief of artillery of the Third Corps. The reason probably was that under the governing law the artillery of the Army of Northern Virginia was entitled to three general officers only, or one for every eighty guns. As Pendleton and Long already held that rank, there was place for Alexander but not for him and for Walker also.[5] When further changes in artillery command were made subsequently,[6] there was no open complaint, but Pendleton reported that "some of the best officers of this corps," finding promotion slow, were seeking transfer to other arms.[7] This was an unwelcome state of affairs because the artillery officers with the rank of company or field officers were of an average competence definitely above that of infantrymen or cavalrymen of like rank.[8]

Although battles were not fought and reorganization of the infantry on the Rapidan did not have to be undertaken, the winter was far from quiet. As will appear in more detail,[9] it was an alternation of excitement and misery. When the commanding General was not present to repress jealousies, they began to develop among old comrades. Ugly disputes eclipsed gallant deeds. Much the worst strife was in the absent First Corps. The new experiences of that command, in combat and in controversy, did more than the previous two years of campaign to show the character, the capacities and the limitations of James Longstreet. Any element of mystery that had clung to him by reason of habitual silence was stripped off him by his own pen.

After much hesitation,[10] Bragg began in October, 1863, the partial investment of Chattanooga, Tenn., but he made little progress beyond that of rendering the Federal lines of supply somewhat hazardous. Bragg's adversary, Maj. Gen. W. S. Rosecrans, decided that the simplest means of securing himself against interruption of the regular issue of rations and ammunition would be to place a strong Union force farther down the river on Bragg's flank. When Maj. Gen. Geo. H. Thomas succeeded Rosecrans on Octo-

[5] *O. R.*, 29, pt. 2, p. 839 ff. The Army was organized for 276 guns but had 244 (*ibid.*) By April the number was reduced to 238 (*O. R.*, 33, 1265).
[6] Alexander was not appointed until Mch. 1, 1864, to rank from Feb. 26, 1864 (*Wright*, 130). Walker was promoted Mch. 1, 1865, to rank from Feb. 18, 1865 (*Wright*, 131–32). See *infra*, Chapter XXXI.
[7] *O. R.*, 33, 1193.
[8] See Early's observation after Cedar Creek, *infra*, Chapter XXX.
[9] See *infra*, Chapter XVII.
[10] Cf. *Longstreet*, 461 ff.

ber 20, he proceeded to carry out Rosecrans's plan.[11] Until this was done at Brown's Ferry on the night of October 26-27,[12] Bragg had turned a deaf ear to all reports that the Federals were moving against him.[13] After he saw how well they could protect their supply line from the position they had taken at Brown's Ferry, he decided that he must recover the ground. On the 28th of October he was on Lookout Mountain and was discussing with "Old Pete" plans for an attack on the Federals when a courier arrived with news that a large Union force was advancing toward the mountain from the West.[14] Bragg had been complaining that signalmen of the First Corps had been transmitting extravagant reports, and he turned to berate the courier for falsifying the news about the Federals. The courier had a realistic answer. "General," he said, "if you will ride to a point on the west side of the mountain, I will show them to you."[15] Bragg had to comply with that request and he invited Longstreet to go with him. Soon they saw below them a long blue column which they subsequently identified as parts of the XI and XII Corps which had been sent from Meade's Army and were under the command of Maj. Gen. Joseph Hooker.

Sight of this force ended all talk of an attack on the Unionists who had established themselves at Brown's Ferry, but Longstreet's fighting blood was stirred. After studying the Federal position, he decided that a night attack might destroy the Federal rearguard, which went into camp three miles from Hooker's main force. "Old Pete" accordingly sent for Micah Jenkins, then in temporary command of Hood's Division, and explained to the young officer what was to be done by him and by Evander Law, who was to command a detached Brigade.[16]

About 8 o'clock that evening, October 28, Longstreet received word that Bragg approved the plan and had released McLaws's Division from the lines in front of Chattanooga so that it could participate in the attack on Hooker's rearguard.[17] Longstreet reasoned that McLaws could not cross Lookout Mountain in time to participate in a night attack. On the other hand, Longstreet was

---

[11] O. R., 31, pt. 1, p. 42.
[12] O. R., 31, pt. 1, pp. 77-78. This expedition was under Brig. Gen. W. F. Smith, who last was encountered in these pages as commander at Carlisle, Penn., when "Jeb" Stuart threatened to bombard the town. See *supra*, p. 138.
[13] See *Horn*, 293.        [14] At that point the Southwest.
[15] *Longstreet*, 474.        [16] O. R., 31, pt. 1, pp. 217-18.
[17] *Ibid.*, 218.

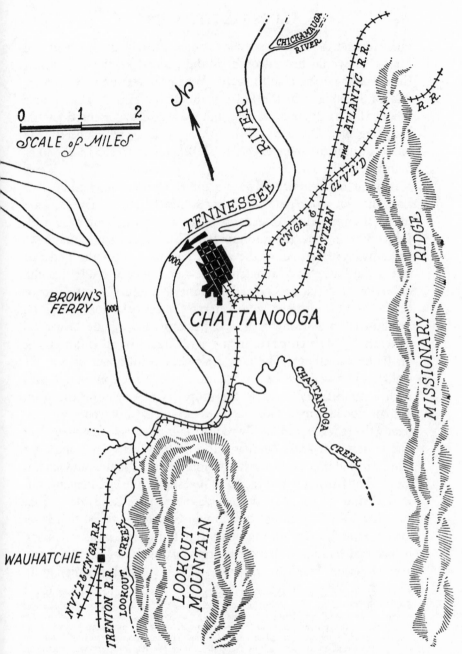

The Vicinity of Chattanooga, Tenn., with special reference to Longstreet's operations around Wauhatchie, Oct. 28–29, 1863—after *O. R. Atlas.* Plate XLIX-1

satisfied that if McLaws's troops waited till daylight to reinforce him, they would be destroyed by the Federal artillery, to which they would not be able to reply. Whatever was done, therefore, had to be done with the Division under Jenkins.[18] That young officer was as diligent as able, but he was inexperienced in the handling of a Division and he was, it will be remembered, the bitter rival of the most experienced Brigadier of Hood's old command, Evander Law.

In their night attack, always a difficult operation, Jenkins and Law did not work together. Law suffered lightly. The Brigade under the immediate direction of Jenkins and its senior Colonel, John Bratton, fought admirably but sustained 356 casualties.[19] In Longstreet's report of the affair, which some of the Federals styled the Battle of Wauhatchie, the assertion was made that the difference in casualties showed a "want of conduct" on the part of Law. As Law's troops were veterans, their behavior had to be attributed "to a strong feeling of jealousy among the brigadier-generals."[20] The corps commander reiterated in an endorsement on Jenkins's report: "The only real weak point about us was the jealousy between the two brigades. . . . This I considered, and with a momentary doubt at the propriety of executing the plan, but concluded after a moment's hesitation that my troops were so steady that they would hardly require commanders after they were in position."[21] Years later, when animosity between Longstreet and Law had become bitter and venomous, the Lieutenant General stated that Jenkins was directed to investigate the circumstances of Law's failure [22] and, after a time, was able to present evidence that Law had said "he did not care to win General Jenkins' spurs as a major-general." On hearing this, wrote Longstreet in his memoirs, he ordered Jenkins to prepare charges against Law but, in the preoccupation of another campaign, Jenkins asked permission to

18 *Ibid.* This is merely a paraphrase of the language of Longstreet's report, which was dated Mch. 24, 1864. The account in *Longstreet,* 475–76, which is almost completely at variance with the official report, represented Bragg as promising to send McLaws to support Jenkins. Bragg's failure to do this, said Longstreet, led to an abandonment of the plan, but as he, Longstreet, failed to notify Jenkins that the action was not to be opened, Jenkins proceeded to attack. In this General Longstreet's late memory was wholly in error. Had Bragg promised a second Division in time for use on the night of the 28th, and had he failed to send it, then Longstreet, writing in March, 1864, would have been certain to say so. In his memoirs, General Alexander, who was on the line at the time, made no mention of the proposed employment of McLaws.
19 *O. R.,* 31, pt. 1, p. 233.      20 *Ibid.,* 218.
21 *Ibid.,* 219.      22 Cf. *O. R.,* 52, pt. 2, p. 557.

defer the matter.[23] In Jenkins's own private correspondence, the only reference to Law's part in the fight was a statement that the Brigades under Law failed to prevent the enemy's passage around his left.[24]

Besides Law, the commander of the Texas Brigade, Jerome B. Robertson, was blamed by Longstreet for failure in the affair at Wauhatchie. Longstreet thought the Brigadier incompetent and, while he had no tangible evidence, he believed that Robertson might have been responsible for the abandonment by the renowned Texans of the position entrusted to them. As the ambitious and exacting Jenkins complained more than once that Robertson was not qualified for his duties, Longstreet went to Bragg about him. The commanding General suggested that Robertson be brought before an examining board. Longstreet understood Bragg to give assurance that when the board was ordered, Robertson would be relieved of command, but this was not done until Longstreet formally renewed a request that Robertson be not left with the troops. Six days later, at the beginning of a movement presently to be described, the suspension of the board's sittings led Bragg to restore Robertson to his old post.[25]

The equities are not easily established in the case of Jerome Robertson or in the controversy between Law and Jenkins, but the effect was to impair a Division which had been, all in all, probably the finest combat force in the Army of Northern Virginia. An absence of a month and a half from that Army had sufficed to produce dissension, talk of incompetence, and a whisper of something morally worse than lack of co-operation!

The next move of Longstreet was to deepen these differences and to spread dissatisfaction to McLaws's command. For reasons that have not been clear to others, if indeed they were plain to him, General Bragg decided to weaken further a weak army in the face of a strong adversary and to send Longstreet to deal with Gen. A. E. Burnside, who was guarding East Tennessee with a force of some 22,200 men [26] based on Knoxville. Longstreet was as anxious to leave Bragg as the commanding General was to be rid of him, and he probably was hopeful that an opportunity for

23 *Longstreet*, 477.
24 J. F. Thomas's *Career and Character of General Micah Jenkins*; letter of Oct. 29.
25 *O. R.*, 31, pt. 1, pp. 466–67.
26 *O. R.*, 31, pt. 1, p. 680. Cavalry numbered 8600, infantry 13,600.

independent action still might be offered. As soon, therefore, as Longstreet heard that he was to be detached, he put forward his standard counter-plan, the one he had urged on Lee in the spring and again in the late summer—that the main army assume a strong defensive position and permit him to undertake an offensive. Specifically, this time, he suggested that the entire Army of Tennessee, including his own forces, withdraw to Chickamauga, and that Bragg recall the troops in East Tennessee. Then, when concentration had been effected, Longstreet was to march to Knoxville and crush Burnside. That done, Longstreet could return to Chattanooga before the approaching Army of Sherman could get there; or else Longstreet could move into Kentucky against the enemy's lines of communication.[27] Bragg did not approve of this but he believed an operation against Burnside would be a relief to him,[28] and he prepared to send Longstreet to Knoxville with such additional troops as could be spared.

The force that left the Chattanooga line November 5-6[29] and proceeded slowly to Sweetwater consisted of about 12,000 men of all arms. Longstreet considered it scarcely more than half as strong as it should be for the mission. As he started on his journey, he wrote Simon Buckner: "Twenty thousand men, well handled, could surely have captured Burnside and his forces. Under the present arrangement, however, the lines are to be held as they now are [at Chattanooga] and the detachment is to be of 12,000. We thus expose both to failure, and really take no chance to ourselves of great results."[30] Inefficient staff work, lame transportation and apparent lack of co-operation at Army Headquarters deepened Longstreet's discouragement. On November 11-12, he dispatched letters and telegram in which he wrathfully set forth his deficiencies. Said he: "The delay that occurs is one that might have been prevented, but not by myself. . . . As soon as I find a probability of moving without almost certain starvation, I shall move, provided the troops are up. If the troops that are opposed

[27] *Longstreet*, 480-81.
[28] At least this seems the fair interpretation of Bragg's curious language of October 31 in a dispatch to Jefferson Davis: "The Virginia troops will move in the direction indicated as soon as practicable. This will be great relief to me." The other interpretation, of course, is that Bragg thought it would be a relief to be rid of Longstreet. For the attendant circumstances see *Horn*, 294-95, to which the writer is indebted for this quotation.
[29] *O. R.*, 31, pt. 2, p. 637.
[30] *Longstreet*, 484-85; *O. R.*, 52, pt. 2, p. 560.

KENTUCKY

VIRGINIA

BRISTOL

CARTER'S DEPOT

CUMBERLAND GAP

ROGERSVILLE

RIVER

LEESBURG

GREENEVILLE

BEAN'S STATION

RUSSELLVILLE

HOLSTON

TENN. & GA. R.R.

NORTH CAROLINA

KNOXVILLE

CAMPBELL'S STATION

EAST

LENOIR'S

RIVER

LOUDON

SWEETWATER

R.R.

ATHENS

TENN. & GA. R.R.

CLEVELAND

TYNER'S ST'N.

CHICKAMAUGA ST'N.

RINGGOLD

TUNNEL HILL

DALTON

SOUTH CAROLINA

GEORGIA

CHATTANOOGA

TENNESSEE

W. CHICKAMAUGA CR.

MIDDLE CHI'M'G.

CHI.'M'G.

ALA.

N

0  10  20

SCALE of MILES

Region of Longstreet's Operations from Wauhatchie, Tenn. to Abingdon, Va., winter of 1863–'64—after O. R. Atlas, Plates CXLII and CXLIX

to me are in a demoralized condition, as your letter intimates, without being beaten in battle, what must be the condition of those of General Rosecrans' army?"[31] Bragg, in answer, professed himself astonished. "The means being furnished," said he, "you were expected to handle your own troops, and I cannot understand your constant applications for me to furnish them."[32]

Longstreet pushed on but, in retrospect at least, he considered himself persecuted. In his memoirs he wrote: "It began to look more like a campaign against Longstreet than against Burnside."[33] At last, on the 14th, contact was established with the enemy; on the 15th–16th the prospect was for a battle near Campbell's Station, thirteen miles Southwest of Knoxville. In the hope of weakening a numerically superior foe, Longstreet deployed with care, but the enemy slipped away. Again, as at Wauhatchie, there were rumors of a lack of concert between Law and Jenkins. In Longstreet's report, he quoted Jenkins as saying there was some mismanagement on the part of Law.[34] Years afterward, Longstreet revived a contemporary report that Law could have attacked successfully but refrained from doing so because the credit would go to Jenkins.[35] Criticism was not altogether one-sided. A supporter of General Law maintained that Longstreet's own slothfulness was responsible for the enemy's escape.[36]

By the 17th of November, the Confederate van was within range of Knoxville, but much time was lost in studying the unfamiliar position of an adversary who awaited attack. Said Longstreet later: "He had as many [men] as we in a strong position fortified. We went to work, therefore, to make our way forward by gradual and less hazardous measures, at the same time making examinations of the enemy's entire positions."[37] First Jenkins and then McLaws thought he had found a weak spot in the enemy's strong earthworks, but both officers had to admit themselves mistaken.[38]

Longstreet proceeded with no suggestion of haste and with some maneuvers that suggested his unfruitful operation of the previous spring against Suffolk. He might, indeed, have demonstrated in-

[31] O. R., 31, pt. 3, pp. 680–81.          [32] Ibid., 686.
[33] Longstreet, 488.          [34] O. R., 31, pt. 1, p. 458.
[35] Longstreet, 494–95. Alexander did not mention this episode, but Sorrel said, op. cit., 207: ". . . the five brigades of this fine command were practically paralyzed by the differences" between Jenkins and Law.
[36] Oates, 334.          [37] O. R., 31, pt. 1, p. 459.
[38] Ibid., 459.

definitely had he not received on the night of November 23 a letter Bragg had written on the 22nd. In this communication, Bragg stated that 11,000 reinforcements were moving to Longstreet, but that if it was practicable to defeat Burnside, it should be done at once.[39] Bragg said little concerning operations on his own front, but earlier in the day Longstreet had heard that the Federals at Chattanooga had moved out of their defenses and had attacked Bragg.

The situation suddenly had become more complicated. If Bragg worsted the Federals, who now were under the vigilant direction of Maj. Gen. U. S. Grant, the outlook at Knoxville would be bright. Longstreet might get further reinforcements and, at the least, would have his rear safe from all serious threat. Were Bragg defeated, Longstreet's troops at Knoxville might be caught between two forces. In that event, if Longstreet were lucky enough to escape destruction, he would be compelled to retreat into East Tennessee. A different prospect, surely, this was from the picture of victory that Longstreet had painted two months and a half previously, when he had bidden farewell to Lee!

Two Brigades of cavalry from Southwest Virginia—one of them under "Grumble" Jones—reached Longstreet on the 27th–28th. About 3500 men of Bushrod Johnson's and Archibald Gracie's Brigades of Buckner's Division had arrived from Bragg's Army.[40] Longstreet had all the force he could hope to get for an attack on Burnside, and he had, in addition, disquieting reports of a battle between Bragg and Grant at Chattanooga. "There seemed to be so many reports leading to the same conclusion," Longstreet subsequently explained, "that I determined that I must attack, and, if possible, get possession of Knoxville."[41]

An offensive was recommended, also, by Brig. Gen. Danville Leadbetter, who arrived at Longstreet's headquarters to counsel on the technical problems involved in the projected assault. Leadbetter had been graduated No. 3 in the class ahead of Braxton Bragg's at West Point[42] and he had been conspicuous in the building of coast defenses prior to his resignation as Captain of Engi-

---

[39] O. R., 31, pt. 3, p. 736.
[40] O. R., 31, pt. 1, p. 532. General Johnson stated that he reported to Longstreet in person on the 28th. Gracie's Brigade, he said, had preceded him. The van of Johnson's force, in bad condition, on the 24th had reached Loudon, which is approximately twenty-two miles Southwest of Knoxville by rail. O. R., 31, pt. 1, p. 532.
[41] Ibid., 460; cf. Longstreet, 502.    [42] Cullum No. 844.

neers in 1857. Porter Alexander, who did not like him, said of Leadbetter: ". . . being the oldest military engineer in the Confederate service, [he] was supposed to be the most efficient. . . . Coming to Longstreet as he did, with the prestige of being on the staff of the commanding-general, and especially charged with the decision of all questions of military engineering, it is perhaps not strange that Longstreet was quick to adopt his suggestions . . ." [43] Leadbetter, moreover, had been at Knoxville while the Confederates were holding and fortifying it. He pressed for early action,[44] and, in the judgment of some of Longstreet's officers, too lightly brushed aside the objections they raised to some of his proposals. At length, after changing his mind abruptly, Leadbetter recommended an assault on an earthwork, known to the Confederates as Fort Loudon and to the Federals as Fort Sanders. This was at the northwest corner of the Union defenses of the town. On high ground, commanding the westward road to Kingston, the fort had stout earthen bastions and a ditch of undetermined depth.[45] Longstreet himself did not believe that the ditch was deeper than 3 feet at some points or more than five or six feet wide, but his judgment was based primarily on a glimpse he had, from a distance, of a soldier who climbed down the parapet and walked across the ditch.[46]

For the assault, "Old Pete" set November 28, but he postponed the attack a few hours because of foggy weather and then, at McLaws's suggestion, deferred it until daylight of the 29th. McLaws urged this delay in order that the troops might move up during the night of the 28th, dig rifle-pits and have ground from which they could make a quick dash for the Federal position.[47] In detail, the plan was to open suddenly with artillery at dawn and to demoralize the enemy with a heavy fire. Then two of McLaws's Brigades, in columns of regiments, were to deliver the assault, which was to be directed against the northwest face of the fort. McLaws was admonished to see that the assault was delivered "with a determination to succeed." [48] His advance was to be followed in échelon on the left by Jenkins; but in the event that McLaws failed, Jenkins was to be deployed in such a manner that part of his troops could move to the right of McLaws and take the

[43] *Alexander*, 485.                    [44] *O. R.*, 31, pt. 1, p. 460.
[45] For a more detailed and technical description, see *Alexander*, 483.
[46] *O. R.*, 31, pt. 3, p. 757.            [47] *Ibid.*, pt. 1, p. 486.
[48] *O. R.*, 31, pt. 3, p. 756.

fort from the rear. The enemy then was to be driven through the town.[49]

As Micah Jenkins made his dispositions, his zeal and his military instincts led him to mount and to start for McLaws's headquarters to be sure their co-ordination was complete. On the way, Jenkins met Brig. Gen. Archibald Gracie, Jr., who had been in Knoxville before Bragg had withdrawn troops from the town. Eagerly Jenkins asked about the ditch and the parapet at Fort Loudon. Gracie's reply was that when he was there, the ditch was four or five feet deep. Jenkins had observed that bales of cotton had been placed on the parapet, and from that fact he calculated that the distance from the floor of the ditch to the top of the parapet would be eleven or twelve feet. The face of this parapet was slippery clay.

Alarmed at this prospect, Jenkins hastened to McLaws and suggested that the assaulting party carry fascines to fill the ditch. McLaws shook his head: Fascines might be some protection against infantry fire,[50] but the men knew nothing about them. Although he did not so inform Jenkins, he had searched for material with which to fill the ditch and had found nothing that would serve the purpose.[51] The troops must trust to luck in getting around or over the parapet. To Jenkins, such a view seemed overconfident. As soon as he had opportunity, he wrote Longstreet what had occurred and he asked particularly whether the fort was closed in the rear. The tone of Jenkins's letter was courageous but he could not forbear reference to the possibility of having to re-form his men in the event of a repulse.[52]

Longstreet was devoted to Jenkins. Next to Pickett, perhaps, he esteemed the ambitious young South Carolinian more highly than he did any of his subordinates; but he did not like the undertone of misgiving. He answered the letter promptly, explained that the fort was not enclosed, and gave his estimate of the shallowness of the ditch and the inconsiderable height of the parapet. Then, metaphorically, he stood Jenkins before him for an exhortation that was almost a scolding: "Keep your men well at their work, and do not listen to the idea of failing and we shall not fail. If we go in with the idea that we shall fail, we will be sure to do so. But no men who are determined to succeed can fail. Let me urge

49 O. R., 31, pt. 1, pp. 460–61, 486–87: Longstreet, 502–03.
50 O. R., 31, pt. 1, p. 488.    51 Ibid., 489, 490.
52 O. R., 31, pt. 3, p. 756.

you not to entertain such feelings for a moment. Do not let any one fail, or any thing." [53]

This was not the sole vexation that Longstreet had in addition to those that normally attend preparation for battle. From numerous sources, rumors had come on the 28th that Bragg had been engaged heavily at Chattanooga in a battle of undetermined result. During the evening, Longstreet received a letter in which McLaws mentioned these relations and asked whether the attack on Knoxville should not be deferred until the outcome at Chattanooga was known. The Georgia division commander explained: "If the enemy has been beaten at Chattanooga, do we not gain by delay at this point? If we have been defeated at Chattanooga, do we not risk our entire force by an assault here? If we have been defeated at Chattanooga, our communications must be made with Virginia. We cannot combine again with General Bragg, even if we should be successful in our assault on Knoxville. If we should be defeated or unsuccessful here, and at the same time General Bragg should have been forced to retire, would we be in condition to force our way to the army in Virginia?" [54]

Longstreet had received more and worse reports than had come to the ears of his subordinates. He had been informed unofficially that after a struggle with the Federals, Bragg had been compelled to retreat to Tunnel Hill. None of this news had Longstreet been willing to accept as true. He reasoned that even if the reports of defeat at Chattanooga were correct, the safety of his own Army depended on the success of the attack on Knoxville, which attack, in turn, hung on the co-operation of the officers. He so replied to McLaws and concluded with this language: "It is a great mistake to suppose that there is any safety for us in going to Virginia if General Bragg has been defeated, for we leave him at the mercy of his victors, and with his army destroyed our own had better be also, for we will be not only destroyed but disgraced. There is neither safety nor honor in any other course than the one I have chosen and ordered." Then, at the suggestion of General Leadbetter, who continued to push for immediate action, Longstreet added a postscript: "The assault must be made at the time appointed, and must be made with a determination which will insure success." [55]

[53] O. R., 31, pt. 3, p. 757.
[55] O. R., 31, pt. 1, p. 494.

[54] O. R., 31, pt. 1, pp. 491–92.

After that, there could be no hesitation or further argument on the part of McLaws, but it was ominous that both the division commanders, men of unquestionable courage, felt so much concern that they expressed their doubts to their chief. This never had happened before on the eve of an attack. If Longstreet observed that fact, he did not permit it to show in his action. He made no alteration in his plans except to direct that the attack on Fort Loudon be made without extensive artillery preparation and that the men go forward a little earlier, perhaps, than had been contemplated.[56] The tactics were to be those of surprise.

Obediently the infantry commanders advanced their sharpshooters at 10 P.M., captured the enemy's pickets and had their men dig new rifle-pits within easy range of the fort.[57] At dawn, about 6:30,[58] a signal gun was fired at each of three widely separated stations. A few batteries went into action briefly to encourage the infantry.[59] All along the line, the sharpshooters opened and fired at every head they could see in the half-darkness above the parapet of Fort Loudon. Then, in two columns, nine regiments of McLaws's veterans rushed forward. In rear of the left column was Anderson's Brigade of Hood's Division, Micah Jenkins's command, which was to attack the line to the left of McLaws's men.

When the troops were close to the fort, but not yet under fire, there was a commotion in the front lines, oaths and the sound of falling men. The cry to "Halt" went up. Soon, word was passed through the companies of the van that the file leaders had stumbled over telegraph wire that had been stretched among stumps left as an obstruction.[60] In a few minutes, most of the men who had fallen over the wire picked themselves up and pushed forward, but the wildest of rumors spread to the rear that the

---

56 This statement has to be qualified. Alexander (*op. cit.*, 486–87) spoke of the receipt of orders after 9 P.M. of the 28th to withhold the fire of most of the guns he had put into position. This modification of orders Alexander considered a mistake. Years afterward, he wrote that "all preparations were thrown away and all advantages sacrificed for the illusive merits of a night attack, decided upon by Longstreet after dark on the 28th" (*op. cit.*, 486). The reports of the division commanders contain no reference to any change of the time set for the delivery of the attack.

57 *O. R.*, 31, pt. 1, pp. 489, 528.     58 *O. R.*, 31, pt. 1, pp. 277, 344.

59 *Alexander*, 487.

60 Although the chief Federal engineer, Capt. (later Brig. Gen.) Orlando M. Poe reported three times at length on the operations at Knoxville, he did not describe in any detail the extent of his use of wire. He merely mentioned (*O. R.*, 31, pt. 1, p. 298) that he made a cheval-de-frise of pikes and fastened "the pikes in place with telegraph wire." In a later paragraph he remarked that confusion was created in Confederate ranks "by passing through the obstacles of stumps, wire entanglements, and brush in front of the fort." Gen. B. G. Humphreys (*ibid.*, 521) reported that his advancing troops encountered at the ditch a "network of wire."

troops had reached impenetrable entanglements where they were being slaughtered.

Sooner than the rumor spread, McLaws's men were in the ditch of Fort Loudon. It was slippery with half-frozen mud. Above it rose forbiddingly the parapet, itself icy and wet. A few Federal cannon shot swept the ditch and mowed men down, but the fallen were hidden under the feet of other hundreds who were sliding down the counterscarp and crowding the ditch. McLaws's columns had converged too closely. Anderson's Brigade was piling on top of them. The ditch was jammed, a trap, a grave trench. Daring, sure-footed men who climbed to the top of the parapet were hurled back dead or were seized from within the fort. A standard bearer was dragged into the fort by the neck;[61] a small detachment crept through an embrasure—to be seen no more.[62] From one Union flank position a heavy fire was concentrated on the ditch. Lighted shells were tossed over the parapet and fell where every fragment tore flesh. Axes and billets of wood followed.[63] The defense was too powerful. Assault was hopeless. If the men remained there, every one of them would be killed.

Word of this reached McLaws. He set out to find Longstreet, who was riding forward with the reserve Brigades of Jenkins and of Bushrod Johnson. Before McLaws could reach the commanding General, Maj. James M. Goggin rode up to Longstreet with a wild report that the wire around the fort was impenetrable without axes and that the men in the assault had not one axe among them. It was useless, said Goggin, to attempt to go on.[64] The General immediately ordered the recall. Both Jenkins and Bushrod Johnson pleaded for an opportunity to use their reserves and to overwhelm the fort, but Longstreet would not listen. The attack had failed. Get out the survivors and stop the fight. That was his order. It was obeyed, but many of the men refused to climb up the counterscarp and to run back to the Confederate lines. Surrender was better than a fatal bullet in the back.

From the ditch, soldiers began to wave handkerchiefs, but almost before the Federals ceased fire, a staff officer from Robert Ransom's cavalry command placed a sealed envelope in Long-

[61] O. R., 31, pt. 1, p. 353.              [62] Alexander, 488.
[63] O. R., 31, pt. 1, p. 521.              [64] Longstreet, 505.

street's hands. It had come a long, long way over mountain roads and it contained this unhappy news:

Richmond, November 27, 1863.

Major-General Ransom,
   Bristol [Va.-Tenn.]
(To be forwarded)

If you are not in communication with General Longstreet, endeavor to open it and inform him of all matters on your front; also, that General Bragg has fallen back before superior forces at Ringgold and hopes to make a stand there, and that his cooperation is necessary and the greatest promptitude required.

Jeff'n Davis [65]

By all reports received from other sources that day and the next, Longstreet had confirmation of worse things than Davis stated in the telegram. Bragg had prepared the road to ruin when he had permitted Rosecrans to open short and sure lines of supply at Chattanooga. The dispatch of Longstreet to Knoxville and the subsequent detachment of Bushrod Johnson to reinforce Longstreet had weakened Bragg on a long, concave line. Himself of doubtful military competence, Bragg had faced in Ulysses Grant an able, self-reliant and aggressive adversary who had in William Sherman and George Thomas two lieutenants of unusual capacity. As a result of these circumstances and of incredibly bad tactics, Bragg had lost Lookout Mountain on the 24th of November and the next day had sustained a heavy defeat on Missionary Ridge, East of Chattanooga. His casualties of 2500 were not excessive, but his loss of forty guns was serious, and his men's loss of confidence in him was worse. On the night of the 26th, Bragg retreated to Ringgold and there beat off pursuers. He then retired toward Dalton, Georgia, twenty-seven miles Southeast of Chattanooga, and was about to ask to be relieved of command [66] when Longstreet received through Ransom the order to co-operate with his defeated chief.[67]

[65] O. R., 52, pt. 2, p. 564. It has been stated frequently that the dispatch received by Longstreet on the 29th of November was directly from Davis, but no such letter appears in the *Official Records* or in *Rowland*. Longstreet's description of the message in his memoirs (p. 507), and in his dispatch to Bragg (O. R., 31, pt. 3, p. 761) applies to the telegram here quoted. Davis at the time was en route to Atlanta from Alabama.

[66] O. R., 31, pt. 2, p. 682.

[67] This brief sketch of Bragg's operations is not taken from the sources but from *Alexander*, 473 ff., and from *Horn*, 297.

By the magnanimity of General Burnside, time was allowed "Old Pete" to consider the course this evil news and the message from the President imposed. The Federal commander generously sent out a flag of truce and offered the Confederates time in which to bring off their dead and to remove their wounded from the ditch. Longstreet gratefully accepted [68] and found that he had lost heavily. In the assault, 129 had been killed and 458 wounded. The missing numbered 226. This gave a total of 813.[69] The removal of the numerous wounded took so many hours that the truce was extended till nightfall.[70] Before it expired, Longstreet had made and then had modified his decision on the strategy of the next move. His first impulse was to abandon the attempted siege at once, and to move immediately toward Bragg's lines. With this in view, he ordered his trains to start for the rear and he telegraphed Bragg for information concerning a line of march which he said he could begin the next day or the next after that.[71]

This plan was changed by the arrival during the afternoon of a message from Bragg through Maj. Gen. Joseph Wheeler. Although the telegram was dated November 26, it was the first clear expression Longstreet had of the commanding General's wishes. Said Wheeler in his telegram: "General Bragg desires me to say he wishes you to fall back with your command upon Dalton if possible. If you find that impracticable, he thinks you will have to fall back toward Virginia. At all events he desires that you order all the cavalry to Dalton." [72]

In the statement of alternatives, Longstreet read a doubt in Bragg's mind whether the road to Dalton would be open. Until that was more nearly established, one way or the other, Longstreet decided to recall his trains.[73] Still later in the day, two messengers from Bragg arrived with the same message: Bragg had reached Dalton; Longstreet must rely on his own resources.[74]

Longstreet was beginning to think by this time that he could perhaps render the largest help to the Army of Tennessee by remaining where he was, by threatening Burnside and by drawing to Knoxville part of Grant's forces that otherwise might be thrown

[68] Longstreet, 507.      [69] O. R., 31, pt. 1, p. 475.
[70] O. R., 31, pt. 1, p. 270; Alexander, 489.
[71] Longstreet, 507; O. R., 31, pt. 3, p. 761.
[72] O. R., 31, pt. 3, p. 760.      [73] O. R., 31, pt. 1, p. 461.
[74] Ibid. If these couriers or staff officers brought any written communication, it has not been found.

against Bragg.[75] In this belief but still in perplexity of mind, he called on the evening of the 29th a council of war and summoned to it McLaws, Jenkins, Bushrod Johnson, Kershaw and Porter Alexander. To these officers the question was put: Should the Army attempt to join Bragg or should it change its base to Southwest Virginia? The only recorded answer is that of McLaws. He doubted whether the troops could reach Dalton otherwise than by remote, difficult roads through a country where neither food for the men nor forage for the animals could be procured. It was better on every count, McLaws thought, to remain in East Tennessee where the force could threaten the Federals, occupy many of them, and subsist on the supplies of a region predominantly hostile.[76]

This appears to have been the prevailing view. As it accorded substantially with his own conclusions, it shaped Longstreet's action. He remained in front of Knoxville, holding Burnside, until he received from a captured Federal dispatch positive intelligence that Maj. Gen. W. T. Sherman was approaching to relieve the garrison.[77] Then, on the night of the 3rd of December, the trains were put in motion northeastward with a heavy escort. The remainder of the infantry followed on the night of the 4th.

As Longstreet turned his back on Knoxville, and followed his men along the muddy road, all informed Southerners, outside his own circle, felt that he had sustained a humiliating defeat. In that mirror of Confederate gossip, the diary of Mrs. James Chesnut, Jr., the opinion of a multitude was reflected: "Detached from General Lee, what a horrible failure is Longstreet!" [78] At Chickamauga, he had been the Longstreet of Second Manassas, but at Knoxville he was back in front of Suffolk. The entire war had witnessed no repulse more complete, by a force of insignificant numbers. In Fort Loudon, at the time of the assault, were less than 250 men [79] under a Lieutenant of Artillery, Samuel L. Benjamin. With casualties of eight killed and five wounded, this garrison was responsible for much of the loss of 813 sustained by the Confederates. Although units farther along the Union line deserved more credit than was given them, the little garrison of

[75] O. R., 31, pt. 1   461.          [76] O. R., 31, pt. 1, pp. 499–500.
[77] O. R., 31, pt. 1  p. 462.          [78] Mrs. Chesnut, 265.
[79] The number may have been increased somewhat during the fight. See the report of Brig. Gen. Edward Ferrero, O. R., 31, pt. 1, p. 353.

New Yorkers, strengthened by a few men from Michigan and Massachusetts, had taken 225 prisoners from some of the most renowned regiments of the famous First Corps of the Army of Northern Virginia! [80]

The advance of these veteran troops had been organized carelessly. They had converged in too narrow a zone. Supports had crowded upon them. The whole plan of action had been clumsily executed. Longstreet himself had ordered the fight abandoned on the strength of a wild report by a staff officer. For this decision, which was made in a spirit almost of panic, Longstreet accepted blame when he wrote his memoirs. With somewhat curious phrasing, he admitted that he was demoralized at the time.[81] In his contemporary report, the Lieutenant General left the impression that the recall was ordered after the men broke for the rear.[82]

On the day of the frustrated assault and at the council of war that evening, Longstreet said nothing, so far as the record shows, to indicate that he held McLaws responsible for the failure. When Longstreet had reached East Tennessee and had reflected upon the failure of the campaign, he decided that the fault was not his but that of his senior division commander. McLaws, he told himself, had not co-operated with him acceptably during the Knoxville campaign. Longstreet wrathfully concluded, also, that McLaws had not shown confidence in the plans of operations or in the leadership of his chief. McLaws's letter of the 29th of November,

[80] The report of Lieut. Samuel L. Benjamin (*O. R.*, 31, pt. 1, pp. 341–44) might be read to advantage by every soldier as an example of the manner in which the splendor of a great exploit can be ruined in the telling. A modest report by Benjamin would have compelled his superiors to praise him. As it was, he said so much for himself that he left little for anyone else to add. He concluded with a sneer at the commander of the nearest infantry, who gave him substantial help, even though the Brigadier General in question remained, as Benjamin wrote, "in the little bomb-proof" (*ibid.*, 344). Benjamin was a native of New York and a West Pointer of the class of 1861. At the time of this defense of Fort Loudon, he was 24, but he was not promoted Captain until June 13, 1864, and he never was advanced above the rank of Brevet Lieutenant Colonel.

[81] *Op. cit.*, 507: "It is not a part of my nature to listen to reports that always come when stunning blows are felt, but confidence in the conduct of the war was broken, and the efforts of those in authority to damage, if not prevent, the success of work ordered in their own vital interest: a poor excuse for want of golden equipoise in one who presumes to hold the lives of his soldiers, but better than to look for ways to shift the responsibility of a wavering spirit that sometimes comes unawares."

[82] "When within about 500 yards of the fort I saw some of the men straggling back, and heard that the troops could not pass the ditch for want of ladders or other means. Almost at the same moment I saw that the men were beginning to retire in considerable numbers, and very soon the column broke up entirely and fell back in confusion. I ordered Buckner's brigade halted and retired, and sent the order for Anderson's brigade of Hood's division, to be halted and retired, but the troops of the latter brigade had become excited and rushed up to the same point from which the others had been repulsed, and were soon driven back" (*O. R.*, 31, pt. 1, p. 461).

urging that the assault on Fort Loudon wait on news from Bragg, probably was one only of several such incidents that stuck in Longstreet's memory.

An exasperating climax was reached on the 15th of December. Three days previously, at Rogersville, where he had established his forces, Longstreet had received word that three Brigades of Federal cavalry and one of infantry were at Bean's Station. Longstreet determined to move down and capture this force. His infantry and "Grumble" Jones's troopers did their part admirably, but the cavalry of Maj. Gen. William T. Martin was mishandled and of small service. The enemy slipped away, with no worse loss than that of some wagons. Pursuit was attempted but was futile, Longstreet maintained, because Evander Law was slow and Lafayette McLaws was loath to move before bread was issued the hungry men.[83]

As soon as the Confederates returned to their camps, Longstreet sprung a sensation that was to trouble him for many a day. In a few brief sentences he relieved McLaws of command, directed that officer to proceed to Augusta, Georgia, and placed the Division under the senior Brigadier. McLaws apparently had no intimation that this was to happen to him and he wrote immediately to ask the reason. Longstreet's A.A.G. replied: "I am directed to say that throughout the campaign on which we are engaged you have exhibited a want of confidence in the efforts and plans which the commanding General has thought proper to adopt, and he is apprehensive that this feeling will extend more or less to the troops under your command. Under these circumstances, the commanding General has felt that the interest of the public service would be advanced by your separation from him, and as he could not himself leave, he decided upon the issue of the order which you have received."[84] Longstreet did not state what he affirmed later —that he refrained from arresting McLaws because he thought the Major General could be used elsewhere.[85]

McLaws had been a Major General since May 23, 1862, and had been in nearly all the principal battles of Lee's Army. He was not accounted among the ablest of the division commanders, but he was respected as a man and a soldier. To relieve him of com-

---

[83] Longstreet's account is in *O. R.*, 31, pt. 1, pp. 463–64; McLaws's is in *ibid.*, 494–95, Martin's in *ibid.*, 546. The action is well summarized in *Alexander*, 490–91.
[84] *O. R.*, 31, pt. 1, pp. 497–98.      [85] *Ibid.*, 503.

mand was to startle thousands of Southerners. McLaws did not linger for argument at headquarters. He departed overland for home the next day [86] and after arriving there, he forwarded to the Adjutant General the correspondence that had passed. He insisted: "I have differed in opinion with General Longstreet concerning many things, but that this difference has influenced my own conduct or that of the troops under my command, I utterly deny. I therefore respectfully request that my division be restored to my command." [87]

This was written on the 29th of December. By that date, Longstreet had decided to undertake to make good his complaint against McLaws by the presentation of formal charges and specifications. McLaws's alleged general lack of co-operation during the campaign, as set forth in his answer to McLaws's first inquiry, was ignored now. All three of the specifications were drawn from McLaws's failure to take precautions in the assault on Fort Loudon. Not a word was said in the specifications or in the covering letter of anything that McLaws did or failed to do at Bean's Station, or at any other time than on November 28–29.[88]

McLaws was as jealous of his professional reputation as he was of his private good name. He struck back hard. In a letter he evidently designed to be circulated among his friends in Richmond he said: "The charges were forced on [General Longstreet] by public opinion and he attempted to make me a blind to run public inquiry off from his complete failure in the whole Tennessee campaign—then forwarded his charges but did not ask that a court be ordered to investigate them. . . . The difficulty with Gen. L. and myself commenced at Chickamauga when I, not believing that he was a greater man than Genl. Bragg kept aloof from the coalition which was forming against him, headed by Genl. L. Genl. L. was next in command and independent of the want of delicacy in his heading a conspiracy I thought it was no time to be spreading dissensions among the troops by the ambitious movements and aspirations of the chief commander. I knew General Bragg to be honest and capable and to be free[r] from the influence of cliques than any other General, and his past distinguished services under very trying circumstances and with a pow-

[86] Ibid., 498.
[88] O. R., 31, pt. 1, pp. 503–04.
[87] O. R., 31, pt. 3, p. 881.

erful combination of political generals against him warranted the belief that in a favorable state of affairs, he would be all that could be desired.

"But Genl. L. has never forgiven me my not joining that clique the object of which was to place him in command of the Army of East [sic] Tennessee.

"When it is considered that Genl. L. failed to assault the enemy before reaching Knoxville, and his long delay before the place, was the cause of much of Bragg's disaster at Chattanooga, and that he has nothing to recommend him as a commander but the possession of a certain bullheadedness, it is mortifying when one feels that he is allowed to tyrannize, as he is doing." [89]

On this basis, McLaws continued to press for trial before a court martial and for restoration to his command. If held, this court martial was not to be the only one of importance that would be convened at the instance of the Lieutenant General. In the opinion of Longstreet, Jerome Robertson had indulged at Bean's Station in some pessimistic utterances which Longstreet took to be part of an effort to dodge heavy duty. In the letter that carried the charges against McLaws, there was an arraignment of Robertson for specified remarks "calculated to discourage . . . the said regimental commanders and weaken their confidence in the movement then in progress" and, in general, "to prevent that hearty and hopeful co-operation necessary to success." [90]

Longstreet was not unconscious of the fact that the filing of charges against two of his senior officers was almost as much a reflection on him as on them. At the moment he was in the depths. Gone was the desire to direct an army of his own; gone, too, was the confidence in which he had come to Tennessee. On the day that he forwarded the court martial charges, he wrote the Adjutant General that he was cut off from communication with Bragg and desired to be "assigned as part of some other officer's command, whom I may reach with less trouble and in less time." He went on to say that if East Tennessee was to be held for future operations, he wished them to be under another commander. In the event a senior officer were named, he would give him full aid. Were only a junior available, "it will give me much pleasure to

[89] Lafayette McLaws to Miss Lizzie Ewell, MS, Feb. 24, 1864—*Ewell MSS.*
[90] *O. R.*, 31, pt. 1, p. 470.

relinquish in his favor, and aid him by any suggestions that my experience may enable me to give." Grimly he went on: "I regret that a combination of circumstances has so operated during the campaign in East Tennessee as to prevent the complete destruction of the enemy's forces in this part of the State. It is fair to infer that the fault entirely is with me, and I desire therefore, that some other commander be tried. . . . I believe that this is the only personal favor that I have asked of the Government, and I hope that I may have reason to expect that it may be granted." [91]

Longstreet doubtless wrote this in humiliation, but if he expected the President or the War Department to placate him with soft words and compliments, he was disappointed. The first response he had from Richmond was telegraphic notice from the Adjutant General's office that it was doubtful whether he could relieve an officer from duty and send that individual beyond the limits of the command. In the case of McLaws, it would have been permissible to have arrested and held him for the action of the Department. Longstreet would do well to recall McLaws for that purpose. General Cooper added only the small consolation that Longstreet had all the authority of a department commander.[92] In Richmond, Mr. Davis took a serious view of the charges against McLaws and deferred the question of whether Longstreet's request to be relieved of responsibility in East Tennessee should be granted.[93] The admonition to recall McLaws was disregarded by Longstreet, but the trial at length was set for February 3. McLaws arrived that day and asked that the proceedings be opened.[94]

Maj. Gen. Simon B. Buckner had been named President of the court. Brig. Gen. B. G. Humphreys was one member.[95] The others are not now known. Through some mistake on the part of Buckner or his Judge Advocate, the court was allowed to adjourn indefinitely. A leave of absence was given a member without the consent of the War Department. It was February 12 when the trial began.[96] McLaws had prepared for it with much care and he had the better of it. The first specification was that he did not prop-

[91] O. R., 31, pt. 1, pp. 467–68          [92] O. R., 31, pt. 3, p. 893.
[93] Ibid., pt. 1, p. 469.
[94] McLaws to Miss Lizzie Ewell, MS, Feb. 25, 1864, loc. cit.
[95] O. R., 31, pt. 1, p. 506.
[96] L. M. Blackford to his mother, MS. Feb. 12. 1864—Blackford MSS.

erly advance his sharpshooters on the night of November 28. Next it was charged that McLaws did not organize a select storming party in front of Fort Loudon. Around the third specification, the legal battle raged vehemently. Longstreet's allegation was that McLaws assaulted Fort Loudon where the ditch was impassable, that McLaws failed to provide ladders or other means of crossing the ditch, and that he did not notify his officers the ditch on the west side of the fort "was but a slight obstacle to his infantry." [97] In the testimony on this specification, all the officers who had made reconnaissance of the fort insisted that the ditch to the West was shallow.[98] The contention of Longstreet was that McLaws's attack had not been directed to that point but to a part of the ditch where the parapet was much higher.[99]

Apparently the trial was interrupted and prolonged.[100] Before all the evidence in the case had been taken, Longstreet had to justify his complaint against Jerome Robertson. The charge was drawn and was filed on the 26th of January, 1864,[101] but if it was brought to trial, the record has not been found. Robertson, a physician by profession, was not stripped of his rank, though he was suspended again from his famous command.[102] Much later, in June, he was ordered to take immediate command of the "reserve forces of the State of Texas." [103] His transfer marked his final disappearance from the First Corps. Inasmuch as Longstreet had relieved Robertson of command in November and then had seen the Brigadier restored, he doubtless was glad to be rid of the Texan.

The case of Evander McIver Law proved more difficult. Longstreet did not attempt to try Law for the alleged failure to support Jenkins at Wauhatchie when the attack was made on Hooker's rearguard. Subsequently, during the retreat from Knoxville, Jenkins charged Law with "mismanagement" in a minor affair at Campbell's Station.[104] This, too, was overlooked because of cir-

97 *O. R.*, 31, pt. 1, pp. 503–04.   98 *Ibid.*, 488.
99 For the depth of the ditch and the height of the parapet at several points, see *ibid.*, 504, 519, 521. These statements were by officers who participated in the advance.
100 Col. Osmun Latrobe noted in his diary that he was on the stand Mch. 15, 1864, as a witness in the case.
101 *O. R.*, 31, pt. 1, p. 470.
102 *Longstreet*, 548. L. M. Blackford in a MS letter to his mother, Jan. 22, 1864, described Robertson as a man of strong sense, kindly and warm impulses, and genial manners, but not a man "much cultivated or polished." Although of established courage, Robertson was not "considered a good officer."—*Blackford MSS.*
103 *O. R.*, 34, pt. 4, p. 692.   104 *O. R.*, 31, pt. 1, p. 458.

cumstances that were unusual if not unique. About the 19th of December, 1863, Law tendered his resignation, through Longstreet's headquarters. It was his purpose, Law was alleged to have intimated, to transfer to the cavalry and to procure a command in that service. Law's own subsequent explanation was that Longstreet had recommended Jenkins's promotion after promising that Hood's Division should go to Law.[105] While action on the resignation was pending, Law asked leave of absence.[106] It is entirely probable that "Old Pete" granted this leave without any urging, perhaps even with alacrity, because he must have shared the belief[107] that Hood's old Division never would have its former value as a combat unit so long as both Jenkins and Law served with it. Longstreet was, in fact, so much obliged to Law for resigning that he listened sympathetically to an odd request the young man made. Law stated that he was going to Richmond and would like to carry his resignation with him and to present it in person. This was not the normal procedure in such cases, but it was not contrary to regulations. Longstreet returned the paper to Law and no doubt wished him luck. The way appeared to be opened for the promotion of Micah Jenkins.

After Law left East Tennessee with his resignation in his pocket, Longstreet began to hear strange tales about the fine Alabama regiments in Law's command. It was reported to him that certain officers of Law's Brigade were circulating a petition to the War Department for transfer to their native State. Law was said to have engineered the leave of absence in order that he might go to Richmond and exert his influence to have the petition granted. Longstreet was outraged. He had the names of witnesses collected and he proceeded to draw up charges against Law of "conduct highly prejudicial to good order and military discipline" in obtaining leave under false pretenses, in deceiving his commanding General and in creating discontent among his troops.[108] Soon it was reported to Longstreet that Law had gone to Richmond but had not presented his resignation. Immediately Longstreet filed new charges that Law took the resignation from headquarters "and did purloin or clandestinely do away with said communication, thereby abusing the confidence of his commanding General

[105] Oates, 338.
[107] Cf. Sorrel, 182–83.
[106] O. R., 31, pt. 1, p. 471.
[108] O. R., 31, pt. 1, p. 471.

aforesaid, and robbing the War Department of its true and proper official record." [109]

What actually happened, according to Law's counsel, was this: When Law reached Richmond he found in the city his wounded former chief. Hood was aware of Law's long, honorable service and of the South Carolinian's hold upon the Alabama troops. In order to save the service of Law to the Confederacy, Hood prevailed upon Law to give him the resignation, which he showed unofficially to the Secretary of War but did not present formally. [110] Law assumed that failure to tender the resignation left him in command of his troops. He accordingly returned and, his counsel explained, soon found most of his officers so discontented that they were circulating a petition for return to Lee or for transfer to Mobile. Law duly approved this petition and forwarded it to Longstreet, who was greatly offended by the paper. It was at this stage of the controversy, according to Law's attorney, that Longstreet ordered the arrest of Law for purloining or destroying a record. [111] This allegation was considered extreme. Although the War Department nowhere used the word "persecution" in referring to Longstreet's charges, the Department was, in the next phase of the controversy, to take a stern position. [112]

These vexatious cases of McLaws, Robertson and Law showed a weakening, if not a demoralization of Longstreet's command, but they were not the full measure of "Old Pete's" tribulations that winter. In February, Congress passed an act to provide for the appointment of an additional General of full rank for the command of the Trans-Mississippi Department, should the President deem the choice of such an officer necessary. [113] The measure was designed solely to give adequate administrative and military powers to Kirby Smith, who had been in the Trans-Mississippi Department for a year. In spite of this, Longstreet felt himself aggrieved that Smith, "of lower rank than mine," was appointed "to hold

[109] O. R., 31, pt. 1, p. 472.
[110] Oates, 338–39. General Oates was of opinion that Hood destroyed the resignation, but Cooper wrote: ". . . it was presented by a friend of General Law unofficially to the Secretary of War, and never came through the regular channel as an official paper" (O. R., 31, pt. 1, p. 471).
[111] Oates, 339.
[112] O. R., 31, pt. 1, p. 472. See also, infra, Chap. XVII.
[113] The same act provided for the appointment of additional Lieutenant Generals where required for the command of any of the military departments. 3 Journal C. S. Congress, pp. 688, 716, 749, 760, 784, 789; 6 ibid., pp. 838, 849, 860.

rank above." [114] The difference in rank was that Smith's name had appeared immediately after Longstreet's on the list of nominations for Lieutenant General, though both held the same commission from the same date.[115] Further, Longstreet had been Major in the "old army" from July 19, 1858 [116] and Smith from January 31, 1861,[117] but Smith was a Major of the line and Longstreet a Paymaster. Longstreet late in life wrote that he thought his resignation was proper when he was passed over in this manner, but that he decided he should "stay and go down with faithful comrades of long and arduous service." [118]

If this quotation correctly recorded the General's state of mind, it would indicate Longstreet's conviction in the winter of 1863–64 that the Southern cause was lost. His contemporary correspondence does not leave that impression. On the contrary, after his periods of doubt and humiliation, he swung in February and March, 1864, to the other extreme. Subsequently, he explained that "the disaffected"—meaning McLaws, Robertson and Law— "were away, and with them disappeared their influence." His little army, he said, "was bright and cheerful and ready for any work to which it could be called." [119] Actually, his change of mood appears in the records prior to the time the court martial of McLaws commenced and, probably, while both Law and Robertson still were in East Tennessee. The tone of Longstreet's dispatches became aggressive. He returned eagerly to the same sort of planning in which he had indulged in the spring and again in the late summer of 1863. It is futile to inquire, on the basis of extant evidence, whether this sudden activity was itself a confession of failure or the expression of his purpose to make a new record that would efface the old. This much is clear. In his planning he showed less of undisguised striving for leadership and more of regard for the co-operation of others—as if he had learned his lesson!—but he scarcely displayed more of wisdom concerning the practicality of the strategical combination he urged.

Bragg had relinquished command of the Army of Tennessee on December 2.[120] "Joe" Johnston took Bragg's place on the 16th

---

[114] *Longstreet,* 524.
[116] *Cullum* 1164.
[118] *Longstreet,* 525.
[120] *O. R.,* 31, pt. 3, p. 775. For the circumstances, see Don C. Seitz, *Braxton Bragg,* 400 ff.

[115] 2 *Journal C. S. Congress,* 462.
[117] *Cullum* 1255.
[119] *Ibid.*

but found himself confronted by superior force. So was Longstreet. Between them, in effect, were two Federal armies, Grant's at Nashville and Thomas's at Chattanooga.[121] Longstreet felt that he could do nothing where he was unless the enemy obligingly came up and attacked him. The only course he could follow, as he saw the situation, was to mount the whole of his command, move into Kentucky and seize the Louisville and Nashville Railroad. This he thought he would be able to hold long enough to force the Federals to withdraw from Tennessee, which Johnston then could occupy. On February 21, Longstreet suggested this plan to Lee and concluded with these words: "The only way to mount us is by sending us 5,000 mules from Virginia, 2,500 from Georgia and 2,000 from South Carolina; I have 5,000. Of these I can get along with about half, by taking no wagons except for ammunition; we will be able to get enough for other purposes from the enemy. We have no time to spare, and the whole thing should be kept from other parties." [122]

The next day Longstreet presented the plan to the Secretary of War in a detailed letter. Evidently the General overnight had become more mindful of the obstacles to the execution of his plan, or else he felt he should explain to Mr. Seddon the technical considerations he did not think it necessary to mention to Lee. Briefly Longstreet admitted that he could not accumulate sufficient forage for the march to Kentucky. Besides, "we will require," he warned, "many horse and mule shoes, many saddles and bridles and spurs, and a large depot of corn at Abingdon and Bristol to start upon." [123]

It was entirely beyond the resources of the Southern government to convert Longstreet's command into mounted infantry. Before Longstreet could be brought to see this, his enthusiasm for his plan led him to inquire directly of the President by telegraph whether he could undertake the movement. The answer came back in a singularly stiff message from the Adjutant General, with whom Longstreet was not on friendly terms. Cooper said: "The Department cannot determine the propriety of your movements; that rests in your discretion. It is advisable, however, that the court-martial in General McLaws' case assemble as soon as it can

121 In addition, Sherman was at Memphis. See *Horn,* 319.
122 *O. R.,* 32, pt. 2, p. 790.     123 *Ibid.,* 791–92.

properly do so. Report your determination, and communicate it, also, to the president of the court." [124]

In the face of this snub, Longstreet continued to press for his plan until the beginning of the second week in March.[125] Then he concluded that the animals and forage were unprocurable, but he would not surrender the idea of an offensive against the Louisville and Nashville Railroad. His new plan was that Beauregard should move from South Carolina and should unite with him at Abingdon, Virginia. Thence the two commands would advance, via Pound Gap, against Louisville, Kentucky. Longstreet hoped then to hold the Federal lines of supply long enough to compel a Federal retreat. Thereupon, Johnston was to advance behind the retreating Unionists. Junction of the three Confederate armies would give them superior force.[126]

This plan assumed that Beauregard could take all the infantry from Charleston and could march them 300 miles to Louisville. A further assumption was that the combined troops of Longstreet and of Beauregard could be subsisted and foraged en route and would be strong enough to beat off attacks in Kentucky until Johnston arrived. Broad as were these assumptions, Longstreet on the 8th of March [127] left his command and journeyed to Richmond to join Davis, Lee, Bragg and War Department officials in a discussion on March 14 [128] of this and other proposals for a counterstroke against the Federals in Tennessee. At the conference, Longstreet's original plan to mount his troops received scant attention, but his scheme of a triple concentration was examined carefully. He scored heavily, he thought, by showing that Bragg previously had pronounced impractical a plan that officer now advanced for a junction of Johnston and Longstreet in Middle Tennessee.[129] When the council adjourned without announcement of Davis's decision, Longstreet was of opinion that the President favored the return of Longstreet's forces to the Army of Tennessee before anything further was attempted.[130] The spirit of the meeting, in Longstreet's opinion, had been cold, if not positively uncivil to Lee

[124] O. R., 32, pt. 2, p. 818.

[125] Ibid., 809; pt. 3, pp. 582, 587, 590, 595, 598.

[126] Cf. O. R., 32, pt. 3, p. 627.        [127] Latrobe's MS Diary, Mch. 8, 1864.

[128] Cf. O. R., 32, pt. 2, p. 641. For the reason of Bragg's presence in Richmond at this time, see infra, p. 315.

[129] Longstreet, 545–46; cf. O. R., 32, pt. 2, pp. 595, 614.

[130] O. R., 32, pt. 3, pp. 627–28.

and to him,[131] and after he left the room with Lee, he probably invoked his old commander to support his plan and to take direction of the Army he hoped to see organized in Southwest Virginia. From Richmond, Longstreet journeyed to nearby Petersburg to visit his wife and to have his first look at the five-months-old son he had named Robert Lee, but he must have allowed himself little time with his family. His plan was uppermost in his mind. He devoted hour after hour to letters in which he explained to Beauregard, to Davis and to Lee what he thought the strategy of the Southern Army should be in Tennessee and Kentucky. The fullest of his letters was to Davis. In detail Longstreet argued again for a joint advance into Kentucky by his troops and Beauregard's. After they had forced a Federal retirement, Johnston was to follow the retreating enemy or was to reoccupy Tennessee.[132] In describing all this, Longstreet was explicit, but he said afterward that he believed little attention would be paid his views by Davis and by Bragg, both of whom he thought hostile to him. Consequently he sent Lee a copy of his letter to Davis, and he again besought Lee to sponsor the plan and to take command of the expedition when it was ready to move into Kentucky.[133]

By March 18, Longstreet was back in East Tennessee [134] and was on the down curve of his emotional crisis. Disappointment of every sort met him. Troops were on short rations. Corn for the animals arrived so slowly and in such small quantities that Longstreet doubted whether he could keep his horses and mules alive.[135] He continued to believe that strong action in Kentucky would end the war in '64,[136] but all the answers to his appeals were discouraging. Davis replied in terms that Longstreet considered a rebuke.[137] The President pointed out, among other things, that one of the railroads Longstreet proposed to use for Beauregard's troop movements was employed in the transport of corn.[138] Davis's preference for the union of "the two wings of the Army of

---

[131] *Longstreet*, 546.      [132] *O. R.*, 32, pt. 3, pp. 637–41.

[133] *Ibid.*, 641–42. There is no direct evidence that Longstreet conferred with Lee about this operation while they were in Richmond, but the tone of the letter of March 16 strongly suggests a previous discussion with Lee.

[134] *Latrobe's MS Diary*, Mch. 18, 1864.

[135] *O. R.*, 32, pt. 3, pp. 648, 655.      [136] *Ibid.*, 655.

[137] *Longstreet*, 547. There was nothing in Davis's letter (*O. R.*, 32, pt. 3, p. 674) that could be regarded, in Longstreet's words, as "a rebuke of my delay" in Petersburg; but the President's language undeniably was stiff.

[138] *O. R.*, 32, pt. 3, p. 675.

Tennessee" was reiterated.[139] Beauregard reported himself unable to supply animals or equipment and questioned the soundness of the plan Longstreet proposed.[140] Johnston did not think an advance should be undertaken. He believed that Longstreet should remain close enough to reinforce the Army of Tennessee if a battle was in prospect.[141] Lee agreed that either a concentration on Johnston's line or an advance into Kentucky was feasible, but he thought the heaviest Federal blow might fall in Virginia [142] and he said frankly that he would not advocate an advance into Kentucky if Johnston, who knew the ground and the circumstances, was opposed to it.[143]

"Old Pete" held to his opinion with the stubbornness that made some of his comrades think of him as German in his mentality; but he soon had other and scarcely less humiliating matters to deepen his distress. He was anxious that men of his own choice be named to succeed McLaws, whom he did not wish to return, and Hood, who would be incapacitated for months. Longstreet's choice for Hood's Division continued to be Micah Jenkins, whose promotion he previously had sought. If Jenkins was advanced, Longstreet wanted "Joe" Kershaw to succeed to McLaws's Division. In the event only one vacancy occurred, Longstreet wished Jenkins to have it.

At the outset, almost before the court martial of McLaws was under way, an obstacle to the execution of Longstreet's plan was presented in the person of Charles W. Field. That fine officer at length had recovered sufficiently from the wounds received at Second Manassas to resume field duty, though he still was crippled. Field had not served under Longstreet after the transfer of A. P. Hill's Division to Jackson's command, but for reasons of its own the War Department on February 12 ordered Field to join Longstreet for assignment to duty with Hood's Division.[144] The same day, Field was promoted Major General,[145] which automatically under his orders gave him command of the Division.

If Longstreet had any advance notice of this, the records do not show it. At the moment he made no protest at the assignment of

139 Ibid., 676.                               140 Ibid., 656.
141 O. R., 52, pt. 2, p. 643.                  142 O. R., 52, pt. 2, p. 649.
143 O. R., 32, pt. 3, p. 736.
144 O. R., 32, pt. 2, p. 726. Field had served, while convalescent, as Superintendent of the Bureau of Conscription. O. R., 25, pt. 2, p. 824; IV ibid., 2, 568.
145 Wright, 37.

"an outsider" to the command of a Division which the senior Brigadier, Jenkins, was qualified to lead. Hopeful of doing by indirection what the promotion of Field kept him from doing directly, Longstreet tried this arrangement: With him, on temporary duty, was Maj. Gen. Simon Buckner, a capable and experienced soldier whose whole career had been spent in the Mississippi Valley. There was no reason to assume that Buckner would wish to go to Virginia. Besides, Hood's Division was larger than Buckner's and was in need of an active commander. Field was crippled. When the orders came to assign Field to Hood's Division, which would stop Jenkins's advancement, Longstreet transferred Buckner to command Hood's Division and put Field in charge of Buckner's troops. If, subsequently, Buckner was called to other duty, the direction of Hood's Division would be vacated in favor of Jenkins who was eager for promotion to regular command of that Division.[146]

After Longstreet had assigned Buckner and Field he reported his action to the War Department and added blandly: "I have felt the less hesitation in this as General Lee suggested such assignment of General Buckner." [147] As soon as his letter reached Richmond, the Adjutant General telegraphed disapproval. "The order from this office," said Cooper, "assigning Field to [Hood's] Division will be carried out." [148] Longstreet was not to be outdone. Command of McLaws's Division was vacant so long as its former head was suspended. If Field were put in McLaws's place, command of Hood's Division still might be retained for Jenkins. Accordingly Longstreet telegraphed the Adjutant General: "Would it meet the views of the Department to assign Major General Field to the Division lately commanded by Major General McLaws?" [149] The answer came the same day: "It does not suit the views of the President to assign Major General Field to the Division lately commanded by Major General McLaws. He is to take the Division to which he was assigned in orders from this office." [150]

Longstreet said no more at the time, but as the days passed, his indignation mounted. On March 20, in circumstances not plain

146 O. R., 32, pt. 2, p. 802. Jenkins, said L. M. Blackford, was exceedingly ambitious to receive command of Hood's Division "and it shows with repulsive plainness." MS Letter of Feb. 12, 1864—Blackford MSS.
147 O. R., 32, pt. 2, p. 802.        148 O. R., 32, pt. 2, p. 583.
149 Ibid.        150 O. R., 32, pt. 3, p. 583.

from the records, he wrote a wrathful letter in which he asked to be informed of "the distinguished services rendered by [General Field] and the high recommendations of his commanding officers which have induced the Government to make this unusual promotion and assignment." [151] This was a challenge of the sort Jefferson Davis never ignored. His was the constitutional right to appoint general officers; it was the duty of his military subordinates to accept his choice. General Cooper was directed to administer a strong rebuke. The Adjutant General did not fail to execute his instructions. He wrote Longstreet: "The advice you have asked [concerning Field's service] is considered highly insubordinate and demands rebuke. It is also a reflection upon a gallant and meritorious officer, who has been severely wounded in battle in the cause of the Confederate States, and is deemed unbecoming the high position and dignity of the officer who thus makes the reflection. The regulations of the Army, with which you should be familiar, prescribe that appointments of general officers are made by selection—selection by whom? Of course by the Executive, by whom appointments are made under the constitution. The regulations referred to do not require the recommendation of general officers for the procurement of such appointments, and your inquiry is a direct reflection upon the Executive." [152]

This came when Longstreet's mission was nearing its end. The tone of this rebuke, which approached a reprimand, had not been the temper of all officialdom toward Longstreet. He and his men had received on February 17 the thanks of Congress for "sharing . . . the arduous fatigues and privations of many campaigns in Virginia, Maryland, Pennsylvania, Georgia and Tennessee, and participating in nearly every great battle fought in those States." Longstreet was commended for displaying "great ability, skill, and prudence in command," and the men for "the most heroic bravery, fortitude, and energy, in every duty they have been called upon to perform." [153] Had these thanks been more specific. they might well have dwelt on what Longstreet and his veterans had achieved at Chickamauga. Although Longstreet had little or no part in planning that battle, he had done much to win it.

When this is stated, it covers substantially everything that can be

151 O. R., 32, pt. 3, p. 738.          152 O. R., 32, pt. 3, p. 738.
153 O R., 31, pt. 1, pp. 549–50.

said to Longstreet's credit in Tennessee. He had done poorly in all the actions he had directed independently. His administration had been as luckless as his combat. While serving under Lee, the one serious difficulty Longstreet had with subordinate commanders had been that involving A. P. Hill,[154] but in Tennessee, during five months of detached service, one Major General and two Brigadiers had been ordered before courts martial. A famous Division had been crippled because of rivalries between two of its brigade commanders. The return of Micah Jenkins had been followed by strife. Concerning all of this Longstreet never wrote a line to indicate that he considered himself at fault.

That was not all. With his command disorganized and his achievement in tragic contrast to the hopes he had cherished before he left Virginia, Longstreet remained confident that he could shape the soundest strategy for a campaign that would save the Confederacy and terminate the war successfully in 1864.[155] To this confidence in himself as a strategist Longstreet tenaciously held. He did not ignore the assertion of Lee that "the great obstacle everywhere is lack of supplies,"[156] but he did not permit that to curb his argument. In advocating the recovery of Kentucky, he was maintaining what all the Southern commanders considered desirable. If Kentucky was to be regained by the Confederates without previously defeating the Federals in Tennessee, the one point of departure for an army would be Southwest Virginia. The objective would be the Louisville and Nashville Railroad. This was unshakable logic, a perfect paper basis for a campaign. Practicality was lacking. The mounting of Longstreet's men on mules scarcely would have been possible at a time when the shortage of horses and mules was one of the most acute of the Army's problems. If by incredible effort, mounts could have been provided, the supply of forage in a country remote from the railways would have been impossible. The route of Longstreet's advance would have been littered with dead mules and dismounted men.

Longstreet's alternative plans for the convergence of all the infantry in the Southeastern States of the Confederacy were by no

154 See Vol. I, p. 664 ff.
155 Cf. Longstreet to Cooper, Mch. 19, 1864: "If our armies can take the initiative in the spring campaign they can march into Kentucky with but little trouble and can finish the war in this year" (O. R., 32, pt. 3, p. 655).
156 O. R., 52, pt. 2, p. 649.

means original with him. They were part of what might be termed the prevailing strategical theory of the South. All military men of experience accepted without argument the doctrine that the Confederate armies should be concentrated, but the administration consented to dispersion because the people of each State demanded protection from the invader. Seapower made it possible for the Union leaders to take advantage of the Confederacy's mistaken policy. By threatening at all times to land troops at any point between Albemarle Sound and Savannah, the Federals could immobilize a great part of the Confederate Army. Where Longstreet's planning was original it was not practical, and where it was practical it was not original. He personified the familiar danger to the effective organization of an Army, the danger that a competent executive officer will destroy his usefulness by regarding himself as a great strategist.

# CHAPTER XVII

## WINTER TESTS TEMPER

BY COMPARISON with conditions Longstreet found in Tennessee, the army command in Virginia seemed a happy fellowship, but during the months of "Old Pete's" absence, some of Lee's other lieutenants had probably more of contention and of heartburning than they had known at any time since the spring of 1862. Of different nature, but manifestly serious was the threat for a few days early in December, 1863, that the man whose tact, courage and character held the Army together would himself be sent to Georgia to succeed Bragg. The President was frankly desirous that Lee assume command in the Mississippi Valley after the Confederate defeats in front of Nashville. It was only by definite expression of his desire to retain his old association that Lee escaped an assignment which would have placed him, not Joseph E. Johnston, in front of Sherman. Had Lee gone, the Southern government might have discovered, quickly and unhappily, the extent to which the morale not less than the strategy of the Army of Northern Virginia depended on him.[1]

As for Bragg, after the President reluctantly had concluded that the man who lost Lookout Mountain and Missionary Ridge was not qualified to command one Army, he decided to give that unsuccessful officer command of all the Armies. On Feb. 24, 1864, Bragg was "assigned to duty at the seat of government" and, under the direction of the President, was "charged with the conduct of the military operations in the armies of the Confederacy."[2] The post, which vaguely resembled that of a modern chief of the general staff, was one which Lee had found impossible in the spring of 1862.[3] Bragg was to surprise everyone by his discharge of his new duties, which better fitted his abilities than did field command. He was to conduct himself with moderation in the re-

[1] For the details, see 6 Rowland, 63; O. R., 29, pt. 2, p. 866, and the references cited in 3 R. E. Lee, 207 ff.
[2] O. R., 33, 1196.                                          [3] See 2 R. E. Lee, 4 ff.

established position and was to perform more than one service of large value without disturbing the organization of the Army of Northern Virginia. At the time of his appointment, deliberate restraint in references to him suggests that he was considered a potential irritant.[4]

If the crisis of Lee's transfer and Bragg's promotion was passed without hurt to the men on the Rapidan, the progressive decline in the rations of the troops and in the forage of the animals brought to the camps a spectre of starvation. An acute shortage of subsistence in January, 1864,[5] compelled Lee to say, "Unless there is a change, I fear the army cannot be kept effective and probably cannot be kept together." [6] Hunger was the normal condition of man and mount.[7] Not a tree among the camps had bark below the point to which a half-starved horse could raise his mouth.[8] For their lack of food, the men damned the commissaries; for the weakness of their horses, artillerists and troopers blamed the quartermasters. No Southerner, unless it was Colonel Northrop, would admit that the food and the fodder actually were unavailable.

In this want and suffering, the Army had to recruit or re-enlist its cavalry.[9] A proposal to bring from South Carolina some regiments which had enjoyed an easy life provoked bitter complaints [10] on their part. Col. James Conner, a loyal South Carolinian, answered for the men who had fought under Hampton and "Dick" Anderson: "I am disgusted, mortified, ashamed that men born in the State should behave thus, and men of position, education and character. This makes it the more to be despised. Talk about Foxe's Book of Martyrs, the 'Drags' will add a chapter to martyrology that will be more harrowing than any yet written. Sweet youths, won't they have a nice time of it? Not a thing to be bought with money; only one small ration a day such as their darkies at present would not eat . . ." [11] A year before, certainly two years previously, it would not have been necessary to write that. Worse even than the task of recruiting the cavalry was that of filling the

---

[4] In spite of apprehension that they would clash, Bragg and Secretary Seddon appear to have co-operated without difficulty. Contrast 2 *R. W. C. D.*, 184, with *O. R.*, 51, pt. 2, p. 865.

[5] *O. R.*, 33, 1061, 1064 ff., 1076, 1087, 1115, 1117; *ibid.*, 51, pt. 2, p. 808.

[6] *O. R.*, 33, 1114.         [7] For details, see 3 *R. E. Lee*, 246 ff.

[8] *Ibid.*, 252.

[9] *O. R.*, 33, pp. 1152–53, 1155, 1162–64, 1170; *ibid.*, 51, pt. 2, p. 835.

[10] 2 *R. W. C. D.*, 176; *O. R.*, 33, 1231, 1243.

[11] *Conner*, 128.

gaps in the infantry. The veterans re-enlisted,[12] but to catch the skulkers, a new conscription act had to be passed.[13] Some State judges so captiously disputed the constitutionality of various military laws that the writ of habeas corpus had to be suspended.[14]

Certain army officers, like these jurists, began to balk. Harvey Hill, it will be remembered, on the 15th of October, 1863,[15] was relieved by Bragg's order of duty with the Army of Tennessee.[16] In the official correspondence that preceded the order, Bragg had said of Hill: "Possessing some high qualifications as a commander, he still fails to such an extent in others more essential that he weakens the *morale* and military tone of his command. A want of prompt conformity to orders of great importance is the immediate cause of this application." [17]

Hill thought that the reason for his removal from command was his participation in the round robin against Bragg,[18] and he called on the War Department for a copy of Bragg's complaint. Next, Hill demanded that a court of inquiry be detailed to investigate the charges. He succeeded in learning what Bragg had said of him, but he was told that a court was not necessary.[19] Prediction, freely made, of a duel between Hill and Bragg came to nothing.[20] Instead of trying to kill Bragg, the aggrieved Lieutenant General sought service elsewhere. In doing this he stipulated that the position be one equivalent to his rank of Lieutenant General. This insistence disclosed a newly developed quality of his mind. Neither as Brigadier nor as Major General had he given any recorded evidence that he was dissatisfied with his commission or with any field command. Now that he was a relieved corps commander, he became jealous of his rank.

Under the interpretation given in the case of Gustavus W. Smith to the law concerning the appointment of Lieutenant Generals,[21] corps command was the only service in keeping with Hill's rank. The Adjutant General accordingly had to advise Hill on the 16th of November, 1863, that there was no command to which he then

[12] *O. R.*, 33, 1145, 1149 ff.
[13] Feb. 17, 1864, IV *O. R.*, 3, 178. For reserves, the age limits were extended from 17 to 50. Details of the measure are discussed in A. B. Moore, *Conscription and Conflict in the Confederacy*, 308.
[14] *Ibid.*, 187; IV *O. R.*, 3, 203, 235.        [15] See *supra*, p. 236.
[16] *O. R.*, 30, pt. 2, p. 149.        [17] *Ibid.*, 148.
[18] 6 *Rowland*, 81.        [19] *O. R.*, 30, pt. 2, pp. 149–53.
[20] 2 *R. W. C. D.*, 106.        [21] See Vol. II, p. 420.

could be assigned without displacing officers then with troops. Cooper went on: "Until a suitable opportunity is offered for placing you on duty according to your rank, you will consider yourself authorized to dispose of your time in such manner as may best suit your convenience, reporting your address monthly to this office." [22]

When Hill went obediently home in accordance with these in- structions, his appointment as a Lieutenant General had not been confirmed by the Senate. That body, in fact, had not met since he had been named in July, 1863. It reassembled on December 7 and from time to time received presidential messages. None of these covered the nomination of Harvey Hill. On Jan. 8, 1864, Mr. Davis submitted for confirmation by the Senate the names of four- teen Major Generals and fifty-six Brigadier Generals. [23] No officer was listed for promotion to Lieutenant General. About four weeks later, the President advanced John B. Hood to that rank and immediately sent the nomination to the Senate, which confirmed it promptly. [24] As Hood had been Hill's junior as a Major General by more than six months, [25] this nomination could be considered tacit notice that the name of Hill would not be presented at all.

Hill soon had opportunity of raising the issue. The second week in February, General Beauregard, then at Charleston, South Caro- lina, felt that he should go into Georgia and Northern Florida to deal with a Federal force that had landed on the 7th at Jackson- ville, Florida. [26] Beauregard felt the need of a more capable and experienced commander in South Carolina than he then had among his immediate subordinates, and he telegraphed the War Department a suggestion that Hill be assigned. [27] After sending the message, he reflected that Hill's rank as Lieutenant General might be a barrier to appointment to a military post that did not carry with it the equivalent of corps command. Beauregard ac- cordingly telegraphed again to say that if this were the case, Lafayette McLaws would be equally acceptable. [28]

[22] O. R., 31, pt. 3, p. 701.
[23] The message was dated January 5. See 3 Journal C. S. Congress, 530–31.
[24] Promoted Feb. 1, 1864; nomination presented February 2, confirmed February 4 (Ibid., 658, 675).
[25] Wright, 26, 30.
[26] This was the beginning of the so-called Olustee campaign which culminated in the Confederate victory of February 20 at Ocean Pond, for which see 4 B. & L., 77 ff and the narrative of J. J. Dickison in 11 C. M. H., Fla., 56 ff. The reports are in O. R., 35, pt. 1, p. 274 ff.
[27] O. R., 35, pt. 1, p. 581.          [28] Ibid., 581.

This request from Beauregard came, after some delay, to the desk of the President, whose administrative interest was intrigued by the involved question of rank. After pondering the circumstances, Davis wrote: "It seems to me better to assign General Hill [to Charleston] as a major-general and explain to him that thus only could we employ him at this time and at that place." There was at the moment some consideration of Beauregard for service at Mobile. Lest that possibility carry the implication that Hill would succeed to the command of the South Atlantic Coast, Davis made reservation that if Beauregard went to Alabama the dispatch of Hill to Charleston, even as a Major General, would be "subject to other views." [29]

Cooper consequently had the difficult task of informing Harvey Hill that if he wanted field service, he would have to accept it at his previous rank. The Adjutant General did not do well with the letter which conveyed this unpleasant and, for the Confederacy, unprecedented announcement. Cooper's final draft was not even logical. He reminded Hill that Lieutenant Generals were available only for the command of corps. Then he proceeded with a flourish to say: "The President, desiring that the public should not hereafter lose the service of an officer whose zeal and gallantry have been so conspicuous as your own, has deemed it better not to ask for your confirmation in the rank of lieutenant-general, in order to leave you in that to which you have already been confirmed, and has directed me to offer to you service as a major-general in the Department of South Carolina, Georgia, and Florida. You will, therefore with as little delay as practicable, repair to Charleston and report to General Beauregard commanding that Department." [30] Either through negligence or else to cover the uncertainty of rank, Cooper addressed this simply to "General D. H. Hill." [31]

When Hill received this remarkable letter, he replied immediately by telegraph that the command at Charleston was "impractical" at present, and that if delay were prejudicial, the post should not be kept vacant for him.[32] Having done this as became a conscientious soldier, Hill was not satisfied to point out that Cooper had said nothing of the reason why he was left without a Corps. He remembered that his ad interim commission as Lieutenant

[29] O. R., 42, pt. 3, p. 1165.      [30] Ibid.
[31] Cf. ibid., 1169.      [32] O. R., 53, 312.

General would not expire until the current session of Congress ended without submission of his name for the Senate's confirmation. For this reason, he could not be ordered to Charleston as a Major General until, by the adjournment of Congress without acting on the case, he ceased to be a Lieutenant General. Further, Hill observed from Cooper's letter that he was not ordered to Charleston; he merely was offered command there, though the offer was followed by instructions to proceed to the station.

As Hill was not under compulsion to go to the Carolina city, and could not be compelled to act at his old rank till deprived of his new, he reached this odd conclusion: He would get his brother, Col. W. R. Hill, to carry to Richmond a letter in which he would inform the Adjutant General that he would not accept the appointment in Charleston unless his formal assignment to duty was accompanied by a statement of the government's full confidence in him.[33] The letter, which was dated February 23, was explicit enough. Hill reviewed what he considered to be his mistreatment at the hands of Bragg and the facts of his demotion and of the appointment of Hood, though he admitted "cordially" that Hood's claims to promotion were superior to his own. From all the relevant circumstances, Hill went on, the inference would be that "the subject of such treatment has been found wanting either in mental capacity or in soldierly qualities." Hill then shaped these sharp sentences: "In this great struggle for independence, I waive all considerations of wounded sensibility as an officer and a man, and would cheerfully serve in any capacity in which I could be useful; but the usefulness of an officer is essentially dependent upon the confidence felt in him by his men, and in my case this must be impaired, if not destroyed, by the facts above alluded to. It is reasonable to suppose that the soldiers will view with distrust one who has been treated as no other Confederate officer has been." The language that was to frame the issue followed: "Unless, then, the assignment to duty be accompanied by an unequivocal expression of undiminished confidence in my capacity, gallantry, and fidelity, I can accept no position that may be tendered."[34] The letter concluded with assurance that Hill would repair forthwith to Charleston to await reply. A telegram followed the next day to like effect but with reiterated notice that unless the "clear record

[33] Cf. *O. R.*, 42, pt. 3, p. 1169.      [34] *O. R.*, 53, 313.

promised me" were forthcoming, the command would be "impracticable." [35]

This curious demand was duly laid before the President. In answer to it, Davis said that he could see no reason for not granting Hill's request. He would see the Adjutant General about the matter, said the President. The next day Colonel Hill called on General Cooper, who, by long experience, was an adept in the art of assuagement. He had a high opinion of Hill's martial virtues and he unhesitatingly said that anything which would soothe the soldierly pride of so gallant a man would be done. Hill could write or even telegraph a draft of such orders as he wished.[36] In saying this to Colonel Hill, who was not a professional soldier, Cooper almost certainly took it for granted that Harvey Hill would recognize the limitations of what could be said in official orders. Cooper assumed, also, that both the Hills would understand that as the order for Harvey Hill's assignment had originated with the President, anything that Hill wished to be included in the order would have to be submitted to the Chief Executive.

Colonel Hill did not so understand the interview. He thought that Cooper made specific promise to meet Harvey Hill's terms and he informed his brother to that effect.[37] Harvey Hill accordingly went to Charleston, whence Beauregard was anxious to leave for Florida. Pending the receipt of orders which Hill expected to be a vindication of his military reputation, he refrained from assuming command, but he assured Beauregard that if an attack were threatened or made, he would go to the scene and advise the local commander.[38]

At length a letter from the Adjutant General reached Hill. It bore the date of February 29. Instead of rendering the demanded tribute to Hill's "capacity, gallantry and fidelity," the Adjutant General explained that the President had examined Hill's letter and the text of the original written offer of the command at Charleston. Said Cooper: ". . . the President can see no necessity for yielding to your wishes and therefore declines to accede to your demand. He would scarcely have offered you the command in question if he did not feel confidence in your capacity, gallantry

35 *Ibid.*                              36 *O. R.,* 42, pt. 3, p. 1168.
37 This is the clear inference from the correspondence between Harvey Hill and Cooper (*O. R.,* 42, pt. 3, pp. 1167–68).
38 *O. R.,* 35, pt. 1, p. 323.

and fidelity, and does not conceive it is necessary to announce the same in orders." [39]

What had happened probably was that until they scrutinized Hill's letter in detail, neither the President nor the Adjutant General had realized to what lengths Harvey Hill had expected them to go. When the stiffness of Hill's terms was perceived, Davis was unwilling to put laudation into orders. As Cooper later reminded Hill, "to express in orders 'undiminished confidence' in an officer would be unprecedented in military history." [40]

Hill, for his part, believed that the President originally had intended to comply with the conditions laid down but had undergone a change of mind. If insistence upon commendatory orders was without precedent, so, Hill retorted, was the treatment he had received.[41] He charged bad faith on Davis's part,[42] and insisted on compliance with what he consistently termed the "promise" of the President.[43] Until he received this, he said, he would not assume command at Charleston. Beauregard, who was about to leave South Carolina on another mission, was satisfied that if positive orders were given Hill to assume command, that officer would do so "with alacrity." [44] Hill himself had said as much,[45] though he believed Davis was trying to force him to resign.[46] The President wrote nothing to justify this suspicion, but when he had reviewed all the facts, he settled the case on April 23 with this endorsement: "If General Hill does not willingly accept the offer of command, it is not deemed well for the service to force him to such high and responsible duty as that proposed." [47] Hill therefore went home,[48] and with the exception of one brief period of service, hereafter recorded,[49] he had for a long time no other duty than that of reporting monthly that he was awaiting orders.[50] His friends shared his belief that the President held him, more than anyone else, responsible for the agitation against Bragg after the Battle of Chickamauga.[51]

About the time Harvey Hill left the Department of South Caro

[39] O. R., 42, pt. 3, pp. 1165-66.
[41] Ibid., 1168-69.
[43] O. R., 42, pt. 3, p. 1167 ff; ibid., 35, pt. 2, p. 370; ibid., 53, 324, 327.
[44] O. R., 35, pt. 2, p. 434.
[46] O. R., 53, 314.
[48] Ibid., 1170.
[50] O. R., 40, pt. 2, p. 650; ibid., 42, pt. 3, p. 1170.
[51] See 21 S. H. S. P., 144.

[40] O. R., 42, pt. 3, p. 1167.
[42] O. R., 53, 314.
[45] O. R., 42, pt. 3, p. 1169.
[47] O. R., 42, pt. 3, p. 1169.
[49] See infra, Chapter XXIII.

lina, Georgia and Florida, in April, 1864, there arrived in Savannah another officer who had held high rank in Virginia. This was Maj. Gen. Samuel Jones, 44 years of age and a West Pointer of the class of 1841,[52] who has not appeared conspicuously in these pages. He had been Chief of Artillery under Beauregard at Manassas[53] and for his service then had been promoted Brigadier General to rank from the day of the battle.[54] Subsequently Jones had relieved Bragg at Pensacola and then had commanded a Division in Kentucky and Tennessee. His commission as Major General bore date of March 14, 1862, and made him senior to any of the division commanders with the Army of Northern Virginia in the winter of 1863–64.

After a brief tour of duty in charge of the Department of East Tennessee in the autumn of 1862, Jones somewhat reluctantly[55] had assumed command of the Department of Western Virginia about the 1st of December, 1862.[56] Strictly speaking, Jones did not then become an officer of the Army of Northern Virginia, but as his Department was under the supervision of the commander of that Army, Jones was one of Lee's lieutenants. He was by birth and manner a gentleman and he had excellent training as a professional soldier. His appearance was alert and dignified, his lips firm, his eyes penetrating.[57] There was every reason to hope that he would be successful in the defense of a region which included the major iron, lead and salt mines of the Confederacy and, in addition, the railroad and the mountain pass that linked Virginia and Tennessee.

Expectations were not realized. From his headquarters at Dublin, in Pulaski County, Virginia, Jones had to direct a Department which, as he wrote subsequently, "has had the reputation of being cursed with intrigue and political plotters ever since the war commenced."[58] He found politicians among the soldiers, but few soldiers among the politicians. Some of his troops, like those of General Imboden, insisted that they were recruited for

---

[52] *Cullum* No. 1077. Jones was born at Woodfield, Powhatan Co., Va., Dec. 17, 1819. See the foreword to his *Siege of Charleston*, p. 7.
[53] See Vol. I, p. 97.                    [54] *Wright*, 59.
[55] *O. R.*, 29, pt. 2, p. 644; *ibid.*, 33, 1173.
[56] The exact date has not been determined. In 3 *C. M. H.*, 615, it is given as December 4, without citation of authority. Assignment of Jones's A.A.G. was made Nov. 27, 1862 (*O. R.*, 51, pt. 2, p. 652).
[57] The photograph of him in his *Siege of Charleston* is the best.
[58] *O. R.*, 29, pt. 2, p. 344.

service in a given district. They resented and scarcely would obey orders to go elsewhere.[59] Jones felt that he could not hold Southwest Virginia and part of East Tennessee with the few troops allotted him [60] and he kept a tight grip on his forces in the face of many calls to send part of them elsewhere.[61]

These traditional shortcomings of the detached commander would have been forgiven Jones had he been successful in dealing with Federal raids into Southwest Virginia. When he failed in this [62] and appeared slow to advance,[63] even the patient Lee lost faith in his aggressiveness.[64] Discontent with Jones's administration spread in Southwest Virginia.[65] A panicky report of a little action at Droop Mountain, Nov. 6, 1863,[66] led lawmakers from Southwest Virginia to clamor for better protection.[67] Jones could reply only that Longstreet in East Tennessee had assumed command of all the troops previously in the Department of Western Virginia.[68] This exchange was followed by a wholly unjustified attack on Jones for holding up supplies destined for Eastern Virginia.[69]

A change of commanders seemed imperative. Largely at the instance of Lee,[70] a decision was reached by February 11, 1864, to relieve Jones.[71] His manful reply—in contrast to the usual protests of the displaced—was that "I await the orders of the President, feeling confident that he will not assign me to any duty which I will not perform cheerfully and to the best of my ability." [72] The President endorsed this with the cordiality he always showed to those who met him halfway and obeyed his orders readily. Said Davis: "The expressions of General Jones are such as I anticipated from him, and he may be assured that I appreciate the embarrassments which have surrounded him and the zeal and fidelity with which he has acted." [73]

When it was suggested that Jones's successor might come from

[59] O. R., 33, 1085.
[60] O. R., 29, pt. 2, pp. 809–10, 820. Cf. ibid., 33, 1092, 1155.
[61] O. R., 27, pt. 3, pp. 858, 877, 986, 989, 991, 995 ff, 1017, 1021, 1022 ff, 1032; ibid., 29, pt. 2, pp. 750, 778, 800–01, 805, 807–08, 897; but see also 27, pt. 3, p. 974.
[62] O. R., 27, pt. 2, pp. 941, 948, 953 ff, 961, 962; ibid., 29, pt. 2, pp. 709, 750.
[63] O. R., 29, pt. 2, p. 758.
[64] O. R., 29, pt. 1, pp. 408–09.      [65] Ibid., pt. 2, pp. 644–45, 767.
[66] Ibid., pt. 1, p. 527; pt. 2, pp. 825, 834–35.
[67] O. R., 33, 1106 ff.      [68] O. R., 33, pp. 1107, 1130.
[69] O. R., 29, pt. 2, p. 911; ibid., 33, 1123.
[70] O. R., 33, 1085–86.      [71] O. R., 51, pt. 2, pp. 813, 816, 820.
[72] O. R., 33, 1172.      [73] Ibid., 1173.

the Army of Northern Virginia, Lee appraised some of his own lieutenants in reviewing possible appointees. Ewell, said Lee, might find the duties more unsuitable than those the commander of the Second Corps then was discharging. Lee continued: "I have also great confidence in the ability of Generals Early, Rodes, Edward Johnson, and Wilcox. Of the brigadiers, I think General [John B.] Gordon of Alabama one of the best." Simon B. Buckner and Robert Ransom were mentioned.[74] The President's final choice was Maj. Gen. John C. Breckinridge, former Vice President of the United States. How admirably Breckinridge discharged his duties and co-operated with the Army of Northern Virginia, later chapters will show.[75] Jones was sent to Savannah and then to Charleston, where he remained in command till Lt. Gen. W. J. Hardee arrived and took charge in the autumn of 1864.[76]

The difficulties of Samuel Jones, of Harvey Hill and of Longstreet were more serious than any that arose in the winter of 1863–64 among the troops immediately under Lee; but even where his example was hourly before the eyes of his subordinates, there were jealousies and the unhappy differences that always arise where men are confined in winter quarters. One of these instances —a minor affair—concerned the promotion of Col. Edward A. O'Neal, which Lee would not approve.[77] More serious troubles developed around "Jube" Early.

On Ewell's recovery from his sickness, immediately after the Mine Run campaign, Early issued an order in which he thanked the Corps and praised its behavior amid hardships.[78] His relief from active field duty, whether welcome or not, was brief, because the restless and troublesome Federal commander, Brig. Gen. W. W. Averell, undertook on December 8 a long raid through the Allegheny Mountains to the Virginia and Tennessee Railroad. Averell reached•that supply line at Salem, Virginia, on the 16th, destroyed a large quantity of cereals [79] and tore up several bridges and some miles of track.

It was certain that Averell would attempt to return to North-

---

[74] O. R., 33, 1124.

[75] For Breckinridge's assignment, see O. R., 33, 1198.

[76] O. R., 33, 1255; 6 Rowland, 340, 9 ibid., 275–76. For Jones's farewell to his troops, Mch. 5, 1864, see ibid., 1210.

[77] All the circumstances are explained in 3 R. E. Lee, 221–22 and, for that reason are not repeated here.

[78] O. R., 29, pt. 2, pp. 859–60.          [79] O. R., 29, pt. 1, pp. 921, 924, 928.

western Virginia by roads that passed West of Staunton and led through the country where Robert Garnett and then R. E. Lee had fought in the summer of 1861. If Confederate forces moved swiftly under competent command and in superior force, Averell might be captured. Early was assigned this exciting task. He hurried to Staunton and dispatched orders furiously, but bad weather slowed the march of his troops. Lack of correct information concerning the movements of the Federals led him to dispatch his main cavalry force in the wrong direction. The enemy got off unscathed.[80] Early wrote a sour, disappointed report, which was accepted by Lee as an adequate explanation of the reason nothing was accomplished.

Now that "Old Jube" was in the Shenandoah Valley, he was directed to stay there temporarily and to undertake to collect supplies from counties on the south branch of the Potomac.[81] Diligently enough Early made his preparations and on the last day of the year sent Fitz Lee from Mt. Jackson toward Moorefield and Petersburg. The mountain roads were so steep that where they were ice-covered they were impassable for vehicles. Fitz accordingly had to leave his artillery and wagons. He pushed on and captured a considerable ordnance train and a drove of cattle, but that was almost the measure of his achievement. The weather was more than his men could endure.[82] Again General Early was disappointed, though he was not disposed to criticize young Lee. As Early had shared the march, he was satisfied that Fitz's troopers and horses had done all he could have demanded of them.

The case was otherwise, Early felt, with many of the irregular cavalry units that operated in Western Virginia. In particular, he concluded that the greater part of Imboden's Brigade of approximately 1000 men [83] was unreliable. Imboden himself was absent at the time; Col. George H. Smith, who was in command, did his utmost to hold his men to the mark, but they had been too long in the same region under lax discipline. Early professed himself much inconvenienced.[84] In the absence of Imboden, said the Major General, even the necessary reconnaissances were not made.[85] At length when a Lieutenant of Imboden's Brigade killed

80 O. R., 29, pt. 1, p. 970.  81 O. R., 29, pt. 2, p. 889.
82 O. R., 33, 7, 1061.  83 O. R., 33, 1192.
84 O. R., 33, 1067.  85 Ibid., 1086.

a Sergeant in Staunton, Early exploded violently in complaint to Colonel Smith.[86]

It was one of Early's vices that when an incident of this sort occurred, he would not act and forget. He would act and continue to talk. Imboden's command. Early insisted with bitterness, included a large number of men who were deserters from other arms of the service. In private conversation "Old Jube" asserted, frequently and vehemently, that Imboden's Brigade was inefficient, disorganized, undisciplined and unreliable.[87] "Old Jube," in short, acquired a violent dislike of the troopers who garrisoned the Valley and probably, without being aware of it, became prejudiced against cavalry in general. Certain it is that he made no effort to acquaint himself with that arm or to study its place in tactical co-ordination. For this neglect, whatever its origin, he was doomed to pay.

When Imboden returned to duty, he heard of Early's sarcasms and he resented them. "Old Jube" never said anything in Imboden's presence that gave offense or raised a personal issue, but by February 12 the Brigadier was so outraged that he decided to protest formally to the commanding General. In a well-written, dignified letter, Imboden reviewed the circumstances as he saw them. He proceeded: ". . . the fact that [General Early] is my commanding officer justifies me in the effort I now make to defend myself and command against sneers unofficially and publicly made which are calculated if true to bring me and my command into disrepute and contempt. I hope to be able to prove that General Early has done me and my command gross injustice by yielding to the promptings of prejudice rather than reason."[88] Imboden accordingly asked a court of inquiry and stipulated that the finding of the court, adverse or favorable, should be published in the Valley.[89]

Early endorsed this with the observation that "the extent of [his] remarks" concerning Imboden's force was "very greatly exaggerated," but he reiterated his belief that the command was "in a very bad state of discipline." He would be most reluctant, he said, "to have to rely on it in any emergency." Citing the recent murder, he expressed conviction that he had not injured the

86 *Ibid.*, 1168.                    87 *O. R.*, 33, 1167, 1168.
88 *O. R.*, 33, 1167.              89 *Ibid.*, 1168.

Brigade in public estimation because the opinion was general that the cavalrymen were "inefficient and indisciplined." Early concluded by recommending the court of inquiry, which he hoped would result in improvement of Imboden's troopers.[90] This correspondence was read by Lee in the memory of the delay at Hancock during the Gettysburg campaign.[91] He had not been impressed favorably by what he had seen of Imboden's men,[92] but he knew that nothing coul' be gained and that much might be lost by angry exchange at a court of inquiry. Lee promptly notified Imboden that he did not think a court "advantageous."[93] There the matter rested, but it was not without value and warning: "Old Jube" had snarled and had sneered privately from the beginning of the war; now he was careless, if not loud, in his condemnation of those he did not approve. It was not a change of character that would improve leadership in the Second Corps.

A controversy between Early and Tom Rosser was avoided by curious circumstances. Rosser was so deeply in love that he scarcely could endure separation and, during the winter, he had Mrs. Rosser come to Staunton. This was not exceptional. Mrs. Powell Hill had lingered overlong on the Rappahannock in the spring of 1863.[94] As for Mrs. John B. Gordon, it had become a tradition in the Army that when she was seen on her way to the rear, action was about to open. Mrs. Rosser consequently had good precedents, but while she was in Staunton, her husband did something that displeased Early. The only specific reference to it is a line in a letter from Early to Lee: "The affair I mentioned to you of his [i.e., Rosser's] coming here after his wife."[95] Whatever the circumstances, they prejudiced Early against Rosser.

While the matter was still unpleasantly fresh in Early's mind, a new raid was undertaken, January 28, 1864, against Moorefield and Petersburg in Hardy County, Western Virginia.[96] Imboden was left behind; Rosser was senior officer of the cavalry; the infantry were Thomas's Brigade of Wilcox's Division, which had been detached for duty in the Shenandoah Valley. This time, the weather was favorable.[97] When the slow-plodding infantry came

[90] O. R., 33, 1168.
[91] See supra, p. 48.
[92] O. R., 33, 1086.
[93] Ibid., 1168.
[94] Cf. supra, p. 73.
[95] O. R., 33, 1166.
[96] By the division of Hardy County, Petersburg is now in Grant County.
[97] Early, 340.

in sight of the beautifully situated town of Moorefield, they were as enthusiastic as if they had been on their way northward in the summer of 1862.[98] Rosser had the best of luck and captured ninety-three loaded wagons, fifty of which were removed safely.[99] His conduct was in every way so admirable on the raid that "Jube" forgave him and urged confirmation of Rosser's appointment as Brigadier which, for some reason, had been delayed in the Senate.[100] Early's wish, which Lee and Stuart shared, at length was realized. The nomination of Rosser, along with scores of others, was confirmed on the last day of the session of Congress.[101] Rosser's career went on in high promise with the encouragement and sometimes with the scolding of "Jeb" Stuart.[102] The morale of the Brigade was excellent. All the men re-enlisted in a manner that gave Stuart a text for the exhortation of other commands.[103] In the Valley, Rosser himself began to take on some of the romance of Turner Ashby.[104]

If Early was pleased over Rosser's rise and was unrepentant of his sneers at Imboden's troops, his difficulties with these two were not comparable in evil potentialities to the change that now began to take place in the relation of Early with his oldest, most devoted friend in the Army, "Dick" Ewell. After the raid on Moorefield, Early expressed a desire to take a brief leave and to go home to Franklin County, Virginia, in order to crush, as he felt he could, some subversive influences there.[105] By the end of February, he was back at Orange and ready to resume command of his Division under Ewell.[106] "Old Bald Head" was not then in good physical condition. While his sickness prior to the Mine Run Campaign had been brief, his general enfeeblement had given deep concern to Army Headquarters. During the Bristoe operations, Lee was in daily fear that Ewell would wear himself out or collapse under his duties.[107] In spite of Ewell's surprising agility on horseback, his wooden leg was of poor design [108] and made his movements uncertain. When it was suggested in Richmond that Ewell, in-

98 *Ibid.,* 336.                               99 *O. R.,* 33, 44.
100 *O. R.,* 33, 1166. Cf. *ibid.,* 1174. The explanation may be given in Rosser to his wife, MS, Dec. 24, 1863—*Rosser MSS.*
101 3 *Journal C. S. Congress,* 809.
102 *Cf.* Stuart to Rosser, MS, Feb. 10, 1864, on the importance of wise appointments within the Brigade—*Rosser MSS.* For Rosser, see *infra,* p. 383 ff.
103 *O. R.,* 33, 1170.                    104 Cf. *Mrs. McDonald,* 200.
105 *O. R.,* 33, 1166.                    106 *O. R.,* 51, pt. 2, p. 822.
107 *O. R.,* 33, 1095.                    108 *Conner,* 113.

stead of Lee, might be sent to succeed Bragg at Dalton, Lee had to answer: "General Ewell's condition, I fear, is too feeble to undergo the fatigue and labor incident to the position." [109] A proposal by the Adjutant General that Ewell go to Tennessee and take Longstreet's command, and that Longstreet return to Virginia to direct the Second Corps, Lee disapproved on many grounds. [110] Among them, undoubtedly, was the same feeling that Ewell might not be able to endure hard field service. Whenever Lee had to leave the Rapidan, "Old Bald Head" as senior officer assumed command of the Army, but the work at headquarters was arranged to trouble him little. Usually, decisions not of the first magnitude were made by the staff and were reported to the acting commander. [111]

Ewell accepted this arrangement without concern or questioning and contented himself with his old routine. About the middle of January he had a bad fall when his horse slipped in the snow He made light of the accident, [112] but Lee did not. As it happened, Ewell almost simultaneously had received some inquiry from the Secretary of War, probably concerning another command, and while the crippled lieutenant still was suffering from his shake-up, he sent Lee a copy of Seddon's letter and of his reply to it. [113] The acknowledgment that came to Ewell had the candor of a General whose first duty was to keep his Army in condition to fight. Lee commended the spirit of Ewell's answer and declined to express an opinion on the future course of the Lieutenant General. That, Lee said, Ewell had to do on the advice of physicians. The whole undertone of Lee's counsel was one of doubt whether the chief of the Second Corps could meet the strain of open campaigning. [114]

Ewell chose to continue where he was and to give to the country his best. The same choice was that of Mrs. Ewell, who never was willing to admit her husband's disability. In her influence over him, some of those around Ewell thought they saw another evidence of what they began frankly to consider a decline of mental as well as of physical power. Doubtless they confused the

[109] *O. R.*, 29, pt. 2, p. 861.      [110] *O. R.*, 33, 1074–75.
[111] *O. R.*, 51, pt. 2, p. 793 ff; *ibid.*, 33, 1192–93.
[112] *Hamlin's Ewell*, 123.
[113] Unfortunately, neither the letter of the Secretary nor the answer of Ewell has been found. From the date it is possible that the correspondence related to the transfer of Ewell to succeed Longstreet in East Tennessee.
[114] *O. R.*, 33, 1095–96.

WINTER TESTS TEMPER 331

psychological effect of the loss of a leg with that of the acquisition of a wife. Mrs. Ewell had become engaged to "Old Bald Head" as early as the winter of 1861–62, though her son by her first marriage doubted if she ever would have married the General had he not been wounded seriously.[115] Once she married him, she managed him, and not him only. Said Col. James Conner, who saw both the General and the lady at close range: "She manages everything from the General's affairs down to the courier's who carries his dispatches. All say they are under petticoat government."[116] During the late autumn of 1863, Mrs. Ewell had joined her husband on the Rapidan and had established herself in the cold, empty mansion of Jeremiah Morton, who had removed from the scene of conflict.[117] With her was her daughter Harriet, described "as a dark skinned, dark eyed clever girl, but not pretty, a very large head and a stout, rollabout figure."[118] Miss Brown played the harp[119] and had charms which, as presently will appear, had won a soldierly heart.

Besides the daughter and the husband, Mrs. Ewell had at her bleak, outpost mansion[120] her able son, Campbell Brown, who was one of Ewell's assistant Adjutants General. The interest of Mrs. Ewell in the welfare and advancement of husband and of son was equal. That she was intelligent and agreeable and had been a beauty in her youth, all agreed; but that she was overzealous and too active, at least one observer at headquarters was convinced. Said Col. James Conner: "Mrs. Ewell [has] the best intentions in the world no doubt, and the very cleverness which would at other times render her agreeable has only tended to make her more and more unpopular."[121] Her opportunity for furthering the interest of her son appeared to be offered in the bill long before Congress for the expansion of the general staff of the Confederate Army. Passage of this measure as drawn would give Ewell's A. A. G. the rank of Colonel. "Old Bald Head" was alleged to be determined that this promotion should not go to "Sandie" Pendleton but to

115 Campbell Brown's MS Military Reminiscences, 26.
116 Conner, Feb. 19, 1864, op. cit., 116.
117 Ewell to Col. B. S. Ewell, Feb. 18, 1864, Hamlin's Ewell, 125.
118 Conner, 113.
119 Campbell Brown, op. cit., 26, recorded his efforts to smuggle the instrument from Nashville after the Federal occupation.
120 Cf. Ewell: "I am a little too far from Orange Court House to see much of the army—may be said to be on the outpost" (Hamlin's Ewell, 126).
121 Conner, 116.

Campbell Brown. Amused junior staff officers thought they could see how Ewell was maneuvering to procure transfer and promotion for "Sandie," in order to get a clear field for Campbell Brown.[122]

One night around a campfire, some of the staff of the Second Corps were discussing their prospects of advancement or replacement. Thomas T. Turner, one of the General's aides, spoke up. "Old Ewell told me he had never exposed Campbell but once and then was so miserable until he came back he did not know what to do: 'If anything had happened to him, I could never have looked at his mother again, sir.' " Turner added: "Hang him, he never thinks of my mother, I suppose, for he pops me around, no matter how hot the fire is."

A few minutes later, Turner arose and went off. Another staff officer took up: "Well, Turner is safe, but I am in a tight place. Campbell Brown hangs on to his mother's petticoats and Turner is engaged to the little Brown girl and she will prize him up, and I have to fight against the pair!" [123] All this talk was humorously exaggerated, of course, and was ended when the bill for the enlargement of the general staff passed Congress but received a pocket veto.[124] The affair, while amusing, was not without an ominous aspect. It boded no good for the Second Corps or for the campaign of 1864 when so able and fairminded a man as James Conner could speak of Ewell as a "fond, foolish old man . . . worse in love than any eighteen-year older that you ever saw." [125]

The veto of the general staff bill had just been announced when "Jube" Early came back from the Shenandoah Valley to resume command of his Division. As senior Major General of the Second Corps, Early of course realized that if Ewell were disabled, he would assume command temporarily, perhaps permanently. Early did not know that the commanding General, while esteeming him highly, was to report before many weeks that if a Major General had to be detached from the Army, Early could be spared better than Edward Johnson could be, for the reason that either John B.

[122] Conner, op. cit., 116, did not mention "Sandie" by name or refer to Ewell's efforts to have Pendleton promoted to the line, but, as will appear infra, young Pendleton soon was tendered a commission as Brigadier General. This scarcely would have been offered him without Ewell's approval.
[123] Conner, 116.
[124] See J. D. Richardson, ed. . . . Messages and Papers of the Confederacy, Vol. 1, p. 457. Cf. IV O. R., 3, 316, 353.
[125] Conner, 116.

Gordon or Robert Hoke was qualified to succeed Early.[126] In her turn, the clever Mrs. Ewell reasoned that if her husband was thought to be incapacitated for duty, Early would supplant him, and she soon became suspicious of "Jube." There is no record of any clashes between her and Early, but she undoubtedly developed a dislike for him. She was impervious to the retarded but developing social graces of the bachelor General, graces that Lee himself had announced in a letter to Margaret Stuart: "General Early has just returned from a visit home, and is handsomer than ever. He looks high in his new garments, and the black plume in his beaver gives him the air of a gay cavalier." [127] If Mrs. Ewell observed, she probably sniffed.

It is impossible to say whether she had any direct part in a curious and obscure incident that occurred some weeks later. For reasons not now determinable, Ewell found Early so much at fault that he had temporarily to arrest him, April 27,[128] for conduct "subversive of good order and military discipline." The controversy reached General Lee, who dismissed it with a statement that Early was at fault and that harmony among officers was imperative.[129] Restraint must have been shown by all those involved in the affair, because no echo of it appears in the records. Whatever the details, outwardly they made no difference in the relations of Early and Ewell. Inwardly, the affair did nothing to lower Early's self opinion. He never had been more ambitious and more confident of himself or more intolerant of others, than he was as the spring of 1864 approached.

The Army itself, the always-impersonal but always-observant Army, was as confident as Early. What thousands believed, Dodson Ramseur wrote on April 15: "I feel so hopeful about the coming campaign. I have never felt so encouraged before." [130] He was influenced, no doubt, by the events which, in the opinion of the troops, indicated that the Army of the Potomac lacked initiative. The campaign on Mine Run had been followed in February by a curious affair at Morton's Ford on the Rapidan. On the 6th, the Federals pushed a Brigade of the 3rd Division of the II Corps across the river and, after a fight, overwhelmed the guard of a

126 O. R., 33, 1321.
127 See D. S. Freeman, "Lee and the Ladies," Scribner's Magazine, Nov. 1925, Vol. 78, No. 5, p. 466.
128 Hotchkiss' MS Diary, 337.        129 Old Bald Head, 167–68.
130 To his wife, MS—Ramseur MSS.

Lieutenant and twenty-five men. The Federals then advanced as if they intended to capture the high ground in rear of the ford. A second and then a third Brigade crossed to support the attack.[131]

By chance, Steuart's Confederate Brigade that morning was relieving two of Doles's and two of Ramseur's regiments that were on picket.[132] This gave the Confederates double the infantry they normally would have had in the vicinity. Artillery was disposed immediately to dispute the Unionists' advance.[133] Ewell, notified of the crossing, had an advantage, for once, by what he had termed his residence at an outpost.[134] Arriving promptly at the ford, he directed an easy defense with his old-time skill. The next dawn showed the Federals back on the left bank of the river; by the morning of the 8th they disappeared from the ford.[135] Lee regarded the foray as "only intended to see where we were and whether they could injure us," [136] but Ewell's men were pleased,[137] and the Army felt its old sense of superiority to the enemy.

At the end of February, Federal cavalry made on Richmond an attack which the Confederates styled "Dahlgren's Raid" though the senior officer was not Col. Ulric Dahlgren but Brig. Gen. Judson Kilpatrick. The aim of the enterprise was to release the Federal prisoners in the Confederate capital and to march them within the Union lines at Williamsburg.[138] Boldness and a measure of skill were shown in the advance, which reached the intermediate line of the Richmond defenses, but it was repulsed with some loss.[139] The raid served the Confederates usefully in this respect: Those who examined the body of the slain Colonel Dahlgren reported that they found on it papers in which the raiders were instructed to burn Richmond and to kill President Davis and his cabinet.[140] Evidence of this purpose inflamed to new fury the fighting spirit of the South.

[131] O. R., 33, 114.
[132] O. R., 33, 142.
[133] Ibid.
[134] See supra, p. 331.
[135] O. R., 33, 141.
[136] See 3 R. E. Lee, 218.
[137] Cf. Col. H. C. Cabell, O. R., 33, 1170.
[138] O. R., 33, 174.
[139] Men, 340; horses, 583; O. R., 33, 188.
[140] One manuscript, signed by Dahlgren, exhorted his soldiers not to "allow the rebel leader Davis and his traitorous crew to escape" (O. R., 33, 178). The other document, unsigned, included the admonition: "The men must keep together and well in hand, and once in the city it must be destroyed and Jeff. Davis and cabinet killed. Pioneers will go along with combustible material" (ibid., 179). For the evidence that the originals of the published papers had been found on Dahlgren's body, and for references to the various accounts of the raid, see 3 R. E. Lee, 219 n. 10 and 12. Needless to say, if Dahlgren's orders to his men were authentic and official, they were drafted without knowledge or approval of General Meade.

Efforts, also, to recover some of the towns on the tidal estuaries of Eastern North Carolina served to strengthen further the confidence of the Army. Late in January, under orders from Lee's headquarters, Maj. Gen. George E. Pickett undertook to capture the town of New Berne.[141] He was allotted infantry who seemed entirely adequate for the purpose and, in addition, he was to enjoy the co-operation of a force of naval commandos,[142] under Col. J. Taylor Wood, one of the most daring of Confederate leaders. Through poor planning and probably because of a defective intelligence service [143] and the slowness of Brig. Gen. Seth M. Barton, the expedition failed.[144]

Brig. Gen. R. F. Hoke, who participated in the attack on New Berne, was left temporarily near the scene of this futile action in the hope that means might still be found of seizing New Berne or of capturing Plymouth, which lies on the south bank of the Roanoke River, close to the point where it empties into Albemarle Sound.[145] While Hoke waited and assisted in many ways, Braxton Bragg developed a plan for the surprise of Plymouth. Hoke was to take the lead. With him were to work the crew of the Confederate ram *Albemarle* which was then nearing completion farther up the Roanoke River. Tactfully Bragg disposed of Pickett by explaining that the expedition had been entrusted to General Hoke "so as not to withdraw you from a supervision of your whole department at this critical time." [146]

Ample force and detailed instructions were given Hoke, though a large measure of discretion was left him.[147] He proceeded with vigor and skill to the discharge of a task he correctly understood. His advance began April 17. On the 20th, by the shrewd use of his artillery and with the valiant employment of the new ram, he

141 *O. R.*, 33, 1061. Davis at one time thought he might direct the expedition in person (*ibid.*). For Pickett's assignment, Sept. 23, 1863, to the command of the Department of North Carolina, see *O. R.*, 29, pt. 2, pp. 706, 773.

142 Needless to say, the word "commandos" was not part of the soldiers' vocabulary of 1864, though the term "ranger" was. This particular contingent had no special designation. Usually, when Taylor Wood went on an expedition he took what were described as "picked men."

143 Cf. *O. R.*, 51, pt. 2, pp. 863–64, 877.

144 See Pickett's account and his criticism of Barton in *O. R.*, 33, 92–94, and Barton's report and defense, *ibid.*, 97. The fullest account of Colonel Wood's exploit in capturing the U. S. S. *Underwriter*, which he was compelled to burn, is by Commander B. P. Loyall in 27 *S. H. S. P.*, 136 ff and in 5 *N. C. Regts.*, 325 ff. Wood's brief post bellum account is in 8 *Rowland*, 543. A court of inquiry in Barton's case was requested by General Lee but apparently was not held (*O. R.*, 33, 1186–87).

145 *O. R.*, 33, 1245. For Lee's subsequent observations on the recall or retention of Hoke in North Carolina, see *ibid.*, 1266, 1273, 1278.

146 *O. R.*, 51, pt. 2, p. 857.    147 *Ibid.*, 857–58.

forced the surrender of Plymouth and its garrison. Confederate casualties were few. Those of the enemy, prisoners included, reached 2834. Booty was large.[148] The country was thrilled. Davis telegraphed Hoke his congratulations and added: "You are promoted to be a major-general" as from the date of the battle.[149] Congress voted formal thanks to Hoke and to Commander James W. Cooke, who handled the *Albemarle*.[150] Lee wrote the President: "I am glad of General Hoke's promotion, though sorry to lose him, unless he can be sent to me with a Division." [151] Circumstance was to deny Hoke time in which to complete the capture of Washington or of New Berne, against which he moved, but he was more than ever a marked young soldier.[152] Little or no credit was given to Bragg, who did the basic planning and collected the troops when it seemed impossible to find men enough for the expedition.

Insistent appeals by Lee for the return of Hoke's Brigade and of the other troops loaned for operations in Southern Virginia, the Carolinas and Tennessee were based on the certainty that the Federals would advance from the Rapidan as soon as the roads were dry.[153] These appeals were not entirely futile. By the time of Hoke's victory at Plymouth, Longstreet was on the way back to his old place in the line of battle. Davis and Bragg had become convinced at the beginning of April that Johnston would not assume the offensive in Tennessee, and they accordingly saw no reason for retaining Longstreet in East Tennessee. On April 7, he was ordered to Charlottesville, whence he could be advanced either to Lee on the Rapidan or to the defense of the Richmond-Petersburg area.[154] Lee was notified the next day that Longstreet was returning. The reason, as it concerned Johnston, was given in restrained terms.[155]

Orders to move to Charlottesville reached Longstreet on the 11th of April at Bristol.[156] He soon got his troops started, but

---

[148] *O. R.*, 33, 296 ff; *ibid.*, 51, pt. 2, 870. No detailed Confederate reports were filed. The narrative in 5 *N. C. Regts.*, 175, is perhaps the best available. In *ibid.*, 315, is an account of the construction and service of the *Albemarle*. See also, W. H. Morgan, *Personal Reminiscences*, 180 ff.

[149] *O. R.*, 51, pt. 2, p. 874.          [150] *O. R.*, 33, 305.
[151] *Ibid.*, 1321.

[152] *O. R.*, 33, 1329–30; *ibid.*, 51, pt. 2, pp. 879, 880, 882.
[153] Cf. *O. R.*, 33, 1255, 1265–66.

[154] *O. R.*, 32, pt. 3, p. 756. Maj. Gen. Simon B. Buckner was put in command of East Tennessee.

[155] *O. R.*, 51, pt. 2, p. 1076.          [156] *O. R.*, 33, 1054.

because the railroads could transport only 1500 men a day, he was slow in reaching the Piedmont region of Virginia.[157] As the troops detrained at Charlottesville, Longstreet wished them to be transported to Petersburg,[158] but they were marched to more convenient camping-grounds near Gordonsville.[159] There, to all observers, the decline in the size of the Corps and the depreciation of its equipment were manifest and serious. Longstreet, who reached Charlottesville on the 14th,[160] received all the help Army Headquarters could give him in making good his losses.[161] Law's Brigade had been kept in Tennessee, with its commanding officer in arrest,[162] but Lee prevailed on the War Department to order these excellent troops to unite with the Division.[163] In directing that the Brigade move to Charlottesville, the Adjutant General sent instructions that Law be restored to command. The charges against Law, said Cooper, would not be considered further.[164]

When Longstreet learned that Law was again at the head of the troops, he telegraphed the Adjutant General to know whether his second charges against the Brigadier had reached Richmond.[165] The answer was that they had been received but had not been entertained, and that Law had been restored to his post.[166] This reply was sent to Longstreet through Lee's headquarters, as if to remind the Lieutenant General that he no longer was a department commander and, as such, authorized to communicate direct. Transmission of the paper "through channels" gave Longstreet an opportunity of putting formally before the commanding General his version of the conduct of Evander Law. In a stiff letter, the Lieutenant General blamed Law for failure at Wauhatchie[167] and at Campbell's Store[168] and added that other "charges of a very grave character"—doubtless those relating to the resignation —had been preferred against Law. Longstreet thereupon delivered an ultimatum of a sort he knew his chief would support. Said Longstreet: "If my efforts to maintain discipline, spirit, and zeal

[157] O. R., 33, 1286.          [158] O. R., 33, 1286.
[159] Specifically, at Mechanicsville, which will not be confused with the more famous village of the same name in Hanover County, near Richmond. See O. R., 33, 1307; ibid., 36, pt. 1, p. 1054.
[160] O. R., 36, pt. 1, p. 1054.          [161] O. R., 33, 1321.
[162] Cf. O. R., 32, pt. 3, p. 652. See supra, Chap. XVI.
[163] O. R., 33, 1286.          [164] O. R., 32, pt. 3, p. 793.
[165] O. R., 31, pt. 1, p. 473.          [166] Ibid.
[167] Longstreet wrote "Lookout Mountain," but fixed the date as October 29, 1863.
[168] O. R., 31, pt. 1, p. 475.

in the discharge of official duty are to be set aside by the return of General Law and his restoration to duty without trial, it cannot be well for me to remain in command. I cannot yield the authority of my position so long as I am responsible for the proper discharge of its functions. It is necessary, therefore, that General Law should be brought to trial upon the charges that have been preferred against him, or that I be relieved from duty in the Confederate States service." Then Longstreet sharpened his ultimatum unmistakably with this bold sentence: "I have ordered the rearrest of General Law upon his return." [169]

Army Headquarters, of course, were not prepared to have Longstreet resign at a time when Ewell was in precarious health and the enemy was expected to launch an offensive any day. Accordingly Longstreet learned that Lee had forwarded his ultimatum to Richmond and had recommended that a court martial be ordered, though doubtful whether it was expedient to open the hearing at the time. "If it is thought unadvisable to do so," Lee concluded, "I would recommend that General Law be relieved from duty until an investigation can be had." [170] By the date this paper reached the President's desk, much was to happen that changed the emphasis and softened the ultimatum, but, at the last, putting the immediate issue temporarily aside, Davis was to say: "General Longstreet has seriously offended against good order and military discipline, in rearresting an officer who had been released by the War Department, without any new offense having been alleged." [171] Law was not to be without defenders. When Whiting heard that the young Brigadier was in trouble with Longstreet, he wrote Beauregard and urged that Law be procured for service in the Carolinas. Said Whiting: "[General Law is] a most capital officer and one of the best men in battle I ever saw." [172] Of this proposal, Longstreet knew nothing. Had he known of it, he probably would have released Law to Beauregard with pleasure.

In Longstreet's case, in Early's and in Ewell's—to say nothing of Sam Jones's and Harvey Hill's—the winter had wrought curious reversals. Edward Johnson, Hoke and Rosser had gained in reputation. In addition to these three. no less a person than the Army's Chief of Artillery received new prestige. The men and

[169] O. R., 31, pt. 1, p. 475.
[171] Ibid., 474.
[170] Ibid., 473.
[172] O. R., 33, 1314.

the guns in the keeping of General Pendleton changed little during the winter, though the appointment of corps chiefs with the rank of Brigadier helped in administration. General Pendleton himself made a long tour of the South to inspect Johnston's artillery and to prepare a plan for its more effective use. Upon his return and presentation of his findings, he was sent to Dalton to explain them in detail to General Johnston.[173] In discharge of this mission, Pendleton achieved what some would have pronounced impossible: he pleased both the Administration and General Johnston. So favorably did he impress Davis that later in the year, after the death of Lieut. Gen. Leonidas Polk, the President was to ask Lee whether Pendleton would be a qualified successor. Lee was to be compelled in honesty to say: "As much as I esteem and admire General Pendleton, I could not select him to command a corps in this Army. I do not mean to say that he is not competent, but from what I have seen of him, I do not know that he is. I can spare him if, in your good judgment, you decide he is the best available." [174] Pendleton was destined to stay and mildly to share the adventures of his juniors, who left him little to do. With the battalion and battery chiefs, the great question-mark of the campaign was not whether Pendleton went or remained, but whether the horses would survive hard work, poor shoeing and half-feed.

The cavalry raised that same question, but, for the rest, they were, of all the confident arms of the service, the one that approached the spring battles with least reason to be concerned over command. Stuart was in flawless health and, surely, more qualified by experience than ever he had been to direct the two Divisions. They were well led and had, in the main, those Brigadiers who best had earned leadership.

These, then, to summarize, had been the changes during the winter of 1863–64 in the Army command:

Longstreet had failed in a semi-independent command and had failed equally to maintain peace in his Corps; his interest in strategy continued despite discouragements; a bitterness toward the administration had developed in his heart. He was less the imperturbable "Old War Horse" and more the aggrieved, restive lieutenant who thought all the authorities, except Lee, arrayed against him.

[173] See *Pendleton*, 314–21.    [174] *Lee's Dispatches*, June 15, 1862, p. 242.

Of Longstreet's three division commanders, McLaws was fighting to be restored to his post. His fate was uncertain, because the War Department had not yet passed on the findings of the court. Hood was promoted and transferred to another Army and was succeeded not by Micah Jenkins, as Longstreet wished, but by a soldier, Charles W. Field, who had never led a Division in action and had not served in the field since Second Manassas. Pickett, the third of the division leaders, was in charge of the Department of North Carolina and was out of touch with the Corps.

Ewell of the Second Corps was not in good condition physically. There was some question whether he was mentally the man he had been before his wound or, in spirit, the fighter he had been before his marriage. His senior lieutenant, Early, was in a strange, confident, perhaps overbearing state of mind. Rodes had not developed, though he had not lost the good opinion of the commanding General.[175] Edward Johnson had done well at Mine Run and had earned the good opinion, in particular, of the commanding General of the Army. Some suggestion had come from Richmond that Johnson was needed elsewhere, and in circumstances that might have led to his promotion to Lieutenant General. Regretful as Lee was to deny "Old Allegheny" such a post, he had to tell the President that he could not spare Johnson.[176]

In the Third Corps, Powell Hill had sustained the humiliation of Bristoe Station, but otherwise had spent a quiet winter. All his division commanders—Anderson, Heth and Wilcox—were present with their troops. None of the three had been given opportunity of acquiring new fame or of demonstrating higher qualities of command than were credited to them. The Corps was competently directed. There was no reason to hope it would be brilliantly led in the operations about to open.

Grim those operations would be, and against an adversary more powerful than ever, more seasoned and more belligerently led. Ulysses Grant, the man who had beaten Albert Sidney Johnston and John Pemberton and Braxton Bragg, had come East as General-in-chief of the Union forces, and had established his headquarters with the Army of the Potomac. Had he been in Hooker's place a year previously, he would have faced Jackson and Pender,

---

[175] Cf. Lee, Jan. 31, 1864: "[Rodes] has commanded his division with success and ability" (O. R., 33, 1133).
[176] O. R., 33, 1321.

the old Second Corps in its glory, and the First Corps before the frustrated Longstreet had shaken its command. Now Longstreet was changed, Ewell enfeebled, Early arrogant and Hill, after eleven months, still not established in reputation as a corps commander.

# CHAPTER XVIII

## THE WILDERNESS TAKES ITS TOLL

THE RECALL of the First Corps was the last step that could be taken to reinforce the Army of Northern Virginia against the expected offensive by the powerful Federal forces under Grant. Other duties delayed until April 29 the formality of a visit by Lee and the headquarters staff to the pleasant fields near Gordonsville where "Old Pete's" veterans were awaiting them.[1]

Officers who attended Lee on this inspection were those familiar to Longstreet, but among them, probably, was one newcomer of established reputation. This was Maj. Gen. Martin L. Smith, who had been sent to the Army as Chief Engineer.[2] Smith, a New Yorker by birth and a professional soldier,[3] had been the engineer who developed the defenses of Vicksburg. That he was a man of intelligence and character, his fine face and bearing made plain. How high his abilities were in field engineering, events must show.[4]

To welcome Lee and Smith and the staff, the First Corps now could muster no more than 10,000 men of all arms,[5] but it did its dilapidated best to make itself presentable to Lee. Said one participant, somewhat proudly: "Guns were burnished and rubbed up, cartridge boxes and belts polished, and the brass buttons and buckles made to look as bright as new. Our clothes were patched and brushed up, so far as was in our power, boots and shoes greased, the tattered and torn old hats were given here and there 'a lick and a promise,' and on the whole I must say I think we presented not a bad-looking body of soldiers."[6] As the reviewing party went

---

[1] Cf. *O. R.*, 33, 1321.

[2] For the circumstances of his appointment, at a time when General Lee wished to have Custis Lee as engineer, see 3 *R. E. Lee*, 262; *O. R.*, 33, 1245, 1265, 1287; *ibid.*, 51, pt. 2, p. 848.

[3] *Cullum* No. 1126; graduated sixteenth in the class of 1842.

[4] See *Mrs. Daly*, 124, with a fine quotation from Col. A. C. Haskell; 6 *C. V.*, 530, an appreciative sketch; and *Alexander*, 505.

[5] "A liberal estimate," said Walter Taylor. Cf. *Longstreet*, 553.

[6] *Dickert*, 340. The date is confirmed by Col. Osmun Latrobe's Diary

down the ranks of the two Divisions, which had the battalions of artillery on the flanks, Charles Field, 36 years of age, was in the place of Hood. At the head of McLaws's Division was its senior Brigadier and prospective new commander, Joseph W. Kershaw, who was 42 and was known to all the veterans. He had been a Brigadier General since February, 1862,[7] and had been distinguished in almost every battle he had shared.[8] Pious.[9] intelligent, a clear blond of high-bred, clean-cut features, he had the bearing of command and a clear voice that seemed to inspire courage when it was raised in battle.[10] Of the Brigadiers in the First Corps, the only stranger to Virginia was John Gregg, who had been assigned to command the famous Texas Brigade in succession to Jerome Robertson. Commissioned a Brigadier General in September, 1862, he had served in the Gulf States, with Johnston during the Vicksburg campaign and under Longstreet at Chickamauga. Without professional training in arms, he had the spirit of a "born soldier." [11]

All these officers rejoiced to see their gray General on his gray horse, and they cheered him wildly as they passed in review.[12] Longstreet, too, was happy to be with his old chief again, and he doubtless showed his satisfaction, but his new penchant for strategy was stronger than any personal consideration. At first opportunity, he urged—to quote his somewhat vague words—that the "preliminaries of the campaign should be carefully confined to strategical maneuver." [13]

The next few days were tense for lieutenant and for chief. From the signal station on Clark's Mountain, as the month of April drew to its close, the commanding General viewed the verdant valley of the Rapidan. Its green was now that of forest and of neglected field, not that of springing grain. A rich agricultural country was in neglect. Fences were gone; barns had vanished into the fires of soldiers; live stock had been slain and eaten or removed to the rear; as at Fredericksburg, wide-spreading woodland had

---

7 *Wright*, 70.
8 For his earliest experiences as a commander, see *Miss Brock*, 29; *O. R.*, 53, 147, 156; *Richmond Dispatch*, Apr. 26, 29, May 1, 1861; *Richmond Examiner*, May 4, 1861; *O. R.*, 2, 451, 500, 522, 943.
9 See *Mrs. Chesnut*, 102.        10 Cf. *Sorrel*, 233.
11 *Wright*, 88; 11 *C. M. H.*, Texas, 234.
12 See *Alexander*, 493–94.
13 *Longstreet*, 551.

been stripped of trees. War was on the land. Grace and thrift and all man's efforts to beautify and to fructify were mocked.[14]

After Lee had studied this scene with his glass, he said what the whole Army had concluded: "I think those people over there are going to make a move soon." Then, turning to young B. L. Wynn, who was in charge of the signal station, he asked: "Sergeant, do you keep a guard on watch at night?" When Wynn answered in the negative the General said: "Well, you must put one on."[15]

Strange things the guard saw. On the 2nd, there was smoke in unusual volume along the north bank of the Rapidan. Officers summoned to the signal station by Lee were told that the Federals probably would proceed down the Rapidan.[16] That night moving lights were observable.[17] The next day, dust clouds and marching columns were visible.[18] So sure were some of the Confederate commanders of an advance with the dawn of the 4th that they ordered the men to prepare three days' rations[19] which, as usual, the soldiers of stoutest appetite forthwith consumed. One private defended this practice in words that became part of the lore of the Army. He said he did not want the trouble of carrying three days' rations and he did crave "one meal occasionally that wasn't an empty form."[20] With the cooking of rations went another preliminary of action: Even the units that always were most skeptical of the familiar "signs of a fight" and therefore slowest to part with their belongings, sent their baggage to the rear. An artillerist explained: "The packing was not done in 'Saratoga trunks,' nor were the things piles of furs and winter luxuries. The 'things' consisted of whatever, above absolute necessaries, had been accumulated in winter quarters; a fiddle, a chess-board, a set of quoits, an extra blanket, or shirt, or pair of shoes, that any favored child of Fortune had been able to get hold of during the winter."[21]

About 12 o'clock on the night of May 3-4, the signalmen on Clark's Mountain could catch glimpses of troops passing in front of distant campfires far across the Rapidan. Army Headquarters were notified at once. Promptly the returning signals spelt out

[14] McHenry Howard, 267.          [15] Wynn in 21 C. V., 68.
[16] O. R., 36, pt. 1, p. 1070.
[17] McHenry Howard, 268, though that author thought there might be an error of one day in his chronology.
[18] Ibid., 268.          [19] C. M. Wilcox in Annals, 487.
[20] W. M. Dame From the Rapidan to Richmond (cited hereafter as Dame), 72.
[21] Dame, 64.

the question that was uppermost in the mind of everyone at head-quarters: Were the lights moving toward Germanna Ford or toward Liberty Mills?[22] That was to say, was Grant attempting to turn the Confederate right and proceed in the direction of Fredericksburg, or was he undertaking to pass the Southern left and to move on Gordonsville?[23] Although Lee had concluded on the 2nd that Grant would seek to turn the Confederate right, the Southern leader wanted verification. The signal station could not supply it. Lee consequently acted on the larger probability. He had the station flash to the right: "General Ewell, have your command ready to move at daylight."[24]

Dawn ended doubt: The enemy was moving toward Germanna and Ely's Ford and moving, apparently, with all his forces. The dust clouds spread across the horizon to the eastward. From every vantage-point the picture was the same—heavy columns of cavalry, endless files of infantry, wagon trains that spread their white sheets for miles on every road. Confederates looked and guessed at the strength of the moving Army. It numbered, in reality, 102,000 officers and men present for duty.[25] When reinforcements immediately at hand—Burnside's IX Corps—overtook the Army of the Potomac, its effective strength would be at least 116,000.[26] To oppose this host, the Confederates had eight Divisions of infantry, the weakest of which, Early's and Johnson's, mustered about 4000 men each. Probably the strongest was that of Cadmus Wilcox, 7200 muskets.[27] Of all arms, the Confederate effective total was approximately 64,000.[28] These grim odds made it necessary that each musket do the service of two. The more intelligent of the men were conscious of this. Although the old, cheerful banter was audible, as the troops made ready to start their march, a returned prisoner of war, still on parole, thought the Army worse

[22] 21 C. V., 68.
[23] Grant, like his predecessors, had debated the question. The considerations that weighed with him were set forth in his final report (O. R., 36, pt. 1, p. 15). His decision to move by his left flank and to march around the Confederate right was due primarily to the greater convenience of available bases. In addition, by this maneuver Grant would be moving in the direction of his principal co-operating column, which was to advance on Richmond from the East. Had he proceeded by his right flank, said Grant, he would have been moving away from that column.
[24] 21 C. V., 68.
[25] As of Apr. 30, 1864, exclusive of the IX Corps of Burnside (O. R., 36, pt. 1, p. 198).
[26] Longstreet, 552, quoting Badeau, made the various deductions. Aggregate present were in excess of 127,000 (Ibid.).
[27] Annals, 493; Early, 345.                    [28] Alexander, 497; Longstreet, 553–54.

equipped and not in as good spirits as it had been before Gettysburg. It was ready to fight; it sensed the most difficult of all its struggles.[29] A new resentment the grayjackets had, too. Col. James Conner stated it precisely: "Our papers mentioned as an extract from the Northern papers that Grant had ordered all Sutler wagons to leave the army. You would have been amused to hear our men's indignation. They swore it was the meanest, cheapest trick that ever was done. They had looked with so many fond anticipations to plundering the Sutler wagons that Grant's order was regarded as cheating them of their just dues."[30]

Damning so inconsiderate an adversary, the infantry of Lee's Army began their counter-movement on the 4th of May. Ewell marched by the turnpike, often called the "Old Stone Road," that ran from Orange to Fredericksburg;[31] Hill conducted Heth's and Wilcox's Divisions by the Orange Plank Road, and left "Dick" Anderson to guard the upper fords of the Rapidan until it was certain the whole of Meade's Army [32] was moving eastward. Longstreet's start was at 4 P.M. toward Brock's Bridge. Thence his route was to be by way of Orange Plank Road and the Catharpin Road.[33]

Before Longstreet's men left their camps, they tore down all the officers' tents, by orders, and cut them up for distribution among themselves. There would be no further use for tents that year! [34]

[29] This was Kyd Douglas's opinion, for which see *Douglas*, 274. It is impossible to distinguish clearly between what observers thought to be the spirit of the Army before the opening of the campaign of May, 1864, and what they knew to be its morale after a month of fighting. Stiles, *op. cit.*, 241, stated clearly the different theories on this point.

[30] *Conner*, 126. The Federal order, Army of the Potomac G. O. 17, II, Apr. 7, 1864, was issued by Meade in stiffest terms: "All Sutlers and their employés will leave the army by the 16th instant, and should Sutlers be found with the army after that date, their goods will be confiscated for the benefit of the hospitals, and their employés will be placed, by the provost-marshal-general, at hard labor" (*O. R.*, 33, 817).

[31] *O. R.*, 36, pt. 1, p. 1070. Ewell left his camps about noon.

[32] It will be recalled that Lieut. Gen. U. S. Grant now had command of all the United States land forces but maintained his headquarters with the Army of the Potomac. The broad strategy of that Army's movements was determined by General Grant but, said he, "I tried, as far as possible, to leave General Meade in independent command of the Army of the Potomac." Grant explained: "My instructions for that army were all through him and were general in their nature, leaving all details and the execution to him. The campaigns that followed proved him to be the right man in the right place" (*O. R.*, 36, pt. 1, p. 18). Strictly speaking, then, the Army of the Potomac was "Meade's Army," but more and more frequently as days passed, the Confederates styled it "Grant's Army."

[33] *O. R.*, 36, pt. 1, p. 1054. Inquiry has failed to disclose any tradition concerning the origin of the odd name of this road. It probably was the extension from one of the Potomac or Rappahannock ports of a short road that reminded seamen of the short ropes, or cat-harpings, used "to brace in the shrouds of the lower-masts behind their respective yards." Locally, the pronunciation placed the accent on the "thar." It is "Cay-thar-pin," not "Cat-har-pin'," though one old Negro was found who said that in his youth the road was called the "cat-hoppin'."

[34] *Caldwell*, 124.

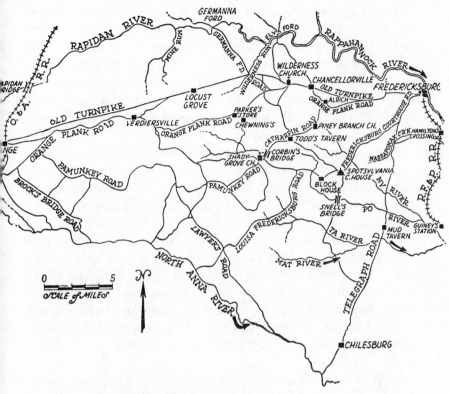

Terrain of the Wilderness-Spotsylvania operations of May 4–21, 1864—after an original map in the Confederate Museum, Richmond, Va.

The cavalry covered the advance but concentrated on the right in the hope of enveloping the enemy.[35]

Once the men knew they were marching to meet the foe, their spirits rose. "I did not hear a despondent word, nor see a dejected face among the thousands I saw and heard that day"—so testified a young artillerist.[36] Among the ranking officers, if better knowledge of the adverse odds created misgiving, no evidence of it was recorded. Longstreet was concerned only over the possibility that the enemy might be drawing the Army to Fredericksburg which, in the existing situation, he did not consider a strong position. He wrote Lee, "Can't we threaten his rear, so as to stop his move?"[37]

After an undisturbed bivouac,[38] the Army on the morning of

35 H. B. McClellan, 406.        36 Dame, 71–72.
37 O. R., 36, pt. 2, p. 947.
38 Annals, 488; O. R., 36, pt. 1, pp. 1054, 1070.

May 5 resumed its March to confront an enemy who now was on the south side of the Rapidan and was moving toward the Wilderness. Across the "P'ison Fields," as the region immediately West of the forest was styled,[39] the Confederates advanced. Ewell's orders were to regulate his march on the turnpike by that of Hill on the Orange Plank Road. If practicable, a general engagement was to be avoided until Longstreet arrived [40]—an order singularly reminiscent of the first day at Gettysburg.[41]

The proximity of the Federals was evident, but it was not yet apparent that the operation undertaken by General Grant on the Rapidan was part of the farthest reaching offensive the enemy ever had launched in Virginia. Before the Confederates had started their march from their camps around Orange, word had been received of the landing at West Point, May 1, of a Federal force which was thought by some to be the vanguard of an army that would move on Richmond.[42] It was the presence of these troops at West Point, among other considerations, that had prompted Longstreet to warn his chief not to be drawn to Fredericksburg. Soon the report was that Maj. Gen. B. F. Butler, with a large naval escort and a river full of transports, was moving up the James toward Richmond.

Butler's expedition was not to be the only one in support of Meade. Maj. Gen. Franz Sigel had orders to march southward up the Shenandoah Valley. The instructions of Brig. Gen. George Crook were to advance into Southwest Virginia and do all possible damage to the Virginia and Tennessee Railroad.[43] Daily, after May 5, as Lee's lieutenants grappled with the main army of the most determined Federal commander they yet had encountered, new details of the other contests were to reach them. The Union strategy was reminiscent of that of May, 1862, when Banks was in the Valley and McDowell mustered at Fredericksburg while McClellan marched on Richmond. In the new crisis, the Confederate President did his utmost, but he put much of the weight of decision as well as the burden of defense on the shoulders of the commander of the Army of Northern Virginia. A lengthy

[39] L. M. Blackford to his mother, MS, Aug. 16, 1863—*Blackford MSS.*
[40] *O. R.*, 36, pt. 1, p. 1070.　　　　[41] See *supra*, p. 86.
[42] *O. R.*, 36, pt. 2, p. 327. This was Col. Guy V. Henry's Brigade of Maj. Gen. Q. A. Gillmore's X Corps.
[43] For General Grant's exposition of his plan, see *O. R.*, 36, pt. 1, p. 15 ff.

telegram from Davis to Lee describing the situation on James River was concluded thus: "With these facts and your previous knowledge, you can estimate the condition of things here, and decide how far your own movements should be influenced thereby." [44]

The first decision of the commanding General was represented by the swift advance of his main Army to meet the enemy. As the columns moved forward on the morning of May 5, the heavy dew of a cool night [45] and the low-hanging fog [46] disappeared under the rising sun. The day grew warm.[47] Hill continued on the Plank Road, which on that stretch curved to the Northeast. Ewell held to the old turnpike, which ran more nearly East. At 10 A.M., the distance between the troops on the two roads was about two and three-quarter miles. An hour later, the advance of Ewell's Corps, which happened to be John M. Jones's Brigade of Johnson's Division, was ordered to halt.

The message that always made hearts beat faster was passed down the files: Federals were ahead. They were moving across the old turnpike along the route that led from Germanna Ford to the Orange Plank Road. A clash might occur at any moment. Ewell was mindful of his orders to regulate his advance by that of Hill and, if practicable, to avoid a general engagement before the arrival of Longstreet. As the Second Corps was then a considerable distance ahead of Hill's column on the Plank Road, Ewell thought proper to suspend his advance, to form line of battle, to report his situation to headquarters, and to await further instruction. "Sandie" Pendleton hurried across to the Plank Road, found Lee with A. P. Hill,[48] and brought back word that Ewell was to adhere, if feasible, to previous orders.[49]

The enemy was no respecter of such orders. Soon after "Sandie" returned from G.H.Q., the Unionists began what appeared at first to be merely a demonstration against John M. Jones. To his support Ewell moved up Battle. On the right of Battle was placed the Brigade of George Doles. These officers were told to avoid involvement and, if pressed, to retire slowly.[50] Advanced artillery sections [51] were withdrawn to safety. They were of no use where

44 O. R., 51, pt. 2, p. 887.          45 O. R., 36, pt. 1, p. 222.
46 O. R., 51, pt. 2, p. 890.          47 Hotchkiss' MS Diary, 339.
48 4 B. & L., 241.                     49 O. R., 36, pt. 1, p. 1070.
50 O. R., 36, pt. 1, p. 1070.
51 Milledge's Battery, O. R., 36, pt. 1, p. 1085.

they were. The Wilderness engulfed everything. Gunners could find no targets in that maze of budding greenery.[52]

Scarcely had the fieldpieces rumbled toward the rear than a furious assault was made on Jones's front and on his right flank.[53] It was almost a surprise to Jones's men and it had behind it strength as well as impetuosity. In a few minutes, Jones's troops broke. Their commander was killed as he attempted to rally them.[54] As they went through the line of their support, they threw into confusion the ranks of Battle's Brigade.

A sudden and dangerous crisis was upon the Second Corps. The other Brigades of Johnson's Division were too far to the left to be of immediate use.[55] Rodes was half deployed, though Daniel's Brigade was available.[56] That left only "Jube" Early's men, who had been the rear Division on the march.[57] Fortunately, that Division was well closed. To bring it quickly into action, "Dick" Ewell galloped back [58] on a mount which, said one observer, bounded "like a deer through the dense underbrush." [59] By the side of John B. Gordon, the corps commander drew rein. "General Gordon," piped Ewell excitedly, "the fate of the day depends on you, sir!"

Gordon, at the moment, was among the men of one of his regiments who, as always, had crowded up to hear what their leaders had to say. For their benefit, much in the spirit of his stand at Sharpsburg,[60] Gordon answered boldly: "These men will save it, sir!" Immediately he wheeled the regiment into line and soon he delivered a counter-attack.[61] The boldness of it made the enemy hesitate. A similar thrust by Junius Daniel of Rodes's Division con-

---

[52] Hotchkiss noted in his *Diary*, May 18, p. 345, that the trees were in full foliage. He probably would not have made the entry had the leaves matured many days before that time.

[53] Grant and Meade had reached the old turnpike and, seeing their opportunity, had ordered G. K. Warren to attack at once with his V Corps (*O. R.*, 36, pt. 1, p. 539). Sedgwick's VI Corps was placed on Warren's right.

[54] McHenry Howard, *op. cit.*, 273, quoted a current report that Jones, disdaining flight, was shot "while sitting on his horse gazing at the approaching enemy." Ewell reported (*O. R.*, 36, pt. 1, p. 1070) that Jones and his aide, Capt. Robert D. Early, "fell in a desperate effort to rally their brigade."

[55] For the operations of Steuart's Brigade, see 14 *S.H.S.P.*, 146.

[56] Ramseur had been left on picket when the Corps advanced on the 5th (*O. R.*, 36, pt. 1, p. 1070).

[57] Gordon noted, *op. cit.*, 237, that his was the rear Brigade of the Corps.

[58] He doubtless was riding Rifle, "a flea-bitten gray" who, said Robert Stiles, "was singularly like him—so far as a horse could be like a man" (*Stiles*, 244).

[59] *Gordon*, 238.          [60] See Vol. II, p. 211.

[61] *Gordon*, 239.

fused the Federals. Ewell gained time enough to form a new line and to recover shortly the ground lost by Jones.[62] In this grim work, Battle's Brigade, which had recovered quickly from the impact of Jones's rout, bore a conspicuous part.

The situation was eased. Meade's attack had been stopped. Later in the day, thrusts were delivered and parried with no material gain or sacrifice of ground. The Confederates' heaviest loss, after that of John M. Jones, was in the mortal wounding of one of the new Brigadiers, Leroy Stafford,[63] and in the serious injury of Brig. Gen. John Pegram, who was shot in the leg.[64] Many a humbler soldier fell in a battle "no man saw or could see" [65] because of the blinding tangle of the Wilderness.

As combat lost its violence on the old turnpike, it rose in wrath on the Orange Plank Road. Along that highway, Hill advanced with his artillery and with Heth's and Wilcox's Divisions. Anderson was still to the rear. About the time the men of the Third Corps passed Parker's Store, they encountered a small force of Federal cavalry, which they drove before them as they proceeded toward the familiar junction of the Brock Road.[66] A little later they heard on their flank the echo of Ewell's action but it had the sound of an intermittent fire equal to that of a vigorous infantry skirmish.[67] About 1 o'clock they halted in the face of a challenge by Federals who were organizing on the Brock Road, or close to it, a line perpendicular to the Plank Road.[68] Skirmishers were thrown out on a wide front. Soon the pop-pop of rifles announced that they had found the Union skirmish line.

Little happened until about 3 o'clock. Then a staff officer from Lee's headquarters found Harry Heth and explained that the commanding General was anxious that Heth occupy the Brock Road if this could be done without bringing on a general engagement. Heth answered that the Federals held the road in strength.

---

[62] O. R., 36, pt. 1, p. 1070.
[63] O. R., 36, pt. 1, pp. 1028, 1070.
[64] Ibid., and Early, 346.
[65] O. R., 36, pt. 1, p. 218.
[66] These cavalrymen were Col. John Hammond's 5th New York and Col. John B. McIntosh's 3rd Pennsylvania (O. R., 36, pt. 1, p. 876).
[67] Annals, 489.
[68] The first Federals were Brig. Gen. Geo. W. Getty's 2nd Division of Sedgwick's VI Corps, who were supported after 2 P.M. by part of Hancock's II Corps and, late in the afternoon, by Brig. Gen. James Wadsworth's 4th Division and by Brig. Gen. Harry Baxter's 2nd Brigade of Brig. Gen. John C. Robinson's 2nd Division, Warren's V Corps. These troops had been hurried into position by General Meade, who realized the importance of holding the junction of the Brock and Orange Plank Roads. For the details, see Meade's report, O. R., 36, pt. 1, pp. 189-90.

Whether he could drive them from it could be determined only by using his entire Division. He had no way of knowing in advance whether that would precipitate a general engagement, but Heth added, with reference to Lee, "I am ready to try if he says 'attack'." [69] Before anything more could be determined, the bluecoats themselves attacked confidently and furiously, as if they knew they had superiority of men and of metal.

Defense was stern. The enemy, repulsed and pursued, turned on the Confederates and drove them back to the open fields of the Tapp Farm on the northern side of the Plank Road. South of the highway, the Confederates were pushed farther into the woods. So heavy were the attacks on Heth and on Wilcox that some of their Brigades had to be shifted from positions where the pressure already was as heavy as a thin line seemed capable of resisting. [70] It was a desperate struggle. At one time, the only troops not engaged in the wild fighting were 125 Alabamians who were acting as guard over the prisoners. Even this detachment had to be called to repulse the assault. In the opinion of Porter Alexander, who had seen most of the battles, none of them had been fiercer. [71] At nightfall, the enemy still was in firm possession of the Brock Road, but in the mad exchanges of the furious day he had done no more than hold his own. When weary Southern commanders could draw breath, they exchanged congratulations. Ewell sent to headquarters his special commendation of John B. Gordon and of Junius Daniel. [72] Lee had praise for Cooke and Kirkland of Heth's Division, [73] and for all those who had repulsed the enemy in the struggle on the Plank Road. Strong as the enemy had shown himself to be, the Confederates must retain the initiative. The decision at Army Headquarters, reached before 8 P.M., was to turn the left of the enemy, if it was not too far extended and, if it was, to try to cut him off from his base by enveloping his right. Indications were that the attack on the left would prove the more promising. Ewell consequently was told to be prepared to shift troops to the Plank Road in the event he could accomplish nothing near the river. [74]

[69] *Heth's MS Memoirs*, 154 ff.
[70] A writer in 3 *N. C. Regts.*, 118, noted that the condition of the trees after the battle showed that the Federal aim was much too high.
[71] *Alexander*, 501. The action on the Plank Road, May 5, is described so fully in 3 *R. E. Lee*, 278 ff., that it has not seemed necessary to repeat the details here.
[72] *O. R.*, 51, pt. 2, p. 890.          [73] 3 *N. C. Regts.*, 118.
[74] *O. R.*, 36, pt. 2, p. 952.

An immediate question was whether anything should be done to untangle the front of Heth and of Wilcox. At many points immediately West of the Brock Road, troops of the Third Corps were prone in the undergrowth, not more than fifty yards from the enemy. The wounded could not be removed, there or on the front of the Second Corps, because of the continuing fire.[75] Both Heth and Wilcox were much concerned. Wilcox's belief was that a skirmish line should be left where the fighting of the day had ended and that a new line should be formed in rear.[76] Heth thought he should collect his men on one side of the Plank Road, while Wilcox did the same thing on the other, and that they then should form a line of battle.[77] Wilcox, in his anxiety, rode at once to Lee, who received him with a compliment on the performance of the two Divisions on the Plank Road. Lee went on to explain that Anderson's Division was due to reach Verdiersville that night; "but," said Lee of Anderson, "he has been instructed to move forward; he and Longstreet will be up, and the two Divisions that have been so actively engaged will be relieved before day." [78] Wilcox had to content himself with this. Later in the evening, he was approached by one of his soldiers who had a startling tale. The man said that he had lost his way, had run into the Federals, had escaped them and had hurried back to say there was not a Confederate between the General and the Federal skirmishers. "Wilcox evidently did not believe a word of it," said the soldier, "and was not over polite in letting me know it." [79] Probability is that Wilcox credited more of the story than he was willing to let the soldier perceive.

Heth went to Hill instead of to Lee. The corps commander was sick, as he had been on the first day at Gettysburg. He was bundled up on a camp stool by a fire, but he shook his lieutenant's hand cordially and with the charm of manner that always fascinated his subordinates.

"Your Division," he began, "has done splendidly today; its magnificent fighting is the theme of the entire Army."

Heth's manners were as polished as Hill's and his tact was even finer, but this time anxiety made him almost brusque: "Yes, the Division has done splendid fighting, but we have other matters to

[75] *Caldwell*, 130; *McHenry Howard*, 278.
[76] Wilcox in *Annals*, 494.          [77] Heth's *MS Memoirs*, 154.
[78] *Annals*, 495.                    [79] *N. C. Regts.*, 47–48.

attend to now." With no further preliminary, he described the state of affairs and made his proposal that he and Wilcox take opposite sides of the road and draw a new line. Heth was emphatic in warning: "A skirmish line could drive both my Division and Wilcox's, situated as we now are. We shall certainly be attacked early in the morning."

Hill was reassuring: "Longstreet will be up in a few hours. He will form in your front. I don't propose that you shall do any fighting tomorrow; the men have been marching and fighting all day and are tired. I don't wish them disturbed."

Heth went away but he was not satisfied. He came back again to receive the same answer. Wilcox called, also, and heard from Hill substantially what Lee previously had told him. Unhappy and full of foreboding, Heth returned a third time to argue with Hill. This time, the Lieutenant General became vexed. "Damn it, Heth," he said, "I don't want to hear any more about it; the men shall not be disturbed."

This was final. Heth's only recourse was an appeal to Lee, but he could not find Army Headquarters.[80] He and Wilcox awaited with gnawing, time-dragging anxiety the arrival of Longstreet who was to take up, they understood, a designated line; but 1 o'clock, 2 and at last 3 passed with no word that the First Corps was approaching. Finally, the two Generals sent back for the Third Corps pioneers in the desperate hope that the men with pick and shovel might be able to throw some dirt in front of the two Divisions before the expected attack was delivered.[81]

The night had been clear and cloudless, though the darkness in the woods had been complete.[82] Before 5 o'clock, the East reddened. A Brigadier of Longstreet's Corps, which was pressing forward, saw the roseate sky and exclaimed, "There is the sun of Austerlitz!"[83] In the Wilderness, when the light came, the pioneers soon were visible to the enemy, but they were not subjected long to the fire of alert skirmishers or to the imprecations

---

[80] *Heth's MS Memoirs,* 154 ff. For confirmation of Hill's remark, "Let the tired men sleep," see 2 *N. C. Regts.,* 173.
[81] *Annals,* 495. It scarcely need be pointed out that the absence of the pioneers from the front was itself evidence of defective staff work, more in keeping with the amateurish staff work of Mechanicsville than with the maturity of the Wilderness. See Vol. I, p. 513. For a critique of the handling of Hill's and Ewell's men, see *infra,* p. 442.
[82] *Annals,* 495.
[83] 5 *Land We Love,* 483.

of the Southern officers.[84] At 5 o'clock, on the stroke, the Federals began a careful [85] but a determined advance.[86]

As most of Wilcox's men were slightly in advance of Heth's front,[87] they first received the shock. Scattered as they were, they soon were driven.[88] They did not run fast or far,[89] but they ran. Heth's troops, according to General Wilcox, did not wait for the onslaught. They made for the rear at once to form their line. Wilcox himself hurried to General Lee and, at the instance of the commanding General, went down the Plank Road to find Longstreet, who was assumed to be approaching from the direction of Parker's Store.[90] In the eyes of brave men who kept their heads and stopped to load and fire, the break of two veteran Divisions was a disgrace. Cowards simply ran till they were out of range. A Lieutenant on foot easily kept pace with a pompous Brigadier on horseback until both were beyond the whining miniés. Then, for the first time, the Lieutenant spoke. "General," said he, "how goes the fight?"

The General's urbanity returned with his safety. He raised his cap politely. "We are driving them handsomely, Lieutenant, very handsomely." [91]

There was no jesting at Army Headquarters. Powell Hill was too ill to do more than share the tense anxiety. The burden fell on Lee and his staff, who were on the ridge of the Tapp Farm, close to the guns of Poague's Battalion. Toward that high ground the enemy was moving steadily and almost unopposed. Farther northward, up a swale, the Unionists were working their way into the space that unavoidably had been left between Hill's left and

[84] Annals, 495.          [85] Caldwell, 133.
[86] This attack was delivered under orders from G.H.Q. by Maj. Gen. D. B. Birney's 3rd Division and Brig. Gen. Gershom Mott's 4th Division of Maj. Gen. W. S. Hancock's II Corps, and by Brig. Gen. George W. Getty's 2nd Division of Maj. Gen. John Sedgwick's VI Corps. In support were two Brigades of Brig. Gen. John Gibbon's 2nd Division of the II Corps (O. R., 39, pt. 1, p. 321). As of April 30, the II Corps had "present for duty equipped" 28,333. If Getty's Division had one-third of the corresponding strength of the VI Corps of three Divisions, it counted about 8000 men of all arms (O. R., 33, 1036). After 8 A.M., Hancock had, in addition, Brig. Gen. Thomas G. Stevenson's 1st Division of Maj. Gen. A. E. Burnside's IX Corps, and Brig. Gen. James Wadsworth's 4th Division of Maj. Gen. G. K. Warren's V Corps. These two Divisions probably had a combined strength of 8700 (O. R., 36, pt. 1, pp. 198, 915).
[87] Annals, 495.
[88] Caldwell, op. cit., 133, stated that the first break in Thomas's Brigade which had belonged to the old "Light Division."
[89] Wilcox insisted (Annals, 497) they withdrew 300 yards only, though Hancock maintained (O. R., 36, pt. 1, p. 321) that the Confederates were "driven in confusion through the forest for about 1½ miles."
[90] Annals, 496.          [91] 4 Land We Love, 345.

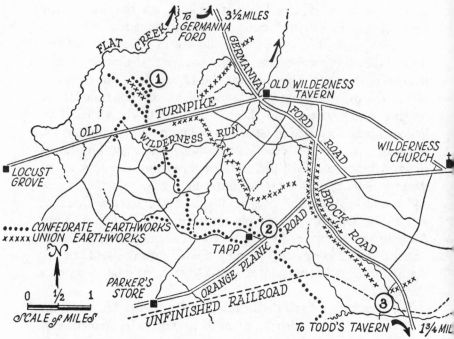

Trench system at the close of the Battle of the Wilderness, May 7, 1864. As here figured, the works are those that were in existence at the time of Grant's movement to Spotsylvania. It is impossible to say when all the different parts of these works were constructed. Numerals indicate: 1, The scene of Gordon's attack, late afternoon of May 6; 2, area of Heth-Wilcox action, morning of May 6; 3, jump-off of Longstreet's flanking column, late forenoon, May 6, 1864. After *O. R. Atlas*, Plate LV–1

Ewell's right. The crisis was instant and desperate. Unless Longstreet came up quickly and opened with vigor, the centre of the Army would be penetrated, the Third Corps would be rolled up, and what remained of it would be hurled back on Ewell toward the Rapidan. There had been no danger more acute since the day the Federals had shattered the Confederate line at Sharpsburg.

Not long did leaders have to hold their breath. Up the Plank Road in parallel columns,[92] the First Corps was moving fast. "Here they come!" cried the delighted artil'erists, and they yelled in their highest key [93] to greet the veterans of Hood's old Division, now under Field, who formed the van on the left. Barksdale's famous old Mississippi Brigade headed Kershaw's Division on the right-hand side of the road.[94] Longstreet was close to the

[92] Col. Charles S. Venable in *Longstreet*, 571.
[93] *Dame*, 84–85.                   [94] 5 *Land We Love*, 484.

front, and as he began to meet the fugitives, he halted his troops. A quick sweep of the ground from the crest of a low ridge showed him the situation. Quickly he ordered Gregg to establish the line to the North of the road while Humphreys, Barksdale's successor, placed his regiments in line South of the road.

It was John Gregg's red hour, his first great opportunity. As the Texans were forming under his eye, he saw approaching him the commanding General and several staff officers. Lee already had greeted the first of the Texans who had moved out into the field to form the left flank of the First Corps' line; but in the excitement, when he drew rein, identification was confused. "General," said Lee, "what Brigade is this?"

"The Texas Brigade," was the proud answer.

"I am glad to see it! When you go in there, I wish you to give those men the cold steel. They will stand and fire all day, and never move unless you charge them."

"That is my experience," answered Gregg.

At that moment, an aide from Longstreet arrived: "Advance your command, General Gregg," he said.

Gregg drew in his breath and shouted: "Attention, Te..a. Brigade! The eyes . . . of General Lee . . . are . . . upon you! Forward . . . march!"

Lee lifted his hat and raised himself in his stirrups. There was manifest anxiety in his brief answer: "Texans always move them!" The men nearest him began to cheer; his words were passed down the line; the cheer spread. "I would charge hell itself for that old man," cried one courier, with weeping eyes, as he paused between yells.[95]

Longstreet probably heard no part of this exchange. He may not even have heard the shouts and the cheering from the left when the Texans cried "Lee to the rear" and swore they would not go forward until "Marse Robert" went to a place of safety.[96] In a short time, Lee rode up, attended by his staff, to the knoll where Longstreet was waiting for his troops to complete their formation.

[95] 5 Land We Love, 484. It is difficult to fit this little-known incident into the events of the early morning of May 6, but the assumption seems reasonable that the exchange with Gregg occurred after Lee's meeting with the first of the Texans and before the episode of "Lee to the rear." The account here quoted from The Land We Love was said by Miss Lucille Gregg to be written by "Major Campbell of General Gregg's staff."

[96] All the details and the references to the various conflicting accounts of this first "Lee to the rear" appear in 3 R. E. Lee. 287-88.

The commanding General manifestly was intensely excited, more excited, in fact, than ever his staff had known him to be.[97] At first opportunity, Colonel Venable whispered to Longstreet that he had experienced the greatest difficulty in persuading Lee to leave the Texans: would Longstreet please prevail on Lee to go farther to the rear? Longstreet spoke up with affectionate bluntness and said, in effect, that if the commanding General intended to direct the First Corps, he personally would be glad to ride to a place of safety.[98]

"Old Pete" watched for a moment, perhaps, as Lee reluctantly went a few hundred yards farther to the westward, and then the corps commander turned to his task. He was at his combative best. A request that he send Hill a Brigade of Anderson's arriving Division was met with an unhesitating "Certainly, Colonel, which one will you take?"[99] That settled, Longstreet began to organize a front line. The most shaken of the withdrawing Third Corps troops already had passed through Longstreet's troops amid the jeers and laughter of the veterans. "Do you belong to Lee's Army?" the soldiers of Field and Kershaw yelled. "You don't look like the men we left here," they cried, and again, "You're worse than Bragg's men."[100] Then, without a break or a waver, the arriving regiments prepared to receive the enemy. A staff officer who had seen Longstreet's men in all their battles said afterward that he thought "the steadiness and inflexible courage and discipline" with which the First Corps formed under fire in the forest and permitted the two Divisions of the Third Corps to pass through its ranks were "perhaps its greatest performance."[101] Soon the stoutest of the soldiers of Hill were forming in the rear—the men who had yielded slowly and sullenly to the enemy and had stopped often to load and to fire.

As Heth's and Wilcox's Divisions were rallying, Longstreet's were making ready for the shock. There was no time to trim a line, to throw out skirmishers and then to counter-attack. Federals were almost on the heels of every fugitive.[102] Down the line

[97] 5 *Land We Love*, 483.

[98] *Longstreet*, 560–61, nd Venable in 14 *S.H.S.P.*, 526, are at variance concerning this episode. Because Venable wrote in 1873 and Longstreet about 1895, Venable is followed, but Longstreet's statement of his remark to Lee has been accepted as substantially correct.

[99] Col. W. H. Palmer in W. L. Royall, *Some Reminiscences*, 28.

[100] 2 *N. C. Regts.*, 665.                    [101] *Sorrel*, 235.

[102] *Cf.* Kershaw, *O. R.*, 36, pt. 1, p. 1061.

dashed Kershaw, a flawless rider. "Now, my old Brigade," he cried, "I expect you to do your duty!" [103]

Nowhere did the enemy fall back. He halted, he lay down, he hid behind stumps or trees—but he kept sending those vicious minié bullets through the forest. Longstreet's spirits and activity mounted with the danger. He rode straight to the front and shouted his commands in a voice that rose above the battle. To Kershaw, his word was to pick brave officers as guides and color-bearers. Now on the left, now on the right, exhortation was mingled with orders. "Old Pete's" very presence seemed to strengthen his men. Soon he had a line from which volley after volley was poured into the enemy. Said one of his artillerists later, "Longstreet, always grand in battle, never shone as he did here." [104]

For a while there was a furious exchange from stationary lines. Then slowly, but with supreme resolution, Kershaw began to advance. Field was ready on the other side of the road. Lee had assisted in getting Law's Brigade into action. "Alabama soldiers," he had cried with flashing eyes, as he pointed to the front, "all I ask of you is to keep up with the Texans." [105] Boldly the Texans were moving forward. They had "put General Lee under arrest," they said, "and had sent him to the rear." [106] Now they would redeem their promise to drive back the enemy. The rest of Field's Division, with Benning directly behind Gregg, supported the counter-thrust. [107]

Every step of ground was contested. The enemy had sensed victory and held stubbornly to his gains, but even the fine troops of Hancock's II Corps could not withstand the cunning and the fury of that assault. Backward toward Heth's position of the previous night, back toward the ground occupied by Wilcox, the veterans of Longstreet pushed the Union regiments. [108] The front was not unduly wide for the advance of two Divisions. [109] Resistance gradually weakened. By 9:45, or about that time, the opposing

[103] Dickert, 346.
[105] 14 C. V., 111.
[107] Field in 14 S.H.S.P., 544.
[108] O. R., 36, pt. 1, p. 1055.

[104] J. C. Haskell's MS Rems., 85.
[106] Dame, 143.

[109] The Federals themselves never were quite certain by what twist of circumstance they seemed unable to attack on a wider front. See Francis A. Walker, History of the Second Army Corps, 424 ff; A. A. Humphreys, The Virginia Campaign of 1864 and 1865, (cited hereafter as Humphreys) 39 ff.

forces were approximately where the day's fighting had started.[110] A hot fire continued, but neither side attempted for the moment to drive the other.

Lee was not content to have the situation remain one of wasteful exchange of lead. Nor was Longstreet willing to end his battle in stalemate. Strategically and tactically, a Confederate attack was dictated. Force for it was at hand, because "Dick" Anderson's Division of the Third Corps had arrived at the front.[111] Expert reconnaissance was assured also. Lee had placed at Longstreet's service the new Chief Engineer of the Army,[112] Martin Smith, whom Longstreet knew well and trusted freely. Before the advance had halted, Smith and some assistants had been sent out to examine the enemy's position. Now, about 10 o'clock, Smith reported that the Federal left extended a short distance only to the South of the Plank Road. It would be entirely feasible, Smith said, to turn that flank. The forest would conceal the Confederate troop movement.[113] Longstreet listened intently and pondered. He would try it! What was more, if he were facing a gap in the Federal line, instead of the actual left of the Federal position, then he would find the extreme left and turn that, too. Smith was directed to take a small party, to reconnoitre beyond the Brock Road and to find a way of getting beyond the farthest position of the Federals.[114]

Around Longstreet, when Smith came and went again, were several of the general officers of McLaws's old Division. They must have heard what Smith reported. W. T. Wofford, one of the ablest of the Brigadiers, suggested that a column move by the right flank until it reached the cut of the unfinished railroad from Orange to Fredericksburg. This cut, said Wofford, would be an excellent place from which to start the attack on the flank of Hancock.[115]

[110] The hour is difficult to determine with precision. From the reports, one gets the impression that the vigor of the Federal defense diminished about the time Hancock directed Birney to move as many troops as could be spared to repair the gap caused by the rout of Brig. Gen. Lysander Cutler's Division on the left of the V Corps, which was to the right of Hancock. The time of the arrival of the news of Cutler's reverse was given by Hancock as 9:45 (*O. R.*, 36, pt. 1, p. 322).
[111] It reported about 8 o'clock from its rearguard duty on the upper Rapidan, *Longstreet*, 561.
[112] *Ibid.*         [113] *O. R.*, 31, pt. 1, p. 1055.         [114] *Longstreet*, 562.
[115] *O. R.*, 36, pt. 1, pp. 1061–62. This railroad, it will be remembered, had a part on May 1, 1863, in the tactical arrangements for Jackson's advance. See Vol. II, pp. 534–35. After the war, the line was completed and was operated as the Piedmont, Fredericks-

The plan had practicality. Longstreet was sure of that, but for the moment he was not certain where all his troops were. They had become scattered during their advance through the mazes of the Wilderness. Anderson's men might be mingled with Kershaw's and with Field's. While Longstreet was wrestling with this confusion, he had opportunity of explaining his plan in a brief conference with Lee, who had been nearby during most of the action.[116] Lee approved. Longstreet then summoned his A.A.G., Lieut. Col. Moxley Sorrel. "Colonel," he began, "there is a fine chance of a grand attack on our right." The General went on: "If you will quickly get into those woods, some Brigades will be found much scattered from the fight. Collect them and take charge. Form a good line and then move, your right pushed forward and turning as much as possible to the left. Hit hard when you start, but don't start until you have everything ready. I shall be waiting for your gunfire, and be on hand for further advance." [117]

Off went Sorrel in full consciousness that his great opportunity had come. In about an hour, working with the help of "Billy" Mahone and others, Sorrel had in line "Tige" Anderson's Brigade of Field's Division, Wofford's Brigade of Kershaw's command, and Mahone's Brigade of Anderson. With these two Brigades of the First and one of the Third Corps, Mahone, as Senior Brigadier, started by the right flank through the woods.[118] Longstreet then had immediately in front of the foe only the troops of Benning, Law and Gregg of Field's Division,[119] but Micah Jenkins's Brigade of that Division,[120] three Brigades of Kershaw and three of "Dick" Anderson were close at hand. If Mahone turned the flank of the Federals, Longstreet would have ample force to press them in front and to prepare for the second and perhaps larger turning movement on which Smith was to report.[121] "Old Pete's" hopes were

burg and Potomac. Before its final abandonment, it was renamed the Virginia Central, though, of course, it nowhere used the right of way of the old Virginia Central, which had become the main line of the Chesapeake and Ohio.

[116] Longstreet to Lee, May 19, 1864, *Sorrel*, 241. Col. J. C. Haskell (*MS Rems.*, 85 ff) said that Mahone and Jenkins also shared in this conference, which he described as "long"; but as the Colonel confused the events of the first and of the second advance, his account has not been followed.

[117] *Sorrel*, 236.

[118] *Sorrel*, 237; *O. R.*, 36, pt. 1, p. 1055. The impression created by Sorrel would be that he commanded the troops as they advanced, but Longstreet, in recommending Mahone's promotion, said that Mahone was in charge (*O. R.*, 40, pt. 3, p. 775).

[119] *O. R.*, 36, pt. 1, p. 1055.

[120] Field had five Brigades (*O. R.*, 36, pt. 1, p. 1022).

[121] In *Longstreet*, 562, the list of the troops not in line of battle is incomplete

high, but his caution as a leader showed itself. He did not confide to Field, and perhaps not even to Kershaw, who was nearby and more intimate, all that he intended to do.[122]

Intently, at his post of command on the Plank Road, Longstreet and some of his subordinates awaited the sound of fire from their right flank. As minutes passed without a burst of fire from the direction where the enemy's pickets would be covering an extended flank, it seemed certain that Mahone's march had escaped detection. A little longer and the flanking column could be assumed to be taking position in the cut of the unfinished railroad. At length there came the challenge of skirmish fire and then the roll of a volley. The attack had begun! Let the troops in line on either side of the Plank Road redouble their fire, press the enemy and occupy him while the flank attack developed. Send word to all the commanders of the reserve to prepare to advance.

Everything proceeded as perfectly as on the great day at Second Manassas or on that triumphant December afternoon at Fredericksburg. The roar from the right gave reassurance that the three Brigades were advancing. In front, perpendicular to the Plank Road, the enemy was beginning to yield ground. Soon he broke [123] as if he sought cover. The fire from the flank was approaching the Plank Road. Victory was in the air, which now was hot as summer [124] and heavy with the smoke of battle and of burning forest.[125] Ample time there was, also, in which to make the victory complete. The hour scarcely was past 11, though it was climbing toward Longstreet's high noon.[126] Not many miles away, in that same Wilderness and on a May day, too, Jackson had turned the Federal right beyond that same Plank Road. Now Longstreet was to roll up their left in an action as decisive. Perhaps, after all, that long winter in East Tennessee was to be rewarded. Never had the prospect been fairer! The enemy's plight, Longstreet told himself, was that of "utter rout with heavy loss." [127]

Back to Longstreet now came General Martin Smith. The

---

[122] It is manifest from Longstreet's reference in his memoirs (op. cit., 565) that Field was not informed of the larger plan.
[123] O. R., 36, pt. 1, p. 1055.     [124] Jed. Hotchkiss' MS Diary, 339.
[125] Longstreet, 562.
[126] Alexander (op. cit., 505) timed the advance at 11 A.M. Wilcox (Annals, 498) said it was a little after 12 M.
[127] O. R., 36, pt. 1, p. 1055.

engineer had located the extreme Federal left, and he suggested a route that would carry a flanking column beyond the Brock Road. Longstreet was highly pleased. He decided to repeat the maneuver of the early morning and to entrust this operation to Smith who, said he, "was a splendid tactician as well as a skillful engineer, and gallant withal."[128] Smith was directed to take some of the troops that already had advanced beyond the flank, and with these he was to move southward and then was to proceed to the East of the Brock Road.[129] Kershaw was to push forward with his Division; Micah Jenkins, who was chafing in reserve, was to co-operate with Kershaw. It would be an opportunity for Jenkins. His chief, Field, still was engaged on the northern side of the Plank Road and need not be disturbed. Longstreet already had ridden over to Field's front and had applauded the Division's fine advance.[130]

Kershaw had ridden ahead on the Plank Road after the break of the enemy, and he now was in advance, but Jenkins was summoned and soon was by the side of Longstreet. Close behind Jenkins marched his men who wore new uniforms of a gray so deep that they appeared dark blue or almost black in the forest.[131] Jenkins was jubilant. When his troops came up, during his conversation with his chief, Jenkins called for a cheer for Longstreet. The Carolinians for the moment drowned the sound of the firing.[132] Longstreet, much pleased, bade Jenkins ride forward with him toward the Brock Road. The younger soldier did not attempt to repress his exaltation of spirit. With boyish candor he told his chief: "I am happy; I have felt despair for the cause for some months, but am relieved, and feel assured that we will put the enemy back across the Rapidan before night."[133]

Next, Moxley Sorrel, equally happy, rode through the woods and along the road to report what Longstreet already knew—that the flanking movement had driven and had broken the enemy on the Confederate right.[134] Longstreet congratulated the young man and perhaps made the resolution he soon executed to recommend

[128] *Longstreet*, 563.
[129] This is almost certainly the meaning of Longstreet's reference (*op. cit.*, 563) to Wofford's Brigade. On first reading, one is apt to get the impression that Longstreet was confusing, in his memoir, the first and the second flanking movement of the day.
[130] 14 *S.H.S.P.*, 545.
[131] *J. C. Haskell's MS Rems.*, 86.                          [132] *Ibid.*
[133] *Longstreet*, 563. See also *infra*, n.          [134] *Sorrel*, 291.

Sorrel for promotion to Brigadier General as a reward of valor.[135] The young staff officer joined the cavalcade that was moving toward the Brock Road. From the direction of that road there now approached another group of riders. Kershaw was one of them. William T. Wofford was another. Staff officers and couriers attended them. As their horses came head on toward Longstreet's mounts, the riders drew rein for new congratulations.[136] Wofford in particular could add to the gratifying detail because his fine troops, pursuing vigorously, had driven ahead and at that moment were North of the Plank Road.[137]

Longstreet explained briefly the part Kershaw's and Jenkins's men were to have in the final operation. While Smith swept northward, to the East of the Brock Road, Jenkins was to move by the flank up the Plank Road. Kershaw was to pass through the woods on the right of the road. Field was to remain on the left where he still was fighting. The attack was to be pressed by all available troops. Grant's Army was to be pushed toward Fredericksburg.[138] All this Longstreet made clear, and then, in his most cheerful manner of the battlefield, he touched his horse and started forward again. Kershaw and Jenkins dropped back a few paces to the head of Jenkins's Brigade, and, following their chief, intently reviewed the details of their part in the attack.

Longstreet was now almost within musket range of the Brock Road[139] and was passing the positions that had been reached by Mahone and "Tige" Anderson in their advance from the right flank. The Virginians and the Georgians were in line of battle parallel to the Plank Road and about sixty yards from it. Wofford's Brigade was on the opposite side of the road somewhat farther to the East.[140]

Whether Longstreet saw any of these troops is not certain, but he had abundant reason to be proud of them. Mahone's Brigade, to be sure, belonged to the Third Corps under the reorganization, and it had wintered on the Rapidan, but in earlier days it had been part of the First Corps. Wofford and "Tige" Anderson had shared the hardships and the disappointments of the campaign in East Tennessee, and were having their compensation. In their first

[135] The letter of recommendation (*Sorrel*, 241) was dated May 19, 1864.
[136] *O. R.*, 36, pt. 1, p. 1062.
[137] *Ibid*.
[138] *Ibid*.
[139] *Ibid*.
[140] *O. R.*, 36, pt. 1, p. 1055.

battle after their return to Virginia, they had equalled their greatest exploits. There was augury in this initial victory, a victory which now gave every promise of a triumph that would drive the enemy back to the fords of the Rappahannock. Jackson, in his dying delirium, had been pushing the enemy to United States Ford. What he had babbled of doing, the First Corps must do!

At that moment, to the left of the road, Longstreet heard the sound of two or three rifles close at hand. Ahead of him, a few stragglers from the direction of Wofford's advance ran across the road toward Mahone's position. There was an instant of uncertainty. Then came shots from the woods on the right. Longstreet did not follow the rule of caution. Instead of throwing himself from his horse on the opposite side, he instinctively turned the animal's head toward the fire and started to dash forward to stop it.[141] A savage volley greeted him. The impact of a heavy bullet lifted Longstreet from his saddle, into which he fell back uncertainly the next instant. Micah Jenkins and two others were struck mortally. At the flash of the volley, Jenkins's men turned to the right, formed a rough line and lifted their rifles. Instantly "Joe" Kershaw dashed among them. "They are fri-e-en-nds," he cried in a voice that everyone heard. The words scarcely were out of his mouth before the disciplined men of the Brigade threw themselves flat on the ground to escape another volley.[142] There was none. Mahone's men, who had done the firing, quickly recognized their mistake. Some of them rushed out to voice their regret and to render such aid as they might.[143]

By this time, Longstreet had been taken from his saddle and had been placed by the roadside. His condition manifestly was serious. A minié ball had entered near the throat and had crashed into the right shoulder. Hemorrhage was severe, though the Medical Director of the Corps soon was at hand to stanch it.[144] So

---

141 *Conner*, 133.    142 *O. R.*, 36, pt. 1, p. 1062.
143 *Ibid*. This description follows the narrative of Kershaw, *loc. cit.*, which seems to have been neglected by writers on the Battle of the Wilderness, though Kershaw's is the only clear, contemporary account by an eye-witness. Longstreet's statement (*op. cit.*, 563 ff) is interesting because it shows that the shock of his wound, as in many such cases, produced complete amnesia concerning the event itself and the happenings of the minutes preceding it. The General stated that the fatal volley was delivered almost as soon as Jenkins had expressed recovery of faith in victory. Kershaw's account shows that some time elapsed between Jenkins's remark to Longstreet and the volley. Unfortunately, Kershaw's report is without date. Its form suggests that it was not written in the regular manner of reports prepared on circular orders, but it manifestly preceded Longstreet's account by many years.
144 *Sorrel*, 238.

great was the vitality of Longstreet that he blew the bloody foam from his mouth and whispered instructions: "Tell General Field to take command, and move forward with the whole force and gain the Brock Road." [145] The divisional leader was at the side of his wounded chief almost as soon as the words were uttered.[146] Solicitously Field inquired if he could give any relief. Longstreet replied that he would receive attention from others: Field must press the enemy.[147] Soon "Dick" Anderson and then the commanding General rode up. To them, as fully as his clogged throat and shaken vocal organs permitted, Longstreet explained his plan.[148]

Lee undertook to direct the execution of it, but the troops were scattered widely. Confusion ruled the field. Time was required to draw the lines and to make the deployment. The enemy meanwhile strengthened his front. Late in the afternoon, when the Confederate right wing attacked, it was repulsed almost before it got under way.[149]

Before the futile attack was delivered, the news of the wounding of Longstreet had spread among the troops on the Plank Road. He was carried promptly to the rear in "tolerable comfort" [150] past soldiers who recognized his bulky form, though his hat was over his face. "He is dead," some of them said, "and they are telling us he is only wounded." Longstreet heard them and gamely, with his left hand, lifted his hat from his face. He said afterward that the answering cheers of the troops eased somewhat his pain.[151] Once in an ambulance, boots and coat were removed by staff officers whose distress made their hands tremble. Osmun Latrobe, himself wounded, hastened to join his chief [152] and seemed to forget his own hurt in trying to alleviate Longstreet's.[153] The General was quiet in his pain. Once, as he lay on his back, he used his uninjured hand to raise his blood-soaked undershirt from his chest. "He is not dead," one observer told himself, "and he is

---

[145] Col. John W. Fairfax in *Longstreet*, 567; *J. C. Haskell's MS Rems.*, 87.
[146] 14 *S.H.S.P.*, 545.          [147] Field in *Longstreet*, 567.
[148] *Longstreet*, 565; *Alexander*, 506.
[149] *O. R.*, 36, pt. 1, pp. 324, 1062. General Longstreet apparently remained of the opinion that if the offensive had been pressed immediately, a decisive victory would have been won, though he did not so state in plain terms (*op. cit.*, 564–65). Alexander (*op. cit.*, 507) concluded that large results might have attended an attack early in the afternoon but that the assault of 4:15 was unwise and costly.
[150] *O. R.*, 51, pt. 2, p. 893.          [151] *Longstreet*, 566; *Dame*, 91.
[152] *MS Diary*, May 6, 1864.          [153] *Stiles*, 247.

calm and entirely master of the situation—he is both greater and more attractive than I have heretofore thought him." [154]

While Longstreet was being carried to the rear, Micah Jenkins was dying. A bullet had penetrated his brain. Half conscious, he scarcely seemed in spirit to leave the contest. He "would cheer his men and implore them to sweep the enemy into the river till he was too weak to talk." [155] Babbling of the battle, he died without knowing he had been hit. He was 28 years of age. Others had been lost that day of rank less exalted but of long service in the Army. Col. Van Manning of the famous Third Arkansas that had shared in John R. Cooke's defense at Sharpsburg was wounded and captured.[156] James D. Nance, Colonel of the Third South Carolina, was killed. Few were more lamented by a Brigade that had many capable fighting men. In the judgment of some of them, Colonel Nance was "the best all round soldier" of the Brigade.[157] Dead, too, was Col. J. Thompson Brown, who had been senior officer of the Second Corps artillery at Gettysburg.[158] Still another excellent soldier who fell that day was Col. C. M. Avery of the Thirty-third North Carolina, Lane's Brigade, who set an example of high courage in resisting the first Federal onslaught of the 6th.[159]

At the moment, the loss of these men scarcely was mentioned beyond the Brigades. All thought, all talk, was of Longstreet. He, the "Old War Horse," had fallen in the Wilderness that had witnessed the mortal wounding of Jackson. The two disasters had been almost precisely a year apart. Every soldier who remembered Chancellorsville observed the similarities and wondered whether Longstreet would have the fate of Jackson. Four surgeons, including the Medical Director of the Army, made a

---

[154] Ibid.
[155] J. C. Haskell's MS Rems., 88. Cf. Conner, 133.
[156] Oates, 344.
[157] Dickert, 353. A sketch of Colonel Nance was republished by Dickert. The Colonel was in his twenty-seventh year. Equally lamented was Lieut. Col. Franklin Gaillard, who was in command of the Second South Carolina. Both Gaillard and Nance, in the words of General Kershaw, were "gentlemen of education, position and usefulness in civil life and [were] highly distinguished in the field" (O. R., 36, pt. 1, p. 1062).
[158] He was born in Petersburg, Virginia, Feb. 6, 1835, the son of a leading lawyer, and was himself engaged in the legal profession when the war began. His career is sketched briefly in 8 C. V., 25–26. For General Pendleton's tribute to him, see O. R., 36, pt. 1, p. 1040. General Long, ibid., 1085, wrote of Brown: "He not only exhibited the highest social qualities but was endowed with the first order of military talents. On every field where he was called to act he was distinguished for gallantry and skill."
[159] 2 N. C. Regts., 570.

preliminary examination and concluded that the wound was "not necessarily fatal." [160] In relation to the command of the Army, the loss of Longstreet, even temporarily, might be as serious as the fall of "Stonewall," because the leadership of the other Corps was shaken. Besides the illness of Powell Hill, the Army that day witnessed a development that raised anew the question whether Ewell was qualified to command in the field.

It was a curious development, for which there scarcely was a parallel in the history of the Army. During the night of May 5-6, John Gordon had sent out scouts to ascertain the position of the enemy near his front, which was on the extreme left of the Confederate line.[161] About dawn, these men returned with an astonishing story: The Federal flank, they said, was in the woods a short distance ahead. Gordon's left considerably overlapped the Union right. This seemed scarcely credible. In so important an operation, close to the scene of the catastrophe that Hooker had suffered by leaving his flank in the air, it did not seem possible that the careful Meade had committed the same blunder.

Confident of his scouts' sincerity but skeptical of their findings, Gordon ordered another examination of the ground. In an hour or two, the second scouting party was back with full confirmation of the first report and with the further assurance that, except on the main line itself, no supports were within several miles of the Federal flank. Still Gordon's judgment refused to accept what his fighting impulse prompted him to hope. He mounted and, with some of the men who had made the previous reconnaissance, he went forward to see for himself. A rapid ride convinced him that no Federal supports were directly ahead or close to the Rapidan and within striking distance. Near the point where the scouts said the Union line terminated, Gordon left his horse and crept forward. He was amazed at what he beheld: "I was shown the end of General Grant's temporary breastworks. There was no line guarding this flank. As far as my eye could reach, the Union soldiers were seated on the margin of the rifle pits, taking their breakfast. Small fires were burning over which they were boiling their coffee, while their guns leaned against the works in their immediate front." [162]

160 O. R., 51, pt. 2, p. 893. James Conner, op. cit., 133, from the outset, took a more optimistic view. See infra, p. 442 and Chapter XXXI.
161 O. R., 36, pt. 1, p. 1077.          162 Gordon, 243-44.

This sight inflamed Gordon's spirit. His great opportunity had come. An attack on that flank of the Federals would overwhelm it. As rapidly as he could, Gordon hurried to corps headquarters, where he expected to find both Ewell and Early. It was then not quite 9 o'clock.[163] The Federals already had attacked Pegram's Brigade,[164] which had repulsed them savagely. So certain were Pegram's men [165] of their ability to beat off any further attack that when Early offered to relieve them, they asked him to let them stay and fight.[166] Early's concern and Ewell's, for this reason, was not for their front but for their left flank. Scouts had brought reports that Federal infantry were between Gordon and the river. Another report, though of the vaguest sort, was that Burnside's IX Corps, which was following Meade's advance, had crossed the Rapidan and was taking position in rear of the Federal right, the very ground that Gordon and his scouts had found unoccupied. Neither Ewell nor Early had undertaken to make personal reconnaissance, or even to have staff officers establish the facts. Assuming the truth of the report that a column was preparing to attempt a turning movement from the extreme Federal right, Ewell had told Early to watch for this column and to keep it from getting to the Confederate rear. Robert Johnston's Brigade,[167] which had been detached, was sent to Early to strengthen this defense of the left rear. Early probably was absent from headquarters,[168] posting Johnston's men, when Gordon arrived.[169] On reaching headquarters, or immediately after Early's return, Gordon described the condition on his front and asked permission to attack with his Brigade, which was idle.[170]

Early opposed. It was too dangerous a move, he said. With a Union column on the left and Burnside in rear of the Federal

163 Ewell stated that it was "about 9" that Gordon's plan was presented through Early (O. R., 36, pt. 1, p. 1071).
164 Hotchkiss' map (O. R. Atlas, Plate LXXXIII, I) placed Pegram immediately on Gordon's right, but Ewell's report (O. R., 36, pt. 1, p. 1070) put Hays between Gordon and Pegram at the close of the fighting on the 5th. No mention was made by Ewell of any change of dispositions on the morning of the 6th.
165 They now were under Col. John S. Hoffman of the Thirty-first Virginia.
166 Early, 347.
167 This Brigade, of Rodes's Division, it will be remembered, previously had been Iverson's and, before that, Samuel Garland's.
168 The reason for doubt is Ewell's statement (O. R., 36, pt. 1, p. 107), that he got word from Gordon "through General Early in person." From Gordon, 255, one would infer that Gordon reported directly to Ewell and waited to discuss the movement in Early's presence.
169 Early, 348.
170 Gordon, 255; O. R., 36, pt. 1, p. 1077.

flank, an attack might be repulsed. If the enemy then assumed the offensive, the Second Corps would have no reserves to throw into the defense. The Corps, indeed the whole Army, might be involved in disaster.[171] Early's argument was based on the domineering assumption that his intelligence reports were correct and those of Gordon were in error, though Gordon had verified brigade reports and Early had done nothing to substantiate those he had received.

Ewell was puzzled. In much the same mood as at Gettysburg, he hesitated. Early asserted afterward that Ewell agreed with him.[172] Ewell himself reported that he could not decide on the move, one way or the other, without personal examination, which he resolved to make later in the day.[173] He was not to be brought to a more positive frame of mind, even though Gordon offered impetuously to assume all the blame in the event of failure.[174]

After Ewell deferred a decision, he directed the repulse of a few thrusts at different points on his front, but he sustained no attack worth mentioning in the same sentence with the fighting on the Plank Road. He wrote subsequently that his examination of the ground in front of Gordon was made "as soon as other duties permitted." Of the nature of those duties and of "other unavoidable causes" that delayed the assault Gordon pleaded with him to make, Ewell gave no details.[175] While Longstreet fought and fell, and Lee painfully put confused lines in order for an advance against the Federal left, Ewell did little or nothing to clarify conflicting intelligence reports. It is not know when or to what extent he made reconnaissance of his own.[176] Perplexed or weary or hypnotized for the moment by the confident insistence of Early, he permitted the fateful afternoon to pass without an offensive blow.

Toward sunset, about 5:30, Ewell saw the commanding General draw rein at corps field headquarters. Lee had passed one of the most anxious days of his military career and now, still shaken by the narrow escape of the morning, the fall of Longstreet and the repulse of the last attack on the Federal left, he came to ask if something could not be done by Ewell to relieve the pres-

---

[171] Early, 348.  
[173] O. R., 36, pt. 1, p. 1071.  
[175] O. R., 36, pt. 1, p. 1071.  
[172] Early, 348.  
[174] Gordon, 255–56.  
[176] The only reference to any "personal examination" by Ewell is the vague line in his own report. Neither Early nor Gordon mentioned it.

sure on the other Confederate flank. By redeeming chance, Gordon was at headquarters when Lee called for action. The young Brigadier listened for a time while his seniors discussed the situation, and at last he told Lee of the situation he had found on the Federal right during the morning and of the plan he had proposed for rolling up that flank.

Immediately "Old Jube" renewed with vigor the objections he had raised when Gordon first had reported. Gordon stood his ground squarely and described to Lee what he had seen. Lee had confidence in Gordon and wished to know why,[177] in the circumstances, the assault had not been delivered. The answers must have been so feeble that Lee considered silence the best rebuke. In a few words he ordered the attack and expressed confidence that the Confederates could wreck as much of the line as they could reach before darkness.[178]

Now that the commanding General assumed responsibility for the attack, Ewell and Early gave Gordon the fullest support. "They did all in their power," Gordon attested, "to help forward the movement when once begun." Early continued to have misgiving and thought soon after the attack was launched that it was failing, but he threw in additional troops to aid Gordon who, at the outset, had only his Brigade and that of Robert Johnston.[179]

The result was all that Gordon had promised. Surprise was complete. As soon as the Confederates were astride the Federal flank, regiment after regiment gave way. Gordon's men pronounced the advance the "finest frolic" they had enjoyed during the war.[180] Steadily and rapidly they moved along the line till darkness and the crossfire of their own comrades to the westward halted their advance. By that time, Gordon had two Federal Brigadiers and several hundred prisoners to his credit. On the ground his men counted more than 400 fallen Federals. The casualties in Gordon's Brigade were about fifty. "I must be permitted," said Gordon in his report, ". . . to express the opinion that had the movement been made at an earlier hour and properly supported . . . it would have resulted in a decided disaster to the

177 See *supra*, p. 325, with reference to Samuel Jones, and *O. R.*, 33, 1124.
178 *Gordon*, 258.
179 Cf. *Early*, 349. For Early's subsequent assertion that during the afternoon he suggested the advance, see *infra*, p. 443.
180 *Gordon*, 250.

whole right wing of General Grant's army, if not in its entire disorganization."[181]

The darkness that had halted Gordon was weird and affrighting. On the Confederate left, there was a strange silence except when some wounded man screamed in his misery, or begged for water, or cried out for litter bearers who had passed him by. Before the darkness became complete, keen eyes saw shattered trees, saplings bent double, and bloody strips of garments caught on bushes.[182] Farther to the right, where the battle had been more furious, there was sound, not silence, and the fantastic light of forest fires that a brisk wind [183] was spreading fast. Dead trees in the woods were aflame like torches. Often, as soldiers watched, fire would run along limb after limb till the whole tree was outlined in blaze. The reflection of the fire gave the clouds a sickening yellow cast.[184] As the flames advanced there was a low swell of sound, a crash of limbs as if the artillery still were in action. The nearer men ventured to the fire, the louder were the frantic cries of the wounded who could not creep away as fast as the flames approached. Some of the wounded could not drag a broken back, or crawl with shattered limbs. These men could only pray and plead for succor or frantically seek to clear an open space around them as the fire drew nearer every minute. It was in vain. Two hundred of them soon were suffocated or were burned to charred trunks of flesh.[185] The transformation of the forest was incredible. At dawn it had been an impenetrable maze of greenery; now, after the fire swept on, there were long, black-bordered aisles [186] and a smouldering floor—a hideous temple of Mars.

The sacrifice had been bloody. John M. Jones and Micah Jenkins were dead. Leroy Stafford was dying. John Pegram and Henry Benning [187] were wounded. Powell Hill was so sick that he might not be able to exercise command the next day. Ewell seemed unable to reach a decision. Longstreet, the strongest and the most dependable of all the lieutenants, was the victim of a wound that might kill him and certainly would incapacitate him for the months of decisive fighting with this new and stubborn adversary, Grant.

181 O. R., 36, pt. 1, p. 1078. For a critique of this episode, see *infra,* pp. 443–44.
182 *Gordon,* 266–67.                                  183 *Ibid.*
184 *Neese,* 262.                                      185 O. R., 36 pt. 1, p. 218.
186 *Caldwell,* 138.                                   187 14 *S.H.S.P.,* 544.

# CHAPTER XIX

## THE ADVANTAGE OF AN EARLY START

To MEET Grant's next attack, whenever and wherever delivered, the Confederates must have the best procurable successor to Longstreet. The senior division commander of the First Corps was Lafayette McLaws. By odd chance, the court martial findings in his case, long delayed and much disputed, were announced on May 4, the very day the offensive on the Rapidan commenced. The court found him guilty on one specification only, that of not "providing means of crossing the ditch" at Fort Loudon.[1] Many circumstances, said the tribunal, exonerated McLaws "from any high degree of criminality" in this failure, because there were reasons to believe the obstacle a light one. McLaws's real offense, in the judgment of the court, was in failing to appreciate the full weight of the responsibility resting on him in directing the assault. His punishment was to be suspension from rank and command for sixty days.[2] This was so light a judgment for so heavy an alleged offense that it was, in effect, a vindication of McLaws and a humiliation to Longstreet; but the War Department was unwilling to have even that mild sentence stand. The findings were disapproved on the ground of irregularity of procedure and on the further ground that the verdict was not sustained by the evidence.[3] At Bragg's instance, McLaws on May 7 was directed to rejoin his command.[4] Notice of this order was not telegraphed Lee at once. Consequently Lee did not know on the day after Longstreet's wounding that McLaws was to return and, by seniority, was to assume temporary command. The acting commander of McLaws's Division, Joseph B. Kershaw, was not yet a Major General and could not be considered for corps command. Nor could Charles W. Field, head of the other Division of the First Corps, be advanced. He was of appointment too recent and of experience

1 See *supra*, p. 300.    2 O. R., 31, pt. 1, pp. 505–06.
3 O. R., 31, pt. 1, p. 506.    4 O. R , 36, pt. 2, pp. 955, 966.

too limited.[5] Pickett, second in seniority among the division com-manders of the Corps, apparently was not mentioned as a possi-bility.

First intimation of what was in the mind of the commanding General was given Moxley Sorrel. Early on the morning of the 7th, the A.A.G. was summoned to headquarters and was con-ducted by Lee to the shade of a large tree, where they would not be overheard. Then Sorrel was told that "Dick" Anderson, Edward Johnson and Jubal Early were under consideration. Which of the three did Sorrel think would be best suited?

Sorrel thanked the General for his confidence and began can-didly to appraise the men. Early, said the young Colonel, prob-ably was the ablest of them but would be the most unpopular with the Corps. The jibes and sarcasms of Early had created resent-ments that would be voiced in the event he were named to the command.

"And now, Colonel," said Lee, "for my friend Ed. Johnson; he is a splendid fellow."

"All say so, General," replied Sorrel, "but he is quite unknown to the Corps. His reputation is so high that perhaps he would prove all that could be wished, but I think someone personally known to the Corps would be preferred."

By elimination, this made Sorrel's recommendation Richard H. Anderson who, it will be remembered, had commanded a Division under Longstreet for about ten months, until transferred to the Third Corps. Sorrel felt that Anderson was not aggressive and might be indolent, but he also knew the South Carolinian to be brave, prudent and intelligent.[6] Without weighing good qualities against bad, Sorrel took up in Anderson's behalf where he had stopped in objecting to Johnson. "We know him," said Sorrel of Anderson, "and shall be satisfied with him."

"Thank you, Colonel," said the General, "I have been inter-ested, but Early would make a fine corps commander."

That seemed to settle it. Sorrel went away in the conviction that Lee believed Early the best qualified man and that "Old Jube" would be named. Instead, later in the day, this order was issued: "Maj. Gen. R. H. Anderson is for the present relieved from duty with Hill's Corps, and assigned to the temporary com-

[5] *Sorrel,* 242.                    [6] *Sorrel,* 247.

ınand of Longstreet's Corps. Brig. Gen. William Mahone, in the absence of Maj. Gen. Anderson, will assume command of his Division." [7]

It was welcome news to the First Corps and was entirely defensible because Anderson, next to McLaws, was the senior Major General of the Army.[8] He had been transferred to the Third Corps some months before the Divisions of Hood and of McLaws had gone to Tennessee, but he was remembered and beloved. That had been demonstrated the previous day. His old Brigade of South Carolina troops had passed long previously to the command of Micah Jenkins,[9] and had not seen him for months until he came upon the men as they were sitting on the ground, in the Wilderness, after the fall of Jenkins. As soon as the men observed Anderson riding up the line, past the left of the Brigade, they rose with a yell to welcome him. They had to be silenced because the enemy was close at hand, and they silently resumed their places without grumbling; but as Anderson passed, they took off their hats and threw them into the air. Close to the centre of the Brigade Anderson drew rein, turned to the troops, removed his hat and said simply: "My friends, your silent expression makes me grateful for your kind remembrance. I thank you sincerely." He could say no more because of tears. The men wept, too, without abashment.[10] They rejoiced the next day to know that he and not another officer temporarily would succeed the wounded Longstreet.

Before another twenty-four hours passed, they had reason to be proud, for the Army's sake, that Anderson was their commander. The reason for their satisfaction was one of the most instructive episodes in the Army's history. Grant had attacked at 5 A.M. on the 6th, but he permitted the bright [11] morning of the 7th to pass with scarcely an exchange of picket fire. He had not been so badly hit the previous day that he had to rest and lick his wounds; consequently, the assumption was that he had begun, or soon would begin, another move. Ewell sent a report early in the day that

---

[7] O. R., 36, pt. 2, p. 967.     [8] Cf. Field in 14 S.H.S.P., 546.
[9] The organization was the same except that the Fourth South Carolina no longer was in the Brigade.
[10] Clipping of war date, apparently from a South Carolina newspaper—*Anderson MSS.* The General evidently cherished the memory of this reunion because, in days of adversity after the war, this clipping was one of the few papers he preserved.
[11] Jed. Hotchkiss' MS Diary, 341.

indicated this: The enemy's lines in front of Early on the extreme
Confederate left had been evacuated, Ewell said, as far as the
old turnpike. No effort had been made by the Federals to bury

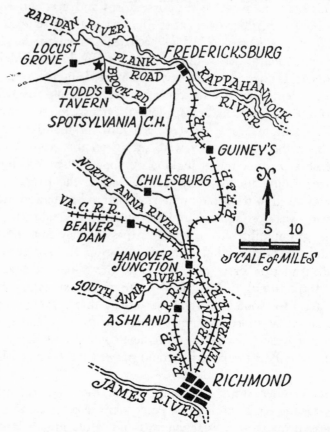

Grant's alternative Routes to Richmond from the Battleground of May 5–6, which is
marked by a star. In addition to the route to Fredericksburg and that to the line of the
R.F.&P. Railroad, via Spotsylvania Court House, several roads to the Virginia Central
Railroad were available to the Federals

their dead or to collect the arms that were strewn over the ground.
As this was the condition found at 7 A.M.,[12] on the flank covering
the road from the Rapidan, the enemy evidently had abandoned
during the night this line of supply via Germanna Ford. He could
open a new supply line by way of Fredericksburg, or he could proceed southward in the direction of Richmond and undertake to
procure supplies from the lower Rappahannock River or down

[12] *Early*, 350; cf. *O. R.*, 36, pt. 2, p. 970.

the R. F. & P. Railroad from Fredericksburg. This sketch shows the alternative routes.

If the enemy were moving to Fredericksburg, he would cover

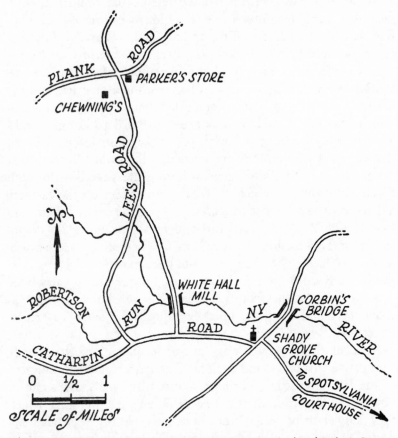

"Lee's Road," more properly "Pendleton's Road," from the Vicinity of Parker's Store to the Catharpin Road West of Shady Grove Church—after an original in the Office of the Engineer Corps of the United States Army, copied by the Virginia Conservation Commission

both the Plank Road and the old turnpike and would advance down them. In the event his objective were the railroad and the direct approaches to Richmond, his road would be by way of Todd's Tavern and Spotsylvania Court House. Without any evidence of a choice by the enemy between these routes, Lee considered the probability of a move on Spotsylvania so great that early in the day he directed General Pendleton to cut a road from

the Confederate right to the main road from Orange to Spotsylvania, in order that a swift flank march, if necessary, could be
made to the Court House by the shortest route.[13]

As for reconnaissance, the Confederate cavalry could not ascertain what was happening on the road directly in rear of the Union
line, but Stuart was operating around Todd's Tavern. His first
report of the day, sent at 9:30 A.M., was that the enemy's mounted
troops had been at the tavern that morning and at the time of
writing were on the Brock Road between the Union left and the
tavern.[14] About 1:30, "Jeb" forwarded from Fitz Lee a note in
which that officer said he was about to fall back from Todd's
Tavern. This deepened the suspicions of the commanding General
that the next move of the enemy would be toward Spotsylvania
Court House.[15] Still later, general headquarters received through
Ewell a dispatch in which a cavalry commander on the extreme
left reported that the Federals about 1 P.M. had removed their pontoon bridge at Germanna Ford and had gone hurriedly downstream in the direction of Ely's Ford.[16] When Stuart wrote again,
it was 3 o'clock. The enemy was not then moving on that part of
the Brock Road nearest Todd's Tavern, but the blue cavalry were
demonstrating in the vicinity of Shady Grove Church, which was
about three and a quarter miles Southwest of Todd's Tavern by
direct road.[17]

None of these reports was conclusive, but all of them were
cumulative. Another and a significant item was communicated
in the late afternoon. Through a strong marine glass, some of
Powell Hill's staff officers had been looking at a building which
they judged to be Grant's headquarters. Nearby was what appeared to be a park of heavy artillery. During the afternoon, these
guns were limbered up and were started to the Federal left—in
the direction of Spotsylvania Court House.[18] This final addition
to his cumulative evidence was decisive with Lee. By 7 P.M. he
issued orders for "Dick" Anderson to take Kershaw's and Field's

---

[13] O. R., 36, pt. 1, p. 1041. The location of this road has been much discussed, but
must be, at least in part, the route described in Lee to Ewell, May 8 (O. R., 51, pt. 2, p.
902) as a road which "has been cut through the pines in rear of the artillery position,
crossing the Plank Road to White Hall Mill, where you will fall into Anderson's route to
Shady Grove Church." That route corresponds to the one sketched on page 377.
[14] O. R., 36, pt. 2, p. 969.
[15] Ibid., 970. The contents of the note are suggested in O. R., 51, pt. 2, pp. 897–98.
[16] O. R., 36, pt. 2, p. 968.          [17] O. R., 51, pt. 2, p. 897.
[18] Col. W. H. Palmer in William L. Royall, Some Reminiscences, 35.

Divisions and to start before 3 A.M. for Spotsylvania.[19] Later reports of the rearward movement of Union wagons on the road to Culpeper did not shake the conviction of Lee that the enemy was moving toward Spotsylvania Court House and that the Confederates must get there first.[20]

"Dick" Anderson was chosen for this movement because his troops were farthest on the right and could start more readily. The whole operation, in fact, could be a swift side-slip to the right. Anderson always had been diligent in following the enemy. One of the favorite stories of Moxley Sorrel described that quality. On the retreat from Gettysburg, Sorrel had reported to the commanding General that Hill was marching rapidly toward the pontoon bridge across the Potomac. Lee had enquired whose Division was leading the Corps. When Sorrel had replied that Anderson was, Lee had answered: "I am sorry, Colonel; my friend Dick is quick enough pursuing, but in retreat I fear he will not be as sharp as I should like."[21] Now Anderson was in pursuit, an exceedingly critical pursuit. If he did not reach Spotsylvania ahead of the enemy, the Army of Northern Virginia might not be able to interpose between Richmond and the Federals. Orders gave him discretion in starting for his objective: He was to withdraw from the lines as soon as practicable after nightfall and was to move his troops to some point where they could rest, though they must keep quiet and must not light fires lest they attract the enemy's attention. Before the designated hour of 3, they were to take the road for Spotsylvania.[22] As the march was at least eleven miles from the right flank of the First Corps, Anderson decided before he moved his men from their battle position that he would begin his movement at 11 o'clock.

Shortly after nightfall, General Pendleton and one of his aides arrived at headquarters of the First Corps. He had come, the artillerist explained, because Lee had directed him to send an officer who could guide Anderson along the road cut that day through the forest. Pendleton had taken the precaution of riding over in

[19] O. R., 36, pt. 1, p. 1041; ibid., pt. 2, p. 968.
[20] O. R., 36, pt. 2, p. 971; cf. 3 R. E. Lee, 303.
[21] Sorrel, 172.
[22] Anderson to Capt. E. B. Robins, Sec. Mil. His. Soc. Mass., MS, May 14, 1879—Anderson MSS. In this letter, General Anderson did not mention the latest hour fixed for his departure, nor did he state some of the facts set forth in Pendleton's report, supra; but as Pendleton's report was written in February, 1865, it has been accepted for details that might have been forgotten by Anderson fifteen years after the event.

person to describe the road in the presence of Anderson and of the officer, so that no misunderstanding could arise. Anderson thanked Pendleton and informed him that the Corps would start its movement at 11 o'clock. Arrangement was made, also, that First Corps artillery units, which were widely stationed, should fall into the column when and where they reached it.[23]

Soon after Pendleton left, Anderson began to shift his men from the line to the vicinity of the new road. He subsequently recorded: "I found the woods in every direction on fire and burning furiously, and there was no suitable place for rest."[24] The new road, moreover, was narrow. Stumps remained above the ground level. Some of the trunks of trees had not been removed. Progress over it would be slow. Its condition was bad for its entire length. Upon ascertaining this, Anderson promptly decided that he would forego the hours of rest authorized by Army Headquarters. He would push on, now that he was moving, until he was close to his objective. It was a soldierly resolution that made history and it was put into execution while the air was vibrant with sound. On the right, among Anderson's own men, someone cried "Three cheers for General Lee!" Instead of cheers there was the weird rebel yell, rendered all the more weird by the night and the burning forest. Down the line from Brigade to Brigade it swept to the left. Again it was raised; again it was carried to the river; still again the troops on the right raised the yell, which was hurled at the enemy and, at the last, was thrown across the Rapidan to die in its echoes over the fields of Culpeper and of Stafford. It was, said one chronicler, "The grandest rebel yell of the war."[25] Wrote another: "It seemed to fill every heart with new life."[26]

The First Corps needed that stimulus on the march they were then beginning. Through the darkness of the forest, along the wretched road, the men of Kershaw and of Field had to feel their way. To them it was a long, long night broken only by the brief halt at the end of 50 minutes and by the usual vexatious starts and stops of the march. About dawn,[27] as the troops approached a

23 *O. R.*, 36, pt. 1, p. 1041.
24 Letter to Capt. E. B. Robins, *loc. cit.*, with the punctuation conformed to current usage. Part of this letter is reproduced in *Irvine Walker*, 162.
25 3 *N. C. Regts.*, 119.
26 *Caldwell*, 135–36; G. C. Underwood, *History of the Twenty-Sixth North Carolina*, 81.
27 *O. R.*, 36, pt. 1, p. 1056—a garbled entry. Alexander said the halt was "about daylight" (*op. cit.*, 510). Anderson (*loc. cit.*) fixed the time as "a little after daylight." Sunrise was at 5:06.

grove and open fields, Anderson had the column turn out of the road to rest and to eat breakfast. The Court House was then distant about three miles.[28] Already the sound of firing was drifting down from the North. The clash might be two miles away, but no farther. There was no Confederate infantry in that direction and at that distance, but some of "Jeb" Stuart's men were in that vicinity. Much might depend on whether their foe was infantry or cavalry.[29]

When the men "fell in" again, after an hour,[30] the fire was as vigorous as before and perhaps nearer. Haskell's Battalion of artillery, which had halted in advance of the infantry, was the first to receive any information of what was occurring. Down the road there rode rapidly toward the battalion a courier who drew rein and called for the commanding officer. Major Haskell stepped forward. As good luck would have it, the courier was a fine young Baltimore boy of the distinguished name of Pegram. He knew Haskell and in the belief that the paper called for action, he gave the Major an unsealed dispatch addressed to "General Lee or General Longstreet." Because it was unsealed and urgent, Haskell opened and read the message. In it, "Jeb" Stuart asked for artillery support and said that he was hard pressed by the enemy. Haskell endorsed the envelope with notation that he had read the dispatch and was going forward. Then he returned the dispatch to the courier and immediately started the battalion. In a few minutes it disappeared on the road to Spotsylvania.[31]

Anderson probably received the dispatch from Pegram's hands a little farther down the road, but he had no knowledge of the size of the enemy's force or of the distance the Federals had advanced after Stuart had written. All Anderson could do was to advance to the sound of the firing. About 7 o'clock, the head of his leading Division, which was Kershaw's, approached a crossroads where stood a queer structure of squared logs known as the Block House.[32] At a distance of 1½ miles, on a road that formed an arc to the North and East, was the village of Spotsylvania. Northward from the Block House a road crossed the farm of one of the Spindler family and joined the Brock Road which ran

---

[28] Alexander (op. cit., 510) stated that the halt was near the Po River and at this distance from Spotsylvania. If he was correct in both particulars, the men rested North of the Pritchett House and about half a mile West of the river.

[29] Alexander, 510.　　　　　　　　　　[30] O. R., 36, pt. 1, p. 1056.

[31] J. C. Haskell's MS Rems., 90 ff.

[32] On the Michler map of 1867, the occupant's name is given as A. Perry.

through the Wilderness and past Todd's Tavern to the Court House.[33]

Down this Spindler road from the North, the front unit of Kershaw's Brigade saw an old man riding furiously. By garb and appearance he evidently was of station, but he was bareheaded and without shoes. When he reached the infantry, he said breathlessly that the Confederate cavalry were up the road. Union infantry were forming for a charge. The Southerners must have help, and have it quickly![34]

Word soon came directly from Fitz Lee that he was fighting in the direction of the Brock Road and most urgently needed assistance. He did not know that Anderson was approaching but he asked that the first troops met by the courier should come to his aid with all speed.[35] The call was not one that a soldier of Anderson's character would disregard or even debate in his own mind. He immediately ordered Kershaw's Brigade[36] and Humphreys's to file off to the left and to go to Fitz Lee's relief. Ahead of them, to the North, but perhaps not visible at the moment, were piles of rails, thrown together at intervals by other soldiers who had torn down the fences to provide these insecure but useful field defenses. Toward this shelter, the infantry had not advanced far when a cavalryman rushed up to the leading regiment: "Run for our rail piles," he shouted, "the Federal infantry will reach them first, if you don't run!" Kershaw's veterans sprang forward without waiting for a command. They reached the rail-piles safely but afterward they swore that the bluecoats were only sixty yards away, and were moving forward, when they crouched behind the rails and opened fire.[37]

By a narrow margin, then, had Anderson won that race, if, indeed, he had won more than the first heat! The Federals were forming to the northward in columns of regiments. Before many minutes had passed, they advanced in four lines. Steadfastly, gallantly, they pressed straight to the weak line of rails, and there, for

[33] Alexander, 510–11.

[34] Dickert, 357. Anderson stated in his letter to Capt. E. B. Robins that Field's Division was in advance, but the contemporary diary of the First Corps (O. R., 36, pt. 1, p. 1056) recorded that Kershaw's Division was leading the Corps.

[35] Irvine Walker, 163.

[36] Temporarily under Col. John W. Henagan of the Eighth South Carloina who, by a slip of the pen, was mentioned in Alexander, 511, as Colonel Kennedy.

[37] Dickert, 357–58.

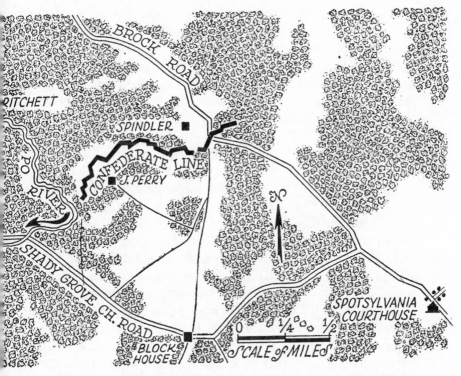

Scene of the Meeting Engagement of the Confederate Cavalry and the V Federal Corps, May 8, 1864. The Confederate works shown in this sketch were the final line. That of the opening action was much simpler and shorter, but the location probably was the same. After Michler's map of Spotsylvania Court House, 1867

once they crossed bayonets.[38] The repulse, which was costly to the Unionists, might not have been possible if Haskell had not been at hand. He had met Stuart when he had reached the Block House and, at the cavalryman's order, had taken position where he could command the approaches from the North. At one time, Haskell was without support, but he had adjusted wisely the fire of his batteries and had held his ground till Kershaw arrived. Now Haskell was having his revenge, though his ammunition was low.[39]

Almost before the South Carolinians and Humphreys's Mississippians had taken position on the Spindler farm, word had come to Anderson that Rosser's Brigade was at Spotsylvania Court House

38 Alexander (*op. cit.*, 511) stated that prisoners said they had been told the Confederate line was composed of dismounted cavalry who, having no bayonets of their own, would not stand a bayonet charge.

39 *J. C. Haskell's MS Rems.*, 91–92.

and was facing an impossibly superior force of cavalry. Rosser too must have help! Stuart sent what he could, by withdrawing some of Fitz Lee's men after the arrival of the infantry to resist the attack from the North. Further assistance for Rosser must come from Anderson. Again Longstreet's temporary successor acted with vigor and decision. The remaining Brigades of Kershaw's Division, Wofford's and Bryan's, were designated to reinforce Rosser. From someone who knew the terrain, Anderson learned that the direct approach to Spotsylvania would be exposed to fire across an open field. Consequently, he had the two Brigades make a detour so that they would approach the Federal flank from the South.[40]

Two battles, then, were to be "Dick" Anderson's—one to the North and one to the East of the Block House—and both of them serious! The Federal infantry in front of Kershaw's and Humphreys's Brigades showed no inclination to break off the fight after a single repulse. They were in great strength. Prisoners said they belonged to the V Corps. If the whole of that Corps was deploying, the two Confederate Brigades fighting behind rails on the edge of a pine thicket would need stout reinforcement. Field's Division was coming up: let part of it move toward Spotsylvania Court House; the remainder must extend Kershaw's line to the left and westward.[41]

Almost before Anderson's left could be strengthend, the whole line was assailed. Once again the enemy was beaten off easily. In another assault, the blue troops found cover within 300 or 400 yards of the Confederate right, and there they began to intrench.[42] After that, as the minutes passed, it was manifest that the Federals

---

[40] The diary of the First Corps (*O. R.*, 36, pt. 1, p. 1056) merely stated that the Brigades were "sent against the Court House by a detour." Brig. Gen. J. H. Wilson, who commanded the Federal cavalry Division that occupied the Court House, said in his report that he heard "a large force of infantry was moving up the road from Snell's Bridge" (*O. R.*, 36, pt. 1, p. 878). This makes it highly probable that the advance of Wofford and of Bryan was southeastward from the Block House to the McKenny farm, about one mile North of Snell's Bridge, and thence up the road from Snell's Bridge to the Court House. The distance from the Block House by this march would have been slightly under three miles. It is difficult to think of any other "detour" except through thick woods.

[41] Field made no report on the campaign. The only brigade report for May 8 in his Division is that of Brig. Gen. (then Col.) John Bratton, who succeeded to the command of Jenkins's Brigade (*O. R.*, 36, pt. 1, p. 1065). Bratton stated that he advanced toward Spotsylvania and then returned and took position on Kershaw's right; but the formation of the Federal right, which was reported adequately, makes it certain that part of Field's Division and later probably the whole, was on the left of Kershaw.

[42] This is merely a rewriting of Alexander's narrative (*op. cit.*, 512), which is defective in the manner indicated in the next note but is the only detailed account by an eye witness on the Southern side.

steadily were extending their lines to the westward, opposite the Confederate left. The infantry who filed into position indulged in some noisy rifle fire but, as minutes passed, they did not attempt any serious assaults.[43] At touch and go the situation remained—two Divisions against four, though the Confederates did not know the exact odds. A bold front, stern resistance by the infantry, the most stubborn artillery fire and about the hardest fighting ever done by the cavalry kept the enemy at a distance. He must be held there till the remainder of Lee's Army arrived.

Anderson's boldness and resolution, like those of many a leader, had their reward. Rosser had been driven from Spotsylvania, but the Federal commander had become alarmed at the reports that Confederate infantry were approaching from the South. The Union troopers were recalled from their pursuit of Rosser and soon were withdrawn by the road to Fredericksburg. Although the Confederates did not know it at the time, they owed this relief to the fact that the new commander of the Union Cavalry, Maj. Gen. Philip H. Sheridan, had not been informed of changes made by Army Headquarters in the disposition of his troops. Sheridan consequently had become concerned over the safety of the cavalry units at Spotsylvania and had ordered their recall.[44] Had there been satisfactory liaison between Federal G.H.Q. and the cavalry, Anderson might not have recovered Spotsylvania. As it was, he soon felt safe in sending for the infantry he had advanced to the Court House. With these men he was able to spread both flanks[45] and to prevent immediate overlapping by the enemy. In all of this Anderson had the help of Porter Alexander, chief of artillery of the First Corps, who so disposed his guns that every one of them could be brought to bear on the Federals.[46]

---

[43] Ibid., 512. Alexander confused the Federal flanks and the order of battle of the V Corps, though the mistakes are of no importance in the study of the engagement. Maj. Gen. John C. Robinson's 2nd Division delivered the first attacks. After their repulse, Brig. Gen. Charles Griffin moved his 1st Division into line on the right of the 2nd Division (O. R., 36, pt. 1, p. 594). The 4th Division, formerly Wadsworth's and now under Brig. Gen. Lysander Cutler, formed on the right of Griffin (ibid., 611). Cutler reported that during the afternoon, Brig. Gen. Samuel Crawford moved the 3rd Division to the right of the 4th (ibid., 611). From right to left, then, the final order of battle was: Crawford, Cutler, Griffin, Robinson; but the order of arrival and of the extension of line to the right was: Robinson, Griffin, Cutler, Crawford.

[44] O. R., 36, pt. 1, p. 789. The cavalry at Spotsylvania were the Third Division of Brig. Gen. James H. Wilson. For his report, see ibid., 878.

[45] Alexander (op. cit., 511) noted that Wofford and Bryan rejoined Field. Presumably they were placed on the left of Kershaw, but Bratton stated after he was moved from the Court House he was put on the right of Kershaw (O. R., 36, pt. 1, p. 1065).

[46] Alexander, 512. This statement was made by General Alexander with much modesty.

Not for long could "Dick" Anderson tell himself that all was well. During the early afternoon, there were indications that the Federal left flank was being prolonged in the direction of Spotsylvania Court House, over ground thickly covered with woods. Little could be seen, but there was a discernible stirring. Troops were being deployed. Federal artillery commanders were trying to find fields of fire. This time, surely, if the Unionists struck heavily on the Confederate right before the arrival of reinforcements, Grant could turn that flank. The Southern batteries might cover part of the line of advance, but Kershaw's and Field's men could not be spread more thinly. Stuart's cavalry had their hands full. Manifestly the outcome might hang on a few hours, on minutes even. If the Unionists attacked in overpowering strength at once, the day was lost; but if the battle-tried veterans of Lee's Second or Third Corps arrived in time, the Confederates would block effectively the road to Richmond.

As the hot afternoon passed slowly, the heat seemed to be a third belligerent. In the fields that faced the Federals in the woods, the Confederates scarcely could believe that May sun could be so furious. An hour under its rays seemed as long as a day should be. Back on the road from the Wilderness, Ewell's men were marching to Anderson's assistance under the eyes of the commanding General himself, but they had "a very distressing march through intense heat and thick dust and smoke from burning woods." [47] The Federals fared no better. If they were less exposed to the sun, they were on unfamiliar ground and were tired after a night-long march.[48]

About 5 o'clock, the edge of the woods in front of Anderson's right became alive with Federals. In front of the left, also, there was activity. Soon the fire quickened. Scattered cheers were audible. The bluecoats were coming! At the sight of them, the weary artillerists found strength to ram home the charge and to send it roaring into the ranks. Infantrymen behind the rails and in the shallow trenches took their stations, looked to their rifles, and waited for the enemy to get within easy range. This advance would decide the day, one way or the other!

On the centre, the attack was half-hearted; on the right the

---

[47] Ewell in O. R., 36, pt. 1, p. 1071. For the route, see ibid., 51, pt. 2, p. 902.
[48] Humphreys, 65.

enemy threatened to turn the flank and to get in rear of Kershaw. Vigorous as was the fire of the artillery, it could not halt the enemy. The prospect was ominous when the Confederates had, once more, their old-time battlefield luck. Ewell arrived! His front Division, Rodes's, was thrown forward at once to the right of Kershaw,[49] That was enough. As soon as the Federals realized that the Southern front was stronger, they withdrew. Part of Rodes's Division pursued. Cullen Battle, leading his Brigade, pushed on 600 yards and struck the enemy's works. The famous old Sixth Alabama and part of the Sixty-first threw themselves over the low parapet and came to grips with the enemy, but they were too few in number. The flag of the Sixth was taken; about fifty men from the two regiments were captured;[50] the others recoiled. General Battle still believed that he could drive the enemy farther. Seizing the flag of the Third Alabama, he called to the men around him to go forward. For once, they would not respond. Dodson Ramseur, who had shared the attack,[51] now came up and added his efforts to Battle's in an attempt to get the troops to charge. It was to no purpose. Battle said the next day that long marching, constant labor and their rapid advance had exhausted his men. At the moment he was angry and humiliated,[52] but he need not have been. Rodes's advance had decided the doubtful action. The enemy attacked no more that evening. Ewell put Johnson's Division on obscure, night-covered ground to Rodes's right. Early's old Division was held in reserve.[53]

Anderson had won his battle. It was because he had started early.[54]

[49] *O. R.*, 36, pt. 1, pp. 1056, 1071.  [50] *O. R.*, 36, pt. 1, p. 561.
[51] *Ibid.*, 1081.  [52] *Ibid.*, 1084.
[53] *Ibid.*, 1042, 1071, 1093. This and all other accounts of the action of May 8 are unsatisfactory because of the absence of reports by officers who participated most actively in the fighting. Maj. Gen. Horatio G. Wright, who succeeded Maj. Gen. John Sedgwick in command of the VI Corps, wrote no report. Reference in subsidiary reports to the advance of the Corps in the afternoon are vague. No report was filed by Brig. Gen. S. W. Crawford, who headed the 3rd Division of the V Corps. His subordinates were equally negligent. It consequently is impossible to say when Crawford was moved from the right to the left of the V Corps. He undoubtedly was on the left when Rodes attacked (cf. *O. R.*, 36, pt. 1, p. 541), because the colors taken by a detachment of Griffin's Division serving with Crawford were those of the Sixth Alabama, which attacked on the right of Kershaw. See *ibid.*, 545, 561, 567.
[54] For a critique, see *infra*, p. 444.

# CHAPTER XX

## FROM MULE SHOE TO BLOODY ANGLE

THROUGH THE MORNING of the hot 9th of May, the Confederate soldiers around Spotsylvania kept one eye on the enemy, who seemed to be taking a day of rest, and the other eye on their earth-works, which were being strengthened hourly [1] against an adversary whose units were being identified rapidly. Examination of prisoners had shown the Southerners where the various Corps had advanced and where they had fought. Grant had started on May 3-4 from his camps North of the Rapidan and had moved with three Corps of infantry, the II, V and VI, and with a cavalry Corps of three Divisions. The IX Army Corps, which was inde-pendent of Meade and under the direct orders of General Grant, was to follow the main force. Grant's plan was to strike far enough down the Rapidan to avoid the defenses on Mine Run.[2] Once across the Rapidan, he intended to hold the Army of Northern Virginia while Gen. B. F. Butler's Army from the lower Peninsula moved up James River in an effort to capture Richmond. If Butler failed, Grant purposed to hammer Lee so hard and so steadily that the Confederate commander would have to retreat or, at the least, would have to keep the Southern forces together without detach-ing any of them for another invasion of the North.[3]

Grant had been immensely relieved that the crossing on the 4th had been unopposed, because he had expected a desperate struggle at the fords.[4] Spared that, he had advanced confidently into the Wilderness and had headed westward to meet Lee. On the 5th, when the march was resumed, the troops that attacked Ewell on the old turnpike were the V Corps of Maj. Gen. G. K. Warren. The fight on the Plank Road had been opened by a Division of Maj. Gen. John Sedgwick's VI Corps and had been pressed by the II Corps, under Maj. Gen. W. S. Hancock. It was Hancock who, on the morning of the 6th, attacked Heth and Wilcox along the

[1] Jed. Hotchkiss' MS Diary, 341; Alexander, 513.
[2] See supra, p. 274, and O. R., 36, pt. 1, p. 189.
[3] Ibid., 17.                    [4] Ibid., 18.

Plank Road and drove them back on Longstreet. The V and VI Corps fought that day against Ewell, but made little progress. Gordon's attack that afternoon, as the Confederates knew already, had been directed against the right flank of Sedgwick's Corps. That same day, May 6, Burnside's IX Corps had arrived in the Wilderness, but instead of placing itself in rear of the right of the VI Corps, as "Jube" Early had insisted it had done,[5] it had undertaken to get a position between Warren's left and Hancock's right and to attack there.[6]

The movement of the Army of the Potomac toward Spotsylvania had been prompted by what Grant had seen of the strength of the Confederate field works on the morning of the 7th of May. He had concluded then that Lee's Army no longer would face him in the open field but would await attack. "I therefore determined," the Union chief explained later, "to push on and put my whole force between [Lee] and Richmond."[7] The V Corps had been advanced for the march on Spotsylvania and had been the force against which Fitz Lee was fighting when "Dick" Anderson arrived.[8]

While few of these details of Grant's plan were known to the Confederates, no thoughtful officer in gray could overlook the fact that on the 5th, on the 6th, and again on the 8th, when contact had been established, the aggressor had been the Federals. This new commander, Grant, manifestly believed in the offensive. He was trying persistently to wrest the initiative from the Southerners. Burnside, in December, 1862, had crossed the Rappahannock on the 11th and had retreated on the night of the 15th–16th.[9] Hooker had passed the river on April 29, had returned into the Wilderness on the afternoon of May 1, and had recrossed the Rappahannock during the dark hours of May 5–6.[10] In contrast, this new adversary on the fifth day of his offensive was farther South than he had been since crossing the Rapidan.

This was by no means the full measure of Grant's aggressiveness. Although Butler's operation against Richmond was not being conducted skillfully, it involved gravest danger to the capital. Beauregard and Robert Ransom had been summoned to cope with it, but there was divided command and all the resultant confu-

5 See *supra*, p. 369.          6 *O. R.*, 36, pt. 1, p. 906.
7 *O. R.*, 36, pt. 1, p. 19.      8 *Ibid.*, pp. 191, 540–51 .
9 See Vol. II, pp. 332, 381.    10 *Ibid.*, pp. 524, 532, 644.

sion.[11] From Winchester on the 9th Maj. Gen. Franz Sigel was starting in the hope of forming a junction high up the Shenandoah Valley with troops of Brig. Gen. George Crook, who was in command of the raid against the Virginia and Tennessee Railroad.[12] Crook that morning met on Cloyd's Mountain, near Dublin, Pulaski County, a small Confederate force and worsted it. For a day or two, the railway was to be at his mercy.[13]

More menacing than this was a cavalry raid launched that day by Sheridan but, at the moment, unknown to the Confederate infantry around Spotsylvania. As they dug dirt under a sun that July would not have disowned, the Southerners talked of cavalry, but more of their own than of Sheridan's. Many of the Confederate infantrymen had twisted their jealousy into a contempt for the mounted arm. Artillery with equal readiness mocked the men who had nothing to haul with horses except themselves. Now there was a change of feeling. Let an artillerist confess it in reviewing the defense Stuart's men had made on the 8th before the arrival of any infantry: ". . . This Spotsylvania business was a 'white day' for the cavalry. When the Army came to know of what the cavalry had done, and of how they had done it, there was a general outburst of admiration—the recognition that brave men give to the brave. . . . Everybody was satisfied the cavalry would do, they were 'all right.' We couldn't praise them enough, we were proud of them. The remark was even suffered to pass, as nothing to his discredit particularly, that our 'Magnus Apollo,' General Lee, himself, had once been in the cavalry, and no one resented it now. We knew that it was when he was younger . . ."[14]

If the cavalry were to be congratulated on their fight of the 8th, at least two men of rank in the infantry were to be wished the best of success in new positions. The circumstances of their advancement were unhappy. Powell Hill's malady had grown worse rather than better. By the 8th he was so ill that he could not sit up. On the march that day, Jubal Early had been notified that he was assigned, during Hill's disability, to the command of the Third Corps. Anderson's appointment in Longstreet's place had left only Heth and Wilcox as divisional leaders of Hill's Corps.

[11] O. R., 36, pt. 2, p. 978 ff.
[12] O. R., 37, pt. 1, p. 407. On the 11th, Sigel reached Woodstock (ibid., 427).
[13] Crook's report is in ibid., 9. The Confederate reports are in ibid., 44 ff.
[14] Dame. 100, 106.

Neither of these two was sufficiently seasoned for the handling of a Corps. Early appeared to be, and had done well with Ewell's command during the Mine Run operations.

Transfer of Early meant, of course, that his Division had to pass to other hands. He had, it will be remembered, three Brigades only, because Hoke's had not yet rejoined. Of the three commanders of Brigades, John Pegram was wounded. That left Harry Hays and John B. Gordon. The commission of Hays antedated that of Gordon by more than eleven months,[15] but Lee believed Gordon better qualified for higher command. Besides, Lee wished to recognize Gordon's exploit of the 6th in turning the right flank of the VI Corps. Already, in a ride with the commanding General on the morning of the 7th, Gordon had heard from Lee's own reserved lips how highly "Marse Robert" esteemed what he had done.[16] Now Gordon was to have recognition almost unique. In order that Gordon might assume command of Early's Division, Hays was transferred from Early's Division to Johnson's and was entrusted with Stafford's Louisiana Brigade in addition to his own. This increased Hays's prestige at the same time that it assured competent leadership for the soldiers of the fallen Stafford. To take the place of Hays's Brigade in Early's Division, Ewell was directed to transfer to Early's Division the Brigade of Robert D. Johnston or some other of the five Brigades of Rodes's Division.[17] Old soldiers might have asked themselves whether so many changes ever had been made by Army Headquarters to give a Brigadier General a Division.

This was, of course, a most notable compliment for Gordon, but when it was taken with the other changes necessitated by four days' fighting, it disclosed a startling shift of command. The record of five days now stood: One Lieutenant General wounded and another incapacitated by sickness; two divisional commanders elevated, at least temporarily, to corps command; two Brigadiers entrusted with Divisions; three Brigadiers killed or mortally wounded; two others seriously wounded; at least six Brigades passed into the hands of senior Colonels.[18]

15 This comparison is with Gordon's second appointment of May 11, 1863, and not with the appointment of Nov. 1, 1862, which was not confirmed because no vacancy existed.
16 *Gordon*, 267.                    17 *O. R.*, 36, pt. 2, p. 974.
18 These were successors to J. M. Jones, Jenkins, Pegram, Benning, Gordon and Mahone. The Brigade of Stafford is not counted because it had been consolidated with Hays's.

So stood the command on May 9. As the hours dragged by without action, the Third Corps arrived and took position on the right of the Second, in the immediate vicinity of Spotsylvania Court House. At the moment, there were no Unionists in front of this Corps, except at a distance on the Fredericksburg Road,[19] but the extension of the Federal front opposite the Confederate right was expected. The new chief engineer of Lee's Army, Maj. Gen. Martin Smith, was laying out a line which, when completed, would anchor the flanks on the steep banks of the little river Po and would make the most of such natural advantages as the ground offered.[20]

In the afternoon, while this line was taking form, there were some indications that the enemy might be planning a move against the Confederate left. Skirmishers in front of Anderson shook off their sleepiness and opened an annoying fire. Federal troops were said to be operating well beyond the Confederate left flank and also across the Po. To combat those North of the stream, Early was ordered to move one of his idle Divisions and was instructed to dispatch another Division the next morning by a detour to deal with the troops on the south side of the Po. All this was done according to order. When Heth attacked in the vicinity of White's Shop on the morning of the 10th, first indications were that he might have a heavy, all-day battle, but soon the fighting slack-ened. The enemy seemed intent on retreat rather than on combat. Then, in the early afternoon, close to the Po, the enemy made a resolute stand. Heth attacked, met with a repulse, advanced again with the same result, went forward a third time and, as he thought, at last drove a stubbornly resisting enemy back across the river.

"Jube" Early was much pleased. The Division, he said after-ward, "behaved very handsomely." [21] It did, but it misunderstood the operation in which it was engaged. The whole of the Federal II Corps had moved to the south side of the river as a result of a curious observation by Grant on the afternoon of the 9th. Together with Meade and Hancock, he was on the right of the Federal line when a Confederate wagon train passed temptingly close along a road on the south bank. A few shots from a Union battery sent the train off in such great disorder that Grant thought a Division,

19 *Early,* 353.
20 For a description of these defenses, see 3 *R. E. Lee,* 309 ff.
21 *Early,* 354.

crossing swiftly, might capture it. After a Division had reached the south bank, where it had no luck in overtaking the wagons, Grant concluded that the whole Corps, if thrown to the same side of the stream, might outflank the entire Confederate position. Had the Corps moved at an hour when it could have delivered a surprise attack, it might have done great mischief, but its movement on the 9th gave away the plan. On the 10th, before the Corps could deploy, it was confronted by two Divisions and then was recalled for another mission. Withdrawal during the forenoon consequently was under orders and not under the compulsion of attack. The final fight of the afternoon had been with Brigades that were covering the departure of the last of the three Divisions.[22] All that was accomplished by the action was the maiming and killing of good soldiers. On the Confederate side, the most serious individual losses were those of Brig. Gen. Harry Hays and of Brig. Gen. H. H. Walker, who had succeeded to the command of the Field-Brockenbrough-Mayo Brigade.[23] Hays would recover easily, but Walker was so badly wounded in one foot that amputation was necessary [24]—another casualty that would require a new appointment or the consolidation of two Brigades.

Upon the wounding of Walker and the withdrawal of the Federals, the battle quickly shifted. Three times during the afternoon the enemy attacked on the front of Anderson and once so seriously that the Texas Brigade was forced temporarily to withdraw.[25] After the third repulse, most of the V Corps appeared to have had fighting enough for the day, but Hancock's II Corps made another assault in which some of Warren's men participated. This, too, failed.

From the Confederate centre, Ewell's men had watched as much as they could observe of the combat to the left of them and, no doubt, after the manner of soldiers, had felt that they could have done better than the First Corps in repelling the attack; but in the mind of ranking officers of the Second Corps, there was no complacency over their position. When Ewell's men had formed on the right of Anderson, on the afternoon and evening of May

22 Hancock's report in O. R., 36, pt. 1, pp. 330–31. The account in Francis A. Walker's History of the Second Army Corps, 447 ff., is admirable and is intelligently critical.
23 O. R., 36, pt. 1, p. 1029.
24 Early, 354.
25 Alexander, 515; Field in 14 S.H.S.P., 547; Dame, 168.

8, in a manner to be described later, they began to fortify an awkward and irregular salient to the northward. Its apex was almost
a mile from the point of divergence of an east-and-west line. The
extreme width was about 1200 yards. This manifestly was a difficult position, though defensible with artillery, but evacuation of
it would have left within reach of the Federals two stretches of
open ground from which Ewell thought the enemy could command the Southern line.[26] Further, if the salient were abandoned,
a stretch of the Shady Grove Road much needed for the movement of men and supplies would be so exposed that the Confederates could not use it.[27] The decision consequently was to hold
the salient with ample artillery and infantry, but to construct a
second line across the base.[28] For reasons never satisfactorily explained, work on this line was deferred. In the salient from left
to right was part of Rodes's Division and the whole of Johnson's.
To the right of Johnson, beyond the salient and in the direction of
Spotsylvania Court House, was Wilcox's Division.

On the western face of the salient, George Doles's Georgia Brigade of Rodes's command held an incomplete work and, about
150 to 200 yards in front of it, a main line in the form of a lesser
salient that looked out on approximately 200 yards of open ground.
Beyond this field, to the westward and northwestward, was woodland. Through the woods and straight to the Confederate works
ran a road from the Shelton or Scott house about half a mile distant.[29] In support of Doles was the Third Company of the Richmond Howitzer Battalion.

Over troops and guns and ground, Doles had cast a vigilant eye.
He must have realized that his position was dangerously vulnerable, because that afternoon of the 10th, when artillery fire was
directed against him, he placed most of his men behind the front
line of works. Rifles were loaded. Bayonets had been affixed.[30]
The men were admonished to keep well covered. Sharply at 6
o'clock, the Federal bombardment ceased. Five minutes of silence
passed. To Doles and his men, the end of the day's combat may
have seemed at hand. Another hour and a half would bring darkness, food perhaps, and then sleep.

26 *O. R.*, 36, pt. 1, p. 1071. For the circumstances in which this position was occupied
by the Second Corps, see *infra*, p. 445 ff.
27 Col. C. S. Venable in 14 *S.H.S.P.*, 527.    28 *O. R.*, 36, pt. 1, p. 1072.
29 See Gen. Emory Upton's description in *O. R.*, 36, pt. 1, p. 667.
30 *O. R.*, 36, pt. 1, p. 668.

At 6:10 there was a breaking of branches and the thump of many feet. As startled Georgians looked over the parapet, a wild cheer rose from the edge of the woods, 200 yards away. Out from among the green trees swept one line. Close behind it was a second. A third emerged almost immediately. There scarcely was time for a volley before the Federals were at the parapet. The boldest of those who sprang over the work were shot. Hundreds of other bluecoats poured into the trench. A furious hand-to-hand clash followed, but not for long. The Georgians were outnumbered. They broke off the fight; they ran toward the second line; scores of them, surrounded, had to drop their guns and hold up their hands.[31]

By this time, the alarm had spread far. The Howitzer Battery had opened already. It fired while the enemy was in front; it continued to fire when the enemy, moving to left and to right, got on its flanks. Even when the Federals reached their rear the men of the battery poured in canister, nor did the Richmond artillerists halt until it was manifest they were doing less damage to the enemy than to their friends, who were beginning to rally. At last the guns were overrun. The heroic Captain, B. H. Smith, and twenty-four of his men were captured by the side of their pieces.[32]

Quick action was taken by the Confederates to mend the break. Battle's Alabama Brigade was put in line directly ahead of the attacking Federals. Gordon and Johnson closed on the Federal flanks.[33] As soon as the advance reached the captured battery, artillerists from Cutshaw's Battalion rushed forward, manned the guns and used them against the enemy.[34] Farther up the main salient, the Confederates saw other lines deploying for an assault, but they opened on these with abundant artillery before the Federals came dangerously close. Almost at once, the bluecoats, who were in thinner timber, withdrew out of range. This discouraged the column that had broken into Doles's lines. For a few minutes it fought to retain its ground. Then the Unionists ducked over the parapet and ran for their own lines. Although they left about 100 dead in the trenches and many on the open ground, they had sent

31 *Ibid.*, 668.          32 *O. R.*, 36, pt. 1, p. 1089.
33 *O. R.*, 36, pt. 1, p. 1072.
34 This was the work of Capt. Asher W. Garber's Staunton Artillery (*ibid.*, 1044, 1086, 1087; 33 *S.H.S.P.*, 342). After the recovery of the battery, Maj. David Watson, who had helped defend it, shared in working one of the pieces until struck down with a wound of which he subsequently died (*O. R.*, 36, pt. 1, p. 1089).

to the rear a disputed number of Confederates. Men of Doles's Brigade said that 300 had been captured.[35] The Federal commander reported the total as 1000 to 1200.[36]

This affair created much talk in both armies. Confederate commanders had praise for the valor of the defense and the promptness of the recovery, but some of the officers became more concerned than ever for the safety of the principal salient which the soldiers by this time had dubbed the "Mule Shoe." Federals commended the fine planning and the vigorous assault. The operation was directed by Col. Emory Upton, 24 years of age, who commanded the Second Brigade of Horatio Wright's 1st Division of the VI Corps. For the excellence of his conduct, which accorded with his record, Upton was recommended immediately by General Grant for promotion to the rank of Brigadier General.[37] The troops that were to have advanced simultaneously on Upton's left belonged to Brig. Gen. Gershom Mott's 4th Division of Hancock's II Corps. Mott made no report. One of his Brigadiers explained that the advancing force was enfiladed by artillery and was compelled to withdraw.[38] This explanation, if given verbally by Mott, scarcely was acceptable to Army Headquarters. Meade blamed Mott for the failure of the attack.[39] Charles A. Dana, Assistant Secretary of War, who was then with the Army, telegraphed indignantly that "we were disgraced" by the retreat of Mott's Division.[40]

Use of that word "disgrace" to describe a failure to advance was itself an indication of the new and more stubborn spirit of the Union Army. The morning after Upton attacked, General Grant wrote the Chief of Staff regarding the situation at the end of six days of fighting. Not a word was said of the assault of May 10, as if that had been a casual incident. The resolution of Grant showed itself in the final clause of this sentence: "I am now sending back to Belle Plain all my wagons for a fresh supply of provisions and ammunition, and propose to fight it out on this line if it takes all summer."[41] Of this determined spirit on the part of their adversary, the Confederates did not yet have the full measure, but they had seen enough by the 11th of May to make them certain

35 *Thomas*, 14.                          36 *O. R.*, 36, pt. 1, p. 668.
37 *O. R.*, 36, pt. 2, p. 695.            38 *O. R.*, 36, pt. 1, p. 487.
39 *O. R.*, 36, pt. 1, p. 191.           40 *Ibid.*, 66.
41 *O. R.*, 26, pt. 1, p. 4.

they faced the hardest campaign in their military experience. It was, perhaps, because of this unvoiced conclusion on the part of the individual fighting man that the Army went earnestly to work to improve the earthworks and, still more, the abatis.[42]

No fighting interrupted the labor on the works during the morning of the 11th. The enemy made no move. Digging dirt was, moreover, less arduous than it had been for several days. Temperature was lower. Showers laid the dust. During the early afternoon, as the rain became steady,[43] the Federals began to stir. On the Confederate left, the enemy made demonstrations that suggested another crossing of the Po similar to that of the 9th. General Early was directed to send troops to that quarter and to occupy the strategic crossroads at Shady Grove Church.[44] Obediently, "Old Jube" started two Brigades of Wilcox's Division. The only other shift of position was in the extension westward and northward of Wilcox's left so that it joined the right flank of "Maryland" Steuart's Brigade on the east side of the "Mule Shoe." [45]

To that "Mule Shoe" late in the afternoon rode the commanding General. He was met at the Harrison House, near the base of the salient, by Ewell and Armistead Long, chief of artillery of the Second Corps. With such help as these and other officers could give him, the commanding General had to sift contradictory intelligence reports from three sources. Outposts on the Confederate left, as indicated already, warned that the enemy was seeking to turn that flank by crossing the Po and sweeping to the East. From the Confederate right came reports based on observations made at a church which commanded a wide view of the roads in rear of the Federal left.[46] The substance of this information was that the enemy seemed to be moving away from the line. Several observers at the church were satisfied the enemy was withdrawing

42 Cf. *McHenry Howard*, 290: "The men fell to work with increased energy."
43 Some differences appear in the description of the weather on the afternoon of May 11, but they are not important. See *McHenry Howard*, 293; Ewell in *O. R.*, 36, pt. 1, p. 1072; *Richmond Howitzers*, 3, 52.
44 *Early*, 355.
45 6 *S.H.S.P.*, 73. Maj. McHenry Howard (*op. cit.*, 292-93) was of opinion that nothing, except perhaps a picket-line, joined Johnson's right and Wilcox's left, which was held by Lane's Brigade. If Howard merely forgot the arrival of Lane on Steuart's right, that is entirely understandable; but if Lane moved up the salient and the A.A.G. of Johnson's right Brigade did not know it at the time, the defenders of the salient were chargeable with serious negligence.
46 This edifice must have been the one on Michler's map slightly more than half a mile South of the Court House.

his left toward Fredericksburg.[47] Somewhat to the same effect was the intelligence forwarded by Gen. "Rooney" Lee, who had returned to duty and was in rear of the Federal left. He stated that the Federal wounded were being sent to Belle Plain and that wagons had been moving in the rear of the Union Army all night of the 10th–11th.[48]

In the evening, Heth, whose headquarters were in the church near the Court House, had the pleasure of welcoming the sick Hill and, a little later, the commanding General. In the free conversation that then began, some of the officers declared that Grant was slaughtering his troops by throwing them against earthworks. Lee was not of that mind. "Gentlemen," he said, "I think General Grant has managed his affairs remarkably well up to the present time." He turned to Heth: "My opinion is the enemy are preparing to retreat tonight to Fredericksburg. I wish you to have everything in readiness to pull out at a moment's notice, but do not disturb your artillery till you commence moving. We must attack these people if they retreat."

Hill spoke up: "General Lee, let them continue to attack our breastworks; we can stand that very well."

"General," Heth said, "you witnessed Burnside's attack on me this morning." When Lee said he had, Heth gave his losses and his estimate of Federal casualties. Then the conversation became more general for a minute, but Lee wished to emphasize one truth: "This army cannot stand a siege; we must end this business on the battlefield, not in a fortified place."[49]

While these words raised before Heth's eyes the picture of a siege of Richmond, Lee rode to the Harrison House on Ewell's sector of the "Mule Shoe." The guns were deep in the woods, from which it would be slow work to extricate them in the darkness along narrow, winding roads. It would be necessary, Ewell was told, to withdraw the advanced guns before nightfall and to place them where they could be started when the direction of the enemy's march could be determined.[50]

As soon as the commanding General left, Armistead Long, Corps Chief of artillery, began to send to the rear the exposed

[47] 6 S.H.S.P., 74.
[48] O. R., 51, pt. 2, pp. 916–17. Cf. Grant's dispatch of May 11 quoted supra in the text.
[49] Heth's MS Memoirs, 158 ff.
[50] O. R., 36, pt. 1, pp. 1044, 1086.

artillery. Of this movement, Ed. Johnson was not informed by Ewell. The first Johnson knew of it was when he saw guns going to the rear.[51] As other infantrymen on the right face of the salient observed the batteries limber up and depart, there was some sur- prise and apprehension, but the men who thus were left without support of the "long arm" told themselves that other guns would take the place of those withdrawn.[52] Only eight fieldpieces, in two of Cutshaw's batteries, remained in the "Mule Shoe." Twenty- two [53] were halted near the Court House and about a mile and a half in rear of the salient.[54]

Guns of the First Corps were handled differently. Porter Alex- ander did not relish the idea of withdrawing all artillery support from positions close to the enemy. Instead of moving the pieces to the rear that night, he visited each of his batteries in turn, had all the ammunition chests mounted, and placed all the equipment where it could be pulled quickly to the rear with minimum noise over roads he took pains to clear.[55]

By the time Alexander had done this and Long had shifted his guns from the salient to their temporary camp, the weather had grown worse. The night air was raw and penetrating, the rain was cold. Where fires could be lighted, the men huddled disconso- lately around them. Pickets were shivering and miserable and became wetter, if possible, every time they moved under the new leaves of the underbrush.[56] It added nothing to the comfort of the dripping Southerners to hear above the patter of rain the music of Federal bands.[57] In that saturated blackness, polkas were wails and marches were dirges. "There was," a sharpshooter remem- bered, "a nameless something in the air which told every man that a crisis was at hand." [58]

Long before midnight, the pickets outside the right face of the salient heard other sounds than those of music from the Federal front. A steady rumble was audible, though its nature could not be determined. The well-trained skirmishers of Steuart's Brigade

51 O. R., 36, pt. 1, p. 1079.      52 McHenry Howard, 293.

53 Alexander, 518.

54 7 S.H.S.P., 535. One section of Page's Battalion was detached that night to escort a wagon train (O. R., 36, pt. 1, p. 1044).

55 Alexander, 518.

56 4 B. & L., 170. Reports of this bad weather are vague, though vehement. From its duration, the storm evidently was a protracted nor'easter of the sort usually described in Virginia as "the long spell in May."

57 21 S.H.S.P., 252.      58 21 S.H.S.P., 245.

immediately reported that something was astir. Two of the brigade staff at once went out toward the skirmish line and stood listening for half an hour on the parapet. Reports were correct. The enemy must be moving. Only that could account for the slow, steady rumble. It sounded like a waterfall or the grinding of some powerful machine.[59] Thousands of men evidently were in motion. There was no way of ascertaining, as yet, whether they were proceeding to the right or were massing for an attack on the "Mule Shoe."

Steuart was notified. He promptly concluded that the enemy's movement was preliminary to an assault on the salient, and he so advised Johnson, whom he requested to return the artillery that had been withdrawn.[60] It is possible that like information came to Johnson from his other brigade commanders, but John M. Jones's and Stafford's men had lost their experienced leaders and perhaps were lacking in vigilance. Walker's Brigade was on the extreme left of the divisional front, next Doles, and may not have heard so plainly the mysterious sounds of motion.[61]

Whatever the extent of Johnson's information, it sufficed to arouse all of his soldierly alarm. He at once wrote Ewell that the enemy was massing in his front and he repeated Steuart's request that the artillery be returned at once.[62] This note reached Ewell shortly after midnight. Johnson's staff officer who delivered the message did not feel that Ewell was sufficiently alive to the danger, and on returning to Johnson, the young officer prevailed on Johnson to ride in person to Ewell.[63] By this time, probably, Ewell had started Johnson's first message to Long by courier. A little later Johnson was told that the artillery would be back in position not later than 2 A.M.[64]

The message from Ewell to Long, either by the first courier or by a second whom Johnson dispatched with his usual care, did not reach the corps chief of artillery till 3:30.[65] Within ten minutes

[59] McHenry Howard, 294.                    [60] Ibid.
[61] In his account of the battle (21 S.H.S.P., 235) General Walker did not mention any sound of movement before dawn.
[62] O. R., 36, pt. 1, p. 1072. In this reference, Ewell did not mention the request by Johnson for a return of the artillery, but Wilcox wrote (6 S.H.S.P., 74) that Johnson twice told him the return of the batteries was asked. See also Col. Thomas H. Carter in 21 S.H.S.P. 240.
[63] O. R., 36, pt. 1, p. 1072; 33 S.H.S.P., 336–37. There are some irreconcilable, though minor differences in the later narratives of this episode.
[64] 21 S.H.S.P., 253.
[65] 21 S.H.S.P., 240; O. R., 36, pt. 1, p. 1086. For a critique of this delay, see infra, p. 446.

after that, Long's instructions for the dispatch of batteries to the salient were given Maj. Richard C. M. Page, who commanded one of the battalions of artillery that had been hauled from the salient the previous evening.[66] Page got the guns under way with promptness and speed.[67]

About the time Page started, a staff officer of Johnson's was going the round of the Brigades and was telling the officers of the day to arouse all the Colonels and to have them awaken the men, who must see that their rifles were in good order.[68] From Jones's Brigade and possibly from others, a regiment moved out to relieve the pickets.[69] One regiment of Jones's former command already had been detached.[70] Consequently till the Forty-second Virginia returned from picket duty, three regiments of the Brigade would be missing. The Brigade had six, but most of them were pathetically small, as well as half demoralized by the death of Jones and the lack of a competent successor.[71] Like all the other regiments in the salient, they were depressed by the chill weather, which now had developed into a thick and chilling fog.

This fog clung close to the ground,[72] until about 4:30. Then it began to lift slightly.[73] Objects close at hand were dimly visible, though if an attack were delivered, friend scarcely could be distinguished from foe.[74] Ten minutes later, as dawn reluctantly spread, there came a sudden burst of fire from the direction of the Landrum House, which was approximately 550 yards North and slightly East of the apex of the salient. To those who knew that the reserve picket was there, this fire was ominous; but, as yet, nothing was visible.[75]

Soon, from the northwest face of the salient, the approaching tramp of many men could be heard.[76] A moment more and from a distance of about 300 yards there came a mighty cheer,[77] and then the sight of bluecoats advancing in a dense mass on the salient.[78] Waiting Confederates rose and gave the enemy a volley. From part of the front of Jones, numbers considered, it was an effective volley, but from Walker's Brigade it was feeble. Powder had been dampened during the night. Officers had not taken pains

[66] Page in 7 S.H.S.P., 535, 536.
[67] O. R., 36, pt. 1, p. 1044.
[68] 21 S.H.S.P., 252.
[69] Ibid., 243.
[70] Ibid., 251.
[71] McHenry Howard, 292.
[72] 21 S.H.S.P., 234.
[73] O. R., 36, pt. 1, p. 358.
[74] O. R., 36, pt. 1, pt. 1087.
[75] Cf. O. R., 36, pt. 1, p. 358.
[76] Gen. James A. Walker in 21 S.H.S.P., 235.
[77] O. R., 36. pt. 1, p. 385.
[78] Ibid.

to see that the charges had been drawn and dry cartridges rammed home.[79]

Johnson by this time had sensed the point of extreme danger and had ridden up to that part of the line nearest the Landrum House. Dismounting, he hobbled about with the help of his long stick and exhorted the men to fire fast. The artillery was coming to help, he said; it soon would be there. When, presently, he saw Page's guns moving up, he sent back to order a gallop.[80] To some eyes, the guns had appeared to move slowly,[81] but at Johnson's word, the drivers lashed the teams. Bouncing and careening, the artillery rushed forward and began to scatter to assigned positions.[82] Capt. William Page Carter [83] was in the lead and pushed his battery straight toward the apex of the salient. As the first gun unlimbered, Carter sprang forward to help load it. One round was discharged at the advancing enemy. "Stop firing that gun," a voice shouted. Captain Carter turned . . . and looked into a score of rifles held by determined men in blue. The enemy already was in the salient and was in rear of guns and infantry.[84]

Federals appeared everywhere the startled Confederates looked. Breaking over the parapet opposite the Landrum House,[85] the Union soldiers quickly found the gap in the front of Jones's Brigade, poured through, got behind the "Stonewall" Brigade on the northwest face of the salient without a direct assault,[86] and captured nearly the whole of that famous command. Simultaneously, plunging ahead, the Federals overwhelmed Jones's men and seized Ed. Johnson himself. He barely escaped death because he con-

[79] 21 *S.H.S.P.*, 236.      [80] *O. R.*, 36, pt. 1, p. 1080.
[81] *McHenry Howard*, 296.

[82] *O. R.*, 36, pt. 1, p. 1080; 7 *S.H.S.P.*, 536. In his report, Ewell said (*O. R.*, 36, pt. 1, p. 1072) that "different artillery was sent back to the salient," but, in part at least, he was mistaken. Page's Battalion had occupied until the previous evening the "toe" and the right of the "Mule Shoe" (21 *S.H.S.P.*, 240). Page's defense (7 *S.H.S.P.*, 535 ff) showed that he knew thoroughly the ground within the salient, and that before starting from camp he told his battery commanders where to go. Neither Johnson in his report (*O. R.*, 36, pt. 1, p. 1080), nor Long in his (*ibid.*, 1086), had any fault to find with Page. On the contrary, both commended him. So did Pendleton (*ibid.*, 1044), who stated that Page "moved up with extraordinary speed and arrived at the proper point, but not in time to arrest disaster." As Ewell, even after his physical decline, never was a man to blame others falsely to protect his own reputation, it is probable that he overlooked the retention in the salient overnight of eight guns of Cutshaw's Battalion. He may have thought that Cutshaw should have been returned to the "Mule Shoe."

[83] Brother of Col. Thomas H. Carter and in command of the Colonel's famous King William Artillery.

[84] 21 *S.H.S.P.*, 240. At a little distance, Lieut. Charles L. Coleman of Capt. Charles Montgomery's battery fell mortally wounded in the midst of the confusion. To a gunner's cry, "Where shall I point the gun?" the Lieutenant answered, "At the Yankees." He spoke no other words before he died.

[85] *O. R.*, 36, pt. 1, p. 335.      [86] 21 *S.H.S.P.*, 236.

Final Confederate Works at the "Mule Shoe" or "Bloody Angle," continued southward to Spotsylvania Court House. The numerals indicate: 1, immediate objective of attack by Upton, May 10; 2, "the Apex," approximate point of Federal penetration, May 12; 3, "Gordon's Line" or "Incomplete Line," styled by the Federals the "Second Rebel Line"; 4, the line constructed May 12 and occupied that night; 5, "Heth's Salient." After the Michler map of 1867

tinued his efforts to rally his soldiers and ignored repeated demands that he surrender.[87] To the right of the salient, where a stronger resistance was offered, part of "Maryland" Steuart's Brigade, including its commander, were made prisoners. All eight of Cutshaw's guns and twelve of Page's fourteen were taken.[88]

After this brilliant coup de main, thousands of the men pressed southward down the salient in pursuit of the Confederates who escaped. The Federals met with little resistance until they reached, midway of the salient, about 5:30 A.M. an incomplete line of the existence of which they had no previous knowledge.[89] Already they had achieved much. In three quarters of an hour they had captured two general officers, more than 2000 men and twenty guns.[90]

The Confederates who met the advancing bluecoats at the incomplete line were men of Early's old Division, which John B. Gordon was directing. Gordon's orders had been to support either Johnson or Rodes. Accordingly, Gordon had placed his three Brigades—one of them new to the Division—on the left side of the salient, near the McCoull House,[91] in rear of Rodes's right and Johnson's left. During the night of the 11th–12th, after Johnson notified him that the Federals were massing in front of the salient, Gordon had sent Pegram's Brigade to Johnson, who posted Pegram's men near the left of the Division. His other troops Gordon had disposed where he thought they could be most quickly available in accordance with his orders. When the attack had opened, he threw Johnston's Brigade forward. After it was repulsed quickly to the North of the McCoull House. Gordon, "with that splendid audacity which characterized him," [92] ordered three regiments of his old Brigade to deploy and to demonstrate. So admirably did these troops do their part that the Federal advance was checked momentarily.[93]

[87] McHenry Howard, 301.
[88] O. R., 36, pt. 1, p. 1044.
[89] O. R., 36, pt. 1, p. 336.
[90] The number of prisoners was much disputed. Ewell (O. R., 36, pt. 1, p. 1072) put the figure at 2000. Meade (ibid., 192) gave the number as "over 3000." Hancock (ibid., 335) said that "nearly 4000" were taken.
[91] This residence, mentioned in many descriptions of the battle, was situated about 200 yards from the northern end of the "Mule Shoe" and approximately 300 yards from the western face of the salient. See Hubert A. Gurney, A Study of the McCoull House and Farm, MS. Fredericksburg and Spotsylvania National Military Park. Mr. Gurney established the fact that the family's name was McCoull and not McCool, or McColl, as it appears on older maps.
[92] Col. C. S. Venable in 14 S.H.S.P., 529.   [93] O. R., 36, pt. 1, p. 1079.

Gordon meantime recalled Pegram's Brigade,[94] and with this and his other troops, he undertook, in a confusion that approached chaos, to form a line of battle. His instinct then, as always, was to attack, but he left the deployment to his Colonels. He was waiting a short distance from his men when one of many minié balls, whistling through the heavy air, struck his uniform coat just above his sword belt. Gordon checked his alarmed horse and felt his spine.[95] "General," cried an aide who was slouching on his mount, "didn't that ball hit you?"

"No," answered Gordon, perhaps drawing his ramrod back a little more erect. "But suppose my back had been in a bow like yours? Don't you see that the bullet would have gone straight through my spine? Sit up or you'll be killed."

The jerk with which the young officer lifted himself in the saddle [96] probably brought a smile to Gordon's soldierly face, but the imminence of disaster left no time for banter. Gordon thought the fate of the Army was in the balance. Grant had broken the front. If he were not checked, the Confederate Army would be divided. At any cost, and as soon as the officers possibly could get their men in position, the Division must charge, halt the enemy and drive him back.[97] Gordon waited as long as he could master his impatience and then he touched his horse and started through the woods to dress the line. Near the flank of Pegram's Brigade was a familiar figure on a gray mount. At the sight of him, Gordon pulled in his animal and saluted. "What do you want me to do, General?" he asked and began to explain what he was planning.

With few words, grim but calm, Lee told him to proceed. Again Gordon saluted and started away, but he observed that Lee did not leave the front. Instead, hat off, the commanding General rode to the centre of the line, which now was nearly complete, and there he headed his horse up the salient, in the direction of the advance the Division was to make. Gordon had heard, of course, that Lee wanted to join the charge of the Texans on May 6, and he suspected immediately that Lee intended to do the same thing now. Back, swiftly, Gordon rode and confronted his chief: "General

94 It scarcely had reached Johnson's sector before it was summoned back to Gordon. See the experiences of a member of the Brigade in 21 *S.H.S.P.*, 245.
95 21 *S.H.S.P.*, 246.     96 *Gordon*, 277.
97 *Ibid.*, 277-78.

Lee, this is no place for you. Go back, General; we will drive them back!" His voice was pitched above the din of the fight; he spoke so that his men might hear. They gathered quickly around the two horsemen. Gordon continued in the tones that always excited his troops: "These men are Virginians and Georgians. They have never failed. They never will. Will you, boys?"

"No, no," the men shouted.

Lee appeared to be determined, though he was not under the tense excitement of the morning at the Tapp House when Heth's and Wilcox's men had broken. The troops were calling to him now to "go back." Lee would not move. Impulsively Gordon guided his horse between Lee and the enemy and then, in desperation, he reached for Traveller's bridle. He caught it, but in a moment, as men and horses were mingled, he had to drop it. A second later, he saw a sergeant take the animal and lead it toward the rear. Lee said nothing but did not resist. Gordon could turn again to his troops. They were ready. "Forward! Guide—right!" he shouted.[98] Soon the line was moving steadily, irresistibly, up the salient. With his men, all determination, all ardor, rode the young General. He was, said his men, the most superb-looking soldier they ever had seen.[99]

Gordon's line was too short to cover the width of the salient. On his left, where the Federals now seemed to be concentrating their fire,[100] Rodes came into action by changing the front of Daniel and then of Ramseur from West to North. The right of the First Corps was moved by the right flank up the salient to occupy the ground left vacant by the shift of Ramseur.[101] In a spirit that matched that of Gordon's Brigades, the North Carolinians swept up the salient, from traverse to traverse, and through the woods to the East of the works. It was, said Ewell, a "charge of unsurpassed gallantry."[102] But it could not drive the Federals from the northeastern tip of the "Shoe."[103] To strengthen the counter-attack, Nat Harris, a new Brigadier, brought up his Mississip-

[98] For the sources and the different versions of this "Lee to the rear," see 3 R. E. Lee, 319, n. 74.

[99] 21 S.H.S.P., 246.　　　　　　　　[100] O. R., 36, pt. 1, pp. 359, 1072.

[101] Ibid., 1072, 1082.

[102] Ibid., 1072. For Ramseur in the winter and spring of 1863–64, and for other accounts of his fine conduct at Spotsylvania, see O. R., 33, 1145; ibid., 36, pt. 1, pp. 1072, 1073, 1082; ibid., 51, pt. 2, p. 973; 1 N. C. Regts., 255–56, 278; 3 ibid., 51; 18 S.H.S.P., 242; 5 Land We Love, 6.

[103] O. R., 36, pt. 1, p. 1073.

pians and led them forward to Ramseur's right with the valor that had made him conspicuous as a Colonel.[104] Mahone followed Harris.[105] Then, after about two hours, McGowan was placed in rear of Ramseur and Harris.[106]

Still later, to relieve some of the exhausted troops,[107] Bratton's and Humphreys's Brigades of the First Corps were sent to the salient.[108] Their fire seemed merely to heighten the fury of the fight. "The trenches, dug on the inner side, were almost filled with water. Dead men lay on the surface of the ground and in pools of water. The wounded bled and groaned. . . . Abandoned knapsacks, guns and accoutrements were scattered all around. . . . The rain poured heavily, and an incessant fire was kept upon us from front and flank The enemy still held the works on the right of the angle, and fired across the traverses. Nor were these foes easily seen. They barely raised their heads above the logs, at the moment of firing." [109]

Before that fire and under the blast of artillery that had been brought nearer the battle line,[110] many officers and men went down. Robert Johnston had fallen early; Daniel had been mortally wounded; McGowan was shot again; Ramseur received a ball through his arm; James A. Walker was removed from the field dripping blood; Abner Perrin was killed.[111] Men less distinguished were no less conspicuous. Private soldiers came willingly to the traverses and fought over them or around them with clubbed gun and with bayonet. Bullets came in torrents. In resisting occasional Federal attemps to regain a traverse or a stretch of the works, even the dead did duty: Often the soldiers placed the hand of a fallen comrade in such a position that, when it stiffened, it would hold their cartridges.[112] In all the bloody fighting of the two armies there never had been such a struggle as this. Where the bluecoats were driven out of part of the works near the apex of the salient, they took shelter under the trench and threw bayoneted rifles over the parapet. Sometimes, too, when a Confederate leaned over the works, the Federals would grab him, pull him down and kill

104 *Ibid.*, 1092.
106 *O. R.*, 36, pt. 1, pp. 1073, 1092, 1094.
107 *O. R.*, 36, pt. 1, pp. 1073, 1092, 1094.
108 *O. R.*, 36, pt. 1, p. 1057.
110 *O. R.*, 36, pt. 1, pp. 336, 360.
111 *O. R.*, 36, pt. 1, pp. 1030, 1073, 1094.
112 18 *S.H.S.P.*, 242.

105 *N. H. Harris*, 28.

109 *Caldwell*, 143.

him or send him to the rear. A Union commander recalled afterward: "Many were shot and stabbed through crevices and holes between the logs; men mounted the works, and with muskets rapidly handed them kept up a continuous fire until they were shot down, when others would take their places and continue the deadly work." [113]

On the right of the salient, Gordon with the help of part of Wilcox's Division of the Third Corps drove the enemy almost to the apex. In the midst of this fury, the dark and rainy sky did not tell by its shadows when noon passed, but before that hour, artillery action had opened all along the line and then had died vainly away.[114] Opposite the front of the First Corps there was a prolonged and violent exchange of infantry fire between forces invisible from the Confederate line—confused Federal troops the Southerners thought they were.[115] To the right of the salient, an attack by the IX Corps was delivered and was repulsed with ease. An attempt to organize a counter-stroke failed.[116]

By midafternoon, many of the soldiers were so weary that they went through the motions of combat and scarcely knew what they were doing. To some, an agonizing wound offered a welcome escape from the torture of the trenches. Death seemed preferable to another hour of din and stench and blood. Old soldiers stared and looked blank, as if the fury of the fight had driven them mad. Others kept their heads. One man incredibly ceased fire, examined leisurely a captured knapsack, stripped, put on the clean clothing he found in the case, and then cheerfully resumed his duty as a sharpshooter.[117] Even men of this stamp, immune to the horror around them, said afterward that the entire war had offered no scene to equal that fight at the apex of the salient. All the troops, even the survivors of the Brigades who met the first onslaught, were told they must remain at the front till a line across the base of the salient was strong enough to afford adequate defense. That order seemed a death sentence. Work on the new line was difficult. Men with pick and shovel made slow progress

[113] Maj. Gen. Lewis A. Grant, 2nd Brig., 2nd Div., VI Corps, in 4 *M.H.S.M.*, 269. He unintentionally exaggerated the stabbing. The Medical Director of the Army of the Potomac reported fourteen bayonet wounds only during the operations of May 8–21 (*O. R.*, 36, pt. 1, p. 237).
[114] *O. R.*, 36, pt. 1, p. 1057.
[115] Gen. John Bratton in *O. R.*, 36, pt. 1, p. 1066.
[116] For the details, which are not particularly instructive. see 3 *R. E. Lee*, 322–24.
[117] *Worsham*, 217–18.

while vagrant minié balls and occasional shells swept far down the salient. Till darkness, till 9 o'clock, the bitter exchange of fire continued. Ten o'clock scarcely brought a slackening. At 11, word was, "Not yet." It was past midnight when the survivors, staggering and wild-eyed, fell back to the new line.[118]

They had bought at heavy cost a reestablishment of the front. Killed, wounded and captured Confederates must have exceeded 5000 that day. Included were some of the best troops and ablest leaders of the Army. Edward Johnson had resisted to the last and then with good heart ate a breakfast provided by his old friend Seth Williams.[119] It was typical of Johnson's swiftly won position in the hearts of his men that some of them credited a tale that he had stopped on his way to the rear, had brandished his staff and had sworn he would not move another foot unless the Provost Marshal's Guard stopped prodding with bayonets his weary men.[120] "Maryland" Steuart did not fare so well. He surrendered his sword to Col. James A. Beaver of the 148th Pennsylvania and then found himself in a milling mass of prisoners and Federals. At length, he was sent to Maj. Gen. W. S. Hancock, who had known him in the old Army. Hancock extended his hand and greeted him: "How are you, Steuart?" Proudly Steuart answered: "Under the circumstances I decline to take your hand." Hancock shot back: "And under any other circumstances, I should not have

[118] O. R., 36, pt. 1, p. 1073. The paucity of Confederate reports on the action of May 12 makes the determination of positions difficult. Michler's map, while accurate enough for general purposes, shows the completed trench system around Spotsylvania and not merely the works used on May 12. Confusion is created, also, by the reference of various writers to the "second line," to the "incomplete line," to "Gordon's line," and to the "final line" or "line across the base of the salient," which also is mentioned as "incomplete." The evidence, when sifted, leads to these conclusions: (1) the "second line," the "incomplete line" and "Gordon's line" are the same, and are the line figured on the Michler map as running roughly East and West between the McCouli House on the North and the Harrison House on the South; (2) the "final line," which is the one across the "base of the salient," is about 1500 feet South of "Gordon's line," though there is a possibility that this "final line" may have been extended and strengthened subsequent to the 12th of May; (3) acceptance of these conclusions necessitates the rejection of Ewell's inferential figure (O. R., 36, pt. 1, p. 1073) of the distance between the front and final lines of the salient as erroneous by about 360 yards. Colonel Venable's statement in 8 S.H.S.P., 107, concerning Gordon's construction of this final line must be rejected, also, as a confusion of that line with the one Gordon previously had constructed. In these conclusions, Ralph Happel, historical aide of the Fredericksburg and Spotsylvania County Battlefields Memorial National Military Park, concurs after a careful examination of the ground. Mr. Happel was kind enough to supply, also, the information that the McCoull House faced a little South of West, which fixes the position of Evans's Brigade. This is a matter of some importance in following the course of Gordon's counter-attack. Particular attention is called to the fact that the sketch in early editions of R. E. Lee, Vol. 3, p. 323, represented "Gordon's line" as the final line.

[119] McHenry Howard, 283 n, 301.          [120] Casler, 328.

offered it." [121] After that, Steuart passed unceremoniously into the custody of the Provost Marshal.[122] Steuart would be missed; even more would Johnson be. To replace the two slain Brigadiers, Abner Perrin and Junius Daniel might not be an easy task. The wounded Generals and their maimed subordinates would be slow to take the field again, because the injuries of the day had been deplorably serious.[123] No wonder, after those ghastly hours, the Confederates spoke, not of the "Mule Shoe" but of the "Bloody Angle." [124] A Division, in effect, had been destroyed. By this battle and by the struggle in the Wilderness, the command of the infantry, which had been weakened at Gettysburg, now was shattered to a degree no one realized at that time. Nor was the only loss of the fatal month of May sustained in the dripping forests of Spotsylvania. News as dire as any from the ghastly salient had reached headquarters on the 12th from Richmond.

[121] *O. R.*, 36, pt. 1, p. 359.          [122] *McHenry Howard*, 301
[123] Of the 3,560 Federal wounded, not more than one-fourth were able to walk back to the hospitals. Shock was much more serious than after the Battle of the Wilderness (*O. R.*, 36, pt. 1, p. 231).
[124] The critique of this operation appears *infra*, p. 446.

# CHAPTER XXI

## "I HAD RATHER DIE THAN BE WHIPPED"

INTO THE DESPERATE fighting of the Wilderness and of Spotsylvania, the cavalry had entered with its organization changed to
conform to the return of "Rooney" Lee. When he had been captured at Hickory Hill, while recuperating from the wound received at Brandy Station,[1] he had ranked as a Brigadier General.
In January, it will be recalled,[2] John R. Chambliss, Jr., had been
given "Rooney's" Brigade. Now that the second son of the commanding General was an exchanged prisoner, provision had to
be made for him. He was too able an officer to be left without a
command. The prompt decision of the War Department was to
advance him to the rank of Major General and to supply a Division by reducing the Brigades of all the Divisions to two each. Exception was made in the case of Wade Hampton because he was
receiving South Carolina reinforcements that could not be placed
acceptably in another Division. His command, therefore, was
Pierce Young's, Tom Rosser's and Calbraith Butler's Brigades.
Fitz Lee's Division was reduced to Lomax's and Wickham's Brigades. "Rooney" Lee had his own old command, now Chambliss',
and James Gordon's North Carolina regiments.[3] The commission
of the new Major General was issued as of April 23, 1864.[4] If
there was dissatisfaction or any cry of nepotism, it is unrecorded.

None of Stuart's Brigades now was directly under the man
who had commanded it a year previously; few of his personal staff
had served with him that long. Von Borcke was in Richmond but
had not recovered sufficiently to resume his duties. Channing Price
was dead. Pelham was no more. Norman FitzHugh was Quartermaster of the cavalry. William Blackford had resigned to become
Lieutenant Colonel of a regiment of engineer troops. John Esten
Cooke remained but was not happy. Henry McClellan was the
backbone of the staff. Probably the most useful recent addition,

---

[1] 3 R. E. Lee, 32, 139, 189, 211.  [2] Cf. Wright, 136.
[3] O. R., 36, pt. 1, p. 1027.  [4] Wright, 38.

certainly the one closest to Stuart, was the Assistant Inspector General, Maj. Andrew Reid Venable, almost universally called Reid Venable.[5] With these men and some younger aides, "Jeb" was content, but headquarters lacked the old hilarity, the old buoyancy of spirit even. The war was becoming too serious! Grant's new cavalry commander, Phil Sheridan, was flinty. He had novel conceptions of fire power and of the function of mounted troops, and he took excellent care of his horses. His fighting was hard and intelligent.

In the first stages of combat in the Wilderness, the Confederates met their stronger adversary with vigor. Stuart himself went to the picket line as soon as he learned on the 4th that the enemy was advancing toward the Rapidan. The next day he conducted in person the advance of Hill's Third Corps and thereby missed a brisk fight between Rosser and part of J. H. Wilson's and David Gregg's Divisions. Rosser acquitted himself with great honor, though the strain on his weak, thin horses must have been dangerously severe.[6] On the 6th and the 7th, the butternut cavalry again were assailed by superior force on the Confederate right. Most of the fighting was on foot.[7] All of it was furious.[8]

The rolling character of those clashes carried the opposing mounted forces toward Spotsylvania Court House where, on the 8th, Stuart's men stood off the Union cavalry and an increasing force of infantry until the arrival of Anderson and the First Corps. Insofar as the details of that action relate to the general course of the campaign, they have been described already.[9] One incident of Fitz Lee's struggle against Wilson at the Court House became part of the proudest record of the cavalry. Capt. P. P. Johnston's four-gun battery of Maj. James Breathed's Battalion of the Horse Artillery had been advanced boldly in order to cover the retirement of the dismounted men and the led horses. While the battery was blazing away, a strong line of battle approached. Seeing no support of the Confederate artillery, the Union infantry rushed for-

---

[5] For a fine sketch of him see W. Gordon McCabe in 37 *S.H.S.P.*, 61 ff.
[6] Wilson's report is in *O. R.*, 36, pt. 1, pp. 876–77. See also H. B. *McClellan*, 406, with a reference to 11 *Moore's Rebellion Record*, 452. It is much to be lamented that no official reports of the Confederate cavalry for May 5–12 are known to be in existence. The best authority is H. B. McClellan, but he was brief in his treatment of the operations of these days.
[7] *Cf.* Gregg in *O. R.*, 36, pt. 1, p. 853.
[8] *Ibid.*, 788–89, 811, 857.      [9] See *supra*, p. 381 ff.

ward to capture it. Major Breathed ordered Johnston to withdraw one section of the battery and to entrust the other to him. Johnston refused to leave the ground while any of his guns remained there. At length the Federals approached so close that all the pieces were in danger. Three of them got off narrowly. With the last of the three went Johnston, most reluctantly and only because he had received a wound. Breathed at the moment was on his horse and had all the men of the fourth gun ready to move it. The oncoming Federals, seeing their prize about to vanish, opened a fusillade. Most of the horses and the drivers of the lead and swing teams were killed or wounded. The driver of the wheel team received a bullet that shattered his arm. Instantly Major Breathed sprang from his mount and, under a heavy fire, cut the traces of the injured horses. That done, he leaped into the saddle of a wheel horse and, with the two animals, drove the gun into the Confederate lines.[10]

Stuart himself had not been at the front when this action opened, but he had done his utmost to get the arriving First Corps into position, and at Anderson's request he directed operations on the left of the line.[11] Early the next day, May 9, Stuart received news that Sheridan's cavalry had moved to Hamilton's Crossing and had proceeded to the Telegraph Road on which they had turned southward. This maneuver had been executed at the farthest outposts of Stuart, but it was reported promptly. Wickham's Brigade, the nearest, at once undertook pursuit of the enemy. "Jeb" already had taken James Gordon from Hampton and he had to leave Rosser and the cadre of Young to cover the flanks of Lee's Army. Few as were his available men, Stuart [12] spurred toward the Telegraph Road. At Mitchell's Shop, he and Fitz Lee, with the Brigades of Lomax and Gordon, joined Wickham. That officer had an altogether creditable report to make of vigorous attacks on the Union rearguard.[13] Federal strength, said the residents, was immense. The column from van to rearguard covered thirteen miles of road.[14]

Sheridan had turned now from the Telegraph Road and had taken the route to Beaver Dam on the Central Railroad. Bad news

[10] This account merely paraphrases that of H. B. McClellan, *op. cit.*, 407–08.
[11] *Ibid.*, 407.  [12] *O. R.*, 36, pt. 2, pp. 970–71.
[13] H. B. McClellan, 409–10; *O. R.*, 36, pt. 1, pp. 812, 857, 861.
[14] *O. R.*, 36, pt. 1, p. 789.

this was, because Lee had his advance base at that point and probably did not have many troops there to defend it. That was not the worst prospect. If Sheridan merely were making a raid on Beaver Dam, he scarcely would have taken so many troops with him. He might be proceeding toward Richmond. If so, at least a part of the Confederate cavalry must interpose between him and the capital, though the main defense of the city must be made by its garrison. Reasoning in this manner, Stuart concluded that Fitz Lee with three Brigades should follow the enemy at least for a few hours, while he himself took Gordon's Brigade and made for Davenport's Bridge on the North Anna, whence he could move in any direction to ascertain whether Sheridan was advancing on Richmond.[15]

With Gordon's reliable North Carolina troopers, "Jeb" rode through the night toward Davenport's Bridge. Perhaps he saw against the sky to the South of him the glare of a conflagration, but if so, there is no record of the fact. Early in the morning of the 10th, Stuart crossed the North Anna at Davenport's Bridge and pushed southward to Beaver Dam Station. There he rejoined Fitz Lee and again concentrated his men, who numbered between 4000 and 5000;[16] but what he saw at Beaver Dam sickened him. Several units of Sheridan's command had reached the advanced base during the night. They had lighted fires after they had reached the station and thereby had given warning to the few Confederates who had custody of the supplies nearby. These guards ignited the inflammable structures that protected bacon, meat and miscellaneous stores from the weather.[17] About 915,000 rations of meat and 504,000 of bread were consumed by fire while Southern boys lay hungry in the woods around Spotsylvania.[18] A grievous blow this was, one which compelled the commissary bureau to order a general impressment of food with a pledge to pay cash for it, or to return it in kind.[19] Nor was this the full measure of loss and hardship. What the guards at Beaver Dam could not burn, Sheridan's

[15] H. B. McClellan (op. cit., 410) is authority for these movements, but not for the reasoning that prompted them. It is possible that the inferences here drawn from Stuart's division of force may credit him with a broader strategic plan than he formulated on the 9th, but all his subsequent movements indicated that he sought to maintain contact with the enemy and at the same time to cover Richmond.

[16] H. B. McClellan, 410.                    [17] O. R., 36, pt. 1, p. 812.

[18] O. R., 51, pt. 2, pp. 909-10. This is the Confederates' estimate. Sheridan's naturally was higher.

[19] O. R., 51, pt. 2, pp. 910-11.

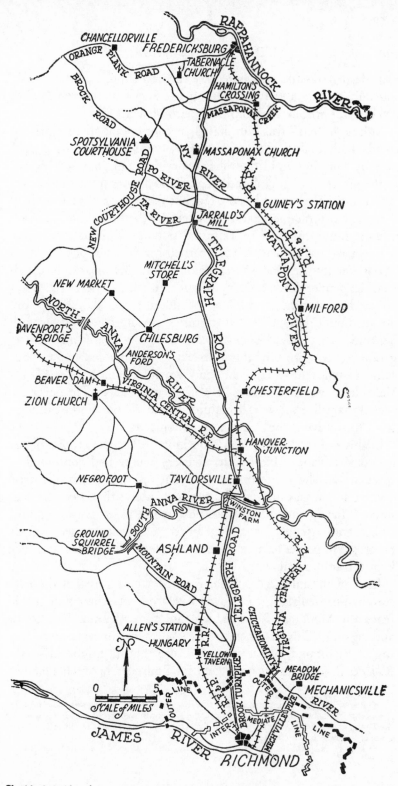

Sheridan's Raid and Stuart's Pursuit, May 9–11, 1864—after A. H. Campbell's Map of Portion of Eastern Virginia, 1864

men destroyed—the army's reserve medical supplies,[20] more than 100 railway cars and two locomotives. Sheridan recovered, also, 378 Federal prisoners, whom he carried off with him.[21]

Although "Jeb'" was humiliated, of course, that an enterprising enemy had reached the advance base, nothing was to be gained now by camping amid the ashes. Sheridan had gone southward, in the direction of Richmond. The Confederates must follow and defeat him. They must hasten, too, but they need not go so swiftly that their commander could not overtake them. He had to spare a few minutes to visit Col. Edmund Fontaine's plantation, where Mrs. Stuart was a guest. "Jeb" yearned for the sight of her. With Major Venable he rode over to Colonel Fontaine's mansion, which gave its name, Beaver Dam, to the station.[22] There, by God's mercy, he found her and his two children safe and well. He did not dismount, but had a few minutes' private conversation with her and, at its close, kissed her and bade her a most affectionate good-bye. Sombre thoughts pursued him as he rode away. For some distance he was silent, and when at length he spoke to Venable it was of a theme he seldom mentioned. He never expected to outlive the war, he confided to the Major, and he did not want to survive if the South were conquered.[23]

In this fighting spirit, "Jeb" continued to receive reports of the Federals' advance. He pondered every report and continued to speculate on Sheridan's possible alternatives, though his own freedom of action was limited. Southerners' horses that had been half starved during the winter were now too weak to pursue rapidly. Confederate troopers were exhausted for lack of sleep. Only Stuart's will power and his encouragement of his officers and men kept the column moving.

Most of the information that reached Stuart was that the Federals had moved southward toward Negro Foot, where they would reach the Mountain Road, which ran from Richmond to Louisa and beyond. This left open the possibility that Sheridan was aiming at Richmond, but it suggested also that he might strike the R. F. & P. and the Virginia Central Railroads between Hanover

[20] O. R., 36, pt. 1, p. 790.     [21] O. R., 36, pt. 1, p. 777.
[22] Rosewell Page, Jr., informed the writer in 1943 that the house was standing then. It was distant about a mile and a half from the station. Neighborhood tradition was that the Fontaine estate originally ran down to the station, which was on the railroad of which Colonel Fontaine was President.
[23] Maj. A. R. Venable, Jr., to Gen. Fitz Lee, MS, June 7, 1888 (cited hereafter as Venable).

Junction and Richmond.[24] Stuart consequently divided his forces again: Gordon must hang on the rear of the enemy; Fitz Lee with Lomax and Wickham must move by way of Hanover Junction and get across Sheridan's path.

The pursuit was without incident but was slow for another reason than that of the weakness of the mounts. By felling trees, Union troopers barricaded the Richmond road and, as a result, compelled Stuart to change his route.[25] He kept toward Hanover Junction and planned to turn southward at that point toward Ashland. Difficult as the pursuit was becoming, Stuart was not without hope of defeating the Federals. He reasoned that if they advanced on Richmond, he could assail their rear while the garrison of the capital contested their advance. In event the bluecoats contented themselves with cutting the railroads near the capital and then sought to escape, the Confederates would press their rear. The enemy was not to be despised, but he was not invincible. Stuart telegraphed Bragg: "His force is large, and if attack is made on Richmond it will be principally as dismounted cavalry, which fight better than enemy's infantry." [26]

The hot day [27] wore the stoutest rider. By the time Stuart reached Hanover Junction, not long before 9 P.M., he had news that the head of the enemy's column had arrived at Ground Squirrel Bridge on the South Anna at 4:15 that afternoon.[28] This report placed Sheridan's men within nineteen miles of Richmond and it sharpened Stuart's desire to push straight on. It was too much to ask of his men. Even Fitz Lee, who would ride neck to neck with Stuart anywhere, had to request that the troopers be allowed a few hours' sleep. "Jeb" consented, but his sense of duty would not permit him to give the men more time than their condition made imperative: they might rest but they must mount and start by 1 A.M. To make certain they observed the time, Stuart directed that Henry McClellan accompany Lee's command to their bivouac, stay awake and see that the whole force start at the appointed hour.[29] Stuart himself rode on to Taylorsville, two and a half miles South of Hanover Junction, and there he stretched out under the same blanket with Major Venable.[30]

After what must have seemed a few minutes only, "Jeb" awak-

24 O. R., 51, pt. 2, p. 911.
25 O. R., 51, pt. 2, pp. 911–12.
26 O. R., 51, pt. 2, p. 912.
27 O. R., 36, pt. 1, p. 812.
28 O. R., 51, pt. 2, p. 912.
29 H. B. McClellan, 411.
30 Venable.

ened. Henry McClellan was standing by his side and was calling his name. As always, Stuart was himself at the first word. Instantly he grasped McClellan's report that Fitz Lee's column was moving at the appointed hour. "Jeb" waited no longer than was necessary for his staff to bestir themselves. "General," one of his officers said, "here's McClellan, fast asleep; shall I wake him?" McClellan had, in fact, spread himself on the ground the moment he had completed his report. He was not yet asleep, but Stuart thought he was. "No," the General said in answer to the question, "he has been watching while we were asleep." Stuart added: "Leave a courier with him, and tell him to come on when his nap is out." [31]

Down the Telegraph Road Stuart made his way. When he crossed the South Anna he was on ground associated with the first of his great adventures under Lee. To the left on the road, as "Jeb" proceeded southward, was the Winston Farm on which [32] the cavalry had camped the night before the "ride around McClellan." That had been twenty-three months previously, lacking one day, and it had been the adventure that had brought him what he most desired, fame for himself coupled with service to the country. The one without the other was not complete. He had the fame; he still believed the South would win independence . . . but those mounted Federals were stronger and more daring than ever they had been. They were close to Richmond now; he told himself, in his romantic manner, that he must save the women and children of the city.

Opposite Ashland, close to the point where he had met Jackson at the beginning of the Seven Days, Stuart learned that the enemy had raided the town during the night. A locomotive and a train of cars had been destroyed. Several government storehouses had been burned. For six miles the Federals had torn up the track of the R. F. & P. and had smashed the culverts. [33] Hearing this, Stuart lost no time. A squadron of the Second Virginia dashed into the town and speedily drove out part of the First Massachusetts, which it found there. [34]

The issue was at hand! If some of Sheridan's troops were this

---

[31] H. B. McClellan, 411.                    [32] See Vol. I, p. 182
[33] O. R., 36, pt. 1, pp. 777, 790. The length of track is given by Sheridan. By Gen. H. E. Davis it is described only as "quite a section" (Ibid., 857).
[34] H. B. McClellan, 411; O. R., 36, pt. 1, p. 857.

close to Richmond, the others would be encountered quickly. By pushing the Confederate horses, Stuart might take the Federals in rear while they were attacking the Richmond defenses. The alternative prospect was affrighting: Failure by Bragg's troops to hold the earthworks around the city might make it possible for Sheridan to accomplish what Dahlgren had attempted—to release the prisoners and to burn the capital. Press on, then, toward Richmond! Although "Jeb" urged the troopers forward, he did not appear to be excited. Henry McClellan remembered: "As I rode by his side we conversed on many matters of personal interest. He was more quiet than usual, softer and more communicative." [35]

Major McClellan was one of the few friends of Stuart, made during the war, who was acquainted with the secret that "Jeb" hid behind his brigand-like whiskers. Fellow-cadets at West Point had known that secret, of course, and with the frank brutality of youthful comradeship had mocked it when they had given him the nickname, "Beauty." Truth was, Stuart had a chin "so short and retiring," in McClellan's words, "as positively to disfigure his otherwise fine countenance." [36] Doubtless that had been the reason Stuart had grown a beard as soon as he could. If, in addition, consciousness of the assumed mark of "weakness" had spurred him to greater daring in war, nobody was aware of his sensitiveness concerning his caving chin. Least of all would there have been time for thought on such a subject that morning of the 11th of May.

About 7 A.M., the sound of firing was heard from the direction of Ground Squirrel Bridge on the South Anna. An hour later, the head of the Southern column reached the Yellow Tavern, where the Mountain Road from Louisa and the Telegraph Road from Fredericksburg join the Brook Turnpike, which runs to Richmond. If Sheridan were ahead of Stuart, the Federals would have moved, in all probability, by one of those roads or the other. Natives said the bluecoats had advanced by neither. Instead, residents had a rumor that the enemy had gone westward toward James River. Stuart decided to move in that direction, if the rumor were authenticated; but before he did anything else he wrote Bragg a brief dispatch in which he described the situation.

[35] *H. B. McClellan*, 411.          [36] 8 *S.H.S.P.*, 450.

"Repeat this to General Lee, Guiney's Station," he concluded. "To General Lee" . . . thither for many months his observant, accurate reports of the enemy's movements had gone. It was proper, for the guidance of his chief, that this one, also, perhaps the last before the battle, should be sent Lee.

This dispatch was hurried to Richmond by courier. Then Stuart examined the ground around Yellow Tavern and considered his tactical problem. As Sheridan had not preceded him, "Jeb" had now to abandon the plan of attacking the Federals in rear while Bragg stopped them in front. As an alternative, the Confederates could form a line of battle and meet the Union cavalry when it approached, or they could take a flank position and assail Sheridan as he advanced on Richmond. Manifestly, if the Richmond fortifications could be held by the forces Bragg might muster, it was far better to strike the enemy's flank than to repulse a frontal attack by a superior force. Major McClellan, then, must ride into Richmond, see Bragg, and ascertain whether the General could hold the defenses.[37]

As the morning passed, the enemy's scouting parties began to appear. By approximately 11 o'clock, all the indications were that Sheridan's main force was taking position.[38] Stuart, watching closely, had to make his dispositions without sure knowledge, as yet, of what he could expect of Bragg. Consequently Stuart had to compromise between a frontal and a flank position. He placed Wickham on his right, with most of the Brigade parallel to the Telegraph Road. Lomax was on the left with his flank West of the road and almost at right angles to it.[39] Gordon was assumed to be engaged with the enemy's rearguard. Two Confederate Brigades had to contend against the undetermined strength of Sheridan.

These arrangements by Stuart exposed to seizure the Brook Turnpike between the Confederate right and the outer defenses of Richmond. Quickly a Federal force swung around and reached

[37] H. B. McClellan, 412.

[38] Curiously enough, none of the published reports gave the time of the arrival of the Federals at Yellow Tavern. Col. Thomas C. Devin stated (O. R., 36, pt. 1, p. 834) that his Brigade reached Allen's Station, now Glen Allen, at 11 A.M. He subsequently received orders to move to the vicinity of Yellow Tavern, where he found part of the reserve Brigade. It is assumed in the text that the arrival of other Federal units at Yellow Tavern was about simultaneous with the appearance of Devin at Allen's.

[39] In the absence of reports, there is uncertainty regarding Stuart's first position, but this uncertainty is confined to the right.

the Pike and the junction of the Telegraph and Mountain Roads.[40] If Stuart was to hold a flank position, this maneuver did not interfere materially with his plans. He was more concerned, at the moment, over the safety of his position on the Telegraph Road, which was held by a thin line of dismounted men. The first Federal attack there was beaten off by the Fifth Virginia in a hand-to-hand grapple that stirred both Stuart's pride and his apprehension. Henry Pate commanded the Fifth, an able man and a furious fighter. Between him and Stuart had developed a bitterness of feeling not unlike the first stage of the feud with "Grumble" Jones. If Pate failed to repel the next attack . . . but Stuart did not wait on "if." He rode over to Pate's position and up to the point where the officer was sitting. Stuart gave the Colonel some instructions and then asked him to hold the position until reinforcements could be sent. Pate got up and looked squarely at the General from whom he was estranged. "I will do it," he said— that and no more. Stuart thanked him and commended him for his firmness. The Colonel listened and then walked over to "Jeb" and held out his hand. Gladly and cordially Stuart grasped it and, on the instant, effaced all difference.[41]

By this time, the Federals were demonstrating again. Stuart rode back to his staff, who were lying down under a hill, [42] whence, for a time, he tried to direct the defense. Momentarily it became more difficult. Now at one point, not a few hundred yards off, the enemy assailed the line in an effort to find the weakest spot. Then the "feeling out" was shifted. This went on and on. Southern losses mounted. Pate again had to beat off the hard-striking, persistent bluecoats who justified Stuart's compliment that they fought better, dismounted, than did the Union infantry. When at length the Federals recoiled, Pate had made good his promise to Stuart, but in doing so he had yielded his own life.

Soon after news of the fall of Pate reached Stuart, the faithful Henry McClellan came back, about 2 o'clock, from Richmond. He had found the Brook Turnpike occupied by the enemy but he had made a detour across the fields and brought Stuart a message from Bragg. That officer had 4000 local defense troops and convalescents.[43] In addition, Bragg had ordered three Brigades from

40 This was done by Devin's Brigade. See O. R., 36, pt. 1, p. 834.
41 Venable.                                      42 Ibid.
43 McClellan (op. cit., 412) described them as irregular troops.

the south side of the James, where Beauregard was opposing Butler. With this force and the garrison artillery, said Bragg, he
thought he could hold the fortifications.

Stuart was pleased with this report and much relieved by it. He
concluded that the worst was over, though he expected to be compelled to repulse more attacks, and he told his chief of staff that
he would hang on Sheridan's flank. If the troops in the Richmond
defenses delivered a strong attack, he could take the offensive and,
with good fortune, could cripple the blue cavalry. This was uppermost in Stuart's mind, but he was grieved by the death of Pate and
was quick to tell McClellan how fine a fight the Colonel had
made.[44]

For an hour and more, Stuart sat talking with McClellan,
Venable, Lieutenant Hullihen and other members of his staff.
All along the line, up the Telegraph Road and then across the
field to the left, there was a lull in the fight. Nobody was deceived
by it. In particular, Lomax's men in the field were on the alert,
because theirs was the most vulnerable position. In front of it,
a little brook and a succession of fences gave some security. Next,
defensively, was a fringe of woodland on the northern side of
which dismounted pickets were stationed. Behind this wood was
a field, which rose somewhat to the southward, where Lomax's
line of troopers on foot was drawn. That line, unhappily, was
thin and had no protection on the extreme left except two guns of
the horse artillery and, probably, a small mounted reserve of the
First Virginia Cavalry.[45] If the flank were turned or the line
broken, the left would be thrown back on the right,[46] which
might be routed.

A stir in the woods and on the fields held by the Federals was
observable at 4 o'clock. Soon the Union troopers began a deliberate advance on the centre and right. At the first evidence of
renewed attack, "Jeb" called some of his staff to join him, and
with them he rode to a gun on the top of the hill above the road.
By the time he got there, artillerists who had been under heavy
fire were half demoralized. Dead horses and slain comrades ringed

[44] H. B. McClellan, 412.

[45] It is not certain that this detachment was in rear of the left, but that seems to be
the logical position for the mounted reserve. Moreover, when Custer attacked, the counter-
charge by this reserve was too prompt to have been delivered by men who had been summoned from any distance.

[46] O. R., 36, pt. 1, pp. 817–18.

them. Stuart remained in the saddle and in his gay, confident manner, encouraged the soldiers. Presently Reid Venable spoke up: The General was exposing himself needlessly on horseback, a conspicuous target, while men sheltered behind fences and stumps were being killed. Stuart answered laughingly, "I don't reckon there is any danger!" [47] Apparently there never had been any. He had been fighting for three years and never had been touched by a Federal missile, though his uniform had been cut by bullets.

After a few words more, "Jeb" told Venable to ride with him to the left. They found in front of them a broken line and other men who seemed, like the gunners, to be close to the limit of organized resistance. Lomax was doing everything he could to rally them. As always, Stuart reasoned that the best way to defend was to attack, and he told Venable to remain there and help Lomax organize a counter-thrust. Alone, Stuart rode to the extreme left,[48] which had not yet been involved in the new fighting that had swept the front. Whistling as he went, and doubtless seeking to spread confidence among the men, Stuart drew rein at a fence in the woods nearly at the point where the left flank was "in the air."

With no formality, "Jeb" placed the head of his horse over the fence between two privates of the First Virginia, J. R. Oliver and Fred L. Pitts.[49] There he waited for the next assault. Soon it came. With a roar, three mounted Michigan regiments of Custer's Brigade advanced from the North. Two of the regiments kept together to assail the left centre; one advanced against the extreme left. When within 200 yards this regiment, the 1st Michigan, broke into a gallop and, with a yell, rode straight for the guns. The Southern artillerists kept up their fire as long as they could, but the fury of the charge was too much for them. They abandoned their guns and fled.[50]

The fierce attack of the 5th and 6th Michigan, though not designed to be pressed home,[51] sent nearly the whole of the left and

---

[47] *Venable.*          [48] *Ibid.*
[49] J. R. Oliver in 19 *C. V.*, 531. This late account does not agree in some particulars with that of Capt. G. W. Dorsey, but there is no reason to question the accuracy of Mr. Oliver's memory of this part of the incident. For the particulars of the charge, the narrative of Captain Dorsey is followed. His statement appeared in *H. B. McClellan*, 413–14. A later, abbreviated version, mentioning Pitts, was given in Theodore S. Garnett, *J. E. B. Stuart . . .*, pp. 45–46.
[50] *O. R.*, 36, pt. 1, p. 818.          [51] *Ibid.*

part of the left centre reeling back toward a ravine about 400 yards to the rear. In pursuit, the 5th Michigan dashed by Stuart and his companions. Out from his holster "Jeb" jerked his pistol and began to fire at the Federals. Quickly they were past, but soon they roared back. They had met not only the fire of the dismounted men in the ravine but also the shock of a counter-charge by the First Virginia. As the returning bluecoats came along the fence where Stuart was waiting, he called to the troopers around him: "Steady, men, steady; give it to them!"[52] He emptied his own pistol and, but for the fence, probably would have dashed among the Federals with his sabre. Soon the recoiling bluecoats were gone, except for a few who had lost their horses at the farthest point of the advance and now were trying to get to the rear. At the moment when he would have shouted a new command, Stuart felt a sudden shock that almost threw him off balance. His head dropped; his hat fell off.[53] Instantly he put his hand to his side.

"General," cried one of the boys at the fence, "are you hit?"

They crowded around him and scarcely observed the Federal trooper, almost the last of the dismounted men, who ran off down the fence with the smoking pistol that had fired the one bullet that hit Stuart.[54]

"Are you wounded badly?" an anxious voice inquired.

"I am afraid I am," said Stuart calmly, "but don't worry, boys: Fitz will do as well for you as I have done."[55]

Then, to a courier, who rode up at that moment, the wounded General said: "Go and tell General Lee and Dr. Fontaine to come here."[56]

By this time, Capt. G. W. Dorsey had reached Stuart's side and had taken the rein of the General's horse to lead it to the rear. Stuart's mount was not accustomed to being led. It became excited and unmanageable. Stuart himself was in too much pain to control the animal and was compelled to ask Dorsey to help him down. Dorsey was loath to do this, because the Federals

[52] 4 B. & L., 194.  [53] Ibid.
[54] General, then Colonel, R. A. Alger of the 5th Michigan Cavalry reported that the man who shot Stuart was Private John A. Huff, Co. E, 48 years of age, who had served two years in Berdan's Sharpshooters and, on discharge, had enlisted in the cavalry command. Huff, who had won a prize as the "best shot" in his old regiment, was mortally wounded, May 28, in the fight at Haw's Shop (O. R., 36, pt. 1, pp. 828–29).
[55] 19 C. V., 531. Reservation has to be made concerning the literal accuracy of this quotation.
[56] 4 B. & L., 194.

might charge again, but Stuart insisted on dismounting from the restive horse. As carefully as they could, Dorsey and some of the men lifted Stuart from the saddle and placed his back against a tree. A moment later Stuart heard Dorsey tell Fred Pitts to go and get another horse for the General. That stirred "Jeb." The Captain must leave him, he said, must collect the men and must repel the enemy. It did not matter about himself. He feared he was mortally wounded and past all service.

Gus' Dorsey balked at this order. Impulsively he said he had rather die than leave the General in that exposed position. He must stay by Stuart's side till a place of safety was reached.[57] Friendly dispute was halted by the arrival of Fred Pitts with his horse. It was while Stuart was being put astride the private's mount, or soon after he was started for the rear, that Fitz Lee dashed up. He had come the whole length of the line at the top speed of his light gray and scarcely could voice his distress over the injury to his alter ego. Now that Stuart was wounded, Fitz was the senior officer on the field, the man who must direct a difficult and doubtful battle. Stuart did not permit him to waste time on sympathy. "Go ahead, Fitz, old fellow," he said, "I know you will do what is right!"[58] Young Lee had to leave with that assurance which, through a long, adventurous life, remained, as he said, his "most precious legacy."[59]

Escorted by Dorsey, Pitts and others, Stuart kept a doubtful seat on Pitts's horse till he was almost beyond the probable sweep of another charge. There he made his companions halt. The enemy, he said, must be held and then driven. Dorsey must go back and help to get the men together. Sheridan must be kept from Richmond. This time Captain Dorsey could not resist orders. He placed Stuart in the intelligent care of Private Charles Wheatley[60] and, with a regretful farewell, returned to the firing line.[61] Stuart waited quietly till Wheatley found an ambulance. Then he gave such feeble help as he could while his companions placed him in

[57] H. B. McClellan, 414, on the basis of a statement by Captain Dorsey.
[58] 1 S.H.S.P., 102. This is Fitz Lee's own account of their brief exchange, the time of which can be approximated but cannot be fixed positively by the statement of the anonymous courier in 4 B. & L., 194.
[59] 1 S.H.S.P., 102.
[60] In the account Captain Dorsey sent Theodore S. Garnett of this incident, reference was made to the service rendered, also, by Corporal Robert Bruce, but in what capacity, Dorsey did not explain.
[61] H. B. McClellan, 414.

the vehicle. For the moment it seemed wise to leave the ambulance where it was. Shortly afterward, when Major Venable came up, he ordered the conveyance moved to the lowland near the bridge and entirely out of range.[62]

Stuart consented but he remained the General. As he crossed the field, he saw numbers of disorganized men who were making for the rear though the pursuit by the Federals had been halted temporarily. Prostrate, "Jeb" wrathfully cried, as loudly as he could: "Go back, go back and do your duty, as I have done mine, and our country will be safe. Go back, go back!" Then, in complete self-revelation he shouted: "I had rather die than be whipped." [63] Not until he had reached the shelter of the depression, beyond the battleground, did he speak again of his own injuries. His surgeon, Dr. J. B. Fontaine, who probably reached him while the ambulance was in motion, carefully turned him on his side as Private Wheatley continued to hold the General's head in strong and friendly arms. While the brief superficial examination was being made, Stuart spoke to Lieut. W. Q. Hullihen of his staff, a young officer to whom he had given an odd nickname. "Honey-bun," he asked, "how do I look in the face?"

"General, you are looking right well. You will be all right."

"Well, I don't know how this will turn out; but if it is God's will that I shall die, I am ready." [64]

The Surgeon must have realized, after examination of the wound, that Stuart had been shot through the abdomen, probably through the liver, and that the prognosis was hopeless.[65] All the Doctor said at the moment concerned Stuart's immediate condition: The General was in danger of prostration from shock. He must take a stimulant. Stuart demurred. He never had tasted whiskey, he said, because he had promised his mother he would not. Major Venable, as his closest friend present, at once tried to explain that the circumstances made the pledge inapplicable. Stuart, again on his back, lifted his hands to Venable and asked

[62] Venable.
[63] H. B. McClellan, 415, doubtless on the authority of one of the staff officers then with Stuart. The similar remark quoted infra by Venable suggests the possibility that the two exhortations are different versions of the same incident, but the circumstances appear to have been somewhat different.
[64] H. B. McClellan, 415.
[65] For a surgical view of Stuart's wound, see the note by Lt. Col. I. Ridgeway Trimble, U. S. Army Medical Corps, Appendix III.

the Major to raise him up. Venable did so. Stuart then said earnestly: "Old fellow, I know you will tell me the truth; tell me, is the death pallor on my face?"

The Major scrutinized the bearded countenance before him. "I hope not," he said, "there is some flush on your forehead." [66]

Stuart was encouraged by this. He agreed to take the stimulant and, once again in command, he repeated substantially to the men who gathered about what he had said to the fugitives on the field: "Go back to the front, I will be well taken care of. I want you to do your duty to your country as I always have through my life." [67]

Those words, if the time of their utterance is reported correctly, were his farewell to the field. The next move was in the ambulance toward Richmond. Custer's attack on the left and the heavy demonstration on the centre and on the right had made two battles of one. Part of the conflict continued North of Yellow Tavern. Another phase of the conflict was carried to the outer line of the Richmond defenses and then toward the Chickahominy River between the outer and the intermediate lines.[68] This was a dramatic advance and one that made the pulse of the Federals beat faster because, when they halted and commanded silence, they could hear plainly the tocsin in Richmond.[69]

To avoid these Federals, who still controlled almost the whole length of the Brook Turnpike, the ambulance and its dolorous escort had to make wide detours over poor and unfamiliar roads. On the way Stuart suffered cruelly. No relief could be given him. He had to grit his teeth and hold fast to the eternals until, long after dark, he was lifted from the vehicle in front of the home on Grace Street of his brother-in-law, Dr. Charles Brewer.[70] By that time, official Richmond and most of Stuart's private friends knew that he had been wounded, though the seriousness of his condition was not realized by all.[71] The faithful von Borcke, who had not yet recovered from his wound, undertook to telegraph Mrs.

[66] *Venable,* with Venable's reply changed to direct discourse.
[67] *Venable.* See note 63 *supra.*
[68] *O. R.,* 36, pt. 1, p. 777.
[69] *Ibid.,* 834.
[70] H. B. *McClellan,* 415–16; *Venable.* The frame dwelling of Doctor Brewer, which remained standing until the early years of the century, was on the north side of Grace about midway between Jefferson and Madison Streets. On the building now (1944) occupying the site, a stone tablet records the association with Stuart.
[71] Cf. 7 *S.H.S.P.,* 141.

Stuart at Col. Edmund Fontaine's home, though the message had
to be relayed by a remote circuit to reach her.[72]

The night was one of misery for "Jeb"—the same night of foreboding that witnessed the withdrawal of the artillery from the
"Bloody Angle," the mysterious sounds from the Federal lines, and
the fantastic concerts by half-drowned Union bands. In the same
dawn with that of the battle for the salient, "Jeb" Stuart rallied
his courageous spirits to face that "last enemy, Death."

He had, as reinforcement, the best medical men of the city,[73]
but they knew he was beaten. Staff officers came, also, to comfort
him and to execute his final orders. Henry McClellan, on a weary
horse, had fallen behind Stuart on the ride to the left the previous
afternoon, and when he had heard of the wounding of Stuart, he
had not dared to violate the oft-repeated injunction that in such a
contingency he must report to the officer next in rank and must
assist him. McClellan had found Fitz Lee and had remained with
him till the action ended. Now that he had come to Richmond
with dispatches to Bragg, he stole time for a visit to his chief.[74]
Stuart was glad to see the dependable McClellan, and when he had
moments of relief from his paroxysms of pain, he talked with
composure of the duties that remained to be discharged. His first
care was for his official papers. They must be forwarded through
channels for proper deposit. Stuart's personal effects must be sent
his wife. As for the horses, "I wish," he said to McClellan, "for
you to take one of my horses and Venable the other." True horseman to the end, he asked, "Which is the heavier rider?" McClellan answered that he thought Venable was. "Then," said Stuart,
"let Venable take the gray horse, and you take the bay."

He paused and ran over in mind the other dispositions he had
to make. His next instruction was a curious one: "You will find
in my hat a small Confederate flag which a lady of Columbia,
South Carolina, sent me, with the request that I would wear it
upon my horse in battle and return it to her. Send it to her."
McClellan knew nothing of this and never had seen such a flag in
Stuart's hat, but he did not interrupt the difficult speech of the

---

[72] 7 S.H.S.P., 108. A report was circulated at the time that some friend sought to
allay Mrs. Stuart's first fears by telegraphing her that the General was "slightly wounded."
This information was alleged to have delayed her departure from Colonel Fontaine's
because she did not believe an emergency existed. For a complete denial of this story, see
ibid., 140.

[73] 7 S.H.S.P., 107.                        [74] H. B. McClellan, 414, 416.

General to ask for explanations.[75] After another pause, perhaps a battle with overmastering pain, Stuart went on: "My spurs, which I have always worn in battle, I promised to give to Mrs. Lilly Lee of Shepherdstown, Virginia.[76] My sword I leave to my son."

In this manner he concluded his business, but not without a fitting accompaniment. Across the railroad tracks on Broad Street, and from the direction of the Chickahominy, there rolled the sullen sound of cannon fire. Eagerly Stuart asked what was happening. McClellan told him of Sheridan's advance between the outer and the intermediate line and described how the Richmond garrison and the cavalry Corps were seeking to trap the enemy. "God grant that they may be successful," Stuart answered with his old eagerness. Then he checked himself, turned his head and said with a sigh: "But I must be prepared for another world."[77]

Even with that resolution, he could not shift his attention from the familiar sound of an artillery exchange. McClellan thought that "Jeb" in spirit was fighting the battle by the side of Fitz Lee and was conscious of the younger General's need of competent assistance on the field. "Major," said Stuart presently, "Fitz Lee may need you." McClellan obediently arose, looked once more at the bearded face and the glassing blue eyes, pressed Stuart's hand and left the room—only to meet the President at the door. As the Major voiced his apology and started for the street, "Jeb" greeted his new visitor with outstretched hand. Davis grasped it and inquired, "General, how do you feel?"

"Easy," said Stuart in an even voice, "but willing to die if God

[75] McClellan, op. cit., 416, wrote: ". . . upon examining [Stuart's hat] the flag was found within its lining, stained with the sweat of his brow; and among his papers I found the letter which had conveyed the request."

[76] Through the kindness of Sam H. Hendricks of Shepherdstown, W. Virginia, Mrs. F. V. Chappell of Sea Orchard, Waterford, Conn., formerly Caroline Hanson Simpson, has given the writer the history of these spurs. They were the property of her grandfather, William Fitzhugh Lee, an officer in the "old army" and one of Stuart's close friends on frontier duty. As soon as Lee could do so, he hurried eastward, in 1861, entered Confederate service and became Lieutenant Colonel of the Thirty-third Virginia Infantry. In leading a charge of that famous regiment at First Manassas, he was mortally wounded. (E. J. Lee, Lee of Virginia, 514–15). His widow, who had been Lilly Parran, daughter of Dr. Richard Parran of Shepherdstown, gave the spurs to Stuart. The wish of "Jeb" concerning them was fulfilled. They were returned to "Mrs. Lilly," who had one daughter, Laura, later the wife of Lieut. William A. Simpson, U. S. A. To one of the children of this union, William Fitzhugh Lee Simpson, U. S. A., his grandmother bequeathed the spurs in 1916. Major Simpson was then on duty in Mexico with Gen. J. J. Pershing, and in 1917 he went to France with one of the first American contingents. He died within a few months and received burial on French soil. Although diligent inquiries were made concerning the spurs, nothing was learned of them after his death. They have to be reckoned among the lost relics.

[77] This is almost verbatim from H. B. McClellan, 416–17.

and my country think I have fulfilled my destiny and done my duty." [78]

The President had the good taste not to stay long. After his departure,[79] Stuart had seizures of intensest pain. At moments he was close to delirium, shouting orders and demanding that couriers make haste; and then, fully conscious, he would ask whether Mrs. Stuart had arrived or whether anyone knew when he might expect her. One thing still disturbed him. He had been alone when he had that last reconciling interview with Henry Pate and he was not sure anyone knew how splendidly the Colonel had behaved. He called for Reid Venable and, in intervals between the agony of his wound, he stumbled through his story. Pate's conduct, he said, "was one of the most heroic acts of the war." The wounded General continued brokenly: "I rode up to him . . . to ask him to hold it until . . . reinforcements could be sent to him. . . . He arose and said . . . 'I will do it!' On my complimenting him . . . for his gallantry . . . Pate came to me and offered me his hand . . . and we there . . . under that deadly fire . . . were made friends. . . . I want you, Major . . . to let his friends know of my commendation of his gallant conduct . . . for in a few minutes afterwards . . . he was shot down . . . yielding his life . . . for his country." [80]

That long tribute must have relieved his mind, but as the afternoon slipped by, his paroxysms were more excruciating, his lucid intervals fewer. When he could control his mind, he helped to apply to his side the ice that seemed to ease his pain.[81] Several times, as he roused, he asked for Mrs. Stuart. After he realized that she might not reach Richmond that day because the raiders had severed communication,[82] he asked Doctor Brewer whether he could survive the night. The physician answered honestly that death was near. Stuart nodded as if he had received an order to go forward: "I am resigned if it be God's will; but I would like to see my wife. . . . But God's will be done." He passed then to the frontier between life and death, though when he spoke it still was to ask if Mrs. Stuart had come. Once when he broke through

---

[78] *Ibid.*, 417.
[79] This is not the established sequence of visits but seems the most probable.
[80] *Venable.*                              [81] 7 *S.H.S.P.*, 108.
[82] It will be recalled that a somewhat similar situation had delayed Mrs. Jackson's arrival at the bedside of her husband. See Vol. II, pp. 671–72.

the maze that enveloped him, he saw that Brewer was by his side and was taking his pulse. He spoke as clearly as a clouded mind made possible: "Doctor, I suppose I am going fast now. It will soon be over. But God's will be done. I hope I have fulfilled my destiny to my country and my duty to God."

Clergymen as well as physicians were in the next room. When it became apparent, after 7 o'clock, that his end was at hand, two ministers came to his bedside. At his request they prayed and then they sang the hymn he asked, "Rock of Ages, cleft for me." He made a pitiful effort to join in the singing and then again he turned his head toward Brewer. "I am going fast now," he repeated, "I am resigned; God's will be done." Then, in spirit, he rode off to New Adventure.[83]

It was 7:38, they thought, when he drew his last breath. About 11:30, having made a difficult and heartbreaking journey by special train and by ambulance, Mrs. Stuart reached the Brewer home. The pervasive, mournful silence told her the worst.[84] Her grief was the South's. Stuart already had received the thanks of Congress.[85] He had now the tribute of President, of press and of cabinet, and as impressive a funeral, May 13, as the war-wrung Confederate capital could give.[86] More impressive still was the tribute written by one of his adversaries, Brig. Gen. James H. Wilson. In his report of the operations of May–June, 1864, prepared when the war was nearly over, Wilson wrote of Yellow Tavern and of the death of Stuart: "From it may be dated the permanent superiority of the national cavalry over that of the rebels." [87]

Other military writers made their estimate of Stuart.[88] Most of his own men agreed with "Grumble" Jones's honest if furious statement that Stuart, whom he hated to the last, was the first of all cavalry commanders. Even critical officers shared Sedgwick's opinion that "Jeb" was "the greatest cavalry officer ever foaled in America." [89]

83 7 S.H.S.P., 109.
84 All essential details are given in 7 S.H.S.P., 140–41. Some additional facts, not all of them accurate, are given in W. W. Blackford's MS Memoirs, 367–68.
85 As of Feb. 17, 1864; O. R., 27, pt. 2, p. 712; ibid., 51, pt. 2, p. 821.
86 An adequate account will be found in 7 S.H.S.P., 109. Burial was in Hollywood Cemetery, Richmond, where his ashes still rest.
87 O. R., 36, pt. 1, p. 789.
88 That of Longstreet, op. cit., 573, and that of Douglas, 280, are just and penetrating but the best and most intimately detailed, in all its parts, remains that of John Esten Cooke in Wearing of the Gray, 2–43.
89 Wearing of the Gray, 39.

In superlatives of this sort, the commanding General of the Army of Northern Virginia did not indulge, but Lee had looked to Stuart for service of the sort "Jeb" had described in a letter to John R. Chambliss, April 4, 1864. Stuart had said then: "Bear in mind that your telegrams may make the whole Army strike tents, and night or day, rain or shine, take up the line of march. Endeavor, therefore, to secure accurate information. . . . Above all, vigilance! vigilance! vigilance!" [90] That had been more than an exhortation. It had been an ideal. By Stuart's own fulfilment of that ideal of the outpost officer, more than by any other, Lee had judged him. When the formal announcement of Stuart's death was made in general orders, Lee was to say: "Among the gallant soldiers who have fallen in this war, General Stuart was second to none in valor, in zeal and in unfaltering devotion to his country. His achievements form a conspicuous part of the history of this Army, with which his name and services will be forever associated. To military capacity of a high order and all the nobler virtues of the soldier he added the brighter graces of a pure life, guided and sustained by the Christian's faith and hope." [91]

That was for the record and for the inspiration of Stuart's lieutenants who were to prove, with inferior weapons and broken-down horses, that Stuart had been as great a teacher as he was a leader of cavalrymen. Before the laudatory general orders were issued, or "Jeb" had breathed his last, Lee had spoken in the fullness of grief a few unpremeditated words that showed how lofty was the estimate he put on Stuart. In the midst of the fighting for the "Bloody Angle," some one placed in Lee's hands a telegram. He opened it, read it and had to get a firm grip on his emotions before he trusted himself to speak. "Gentlemen," he said to the officers around him, "we have very bad news. General Stuart has been mortally wounded." Lee paused and then exclaimed: "He never brought me a piece of false information!" [92]

Reliable information of the sort that Stuart sent him, Lee seldom needed more than during those baffling days around Spotsylvania. Only during the Gettysburg campaign had he been more completely in the dark. Never had the Army had so few discerning eyes. Daily the grim list of fallen leaders was lengthened—Long-

[90] O. R., 33, 1257–58.        [91] O. R., 36, pt. 3, p. 800.
[92] W. Gordon McCabe in R. E. Lee, Jr., 124–25 and in 37 S.H.S.P., 68.

street wounded, Powell Hill sick, Ewell in danger of collapse under his burdens, Edward Johnson in the hands of the enemy, nine of the Brigadiers killed, wounded or captured, some of them among the best; and now "Jeb" Stuart dead. The Wilderness might be the graveyard of the Army command.

# CHAPTER XXII

## THE DEBITS AND CREDITS OF MAY

THE NEWS of Stuart's death was announced at field headquarters on the 13th, but it did not become generally known to the troops until the 14th.[1] "It caused indescribable feeling in the Army," Moxley Sorrel wrote years afterward.[2] Distress was the deeper because of the strain of a week's fighting on the nerves of ill-fed soldiers. For the relief of nerves and the rest of exhausted men the rain of the 11th–12th fortunately continued through the 15th and into the 16th.[3] "It looked," said George Neese, "as if Heaven were trying to wash up the blood as fast as the civilized barbarians were spilling it."[4]

While the Southerners peered from muddy trenches through the dripping forest at the dim position of an enemy held captive by mud, a few appointments were made for the command of leaderless troops. John B. Gordon was promoted Major General as a reward for his attack on May 6 and for his service in the "Bloody Angle."[5] When Hill's recovery permitted the return of Early to the direction of his own Division, Gordon's old Brigade was transferred to what was left of Edward Johnson's command, at the head of which Gordon was placed.[6]

Johnson's wrecked Division, needless to say, contained the Stonewall Brigade and the old Second Brigade of the Army of the Valley. Some of the regiments of Johnson's original Brigade had been incorporated with the Second, and had been commanded in the Wilderness by John M. Jones. Steuart's Virginia units of 1864 had been Taliaferro's in 1861.[7] So many men of these organizations had been captured in the "Bloody Angle" that the rem-

[1] *Hotchkiss' MS Diary*, 345.　　　　　　[2] *Sorrel*, 248.
[3] *Hotchkiss' MS Diary*, 343, 345; O. R., 36, pt. 1, p. 72.
[4] *Neese*, 268.　　　　　　[5] *Wright*, 38.
[6] Cf. O. R., 36, pt. 3, p. 814.
[7] Specifically, Walker's had been the Stonewall Brigade intact. John M. Jones's included the Twenty-first, Forty-second and Forty-eighth Virginia, which had constituted the Second Valley Brigade, and the Twenty-fifth and Forty-fourth of Johnson's original Brigade. The Virginia regiments of Taliaferro, transferred to Steuart, were the Tenth, Twenty-third and Thirty-seventh. Cf. 43 *S.H.S.P.*, 156, 100, and O. R., 36, pt. 1, p. 1023.

nants could not operate as Brigades. Grievous as was the necessity, the Stonewall Brigade, Jones's and Steuart's Brigades [8] had to be consolidated. When orders to effect this were issued on the 14th of May, Army Headquarters did not know who was the senior officer of the three Brigades.[9] Even after they were consolidated, they remained pathetically small. John Casler's company of the Thirty-third Virginia consisted of the Captain and three privates. One of these was a cavalryman who had lost his horse.[10]

Many assignments of new officers had to wait until combat absorbed less of the attention of Lee, but one thing that could not be delayed was action in the case of Lafayette McLaws. It will be remembered that after the charges against General McLaws had been dismissed on May 4, General Bragg had recommended that the Georgian be ordered to rejoin his command.[11] Whether Bragg was influenced to do this because McLaws had supported him after Chickamauga, there is no evidence. Nor is there anything to indicate that General Cooper's prompt acceptance of Bragg's recommendation [12] was due to the fact, obvious from correspondence, that Cooper had no fondness for Longstreet. As it chanced, McLaws was employed for a few days in dealing with a raid in Southside Virginia. When this ended on May 17,[13] his orders to return to his command would have been effective; but Bragg properly decided to put the facts before General Lee in a telegram that has been lost. In framing a reply, Lee had to reason that if Longstreet recovered and resumed command, as there now was every reason to believe he would, he and McLaws could not work together. Moreover, Joseph Kershaw was handling McLaws's old Division with skill and success. It had to be admitted, further, that McLaws's record as a divisional commander had not been one of uniform promptness and of average success. Finally, it might be that McLaws was becoming a fault-finder. Men of that type Lee did not like to have around him. To Bragg's telegram, therefore, Lee dispatched this reply: "I request that Gen. McLaws be not ordered to this Army, but assigned to duty elsewhere." [14] That

8 Less the First and Third North Carolina, which were transferred to W. R. Cox's Brigade (1 N. C. Regts., 153). All except thirty men of the First North Carolina had been captured (ibid). For Cox's Brigade, see infra, p. 512.
9 O. R., 36, pt. 2, p. 1001.     10 Casler, 331.
11 O. R., 36, pt. 2, p. 955. See supra, p. 373.
12 O. R., 36, pt. 2, p. 966.
13 O. R., 36, pt. 2, p. 174.     14 Lee's Dispatches, 182.

settled the case. McLaws was sent to the Department of South Carolina, Georgia and Florida and was assigned, May 25, to command of the District of Georgia.[15] There he remained till the final retreat.

A second question of command that would not wait for more merciful days was that of a successor to "Jeb" Stuart. Hampton was the oldest of the three Major Generals of cavalry and had more prestige than either of the others. Seniority was his by a narrow margin.[16] In combat, he undeniably was the peer if he was not the superior of Fitz Lee, though Hampton was not so resourceful as Fitz in finding provender for the horses. Fitz, on the other hand, had been closer to Stuart personally and had much of "Jeb's" joy of battle. The difficulty was that Hampton and Fitz Lee were secret rivals. They never were pitted against each other. Outwardly they were on good terms. At heart, Fitz Lee represented and Wade Hampton challenged the Virginia domination of the cavalry Corps, and, some would say, of the entire Army of Northern Virginia. Advancement of one man over the other might, at the moment, be demoralizing. Time must try and perhaps time would resolve the differences between the two. In the same orders that announced the consolidation of three of the Brigades of Johnson's Division, Lee directed that "until further orders, the three Divisions of cavalry serving with this Army will constitute separate commands and will report directly to and receive orders from these headquarters."[17] This was a heavy burden to add to the overloaded shoulders of the commanding General. It was, moreover, a dangerous gamble in co-ordination, even though the chief of one Division was the son and the chief of another Division the nephew of the man to whom they were to report. The risk had to be taken. There appeared at the moment to be no sound alternative.

Not all the news of those mid-May days was as gloomy as the weather or as grim as that of promotion to fill dead men's saddles. Within less than a fortnight after General Grant had launched offensives in Southwest Virginia, in the Shenandoah Valley and

[15] O. R., 35, pt. 2, p. 513.
[16] Hampton had been promoted Brigadier more than two months before Fitz Lee (Wright, 82, 86), but both had been made Major General to rank from the same day (Wright, 35). On the list of nominations sent Congress, Jan. 8, 1864, Hampton's name immediately preceded Lee's (3 Journal C. S. Congress, 530. Cf. ibid., 618).
[17] O. R., 36, pt. 2, p. 1001.

up the James River, all three of these subordinate operations had been ended or frustrated. Sheridan's raid lost its momentum after the action at Yellow Tavern. His troopers hammered feebly at the northeastern face of the Richmond defenses and then rode away down the James.[18] This raid and all the subsidiary operations of the Federals were brought to naught without the dispatch from Lee's Army of any troops besides the two small Divisions of cavalry that Stuart had used against Sheridan.

There could have been no detachment of infantry. On the contrary, Lee was doing everything possible to procure reinforcements from the other fronts,[19] because he felt sure Grant's attack would be renewed as soon as the rain ceased, though he himself wished, as always, to take the offensive.[20] By the afternoon of the 16th of May, the roads began to dry.[21] The sunshine of the 17th, which was unusually warm for the season,[22] hastened the process. Grant did not wait another day. He ordered Hancock to attack again at the "Bloody Angle," the apex of which the Federals had evacuated on the night of the 14th [23] as not worth holding. In the new assault on the line across the base of the angle, Hancock was to have on his right the support of the VI Corps.[24]

Promptly at 4 A.M. on the 18th, the advance began,[25] but so much time was lost in occupying the undefended first and second lines of the original Confederate position [26] that it was 8 o'clock before the Confederate artillerists, who had been told to expect an attack,[27] observed a stir on the abandoned works. Pickets and skirmishers were recalled. Gunners took their stations at the twenty-nine pieces that commanded the ground the enemy must cross.[28] Orders were to fire round shot where the enemy was in the woods and shell where he could be seen. This fire was slow compared with that of the enemy. At length the Federals cleared the thickest of the woods. The Confederates scarcely could believe their eyes or realize that a frontal assault on the line was to be made by the enemy. "This infantry . . ." said one witness, "stepped out rapidly with their muskets at a 'right shoulder shift,'

18 O. R., 36, pt. 1, pp. 791–92.          19 For the details, see 3 R. E. Lee, 332 ff.
20 Cf. Lee's Dispatches, 183–85.          21 O. R., 36, pt. 1, p. 72.
22 Hotchkiss' MS Diary, 345.          23 O. R., 36, pt. 1, p. 361.
24 O. R., 36, pt. 1, p. 337.          25 O. R., 36, pt. 1, p. 337.
26 Ibid. and 33 S.H.S.P., 332.          27 Cf. O. R., 36, pt. 1, p. 1087.
28 Ewell (O. R., 36, pt. 1, p. 1073) said the number was thirty, but both Pendleton (ibid., 1046) and Long (ibid., 1087) reported twenty-nine in position.

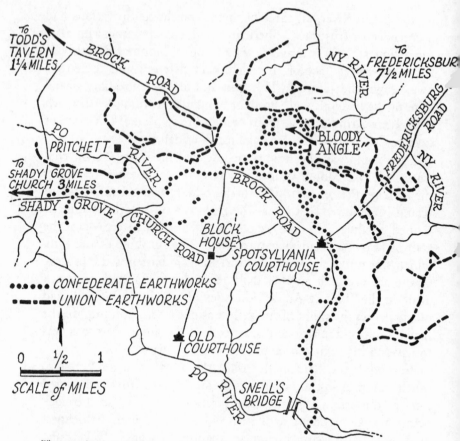

The completed Trench System around Spotsylvania Court House, May 19, 1864. It is impossible to determine accurately how the lines were extended day by day. After the Michler map of 1867.

in successive lines, apparently several brigades deep, well aligned and steady, without bands, but with flags flying, a most magnificent and thrilling sight, covering Ewell's whole front as far as could be seen." [29] The moment the Unionists came within shrapnel range, orders were given to shift the fire to case shot and to shell. This confused the gallant lines but did not halt them. Soon the Federals broke into a double-quick. Hotter grew the artillery fire; nearer raced the enemy. A few score yards, a round or two, and then orders to serve canister along with the shrapnel.[30] By this time the Federal lines, badly torn, were at the abatis. Brave

[29] Col. W. E. Cutshaw in 33 S.H.S.P., 333.　　　　　　[30] Ibid.

men tried to tear it away or to push through it,[31] but the short range artillery fire was past endurance now. The lines hesitated and broke. Thousands of men ran back toward the shelter of the trees. Almost as soon as the enemy disappeared into the woods, the Confederate artillery ceased fire, not to spare life but to save ammunition.[32] By 10 o'clock, with grievous casualties and the worst wounds of the entire campaign,[33] Hancock abandoned the attack.[34] General Long was entirely justified in saying, "This attack illustrates the immense power of artillery well handled." [35] George Meade, beyond the woods, was more realistic: ". . . we found the enemy so strongly entrenched that even Grant thought it useless to knock our heads against a brick wall . . ." [36]

The next day, May 19, there were several showers [37] and a consequent threat of another period of inactivity. Evidence accumulated that the enemy was shifting to his left again. An ominous and a threatening move that might prove to be. Unless met as Grant's flank march of May 7 was, the side-slip might put the Federals between Lee's Army and Richmond. The utmost vigilance was demanded. Such scant intelligence as was available suggested that the Federals might be abandoning their positions opposite the Confederate left, which Ewell now held.[38] Ewell accordingly was ordered to demonstrate on the 19th and to ascertain whether the Federals still were in his front.

As the Second Corps now had been reduced to approximately 6000 men, Ewell did not relish the prospect of a frontal demonstration that might become a costly attack. He therefore asked if Army Headquarters objected to a flank operation as a substitute. It was acceptable.[39] With that assurance, Ewell made preparations to move around the Federal right. He decided to take the whole of his infantry but to move six guns only.[40] Why Ewell limited his artillery to this extent, he never explained.

Not long after 12 M. of the 19th, with Ramseur's Brigade in front [41] Ewell had the Second Corps and the six guns of Braxton's

[31] O. R., 36, pt. 1, p. 338.
[33] Ibid., 232.
[35] Ibid., 1087.
[37] Hotchkiss' MS Diary, 345.
[38] The First Corps had been shifted on the 14th-15th to the extreme Confederate right (O. R., 36, pt. 1, p. 1057).
[39] Ibid., 1073.
[40] Ibid., 1088.
[32] 33 S.H.S.P., 333.
[34] O. R., 36, pt. 1, p. 338.
[36] 2 Meade, 197.
[41] Ibid., 1082.

Battalion proceed by a detour toward the Ny. The time of day prescribed a swift advance if Ewell was to get around the Federal flank before darkness. After a march of two or three miles, the roads were found to be so bad that Braxton was turned back. If this was not done by Ewell's order, it must have been with his approval,[42] certainly with his consent. Unhindered, then, by slow-moving guns but stripped of all artillery support, Ewell pushed on. About 3 o'clock, he crossed the Ny.[43] Half an hour later,[44] as Ewell naively stated it, he "came on the enemy prepared to meet [him]."[45]

Neither side was ready for a meeting engagement, but the militant instinct of Dodson Ramseur told him he would be overwhelmed if he waited for the enemy to assail him. He offered to attack at once. Rodes or Ewell or both authorized him to do so. He rushed forward and furiously drove the enemy until he found that his flanks were being enveloped. Ramseur then shook himself loose, skillfully retired about 200 yards and re-formed his line. By that time, Gordon had the survivors of Johnson's Division in line on the left of Ramseur, but another flanking movement soon pushed Gordon and consequently Ramseur back to the ground from which the North Carolinian had started his attack. The Federals pressed their advantage. They might have overwhelmed Ramseur and perhaps might have routed the Corps had not two things happened. First, on the left of Ramseur, the Brigade of the wounded John Pegram, Early's old Division, was advanced by its temporary commander, Col. John S. Hoffman, with fine élan at the moment the left of Ramseur's Brigade was threatened again.[46] This relief might not have been enough to prevent defeat had not Wade Hampton been at hand. He had received orders to cover Ewell's movement and he prudently had carried a battery of horse artillery with him. When Ewell's confused plight was close to disaster, Hampton's guns helped to hold off the enemy until nightfall.[47]

[42] Both Long (O. R., 36, pt. 1, p. 1088) and Pendleton (ibid., 1046) wrote that Braxton "was ordered to return." They did not state by whom the order was issued. Ewell said only (ibid., 1073) that his advance was "through roads impassable for my artillery." Col. C. S. Venable brought the responsibility somewhat closer to Ewell when he wrote, in 1873, "that on account of the difficulties of the way through the flats or the river, [Ewell] had not taken his artillery with him" (14 S.H.S.P., 533).
[43] O. R., 36, pt. 1, p. 1082.
[44] Ibid.
[45] Ibid., 1073.
[46] O. R., 36, pt. 1, p. 1083.
[47] 14 S.H.S.P., 533.

Ewell then was able to withdraw. He had demonstrated that the Federals still occupied the right of their line, and, as the event proved, he delayed for twenty-four hours the start of the II Corps on another turning-movement,[48] but he had paid with 900 casualties.[49] The Federals whom Ewell first had encountered were the new 4th Division, former heavy artillerists, who had been attached under Brig. Gen. Robert O. Tyler to Hancock's II Corps. These troops had done admirably and had received all needed support from Birney's 3rd Division [50] and from the Maryland and the Heavy Artillery Brigades of the V Corps.[51] The Federals were much gratified by the repulse of an attack which they took to be designed to gain possession of the Spotsylvania-Fredericksburg highway.[52]

With this unhappy affair, the ghastly fighting around Spotsylvania Court House came to its conclusion. Grant now had undertaken a farther advance by his left flank. A race similar to that from the Wilderness to Spotsylvania was beginning. Insofar as this again was to challenge the command of the Army of Northern Virginia, the one encouraging circumstance was that Powell Hill had sufficiently recovered from his illness to resume direction of the Third Corps on the 20th.[53]

Nothing that happened to the command during the Wilderness-Spotsylvania battles was comparable, in seriousness, to the unparalleled losses that had been sustained. If the repair of these losses had not occupied the full thought of Lee during every hour he could spare from the direction of operations, appraisal of individual performance during the campaign would have shown, as usual, much that was admirable and at least as much that was mediocre.

For Longstreet's brief part in the campaign, there could be nothing but praise. Charges made subsequently that he was slow in his advance to the Wilderness rest on no sure foundation. Primarily the question is whether he was wise in allowing his men

[48] O. R., 36, pt. 1, p. 340.          [49] Ibid., 1073.
[50] Ibid., 338.
[51] Commanded, respectively, by Col. Richard N. Bowerman and Col. J. Howard Kitching (ibid., 542).
[52] O. R., 36, pt. 1, p. 192.
[53] Ewell (O. R., 36, pt. 1, p. 1073) gave this as the date of Early's return to command in the Second Corps. The orders from Army Headquarters were dated May 21 (O. R., 36. pt. 3, p. 814).

as many as five or six hours of sleep on the night of May 5–6. The probability is that the troops fought the better on the 6th because of that rest. A further charge that Longstreet refused to accept the service of an engineer sent to guide him was untrue.[54] Once Longstreet was on the field, his management of his men and his entire conduct were at his top pitch of performance. If his behavior in the Wilderness was an indication of what was to be expected of him, his recently developed penchant for strategy had not marred him as an executive officer under Lee.

Ewell's record in the Wildnerness might have prompted the patient Lee to make the same criticism he subsequently passed on that officer's action at Gettysburg—that he could not get Ewell to act with decision.[55] The command of the Second Corps on the 5th of May was undistinguished. On the 6th, so far as Ewell was concerned, indecision cost the Army the superb opportunity offered by the exposure of Grant's right. An attack on that flank, delivered while Longstreet was rolling up the left, might have involved a complete defeat of the Union forces. This was the first and only time during the campaign that both flanks were found to be vulnerable simultaneously. Ewell failed at that great hour because he could not make up his mind when his subordinates were divided in opinion.

Chance or a psychosomatic malady left Powell Hill unable, after the first day's fighting, to exercise field command. He did not recover until the most serious fighting was over at Spotsylvania, but he did his utmost to keep in touch with his troops. In the most desperate hours at Spotsylvania he was as near the firing line as his ambulance could be driven. The one decision he made on May 6, when he already was sick, was unwise and might have been fatal. It was proper, of course, to provide for Heth's and Wilcox's men such sleep as they could hope to get in the presence of the enemy. No small part of Hill's success as a division commander had been due to the care he took of his troops' physical well-being; but on the night of May 5, his alternatives were not those of allowing the men to sleep and of forcing them to intrench. He could easily have left a strong picket in the woods and could have moved the Divisions of Heth and Wilcox back to a point

---

[54] For the evidence on these allegations, see 3 R. E. Lee, 283, n. 69.
[55] See supra, pp. 172–73; Marshall, 250.

where they could have formed a new line. The pioneers then could have dug a fire trench. Lee evidently thought Hill erred in doing nothing to protect the men from a sudden onslaught. In fact, Heth believed that Lee never forgave him and Wilcox for failing to protect their front. Once in the winter of 1864-'65, Heth brought up the subject in conversation and explained to Lee how he and Wilcox had sought to get Hill to act. Lee was unconvinced that they had done their utmost. "A division commander," said Lee, "should always have his Division prepared to receive an attack." Heth answered: "That is certainly so, but he must also obey the positive orders of his superiors." Lee said no more.[56]

The divisional command in the Wilderness had been competent but no more than that. Johnson had done well on the 5th of May. Kershaw had fulfilled expectations and Field had exceeded them on the 6th. The other Major Generals had not shone. In particular "Jube" Early's refusal to believe John Gordon's report concerning the Federal right flank was not creditable. It was not even openminded. Early was satisfied that his intelligence reports accurately reflected the situation on the Union right and that Gordon was wholly wrong in thinking the flank unprotected. In that belief, Early would not verify either set of reports. He may have tried to browbeat both Gordon and Ewell. More than that, Early in later writings disparaged Gordon's performance and persisted to the end of his days in asserting that Burnside was in rear of the Federal right until afternoon,[57] though the contrary was demonstrable from the records.[58]

Perhaps the strangest part of the whole affair was Early's statement that Gordon's attack before sunset was suggested by Early himself. Not one word did Early say of Lee's visit to the Confederate left,[59] which visit, according to Gordon, alone was responsible for the order to deliver the attack.[60] Ewell, for his part, reported that "after examination" of the ground, he "ordered the attack" and placed Johnston's Brigade in support of Gordon.[61] Lee's judgment was expressed in his prompt shuffling of commands to give Early's Division temporarily to Gordon, who was

[56] Heth's MS Memoirs, 155.  [57] Early, 348 ff.
[58] See Gordon, 258 ff; 3 R. E. Lee, 297, n. 35.
[59] Early, 348.
[60] Gordon, 258.  [61] O. R., 36, pt. 1, p 1071.

promoted eight days later to the rank of Major General. This was an honor due Gordon. He shared with "Old Pete" the laurels of the Battle of the Wilderness. In recognizing Gordon's service, Lee did not disparage or rebuke Early. On the contrary, to "Jube" was entrusted the Third Corps during the illness of Hill. In view of this and of other distinction soon to be accorded Early, it is difficult to escape the conclusion that Lee thought Ewell, not Early, to blame for failure to act promptly on Gordon's report of as glorious an opportunity as Jackson had found the previous year in that same treacherous Wilderness.

To turn now to Spotsylvania, the heroes of the first day were "Dick" Anderson, "Jeb" Stuart, Fitz Lee and Tom Rosser. Had not the cavalry fought stubbornly and shrewdly on the 8th of May, the First Corps would not have been able to recover the Court House and the crossroads; but if Anderson had not started early, the cavalry would have been defeated before he could have reached the scene. It is regrettable that neither Fitz Lee nor Rosser prepared a report of the day's occurrences. The glimpses a student gets from the statements and memoirs of other officers make him wish he knew more of the tactical dispositions of the cavalry before the arrival of Anderson. They fought dismounted and behind makeshift defenses of piled rails, but of their density of line and kindred interesting details, nothing is known except by the analogy of later action.

The co-operation of Anderson was cool, well balanced and prompt, though deliberate. He was as calm, outwardly, as if he were directing a regiment on a field where all the advantage was his. The modesty of his nature kept him from asserting anything more concerning his march to Spotsylvania than that, after starting, he kept moving because he did not find a suitable place at which to rest. This may have been the literal fact, but behind it was the soldierly spirit which applies almost instinctively this sound principle: when on the march, the best insurance against the accidents of the road is an early start. An extra hour allowed at the beginning will compensate for an hour unexpectedly lost en route.

Anderson maintained after the 8th the excellent rating he won that day, but his opportunities and his risks were less than those of the commander on his right, the unique "Dick" Ewell. It is not easy, on the strength of the evidence that remains, to appraise Ewell fairly for the period from May 10 to the end of the operations around Spotsylvania. Most of the criticisms of his handling of his Corps spring from the existence and form of the "Bloody Angle."' The proximity of woods within 200 yards of the works made possible the attack of Upton on Doles; the narrowness and bad roads of the salient prompted the commanding General to order the artillery withdrawn on the evening of the 11th. Had the line been drawn farther southward, the difficulty of communicating between the flanks would not have been comparably so serious a matter as the loss of a Division was.

All this is obvious but it also is hindsight. The question as it concerns Ewell is primarily whether his part in drawing and then retaining the salient was such that he has to share the blame along with the commanding General and the Chief Engineer. In the absence of reports by Lee and by Martin Smith, the story of the choice of the salient has to be gleaned from the personal narratives that supplement Ewell's few references.

The principal witness is Capt. W. W. Old, later a lawyer of distinction, who was Edward Johnson's aide. Captain Old, writing in 1905, described how Johnson, on the evening of the 8th was ordered to place his Division on Rodes's right. To do this, Johnson had to proceed through the woods in gathering darkness with no guide. After a thicket was passed, campfires were discerned almost directly ahead. Said Captain Old: "The ground was examined, and General Johnson found we were on the brow of a ridge, which turned somewhat shortly to the right. The campfires in our front seemed to us to be considerably below the plane of our position, as they were in fact. It was now quite late in the night, and General Johnson deflected his line and followed the ridge, so far as it could be distinguished in the darkness." [62]

Captain Old explained subsequent dispositions and added: "My recollection is that on the 9th of May the engineer officers, with General M. L. Smith at their head, went over the line and considered it safe with artillery." [63] This statement is confirmed in part by Johnson, who mentioned in his report "the salient—a point which with artillery was strong, but without it weak." [64] Col.

[62] 33 S.H.S.P., 20–21.          [63] Ibid.
[64] O. R., 36, pt. 1, p. 1079.

Thomas H. Carter was of opinion that if the salient was defended by artillery, with infantry in support, it was "absolutely impregnable against successful assault." [65]

If this is approximately a correct statement, then Ewell is not to be blamed for the choice or occupation of the salient. Failure to complete the support line earlier must be charged against the Chief Engineer who was directed to fortify the new line but probably was unable to do so promptly because of an enfilading fire and the weariness of the troops.

For the withdrawal of the artillery from the salient, the blame rests on the commanding General, not on Ewell. There is no reason to doubt the statement of Campbell Brown that he heard Lee give the order to Long in the presence of Ewell.[66] Lee was prompted, of course, by outpost statements of enemy shifts of grounds; but the case was one in which the intelligence officers were accurate in reporting the movement of wagons to the rear and wrong in the interpretation of the movement. What the Confederate officers mistook for the preliminaries of a withdrawal or a new flanking operation was, in reality, the evacuation of wounded and the dispatch of vehicles for additional supplies.[67] Lee was conscious of his mistake, after the attacks of the 12th had been delivered, and, as always, was instant in assuming responsibility for it.[68]

The next question concerns the time required to bring back the guns. Johnson's request was sent Ewell, was endorsed by Ewell and was transmitted to Long by one of Johnson's couriers. The dispatch was not forwarded to Lee. He knew nothing of Johnson's concern or of the situation at the salient until, after having arisen about 3 o'clock, he heard the firing.[69] The courier, meantime, had much difficulty in locating Long's headquarters. Johnson's messenger, in fact, had been so slow in returning that "Old Allegheny," suspecting something was amiss, had sent a second after him. It is not certain whether the first or the second of these couriers reached Long. In either case, approximately three hours and forty minutes elapsed before a most urgent request from

[65] 21 S.H.S.P., 240.   [66] O. R., 36, pt. 1, p. 1088.
[67] See supra, p. 398.   [68] 33 S.H.S.P., 24.
[69] 14 S.H.S.P., 529. This is the unqualified statement of Col. C. S. Venable, who was at Lee's headquarters on the night of the 11th-12th.

Johnson passed through corps headquarters and reached the officer, distant about 2 miles, who was to return the artillery.[70]

To say this is to make it virtually certain that the late return of the artillery, which may have been responsible for the loss of the salient, was attributable to the slow transmission of orders. In one sense, then, a courier probably cost the Confederacy the greater part of the casualties of the "Bloody Angle"; in a sense more nearly accurate, the disaster was due partly to a slow and awkward method of transmitting orders. Ewell's responsibility for this was no greater and no less than that of any commanding officer who fails to correct what manifestly is wrong.

Ewell's mishandling of the demonstration against the Federal right on the 19th of May was not subject to any of the reservations and allowances that have to be made in any fair examination of his conduct at the "Bloody Angle." It is doubtful whether, on the 19th, Ewell was justified in attempting an elaborate turning-operation simply to ascertain whether the enemy still was in his front. As he asked and procured the consent of the commanding General to this adventure, some of the blame must be put on Lee. For ordering or approving the continuance of the march without the guns of Braxton's Battalion, Ewell must be held accountable. In the absence of all information concerning his reasons, he can be charged with nothing more specific than an error of military judgment.

Small though the action of the 19th was, when compared with the battles of the 5th, 6th and 12th, its events must have been regarded at Army Headquarters as cumulative evidence that Ewell's mental powers were failing or else that the strains of the campaign were exhausting him dangerously.[71] He was at the front daily,[72] and he was as devoted as ever he had been, but he was not the Ewell of 1862.

If it has to be concluded that Ewell was not equal to the de-

70 The timing is not difficult. Johnson reported that he sent the information to Ewell "about 12, or between 10 and 12 o'clock on the 11th" (*O. R.*, 36, pt. 1, p. 1080). Col. Thomas H. Carter stated in 1893 that he received the order 20 minutes before daybreak (21 *S.H.S.P.*, 240). More specifically, Long wrote (*O. R.*, 36, pt. 1, p. 1086) that he received at 3:30 A.M. Johnson's note which Ewell had endorsed (*O. R.*, 36, pt. 1, p. 1086). Major Page stated that he received orders about 3:40 to move back to the salient (7 *S.H.S.P.*, 535).
71 See *infra*, p. 498.                    72 *Jed. Hotchkiss' MS Diary.*

mands of the campaign, it should be said in the same sentence
that, next to Anderson, the most conspicuous figures of the operations around Spotsylvania were three of Ewell's lieutenants. "The
restoration of the battle on the 12th . . ." wrote Col. Charles S.
Venable, "was a wonderful feat of arms in which all troops engaged deserve the greatest credit for endurance, constancy and
unflinching courage; but without unjust discrimination, we may
say that Gordon, Rodes and Ramseur were the heroes of this
bloody day." [73] That scarcely can be disputed.

Gordon, as the designated reserve, acted with sound judgment
and with the utmost speed. A less courageous man, or a man of
less daring, would have considered his duty done if he had retreated to a respectable distance and then had drawn a defensive
line. Gordon, instead, threw forward offensively the first troops
he met, then formed a line as far to the front as he could, and
immediately attacked. Whether or not he reasoned that he would
find the enemy in confusion, he did so find them. All the numerous Federal reports spoke of the counter-attack as one before which
the II Corps had to withdraw.

Rodes's conduct, like his military bearing, [74] was flawless. In
the crisis, which allowed no time for deliberate reflection, he displayed the soundest economy of force. His tactics were those of
protecting his flank by drawing a line perpendicular to the west
front of the salient, while the greater part of his Division fought
its way up the earthworks. The achievement was reassuring proof
that Rodes had learned much since Gettysburg in the handling of
a Division.

Ramseur, the youngest of the three, showed once again his remarkable leadership in offensive combat. Seldom in the war had
one Brigade accomplished so much in fast, close fighting. He deserved the compliment he received when General Lee sent for
him to thank him. Nor could he be blamed if, at 27, he confided
to his wife that Ewell said he was the hero of the day. [75] After
Ramseur was wounded, Col. Bryan Grimes handled the Brigade
in a manner to mark him as ripe for promotion. [76] Nat. Harris
probably was next to Gordon, Rodes and Ramseur in the praise he

[73] 14 S.H.S.P., 532–33.                    [74] Stiles, 261.
[75] Ramseur to his wife, MS, May 30, June 4, 1864—Ramseur MSS. For the continuance
of the sketches of Rodes, Gordon and Ramseur, see infra, pp. 511 and 558 ff.
[76] Grimes, 52.

merited for his behavior on the 12th. Harris, in his thirtieth year, was a well-educated Mississippi lawyer who had raised a company and had served in every capacity with the Nineteenth Mississippi from Captain to Colonel. He was steady and hard hitting.

Encouraging as were these performances, it has to be repeated that too many of the apt pupils were being killed. The schoolmaster of the Army, the commanding General, had to be ceaselessly active in seeking new students, in giving instruction to those who survived, and in correcting the exercises of others. He explained much of his method one day near Spotsylvania while urging Powell Hill not to be severe with a Brigadier who had blundered: "I cannot do many things that I could do with a trained Army. The soldiers know their duties better than the general officers do, and they have fought magnificently. You'll have to do what I do: when a man makes a mistake, I call him to my tent, talk to him, and use the authority of my position to make him do the right thing the next time." [77] It was a limping rule, but Lee could apply no other.

[77] See the reference in 3 R. E. Lee, 331.

# CHAPTER XXIII

## A New Struggle for the Railroads

THE PERIOD of Lee's grapple with Grant in Spotsylvania County was one of exciting contest for Richmond and its railroad connections. In their contest Pierre Gustave Toutant Beauregard reappeared, Beauregard *Felix* as some now styled him. His consistent good luck justified the *nom de guerre*. At Shiloh, after Albert Sidney Johnston fell, Beauregard, as the officer next in rank, held the advantage at the end of the first day's fighting. He retreated at the close of the battle of the second day, but he escaped blame for the defeat. In the subsequent operations around Corinth, he lost little reputation. Compelled by sickness to ask for relief, he received on his recovery his old command at Charleston, South Carolina, to which responsible post was added supervision of the long front of Georgia and of Florida. In the campaign of 1863, he conducted an excellent defense of Charleston against an adversary who controlled the waterways.

It might have seemed, in April, 1864, that Fortune was abandoning him. A worse assignment scarcely could have been devised than the one Mr. Davis gave him of protecting Southern Virginia and North Carolina from an invasion the Federals openly were preparing to launch. Beauregard may have been a poseur, but he certainly was a patriot. On the 14th, in answer to an inquiry from Bragg whether his health permitted him to take the field, he gave assurance he was "ready to obey any order for the good of the service." [1]

As it was not then certain where the blow would fall on the seaboard, he was ordered to Weldon, North Carolina,[2] but was delayed a few days at Charleston to await the arrival of Maj. Gen. Samuel Jones, who was to act in his place.[3] On the 20th of April Beauregard bade farewell to his officers and soldier in an address that differed incredibly, as to temper and tone, from the one he

[1] 2 *Roman*, 193.
[2] *O. R.*, 33, 1283. For Jones's appointment, see *supra*, p. 325.
[3] 2 *Roman*, 193–94.

had penned three years previously at the time he had been summoned to Virginia.[4] Then he had been flamboyantly oratorical. This time he merely asked support for Jones, who, he explained, was relieving him temporarily. He concluded: "Should you ever become discouraged, remember that a people from whom have sprung such soldiers as those who have defended Wagner and Sumter can never be subjugated in a war of independence." [5]

At Weldon, which he reached April 22,[6] Beauregard announced that he assumed command of the Departments of North Carolina and Cape Fear.[7] Almost at once, on his own initiative and apparently without authorization from Richmond, he renamed the consolidated areas the Department of North Carolina and Southern Virginia.[8] Within this large area and adjacent to it, he found military jurisdiction confused. Chase Whiting commanded on the Cape Fear. North of that, most of the best troops in Eastern North Carolina were about to be concentrated in front of New Berne, where Robert Hoke, under the direct orders of Braxton Bragg, was hoping to duplicate his fine success at Plymouth.[9] These operations were in the Department of North Carolina, the charge of Maj. Gen. George E. Pickett, whose headquarters were in Petersburg, Virginia.[10] To what extent Pickett was responsible for affairs between the James and Appomattox, Beauregard manifestly did not know. Beauregard's own statement on assuming command was, in effect, that the northern boundary of the new Department was "the James and Appomattox Rivers." [11] As these streams came together at City Point, South of Drewry's Bluff, the important "water gate" of Richmond, Beauregard's language left in doubt the control of the heavy fortifications at the Bluff. Directly North of the James, the Department of Richmond was about to be transferred from Arnold Elzey to Robert Ransom.[12] The commander of that Department would be independent unless, of course, Ransom took the field in co-operation with Beauregard. In that event, as senior, "Old Bory" would exercise command. Beyond the Department of Richmond was the domain of General

---

[4] See Vol. I, p. 1.  
[5] 2 *Roman*, 194.  
[6] *O. R.*, 51, pt. 2, p. 872.  
[7] *Ibid.*, 33, 1307.  
[8] 2 *Roman*, 195; *O.R.*, 33, 1292. See Whiting's note in *O. R.*, 33, 1305.  
[9] See *supra*, pp. 335–36; 2 *Roman*, 196 ff; *O. R.*, 51, pt. 2, p. 882.  
[10] Pickett had been assigned Sept. 23, 1863 (*O. R.*, 29, pt. 2, p. 746 and *supra*, p. 335).  
[11] *O. R.*, 33, 1307–08, but see *ibid.*, 51, pt. 2, p. 872.  
[12] *O. R.*, 33, 1312.

Lee, whose control of affairs, in an emergency, was recognized to the Southern limit of W. H. C. Whiting's Department. Beauregard's command, in a word, scarcely could have been more complicated or less clearly defined.

The military problem had unhappy qualities of a nature more dangerous. Bragg's estimate of the situation was explained by one of his staff officers, who came promptly to Weldon to inform Beauregard.[13] The War Department at that time was anticipating Grant's offensive on the Rapidan and an advance up the James or inward from the Peninsula or from the Southside by a force that Maj. Gen. A. E. Burnside was expected to command. His objective might be Richmond, Petersburg, the railroad between the two, or the line that joined Petersburg and Weldon.[14]

Great superiority of force was known to be on the side of the Federals. The one hope of reducing these adverse odds lay in the probability that the Unionists would draw troops from the South Atlantic coast for the advance into Virginia or upper North Carolina. Were that to occur, prompt and proportionate reduction of force could be made by the Confederates. Beauregard himself already had admitted that in these circumstances, two Brigades could be withdrawn from his old Department for service in the assailed states.[15] If he was willing to set that figure, the War Department would accept it as the minimum and would call to the new theatre of war as many additional troops as the size of the garrisons and the inactivity in South Carolina, Georgia and Florida justified. The instant and alarming question was whether the maximum withdrawal of men from the Southern coast would be sufficient to hold Richmond, Petersburg and the railroad leading from them into the Carolinas. Lee was insisting with the fullest of his polite firmness that the troops "borrowed" from the Army of Northern Virginia should be returned. Besides these, there would not be many for Beauregard.

After the almost universal manner of commanders who leave one post for another, "Old Bory" at Weldon did not think the situation at Charleston as dangerous as it had appeared from the Battery. Consequently he began to consider whether he could not summon the stronger, rather than the weaker Brigades, from

[13] O. R., 33, 1317. No memorandum of this interview has been found.
[14] See the sketch of the military geography of this region in Vol. I, p. 697 ff.
[15] O. R., 35, pt. 1, p. 116.

Principal Southern Railway Connections of Richmond, May, 1864. Included are the
northern and northwestern connections, the R.F.&P. and the Virginia Central—after
*O. R. Atlas*, Plate CLXIII.

South Carolina. Alfred Colquitt's Brigade was the one that could
be moved from Charleston with least risk to the city; but on the
same island with Colquitt was Johnson Hagood, who had a large,
fine Brigade that had never been in Virginia. It would be better,
Beauregard reasoned, to take Hagood than Colquitt. If, further,
the Federals reduced force in front of Charleston, it might be possible to release for service in Virginia or in North Carolina the
powerful Brigade of Henry A. Wise, which had sustained few

casualties. By bringing forward these troops and concentrating those already in his new Department, Beauregard believed he would be able to strike the rear of the Army Burnside was expected to lead inland. That was to be Beauregard's basic plan. Bragg was so advised.[16]

The assumption that the Federals were about to advance inland was strengthened in a few days by a succession of excellent intelligence reports from the Peninsula and from the Southside.[17] Thoughtfully Beauregard transmitted to Bragg the names of half a dozen Federal Generals who had commanded on the South Atlantic so that, if the Department heard that these men had troops in Virginia waters, it would know they had been withdrawn from South Carolina, Georgia or Florida. In the letter that carried this information, Beauregard asked for maps of the region North of James River in the event he had to operate there. He added civilly that if he should be placed under Lee, "I would take pleasure in aiding him to crush our enemies and to achieve the independence of our country."[18] Perhaps it was well for Beauregard that he never knew in what spirit this remark was received. Because of the diversity of the information and requests in his letter, the paper went the rounds of the War Department and came at length to the President's desk. He endorsed it with some remarks about maps and bridges and then wrote: "I did not doubt the readiness of General Beauregard to serve under any General who ranks him. The right of General Lee to command would be derived from his superior rank."[19] From that endorsement anyone would have been safe in saying that a situation which brought Beauregard close to Richmond would have in it an explosive. The pride of either man might set it off.

Developments came swiftly. With Beauregard's counsel after a friendly visit, Hoke matured his plans for the capture of New Berne.[20] Brig. Gen. Johnson Hagood moved his Brigade from James Island and started northward by train to reinforce Lee; the Brigade of Henry A. Wise prepared to follow; in Petersburg, George Pickett was directed to proceed to Hanover Junction and to assume command there of two of his Brigades.[21] This was on

16 *O. R.*, 51, pt. 2, p. 876.       17 *Ibid.*, 877, 880, 881.
18 *O. R.*, 33, 1327.       19 *Ibid.*, 1327–28.
20 *O. R.*, 51, pt. 2, pp. 880, 882. Beauregard met Hoke at Kinston.
21 *O. R.*, 36, pt. 2, p. 950; *ibid.*, 51, pt. 2, p. 886. Pickett's other Brigades were with Hoke in North Carolina.

May 4. Before Pickett could pack his kit and comply, scouts and signal parties notified him on the morning of the 5th that the new invasion had begun. James River below City Point was full of transports—four, twenty, forty, fifty-nine—the number rose hourly. Barges were in tow; some of the vessels had horses aboard; Negro troops as well as white were to be seen; monitors and gunboats formed an escort.[22]

Pickett read and reflected. Strictly speaking, he no longer was in command of the Department,[23] which Beauregard that day made a District[24] of the enlarged Department. Although ordered elsewhere, Pickett could not leave or refuse to act. Until Beauregard arrived, he must continue to direct a force that scarcely could offer even the form of resistance. All the troops at his disposal were one regiment of infantry, the City Battalion of Petersburg, the militia, and the Washington Artillery, twenty-one guns, that had been wintering near the city. Not one cavalryman, to his knowledge, could Pickett employ close to the city.[25] The nearest mounted men subject to his orders were 150 on the Blackwater, perhaps thirty miles to the Southeast.[26] Nor did Pickett know what forces were between Petersburg and Richmond. He must have been aware that Drewry's Bluff had a garrison; but beyond that, though the distance to Richmond was no more than an oft-traveled twenty-two miles, he was in ignorance.[27] His first step, of course, was to notify Beauregard, but as his immediate superior was farther from Richmond than he was, he communicated directly with the War Department. Upon the receipt of every new report from the signal stations, he telegraphed Richmond. Beauregard notified him promptly to remain in command, to assume direction of troops arriving from the South en route to Richmond and, in particular, to halt Hagood's Brigade, which was soon to reach Petersburg.[28] As for himself, Beauregard telegraphed, he was sick and was unable to come to Petersburg that night.[29]

This information from Beauregard was not of a sort to raise Pickett's hopes greatly, but, at the least, it was explicit; it was something. The War Department, in contrast, seemed preoccupied. All day on May 5 Pickett transmitted messages; all day he

22 O. R., 36, pt. 2, pp. 955–56; ibid., 51, pt. 2, pp. 892–93.
23 Walter Harrison, 124.      24 O. R., 51, pt. 2, pp. 891–92.
25 O. R., 36, pt. 2, p. 957; ibid., 51, pt. 2, p. 896.
26 Ibid., 51, pt. 2, p. 896.      27 O. R., 36, pt. 2, p. 958.
28 O. R., 36, pt. 2, pp. 956–57.      29 Cf. ibid., 51, pt. 2, p. 89x

waited in vain for a single reply. In desperation, during the afternoon he put a courier on a railroad train and sent him with a dispatch to the Adjutant General. The next day, as a matter of record, the paper was returned to the War Department by General Bragg. Across it in pencil was written the one word, *seen*.[30]

Uncounselled and unaided, Pickett hoped that the Navy Department would carry out suggestions he previously had made for the use of torpedoes and of the ironclads above the obstructions in James River;[31] but no word came from the James or the lower Appomattox of the appearance of any Southern warship to challenge the enemy. Pickett could only chafe and wonder and take such small precautions as his force permitted. He sent out his regiment of infantry to that side of the Petersburg defenses nearest the road from City Point; he recalled his little cavalry force from the Blackwater;[32] and he asked Capt. John Scott, a cavalryman who reported for service, to collect a few men and with them to hover in front of the enemy.[33] The Federals were known to have landed on the 5th, but precisely where, Pickett could not ascertain until almost nightfall. Then it was reported that the greater part, perhaps nearly all the invaders, were going ashore at Port Walthall, which was North of the Appomattox.[34] Debarkation there would indicate that the immediate objective of the Federals was not Petersburg but the railroad between that city and Richmond.[35]

During the night of May 5-6, new reports reached Pickett of probable landings by the enemy at Bermuda Hundred,[36] but he could do little and plan little because he did not even know whether the War Department intended to defend the railroad between Richmond and Petersburg.[37] All the information that came to him he forwarded at once to Bragg, though he could not be sure his telegrams were received. It was, in a word, a black night for George Pickett, as black as it was for the soldiers of Heth and of Wilcox, who then were lying in the woods that faced the Brock Road near the Tapp House in the Wilderness.

The Federals, if well led, would advance the next morning. Unopposed, they could wreck railroads, seize Petersburg, threaten

[30] *O. R.*, 36, pt. 2, p. 957.          [31] *O. R.*, 36, pt. 2, pp. 956, 957.
[32] *O. R.*, 51, pt. 2, p. 896.
[33] Scott collected a total of 30 men, only one of whom was a soldier. See the Captain's narrative in *Annals*, 380.
[34] *O. R.*, 36, pt. 2, p. 958.          [35] See the map, p. 479.
[36] *Ibid.*, 965.          [37] *O. R.*, 51, pt. 2, p. 895.

Richmond. It was a crisis as acute as any the dreadful war had brought. A defenseless region awaited the invader as if it had been a rich mansion with its door unlocked and unguarded. At the darkest hour of foreboding, about 3 o'clock [38] on the morning of May 6, there rolled into Petersburg over the tracks of the Petersburg and Weldon Railroad a train aboard which were 300 infantrymen of the Twenty-first South Carolina, Hagood's Brigade. Few as they were, they represented a northward troop movement which, if continued in strength, might bring sufficient men to Petersburg to save the city. At the moment Hagood's men could not assist Pickett in opposing the forces that had landed at Bermuda Hundred. In obedience to new orders received from Richmond, Pickett had to permit the train to proceed toward Richmond,[39] but he could count on the employment of these South Carolinians against the enemy somewhere. Hope of saving Petersburg hung on the troops that would follow Hagood's van.

Tangible assistance of a second sort reached Pickett before many hours. On the morning of May 6, D. H. Hill arrived in Petersburg. He came in the odd capacity of volunteer aide to Beauregard, because he had learned of the mounting danger and had tendered his services. Beauregard sent him to explain the opinions of the Department commander and to render such help as was possible.[40] Another gain was the reopening of the telegraph to Richmond.[41]

These two occurrences raised hopes a little. Pickett could take counsel with an able combat officer and with the War Department, which now seemed conscious of the desperate need at Petersburg. During the forenoon, Bragg authorized Pickett to halt the remaining units of Hagood's Brigade, as they arrived from the South, and to use them against the enemy who, Pickett thought, would that day seek to cut the Richmond-Petersburg Railroad.[42]

38 The time is estimated from the fact that these troops are known to have reached Drewry's Bluff, about fifteen miles North of Petersburg, approximately at 5 A.M. (O. R., 36, pt. 2, p. 239.)

39 O. R., 36, pt. 2, p. 255. For evidence that Pickett did not feel that he was authorized to halt Hagood's troops at Petersburg, see O. R., 51, pt. 2, p. 895.

40 O. R., 36, pt. 2, pp. 960, 965.

41 Pickett was concerned lest the telegraph line be broken and he was urgent that, if necessary, communication should be maintained by a longer circuit (O. R., 51, pt. 2, p. 895).

42 Ibid. No telegram from Bragg to Pickett authorizing the detention of Hagood has been found, but it is manifest from Pickett's dispatch to Bragg, O. R., 51, pt. 2, p. 897, that Bragg directed that Hagood be sent to Port Walthall Junction. Beauregard was credited in 2 Roman, 198, with saving Petersburg by insisting that Hagood be held South of James River.

All of Pickett's information was to the effect that the Federals had not yet reached the railway, which was about two and a half miles from their landing place, but reports of their advance were being received.[43] In this situation, which was cracking toward calamity, Pickett could do nothing more than ask officials of the Petersburg and Weldon when they expected more cars from the South.

Before noon, as if in answer, another train groaned its protesting way into Petersburg from Weldon. Its passengers were six companies, 300 bayonets, of Hagood's Brigade, and they were under Col. R. F. Graham, of the Twenty-first South Carolina.[44] In accordance with Bragg's orders, Pickett directed Graham to march to Port Walthall Junction. A battery was sent with him.[45]

Accustomed as were the Confederates to fighting against oppressive odds, their commander might have thought it farcical to send 600 men to oppose an army estimated at 40,000.[46] Gideon himself would have quailed in the face of such odds. Still, orders were orders. Miracles sometimes did occur, or, at the least, deliverance appeared to be miraculous. Graham and his South Carolinians must march against the host of the invader. Obediently, willingly, they crossed the Appomattox, climbed the ridge North of it, and then through the pleasant May weather marched to Swift Creek and beyond.

At length, after 4 o'clock on the same 6th of May, they reached a point on the Turnpike opposite Port Walthall Junction, a discouraged station past which a frail track ran to the lower Appomattox.[47] The main line to Richmond was distant from the highway only a quarter of a mile to the eastward. A glance showed the rails intact. Another glance disclosed the presence of troops, but they wore gray coats, not blue, and they carried the Stars and Bars. In surprise and curiosity, Graham set out to ascertain who they were. They proved to be none other than men of his own regiment, the van that had reached Petersburg during the night. Proceeding to Drewry's Bluff, they had detrained there and had marched back to meet the anticipated attack at the Junction.[48]

---

43 *O. R.*, 36, pt. 2, p. 965; *ibid.*, 51, pt. 2, p. 895.
44 *O. R.*, 36, pt. 2, p. 255. Colonel Graham is incorrectly styled Col. Mercer in *O. R.*, 51, pt. 2, p. 895. The hour of Graham's arrival at Petersburg is inferred from the time he reached Port Walthall Junction, about 4:45 P.M.
45 *O. R.*, 51, pt. 2, p. 895.       46 *Ibid.*, 895, 896.
47 See the map *infra*, p. 479.       48 *O. R.*, 36, pt. 2, p. 255.

Hagood's first two contingents incredibly were reunited and were in position before the enemy struck, but they had not a moment to relax and to greet one another. Scouts and pickets reported that the enemy was close at hand and in great strength. An attack might be delivered at any moment.

Graham cast about for cover. It was near at hand. About 300 yards East of the railroad was a sunken road which joined the Petersburg Pike South of the Junction. Up the sunken road, on Graham's left, was a ravine.[49] On the right was a wood the enemy might hesitate to enter.[50] Into this position, with a prompt decision that would have done credit to a veteran, Colonel Graham moved his 600 men. They scarcely had time to load before the bluecoats began an advance upon them. Fieldguns boomed in support of the Union infantry. Graham's troops held to the bank of the road, fired furiously and drove back the attacking force. Again the Federals formed for an assault, which this time they manifestly intended to deliver against the Confederate left. Graham thinned his line, concentrated on his threatened flank, and again repulsed the enemy.[51] So furious was the fire of the few guns that it was audible in Petersburg.[52]

After the repulse of the second assault, the South Carolinians held their ground and watched the fields and woods. Prisoners said that the attacking column was Heckman's Brigade, Massachusetts and New Jersey troops of "Baldy" Smith's XVIII Corps [53] —the first positive identification of that Corps as part of the new Army.[54] Soon there was movement, but not by Heckman: Before nightfall, down the road from Drewry's Bluff, there marched a small Brigade to reinforce the Carolinians. Its presence near the fort on the river may have been known to Lt. Col. A. T. Dargan, the officer who had conducted part of the Twenty-first South Carolina to the Bluff; but to others the arrival of 800 good soldiers was a surprise, almost the miracle that pious souls had come to expect.

The Brigade, unknown in Eastern Virginia, might veritably have seemed to have dropped from heaven. Its commander was an experienced soldier, Brig. Gen. Bushrod R. Johnson, who had

49 Evidently one that led down to Ashton Creek.
50 O. R., 36, pt. 2, p. 251.               51 Ibid., 255–56.
52 Owen, 311.                                53 O. R., 36, pt. 2, p. 251.
54 Brig. Gen. Charles A. Heckman commanded the 1st Brigade of Brig. Gen. Godfrey Weitzel's 2nd Division (O. R., 36, pt. 2, p. 16).

fought under Longstreet at Chickamauga and subsequently had served with him in East Tennessee. Johnson and his Tennessee troops had been ordered by Bragg, late in April, to move from the Virginia-Tennessee border to Richmond in order to share in the city's defense.[55] Before Johnson had been able to do more than unload his baggage, he had been directed on the night of May 5–6 to cross immediately from Chafin's Farm to Drewry's Bluff. He had arrived at 3 A.M. and two hours later had received the first contingent of Hagood's Brigade. Later in the morning, while he was riding about to learn something of the terrain, telegraphic orders had been received for the dispatch of Hagood's Brigade to Port Walthall Junction if a train were available. No cars and locomotive were at hand, but after some slow telegraphic exchanges in Johnson's absence, Hagood's men were started on foot for the Junction. About 11 A.M. Johnson received a message from the commander of the Department of Richmond, Maj. Gen. Robert Ransom, his immediate superior, to move to the Junction Hagood's Brigade and, if need be, his own. Ransom continued: "The railroad must not fall into the enemy's hands. Rapidity is necessary. Act at once. If the enemy be at Port Walthall Junction dislodge him." [56]

Johnson read and wondered. "This," he wrote afterward, "was the first intimation I had that the enemy was threatening the railroad." [57] He made the best of his belated orders, put his column in motion and, after a doubtful pause, he pushed on to the Junction when he heard the sound of firing there. At the scene of Graham's fight, when he ascertained what had happened, Johnson assumed command and extended the line to the right.[58]

Nothing quite like this small concentration, in an hour of extreme danger, ever had occurred previously in Virginia. The vital railroad between Richmond and Petersburg, at its most vulnerable point, now was in the keeping of 1400 to 1600 men,[59] some of whom had prevented a break in the track. The astonishing fact was that none of these soldiers ever had performed a day's

---

[55] The dates neither of Bragg's orders nor of Johnson's departure from the vicinity of Zollicoffer, Tenn., appear in available records. On May 2, Johnson and his men were in movement. See *O. R.*, 52, pt. 2, p. 664.
[56] *O. R.*, 36, pt. 2, p. 239.
[57] *Ibid.*                                    [58] *Ibid.*
[59] Johnson stated (*ibid.*) that he arrived at Drewry's Bluff with 1168 men. Hagood (*ibid.*, 251) reported that Johnson had 800 muskets on the morning of May 7.

field service in Virginia. All of them were newly arrived from other States. To this narrow margin of men and of time was the Confederacy reduced!

At the Junction, after Johnson's arrival, there may have been, by comparison, a sense of lessened danger; but in Petersburg, Pickett had notice of another serious threat. Word came from the vicinity of the Blackwater that 3000 Federal cavalry with eight guns were on the move westward from Suffolk. They were preparing, said the commander of the Confederate outpost, to form "a junction with the force which landed on the James River." [60] To a soldier of Pickett's experience, it must have been apparent that these Union cavalrymen might be seeking to cut the railway between Petersburg and Weldon, precisely as the Army which had landed at Bermuda Hundred was endeavoring to sever connection between Petersburg and Richmond. To oppose these raiders, no Confederate cavalry other than James Dearing's small Brigade could be made available and this had been scattered and was not yet concentrated. [61] If the enemy reached the Petersburg and Weldon tracks, in the face or in the absence of Dearing's Brigade, then the Confederate troops that were hurrying northward would be detained. Any such delay might entail the defeat of the men in front of Port Walthall Junction. Much would depend, to be sure, on the time of the start by the Federals who, from the mid-stretch of the Blackwater, would have to cover approximately thirty-seven miles to reach the nearest point on the Petersburg and Weldon Railroad. [62] With little or no information at hand concerning the trains then moving, it was impossible for Pickett to reach any conclusion except that the race between the cavalry and the carrier might be close.

The first heat was won by the railway. After dark on the 6th, when the action at Port Walthall Junction had ended, a train brought to Petersburg Brig. Gen. Johnson Hagood and the remaining units of the Twenty-fifth South Carolina. Hagood, a forthright soldier, marched directly from the railroad track to reinforce his men at the Junction. Behind his train rolled another, aboard which was the Twenty-seventh South Carolina. This regi-

[60] O. R., 51, pt. 2, p. 897.
[61] Cf. O. R., 36, pt. 2, pp. 275, 972. The Brigade consisted of the Seventh Confederate, the Eighth Georgia and the Fourth and Sixty-fifth North Carolina (O. R., 36, pt. 2, p. 208).
[62] Zuni to Stony Creek.

ment, also, immediately started on foot for the area of the Federal advance to the Richmond-Petersburg Railroad.[63] Before daylight, the whole of Hagood's command had reached the Junction and

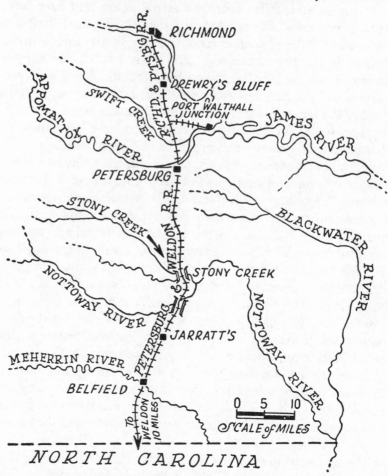

The Richmond and Petersburg and the Petersburg and Weldon Railroads, 1864. The sketch shows the bridges of the Petersburg and Weldon at Stony Creek and at Nottoway River, North of Jarratt's, destroyed in Kautz's Raid. After A. H. Campbell's Map of Virginia South of James River, 1864

had raised the defending force to a total of 2668 infantry under the informal command of D. H. Hill, who, at Pickett's request, had gone to the scene to advise Johnson and Hagood.[64] With all his old spirit of combat, Harvey Hill examined the ground and

[63] O. R., 36, pt 2, p. 251.          [64] Ibid., 240.

suggested dispositions his less experienced juniors in the service cheerfully made.

Although the situation, for these reasons, was vastly better than it had been twenty-four hours previously on the Petersburg Pike, the crisis of communication was acute along the entire front from Richmond to the Roanoke River. In the capital, the tocsin was sounded all day of the 7th to bring the last of the militia to the ranks.[65] War and Navy Departments engaged in an exchange over the alleged failure of the Army Engineers to remove obstructions from the James River in order that the warships might descend and engage the enemy.[66] One of the last three available infantry Brigades of the city garrison already had been sent across the James to Drewry's Bluff. This Brigade was Archibald Gracie's, which a few days previously had come to Richmond with Bushrod Johnson.[67] Command remained in confusion. Pickett in Petersburg was aware of Beauregard's sickness [68] and was increasingly apprehensive, as the morning passed, of the danger to the Weldon Railroad.[69] Beauregard himself had received by telegraph a flattering expression of the President's desire that he proceed to Petersburg, when his physical condition permitted, to direct operations. The General had replied that he hoped to leave on the 7th, but he remained at Weldon.[70] There he continued to do what he could to expedite the movement of Wise and of the troops that had been designated for the attack on New Bern. In obedience to orders, Hoke had abandoned his expedition against that town and was hurrying his troops to the railroad.[71]

While these forces slowly or swiftly were converging on the Richmond-Petersburg line, Bushrod Johnson at the suggestion of Harvey Hill was employing on the 7th simple combat tactics that had been used with success many times in the Army of Northern Virginia. A heavy screen of skirmishers was thrown out from Port Walthall Junction to meet the enemy; when he showed fight, the skirmishers engaged and held him until he disclosed by his

[65] 2 R. W. C. D., 202.
[66] O. R., 36, pt. 2, p. 971; ibid., pt. 3, p. 829; O. R., 51, pt. 2, p. 946.
[67] Cf. O. R., 36, pt. 2, pp. 965, 966. Gracie's Brigade consisted of the Forty-first, Forty-third, Fifty-ninth and Sixtieth Alabama (ibid., 207). The other Brigades left in the Richmond defenses were William R. Terry's, formerly James L. Kemper's, and Eppa Hunton's. Both of these belonged to Pickett's Division
[68] O. R., 51, pt. 2, p. 898.          [69] Ibid., 899.
[70] Ibid., 894.          [71] O. R., 51, pt. 2, pp. 888–89, 891.

movements something of his strength and his design.[72] The Confederate skirmishers' task was not difficult. Bluecoats showed neither dash nor originality in the deployment. When they made their main assault, which was not delivered until about 2 o'clock, Johnson drew back his line to the railway cut where Hagood repulsed first a frontal and then a flank attack. By 4 P.M., the firing, except for some sharpshooting, was at an end. The one achievement of the Federals was the severance of the telegraph wires and the tearing up of some 300 to 500 yards of railway track during the brief time they held it.[73] In repelling them, Johnson lost 184 men, nearly all of whom belonged to Hagood's Brigade.[74] Hagood estimated the Union casualties at 1000, but they were in reality 289 in three attacking Brigades.[75] The Confederates were well satisfied. Johnson had praise for the manner in which the newly arrived Carolinian handled the Brigade,[76] but he [77] and Hagood [78] felt that the repulse was due in large degree to the leadership of Harvey Hill.[79]

After the close of this little action, the final contingent of Hagood's Brigade reached the battleground and raised the total strength of the Confederates to about 3500.[80] This reinforcement encouraged the defenders of the railroad, but instructions from the rear now began to hamper them. Johnson received suggestions from Pickett that if the forces at Port Walthall Junction could not hold their position, they should return to Swift Creek, two miles southward. In one message Pickett stated that he must retain for the defense of Petersburg the first contingent that arrived from the South. The next telegram called for dispatch of one of Johnson's regiments to the city, but assurance was given that whenever new troops arrived, they would be forwarded to the Junction.[81] Johnson had been receiving his instructions from Ransom in Richmond and apparently he did not know whether he should accept orders from Pickett. Besides, it is likely that Johnson knew a retreat to Swift Creek would expose to the Federals another stretch of the

---

[72] Cf. O. R., 36, pt. 2, p. 240.
[74] Ibid., 241, 253.
[76] Ibid., 240–41.
[73] O. R., 36, pt. 2, p. 124.
[75] Ibid., 125.
[77] Ibid., 240.
[78] Johnson Hagood, Memoirs of the War of Secession (cited hereafter as Hagood), 221–23.
[79] The more important of the reports appear in O. R., 36, pt. 2, pp. 124, 239, 251. In ibid., 51, pt. 2, p. 901, Johnson epitomized the story of the action in a telegram to Ransom. The recollections of Hagood are in op. cit., 223.
[80] Ibid., 242.
[81] O. R., 36, pt. 2, p. 242.

railroad he was trying to defend. He paid no attention to the first and the second telegram from Pickett, but when a third message conveyed direct orders to retire to Swift Creek, Johnson moved at midnight of the 7th–8th.[82] His tired men were on the road at the same time that "Dick" Anderson was struggling through the smoke-covered road in the Wilderness en route to Spotsylvania Court House.[83]

If Pickett learned before morning of the 8th that Johnson's men were safely on the line of Swift Creek, he scarcely could have felt that he had reduced greatly the risk of losing Petersburg. He thought he saw indications of an early direct assault on the city.[84] In addition, he had new instructions from Beauregard not to bring on a general engagement. That was the reason for the insistent recall of Johnson to Swift Creek. The strong southern bank of that stream, Pickett reasoned, could be held until the arrival of reinforcements.[85]

When those additional troops would reach Petersburg, Pickett did not know. Railroad officials had expected at least eight trains from Weldon on the 7th.[86] Three had arrived, but during the early afternoon, telegraphic communication with Beauregard had failed.[87] Alarmed by this, Pickett or the railroad authorities had sent a scouting locomotive down the exposed Petersburg and Weldon Railroad. The crew had proceeded about nineteen miles South of Petersburg to the vicinity of Stony Creek. There they found that the Federal cavalry raiders from the Suffolk area, under Brig. Gen. August V. Kautz, had reached and had burned the railway bridge before troops from Weldon had arrived to defend it.[88] This structure was of frame and 110 feet in length.[89] It could be rebuilt quickly but, during the critical days immediately ahead, Beauregard could not move troops by rail directly to Petersburg. The enemy had won the race. Richmond's main line of supply, up the coastal plain, was severed North and South of Petersburg. Before it could be reopened, anything might happen in the face of the adversary at Bermuda Hundred. That opponent now was

82 Ibid.
84 O. R., 36, pt. 2, p. 242.
86 Cf. O. R., 36, pt. 2, p. 172.
87 Ibid. All these references are to dispatches from Pickett to Bragg. No report of operations during these critical days was filed by General Pickett.
88 O. R., 51, pt. 2, p. 899. Kautz's cavalry Division had completed this work of destruction about 4 P.M. (O. R., 36, pt. 2, p. 172).
89 Ibid.

83 See supra, p. 380.
85 O. R., 51, pt. 2, p. 899.

known to have two Corps, the X and the XVIII, opposite the Richmond and Petersburg Railroad. Prisoners said, also, that the entire force was commanded, not by Burnside, as the Confederates had anticipated, but by Maj. Gen. Benjamin F. Butler, "Beast" Butler to the more vehement Southerners. Some there were who doubted whether so important a field command had been entrusted to a "political General" of limited experience.[90] Whether Butler was competent or not, the Confederates still thought he had 40,000 men with him—ten times as many as stood in his front.[91]

Surprisingly, the next day, the 8th of May, Butler did not take advantage of his superior numbers. He remained idle within easy striking distance of the Richmond-Petersburg Railroad, though he readily could have destroyed several additional miles of its track. By this blunder on his part, the Confederate commanders gained a day in the northward movement of the troops still in North Carolina. The expedient of the Southern authorities was to hasten the advance of the soldiers as far northward as the break in the line near Stony Creek. There the regiments were to be detrained and marched to cars that were being assembled North of the burned bridge.

Behind this arrangement and all other aspects of the concentration to save Richmond from Butler's Army, the driving power was that of Braxton Bragg. He was scouring the entire South Atlantic seaboard for reinforcements, and he was ceaselessly urging Whiting and Beauregard to speed traffic on the railway.[92] Beauregard was pleased to be able to tell Bragg that he had anticipated a call for timbers with which to reconstruct the burned bridge at Stony Creek. Further, Beauregard announced that he

---

[90] Cf. Archibald Gracie, Jr., in O. R., 51, pt. 2, p. 973.

[91] Confederate intelligence reports were not greatly in error when they credited Butler with a total of 40,000. His monthly return for May showed about 44,000 officers and men present in his Department. Where the Confederates made their mistake was in the exaggeration of the number he had with him in the field. The strength of the X and XVIII Corps, including Brig. Gen. Edward W. Hinks's Division of Negro troops, was about 21,000 present for duty. Separate siege artillery, numbering 1360, did not report until May 13 (O. R., 36, pt. 2, p. 739). Kautz's cavalry had a roster of 5500, but on a separate return (O. R., 36, pt. 2, p. 175), Kautz credited himself with only 2900 equipped for duty. In addition, Butler had 1200 unattached cavalry, whose station is not given. A safe estimate of the force actually at Butler's disposal at Bermuda Hundred and City Point as of May 8 is 22,000. For his departmental return, May, 1864, see O. R., 36, pt. 3, p. 427.

[92] Cf. O. R., 51, pt. 2, p. 904.

was sufficiently recovered to proceed to Petersburg. "The water," he said naively in an official telegram, "has improved my health." [93] This benefit had come opportunely. President Davis was preparing to name Robert Hoke to command on the Petersburg front in the event that Beauregard's indisposition continued.[94]

The day of inaction at Port Walthall Junction was not one of relief on the Petersburg and Weldon Railroad. South of Weldon, the Confederates could make the most of poor equipment and limited rolling stock; North of Weldon, bad conditions grew worse. Early on the 8th Kautz attacked the defenders of the railroad bridge across the Nottoway River, about six miles North of Jarratt's Depot and five miles South of Stony Creek. While Kautz engaged the garrison, he set the structure afire. In twenty minutes the ruined bridge fell into the river. This was a more serious blow by far than the destruction at Stony Creek, because Nottoway Bridge was 210 feet in length. Troops could march around the long break, but for an indefinite period, all supplies sent up the Petersburg and Weldon must be unloaded South of the Nottoway, hauled by wagon to Stony Creek, and reloaded there [95]—an added burden on overworked Quartermasters.

Still another difficulty was presented now by Pickett. His military judgment began to show the effect of strain. Although he had ordered Bushrod Johnson on the night of the 7th to evacuate Port Walthall Junction and to take position on Swift Creek, Pickett on the 8th directed D. H. Hill to march the troops back to the Junction. Johnson was notified of these instructions and was told to keep in communication with troops that had come to Drewry's Bluff from Richmond, but Johnson was to continue to report to Petersburg.[96] Fortunately, there was good understanding between Hill and Johnson, who had become acquainted during the Chicka-mauga campaign. Doubtless with Hill's approval and possibly at his suggestion, Johnson sent several detachments during the day to the Junction to reconnoitre and to collect arms from the field. The main body he retained on Swift Creek in the belief, probably, that if he went to the Junction, he would be ordered back again.[97] He employed his men usefully enough on the 8th, under good

[93] O. R., 51, pt. 2, p. 903.          [94] Ibid., 902.
[95] O. R., 51, pt. 2, p. 906. Kautz's report is in O. R., 36, pt. 2, pp. 172–73.
[96] O. R., 36, pt. 2, p. 975.          [97] See O. R., 36, pt. 2, p. 242.

engineering direction, in digging a line of rifle pits South of the creek.[98]

More trouble was brewing. During the forenoon of the 9th, Federal gunboats bombarded Fort Clifton, a semi-permanent work on the right of the position at Swift Creek. With the help of a few of Johnson's Tennesseans, this attack was repulsed easily, but while it was in progress, the enemy appeared in considerable strength immediately North of Swift Creek.[99] Pickett promptly reminded Johnson that reinforcements were en route from Weldon and that Beauregard wished a general action deferred, if possible, until these troops arrived.[100]

The zone of action now widened. Because Butler at Bermuda Hundred was a continuous threat to the southern face of the Richmond defenses, General Ransom already had sent Seth Barton's Brigade to reinforce Gracie and the garrison of Drewry's Bluff. Ransom then had crossed the river and had established his own field headquarters near the heavy works that overlooked the James. From the Bluff, rumor spread to Richmond on the morning of the 9th that the enemy was advancing toward the fort and already was within two miles of the outer works.[101] Bragg was conspicuously disdainful of rumor,[102] and he was skeptical now, but he saw in the reported Federal advance both a danger to Drewry's Bluff and an opportunity of delivering a blow. About noon on the 9th, Bragg telegraphed Pickett an order to push forword all troops as fast as they arrived from the South, in order that they might recover the lost position at Port Walthall Junction and reopen the line to Richmond. If Butler advanced on Drewry's Bluff, the Confederates in the Petersburg area must assail him in rear from the Junction. Bragg added that Hoke, on arrival, would take command North of the Appomattox.[103] Pickett immediately transmitted this dispatch to Johnson, with orders to "move forward at once and see what the enemy are doing."[104] In the judgment of Pickett, there was small prospect of the early arrival of Hoke, because of the burning of Nottoway Bridge. Pickett so advised Bragg.[105]

At 1:10 there came new and imperative instructions from Bragg: The enemy was moving on Drewry's Bluff; all the troops at Pick-

98 *Ibid.*, 242–43.
100 *Ibid.*, p. 978.
102 Cf. *supra*, p. 282.
104 *Ibid.*

99 *O. R.*, 36, pt. 2, p. 243.
101 *Ibid.*, 977.
103 *O. R.*, 36, pt. 2, p. 978.
105 *O. R.*, 51, pt. 2, p. 907.

ett's disposal must move out immediately and assail the Federals in rear; this admitted of no delay.[106] Pickett acknowledged this at once, recalled to Bragg's mind the paucity of his force,[107] and then communicated with D. H. Hill and told that officer to advance.[108]

Soon the troubled commander at Petersburg repented these orders. Johnson was weak; indications were that the Federals were about to attack at Swift Creek. For the moment, in spite of Bragg's imperative, it seemed wise to hold the creek and to ascertain, if possible, whether the enemy was making a feint or a serious thrust. Johnson was so advised.[109] About 3 o'clock, Pickett received Johnson's acknowledgment of attack orders, which, Johnson said, he was obeying. In utmost haste Pickett replied that a countermand had been sent already and that Johnson was to hold the line of Swift Creek if it were true, as reported, that the Federals were advancing on that position.[110]

Johnson, it may be assumed, was as much bewildered by these changes of orders as Pickett was by Bragg's instructions and the enemy's threats. The conclusion of the commander on Swift Creek was that Pickett wished him to make a reconnaissance in force. He undertook it with a part of Hagood's Brigade and sustained a total of 137 casualties to establish the fact, almost obvious, that the enemy was strong and in his immediate front.[111] Stirred by the Confederate advance, the Federal sharpshooters stung like hornets. Later in the afternoon the Unionists made a strong demonstration, but they had to fall back from the strong Southern position.[112] At the other end of the exposed section of the Richmond-Petersburg Railroad, the advance on Drewry's Bluff did not materialize. Ransom was easy in his mind and was of the opinion that the enemy was seeking only to destroy the railroad.[113] His chief concern was over the difficulty of communicating with Bushrod Johnson, whom he considered still under his command.[114]

The end of the day left Pickett the most harassed of all the

---

106 *O. R.*, 36, pt. 2, p. 979.           107 *O. R.*, 51, pt. 2, p. 907.
108 *O. R.*, 36, pt. 2, p. 979.
109 *Ibid.*, 243. In the dispatch next mentioned in the text, Pickett gave the only explanation that has been found for these orders.
110 *O. R.*, 36, pt. 2, p. 979.
111 *Ibid.*, 244. A more detailed account appears in *Hagood*, 228–29.
112 *O. R.*, 36, pt. 2, p. 244. *Cf.* Maj. Gen. Q. A. Gillmore, *ibid.*, 35: "We found this creek impassable for any kind of troops. The bridges were all guarded by artillery and infantry, the latter occupying both banks of the stream."
113 *O. R.*, 51, pt. 2, p. 908.           114 *O. R.*, 36, pt. 2, p. 980.

commanders on the Southside. He expected to be attacked the next morning from Swift Creek, from City Point and from the South,[115] and he could not understand why no effort seemed to be made to push northward the troops that had been delayed by the burning of the bridges.[116] On the night of the 8th, he had sent trains to the northern end of the break in the Petersburg and Weldon Railroad. For eighteen hours and more the locomotives and cars had waited,[117] but not one contingent had arrived. His appeal to Bragg in the early afternoon had been desperate: "Why do not the forces at Jarratt's and below march up and drive off the enemy? This delay is criminal." [118]

[115] *Ibid.*, 979; *O. R.*, 51, pt. 2, p. 907.          [116] *O. R.*, 51, pt. 2, p. 907.
[117] *Ibid.*, 906.                                       [118] *Ibid.*, 907.

# CHAPTER XXIV

## BEAUREGARD PLANS AGAIN (STYLE OF 1861)

BEFORE 9 O'CLOCK [1] on the morning of May 10—the day of Upton's attack on Doles at the "Mule Shoe"—Beauregard reached Petersburg by way of Raleigh, Greensboro and Danville. He brought his good luck with him. From the South, over repaired tracks and by marches around the destroyed bridges, more of the long delayed reinforcements came that day to the city. Hoke arrived. So did his old Brigade, three regiments of Wise, and two of Matt Ransom. On the road, due to detrain that day, were Clingman's Brigade and four regiments of Brigades already on the ground. By 9 A.M., the accession of strength was 4900 infantry, [2] or more men than previously had been collected, with haste and anguish, for the defense of the southern end of the Richmond-Petersburg Railroad.

These newly arrived troops Beauregard, with his old self-confidence, prepared at once to organize. Hoke was to have one Division. Pickett was relieved of his command of the Military District in order to be assigned to the other Division. [3] To each of these Divisions, Beauregard attached an extemporized battalion of artillery. He could proceed, for the moment, without concern, because the Federals North of Swift Creek gave little trouble. They demonstrated during the morning, but made no attack. By noon, they had retired from the vicinity of the stream. [4] Before the day was over, Beauregard was able to telegraph Bragg: "Hope to be in position for offensive tomorrow night. Will inform you in time from [sic] General Ransom." For that matter, Ransom himself was distinctly stronger, though at the expense of the Richmond garrison. To Barton's Brigade of 1600 and Gracie's of almost the same size, [5] he was adding at Drewry's Bluff Hunton's Brigade of 1600 from the defenses of the capital. [6] This would give Ransom

---

[1] O. R., 51, pt. 2, p. 915.   [2] Ibid.
[3] Ibid. Brig. Gen. Henry A. Wise was put in command of the District (O. R., 36, pt. 2, p. 987).
[4] O. R., 36, pt. 2, p. 36.   [5] O. R., 36, pt 2, p. 988.
[6] Ibid., 985.

almost 5000 men, to which number a large part of those arriving at Petersburg were to be added. Thus emboldened, Ransom was making a reconnaissance in force with Barton's and Gracie's Brigades to locate the exact position of the enemy's van, which was reported on Winfree's Farm opposite Chester.[7] Nearer Petersburg, the enemy continued on the morning of the 10th to demonstrate but made no serious attack. Before noon, the Federals withdrew from Swift Creek.[8]

Beauregard, expecting his usual good fortune, was thinking he saw some evidences of possible Union withdrawal from Bermuda Hundred when, during the night of May 10-11,[9] the telegraph brought this message:

War Department, C.S.A.,
Richmond, Va., May 10, 1864

General G. T. Beauregard:

This city is in hot danger. It should be defended with all our resources to the sacrifice of minor considerations. You are relied on to use every effort to unite all your forces at the earliest practicable time with the troops i.. our defenses, and then together either fight the enemy in the field or defend the intrenchments. Our lines are a little in front of Drewry's Bluff, crossing the railroad and turnpike.

J. A. Seddon,
Secretary of War [10]

If Beauregard did not already know it, he soon learned what was behind this message: Sheridan's powerful cavalry Divisions had reached the Virginia Central Railroad, had torn up the track and had headed in the direction of Richmond, which had been stripped of almost all its defending infantry in order to protect Drewry's Bluff and the Richmond and Petersburg Railroad. The danger was not overstated by Seddon. No help could be sent from Lee's Army, except for that which cavalry could give. Beauregard's forces, including those at Drewry's Bluff, were the sole hope of the city. Divided, the troops of Beauregard could save neither Richmond nor Petersburg. Brought together close to the capital's defenses, which extended to the south side of the James, the troops under Beauregard might be able to deal successively

[7] O. R., 36, pt. 2, p. 914. Federal reports of this affair are in ibid., 36, 46 ff.
[8] Ibid., 36.
[9] The time is fixed by Seddon to Beauregard, May 11 (O. R., 36, pt. 2, p. 991).
[10] O. R., 36, pt. 2, p. 986.

with Sheridan or Butler or, behind the fortifications, with both simultaneously. This was the military logic that shaped the Secretary's telegram.

It was Beauregard's intention to form a junction with Ransom and to assail Butler. To that extent the anxious message from Richmond conformed in part to Beauregard's view of the strategic situation; but he did not like to be tied to a specific plan regardless of other opportunities and obligations. Although Beauregard ordered Hoke the next morning, May 11, to march with six Brigades for Drewry's Bluff, he kept an open ear for confirmation of rumors that the Federals were preparing to leave Bermuda Hundred, and he did not hasten the column's advance. After Hoke started at 1 P.M.,[11] Beauregard heard a rumor from some source that Butler was reembarking. A message was sent to Hoke to undertake a forced reconnaissance toward the river and to press the Federals if they were evacuating. Assurance was given Hoke that Beauregard would come in person, should necessity require, to direct the fighting.[12] Bragg was notified of this change of orders and was requested to inform Beauregard if the move was contrary to his views.[13]

Instead of a reply from Bragg, there came another message from Seddon, who said: "Division of your forces is earnestly objected to. It is decidedly preferred that you carry out the instructions given last night, and endeavor to unite all forces." [14] To this Beauregard replied that the division of force was temporary, and that upon statement of the Secretary's objections, his wishes, if practicable, would be executed.[15] Seddon reiterated that all the troops should be concentrated without delay.[16] Beauregard then countermanded the order to Hoke, but he appealed to Bragg and insisted that he receive "orders only from one source, and that from the general commanding." [17] Another exchange with Seddon followed. The Secretary professed himself much pained; Beauregard protested that he had foregone his needed sick leave and was willing to make the utter sacrifice of his shattered health,

[11] *Hagood,* 232.
[12] See Beauregard to Davis, *O. R.,* 36, pt. 2, p. 920.
[13] *O. R.,* 51, pt. 2, p. 919.          [14] *O. R.,* 36, pt. 2, p. 991.
[15] *Ibid.*
[16] This dispatch probably is missing from the tangled correspondence of the day, though it possibly is the message in *ibid.,* 992, that begins: "Your second telegram," etc.
[17] *O. R.,* 51, pt. 2, p. 920.

LEE'S LIEUTENANTS

but that if his course was not approved, he wished to be relieved at once.[18] In the end, the reconnaissance toward Bermuda Hundred, if made at all, showed that the Federals were as numerous and almost as far advanced as ever they had been. Hoke with six Brigades moved northward and formed a junction with Ransom about two miles below Drewry's Bluff.[19]

Pickett did not participate in this movement. He had reported sick on the evening of the 10th and on the 11th had kept to his quarters.[20] In the belief that Pickett might not recover promptly, Beauregard telegraphed for Chase Whiting to come from Wilmington to Petersburg and to take command of the field forces there.[21] Whiting had been eager to join his old chief;[22] Beauregard was no less anxious to use in the field an officer for whose abilities he continued to have high admiration. Pending the arrival of Whiting and of troops still on the road from Weldon, Beauregard remained in Petersburg, though the harassed War Department manifestly wished him to proceed immediately to Drewry's Bluff.[23] He lingered, he said, because he wanted to hasten the advance of the troops still en route, but he probably waited, also, because he had a taste for independence, for suspense, and for dramatic appearance at the climax of a scene. His arrival must mean action.

The day of the "Bloody Angle" and of Stuart's death, May 12, was one of taut anxiety along the James. Sheridan was between the outer and the intermediate lines of the Richmond defenses. To combat him, Ransom was recalled from Drewry's Bluff.[24] Two Brigades were hurried back across the James to aid in manning the earthworks that girdled the capital.[25] More could be sent, Hoke encouragingly reported, if all went well at the Bluff the next day.[26] With depleted forces but with firm resolution, Hoke, who was left in command at Drewry's Bluff, faced a somewhat hesitant attack on his front [27] and had to prepare, also, to deal with

[18] O. R., 36, pt. 2, p. 992.
[19] O. R., 36, pt. 2, pp. 990, 991; Hagood, 231–32.
[20] O. R., 51, pt. 2, p. 920.
[21] 2 Roman, 200.
[22] O. R., 33, 1314.
[23] Cf. O. R., 51, pt. 2, pp. 920, 921.
[24] O. R., 36, pt. 2, p. 995.
[25] O. R., 36, pt. 2, p. 924.
[26] O. R., 51, pt. 2, p. 924.
[27] This advance was by Brig. Gen. Wm. T. H. Brooks's 1st and Brig. Gen. Godfrey Weitzel's 2nd Division of the XVIII Corps and Brig. Gen. John W. Turner's 2nd Division of the X Corps. The entire force was under Maj. Gen. Wm. F. Smith, commander of the XVIII Corps. Cf. O. R., 36, pt. 2, p. 113.

what he assumed at the moment to be a threat against his right and rear by Kautz's cavalry. In forwarding an early report of the Federals' movements, Hoke told Bragg: "I will know fully soon and will report to you. I shall fight them if met from all sides." [28] He meant it. Naturally a fighter, he had gained vastly in self-confidence by his successful attack on Plymouth. He might need all his faith in himself. The enemy was across the Richmond-Petersburg Turnpike;[29] Confederate orders were to hold the railroad [30] as well as the defenses of Drewry's Bluff. Beauregard, at the opposite end of the railway, received from the South a part of the two Brigades for which he was waiting and he announced to Bragg, late in the evening, that he would leave for Drewry's Bluff after the arrival of the remainder of one of these Brigades, which probably would reach Petersburg the next day.[31]

On the morning of the 13th the situation on all the Virginia fronts was gloomy. The defenders of the "Bloody Angle" had limped furiously back to their line across its base. In the Shenandoah Valley, Sigel was moving southward in force superior to any the Confederates could hope to concentrate against him. Brig. Gen. George Crook and Brig. Gen. W. W. Averell, who often had made trouble for the Confederates in Western Virginia, were on a raid in Southwestern counties and, after a bloody little fight on Cloyd's Mountain, were destroying bridges and trackage on the Tennessee Railroad.[32] That railway had to be added to the four that already had been cut.[33] Although the Confederates were not quite sure of it, early in the day, the Federal cavalry were seeking to cut the last two railways within the Confederate lines, the Richmond and Danville and the Southside. Kautz's troopers were operating against those lines and not, as Hoke had thought, against the rear of the defenses at Drewry's Bluff.[34]

Black as was this situation in a devastated land, where food reserves were available for a few days only, a change was discernible on the 13th in two respects: First, Sheridan had ridden down the James and had given no evidence of a purpose to resume his attack that day. Second, the Confederates no longer were think-

28 *O. R.*, 51, pt. 2, p. 924.  29 *O. R.*, 36, pt. 2, p. 997.
30 *Ibid*.  31 *O. R.*, 51, pt. 2, pp. 923–24.
32 See the reports in *O. R.*, 37, pt. 1, p. 9 ff.
33 That is, in order, the Richmond and Petersburg, the Petersburg and Weldon, the Virginia Central and the R. F. & P.
34 See Kautz's report, *O. R.*, 36, pt. 2, p. 173.

ing in terms of defense. An offensive plan for the Southside had taken shape in Bragg's mind. It was that Hoke should engage the Federals in his front while Beauregard moved up swiftly from Petersburg and formed a junction.[35] Beauregard was ordered to march at once to Hoke and to leave only a garrison behind him at Petersburg.[36] Hoke gave prompt and repeated assurance that he would co-operate with Beauregard. No message had been received from Beauregard, said Hoke, but he would know of the General's advance by the firing and he would join the battle.[37] As the day passed with no report from Beauregard, it was correctly assumed that Kautz's raiders had cut the telegraph line on the Richmond and Danville Railroad, by which Beauregard had maintained somewhat uncertain communication with Richmond.[38]

While waiting vainly for Beauregard to announce his approach, Hoke fought all day against an enemy who, with an overlapping front, captured a part of the outer line of the Drewry's Bluff defenses. Luckily, the Federals could not exert equal pressure at all points.[39] Had they done so, they might have captured the whole of the field works before nightfall. At 7:30 P.M., Hoke asked if troops could not be moved down the Richmond and Petersburg Railroad to attack the enemy. If they were sent directly to Drewry's Bluff, Hoke telegraphed Bragg, "we can push through their lines and join General Beauregard and then attack their whole force." [40] This could not be attempted for the all-sufficient reason, among others, that no troops were available in Richmond. Fortunately for Hoke, the Federals undertook no twilight offensive. Where they were out of range, they cooked their suppers and prepared to bivouac.

---

35 It is possible to interpret Hoke's dispatches, which alone are available, as indicating that Bragg proposed an attack by Beauregard on the enemy's rear; but Bragg to Beauregard, May 13, 1864 (O. R., 36, pt. 2, p. 927), said "Move at once to Hoke" with no mention of an attack on the enemy's rear. Nor did Hoke anywhere speak of an attack of this character. On the contrary, his dispatch of 7:30 P.M., quoted in the text, *infra*, referred to a joint attack, presumably on a single front.

36 O. R., 51, pt. 2, p. 927.          37 O. R., 36, pt. 2, p. 999.

38 Cf. O. R., 51, pt. 2, p. 927.

39 The reason, as given in the report of Maj. Gen. William F. Smith, was that "if the line was held in force by the enemy, it could not be carried by assault" (O. R., 36, pt. 2, p. 115).

40 O. R., 36, pt. 2, p. 999. In 6 C. V., 213–14, is a story that courier "Hal" R. Wood of Hoke's headquarters put on a Federal uniform at Hoke's request and then rode to Butler's headquarters and "reported" that Confederate troops in great strength were landing on the Federal right and rear. Wood is said to have performed this mission and to have ridden swiftly off before he could be questioned. To this, according to the story, was due the halt in the Federal advance on the right. Nothing in the Official Records confirms any such possible explanation of the Federals' halt.

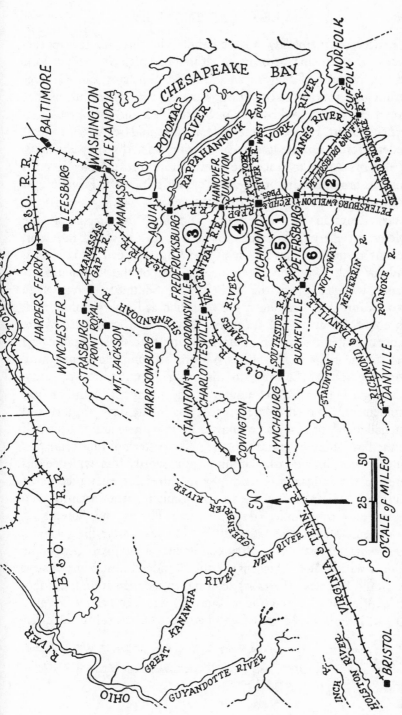

Railroad Connections of Richmond, within the Commonwealth of Virginia, May, 1864. The numerals show the order in which and the approximate point at which all the lines leading to Richmond were cut in May, 1864. The Richmond-York River Railroad, leading East from the capital, was useless. Part of its track previously had been removed. After J. W. Randolph's Map of Virginia, 1860

A decision manifestly was at hand. The time for the appearance of the principal actor in the drama had arrived. At 3 o'clock on the morning of May 14, in the midst of a hard rain, General Beauregard rode up to the Drewry mansion near the bluff of that name. He had moved by way of Swift Creek and then past Chesterfield Court House, where he had met and scattered a small Federal force. On the last lap of his ride, he had skirted the flank of Butler's Army to reach the Confederate fortifications.[41] With him he brought part of A. H. Colquitt's infantry Brigade and some of the Third North Carolina cavalry.[42]

As always in such a setting, "Old Bory" was cap-a-pie the soldier, all energy, altogether for action. In disdain of the hour, he sent immediately for his own Chief Engineer, Col. D. B. Harris, and for Col. Walter H. Stevens, engineer of the Richmond defenses, who had spent the night on the Southside. From these two, Beauregard ascertained the condition at Drewry's Bluff, and, no doubt, from the well-informed Stevens he learned also of the general strategic situation. Before leaving Petersburg, Beauregard had given orders to W. H. C. Whiting to complete a concentration he expected to be ample for disposing of Butler. Consequently, Beauregard gave little attention, at the moment, to the tactical problem on his own front. Precisely as in the days of glory and unchallenged primacy at Manassas in 1861, he indulged himself in the fashioning of grand strategy. The pattern of four years previously was unchanged. Nothing, apparently, had widened his sense of the militarily practical, or modified his early theories of logistics. "His plan," wrote his biographer, "was instantly conceived and communicated to Colonels Harris and Stevens." [43] Beauregard's own account, written nine years after the incident, was characteristic: ". . . after conferring with them about one hour, I sent [Colonel Stevens] to the President, to tell him that, if he would that day (the 14th) send me 10,000 men from the troops about Richmond (5000 under Ransom) and Lee's army, I would attack Butler's 30,000 men (who had been successful in the after-

[41] 2 Roman, 211; Beauregard to Henry A. Wise. Oct. 3, 1873, in 25 S.H.S.P., 206; O. R., 36, pt. 2, p. 1002.
[42] Beauregard, 25 S.H.S.P., 206, spoke of "Col. Baker's Reg't of Cavalry." Identification is from O. R., 36, pt. 2, p. 1021.
[43] 2 Roman, 201.

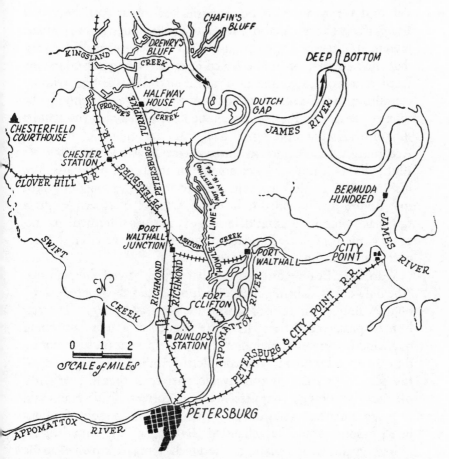

The District between Drewry's Bluff and Petersburg involved in the operations of May 5–17, 1864—after O. R. Atlas, Plate LXXVII–2 and 3

noon of the 13th in taking over the outer line of defenses) [and] capture or destroy them by 12 [o'clock] on the 15th. I would then move to attack Grant on his left flank and rear, while Lee attacked him in front, and I felt sure of defeating Grant and probably open the way to Washington where we might dictate *Peace*!!" [44]

With this plan, which had not then been written out, Colonel Stevens went immediately to Richmond. The President was both

[44] 25 *S.H.S.P.*, 206. In 2 *Roman*, 201, is a more elaborate description of the plan. It is stated there that Beauregard asked 10,000 men from Lee and 5000 from Ransom. As will appear in the text, *infra*, Beauregard wrote Bragg that Lee should send "temporarily to this place 15,000 of his troops."

sick and weary and was not accessible at so early an hour, but Bragg received Stevens and listened to the great design the Colonel presented. Stevens had been instructed by Beauregard to request that the necessary orders be issued at once.[45] Bragg of course refused to act on so complicated and doubtful a question without consulting Mr. Davis. As a courtesy to a comrade, pending the moment when the President could be informed, Bragg thought he should hear what Beauregard had to say in support of the plan. Accordingly he ordered his horse and rode at once to Drewry's Bluff, where Beauregard welcomed him and began a discussion of his proposal. In their consideration of it, Bragg soon discovered that Beauregard intended to have the Army of Northern Virginia fall back to the Richmond defenses, to the city's intermediate line, even, while heavy detachments from that Army were sent to support the attack on the Southside.[46]

Years later Beauregard insisted that Bragg agreed the plan was "the only one which might save Richmond and the Confederacy," but that Bragg "still refused to issue the necessary orders." [47] Bragg himself preserved little of his correspondence of those absorbing days, and he wrote no memoirs. In a contemporaneous memorandum for the President,[48] he completely riddled Beauregard's entire plan. It scarcely is conceivable, therefore, that Beauregard's memory of Bragg's acquiescence was correct. The plan, said Bragg, postulated a delay during which the scanty supply of rations in Richmond would be exhausted. So long a time would be required, in the second place, to execute Beauregard's plan that the Unionists could intrench themselves in front of Drewry's Bluff and thereby overcome the advantage the reinforcements would give the Confederates. Again, argued Bragg, the delay and concentration "involved the almost certain fall of Petersburg." Fourth, to quote Bragg's own concise statement, "the retreat of General Lee, a distance of 60 miles, from the immediate front of a superior force with no less than 8000 of the enemy's cavalry between him and the Chickahominy, to retard his movement, at least endangered the safety of his army if it did not involve its destruction."

[45] 25 S.H.S.P., 207.
[46] In 2 Roman, 201, this was presented as part of the plan from its conception. Perhaps this was the fact, but Beauregard himself, reviewing the plan in his letter to Wise, did not so present it. The letter to Wise antedated the publication of Roman by approximately ten years. See also note 50, infra.
[47] 25 S.H.S.P., 207.       [48] Dated May 19, 1864.

Even if the retreat were successful, Bragg went on, the retreat would lower the morale of Lee's Army and would involve the loss of the Shenandoah Valley, of other regions on which the South must depend for supplies, and of the strategically valuable Virginia Central Railroad. Finally, said Bragg in comment on the plan, the reconcentration was unnecessary because Beauregard had by this time sufficient force, if promptly and vigorously used, to crush Butler's Army.[49]

Beauregard would admit none of this. Subsequently he wrote that he said to his visitor: "Bragg, circumstances have thrown the fate of the Confederacy in your hands and mine; let us play our parts boldly and fearlessly! Issue those orders and I'll carry them out to the best of my ability. I'll guarantee success!"

This did not appeal to Bragg. He merely said that he would lay the facts before the President.[50] Then Bragg rode off.

In a short time Davis himself came to the Bluff and listened attentively to the grandiose plan of Beauregard. Like Bragg, the President could see nothing practicable in the proposal. All he promised Beauregard was that he would send back to the South-side Ransom and all the troops who could be spared from the Richmond garrison.[51]

Doubtless both Davis and his military adviser were steeled by the emergency to the swift and unceremonious rejection of a scheme that was basically and irredeemably wrong in its logistics and in its psychology. The crisis could not wait on theory or theatricals. A desperate moment in the life of the Confederacy had been reached. The previous night Kautz had torn up part of the track of the Richmond and Danville Railroad. On the 14th some of his troops struck the Southside line [52] and thereby severed the last railroad that connected Richmond and Petersburg with any large section of the Confederacy. The military depots of Richmond, as well as the city itself, now would receive no supplies other than those brought by wagon from nearby districts that were occupied, in large part, by the enemy. Nor was Richmond

---

[49] *O. R.*, 36, pt. 2, pp. 1024–25.

[50] In the previously quoted letter to Wise, 25 *S.H.S.P.*, 207, Beauregard said that Bragg promised to return to Richmond at once and to get the President to issue the orders; but here again, Bragg's fundamental and continuing opposition to the plan makes it virtually certain that in this particular, also, the memory of General Beauregard was at fault.

[51] 25 *S.H.S.P.*, 207.      [52] *O. R.*, 36, pt. 2, pp. 173–74.

itself sufficiently secure for risks to be taken. Even if Butler were held, Sheridan with his powerful cavalry still lingered at Haxall's Landing below Malvern Hill,[53] and might advance at any time and penetrate defenses that were far too extensive to be held in strength against a mobile adversary. As most of the Confederate cavalry had to be employed with Lee's desperately threatened Army, the alternative to Beauregard's grandiose plan was clear: Butler must be destroyed and a part, at least, of the troops confronting him must be sent back to the north side of the James.

Beauregard did not understand, or else did not believe, that Sheridan might return at any time and assail the capital. In contrast to the excited men in Richmond, Beauregard began the duties of the 15th in a composed and leisured state of mind. All was quiet at dawn. The enemy, as he saw it, was not pressing. There was time for Whiting to collect the delayed wagons of his troops in Petersburg and to advance to join the Confederates at Drewry's Bluff. It would be better to allow Whiting the whole of the 15th and the greater part of the 16th for his preparations to march to Beauregard. The 17th would be a suitable day for the battle.

In a brief dispatch to Bragg in Richmond, Beauregard mentioned these dates and requested the help of the Confederate gunboats and the presence of General Ransom.[54] Perhaps Beauregard would have been surprised to know the magnitude of the sensation his telegram created at the capital. Secretary Seddon at 10 A.M. hurried the message to the President with the endorsement that, in his judgment, the delay in Beauregard's advance would be fatal. Davis was less alarmed but was anxious that the attack be delivered the next day, May 16.[55] Whatever Bragg thought and said, he at once sent Beauregard this moderately phrased telegram: "Whiting is urged to join you earliest moment with his whole force. It is hoped you may receive him in time to attack tomorrow. Time is all-important to us, as the enemy gains more by delay than we possibly can. Sheridan's cavalry, with reinforcements, will again threaten the city very soon, which is almost stripped of troops to aid you." [56]

Before this telegram reached the headquarters of Beauregard, he had found, as he afterward explained, that Whiting would have

[53] O. R., 36, pt. 1, p. 779.          [54] O. R., 36, pt. 2, p. 1004.
[55] Ibid.                               [56] O. R., 51, pt. 2, p. 934.

an impossibly long one-day route to follow in marching to join him while avoiding Butler. Instead of forming a junction and assailing the enemy with superior force in front, it would be better, Beauregard reasoned, to leave Whiting South of Butler. Then Whiting could attack the Federals in rear while Beauregard moved against them near Drewry's Bluff. By this arrangement, Beauregard believed he could envelop and destroy the enemy and achieve triumph at the gates of the capital.

Accordingly, at 10:45 A.M., Beauregard drafted instructions to Whiting to assault the enemy from the South on the morning of the 16th.[57] While these instructions were in the hands of the copyist, Beauregard received Bragg's dispatch. To Whiting's letter the disappointed Beauregard merely added a postscript: "I have just received a telegram from General Bragg, informing me that he has sent you orders to join me at this place. You need not do so, but follow to the letter the above instructions." [58] Beauregard knew this would not surprise Whiting. Already that officer had been told to disregard any instructions that did not come through Beauregard's headquarters.[59]

The next task Beauregard set for himself was to see that Bragg did not again interfere with his plans. Promptly Beauregard advised Bragg that Whiting had been told what to do. "Please telegraph [Whiting] to follow [my instructions] by Colonel Logan. Yours may conflict with mine." [60] Correspondence of this sort was an art in which Braxton Bragg had enjoyed long experience and had acquired much skill. He was not to be caught off guard by a brother officer who was notoriously less adept with pen than with tongue. Bragg answered at once: "My dispatches of this morning to you and General Whiting were by direction of the President and after conference with him." [61]

Beauregard did not let this stop him. He informed Bragg: "Change of plan since the President was here necessitated a corresponding change in Whiting's instructions, which I have ordered accordingly." [62] For the President—and doubtless for the record —Beauregard wrote a detailed account of why he changed the instructions to Whiting.[63]

Then Beauregard prepared and in the early afternoon delivered

57 O. R., 36, pt. 2, p. 200.
58 Ibid.
59 25 S. H. S. P., 207.
60 O. R., 51, pt. 2, p. 934.
61 Ibid., 934.
62 Ibid.
63 Ibid., 1077.

to his divisional commanders full orders for their participation in the battle of the next day.[64] He was satisfied that his plan was sound. As he later pictured the anticipated result: "Butler thus environed by three walls of fire with the defeated troops, could have no recourse against substantial capture or destruction, except in an attempt at partial and hazardous escape westward, away from his base, trains, or supplies."[65]

Two obstacles only did Beauregard admit. One was the possibility of stubborn resistance by the Federals. The other, as he stated it in retrospect, was that in a hastily organized force his officers and men would be unacquainted. Said he: "The moral force which tells so significantly of the unity which springs from old association was entirely wanting . . ."[66] He did not overstate the troubles that sprang from his inability to reorganize his Divisions prior to the 15th. That day, at first opportunity, he named Ransom, Hoke and Alfred Colquitt to the three commands, which varied in strength from two to four Brigades that never had fought together.[67] Colquitt was an old acquaintance, but Hoke and Ransom, according to Beauregard's official biographer, had not been known to the Army commander until the opening of the campaign.[68] This was not the full measure of Beauregard's embarrassment. Before he had left South Carolina, he had remarked in a letter to Gen. J. F. Gilmer: ". . . not those officers who stand the highest in the estimation of the War Department are sent here permanently. In fact, this has been called 'the Department of Refuge.'"[69] Beauregard might have added, after he came to Virginia, that along with some able men like Hoke and Ransom, his subordinates included an undue number of Brigadiers who had been tried in the Army of Northern Virginia and had been found wanting.

A third potential liability, of which Beauregard had no forewarning, was in the brain of Chase Whiting. That fine engineer, it will be recalled, had solicited field command under Beauregard, but now that he had it, he seemed to be appalled by its responsibilities. At Wilmington he always had been apprehensive of

[64] O. R., 36, pt. 2, pp. 200–01.      [65] Ibid., 200.
[66] Ibid.
[67] O. R., 36, pt. 2, pp. 1004–05. Beauregard put in separate Divisions the Brigades of Corse and of Kemper, and of Gracie and of Bushrod Johnson, which Brigades previously had belonged, respectively, to Pickett's and to Bushrod Johnson's (Buckner's) Divisions.
[68] 2 Roman, 203.      [69] 2 Roman, 192.

attack, and he brought like anxiety of mind to Petersburg. That city, he insisted, and not Drewry's Bluff would prove to be the Federal objective,[70] and he was working ceaselessly, under immense strain, day and night, to protect the city. On the 14th and 15th, though his concern was extreme, his orders and dispositions were sensible and timely.[71] He was able to lean heavily on D. H. Hill, who had remained to counsel Pickett's successor.[72]

Whiting had not liked the proposal that he abandon Petersburg, if necessary, and join in the defense of Richmond.[73] When he received Beauregard's later orders to prepare to attack the rear of Butler's Army on the 16th, he was pleased. "This suits better," he wrote Hill,[74] and he telegraphed Bragg: "All right. Got the orders I want now. Will try my best."[75] The tone of that was confidently encouraging. It never occurred to Beauregard, as far as the records show, that Whiting's state of mind might hamper the attack for which his plan was now complete.

For the front of Drewry's Bluff, the plan simply was to take the offensive on the Confederate left and to cut off Butler's Army from its base at Bermuda Hundred. While Robert Ransom was directing this attack, Hoke was to demonstrate on the Confederate right and was to hold the Federal left so that it could not send reinforcements to the assailed Federal right. When the Union right had been broken, Hoke was to advance. Colquitt, with his extemporized Division of two Brigades, was to constitute the reserve, which would be stationed near the centre.[76] Whiting was to advance at daylight on the 16th from Swift Creek to Port Walthall Junction and was to wait there until he heard the sound of an engagement. Then he was to press rapidly by the shortest

70 *O. R.,* 36, pt. 2, pp. 1005–06; cf. *ibid.,* 51, pt. 2, p. 935.
71 Cf. *O. R.,* 36, pt. 2, p. 1008.          72 Cf. *ibid.,* 1009.
73 After the campaign and more fully after the war, D. H. Hill and Henry A. Wise maintained that Bragg ordered the evacuation of Petersburg, which was saved to the Confederacy only because Whiting, with Wise's approval, refused to obey the order. The details, as Wise understood them, are set forth in *O. R.,* 36, pt. 3, pp. 859–60, and in 25 *S.H.S.P.,* 10. All the circumstances render it practically certain that the references are to the orders Bragg sent to Whiting when he learned, on the 15th, that Beauregard intended to delay the battle until May 18. Manifestly Bragg's orders were misunderstood or perhaps were badly expressed. He did not intend to direct that Whiting move to Richmond but that Whiting unite with Beauregard. While this might have involved the temporary occupation of Petersburg by the enemy, it was substantially the plan of concentration that Beauregard himself approved and intended to execute until he found that Whiting's march to Drewry's Bluff would be unduly long. Beauregard himself thought that Hill mistakenly was referring to Bragg's orders to Whiting (*O. R.,* 51, pt. 2, p. 967).
74 *O. R.,* 36, pt. 2, p. 1009.
75 *O. R.,* 51, pt. 2, p. 935.          76 *O. R.,* 36, pt. 2, pp. 200–01.

road in the direction of the heaviest fire and was to fall on the flank or rear of the Federals. Dearing's cavalry were to cover Whiting's advance.[77]

The day for the execution of the plan dawned in Richmond with no indication that Sheridan was preparing to resume his attack on the capital. Across the river, Hoke's artillery, at earliest dawn, opened vigorously. His infantry, in line of battle, waited for the column of attack to get in position.[78] Then, at 4:45 A.M., Ransom began the advance of his Division,[79] only one Brigade of which was under a general officer.[80] Fog delayed and confused,[81] but Ransom's men pushed vigorously ahead and, in about an hour, carried the first line of Federal fortifications, which consisted of rifle-pits and breastworks.[82] Five stands of colors, a Brigadier General and about 400 other prisoners fell into Ransom's hands.[83]

It was an encouraging start but it had been costly. In the fog, some of the troops had been scattered; the ammunition of some units had been dangerously reduced; casualties had been heavy. Ransom could see nothing in his front. Visibility was at zero [84] It seemed necessary to halt and to re-form his line. In order not to delay in this manner the general advance, Ransom sent Beauregard a request for one of the two nearby reserve Brigades.[85] Beauregard sent Colquitt's Brigade, but with the stipulation that it should be returned when no longer indispensable.[86]

Before Colquitt's troops or fresh ammunition reached the attacking column, Ransom heard that Hoke's left was being driven back by the enemy. To aid his comrade and to protect his own right, Ransom started troops at the double quick.[87] They never got to the exposed point.[88] Instead, under brigade officers who did not know how to handle them, they began what developed into a confused drift to the right.[89]

In the centre, the direction of this drift, Hoke's left Brigade,

[77] Ibid., 200.                                    [78] O. R., 36, pt. 2, p. 237.
[79] Gracie's, Kemper's, Barton's and Hoke's old Brigades.
[80] This was Gracie's. Col. William R. Terry commanded Kemper's Brigade. Gen. Seth M. Barton's troops were under Col. B. D. Fry. Direction of Hoke's former Brigade was by Lt. Col. William G. Lewis (O. R., 36, pt. 2, pp. 201, 207). As it happened, all three of these field officers were capable men.
[81] Ibid., 200, 212.                          [82] Ibid., 212.
[83] Ibid., 213.
[84] Ibid., 212; C. T. Loehr in 19 S.H.S.P., 103–04.
[85] O. R., 36, pt. 2, p. 212.
[86] Ibid., 201.                                    [87] Ibid., 202.
[88] Hagood, 244.                              [89] O. R., 36, pt. 2, pp. 212–13.

which was Hagood's, had advanced promptly in line,[90] had captured five guns and had overrun the Confederate outer lines previously seized by the Federals.[91] After the recovery of these works, Hoke had ordered Hagood to connect with Ransom on the left.[92] In this maneuver, part of Hagood's command advanced too far to the front and, in the face of a hot fire, had to fall back to the line of the Brigade.[93] By the time this withdrawal was undertaken, the Federals were assailing the right flank of Johnson's Brigade, which was West of Hagood. The Tennesseeans of Johnson held their ground firmly but they required part of the vanishing reserve.

As the right centre of Hoke was pounded by the Federals, Beauregard ordered the division commander to advance the two Brigades on the right, those of Clingman and Corse. These troops, successfully driving the enemy, created a gap between Clingman's left and Johnson's right. So dangerous was this situation that Hoke had to pull back the advanced right. In retiring, the extreme right Brigade became isolated. Thereafter, neither Clingman nor Corse shared in the battle.[94]

As far as this confused fighting could be seen, its development had been observed by Beauregard. He had begun at 5 A.M. to forward telegraphic reports to the War Department. The first of these had announced the opening of the action. "Our trust," the General had written, "is in God, the valor of our troops, and the justness of our cause."[95] He sent other messages at intervals and, for a time, he appeared confident.[96] After Ransom had halted and Hoke had become heavily engaged, Beauregard had undertaken to relieve the Brigades in the centre. This "slight modification of the original movement," he later described thus: "Ransom was ordered to flank the enemy's right by changing the front of his right Brigade to support it by another in échelon, to advance a third toward Proctor's Creek, and to hold a fourth in reserve."[97] Ransom doubtless understood this, because he was a professional soldier, but his subordinates had been incapable of executing the movement. Consequently Ransom had been compelled to report that he needed to straighten his lines.[98]

90 Johnson was on Hagood's right; next Johnson stood Clingman; the extreme right was held by Corse.

91 O. R., 36, pt. 2, pp. 202–03, 237.

93 Ibid.; O. R., 36, pt. 2, pp. 203, 237.

95 O. R., 36, pt. 2, p. 938.

97 Ibid., 202.

92 Hagood, 246.

94 O. R., 36, pt. 2, p. 203.

96 O. R., 36, pt. 2, pp. 196–97.

98 Ibid.

About 8 o'clock, while the Confederate left was idle and only Hagood and Johnson were in close action, the sound of firing was heard from the South, the direction of Whiting's expected advance. The noise continued for a time and then it died away.[99] Beauregard took this to mean that Whiting was advancing in the face of little or no opposition. Subsequently Beauregard explained that his belief in the approach of Whiting was one of the considerations that weighed with him when he decided, about 10 A.M., that he would not order Ransom to resume the offensive on the left. Said the commanding General: "I withheld an order . . . for the following reasons: The right was heavily engaged; all of the reserves had been detached right and left at different times; the silence of Whiting's guns . . . gave reasonable hope that he had met no resistance and would soon be on." [100]

Fact was, the movement to cut off Butler from his base had yielded a little ground, a few guns and some hundreds of prisoners and then had come to a halt in the face of stiff resistance. Hagood and Johnson could continue their fight, though it would be costly and might be futile, but Ransom was balked and was aware of it. "Ransom," wrote Beauregard, "not only reported the enemy in strong force in his front, but expressed the opinion that the safety of his command would be compromised by an advance." [101]

Thus it developed that Whiting's co-operative movement, which had been a minor part of the plan, grew in importance with the passage of the hours until it became the contingency on which success was believed to hang. At 9 o'clock and again at 9:30, Beauregard sent Whiting this message by courier: "Press on and press over everything in your front, and the day will be complete." [102] For the execution of those orders, Beauregard had to wait, and none too happily at that. He probably was not pleased to learn, among other things, that President Davis had arrived and was watching the action.

Eleven o'clock, noon, one o'clock brought no change of any importance on the front, no news of Whiting's approach. About 1:45, while the President and General Beauregard were standing on the works, the long-awaited sound of renewed firing was heard

[99] *Ibid.*, 197, 202.                     [100] *Ibid.*, 202.
[101] *O. R.*, 36, pt. 2, p. 202.           [102] *Ibid.*

from the direction of Whiting's advance. "Ah, at last!" said Davis with a smile. He listened more intently and waited till hopeful seconds lengthened to doubting minutes. Not another sound came from the South or Southwest.[103]

Beauregard concluded, regretfully, that Dearing's cavalry, not Whiting's infantry, was responsible for the firing, but he remained until 4 o'clock. Then, as he explained in his report, he "reluctantly abandoned so much of his plan as contemplated more than a vigorous pursuit of Butler" to the Union fortified base.[104] An effort was made to extend Hoke's flank and to enfilade the Federals with artillery, but a heavy rain and a vigorous challenge by the enemy delayed the advance until darkness approached. ". . . Upon consultation with several of my subordinate commanders," Beauregard reported, "it was deemed imprudent to attack, considering the probability of serious obstacles and the proximity of Butler's intrenched camp."[105] He had to content himself for the moment with his five captured colors, his five guns and his 1388 prisoners as compensation for 2506 casualties.[106] His decision against further attack that day was confirmed by the return from Whiting's headquarters of Lt. Col. T. M. Logan, one of Beauregard's acting staff officers, who reported that he did not believe Whiting would advance that day.[107]

The next morning brought to *Felix* Beauregard a measure of his old good luck. He discovered that Butler had retreated to the Bermuda Hundred lines where, it soon developed, the Federal commander was "corked" as if in a bottle.[108] To Beauregard came

---

[103] *Owen*, 318; *O. R.*, 36, pt. 2, p. 203. Beauregard wrote of "brief firing," but Owen said that one shot only was heard.
[104] *O. R.*, 36, pt. 2, p. 204.
[105] *O. R.*, 36, pt. 2, p. 204.
[106] *Ibid.*, 204, 205, 206. Butler's casualties for May 16 were not reported separately. For May 5–31, with the Battle of Drewry's Bluff much the heaviest action, they were 5958 (*O. R.*, 36, pt. 2, p. 18). Personal narratives of the engagements are few. Among them are C. T. Loehr, 19 *S.H.S.P.*, 100 ff; David E. Johnston, *The Story of a Confederate Boy*, 249 ff; W. H. Morgan, *Personal Reminiscences, War 1861–65*, p. 195 ff; B. W. Jones, *Under the Stars and Bars*, 167 ff. The last named work contains letters that cover the whole of Beauregard's campaign.
[107] Logan in 2 *Roman*, 559–60.
[108] *O. R.*, 36, pt. 1, p. 20; *ibid.*, pt. 2, p. 204. The phrase about the bottle and the cork was General Grant's. In resisting Beauregard's attack on May 16, Smith's XVII Federal Corps had been on Butler's right and Gillmore's X Corps on the left. Smith's front was broken by Ransom's attack and was confused a little later by the unintended withdrawal of a Brigade (*O. R.*, 36, pt. 2, p. 115). Gillmore suffered chiefly from an endless succession of orders from Butler who, apparently, did not understand what was occurring (*ibid.*, 38–39). Both Corps probably had plenty of fight left in them when the bewildered commanding General ordered them to withdraw to the fortified lines.

also, on that same 17th, between 9 and 10 A.M.,[109] Whiting's two Brigades that were to have attacked the rear of the enemy. They arrived with ranks almost full and with the men in condition for a battle, but they were under the informal command of Harvey Hill, not of Chase Whiting.

Behind the change of commanders was a strange, strange story. Early on the morning of the 16th, in obedience to orders, Henry A. Wise's Virginia Brigade and James G. Martin's North Carolina regiments had assembled at Dunlop's Station for the prearranged advance. Whiting kept them waiting an hour before he started them northward.[110] He rode in person with them and, at his own request, had D. H. Hill at his side as counsellor.

When the enemy's pickets were flushed on Timberry Creek, Whiting asked Hill to take charge of the advance while he watched the right. Hill of course undertook to do this and met with the most cordial reception from General Wise, who, said Hill, "carried out all my suggestions as though they were responsible orders." [111] With all the skill acquired in many battles and with all his old combativeness, Hill maneuvered the fine and willing troops of Wise and soon had the enemy in rapid withdrawal. A few minutes later, to his amazement, he found the Confederates moving back on the Swift Creek Road. At once Hill rode to Wise and asked the reason. Wise said that he had been ordered by Whiting to retire to a line that officer would designate.

Hill wheeled his horse and hurried off to Whiting, whom he urged to return the troops to a good position they had occupied in the railroad cut near Port Walthall Junction.[112] Whiting agreed to do so, though later, it would appear, he had no remembrance of ordering either the withdrawal or the return.[113] His concern was that he had received no message from Beauregard, that he was in a strange position, that the enemy was threatening him,[114] and that the sound of firing from the direction of Drewry's Bluff was not heavy. He had been instructed to advance, he said, when the firing was heavy. This was not. Beauregard might be ending his fight. Petersburg might be in danger.[115]

Hill soon learned that the report of an impending attack by the

[109] O. R., 36, pt. 2, p. 259.
[111] Ibid., 210.
[113] Ibid., 257.
[115] 23 S.H.S.P., 190.

[110] 25 S.H.S.P., 11.
[112] O. R., 36, pt. 2, p. 211.
[114] Ibid.

Federals had no foundation. The bluecoats, he was sure, had only a small regiment in Whiting's front, and he so wrote the commander. Then Hill went to Martin's field headquarters. While he was there, Whiting rode up to Martin and ordered him to call in his skirmishers.

"General Whiting," said Hill, "you cannot occupy this place if you withdraw your skirmishers."

"You don't think I intend to remain here?" Whiting asked.

Bluntly, perhaps bitterly, Hill replied that he did not know what Whiting intended to do.

Without further explanation, Whiting bade Martin retire the Brigade as soon as the skirmishers reached the line.

Naturally Martin suggested that the Brigade move back while still covered by the skirmishers.

"It makes no difference," said Whiting, "there is no enemy in our front."

The withdrawal began and soon resulted in a wretched tangle of wagons and troops, artillery and ambulances on the Petersburg Pike. Hill observed this. He had said nothing and had attempted nothing after Whiting ordered Martin back, but he could not endure to see good soldiers exposed to possible panic or slaughter. Briefly he warned Whiting that a Federal cavalry regiment, which was within sight, might play havoc in the confused column. "What ought I to do?" asked Whiting.

"I wrote you two hours ago," Hill replied, "to press the Yankees." [116]

"I did not receive your note," answered Whiting.

This was more than Hill could endure. "Fearing," Hill wrote afterward, "that General Whiting might be embarrassed by the seeming divided responsibility of my presence, and feeling that I could accomplish nothing more, I retired to Dunlop's house, when I learned that the troops were ordered to recross Swift Creek." [117]

By that time, Whiting had received his first news of the day from Beauregard. A little later he heard, through General Dearing, of the progress of the battle at Drewry's Bluff to 1 P.M. Then, at 7:15 P.M., Whiting opened a dispatch of 4:15 from Beauregard.

[116] This exchange is here changed to direct discourse from the clear sentences in Hill's report (O. R., 36, pt. 2, p. 211).

[117] O. R., 36, pt. 2, p. 211. The account given by Lt. Col. (later Brig. Gen.) T. M. Logan in 2 Roman, 557 ff, is substantially the same.

To this, Whiting replied tersely "Too late for action on my part."
In recording this subsequently, Whiting added: "My personal
presence was absolutely required in Petersburg, and not having to
clear the road, I hoped to be able to join the General readily on the
17th." [118]

Whiting spent the night sleeplessly, and at 3 A.M. he got still
another note from Beauregard. This time the commanding General again ordered him to advance at daylight and to form a junction at Drewry's Bluff. The troops, Whiting later reported, "moved
out, after some consultation with the generals, under the command of General D. H. Hill, I having relinquished it to him in
consequence of the dissatisfaction expressed by Generals Wise and
Martin with my movements and orders of the preceding day,
deeming that harmony of action was to be preferred at that time
to any personal consideration, and feeling at the time—as, indeed,
I had felt for twenty-four hours—physically unfit for action." [119]

The reason, in the judgment of the Army, was that Whiting was
drunk. This was the conclusion of Henry A. Wise, who was near
him several times during the day.[120] Johnson Hagood was not
with Whiting's column but he probably was repeating another
current explanation when he said that Whiting's condition "was
due to the unfortunate use of narcotics." [121] Harvey Hill, on the
other hand, reported that he "saw no evidence of alleged intoxica-
tion." [122] Whiting's aide certified that he was with Whiting from
the time of the General's arrival in Petersburg through the 16th.
During that time, said the staff officer, Whiting did not drink any
spirituous liquor.[123] In his own behalf, Whiting certified on his
honor that for the period of operations around Petersburg he drank
nothing except water and coffee. From the First Battle of Manassas, he said, it had been his rule never to touch spirits when the
enemy was in his front.[124]

Beauregard was more than generous to his friend. He expressed
regret that Whiting's brother officers should have thought their
commander drunk.[125] In his own report, Beauregard said only

[118] O. R., 36, pt. 2, p. 258.          [119] Ibid., 258–59.
[120] O. R., 36, pt. 2, p. 1026; ibid., pt. 3, p. 812.
[121] Hagood, 236.
[122] O. R., 36, pt. 2, p. 211.          [123] Ibid., pt. 3, p. 845.
[124] Ibid., p. 312.          [125] O. R., 36, pt. 2. p. 1026.

that Whiting's "premature halt" before obstacles that should not have deterred the column from Petersburg was one of the reasons the "more glorious results" of the victory were lost.[126] Nobody seems to have reasoned that Whiting may have given the full and true explanation when he said that he had not taken off his clothes or rested from the time of his arrival in Petersburg during the forenoon of the 13th. He may have been of the type, wholly familiar in war, that loses through prolonged loss of sleep all grip on the mental faculties.

Whiting immediately asked to be relieved and, when Harvey Hill temporarily was assigned to command his scratch Division, he prepared to resume his station at Wilmington.[127] Before he left Petersburg, Whiting wrote Beauregard that he was returning to complete the fortifications around the Carolina city. He added: "When I shall have laid out all that is necessary to be done there, if you do not join in the censure to which I am now unfortunately subject here, I will be glad if you will call me to your side."[128]

For Whiting's failure, none of the responsible leaders blamed Beauregard, but some of them felt that in an effort to execute a spectacular coup, Beauregard had neglected the sure way to success, which they held to be that of bringing Whiting to Drewry's Bluff early so that the united superior forces could fall on Butler and destroy the Union Army. Col. L. B. Northrop was open and vehement in denunciation of Beauregard for blunders which, he said, were ruining the South. The hero of Sumter, said the Commissary General, was a charlatan![129] How much of this criticism reached Beauregard, it is not easy to say; but he possessed friends in Richmond who retained their belief in him and he had a "good press."[130] His self-confidence did not appear to be shaken in the slightest.

Perhaps it was no more than coincidence, but while the Confederate capital was echoing comment, favorable and hostile, Beau-

126 O. R., 36, pt. 2, p. 204.       127 O. R., 36, pt. 3, p. 811; ibid., 51, pt. 2, p. 939.
128 O. R., 36, pt. 3, pp. 824–25.
129 2 R. W. C. D., 215. In 1879, Davis and Northrop had some reminiscent correspondence regarding the movements of Whiting, but the memory of Davis was so much less accurate than he thought it to be, and Northrop's venom was still so unrelieved that the statements of the two have not been incorporated in the text. See 8 Rowland, 194, 337–38, 418. Similarly the account of Drewry's Bluff in 2 Davis, 511, is too inaccurate to be of use.
130 Cf. Richmond Dispatch, May 18; Richmond Enquirer, May 20, 1864.

regard on the 19th transmitted to General Bragg a letter, which, as the recipient promptly observed, bore date of May 14. In this communication Beauregard set forth at length his full plan for the withdrawal of Lee to the Richmond defenses and for successive concentrations against Butler and Grant. If this paper was completed on the 14th, Beauregard did not explain to Bragg why the delivery of so important a document was delayed four or five days. Bragg evidently thought the paper was written to show the world that Beauregard—as after the First Battle of Manassas—had fashioned a great design which the administration had rejected. Not to be outdone in maneuvers of this nature, Bragg promptly drew up the list, already summarized,[131] of the objections to Beauregard's plan.

Another strange aftermath of the battle of Drewry's Bluff was Beauregard's treatment of Robert Ransom. The day after the action, Ransom was recalled to his regular duties as officer in charge of the Department of Richmond. In relieving him, Beauregard issued a special order in which "the commanding General takes occasion to express his cordial appreciation of General Ransom's brilliant conduct in the battle of yesterday, and his great regret in relinquishing his valued service at this moment." [132] Ransom proceeded to write a brief matter-of-fact report [133] which he filed through the headquarters of Beauregard.

Almost a month later, in Beauregard's report of the engagement, Ransom's conduct was presented coldly and, at the end, was described along with Whiting's delay as one of the two reasons why "more glorious results" were not attained.[134] In the knowledge that the tone of the report clashed with the praise of the special order on the relief of Ransom, this was written: "When [the order] was issued I still assumed that [Ransom] had properly felt and estimated the obstacles and hostile force reported by him in his immediate front, and that his reports were to be accepted as maturely considered and substantially accurate. Subsequent investigation, necessarily requiring time, has, I regret to say, brought me to a different conviction." [135] Reading this, Ransom and his friends might have felt themselves justified in contending that

131 See supra, p. 480.                    132 O. R., 36, pt. 2, pp. 1017–18.
133 Ibid., 212–13.                        134 Ibid., 202–03.
135 Ibid., 205.

Beauregard had discovered the need of a scapegoat. Perhaps that would have been unjust to Beauregard. He was convinced now, as always, of his rightness as a tactician and as a strategist. In a swiftly changing crisis, he already had new plans for his own army and for Lee's which now was moving from the battleground of Spotsylvania.

# CHAPTER XXV

## The End of the Old Organization

ON THE BLOODY FRONT where Lee's lieutenants had faced Grant for almost a fortnight it was apparent by the morning of May 21 that the Federals had undertaken another side-slip. Again they were trying to get between Richmond and the Army of Northern Virginia; again the leaders of that Army were determined to interpose. For a number of sound reasons of strategy,[1] the next line of defense appeared to be the North Anna River, twenty-three miles North of Richmond. On the deep bank of that river, the Southerners would have a good prospect of repulsing any direct attack, and from the North Anna, if the enemy sought to assail Richmond from the Northeast, by way of the Mattapony, the Southern Divisions could be shifted readily to the Pamunkey.[2]

To nerve-weary leaders, the departure from Spotsylvania seemed slow[3] but the maneuver was executed cleanly, with no loss and with little straggling. The corps commanders were entitled to a credit for this, because two of them scarcely were able to discharge their duties. Powell Hill probably had reported for duty too soon after his illness.[4] Ewell managed to ride with his men, though his collapse was apprehended by Lee.[5] Only Anderson, the least experienced of the three, remained in good physical condition.

On the North Anna, which was reached May 22,[6] after a "severe and weary march,"[7] the Confederates had a few hours of rest and then, on the 23rd, they had to repel an attack on their left by the strong V Corps. The task of beating off the Federals chanced to fall on Hill's men and principally on Wilcox's Division, which sustained 642 casualties.[8] That night or the next day, Lee was

---

1 They are given in detail in 3 R. E. Lee, 340–42.
2 Pendleton, 335.    3 O. R., 36, pt. 3, pp. 814–15.
4 O. R., 36, pt. 3, p. 815.    5 See infra, p. 498.
6 O. R., 36, pt. 3, p. 823.    7 Ibid., pt. 1, p. 1073.
8 Wilcox's MS Report of the Richmond Campaign (cited hereafter as Wilcox's MS report), p. 48. For an interesting description of part of the ground of the Federal crossing, and of the curious "shelfing" of Jericho Ford, see O. R., 36, pt. 1, p. 238.

assailed by an intestinal ailment that had the usual effect of sharpening his temper and of shaking his control of it. Never, said his staff, was he comparably so difficult as during a sickness. When he rode to the front of the Corps and saw what had happened, he gave Powell Hill what was, perhaps, the stiffest rebuke ever administered to any of his general officers during the war. "Why," Lee demanded, "did you not do as Jackson would have done— thrown your whole force upon those people and driven them back?" [9] Hill had no answer. If the question had been put by Jackson, there might have been a scene. Against Lee's judgment, no matter how unfavorable, Hill never protested.

For the disappointment of this affair, there were two compensations. The first, a permanent one, was the arrival of the only reinforcements the Army had received, except for Robert D. Johnston's Brigade,[10] since the opening of the campaign. Pickett's Division returned and found a place temporarily with the Third Corps.[11] Hoke's old Brigade was reassigned to Early's Division. Maj. Gen. John C. Breckinridge, whose physical magnificence won much admiration, had defeated Sigel in a manner presently to be described [12] and had moved to Lee from the Shenandoah Valley with two Brigades. For the time being, these troops were placed directly under Lee's orders.[13] In the aggregate, the three commands counted about 8000 muskets.[14] A second, if momentary, compensation for the rough handling of Wilcox's Division on the 23rd was a succession of Federal maneuvers, by which Grant got astride the North Anna on either side of the strong position at Ox Ford held by "Dick" Anderson. The Union commander could not reinforce one wing from the other without crossing the river twice.[15] The opportunity of smashing one wing of the Federal Army was better far than any that had been offered since the opening of the campaign, but Lee was too sick to direct the attack. Had Jackson been alive or Longstreet unwounded, either of them

9 Hotchkiss in 3 C. M. H., 460. Major Hotchkiss did not mention this episode in his MS Diary. He evidently heard of it later.
10 It had rejoined the Second Corps May 6 (O. R., 36, pt. 1, p. 1071).
11 O. R., 36, pt. 1, p. 1058.      12 See infra, p. 515.
13 Cf. O. R., 51, pt. 2, p. 957.
14 Alexander, op. cit., 530, gave the figure as 9000.
15 O. R., 36, pt. 1, pp. 918, 1030-31. General Grant, in his report (ibid., 21), amusingly dismissed his singular blunders with the statement: "Finding the enemy's position on the North Anna stronger than either of his previous ones, I withdrew on the night of the 26th."

could have handled the operation. As it was, Lee did not even attempt to deputize one of his corps commanders to make the effort. All he could do was to say from his cot: "We must strike them a blow—we must never let them pass us again—we must strike them a blow." [16]

Because of Lee's illness and the impairment of command, Grant was able to withdraw unhurt the two wings of his army that had been separated by Anderson's unshakable grip on high ground.[17] On the 27th of May, the whole of the Union Army was back on the north bank of the river and once more was marching by its left flank in the hope of getting between Lee and Richmond. This time it was manifest that the shift would bring the Federals embarrassingly close to the defenses of the Confederate capital. If it was possible, the enemy must be defeated before warfare became stationary. The alternative Lee soon was to state in grim words to Jubal Early: "We must destroy this Army of Grant's before he gets to James River. If he gets there it will become a siege, and then it will be a mere question of time." [18]

To catch a numerically superior adversary on the march or in some rare situation favorable to an attack, the Confederates had to be mobile and alert as well as strong. Every general officer in charge of troops had to be ready to strike instantly. This, unhappily, was more than the stricken command could hope to be. By the worst of fortune, while Lee himself was ill, Ewell was stricken with an acute intestinal malady. On the 27th, the very day the new Federal movement began, Ewell was so ill that he had to ask Early to handle the Corps.[19] This was not unexpected at Army Headquarters. For months Lee had been uneasy about Ewell, who recklessly slept on the ground and exerted himself ceaselessly. In Ewell's place, Early could serve, as he had during the Mine Run campaign, but it was dangerous business to be changing officers ceaselessly while critical operations were in progress! On the 28th and 29th, Ewell still was so prostrate that he had to remain in his tent.[20] As serious operations by that time again were imminent,

[16] 14 S.H.S.P., 535.   [17] Details are given in 3 R. E. Lee, 358 ff.
[18] Early in J. William Jones, Personal Reminiscences . . . of Gen. Robert E. Lee, 40.
[19] Hotchkiss' MS Diary, 349. Mrs. Ewell wrote June 8 that his affection had "something of the nature of scurvy, consequent on salt meat and terrible exertions" (Hamlin's Ewell, 127). Ewell himself (O. R., 36, pt. 1, p. 1074) stated simply that he had a "severe attack of diarrhea."
[20] O. R., 36, pt. 1, p. 1074.

the Second Corps had to be put formally under Early's command. Ewell was given indefinite leave in order that he might have the benefit of rest and of medical treatment until he was able to resume his post. Characteristically, Ewell declined to avail himself of this leave. He was resolved, as always, to remain with his men and, to the limit of his strength, to discharge his duties.

The Army by that date, May 29, had been moved from the North Anna to the vicinity of Totopotomoy Creek. With superlative care, in spite of his sickness, Lee disposed the three Corps where they covered all the approaches to Richmond from the Pamunkey River, which Grant was expected to cross.[21] A forced reconnaissance by cavalry was ordered that day to determine whether Federal infantry had passed the stream. Wickham's Brigade of Fitz Lee shared this task. Hampton's Division supplied Rosser's Brigade and, from Calbraith Butler's reorganized Brigade, the Fifth South Carolina and half of the Fourth.[22] After much negotiation these 1100 finely equipped, well mounted men, who never had been in action, had been brought to Virginia.[23] Butler was not yet with them;[24] the Colonels were as inexperienced in combat as were the troopers. The Federals heard later that in welcoming these green cavalrymen, the ragged veterans of the dead "Jeb" Stuart's command jeered and joked till the Carolinians were mad enough to give their lives in order to prove they could and would fight.[25] In a seven-hour fight,[26] through woodland so thick that most of the fighting had to be on foot,[27] the Carolinians did their share in repulsing the 2nd Federal Cavalry Division. Then, perhaps at too long a range, the newcomers poured remembered volleys into the enemy when he returned to the attack with the support of Custer's Brigade of the 1st Division.[28] The Carolinians had difficulty in breaking off the engagement, but when Hampton himself rode forward and took them in hand, they reached their horses and rode off like veterans.[29] They had so much fire-power that Custer reported them as regiments of mounted infantry;[30] Sheridan insisted that they numbered 4000 and carried long-range

21 O. R., 36, pt. 1, p. 1031; pt. 3, pp. 837–39.
22 Wells, 155, 167. Some regiments of W. H. F. Lee's Division came up later in the day.
23 See James Conner's remarks, supra, p. 316.
24 He reported on the evening of the 28th (Wells, 158, 170).
25 Ibid., 165.                              26 Ibid., 154.
27 O. R., 36, pt. 1, p. 821.                28 Ibid., 854; H. W. Wingfield, 40.
29 Wells, 158–59.                           30 O. R., 36, pt. 1, p. 821.

rifles.[31] The distinction won that day in the Battle of Haw's Shop [32] was valiantly earned by the recruits and was acknowledged quickly by the old troopers. All of them shared one other satisfaction that 29th of May. To the lore as well as to the glory of the cavalry corps a treasure of understatement was added. As the Ninth Virginia rode off the field, in gathering twilight and under a heavy and wrathful musketry fire, a trooper looked long and eagerly at the flashing rifles. "Lor's," said he, "they beat the lightning bugs!" [33]

This costly reconnaissance made it virtually certain that Grant was crossing his infantry as well as his cavalry over the Pamunkey.[34] All indications were, in addition, that Benjamin F. Butler was releasing troops from his "bottle" at Bermuda Hundred and was reinforcing the Army of the Potomac. The first suggestion of this transfer had reached Lee's headquarters, May 18, in a Northern newspaper of the 13th. Butler's two Corps, it was said in a Washington dispatch, would be called to service with Grant because "they are not strong enough to take Richmond, and too strong to be kept idle." [35]

To the Confederate commanders this seemed so soundly logical that they undertook at once to ascertain the truth through Beauregard, who was best placed to observe any withdrawal from his front. As late as May 23, Beauregard thought Butler might be increasing instead of decreasing force.[36] By the 29th Beauregard believed the enemy at Bermuda Hundred might have sent 4000 troops to Grant,[37] but he did not think the situation justified any diminution of his own command.[38]

Expression of this opinion was regarded by the President as contrary both to Beauregard's previous views and to the General's most recent exercise in theoretical strategy. Two days after the Battle of Drewry's Bluff, Beauregard had proposed that if the Army of Northern Virginia would retire to the Chickahominy River, he would detach 15,000 men, join Breckinridge, fall on Grant's flank and, while Lee attacked in front, destroy the Army

[31] Ibid., 793.   [32] Sometimes styled the Battle of Enon Church.
[33] G. W. Beale, 158.   [34] O. R., 36, pt. 1, p. 1031.
[35] O. R., 51, pt. 2, pp. 952–53. The quotation may be Lee's epitome and not the precise language of the newspaper report.
[36] O. R., 36, pt. 3, pp. 818–19, 826; ibid., 51, pt. 2, p. 953.
[37] O. R., 36, pt. 3, p. 849; ibid., 51 pt. 2, pp. 964–65.
[38] Ibid.

of the Potomac. Then Butler could be overwhelmed. In submit-
ting this plan, Beauregard had sought to safeguard his command
by saying that until the time for its execution arrived, and his lines
had been strengthened, he could not release more than 5000 men
to reinforce Lee's Army.[39] Davis maintained, in comment on this
plan, that if Beauregard could detach 15,000 men for a flank attack, the General certainly could spare 10,000 to aid Lee.[40] A little
later the President changed his mind momentarily, a thing he
seldom did. He concluded that if Beauregard were holding on the
Southside as many Federal troops as Beauregard thought, the
forces opposite Butler were well employed.[41]

The patient Lee, striving always to be just, assumed that Beauregard knew the needs on the Richmond-Petersburg line,[42] but he
reasoned that if the Army of Northern Virginia could not resist
Grant, the forces under Beauregard and the small garrison of Richmond could not save the city.[43] Co-operation, Lee thought, was
demanded immediately. To assure it wherever it would suit Beauregard, he urged a conference with that officer.[44] Early in the evening of May 29, Beauregard came to field headquarters and reviewed the situation on his sector. He held to his belief that not
more than 4000 Union troops had been detached from Butler's
army and he maintained that his own force, which he estimated
at 12,000 infantry, could not be reduced further without creating
more danger for Richmond than was averted.[45] In asserting this,
Beauregard, as always, was graciously courteous, but he could not
be committed to any specific detachment of force. If he said anything about his previous plan for coming to the assistance of Lee
with the greater part of his little army, no record of that fact survives.[46] When Beauregard left, it was manifest at Headquarters
of the Army of Northern Virginia that any action would have to
be fought without assistance from the south side of the James.[47]

On the 30th, the crisis was heightened. All the indications were

---

[39] O. R., 36, pt. 2, pp. 1021–22, pt. 3, pp. 818–19.
[40] O. R., 51, pt. 2, p. 945.       [41] O. R., 51, pt. 2, p. 966.
[42] Lee's Dispatches, 208–09.        [43] Ibid., 209.
[44] Ibid., 204.
[45] Lee's Dispatches, 205. This brief telegram from Lee to Davis is the only report of
the conference, but Beauregard's argument may be elaborated from O. R., 36, pt. 3, p.
349 and ibid., 51, pt. 2, pp. 964–65.
[46] In 2 Roman, the period of Beauregard's activities from May 17 to June 9, 1864, was
covered in less than two pages (222–24). The conference of May 29 received no mention.
[47] Lee's Dispatches, 205.

that Grant once more was extending his left and was aiming to rest that flank on the Chickahominy.[48] The Federal commander could do this without giving up any of the ground he held on the right, because most of the heavy losses he sustained after May 4 had been made good.[49] The Army of Northern Virginia probably had not received as reinforcements more than half as many soldiers as it had lost.[50] Lengthening of line, therefore, meant that unless Beauregard sent aid, parts of the Confederate front would be so stripped that they could not be held in reasonable safety.

The one possible hope of preventing an eastward extension of Grant's left, before the arrival of Southern reinforcements from some quarter, was to strike the enemy hard enough to halt him. An opening seemed to be offered the Second Corps near Bethesda Church. "Jube" Early was given discretion to develop the opportunity.[51] He did so, head on, without proper reconnaissance or co-ordination with the First Corps.[52] The result was a bloody repulse [53] that cost the life, among many, of Col. Edward Willis of the Twelfth Georgia, who was acting commander of Pegram's Brigade. Willis had earned promotion long previously and doubtless would have received it within a few days. For his memorial, he left the Army as courageous a statement as ever fell from a soldier's lips: "I am no more afraid to die than I was to go into the battle." [54]

After Early's attack failed, it was safe to assume that Grant would continue to extend his left as fast and as far as fitted his plan. Because of the roads meeting at Old Cold Harbor, that familiar village seemed a logical objective. In addition, the Confederates had good reason to believe that a large part of Butler's troops would reach West Point on the 30th.[55] A rapid march of

---

[48] O. R., 36, pt. 3, p. 851.

[49] Present for duty, May 31, were 107,433 officers and men. The IX Corps of 19,930 (O. R., 36, pt. 3, p. 426) was included, but the troops arriving from Butler's Army were not. This total compared with 102,869 on April 1, exclusive of the IX Corps (O. R., 36, pt. 1, p. 198). C. A. Dana, Assistant Secretary of War, stated May 28, 1864, that reinforcements received to that date were "not quite 20,000" (O. R., 36, pt. 1, p. 80).

[50] Casualty lists are fragmentary for these operations. The estimated total for Lee's Army, from May 4 to June 14, is 25,000. See 3 R. E. Lee, 446.

[51] O. R., 36, pt. 3, pp. 851, 854.

[52] O. R., 51, pt. 2, p. 975; Early, 362.      [53] Ibid.; 33 S.H.S.P., 59.

[54] Hotchkiss' MS Diary, 351; Thomas, 228–29. For other references, see 3 R. E. Lee, 370, n. 35. Lee's belief in Willis's qualifications for brigade command had been expressed as early as May 20, 1863 (O. R., 25, pt. 2, pp. 810–11).

[55] Lee's Dispatches. 207; O. R. 51, pt. 2, pp. 971.

one day would bring this large force to Grant's left, or to some other point where units of the X and XVIII Corps could relieve troops that might be regrouped at Cold Harbor. The Confederate front might be broken where the momentum of the attack might carry the Federals into the streets of Richmond.

To aid in covering the approaches to the capital, all the mobile elements of the small garrison had been employed. Days before, commands from as far distant as Florida had been hurried to Richmond.[56] Western Virginia and East Tennessee could not yield another company in time to be of service. Representations of Beauregard still were such, concerning the force in front of him, that the War Department hesitated to issue a peremptory order for the detachment of part of his men to assist the Army of Northern Virginia.

Lee made a final, direct appeal in a telegram to Beauregard. The answer came back promptly: "War Department must determine when and what troops to order from here. I send to General Bragg all information I obtain relative to movement of enemy's troops in my front. Have you been attacked today?"[57] This refusal on Beauregard's part to assume responsibility for transfer of men to meet the reinforcement of Grant left no recourse except the President. About nightfall of the long May day, this telegram, decoded, was placed in Davis's hands:

Atlee's, May 30, 1864—7.30 P.M.

His Excellency Jefferson Davis,
                    Richmond:
General Beauregard says the Department must determine what troops to send for him. He gives it all necessary information. The result of this delay will be disaster. Butler's troops (Smith's corps) will be with Grant tomorrow. Hoke's division, at least, should be with me by light tomorrow.

R. E. Lee[58]

Never had such a message as that come to the President from Lee. Often the General had said that this evil *might* occur, or that he feared possible calamity from such and such a mistake. Here the language contained no reservation, no proviso. It was plain use of the unqualified future tense: "The result of this delay

---

56 *O. R.*, 36, pt. 3, pp. 825, 832, 834, 836.
57 2 *Roman*, 563.          58 *O. R.*, 36, pt. 3, p. 850.

will be disaster." Davis lost no time. Bragg was summoned. The two agreed that Hoke and his 7000 men must be sent immediately to Lee, no matter what Beauregard said. If the Division was to reach Lee the next day, it must proceed part of the way by train.[59] Bragg hurried off to telegraph instructions to Beauregard and to arrange for the transportation.[60] In the form in which the order was transmitted, it left no room for discretion, argument or delay. It was peremptory: "By direction of the President," Bragg began, "you will send Hoke's division, which you reported ready, immediately to this point by railroad . . ." [61]

Bragg and Davis must have been surprised at the next development. Sometime after 11 P.M.[62] Bragg received from Beauregard a telegraphic dispatch marked 10:15, which was a quarter of an hour ahead of the time at which Bragg had sent the order. In his dispatch Beauregard said that he had received from Lee a call for reinforcements which he felt authorized in sending under previous instructions from the President. The Division of Hoke, said Beauregard, was ordered to report to Lee. As soon as the enemy's movements permitted, Johnson's Division would follow. Beauregard would accompany it.[63]

These messages were the pistol shot that started Hoke's lean men in a race to overtake the troops from Butler that had been sent to Grant. Southern scouts and signalmen had not been behindhand in discovering and reporting the Federal movement. On the 27th, Maj. Gen. "Baldy" Smith had been ordered to concentrate in rear of the lines at Port Walthall the two Divisions of white troops of his XVIII Corps and two Divisions of Gillmore's X Corps.[64] By 11:30 A.M. of the 29th, virtually all these men and their equipment—nearly 16,000 infantry, about 100 cavalry and sixteen field guns—were embarked at Bermuda Hundred.[65] This flotilla was observed, of course, as it descended the James. By the morning of the 30th, Beauregard knew and notified Richmond that seventeen vessels had passed downstream. The chief error of the signalmen who reported these transports was in estimating the

---

[59] O. R., 51, pt. 2, p. 969.                    [60] Ibid.
[61] O. R., 36, pt. 3, p. 857.
[62] Evidently the message had not been received when Davis telegraphed Lee at that hour (O. R., 51, pt. 2, p. 969).
[63] O. R., 36, pt. 3, p. 857.
[64] O. R., 36, pt. 1, p. 998; ibid., pt. 2, p. 40.
[65] Ibid., 36, pt. 1, p. 998; ibid., 36, pt. 3, p. 320.

number of men aboard at 7000, or less than half the actual force.[66] Confederate expectations of a landing at the White House on the 30th [67] were fulfilled: Smith at 11 A.M. reached that point and began to disembark.[68] He was at that time sixteen miles by road from Cold Harbor. Hoke, the next morning, May 31, received his first train near Chester station in time to start Clingman's Brigade for Richmond at 5:15. Before 9 A.M., a total of five trains were moved. A sixth was then being loaded. The seventh and last was to be dispatched from Chester shortly after the hour. By rail and by road, Hoke had eighteen miles to go, or two miles more than Smith and the opposing Federal force had to cover after they completed debarkation. The odds were against Hoke.

To hold the crossroads of Cold Harbor until the arrival of Hoke, the cavalry of Fitz Lee had been posted. Through the morning of the 31st, the Confederate troopers had nothing to do. In the early afternoon, Fitz Lee heard that Clingman's Brigade of Hoke's Division had arrived within two miles of Gaines' Mill and had halted there. A little later Fitz's outposts sent word that the blue cavalry were approaching. The young Confederate prepared for a fight, notified the commanding General of the situation. and asked if Clingman might not be ordered in support.[69]

Clingman came, but so did the Federals and in a strength sufficient to drive him and Fitz Lee's troopers from the crossroads. Fitz thought the Union cavalry had infantry behind it, but he could not be sure. Nor had he any means of knowing whether, if blue infantry were at hand, they were Smith's men.[70] The action, in either event, gave Cold Harbor temporarily to the Federals. Lee, the senior, was not willing to leave the village to the enemy, or its recovery to Hoke's Division when all of that command arrived. The commanding General decided to anticipate the Federals, if he could. Instead of taking a chance that they might turn his flank, he would undertake to roll up theirs. This decision showed characteristically his innate daring. Until that day a defense of the extended line had seemed impossible. Now that even

[66] O. R., 51, pt. 2, p. 971.                    [67] Ibid.
[68] O. R., 36, pt. 1, p. 998; ibid., pt. 3, p. 410.
[69] O. R., 36, pt. 3, p. 858.
[70] Ibid. The Federals were Brig. Gen. A. T. A. Torbert's 1st Division of the Cavalry Corps. Torbert reported that he drove Fitz Lee and Clingman three-quarters of a mile from Cold Harbor and that he captured four officers and sixty-one men of Clingman's command (O. R., 36, pt. 1, pp. 805–06).

LEE'S LIEUTENANTS

7000 muskets were to be added to his force, Lee shifted at once
from defense to offense. Anderson was ordered to leapfrog Early
and then to side-slip to the right until he touched the left of Hoke,
whose entire Division would be in position before daylight on
June 1.[71] To assure co-operation, Anderson was given control of
Hoke's forces.[72]

Anderson attacked early on the morning of the 1st. In the first
encounter, Kershaw's old Brigade was led by the inexperienced
Colonel of the Twentieth South Carolina. This officer, Lawrence
M. Keitt, was a man of high political and social distinction in his
own State but he had seen little action. When his regiment came
to Virginia late in May[73] and joined Kershaw's leaderless Brigade, Keitt's seniority gave him command. Now in his first battle,
he rode recklessly forward on horseback. His regiment broke. In
an effort to rally it, he fell mortally wounded. The panic spread
to other units of the Brigade.[74] Anderson's advance came quickly
to a halt. Hoke's men did virtually nothing in what had been expected to be a general attack.[75] Had the Federals delivered a vigorous counter-attack then, the Confederate right wing might have
been shattered, but the bluecoats seemed content to remain in their
entrenchments and to await developments. Truth was, Sheridan's
unsupported cavalry alone defended their light field works until
10 A.M. Then Wright's VI Corps moved in from the left and took
over the line. The Union cavalry shifted to the right.[76] Smith's
XVIII Corps had not then arrived.

After their repulse on the morning of June 1, the Confederates
in their turn began to put between them and the enemy every tin
cup of dirt that could be scraped from the loamy soil.[77] It was well
that they sensed danger and fortified against it, because, at 4 P.M.,
the Federals launched a furious attack. Behind it now was abundant strength. Smith had arrived at noon with about 10,000 men[78]
and joined the VI Corps in the assault. Union troops pushed the
attack until they separated Anderson's right and Hoke's left; but

[71] For the details and a sketch of the order of battle, see 3 R. E. Lee, 375–76.
[72] O. R., 36, pt. 3, p. 858; O. R., 51, pt. 2, p. 974.
[73] Dickert, 367. For Keitt, see Mrs. Chesnut, 68, 258; O. R., 36, pt. 2, pp. 850, 1012.
A sketch, with an excellent bibliography, will be found in D. A. B.
[74] Stiles, 274.
[75] Dickert, 369–70; Hagood, 255–57; Clingman in 5 N. C. Regts., 198 ff.
[76] O. R., 36, pt. 1, p. 794. These movements are stated in terms of the Confederate,
not of the Federal, position.
[77] Hagood, 258.                    [78] O. R., 36, pt. 1, p. 999.

the labor of the midday hours had piled the dirt high enough to stop the Federals before they had penetrated far. The enemy still occupied the village of Old Cold Harbor, though he could not break or turn the Confederate right.[79]

Narrowly Lee's lieutenants had saved their flank and, probably, their capital. They did not know that they perhaps owed their safety to two bits of good fortune. One was General Smith's inability to get his troops ashore quickly at the White House where dockage was almost nonexistent. He landed personally and opened headquarters at 11 A.M., May 30, but he did not begin his march till 3:30 P.M. of the 31st. Then came the second bit of good luck for the Confederates. Through a blunder by General Grant or by Gen. John A. Rawlins, the orders for Smith's advance directed him to "New Castle" on the Pamunkey, instead of Cold Harbor.[80] Smith had reached Bassett's House near Old Church about 10 P.M. The next morning, June 1, Army Headquarters ordered him to New Castle Ferry. Arriving at that point, he did not find any troops, though he had been told to place himself there between the V and VI Corps. When finally he was told to move to Cold Harbor, the hot morning was so far advanced that he did not arrive in time to make possible a swift counter-attack after the repulse of Kershaw's Brigade.[81] Had Smith not been misdirected twice, he probably could have overcome his slow debarkation and could have attacked early on the 1st along with the VI Corps.

This double good fortune was the first the Confederates had enjoyed since that May night when "Dick" Anderson had found no suitable resting place in the Wilderness and had marched on toward Spotsylvania. Now that Fortune favored the Confederates, she smiled still again. On the 2nd of June, the centre of action shifted toward Cold Harbor.[82] Confederate troops were moved there and were placed still farther to the right until, at nightfall, Wilcox's Division was within half a mile of the Chickahominy.[83] The chief distresses of an anxious day were the wounding of James H. Lane and the death of George Doles, one of the best Brigadiers of Rodes's Division, indeed, of the Second Corps.[84]

[79] O. R., 36, pt. 1, p. 1049; Hagood, 258–59. All the details and the full references are given in 3 R. E. Lee, 379–80.
[80] O. R., 36, pt. 1, p. 998.       [81] O. R., 36, pt. 1, p. 999.
[82] For Anderson's expectation of a renewal of the attack on the morning of June 2, see O. R., 51, pt. 2, p. 976.
[83] Wilcox's MS report, 48.       [84] 9 S.H.S.P., 244; 6 C. M. H., 413–14; Thomas, 47.

In these operations, with exhausting effort and dark risks, the movements of the enemy were completely anticipated. General Grant lost patience. He decided to lower his head, as it were, to put his full weight behind his blows, and to beat down his adversary. At dawn on the morning of June 3 he attacked along the whole line in the blind, brutal action known as Second Cold Harbor. At one point, he temporarily made lodgment in Confederate lines held by some of Breckinridge's troops [85] but on the greater part of the front, his assaults were beaten off so easily that the battle was over before some of the Confederates knew that an effort had been made to break the line. "The writer of these memoirs," said General Hagood, "situated near the centre of the line along which this murderous repulse was given, and awake and vigilant of the progress of events, was not aware at any time of any serious assault having been given." [86] Eight minutes sufficed to show the men of three Union Corps that farther advance would be suicide.[87] Spasmodic fighting broke out later on different parts of the line, but it never became threatening. At the price of not more than 1500 casualties, the Army of Northern Virginia killed or wounded 7000 of Grant's men.[88] The only injury in the Confederate high command was the wounding of E. M. Law.[89]

So weary was the Army of the Potomac and so dispirited by this defeat that Grant had to give the men rest while he decided on his next step. He had extended his left flank until he now was close to James River and he had to consider whether he would continue to fight North of that stream or would cross it and renew on the Southside his attempt to outflank Lee. To the open-field slugging in which he had engaged for a month, a period had been set. "I have always regretted," Grant wrote afterward, "that the last assault at Cold Harbor was ever made." He explained: ". . . no advantage whatever was gained to compensate for the heavy loss we sustained. Indeed, the advantages other than those of relative losses, were on the Confederate side." [90]

During this pause in the fighting, time was found for another reorganization of the depleted Army of Northern Virginia. It was a necessary, an imperative reorganization. In spite of the stress

[85] See 23 S.H.S.P., 193.　　[86] Hagood, 260.
[87] 4 B. & L., 217.
[88] These are the figures of General Alexander (op. cit., 542).
[89] 7 C. M. H., Ala., 424.　　[90] 2 Grant's Memoirs. 276.

of battle and the sickness of General Lee, new commanders had to be provided immediately for many units. Otherwise the casualties in the high command during the bloody month of May would cost the Army both discipline and leadership. The humiliating repulse of Kershaw's Brigade on the 1st of June had shown what might be apprehended even of veteran troops if they lacked a competent Brigadier.[91]

In facing with reduced personnel the perennial task of finding qualified leaders, the commanding General fortunately had the benefit of a helpful new act of Congress.[92] This authorized the appointment, with the Senate's approval, of Brigadier Generals, Major Generals and Lieutenant Generals to hold rank and command "for such time as the temporary exigency may require" and then to revert to their regular status. If an error were made in the hurried selection of a new Brigadier, there would be opportunity of correcting it by the direct if unpleasant process of declaring the particular emergency past. Besides, the new law permitted appointments to fill vacancies that otherwise would last as long as the illness or other physical incapacity of a general officer continued. The statute, in short, offered so much potential benefit that some appointments probably were delayed in order to await the passage of the bill.[93]

As authorized by this act, it seemed proper, first of all, that "Dick" Anderson should be given the temporary rank of Lieutenant General while commanding the First Corps during the absence of Longstreet, who now was recovering, though slowly. Anderson had won advancement by his famous march to Spotsylvania. He had fought prudently and intelligently there. Although Lee had directed him much more closely than the commanding General would have thought of doing in the case of the senior corps officers,[94] Anderson had shown no lack of stalwart qualities for his new post. If he was not brilliant he was dependable. At Cold Harbor, June 1, his handling of the Confederate advance and subsequent defense had not been good, but the fault may have been

[91] Two days before the break of the Brigade, Lee had urged Anderson to seek a good commander for it (O. R., 36, pt. 2, p. 851).
[92] Signed May 31; IV O. R., 496. For some of its antecedents, see ibid., 457 and O. R., 51, pt. 2, pp. 973–74.
[93] It had been introduced in the House May 12, 1864, and had been contested. See 7 Journal C. S. Congress, 56, 83, 84, 100, 124, 127, 128, 133, 151; 4 ibid., 133, 154.
[94] Correspondence with Anderson is much the most extensive in O. R., 36, pt. 3, p. 814 ff for the period after May 21 when the Army was in movement.

Hoke's. Nobody took time, in that red emergency, to determine why the North Carolinian did not give more assistance to the veteran now made Lieutenant General.

Another Lieutenant General was to be named, because it was manifest that Ewell could not resume safely his duties as commander of the Second Corps while the Army was in a furious field campaign. The danger was too great that Ewell might fall from his horse or succumb to sickness at a critical moment. He must be given an easier post until the battles of the summer were past. This did not suit Ewell and it acutely displeased Mrs. Ewell. After his illness at the end of May, the Lieutenant General reported for duty before he should have done so. He remained with the troops a week when he should have been resting; then he appealed to the President, had a long and none-too-pleasant interview with Lee and, in the end, reluctantly accepted direction of the Department of Richmond.[95] This transfer from field duty was a worse wound to "Old Bald Head" than the loss of his leg at Groveton, but in it there was no discredit to him. If he had not shown uniformly, after his return to the Army at the end of May, 1863,[96] the dash and decision that had marked him under Jackson, the reason was simply that he was never the same man in body or in mind after the amputation. Transfer of Ewell dictated the promotion of Early to Lieutenant General on the same temporary footing with "Dick" Anderson. This was considered by Lee an act of justice and was not delayed. For the period of Ewell's incapacity, at least, Early became Lieutenant General as of May 31.[97]

These two notable promotions left vacancies in Early's and in Anderson's Divisions. For those positions, the decision of Lee was prompt and probably was not doubtful. Anderson's senior Brigadier, William Mahone, was entirely qualified for promotion, though his opportunities in the field had been fewer than might have been assumed for a man who had been a Brigadier from

[95] *O. R.*, 36, pt. 1, p. 1074; *ibid.*, pt. 3, p. 863; *ibid.*, 40, pt. 2, p. 646; *Conner*, 143; *Hamlin's Ewell*, 127–130.

[96] See Vol. II, p. 705.

[97] *Wright*, 19. In orders of June 4, the promotion of Anderson was announced ahead of that of the other new Lieutenant Generals but Early was nominated and confirmed May 31 to rank from that date (4 *Journal C. S. Congress*, 127, 128). Anderson was nominated and confirmed June 1 to rank from May 31 (*ibid.*, 135, 136). It might have been argued, therefore, that Early ranked Anderson at their new grade though Anderson had been Early's senior as Major General; but when there was a prospect later in the summer that the two might operate together, Early was regarded as junior. See *infra*, p. 574.

November 16, 1861.[98] Early's successor was Dodson Ramseur.[99] This might have been a surprise, because Ramseur had been a Brigadier of Rodes and not of Early, but John Pegram's wounds and Gordon's promotion had left in Early's Division no officer then qualified for promotion. Ramseur had won the honor by a career of consistently fine, hard fighting. The young North Carolinian first heard the rumor of his new rank a few days after the observance of his 27th birthday.[100] He wrote his wife that if the rumor was true he would endeavor to do his whole duty. Then he added in his boyish manner, "I will be the more rejoiced on your account, first, because you will be pleased at the honors conferred on me, and, second, because I'll not be so much exposed. If I am a Division Commander now and stay further off from the line, I'll tell you of my escapes. I have had three horses shot under me, and disabled, one of these was struck three times; in addition to these the pony was also slightly wounded in the leg but not disabled. My saddle was shot through the pommel. I got four holes through my overcoat besides the ball which passed through my arm. I tell you these things, My Darling Wife, in order that you may be still more grateful to our Heavenly Father for his most wonderful and merciful preservation of my life." [101]

Besides these two appointments to temporary rank as Major Generals, Joseph B. Kershaw's command of McLaws's Division was made permanent. This action strengthened the First Corps and rewarded the admirable service of one of the ablest of the South Carolina general officers. All three of these appointments, Mahone's, Ramseur's and Kershaw's, were fortunate. Several times Lee had lamented that his inability to get rid of a mediocre senior had prevented the advancement of a much abler junior. In these instances, except as McLaws unhappily was involved, both Major Generals and Brigadiers deserved promotion. None of them might prove a Jackson or a Longstreet but none of them was apt to fail.

Permanent promotion as Brigadier General went to Col. Bryan Grimes, who was assigned to the command of the dead Junius Daniel's North Carolina troops. This advancement came because Grimes was in line of promotion, was qualified and had been

98 *Wright*, 66.                    99 *O. R.*, 36, pt. 3, pp. 873–74.
100 Ramseur to his wife, MS, May 31, 1864—*Ramseur MSS*.
101 To his wife, MS, June 4, 1864—*Ramseur MSS*.

much distinguished at the "Bloody Angle." His comment on the death of his Brigadier bespoke his own character: "[Daniel] was an excellent officer, and although I probably gained a brigade by his death, I would have preferred to remain in statu quo rather than his services be lost to the country."[102] The able, diligent and always courageous Col. James Conner at last had sufficiently recovered from an old wound to take the field. Most appropriately he was made a Brigadier General and was assigned temporarily the Brigade of the wounded Samuel McGowan.[103] To Rufus Barringer, a cavalry Colonel of excellent record, went the insignia and the commission of a Brigadier General, and the fine regiments of James B. Gordon, who had been killed at Yellow Tavern.[104] Of temporary Brigadiers, five were named: Col. William R. Cox of the Second North Carolina to take Ramseur's Brigade, Col. Thomas F. Toon of the Twentieth North Carolina, to handle the men of the injured Robert Johnston, Lt. Col. William G. Lewis of the Forty-third North Carolina to direct John Pegram's Brigade while that officer was wounded,[105] Col. Zebulon York of the Fourteenth Louisiana to lead the combined Louisiana Brigades till Harry Hays recovered,[106] and Lt. Col. R. D. Lilley of the Twenty-fifth Virginia to command Early's old Brigade.[107] All these were solid men of character but, with the exception of Cox, they scarcely could be termed conspicuous. They were simply the best that could be chosen quickly and without manifest unfitness from an officers' corps that had no superfluity of talent after the loss of so many able officers.

How much the Army command had suffered in the Wilderness and at Spotsylvania, no statistician set forth at the time. The list was longer than in any previous campaign; the summary was nothing short of terrifying:

102 *Grimes,* 52–53.
103 After his fine conduct at First Manassas (see Vol. I, p. 95), Conner was promoted Major. In June, 1862, he became Colonel of the Twenty-second North Carolina, but was wounded badly in the leg at Mechanicsville, on the 26th of that month. While invalided, he served as a member of the Military Court of the Second Corps. It was to this experience that history owes the intimate sketches of Ewell in 1863–64. Cf. *Conner,* 7 ff and *supra,* p. 331.
104 *O. R.,* 36, pt. 3, p. 873.
105 4 *C. M. H.,* 328.
106 *Ibid.,* pp. 873–74.
107 Lilley's promotion and assignment were not announced in the orders of June 4: 1864, but the nomination was presented and confirmed with the others, June 2, 1864 (4 *Journal C. S. Congress,* 144). For his assignment and a brief sketch see 3 *C. M. H.,* 627–28.

General Officers of the Army of Northern Virginia Whose Troops
were Present Throughout the Campaign, May 4–June 3, 1864 [108]

|  | Present | Killed | Wounded | Captured |
|---|---|---|---|---|
| Army Headquarters ... 1 | | — | — | — |
| First Corps ...........11 | | 1 | 3 | — |
| Second Corps .........16 | | 4 | 4 | 2 |
| Third Corps ..........16 | | 1 | 5 | — |
| Cavalry Corps ........11 | | 2 | — | — |
| Artillery ............. 3 | | — | — | — |
| Total ............58 | | 8 | 12 | 2 |

The killed were: First Corps, Micah Jenkins; Second Corps,
Junius Daniel, George Doles, John M. Jones and Leroy A. Staf-
ford; Third Corps, Abner Perrin; Cavalry Corps, "Jeb" Stuart
and James B. Gordon. The following sustained wounds severe
enough to incapacitate them for command, temporarily or per-
manently: First Corps, James Longstreet, E. M. Law and Henry L.
Benning; Second Corps, Harry Hays, Robert D. Johnston, John
Pegram and James A. Walker; Third Corps, John R. Cooke,
James H. Lane, Samuel McGowan, Edward L. Perry and Henry
H. Walker. The captured Generals were Edward Johnson and
Geo. H. Steuart. By rank the casualties ran in this manner: Killed,
one Major General and seven Brigadiers; wounded, one Lieutenant General and eleven Brigadier Generals; captured, one Major
General and one Brigadier. In addition, the commanding General
had been almost incapacitated by diarrhoea for a week; one corps
commander, Hill, had been too sick for almost a fortnight to
direct his troops; and another corps chief, Ewell, had been failing
so steadily in vigor that he had to be relieved of duty. In the First
and in the Second Corps, two experienced divisional leaders, R. H.
Anderson and Early, had been separated from their commands
and Corps, for a part of the campaign, in order to direct other
Corps.

These changes were more far reaching than anyone seems to
have realized at the time. Faith in the Army itself was so unshakable that the President, the War Department and General Lee
apparently believed the normal process of training would be re-

108 This excludes Pickett's Division, Breckinridge's command and Hoke's old Brigade
as well as Beauregard's command and the units of the Richmond defenses.

versed: Instead of the Generals instructing the troops, the veterans would school their new commanders. Within the limits of the tactics of every-day combat, this might prove true, but it could not be true of discipline and morale in a time of continuing discouragement and waning hope. Nor could the changes have been made at a time much more critical. A new development, a stern challenge, was to be expected daily. When Grant launched another direct drive on Richmond or undertook a turning operation South of the James, liaison with Beauregard and his newly arrived troops would be imperative. At a time when experience would be required to effect swift co-operation, two of the Corps of Lee's Army would be in the charge of men who had exercised that command less than a month.[109] Of the nine Divisions, two in the First Corps were under promising men, Kershaw and Field, though they scarcely could be regarded as fully seasoned at their higher rank. Two of the divisional leaders of the Second Corps were entirely new to that duty, Gordon and Ramseur. One of the three divisional chiefs of the Third Corps, Mahone, had never acted in that capacity for any length of time before the 8th of May. The only Major Generals left with the Army who had led Divisions as recently as Gettysburg, eleven months previously, were Pickett, who now was returning from detached service, Rodes, who had done admirably in Spotsylvania county, and Harry Heth, who carried some new odium for the events of May 6. None of these older Major Generals had directed as many as four Brigades in any hard action before Chancellorsville.[110]

The battles of a single month had put 37 per cent of the general officers of the Army of Northern Virginia hors de combat. Except as Lee himself embodied it, the old organization was gone!

[109] In addition, it will be remembered, Early had the Second Corps briefly in November-December, 1863.

[110] If Pickett at Fredericksburg be regarded as an exception, it will be remembered that he had virtually no active combat on the 13th of December, 1862. See Vol. II, p. 395.

# CHAPTER XXVI

## THREE MORE FEDERAL DIVERSIONS

AFTER ANNOUNCEMENT on June 4 of the promotions to succeed irreplaceable men, seven days of stench [1] and sharpshooting,[2] thirst and heat passed at Cold Harbor without any heavy attack by either belligerent. On other fronts in Virginia, the week brought alarms and advances. Had detached judgment of it been possible, the general strategic situation might have suggested that Grant was directing from the vicinity of Richmond three such minor offensives as he had launched a month previously on the Rapidan. The first of these was in the Shenandoah Valley. There, Maj. Gen. Franz Sigel had been relieved of command May 19,[3] after he had been defeated at New Market, May 15, by Gen. John C. Breckinridge. The force under Breckinridge had consisted of John Echols's and Gabriel Wharton's Brigades, to which, in the emergency, the small cadet corps of the Virginia Military Institute had been added. This combined force, with some artillery, had marched northward, down the Valley, in support of Imboden's cavalry, who were skirmishing with Sigel's van. When battle was joined near New Market, the cadets had fought with a disciplined courage and a consistent élan that had added to the prestige of the remarkable school without which the Army of Northern Virginia could not have had competent regimental command in the first year of the war.[4] Seldom did a small victory have so large an effect. Had Sigel not been driven back when he was, the Valley of Virginia might have been occupied by the Federals before the wheat crop was harvested. Hunger would have come sooner. In addition, the western end of the Virginia Central Railroad would have fallen into hostile hands. The prospect of losing that supply line might have compelled Lee to send part of his Army to the

---

[1] Cf. 2 *R. W. C. D.*, 226: "A deserter says Grant intends to *stink* Lee out of his position, if nothing else will suffice."
[2] In *N. H. Harris*, 30, it is stated that the daily loss of the Brigade from artillery and sharpshooters was ten or fifteen men.
[3] *O. R.*, 37 pt. 1, pp. 492, 508.　　　　[4] See Vol. I, p. 708 ff.

Valley while pressure at Spotsylvania was heaviest.[5] Short as was the time saved by the Battle of New Market, it was invaluable.

Now, in the first week of June, Sigel's successor, Maj. Gen, David Hunter, was moving rapidly up the Shenandoah. On the 6th, at Piedmont, seven miles Southwest of Port Republic, the Federals attacked and defeated a scratch force of about 5000 under "Grumble" Jones. About 1000 Confederate prisoners were taken. In a tragic end to a tragic life, Jones himself was killed.[6] The next day, June 6, Hunter gained without opposition a prize for which many a Union soldier previously had shed blood in vain: Staunton was occupied.[7] There, on the 8th, Hunter was joined by the tireless George Crook, who was returning from his raid on the Virginia and Tennessee Railroad. As he approached Staunton, Crook destroyed all the railroad West of that city. These combined forces of Hunter and Crook were in position to do vast military mischief. To delay them and to form a nucleus for future resistance, Breckinridge and his 2100 men were started from Cold Harbor on the 7th of June for Lynchburg,[8] whence they could move to the upper Valley or dispute a crossing of the Blue Ridge.

Before a decision could be reached in Richmond for any larger action against Hunter, the Southern cavalry discovered the second diversion: Sheridan had gone on another raid. On June 7, he had crossed the Pamunkey at New Castle Ferry and had camped that night at Dunkirk and Aylett's on the Mattapony.[9] Wade Hampton, who reported this movement, reasoned that Sheridan would strike for Gordonsville and Charlottesville.[10] It was manifest, also, that Sheridan might be moving to effect a junction with Hunter in the Valley,[11] or perhaps East of the Blue Ridge. Experience in May had warned that a heavy raid by Sheridan called for the sternest and most immediate counteraction. At headquarters near Atlee, Wade Hampton received orders on the 8th to prepare three days' rations and to proceed after the enemy with his

[5] The bibliography of New Market is extensive, though official reports are few. The most extensive study is E. Raymond Turner, *The New Market Campaign, May 1864.* Several addresses and late narratives are to be found in Col. William Couper's indispensable *One Hundred Years at V. M. I.* An extended account, with a detailed map, appears in Col. J. C. Wise's encyclopedic *Military History of the Virginia Military Institute from 1839 to 1865.* The reports and correspondence are in *O. R.,* 37, pt. 1, p. 76 ff.

[6] *O. R.,* 37, pt. 1, pp. 95, 747, 758: *ibid.,* 51, pt. 2, pp. 905, 981–82; *Annals,* 172–74, [7] *Ibid.,* 95, 153.

[8] *O. R.,* 37, pt. 1, p. 755 ff; *Lee's Dispatches,* 219.

[9] *O. R.,* 36, pt. 1. D. 1034.    [10] *Ibid.,* 1095.

[11] *O. R.,* 37, pt. 1, p. 754.

own and Fitz Lee's Divisions.[12] This order, incidentally, was an approach to a reorganization. After Stuart's death, it will be remembered, Lee had notified each of the cavalry Divisions to report directly to him.[13] This was ordered, almost certainly, to avoid a choice between Hampton and Fitz Lee as successor to the dead commander of the cavalry Corps. Now that the Divisions of these rivals had to operate together at a distance from Richmond, there was no safe alternative to applying the army regulation which entrusted command to the senior. This gave Hampton the greatest opportunity that had come to him during the war.

No large expenditure of time and effort was involved in preparing rations and horse-feed. The men received a pound and a half of hardtack and eight ounces of bacon. That was all. For the horses no more corn was issued than could be fastened in a bag to the saddle.[14] By daylight of the 9th of June, the column was in motion. It must proceed steadily, Hampton resolved, until grazing land was reached about noon. After two hours' rest then, the troopers should take the road again and march till midnight. Another two hours of rest would follow.[15]

While Hampton was en route that 9th of June, a critical alarm reached G.H.Q. from Petersburg, through Bragg's office. A third diversion had begun: a surprise attack was being delivered on that city. Beauregard had telegraphed that he had sent to the Petersburg defenses all the men he could spare from the Howlett Line. He went on: "Without the troops sent to General Lee I will have to elect between abandoning lines on Bermuda Neck and those of Petersburg."[16]

In midafternoon of the 9th of June, then, the high command of the Army of Northern Virginia faced this situation: Grant with his powerful host was directly in front; Hunter was in Staunton and was preparing to march on Lexington,[17] though his objective was not then known at headquarters. Sheridan was beyond the Mattapony and presumably was headed for the Virginia Central Railroad and jossibly for a junction with Hunter. The sudden activity around Petersburg did not appear to the commanding General to be more, in itself, than a reconnaissance, but there was

---

12 *Wells*, 188. W. H. F. Lee's Division was left with the main army.
13 See *supra*, p. 436.        14 *Wells*, 188; *Brooks*, 238.
15 *Brooks*, 238.              16 *O. R.*, 36. pt. 3, p. 884.
17 *O. R.*, 37, pt. 1, p. 96.

LEE'S LIEUTENANTS

no way of determining what adventure might follow the reconnaissance.[18]

To cope swiftly and vigorously with these three diversions was a grim assignment for a tired, weakened Army. The nearest of the three operations proved the easiest to combat. A clumsy, half-hearted attack on Petersburg was repulsed by the effort of Confederate troops, old civilians, boys too young for military service, and jail prisoners released on their promise to fight. Their adversaries proved to be Kautz's cavalry and small contingents of the X and XVIII Corps.[19] The cavalry attacked the intrenchments with some spirit but the infantry did nothing more than make a feeble demonstration. During the hours of darkness the whole of this attacking force withdrew.[20]

Hampton, that night of the 9th, followed the long road toward Louisa Court House and, after the brief rest, had his men on the road before dawn. During their first day's march the troopers for some reason had thought they were going to raid Washington and they found much pleasure in the prospect; but they had not gone many miles on the 10th before they understood that they were moving to cross swords with Sheridan again.[21] The day was hot. Drought made the dust so thick that the rear ranks had to grope their way. One rider recorded: ". . . The only water obtainable for man or beast was from small streams crossed, and this, churned up by thousands of hoofs, was almost undrinkable."[22] Men and mounts suffered but they staggered on until nightfall of the 10th found Hampton's Division in Green Spring Valley, the loveliest section of Louisa County. On the thick grass of wide pastures, the soldiers stretched themselves. The horses feasted. In a setting less Elysian, Fitz Lee went into camp at Louisa Court House about eight miles to the eastward.[23]

Hampton's superb endurance served him well that night. Although he had ridden all day of the 9th and of the 10th, he still was able to keep awake the second night and to collect information

---

[18] Lee to Beauregard; 2 *Roman,* 566. Cf. *O. R.,* 51, pt. 2, p. 1002.

[19] About 1200 of Kautz's cavalry, 1800 infantry of the X Corps and 1200 or 1300 of Brig. Gen. Edward W. Hinks's Negro troops of his 3rd Division of the XVIII Corps (*O. R.,* 36, pt. 2, pp. 287, 309).

[20] *Ibid.,* 289. For the reports of the "Battle of the 9th of June," as it was styled, see *O. R.,* 36, pt. 2, p. 272. Beauregard's dispatches are in *ibid.,* pt. 3, pp. 884–85. The principal authorities are listed in 3 *R. E. Lee,* 399, n. 47.

[21] *Wells,* 194.   [22] *Wells,* 193.

[23] *O. R.,* 36, pt. 1, p. 1095. This is Hampton's report and is the principal source.

about the enemy's movements. He learned to his immeasurable relief that his horses, on the shorter arc, had carried their riders to the Virginia Central ahead of the enemy. The railroad was

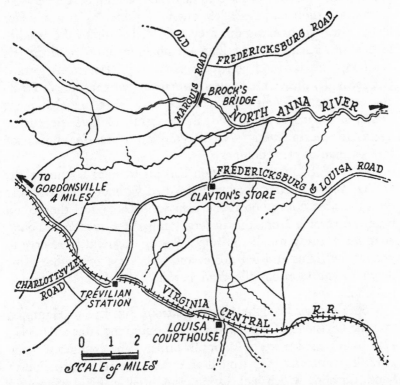

Vicinity of Louisa Court House and Trevilian Station. Carpenter's Ford, mentioned in the text, was slightly more than five miles down the North Anna from the right edge of the sketch. After A. H. Campbell's Map of a Portion of Eastern Virginia, 1864

intact and was in operation, but its safety had been assured by the thinnest of margins. Union cavalry already had crossed the North Anna at Carpenter's Ford.

Carefully Hampton questioned natives and studied his map, which supplied some detail.[24] From the ford, a convenient route for Sheridan led to Clayton's Store. There the enemy was offered two roads to the Virginia Central. One of these ran Southwest to Trevilian Station. The other proceeded southward to Louisa Court

---

[24] A. H. Campbell's "Map of a Portion of Eastern Virginia" between the Rappahannock and the James, East of the Blue Ridge, was approved April 22, 1864. A copy probably was in the hands of Hampton by June.

House, where Fitz Lee was bivouacked. Hampton's conclusion was to proceed with his own Division up the road from Trevilian to Clayton's Store and to have Fitz Lee move toward the same point from Louisa. Their columns then would be converging. Hampton's right and Lee's left might be protected in a measure by the thick woods along the Trevilian Road [25] and by the rapidity of this convergence. If Sheridan attempted to slip beyond the left of Hampton's Division and to proceed by inferior roads toward Gordonsville, the Confederate commander felt that he would be able to drive the enemy back to Clayton's Store. At that point Hampton hoped to close and, if successful, to hurl the enemy against the North Anna.[26] Needless to say, this was, for an inferior force, a plan of great boldness.

By dawn of June 11, Hampton had his troopers in the saddle. He had seen to it that they were aroused without bugle call and with the least noise; but as the men waited in ranks they could hear the reveille from the Federal camps.[27] Butler and Young were made ready for the advance. Rosser was held in reserve to protect the trains and led horses and to cover a route that came down to the Gordonsville road beyond the left of Hampton's position.

Soon a courier brought a message from Fitz Lee to Hampton that the Division at Louisa was moving out to the attack. Quickly Hampton passed word to Calbraith Butler. The younger General gave the command. Off trotted an eager squadron of the Fourth South Carolina which had distinguished itself at Haw's Shop. In a few minutes, shouts and an exchange of fire showed that the enemy had been encountered.[28] Hampton then dismounted the remainder of Butler's men and sent them forward in line of battle.

Before the steady advance of these troops, the enemy gave ground until he reached his supports. There he stood and returned the men from the Palmetto State as good as they sent. Immediately and smoothly, Hampton sent Young to reinforce Butler.[29] Because Fitz Lee simultaneously was moving up the road from Louisa Court House, Hampton felt confident that he would effect

[25] *Wells*, 196.
[26] *O. R.*, 36, pt. 1, p. 1095; *Wells*, 195–96.
[27] *Wells*, 194.
[28] *Wells*, 197.
[29] *O. R.*, 36, pt. 1, p. 1095.

junction in a short time and then could strike with all his troops and drive Sheridan back to the river.[30]

At that promising moment, Hampton received startling intelligence. The enemy was in his rear. At first Hampton doubted the verity of the report, but he quickly found it true. George A. Custer's advancing Brigade had engaged Wickham's men who formed the left of Fitz Lee's line on the road from Louisa to Clayton's Store. When Wickham had pulled back to ascertain the situation, the Federals had renewed their advance. As the Union left was strong, Custer had been ordered to proceed through the woods by a road which was thought by his immediate superior, Brig. Gen. A. T. A. Torbert,[31] to lead almost directly to Trevilian Station.[32] The road actually came into the Gordonsville highway about a mile and a quarter from the station,[33] but that merely isolated and did not deter Custer. He hurried westward and soon found himself among Hampton's wagons. Nearby were about 800 of Butler's led horses.[34] This fine booty Custer was collecting when Hampton was told what had happened. The Southern commander had, of course, to break away from the advancing Federals on the Trevilian-Clayton Store Road and to devote his fire to Custer.[35]

There followed as bewildering a fight as the Confederate cavalry ever had waged. At one moment Hampton's withdrawal appeared to be a rout; at another, Custer seemed in danger of destruction. Fitz Lee closed on him from the East, Rosser from the West, and Butler from the North. In the end, the Confederates recovered all their lost horses and vehicles and captured some of the Federals', among which was the headquarters wagon and records of Custer,[36] who contrived to hold Trevilian Station and the adjoining track. Fitz Lee was driven toward Louisa and was separated for the night from Hampton; but Custer had been so badly crippled and the entire Union force so roughly handled that Sheridan did not press the fight.

The next afternoon Sheridan undertook what he was pleased

30 O. R., 36, pt. 1, p. 1095.
31 Commanding the 1st Division of the Cavalry Corps.
32 O. R., 36, pt. 1, pp. 807, 823.
33 According to Campbell's map. Torbert (ibid., 808) reported the distance as two miles.
34 Ibid., 823.                                    35 Ibid., 1095.
36 O. R., 36, pt. 1, p. 1095. Some informative details will be found in Neese 284 ff and in D. A. Grimsley, Battles in Culpeper County, 32 ff.

to call a reconnaissance of a position west of Trevilian, across the Gordonsville and the Charlottesville roads, where Hampton had entrenched the reunited Divisions.[37] Several furious attacks by the dismounted bluecoats were repulsed at heavy cost to them. The Union commander then decided that his own losses, the depletion of his ammunition and the shortness of his rations made it unwise for him to continue an attempt to join Hunter.[38] That night, having destroyed part of the railroad track, Sheridan abandoned the campaign, and recrossed the North Anna. After giving men and mounts a rest, he started back on a wide sweep for Grant's Army.[39]

Although the heavy Confederate losses at Trevilian Station included a painful wound for Tom Rosser,[40] the operation could not be regarded otherwise than as a Southern victory.[41] It was the most encouraging small action to that date in Virginia during 1864 and it equalled Stuart's final performance.

Insofar as the Battle of Trevilian Station involved Hampton's leadership, it showed him capable and careful. At least one observant cavalryman, with some flair for historical fact, had concluded already that the difference between Stuart and Hampton was this: " 'Jeb' would attempt any necessary task with whatever force he had at hand, and sometimes he seemed to have a delight in trying to discharge his mission with the smallest possible number of men; Hampton believed in superiority of force and exerted himself to concentrate all the men he could at the point of contact." [42] In his heart, Hampton probably had felt from the beginning of his command the sentiment he was to voice a few months later in a letter to his sister: "We gain successes but after every fight there comes in to me an ominous paper, marked 'Casualties,' 'killed' and 'wounded.' Sad words which carry anguish to so many hearts. And we have scarcely time to bury the dead as we press on

---

[37] O. R., 36, pt. 1, p. 797. Fitz Lee was not able to rejoin Hampton until noon of the 12th (ibid., 1095).

[38] Torbert (ibid., 809) was somewhat more candid than Sheridan (ibid., 796–97) in stating the reasons for retreating.

[39] Ibid., 797–98.

[40] O. R., 36, pt. 1, p. 1096. Lee's regrets at the wounding of Rosser were expressed in a letter of July 28, 1864—Rosser MSS.

[41] Losses never were stated with any approach to accuracy. In Hampton's Division they were 612 (ibid., 1096). If those of Fitz Lee's Division, which was more lightly engaged, were 75 per cent of Hampton's, the total was not much under 1100. Sheridan reported only (ibid., 802) that from May 4 to July 30, his casualties were 4883.

[42] F. M. Myers, 291.

in the same deadly strife. I pray for peace. I would not give peace for all the military glory won by Bonaparte . . ."[43]

A man who had that view of war, but displayed on the field of battle highly intelligent leadership and the most unflinching courage, could not fail to impress his soldiers. Increasingly he won favor as the best procurable successor to the lamented "Jeb." Some of the troopers, in fact, thought then and thereafter that Hampton had been named to command of the cavalry Corps immediately after Stuart died.[44] Fitz Lee, of course, knew that this was not the case and he may have cherished still the ambition to take the place of his beloved Stuart; but if Fitz hoped to outshine Hampton, he was too good a soldier and too honorable a patriot to withhold full support. In Hampton's report on Trevilian Station and the operations that followed the battle, this was written: "Maj. Gen. Fitzhugh Lee co-operated with me heartily and rendered valuable assistance."[45] That may not have been warm by comparison with Stuart's praise, but it showed, at the least, that Hampton and Fitz Lee could work together.

The larger effect of Hampton's victory was to dispose of the second diversion undertaken by Grant and to simplify the abatement of the third threat, that offered by Hunter's advance up the Shenandoah Valley. On the day of the first grapple at Trevilian Station, June 11, General Hunter entered weakly defended Lexington.[46] As this completed the occupation of the strategic region West of the Blue Ridge, it was prudent to assume that Hunter would undertake to move East of the mountains. His position and movements could not be determined with certainty because the telegraph had been cut.[47] There had been annoyance in Richmond over his raid, and natural reluctance to detach more troops to deal with him; but when it became manifest that action against Hunter had to be taken, the decision was to do this effectively. If the capture of Richmond was to be risked at all, then the forces sent to drive Hunter from the Valley should be strong enough to pur-

[43] Wade Hampton to his sister, MS, Oct. 5, 1864. This revealing item from the Hampton MSS was placed most courteously at the writer's disposal by James C. Derieux of Columbia, S. C.

[44] Grimsley, op. cit., 35–36. Hampton's own headquarters contributed in an order of June 2, probably by inadvertence, to create the same impression. The order is marked "Hdqrs. Cavalry." Hampton is mentioned as "the major general commanding" (O. R., 36, pt. 3, p. 867).

[45] O. R., 36, pt. 1, p. 1097.          [46] O. R., 37, pt. 1, pp. 96–97.

[47] Early, 371.

sue him and, if possible, to threaten Washington.[48] For this large enterprise an entire Corps would be required.

The honor and the responsibility of the mission went to "Jube" Early. Although no reasons for this choice were given, one of them undoubtedly was that many of the troops of the Second Corps were units associated with Confederate successes in the region to which Early was to move. The old "Army of the Valley" belonged to the Second Corps: its presence on the Shenandoah would be reassuring. Furthermore, Early was a man of independent mind, entirely self-reliant and with an aptitude for strategy.[49] He was not a Jackson nor even a Longstreet, but he had some knowledge of the Valley and he appeared to be the most available man.

Verbal orders were given on the 12th, the second day of the Battle of Trevilian Station, for Early to hold in readiness the Second Corps and two of its battalions of artillery for detached service. Written orders followed later in the day. Before the first glint of dawn on the 13th, Early's men were moving. He had scarcely more than the bone of the famous old Corps. Eight thousand muskets were all he could count. Of the twelve Brigadier Generals in command at the opening of the Wilderness campaign, one only, Cullen Battle, remained in charge of the same troops. Ramseur and Gordon had been promoted; all the others had been killed, wounded or captured within less than six weeks.[50] New as were brigade officers, thin as were the ranks, the spirit of the Corps was as high as ever.

By steady marches,[51] but in complete ignorance of what Hunter was doing, Early reached and passed the battlefield of Trevilian Station. On the 16th, when the column was approaching the Rivanna River, Early rode ahead to Charlottesville. There, for the first time, he was able to establish communication with John C. Breckinridge, who, it will be remembered, had been ordered to Lynchburg as soon as Hunter had reached Staunton.[52] Breckinridge had gone to Rockfish Gap, where the tunnel of the Virginia Central passes through the Blue Ridge,[53] and there he had awaited

[48] See Lee's explanation, July 19, 1864, in *O. R.*, 37, pt. 1, p. 346.
[49] *Cf.* John W. Daniel in 22 *S.H.S.P.*, 326-27.
[50] *Early*, 372. Cullen Battle is not mentioned by name in Early's summary, but he was the remaining unwounded Brigadier.
[51] *Cf. O. R.*, 51, pt. 2, pp. 1012-13. [52] See *supra,* p. 516
[53] *O. R.*, 37, pt. 1, pp. 753, 755 ff; *ibid.,* 51, pt. 2, p. 1002.

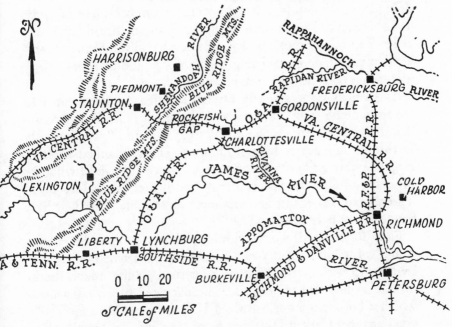

Sketch of Virginia from Richmond to the Allegheny Mountains and from the Rappahannock River to the Southside Railroad, to illustrate the first stages of Early's advance, June, 1864

Hunter. When the Federal commander moved as if he intended to cross the mountains South of Rockfish Gap, en route to Lynchburg, Breckinridge returned to that city and organized its defense as best he could.[54] Besides his two small Brigades of infantry, Breckinridge had the corps of cadets of the Virginia Military Institute.[55] In front of the enemy were two small, badly mounted and poorly armed forces of Confederate cavalry. One of these was under a newly commissioned Brigadier of some experience and of definite capacity,[56] John McCausland, 27 years of age, who had commanded the cavalry in Southwest Virginia after the death of Albert Jenkins.[57] The other force was Imboden's which, in spite of that devoted officer's efforts, was in bad condition. Breckinridge reported promptly to Bragg: "The cavalry under Imboden [are]

<hr/>

54 Cf. *O. R.*, 40, pt. 2, p. 658. Hunter crossed the mountains on the 15th (*O. R.*, 37, pt. 1, p. 98). Breckinridge arrived in Lynchburg that day (*O. R.*, 40, loc. cit).
55 *O. R.*, 37, pt. 1, p. 91; J. C. Wise, *Mil. Hist. V. M. I.*, 358–59.
56 Cf. *Early*, 373–74, 376.
57 For McCausland, a graduate of the Virginia Military Institute, see 2 *C. M. H.*, West Virginia, 135 ff.

doing less than nothing. If a good officer cannot be sent for them at once they will go to ruin." [58] Robert Ransom already had been ordered to take command of all the cavalry in the Department.[59] To that extent, need was being met, but beyond that, Breckinridge was facing odds he could not hope to beat.

As soon as General Early ascertained this, he determined to requisition all nearby rolling stock of adjacent railroads and to use it in moving the troops to Lynchburg. "Old Jube" was furiously in earnest and was to balk at nothing. He telegraphed Breckinridge: "I have authority to direct your movements, and I will take the responsibility of what you may find it necessary to do. I will hold all railroad agents and employés responsible with their lives for hearty co-operation with us." [60]

Early followed his words with his person as soon as the railway would carry him, but it was 1 P.M. of the 17th when he reached Lynchburg with part of Ramseur's Division. "Jube" found Breckinridge in bed and for the time incapacitated by an old wound which a fall from a horse at Cold Harbor had made angry.[61] By good chance, Harvey Hill was in the city and, at Breckinridge's instance, had put the troops to fortifying. Early was not among the enthusiastic admirers of Hill, but he telegraphed for permission to assign the North Carolinian to the temporary leadership of Breckinridge's troops. "It is of the utmost importance," said Early, "to have another commander than the senior brigadier." [62] The formal appointment of Hill was not considered necessary by a hostile administration because the invalided Arnold Elzey, who had been in Staunton, vainly attempting to reorganize the Maryland Line,[63] was ordered to Lynchburg.[64] He had not yet arrived, but one of Early's own former officers, Brig. Gen. Harry Hays, was recovering in Lynchburg from a wound received at Spotsylvania, and he of course tendered his experienced services.[65]

[58] O. R., 40, pt. 2, p. 658.    [59] Ibid., 646, 760, 762, 764, 765.
[60] O. R., 37, pt. 1, p. 763.

[61] O. R., 51, pt. 2, p. 1020. For the accident at Cold Harbor, where Breckinridge's horse was killed by a round shot while the General was astride him, see ibid., 983, and 7 S.H.S.P., 317.

[62] O. R., 51, pt. 2, p. 1020. The senior Brigadier with Breckinridge was John C. Vaughn, a native of Grayson County, Virginia, 40 years of age, who had been appointed from Tennessee, Oct. 3, 1862 (Wright, 90–91). For Vaughn's report after the engagement at Piedmont, see O. R., 51, pt. 2, p. 990.

[63] O. R., 40, pt. 2, p. 650.

[64] Ibid., 662 and ibia., 37, pt. 1, p. 765. Elzey had gone back to Richmond from Staunton.

[65] Early, 374.

With these commanders and those of Ramseur's Division, Early surveyed the trenches that had been dug and decided that they were too close to Lynchburg to protect it from the Federal artillery. A more advanced line was taken and was occupied by Early's troops, who now were reinforced by the arrival of other trains. The van of the enemy challenged with its artillery the veterans of the Second Corps on the 17th of June but did not assail them.[66]

"Jube" was not afraid of Hunter, but the Orange and Alexandria Railroad brought up the remaining Confederate troops so slowly from Charlottesville on the 18th that Early held to the defensive. A few small-scale attacks were made on him during the afternoon and were repulsed easily. Before the day was over, all the remaining troops of Early had arrived. Ransom and Elzey had reported. Breckinridge would be well enough to resume command on the morrow.[67] Early accordingly made his preparations to attack on the 19th, only to learn, soon after midnight, that Hunter was in retreat. At dawn pursuit began. Early pushed it to the limit of lungs and vigor and at the town of Liberty, Bedford County,[68] he skirmished with the rearguard of the retiring Federals. That was all "Jube" could do.[69] He had saved Lynchburg and the Southside Railroad; he had ended the third Federal diversion; he had not destroyed Hunter.[70]

[66] *Early*, 374-75.
[67] Cf. *O. R.*, 37, pt. 1, p. 766.
[68] Now Bedford City
[69] *Early*, 376-77.
[70] Details of the Battle of Lynchburg will be found in an article by Charles M. Blackford, 30 *S.H.S.P.*, 279 ff.

# CHAPTER XXVII

## Toward Immobilized Command

THE DAYS OF THE OPERATIONS in front of Lynchburg had witnessed a new climax in the struggle for Richmond. From the sequence of events, that climax might have seemed one to which both Lee and Grant had been building. Hunter's victory over "Grumble" Jones at Piedmont had occurred on the 5th. Sheridan had started on the 7th to join Hunter and to cover that officer's advance to a junction with Grant.[1] The 8th of June had witnessed the meeting of Hunter with Crook in Staunton.[2] Kautz, on the 9th, had threatened Petersburg. The 10th was the date of Hampton's arrival near Trevilian Station and of his decision to attack Sheridan.[3] While the cavalry were fighting the next day, Hunter was entering Lexington. Early's orders to move against Hunter bore date of the 12th.

These were the preliminaries. The next day, June 13, as the Second Corps was beginning its long march up the Virginia Central Railroad, the troops who remained on the line at Cold Harbor ascertained that the enemy had left their front. Grant had undertaken another shift. The probability that the Federal commander might move to the South of James River had been recognized,[4] but his departure was into the baffling, heavily wooded country where Lee had fought McClellan in 1862. "Our skirmishers," Lee reported to Davis as he started the pursuit of the Federals, "were advanced between one and two miles, but failing to discover the enemy were withdrawn, and the army was moved to conform to the route taken by him."[5] While Grant made the most of the day's march that either adversary could steal on the other in that difficult terrain, Lee searched for him. By the afternoon of June 14, but not before that time, the Confederate command knew

[1] O. R., 36, pt. 1, p. 795.                    [2] O. R., 37, pt. 1, p. 96.
[3] O. R., 36, pt. 1, p. 1095.
[4] For the evidence that the crossing of the James was anticipated, see 3 R. E. Lee, 399, 404, 439 and the references there cited.
[5] O. R., 36, pt. 1, p. 1035.

528

Grant's approximate position and perceived how readily the Union Army could move over the James to Petersburg.[6]

The next day, June 15, the date of Hunter's crossing of the Blue Ridge and of Breckinridge's arrival in Lynchburg,[7] Petersburg, not Richmond became the theatre and Beauregard's troops, rather than Lee's, the actors. Two small[8] regiments of Dearing's cavalry were attacked by Kautz's cavalry before 8 A.M.,[9] on the road leading from City Point to Petersburg. With the aid of Graham's Battery,[10] which commanded a good field of fire,[11] Dearing was able to repulse Kautz and to send word to his chief. Beauregard had at that time on the entire front opposite Bermuda Hundred and in front of Petersburg a force he estimated at slightly in excess of 5400.[12] Of these men, about 2200 of all arms, consisting of a part of Henry A. Wise's Virginia Brigade and some local troops, defended Petersburg.[13]

On receipt of the news of the enemy's approach, Wise's men were concentrated immediately on the sector of the Petersburg earthworks that faced the approaching Federals. Fighting opened quickly. The defenders of the city stoutly resisted parts of the XVIII Corps which included a Division of Negro troops.[14] With varying fortune and no great show of initiative on the part of the assailants,[15] the day passed. Wise's men held their light fortifications until driven from some of them late in the evening.[16] The Virginia troops then closed on the second line and prepared to renew the contest at dawn.[17] To aid them, Beauregard stripped almost naked the front opposite Bermuda Hundred,[18] and he appealed in loudest terms for help from Lee.

As soon as it had seemed probable on the 14th that Grant might cross the James, Hoke's Division, which was on the north side of the river, had been moved by Lee's orders to the pontoon bridge above Drewry's Bluff.[19] While Wise's fight was in its first stage on the 15th, Hoke was put in motion for Petersburg.[20] His leading Brigade, Hagood's, arrived not long after the Federals had

[6] Lee's Dispatches, 227–32.       [7] See supra, p. 525.
[8] 2 Roman, 229.
[9] O. R., 40, pt. 1, p. 720; Wise in 25 S.H.S.P., 13.
[10] 25 S.H.S.P., 13.                [11] O. R., 40, pt. 1, p. 729.
[12] 2 Roman, 230.                   [13] 25 S.H.S.P., 13.
[14] O. R., 40, pt. 1, pp. 705, 721. [15] 2 Grant's Memoirs, 295, 298.
[16] O. R., 40, pt. 1, p. 705.       [17] 25 S.H.S.P., 13.
[18] Ibid., and 2 Roman, 230.        [19] Lee's Dispatches, 233.
[20] O. R., 40, pt. 2, p. 658.

stormed part of the outer line. Remaining units of the Division reached the front during the night.[21]

Richmond and Petersburg, either or both, now were in acutest danger. Grant had the initiative, had superior force and had alternatives of action his opponent could understand but might not be able to oppose with success. Anything might happen, and happen swiftly, once that fine Union Army had shaken itself loose and could strike where it chose.

Beauregard and Lee faced different aspects of the same difficult problem. The commander on the Southside had believed from the 15th onward that Grant was moving large forces across the James. For Beauregard the question was whether, in the face of heavy attacks, he could retain his long lines with his small forces until larger help came from Lee. The conclusion of Beauregard was that the assaults would continue to be powerful and that, if he were able, at all, to hold Petersburg till relief came, it would have to be by abandoning and not merely by stripping the "Howlett Line."[22]

Lee, in his turn, had responsibility for Richmond as well as for Petersburg, and he did not feel that he could reinforce Beauregard heavily at the expense of the scanty Divisions defending the capital, until it was certain that the principal attack was to be against Petersburg. It seemed probable, from the first intelligence reports, that those of Butler's troops who had been sent to Grant were being returned. If they were all who faced Beauregard, he could checkmate them with moderate assistance. In the event that Grant was detaching heavily from his own Army to assist Butler's, then Beauregard must have larger reinforcement. The instant essential was to ascertain whether any of Grant's troops, as distinguished from Butler's, were on the south side of the James.

This was the subject of an anxious exchange of many telegrams on the 16th.[23] Early in the day, Beauregard could not procure information; Lee could not act without it. To save Petersburg, the Confederate rearguard in front of Bermuda Hundred had in mid-morning to evacuate the second line.[24] Before the men with-

---

[21] 2 *Roman*, 230.
[22] It is not certain when this name was given the Confederate line across Bermuda Hundred Neck.
[23] For the details, see 3 *R. E. Lee*, 411 ff.
[24] *Lee's Dispatches*, 245.

drew from Battery Dantzler, which had been completed a short time previously at the Howlett House, they carefully buried and concealed the guns and mounts.[25] The enemy, moving into the abandoned works, did not have the enterprise to search for the missing artillery.

Troops of Johnson's Division, who were started for Petersburg during the night of the 15th–16th,[26] were able to reach the city's defenses in time to support Wise and Hoke. According to General Wise, a mistake was made by Johnson in not filling a gap on the Confederate left,[27] where the pressure was increasing hourly; but in the brisk fighting little ground was lost until late afternoon. Then the Confederates had to face so heavy an assault that they abandoned another part of their works.[28] In spite of this withdrawal, the defenders of Petersburg were not discouraged. One participant wrote years later: "We had practically nothing to eat, almost no water to drink, and no sleep at all except such little as we could snatch from the few intervals of calm. . . . It had been a time that called for every ounce of endurance there was in us. But the boys during all the weary hours of suffering with hunger and thirst did not complain. . . . Our casualties were not heavy for such a tremendous amount of real fighting. The old earthworks, though very poor protection, saved many of us. We could lie flat down to load our rifles and then quickly rise and 'give it' to the bluecoats." [29]

During these stubborn exchanges, which continued through the day and into the night,[30] Army Headquarters were transferred to the south side of the James. First corps units were moved there to meet any new threat and to recover the Howlett Line, which had protected the railway. These transfers put on the Southside a total of about 22,600 of Lee's troops and left North of the James Powell Hill's Third Corps, Kershaw's Division of the First, and most of the cavalry—an aggregate of approximately 21,000.

As night of the 16th approached, the unsettled question remained: It had not been possible to ascertain whether Butler alone,

[25] 2 Roman, 231.          [26] Ibid.
[27] 25 S.H.S.P., 14.
[28] O. R., 40, pt. 1, p. 168. This attack at 6 P.M. was delivered by Hancock's II and Burnside's IX Corps, while Smith's XVIII demonstrated. The works taken by Hancock's men, who did most of the fighting, were in front of and to the left of the Hare House (Ibid., 306).
[29] MS Memoirs of W. B. Freeman.          [30] 2 Roman, 232.

or Butler with large help from Grant, was attacking Petersburg. No helpful intelligence had come from the Richmond sector. Near the end of the day's struggle, in answer to repeated inquiries from G.H.Q.,[31] Beauregard reported the presence of Hancock's II Corps, but beyond that he confessed: "No satisfactory information yet received of Grant's crossing James River." [32] That news had to be weighed. Although an enterprise shared by Hancock was apt to be serious, there still was a chance that Grant was perpetrating a ruse and that he would strike at Richmond when he thought Lee's back was turned.

The 17th of June, the date of Early's arrival in Lynchburg,[33] brought new suspense to the Confederate capital and long hours of exciting adventure and gnawing uncertainty on the Southside. Veteran troops of the First Corps, under the calm and competent direction of "Dick" Anderson, had no difficulty in clearing Butler's X Corps from most of the ground that had been seized by the Federals when Beauregard had sent the defenders to Petersburg. The final advance against a strong point on the Clay Farm was reminiscent of 1862. After Anderson had ordered an assault by Pickett and Field, the engineers reported that they believed they could mask the position and that they consequently did not think an assault necessary. Lee promptly sent a countermand to Field, but before the messenger reached the other Division, Pickett had started forward. The nearer units of Field could not deny themselves a hand in what promised to be a brisk fight. In defiance of orders, a large part of Field's men joined the assault in a spirit of which their old commander, John Hood, would have been proud. Pickett's men advanced as if the hill at Mrs. Clay's Farm were another Cemetery Ridge. After they had reached their objective and had driven the Federals, Lee sent congratulations to Anderson on the fine conduct of the men of the First Corps. Said the commanding General: "I believe that they will carry anything they are put against. We tried very hard to keep Pickett's men from capturing the breastworks of the enemy but couldn't do it." [34]

Beauregard had a more difficult day. During the early forenoon of the 17th he was unable to identify any troops in his front besides

[31] 2 Roman, 571; O. R., 40, pt. 2, p. 659.
[32] O. R., 51, pt. 2, p. 1079.
[33] Early, 373.
[34] Walter Harrison, 130–31. See also R. H. Anderson in O. R., 51, pt. 2, p. 1019.

the two Corps he had reported the previous evening. He concluded that the strength of these two and the superiority of their position would force him to take up a shorter line close to Petersburg, but his old fondness for proposing an offensive with troops taken from another Army would not down. His first telegraphic dispatch of the morning to the commanding General included in a new form the familiar proposal that Lee give him sufficient reinforcements to "take the offensive [and] get rid of the enemy here." [35] Almost before the message was dispatched, the situation indicated that the enemy might "get rid" of Beauregard. An early assault by part of the IX Corps carried the sweating Unionists into the Confederate works near the Shands House. Four guns, five colors and about 600 prisoners were captured.[36] Steady Federal attacks followed this success. Beauregard fought shrewdly and beat back repeated assaults, but he realized he was nearing adversely the end of a desperate gamble. He telegraphed Lee: "We greatly need reinforcements to resist such large odds against us. The enemy must be dislodged or the city will fall." [37]

This warning followed dispatches from Beauregard and from other officers who had been working ceaselessly to answer the wearisome, perilous question of Grant's movements. During the forenoon, an effort was made at Lee's Headquarters to ascertain the truth of prisoners' statements on the Petersburg front that Warren's V Corps had left White House on the 10th for an unknown destination.[38] Beauregard later telegraphed the boast of another prisoner, who asserted that 30,000 of Grant's men were South of the James.[39]

All the reports of the morning and early afternoon confirmed the probability that a greater part of Grant's Army had crossed the James. On the basis of information received prior to 4:30 P.M., Powell Hill was ordered to march the Third Corps to Chafin's Bluff, whence he could move quickly to defend Richmond or could cross the James and proceed to Petersburg.[40] Kershaw's Division, which had been waiting at Chafin's Bluff, was ordered

[35] O. R., 51, pt. 2, p. 1079.
[36] O. R., 40, pt. 1, pp. 522, 545. The burden of this assault was borne by Brig. Gen. Robert B. Potter's 2nd Division.
[37] O. R., 51, pt. 2, p. 1079.
[38] O. R., 51, pt. 2, pp. 1079–80; ibid., 40, pt. 2, p. 664.
[39] O. R., 51, pt. 2, p. 1080.
[40] O. R., 40, pt. 2, p. 662.

to the Howlett Line.[41] As a matter of military instruction, desperate but brilliant, it was much to be regretted that virtually none of Lee's lieutenants, outside his personal staff, witnessed this demonstration of his methods of sifting and interpreting his intelligence reports.

During the late afternoon of the 17th, Beauregard sent to headquarters the most detailed information he yet had been able to get from prisoners. Federals in his hands said that the II, IX and XVIII Corps were in action on the Petersburg front and that the V and VI were advancing. Long experience in dealing with prisoners' statements had made the commanding General skeptical about reports that contained more knowledge of operations than the average enlisted man would be likely to possess. Lee felt that all assertions by prisoners of great strength on any sector should be gauged by the pressure the enemy did or did not exert there. In this instance, the new reports were corroborative but not conclusive. No further Confederate troop movements were ordered immediately.

From Beauregard, about night, came next a dispatch that was the more serious because it was not theatrical. The General informed G.H.Q. that increasing numbers in front of his inadequate and over-extended forces would compel him that night to withdraw to a shorter line. "This," said he, "I shall hold as long as practicable, but, without reinforcements, I may have to evacuate this city very shortly." Beauregard concluded: "In that event I shall retire in the direction of Drewry's [42] Bluff, defending the crossing at Appomattox River and at Swift Creek." [43]

This warning seemed to indicate more pressure than had been observable previously, the pressure that would be exerted by a powerful adversary who was prepared and determined to reach his objective. Beauregard, it appeared to Lee, now was genuinely in need of further reinforcement. Kershaw therefore was directed to proceed down the Petersburg Pike at dawn and to join Beauregard. Powell Hill received orders to advance the Third Corps to the same road via the pontoon bridge above Drewry's Bluff, to

[41] For the doubt concerning the time of Kershaw's transfer to the Southside, see 3 R. E. Lee, 419, n. 141.
[42] Beauregard and many other officers consistently misspelt this familiar Virginia name and rendered it Drury's.
[43] 2 Roman, 234–35.

halt on the highway, and to await developments.[44] Obediently, at midnight, June 17-18, Hill was in motion to cross the bridge. No troops besides Lee's cavalry and the garrison of Richmond remained North of the James.

The next few hours were decisive. Beauregard had received no relief from the attacks that had begun disastrously at dawn of the 17th. Toward evening the assaults became more furious. About dusk [45] a desperate attack by a Division of the IX Corps breached another section of the line and took Battery 14, which had been held by part of Wise's command. The arrival of Archibald Gracie's Brigade prevented deep penetration,[46] but a necessary counter-attack by Mat Ransom's North Carolina Brigade cost it many lives.[47] By the time Ransom's men threw the Federals out of the salient they had taken.[48] Beauregard was poised for a withdrawal to new positions that had been staked out by his capable chief engineer. The plan was to move back to this ground as soon as the firing ceased and to throw up sufficient earthworks before dawn to hold off the enemy till reinforcements could arrive.

Chance favored Beauregard's resolution. About the hour the North Carolinians were grappling with the IX Corps, a Federal courier, bearing a message from Burnside to Meade, lost his way and rode into the Confederate lines. The paper in his charge showed that the IX Corps was nearly exhausted and would not be able to renew the attack before daylight.[49] Encouraged by this news, Beauregard had the campfires piled high and the picket line advanced. Then, under strictest injunction of silence, his men moved to the rear and went to work on the construction of a new inner line.[50]

While the defenders of Petersburg were raising these works, conclusive news had reached Army Headquarters. "Rooney" Lee, who commanded the cavalry advance in the vicinity of Malvern Hill, had been ordered on the afternoon of the 17th to ascer-

[44] 4 S.H.S.P., 190; O. R., 40, pt. 2, p. 663.
[45] Burnside's report (O. R., 40, pt. 1, p. 522) would indicate that the principal attack was ordered about 4 P.M. Brig. Gen. James H. Ledlie, whose 1st Division of the IX Corps delivered the assault, stated that he received at 5:30 P.M. the orders to form for the assault (Ibid., 532).
[46] 2 Roman, 232.                    [47] 3 N. C. Regts., 622.
[48] O. R., 40, pt. 1, p. 533.
[49] 2 Roman, 233. No copy of this dispatch has been found in O. R.
[50] Ibid. The recollection of W. B. Freeman, op. cit., was that Negro laborers had been throwing up dirt for this line and that considerable progress had been made before the soldiers began to dig.

tain, if possible, what had "become of Grant's army";[51] but the son of the commanding General had not let reconnaissance wait on orders. At the very time that instructions were being drafted for him, he had on the road to Chaffin's Bluff a courier with a detailed report. During the night this was placed in the hands of the senior Lee. It contained information that the enemy had a pontoon bridge across the James at Wyanoke Neck and that the rear of the enemy had left Doctor Wilcox's the previous night after posting a notice that Petersburg, with twenty-two guns and 3,000 prisoners, had been captured.[52]

This information from "Rooney" Lee removed the last doubt from his father's mind. Grant evidently had shifted the entire infantry battle to the Southside. If his "left flank movement" had not succeeded North of the James, he would renew it where there would be no broad river to halt him.[53]

Regrouping of the Confederate forces began immediately. Kershaw's orders stood: he was to proceed to Petersburg to reinforce Beauregard's weary men. Powell Hill was to follow Kershaw. One Brigade of cavalry was to be transferred to the Southside. On the Lynchburg front, "Jube" Early was to push his offensive or, if that proved impossible, was to return to Petersburg.[54] Army Headquarters were to be moved there. As this involved Lee's entrance into Beauregard's Department, the possibility of complications had been anticipated and obviated. On June 15, the Secretary of War had instructed all officers exercising separate commands in Virginia and in North Carolina to report to General Lee and to receive orders from him.[55]

By the movements undertaken on the night of the 17th–18th, adequate reinforcements were assured the defenders of Petersburg. The diary of the First Corps for the 18th of June read as

[51] O. R., 40, pt. 2, p. 663.
[52] O. R., 51, pt. 2, p. 1080. Doctor Wilcox's plantation was directly East of the Westover estate and South of the River Road. The residence was on high ground East of the road that still (1944) runs to Wilcox's Landing. Strictly speaking, "Rooney" Lee was mistaken in saying that the pontoon bridge was from Wyanoke Neck to the Southside. According to all the other reports and to the evidence of the ground itself, the crossing was from Wilcox's Landing to Windmill Point.
[53] It does not appear to have been recognized generally that from May 7, 1864, to April 1, 1865, General Grant's maneuver was consistently that of outflanking the Confederate right. He began this in the Wilderness; he succeeded in it, finally, at Five Forks. For some reason, General Grant thought that his movement South of the James might be considered the course of desperation. Consequently he took pains to assert that from the beginning it had been part of the plan he intended to follow in event he could not destroy Lee's Army North of the James. Cf. O. R., 36, pt. 1, p. 22.
[54] O. R., 40, pt. 2, pp. 667, 668; Lee's Dispatches, 249 ff.
[55] O. R., 40, pt. 2, p. 654.

confidently as of old: "At 3 A.M. Kershaw moves for Petersburg, followed by Field, Pickett occupying the whole Howlett line. We arrive at Petersburg and Kershaw relieves Bushrod Johnson's division, Field taking position on Kershaw's right." [56] The reality was as dramatic as the narrative was commonplace. Beauregard's men had labored all night on the new works, which consisted of simple trenches, with the ditch behind them. Eight hundred yards closer to the city than were the abandoned fortifications, the new line was the chord of the arc of the original defenses.[57] A night's labor on this line had completed the exhaustion of Beauregard's troops. When they saw the glint of the morning sun on the bayonets of Kershaw's Division and realized that they at last were to have relief, they wept and cheered. To the end of their days, they kept fresh in memory the picture of that advancing relief column on the hill of Blandford Cemetery.[58] As for Petersburg folk, their supreme hour came that afternoon, June 18, when Hill's Corps marched through the city to take position on the line. One woman wrote that night in her diary: ". . . what regiment should come first but our own gallant Twelfth Virginia—but oh! so worn with travel and fighting, so dusty and ragged, their faces so thin and drawn by privation that we scarcely knew them." [59]

As these and other veterans of the Army of Northern Virginia placed themselves between Petersburg and the enemy, danger of a sudden catastrophe passed. Beauregard's spirits underwent their usual swift change. From deepest concern he was lifted to optimism. After showing Lee the ground visible from a high point near the city reservoir, Beauregard proposed to the commanding General that an attack be made on Grant's flank and rear as soon as Hill's and Anderson's Corps arrived. Lee of course rejected all idea of throwing his weary and weakened Divisions immediately against so strong and well placed an adversary.[60]

[56] O. R., 40, pt. 1, p. 761.

[57] Students of the Petersburg campaign may find it worth while to remember that this line of June 18, which was the main defense of Petersburg till the close of operations, continued to be styled "the trenches," though greatly elaborated and strengthened. See Hagood in 16 S.H.S.P., 400.

[58] Cf. MS Memoirs of W. B. Freeman.

[59] David Macrae, The Americans at Home, 1, 170.

[60] In 2 Roman, 247, where this incident is recorded, the author of that work expressed for himself, and doubtless for General Beauregard, disapproval of Lee's refusal to order an offensive on the 18th. Roman voiced equal regret that Lee had not supplied needed reinforcements in time to prevent the occupation by the Unionists of a strong line. Neither General Beauregard nor Colonel Roman appears to have had an understanding of the condition of the Army of Northern Virginia after more than six weeks of hard campaigning.

Although "No" was said to him on that memorable 18th of June, Beauregard soon learned why Lee's old lieutenants swore "Marse Robert" never lost an opportunity of delivering a blow when he saw a fair opening. For four reasons, it was difficult to strike soon or heavily at Petersburg. The Army's task was vastly complicated. Because of the strength of Grant's position and the weight of Federal numbers, the Confederates, in the first place, could not afford to attack the Union entrenchments unless the necessity was desperate.[61] At the same time, the Army of Northern Virginia had to defend the approaches of Richmond as well as of Petersburg and, third—cost what it might—the Army must keep open lines of supply from the South. "If this cannot be done," Lee said, "I see no way of averting the terrible disaster that will ensue." [62] From this statement Lee perforce had to except the Petersburg and Weldon. That line manifestly was doomed,[63] though sound logistics demanded its protection and use as long as this could be done without excessive loss of life. Whenever other railways were assailed by the enemy's raiders, they must be defended to the limit by the Confederate cavalry. Finally, in the planning and execution of this difficult military course, the Confederates were crippled by lack of men and by loss of leaders. As early as the end of May, many regiments had been reduced in size to companies, and Brigades to regiments  One captain reported that he began the campaign in the Wilderness with seventeen men. On May 30, he had one left. His regiment had sixty-eight muskets. He commanded it.[64] There probably was not a Division as large in June, 1864, as Branch's or Lawton's Brigades had been two years previously.

One after another, between June 18 and July 30, these four obstacles to offensive strategy presented acute strategic problems. The first test came almost before the tired troops had begun to recover. On June 21–22, the launching of another cavalry raid under Brig. Gen. James H. Wilson [65] was accompanied by an infantry demonstration against the Weldon Railroad near Petersburg. Wilson got away on the errand of mischief, but Maj. Gen. William Mahone [66] found a gap between the II and VI Corps,

---

61 Lee's Dispatches, 254–55.  
63 Ibid.  
65 O. R., 40, pt. 1, pp. 620, 730.  
62 O. R., 40, pt. 2, p. 690.  
64 Wingfield, 40.  
66 He had succeeded, it will be remembered, on May 7 to the command of "Dick" Anderson's Division.

SWIFT CREEK

RICH'D-PRSBG. R.R.

CITY POINT R.R.

CITY POINT

JORDON'S POINT RD.

APPOMATTOX

PRINCE GEORGE C.H.

ZOMINE ROAD

RIVER

NORFOLK & PETERSBURG R.R.

BLACKWATER SWAMP R.R.

S RD.

FORD RD.

SOUTHSIDE R.R.

SOUTHSIDE ROAD

PETERSBURG

SQUIRREL LEVEL ROAD

GLOBE TAVERN

BAXTER RD.

DISPUTANTA

HATCHER'S RUN

BURGESS' MILL

OAK ROAD

GRAVELLY

PLANK

RUN

REAMS STATION

SUSSEX or BAXTER RD.

ITE

SCOTT'S RD.

VAUGHAN'S ROAD

MONK'S NECK BRIDGE

ROWANTY CREEK

JERUSALEM PLANK ROAD

NWIDDIE 'URTHOUSE

DTON

SAPPONY

STONY CREEK

FLAT POOL ROAD

HALIFAX ROAD

PETERSBURG & WELDON R.R.

CROSS ROADS

NOTTOWAY RIVER

SAPPONY CREEK

GREENSVILLE ROAD

APPONY HURCH

STAGE ROAD

SAPPONY CHURCH

STONY CREEK DEPOT

SUSSEX C.H.

NOTTOWAY RIVER

JARRATT'S DEPOT

0    2½    5

SCALE of MILES

ncipal Watercourses and Roads between the Appomattox and the Nottoway Rivers, in the Zone of the st active Maneuver of the Summer and Autumn of 1864. It will be noted that two churches bearing the name Sappony were to the West of Stony Creek. After *O. R. Atlas*, Plate XCIII–1

plunged into it, took 1600 prisoners and returned to the lines with them. In this affair, Perry's Florida Brigade particularly distinguished itself.[67]

The next opening appeared to be on the Federal right, but an attack there, June 24, was abortive,[68] and was almost forgotten in excitement over the wide range of Wilson's cavalry raid, in which Kautz participated. After tearing up a long stretch of track eight miles below Petersburg, the raiders struck westward and did much damage to the Southside Railroad and still more to the Richmond and Danville, though a gallant defense saved the indispensable bridge over Staunton River.[69]

At that stream, which was the western limit set by Meade's orders,[70] Wilson wheeled and made for the Petersburg and Weldon at Reams's Station, to which he thought the Union lines would have been extended by the time he returned.[71] On Wilson's race through Midland Virginia, "Rooney" Lee's Division had pursued and several times had engaged the enemy but had not inflicted heavy loss. Wade Hampton had won on the 24th a brilliant action at Samaria Church, North of the James,[72] and did not reach the Southside as soon as had been hoped, but on the 28th his Division joined W. H. F. Lee.[73] As senior, Hampton took command and proceeded to drive the enemy to Sappony Church. After scattering the Federals there, Hampton pushed the larger part of them to Reams's Station, where Mahone was awaiting them. Fitz Lee was at hand to take the Federals in flank. Virtually surrounded, Wilson had to burn his wagons, spike or dismount his guns and cut his way out.[74] This fine Confederate success yielded more than 1000 prisoners in addition to the thirteen abandoned guns; but the defeat of the raiders did not alter the fact that they had

[67] O. R., 40, pt. 1, p. 750. All the details will be found in O. R., 40, pt. 1, pp. 326–27, 328–39, 366–67. The heaviest of Mahone's blows fell on the 2nd Division of the II Corps. A brief but dramatic account of this affair is given in W. Gordon McCabe's admirable "Defence of Petersburg" (2 S.H.S.P., 274–75).

[68] See infra, p. 554.

[69] Near the present Randolph and on the line between Charlotte and Halifax counties. The defense of this bridge by Capt. B. L. Farinholt was one of the most stirring small fights of the war. Farinholt's report is in O. R., 40, pt. 1, p. 764. A longer, post bellum narrative appears in 19 S.H.S.P., 201 ff. Still another account will be found in 2 C. V., 19. The official Federal report, by General Wilson, is in O. R., 40, pt. 1, pp. 626–27.

[70] O. R., 40, pt. 1, p. 29.          [71] Ibid., 628.

[72] See infra, p. 550.

[73] Wells, 238. For an amusing account of the regret of some troopers over moving to the Southside, see F. M. Myers, 307–08.

[74] O. R., 40, pt. 1, p. 629. An excellent account is that of McCabe, loc. cit. Numerous other references are given in 3 R. E. Lee, 456.

destroyed sixty miles of railway,[75] some of which could not be repaired within a month.[76] This was the grimmest of all warnings that a superior Federal cavalry force at any time might interrupt and, with good fortune, destroy communications on which the very existence of the Army depended.

Gloom was relieved by the news of Early's advance into Maryland, the details of which are to be described later. In other respects, the daily incidents of trench warfare at Petersburg soon showed how grievously the numerically inferior Confederate Army was to suffer from attrition when it was chained down and unable to employ the offensive strategy that had won it many battles. On the left of the Confederate line, which was within easy and precise range of the Federals, sharpshooting became costly and began to be demoralizing. To lift one's head above the parapet in daylight was almost equivalent to suicide. "There is the chill of murder about the casualties of this month," said one Brigadier as he later reported the losses of July.[77] Second, by the time the hot days grew torrid,[78] both sides began to use mortars in the hope of dropping projectiles into the opposing trenches. The fire seldom was accurate enough to do great damage but the constant danger added to the miseries of life.[79]

After the 1st of July,[80] mysterious and concealed activity on the Federal front indicated that the enemy was mining in the vicinity of Elliott's salient on the line of Bushrod Johnson's Division, in front of Blandford Cemetery. Countermining was begun before many days and was pressed under strict orders.[81] By July 21, the Southern miners heard plainly underground the sound of the picks and shovels of the Union sappers,[82] but nowhere could the Confederates break into the enemy's gallery. The troops became restless and anxious.[83] To reassure them and to protect the position, a cavalier line, so called—an elevated retrenchment—was con-

[75] O. R., 40, pt. 1, p. 630.
[76] Ibid., 31; O. R., 51, pt. 2, p. 1029.
[77] O. R., 40, pt. 1, p. 767.
[78] Cf. O. R., 36, pt. 1, p. 255. Fortunately for the sick and wounded, the nights were cool with heavy dew.
[79] Alexander, 560.
[80] Ibid., 564.
[81] O. R., 40, pt. 3, p. 777. For details of mining operations, then and subsequently, see also W. W. Blackford's MS Memoirs, 382, 393; Alexander, 565 ff; O. R., 42, pt. 1, p. 884 and T. M. R. Talcott in 5 Photographic History of the Civil War, 292.
[82] O. R., 40, pt. 3, p. 790.
[83] 3 N. C. Regts., 308–09.

structed in rear of the main line and was nearing completion late in July.[84] A short third line had been started.[85]

While the lines were agog with talk of shafts and tunnels, reports from the Northside indicated that Federal infantry were being assembled there. Although Army Headquarters did not believe the enemy intended to begin an offensive on the Richmond front, "Joe" Kershaw and his Division were sent back across the James on the 23rd of July to the outer defenses of the capital.[86] There, on the 27th and 28th, veterans of the First Corps met what General Grant had intended to be a surprise, diversionary attack to cover a new raid by Sheridan against the Virginia Central Railroad.[87] The fighting not only was confused in itself but also because of the absence of any clear definition of the relative authority of "Dick" Anderson and of Ewell as commander of the Richmond defenses.[88] After the advanced Confederate regiments had been driven in with the loss of four guns,[89] part of Kershaw's Division attacked successfully on the 27th,[90] though the operation was contrary to Ewell's judgment.[91] On the 28th, Kershaw's men had to retreat in greater haste than glory[92] and with the loss of 300 prisoners and several colors.[93]

Unhappy as were the details, this affair at Deep Bottom[94] served a useful purpose for both Armies. It prevented a raid by Sheridan,[95] which the Confederates would have experienced difficulty in opposing. At the same time the demonstration compelled Lee to transfer so many of his troops to the Northside[96] that Grant thought the time ripe for a direct attack on Petersburg.[97] On the morning of July 30, at dawn, the Confederate works at Elliott's Salient were blown high into the air by 8000 pounds of powder from magazines established after mining 510 feet.[98] By the explosion at least 278 men were killed instantly or buried under hundreds of tons of earth. but the Federals who quickly rushed into

---

[84] 3 N. C. Regts., 141, 142, 362; O. R., 40, pt. 1, pp. 775, 788; ibid., pt. 2, p. 714.
[85] Ibid., pt. 1, p. 778.                    [86] O. R., 40, pt. 3, p. 794.
[87] O. R., 40, pt. 1, pp. 308–09.            [88] O. R., 40, pt. 3, pp. 813–15.
[89] O. R., 40, pt. 1, p. 800.                [90] Dickert, 390.
[91] O. R., 40, pt. 3, p. 811.                [92] Dickert, 390.
[93] O. R., 40, pt. 1, p. 310.

[94] It sometimes was described as the fight of Darbytown, Strawberry Plains and New Market Road (O. R., 40, pt. 1, p. 2).
[95] Ibid., 16.                               [96] Ibid., 761.
[97] Ibid., 17.

[98] For the size and position of the mine and of its crater in relation to the Confederate works and countermines, see O. R., 40, pt. 1, p. 788; pt. 3, p. 820.

the crater of the mine were slow and hesitant in assailing the breached line. The Confederates on either side of the crater, and particularly to the South of it, rallied quickly and held their works.

In support of the stubborn infantry, nearby gray batteries had a perfect target.[99] Mahone's Division was ordered from the right to form in rear of the captured position and to prepare to storm it. Attempts by the Federals to advance from the crater toward Blandford Cemetery were made gallantly by a few detachments under spirited officers, but the principal effort to break through the defenses did not progress more than fifty yards down the covered way.[100] By 10 o'clock Mahone's Division, admirably led, recovered most of the trenches the Federals had occupied. Shortly after 1 P.M. the last stretch of line in Federal hands was regained. Those Union soldiers who escaped death or capture again took refuge in the crater and either surrendered or ran the gauntlet back to their own lines.[101] With twenty flags,[102] perhaps 1500 prisoners,[103] and at least 3500 Federals killed and wounded to offset their own gross losses of 1500, the Confederates had won a unique victory. Lee reported simply: "We have retaken the salient and driven the enemy back to his lines with loss." [104] Grant telegraphed the Chief of Staff: "It was the saddest affair I have witnessed in the war. Such opportunity for carrying fortifications I have never seen and do not expect again to have." [105]

To many a Confederate soldier, it has to be recorded, the Battle of the Crater, that hot 30th of July, connoted warfare of a more savage character because of the employment of Negroes against them. The change of mental attitude was startling. A wise and humor-loving matron of a ward at Chimborazo Hospital in Richmond wrote that until that struggle in front of Petersburg, she had not found the sick or wounded Confederates bitter toward the enemy. They would assert endlessly the superiority of the troops of their State over any other Confederates, but of the Federals the

[99] One of the most interesting of the unpublished accounts of this familiar battle is that of Col. J. C. Haskell, *op. cit.* For the mishandling of Davidson's Battery, see *Ham Chamberlayne*, 232 ff, 251, 258; *O. R.*, 40, pt. 1, pp. 789, 791.

[100] *O. R.*, 40, pt. 1, pp. 91, 93, 115; *J. C. Haskell's MS Rems.*, 97.

[101] For the details, see 3 *R. E. Lee*, 469–77.

[102] *O. R.*, 40, pt. 1, p. 753.

[103] Mahone had 1101, but Johnson (*O. R.*, 40, pt. 1, p. 793) left blank in his report the number taken by his Division.

[104] *O. R.*, 40, pt. 1, p. 752.        [105] *O. R.*, 40, pt. 1, pp. 17, 134.

usual remark was, "They fit us, we fit them." Now it was differ
ent. The explosion of a mine was a "mean trick," the use of
Negro troops an infamy. The wounded for the first time cursed
their enemy. "Eyes gleamed, and teeth clenched as they showed
me the locks of their muskets, to which the blood and hair still
clung, when, after firing, without waiting to re-load, they had
clenched the barrels and fought hand to hand." [106] It had been a
desperate day in a cause daily more desperate.

[106] Phoebe Yates Pember, *A Southern Woman's Story*, 105–06. This little known
volume is one of the most fascinating of Confederate books.

# CHAPTER XXVIII

## ATTRITION IN A CHANGED ARMY

AN EXCHANGED prisoner of war, reading in the Richmond papers of the Battle of the Crater, would have encountered so many unfamiliar names that he might have concluded Lee had a new Army. The trenches destroyed by the explosion of the mine were occupied by Elliott's South Carolina Brigade: it had come to Virginia in May under an officer who was promoted Brigadier on the 28th of that month.[1] Nearby was Gracie's Brigade, which had been associated with none of the great contests of the old Army of Northern Virginia.[2] Wise's Brigade, which participated most gallantly in the action of July 30, had been absent for months from Virginia. All these troops were commanded by Maj. Gen. B. R. Johnson. With him the public had been so completely unacquainted prior to May that some might have thought the initials incorrect, and the soldier "Old Allegheny" Johnson. After the Battle of Drewry's Bluff, Bushrod Johnson was promoted to divisional rank [3] at the instance of Beauregard,[4] who had felt himself in great need of officers of that rank.[5] Strictly speaking, Johnson thus became a Major General in Beauregard's Department, but after June 15 he had passed under Lee's command.

What was true of the unfamiliarity of Virginians with Johnson's Division—Wise's, Mat Ransom's, Stephen Elliott's and Archibald Gracie's Brigades [6]—was true in large part of Hoke's Division. Hagood's South Carolina Brigade was one of those, it will be

---

[1] *Wright*, 138. The date of Elliott's arrival in Virginia does not appear from available records. He was commanding at Fort Sumter May 4, 1864, as a Lieutenant Colonel (*O. R.*, 35, pt. 1, p. 207) but was relieved temporarily about that date (*ibid.*, pt. 2, p. 472). First specific mention of him in the accounts of Virginia operations was on June 2 (*O. R.*, 36, pt. 2, p. 265), though it was manifest from this reference that he had been on duty for some days. In 5 *C. M. H.*, 391, it is stated that he was ordered to Virginia in May as Colonel of Holcombe's Legion. The memorial address of Sept. 8, 1866, by William Henry Trescot, gave no date. Probabilities are strong that Elliott went to Virginia during the heavy troop movement of early May.

[2] See *supra*, p. 463.  [3] May 26; *Wright*, 38.

[4] *O. R.*, 36, pt. 3, p. 820; *ibid.*, 51, pt. 2, p. 947.

[5] *O. R.*, 51, pt. 2, p. 954.

[6] At the Crater, Gracie was detached from the Division and Alfred Colquitt's Brigade of Hoke's Division was under temporary assignment to the Division (*O. R.*, 40, pt. 1, pp 787, 793).

remembered, that had come to Virginia during the emergency of Butler's attack.[7] Another Brigade of the Division, Brig. Gen. Thomas L. Clingman's, consisted of North Carolina troops that had served on the Southside but had not fought as a unit of the Army of Northern Virginia until the Second Battle of Cold Harbor. Kirkland's fine Brigade of Hoke's Division was a familiar one that had suffered cruelly at Bristoe Station.[8] Colquitt's Brigade, the fourth unit of Hoke's Division, had left Virginia after Chancellorsville[9] and had fought in Florida with distinction. It had been returned for the critical summer campaign.[10]

Two of the eight infantry Divisions thus were in large part new to Lee's Army. Of the eight Brigades of these two Divisions, the commanders of two only—Colquitt and Kirkland—had been schooled under the commanding General. One of these two, Colquitt, had not shone in his last previous campaign in Virginia. Still other officers of untested skill as brigade commanders had now to be promoted to fill vacancies that could not remain open. The list of Brigades needing competent direction was long.

To simplify the weary, recurrent task of finding new leaders, there now were few juniors of shining promise. No successor had been named to Abner Perrin, whose Alabama Brigade had been Cadmus Wilcox's. Second, "Rans" Wright was absent from a famous Brigade that required a temporary commander of appropriate rank and prestige. Next, James L. Kemper had been exchanged as a prisoner of war but had been so much weakened by the wound received at Gettysburg that he had been assigned to the command of the Virginia reserves.[11] Still again, W. W. Kirkland had fallen at Cold Harbor with an injury that would involve long absence from his North Carolinians.[12] In the same battle, George Doles lost his life and left one of the best Brigades without a leader.[13] A sixth vacancy had been caused by the death of "Grumble" Jones at Piedmont.[14] The addition of scattered cavalry regiments to the Army of Northern Virginia made a seventh nomination for brigade command desirable. An eighth and a ninth were necessary to fill the places of the promoted Hoke and of the dead Micah Jenkins.

[7] See *supra*, p. 454 ff.
[9] See Vol. II. pp. 664, 710.
[11] *O. R.*, 36, pt. 2, p. 1012.
[13] See *supra*, p. 507.

[8] See *supra*, p. 245.
[10] 6 *C. M. H.*, 406.
[12] 3 *N. C. Regts.*, 246.
[14] See *supra*, p. 516.

Some of these vacancies, it will be observed, had been continued beyond the reorganization of June 4 because circumstance then had prompted delay or else because senior Colonels were doing well enough to justify a trial before final decision was made. Most of the other cases were those of the tragic attrition already described, the attrition that had been increasing rapidly since May. More frequent battles at close quarters had prompted officers to take more desperate personal risks when their men fought somewhat less well and the Federals fought better. As soon as one series of vacancies was filled, another was created. Generals were being killed more rapidly than they could prudently be selected. Successors to some of the fallen leaders were not to be had. Although three promotions were announced in orders of June 27, there could be no full reorganization. Appointments had to be made when— but not until—reasonably well qualified men could be found. On occasion, Brigades had to be entrusted to men of limited competence in the hope that the experience of the divisional commander and of the men themselves would make good the deficiencies of the new Brigadiers.

The one alleviating aspect of the deficiency of men qualified for promotion was the operation of the new law for temporary appointments. If, for instance, the wounds sustained by Brig. Gen. Stephen Elliott at the Crater proved as serious as was feared,[15] it would not be necessary to leave his South Carolinians in the hands of the senior Colonel for the whole period of Elliott's invalidism in the event the Colonel did not have the stature the post required. A temporary Brigadier could be named—to remain, if he succeeded, to receive another command if he showed ability and the absent General recovered, or to return to his former rank should he fail.

The appointment to "Rans" Wright's Brigade was a unique example of the operation of this law and of the swift attrition that was wrecking command. Capt. Victor J. B. Girardey had served with high courage and marked capacity as an aide to Wright,[16] and, on May 21, received transfer from Wright's staff to the Adjutant General's Office.[17] This must have been a device for shifting him from the brigade to the divisional staff because, by

[15] O. R., 42, pt. 2, pp. 1156–57, 1183, 1232.
[16] 6 C. M. H., 420–21; cf. O. R., 25, pt. 2, p. 641; ibid., 27, pt. 2, p. 626.
[17] O. R., 36, pt. 3, p. 813.

the date of the Battle of the Crater, he was a fixture on the staff of Mahone. In organizing and timing the attack of Mahone's Division, that day, Girardey won the admiration of the entire Army. As a reward, he received a distinction never given any officer of Lee's command, promotion at a single jump, four days after the action, from a captaincy to the temporary rank of Brigadier General,[18] in command of Wright's Georgians. Girardey had every promise of being a brilliant officer, but before he had served a fortnight in the place of his absent former chief, he was killed.[19]

To Perrin's command, under the same act, one of his Colonels, J. C. C. Sanders of the Eleventh Alabama, was promoted June 7 [20] with temporary rank. Sanders's commission ended August 21 in a wound from which he died in a few minutes. He was 24 years of age.[21] Still another promotion in accordance with the statute for the temporary commission of general officers went to William R. Terry. He had handled Kemper's Brigade during its commander's captivity and invalidism and had earned the wreath that was to surround the three stars on his collar.[22] For the post of the wounded Kirkland, one of his stoutest Colonels, William McRae of the Fifteenth North Carolina, was advanced to the rank of temporary Brigadier.[23] This was a wise appointment. Within a fortnight, it was said, McRae "changed the physical expression of the whole command, and gave the men infinite faith in him and themselves, which was never lost. . . ." [24]

Doles's Brigade went to Philip Cook, 47 years of age, Colonel of the Fourth Georgia, a lawyer who had enlisted as a private, had served as Adjutant and, as a result of the election of 1862, had risen to the rank of Lieutenant Colonel.[25] Cook was a fighter—all agreed on that—and by long service he was entitled to permanent rather than temporary rank as Brigadier.[26]

To "Grumble" Jones's weakened command, Col. Bradley T. Johnson was appointed [27] as temporary Brigadier. Why this able Marylander, then in his 35th year, so long was denied advancement is among the Confederate mysteries. He was, to be sure, a

[18] O. R., 42, pt. 2, pp. 1156–57.
[19] Aug. 16, 1864; Wright, 145; O. R., 42, pt. 2, pp. 210, 215, 301.
[20] Wright, 143.                                   [21] / C. M. H., Ala., 444.
[22] O. R., 40, pt. 2, p. 694.
[23] O. R., 40, pt. 2, p. 694. For accounts of his earlier achievements see O. R., 19, pt 1, p. 870; 3 N. C. Regts., 27; 4 C. M. H., 330–32.
[24] 2 N. C. Regts., 385.                           [25] 6 C.M.H., 406–07; Thomas, 51.
[26] Aug. 8, 1864; Wright, 122.                     [27] June 28, 1864; Wright, 143.

lawyer and not a professional soldier, but many another lawyer of military skill less marked had been made a general officer. "Stonewall" Jackson several times had urged the promotion of Johnson, for whom he had genuine admiration.[28] The Maryland Colonel probably had suffered from the typical émigré jealousies of officers from his own State. Now, at last, he received the distinction he long previously had earned. From his vigorous record, there was every reason to believe he would prove an efficient officer.[29]

Another commission as Brigadier General, with similar assignment to the mounted arm, went to Col. Martin W. Gary of South Carolina. Thirty-three years of age, a Harvard graduate and a lawyer already conspicuous in the politics of the Palmetto State, "Mart" Gary had risen to the command of the infantry of the Hampton Legion and, in March, 1864, had led in re-equipping it as mounted infantry.[30] Subsequent recruitment in South Carolina and the concentration of scattered small units had added to the cavalry corps men enough to organize a small Brigade. To this, by reason of hard service and harder fighting, Gary was appointed as a "permanent" general officer.[31] He justified the appointment forthwith by his bearing and conduct in Hampton's fight at Samaria Church.[32]

To Hoke's old Brigade was assigned as Brigadier the vigorous Colonel who had commanded it at Rappahannock Bridge and had fought there till overwhelmed, Archibald C. Godwin of the Fifty-seventh North Carolina.[33] He now had been exchanged and had not been too grievously shaken by his imprisonment to resume field duty. Accordingly, he was promoted to lead the troops with whom his record had been high.[34]

Promotion of the same sort went to Col. John Bratton of the Sixth South Carolina. This young physician, now 33, had been

[28] 2 *C. M. H.*, Maryland, 177 ff.
[29] The following are the principal references to him, chronologically arranged, from the *Official Records:* 51, pt. 2, pp. 127, 570, 591, 781, 968; 12, pt. 2, p. 664; *ibid.*, 27, pt. 2, p. 534; *ibid.*, 29, pt. 2, p. 727; *ibid.*, 33, 202, 1089, 1011; *ibid.*, 37, pt. 1, p. 768. See also *Richmond Enquirer*, Aug. 26, 1862, p. 2, col. 2–3; *DeLeon B. B. B.*, 197–98, 317; 12 *S.H.S.P.*, 504. For a sketch of Johnson's remarkable wife, see 9 *C. V.*, 321–25. The account of Johnson's life in 2 *C. M. H.*, Maryland, 174 ff is adequate.
[30] *O. R.*, 33, 1231.
[31] *Wright*, 121; as of June 14, 1864. For important references to him in chronological order, see *O. R.*, 11, pt. 3, p. 648; *ibid.*, 12, pt. 2, p. 606; *ibid.*, 51, pt. 2, p. 837; *ibid.*, 36, pt. 2, pp. 960, 1023.
[32] *O. R.*, 36, pt. 1, pp. 1096–97; *ibid.*, 40, pt. 2, p. 688.
[33] *O. R.*, 29, pt. 1, p. 624.
[34] August 9, 1864; *Wright*, 122.

recommended by "Dick" Anderson as early as the end of May, 1862 for commission as Brigadier General,[35] but he had served in Micah Jenkins's Brigade where promotion was slow. Now he had the Brigade, still strong in numbers and indomitable in spirit.[36]

It was improbable, of course, that all these men would succeed as brigade commanders. Not one of them had been a professional soldier. A majority of them had been antebellum lawyers. They simply seemed the logical appointees or those that appeared most likely to develop, or to escape failure. Outside the Army of Northern Virginia many general officers were available and were awaiting assignment,[37] but except those mentioned already, none was summoned to fill a vacancy. Lee doubtless reasoned that if they were qualified, positions would have been found for them in the armies that had dropped them. For the South as a whole, the shortage, in a word, was in competence of officers, not in their rank.

Had time and rest from the strain of battle permitted a review of what had been achieved from the arrival at Cold Harbor, May 31, until the Battle of the Crater had been won, two names only besides that of the commanding General would have been found to possess new lustre. One of these names was Wade Hampton's. All that had been said of the difference between him and Stuart was being confirmed. The South Carolinian lacked the glamour the Virginian had in the eyes of the hard-riding young troopers of 1862, but Hampton appealed more strongly to the temper of 1864. If Stuart had the admiration of new soldiers, Hampton had the respect of veterans. The operations in Spotsylvania, the contest at Haw's Shop, the Battle of Trevilian Station—these and all the minor clashes of reconnaissance and patrol had been handled without material blunder.

On the 24th of June, Hampton had added another solid credit. He had kept between Sheridan and the Confederate capital and repeatedly he had offered battle while the Unionists were retreating from Trevilian Station.[38] Not until Sheridan had completed the circuit of the Richmond defenses and had rested and refitted

[35] 13 S.H.S.P., 132, 133.
[36] O.R., 40, pt. 2, p. 694. For the references to Bratton's service, in addition to that from 13 S.H.S.P., see O. R., 11, pt. 1, p. 567; ibid., 36, pt. 1, pp. 1057, 1065 ff.
[37] O. R., 32, pt. 2, p. 817.        [38] O. R., 36, pt. 1, p. 1096.

his men did he again challenge Hampton. At the first threat on the 23rd, the South Carolinian took position to intercept an advance up the north bank of the James via Charles City Court House and Westover.[39] When the Confederate pickets were driven in the next morning, Hampton decided to attack immediately. "Mart" Gary was moved to one flank of the enemy; John Chambliss was maneuvered into position next Gary in the vicinity of Nance's Shop. Fitz Lee's men and most of the remaining troopers were dismounted and were sent forward against the enemy's light field works while Gary and Chambliss assailed the flank. After the enemy was driven by this onslaught, two mounted units that had been reserved for the purpose were sent in pursuit.[40] More than 150 prisoners were taken at a gross loss that probably did not equal that number.[41] The bluecoats worsted in this fight proved to be the Division of David Gregg, who was covering the movement of a heavy wagon train. Sheridan professed himself more than satisfied at getting off so lightly.[42]

Coming after the fine action at Trevilian, this engagement of Samaria Church confirmed belief that the discretion of Hampton could be trusted. The awkward arrangement by which all three of the cavalry Divisions had been reporting directly to the commanding General after the death of Stuart was abandoned finally on the 11th of August, when it appeared that Hampton would be required to undertake a mission in which he would need the largest authority.[43] Once the decision was made to place the mounted forces under Hampton, it was done without any restrictions: Hampton was "assigned to the command of the cavalry of this Army." By the next sentence, "Division commanders will report to him accordingly."[44] Hampton's appointment to general direction of the cavalary left his Division under the command of its senior Brigadier, Calbraith Butler, who was endorsed by Hampton as qualified for the duty. Butler remained in charge of the Division without formal order or immediate promotion.[45]

In business-like spirit, Hampton immediately proposed that a

[39] *Ibid.*   [40] *Ibid.*, and *O. R.*, 40, pt. 2, p. 688.
[41] Hampton's loss in his Division was sixty-five. Casualties in the other units were not reported. Federal killed, wounded and missing were 357 (*O. R.*, 36, pt. 1, p. 856).
[42] *O. R.*, 36, pt. 1, pp. 798–99.   [43] See *infra*, p. 575.
[44] *O. R.*, 42, pt. 2, p. 1171. For Lee's praise of Hampton's conduct in the action of June 24 at Samaria Church, see *O. R.*, 36, pt. 3, p. 903; *ibid.*, 40, pt. 1, pp. 750–51.
[45] *O. R.*, 43, pt. 1, pp. 996–97.

Bureau of Cavalry be established under the Adjutant General. This suggestion Lee at once approved. As chief of the Bureau, Lee recommended the appointment of Ewell, who, said the commanding General, "besides possessing great merit, . . . has great claims."[46] Ewell balked. If the interests of the service permitted, he said, he much preferred active duty. He had been in the field for almost a quarter of a century, he explained, and had "no experience whatever as a bureau officer."[47] From this correspondence he omitted all reference to the fact that General Joseph E. Johnston had applied for his services.[48] "Unfortunately," Ewell wrote his brother, "Lizinka [Mrs. Ewell] went to see Bragg about it while I was away." Ewell continued sadly: "She learned that the authorities declined to make the transfer. I regretted her going very much, as I wanted the chance to give the authorities a plain statement of my case, and if developments authorized it, to hand in my resignation. I would at once have telegraphed to General Johnston for a command on being relieved, but I understood that [A.P.] Stewart had been appointed at General Johnston's request, and of course it was too late. My position here is without troops, merely a polite way of being laid on the shelf. For what reason I cannot tell. Had I thought General Johnston wanted my services I would have gone in spite of everything."[49] None of this probably was known at the time to Hampton.

Equal with Hampton in distinction during May–July, 1864, was William Mahone. His was proving an exceptional career. Many officers who were competent, even conspicuous, at a particular rank in Confederate service, failed when they were given larger duties. Mahone reversed this. A Brigadier of no shining reputation, with achievements scarcely above the army average, he proved himself within three months one of the ablest divisional commanders the Army ever had. He appears in the records as a man never aroused to his full potentialities until he felt he had duties that challenged all he knew, all he could learn, all he could do. Small in person, he was so thin that when his wife heard he had received a flesh wound, she said, "Now I know it is serious, for William has no flesh whatever."[50] In garb he put comfort above convention. One comrade wrote of him: "On a certain hot

46 *O. R.*, 42, pt. 2, p. 1173.                   47 *Ibid.*, 1174.
48 June 22; *O. R.*, 38, pt. 4, p. 785.          49 *Hamlin's Ewell*, 130.
50 *Sorrel*, 267.

summer's day that I recall he was seen, a Major General indeed, but wonderfully accoutered! A plaited brown linen jacket, buttoned to trousers of same material, like a boy's; topped off by a large Panama hat of the finest and most beautiful texture, met our eyes, and I must say he looked decidedly comfortable." [51] With Mahone's headquarters moved his cow, to whose back by varied gear his cooking utensils were attached.

In action, these oddities of "Little Billy" vanished. There was about him, said Col. J. C. Haskell, a "cool promptness and dash peculiarly his own" [52] and, along with these qualities, a sharpened power of organization and a keen military perception.[53] Anderson's old Division, which Mahone now led, seldom had been called to exceptional service, but Mahone made the men, within three months, what Hood's and A. P. Hill's Divisions had been at their best, the spearhead of attack. Gratefully after the flank movement of May 6 in the Wilderness, the wounded Longstreet had recommended Mahone's promotion "for the distinguished skill and gallantry displayed." [54] In like spirit, after the Battle of the Crater, Lee had Mahone's temporary commission as a Major General made permanent.[55] Mahone, beyond doubt, was the military "discovery" of those summer days in front of Petersburg, precisely as John B. Gordon had been the "discovery" of the campaign in Spotsylvania.

The old Army that included two new Divisions and two new Major Generals of high promise had, also, from the time of the crossing of the James, what it never had counted in its personnel: a full General under the direction of the commanding General. In one sense, the Army of Northern Virginia was operating in a Department that chanced to have a General of highest rank in

[51] *Ibid.*, 267–68.  [52] *J. C. Haskell's MS Rems.*, 101.
[53] He was, it will be remembered, a V.M.I. graduate, President of the Petersburg and Norfolk Railroad, and was in his thirty-eighth year. See Vol. I, p. 557.
[54] *O. R.*, 40, pt. 3, p. 775. See *supra*, p. 361 ff.
[55] August 3, to rank from the date of the battle, July 30, 1864 (*Wright*, 39). Because of the long delay in promotion to permanent rank, there had been some soreness on Mahone's part and a threat to refuse the honor when it came. "You cannot think of declining," said A. P. Hill. After the war, Jubal Early took offence at a published remark by Mahone and made a venomous attack on that officer. Mahone was accused by Early of shirking action and of indulging in shameless self-advertisement. Brig. Gen. David A. Weisiger subsequently joined Early in assailing Mahone. For detailed references, see N. M. Blake, *William Mahone of Virginia*, p. 68, n. 212. It is enough to say, in answer to this abuse, that the commendation of Lee, Longstreet and A. P. Hill would not have been voiced if there had been the least question of Mahone's courage or competence. All the libel of him as a soldier was the result of personal or political dislike.

charge of operations. For practical purposes, Beauregard became temporarily a corps commander, but because of his rank and prestige he enjoyed a privileged status. During the first stage of the Cold Harbor operations, when Lee in desperation was seeking to get troops from the Southside, he had proposed that Beauregard leave a guard on the Howlett Line, move his forces to the Richmond line and take command of the right wing of the combined Army.[56] "Old Bory" had replied cannily, "I am willing to do anything for our success, but cannot leave my Department without orders of War Department."[57]

That message had epitomized Beauregard's position during the anxious first fortnight of June: he had been subordinate, reasonably well informed of most developments on his front and aware of his obligations, but he was determined always that responsibility for major decisions should rest on the War Department.[58] To his credit it could be said that he had been among the first to be convinced that Grant was to cross the James.[59] During the progress of the movement to the Southside and while the absorbing battle of June 15–17 was under way, Beauregard could not ascertain quickly the composition of the forces opposing him, and he was more than normally mercurial in his fluctuation of hope and misgiving. In directing the combat in front of Petersburg, before Lee's arrival, he was at his best. For the time his theatrical manner disappeared, not to be resumed until Lee was at hand. Then, it will be recalled, when the burden of decision was on someone else, he was instant in proposing an offensive.[60]

Beauregard could be useful, but he must be handled with some care. That came to be the view of Army Headquarters and of the War Department. Gossip in Richmond was that he was in disgrace but was allowed to remain in command because of his reputation and the influence of his friends.[61] On June 24 blame for the failure of an attack launched against the extreme left of the Union line, South of the Appomattox, fell on Beauregard, because the plan was his.[62] Hoke, who was acting under Beauregard's instructions, was quick to shift the blame to "Tige" Anderson's Brigade of Field's Division. A controversy that pitted "Beauregard's Army" against Lee's might have been precipitated. It was avoided by the

[56] O. R., 36, pt. 3, p. 864.
[58] Cf. O. R., 36, pt. 3, pp. 849–59.
[60] See *supra*, p. 537.
[62] O. R., 40, pt. 1, pp. 804–05.

[57] 2 *Roman*, 563.
[59] *Ibid.*, pp. 878 ff, 886.
[61] 2 R. W. C. D., 233, 236, 238, 249.

prompt veto of Lee on further agitation. "There seems," he said, "to have been some misunderstanding as to the part each Division was expected to perform." [63] That precluded further argument.

Another quarrel was threatened late in July by a complaint on the part of Braxton Bragg that the Third North Carolina cavalry, ordered to Richmond in April, had been detained in its native State without authority for three weeks. When this letter was forwarded to Beauregard for comment, he took it to be a personal reflection on himself. After explaining the facts, he demanded a court of inquiry. Beauregard had the better end of the dispute, together with the documentary proof of his contention, and he doubtless would have delighted to prove Bragg in error. Again it was the patient commanding General who intervened. Beauregard's explanation was satisfactory, said Lee, who added: "I hope no court will be considered necessary." [64] Secretary Seddon employed his good offices, also. In due time, Bragg explained that he meant his protest to be general. As it might be construed as a reflection on Beauregard, he asked to withdraw the offending letter from the files.[65] Beauregard thereupon recalled his application for a court.[66] Neither in this affair nor in that of the abortive action of June 24 was Beauregard unpleasantly or unreasonably aggressive; but he showed himself in the contemporary vernacular most distinctly "touchy." Such men, if in high position, did not usually remain long with the Army of Northern Virginia. They quietly were sent to another field. As it happened, while Beauregard lingered, a recent and welcome accession to the Army's corps of officers, Maj. Gen. Martin L. Smith, decided to ask for permission to return to the Gulf States. This was granted by the War Department to the regret of Lee and of all who knew of the professional and personal excellencies of Smith. He was succeeded by Col. W. H. Stevens as Chief Engineer of the Army.[67]

Two other conditions on the half-immobilized front of the Army deserved a consideration they did not receive at a time when eyes and mind alike were fixed on the rising parapets of red earth a few hundred yards away. The Army itself was as much changed as its command. Many of the old, experienced units had been so reduced by casualties that they had lost their offensive power. Inexperienced and reluctant conscripts, in many instances, took the

---

[63] O. R., 40, pt. 1, p. 799.　　　　[64] O. R., 40, pt. 3, pp. 801–03.
[65] O. R., 42, pt. 2, pp. 1178–79.　　　[66] Ibid., 1201.
[67] O. R., 40, pt. 3, pp. 787–88; 6 Rowland, 299–300; 6 C. V., 530.

place of veteran volunteers. The infantry who remained in the trenches around Petersburg included a larger percentage of Carolinians than ever had been mustered in Lee's Army—fifty-nine regiments and battalions in a total of 161.[68] This most assuredly involved no loss of devotion or of valor, but it was to prove seriour when some of these men, nostalgic and half-starved, heard thar their homes were threatened by invaders who previously had not penetrated to the interior.

The other new condition was the absence of the Second Corps. From the date of the Battle of Cedar Mountain, August 9, 1862, until Early marched toward the Valley on the 13th of June, 1864, the Second Corps never had been detached for more than a few days, except during periods of inactivity such as that which followed the Maryland Expedition. In every heavy battle of that long period, the Second Corps had borne its full part. Now it was gone. With it had moved not only the rifle-strength of sixty-four regiments and battalions[69] but also three division commanders who, in the Spotsylvania campaign, had much distinguished themselves. Any organization would be the weaker for the absence of three such men as John Gordon, Dodson Ramseur and Robert Rodes, to say nothing of their new corps commander, Early.

In summary, then, that part of the Army of Northern Virginia in the Richmond-Petersburg area was weakened numerically, recruited uncertainly with less experienced troops, and commanded by an officers' corps that included many incompetent regimental officers and not a few general officers of untested ability. The two new Divisions were under the immediate direction of Beauregard, a General of full rank, whose relations with the Administration and with Lee might involve difficulties. In succession to Stuart, there was every prospect that Wade Hampton might prove himself wholly qualified to command the cavalry. "Billy" Mahone was emerging as a division commander of great offensive skill. Grimly on the other side of the book of battle had to be written three stern entries: the Army was being caged in the Petersburg trenches, the opposing odds were heavier, the absent Second Corps was engaged in a desperate gamble now to be described.

[68] See the organization in *O. R.*, 42, pt. 2, pp. 1214–19, 1227. The figures in the text do not include the detached Second Corps.
[69] *O. R.*, 42, pt. 2, pp. 1216–17.

# CHAPTER XXIX

## "Jube" Early Gambles at Long Odds

In pursuing Maj. Gen. David Hunter from Lynchburg on June 19, "Jube" Early's poorly organized cavalry were soon outrun. Lee as well as Early was disappointed that the raiders were so slightly punished.[1] Both the Confederate leaders had been anxious to defeat and, if possible, to destroy Hunter, who had burned V.M.I. and the home of Governor Letcher at Lexington [2] and had countenanced much looting.[3] After three days of futile effort to overtake the Federals on the way to Lewisburg and Western Virginia,[4] Early gave his men twenty-four hours of rest and then proceeded into the Shenandoah Valley by way of Lexington. As Rodes's Division passed through that town, the column was diverted. At length, Rodes had the band of the leading regiment begin a dirge. To this music, some thousands of the men who had fought under "Stonewall" Jackson marched by his grave.[5] It was his last review of them.

In Staunton, which Early reached on the 26th, ahead of his troops,[6] he reorganized his forces and rid himself of batteries too weak to participate in the invasion of the enemy's country. Robert Ransom and his cavalry had been reporting to Breckinridge. They now were placed under Early's own command. Bradley Johnson was designated formally to head "Grumble" Jones's Brigade. To compensate General Breckinridge for the loss of Ransom, and to give the Kentuckian a force in keeping with his rank and abilities, Gordon's Division was assigned to Breckinridge. It developed, further, that Maj. Gen. Arnold Elzey, who had reported in Lynchburg to assist Early, was physically unfit to endure the strain of open campaigning. He was relieved at his own request and was succeeded temporarily by Brig. Gen. J. C. Vaughn. As Vaughn had not been regarded as altogether qualified for the handling of

[1] O. R., 37, pt. 1, p. 766.
[2] Ibid., 97; H. A. Du Pont, The Campaign of 1864, p. 69.
[3] Early, 380 n.          [4] Ibid., 376–79.
[5] 1 N. C. Regts., 275.          [6] Early, 381.

a Division, doubtless Early contemplated from the outset the transfer of command from Vaughn to Brig. Gen. John Echols. This was effected by July 7.[7] Rodes's and Ramseur's Divisions continued to report directly to Early. The two Major Generals could operate advantageously together because a strong personal affection and the fullest confidence existed between them.[8]

Altogether, the infantry, as reorganized in this form, counted 10,000 men.[9] Cavalry and artillery perhaps added 4000. The mounted forces were to prove, in a double sense, the weakness of Early as a commander; his artillery was to be his bulwark. Most of the infantry, though overworked, were in excellent spirits. Ramseur's and Rodes's depleted Divisions were unified and free of any dissatisfaction except that which is voiced in soldiers' habitual complaints and is, for that reason, evidence that their condition is normal.

In Gordon's Division, through no fault of his own, there was a measure of positive and almost vehement discontent. York's Brigade combined what an inspector subsequently termed the "discordant fragments" of the proud old Louisiana Brigades of Harry Hays and Leroy Stafford. Under Terry, it will be remembered, were the survivors of the Stonewall Brigade and of other units of Edward Johnson's Division. In August the inspector wrote: "Both officers and men object to their consolidation into one Brigade. Strange officers command strange troops, and the difficulties of fusing this incongruous mass are enhanced by constant marching and frequent engagements."[10] In this was a new challenge of the demonstrated skill of John Gordon in making his troops believe themselves the special instruments of victory.[11]

A man of equal magnetism and of a person even more magnificent, John C. Breckinridge had in his command a problem of somewhat similar nature. His regiments included many soldiers who had no desire to do battle for anything beyond the mountains among which they lived. They would fight hard when the issue was joined but, left alone in a strange country, they would disappear mysteriously—to reappear, weeks later, at home.[12]

Another condition that might impair efficiency was the fact that

[7] Early, 385.                          [8] See infra, p. 570, n. 73.
[9] Early, 381.
[10] O. R., 43, pt. 1, pp. 609–10; inspection report of August 21.
[11] See Vol. II, p. 656.                 [12] Cf. O. R., 37, pt. 2, p. 591 ff.

about half the infantry, including even company officers, were without shoes. That was no hardship, so far as the weather was involved, but experience in 1862 had demonstrated what injury the stone roads North of the Potomac would do to the feet of unshod men.[13] If Early was to enter the enemy's country again, he must have shoes. While he was seeking them,[14] he would go forward. That was his decision under the discretionary orders of Army Headquarters.[15]

On June 28, the advance from Staunton began. By the 30th, the column was passing New Market. Early was able to write Lee: "[The soldiers] are in fine condition and spirits, their health greatly improved. We will have no trouble about supplies. . . . If you can continue to threaten Grant I hope to be able to do something for your relief and the success of our cause shortly. I shall lose no time." [16]

This was not bravado on the part of "Jube." In disdain of numerically superior Federal forces that could be mobilized quickly, he was resolved to enter Maryland. Said Kyd Douglas afterward: "Jackson being dead, it is safe to say no other General in either army would have attempted it against such odds. . . . The audacity of Early's enterprise was its safety; no one who might have taken steps to oppose or cut him off would believe his force was so small." [17]

The first anniversary of the opening of the Battle of Gettysburg found Early far down the Valley. On July 2, the little Army was in Winchester; the next day contact was established with the enemy for the first time since June 21. Sigel's advance guard was struck and was driven to Harpers Ferry.[18] On the approach of Early, that town was evacuated the night of the 4th but it could not be occupied by the Confederates because the enemy held Maryland Heights.[19] Without hesitation, July 6, Early led the Second Corps into Maryland for its third great adventure.[20] This time there was no glamour, no crowds. If the bands played "Maryland, my Maryland," nobody recorded that soldiers or populace cheered.

13 See Vol. II, p. 150.
15 O. R., 37, pt. 1, pp. 346, 767–68.
17 Douglas, 293–94.
19 Early, 384.
14 Early, 382.
16 O. R., 51, pt. 2, pp. 1028–29.
18 O. R., 37, pt. 1, pp. 175–76.
20 Strictly speaking, it was the fourth time Jackson's old troops had been across the Potomac, but the entry of September, 1862, the return to Harpers Ferry and the hurried march to Sharpsburg may with propriety be regarded as parts of a single operation.

In advancing, the cavalry and some infantry detachments had torn up railway tracks and had wrecked a few minor bridges, but such acts no longer outraged Unionists or enthused Southern sympathizers. Maryland borderers had learned something of the meaning of war.

By the night of the 7th, the needed shoes had been received and distributed. The Army was ready to move.[21] Nothing more serious than rows provoked by an abundance of lemon punch had disturbed the day.[22] With no discernible hangover, the columns went over South Mountain on the 8th and pressed eastward. The 9th, a day of sunshine and rare beauty,[23] saw the advance of part of the force through Frederick and toward a country where friends were numerous.[24]

About 8 A.M. that day, July 9, the van approached the Monocacy River and reported the presence of the enemy. An hour later,[25] Early's infantry came up and, by his orders, halted for deployment. The artillery opened quickly on the opposing batteries. As far as could be ascertained the enemy had a heavy howitzer [26] and some field guns North of the railroad bridge. This Union ordnance commanded the bridge and the crossing of the highway about a quarter of a mile downstream. Below this second bridge, on the eastern side of the river, the Federals were awaiting attack. Two miles North of the railway was the bridge on the Baltimore road. There the Federals were West of the stream as if they were preparing to resist a crossing.

The day was young, the position unfamiliar to most of the officers. "Old Jube," who was not quick to get his direction, decided to take his time and to ascertain where he best could turn a position he did not wish to attack frontally. Skirmishing and long-range fire quickened but nowhere did the opposing forces come to grips. On the Confederate right, where the main line of the Baltimore & Ohio parallels the river, Early was examining the ground, probably about noon, when to his surprise he saw young John McCausland's cavalry Brigade ride down to a river ford, slightly more than a mile below the highway bridge. With little

---

[21] Early, 385.
[22] Hotchkiss' MS Diary, 361.
[23] Worsham, 235.
[24] Hotchkiss' MS Diary, 363. Hotchkiss was speaking more particularly of the district East of the Monocacy.
[25] O. R., 37, pt. 1, p. 196.
[26] It was a 24-pounder (Ibid.).

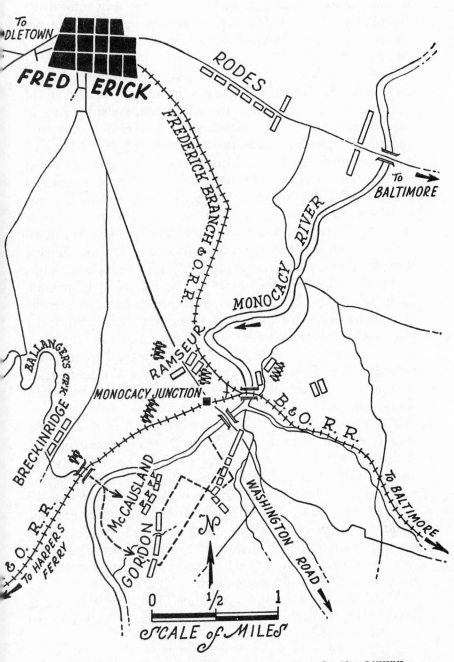

FREDERICK

RODES

FREDERICK BRANCH & O.R.R.

To
BALTIMORE

MONOCACY RIVER

MONOCACY

BALLANGER'S CR'K

RAMSEUR

MONOCACY JUNCTION

BRECKINRIDGE

B. & O. R. R.

To BALTIMORE

B. & O. R. R.

To HARPERS FERRY

McCAUSLAND

GORDON

WASHINGTON ROAD

N

0    1/2    1

SCALE of MILES

Battlefield of Monocacy, July 9, 1864—after Hotchkiss in *O. R. Atlas*, Plate LXXXIII-9

ado, McCausland crossed, dismounted and furiously assailed the Federal line. His men captured a battery, but they were not quite strong enough to drive the enemy. After a hard struggle, they fell back.

"McCausland's movement, which was brilliantly executed," Early said later, "solved the problem for me." [27] He determined to throw the nearest Division, that of Gordon, across the river at the same ford and to complete the turning movement McCausland had begun. Gordon's men had been enjoying the pleasure of watching and of criticizing a battle they did not think they would be compelled to share. They were not pleased to be summoned into the fight, and still less were they pleased to be told, "Take arms!—no time now for blankets, but get into your places at once!" [28] Questioning but obedient, the Division marched down to the ford, splashed through it and started to deploy. Gordon was intrepid as he sat on his horse in his red shirt, with sleeves rolled partly up; [29] but he looked twice and doubtfully at the position Early had ordered him to storm. Said Gordon later: "Across the intervening fields . . . there were strong farm fences, which my men must climb while under fire. Worse still, those fields were thickly studded with huge grain-stacks which the harvesters had recently piled. They were so broad and high and close together that no line of battle could possibly be maintained while advancing through them." [30]

It was too late to turn back. The enemy already was opening fire. In échelon from the right,[31] the Division pressed forward. Although Brig. Gen. Clement Evans fell quickly with a severe wound,[32] the men of Gordon's old Brigade climbed over or knocked down the fences and fought with so much dash that the Federals were compelled to change front.[33] By that time, the Louisiana troops of the Division had advanced within striking distance. Gordon hurled them and Evans's Brigade against the first line, drove it back, stopped long enough to catch breath, and then charged and broke a second line.

Ahead Gordon saw a third, long line. To attack it, he had to expose his men to a flank fire. After brief reflection he determined

[27] *Early*, 387.
[29] *Worsham*, 238.
[31] *Ibid.*, 311.
[33] *O. R.*, 37, pt. 1, p. 351.

[28] *Worsham*, 236.
[30] *Gordon*, 310.
[32] *O. R.*, 37, pt. 1, p. 351.

to keep his two Brigades where they were and to throw the third, Terry s, against the Federals who were delivering the fire on his flank. Although Terry achieved some success in this attack, it was not enough to justify a frontal assault by Evans and York. Further reserves were needed. Gordon sent for them, but when he learned they could not reach him promptly, he decided to have Terry change front and attack the enemy's right while he himself assailed the front with his remaining Brigades.[34]

Silently and alone, Gordon rode to the point where Terry would deploy. Soon he saw a new line of Federals advancing at the double-quick to a fence in front. Up the grade to meet them Terry's veterans were coming. "Hurry up, boys," Gordon called. The soldiers stepped faster and in a few minutes caught a glimpse of the bluecoats. A yell went up from the Southerners at the head of the column: "At them, boys!" they cried.

"Keep quiet," said Gordon, turning in his saddle; "we'll have our time presently."

He had the men in front pull down part of the fence to let the column through and again he led it forward. The men were excited almost to a frenzy at the sight of the enemy running to the fence the Confederates wished to seize, but the front ranks heeded the General's voice "until," said a participant, "about a hundred passed through the fence when the cry went up from the men, 'Charge them! Charge them!'" The same observer continued: "It was useless for General Gordon to try to stop it now—nothing but a shot through each man could have done it—and with a yell we were at the fence."

One volley scattered the Federals, who had not formed a line. The remainder of Terry's Brigade hurried up and added its fire. Evans's veterans and the Louisianians pushed forward now to other music than that of the guns. From the opposite side of the river came the reassuring cheers of the troops of the two other Divisions.[35] Soon they, too, pushed over the Monocacy and joined in the chase.[36] It was, said John H. Worsham, "the most exciting time I witnessed during the war."[37]

The pursuit ended quickly, because Early did not wish to be burdened with more prisoners. As it was, he captured between

[34] O. R., 37, pt. 1, p. 351.
[36] Early, 388.

[35] Worsham, 238-39.
[37] Worsham, 239.

600 and 700, a number almost as great as that of his own casualties.[38] The total loss of the enemy, missing included, was computed at the time as close to 2000,[39] but the return of missing men lowered this to slightly less than 1300. Early's gross loss was under 700.[40]

Another reason for hesitation on Early's part in pushing after the enemy was the discovery of the composition of the forces that had contested the crossing of the Monocacy. The Federal commander proved to be Maj. Gen. Lew Wallace, of the Middle Department, who had a Brigade of the VIII Corps and a small force of cavalry. These troops had been reinforced—and this made every Confederate in the expedition attentive—by Brig. Gen. James B. Ricketts's 3rd Division of the VI Corps, Army of the Potomac. Good news and bad that was! Whatever Early might or might not accomplish after the Battle of the Monocacy, he had achieved one of the objects the high command had in mind: he had forced Grant to detach troops from the Richmond-Petersburg area in order to defend Washington.[41] Desirable as this was, it imposed greater caution on Early. He could not afford to risk his little Army against unknown odds. Besides, he had received from General Lee, by special courier, notice that an attempt might be made to release the Confederate prisoners at Point Lookout, Maryland. Lee's despatch contained the admission that the commanding General himself was not familiar with all the details of this adventure. Early knew nothing of it, and could ascertain nothing, but he had, of course, to be vigilant and mobile in the event he learned that his cavalry could assist the released prisoners.[42]

For these reasons, Early did not follow fast from the Monocacy. He hoped to be able to attack and perhaps to capture Washington, but he was in no wise reckless. On the morning of the 10th—a day of much heat and dust—he resumed his advance and sustained the reputation of the "foot cavalry" by marching his force thirty miles.[43] Breckinridge's Corps, as it now was styled, vigorously set the pace. Ramseur closed the rear. The Marylander, Bradley Johnson, to his life-long satisfaction, was moving with his cavalry toward Baltimore.[44]

[38] *Early*, 388.
[39] *O. R.*, 37, pt. 1, pp. 201–02.
[40] *Ibid.*, 202, 348.
[41] *O. R.*, 37, pt. 1, pp. 347–48.
[42] *Early*, 385; *O. R.*, 37, pt. 1, p. 767; *ibid.*, 40, pt. 3, pp. 749, 753, 759 ff; 20 *C. V.* 69–70; *Lee's Dispatches*, 269 ff; *R. E. Lee, Jr.*, 131.
[43] *O. R.*, 37, pt. 1, p. 348.
[44] *Hotchkiss' MS Diary*, 363.

The next day, July 11, was an historic date in American history. In the winter of 1861–'62, the Confederate outposts North of Manassas had been able to see distant buildings of Washington, but between them and their goal, the defiant Potomac had flowed. Now, with no stream to halt them, the Confederates might march straight to the defenses of the capital and, if they had the strength and the resolution, might storm them successfully. After the war, men said that the charge on the third day at Gettysburg marked "the high-water mark" of the Confederacy, and in the just determination of military values, they were correct; but if proximity to White House, to Capitol and to Treasury be considered strategically the greatest advance, then the honor of it fell a year and a week after Pickett's charge to that strange, bitter, and devoted man, Jubal A. Early, former Commonwealth's Attorney of Franklin County, Virginia.

He pressed the march as vigorously as he had on the 10th. When he and his staff rode past the sweating column, he told the troops that he would take them into Washington that day.[45] They responded with their old yell, but officers soon observed that the heat of the day was exhausting the men. Long before noon, veterans who had endured some of the hardest marches of the Second Corps, were falling out of ranks. "Our Division," wrote the invaluable Worsham, "was stretched out almost like skirmishers, and all the men did not get up until night."[46] Early slackened the pace, but even his zeal and stern orders could not keep the column closed or the men in their place.

When Rodes's troops, who that day were in the van, came at last within sight of the Soldiers' Home and of the city's heavy fortifications,[47] Early had to admit that an immediate attack was out of the question. The most he could do at the moment was to advance his skirmishers while he rested his men and studied the works. As a seasoned soldier, he admired what the Union engineers had accomplished. The works, he wrote a few days later, "consist of a circle of inclosed forts, connected by breast-works, with ditches, palisades and abatis in front, and every approach swept by a cross-fire of artillery . . ."[48] Investment was impossible; assault would be costly; but the fighting blood of "Old Jube" was up. If an attack could achieve results, he would make it.

---

45 *Hotchkiss' MS Diary*, 363.  46 *Worsham*, 241–42.
47 *Ibid.*, 241.  48 *O. R.*, 37, pt. 1, p. 348.

Before he decided where he would try to break the defenses, he ascertained that the whole of the VI Corps and not merely Ricketts's Division had arrived on the Washington front from Grant's Army.[49] In conferring on this news with his division commanders, he reminded them that a decision to fight or to move the little Army had to be made forthwith. Otherwise the passes of South Mountain and the fords of the Potomac might be occupied by the enemy.[50] Such men as John Breckinridge, Robert Rodes, John Gordon and Dodson Ramseur always were inclined to resolve doubts by taking the offensive when there was any chance of winning. Their counsel and Early's decision was to attack at earliest dawn the next morning unless some new development came.

During the night of the 11th–12th, a message was received by Early from Bradley Johnson, who then was close to Baltimore. Johnson's information was that two Corps had arrived from Grant's Army to reinforce Washington.[51] It was thought probable, Johnson added, that the whole Army of the Potomac was in motion northward.[52] This was news to make Early hesitate. Skeptical as he always was of the reports of scouts, he could not disdain a report from an officer of Johnson's standing. Orders consequently were sent the divisional leaders to delay the assault until daylight would show whether the defenses of the Federal capital were manned heavily.[53]

As soon as Early could see in the soft summer dawn the far-spreading line of earthworks, he was at a vantage point and was gazing at them with his binocular. They were lined with troops.[54] If the assault were successful, Early had to tell himself, it would entail such losses that the remnant of his little Army might not be able to escape. Should he fail in the assault, he almost certainly would lose his entire force.[55] In either event, the destruction of a Confederate Army in front of Washington might have a fatally depressing effect on the South. Much as Early wished to attack, much as he regretted the necessity of desisting, he saw no choice.

[49] O. R., 37, pt. 1, p. 348.          [50] Early, 392.
[51] This report doubtless originated in the fact that Ricketts's Division of the VI Corps disembarked in Baltimore while the remaining Divisions proceeded directly to Washington by steamer. See O. R., 37, pt. 1, p. 265 ff and the corps diary in ibid., 270 ff. Grant's account of the detachment is in ibid., 36, pt. 1, p. 28.
[52] Early, 392.          [53] Ibid.
[54] Ibid.          [55] O. R., 37, pt. 1, p. 348.

The odds against him were too heavy. The plan must be abandoned!

Combat orders were cancelled. The troops demonstrated and skirmished in front of Fort Stevens on the 12th and beat off three "feeling out" advances by the enemy. That night they began their retreat to Virginia. "Major," said Early to Kyd Douglas, just before the column slipped away, "we haven't taken Washington, but we've scared Abe Lincoln like hell!"

"Yes, General," Douglas answered, "but this afternoon when that Yankee line moved out against us, I think some other people were scared blue as hell's brimstone!"

John Breckinridge broke in with a laugh: "How about that, General?"

"That's true," Early answered, "but it won't appear in history!" [56]

There were losses along with gains, and regrets as well as booty. Four hundred men wounded at Monocacy had to be left at Frederick for lack of transportation, but all prisoners and all the Army's property were brought back, via White's Ford, to Loudoun County, northern Virginia.[57] Particularly cherished by "Jube" was $220,-000 in cash he had levied on Hagerstown and Frederick.[58] Scarcely less appreciated by "Old Jube" was the report of his cavalry commanders that they had destroyed numerous railroad and highway bridges. "It was believed by the men," Adjutant Worsham recorded, "that we could have gone into the city on the evening of the 11th, if our men had been up, but straggling prevented it." [59] Dodson Ramseur was of substantially the same mind. He wrote his wife after the return to Virginia: "Natural obstacles alone prevented our taking Washington. The heat and dust was so great that our men could not possibly march further. Time was thus given the enemy to get a sufficient force into his works to prevent our capturing them." [60] Early himself was not greatly concerned over his failure to enter Washington, because he thought that was explicable. When he came to write of the campaign, his pains were spent in answering criticism that on his advance he had lingered too long in the lower part of the Shenandoah Valley.[61]

[56] Douglas, 205.        [57] Ibid.; Early, 392–95.
[58] O. R., 37, pt. 1, p. 349.    [59] Worsham, 243.
[60] Ramseur to his wife, MS, July 15, 1864, near Leesburg, Va.—Ramseur MSS.
[61] Early, 394.

Lee was satisfied with the results and was hopeful of still further gains from Early's presence on the frontier.[62]

Had there been any disposition to review critically the Battle of Monocacy, it would have been observed that most of the combat had been the work of a single Division. While Gordon fought furiously below the highway bridge, the forces of Ramseur and of Rodes engaged in nothing more formidable than skirmishing and artillery exchanges. This might have been solely the result of circumstances. If it became a habit for Early to conduct his battles in this fashion, it might imply that he still was, in spirit and in strategical conceptions, a division and not a corps or army commander. The difference between the employment of Divisions in succession, and the simultaneous use of the full strength of all the Divisions might be the difference between defeat and victory. Were he ever so skillful in the use of separate Divisions, a General could not aspire to competence in army command if he thought in terms of Divisions and of divisional fire-power and attack only.

A second weakness of Early's operations, even at this hopeful stage, was the lack of a consolidated command of his cavalry. Robert Ransom, who had been sent to Lynchburg to take charge of the cavalry,[63] had been incapacitated by a return of the physical ailment that plagued him throughout the war. "All my operations," Early said later, "had been impeded for the want of an efficient and energetic cavalry commander." [64] McCausland had several bold exploits to his credit; Bradley Johnson and Harry Gilmor and John Imboden had ridden far, had burned bridges, and, in Johnson's case, had threatened Baltimore. These men's troopers had proved themselves raiding forces of varying discipline and hardihood; but they were not, and without an able leader, a strong disciplinarian, they could not be, a unified body of fighting men in the sense that Hampton's or Sheridan's troopers were. Although Early already had monitory evidence of the feebleness of his cavalry, he did not have the aptitude, if indeed he had the time, to improve that arm.

As soon as Early was back in Virginia, four Federal com-

---

[62] O. R., 37, pt. 1, p. 346. Typical newspaper comment on the basis of first reports was that of the *Richmond Enquirer*, July 20, 1864; but by the 28th that newspaper was bristling with criticism. The expedition, it said, was everywhere and in all particulars a failure.

[63] See *supra*, p. 526.      [64] *Early*, 400.

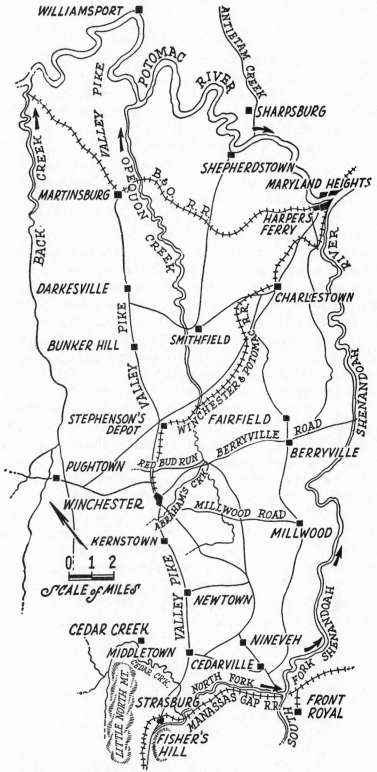

The Lower Shenandoah Valley from Fisher's Hill to the Potomac, Scene of Early's Operations, July–September, 1864—after *O. R. Atlas*, Plate LXXIX-1

manders, Sigel, Hunter, Averell and Crook, gathered their forces to attack him. From Washington, Maj. Gen. Horatio G. Wright [65] pursued into Loudoun County.[66] When "Jube" slipped away to the West, there followed a succession of skirmishes that did not change materially the strategic situation.[67] The first affair of any importance was an advance by Ramseur on the 20th of July. He had been informed by Brig. Gen. J. C. Vaughn that a regiment of cavalry and one of infantry were North of Winchester. As Ramseur had responsibility for the defense of that portal of the Shenandoah, he decided to drive away these intruders. At first he thought to take only a part of his troops, but caution prompted him to move the whole. Near Stephenson's Depot, the scene of Edward Johnson's success over Milroy en route to Gettysburg, Ramseur was attacked suddenly by Averell. To the amazement of everyone, part of Hoke's trusted old Brigade ran and spread confusion among Robert Johnston's troops.[68] In the panic that ensued, a total of 267 unwounded officers and men were captured. On the field, Ramseur was said by his adversary to have left four guns, seventy-three dead and 130 wounded.[69]

This reverse almost broke the heart of young Dodson Ramseur.[70] "I am greatly mortified at the result," he confessed to his wife, and added with bitterness, "My men behaved shamefully." Later in the day he wrote again: "I am sure I did all that mortal man could do. Yet, newspaper editors and stay-at-home croakers will sit back in safe places and condemn me." [71] His brother officers, with whom he was most popular,[72] did their utmost to console him and to explain the circumstances [73] Early felt that Ramseur had not taken "the proper precautions" in advancing. Beyond that he did not criticize his young lieutenant.[74] Lee reported the action simply as one in which Ramseur encountered "a much superior force" and had to withdraw.[75] The wound to the pride of the ambitious and devoted young Carolinian remained.

[65] He had succeeded the fallen John Sedgwick in command of the VI Corps.
[66] *O.R.*, 37, pt. 1. pp. 268–69.
[67] For the details, which are of little interest, see Averell's report (*O. R.*, 37, pt. 1, p. 326; *Early*, 396)
[68] *O. R.*, 37, pt. 1, p. 353; *ibid.*, pt. 2, p. 599.
[69] *O. R.*, 37, pt. 1, p. 327.
[70] *Douglas*, 300; *O. R.*, 36, pt. 1, p. 1081.
[71] Letters of July 23, 1864—*Ramseur MSS.* Cf. *Richmond Enquirer*, July 25, 27, 1864.
[72] Cf. *Gordon.* 64.
[73] *Cf.* Rodes to Ewell, *O. R.*, 37, pt. 1, pp. 353–54.
[74] *Early*, 397.                    [75] *O. R.*, 37, pt. 1, p. 347.

Four days later, July 24, Ramseur had partial revenge in a sharp little action that Early waged on the old battleground of Kernstown. There again a critic might have observed that the battle was fought by Echols's Division which Breckinridge brilliantly led. The other Divisions merely waited to join in the pursuit.[76] It was enough that George Crook was routed with substantial losses,[77] and that the Confederate officers captured on the 20th were recovered.[78]

In pursuit of Crook, who retreated to the Potomac, Early moved his forces to Martinsburg and there gave his men a brief rest. He learned while in Berkeley County that during his advance to Washington, the homes of Alexander Hunter, a State Senator, of Col. A. R. Boteler, and of Col. Edmund Lee, a kinsman of the commanding General, had been burned wantonly by the Federals. "I came to the conclusion," Early wrote afterward, "it was time to open the eyes of the people of the North to this enormity, by an example in the way of retaliation." He went on: "I did not select the cases mentioned, as having more merit or greater claims for retaliation than others, but because they had occurred within the limits of the country covered by my command and were brought more immediately to my attention." [79]

John McCausland with his own and Bradley Johnson's Brigade and a battery of artillery were started on the 29th of July for Chambersburg, Pennsylvania, which Early selected as the object of reprisal. McCausland's instructions were to demand $100,000 in gold or $500,000 greenbacks for the indemnification of the persons whose property had been put to the torch by the Federals. If this indemnity was not forthcoming at once, McCausland was to reduce the town to ashes. The cavalry rode off; Early demonstrated on the line of the Potomac to cover the operation.

About 5:30 A.M., July 30, the Confederate cavalry Brigades entered Chambersburg and presented their demand.[80] The first member of the town council who was told of this was instant in answer: the citizens would not pay 5 cents.[81] Other councilmen

[76] Early, 399; O. R., 37, pt. 1, p. 347.
[77] They were not known to the Confederates but were, in the aggregate, 1,185, of whom 479 were prisoners (O. R., 37, pt. 1, pp. 288–90).
[78] Ibid., 347; Richmond Enquirer, July 27, Aug. 1, 1864. No detailed reports of this action were filed by Early or by any of his subordinates. Among the officers recaptured was Brig. Gen. R. D. Lilley (Ibid.).
[79] Early, 401.  [80] O. R., 37, pt. 1, p. 337.
[81] Ibid., 334.

replied that they were not frightened by the threat: a Federal force was close at hand.[82] General McCausland waited till 9 o'clock [83] and then directed that the town be fired.[84] His order provoked virtual mutiny on the part of some of his officers and men. Col. William E. Peters of the Twenty-first Virginia Cavalry rode to McCausland and asked if the plan to burn the town originated with the commander of the expedition. McCausland showed him Early's instructions. Peters answered that he would break his sword and throw it away before he would obey any such order, as the only persons in Chambersburg were women and children. McCausland, of course, had to put the Colonel under arrest.[85] Other soldiers were of different temper. They would have burned the town even more gladly had they known that Mahone's men were gathering at that very hour in the ravine below Blandford Church, outside Petersburg and were preparing to recover the crater of the mine sprung under the Confederate lines.

As soon as the fires at Chambersburg were well ablaze, McCausland began his withdrawal toward the Potomac. He was prompt to relieve Colonel Peters of arrest,[86] and he doubtless was unaware of the many acts of robbery and of violence subsequently charged against stragglers and thieves in his command. If Early heard the first of these stories he did not credit them. He was quite satisfied with the main result, and for the burning of the greater part of Chambersburg, he never expressed any regret. His one concern was to be sure that the reprisal should not be blamed on his subordinates. In his military autobiography he wrote: "For this act I, alone, am responsible, as the officers engaged in it were simply executing my orders, and had no discretion left them. Notwithstanding the lapse of time which has occurred, and the result of the war, I see no reason to regret my conduct on this occasion." [87]

At the moment, Fate, as well as Gen. W. W. Averell, seemed to pursue McCausland and Bradley Johnson on their return from Chambersburg. After moving toward Cumberland, they had to withdraw to Hampshire County and then to Hardy County.

[82] *Early*, 404.
[84] *Ibid*.
[86] *Ibid*.
[83] *O. R.*, 37, pt. 1, p. 335.
[85] 31 *S.H.S.P.*, 270.
[87] *Early*, 404 n. In his *Memoir of the Last Year of the War* . . . edition of 1867, on which the larger work was based, the closing part of the second sentence read: "I am perfectly satisfied with my conduct on this occasion, and see no reason to regret it" (*op. cit.*, 70 n).

There, at Moorefield, in the belief that they were safe, the Confederate commanders relaxed their vigilance with the familiar result. Averell descended on Johnson's camp in a surprise attack, before daylight, August 7, and routed the Brigade. McCausland's force, on the opposite side of the south branch of the Potomac was driven, also. Averell reported that he captured four guns, 420 prisoners and over 400 horses. Bradley Johnson himself was caught but was able to escape. John McCausland had slept three miles from his camp and, for that reason, escaped.[88]

The affair at Moorefield led to a violent written attack by Bradley Johnson on McCausland. In his denunciation of his immediate superior, Johnson contrasted the strict orders given him by McCausland with the alleged negligence of that officer in failing to discipline the men during the raid. Johnson's account of the misbehavior of some of the troopers confirmed everything the residents of the burned Pennsylvania town were saying. At Chambersburg, on the road, and even on Virginia soil, Johnson charged that men of McCausland's Brigade had been guilty of infamous conduct. Johnson specified: "Every crime in the catalogue of infamy has been committed, I believe, except murder and rape. Highway robbery of watches and pocket-books was of ordinary occurrence . . . Pillage and sack of private dwellings took place hourly." [89]

As between McCausland and Johnson, Army Headquarters at first were inclined to hold the Marylander responsible. Early was instructed by Lee to relieve Johnson of command if the blame rested on the Brigadier.[90] Johnson himself sought a court of inquiry,[91] but "Old Jube" ignored this and did nothing to improve discipline. Although the responsibility was his as head of the forces in the Valley, he seemed powerless to control or to reorganize his cavalry. Later he had reason to lament the bad blood that prevented co-operation between the two young cavalry Generals. Still more painfully was he to discover that looting and robbery by a certain type of soldier are to him what traditionally the taste of human blood is to the tiger. The thief covets more loot. When discipline is debased by robbery, it seldom can be restored. Early was more than conservative when he said of the rout at Moorefield

[88] Averell in O. R., 43, pt. 1, pp. 494–95.
[89] O. R., 43, pt. 1, p. 7; ibid., 994.
[90] O. R., 42, pt. 2, p. 1172; ibid., 43, pt. 1, pp. 551, 568.
[91] O. R., 43, pt. 1, p. 8.

what he should have applied to the whole of the disgraceful Chambersburg raid: "This affair had a very damaging effect upon my cavalry for the rest of the campaign." [92]

Before McCausland and Johnson had rejoined Early with their shamed and shattered men, a major change in the campaign had occurred. The Shenandoah Valley once more had become a major theatre of war. Lee had been convinced by August 4 that Grant was dispatching other troops to aid Wright's VI Corps in assailing Early. On the 6th, in conference with the President, Lee had decided to send Kershaw's Division of infantry and Fitz Lee's cavalry to Northern Virginia to assist the Second Corps. Under "Dick" Anderson, these troops at the outset were to operate East of the Blue Ridge and were to utilize in Early's behalf the familiar geographical relationship between the Northern Frontier District and the lower Valley.[93] To this region, Lee was prepared to move still other units of his weakened Army, if it should develop that Grant was detaching heavily to the same quarter.[94]

Early was gratified at the prospect of having trusted veterans of Longstreet's and Stuart's old Corps in Culpeper and Prince William. He felt some personal concern because Anderson ranked him, but he was relieved by assurance from Lee that no difficulty was expected on this account.[95] "Old Jube" needed Anderson and all additional reinforcement he could get, because news of the enemy's plans was ominous. On the 9th of August, Imboden reported to the Lieutenant General that a heavy Federal concentration was in progress at Harpers Ferry. The information of the cavalryman was that the VI and XIX Corps, as well as Crook's troops, were being assembled and that they were under a new commander.[96] Quickly the outposts learned that Early's adversary was Maj. Gen. Phil Sheridan.[97]

With confident heart and probably in contemptuous spirit,

[92] *Early*, 405. McCausland's account of the raid is in 31 *S.H.S.P.*, 266-70.

[93] See Vol. 1, p. 688. For references to the dispatch of Anderson and Fitz Lee, see 3 *R. E. Lee*, 479.

[94] *O. R.*, 42, pt. 2, pp. 1170-73.

[95] *O. R.*, 43, pt. 1, p. 1006. It will be observed from the correspondence of Early with Anderson (cf., *O. R.*, 43, pt. 2, p. 862), that "Jube" was both tactful and deferential toward his comrade. On Aug. 23, 1864, Anderson concluded with these words a report to Lee on the situation in Northern Virginia: "Consulting solely the best means of success and believing it not to have been your intention that I supersede Early, I have not assumed command but will continue to act in concert with him."—*Anderson MSS.* See *supra*, p. 510.

[96] *Early*, 406.

[97] *Ibid.*, and *O. R.*, 43, pt. 1, p. 995.

Early determined to set the pace and to occupy Sheridan by ceaseless maneuver. On the 10th "Jube" began a succession of marches and demonstrations that puzzled Sheridan and created the impression of far greater force than the Confederates mustered.[98] In this deception Early was assisted by Anderson, who moved into the Valley for a time. Fitz Lee also gave skillful aid both in maneuver and in the attempted reorganization of the disorganized cavalry that had hampered Early from the beginning of his campaign.

On the publication of the news that Sheridan had taken command in the Valley, Gen. R. E. Lee had issued orders for Wade Hampton to proceed to Northern Virginia with that officer's Division,[99] and for this mission had given the South Carolinian general command of the cavalry,[100] but the activity of David Gregg on the James had forced Lee to recall Hampton.[101] Although Hampton could not go to the Valley, it was manifest that relief had to be given Robert Ransom, who had not been able to keep the field. Under orders of August 10, Ransom was ordered to Richmond and was succeeded by one of Fitz Lee's capable former Brigadiers, Lunsford L. Lomax, who was made temporary Major General.[102] In surrendering an assignment he lacked the physical strength to discharge, Ransom showed close knowledge of the various units and suggested many changes. Among these was the transfer of Imboden's men to Wickham's Brigade and the relief of Imboden.[103] Broad reorganization was necessary, said Ransom, to bring Early's cavalry "to anything like a state of efficiency."[104]

Ransom's suggestions were forwarded by Bragg to Early. As Breckinridge through long acquaintance might be better acquainted with the personnel than Early was, Bragg directed that the Kentuckian be consulted. Bragg's own conclusion was: "It is feared that too radical a change may produce dissatisfaction in those commands raised mostly in the country now held by the enemy and cause many desertions. At the same time it is felt that some stringent measures are necessary to secure discipline and prevent disaster."[105] For some reason, Early did not answer this

[98] See Sheridan's contemporary reports (O. R., 43, pt. 1, pp. 18–20), which differed substantially in tone and spirit from his final report.
[99] O. R., 43, pt. 1, pp. 995, 996.
[100] See supra, p. 551.                    [101] Ibid., 999.
[102] O. R., 43, pt. 1, pp. 990, 992, 993, 1001; Wright, 44.
[103] Ibid., 1003–04.        [104] Ibid., 1003.        [105] Ibid., 1008.

letter.[106] Nor, apparently, in the face of new warnings, did he take in hand any reorganization. Whatever was done in that essential had to be undertaken by Fitz Lee, when he was West of the Blue Ridge, or by Lunsford Lomax, who was a stranger to the Valley troopers. Early persisted—it is impossible to say why—in his curious neglect of his cavalry, though he complained often of it.

During the first month of Early's maneuvering, he did not gain a favorable impression of Sheridan. Although "Jube" felt that he offered his opponent numerous opportunities, he believed that Sheridan ignored them. Even when the Confederates were in an exposed position, Sheridan did not attack. "If it was his policy," said Early, "to produce the impression that he was too weak to fight me, he did not succeed, but if it was to convince me that he was not an energetic commander, his strategy was a complete success . . ." [107] Early, in a word, became overconfident. He concluded that Sheridan was lacking in initiative and in boldness. This state of mind is a dangerous one for any commander prior to actual test of his adversary. It was doubly hazardous for Early because after little more than a month, he lost his infantry reinforcement. Anderson and Kershaw were ordered back to the Army of Northern Virginia. On the 14th of September, the experienced troops of the First Corps left the lower Valley by way of Front Royal.[108]

This loss of a well-led, veteran Division did not curb "Old Jubilee." Although conscious that the Federals were strong, Early continued to maneuver and, on the afternoon of September 17, advanced from Stephenson's Depot to Bunker Hill. On the 18th, he moved Gordon's Division and some cavalry to Martinsburg to disperse what was assumed to be a work force engaged in the repair of the railroad. The "workers" proved to be Averell's cavalry Division, which was driven in the direction of Charlestown. Early then retraced his steps. Gordon's Division was bivouacked

---

106 *Ibid.*, 1004.

107 *Early*, 415. It was during this period of operations in the Shenandoah Valley that Col. John S. Mosby and his partisan rangers began their most successful attacks on Sheridan's supply lines. The story of Mosby's gallant raids is intriguing, but as it has been told in much detail by numerous writers, it is not included here.

108 *O. R.*, 43, pt. 1, p. 1027. Sheridan heard on the 15th that these troops were moving toward Front Royal (*ibid.*, 46), but as late as the 20th the Federal commander thought the Division still was at that town (*O. R.*, 43, pt. 2, pp. 102, 119).

at Bunker Hill. Rodes was marched to Stephenson's Depot,[109] where Breckinridge already was.[110] Ramseur's Division was one mile East of Winchester on the road to Berryville. Lomax's cavalry picketed the left, Fitz Lee the right.[111] The strength of this force was reckoned by Early at 8500 infantry, 2900 cavalry and three battalions of artillery [112]—a total of about 12,150. In comparison, though Early of course did not know even the approximate figures, Sheridan had under his command about 48,000 effectives. In the field, Sheridan could muster about 40,000, of whom more than 6400 were cavalry.[113]

This strong Union Army at length was moving. What Early had assumed to be overcaution on the part of Sheridan had been, in reality, obedience to orders from Grant who had told the cavalrymen in August to remain on the defensive while Early had the superiority of force the Federals assumed him to possess.[114] Sheridan had received heavy cavalry reinforcement while waiting, and now that he had vague reports of the withdrawal of Kershaw, he had determined to strike.

Soon after dawn on the 19th of September, Early heard that the Federals had forced the crossing of the Opequon on the Berryville Road, which led to Winchester. "Old Jube" was not entirely unprepared for this news, because he had learned at Martinsburg that Grant had been paying a visit to Sheridan and he had assumed that this presaged early action.[115] Immediately, therefore, Early ordered Gordon to support Ramseur. Then, as quickly as his horse could carry him there, Early rode to the young North Carolinian's position East of Winchester. So plain were the indications of a general attack that Early directed his remaining infantry, that of Rodes and of Breckinridge, to hurry to the ground where Ramseur was standing in furious determination to wipe out the disgrace of recent defeat at the hands of Averell.[116] After Ramseur's line of battle had been examined and approved, the available artillery was placed by Early where he thought it most effectively would cover the approaches to Ramseur's front. The small cavalry Divi-

---

[109] Early, 419.    [110] Ibid., 414.
[111] Ibid.
[112] Fitz Lee had with him one battery of horse artillery. This is included in the estimate of personnel. Early (op. cit., 415–16) did not give the numerical strength of his artillery, but it is here computed at 750 officers and men.
[113] O. R., 43, pt. 1, pp. 60, 61 and note.    [114] O. R., 43, pt. 1, p. 43.
[115] Early, 419, 420.    [116] See supra, p. 570.

sions already were mustering on the flanks. Part of Bradley John-son's weakened command was placed on Ramseur's left to hold the ground leading down to Red Bud Creek until Gordon and Rodes arrived.

Gordon led his men on the field about 10 A.M. Behind him, looking as much the god of war as ever, Robert Rodes advanced with three of his Brigades. Almost before Gordon could be de-ployed on the extreme left, or Rodes could be placed between him and Ramseur, the attack opened on a line to which Ramseur slowly and skillfully had withdrawn.[117] There was no mystery or finesse about this initial Federal advance: it manifestly was an effort to hold Ramseur in front while another column turned his left. Early's black eyes burned at the sight of this. He would meet it and would show young Mr. Sheridan how the Army of Northern Virginia fought! Let Gordon and Rodes outflank the flankers and rout them.[118]

Gordon and Rodes themselves had decided to undertake that maneuver. Before Early's orders reached them, they conferred briefly and started their men forward. Gordon proceeded at once to the front. Robert Rodes turned away to observe his line, which was advancing under well-placed enemy fire. The fine black horse of the General—as familiar to the troops as Rodes himself—be-came restive. Rodes was trying to control the animal when a shell burst near him. A fragment struck the General on the head and knocked him from his horse. Although his heart beat feebly for a few minutes, he knew nothing.[119] His troops had to go on without him. As Rodes's men advanced, Evans's Brigade, the left flank element of Gordon's Division, was checked and driven back, but it was staunchly supported by the artillery until Rodes's absent Brigade, Battle's, came up and attacked as ferociously as at Spotsyl-vania. Swiftly and with heavy loss the enemy was driven back.

The repulse was sharp; the day appeared to have been won, though at heavy cost in the death of Rodes. Said one participant: ". . . we lay down to rest. [Gordon's Division] had been in action only about an hour, and we thought we had gained an easy vic-tory."[120] The situation seemed even less dangerous as the minutes

[117] *O. R.*, 43, pt. 1, p. 47.　　　　　　　[118] *Early*, 421–22.
[119] 16 *C. V.*, 269; 2 *S.H.S.P.*, 26–27; *Gordon*, 321; Diary of Capt. James M. Garnet' in 27 *S.H.S.P.*, 5; *O. R.*, 43, pt. 1, pp. 555, 574.
[120] *Worsham*, 258.

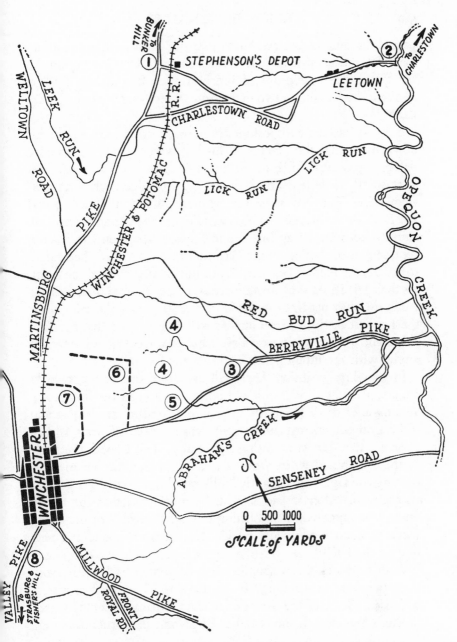

essive Confederate Infantry Positions, Third Battle of Winchester, Sept. 19, 1864. The encircled ~~erals~~ indicate: 1, Bivouac of Gordon and Rodes, night of September 18–19; 2, Scene of Breckinridge's ~~noon~~ action; 3, Ramseur's first position; 4, engaging position of Rodes and Gordon; 5, Ramseur's ~~nd~~ position; 6, Confederate line about 4:30 P.M.; 7, final Confederate line, about 5 P.M.; 8, line of retreat to Fisher's Hill. After Sheridan's Map in *O. R. Atlas*, Plate XCIX–1

passed, because of the arrival of John C. Breckinridge, who had been delayed because he had to repel some Federal cavalry on the Opequon. Early held one of Breckinridge's Brigades on the left and sent the remaining two to the right, which was now his weaker flank.[121]

Scarcely had these dispositions been made when Early saw to his amazement that the cavalry on his left were retiring in disorder before a powerful force of the enemy's mounted troops. As fast as it could be done, Early brought Breckinridge back to the extreme left. With the same fine artillery support that Evans had received, Breckinridge was able to halt the enemy's advance.[122] A simultaneous attack against the left, nearer the front, was being repulsed, also.[123] Then noise accomplished what force had failed to do. As the men of Gordon, Rodes and Ramseur heard the firing on their left flank, they became uneasy. In spite of all their officers could do, they began to make for the rear. About the same time, the heaviest of the Federal attacks was delivered against Breckinridge and the retreating cavalry, who now were almost at right angles with the infantry that had met the frontal attack.[124]

In growing confusion, Early fell back to a line of breastworks close to the town. With his old pugnacity and in the imperturbable manner of all his fighting,[125] he prepared to stand there and to beat off the enemy, but he soon was attacked in front as well as on the left. He was fighting stubbornly on an L, with the angle to the Northeast, when word was brought that the enemy was turning the right. Reluctantly "Old Jube" had to order a general withdrawal. After it had started, he discovered that the troops who were supposed to be turning his right were in reality Ramseur's unshaken regiments which were conforming to the new line on their left.[126]

With eagerness Early sought to send the men back to the positions they were evacuating. It was too late. The spirit of retreat had risen. Some of the troops were close to panic. As they passed through Winchester, the beautiful Mrs. John B. Gordon, as usual,

---

[121] *O. R.*, 43, pt. 1, p. 555.       [122] *Ibid.*, 47, 555.
[123] *Early*, 425. This was George Crook's attack, for which see *O. R.*, 43, pt. 1, pp. 361–62.
[124] *Ibid.*, 47, 427. The Federal attack was that of Gen. A. T. A. Torbert down the Martinsburg Road, with the Divisions of Brig. Gen. Wesley Merritt and Brig. Gen. W. W. Averell.
[125] Cf. *Gordon*, 317.       [126] *Early*, 425–26.

was entirely too near the front. She ran out into the street of the town to exhort the men to rally; and when she found that they belonged to her husband's command, neither the whine of the minié balls nor the approach of the enemy could stop her entreaties. By the narrowest of margins only did she escape capture.[127]

Soldiers who survived the onslaught now rallied South of the town. Then, rapidly, but not in rout, they retreated twenty miles and more to Fisher's Hill which, in Early's opinion, "was the only place where a stand could be made."[128] When he got his troops in position there and could count his casualties, he found that of his little Army of 12,000, he had lost 3611 of his infantry and artillerymen—1818 of them captured—and probably 1000 of his cavalry.[129] This total was almost 40 per cent of the force with which Early had withstood Sheridan's advance. The command had suffered proportionately. Besides Rodes, who was irreplaceable at the moment, Early had lost Brig. Gen. A. C. Godwin of Hoke's old Brigade, in circumstances that duplicated those of Rodes's death. Like Girardey and Sanders, mentioned already, Godwin seemed to have been promoted solely to be slain. He had held his commission forty days.[130] Fitz Lee had been wounded seriously by a minié ball in the thigh[131]—a most deplorable injury because it deprived Lunsford Lomax of experienced help in the reorganization of the cavalry. In addition, Col. Geo. S. Patton of the Twenty-second Virginia, commanding Echols's Brigade of Breckinridge's command,[132] had been left on the field of Winchester with a mortal hurt.[133] On the 13th, the experienced John W. Henagan, Colonel of the Eighth South Carolina, had been captured.[134]

---

127 *Gordon*, 42, 320 ff; 2 *S.H.S.P.*, 28; 32 *S.H.S.P.*, 92; *Douglas*, 311. Perhaps it was to Early's pretended regret that she escaped at all. He knew of her insistence on sharing as far as she could the perils of her husband, and he had said: "I wish the Yankees would capture Mrs. Gordon and hold her till the war is over." Once, when she had arrived in a cloud of dust, which had been attributed to charging cavalry, Early had observed, "Well, I'll be damned! If my men would keep up as she does, I'd never issue another order against straggling" (*Gordon*, 319).

128 *O. R.*, 43, pt. 1, p. 556.

129 *Ibid.* In his report of losses, Early said sixty cavalrymen were killed and 288 wounded. "Many," he wrote, were captured, but he did not attempt to estimate them. In view of the widespread open fighting, 700 would seem a low figure for prisoners and stragglers subsequently caught. Sheridan's Provost Marshal did not attempt to record separately the prisoners taken in the different actions in the Shenandoah Valley.

130 3 *N. C. Regts.*, 421; *O. R.*, 43, pt. 1, p. 552; *Wright*, 122.

131 35 *S.H.S.P.*, 143.     132 *O. R.*, 43, pt. 1, p. 1011.

133 *Ibid.*, 597.     134 *O. R.*, 43, pt. 1, p. 592.

Now, at Fisher's Hill, came another heavy loss of a different character: Maj. Gen. John C. Breckinridge received orders to return at once to his own Department of Southwest Virginia, where his presence was required.[135] Breckinridge had co-operated ably and heartily with Early [136] and he had fought at Winchester as a man who courted death. When Gordon had protested that the Kentuckian was exposing himself needlessly, Breckinridge had turned to his comrade his handsome face, begrimed with sweat and smoke, and had said simply, "Well, General, there is little left for me if our cause is to fail." [137] The departure of Breckinridge and of his troops, after the grievous losses of Winchester, would have made Early's situation hopeless had he not received assurance of the early return of Kershaw, who had not proceeded southward beyond Culpeper.[138] More cavalry were promised also.

While awaiting these reinforcements, Early had to undertake reorganization. Before the blood, so to say, had been washed off his subordinates' faces, he had to introduce some of these men to strange troops. Little choice was his. With Rodes dead and Breckinridge gone, there were three men only in the Army who could be regarded as sufficiently experienced to handle a Division. Two of these were, of course, John B. Gordon and Dodson Ramseur. The third qualified officer was John Pegram. He had been commanding a Brigade under Ramseur but, it will be remembered, had led acceptably a Division in the Army of Tennessee.[139] As quickly as possible, Early gave Ramseur the Division of Rodes. In command of Ramseur's men, Pegram was left as senior Brigadier. To Gordon were transferred the forces previously called Breckinridge's Division but styled Wharton's Division [140] during the time Breckinridge, as corps commander, had been directing both his Division and Gordon's.[141]

This was the best arrangement that could be made. Ramseur's conduct at Winchester had been as brilliant as anything in his career and had been full atonement for any charge of negligence in the affair at Stephenson's Depot.[142] Gordon was never as happy

---

[135] O. R., 43, pt. 1, pp. 1010–11, pt. 3, p. 864 ff; ibid., 51, pt. 2, p. 1040; 7 S.H.S.P., 323.

[136] Early, 429–30.                    [137] Gordon, 322.

[138] O. R., 43, pt. 2, pp. 877, 878, 880.        [139] See supra, p. 238.

[140] After the senior Brigadier, Gabriel C. Wharton.

[141] O. R., 43, pt. 1, p. 574; ibid., pt. 2, p. 877; 7 S.H.S.P., 323.

[142] Early, 397; Douglas, 310; 1 N. C. Regts., 173.

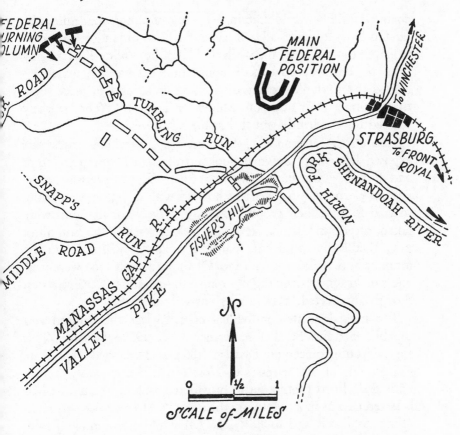

Battlefield of Fisher's Hill, Sept. 22, 1864—after Hotchkiss in *O. R. Atlas,* Plate LXXXII–11

under Early as he had been when Lee was in general command,[143] but he was bold, intelligent and capable of raising the morale of ill-disciplined or discouraged troops. Pegram was an experiment but probably a safe one.

Before Gordon or Ramseur or Pegram had done more than assume their new duties, the woes of the little army were aggravated. "Old Jube" had considered the occupation of Fisher's Hill, which was near Strasburg, as the sole alternative to a retreat southward, up the Valley to one of the gaps opposite Charlottesville or Gordonsville.[144] In this, needless to say, he was correct; but when he took position at Fisher's Hill, he was compelled, as he thought, to occupy the entire distance from the North Fork of the Shenan-

143 Cf. *Gordon,* 317–18.          144 *Early,* 429.

doah to Little North Mountain. This line of almost four miles was far too long for so small a force as Early commanded. In order to cover the front at all, while holding the Valley Pike in any strength, Early decided to dismount Lomax's cavalry, which included the unstable, poorly disciplined units, and to place these troops, under their new commander, on his left.[145] They scarcely sufficed for a skirmish, much less for a battle.

Late on the afternoon of September 22, Sheridan struck this exposed left, swept down it, took up the attack near the centre and forced a disorderly general retreat. The artillerists of the Second Corps had to cover this hurried withdrawal and, in doing so, had to hold their ground too long. Twelve of the guns were taken, a serious loss but, in a more realistic sense, the minimum price that Early could have paid for escape.[146] Casualties in the infantry and artillery were 1235. Of these, almost 1000 were prisoners or stragglers who did not return to the ranks. Cavalry losses, though unreported, were said by Early to be slight.[147]

The most lamented individual casualty was the beloved and capable "Sandie" Pendleton, former A. A. G. to Jackson. This superb young officer on Dec. 29, 1863, had married Miss Kate Corbin, one of the heiresses of Moss Neck,[148] and in May, 1864, he had declined promotion to brigade command because he had believed he was more useful on the staff.[149] After service past reckoning, to Ewell and to Early, he fell while attempting to rally routed troops to form a line South of Fisher's Hill.[150] The next day he died at Woodstock, which by that time was inside the Federal lines. Had he lived five days longer, he would have been 25 years of age.[151]

Staggering, dazed men who had to leave the dying "Sandie" Pendleton in the hands of the enemy were unable to halt for anything more than a rearguard action until September 28. Then they reached Waynesboro, at the foot of the Blue Ridge opposite

---

[145] *Ibid.*, 430; *O. R.*, 43, pt. 1, p. 556.

[146] *Ibid.* General Sheridan's report (*ibid.*, 48–49) should be read with the reminder that battles in execution seldom are as logical as they can be made to appear in subsequent narration.

[147] *Ibid.*, 556.  [148] *Pendleton*, 309.

[149] *Pendleton*, 338.  [150] *Early*, 431; *O. R.*, 43, pt. 1, p. 575.

[151] *Pendleton*, 368 ff; *Douglas*, 312–13. Both these are pathetic accounts of the last hour of this magnificent young man, whom Douglas termed "the most brilliant staff officer in the Army of Northern Virginia."

Rockfish Gap.[152] En route, September 26,[153] the broken Brigades were cheered by the return of Kershaw, who came via Swift Run Gap with about 2700 effectives.[154] By October 5, Rosser's Brigade of 600 cavalry arrived to reinforce Early.[155]

That indomitable Lieutenant General, "bloody but unbowed," wrote later that on the arrival of these reinforcements, who "about made up my losses at Winchester and Fisher's Hill," he determined to take the offensive.[156] In a short time he undertook to do so, with results presently to be described; but, strategically, the chapter that began with the advance to Lynchburg had been ended. Force and results considered, it was a chapter as full of honor as of disaster. Early had succeeded in drawing from the Army of the Potomac the whole of the VI Corps, which was an infantry force larger than his own total strength,[157] had occupied Sheridan and one Division of cavalry from James River, and had compelled the Federals to consolidate against him the troops of Crook and of Averell who might have been engaged in attacks on Confederate supply lines. This was a remarkable achievement for a command that at no stage of operations counted more than 13,200 infantry and about 3700 cavalry. These were the outside figures when Kershaw was in the Valley. Without Kershaw, but counting Fitz Lee, Early never had more than 10,200 infantry and 3700 cavalry, a force steadily and swiftly reduced.[158] Sheridan, as noted already, had 40,000.[159]

The weight of these odds was not realized at Army Headquarters in Petersburg.[160] Even when crediting Sheridan with fewer men than that officer commanded, Lee thought that Early's "reverses," as he termed them, could be "remedied." Said the commanding General, "One victory will put all things right." His chief criticism, voiced only to Early, was "As far as I can judge, at this distance, you have operated more with divisions than with

[152] Early, 432-35; O. R., 43, pt. 1, pp. 49-50, 552, 575-77.
[153] O. R., 43, pt. 1, p. 576; ibid., pt. 2, p. 878.
[154] Early, 435.                [155] Early, 435; O. R., 43, pt. 2, pp. 878-81.
[156] Early, 435.
[157] The VI Corps, as of June 30, had present for duty 18,311 and had an aggregate present of 23,014 (O. R., 40, pt. 2, p. 542). On September 10, Sheridan reported that the Corps had present for duty 12,696 (O. R., 43, pt. 1, p. 61).
[158] The estimate here given is in detail: Second Corps at the beginning of the command, 8000; Breckinridge, 2200; Valley cavalry, 2500; Fitz Lee's cavalry, 1200; Kershaw, 3000, which last figure may be as much as 750 to 1000 in excess of roll-call strength.
[159] See supra, p. 577.                [160] See 3 R. E. Lee, 495.

your concentrated strength."[161] Lee perceived, also,[162] as Early did at length, that next to the heavy odds against which the Valley commander had fought, his defeats had been due to what Early termed "the inefficiency of the greater part of" his cavalry.[163] He did not admit that this inefficiency was attributable, in a measure, to his failure to use a firm hand with his undisciplined troopers. His whole dealing with his mounted forces appeared to be awkward. Early, moreover, was to be charged with some part of the responsibility for a succession of small losses which, in the total, amounted to stern, expensive attrition. In every instance, these casualties resulted from the carelessness or incompetence of one or another of his subordinates, but when costly skirmishes and surprises occur with frequency, there always is a question whether the commanding General has not displayed bad judgment in choosing or in using his lieutenants. Early's most probable answer would have been that he, like Lee, had to make the best of the personnel that was left.

The fullest of apparent failure, with no allowance for the success of his diversion, was charged against Early.[164] Stout as was his heart, he had to admit, after Fisher's Hill, that his troops were "very much shattered, the men very much exhausted . . ."[165] His enemies in the Confederacy did not stop with that. He had created many animosities by his snarling manner and his bitter sarcasms. Now his criticisms came home to him.

Foremost among his adversaries was one of his former Brigadiers, the Governor of Virginia, William Smith. The charges of Smith were the obvious—that Early had been surprised, that his tactics were poor and that he had lost guns. Somewhat more serious was the allegation that the troops no longer believed Early "a safe commander."[166] Lee defended Early and vainly sought the name of an anonymous accuser to whose allegations Smith attached great weight.[167] Smith refused to give names but per-

---

[161] O. R., 43, pt. 2, p. 880.
[162] O. R., 43, pt. 1, p. 559; ibid., pt. 2, p. 891.
[163] O. R., 43, pt. 1, p. 558. Cf. Richmond Enquirer, Sept. 26, 1864.
[164] For comment on Winchester and Fisher's Hill, see Richmond Enquirer, Sept. 22, 23, 26, 1864.
[165] O. R., 43, pt. 1, p. 558.
[166] O. R., 43, pt. 2, p. 894. In contrast, one of Early's junior officers, Capt. James M. Garnett, had noted in his diary, during August (27 S.H.S.P., 1) that Early was, "if possible, too cautious."
[167] O. R., 43, pt. 2, p. 893 ff.

sisted in the correspondence, though he in a degree disqualified himself as a critic by his admission of "some little unfriendliness in my relations with General Early." [168] In a knowledge of the military limitations that had accompanied Smith's personal bravery, professional soldiers might laugh to see him in the rôle of critic. Before the Virginia people, with whom he was most popular, Smith's lack of standing as a professional soldier did not disqualify him. What he was saying, thousands were thinking. For the first time since the Army of Northern Virginia had been reorganized by Lee after the Seven Days, public clamor was rising against one of his senior officers.[169]

[168] Ibid., 894.                       [169] Cf. 18 S.H.S.P., 255–56.

# CHAPTER XXX

## THE DARKENING AUTUMN OF COMMAND

WHILE EARLY was employing in the Shenandoah Valley the Second Corps, Kershaw's Division and Fitz Lee's cavalry, the Confederate Army on the Richmond-Petersburg front consisted of five Divisions of the First and Third Corps, Beauregard's command and two Divisions of cavalry.[1] Most of these thin units had ceaseless trench duty and occasional hard fights in which they scarcely did more than hold off their adversary, who deliberately sought to exhaust them.

It was a grim story. On August 14, at a time when "Old Jubilee" was engaged in his first maneuvers with Sheridan, a strong demonstration was made against the eastern end of the outer defenses of Richmond, where Maj. Gen. Charles Field of the First Corps commanded. He was alert and, in three days of small-scale fighting, he was able to beat off the Federals; but during the fighting of the 16th, two Brigades broke badly. "Not only the day but Richmond," wrote Field, "seemed to be gone."[2] One of these Brigades was that of "Rans" Wright, a veteran command, which was led at the time by its brilliant temporary Brigadier, Victor Girardey.

While Lee in person was planning to disentangle these units of the Confederate left on the Charles City Road, his persistent opponent sought to seize the Weldon Railroad a few miles below Petersburg in the vicinity of Globe Tavern.[3] In Lee's absence, direction of the defense was in the hands of Beauregard. He sent Powell Hill against the Federals with two Brigades of Heth, three of Mahone and three batteries under William J. Pegram. The result on August 19 was a fine local success. Twenty-seven hundred prisoners were taken,[4] but the enemy could not be dislodged

---

[1] The cavalry, it will be remembered, was reduced by Rosser's Brigade, which was sent to Early (*O. R.,* 43, pt. 2, p. 879). As long previously as July, Lee had suggested that Rosser might operate advantageously North of the Virginia Central Railroad (*O. R.,* 37, pt. 2, p. 598; *ibid.,* 40, pt. 3, p. 792).

[2] 14 *S.H.S.P.,* 553.     [3] See the map, p. 539.

[4] These are Powell Hill's figures (*O. R.,* 42, pt. 1, p. 940). Maj. Gen. G. K. Warren, reporting for his own V Corps and for two Divisions of the XI, stated (*ibid.,* 432) that the "missing" for August 18–21 numbered 3152.

immediately from the railroad. Two days later, Hill again under-took to regain the Petersburg and Weldon, by employing Mahone. That officer attacked furiously but in vain. Through a mistake on the part of Hill and Mahone, Johnson Hagood's Brigade was caught inside an angle of the Union line and was shattered. Hagood entered the action with 681 men; he brought out 274.[5] In Nat Harris's small Brigade of 450, no less than 254 were killed, wounded or captured.[6] Heavy as were these casualties, they did not discourage Mahone. He asked and received permission to attack again, but the required fresh Brigades did not arrive in time.[7]

This affair at Globe Tavern, as it was called by both sides, raised a question whether Beauregard in the first instance had employed sufficient force.[8] In the last stages of the fight, there was room for disagreement concerning the reason for failure. Nobody could say that a particular commander had failed, or that any special move had been a mistake. Improved combat by the Federals undoubtedly counted. Odds may of themselves have been an all-sufficient answer, but there had been a time when officers and men would have counted like odds as nothing more than a challenge. The operation, in a word, was disquieting—that and no worse.

Another test followed almost immediately. In a reconnaissance toward Reams' Station, about four and a half miles South of the Tavern, Hampton found the Federal II Corps loosely disposed while tearing up a section of the railroad. By his report of the situation, Hampton so impressed Lee that the commanding General decided to attack at Reams' Station and to do so in numbers adequate to the task, even if the Petersburg trenches had to be stripped to supply the men. On the 24th of August, the blow was struck. Heth and Wilcox attacked in front of the II Corps. Two of Wilcox's Brigades were repulsed roughly, but while Hill's men fought, Hampton slipped to the left of the Federals. There he dismounted his men and assailed the exposed flank. The II Corps was routed. More than 2100 prisoners were taken at a price that probably did not much exceed 720.[9]

[5] O. R., 42, pt. 1, p. 936.                 [6] Ibid., 939.
[7] See the references in 3 R. E. Lee, 487.
[8] Cf. Hill in O. R., 42, pt. 1, p. 940, and Beauregard in ibid., pt. 2, p. 1192.
[9] O. R., 42, pt. 1, p. 940. For the authorities, which on the Confederate side are not numerous, see 3 R. E. Lee, 490, n. 54. A sketch map will be found in ibid., 489. Another is in 3 N. C. Regts., 620.

This Battle of Reams' Station could be accounted a Southern vic- tory, but it did not recover the Petersburg and Weldon Railroad. Nor did it give any permanent assurance that Grant would not seek to destroy the track so thoroughly that even if the Confeder- ates recovered the right of way, they could not use the line. Noth- ing would drive the Union troops away—and keep them away-- except a bloody attack by more troops than Lee could afford to risk. Every aspect of the little battle and of every other engage- ment fought after the Army left Spotsylvania underlined the solemn words the commanding General wrote Secretary Seddon the day before the fight at Reams' Station: "Without some increase of strength, I cannot see how we can escape the natural military consequences of the enemy's numerical superiority." [10]

Apart from a brilliant "cattle raid" by Hampton and Rosser on the 16th of September—a raid that gave hungry Confederates 2468 beeves [11]—there came no action of importance on the Richmond- Petersburg front till the Battles of Winchester and of Fisher's Hill had been fought and lost. Then, while Early was skirmishing around Staunton and Waynesboro,[12] Grant on the 29th of Septem- ber delivered a surprise attack against the Confederate position known as Fort Harrison, on the outer line of the Richmond de- fenses, below Chafin's Bluff. The fort itself was held by so small a force that its loss was no disgrace. Success in holding against Federal assaults the next heavy work to the North, Fort Gilmer, was vastly to the credit of the few defending troops.[13] Although their grip on Fort Gilmer was secure, it was manifest that the loss of Fort Harrison threatened the rear of the works at Chafin's Bluff and thereby endangered the water gate of Richmond. Army Headquarters accordingly decided that the position must be re- covered. For this purpose Field's Division and then Hoke's were sent to the Northside to deliver the assault. The equivalent of a Brigade from Pickett's command was ordered to the vicinity. A

---

[10] O. R., 42, pt. 2, pp. 1199–1200. Cf. ibid., 1228 ff.
[11] For the cattle raid, see Hampton's report, O. R., 42, pt. 1, p. 944 ff; Wells, 287 ff; 22 C. V., 166–67. In this affair an indispensable part was played by one of Hampton's best scouts, Sergt. Geo. D. Shadburne, who deserves a memoir. Some facts about him, probably written by Hampton himself, appear in 3 Land We Love, 349–50. See also Col. U. R. Brooks in Butler's Cavalry and in 22 C. V., 409.
[12] O. R., 43, pt. 1, p. 552.
[13] In addition to the many references cited in 3 R. E. Lee, 501, see 13 C. V., pp. 269, 70, 413–15, 418–20; 21 C. V., 484; 2 R. W. C. D., 295.

Division of cavalry was directed to support any offensive action.[14] Porter Alexander was given twenty-four additional guns and was instructed to direct the artillery in person.[15]

These were preparations on a large scale and they were made under the eyes of the commanding General. With employment of less force, victories had been won in '62. Now, when the assault was delivered on the 30th of September, nothing went well. Through some mistake, "Tige" Anderson advanced beyond his first objective and compelled Field to support him prematurely. Hoke's attack, as at Cold Harbor, was not co-ordinated with that of the other Division. After both had been driven back, Lee called on Hoke's North Carolinians to make another charge. When this was repulsed, they tried a third time, only to fail so tragically that in their withdrawal they did not halt until they were behind cover.[16] Some of Hoke's regiments were wrecked. The Eighth North Carolina, which carried only about 175 officers and men into the first charge, had at the close of action twenty-five men under the command of a Lieutenant, the surviving senior officer.[17] Other regiments suffered almost as severely. There could be no denying the fact that the attack had been a failure and that the operation had been no credit to any of the participating commanders.

While the infantry had been storming Fort Harrison, part of the cavalry under Hampton had been struggling with Federals who seemed to be gambling on the capture of Petersburg or the seizure of the Southside Railroad. This Federal advance was timed shrewdly, but it was resisted on the Vaughan Road with all the tactical resources Hampton could command. He used Calbraith Butler's men to the limit and at the pitch of the emergency he halted and threw into the fight W. H. F. Lee's Division, which was en route to the Northside. With these men, Hampton drove the bluecoats wherever he met them; but he had one contretemps. On the second day of the fighting, September 29, Brig. Gen. James Dearing, who commanded the cavalry of Beauregard's forces,[18] was too sick to take the field. This placed Dearing's troopers under

---

14 O. R., 42, pt. 1, p. 979; 14 S. H. S. P., 555.    15 O. R., 42, pt. 1, p. 859.
16 For the details and the numerous references, see 3 R. E. Lee, 503–04.
17 1 N. C. Regts., 408. Cf. 3 ibid., 213.
18 The Brigade at this date was attached to Butler's Division (O. R., 42, pt. 2, p. 1310).

Col. Joel R. Griffin of the Eighth Georgia. He had in his charge a most important sector, the loss of which would necessitate an extension of line that Hampton with thinned ranks could not afford to make. This was generally known, but it did not avail with Griffin. He lost his entire position, which the bluecoats seized and held.[19]

Hampton must have excoriated him. On receipt of the report of the cavalry commander, even the forbearant Lee felt that an inquiry was essential and that a court martial might be necessary.[20] In spite of Griffin's failure, Hampton was satisfied with the general behavior of his forces. Said he: "The troops behaved as well as possible, and they were well led by their officers." Of his men's counter-attack on September 30 he wrote, "The whole affair was one of the handsomest I have seen, and it reflects the highest credit on the troops engaged in it." [21] This was not an exaggerated appraisal of the action on the Vaughan Road;[22] but—there always was a "but" now—the position wrested from Dearing's Brigade was made the basis of precisely such an extension of front as Confederate Headquarters sought to avoid.[23] It was an extension that could not be met otherwise than at the direst risk.

Before the case of Colonel Griffin was aired or the result of the extension of line apparent, an effort was made to drive the Federals from a small part of the outer line of the Richmond defenses they had won by taking Fort Harrison. The operation was entrusted again to Field and to Hoke, who, as previously, were to be under the direction of the commanding General. According to the simple plan, Mart. Gary's dismounted cavalry and Perry's Florida Brigade were to move secretly until they were East of what had been the outer side of the fortifications when the line had been in Confederate hands. Field was then to dash over the works. On Field's right, Hoke was to attack.

Preparations were made with care. Everything went in accordance with plan on October 7, until it came Hoke's turn to charge. For reasons never explained, he failed to assault. The result was heavy loss for the other units and abandonment of the effort to

19 *O. R.,* 42, pt. 1, p. 947.
20 *O. R.,* 42, pt. 3, p. 1133. The forces operating against Hampton were two Divisions of the V and two of the IX Corps. See Meade's succinct report (*Ibid.,* pt. 1, pp. 31–32).
21 *Ibid.,* pt. 1, pp. 947, 948.
22 The Federals styled it the Battle of Poplar Spring Church.
23 For the details of this extension of front, see 3 *R. E. Lee,* 505.

recover the lost line.[24] To secure Chafin's Bluff from surprise attack, a retrenchment was constructed opposite Fort Harrison.[25] Nothing was said publicly concerning Hoke's responsibility for the failure. Had his record been reviewed, it would have shown at least four and perhaps five instances in which he could have been accused of failing to give his full co-operation in attack. These were: Cold Harbor, June 1; the attack on the Confederate left, near the Appomattox, June 24; the attempt to recover Fort Harrison on September 30, and now this repulse on the exterior line. In three of these four instances, the man with whom Hoke was to co-operate in an attack was Charles W. Field. The other was "Dick" Anderson. In the fifth affair, that at Drewry's Bluff, May 16, Beauregard had placed the blame on Robert Ransom, not on Hoke, but Hoke's activity that day might be subject to reconsideration in the light of what happened later. The record, at best, was not inspiring. Hoke, as a division commander, manifestly was of the type that excels in individual performance, not in teamwork. That charge never could have been brought against him before the Plymouth expedition.[26]

The attack of the 7th of October was the last affair of any importance on the Richmond-Petersburg front prior to two events— one calamitous and the other encouraging—that presently are to be described. To summarize the seven more important clashes during the period between the Battle of the Crater, July 30, and the abandonment of the effort to recover the works adjacent to Fort Harrison, this had been the performance of Lee's lieutenants:

Federal attack of August 14–16: Successfully repulsed by Charles W. Field, but marred by the break of two Brigades.

Affair of Globe Tavern: A Confederate failure in the sense that the enemy seized and held the Petersburg and Weldon Railroad, though he lost more than 3100 prisoners. The action also raised a question whether Beauregard at the outset had used sufficient force.

Battle of Reams' Station, August 24–25: A Confederate success, chiefly through Hampton's effort, without permanent gain.

Cattle raid of September 16: Distinctly to the credit of Hampton and of Rosser.

[24] In 3 R. E. Lee, 507–10, will be found an extended account of this poorly reported action. (The Federals called it the engagement on the Darbytown and New Market Roads. It had no Confederate name.)
[25] It is sketched in 3 R. E. Lee, 510.    [26] See *supra*, p. 335.

Attempt to recover Fort Harrison, September 29: A failure both in co-ordination of attack and in outcome.

Engagement on the Vaughan Road, September 29–October 1: Tactically a fine success for Hampton, for Butler and for W. H. F. Lee, in spite of the break of Dearing's Brigade; strategically a Union victory.

Assault on a section of the Richmond outer line, October 7: A repetition of the failure of September 29.

This was not a record of disgrace but it was a record far below the average achievement of the Confederate command at any comparable period in the Virginia campaigns fought under Lee. Even the small successes of the late summer had been at heavy price in command. On August 16,[27] Brig. Gen. John R. Chambliss was killed in fighting North of James River.[28] Thomas L. Clingman was wounded so severely in the leg, August 19, that his return to the Army was doubtful.[29] In September, Brig. Gen. Goode Bryan resigned because of ill health.[30] On the 1st of October fell Brig. Gen. John Dunovant, who had held commission for slightly more than a month at the head of Calbraith Butler's Brigade of Hampton's cavalry Division.[31] Brig. Gen. John Gregg, he who had led the brilliant charge of May 6 in the Wilderness, was killed October 7, in a clash on the New Market Road.[32] As early as June 11, his famous Brigade had been reduced to 430 muskets, which Gregg had hoped to recruit by visiting the Trans-Mississippi.[33] Denied that privilege, he fought to his last hour.[34] Gregg thus was the fourth general officer Lee lost in a little more than sixty days after the Battle of the Crater. The death of Sanders and that of Victor Girardey have been mentioned already. Add Godwin and Rodes killed in the Valley, and Bryan resigning while his troops were in that region, and the number stricken off the list of active general officers during the same two months was nine.

Another loss was not attributable to death. Until about September 23, Beauregard continued in his somewhat anomalous posi-

---

[27] O. R., 42, pt. 2, p. 213.
[28] Lee wrote Hampton of Chambliss: "His fall will be felt throughout the Army, in which by his courage, energy and skill, he had won for himself an honorable name" (Ibid., 1189).
[29] O. R., 42, pt. 1, p. 858; 4 C. M. H., 301.
[30] As of September 20 (6 C. M. H., 401).
[31] O. R., 42, pt. 1, pp. 947–48; 16 C. V., 183–84; 5 C. M. H., 389–90.
[32] O. R., 42, pt. 1, p. 852.
[33] O. R., 36, pt. 3, p. 894.          [34] 11 C. M. H., Texas, 235–36.

tion as commander of a Department and of the troops he had there before Lee came to the Southside; but with these arrangements, the "Great Creole" was not content. A deeper grievance was the feeling that he, not Early, should have been given command of the forces sent to the Shenandoah Valley. Knowledge of Beauregard's dissatisfaction probably led Davis to arrange a transfer. After a tour of inspection of the defenses of Wilmington and of Charleston, Beauregard was given a supervisory command, the Military Division of the West, which consisted of the five States covered by the commands of John B. Hood and Richard Taylor. Before this assignment was made formally, Beauregard left Virginia in good spirits. Warm affection marked his farewell to Lee and to the staff officers who were not to serve him at his new post. He was glad to go, if not to assume his new duties. There probably was little regret at his departure. A change had come over the man who at Manassas had been anxious to get "Joe" Johnston off the field so that he might have a free hand. Beauregard seemed to be developing a dislike for the responsibility of action. This attitude may have been due to ill health; it may have had its origin in a feeling, scarcely conscious perhaps, that he had a reputation to maintain. If he was concerned over his fame, he manifestly was nearing the end of his usefulness. Every soldier is on the wane from the moment he begins to think more of reputation than of opportunity.[35]

That could not be said of Jubal Early. Regardless of praise or of abuse, he had been unwilling to accept the defeat at Winchester on September 19 and that at Fisher's Hill on the 22nd as the termination of the contest for the Shenandoah. In his camps near Staunton, after Sheridan had withdrawn to Harrisonburg, Early now was meditating a new thrust at his adversary. His impulse to attack was fortified by at least two dispatches from Army Headquarters.[36] In the second of these, Early was told by Lee: "I have weakened myself very much to strengthen you. It was done with the expectation of enabling you to gain such success that you could return the troops if not rejoin me yourself. I know you have endeavored to gain that success, and believe you have done all in your power to insure it. You must not be discouraged, but con-

---

[35] 2 Roman, 274–79; O. R., 42, pt. 2, pp. 1235, 1242 ff; 6 Rowland, 344–45.
[36] O. R., 43, pt. 2, pp. 880–81, 891–92.

tinue to try. I rely upon your judgment and ability, and the hearty cooperation of your officers and men still to secure it. With your united force it can be accomplished." [37]

That was an appeal of a sort to which "Jube" never failed to respond when the signature at the end of the letter was "R. E. Lee, Genl." Besides, reinforcements raised hopes. Kershaw and his fine Division had received a joyful and hilarious welcome on their return to the Valley.[38] Tom Rosser was regarded as a great accession, though, at the time, he could not mount more than 600 men because of the condition of his horses. Fitz Lee was absent, wounded; Brig. Gen. Williams C. Wickham had resigned his commission in order to occupy the seat in the Confederate House of Representatives, to which he had been elected in 1863. He had not been able to attend the first session of the Second Congress.[39] As Rosser was assigned to Lee's Division, which Wickham had been directing temporarily, Rosser's seniority over the Colonels then at the head of the other Brigades gave him command of the Division. This was, of course, in accordance with regulations but it had one unhappy aspect: When Wickham resigned, his Brigade passed to Col. Thomas T. Munford of the Second Virginia, a devoted officer who, it will be remembered, never had received promotion to the rank of Brigadier. Munford had been a Lieutenant Colonel as early as the First Battle of Manassas, when Rosser had been a First Lieutenant.[40] Between the two men, who now must work together, there was blood scarcely less hot than that of "Jeb" Stuart's feud with "Grumble" Jones in 1863.

Rosser did not wait on conciliation or information or anything else. The time of his arrival corresponded to that of Federal withdrawal down the Valley from the vicinity of Harrisonburg to' camps North of New Market, which Early occupied with his infantry on the 7th.[41] By Early's orders,[42] Rosser pressed ahead on the Back and Middle Roads; Lomax proceeded on the Valley Pike The two cavalry commands had several skirmishes on the 8th and on the 9th, at Tom's Brook, not far from Fisher's Hill, they met the strong Federal mounted Divisions of George A. Custer

---

[37] *Ibid.*, 892.  [38] *Gordon*, 331.
[39] 3 *C. M. H.*, 686, 687. He took the oath at the beginning of the second session, Nov. 7, 1864. See 7 *Journal C. S. Congress*, 246.
[40] 3 *C. M. H.*, pp. 639, 658. See *supra*, Vol. I., p. 97.
[41] *Early*, 436.
[42] Early to Rosser, MS, Oct. 7, 1864, 7 P.M.—*Rosser MSS.*

and Wesley Merritt. These hard-hitting blue troopers were under Maj. Gen. A. T. A. Torbert whose orders from Sheridan were "to whip the rebel cavalry or get whipped" himself.[43] The result was the rout of Rosser and then of Lomax with the loss of eleven guns and, Sheridan boasted, of "everything else . . . carried on wheels." [44] Rosser filed no report of this affair which, in the judgment of his critic Munford, was "the greatest disaster that ever befell our cavalry during the whole war." [45] Lomax attributed his part of the defeat to the condition of the artillery horses and to the distance from infantry support of his men who, said he, were "without proper arms or discipline." [46]

Early was not deterred by this minor disaster from pursuing his offensive. He moved to Fisher's Hill on the 12th–13th of October and found the enemy on the north bank of Cedar Creek. After reconnaissance, Early concluded that the Federal position was too strong to be assailed by his small force unless necessity was pressing. Consequently he waited in the hope that his opponent would retire or attack. Sheridan did neither. By the 17th Early had consumed most of his provisions. He was in a country that the Federals systematically had devastated in order that it might be, in Sheridan's words, "a barren waste." [47] No supplies could be procured by Early from farms within hauling distance of his lines. "I was now compelled," Early explained later, "to move back for want of provisions and forage, or attack the enemy in his position with the hope of driving him from it, and I determined to attack." [48]

The course both of the North Fork of the Shenandoah and of sinuous Cedar Creek made a frontal assault impossible. Early, in consequence, had to shape a flank operation. After reconnoitering from Massanutton Mountain, John B. Gordon and Jed. Hotchkiss urged the Lieutenant General to launch this flank movement from his right. This, the two officers said, would involve a difficult night march around the corner of the mountain, South of the river, but it held the promise of an advantageous first blow, perhaps of a surprise. Gordon was so confident of success that he said he would assume responsibility for failure.[49]

43 O. R., 43, pt. 1, p. 431.       44 Ibid., 51.
45 13 S. H. S. P., 134.             46 O. R., 34, pt. 1, p. 613.
47 O. R., 43, pt. 1, p. 50.         48 Early, 438.
49 Gordon, 335.

Early accepted these conclusions. At 2 o'clock on the afternoon of October 18, he met his division commanders and explained to them a plan which he changed in one particular because of information John Pegram brought. "Old Jubilee" had not forgotten that Lee had thought him too much disposed to fight his battles by Divisions rather than with his full strength, and he had determined to throw into the next battle all his troops of all three arms.

In final form, his plan was as follows: John B. Gordon, senior Major General since the death of Rodes, was to take the three Divisions of the Second Corps, was to march in the darkness around the edge of Massanutton, was to cross the Shenandoah at Bowman's Ford and was to move to a house, J. Cooley's, slightly more than a mile and a quarter North of the ford. There Gordon was to deploy for the attack. His immediate objective was to be Belle Grove, a conspicuous farm site, which was believed to be Sheridan's Headquarters. Kershaw's Division was to proceed through Strasburg, turn to the Northeast, cross Cedar Creek at Bowman's Mill and strike northward against the left of the force Gordon was to attack in front. Gabriel Wharton's Division, Breckinridge's old command, was to move up the Pike, secure the bridge across Cedar Creek and join in the attack. Rosser, with his own troopers and Wickham's Brigade, was to engage the enemy's cavalry opposite the Confederate left. Lomax was to proceed via Front Royal, was to co-operate with the forces on the Valley Pike, and was to move to Newtown or to Winchester as circumstance might impel. Payne's small cavalry Brigade was to accompany Gordon and was to make the capture of Sheridan its particular mission. The artillery was to have Hupp's Hill as its station. Rosser, Gordon and Kershaw were to attack in that order at 5 o'clock, just before daybreak. The other columns were to advance when they heard the sound of the firing.[50]

It was an elaborate plan but it did not seem too ambitious for veteran troops. No question concerning any particular aspect of it was raised. Lomax's part in the action appears to have been considered fit employment for half, or nearly half, of the cavalry. Everyone knew, of course, that some of the regiments did not have fifty per cent of their quota of officers, but this was accepted as a

[50] *Early* 440–42.

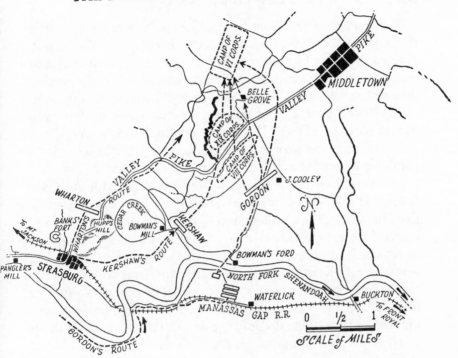

Early's Plan for Attacking the Federal Camps on Cedar Creek, Oct. 19, 1864—after Hotchkiss in *O. R. Atlas,* Plate LXXXII–9

condition which could not be corrected and therefore should be disregarded.[51]

Most of the Generals were confident; some were enthusiastic. Dodson Ramseur was full of excitement, and not solely because of the prospect of the battle. On the night of the 16th, an officer of the signal corps had delivered him a message that had been wig-wagged or flashed from peak to peak down the Valley. The signal read, somewhat mysteriously, "The crisis is over and all is well." This meant that his baby had been born, but whether it was boy or girl, and how the mother had fared, he did not know. He wrote on the 17th in gratitude and perplexity and asked for details. "Tell Sis Mary," he said, "for pity's sake, if not for love's sake, write me a long letter about my little Wife and baby." Then, boyishly he added: "Oh Me! I want to see you so bad!"[52]

51 The fullest reports on the shortage of officers are those filed by the inspectors of Wharton's Division, for which see *O. R.,* 43, pt. 1, p. 595 ff.
52 Dodson Ramseur to his wife, MS, Oct. 17–18. *Ramseur MSS.*

Ramseur's chief and friend, John Gordon, was moving most of the night of October 18–19, by a route that required the men to proceed in Indian file, but they had none of the familiar click and clatter because they had left their canteens and all their cooking utensils behind them. "The long gray line," said Gordon reminiscently, "like a great serpent glided noiselessly along the dim pathway above the precipice." [53] Before dawn the entire Second Corps was waiting in the shadows close to the river, in which, at Bowman's Ford, stood the Federal vedettes on their horses.[54]

Not more than a mile away, opposite Bowman's Mill on Cedar Creek, "Old Jube" was waiting. He had not been able physically to climb to the crag of Massanutton, whence Gordon and Hotchkiss had viewed the Federal camps,[55] but he had not been willing to remain behind at Army Headquarters. Consequently he had marched with Kershaw and, at 3:30 A.M., had come within sight of the Federal campfires across the creek. The moon, which had been full on the 15th, shone brightly, high in the heavens, and lighted the tents of the sleeping enemy. Behind cover, in his sharp voice, Early pointed out to the South Carolinians the position of the Federals and explained the nature of the ground. He knew he had to deal with the VI Corps, which, it will be remembered, Grant had sent Sheridan when Early had threatened Washington. In addition, Early was aware that Sheridan had the VIII and XIX Corps, neither of which was considered redoubtable. To overrun the camps of these troops, and to rout them, Early gave carefully his instructions for advance in column of Brigades. It was a great hour for "Jube," an hour of vengeance for Winchester and Fisher's Hill. A few miles up the Valley Pike, beyond the Federal camps, was Middletown, where Jackson had caught Banks's wagon train that famous 24th of May, 1862. "Old Jack," who had been kind to "Jube" in his strange, half-shy, half-detached way, seldom had enjoyed such an opportunity for surprise as his lieutenant had fashioned for himself now.

"Old Jube" watched closely the passage of the minutes and at 4:30 ordered Kershaw across the creek. No opposition was encountered. As the men formed in column North of the stream Early heard from the extreme left the sound of Rosser's guns and from

[53] *Gordon*, 336.      [54] *Ibid.*, 337.
[55] *Early*, 440.

the right the rattle of Gordon's picket fire at the ford.[56] Everything was proceeding according to plan and time-schedule! "Jube" saw the Carolinians take their position quickly and confidently. His black eyes must have kindled when they started forward. A participant remembered, years after: "As we emerged from a thicket into the open we could see the enemy in great commotion, but soon the works were filled with half-dressed troops, and they opened a galling fire upon us. The distance was too great in this open space to take the works by a regular advance in line of battle, so the men began to call for orders to 'charge.' Whether the order was given or not, the troops with one impulse sprang forward." [57]

Their rush cleared the camp of the VIII Corps and carried them on to an elevation, below Belle Grove, where the XIX Corps was in confusion. Early observed and rejoiced and hurried off to Hupp's Hill, where Wharton and the artillery were to take position. When Early drew rein, the first of the faithful old batteries of the Second Corps was galloping into place. As if to applaud the advance of the artillery, there swelled from the rear of the Federals the furious fire of Gordon's men. Above that soon roared the Union guns in the works Northeast of Hupp's Hill and to the left of the turnpike. This did not disturb Col. Tom Carter, who had long experience in maneuvering his batteries under fire. While "Jube" stood by, the Colonel placed his fieldpieces and soon had the satisfaction of seeing the enemy evacuate the high ground. In a few minutes more, Early joyfully watched some of his own troops—he could not tell which—pour over the works in pursuit of the retreating enemy.[58]

The sun was now rising, but in low places fog hung heavily. Smoke drifted and shifted. Through it, Early could not observe to what line the enemy was retiring, but he rode triumphantly forward and on the next hill met Gordon. The Georgian reported many prisoners and guns. Two of his Divisions were successfully engaged and the third, Pegram's, ordered forward. With few words, Gordon rode off to supervise the further deployment of these three Divisions, which were more than he ever had handled in action.[59] After Gordon left him, Early went down the Pike to

[56] *Early,* 443.                        [57] *Dickert,* 447–48.
[58] These were Kershaw's men, though some of Gordon's, according to Hotchkiss' map, passed directly in rear of the fortifications. See *O. R. Atlas,* Plate LXXXII–9.
[59] *Early,* 444.

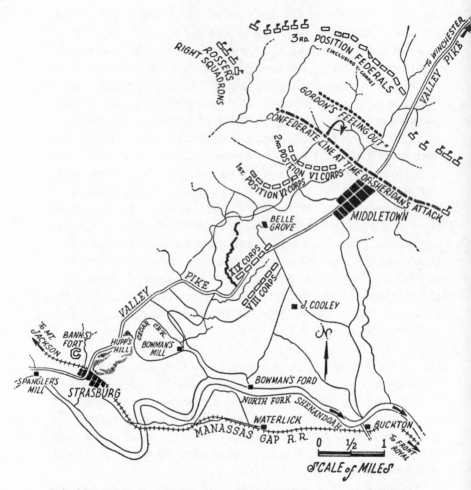

Federal Lines of Battle and Successive Positions of the VI Corps, with sketch of the Confederate line prior to Sheridan's attack at Cedar Creek, Oct. 19, 1864—after Hotchkiss in O. R. Atlas, Plate LXXXII–9

reconnoiter. Before he had gone far, he met Ramseur and Pegram, who told him they were facing the VI Corps, and needed troops to fill a gap on their right. "Old Jube" probably did not observe it, but Ramseur was in the highest spirits. "Douglas," he cried joyously as he passed the Virginian, "I want to win this battle, for I must see my wife and baby!" [60] Early was thinking of reserves,

---

[60] *Douglas,* 317. Gordon (*op. cit.,* 64) quoted Ramseur as saying before the attack began, "Well, General, I shall get my furlough today." After the battle, Gordon felt that this was a premonition, but evidently he misunderstood what Ramseur meant. The North Carolinian was resolved to fight so hard that he would earn his furlough.

not of domestic bliss, and he ordered to the right the Division of Wharton, which had no adversary in its front.[61] In a short time Wharton moved into the gap and advanced. He ran into a heavy fire from the VI Corps, and he fell back to the line of Pegram, but he did not have to beat off a counter-attack.[62]

The VI Corps, which had been driven from its position North of Belle Grove, now was rallying on what became known as the "second position" of the day. Other units of the VIII and the XIX fled to the Northwest of Middletown; Wright's men formed directly West of the town. They endeavored to stay there and for a time they fought hard. It was in vain. They had lost most of their guns in the first Confederate onrush and they could not long resist the concentrated artillery that Colonel Carter brought to bear on them. Between 9 and 10 o'clock, the VI fell back to the "third position" where Crook's troops and the XIX Corps were waiting the next turn of the battle.[63]

By the time Early advanced to examine this position, a bright sun had driven away the fog. As he heard the news of success all along the line, "his face," a staff officer wrote of Early, "became radiant with joy, and in his gladness he exclaimed, 'the sun of Middletown, the sun of Middletown!' "[64] It was his Austerlitz.

"Well, Gordon," he exclaimed when next he met the Major General who was leading brilliantly the Second Corps, "this is glory enough for one day!" Early went on: "This is the 19th. Precisely one month ago today we were going in the opposite direction."

Gordon had abundant reason to remember the 19th of September at Winchester, but his thought was of the battle in progress: "It is very well so far, General; but we have one more blow to strike, and then there will not be left an organized company of infantry in Sheridan's army."

He pointed as he spoke to the front of the VI Corps and explained what he intended to do. Early listened but did not appear

---

[61] *Early,* 445.          [62] *Ibid.*

[63] The time of the withdrawal of the VI Corps given on Sheridan's map (*O. R., Atlas,* Plate XCIX–2), is 9 A.M., but this, needless to say, was approximate. Col. J. M. Warner, 11th Vermont, commanding the 1st Brigade, 2nd Division, and Bvt. Brig. Gen. J. Warren Keifer, 110th Ohio, commanding the 2nd Brigade, 3rd Division (*O. R.,* 43, pt. 1, pp. 201, 226–27), gave the most detailed timing of this phase of the retreat. Their reports indicate that the withdrawal to the position North and Northwest of Middletown was between 9:30 and 10:00 A.M.

[64] Capt. S. V. Southall in *Gordon,* 359.

to be impressed. "No use in that," he said, "they will all go directly!"

Gordon answered: "This is the VI Corps, General. It will not go unless we drive it from the field."

"Yes, it will go, directly." [65]

Writing of this years afterward, Gordon said: "My heart went into my boots. Visions of the fatal halt on the first day at Gettysburg, and of the whole day's hesitation to permit an assault on Grant's exposed flank on the 6th of May in the Wilderness rose before me." [66] Gordon said no more. Nor did Early. What was deep in the mind of "Old Jube" at the moment, history will never know. If he correctly recorded his state of mind in his military autobiography, he believed at the time of the conversation with Gordon that the victory had been won. He did not know that Sheridan had been absent from the battle and, at the first news of it, had been quick to throw himself on his horse and to start for Cedar Creek. It seemed incredible to Early that a Federal Army which had lost 1300 prisoners and eighteen guns [67] would attempt to stand. It had been beaten; it should be in retreat; it soon would be.

After 10 A.M., then, "Jube" waited for the Federals to leave their position Northwest of Middletown. Soon he heard that many of his soldiers and even some of his officers [68] were plundering the deserted camps of the enemy. The General had seen some evidence of this as he had ridden forward after the first rout of the Federals, and he had ordered one of Wharton's battalions to clear the camps. Now he sent back staff officers to stop this renewal of the plundering. Division commanders were instructed to recall their men to the front. General Gordon insisted subsequently that the men who went through the Federal tents in search of clothing, money and food were comparatively few in number. They were not, he maintained, soldiers from the ranks but disabled men who had not been assigned places in action. [69] Neither then nor thereafter

---

[65] This colloquy scarcely can have been reported with literal accuracy. The exchange may have occurred before the VI Corps was driven from its second position; but as Gordon did not mention in his narrative any subsequent withdrawal by the Corps, he may have confused the incidents of the bombardment of the VI Corps in its second position with Early's failure to attack the third position, Northwest of Middletown.

[66] *Gordon*, 342.                                 [67] *O. R.*, 43, pt. 1, p. 561.

[68] *Ibid.*, 562.

[69] See *Gordon*, 365 ff, and particularly 368, for evidence which is late but convincing.

would "Jube" admit this. Both he and Gordon overlooked the fact that if plundering was extensive and was not stopped, it was because of the lack of officers.

As the forenoon passed, the thought of the wreck of his Divisions by absentees began to sap Early's soldierly vigor. His state of mind changed subtly and progressively from one of confidence to one of concern. Further, the appearance of an increasing force of cavalry on his right began to alarm him. Early had on· that flank, immediately available, only the Brigade of Col. W. H. Payne,[70] which counted no more than 300 sabres.[71] Lomax, it will be remembered, had been ordered to proceed by way of Front Royal, to co-operate with the column on the Valley Pike and to move to Newtown or to Winchester as conditions would admit.[72] He had sent word that he had crossed the North Fork of the Shenandoah in the face of some opposition and that he was advancing. Early at once dispatched imperative instructions for Lomax to move as quickly as possible to Middletown, but the commanding General had no assurance when or even whether Lomax could reach the field.[73] Rosser was fighting vigorously and shrewdly on the Confederate left. With a heavy force in his front, Rosser could do little more, Early reasoned, than to hold his own.[74] There was no possibility that he could help on the right and no suggestion that he try.

The uncertainty of Early's mind and his concern over the threat of a cavalry attack were heightened by an unusual confusion on the field. Kershaw and Gordon were hurrying about to organize their line. Early kept changing his post. Because most of his staff officers had been sent to discipline the plunderers, he did not have a sufficient number of competent men at hand to see that his other orders were executed. In one instance, even before the Federals occupied their third position, a headquarters staff officer had decided on his own account not to deliver Gordon one of Early's orders because he concluded that Gordon could not execute it.[75]

---

[70] This consisted of the remnant of Lomax's old Brigade, to which other skeleton regiments had been added. Colonel Payne had assumed command by seniority when Lomax became head of a Division. An excellent officer, Payne was promoted Brigadier as of Nov. 1, 1864, under the act of Oct. 13, 1862, for the appointment of twenty general officers. See Vol. II, p. 256 and *Wright*, pp. 135, 139.

[71] *Early*, 440.

[72] See *supra*, p. 598 and *O. R.*, 43, pt. 1, p. 613.

[73] *Early*, 446; *O. R.*, 43, pt. 1, pp. 562, 613.

[74] *Early*, 446–47.          [75] *Early*, 446.

At last, after hesitant delay and with manifest misgiving, Early ordered Gordon to advance and, with the help of Kershaw, to drive the enemy from the third position; but he instructed his messenger to say that if Gordon found the enemy's line too strong, the assault was not to be made.[76] In the first stage of the advance that then began, an initial repulse of the Second Corps led Early to conclude that Gordon had abandoned the effort.[77] In reality, the fiery Gordon did not regard the repulse as anything more than a preliminary. All Gordon's wishes, all his hopes, all his judgment, were on the side of a furious, smashing assault. If he fell back, it was to renew the assault.[78] Early did not think so, and may not have believed the advance he ordered to be made by Gordon was wise or could be successful.

By successive stages, then, the triumphant Early who had acclaimed the "sun of Middletown" was reduced to confusion and perplexity of mind. He determined to suspend further attack, at least until the arrival of Lomax, and to content himself with securing his prisoners and his captured property.[79] Early's decision to do this was not made known to his subordinates. Said General Wharton afterward: "I supposed we were arranging for a general movement to the front, and expected every minute orders to advance; but no orders came, and there we stood—no enemy in our front for hours, except some troops moving about in the woodland on a hill nearly a mile in our front." [80]

The captured guns were moved across Cedar Creek; the prisoners were started on the long march to Staunton; the advances of the enemy's cavalry on the right were beaten off; [81] Lomax did not arrive or report again. Gordon and some of his officers began to sense a counterstroke and pleaded with Early to strengthen the

[76] *Early,* 447. [77] *Ibid.*
[78] In *Gordon,* 365, appeared the statement that "no such order ever reached us as the one which General Early sent." From the context it is almost certain that Gordon was referring to instructions to assault the third position of the enemy. Early's report (*O. R.,* 43, pt. 1, p. 562) bore out this interpretation; but when Early came to write his military autobiography (p. 446), the changes he made in the text of his previous *Memoir,* p. 108, show plainly that he was not certain what condition prevailed on the battlefield at the time he issued the orders for an attack on the enemy's position. He may have confused orders for an assault on the second position with those for an attack on the third. It consequently is not possible to do more than to make a guess concerning the time at which this order was issued.
[79] So Early in his report of Oct. 21, 1864 (*O. R.,* 43, pt. 1, p. 562). In his late writings, he made no reference to any design to await the arrival of Lomax, and said only: "I determined, therefore, to try and hold what had been gained."
[80] Quoted in *Gordon,* 361. [81] *O. R.,* 43, pt. 1, pp. 562, 581.

left, which manifestly was weak and exposed. All that Early could suggest was that Gordon extend the flank and put more artillery in position.[82]

Nothing else happened until about 4:30. Then, while the Confederates stood idle, though now expecting a blow, the enemy launched a swift, oblique attack exactly where it could do most harm—on the left. So thinly held was this flank that the Federals quickly found what was, in effect, a gap between Evans and York of Gordon's Division.[83] The left offered such resistance as it could, but it collapsed quickly. Knowing their position hopeless, veteran troops started for Cedar Creek.

When Kershaw's and Ramseur's Divisions found that Gordon's men had given way, they, too, started for the rear. Panic began to show itself. Fortunately, the artillery remained under the direction of Colonel Carter, who was as efficient as at Seven Pines or at Sharpsburg. Defiantly his guns covered the first stage of the retreat. Presently, through the efforts of Gordon, of Ramseur, and of every courageous officer who could wield a sword or shout a command, a halt was made. It was not for long. Discipline was shaken. Leaders began to fall. Dodson Ramseur, never more magnificent in battle, received a wound, which he ignored. Soon he felt his horse going down under him. Quickly he changed to another and rode among his men to encourage their stand. The second horse was shot. A moment later a bullet entered his right side and tore through both lungs.[84] Devoted followers hurried him to the rear, but in his absence the temporary line sagged and broke.

This time there was no stopping the men. "They would not listen to entreaties, threats or appeals of any kind. A terror of the enemy's cavalry had seized them, and there was no holding them." So reported Early.[85] He did his utmost to halt the fugitives, but as he saw entire Brigades running for the creek, he had to order to the rear the small commands of Wharton and of Pegram, which

---

[82] *Gordon,* 347.
[83] According to General Sheridan's report (*O. R.,* 43, pt. 1, p. 53), the thin Confederate line had been so extended on the left that it overlapped his right, but the maps indicate that this was little more than a slight refusal of the Southern left with six guns of Capt. Lorraine F. Jones's and Capt. Asher W. Garber's Batteries of Cutshaw's Battalion, Carter's Artillery reserve. See *O. R. Atlas,* Plate LXXXII–9.
[84] *O. R.,* 43, pt. 1, p. 562; 18 *S.H.S.P.,* 257.
[85] *O. R.,* 43, pt. 1, p. 562.

had been on the extreme right and had not been involved in the break.[86]

The artillery maintained its intelligent discipline and continued to cover the mad retreat. Prisoners, captured fieldpieces and most of the Federal wagons had been passed to the south side of the creek before the panic began. Colonel Carter skillfully brought his guns down to the crossing and got them over. Early rode furiously about in an effort to stop the infantry, and he swore that if he could get even 500 men to make a stand, the day could be saved.[87]

Instead of a rally, there came a new alarm. Rosser had been compelled to retire on the left, though he continued to delay slightly the advance of the strong Federal squadrons. At length, as he gave ground, they struck the Valley Pike West of the crossing of Cedar Creek and, dashing on toward Strasburg, got among the wagons and the retreating artillery at Hupp's Hill. Some of the blue troopers pushed on West of Strasburg to Spangler's Mill and broke a bridge which had been damaged and repaired earlier in the day.[88] The guns and wagons between Hupp's Hill and Spangler's Mill thus were at the mercy of the Federals. All the vehicles captured during the morning, some that belonged to the Confederates, and a total of forty-three pieces of artillery, Union and Confederate, were taken.[89]

At Fisher's Hill, whither the escaping teamsters flocked, Early undertook another rally. Failing in this, he had to retreat to New Market and, in humiliation, to report the disaster. In his first telegraphic summary [90] he attributed his defeat to the panic that followed the enemy's attack. By the 21st, when he wrote a more detailed report, Early had convinced himself that the pillaging of the Federal camps was the reason he had not pursued his advantage during the forenoon of the 19th. He wrote: "We had within our grasp a glorious victory, and lost it by the uncontrollable propensity of our men for plunder, in the first place, and the subsequent panic among those who had kept their places . . ." [91]

While Early doubtless believed all this and considered it a suffi-

<hr>

[86] *Ibid.*       [87] *Ibid.; Early,* 449.
[88] *O. R.,* 43, pt. 1, pp. 581–82.
[89] *Ibid.* Early reported on the 21st that his net loss of artillery was twenty-three guns (*ibid.,* 560). For the next extended references to Gordon, see *infra,* p. 628 ff.
[90] *Ibid.*       [91] *O. R.,* 43, pt. 1, pp. 562–63.

cient explanation, he was too intelligent a man and too experienced a soldier not to know that he had blundered ruinously in failing to press the attack against the third line after the VI Corps had left its second position. He showed this with curious naiveté. When he sent his report to Richmond by Jed. Hotchkiss, he admonished the engineer—to quote Hotchkiss' words—"not to tell General Lee that we ought to have advanced in the morning at Middletown, for, said he, we ought to have done so." [92] More bluntly, "Jube" told some of his officers, "The Yankees got whipped; we got scared." [93]

Neither then nor thereafter—such was his peculiar ineptitude for dealing with cavalry—did Early realize how he had weakened himself and had invited disaster by his optimistic detachment of 1700 of his 3900 mounted troops,[94] to operate under vague instructions against the rear of an adversary he hoped to rout.[95] He lamented several times that there was open country on his flank but he never once admitted that he might have given his right a considerable measure of protection by keeping Lomax, instead of Payne, immediately on that flank. Payne readily might have been assigned the more remote mission. His weakness scarcely would have hampered him. Not much more than patrol of the roads that led to Early's rear from the district of Front Royal and Cedarville could have been accomplished by any cavalry force Early could afford to detach. As it was, he sent off, to no good purpose, far more men than he could spare in dealing with an opponent whose mounted forces were powerful and were admirably led.

Through the detachment of Lomax, the fatal delay at Middletown and a certain relaxation of grip after the action was joined, Early lost more than the twenty-three guns and the 1600 prisoners [96] Sheridan captured. Irreplaceable veterans were lost by death and wounds. Brig. Gen. James Conner had been wounded in the preliminaries of October 13,[97] and as the injury was in the same leg that had been injured during the Seven Days, amputation had

[92] O. R., 43, pt. 1, p. 582.          [93] Douglas, 319.
[94] It is not certain whether Early included Payne's 300 in crediting Rosser with 1200 (Early, 451).
[95] Lomax's report (O. R., 43, pt. 1, p. 613) shows that his instructions gave him little opportunity of reaching the battlefield in time to influence the outcome.
[96] So Sheridan reported (O. R., 43, pt. 1, p. 33); the number may be high.
[97] This is the date given by Hotchkiss (O. R., 43, pt. 1, p. 579). In Conner, 168 n, October 14 is mentioned. This may have been the date of the operation which followed the wound.

been necessary.[98] Cullen Battle, another Brigadier of much promise, had been hit during the fight of the 19th.[99] As the bullet had entered the knee, there was small chance that he would recover sufficiently in many months to resume command.[100]

Worst of all was the case of Dodson Ramseur. In spite of unrelaxing efforts to get him off the field, he had to be left in the hands of the enemy. Friends in the Union Army carried him to the headquarters of General Sheridan, where Union doctors labored with a Confederate surgeon to save him. Conscious at intervals in his pain, Ramseur knew that his wound was fatal but he faced the end with the courage that always had mounted with the emergency. As he was dying, he sent messages to his comrade Hoke, to his wife and to the baby he had yearned to see.[101]

A defeat was doubled in cost when it took that superb young combat officer. Other losses of regimental and company officers were so extensive that some commands were almost without leaders. In the ranks the price had not been excessive. Total Southern casualties, exclusive of prisoners, were not thought by Early to exceed 1000, which figure probably was too low.[102] Sheridan estimated his losses as "between 3000 and 4000," [103] but they proved to be 5665.[104]

The battle had not been without fine performance. All phases of the advance had been admirable. Many individual officers had outdone their previous valiant records. In the annals of the artillery of the Army of Northern Virginia nothing had been finer than the manner in which Col. Tom Carter's men had covered the retreat of the infantry. Early was careful in his report to commend the gunners even when he had to condemn the behavior of the men who had won fame as Jackson's "foot-cavalry." He wrote: "The artillery throughout, from first to last, in this as well as in all the actions I have had, behaved nobly, both officers and men, and not a piece of artillery has been lost by any fault of theirs." Then Early added significantly: "I attribute this good conduct on their part to the vast superiority of the officers. Colonel Carter and all his battalion commanders richly deserve promotion."

[98] *Conner,* loc. cit.     [99] *Early,* 450–51.

[100] 7 *C. M. H.,* Ala., 392.

[101] 5 *Land We Love,* 7–8; 18 *S.H.S.P.,* 257; Charles Huger to Mrs. Dodson Ramseur, MS, Nov. 12, 1864—*Ramseur MSS.*

[102] *O. R.,* 43, pt. 1, p. 560.

[103] *Ibid.,* 34.     [104] *Ibid.,* 137

Much more "Old Jube" might have added, but he proceeded logically in his report to his own responsibility. The defeats of his troops, he said, were "due to no want of effort on my part, though it may be that I have not the capacity or judgment to prevent them." He proceeded to tell Lee: "I have labored faithfully to gain success, and I have not failed to expose my person and to set an example to my men. I know that I shall have to endure censure from those who do not understand my position and difficulties, but I am still willing to make renewed efforts. If you think, however, that the interests of the service would be promoted by a change of commanders, I beg you to have no hesitation in making the change. The interests of the service are far beyond any mere personal considerations, and if they require it I am willing to surrender my command into other hands. Though this affair has resulted so disastrously to my command, yet I think it is not entirely without compensating benefits. The VI Corps had already begun to move off to Grant and my movement brought it back, and Sheridan's forces are now so shattered that he will not be able to send Grant any efficient aid for some time. I think he will be afraid to trust the VIII and XIX Corps." [105]

Had "Old Jube" enjoyed access to the records of Lew Wallace's and of Sheridan's Medical Directors, he could have added that he had put out of action between the 1st of July and the 20th of October the equivalent of a Federal Corps or, roughly, as many Federals as he had infantry in any single engagement of the campaign. Not less than 14,500 Federals had to be charged against Early and his Army.[106] After the war, when Early was free to tell all that had happened, he insisted that he had been outnumbered three to one—a fact that could not be made known during the course of the campaign. He was not far wrong in his estimate. Sheridan often had odds of two and a half, or two and three quarters to one. Early did not dwell, as in self-defense he might, on the fact that Lee consistently and most seriously underestimated the force Sheridan employed in the Valley. No other mathematical calculation made by Lee during the war was so much in error.[107]

[105] O. R., 43, pt. 1, pp. 563–64.
[106] Monocacy, 1294 (O. R., 37, pt. 1, p. 202); Winchester, 5018 (O. R., 43, pt. 1, p. 118); Fisher's Hill, 528 (ibid., 124); Cedar Creek, 5665 (ibid., 137). Casualties of the many miscellaneous minor actions are here put at 2000, which is a conservative figure.
[107] Cf. 3 R. E. Lee, 495.

The final explanation given by Early anticipated a natural question: "It may be asked why with so small a force I made the attack [at Cedar Creek]. I can only say we had been fighting large odds during the whole war, and I knew there was no chance of lessening them. It was of the utmost consequence that Sheridan should be prevented from sending troops to Grant, and General Lee, in a letter received a day or two before, had expressed an earnest desire that a victory should be gained in the Valley if possible,[108] and it could not be gained without fighting for it." [109]

That was bravely said, and truly said, but in the darkening autumn of the Confederacy it could not be stated in public, nor would it have been credited if proclaimed. Early had retreated from Washington when it had seemed within his grasp; he had been routed at Winchester, routed at Fisher's Hill, routed at Cedar Creek. That could only mean incompetence, mismanagement and the loss of the confidence of his officers and men. So ran the public indictment. Under it, a disappointed South tried and condemned "Old Jube" and clamored for his head. Few there were to say that Early was acting in accordance with orders and in unquestioning loyalty, personal as well as military, to the chief he so much admired and so little resembled.[110]

[108] The reference evidently is to Lee's dispatch of October 12, 1864, for which see O. R., 43, pt. 2, p. 891. Cf. supra, pp. 595–96.
[109] Early, 452.
[110] For the continuance of the sketch of Early, see infra, p. 635.

# CHAPTER XXXI

## DISCIPLINE AND DESERTION

WHEN THE GRIEVOUS news of Early's rout and Ramseur's death reached Army Headquarters, Lee had with him again his senior lieutenant to share the heavier burden the defeat in the Valley imposed. Longstreet returned the day the battle of Cedar Creek was fought.[1] Although his right arm still was half paralyzed, he had taught himself to write with his left hand and he cherished some hope of ultimate recovery.[2] Long absence from the Army had not destroyed the strategical complex he had developed during the Suffolk campaign. He was fertile in suggestion and vigorous in discipline from the hour he assumed command on the north side of the James[3]—and equally careful to stipulate, when he was to share any of the moves he proposed, that he have ample troops.[4]

For the maneuvers he executed and the more numerous operations he planned, he had a few more of his tested lieutenants. Some of his wounded Brigadiers and some of Hill's had come back to the line. By October the roster of officers did not seem quite so unfamiliar as it had been immediately after the Battle of the Crater. McGowan, Kirkland and Lane had resumed command in August. Archer, much shaken by imprisonment, had been exchanged.[5] A few others came later, but there was no replacing such men as "Jeb" Stuart, Robert Rodes, Dodson Ramseur and some of the brigade commanders who had been killed after the Battle of the Wilderness. "Alas," wrote War Clerk Jones, when he set down the casualties of Third Winchester, "the chivalry have fallen!"[6]

---

[1] O. R., 42, pt. 1, p. 871. For circumstances of his convalescence, see O. R., 51, pt. 2, p. 1017; ibid., 40, pt. 2, pp. 661, 664; pt. 3, pp. 775, 792.

[2] O. R., 42, pt. 3, p. 1140; Sorrel, 265; Southern Generals, 319–20.

[3] For final definition of his authority there, see Lee to Longstreet, MS, Feb. 3, 1865—Fairfax MSS.

[4] The following references cover his principal suggestions and moves to Feb. 25, 1865: O. R., 42, pt. 3, pp. 1222–23 ff, 1267, 1270, 1286–87, 1290; ibid., 51, pt. 2, p. 1056; ibid., 46, pt. 2, pp. 1189, 1192, 1203, 1229, 1233–34, 1253–54.

[5] For details, see 3 R. E. Lee, 496 n. 35.    [6] 2 R. W. C. D., 288.

In the hearts of some of the survivors, hope was dying. Long-street himself was losing faith in victory. He and his division commanders had followed the news of the appointment of their magnetic comrade John Hood to succeed "Joe" Johnston in command of the Army of Tennessee; and early in September, they read that Hood had evacuated Atlanta. All men could see then that the Southern cause was losing in Georgia, and not in Georgia only. Lee had been compelled on October 4 to warn the Secretary of War that Richmond might be captured.[7] November brought the re-election of Lincoln and the assurance of a fight to the finish. Among the less determined, a certain apathy was showing itself. From the trenches of Petersburg an observant young artillerist wrote, "Living cannot be called a fever here but rather a long cata-lepsy."[8]

If this were true among general officers, it was in the nature of the case more widespread among regimental and company officers. Their ranks had been decimated. Losses sustained at Gettysburg in the First Corps had never been made good.[9] Regiments often were commanded by Captains and not infrequently by Lieuten-ants. As conditions grew worse, in the manner presently to be described, the zeal, the ambition, the courage, even, of some company officers were dissipated. They began to think of their safety more than of their cause. Applications for sick leave multiplied. The efforts of the unflinching, conscientious majority were undone by the absence of the despairing and the indifference of the dis-couraged.

Decline in the alertness of command had its inevitable effect on discipline. As early as June, the ghastly fortnight in the trenches at Cold Harbor had marked the first clear evidence that the fight-ing edge of the Army was being dulled by doubt. In a sharper metaphor, soldiers had said then that shooting bluecoats was like fighting mosquitoes: every time one was killed, two more were at the ears.[10] By mid-August, the change of spirit on the part of some of the men was discernible. It was not serious as yet. In action, well-led troops were almost as good as ever they had been. Cadmus Wilcox probably stated the case precisely when he wrote his sister-

[7] O. R., 43, pt. 2, p. 1134.
[8] Oct. n.d., 1864; Ham Chamberlayne, 284
[9] Sorrel, 270.
[10] 14 S.H.S.P., 537; 4 B. & L., 231; 3 R. E. Lee, 384.

in-law: "I sometimes of late think they are not quite so full of ardour as they were the first two years of the war." [11] In another month, Clerk Jones was saying extravagantly: "The poor will not fight for their oppressors, the money changers, extortioners, etc., whose bribes keep them out of service." [12]

One and probably the main reason in the early autumn for the wane in morale was this: The stimulus of victory, which had been the specific for all the ills of the Army, no longer could be applied. After the vain attempt to recapture the lines North of Fort Harrison,[13] the Confederates took the offensive only when opportunity seemed large or necessity compelled. There was no great battle any day but a small battle every day, the contest of the sharpshooters, of the mortar companies and of the other artillerists. During these exchanges, the Confederates could not hope to kill more opponents than the Federals themselves slew. The side numerically weaker of course had the heavier percentage of casualties. Even before the Federal capture of Fort Harrison or the tragedy of Cedar Creek, Lee had written Bragg conservatively: "I get no additions. The men coming in do not supply the vacancies caused by sickness, desertions, and other casualties. If things thus continue, the most serious consequences must result." [14]

When the enemy was challenged, the odds usually were so adverse and the hardships so biting that Confederate morale was lowered, not raised. An exception was the engagement of October 27. The Federals that day attempted to advance on both flanks. Longstreet repulsed them easily on the Northside by deciding correctly where the attack was to fall;[15] Hampton's men on the Southside fought brilliantly at Burgess' Mill [16] and, with help from Heth and Mahone, drove off in confusion two Federals Corps that failed to co-ordinate their attacks. The commander of the Confederate cavalry was anxious to pursue his advantage, but Hill was not willing to leave so long exposed the trenches on the right, which were almost bare of defenders.[17] It was a brilliant addition to Hampton's record, but it was bought at a price of personal

11 Aug. 15, 1864—*Wilcox MSS.*      12 2 *R.W.C.D.*, 288.
13 See *supra*, pp. 592–93.      14 Sept. 26, 1864; *O. R.*, 42, pt. 2, p. 1292.
1o *Longstreet*, 576; 14 *S.H.S.P.*, 559; *O. R.*, 42, pt. 1, pp. 795 ff, 814, 871.
16 The mill was on Hatcher's Run immediately to the West of the Boydton Plank Road. See the sketch on p. 539.
17 The essential details, which are of some interest but are inadequately reported, are given briefly in 3 *R. E. Lee*, 513–14.

anguish almost past endurance. In the action, one of Hampton's sons, Frank Preston, was mortally wounded. The other boy, Wade, galloped to his brother's side.[18] When the General himself arrived, Preston was dying and Wade was gasping from a bullet that struck him while he was ministering to Preston. Their father leaped from his horse, kissed his expiring boy, cried "Look after Wade" and then had to gallop off to direct the battle.[19] When it was over, he said that no son of his must ever be in his Corps again. The younger Wade, on recovery, must join some other command. "The agony of such a day, and the anxiety and the duties of the battle-field—it is all more than mere man can bear." [20]

This notable action of October 27 on both sides of the James was, to repeat, the exception. The infantry did not and could not leave the fortifications often to taste the wine of stimulating success. After the engagement at Burgess' Mill,[21] nothing but a few skirmishes and an occasional reconnaissance relieved the ghastly tedium of the trenches [22] until the end of the first week in December. At that time the Federals undertook on the Petersburg and Weldon Railroad an advance, known later as the Hicksford Raid, which was thought at first to be directed against the vital bridge over the Roanoke. Hampton moved immediately and sought to harass the enemy.[23] Hill's Corps was taken from the trenches and was started southward over bleak, frozen roads. The hard, shivering march was to no purpose. At Hicksford on the Meherrin River the enemy was turned back by the guns that covered the crossing.[24] It was a mismanaged, half-hearted affair on both sides. "We hoped," wrote General Pendleton regretfully, "A. P. Hill might destroy the column thus engaged, but either we were too slow or the inclement weather rendered it impossible." [25] Pendleton and many other Confederates would not admit, if indeed they realized, that the Army was becoming much too enfeebled to march at the old speed in bitter, wintry weather.

18 M. C. Butler, *Address on Wade Hampton*, 17; *Wells*, 328 ff.
19 *DeLeon, B. B. B.*, 161.
20 *Mrs. Chesnut*, 332, 334. The quotation may be Mrs. Chesnut's language, not Hampton's. For a letter of condolence from Lee to Hampton, see 3 *R. E. Lee*, 514 n. 136.
21 It sometimes was called the action of the Boydton Plank Road or of Hatcher's Run.
22 See the chronology in *O. R.*, 42, pt. 1, p. 3.      23 *O. R.*, 42, pt. 1, p. 951.
24 *O. R.*, 42, pt. 1, p. 444. The expedition was conducted by the V Corps and one Division of the II with the support of David Gregg's cavalry Division. Terminal dates were Dec. 7–12, 1864.
25 *Pendleton*, 379.

At Christmas time there was a minor call of the familiar sort that added to the exhaustion of troops without contributing the tonic of victory. On December 22, reports reached Army Headquarters of a raid on Gordonsville by a Federal force estimated at 6000. To meet it, two Brigades were sent from Longstreet's command; Early dispatched Lomax's cavalry.[26] The enemy was driven off promptly; on Christmas Eve the infantry started back; "but," General Bratton reported, "owing to the bad condition of the road did not all reach Richmond till 9 P.M. on 25th of December." [27]

For such limited operations as it was able to undertake, the Army received a short time before the Gordonsville Raid the last accession of strength it could hope to have. Kershaw's Division, or what remained of it, left Early November 15 [28] and by the 21st rejoined its old corps commander North of the James.[29] On the 9th of December, Gordon's and Pegram's troops were started from Waynesboro for Richmond by train.[30] Both Divisions had increased somewhat in strength through the recall of detailed men,[31] the return of convalescents and the assignment of conscripts,[32] but numbers of the drafted men already were deserting.[33] After these units of the Second Corps reached the Richmond-Petersburg front, a deep snow in the upper Valley of the Shenandoah made it reasonably certain that Sheridan could not move. Rodes's Division, under its senior Brigadier, Bryan Grimes, accordingly was ordered back to the main Army.[34] By this movement, General Early was left with no troops except Wharton's fragment of a Division, a few batteries, and a little force of cavalry.

The crippling of Early was not long the gain of Lee. On the 18th of December the telegraph clicked off the ominous intelligence that a powerful Federal fleet had left Hampton Roads, presumably for Wilmington.[35] The next day Beauregard reported that Sherman had demanded the surrender of Savannah. This had been refused, but, said the Confederate commander, the Union Army could march on Charleston. Beauregard asked if Bushrod Johnson's and Hoke's Divisions, which he evidently still consid-

26 O. R., 42, pt. 1, pp. 882–83; pt. 3, pp. 1289 ff.
27 Ibid., pt. 1, p. 883. For Early's commendation of Lomax's part in repelling this raid, see O. R., 43, pt. 2, p. 947.

28 O. R., 43, pt. 1, p. 584.
30 O. R. 43, pt. 1, pp. 586–87.
32 O. R., 43, pt. 2, p. 911.
34 Ibid., and O. R., 42, pt. 3, p. 1272.

29 Cf. O. R., 42, pt. 3, p. 1222.
31 Cf. 2 R.W.C.D., 303.
33 O. R., 43, pt. 1, p. 587.
35 O. R., 42, pt. 3, p. 1278.

ered his own, could not be returned to him.[36] It was impossible to dispatch infantry from Virginia to oppose Sherman in South Carolina, but it was imperative that Wilmington be defended and, if possible, be kept open. It was the only port into which blockade runners had a chance of bringing the supplies on which the life of the Confederacy depended. Hoke's Division, in consequence, was detached from the Army of Northern Virginia. Its movement to the coast of North Carolina, via Danville and Greensboro, was not a ride but a crawl. At the time this spread suspicion of deliberate treachery, but it should have been accepted as warning that the long-threatened collapse of transportation now was imminent.[37] With the long-delayed regiments went their commander, to return no more. Robert Hoke had been a superlative Colonel and an excellent, hard-hitting Brigadier. As a division commander, he had one defect only, but it might have been fatal: he could not or he would not co-operate.[38]

In terms of fighting strength, the loss of Hoke cost the Army in the trenches the equivalent of 70 per cent of the infantry Lee had gained by the return of the survivors of Early's battles,[39] though this did not appear on the official "returns." If inspection reports had told the whole truth, the Army still would have been strong enough to hold, at the least, to a vigorous defensive. As of December 31, the Army was supposed to have present 71,854; but 6155 were credited to Hoke and 3611 to Early. This reduced total strength to 62,088. Because of sickness and lack of shoes or clothing, the difference between the "aggregate present" and the number "present for duty" on the Richmond-Petersburg front was 10,312. Of men of all arms, presumably able to fight, Lee had with him 51,776.[40] Ewell's command added 5358, some of whom were local defense troops and reservists.[41] Meade, on the same date, commanded 83,826[42] and Butler 40,452.[43] The Confederates were outnumbered more than two to one. In equipment, in sub-

[36] O. R., 42, pt. 3, p. 1280.
[37] O. R., 42, pt. 3, pp. 1280, 1282, 1305, 1334, 1344, 1348–49. Hagood, 316.
[38] See supra, p. 593.
[39] As of December 20, Early's three Divisions had 8770 officers and men present for duty. Hoke had 5933 (O. R., 42, pt. 3, p. 1285).
[40] O. R., 42, pt. 1, p. 1362.           [41] Ibid., 1358.
[42] Ibid., 1114.
[43] Ibid., 1123. In these figures for Butler, the Districts of Eastern Virginia and of North Carolina are not included because the 9405 troops in those Districts were not immediately available for action against Lee.

sistence, in regularity of supply and in everything that made for the health, comfort and contentment of the troops, the advantage of the Federals was even greater.

This was a gloomy calculation with which to end a fatal year. There had been nothing during the autumn to renew the faith of the Army in itself, nothing to give it hope for 1865, nothing to relieve the wretched exposure of the trenches where a thoughtless lifting of the head would bring a bullet from a sharpshooter's rifle. Those who did not fall before this fire lived in the shadow of heartbreaking news. "Lee's Miserables," as they sometimes called themselves, knew in their hearts that they had won no shining victory since Chancellorsville, but most of them still believed they could win where they did not face impossible odds. Faith was gone that the Confederates elsewhere could withstand the enemy. Hood had lost at Franklin and then at Nashville; Sherman had occupied defiant Savannah; Fort Fisher resisted successfully an attack on December 24-26,[44] but a Confederate did not have to be a defeatist to admit that the enemy might come again and might seal that last open fort. In the face of this black prospect, the most determined of the soldiers shut their eyes, professed faith in God's approval of their sacrifice, and refused to admit that the Southern cause would be destroyed. Others confessed privately that they did not see how the Confederacy could achieve its independence. Still others began to whisper that the end was near. As long previously as September, J. B. Jones wrote in his diary, "Many of the privates in our armies are fast becoming what is termed machine soldiers, and will ere long cease to fight well—having nothing to fight for." [45] By January, 1865, he might have said this prediction was being fulfilled.

Hunger deepened doubt. The notorious incapacity of the commissary was rendered daily worse by the wider Federal occupation of Southern territory and by the inability of some of the railroads to deliver the little food that could be collected or purchased. In December there had been an acute shortage of meat, a condition that President Davis attributed to "criminal neglect in permitting blockade-runners at the port of Wilmington to come in with little or no freight, leaving army supplies at West India ports waiting for shipment." [46] January witnessed still another crisis.

---

[44] O. R., 42, pt. 1, pp. 989, 993 ff; pt. 3, pp. 1301, 1324.
[45] 2 R.W.C.D., 288.          [46] O. R., 51, pt. 2, pp. 1054-55.

Rain stopped traffic on twenty miles of the Piedmont Railroad between Danville and Greensboro. The Army's reserve of food then was reduced to two days' short rations.[47] February was to bring another time of hunger when, in the severest weather of the winter, men who were engaged in active operations against the enemy had no meat for three days. The Secretary of War then was to read, over the signature of the commanding General: "Taking these facts in connection with our paucity of numbers, you must not be surprised if calamity befalls us." [48] This failure was to force the retirement of Chief Commissary Northrop and the appointment of an able and reasonable man in the person of Brig. Gen. I. M. St. John.[49] He improved the distribution of supplies; there remained the question whether enough could be brought to Virginia from the Carolinas to keep the Army from starvation. No less a question was that of farmers' willingness to sell their products for depreciated currency even if the Quartermaster or the Commissary had the paper money with which to tender payment. East of the Mississippi, unpaid requisitions of the War Department, as of December 29, 1864, had been $181,000,000.[50]

Misery and discontent spread with hunger. The men could not forage because the countryside had been swept bare. Scarcely anything could be purchased by those who had money from home to take the place of army pay that was months in arrears. Many received boxes of provisions from home, but food so sent often was stolen or spoiled in transit, or was left in railway stations that never were cleared of freight and express.

The hunger, the hope, the exhaustion of supplies and the spirit of the men, strong and weak, were exhibited in the "Christmas feast" the women of Richmond undertook to provide. Appeals were directed to farmers and to merchants. The soldiers in the trenches were told to expect the food on New Year's Day. A member of the Eighteenth Georgia now speaks: ". . . our mouths 'watered' till January 1, 1865. On that day all who were able to do so got up very early. The army was to do nothing. The ladies were to do all. They would provide all vehicles, and the 'goodies' would be taken right along the lines and distributed to the half-famished men by dainty hands. And we waited. What a long day

[47] O. R., 46, pt. 2, pp. 1035, 1040.     [48] O. R., 46, pt. 1, p. 380.
[49] For the details, see 3 R. E. Lee, 536.     [50] IV O. R., 3, 975.

that seemed to be! We whiled away the tedious hours by telling stories and cracking jokes! Noon came, then two, four, eight, ten, and twelve o'clock, and still no 'goody' wagon. Being still a little weak, I became tired and lay down and went to sleep with the understanding that those on watch would call me when our dinner arrived. It was after 3 A.M. when a comrade called and told me that a detail had just gone out to meet the precious wagon and bring in our feast. But O what a disappointment when the squad returned and issued to each man only one small sandwich made up of two tiny slices of bread and a thin piece of ham! A few men ventured to inquire, 'Is this all?' But I think they were ashamed of themselves the next moment. After the 'meal' was finished a middle-aged corporal lighted his pipe and said: 'God bless our noble women! It was all they could do; it was all they had.' And then every man in that old tent indulged in a good cry. We couldn't help it!" [51] Another soldier, a North Carolinian, recalled that word was received to "send to the commissary for our Christmas dinner, and when it came we got for Company G one drumstick of a turkey, one rib of mutton, one slice of roast beef, two biscuits, and a slice of light bread." [52]

The daily ration seldom consisted of anything beyond a pint of corn meal and an ounce or two of bacon. A trooper who probably fared better than the average infantryman said of his ration: "What we had was corn pone cooked three days before and raw Nassau bacon (sometimes called 'mule' by the boys, who worshiped it and got so little of it.) I was hungry . . . so hungry that I thanked God that I had a backbone for my stomach to lean up against." [53] When the backbone rebelled, or the ration was not supplemented in some way, the soldiers steadily lost strength and weight. They looked healthy, but if they had to dig and to shovel dirt, they would "pant and grow faint." [54] The Army, in a word, was starving on its feet. [55]

So were the draft animals. No provender could be had around Petersburg or Richmond. After Sheridan devastated the Shenandoah Valley, nothing reached the horses and mules from that

[51] John Coxe in 22 *C. V.*, 359.      [52] 4 *N. C. Regts.*, 204.
[53] 22 *C. V.*, 117.      [54] *Caldwell*, 196.
[55] For a soldier's realistic summary, see 29 *S.H.S.P.*, 290. Of many references to subsistence during the winter of 1864–65, the following may be of special interest: *IV O. R.*, 3, 653, 930, 1137; *O. R.*, 46, pt. 2, pp. 1211 ff, 1250, 1297 ff; 7 *Rowland*, 415; 2 *R. W. C. D.*, 384.

granary. The uncertainties of the railroad service made day-by-day delivery of feed a gamble. For that reason, all horses except those indispensably required for the movement of guns and wagons were kept miles from the front. This had direct and ominous relation to the mobility of the Army. Grant was continuing steadily to build up his left flank. There was danger that he would undertake to turn the Confederate right as soon as the roads ceased to be streams of mud. When that happened, Hampton's mounted Divisions might not be strong enough to resist. More than 20 per cent of the 6200 cavalrymen were without horses of any sort, strong or weak, healthy or sick.[56]

Besides the hunger of soldiers and of horses, the growing consciousness of defeat on other fronts, and the lack of the old stimulus of victory, there was for many of the men in the trenches that ghastly winter a reversal of what had been one of the most potent of all factors in the creation of morale. Letters from homes in remote States once had inspired the soldiers to desperate deeds. Now that Sherman had swept through Georgia and was advancing into the Carolinas, the wives and mothers of many of the soldiers could not communicate. Their fate was pictured in all the imaginative horror that alarm and suspense colored. Other women wrote in a strain incredibly different from that of 1861–62. Maj. Robert Stiles thus stated his observations: "Ask any Confederate officer who commanded troops during the latter part of the war and who was loved and trusted by his men. He will tell you of letters which it would have seared your very eyeballs to read, but that they could not be read without tears, letters in which a wife and mother, crazed by her starving children's cries for bread, required a husband and father to choose between his God-imposed obligations to them and his allegiance to his country, his duty as a soldier . . ."[57]

This beyond doubt was an extreme statement. The letters that did the most harm were not written by women who would draw

---

[56] These were the figures for November (*O. R.*, 42, pt. 3, p. 1236). By the end of December, the total probably was higher. The reduction of the Army's supply of horses is covered fully in 3 *R. E. Lee.* As no new evidence has come to light since the publication of that work, the subject is not reviewed here. Prof. Charles W. Ramsdell, who wrote a valuable article on "General Robert E. Lee's Horse Supply, 1862–65" (*American Historical Review*, v. 35, no. 4, July, 1930), has stated that much material on the subject is to be found in the unpublished papers of the Confederate Quartermaster General in the National Archives.

[57] *Stiles*, 350.

a fine distinction between duty and allegiance. More often they were ignorant letters to ignorant men. The enemy was approaching and might steal the cow; other soldiers had come home to look after their wives and children and had not suffered because of it; [58] exempted landowners and officeholders were enjoying an easy life and were fattening on the poverty of soldiers' families. Of these expressions of confusion, of misery and of despair many letters to soldiers were compounded.[59]

The result of weakened command, lack of victory, loss of hope, hunger, and alarm on the home front was desertion. This had occurred with some frequency in August, 1864,[60] had diminished in September, had risen again in October,[61] had dropped in November, and had mounted anew at Christmas time. Lee in December had attributed this desertion to the low spirit of the Army: "Scant fare, light clothing, constant duty, no recruits have discouraged it." [62] After winter settled on the trenches in January, desertion literally multiplied. The beginnings of this final wave of desertion were on the night of January 9–10, 1865.[63] Within another fortnight, so many conscripts and even volunteers were leaving the ranks that rumors spread of impending desertion en masse. It was said that "Tige" Anderson's Brigade, one of the oldest and staunchest, intended, when next it was paid, to march away—a slander that was at once denounced.[64] The realities were shameful enough. On the Petersburg front, where the opposing picket lines were in easy hailing distance, the temptation to go over to the enemy was too great for many of the weak, hungry and half-frozen troops.[65] This nightly passage of men from the Southern to the Federal lines prompted a final, almost futile amnesty for the return of all deserters [66] and a vain attempt by army commanders to stop the President's reprieves and pardons. Clemency was so general that many an officer was of opinion the soldiers believed they would not be shot for desertion if caught.[7]

Morning reports became a sickening and bewildering story of

58 Cf. O. R., 46, pt. 2, p. 1254.     59 Cf. Mrs. McDonald, 238.
60 O. R., 42, pt. 2, pp. 1175, 1183; C. M. Wilcox to his sister-in-law, MS, Aug. 15, 1864—Wilcox MSS.
61 O. R., 43, pt. 2, pp. 890, 907, 908; 2 R. W. C. D., 302, 308.
62 O. R., 42, pt. 3, p. 1311.     63 O. R., 46, pt. 2, pp. 1033, 1036.
64 O. R., 46, pt. 2, p. 1125.     65 Cf. ibid., 1143.
66 Ibid., 1228, 1229–30.
67 O. R., 29, pt. 2, pp. 806–07, 820; ibid., 51, pt. 2, p. 781; IV O. R., 3, 524; O. R., 42, pt. 2, pp. 1169, 1213; ibid., 46, pt. 2, p. 1258; 2 R. W. C. D., 273.

new desertion. Bushrod Johnson, who commanded the sector of trenches nearest the enemy, wrote that the previous night twenty men had left from a single regiment of Mat. Ransom's Brigade; [68] another night the number was forty.[69] In a fortnight of February, Heth's and Wilcox's Divisions lost 500.[70] "Hundreds of men are deserting nightly," Lee telegraphed the Adjutant General on the 25th, "and I cannot keep the army together unless examples are made of [convicted deserters]." [71] Over a period of ten days in February, for the entire Army, 1094 men disappeared. The greater part of these went home, rather than to the enemy, but they took arms and ammunition with them and they could defy the Provost Marshal's guard. "I am convinced," Lee wrote the Secretary of War at the end of February, ". . . that [desertion] proceeds from the discouraging sentiment out of the Army, which, unless it can be checked, will bring us calamity." [72] There was suspicion, though no proof, that men of different commands had an understanding about desertion and a rendezvous.[73]

By the beginning of March the Chief of the Bureau of Conscription estimated that 100,000 deserters from Southern armies were at large. These figures were disputed [74] as, no doubt, was the unofficial estimate of 60,000 Virginia deserters and a.w.o.l.'s,[75] but the immensity of the evil appalled. After the February weather moderated in March, there was a period of ten days during which desertions diminished to 779.[76] This improvement was temporary. For the next ten days, incomplete reports showed 1,061 desertions. Many of these were attributed to the desire of men to join "light duty" commands near their homes. Allegations were made, but were not credited, that a Brigadier of distinguished record was party to this.[77] From February 15 through March 18, desertions numbered close to 3000, or about one-twelfth of the effective strength of an Army crippled by sickness as well as by absence.[78]

For a time, the record of Longstreet's First Corps as respected desertions was much better than that of any other command of like size, though it had about the normal percentage of the reluc-

68 O. R., 46, pt. 2, pp. 1238–39.    69 Ibid., 1256.
70 Ibid., 1254.    71 O. R., 46, pt. 2, p. 1258.
72 O. R., 46, pt. 2, p. 1265.    73 Ibid., 1261, 1303.
74 O. R., 51, pt. 2, pp. 1064–66; IV O. R., 3, 1119.
75 2 R. W. C. D., 464.    76 O. R., 46, pt. 2, pp. 1292–93.
77 Ibid., 1353 ff.
78 O. R., 46, pt. 2, pp. 1254, 1265, 1293; ibid., pt. 3, p. 1353.

tant, sullen conscripts.[79] This record in standing to the colors was in part a tribute to the stable and vigilant leadership of the Corps, but it was due in at least equal measure to the fact that the men on the north side of the James were somewhat less exposed than were their comrades on the Southside. Nor did they have the same facilities for going over to the enemy. In March, 1865, desertion from the First Corps increased dangerously. Field and Kershaw, especially Kershaw, held their men together with some success, but Pickett's Division, which now was composed largely of conscripts, was disintegrating fast. During a ten-day period, when Kershaw had forty-one deserters, Pickett had 512.[80] A little later, when Eppa Hunton's Brigade was ordered from the Northside to the Petersburg front, a corps staff officer had to send warning that the men should not be kept waiting long in the streets of Richmond. "It was not desirable," said Colonel Latrobe, that this should occur. He meant that if the men were held on the streets, waiting for their train, some would slip away and be seen no more.[81] To reduce the ruinous evil, Longstreet made the interesting experiment of giving to any man who stopped a deserter the promise of a commission in one of the Negro regiments, which then were at the first stage of organization. Some ambitious men were challenged by this offer. In one instance a soldier detected and exposed a plot of seven of his companions to desert.[82] Reward of the faithful and alert may have helped somewhat in preventing desertion, but even the First Corps could not be kept under such firm, vigilant discipline that desertion was stopped.

The senior officers who stood almost helpless in the face of desertion were themselves increasingly depleted in number. Governor "Joe" Brown of Georgia had prevailed on Davis to detach W. T. Wofford and "Rans" Wright for service in their State.[83] Many generals of Brigade still were absent from the Richmond-Petersburg front on account of wounds. Some were seriously sick. In a few instances, no doubt, more of illness was alleged than was experienced, for the plain reason that self-indulgent, ease-loving individuals wished to avoid the mud and misery of the trenches until the approach of the spring campaign. As of January 31, 1865,

79 Cf. O. R., 46, pt. 2, pp. 1265, 1296.    80 O. R., 46, pt. 3, p. 1332.
81 O. R., 46, pt. 3, p. 1343.                82 O. R., 46, pt. 3, pp. 1361, 1367.
83 6 C.M.H., 455, 457.

Longstreet, with thirteen Brigades, had one Major General and seven Brigadiers absent. In the Second Corps, which a Major General was commanding, Rodes's Division was without a regular leader; Early's old Division was under a Brigadier General; one Brigade was without a commander; two other Brigadiers were on leave. The Third Corps was relatively in better condition. Three only of its thirteen Brigadier Generals were absent. In "Dick" Anderson's command of four Brigades, presently to be described, three of the Brigadiers were not with their troops. For the infantry as a whole, three Divisions did not have regular commanders of appropriate rank present. Sixteen of thirty-nine Brigades either had no general officer at their head or else did not have the advantage of his presence.[84] At the end of February the showing was even worse. Of the ten Major Generals of infantry, only four or possibly five were present.[85] Five of the Divisions were commanded by Brigadiers. Of the thirty-nine Brigade commanders, twenty-one were on duty.[86] Seventeen Brigades were under regimental officers.[87]

Qualified men to fill some vacancies could not be found. Several of the weakest Brigades were not supplied with new general officers because, in all probability, the unexpressed purpose of Lee was to unite them with other units. One step down the table of organization, Longstreet urged a specific plan: Regimental vacancies should not be filled, he said, but should be made good by the consolidation of regiments; companies should be reduced to six per regiment; this, he maintained, would involve less disruption of organization than would the formal disbandment of regiments and the establishment of others; surplus officers could be used in the conscription service.[88] This plan was in itself an admission that most of the resources of command had been exhausted.

Ranking officers represented, in the main, the survival of the fittest, but the personality of nearly all the officers below corps

[84] Inspection reports do not agree in all instances with the table of organization in *O. R.*, 46, pt. 2, pp. 1170 ff. If inspection reports were correct, six Major Generals were present and four of the Divisions were under Brigadiers. Twenty-six Brigades were listed under general officers, twelve under officers of lower rank. One Brigade was detached (*Ibid.*, 1179 ff).
[85] There is some uncertainty about Pickett; he may have been sick and absent.
[86] This figure included those who were commanding Divisions.
[87] *O. R.*, 46, pt. 2, pp. 1268 ff. In the cavalry and in the artillery, absentees were not relatively so numerous.
[88] *O. R.*, 46, pt. 2, pp. 1032–33.

command seemed to be submerged after pitched battles gave place to the sombre months of semi-siege. Some of these men became respected figures in the social life of Petersburg or among the worshippers at church, but in the service they no longer shone as individuals. They had lost in the mud of those tangled trenches the glamour that had been theirs at Second Manassas or at Chancellorsville.

Of those who retained their personality against the ugly background, as the winter dragged wretchedly to its close, Longstreet stood out. He had regained the sturdy good health that always contributed to strengthen faith in him as a leader and as a fighting man. The partial paralysis of his right arm still hampered, but he could write swiftly now with his left, and he had as many ideas as ever. Although his loss of faith in victory became more pronounced, he neither voiced it nor permitted it to interfere with his duty. Of his divisional chiefs, Kershaw kept his fine, courageous spirit. Field was holding his Division together with notable success. The other Division of the First Corps, that of Maj. Gen. George E. Pickett, had been placed on the Howlett Line and had been employed as the mobile reserve of the Army under the direct command of Lee. Later, when Longstreet resumed command, Pickett guarded part of the outer defenses of Richmond. His case was somewhat mystifying. Although he was the senior Major General of the Army, Pickett was given no important detached command after his service at Petersburg in May, 1864.[89]

In the Second Corps, tragic change was ceaseless. Early had been left on the Waynesboro-Staunton front, it will be remembered, when the Divisions of the Corps had been ordered back to Petersburg. "Old Jube" had little more than the equivalent of a Brigade of infantry,[90] though it was termed a Division. His thin

[89] References to him in O. R. during the closing months of the war are few. In O. R., 42, pt. 2, p. 1271 is a favorable report, Aug. 30, 1864, of an inspection of his Division. He then was bivouacking with his troops and was said to be vigilant and active in all that pertained to the comfort and efficiency of his command. At that time, Pickett was hampered because so many of his officers were disabled and absent. Further mention of Pickett will be found in O. R., 42, pt. 1, p. 854; ibid., pt. 2, p. 1271; pt. 3, p. 1213; ibid., 46, pt. 2, pp. 1285, 1290 ff; pt. 3, pp. 1325, 1326, 1341 ff, 1345. In the Fairfax MSS is a previously mentioned letter of Feb. 3, 1865, Lee to Longstreet, in which the commanding General clarified the status of Longstreet's command and gave that officer broad control of the troops North of the James. Lee wrote: ". . . I should be very glad to send Pickett's Division to the Northside if I could in any way replace it. But as I believe I told you before, it would require the whole of Gordon's command, leaving us nothing in reserve and nothing to defend our right from Hatcher's Run . . ."

[90] With the artillery, 2932 present for duty (O. R., 42, pt. 3, p. 1362).

cavalry, under Lomax, had to guard a wide area. Defeated and discredited, but conscious that he was obeying the orders of his chief, "Old Jube" held his head high and kept his tongue sharp. At the blackest hour of the darkest winter of the war, he brought a smile to many tightened lips by his comment at the end of an eloquent sermon to which he and his staff devoutly had listened. The minister had closed his book and had launched on his peroration: "Suppose, my Christian friends, that those who have laid for centuries in their graves should arise now and come forth from their quiet resting places; and marching in their white shrouds should pass before this congregation, by thousands and tens of thousands, what would be the result?"

"Ah," said Early in a stage whisper to the officer next him, "I'd conscript every damned one of them."[91]

Because he could not conscript either the dead or the living in sufficient numbers to offer resistance to his adversary, Early was about to face the supreme humiliation of a commander. In it he was to have few sympathizers among those on whom he never had practised the arts of ingratiation. Public interest already had passed from him to John B. Gordon, who was acting commander of the Second Corps on the Richmond-Petersburg front and was gaining steadily in reputation.

Gordon's continuance in that position, his temperament and his propinquity to Lee gave him a special place during the winter. Longstreet was across the James and was not in personal touch with Army Headquarters. Powell Hill was in bad health and was not of the consultative type. Gordon became Lee's principal confidant—as far as any man ever enjoyed that status. The Georgian was continuing to develop as a soldier, though the Second Corps by the end of the year was reduced to 8600 effectives and was the smallest Corps in the Army.[92] His Divisions were in the hands of men of measurable competence. Early's old Division, it will be remembered, had been given to Ramseur. After the death of Rodes at Winchester, Ramseur had assumed command of that officer's

[91] 5 *Land We Love*, 441–42; republished in *Douglas*, 324. For other glimpses of Early after Cedar Creek, see *O. R.*, 43, pt. 1, p. 584; *ibid.*, pt. 2, p. 924; *Wearing of the Gray*, 103; 2 *R. W. C. D.*, 318; *Alexandria* (Va.) *Gazette*, Nov. 25, 1864. In the first of these references, Jed. Hotchkiss estimated, as of Nov. 16, 1864, that from the beginning of that year's campaign in the Valley, "We have marched . . . 1670 miles and have had seventy-five battles and skirmishes."

[92] *O. R.*, 42, pt. 3, p. 1362.

Division. Ramseur's own command then had passed to its senior Brigadier, John Pegram.

This able young Virginian remained at that rank but he exercised all the duties of a Major General.[93] His marriage to Hetty Cary of Baltimore on the 19th of January, 1865,[94] was an event about which the Confederate capital talked excitedly. Kyd Douglas put the union in superlatives: "One of the handsomest and most lovable men I ever knew wed to the handsomest woman in the Southland—with her classic face, her pure complexion, her auburn hair, her perfect figure and her carriage, altogether the most beautiful woman I ever saw in any land." [95] She had long been the affianced of Pegram,[96] but his service in Tennessee and then his active duty with Lee and his wound delayed the marriage. When the day for the nuptials arrived and the President's carriage came for the bride, the horses balked. Old ladies said, too, that she tore her wedding dress as she entered St. Paul's Church, and that she almost lost her veil.[97] About two weeks later, when she was visiting her husband in Petersburg, a review of Pegram's Division was made, in effect, a review by the bride. Lee was at her side. Half a dozen generals were in her train. Again a triumph was marred. Her horse almost knocked down a gaping soldier, but when she reined in the animal and tried to apologize, the man gallantly interrupted. Tearing off his battered hat he said: "Never mind, Miss! You might have rid all over me, indeed you might." [98] This was on the 2nd of February. Four days later her husband was killed in action.[99]

Rodes's Division, after the death of Ramseur at Cedar Creek, was under the direction of its senior Brigadier, Bryan Grimes of North Carolina, who had succeeded previously to the command of Junius Daniel's troops. On February 23, 1865, Grimes was made Major General—the last officer of the Army of Northern Virginia

---

[93] It is generally assumed and is formally stated in 3 C. M. H., 649, that he was promoted Major General, but the Journal C. S. Congress shows neither nomination nor confirmation.

[94] The date has been given variously but this is the one in the parish register of St. Paul's Episcopal Church, Richmond.

[95] Douglas, 325.                              [96] Ibid., 327.

[97] Ibid., 325.                               [98] Douglas, 325.

[99] O. R., 46, pt. 1, p. 381; Douglas, 326–27; DeLeon B. B. B., 168; Ham Chamberlayne, 309; Wearing of the Gray, 553 ff. The Division passed temporarily to Brig. Gen. James A. Walker, who, though still suffering from a slowly mending wound in the arm, returned to lead it (3 C. M. H., 678–79).

to receive promotion to that rank.[100] He was 36 years of age and of quick and fiery temper,[101] but in action he showed judgment as well as skill and courage.[102]

Gordon's Division of the same Corps did not receive a new Major General because Gordon remained at that rank and presumably would return to his old command if Early again led the Corps. During the time Gordon directed the three Divisions, his own was under his successor in brigade command, Brig. Gen. Clement A. Evans. Through Gordon's efforts, the Division was in fighting mood, but it still contained unhappy and uncooperative remnants of famous old Brigades that could not endure amicably the loss of their separate existence. William Terry's Brigade, at the end of February, included the fragments of thirteen Virginia regiments, among which were those of the Stonewall Brigade and other units of Jackson's Army of the Valley. In York's Brigade, led now by a Colonel, were the survivors of no less than ten Louisiana regiments. Those of "Dick" Taylor's Brigade were included.[103]

In spite of the progressive impairment of his health, Powell Hill kept the command of the Third Corps stable to the extent that all three of his division commanders usually were with their troops. Harry Heth had his wife with him in Petersburg and once came under the half-amused suspicion of the commanding General that he did not visit his lines as frequently as he should.[104] Mahone, too, had his wife near the front, but neither Lee nor Hill had to prod him. Since Mahone's ambitions had been aroused by command of a Division, his zeal had been complete and his service brilliant. Between him and his successor in brigade command, David A. Weisiger, serious friction had developed but it did not impair the Division.

Cadmus Wilcox was not happy. The sudden death of his brother, Congressman John A. Wilcox of Texas, February 7, 1864,[105] had left the widow [106] and two children in a distant State without the counsel of her kin. General Wilcox felt that the obli-

[100] *Wright*, 40; *O. R.*, 46, pt. 2, p. 1266.

[101] 1 *N. C. Regts.*, 280.

[102] *Ibid.*, 239, 266-67; 4 *ibid.*, 515. Grimes, J. J. Pettigrew and L. O'B. Branch were connected and had been friends from boyhood (*Grimes*, 127).

[103] Cf. *O. R.*, 46, pt. 2, p. 1271.

[104] This familiar anecdote will be found in 3 *R. E. Lee*, 530. Substantially the same version appears in General Heth's *MS Memoirs.*

[105] 6 *Journal C. S. Congress*, 771.

[106] Née Emily Donelson, daughter of Andrew Jackson Donelson.

gation of directing the education of the boy and girl rested in large part on him, and he accordingly thought often of procuring transfer to the Trans-Mississippi Department.[107] He did not succeed in getting an assignment nearer his young charges and he had a winter of some sickness,[108] but he kept his troops in good condition. Few Divisions had a smaller number of absentees and deserters.[109] In Wilcox's absence, "Jim" Lane commanded the Division, though the North Carolinian preferred his own Brigade.[110] When Wilcox had talked of going to Texas the belief of many officers was that John R. Cooke might succeed him as Major General.[111]

Besides the First Corps North of the James and the Second and Third South of the river, there was a Fourth, though after Christmas, 1864, it contained only four Brigades. This was Johnson's Division—Elliott's, Gracie's, Mat. Ransom's and Wise's Brigades —and was in effect Beauregard's old command from the defenses of Charleston, S. C. Until Hoke had been sent to Wilmington, his Division, also, had been under Anderson.[112] These forces had been assigned Anderson after the departure of Beauregard and the return of Longstreet in order, no doubt, to preserve the separate status of the troops, to assure their proper employment, and to give Anderson a command in keeping with his rank. "Dick" Anderson himself was not in his old, easy mood. Ahead he could see the ruin of the Southern cause. He knew that his men had no faith in the future of the Confederacy and little spirit for the conflict that was certain to be renewed in a few weeks.[113]

107 Wilcox to his sister-in-law, MS, Nov. 21, 1864—*Wilcox MSS*. In this letter, commenting on the reelection of Lincoln, the General said: "It may be it is better for us for with McClellan there might have been a reconstruction of the Union, but with Lincoln such a thing is not possible, and as it is independence that we are after, Lincoln is the best, for with him it is either subjugation or independence."
108 18 *S.H.S.P.*, 421.                    109 Cf. *O. R.*, 46, pt. 2, p. 1173.
110 18 *S.H.S.P.*, 421.
111 Cooke to Mrs. J. E. B. Stuart, MS, Dec. 15, 1864. Cooke gave in this letter an interesting illustration of the religious feeling of his time. He was seeking, he told his sister, to be a consistent Christian and he explained: "Since my marriage I have not sworn, but I find it as yet impossible to bring myself to a full determination to take Christ as my guide in all things"—*Cooke MSS*. The following references may be useful in the study of Cooke's career after Sharpsburg: 3 *N. C. Regts.*, 69; *O. R.*, 18, 1012, 1041; *ibid.*, 27, pt. 3, p. 976; *ibid.*, 29, pt. 2, p. 727; *ibid.*, 33, 1181; *ibid.*, 42, pt. 1, p. 851; pt. 2, pp. 1206-07; 2 *N. C. Regts.*, 449. Of especial interest is the report of August, 1864, in which Col. R. E. Peyton said that he had inspected the Brigade three times after Cooke had assumed command "and each time have found it equal to any in the army in all respects" (*O. R.,* 42, pt. 2, p. 1273).
112 *O. R.*, 42, pt. 3, pp. 1190, 1362.
113 Anderson's MS report of the Petersburg-Appomattox campaign—*Lee MSS*.

The artillery commanders suffered equally with their comrades of the infantry in discomfort and in doubt, but they had fewer casualties. General Pendleton agonized over the death of his son and pride, "Sandie," and he had to struggle hard to keep his thoughts from the tragedy of Fisher's Hill. "To dwell on the loss and on the trying circumstances of his removal, as there is some natural tendency in my mind, would so accumulate grief as to render it painful beyond expression and unfit me for duty." [114] Again: "Our dear Sandie seems as much in my thoughts as the first week of our mourning, and with an inexpressible sense of loss. He comes before me in many scenes: as in his boyhood, student life, and in the Army; when he and I went to Moss Neck; as he stood before me with his beloved bride; as we were at home together last winter. But I must try to think more of him as rejoicing in the Master's likeness and presence, and awaiting us all there." [115] Pendleton occasionally advised on the location of batteries, but he discharged usually the duties of a chief inspector and, as always, he planned essential reorganization. The corps chiefs of artillery—Alexander on the Northside with Longstreet, Lindsay Walker on the Southside with Hill, Armistead Long in the Valley—discharged the active duties wisely and with little friction. After the excessive losses of guns in the Valley, there seemed no good reason for retaining there, weaponless, so fine a combat officer as Col. Tom Carter. With Braxton's and Cutshaw's Battalions, he accordingly was brought back to the Richmond defenses and was put in charge of the batteries of the Second Corps on that front.[116] Stapleton Crutchfield, who had lost a leg at Chancellorsville, was able now to hobble about and was assigned in January to command the garrison of Chaffin's Bluff and the heavy artillery battalion of the Richmond defenses.[117] William J. Pegram, now a full Colonel, continued with the Third Corps on the Petersburg line. In the same corps and with like rank were David McIntosh and William T. Poague.[118]

[114] Pendleton, 377.                    [115] Ibid., 378; Nov. 28, 1864.
[116] The date of Colonel Carter's return has not been established. It was after January 17, probably by March 3 and certainly by March 7. See O. R., 46, pt. 2, pp. 1083, 1208, 1280–81; ibid., pt. 3, pp. 1316–17. The papers of Powel Page, courier to Colonel Carter, show that young Page was at Greenwood Station, March 2. He probably was not far from Colonel Carter then and doubtless was en route to Richmond.
[117] Ibid., 1093, 1194, 1275.
[118] O. R., 46, pt. 2, p. 1177. For a succinct statement of conditions in the artillery at this time, see a Wise, 919 ff.

Because the cavalry needed more horses almost as badly as did the artillery, the officers of that service were gloomy and widely scattered. Lomax was to remain in the Valley, or near it, as long as he could. Tom Rosser was to return to the Richmond front prior to the end of March.[119] Other changes made before that time were a part of events hereafter to be described.[120]

In those events a number of new brigade commanders were to have a share. Through what Moxley Sorrel gratefully remembered as evidence that Powell Hill cherished no grudge against him for the arrest of July, 1862,[121] the commander of the Third Corps applied for the promotion of Longstreet's A.A.G. to head the Brigade of "Rans" Wright which Victor Girardey commanded briefly while Wright was absent.[122] Wright was made temporary Major General at the end of November and, as noted already, was sent to Georgia.[123] Sorrel had joined Mahone's Division in November,[124] but by February 7, 1865 he was down with a chest wound that would incapacitate him for months.[125] Another Georgia Brigade, equally famous, also suffered a change. In succession to command of W. T. Wofford's Brigade [126] a new Brigadier was assigned, in the person of Dudley M. DuBose, former Colonel of the Fifteenth Georgia.[127] George H. Steuart, exchanged prisoner of war, took Armistead's old Brigade, which Col. William R. Aylett had been commanding.[128] Brig. Gen. J. J. Archer did not long survive his release from prison and his resumption of command. Some months after Archer's death on October 24, 1864,[129] Col. William McComb of the Fourteenth Tennessee was promoted to succeed him.[130] The fragments of Bushrod Johnson's Tennessee Brigade were consolidated with Archer's men.[131] Elliott's Brigade of Bushrod Johnson's Division had been entrusted in September, 1864, to Col. William H. Wallace of the Eighteenth South Carolina,[132] who was made a Brigadier in accordance with the act for temporary appointments.[133] Col.

---

119 *O. R.*, 46, pt. 3, pp. 1338–39.  120 See *infra*, p. 656 ff.
121 See Vol. I, pp. 666–67.  122 See *supra*, pp. 546–47.
123 *Wright*, 45.
124 Commissioned under the Act of May 31, 1864, for the appointment of temporary Brigadiers (*Wright*, 147; *Sorrel*, 265–66).
125 *Sorrel*, 275.  126 See *supra*, p. 625.
127 *Ibid.*, 414–15; *Wright*, 147. DuBose was commissioned Dec. 5, 1864.
128 Cf. *O. R.*, 46, pt. 2, p. 1268.  129 *D. A. B.*
130 Feb. 13, 1865 (*Wright*, 124).  131 8 *C. M. H.*, 320.
132 5 *C. M. H.*, 424.  133 *Wright*, 146.

William H. Forney of the Tenth Alabama was promoted and was assigned to Sanders's Brigade, the one in which he had served.[134] James P. Simms, Colonel of the Fifty-third Georgia, was named February 18 as successor to Goode Bryan, who had led Paul Semmes's Brigade.[135] To Young M. Moody, Colonel of the Forty-third Alabama, was entrusted the Brigade of Archibald Gracie, Jr., who was killed in the Petersburg trenches December 3, 1864.[136] Col. W. F. Perry, who had commanded Law's old Brigade for months, was appointed Brigadier on the 16th of March.[137] Some of these were last-minute imperative appointments to assure direction of troops that had to be organized properly when open campaigning began. In more than one instance, perhaps, promotion was not made because the officer was assumed to be competent, but because other aspirants were manifestly, even notoriously unqualified. The springs of command had run dry.

Col. Lindsay Walker received on the 1st of March the commission of Brigadier General of Artillery, which Long of the Second Corps and Alexander of the First already held.[138] Of the cavalrymen, Col. R. L. T. Beale of the Ninth Virginia was advanced January 13, 1865, to the rank of Brigadier and was assigned formally to the Brigade he had been leading ever since the death of John R. Chambliss.[139]

Three other changes of a character more dramatic were made. Worn by hard service and outraged by unjust criticism, James A. Seddon, Secretary of War, insisted upon resigning, January 18, 1865, though he continued on duty till February 6,[140] when Maj. Gen. John C. Breckinridge succeeded him.[141] Simultaneously, the position of the foremost Southern leader was changed. Because of discontent in the General Assembly of Virginia [142] and in the Confederate Congress with the management of the war, the President somewhat reluctantly [143] signed, Jan. 23, 1865, a bill for the appointment of a General-in-Chief to be "ranking officer of the Army and as such [to have] command of the military forces of

[134] O. R., 46, pt. 2, pp. 1174, 1272; Wright, 125.
[135] 6 C. M. H., 436–37. Simms was to rank from Dec. 8, 1864 (Wright, 124).
[136] 7 C. M. H., Ala., 426; appointed March 13, to rank from Mch. 4, 1865.
[137] To rank as of Feb. 21, 1865 (Wright, 126).
[138] Wright, 131–32.          [139] 3 C.M.H., 582.
[140] IV O. R., 1046; 4 Journal C. S. Congress, 525.
[141] For the circumstances, see IV O. R., 1046–48; O. R., 46, pt. 2, p. 1118; 2 R. W. C. D., 334, 395, 396, 401, 415, 423.
[142] O. R., 46, pt. 2, pp. 1084, 1092.          [143] Cf. ibid., 1118.

the Confederate States." [144] This avowedly was a last effort to utilize the abilities of Lee to the fullest, and to give to the whole of a waning cause the prestige of his name and character. Davis unhesitatingly appointed Lee and had the appropriate general order issued on the 6th of February.[145] Had this order been interpreted by the Army of Northern Virginia as notice that Lee would cease to exercise direct control of his old troops, more harm than good would have been done. As it was understood promptly that Lee would remain in command in Virginia and act elsewhere through the Generals in the field,[146] the enlargement of the duties of "Marse Robert" was to the men in the trenches little more than a matter of present pride and vague hope.

The third major change was full of tragedy. Near Waynesboro, on the 2nd of March, 1865, "Jube" Early was attacked again by Sheridan in overwhelming strength. Early's small command was demoralized and in bad order. He had little more than 1000 infantry and only six guns with teams that could haul the pieces through the freezing rain. Tom Rosser collected about 100 cavalrymen to form a skirmish line until Lomax could come from Millboro, about forty miles West of Staunton, where the main force of mounted troops was stationed. "Jube" knew that a long flight would be hopeless, but he took position and prepared to fight because he wished to remove some guns and supplies for which he had no horses. "I did not intend making my final stand on this ground," Early explained afterward, "yet I was satisfied that if my men would fight, which I had no reason to doubt, I could hold the enemy in check until night, and then cross the river and take position in Rockfish Gap; for I had done more difficult things than that during the war." [147]

It was not to be. The small force broke quickly; the enemy got in its rear. "I went to the top of a hill to reconnoitre," Early wrote, "and had the mortification of seeing the greater part of my command being carried off as prisoners, and a force of the enemy moving rapidly towards Rockfish Gap." [148] With General Long and about a score of other companions, Early rode over the mountains

[144] 4 *Journal C. S. Congress*, 432, 443, 446, 448, 450, 453, 454, 457, 458, 477, 478, 482, 486; 7 *ibid.*, 462–64, 476, 495.
[145] *O. R.*, 46, pt. 2, p. 1205. For the correspondence and relevant circumstances, see 3 *R. E. Lee*, 533–34.
[146] *O. R.*, 51, pt. 2, pp. 1082–83.
[147] *Early*, 462.          [148] *Ibid.*, 463.

in an effort to escape. After much hardship and more than one hasty gallop from pursuing bluecoats, Early reached Army Headquarters near Petersburg about the 16th of March. He had left with a Corps; he came back almost alone. His report was made to sympathetic ears. Lee had unimpaired confidence, as he soon had occasion to say, in Early's "ability, zeal and devotion to the cause"; [149] and after hearing the story of the odds his lieutenant had faced, Lee determined to send "Jube" back to the Valley, which Sheridan by that time had left, in the hope that Early would be able to collect and to reorganize scattered troops. There was no thought, apparently, of restoring "Jube" to the command of the Second Corps on the Petersburg front. Gordon was doing admirably. No good reason existed for replacing him. Lee must have reasoned, also, that Early's disasters would make him unacceptable to the troops. Failure overtook this considerate effort to keep Early in the service by employing him in the Valley. A desperate people and an embittered press were unwilling to have the defeated General retained in any position of military trust: If he undertook recruiting in the region of the Shenandoah, they said, he would wreck the enterprise and antagonize the citizens. So great was the clamor that Lee on the 30th of March had to relieve Early of command and send him home to await orders.[150] To this fate had fallen "Old Jube" of Manassas and of Williamsburg, of Cedar Mountain and of Sharpsburg, of Salem Church and of Monocacy.

[149] *Early*, 469.
[150] The essential details will be found in 4 *R. E. Lee*, Appendix IV-1, pp. 507-09.

# CHAPTER XXXII

## The Last Attempts at Grand Strategy

THE MISERABLE, WINTRY WEEKS of desertion and reorganization had witnessed desperate attempts by the Confederates to use the knife of strategy to cut the coils that were enveloping them. After the repulse of Maj. Gen. B. F. Butler's attack of December 23-26 on Fort Fisher, below Wilmington, North Carolina, the Federals returned to Hampton Roads, refitted, changed commanders of the participating troops and steamed back to the mouth of Cape Fear River. This time there was no experimentation with "powder ships" and no bluffing. Preparations were made to reduce and to storm the forts. In doing this, Maj. Gen. Alfred H. Terry, who headed the Federal expedition, enjoyed the full and confident support of Rear Admiral David D. Porter. Fire from the fleet so damaged Fort Fisher on the 14th of January that Union troops pushed their reconnaissance within 600 yards of the main work. The next afternoon the fort with its armament and its garrison fell.[1] After that, control of the mouth of the Cape Fear was secured easily.[2] The defense had been conducted by Braxton Bragg, who had been sent to Wilmington in advance, by Robert Hoke, by Chase Whiting and by the immediate commander of the fort, Col. William Lamb. Both Lamb and Whiting were wounded and captured. Whiting was sent to Fort Columbus, Governor's Island, whence he wrote a furious demand for an investigation of the conduct of Bragg, whom he blamed for the disaster.[3] He did not live to prosecute his charge or to witness the effect on the Southern cause of the loss of the fortifications he had built. Death from his wound ended on March 10 his strange, frustrated career.[4]

---

[1] Bragg (O. R., 46, pt. 1, p. 434) estimated the garrison at 110 officers and 2400 to 2500 men. Prisoners were 112 officers and 1971 enlisted men (Ibid., 399).

[2] O. R., 46, pt. 1, pp. 44, 397 ff.       [3] O. R., 46, pt. 1, pp. 441-42.

[4] The reports on Fort Fisher are in O. R., 46, pt. 1, p. 394 ff. Perhaps the fullest account of the siege is that in 10 S.H.S.P., 350, by Col. William Lamb. His MS Diary and his papers are in the library of the College of William and Mary.

Loss of the mouth of the Cape Fear River destroyed the last contact of the South with the outer world, except for the remote and
undeveloped route through Mexican territory. So desperate had
the situation become that the possibility of peace negotiations was
seized upon eagerly. Francis P. Blair, Sr., had come to Richmond
January 12, the day before the final attack on Fort Fisher began.
As mysteriously as he had arrived, Blair left the city: Millions of
Southerners hoped that he carried with him a draft of a peace
treaty. While the South waited and discussed, and prayed and
doubted, military events moved swiftly against the gasping Confederates. Sherman now had rested his men around Savannah
after their long march through Georgia. His lines of supply were
restored and in smooth operation, by the use of vessels that moved
without molestation down the Atlantic coast and into the Savannah River. It was manifest by the time of Blair's visit to Richmond
that Sherman would march northward into South Carolina. If
the victorious Federal could not be resisted successfully there by
the small force Lt. Gen. W. J. Hardee then commanded[5] at
Charleston, Sherman could advance into North Carolina. There
he could form a junction with the forces that had captured Fort
Fisher and doubtless by that time would have taken Wilmington.
Sherman's reinforced Army then could proceed into Southern Virginia. Were Lee's Army to remain at Petersburg, facing Grant's
troops, Sherman could destroy the last railroads that fed the Army,
and then he could take Lee in flank or rear.[6]

The strategy of such an advance was within the grasp of the
average soldier who, after four years of argument and observation,
had learned most of the realities and some of the probabilities of
military movements. Sherman must be stopped. That was imperative. If he were not halted, all was lost. By no possibility could
"Lee's Miserables" contend against Grant and Sherman combined.
To strengthen opposition to Sherman, more troops must be concentrated. Conner's Brigade, which had been Kershaw's famous
old command, accordingly was sent to South Carolina during the
first week in January at the instance of Gov. A. G. Magrath;[7] but

---

[5] Beauregard still was in nominal command of the "Military Division of the West,"
which included the area between the Appalachians and the Mississippi. See *supra*, p. 595.
[6] The simplest statement of the plans and progress of Sherman is his own in *O. R.*, 47,
pt. 1, p. 17 ff. Grant's review is in *ibid.*, 46, pt. 1, pp. 45 ff.
[7] *O. R.*, 47, pt. 2, pp. 991, 997; *Dickert*, 501.

one Brigade, of course, could not give Hardee, who had only 13,700 troops,[8] sufficient strength to stop Sherman. Pending a decision whether additional infantry could be dispatched from Virginia, more cavalry had to be provided. Hampton believed that his crippled old Division under Calbraith Butler could get mounts if it could go back to South Carolina to seek them. Horses then used by Butler's men might be left in North Carolina. As Mr. Davis already had sanctioned the move, Lee authorized it. Regretfully, also, he authorized Hampton to leave the Army, to visit the Palmetto State and to endeavor to stir the people. "I think Hampton will be of service," Lee told the President, "in mounting his men and arousing the spirit and strength of the State and otherwise do good."[9] On the 19th, formal orders were issued by Hampton for the departure by train of Butler's Division for Columbia, South Carolina.

This detachment of Butler was the final instance in which the Army of Northern Virginia was weakened to strengthen the Confederate cause elsewhere. At the moment, the release of one-third of the cavalry seemed necessary and appeared to involve no heavier risks than had been taken half a dozen times; but the event was to show—as Lee himself saw afterward[10]—that the departure of Hampton's Division hastened the catastrophe.

The secrecy of the operation precluded, of course, any formal farewell to Wade Hampton. None could foresee, for that matter, that he was leaving for the last time the Army with which he had served since the First Battle of Manassas. Had it been possible to honor the departing South Carolinian, he would have deserved the homage of massed regiments, dipping standards and acclaiming hands. In all the high companionship of knightly men, none had exemplified more of character and of courage and none had fewer mistakes charged against him. Untrained in arms and abhorring war, the South Carolina planter had proved himself the peer of any professional soldier within the bounds and opportunities set for a commander who did not have complicated decisions of strategy to make. There is nothing to indicate that he would have failed in higher command. He may not have possessed military genius but he had the nearest approach to it. In his place, while Fitz Lee was

[8] *O. R.,* 47, pt. 2, p. 984.
[9] *Lee's Dispatches,* 317. For Hampton's own view, see his letter of Jan. 20, 1865, to L. T. Wigfall in *Mrs. Wright,* 222.
[10] See 4 *R. E. Lee,* 533.

on the Northside, "Rooney" Lee assumed direction of the cavalry on the Confederate right and reported directly to the commanding General.[11]

On January 22, three days after the issuance of the orders for the transfer of command to "Rooney" Lee, the Federals who had captured Fort Fisher occupied Wilmington.[12] By the end of the month, Maj. Gen. John M. Schofield, with heavy reinforcements, arrived and assumed direction of the Federal Department of North Carolina. Although the Confederates did not know it immediately, Schofield was placed under the orders of Sherman[13]—ominous confirmation of the fear that the stern man who had wasted Georgia would hasten up the Atlantic coast toward the dwindling, shivering Army in the Petersburg trenches and on the bleak and muddy lines below Richmond.

Hope rose for a few days at the beginning of the new month. On the 29th of January, three Confederate peace commissioners had appeared with a flag of truce on the front of the IX Federal Corps in accordance with an unofficial understanding that had been reached as a result of Francis P. Blair's visit to the Confederate capital. For three days indications were that they might not be permitted even to enter the Federal lines, but through the intervention of General Grant,[14] arrangements were made for the commissioners to proceed to Hampton Roads. There, on the morning of February 3, a conference was held between President Lincoln and Secretary of State William H. Seward on one side and, on the other, the Confederate representatives, Vice President Alexander H. Stephens, Senator R. M. T. Hunter and Judge James A. Campbell, former Justice of the Supreme Court of the United States. At the close of a single meeting of four hours' duration,[15] the Southerners left[16] and, that same day, started back for Richmond.[17] On the 6th, in a message to the Congress, President Davis announced formally that the Hampton Roads conference had failed because Mr. Lincoln had "refused to enter into negotiations with the Confederate States, or any of them separately, or to give to our people any other terms or guarantee than those which the conqueror may

11 *O. R.*, 46, pt. 2, p. 1101.      12 *O. R.*, 46, pt. 1, p. 46.
13 *O. R.*, 46, pt. 2, p. 314.      14 *O. R.*, 46, pt. 2, p. 511.
15 *O. R.*, 46, pt. 2, p. 472.
16 The best, succinct narratives of what happened at the conference are those of R. M. T. Hunter, 3 *S.H.S.P.*, 168 ff, and of W. H. Seward, *O. R.*, 46, pt. 2, pp. 471–73.
17 *O. R.*, 46, pt. 2, p. 36*.

grant, or to permit us to have peace on any other basis than our unconditional submission to their rule . . ."[18]

The disappointment came at a time of crisis in everything. Davis's message, it will be noted, was sent Congress when the troops fighting in the open on the extreme Confederate right had been without meat for three days.[19] That was the date, also, on which Breckinridge was confirmed as Secretary of War and the appointment of Lee as General-in-chief was announced.[20] Only two days previously, Lee had been compelled to dissipate the last hope of the Administration that he could hold the lines with diminished forces and could send substantial assistance to South Carolina. This could not be done, Lee said; Hardee or Beauregard or whoever commanded in the Palmetto State must oppose Sherman with such force as could be mustered there.[21]

No peace without surrender, no meat for men battling in wintry weather, no prospect of effective resistance to Sherman—in the face of all this the braver officers and men held together. They heard, before many days had passed, that Beauregard had resumed command in South Carolina,[22] though that meant far less than in the days when his name had magic. Soon the telegraph brought the depressing news that Sherman had entered Columbia, South Carolina, on the 17th,[23] and, as the Confederates believed, had fired the city that night.[24]

It was not known then to many of the commanding officers in Virginia that Beauregard had informed Lee that the Governor of South Carolina could not authorize the militia, consisting of young boys and elderly men, to cross the border into North Carolina.[25] This, said Beauregard, reduced his mobile infantry to about 2500 men,[26] but, as always, he was fertile in suggesting what should be done with the troops of other leaders. The day he reported himself with fewer men than would constitute a strong Brigade, he talked of collecting 15,000 and urged that 35,000 men be assembled at

[18] 7 *Journal C. S. Congress*, 545.
[19] *O. R.*, 46, pt. 2, pp. 1206, 1210. See *supra*, p. 620.
[20] See *supra*, p. 634.
[21] Lee to Davis, MS, Feb. 4, 1865—*Lee MSS*, Duke University.
[22] As of February 16 (*O. R.*, 47, pt. 2, p. 1204). He continued, nominally, to direct the "Military Division of the West."
[23] *O. R.*, 47, pt. 1, pp. 20–21.
[24] Sherman (*ibid.*, 21) insisted that the flames were spread by high wind from bales of cotton the Confederates set afire in the streets. The evidence to the contrary was marshalled in 7 *S.H.S.P.*, 156–58, 185–92; 8 *ibid.*, 202–14; 10 *ibid.*, 109–19.
[25] *O. R.*, 47, pt. 2, pp. 1238, 1256.    [26] *Ibid.*, 1238.

Salisbury, North Carolina, "to crush" the enemy. This done, Beauregard's plan was to "concentrate all forces against Grant and . . .
to march on Washington to dictate a peace." [27]

There had been a time when a dispatch of this sort would have
puzzled the President; later it would have provoked him; now he
contented himself with referring it to Lee [28] while personally he
urged Beauregard to hasten the concentration.[29] In response,
Beauregard maneuvered feebly. It was while he was attempting
to get his troops together that Wilmington fell.[30] After that, military chaos was threatened in North Carolina. Where Beauregard,
Hardee, Hampton, Bragg, Hoke and others had divided control
of troops, it was plain that command must be co-ordinated at
once. Lee had to conclude that Beauregard, in the circumstances,
was not "able to do much." [31] Accordingly, in spite of the President's notorious dislike of Joseph E. Johnston and distrust of that
officer's abilities,[32] Lee, as General-in-chief, asked that Johnston be
ordered to report to him for assignment to duty.[33] On the 22nd
of February, Johnston was given direction of the Department of
Tennessee and Georgia and of the Department of South Carolina,
Georgia and Florida. There was no time for finesse. The order
for the appointment of the new commander included a provision
that Beauregard should report to Johnston "for such duty as
[Johnston] deems most advisable." A telegram to Beauregard
notified him of the content of the order.[34] Johnston was told that
he needed no assurance of Beauregard's "cheerful and zealous
support." [35] Beauregard's own answer was: "In the defense of our
common country I will at all times be happy to serve with or under
so gallant and patriotic a soldier as General Johnston." [36] As for
Bragg, in the event the advance of Johnston brought him where
he could use the troops with which Bragg had marched from
Wilmington, Johnston was told, "of course you will direct their
movements." [37]

[27] Ibid., 1238.
[28] The commanding General observed only: "The idea is good, but the means are lacking" (O. R., 53, 413).
[29] Ibid.; O. R., 47, pt. 2, p. 1246.        [30] See supra, p. 640.
[31] O. R., 53, 412–13.
[32] Cf. O. R., 47, pt. 2, p. 1304 ff—a long detailed review, a denunciation, in fact, of
Johnston's entire military career as a Confederate soldier.
[33] O. R., 46, pt. 2, pp. 1242–45; 53, 412–13; 6 Rowland, 481.
[34] O. R., 47, pt. 2, p. 1248.        [35] Ibid., 1256.
[36] Ibid., 1248.        [37] Ibid., 1257.

In this late scene of the tragedy, there now was another brief interlude of hope. Maj. Gen. Edward O. C. Ord had succeeded General Butler on January 7 in command of the Department of Virginia and North Carolina.[38] Ord was one of the kindest and most unselfish of men [39] and, needless to say, he was desirous of ending the war without further waste of blood and life. He had known before the war "Peter" Longstreet, who now opposed him on the north side of the James. Ord was aware, too, that Mrs. Longstreet and Mrs. Grant had been friends [40] and he was of opinion that if an armistice could be arranged by the commanders, an exchange of visits between these ladies, with an ample escort of officers, might bring an understanding and then an honorable peace. In this hope, Ord found an occasion for a meeting with Longstreet under a flag of truce on February 21 and broached his proposal. Longstreet, of course, welcomed the suggestion and conveyed it immediately to Lee. In a lengthy conference at the White House of the Confederacy on the 22nd—the date of the fall of Wilmington—the idea was approved.

After further exchanges between Ord and Longstreet regarding the essential preliminaries, Lee on March 2 wrote two letters to Grant. One, which was an excuse for the other, raised a question regarding the exchange of political prisoners. The other requested an interview, in accordance with the conversations between Ord and Longstreet, for discussion of a possible military convention. Both letters were forwarded through the lines. On the 4th of March, the day Lincoln delivered his second inaugural, Grant declined an interview on the ground that he had no authority to formulate the suggested convention. "Such authority," he said, "is vested in the President of the United States alone." [41] That was final. It removed all hope of peace by negotiation. Nothing remained for the Army except to resume the fight in the field, provided the men were willing to face the overmastering odds.

That proviso could not be disregarded. So well placed and in

---

38 O. R., 46, pt. 2, p. 61. On Feb. 6, 1865, this command was reduced to the Department of Virginia (Ibid., 421).

39 Cf. Sherman's order on the death of Ord, July 22, 1883. Cullum No. 1002.

40 Longstreet, 584.

41 The circumstances were explained and the correspondence printed conveniently in Longstreet, 582 ff. In O. R., 46, pt. 2, p. 802, are the insistent orders of President Lincoln that General Grant should have "no conference with General Lee, unless it be for the capitulation of General Lee's army or on some minor and purely military matter." Grant's reply is in ibid., 823–24.

formed an officer as Col. Walter Taylor, A.A.G. at Headquarters, had vague misgivings of the morale of the men. "My faith in this old Army is unshaken," he wrote, and again, ten days before the exchange of letters with Grant: "They are trying to corner this old army like a brave old lion brought to bay at last, it is determined to resist to the death and if die it must, to die game." Then he added hastily: "But we have not yet quite made up our minds to die, and if God will help us, we shall yet prove equal to the emergency." [42]

As the winds shifted and the March rain lost some of the wintry chill, two possibilities of breaking the grip of the enemy were considered and, in time, were combined. One was for Joseph E. Johnston to hold off Sherman, to beat the Federals if possible, and to prevent a junction between Sheridan and Schofield. If Johnston failed in this, he was to move his own forces toward Virginia. When this was done, the Army of Northern Virginia was to shake itself loose from Grant and was to march to join Johnston. [43] The two Confederate Armies were then to assail Sherman and, having defeated him, were to turn and attack Grant.

A similar plan of concentration and regrouping had been attempted, on a small scale, by the junction of Ewell and Jackson in the Shenandoah, but 1865 was not 1862. What daring made possible then, exhaustion precluded now. Johnston never had much faith in realization of the scheme because he knew the weakness of his troops, on whom Lee and the Administration placed too much reliance, [44] but the commander in North Carolina worked hard and honestly to checkmate his adversary. [45] The enemy, Johnston soon concluded, was too strong and too advantageously placed to be attacked with any prospect of success. If junction were effected between Sherman and the field force of Schofield, which was under Maj. Gen. Jacob D. Cox, [46] "their march into Virginia," said Johnston on March 11, "cannot be prevented by me." [47]

Lee already had concluded that Johnston's Army could accom-

[42] Letters of Feb. 16 and 20, 1865—*Taylor MSS.*
[43] The first known suggestion of this plan appeared in Lee to Johnston, Feb. 23, 1865, *O. R.*, 47, pt. 2, pp. 1256–57. Details were developed in their subsequent correspondence and in Lee's conferences. See *Gordon* 385 ff; 2 *Davis*, 648.
[44] *O. R.*, 47, pt. 2, p. 1271.    [45] Cf. *ibid.*, 1297.
[46] For his assignment to duty, see *O. R.*, 47, pt. 2, pp. 579–80.
[47] *Ibid.*, 1373.

plish little [48] and he studied more carefully a second plan that fitted into the first. Longstreet,[49] Gordon [50] and Johnston [51] had made the same general suggestion in different forms. It was, in effect, that Lee endeavor to hold Richmond and Petersburg, or Richmond only, with part of his forces, and dispatch the remainder to join Johnston in an attack on Sherman. If the main Federal force in North Carolina were defeated, then the victorious Army could move northward, relieve Richmond and deal with Grant on terms less unequal. Here again, the main defect of the plan was patent: The Confederate lines on the Richmond-Petersburg front already were so lightly held that if any part of the defenders were detached, Grant could storm successfully almost any sector he chose.

Discussion produced at length, through the ingenuity of John B. Gordon, a plan that seemed to overcome this objection. Gordon proposed that at a point he believed vulnerable, he assault the Federal line, break through, take a position in rear, sweep down the Union works and force Grant to abandon the left of his line. Lee then would have a shorter front and consequently could have greater density of force.[52]

Perhaps it was indicative not only of the desperation but also of the distorted military thought of the Confederates, after a winter of hunger and strain, that in planning this they should ignore the certainty of an immediate counterstroke by Grant. They assumed, apparently, that after the Confederates broke through, the Union commander submissively would disregard his own numerical superiority and docilely would take up a shorter line. That was not Grant's way. He would blunder but he always would fight. At the moment, he was thinking of the Southerners' retreat, not of their advance, and of the difficulties he would have in overtaking them. "I felt," said Grant afterward, "that the situation of the Confederate Army was such that they would try to make an escape at the earliest practicable moment, and I was afraid, every morning, that I would awake from my sleep to hear that Lee had gone, and that nothing was left but a picket line." [53] Grant would have asked nothing better than that the Confederates assume the offensive.

48 O. R., 46, pt. 2, p. 1295.      49 See the detailed note in 4 R. E. Lee, 12.
50 Gordon, 389.      51 O. R., 47, pt. 2, p. 1373.
52 All the details are to be found in 4 R. E. Lee, 14 ff.
53 2 Grant's Memoirs, 424.

In curious disregard of this, Lee authorized John B. Gordon to develop his plan for storming the Federal lines and for cutting off the Union left. Formal approval was not given. That would depend, primarily, on what happened in North Carolina, and, in part, on a new and most ominous factor, namely, the probable return of Sheridan's mounted troops to Grant's Army. After the final defeat of Early at Waynesboro, there was no reason why the cavalry of Sheridan should remain in the Shenandoah Valley. He had destroyed all its barns and mills and stables. The Valley could supply no more food to the Confederate Army and scarcely could subsist its own population. Sheridan could afford to leave infantry to guard the desert he had created. He himself, with his strong Divisions, could rejoin the Army of the Potomac, and could prepare for the spring campaign.[54] If Sheridan returned while Butler's Division was in Carolina to oppose the advancing Sherman and Schofield, the Confederates would make the best fight they could, but the odds would be long and might be hopeless. There was little prospect, even, that Lee could get forage enough to retain on the flanks his few mounted troops and to use them against Sheridan.[55]

It was well for Gordon that he had been studying his proposed attack even before it had been regarded at Headquarters as a possible expedient. Events moved swiftly. On the night of the 23rd of March, after the Georgian had explained fully to the commanding General what he intended to do, he was told to assemble his forces and to make the assault on the morning of the 25th. Gordon, it will be remembered, was "a self made" soldier. He had begun as a Captain and had risen to the rank of Major General in the hard school of combat. As he had been brilliantly successful in several battles, he had faith in infantry. Of engineering he knew little and of artillery not enough to distinguish him. In short, his lack of hampering military preconceptions was balanced by his ignorance of the other arms of the service. The plan he had developed after long examination of the ground was to deliver a surprise attack before dawn at a point where the opposing trenches were not more than 150 yards apart. By pretending that they were Federals driven back by the enemy, men in three carefully chosen columns of 100 were to press through the Union line. Then they

[54] O. R., 46. pt. 3, p. 1319.          [55] Ibid.

were to make a rush for small forts which Gordon had satisfied himself were behind the heavy main defenses. While fire from these forts was being poured into the rear of the Federals, strong Confederate forces were to pour through the break and were to advance up and down the trenches. The cavalry would follow and would push to the rear and destroy the enemy's lines of communication. Into the assault, almost half the Confederate infantry on the Southside were to be thrown. On the 24th it was decided to bring Pickett's Division from the Northside and to use it, also, if it could arrive in time. While the attack was being delivered, Longstreet was to demonstrate below Richmond.

All the preparations were made smoothly and with maximum secrecy. By 4 o'clock on the morning of the 25th, Gordon was on the ground of attack. He made a stirring speech to the sharpshooters [56] and then he mounted the parapet opposite the work, Fort Stedman,[57] which his men were ready to storm. By Gordon's side stood the soldier who was to fire a single shot as a signal for the advance. Between the two picket lines was nothing except open ground and the remnant of a cornfield. The Confederate abatis and obstructions had been removed, but not all the materials had been carried away. Although troops were tense and ready for the dash to Fort Stedman, Gordon thought he should wait long enough to remove the debris lest men stumble over it. The handling of the timbers made some noise. Out of the darkness, the voice of a Federal picket called: "What are you doing over there, Johnny? What is that noise? Answer quick or I'll shoot."

Gordon was aghast. Through his mind there flashed the fear of an alarm, picket firing, an awakened enemy, a repulsed charge. The soldier by him was not disturbed. Accustomed to verbal exchanges with the enemy, he shouted back: "Never mind, Yank! Lie down and go to sleep. We are just gathering a little corn. You know rations are mighty short over here."

"All right, Johnny; go ahead and get your corn. I'll not shoot at you while you are drawing your rations."

With no further challenge, the remaining fragments of the

---

[56] *Thomas,* 39–40. A sketch of Fort Stedman and adjoining works will be found in 4 *R. E. Lee,* 15.

[57] For descriptions of the fort, see *O. R.,* 46, pt. 1, pp. 173, 316. It took its name from Col. Griffin A. Stedman, 11th Conn., mortally wounded, Aug. 5, 1864.

obstructions were put aside. The assault now could be delivered. Gordon ordered the signal given. The soldier at his elbow lifted his rifle but did not seem able to pull the trigger. Gordon repeated his order: "Fire your gun, sir!" Still the boy hesitated: he must contrive to play fair with the Federal picket who had not fired on him. In a moment, still gripping his rifle, the Southerner cried: "Hello, Yank! Wake up; we are going to shell the woods. Look out; we are coming!" That satisfied him. He fired. The Confederate pickets, who meantime had crept forward, sprang silently upon the opposing pickets and killed or made prisoners of them without the discharge of another rifle. Experienced axemen sprang over the parapets and, with swift blows, hacked to pieces the sharpened timbers that protected the Union works. Behind them poured the three columns of 100, each man of whom had a white band on his arm. After these troops surged the main body of the infantry.[58]

Surprise scarcely could have been more nearly complete. Passageways were cut through the heavy Federal obstructions.[59] Everything worked to perfection. If Gordon could have known it, as he went with the troops to Fort Stedman, he had anticipated in miniature by fifty years and more the tactics of the breakthrough. Once in the fort, he saw his men spread to left and to right, and he observed a large number of sleepy, bewildered prisoners. It looked as if success would attend the operation on which hung the life of the Confederacy! Besides the infantry, picked officers and men of Stribling's Battalion of artillery had crossed No Man's Land and had turned the four guns of Fort Stedman on the enemy.[60] The ordnance in the adjoining Battery, No. 10, also was brought into service against the Federals.[61] Never had fortune smiled more approvingly on John B. Gordon, whose young wife

[58] All the details, perhaps colored somewhat by time, appear in *Gordon,* 407–10.
[59] In *Thomas,* 38, the Captain of the sharpshooters, Capt. Joseph P. Carson, Fourth Georgia, described the obstruction as follows: "Between the branch and the old fort there were three lines of obstructions as perfect as human ingenuity and labor could devise. The first was composed of pine logs, about eight inches thick, in which holes had been bored at intervals and sharpened spikes inserted. Then logs about twenty-five feet long had been crossed and recrossed and fastened together with wire. About forty steps farther back was the second line, composed of tangled brush with the sharpened butts projecting toward us. The third and last line was composed of fence-rails planted in the ground with their sharpened ends slanted towards us." No other account of the obstructions is measurably so full. Consequently, Carson's account cannot be tested for accuracy by comparing it with the statements of different observers.
[60] *O. R.,* 46, pt. 1, pp. 317, 391.        [61] *Ibid.,* 317.

was listening from her room in Petersburg to the roar of the guns that proclaimed the widening success of the attack.

The sound for which Gordon was listening was not that of Stribling's pleasant music with the twelve-pounders in the fort, nor that of the Federals who were beginning now to send their protesting missiles from the flanks. What Gordon wanted to hear was the crash of guns from the small forts in the rear, the forts to which he had told those columns of 100 to press. If the guns in those earthworks would bring their fire to bear on the Union rear, the victory would be complete.

Presently, from one of the columns a messenger made his way to Gordon. The commander, said the courier, had experienced no difficulty in getting to the rear by pretending that he was a Federal officer, but he had lost his guide and had not found the fort. From the other advance columns came the same report.[62] There followed long, long minutes of uncertainty, confusion and suspense. Then, gradually, a fine initial success became a reversed Battle of the Crater. Before some of Gordon's men realized it, they were confined to a little fort and narrow front of trenches from which they could not advance, though they soon would be subjected to a heavy fire of enfilading artillery. There was no prospect, so far as Gordon knew, of any reinforcements. He had employed in the attack all the men assigned him, and he had been warned that the arrival of Pickett was improbable. Grimly, at dawn,[63] Gordon had to notify Lee that the rear forts had not been reached and that the advance had been halted.[64]

Tenure of Stedman and of the nearby Federal line soon became intolerable. The troops who had occupied Battery 10 could not take Battery 9.[65] A bold contingent of Gordon's men pushed within about 500 yards of Battery 9, only to come under so heavy a drenching of canister that the men had to take refuge in a depression.[66] On the Confederate right, "down the line," Batteries 11 and 12 had been seized in the first onrush. Number 12 had to be abandoned in a short time. As soon as the Federals could see enough to guide their assault, they attacked and recovered Num-

[62] *Gordon*, 411.

[63] Sunrise at Petersburg on the 25th of March, 1865, was at 5:54.

[64] *Gordon*, 411.

[65] The report of Maj. Gen. John G. Parke, commanding the IX Corps, is detailed on all essential facts concerning the defense of the position (*O. R.*, 46, pt. 1, p. 316 ff).

[66] *O. R.*, 46, pt. 1, pp. 356–57.

ber 11.[67] From Fort Haskell, farther southward, a battery of light twelve-pounders held off the attack. Soon all the batteries on a long stretch of line were hurling their projectiles into Fort Stedman and Battery 10.[68] The fort was without bastions and scarcely was higher than the ground in rear of it; Battery 10 was open in rear.[69] In both these vulnerable works, Gordon's men were exposed helplessly. The Southern commander could see also, as morning light spread, that the enemy was massing troops in a cordon around Fort Stedman. An attack for the recovery of the fortifications evidently would be made in a short time.[70] This could not be prevented by anything Gordon could do. Even if there had been opportunity of making another of the bold charges that had brought Gordon renown, his men might not have been willing to deliver it. He may not have known it at the time, but some of his troops, after storming Fort Stedman, had refused to go forward.[71]

Gordon had learned the rewards of tenacity and, doubtless, he would have held Fort Stedman and would have repulsed assaults as long as any of his soldiers would fight. He would have died manfully, if the cause demanded the sacrifice, at the farthest traverse his troops had reached. That was not required of him. About 8 A.M. orders came from General Lee to evacuate the captured works.

There followed a scene that few of the Southern commanders liked to mention afterward. Every man in the ranks could see for himself that the return to the Confederate positions, across the open ground between the lines, would be a challenge of death. The bravest took the chance; the weak and the dispirited defied their commanders and chose surrender. Said a Federal officer who had been captured and held in a bomb-proof at the fort: ". . . officers ordered, threatened, and begged their men to fall back to their old lines in vain."[72] The troops who had taken cover in the depression near Battery 9 had to surrender en masse.[73] When the broken Divisions were back in their red trenches and were able to

[67] Ibid., 318.  [68] Ibid., 375.
[69] Ibid., 316.
[70] For the approximate position of the Federals who were moved forward to deliver this assault, see the map in William H. Hodgkins, The Battle of Fort Stedman, though this map has several inaccuracies. See also Parke in O. R., 46, pt. 1, p. 318.
[71] J. C. G., Lee's Last Campaign, 10.
[72] Maj. Theodore Miller in O. R., 46, pt. 1, p. 359.  [73] Ibid., 357.

estimate their losses, they found they had left behind in the Federal works and in the field between the lines probably 3500 men. Of this total, approximately 1900 were prisoners.[74] In that black hour, there was neither time nor heart to name among the fallen the brave, the well-loved or the renowned. Had the occasion been different, there might have been a line at the least to record the death of William Hood of the Thirty-third North Carolina, he who had climbed a tree for "Old Jack" at Sharpsburg amid whining miniés.[75] Even as it was, they did him such honor as they could and buried him on the field in one of Gen. Mat. Ransom's uniforms.[76]

The action did not end with the return of the Confederates to their lines. As soon as the commanders of the II and VI Corps had heard of the concentrated attack on Fort Stedman, they reasoned that the rest of the line had been stripped and they urged a general assault. Their suggestions were sent to Maj. Gen. John G. Parke of the IX Corps who had ascertained to his surprise, not many minutes before, that General Meade was absent from the front and that he had field command of the Army. In this position of unexpected responsibility, Parke declined to order a general assault.[77] Later in the morning, Meade arrived from City Point, resumed command and directed an attack on the Confederate picket lines in front of the II and the VI Corps. This attack was delivered in the afternoon and was successful.[78] About 650 additional prisoners were captured by the VI Corps.[79] The II Corps took approximately 184.[80] This made the Confederate loss in prisoners that day heavier than in any single day's action on Lee's front after the Bloody Angle.[81] On the entire front, March 25, the Federal losses were 2080 men.[82] Gross Confederate casualties certainly reached 4400 and perhaps 5000. The number of infantrymen pres-

---

[74] O. R., 46, pt. 1, p. 51. For other accounts of the attack and repulse, see 19 C. V., 217–18; 22 ibid., 460–62; 31 S.H.S.P., 19 ff.

[75] See Vol. II, pp. 241–42.  [76] 2 N. C. Regts., 608.

[77] O. R., 46, pt. 1, p. 319.

[78] The general assumption that this advance was made immediately subsequent to the recovery of Fort Stedman is demonstrably incorrect. The itineraries of both the Corps (O. R., 46, pt. 1, pp. 75, 100) show that the attack was made after 12 M.

[79] Ibid., 100.

[80] Grant (O. R., 46, pt. 1, p. 51) stated that the total for the two corps was 834. As Wright accounted for 650, the remainder were Humphreys's prisoners. These would appear to be the official figures, but they may be approximations only. Meade, on the 26th of March, reported the totals for the 25th as: IX Corps, 1949 prisoners; II Corps, 365; VI Corps, 469; total 2,783 (O. R., 46, pt. 1, p. 156).

[81] See supra, p. 434.  [82] O. R., 46, pt. 1, p. 156.

ent in the entire Army, including Ewell's garrison of Richmond, was reduced to approximately 36,000.[83] Whether some of these would fight, leaders had new reason to doubt. Lt. Col. R. M. Stribling, who had taken his artillerists to Fort Stedman and had served the guns there, had no illusions. "This attack," he wrote subsequently, "demonstrated that Lee's army had lost hope of final success, and the men were not willing to risk their lives in a hopeless endeavor . . ."[84] That language stated the case realistically, though perhaps in the long after-light. Deserters, for once, told the whole truth when they said on the night of the 25th, after entering the Union lines, that the "fighting [was] very severe, and the result [was] having a depressing and demoralizing effect on their army."[85]

Gordon's responsibility for the greater part of the day's casualties was not appraised at the time and is not easy to determine now. His repulse was due, in part, to his failure to appreciate the severity of the artillery fire he had to encounter while developing his attack or while retiring in the event of repulse. By his own admission, much of his heaviest loss, in killed and wounded, was sustained when his men were recrossing the open field between the works.[86] In his account of preparations for the attack, Gordon made singularly little reference to the artillery's part in the operation. General Pendleton apparently was not consulted in advance.[87] If General Long, Chief of Artillery of the Second Corps, was asked for counsel, it must have been in vague terms, because Long's subsequent remarks on the operations showed that he did not know what was planned.[88] Besides Long and Pendleton, one of the ablest of all the combat artillerists of the Army, Col. Thomas H. Carter, was at Gordon's service. There is nothing to show that his advice was sought.

Gordon's other serious mistake was in assuming that he could capture easily the "three small forts" in rear of Stedman and could

[83] For the detailed calculation, see 4 R. E. Lee, 6, n. 25.
[84] Gettysburg Campaign and Campaigns of 1864 and 1865 in Virginia, 299.
[85] Grant in O. R., 46, pt. 1, p. 156.
[86] See his letter of Oct. 16, 1880 in 2 Davis, 650 ff.
[87] The only reference in Pendleton, without quotation of any letter, is pp. 395–96, that on the morning of March 25 the Chief of Artillery was notified to meet the commanding General at five o'clock A.M. at the headquarters of Major General Gordon." The explanation that follows this reference suggests strongly, though it does not state authoritatively, that Pendleton had no previous knowledge of the attack. He filed no report on it. Nor did he mention in any published correspondence that he was making any preparations for it.
[88] See Long, 404–05.

use them effectively to blast the Federal rear. The forts were said later, in reviews of the battle, to be non-existent; but two of these probably were what and where Gordon thought they were. In all likelihood, he had seen at a distance some small works that had been constructed by the Confederates in 1862–63 and had been re-faced by the Federals in 1864. The third fort may have been an abandoned Southern battery. There had been little chance that Gordon's men could find these places in the dark. Whether the Federals would have been routed by the fire from the rear positions is a question that cannot be answered.[89] For hundreds of yards on that part of the front, the confusion of old Confederate works, of abandoned Union batteries and of Federal works little used and lightly guarded was enough to bewilder Gordon who had been in the Valley, not in Eastern Virginia, when the Army first took position in front of Petersburg.

While Gordon's mistake is understandable, it seems strange that none of the engineers should have known the approaches and approximate armament of the Union works. The explanation may be that Gordon's error was shared by all. Perhaps, in the misery of a dying cause, the usual care of competent soldiers weakened. Still again, the secret of the operation may have been too restricted, or, finally, Gordon may not have seen fit to confer with other officers. He never wrote at length of the forts. As Lee understood it, Gordon's failure was due to the fact that the "redoubts commanding the line of entrenchments were found enclosed and strongly manned." [90] Gordon later said that the guides had become lost in the rush of the advance columns and that the commanders then had been confused and been unable to find the forts.[91] With this explanation Gordon coupled the non-arrival of Pickett in support,[92] though Gordon, to repeat, had been warned

[89] *Humphreys*, 317–18; W. H. Hodgkins, *The Battle of Fort Stedman*, 13; Maj. Gen. J. F. Hartranft in 4 *B. & L.*, 584. It is difficult, after eighty years, to be certain what Gordon saw, or thought he saw, or where his point of vantage was. O. F. Northington, Jr., Superintendent of the Petersburg National Military Park, is of opinion (1944) that Gordon attempted to reach (1) Union Battery 4, which was refaced Confederate Battery 5 of the old, so-called "Dimmock line," (2) Fort Friend, which was known also as the Dunn House Battery and had been Confederate Battery 8 on the same line, and (3) a position on the Dimmock line that covered Meade's Station. This third position may have been Confederate Battery 10. It was unoccupied at the time of Gordon's attacks, but was used for field guns before the fight at Fort Stedman was over. The armament of Fort Friend was six 3-inch rifles. In Union Battery 4 were three 30-pounder Parrotts.

[90] *Lee's Dispatches*, 344. The context (p. 342) made plain that the "redoubts" were those "in the rear of the enemy's main line," not those on the line.

[91] *Gordon*, 411.            [92] *Ibid.*

that Pickett probably could not reach Petersburg in time to be of help on the morning of the 25th.[93]

To none of this did the army command give thought after the failure of the attack. The nearer, fatal actualities absorbed every mind.

[93] Gordon's request was not made until 2:30 P.M. on the 24th (*Gordon*, 407). Longstreet's effort to expedite the movement of Pickett's Division is set forth in *O. R.*, 46, pt. 3, p. 1345 ff. "Maryland" Steuart was in command of the Division that day.

# CHAPTER XXXIII

## PICKETT AND PEGRAM: A CLOSING CONTRAST

TWO DAYS BEFORE the attack on Fort Stedman, Johnston had telegraphed that Sherman and Schofield had formed a junction at Goldsboro, 120 miles from Petersburg. Johnston stated in fullest candor that his small command could not hinder Sherman's advance to a union with Grant.[1] That had been one reason Gordon's assault had been set for the 25th. Now that Gordon had failed, every general officer and many a man of lesser rank sensed what Lee confided to the President on March 26 in an autograph letter:[2] The time was at hand to evacuate Richmond and Petersburg and to unite with the forces in North Carolina.[3]

The one route to Johnston's lines, with railroad communication all the way, was via the Southside Railroad to Burkeville, and thence parallel to the Richmond and Danville to its terminus. Beyond Danville, the Army could use the Piedmont Railroad, which led to Greensboro.[4] For the marching columns and the wagons, there could be a short cut, if need be, to the Richmond and Danville, by roads to be described later. All rail movement directly West from Petersburg and all delivery of supplies at Petersburg from the Southside Railroad manifestly depended on keeping the enemy from that line of track. For months it had been recognized that the Confederate Army could not subsist many days if Grant seized the railroad at any point beyond the extreme right of the Confederate line, which now rested on Hatcher's Run about three miles west of Burgess' Mill. Grant's strategy had been based on this assurance. Once he was astride the railroad, Petersburg was lost. Ipso facto, Richmond was. If, in addition, the Federal cavalry could swing far beyond the Confederate right and could get across the roads that led to Danville . . .

---

[1] *O. R.,* 46, pt. 1, p. 1055.    [2] *Lee's Dispatches,* 341 ff.
[3] Lee's language to Davis was: "I fear now it will be impossible to prevent a junction between Grant and Sherman, nor do I deem it prudent that this army should maintain its position until the latter shall approach too near" (*Ibid.*).
[4] For a sketch of these railways, see *supra,* p. 477.

This must not be, but the threat now was imminent. Sheridan had done what was expected of him. Set free by Early's defeat at Waynesboro, the Federal commander had moved over the Blue Ridge at Rockfish Gap, had proceeded to Charlottesville and, after tearing up all the railroad trackage within reach, had advanced down the Valley of the James and by one of his long sweeps had reached, on the 19th of March, the White House on the Pamunkey.[5] There he rested his men, but on the day that Fort Stedman was attacked, Fitz Lee sent word that Sheridan again was moving. The destination of this heavy mounted force could be none other than the Federal left.[6] Sheridan therefore must be kept from the Southside Railroad until preparations to evacuate Petersburg had been completed. If possible, he must be held until the roads were firm enough for the weakened teams to haul the wagons which still numbered hundreds.

To oppose Sheridan, who counted some 13,000 sabres,[7] the Confederates could employ Fitz Lee's Division, W. H. F. Lee's and Rosser's, if what remained of Rosser's forces could be termed a Division.[8] The strength of these units probably did not exceed 5500.[9] Butler was gone with his 2200 men.[10] Gone, too, was Hampton, whose leadership had offset odds on many a battlefield. The necessity that had compelled the dispatch of Hampton and Butler to the Carolinas might prove the decisive circumstance of the campaign.[11] There was no way of changing that, but the commanders undertook to make the best substitution they could for the absent Carolinians and Georgians. Fitz Lee was on the left: he must leave Gary there with one Brigade and must bring the others to the right. This would supplement by 900 officers and men the Division of W. H. F. Lee, whose 2500 must bear the heavier part of the fight. Fitz, as senior, would command all. To strengthen this force, a desperate, clumsy proposal made by Longstreet had been adopted at Army Headquarters:[12] Infantry were

---

[5] O. R., 46, pt. 1, pp. 477–80.      [6] See the detailed references in 4 R. E. Lee, 21.
[7] Humphreys, 433: officers, 611; enlisted men, 13,209. In O. R., 46, pt. 3, p. 391, the totals are: officers, 591; enlisted men, 12,835. Both set of figures are "present for duty."
[8] For Rosser's return see supra, p. 633.
[9] As of March 1, Fitz Lee had 1887 present for duty and W. H. F. Lee had 2541. Officers of the two Divisions numbered 283 (O. R., 46, pt. 1, p. 390). To the 4428 men of these two Divisions, Rosser's command should be added. Its strength is not known, but, at the maximum estimate, it scarcely could have exceeded 1000.
[10] This was his strength as of January 10, 1865 (O. R., 46, pt. 1, p. 384).
[11] See supra, p. 639.      [12] Cf. O. R., 46, pt. 3, p. 1357.

to be used in place of cavalry. Pickett's Division [13] was to be made a special mobile force to operate with the two young Generals Lee in protecting the right.

On the 29th of March, four days after the attempted break-through had failed, word passed among the higher officers that Federal cavalry and infantry were moving to the Southwest from Monk's Neck Bridge.[14] Although the line of march of this column was not determinable at once, orders were received by the cavalry for an immediate concentration on the extreme right.[15] Three Brigades of Pickett's men were ordered to proceed ten miles westward on the Southside Railroad, to Sutherland Station, and to detrain there.[16]

The movement was made promptly. From Sutherland, during the night, Pickett marched his troops across Hatcher's Run to the trenches farthest westward. It was a rainy, shivering night. The roads were mudholes; the angry little streams were almost past fording.[17] The next morning, March 30, Pickett, "Dick" Anderson, Harry Heth and perhaps one or two others were called to a conference with the commanding General, who rode out to Sutherland to see them. Reports were that the enemy had reached Dinwiddie Court House, six miles from Monk's Bridge, and that he had artillery as well as infantry and cavalry. Anderson had sent two Brigades on the 29th against this force but he had not been able to shake it.[18] Information may have been received, also, of an advance by Federal cavalry to Five Forks,[19] but if so, this was not credited.[20] Later in the day there was an abundance of evidence that Federal horse were spread widely to the South of Five Forks.

All practicable means of dealing with this advance by Sheridan were considered. Two only of these seemed promising. Harry Heth had hopes that from his widely extended front he might be

13 This Division, it will be recalled, had been moved to the Southside to share in the attack on Fort Stedman, but it had not been used there.
14 *O. R.*, 46, pt. 1, p. 1263.
15 W. H. F. Lee's MS Report of the Appomattox campaign—*Lee MSS; Proceedings . . . of the Court of Inquiry . . . in the case of Gouverneur K. Warren* (cited hereafter as *Warren*), 467.
16 Pickett's MS Report of the Appomattox Campaign—*Lee MSS; Walter Harrison*, 135.
17 *Walter Harrison*, 135.  18 *O. R.*, 46, pt. 1, p. 1263.
19 *Walter Harrison*, 136.
20 Harrison stated it as a fact that Federal Cavalry were at Five Forks, but Sheridan's report and that of Brig. Gen. Thomas C. Devin (*O. R.*, 46, pt. 1, pp. 1102, 1122) show that the Federals did not get nearer than three-quarters of a mile to Five Forks.

able to strike a heavy blow. Pickett seemed to have a better chance. He was told that he was to take his three Brigades, two of Anderson's, and six guns of Col. William J. Pegram's and with these to march to Five Forks, where Fitz Lee then was. W. H. F. Lee and Rosser were to report there, and were to be under the direction of Fitz Lee as senior Major General. Pickett was to be in general command. From Five Forks, with the cavalry in support, he must advance in the direction of Dinwiddie Court House and assail the enemy.[21] If Pickett then could drive the Federals from the Court House, he would frustrate their movement and save the railroad. It was an order in the old spirit of the Army—to disdain odds and to attack.

This was an honor for Pickett but it carried a weight of responsibility as well. Fortune had not been kind to him since that great, bloody day at Gettysburg. His expedition in North Carolina had not been successful; the effort to cope with Butler's advance in May, 1864, had put him in bed; the reputation of his famous Division had been marred by the conscripts who no sooner reached the Army than they tried to desert. Pickett had the companionship of his adoring young wife, but Fame had passed him by. Now, as senior Major General among the officers on the right, detached from Anderson, he was to attempt to deal with Sheridan and with whatever infantry support that furious fighter might have. A victory would be a triumph, but the roads were almost impassable, the men were hungry, the odds were frightful.

Soon after noon on the 30th, General Lee rode grimly back to Headquarters near Petersburg. "Dick" Anderson had his lines to guard. Pickett was his own commander now. As quickly as he could, he started the advance westward from White Oak Road to Five Forks. The distance was only a little more than four miles, but the march was through a flat, drab country of pine woods and small open fields. Several roads led from the South to the flank of Pickett's columns where the men waded through mud and chill water. The enemy made the most of these lines of attack. Col. William Pegram's Adjutant, Capt. W. Gordon McCabe, was accustomed to swifter advances than Pickett approved, and in his diary McCabe wrote: "Our flank being exposed to the enemy, they

[21] Pickett in *Walter Harrison*, 142–43; more detailed references are given in 4 R. E Lee. 31.

harassed us with small bodies of cavalry without intermission. General Pickett, instead of pushing on, stopped, formed a regiment in line-of-battle, and awaited some attack. Much valuable time was lost in this way. A line of skirmishers marching on our flank would have been ample protection." [22] Pickett, himself, thought the march "necessarily slow" because of the constant skirmishing. "In front," he said, "we had to drive the enemy out of the way nearly the whole distance." [23]

About 4:30 P.M.[24] the column reached Five Forks. There, as anticipated, Pickett found Fitz Lee. At that time "Rooney" Lee and Tom Rosser had not reached the rendezvous, which was merely a bare crossroads in the all-engulfing forest where the White Oak crossed Ford Road, and three other trails cut southward to make five forks. Pickett wrote later that he intended to press on that evening toward Dinwiddie Court House; but in consultation with Fitz, he decided because of the late hour, the weariness of the troops, and the absence of the other cavalry, to wait until morning. Two infantry Brigades were thrown out some 1200 yards to protect the column from surprise attack. In advancing they soon had a brisk fight with dismounted cavalry who carried repeating rifles. The Confederates persisted, covered the assigned distance and held their ground. [26] Other Southern units bivouacked in the woods at the forks. Mercifully the rain ceased about dark, but during the night it began to fall heavily again. The infantry were prepared for this, after a fashion. Colonel Pegram and his staff had neither blankets nor food. They had hoped to return that night to their station.[26]

Pickett did not know, as yet, whether the enemy had infantry in support of cavalry who manifestly were numerous. All the bluecoats captured during the day had belonged to the mounted arm.[27] Whatever the composition of the force, it was found at daylight of the 31st to be in a strong position on the road to the Court House. Pickett himself was somewhat stronger. W. H. F. Lee and Rosser, breasting high water, reached Five Forks and

[22] Armistead C. Gordon, *Memories and Memorials of William Gordon McCabe* (cited hereafter as *Armistead Gordon*), 1, 163.
[23] *Walter Harrison*, 143. References to this work, pp. 142–51, are to Pickett's official report, the original of which is in the *Lee MSS.*
[24] 1 *Armistead Gordon*, 163; Pickett said "about sunset."
[25] *Walter Harrison*, 143.            [26] 1 *Armistead Gordon*, 163–64.
[27] *Walter Harrison*, 143.

reported. With their sabres to strengthen those of Fitz Lee's men, Pickett determined to press his advance to Dinwiddie Court House by two roads. About 10 A.M.[28] he began his march. In spite of weather and hunger, the cavalry were in excellent spirits. Instancing this, later in the day, some of "Rooney" Lee's men under Gen. R. L. T. Beale made a crossing at the double-quick, passed through water up to their armpits and carried the position.[29] The infantry, too, were alert and full of fight. Although contact with the enemy was maintained nearly all day, in advances and repulses, and with perceptible losses, there was nothing to indicate that Pickett's men would not or could not cope with the enemy. The spirit of the old Army was apparently as stout as ever.[30] If progress was slow, it was because the Federals fought hard and, when driven southward, soon returned.

By the time the Southerners were within about half a mile of the Court House, darkness had fallen.[31] Pickett had to halt. All his fighting during the day had continued to be with cavalry, most of whom had been dismounted, but sometime after 9 P.M., he learned that Tom Munford's outposts on the Confederate left had captured two infantrymen of Warren's familiar V Corps.[32] They belonged to Bartlett's Division which had pushed westward from the Boydton Plank Road and, at nightfall, held a good position North of Gravelly Run on the left and in the rear of Pickett.[33] Whether or not Pickett knew Bartlett's position,[34] he decided promptly that he should not remain in an advanced position. He had established the fact that the Federal cavalry were in great strength at Dinwiddie Court House and that they had infantry support. In this situation, Pickett felt that he should not expose his forces needlessly. It was better, he concluded, to take position where he could discharge his main duty, which was that of protecting the Confederate right flank and the approaches to the Southside Railroad.

[28] Ibid., 144.
[29] 1 Armistead Gordon, 164.
[30] Cf. W. Gordon McCabe in 1 Armistead Gordon, 173–74.
[31] Walter Harrison, 144–45.
[32] T. T. Munford, Five Forks, the Waterloo of the Confederacy, MS (cited hereafter as Munford MS). This apparently is the longest and most careful of General Munford's numerous unpublished articles in his long controversy over Five Forks.
[33] Cf. Warren in O. R., 46, pt. 1, p. 819 ff.
[34] The report of Maj. Emmor B. Cope (ibid., 821) would indicate that the Confederates South of Gravelly Run did not know of the continuing proximity of a strong force of Union infantry.

Orders consequently were given for a withdrawal at 4 A.M. along the line of the previous day's advance. At the hour fixed for the return march, it was apparent that Pickett's left was threatened,[35] but because of the usual delays of bivouac, it was daybreak, about 5 o'clock on the fateful 1st of April, when the gray column began to move northward through the mud.[36] The enemy almost immediately was on the heels of some of the withdrawing troops, and he kept always in sight or close enough to know what was happening. He did not force a fight or attempt to cut off the guns, which had been started for Five Forks at 2 A.M.[37] The artillery had an uneventful wade through the spring mud and by sunrise parked on the ground they had occupied before the march to Dinwiddie Court House. Hungry artillerists, finding no rations, had to rob their horses of some of the animals' corn. Parched over the fire, this was their breakfast.[38] Pickett probably fared no better. He brought back all his wounded and he watched closely the enemy's movements. The Federals, he concluded, at the moment were not seeking to get to the West of his column but were trying to separate him from the Confederates to the East of him. Subsequently he reported that he sent Lee a telegram to this effect and asked that a diversion be made to prevent his isolation.[39]

When the infantry reached Five Forks during the forenoon, Pickett dispatched his wagons across the protecting shelter of Hatcher's Run. He would have placed the men also on the north bank of the little stream, he said afterward,[40] had he not received a telegram from the commanding General to this effect: "Hold Five Forks at all hazards. Protect road to Ford's Depot and prevent Union forces from striking the Southside Railroad. Regret exceedingly your forced withdrawal, and your inability to hold the advantage you had gained." [41] This was, in a sense, justification of the course Pickett had taken: Lee recognized that the withdrawal had been forced. At the same time, the telegram from headquarters forbade a farther retreat for compelling reasons: If

---

35 *O. R.*, 46, pt. 1, p. 1264.  36 Fitz Lee in *Warren*, 479.
37 Munford, *op. cit.*, 18, wrote that he was not conscious of being pressed while handling Fitz Lee's Division.
38 1 *Armistead Gordon*, 164.
39 *Walter Harrison*, 145; see note 43 *infra*.
40 *Ibid.*, 145.
41 La Salle Corbell (Mrs. George E.) Pickett, *Pickett and His Men*, 386. Although no copy of this telegram is found in any official record, there is no reason to question its authenticity. It has verisimilitude

Five Forks were taken and the enemy were able to reach the railroad, all would be lost. Again, if the small force under Pickett were to abandon Five Forks, the numerically superior Federals with ease could pass westward along White Oak Road, get above the headwaters of Hatcher's Run and turn the Confederate right there. The position at Five Forks was weak, in itself, but strategically it was the most important on that sector. It had to be defended.[42]

Pickett obediently halted at Five Forks. He wrote subsequently that he assumed his telegram concerning his withdrawal had been received at Army Headquarters, that reinforcements would be sent him, and that a diversion would be made in his behalf.[43] On these assumptions, Pickett may not have been vigilant or careful in deploying his troops to meet possible attack that day. He put W. H. F. Lee's cavalry on the right. On his left Pickett placed a regiment, and no more than a regiment, of Munford's Division, to maintain contact with William P. Roberts's numerically weak Brigade, which tenuously connected Pickett with the Confederate right at Burgess' Mill.[44] Roberts's men were stout fighters but, like most of the regiments, they were lacking in field officers.[45] A stronger Brigade should have been in its place.

Between Roberts and Munford's regiment on the left and "Rooney" Lee's Division on the right Pickett deployed his infantry. With its left refused, Mat Ransom's borrowed Brigade of

---

[42] The contrary view, in defense of Pickett, will be found in *Longstreet,* 596 ff.

[43] *Walter Harrison,* 145. It is possible, but it does not seem probable, that Lee's telegraphic orders for Pickett to hold Five Forks covered an acknowledgment of Pickett's request for reinforcements and a diversion. A report from Pickett evidently had reached Army Headquarters that morning, but indications are that it covered only the events of the night. In his full dispatch to Breckinridge on the evening of April 1, Lee described Pickett's report of the night of March 31–April 1, but did not say anything to suggest that Pickett had appealed for assistance. See *O. R.,* 46, pt. 1, pp. 1263–64. Absence of all evidence during the forenoon that Lee had any specific appeal from Pickett for help would indicate that Pickett's memory of events was confused when he wrote his report, or else that his telegram miscarried. It scarcely seems possible that so important a message, if received at G. H. Q., would have been forgotten by Lee, by Walter Taylor, and by others who wrote of the events of April 1.

[44] *O. R.,* 46, pt. 1, p. 1299. General Roberts's command was the Fourth North Carolina and the Sixteenth North Carolina Battalion (*ibid.,* 1276). The Fourth Cavalry, also known as the Fifty-Ninth North Carolina, had served successively in the Brigades of Beverley Robertson, Lawrence S. Baker, James B. Gordon and James Dearing (*Cf.* 3 N. C. *Regts.,* 464 ff). The Sixteenth Battalion was known also as the Seventy-fifth North Carolina Regiment or Seventh Cavalry. It had come to Virginia in May, 1864 (4 N. C. *Regts.,* 71, 85, 89, 370). Brig. Gen. James Dearing having been transferred to Rosser's Old Brigade, Col. W. P. Roberts of the Nineteenth North Carolina was promoted Brigadier General (*Wright,* 125) as of February 21, and was assigned to command the small Brigade (3 N. C. *Regts.,* 466). Roberts was then not 24 years of age.

[45] 3 N. C. *Regts.,* 467.

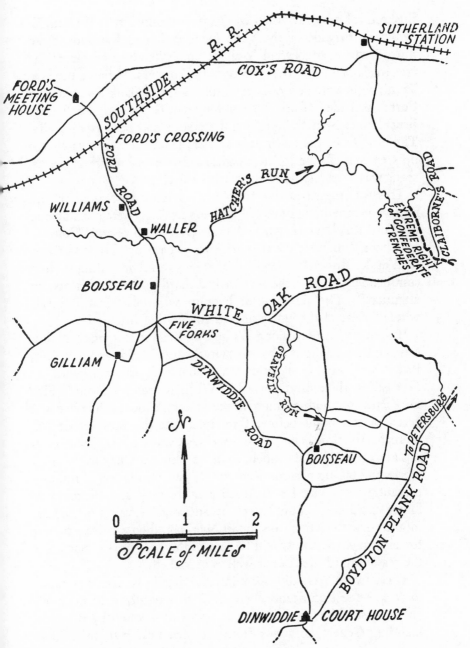

FORD'S MEETING HOUSE

SOUTHSIDE R. R.

COX'S ROAD

SUTHERLAND STATION

FORD'S CROSSING

FORD ROAD

HATCHER'S RUN

WILLIAMS

WALLER

CLAIBORNE'S ROAD

EXTREME RIGHT of CONFEDERATE TRENCHES

BOISSEAU

OAK ROAD

WHITE

FIVE FORKS

GRAVELLY RUN

GILLIAM

DINWIDDIE ROAD

BOISSEAU

To PETERSBURG

BOYDTON PLANK ROAD

N

0       1       2

SCALE of MILES

DINWIDDIE ▲ COURT HOUSE

Approaches to the Southside Railroad from Dinwiddie Court House, with particular reference to the Battle of Five Forks, Apr. 1, 1864—after Michler's Map of 1867

Bushrod Johnson's Division was on the extreme left.[46] William H. Wallace's Brigade of the same Division joined Ransom. Next, toward the right beyond Wallace and extending as far as the crossroads that led to the railway, was George H. Steuart's Brigade. To his right was Terry. Beyond him, as right flank element, was Corse's Brigade.[47] Corse had not fought at Gettysburg, but Terry's Brigade had been Kemper's, and Steuart's had been Armistead's. The descent of those Virginia soldiers from their furious charge up Cemetery Ridge to their pathetic defense of a wooded crossroads was the epitome of their army's decline.

This was the main line from left to right. In rear of the infantry the remaining units of Fitz Lee's Division were posted along the Ford Road, which ran to the railway.[48] As a reserve, North of Hatcher's Run, were the two Brigades of Dearing and of McCausland under Rosser.[49] They had been sent there, according to their commander, because the sore-backed, hard-ridden horses needed attention.[50] The six guns of Pegram were placed at intervals where the wooded country offered any field of fire.

If these dispositions along White Oak Road were made with less care, and were followed by less than the usual field entrenchment, Pickett's reported explanation was elaborated, years afterward, by Fitz Lee in these candid words: "When we moved towards Five Forks, hearing nothing more of the infantry's move which we had heard of the night before, I thought that the movements just there, for the time being, were suspended, and we were not expecting any attack that afternoon, so far as I know. Our throwing up works and taking position were simply general matters of military precaution." [51] Fitz Lee believed that his men and Pickett's infantry could beat off any attack by Sheridan's cavalry. If Federal infantry left their lines to support Sheridan, then a corresponding force from Anderson would be sent to the Five Forks. Such was the reasoning of Fitz Lee as well as of Pickett.[52]

These two officers did not know the details, or else they failed to realize the significance, of a fight that occurred to their left on the 31st. That morning, Anderson was directed by the commanding General to attack from the lines near Burgess' Mill in

[46] *Munford MS*, 20.
[47] *Ibid.;* Mrs. Pickett, *op. cit.,* 388.
[48] *Munford MS*, 24.
[49] *O. R.*, 46, pt. 1, p. 1299.
[50] Rosser in *Philadelphia Weekly Times*, April 5, 1885.
[51] *Warren*, 376.
[52] *O. R.*, 46, pt. 1, p. 1300.

order to protect Pickett's advance toward Dinwiddie Court House. In a second sense, this attack by the Confederate right wing was to be an offensive-defensive and was designed to discourage any attempt by the Federals to penetrate the gap between Anderson's right and Pickett's left. The advance was made in accordance with Lee's instructions, and it was not lacking in vigor. At one time, when Sam McGowan assaulted with the dash of the old "Light Division," there had been hope of success. It had faded quickly.[53] The final result was stated without apology by Bushrod Johnson: "Our troops persistently continued to fight, but were unable to advance, and orders were first sent to hold the position they had gained. It, however, became evident that our troops were being exhausted, and needed reinforcements, of which there was none available." [54] Gloomily, sullenly, the men of Anderson's command returned to their trenches. Losses had been about 800.[55]

Reduced by that number, and with two of his Brigades already assisting Pickett,[56] Anderson manifestly was in no condition to give further aid on the right.[57] Pickett and Fitz Lee, to repeat, apparently did not realize this. They cherished the general belief of the Army—a belief which had helped to create high morale— that the commanding General somehow would contrive to achieve the "impossible," even though, in this case, the line was stretched to the breaking point. Eleven thousand men, in actual fact, were occupying eleven miles of the Petersburg fortifications.[58] Already Lee had been compelled to call on Longstreet to deplete the First Corps North of the James in order to bolster the shaken right.[59] Everywhere on the long front from the Williamsburg Road to Five Forks, the odds were so adverse that no weak point could be strengthened without increasing danger elsewhere.

Besides the overconfidence of Fitz Lee and Pickett, and their lack of understanding of the dread immediacy of the crisis, it is probable that a third consideration, a most human one, led them to assume that "general precaution" sufficed. Tom Rosser had spent a day on the Nottoway River immediately before moving on

[53] For details, see 4 *R. E. Lee,* 34–35.     [54] *O. R.,* 46, pt. 1, p. 1288.
[55] *Ibid.*
[56] That is to say, Matt Ransom's and Wallace's Brigades of Bushrod Johnson's Division.
[57] This state of affairs was understood fully at Army Headquarters. Knowledge of Anderson's plight would have prompted Lee, if he had received Pickett's request for help, to explain immediately that it could not be given by Anderson.
[58] See 4 *R. E. Lee,* 37.     [59] *Ibid.*

March 30–31 to Five Forks. The shad had been running in the stream. With a borrowed seine, the young General had caught many of the fine fish. Some of these he had placed in his head-quarters ambulance and had brought to Five Forks. As soon as he got permission to move his Division North of Hatcher's Run, he arranged that the fish be cleaned and split and placed on sticks in front of brisk fires of dry wood.

In the assurance that this would provide a meal delectable at any time and incredible in the hungry days of bone-gnawing war, he invited Pickett to the shad-bake. Hungry and probably half wet, Pickett gratefully accepted and promised to join his host at the designated place in an hour. Fitz Lee with equal satisfaction accepted.[60] Neither man lost any time in preparing to keep the appointment.

After Fitz Lee mounted, between 12 and 1 o'clock, but before he started for Rosser's headquarters, Tom Munford dashed up and handed him a dispatch from Lt. Wythe B. Graham, of the Eighth Virginia Cavalry, the unit that had been placed in liaison with Roberts's Brigade on the extreme left. Graham reported that part of the North Carolina troopers had ridden into the picket line of the Eighth. They had stated that they had been attacked by over-powering Federals to the East of Five Forks, that their Brigade had been split by this attack, and that some of the Carolinians had been driven back on General Anderson's lines near Burgess' Mill while the men who made the report had themselves retreated west-ward.[61] If this information was correct, then Sheridan had reached the White Oak Road and had destroyed contact between Pickett's mobile force and the left of the Confederate fortifications. The "isolation" dreaded by Pickett was a reality. Reinforcements, if dispatched to him, would have to cut their way through.[62]

[60] Rosser in the *Philadelphia Weekly Times*, April 5, 1885, and in a letter to Capt. A. S. Perham, April 29, 1902. It perhaps should be noted that both these references are given incorrectly in *Irvine Walker*, 229–30. Naturally, Rosser did not describe in his published article the method by which the shad were prepared and cooked. The details given here were and are "standard practice" for the outdoor cooking of shad in Virginia. While such a feast as that prepared by Rosser usually is called a "shad-bake" the process is not that of baking but of broiling.
[61] *Munford MS*, 23–24.
[62] The Federals who had assailed and divided Roberts's Brigade about noon were units of Brig. Gen. Ranald S. MacKenzie's Cavalry Brigade of the Army of the James. They had reached White Oak Road about three miles East of Five Forks. See MacKenzie's report, *O. R.*, 46, pt. 1, p. 1244. Munford (*op. cit.*, 23), quoting Sheridan, is authority for the hour of the attack.

Fitz Lee was either impatiently hungry or uncritically skeptical. He read the dispatch and said merely: "Well, Munford, I wish you would go over in person at once and see what this means and, if necessary, order up your Division and let me hear from you." With that, the chief of cavalry went off. Soon Munford saw Fitz and Pickett riding northward together in the direction of Hatcher's Run, though he knew nothing of their destination or of their reason for being together.

Unannounced departure of the two senior officers of both arms of the service for a point which proved to be approximately two miles from their line [63] left "Rooney" Lee in general command as senior officer, but he was far to the right and had no knowledge that his seniors had left the field. He probably had no information, at the moment, of the skirmish on the left. Among the cavalrymen facing the enemy who had struck Roberts's Brigade, the senior was Tom Munford. He was not yet even a Brigadier in the sense that his commission had been signed and delivered, but in the absence of Fitz Lee, or when that officer was exercising general command, Munford handled Fitz Lee's Division.[64]

This was as much a vindication as it was a responsibility. During the previous winter, when Rosser had been preparing for a raid into Western Virginia, he had called on Munford for a detachment. Because of the condition of his men and of his shoeless horses, Munford had pleaded for time in which to await the arrival from Richmond of promised supplies. As a result of disputes thus provoked, Rosser had placed Munford under arrest and had insisted on a court martial. Munford had been acquitted and Rosser inferentially censured for preferring the charges,[65] but

---

[63] *Munford MS,* 32.
[64] The *Munford MSS* contain positive proof that the promotion of Colonel Munford had been recommended by those whose signatures would assure the commission. "Jeb" Stuart had written Munford's father, George W. Munford, April 24, 1864, that upon the resignation of Williams C. Wickham (see *supra,* p. 596) he would urge Munford for advancement to brigade command. Wade Hampton wrote Munford, June 10, 1866: "I am glad your merit and services were recognized even though that recognition in the shape of your promotion came late. One of my last acts in Virginia was to recommend this promotion." E. J. Harvie, of the War Records Office, wrote Munford, Oct. 2, 1886. that he had found Fitz Lee's recommendation of Mch. 20, 1865, for Munford's promotion to date from Wickham's resignation, which was accepted Nov. 9, 1864. Gen. R. E. Lee, on March 23, had endorsed this favorably and had forwarded the paper to the Adjutant General's Office where it was received Mch. 29, 1865. Space is taken to explain this because of some of the partisans of General Rosser, in the controversy with General Munford, asserted that Munford had no right to the title of General.
[65] 13 *S.H.S.P.,* 143, 144; 32 *ibid..* 11.

Rosser had been quick to restore his reputation. He won much praise for a raid on. Beverly [66] and as he had received applause for a previous raid on New Creek Depot and Fort Kelley,[67] he had been confirmed by the Senate, Feb. 28, 1865, at the rank of Major General.[68] Munford had remained a colonel until the last days, but he, too, was now in command of a cavalry Division. The infantry, in the absence of Pickett, had "Maryland" Steuart as their commander.[69] Colonel Pegram was the ranking artillerist.

None of these men, to repeat, not even Munford after his brief conversation with Fitz Lee, knew that Pickett and the chief of cavalry had quit the lines. The shad bake was at the moment a social secret, but, as food was abundant, the affair was leisured and deliberate as every feast should be. If there was "something to drink" it probably was not shunned. Many officers did not hesitate to indulge moderately even in the presence of the enemy, but if the three preceded or followed their dinner with a little whiskey or brandy, there was no evidence, then or thereafter, that any of the trio got drunk.[70]

Hours slipped pleasantly past. While the Generals still were picking the bones from broiled shad, two pickets reported. They were Rosser's men and they said that the enemy was advancing on all the roads the Division was guarding. Rosser wrote later: "These reports were made to Pickett and to Lee and as the position at Five Forks was considered as well chosen and strong but little attention was given to the·enemy's advance. I was suffering from my wound and as I was not immediately in command of the pickets I took no steps to reinforce them. Indeed the pickets were a part of Colonel Munford's command and I, reporting direct to General Lee, and as he was present, felt little or no concern about them." [71] Perhaps he and his feasting comrades were the less concerned over the pickets' reports because there had not been any sound of action. All appeared to be quiet; the enemy evidently was approaching but he was not attacking. With any skirmishes that might be opened, the officers at the front could deal.

[66] O. R., 46, pt. 1, p. 451.                    [67] O. R., 43, pt. 1, pp. 586, 669 ff.
[68] Wright, 44; commissioned as of Nov. 4, 1864.
[69] He ranked as Brigadier from Mch. 6, 1862 (Wright, 77).
[70] This is to be emphasized because, for many years, before any of the facts about the shad bake were made public in 1885, it was whispered in the South that one or another of the Generals was intoxicated.
[71] Rosser to A. S. Perham, Apr. 29, 1902, quoted in Munford MS, 39.

After 4 o'clock,[72] Pickett asked Rosser for a courier to take a message to Five Forks. Obligingly, Rosser offered two, one of whom, according to Rosser's rule, would ride ahead of but in sight of the second. Pickett prepared his message and gave it to the couriers. They started.[73] Doubtless the conversation around Rosser's hospitable fire was resumed. Soon there came from the South of the Run a burst of infantry fire. In plain view, on the other side of the stream, the Generals saw the leading courier captured by the Federals. At the same moment, a line of bluecoats crossed the road.[74]

That ended the party. With few words but in utmost haste, Pickett took horse and galloped back across Hatcher's Run. South of the stream he continued his pace until he came to the left of a line of cavalrymen who faced eastward on the Ford Road. They were retreating slowly before Federal infantry,[75] who were not 100 yards distant.[76] Directing the Confederates was Tom Munford. He was recognized immediately by Pickett, who inquired: "What troops are these?"

He was told that they were part of Fitz Lee's Division.

Pickett looked again at the Federals. "Do hold them back till I can pass to Five Forks," he said.

A young Captain of the Third Virginia Cavalry, James Breckinridge of the sharpshooters, heard Pickett's appeal and, quickly turning his men, dashed straight at the enemy. The brief counterattack cost Breckinridge's life,[77] but it probably saved Pickett's. The General threw himself forward on his horse, with his head on the farther side from the enemy, and successfully ran the

[72] Rosser in the letter cited *supra* said "Some time after we had finished lunch, I should say three or four o'clock," but Munford insisted (*op. cit.*, 32) that "the attack was begun after 4 o'clock." McCabe's diary (1 *Armistead Gordon*, 165) stated that the attack on Pegram began at 4:30. Prior to that, said McCabe, all had been quiet. Had there been heavy action before that hour, it almost certainly would have been audible at Pegram's post of command. Warren's report (*O. R.*, 46, pt. 1, p. 831) suggested an advance subsequent to 4 P.M. though he did not give the precise time. Sheridan (*ibid.*, 1105) wrote that "the sun was getting low."

[73] Rosser's letter to Perham, *loc. cit.*

[74] *Ibid.* Rosser's earlier account at the Warren Inquiry would indicate that the first news of the presence of the enemy came from a returning courier. If this incident is correctly reported, the courier must have been captured on the Boisseau Farm. In that event, the scene of the shad bake would have been, in all probability, on the property marked "Walla" [Waller?] on the Michler map, or on the Williams Farm.

[75] This was Samuel W. Crawford's 3rd Division of the V Corps.

[76] *Munford MS*, 31.

[77] Munford, *op. cit.*, 32, said: "If there was ever a braver soldier than James Breckinridge, I never saw him."

gauntlet of several hundred yards of furious infantry fire.[78] **Fitz** Lee tried to reach his troops by the same route but found the blue-coats across the road. Fired upon, he turned back and attempted to lead Rosser's men toward Five Forks by the Ford Road. He was repulsed quickly.[79]

The battle that had occurred while the Generals were eating shad was ending by this time. It had been as swift as it had been disastrous. Sheridan had with him three cavalry Divisions of his own command and, as already noted, the excellent small Brigade of Ranald MacKenzie from the Army of the James. In addition, at Sheridan's disposal was the entire V Corps of Gouverneur Warren, 17,000 officers and men.[80] Sheridan's full strength did not fall below 30,000 as against Pickett's 10,000.[81] During the early afternoon, Sheridan had demonstrated with his left against the Confederate right, but that stout wing, well commanded by "Rooney" Lee and "Monty" Corse, had not been shaken. All the while Sheridan was prodding forward Warren's V Corps with which he intended to attack the Confederate left.[82] These Federal dispositions were shaped primarily by the fact that Warren was approaching from the South and Southeast and could strike the Confederate left conveniently. Sheridan intended, he afterward maintained, to drive Pickett westward, but he did not know that the left of the Confederate line was its weakest part.

Deployment of the Federal Infantry for the final attack was bold and unconcealed. Munford, reconnoitering on the Confederate left, observed the preparations and sent courier after courier to report to Pickett or to Fitz Lee that the enemy was making ready to strike. Neither General was to be found; nobody knew whither either had ridden; no instructions had been left for forwarding dispatches. Capt. Henry Lee of the divisional staff vainly rode the whole length of the line without learning any more than the baffled couriers had returned to announce.[83] The little that could be done to make ready for the impending attack was undertaken by the individual commanders and then not always in co-

---

[78] Ibid.

[79] Fitz Lee in the Warren Inquiry, quoted in *Munford MS*, 33.

[80] "Ready for duty equipped" (*O. R.*, 46, pt. 1, p. 62).

[81] When Pickett's mobile force was set up, it consisted of approximately 6400 infantry and 4200 cavalry (4 *R. E. Lee*, 31). From that total the casualties of March 31 and the stragglers have to be deducted. Consequently, 10,000 must be the highest possible figure.

[82] *O. R.*, 46, pt. 1, pp. 1104–05.  [83] *Munford MS*, 25.

operation. Mat Ransom refused, for example, to send any of his guns to an excellent position the acting division commander of the cavalry had found.[84] Said Munford afterward: "All this time Warren's swarming blue lines were plainly visible from the road, forming into line and preparing to assault Pickett's left; Merritt's dismounted cavalry was keeping up a sharp continuous fire along the whole of our infantry front, as if preparing to attack our right, and Custer's mounted Division was demonstrating . . . And I was still without orders."[85] He took position on Ransom's refused left, built a few "pens" of rails, from nearby fences, and awaited the inevitable.

When the attack was launched, it was irresistible on the left. Soon it rolled Ransom back on Wallace, who already was shaken. The sagging Confederate left had to be extended farther northward to prevent a turning movement, but the line was too thin to hold. When Pickett rode on the field, the retreating left was more than half a mile West of the original position taken by the dismounted cavalry.[86] The attack continued after that with little abatement, but Corse's Brigade, which had not been assailed heavily,[87] was held firmly together and was used to rally some of the fugitives.[88] W. H. F. Lee, vigilant as always, beat off Federal charges and, at dark, in good order, slipped away to join Fitz Lee, who remained with Rosser's men North of Hatcher's Run.[89]

Except for Corse's stalwarts, those of Pickett's men who escaped from the field were reduced to panic and were pursued by Sheridan till night forced recall. The number of Confederates captured that afternoon and rounded up on the morning of April 2 by the V Corps was 3244, with eleven flags and one gun, at a cost of 634 casualties.[90] Prisoners taken by the cavalry were not listed fully in reports, but they doubtless reached 2000.[91] It probably was a more costly day than that of the attack on Fort Stedman, more costly than any since May 12 of the preceding year at the Bloody Angle.

[84] Ibid., 26.    [85] Munford MS, 27.
[86] This fact makes it certain that unverifiable details of the action on the left described in Pickett's report (Walter Harrison, 146–47) must rest on somewhat inaccurate information given Pickett after the battle and not on what he himself saw.
[87] 1 Armistead Gordon, 165.
[88] Ibid., 147. This Pickett doubtless witnessed.
[89] O. R., 46, pt. 1, p. 1300.    [90] O. R., 46, pt. 1, p. 836.
[91] Sheridan (ibid., 1105) estimated the total prisoners as "between 5000 and 6000." Grant (ibid., 54) accepted these figures.

To the artillerists, it was a day of disaster not to be recorded solely in terms of four guns lost or of good soldiers captured. After Col. William Pegram had posted his six guns at 10 o'clock, he had lain down on the field and had fallen asleep. He had felt at its keenest, of course, the grief of the South at the death of his magnificent brother John, the General of the family,[92] but he had shown and probably had felt no disappointment that he had himself been kept so long at the rank of Lieutenant Colonel and had not been made a general officer. Heth and "Dick" Anderson separately had asked for his promotion and assignment to command of an infantry Brigade. Powell Hill in these words had endorsed Heth's recommendation of Pegram: "No officer of the Army of Northern Virginia has done more to deserve this promotion than Lieutenant Colonel Pegram."[93] Pegram did not know that when Heth had urged on Lee the advancement of the artillerist, the Commanding General had said: "He is too young— how old is Colonel Pegram?" Heth had answered: "I do not know, but I suppose about 25." Lee had replied: "I think a man of 25 as good as he ever will be; what he acquires after that age is from experience; but I can't understand, when an officer is doing excellent service where he is, why he should want to change."[94] The recommendation was returned, camp gossip had it, with the statement that "the artillery could not lose the services of so valuable an officer."[95] Pegram was made Colonel of Artillery as of February 18,[96] though reports had persisted almost until that time that the higher honor was to be his.[97] It did not matter: he was content . . . even under that tree, on wet ground, and with no food that day except the parched corn taken from the horses.

The frightful crash of Warren's opening volley awakened Pegram with a start. Almost in the same moment he was in his saddle and, with his Adjutant, Gordon McCabe, was racing toward the assailed left. Soon he was among his gunners there. They were firing furiously but in perfect order at Federals who were

92 See *supra*, p. 629.    93 14 *S.H.S.P.*, 17.
94 *Heth's MS Memoirs*, 166.
95 14 *S.H.S.P.*, 17. Lee wrote after the war that the "appointment was not denied for want of confidence in his ability, for no one in the army had a higher opinion of his gallantry and worth than myself" (*ibid.*, 18). The General's words suggest that if the alleged endorsement was not actually written, the feeling at Headquarters was correctly indicated by the attributed language.
96 4 *Journal C. S. Congress*, 612.    97 *Ham Chamberlayne*, 309.

not more than thirty to fifty yards in their front. From those advancing bluecoats there came a continuous hail of bullets.

Pegram admiringly watched the contest in the spirit that led Harry Heth to say that the young artillerist was "one of the few men who, I believe, was supremely happy when in battle." Without deigning to dismount, Pegram then rode out between the guns. "Fire your canister low," he said to his men. A moment after he reeled and fell from his horse. "Oh, Gordon," he cried to his companion, "I'm mortally wounded; take me off the field." [98]

This was exceedingly difficult to do, because the enemy was at the very mouth of the guns. McCabe got his friend on a stretcher, sent him a little distance to the rear and then returned momentarily to the battery. When he came back, he put Pegram in an ambulance and had it started for Ford's Depot on the Southside Railroad.

Both the Colonel and the Adjutant were scarcely more than boys. The imminence of Pegram's death made them "as little children." McCabe wrote three days later: "While in the ambulance I held him in my arms and prayed for him and kissed him over and over again. Once when I prayed that his life might be spared, he said, 'If it is God's will to take me, I am perfectly resigned. I only wish life for my Mother's and sisters' sake.' He said several times—'Give my love to mother and both sisters and tell them I thought of them in my last moments.' Once when in my agony I cried out, 'My God, my God, why hast Thou forsaken me,' he said quickly, 'Don't say that, Gordon, it isn't right.' One thing I love to dwell upon. I bent over and kissed him and said, calling him by his name for the first time in my life, 'Willie, I never knew how much I loved you until now.' He pressed my hand and answered, 'But I did.' Without ceasing, except when I lost my voice in tears, I prayed for him, for comfort for body and soul, and he would simply say, 'Amen.' " [99]

McCabe continued: "At about 10 o'clock we reached Ford's, and I obtained a bed for him . . . I had given him morphine in small quantities until he was easier, and he soon fell into a doze. The enemy advanced on the place about 12 o'clock, and I was left

[98] McCabe's own narratives in 1 *Armistead Gordon*, 165, 169.
[99] W. Gordon McCabe to Miss Mary Pegram, Apr. 4, 1865, *Ham Chamberlayne*, 318–19.

alone with him. I sent off our sabres, horses, spurs, etc., as I felt sure that we would be captured. I shall never forget that night of waiting. I could only pray. He breathed heavily through the night, and passed into a stupor. I bound his wounds as well as I knew how and moistened his lips with water. Sunday morning he died as gently as possible." [100]

His cause was dying with him.

[100] 1 *Armistead Gordon*, 165–66. McCabe concluded: "Thus died the truest Christian, the most faithful friend and the most superb soldier in all the world. He was my Jonathan, pure in heart, brave in deed, chivalric until it bordered on quixotism, generous and unselfish, he was the Havelock of the Army of Northern Virginia. I laid him out, helped to dig his grave, buried him in a blanket and read the Episcopal service over him." Various references to Pegram, more detailed than can be quoted here, will be found in 19 *S.H.S.P.*, 117–18; 27 *ibid.*, 91; 28 *ibid.*, 372; 6 *C. V.*, 271; 22 *ibid.*, 117; *O. R.*, 33, 1173; *ibid.*, 42, pt. 1, p. 851. The fullest sketch is McCabe's in 14 *S.H.S.P.*, 10 ff, but it may be said of Pegram, as of "Sandie" Pendleton, see *supra* p. 584, that he deserves a biography. An interesting comparison between Pelham and Pegram will be found in *J. C. Haskell's MS Rems.*, 109–11.

# CHAPTER XXXIV

## THE COLLAPSE OF COMMAND

THE DAY of the Battle of Five Forks, April 1, was one of intensest anxiety on the front from which Pickett had been isolated. Nothing positive was known at the headquarters of Lee or at those of Powell Hill concerning Pickett's contest until late in the afternoon. Then it was apparent only that a reverse had been sustained and that Fitz Lee had been separated from the infantry. "Dick" Anderson consequently was ordered to send the three remaining Brigades of Bushrod Johnson's command [1] to support the cavalry in defense of the Southside Railroad.[2] By that movement, the three miles of line on the Confederate right from Burgess' Mill to Hatcher's Run beyond the Claiborne Road were, in effect, abandoned. Only one small regiment of sharpshooters was left there.

East and Northeast of Burgess' Mill, for a distance of three and three-quarter miles, Heth's Division held the trenches. The two and a quarter miles on the left of Heth were occupied by Wilcox. Beyond Wilcox as far as the Appomattox, six miles of front were in the keeping of the Second Corps. The Howlett Line, which was comparatively inactive, had been entrusted to the mobile reserve, Mahone's Division. North of the James, Field's and Kershaw's Division of the First Corps, together with the garrison of Richmond and the local defense troops, guarded the strong fortifications.

On receipt of the first news of Pickett's lost battle, Field's Division was ordered to the Southside during the afternoon of April 1 to restore, if possible, the shattered right.[3] Longstreet was directed to come in person with these troops.[4] To all who knew of these instructions, the transfer of 4600 men from the thinly held left was confession that the entire line South of the Appomatox was in danger of rupture even if it were not turned.

---

[1] His own Brigades of Wise and Moody, plus Hunton's Brigade, which had been attached temporarily (*O. R.*, 46, pt. 1, p. 1288).

[2] Details and references will be found in 4 *R. E Lee*, 41.

[3] Cf. *O. R.*, 46, pt. 3, pp. 1374, 1375; see *supra*, p. 671.     [4] *Longstreet*, 602.

Powell Hill sensed this as he went over his front, yard by yard, on the 1st to see that abatis and chevaux de frise and all the other obstructions were in place. The enemy was no more active than usual, though the sharpshooters were exasperatingly close and vigilant. It was after nightfall when Hill returned from the right to Fort Gregg. This was one of a chain of minor defenses so located that if the right were abandoned, a line could be drawn northward to the Appomattox in a manner to cover temporarily the inner defenses of Petersburg. As if studying the possibilities of a stand on that line, Hill remained a long time at Fort Gregg. Then wearily he made his way back to his headquarters.[5] When he had discharged his last duties of the day, he walked across to the Venable Cottage where his beautiful wife and his two baby girls were lodged.

They had shared a winter during which, as for the preceding year and more, Hill had received more than his share of the Army's adversity. Few of his days after his promotion to corps command had been as brilliant as those of the year during which he had led the "Light Division." At Gettysburg, there had been a flash of splendor on the 1st of July, but after that, Hill had a bystander's part in the drama. Falling Waters, Bristoe Station, the stampede of Wilcox and Heth in the Wilderness, his own illness there and at Spotsylvania—all these must have been unhappy memories. Globe Tavern and Reams' Station had brought at least as much honor to "Billy" Mahone as to him. The Crater, too, had been Mahone's battle. Hill had the affection of his men; his magnetism and personality made him one of the most popular officers of the Army. In rare instances, similar to those with Jackson, when he felt that his own punctilious observance of the military amenities was disregarded, he could be stiff, stern, bitter. The third senior officer of the Army he was, and during Longstreet's absence, the second; but he may have felt what others often said privately—that as a corps commander he had not fulfilled expectations.[6]

Ill health, like ill fortune, increasingly had been his lot during

[5] These were located at Indiana, a property on the extension of Washington Street and next the so-called Model Farm.

[6] Sorrel, 91. Perhaps the best character study of Hill is in the sketch by Gen. James A. Walker, 20 S.H.S.P., 376 ff. See 8 ibid., 451; 14 ibid., 452; 19 ibid., 183; 28 ibid., 374. Informative details are given in 16 C. V., 178; 21 ibid., 433; Annals, 694 ff; 1 N. C. Regts. 765; J. C. Haskell's MS Rems., 29; 2 Land We Love, 288–89.

1864-65. After weeks of sickness, he had procured leave in March,[7] had visited kinsmen in the northern part of Chesterfield County [8] and then had spent a day or two in Rchmond. When he heard open talk in the capital of the probable early evacuation of the city he was outraged. For his own part, said he, he did not wish to survive the fall of Richmond.[9] He hurried back to Petersburg, with the approach of the crisis, and before his leave expired, he resumed command, though his sickness clung to him.[10] Now, as he sought sleep after his day of inspection, the guns were rumbling all along the line.

With the passing of the hours, the fire became more violent. Long before dawn, Hill's Chief of Staff, Col. William H. Palmer, knocked and reported that another member of the staff had been to the left and had heard that the enemy had captured part of the line near Rives's Salient.[11] Hill rose, dressed, went to his quarters and asked if any reports had been received during the night from Heth or Wilcox. Nothing had come; no further news had been received of the break in the line to the left. In this assurance, Hill mounted and rode rapidly to Army Headquarters at Edge Hill, the Turnbull House, which was nearly a mile and a half from Indiana.[12] Upon arrival, Hill found some of the members of the military household of the commanding General astir, and he went in at once to Lee, who was lying partly clothed on the bed. With little ceremony, the two began to discuss what could be done to hold the line. They had decided nothing when, abruptly, Colonel Venable broke into the room. Army wagons, he said, were being driven wildly along the road toward Petersburg. An officer occupying a hut far within the lines had said that Federal skirmishers had driven him from it.[13]

Hill sprang up and hastened from the house: he must reach his troops at once and must rally them. In a moment, he was

[7] Probably from about the 20th (11 S.H.S.P., 565), and certainly prior to the 22nd (O. R., 46, pt. 2, p. 1316).
   [8] 19 S.H.S.P., 185.                    [9] Ibid.
   [10] W. Gordon McCabe in 2 S.H.S.P., 302, said of Hill, "much he suffered during this last campaign from a grievous malady," but the nature of it was not explained. Late photographs of Hill show an emaciation that suggests tuberculosis. Such scanty information as exists concerning his earlier periods of sickness indicated, as noted above, p. 442, that his malady was psychosomatic.
   [11] 11 S.H.S.P., 566. This narrative by G. W. Tucker, Hill's sergeant of couriers, is the primary account of the events of the early morning.
   [12] Ibid., 566.
   [13] 12 S.H.S.P., 186. This is another primary account and is by Venable.

mounted and was off. Two of his couriers followed. Venable quickly joined them. The four rode toward the enemy. Soon they had evidence of their own that Unionists already were inside the Confederate lines. Bullets began to whistle; two prisoners were taken; Union soldiers were swarming around the huts that had been used during the winter by Mahone's Division. The only indication of the presence of any troops to oppose the Federals was the sight of an unemployed battalion of Southern artillery on a nearby hill. Hill sent off Venable to place the guns where they could open on the enemy.[14]

With scarcely a pause in his search for his troops, Hill continued across fields and through copses where Federals might be encountered at any minute. Soon his chief courier, George Tucker, spoke up: "Please excuse me, General, but where are you going?"

"Sergeant, I must go to the right as quickly as possible. We will go up this side of the branch to the woods, which will cover us until reaching the field in rear of General Heth's quarters. I hope to find the road clear at General Heth's."[15]

Tucker said nothing. He had kept his Colt revolver in his hand from the time the four of them had captured the two prisoners, and now, touching his horse, he got a little ahead of Hill. The two men[16] silently crossed the Boydton Plank Road, reached the woodland and followed the edge of it for about a mile. Not one person, Federal or Confederate, civilian or soldier, did they encounter. Hill must have felt this was no more than the luck of the moment. "Sergeant," said he to Tucker, as they rode through the woods, "should anything happen to me, you must go back to General Lee and report it."

On they went until they entered a field, beyond which, in a road, a mass of men were visible. Hill raised his field-glass. "There they are," he said simply.

Tucker knew Hill meant that the troops were Unionists: "Which way now, General?"

Hill pointed to the side of woods that paralleled the Boydton Plank Road: "We must keep on to the right."

The sergeant pushed ahead until two-thirds of the distance had

[14] 12 S.H.S.P., 186.
[15] Cf. 2 N. C. Regts., 61.
[16] There is no mention of the second courier in this part of the narrative. He probably had been sent on some mission.

been covered. Then he pulled up his horse to a walk and began to scrutinize the edge of the wood, where a number of large trees stood sentinel. Soon he saw six or eight Federals lurking there. Two of these men, nearer the field than the others, ran together to a great trunk and hid behind it. Both the Federals lowered their guns, one man's rifle under the other's, and both took aim. Tucker flashed a quick glance to Hill, who was riding on the right. "We must take them," said Hill, and he quickly drew his pistol.

"Stay there!" called Tucker, "I'll take them." Then he shouted to the Federals, who were not more than twenty yards away: "If you fire, you'll be swept to hell! Our men are here—surrender."

"Surrender," cried Hill in the same instant.[17]

"I can't see it," one of the Federals shouted back, and as his companion let the stock of the lower rifle down, he called loudly, "Let us shoot them!" [18]

Two shots were fired. One went wild. The other struck the uplifted left hand of Hill, took off his thumb in the gauntlet and entered his heart.[19] As Tucker dodged, and then reached out his right hand to catch the General's horse, he saw Hill on the ground, arms thrown out, motionless.[20]

A few hours later, Col. William H. Palmer rode up to the Venable House and dismounted. His instructions from the commanding General were to break to Mrs. Hill the news of her husband's death, and then to move her and the children across the Appomattox and out of the path of danger that day. So hard an assignment was this that Colonel Palmer hesitated at the front door. From within he heard a clear voice singing, a woman's voice. He knew it. Mrs. Hill was at her housework. The Colonel could not bring himself to knock. Silently he entered the hall. Although the cannonade along the line was heavy, Mrs. Hill heard the reluctant footfall of her husband's Chief of Staff. She turned her eyes to the open bedroom door. The note of her music died in her throat. "The General is dead," she said in a strained, startled voice, "you would not be here unless he was dead." [21]

Worse than death seemed the ensuing events of that frightful

---

[17] 11 *S.H.S.P.*, 568.     [18] 27 *S.H.S.P.*, 33.
[19] 19 *S.H.S.P.*, 184–85.     [20] 11 *S.H.S.P.*, 568.
[21] W. H. Palmer to W. H. Taylor, MS, June 25, 1905—*Taylor MSS.* The writer had supplementary details from Colonel Palmer and from Mrs. Lucy Hill Macgill, daughter of the General. She was too young to have any memories of this incident, but she gave the writer her mother's verbal account of the arrival of Colonel Palmer.

2nd of April to other lieutenants of Lee. Ahead of Field's Division, "Old Pete" Longstreet arrived early at Headquarters. With his unshakable calmness, as soon as Benning's Brigade reached the flank, he deployed it to protect the exposed right.[22] In the absence of Harry Heth, who was cut off temporarily from contact with the remainder of the Third Corps, Longstreet at Lee's instance assumed direction of such of Hill's troops as now began to collect behind their shattered lines.[23]

By 9 A.M., the details of the catastrophe began to take form. The Union VI Corps had delivered at 4:40 A.M. an overpowering attack on Hill's front, had shattered the line held by Heth's and Wilcox's Divisions and had driven the Confederates to right and to left.[24] The hope was that the shattered troops thrown westward would be united with those of "Dick" Anderson. He, as already noted, had been ordered the previous evening to march to support Fitz Lee. Those of Hill's men who had been driven to the left, and to the rear of their captured fortifications, were rallied on Fort Gregg and adjoining works. Still farther to the left, Gordon's picket posts had been taken at 11 o'clock on the night of April 1-2. Much of his first line had been stormed successfully at daylight, but his second line was intact. He could hold it for some hours, with adequate artillery support, even though his men were eight feet apart; [25] and if the contest were worth the lives, he could recover temporarily what he had lost. Gordon was proud that day and not a little harassed in mind, because his beautiful young wife had just been delivered of a new baby; [26] but at the front he was the same determined, competent and inspiring leader.[27]

Neither Gordon nor Lee, nor anyone else now believed that more could be accomplished at Petersburg than to occupy the breaking line until nightfall. Then the whole of the Richmond-Petersburg front must be abandoned. The long-projected effort to unite with Johnston must be made. Dread notice of this necessity was telegraphed to Richmond. Orders were dispatched Mahone on the Howlett Line and Ewell on the Richmond front to start their troops that evening by routes previously determined. The

---

[22] *Longstreet*, 606.                          [23] *Ibid.*, 608.
[24] *O. R.*, 46, pt. 1, p. 903. A clear and succinct account of the developments of the day will be found in *Alexander*, 592.
[25] Cf. *Grimes*, 109.                          [26] *Douglas*, 330–31.
[27] Cf. *Grimes*, 109.

immediate objective was to be Amelia Court House, which was by road thirty-nine miles Southwest of Richmond and thirty-six miles Northwest of Petersburg.[28] This village was chosen because

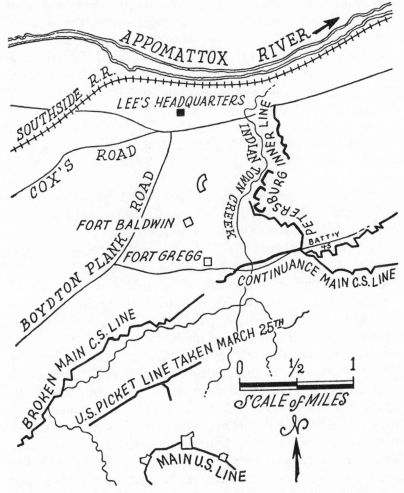

Relation of Fort Gregg to the Main and Inner Confederate Lines Southwest of Petersburg. Shown, also, are the Defenses captured by the Federals at dawn, Apr. 2, 1865. After Michler's Map of 1867

it was approximately equidistant from the major sectors and was on the railroad that would be the Army's principal supply line on any retreat to join the Confederate forces in North Carolina. In

[28] Details and sketch map in 4 *R. E. Lee*, 54. A larger scale map will be found in *O. R. Atlas*, Plate LXXVIII, 1.

addition, part of the reserve artillery ammunition of the Army had been stored at Amelia Court House.[29]

Even after such calamitous days as those of Five Forks and the 2nd of April, the Army was not to march into the night without one more demonstration of its old fighting prowess. This occurred at Fort Gregg, which, to repeat, covered the angle of the "L" on which the Confederates had to keep their grip until nightfall made possible an unassailed withdrawal. If the enemy took Fort Gregg and the adjoining work to the North, Fort Baldwin, he would have between him and Petersburg nothing but the old inner line on the east side of Indian Town Creek. The battle then might be in the streets of Petersburg. Gregg must be held at least until Longstreet could occupy the line from Battery 45 to the Appomattox.

Orders to that end were issued. Come what might, the survivors of Harris's Brigade [30] and of Wilcox's Division, who had gravitated to the fort, must stay there and fight it out.

They did. Although the defenders of Fort Gregg probably numbered not more than 500, they beat off one assault, then another and another till count was lost. Wounded men loaded rifles and handed them with bloody hands to comrades behind the parapet. Artillerists of the First Corps were proud to claim the gunners in the fort as their own.[31] Had not an uncompleted ditch to the northward afforded access to Gregg, its extemporized garrison might have held it all day and might have defied all attacks till ammunition was exhausted. As it was, the few unwounded left in the fort fought hand to hand for twenty-five minutes on the parapet.[32] The Federals had to charge themselves with 714 casualties in return for fifty-seven Confederate dead, 129 wounded prisoners and thirty who were worn and grimy but unhurt.[33] The other Southerners escaped to receive the plaudits of observers and the assurance that their resistance had given "Old Pete" sufficient

---

[29] Cf. O. R., 46, pt. 1, p. 1281; 38 S.H.S.P., 5.

[30] This Brigade was part of Mahone's Division, but had been left on the line when Mahone had moved to the sector opposite Bermuda Hundred.

[31] Alexander, 592–93; Owen, 371 ff.          [32] O. R., 46, pt. 1, p. 1179.

[33] Alexander, 593, with figures corrected, in part, by O. R., 46, pt. 1, p. 1179. The assaults were made by Brig. Gen. Robert S. Foster's 1st and Bvt. Maj. Gen. John W. Turner's 2nd or "Independent" Division of Maj. Gen. John Gibbon's XXIV Corps. See O. R., 46, pt. 1, pp. 1174, 1179, 1215. See also 3 S.H.S.P., 19 ff, 82 ff; 4 ibid., 18 ff; 8 ibid., 475 ff; 9 ibid., 102 ff, 168 ff; 19 ibid., 65 ff; 28 ibid., 265–67; 31 ibid., 56 ff, 370–72; Owen, 371 ff.

time in which to organize a thin but stalwart defense of the works on Indian Town Creek.[34] After the line was stabilized for the day, several of the commanders were called to headquarters that had been moved to the McIlwaine House when Edge Hill was evacuated.[35] The necessity and the plan of the evacuation were explained, but so calm was the manner of the commanding General that none of those who participated in the conference left any record of it. Along the Howlett Line and on the Northside, announcement of the evacuation was delayed as long as possible, though ranking officers, after midday, doubtless had been informed that they would begin their withdrawal that night.[36]

On the extreme right, Anderson and Bushrod Johnson had reached Church Crossing on Ford Road.[37] Nothing had been heard of Pickett. Nor had any Federal infantry been identified. The belief of Anderson was that he had only Sheridan's cavalry in his front, but he did not think he should attack until his men had some rest.[38] By 11 o'clock, word was forthcoming of the break in the line at Petersburg. With the news were orders from Lee for Anderson to proceed to Bevill's Bridge and to cross there. This would protect the bridge and give him temporarily the cover of the Appomattox until the main army arrived.[39] About the time that Anderson received these instructions, he learned, also, that

[34] Gen. E. P. Alexander (op. cit., 593) following Longstreet, 608, expressed the opinion that the stubborn defense of Fo:t Gregg led Grant to delay the final assault, especially as Grant believed, according to Alexander, that Lee would be compelled to retreat that night. It is difficult to find in Grant's report (O. R., 46, pt. 1, p. 54) or in his Memoirs (Vol. 2, p. 449 ff), any basis for Longstreet's and Alexander's contention. Grant delayed, apparently, because he exaggerated the importance of a minor contest of April 2 in the vicinity of Sutherland Station and also because the IX Corps had not been able to carry the second line of defenses held by Gordon. So far from anticipating the evacuation of Petersburg on the night of the 2nd, Grant recorded (2 Memoirs, 453) that he ordered the bombardment to be resumed at 5 A.M. and an assault to be delivered at 6. Gibbon, in his report (O. R., 46, pt. 1, 1174), mentioned the "fearful cost" of the attack on Fort Gregg and Fort Baldwin, but manifestly had no intention of pursuing the attack otherwise than on orders. None came.

[35] 4 R. E. Lee, 51, 53.

[36] Cf. Stiles, 321.

[37] The settlement later was called Church Road.

[38] Anderson's MS Report—Lee MSS, printed in part in Irvine Walker, 210–11. The detailed movements of the troops are given in Bushrod Johnson's report, O. R., 46, pt. 1, p. 1288.

[39] Anderson, loc. cit. This movement will be misunderstood unless it is followed on the map. Lee was to cross the Appomattox at Petersburg and was to strike to the Northwest. He then would approach from the East the north-and-south stretch of the river on which Bevill's Bridge was located. Anderson was to skirt the bend in the Appomattox and was to approach the north-and-south stretch from the West. Lee and Anderson thus wer: to meet at Bevill's Bridge.

one object of the Federal advance against the Confederate right had been attained: The Southside Railroad had been reached.[40] As Anderson could not recover the line or serve any good end by remaining where he was, he began the march prescribed by his instructions.[41]

At nightfall on the 2nd, Anderson was beating off attacks by the pursuing Federal cavalry; Mahone was ready to leave the Howlett Line; from Drewry's Bluff and from the Northside the Naval Battalion, the infantry, and the heavy artillery were preparing to leave positions that some of them had occupied for almost two years. The difficult task would not be that of retiring from these positions, but that of taking from the Petersburg front the Second and Third Corps and Field's Division of infantry, the field artillery and the long, long wagon train. Of these tasks, the movement of the vehicles over bad roads deep in mud always had been considered the most uncertain part of evacuation. It scarcely had seemed possible that the thin, underfed teams could pull the loads that had to be transported. The hope of the Confederacy could be no stronger than the legs of the horses.

Carefully after 8 P.M., the guns were withdrawn. There was no need for silence because the nervous fire of both armies drowned the sound of creaking wheels; but General Pendleton had good reason that night to be proud of the men who handled the guns and the caissons. Artillerists brought out all the mobile ordnance except ten pieces and even took with them some of the mortars. Heavy weapons that had to be left in the redoubts were disabled.[42]

Field's Division quit the feeble works on Indian Town Creek and marched across the Appomattox in perfect order. Those units of the Third Corps that had not been captured or driven westward along Hatcher's Run moved out as part of Longstreet's command. To Gordon was entrusted the command of the rearguard. He rode boldly, as always he did, but with heavy heart. This time he could not be accompanied by the young wife who often had kept close to the Army.[43]

Except for those, like Gordon, who left families or sweethearts

[40] Bushrod Johnson (O. R., 46, pt. 1, p. 1288) said the railroad had been reached by the Federals at Jarratt's Station, but he probably confused the Southside and the Petersburg and Weldon. Sheridan's report (ibid., 1106) showed that the Southside first was struck at Ford's and then at Sutherland Station.

[41] O. R., 46, pt. 1, p. 1288; Anderson's MS Report, loc. cit.
[42] O. R., 46, pt. 1, p. 1280.          [43] Gordon, 423, 454-55.

behind, departure from Petersburg was undramatic. It was not so across the James. In the absence of Longstreet, his comrade Ewell exercised general command.[44] The remaining infantry of the First Corps were under Kershaw. All the other troops were entrusted to Custis Lee, who was embarrassed with the trappings of a newly commissioned Major General, though he had never led troops in any action outside the Richmond defenses.[45] Col. Stapleton Crutchfield, it will be recalled,[46] had the heavy batteries on James River in his charge, and he now led the gunners whose well-kept uniforms and smart red facings gave them the best appearance of the entire Army.[47]

Custis Lee's troops and most of Kershaw's crossed the James on the pontoon bridge below Richmond.[48] Gary's cavalry and some of the units nearest the city marched toward the capital in order to use its bridge. When they arrived, the night was far spent but the town was in a frenzy. Everyone knew that evacuation had been ordered. The slums, the dives, the brothels and the bars had vomited into the streets all the city's thieves and wastrels and gamblers and harlots. The town's few police were overwhelmed. Provost Marshal's guards were occupied in removing the Federal prisoners of war.[49] Convalescent soldiers in the military hospitals were expected to take the place of the regular guards, and they were assembled in Capitol Square for this purpose, but they were unable to disperse the mob. Although an effort was made to pour out all the whiskey in the stores, much of the liquor dumped into the gutters was dipped up and drunk. Much more was found and consumed before the guards could knock the barrels to pieces. Stores were broken open and looted. Every thief who had a den in which he could hide his stealings carried off armfuls, or overflowing wheelbarrows or wagonloads, even. Ewell used his staff and couriers to ride through the crowds and to make a show of

44 Liaison between Longstreet and Ewell had been clumsy in spite of Lee's instructions of February 3 (See *supra*, p. 613, n. 3). When Sheridan approached the city in March, Longstreet complained of the lack of information given him (*O. R.*, 46, pt. 2, p. 1304). On Longstreet's departure for the Southside, April 1, he wrote bluntly to Ewell: "It will be necessary, I presume, for you to come out and take command during my absence" (*Ibid.*, pt. 3, p. 1376).
45 He had been given temporary rank, Oct. 20, 1864, and, on Feb. 7, 1865, had been made Major General in the Provisional Army (*Wright*, 40, 44). Confirmation was on February 4. See 4 *Journal C. S. Congress*, 521.
46 See *supra*, p. 632.                    47 *McHenry Howard*, 367–68.
48 *Ibid.*, 367.                           49 *O. R.*, 46, pt. 1, p. 1293.

force. Kershaw was directed to hurry his leading regiment to Richmond. By these means, disorder was curbed,[50] but fire now succeeded looting. Warehouses filled with tobacco had been set aflame by the Provost Marshal, under previous directions from the government, in order to keep the precious leaf from falling into the hands of the enemy. Flames from these buildings ignited others or else drunken looters started new fires. By daylight a conflagration was sweeping the business district, was approaching the arsenal and was threatening private homes. All the departing Confederate soldiers could do was to behold and lament.[51]

Their Troy was falling, their cause was in its death throes, but some officers and men on the Richmond sector refused to admit the reality even to themselves, and they would have perished before they would have told a comrade that they believed the end of their dream of an independent South had come. Said Col. Alexander Haskell, one of a great family of fighters, "The idea of subjugation never dawned upon us."[52] Another soldier who left the Northside wrote: ". . . not one of us . . . despaired of the end we sought. We discussed the comparative strategic merits of the line we had left and the new one we hoped to make on the Roanoke River, and we wondered where the seat of government would be, but not one word was said about a probable or personal surrender. Nor was the army alone in this. The people who were left behind were confident that they should see us again shortly, on our way to Richmond's recapture."[53]

In the dawn of April 3, such confidence as that expressed by men from the Richmond front was not general among troops who had been at grips with the enemy around Petersburg. Instead, every shade of woe and of despair was in the faces of those who had survived nine and a half months of sharpshooting and of desperate combat. Older officers of wide information were less cheerful than the juniors. While there was widespread relief that the Army once more was able to maneuver,[54] observant and experienced men did not misread the look in the eyes of soldiers who

[50] O. R., 46, pt. 1, p. 1293.
[51] In addition to the references given in 4 R. E. Lee, 162, n. 46, see 16 C. V., 397; 20 ibid., 119; John B. Danforth and Herbert A. Claiborne, Historical Sketch of the Mutual Assurance Society, 146 ff; E. M. Boykin, The Falling Flag, 11–14.
[52] Mrs. Daly, 169.
[53] George Cary Eggleston, A Rebel's Recollections, 232.
[54] Cf. 4 R. E. Lee, 59; Owen, 374.

always in the past had met the test. The progress of the 12,500 infantry from Petersburg was pathetically fatiguing to men whom half-starvation had weakened. It was a slow march, too, because more than 200 guns and 1000 wagons had to be moved over the few roads available to the various columns.[55] As the vehicles crept along, and the troops halted and started and stopped again endlessly, Lee and Longstreet and most of the senior officers with the main force kept a stout heart and a soldierly front. At the Cox plantation, Clover Hill, where the two ranking Generals and their staffs were invited to dine, there was no lack of faith in the ultimate victory and no reluctance in voicing it. "General Lee," said the daughter of the house, "we shall gain our cause, you will join General Johnston and together you will be victorious."

"Whatever happens," the old warrior answered, "know this, that no men ever fought better than those who have stood by me."

Years later, as she recorded this, the matron who had been the girl of 1865 hastened to say of the General's brief reply, "No more, no less, and his words showed that his thoughts were with those ragged veterans, one mile away, resting by the roadside."[56] Longstreet, who still was unable to use his wounded arm in cutting his meat, had little to say on any subject. He enjoyed in silent thankfulness the food of a home that had not been stripped of its plenty.

Officers less exalted and the enlisted men ate by the roadside what was left of the rations they had brought with them from the trenches. Little enough it was, of cornpone and, for some, of bacon, but during the last days around Petersburg hunger had not gnawed every hour of every day. The new Commissary General had contrived in some fashion to get more food and to deliver it to the men.[57] Some reserve supplies had been accumulated at Greensboro, Lynchburg and Danville. It was toward Danville, at the terminus of the railroad from Richmond, that the Army was moving. The line still was in operation. Almost everyone in all the regiments apparently had learned, in one way or another, that railway trains were carrying supplies to Amelia Court House, which the columns would reach on the 4th. Then, if all went well, the troops with replenished haversacks and cartridge boxes

[55] Pendleton in O. R., 46, pt. 1, pp. 1281, 1283; Col. J. L. Corley's MS Report—Lee MSS.
[56] Kate Virginia Cox Logan, My Confederate Girlhood, 70–71.
[57] 4 R. E. Lee, 11.

would march to join "Joe" Johnston, "Little Joe," "The Gamecock." His name still had magic.

In this and like reflections the 3rd of April ended. It had not been an easy day, nor a cheerful one, but it had not been disastrous. The enemy had not overtaken, if, indeed, he was pursuing the main forces. "Dick" Anderson and the cavalry approached Bevill's Bridge before nightfall. While they awaited the arrival of the main Army, Pickett rejoined with fugitives who had escaped capture at Five Forks. A few hundred were the only survivors of the famous Division. To Anderson's dark depression of spirit was added the unhappy news that almost every man of the two Brigades "loaned" Pickett from the command of Anderson had been made prisoner on the 1st of April. The whole of the mobile force that had sought to protect the Confederate right was represented by an unwashed, half-starved, staggering little contingent that had followed the general course of the Appomattox toward Bevill's Bridge.[58]

Those of Heth's and Wilcox's troops who had been driven West in the Federal break-through at Petersburg also reunited the main Army on the afternoon of the 3rd. Under Heth's leadership they had numbered about 1200 when they had reached Sutherland Station on the 2nd, and they fought that day to repulse attacks by Nelson Miles's Division of the II Corps. For a time Heth was successful, but in the afternoon the left flank of his feeble force was turned. Approximately half his men fell into the hands of the Federals. The others had to retreat in disorder.[59] That any of them got away and succeeded in reaching Lee's line of march from Petersburg was due more to the character of the individual soldier than to the persistence of the old-time discipline of the Third Corps. The historian of McGowan's famous Brigade was too candid a man to say that the march had been creditable. He wrote: ". . . the Confederacy was considered as 'gone up,' and every man felt it his duty, as well as his privilege, to save himself. I do not mean to say that there was any insubordination whatever; but the whole left [right] of the army was so crushed by the defeats of the last few days, that it straggled along without strength, and almost

[58] Anderson's report in *Irvine Walker*, 211; Pickett in *Walter Harrison*, 148.
[59] See Miles's report in *O. R.*, 46, pt. 1, pp. 711–12. Sheridan was confused in his narrative (*ibid.*, 1106) of this action. Humphreys's account (*ibid.*, 679) confirmed that of Miles.

without thought. So we moved on in disorder, keeping no regular column, no regular pace . . . there were not many words spoken. An indescribable sadness weighed upon us." [60]

Disheartened as were many of those who bivouacked near the upper crossings of the Appomattox, this much was true: If Ewell succeeded in establishing junction with the main Army, as Anderson, Pickett and Heth had, a difficult convergence would have been completed. The Army of Northern Virginia might count then as many as 30,000 muskets—with which to oppose 100,000.[61]

On April 4, as on so many mornings of hope and adventure in earlier years of their struggle for independence, the troops started early.[62] Most of them were hungry, but not all of those who marched on empty stomachs were without hope. The hungrier they were, in fact, the brighter seemed the prospect of the rations the officers said they would receive at Amelia Court House, their objective for the day. While the column marched, the familiar sound of skirmishing on the left was audible. Sheridan was catching up! He had been able to follow the chord while Confederates had been compelled to move on the arc. That meant fighting, of course, but so long as the Army could outmarch the Union infantry, Sheridan could not do great mischief. Longstreet's men could cope with him until Fitz Lee's troops reached the flank.[63]

At last,[64] the van approached the village of Amelia Court House. The columns were halted along the road. Army Headquarters were opened.[65] There was much stir among commissaries and quartermasters. Hours passed. No rations were issued. Then army wagons were unloaded and were sent off under guard. That meant foraging, which was a confession, of course, that food for men and provender for the animals were not at hand. Truth

---

[60] Caldwell, 226.    [61] O. R., 46, pt. 1, p. 62.

[62] All the difficulties over routes and bridges, which are not essential to this narrative, will be found in 4 R. E. Lee, 61.

[63] The Federal cavalry who skirmished on the Confederate left must have been Ranald MacKenzie's command from the Army of the James. See O. R., 46, pt. 1, p. 1245. Curiously enough, Fitz Lee in his report (ibid., 1300–01) gave no account of his operations on the 4th. Apparently he spent the day in an effort to delay the advance of the V Corps and of Crook's cavalry Division.

[64] For the time of the arrival of the different units, see 4 R. E. Lee, 66, 69.

[65] George K. Taylor, Jr. of Amelia graciously made an inquiry in 1940 to establish, if possible, the location of Lee's Headquarters at Amelia. He unearthed a tradition that Lee spent some time on the 4th in the yard of Mrs. Jane R. Masters. The night of the 4th, according to local tradition, Lee camped on property that belonged at one time to Charles E. Wingo, of Richmond.

finally leaked out among higher officers: Although General Lee had given orders for supplies to be sent to Amelia, they had not been delivered. Nobody knew why.[66] All that could be said to the Army was that General Lee had made an appeal to nearby farmers[67] for food and fodder. The wagons had gone to collect what the residents of the county could spare. Hungry though the men were, they must wait until the wagons returned.

This information, spread swiftly through the ranks, brought to the surface the innate qualities of every man and tested what remained of discipline. Those who were physically feeble began to lose their grip on reality. Soldiers whose weakness was in character, rather than in body, began to slip away in sullen,determination to fight no more for a Confederacy that would let them starve. One of the loyal artillerists specified: "Many of [the men] wandered off in search of food, with no thought of deserting at all. Many others followed the example of the government and fled." [68] In those commands where good fellowship prevailed and discipline had not lost its compulsion, the fatal 4th of April merely was another day of hunger, unwelcome but endurable. Veterans of the old Second Corps still had the spirit to cheer General Lee when he rode past them.[69] The officers of the Twenty-seventh North Carolina resolutely decided to reduce rank and to reorganize their famous old regiment, which had been the rock of Cooke's fight at Sharpsburg,[70] into a battalion of two companies.[71] Field's Division of Longstreet's Corps, now the strongest unit left in the Army, was as firm and as disciplined as in the Wilderness.

The manner and the activity of the ranking officers did not change. Longstreet remained in the village. Heth arrived during the afternoon with the remnant of the Third Corps; Gordon bivouacked five miles east of Amelia;[72] Anderson was close at hand; Mahone was holding Goode's Bridge to await the arrival of

[66] The reason never has been ascertained with certainty, but the evidence assembled in Appendix IV-2 of 4 R. E. Lee, 509 ff, that in 25 S.H.S.P., 269 and that in 9 Rowland, 522, indicate strongly that supplies were not dispatched to Amelia because of delay at Lee's Headquarters in replying on April 2 to a telegraphic inquiry from the Commissary General concerning the disposition of reserve rations in Richmond. This delay was attributable in part to the confusion that prevailed while Headquarters were being transferred from Edge Hill to the McIlwaine House. In part, also, the ruinous delay was due to the fact the Army Headquarters never had a numerically adequate staff.
[67] Text in 4 R. E. Lee, 67.                    [68] George Cary Eggleston, op. cit., 244.
[69] J. R. Stonebraker, A Rebel of '61, p. 95.    [70] See Vol. II, p. 214 ff.
[71] John A. Sloan, Reminiscences of the Guilford Grays, 113; 2 N. C. Regts., 457.
[72] O. R., 46, pt. 3, p. 1385.

Ewell, many of whose troops were unaccustomed to long marches.[73] By no recorded word did any of these leaders suggest that the end was near. Theirs it was to encourage their men and to support the commanding General whose haggard face, despite his calm mien, showed how heavily he appraised the failure to find supplies at Amelia.[74] He knew, though he did not admit to any-one, that when he halted and sent out foraging parties, he lost his one-day lead. Evidence of this might be found in the fact that Federal cavalry had appeared South of Amelia on the afternoon of the 4th though they withdrew at nightfall.[75] If the cavalry were near, the infantry might not be far behind.

A gray 5th of April and a slow spring drizzle [76] probably added little to the misery of the thousands who had slept in the fields and the woods. Rain was nothing: it was bread they must have. The railroad had brought none during the night. No trains, in fact, were being operated. Eagerly, anxiously, the troops awaited the return of the commissary wagons. When the vehicles were hauled wearily back to camp, despair deepened. So little had been col-lected that it scarcely counted. The farmers reached by the forage parties had been visited previously by commissaries and quarter-masters. Barns and storerooms were almost empty.[77] The weak-ened soldiers, now heartsick as well as famished, had to face another day of acute hunger. They must proceed down the rail-road toward Burkeville in the hope of meeting one of the trains of provisions that had been ordered from Danville. If the enemy reached the railroad ahead of the column and severed connection with Danville, then . . .

No time could be wasted on an "if"! Bad news had galvanized the command. Because the day's lead of the Southerners had been lost, they must outdistance the Union infantry. On the main-tenance of the line of supply from Danville, the life of the Army and the Confederacy depended. Surplus wagons must be moved by a different route from that of the infantry. Everything that

73 Some observations of June, 1864, concerning the proposed removal of Bevill's Bridge or Goode's Bridge, as a means of hampering cavalry raiders, will be found in *O. R.*, 36, pt. 3, p. 900.
74 See the references in 4 *R. E. Lee*, 67.    75 Longstreet's MS Report—*Lee MSS.*
76 McHenry Howard, *op. cit.*, 370, said this prevailed on the 4th, but Waldrop, one of the most reliable of the reporters of the weather, recorded the downfall on the 5th. See 3 *Richmond Howitzers*, 57.
77 *Cf.* Lee in *O. R.*, 46, pt. 1, p. 1265: "Nothing could be obtained from the adjoin-ing country."

delayed the march must be left at Amelia. Orders to this effect had been given on the 4th. That day, too, artillery officers had been instructed to reduce the number of guns, to strengthen the remaining teams with horses released from discarded batteries, and to send the surplus ordnance on railroad cars to Danville.[78] Now these orders must be put in execution. Colonel Baldwin must arrange to destroy the reserve caissons and ammunition that had been sent to Amelia during the winter.[79] Cavalry must protect flanks and trains. In every advanced regiment, the long roll must be beaten at once. The choice was speed or doom.

At 1 P.M., off moved the men, though many dragged their feet. As they plodded gloomily toward Jetersville, a station on the railway to Burkeville, the unannounced explosion of the caissons at Amelia sent a flaming column of smoke high in air. Startled soldiers shivered in the memory of the Petersburg mine,[80] but they pushed on. In front was a cavalry screen of "Rooney" Lee's reliable command. Behind it marched Field, Mahone and, presumably, the remnant of Pickett. The Divisions of Heth and Wilcox followed.[81] Then came Anderson's men. As they left Amelia, Ewell was arriving with troops from the Richmond front. His soldiers were not starving but they had not found their commissary trains, which had followed separate and longer roads.[82]

These last units of the converging Army were held at Amelia while the strongest pressed forward to see whether the road to Burkeville was clear. It ran close to the railway for the greater part of the seven miles between Amelia and Jetersville. Beyond the second of these villages, the highway rose slightly to a narrow watershed. On the right of this elevation, as the First Corps approached it, was a branch that led down to Flat Creek. On the left, the railroad passed for half a mile through woodland. The position was not one of great strength, but if it were in the hands of an enemy who sought to bar the road to Burkeville, it might prove troublesome.

Rumors had circulated in some manner that Sheridan already was there. With the commanding General, Longstreet rode forward to see what the woods concealed. Soon there rolled back the

[78] G. O. unnumbered, Amelia C. H., Apr. 4, 1865—*Latrobe MSS.*
[79] *O. R.*, 46, pt. 1, p. 1281.                    [80] *E. A. Moore*, 279.
[81] This is the inference from *Longstreet*, 610, though the fact is not stated explicitly.
[82] *O. R.*, 46, pt. 1, pp. 1294, 1296.

familiar crack-crack of skirmishers' exchange. Grimly the two Generals continued past Jetersville until they met "Rooney" Lee.[83] With the diligence he always displayed, he had reconnoitered thoroughly and he now told his seniors all he knew about the situation ahead. Dismounted Union cavalry undoubtedly were in front. Infantry might be also. It certainly was approaching. The whole Federal Army, said young Lee, appeared to be advancing on Burkeville.[84] Light earthworks had been thrown up along the edge of the woods and, on the Confederate left, to the head of North Buckskin Creek.[85]

This might prove the most grievous intelligence of all! Grant's Army, or a part of it, was across Lee's line of retreat. The road by which the starving Confederates were to receive supplies from Danville was closed to them. A decision had now to be made whether the Southerners should or should not attempt to clear the road. This was a fateful question Lee evidently felt he should not leave to anyone else. His must be the responsibility. Longstreet would have been willing to share, but apparently Lee did not consult him.[86] As "Old Pete" waited silently and the soldiers spread themselves out by the roadside, the commanding General interrogated his son and studied the ground with his field-glasses. He had never been there before and he had no map that showed anything more than the roads and the approximate course of the streams.[87] Consequently, nearby farmers were summoned to describe the country to the southwestward. They knew little and could give no help.[88]

Finally Lee turned to Longstreet: The Federal position was too strong to be attacked. No farther advance could be made toward the Roanoke River by that route. The alternative—Lee did not say the last alternative—must be adopted. At Burkeville, the Southside Railroad crossed the Richmond and Danville, which the retreating Army had been following. The two lines formed an X. Instead of moving approximately from Northeast to Southwest, the column must move westward to the vicinity of Farmville, on the Southside. There the Army might procure supplies sent down from Lynch-

[83] *Alexander*, 595.          [84] *O. R.*, 46, pt. 1, p. 1265.
[85] The best map is Michler's of 1867, on a scale of three miles to the inch.
[86] *Longstreet*, 610.
[87] He undoubtedly used Campbell's preliminary map, 1864, of the "South Side of the James."
[88] *Longstreet*, 610.

burg. Revictualed, the troops then could strike southward again toward the Roanoke.[89] This would be the maneuver:

The distance from Jetersville to Farmville was twenty-three miles. If the Army was to get ahead of its pursuers and meet supplies on the Southside Railroad at Farmville, it must keep the road all the remaining daylight hours and all night. This was the most cruel marching order the commanders ever had given the men in four years of fighting. Unless the columns reached Farmville and received food there before the arrival of the enemy, the proud Army of Northern Virginia would be helpless. "It is now a race for life or death"—that line from a soldier's diary[90] spoke ten thousand words.

Change in the route of march left the infantry and artillery a clear road for approximately five and a half miles from Jetersville to Deatonsville, though this involved crossing of Flat Creek near Amelia Springs. The bridge collapsed, with maddening delay of all wheeled traffic. Infantry forded.

After the troops had dragged their way to Deatonsville, they found themselves on the road the trains from Amelia Court House were using.[91] Through a night that grew blacker as the hours passed,[92] the men groped their way alongside an endless tangle of wagons. Then, as always, the strong and experienced officers of resolute character kept their men under control, but among the more discouraged and weaker units, command collapsed. Drowsiness and nervousness were worse than were hunger and exhaustion.[93] Men staggered as if they were drunk. When some of them tried to talk, they were incoherent. Nerves were so taut that panic spread wildly. An unmanageable black stallion broke loose from a fence and charged down the road with a rail still on his tie rein. His dash started infantry fire. Troops thought they were being subjected to a night attack. Round after round was sent in every direction. When officers at last restored order, panic again produced veritable mania. A third time the adjoining battalions fired into one another and killed and wounded an unascertained number of men. These soldiers had to be left dead

[89] Lee to Longstreet, MS Amelia Springs, 4:30 A.M., Apr. 6, 1865—*Latrobe MSS.*
[90] *Owen*, 376.
[91] *O. R.*, 46, pt. 1, p. 1265.
[92] The moon set at 3:09 A.M. It was three days beyond the first quarter.
[93] *Stiles*, 326.

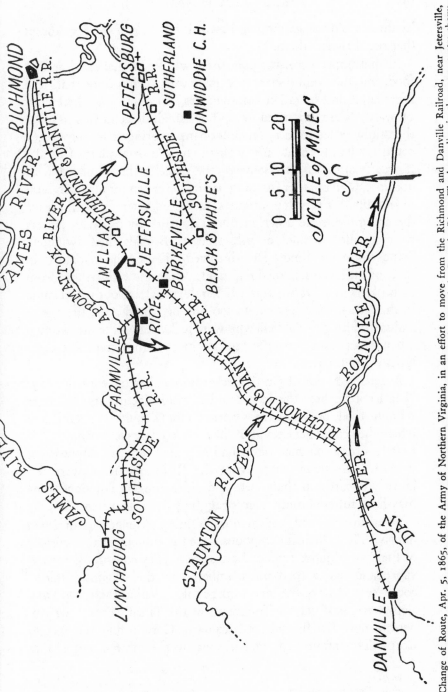

Change of Route, Apr. 5, 1865, of the Army of Northern Virginia, in an effort to move from the Richmond and Danville Railroad, near Jetersville, to the Southside Railroad in the vicinity of Farmville and to turn South again toward the Roanoke River. The heavy line in the upper centre shows the projected march

by the roadside or gasping and groaning in one of the few houses that could shelter them.[94]

In that unprosperous region, there was small chance of getting food, but the condition of the men was so desperate that "the regimental and battalion commanders," to quote Maj. McHenry Howard, "were instructed to send out small detachments to scour the thinly settled country on either flank to bring in whatever they could lay hands on, if only a pig, a chicken or a quart of meal." It was fruitless effort. Some of the detachments returned with nothing. Men of other foraging parties never caught up again with their units.[95] Every few minutes, half-dead veterans would leave the column and lie down in dumb despair. By daylight, officers were appalled to find to what a degree Brigades had dwindled. Some regiments almost had dissolved. Those who remained in some of the less disciplined regiments "were allowed to shoot from their places in the ranks pigs, chickens or whatever of the sort came in their way." Officers would look on or would avert their gaze and say nothing.[96] Soldiers who were lucky enough to bring down a hen or a porker devoured the raw meat as they crept like paralytics along the road.[97]

A veteran Major of Custis Lee's command wrote subsequently: "I did not see how the men could be held together much longer without food, or where the scantiest supply could be obtained or where they could get enough if they scattered in such a country."[98] Ewell's strength, which never had exceeded 6000, already was cut in half.[99] As these troops from the Richmond front were less inured to hardship than were the older combat Divisions, they may have suffered more from straggling and exhaustion.

Even in the best commands, fighting strength diminished hourly. The principal exceptions were the still-powerful Divisions of Field and Mahone under Longstreet. They constituted the advance and had a road unencumbered by the wagons. Officers could keep most of the men in the ranks. Behind these two Divisions were, in order, the fragments of the Third Corps, then Anderson, next Ewell, and, as rearguard, Gordon and the Second Corps. The infantry column thus was weakest in the centre. Fitz

94 *Ibid.*, 327–28.                         95 *McHenry Howard*, 376.
96 *Ibid.*, 377.                              97 *O. R.*, 46, pt. 1, p. 1295.
98 *McHenry Howard*, 377.                     99 *O. R.*, 46, pt. 1, p. 1295.

Lee's cavalry were under orders to support the van and to cover the rear.[100] Wagons not with the troops were moving toward Farmville by the least exposed roads. Some of the vehicles had been destroyed already by the enemy.[101] For tired teamster and for drowsing trooper, for gunner and for foot soldier, for every man of the Army from General to youngest drummer, the decisive 6th of April was dawning.

[100] *O. R.*, 46, pt. 1, pp. 1301–02.
[101] For the attack by Brig. Gen. H. E. Davies, Jr., 1st Brig., 2nd Cav. Div., on the wagons moving toward the Appomattox River, via Prideville, Paineville and Rodophil, see *O. R.*, 46, pt. 1, p. 1145. General Davies asserted that his men on the 5th set 200 vehicles afire before his Brigade was attacked by Fitz Lee and Mart Gary. For Fitz Lee's brief account, see *ibid.*, 1301.

# CHAPTER XXXV

## The Black Day of the Army

THROUGH THE HOPEFUL dawn of a spring day that seemed to mock the miseries of man, the troops struggled on toward the Southside Railroad. This would be reached at Rice Station, which was about seven miles Southeast of Farmville by the highway. Supplies sent to Farmville could be moved to Rice and issued. Orders were that after the advance reached Rice and had waited long enough for the column to close, the leading troops should proceed to Prince Edward Court House. If it were necessary to pass through Farmville en route, rations could be drawn there.[1] The town was believed to be beyond the range of the Federal cavalry operations; but of the enemy's approach to the railroad, little was known. During the night of the 5th-6th,[2] a dispatch from Grant to Ord had been found in the shoe of one of two Federal spies captured in Confederate uniform. This document, which was timed April 5, 10:10 P.M., showed that Grant was at Jetersville. Ord was addressed at Burkeville. In the dispatch, Grant expressed the opinion that Lee would leave Amelia on the night of the 5th and would proceed southward. Ord's instructions were to move at 8 A.M. and to watch the roads between Burkeville and Farmville.[3] All this was black warning to the Confederates that the infantry of the Army of the Potomac were within striking distance and that the Army of the James had reached the very front of attack. As for the Union cavalry, it now was apparent that after the Confederates' approach to Amelia Court House, Sheridan had quit the rear and was operating parallel to Lee's left flank.[4] Powerful Union infantry in rear, Sheridan able to strike the flank of a long column in motion—short of envelopment, a more dangerous situ-

---

[1] Lee to Longstreet, MS, Amelia Springs, 4:30 A.M., Apr. 6, 1865—*Latrobe MSS.* Prince Edward Court House was close to the Briery River, seven miles by air SSW of Farmville.

[2] For an error in previous dating of this incident, see 4 *R. E. Lee,* 79 n. 10.

[3] *Gordon,* 425 ff; original dispatch in *Lee MSS.*

[4] *O. R.,* 46, pt. 1, p. 1301.

ation scarcely could have existed for a starving Army in full retreat!

At Lee's headquarters, this was realized. The anxious commander was as alert as ever he had been and he showed at 57
much the same endurance he had displayed at 40 in crossing the
pedregal in the advance on Mexico City.[5] Some of his staff officers
still were conscious of all that was happening. Others were dazed
by lack of sleep. Longstreet's advantage in moving at the head of
the long, long column had given him some opportunities of rest;
but even if he had been in the tangle of troops and guns and
wagons, he probably would have shown his old, imperturbable
control of nerves. Mahone, Heth and Wilcox, moving with the
van, appear to have been masters of their minds. Gordon certainly
was. The events of the day were to prove that the commanders
who were losing their military judgment under the paralyzing
strain were some of those who had been struggling all night of
the 5th–6th to keep trains and guns and men moving over the
narrow road toward Rice.

The order of march toward Rice had placed Longstreet's wagons
in rear of the First and Third Corps. Anderson and Ewell had
followed. Behind them were all the remaining vehicles with the
column. These wagons were protected by the rearguard, Gordon's
Corps. Slowly, painfully, after Longstreet had gone ahead toward
Rice, the other Divisions toiled over the bad roads that led down
to the two forks of Sayler's Creek. Continuously in this advance,
the toiling infantry had to move out to the left, form line of battle,
and repulse cavalry attacks. The energy of Sheridan's troopers
seemed exhaustless. Driven off, they soon would find another road
up which they could press an attack.

Lee had ridden ahead to expedite the march of Longstreet, because it was imperative that the van make utmost speed.[6] This
left Ewell as ranking officer of all the troops in rear of Longstreet;
but Ewell had no instructions to exercise command beyond that of
the troops he had brought from Richmond. Whatever he did in
any sudden emergency would have to be based on his seniority,
which he always was slow to assert. His was as dolorous a part as
any officer had in that tragic retreat. He who had commanded the
old Second Corps on the road to Gettysburg now had 3000 oddly

[5] See 1 R. E. Lee, 261 ff.          [6] Cf. 2 Grant's Memoirs, 472.

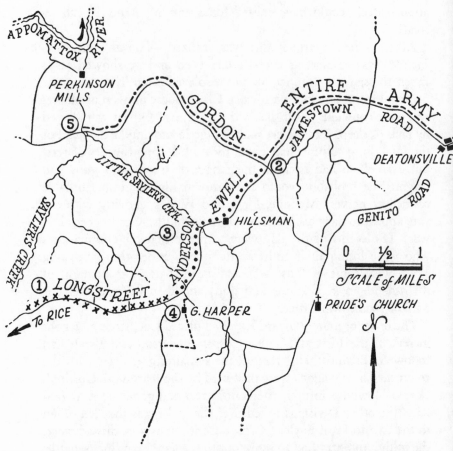

Vicinity of Sayler's Creek, scene of the battle of Apr. 6, 1865. The encircled numerals represent: 1, the line of Longstreet's march to Rice; 2, Forks of the Jamestown Road where Gordon mistook the route of the wagon train for that of the army and turned to the Northwest; 3, Scene of Ewell's stand and surrender; 4, Ground of Anderson's halt and vain attempt to cut his way through; 5, Gordon's battleground. After Michler's map of 1867

assorted, half despairing troops, some of them veterans, some of them clerks from closed government offices in smouldering Richmond.

About 11 A.M., Ewell found the enemy's cavalry stabbing viciously at the·wagon-train. Skirmishers were thrown out. The Federals were repulsed. Wagons between Ewell and Gordon then were started forward so that Gordon, as rearguard, would not have the whole length of the wagon trains of the two Corps between him and Ewell in the event Gordon needed help from the troops ahead. For the passage of these wagons, Ewell and Anderson in succession halted by the roadside.[7] After part of the trains had gone on, Ewell left the remainder between his rear and the van of the Second Corps, while he moved to close on Anderson,[8] who had not resumed his march.

Then occurred the first of the mistakes that showed how exhaustion was destroying command. When "Dick" Anderson halted, he should of course have notified Mahone, who was ahead of him; but by oversight or the mental paralysis of fatigue, Ander. son failed to do this. Mahone, unaware of the halt in his rear, pushed on toward Rice.[9] Across the gap thus created between Mahone and Anderson, the wagons began to roll. Federal cavalry observed them, rushed in, and set some of the vehicles afire. This created much uncertainty and prolonged Anderson's halt until about 2 P.M. Then Anderson started again—only to be stopped once more by a force of Federal cavalry in a strong position on his left front.[10]

His confusion, which was not unnatural in so mystifying a situation, was increased by a message from Gordon. The commander of the rearguard urged that the column push on, as he was being pressed heavily.[11] While Anderson hesitated, Gen. Henry A. Wise impulsively attacked the Federals without consulting his division commander, Bushrod Johnson, whom Wise detested.[12] This bold thrust by Wise shook the enemy but failed for lack of support. Anderson apparently was unaware of the attack or of its outcome. In search of counsel and of reinforcement, he rode back through his column and found Ewell. "Old Bald Head" already had been informed by Fitz Lee of the presence of the enemy on Anderson's line of advance. On the basis of this intelligence, Ewell had directed that the wagons remaining between his rear and the front of the Second Corps turn to the right and follow a road to a less exposed, lower crossing of Sayler's Creek,[13] about two and a half

[7] It is not recorded at whose instance this was done. General orders, according to Lee's report (O. R., 46, pt. 1, p. 1265), were for the units behind Longstreet's Corps "to close upon it as fast as the progress of the trains would permit or as they could be directed on roads farther West."

[8] O. R., 46, pt. 1, p. 1294.

[9] O. R., 46, pt. 1, pp. 1265, 1294; Anderson's report in Irvine Walker, 211.

[10] It seems impossible to determine from extant reports how far the Federal cavalry advanced directly in Anderson's front.

[11] Irvine Walker, quoting Anderson, p. 211.      [12] 25 S.H.S.P., 17 ff.

[13] This was below, i.e., North of the confluence of Sayler's and Little Sayler's Creek.

miles North and slightly West of the point where the Federals were in front of Anderson.[14] In diverting the wagon trains, Ewell failed, precisely as Anderson had, to notify the next unit in the column: no staff officer or courier was posted to tell Gordon that he must keep straight ahead to the Southwest and must close on Ewell, though the wagons had taken the right fork of the road and had started to the Northwest.

The two bewildered and weary Lieutenant Generals, Ewell and Anderson, knew little of the terrain, which was of a character to mystify. Long, frowning ridges ran for several miles toward the Appomattox, as if they guarded deep, swift streams. Instead, the two branches of the creek, except in rainy weather, were small, sluggish and heavily bogged. Lacking acquaintance with Nature's prank in guarding so little with so much, Anderson and Ewell scarcely knew where to expect the enemy next. This did not weaken Ewell's disposition, then as always, to help a comrade. Anderson thought that two Divisions of cavalry were in his front. They could be forced out of the way, he believed, if he and Ewell united their commands and attacked. The alternative was to abandon the wagons and to move to the right, through the woods, in hope of striking a road that would lead to Farmville.[15] "Old Bald Head" thought the wiser course was to move to the right and to seek a road nearer the Appomattox. As he had no artillery, this did not seem an impossible maneuver for his own troops; but he suffered now from a weakness that had shown itself progressively after he had assumed corps command: he would not decide. "I recommended [the march through the woods]," he reported later, "but as [Anderson] knew the ground and I did not, and had no one who did, I left the dispositions to him." [16] Anderson actually had no knowledge of the terrain beyond that of hurried, partial reconnaissance. His training as a soldier of Lee's, rather than the nature of the ground, prompted him to undertake a direct attack to clear the road.[17] In the preparations he now directed, neither he

14 *O. R.*, 46, pt. 1, p. 1294.
15 *O. R.*, 46, pt. 1, p. 1294. If Ewell and Anderson were using Campbell's preliminary map of the Southside of the James, 1864 (see *supra* p. 693), it ended on the very edge of their scene of action.
16 *O. R.*, 46, pt. 1, p. 1294.
17 *Ibid.* Fitz Lee was of opinion that either course would have been practicable had prompt action been taken when the march was first interrupted. For his observations, see *ibid.*, 1302.

nor any of his subordinates except General Wise could display any zest. Initiative was gone. Dispirited movements were mechanical. Men acted as if they were in a nightmare and could not make their muscles respond.

Ewell's troops had started their march up the road to support Anderson when, in an instant, the whole prospect changed. A messenger brought a report that staggered the two Generals: The enemy was in large force in Ewell's rear and was making ready to attack! It was true. Failure to notify Gordon of the change in the route of the wagons had brought acutest danger. Gordon had followed the wagons to the point from which Ewell had diverted them to the Northwest, and he had assumed, naturally, that their route was his, as it had been all day.[18] Soon after he left Ewell's road toward Rice, the enemy closed on the troops from the Richmond front. Federals now faced Anderson from the Southwest [19] and Ewell from the East. The envelopment of both was threatened.[20]

At this intelligence, the exhausted "Dick" Anderson aroused himself. Ewell, said Anderson, would have all he could do to look after the rear; the attack on the flank must be met by Anderson's own troops.[21] The South Carolinian rode off to rally his men; Ewell turned to his front, where Kershaw and Custis Lee feverishly were deploying for defense.[22] On the left, young Lee had his local defense troops and his heavy artillerists who marched and fought as infantry. In rear of Custis Lee's right, Ewell placed the naval contingent, styled a battalion, that had defended some of the James River fortifications. On the right of Ewell's line, stalwart still in their thin ranks, were three Brigades of Kershaw, Brigades that had been, in the day of the Army's greatest prowess, those

18 Kershaw in his report (O. R., 46, pt. 1, pp. 1283–84) stated that "before [his] troops left the ground Gordon's advance appeared, while his rear was engaged with the enemy." He expected Gordon to follow him but apparently did not feel that he was responsible for notifying Gordon of what appeared to him a plain route.
19 See note 10, supra.
20 O. R., 46, pt. 1, pp. 1265, 1294, 1297. The troops on Anderson's flank threatening his front were those of Custer's Division, supported by Devin and Crook (ibid., 1107). In rear of Ewell were two Divisions, the 1st and 3rd, of Wright's VI Corps. Before the action closed, the 2nd Division of the VI Corps arrived. Although "not actually engaged," Wright reported, it "performed an important part by its presence" (Ibid., 906).
21 O. R., 46, pt. 1, p. 1298.
22 Ewell in O. R., 46, pt. 1, pp. 1294–95; Anderson in Lee MSS and in Irvine Walker, 211.

of Barksdale, Tom Cobb and Paul Semmes.[23] These and the other units were as well placed as the ground permitted. In front of them were low, scattered pine bushes for about 300 yards. Then came Little Sayler's Creek, which was not a formidable barrier. East of the stream was a cleared hillside that led up to the Hillsman House.[24]

Before this deployment was complete,[25] the Federals placed two guns [26] and then a large number [27] on the Hillsman farm within plain sight of the Southerners. As Ewell's lack of artillery made a duel impossible, he sheltered most of his men behind a bit of rising ground that served almost as a parapet. Only a few score of the heavy artillerists were exposed, but among these men, the accurate and persistent Federal fire took grim toll.[28] In the midst of this bombardment, which the Federals seemed in no hurry to conclude, Ewell did a curious thing. Although his own men manifestly were soon to be subjected to fierce Federal attack, he rode to his rear to see how Anderson's attempted breakthrough had succeeded.[29]

"Old Bald Head" had not been absent many minutes from his command when the Union infantry began its assault. The strong blue regiments splashed across the creek and broke their way through the pine brush. Straight for Ewell's position the powerful lines pressed. So long was the front that both of Ewell's flanks would be overlapped, but his men did not flinch. The hungry Confederates, green clerks and four-year veterans, waited till the bluecoats were close. Then the Southerners poured into the enemy a volley that had the ring and roar of Fredericksburg. Everywhere

[23] Col. William H. Fitzgerald commanded the survivors of Barksdale's Brigade; Brig. Gen. Dudley Du Bose had Cobb's old troops; those of Paul Semmes now were Brig. Gen. James Simms's. See *O. R.*, 46, pt, pt. 1, p. 1269. For the order of battle on Sayler's Creek, consult *ibid.*, 1295. In the preliminary stage of the fighting, Kershaw had Humphreys and a contingent of dismounted cavalry on the Hillsman farm, but in the first onset Humphreys was forced across the creek. He took position in Kershaw's centre, North of the road (*O. R.*, 46, pt. 1, p. 1284).
[24] *Ibid.* A sketch of this interesting property has been written by M. R. Turner, through whose efforts, with those of others, the Hillsman House has been restored and has been made part of the Sayler's Creek Battlefield Memorial.
[25] *Ibid.*, 1297.                     [26] *McHenry Howard*, 380.
[27] *Stiles*, 330.
[28] *McHenry Howard*, 381; *Stiles*, 330. Stiles stated that the fire lasted "a few moments," but he may not have intended to leave the impression that the whole bombardment was compressed into so brief a time. Ewell reported that the artillery were in action "nearly half an hour" (*O. R.*, 46, pt. 1, p. 1295). Custis Lee (*ibid.*, 1297) said that the enemy shelled and skirmished "for some time, an hour or more" and continued fire until the action ended.
[29] *O. R.*, 46, pt. 1, p. 1295.

the Federals recoiled. Kershaw's men rammed another charge home and waited for a new assault. They knew it would come. The heavy artillerists, being less experienced, sprang up, rushed out, grappled with the enemy and pursued him to the creek. Their commander, Col. Stapleton Crutchfield, went with them—led them probably—and close to the stream fell dead with a bullet through his head.[30] His men could not go beyond the creek. When they started to return to their position, shell tore them.[31]

The Federal left, by this time, already had begun to turn the flank of Simms's Brigade, the right flank element of Kershaw. While this struggle waged uncertainly, Anderson dispatched word that the attack to clear the westward road had begun and might succeed if Ewell's men held on a little longer. Kershaw sent back a message of encouragement [32] and did his utmost to rally Simms's Brigade. Every loyal man in the thin Georgia regiments sought to fire faster. Humphreys's Mississippians gave their last ounce of energy to the battle. They still were hanging on, with front engaged and right flank turned, when a cloud of men in blue appeared in rear of Simms's Brigade.

Kershaw concluded that these troops must have beaten Anderson and now were enveloping the Confederates who were facing the rear. Swiftly, when Simms's Georgians saw themselves almost surrounded, they moved to the left and rear in the hope of escaping. Humphreys and Du Bose undertook the same maneuver. Kershaw defiantly gave them such direction as he could on the confused, fireswept field; but when he had gone about 400 yards, he found his troops melting away. Federal cavalry, he told himself, were crowding the last field and wood by which his Brigades might escape. The last alternative, then, had to be faced: Every man for himself! It was in vain. Within a few minutes, Kershaw, his staff and practically all the survivors of his Division were captured. So far as Kershaw could ascertain later, one man only slipped through the enveloping Federals.[33]

The same fate was Custis Lee's. His troops were exposed on their right by Kershaw's break, were broken in front and soon

---

[30] *McHenry Howard*, 382; Maj. W. S. Basinger in 25 *S.H.S.P.*, 40 ff. Curiously, Stiles made no mention of Crutchfield, otherwise than to remark (*op. cit.*, 332) that his brigade commander was killed.

[31] *O. R.*, 46, pt. 1, p. 1297.     [32] *O. R.*, 46, pt. 1, p. 1284.

[33] *O. R.*, 46, pt. 1, p. 1284.

were enveloped. To save lives which he knew would be wasted by further fighting, the son of the commanding General had to order his men to cease firing.[34] Young Lee, his staff and all his men, except perhaps for a fleet-footed few, became Federal prisoners.

This was not the full depth of catastrophe. Ewell, who so strangely had left his own troops to witness the attack to the westward, had found Anderson and, at the side of the South Carolinian, had awaited the opening of the attack. In minutes humiliatingly few, a staff officer arrived and announced a failure. Anderson later reported it in these brief, pathetic words: ". . . the troops seemed to be wholly broken down and disheartened. After a feeble effort to advance they gave way in confusion and with the exception of 150 or 200 men the whole of General Ewell's and my command were captured." [35]

In reality, it was not quite that ruinous. Whether the remnant of Pickett fought well or abandoned the field was later a subject of dispute.[36] Wise's Brigade forced its way out and, its picturesque commander insisted, it then fired into a wood where another Brigade of Johnson's Division had taken refuge. This command, he said, "raised the white flag and came out to us and formed and marched with us safely off the field, and gained our road past the enemy.[37] Almost all the other of Anderson's troops, with fifteen guns, were captured.[38] Anderson himself, after leaving Ewell, rushed to the front. Together with Bushrod Johnson and a few others, Anderson later escaped through the woods on horseback. Pickett and two of his staff officers rallied a squad which fired bravely into the face of a charging cavalry squadron and delayed it long enough for the trio to outrun their pursuers.[39]

Ewell had not waited for this last scene of Anderson's tragedy.

---

[34] O. R., 46, pt. 1, p. 1297.  [35] Irvine Walker, 211–12.
[36] Henry A. Wise said in 25 S.H.S.P., 18: "We had hardly formed and begun to move in his rear before Pickett's whole command stampeded . . ." Walter Harrison (op. cit., 154) wrote: "We carried nearly as many men into the last fight at Sailor's Creek as we had left to us from Five Forks, and . . . those men behaved as well on that last battlefield as they had ever done in their first flush of glory, or under the better fortunes of an earlier day. I have never seen on a battlefield less disposition in the troops to fall back."
[37] 25 S.H.S.P., 18.
[38] This was the number mentioned by Custer, who (O. R., 46 pt. 1, p. 1132), somewhat to the disgust of Sheridan (ibid., 1108). asserted a claim to all the captured guns. As Sheridan attacked only the commands of Ewell and Anderson, and as Ewell had no artillery (ibid., 1295), all the ordnance must have belonged to Anderson. The list of his batteries, few of which had any guns at Sayler's Creek, will be found in ibid., 1275.
[39] Walter Harrison, 157.

As soon as Anderson galloped off, Ewell turned back toward his command in the desperate hope of leading it through the woods to the North. He recorded the rest: "On riding past my left I came suddenly upon a strong line of the enemy's skirmishers advancing upon my left rear. This closed the only avenue of escape, as shells and even bullets were crossing each other from front and rear over my troops, and my right was completely enveloped. I surrendered myself and staff to a cavalry officer who came in by the same road General Anderson had gone out on. At my request he sent a messenger to General G. W. C. Lee, who was nearest, with a note from me telling him he was surrounded, General Anderson's attack had failed, I had surrendered, and he had better do so too, to prevent useless loss of life, though I gave no orders, being a prisoner." [40]

To this end had come the man who had been Jackson's lieutenant and, in the mind of many, the successor of "Stonewall." Ewell was shattered in spirit and, for the next day or two, scarcely responsible. At least one of his fellow-prisoners, Eppa Hunton, thought that Ewell was anxious to make himself popular with the enemy. "He was," said Hunton, "thoroughly whipped and seemed to be dreadfully demoralized." [41] This wavering in the spirit of a courageous enfeebled man did not hurt his fame or mar the splendor of his soldiers' last fight. Kershaw said: "On no battlefield of the war have I felt a juster pride in the conduct of my command." [42] Custis Lee, who was commended by Ewell, [43] was equally proud of his scratch Division. [44] Everyone had high praise for the Naval Battalion and the Heavy Artillery Brigade from the Richmond defenses. [45]

The capture of Ewell's and of Anderson's troops meant, in the eyes of the commanding General, the loss of two of his four Corps. [46] "General," said Lee to Pendleton, "that half of our Army is destroyed." [47] The other half escaped, though part of it suffered heavy losses in a drama as strange as that of Ewell and Anderson. On Longstreet's arrival at Rice during the early forenoon with the van of the First Corps, he learned of the approach of Ord's Army

40 O. R., 46, pt. 1, p. 1295.   41 Eppa Hunton, 125–26.
42 O. R., 46, pt. 1, p. 1284.   43 Ibid., 1295.
44 Ibid., 1297.
45 Ibid., 1295; McHenry Howard, 384, 388; Stiles, 329.
46 The Third, it will be remembered, had, in effect, been consolidated with the First.
47 Pendleton, 401.

of the James. To meet the expected attack of these troops, Long-street deployed carefully, and at exposed points he threw up light field works. An immediate danger was presented by a report that 600 or 700 mounted Federals already had marched up the road toward Farmville.[48] So small a force as that could be intended only for a mission of destruction—in this case almost certainly the burning of the bridges across the Appomattox. One of these structures was the so-called "High Bridge" of the Southside Railroad, almost directly North of Rice at a distance of four and a half miles. Under that was a wagon crossing. At Farmville itself were another railway bridge[49] and the highway span. These must be saved, cost what they might, because the Army's line of retreat might carry it to the north side of the river.[50] Longstreet chafed in the knowledge that he had no cavalry with which to pursue the "bridge-burners," but before he started any of his infantry on an overhauling mission, Tom Rosser arrived with a small mounted Division. The young cavalry General was directed to picket all the roads and to send out scouts in every direction.[51] As soon as possible after that, "Old Pete" told Rosser to follow and to capture or destroy the venturesome Federals "if it took the last man of his command to do it."[52] Munford, with Fitz Lee's Division and then Gary with his Brigade speedily were sent to support Rosser.

Close to midday[53] they met near the "High Bridge" the Union infantry, which proved to be under Brig. Gen. Theodore Read, Chief of Staff to Ord. Some of Rosser's men dismounted and proceeded to attack the infantry, but before the action had progressed far, the Federal cavalry detachment arrived and boldly charged

[48] Longstreet understood that all these troops were mounted and he so reported (*Lee MSS*). Actually the force consisted of Ord's headquarters mounted escort of eighty men and two regiments of infantry. The whole was computed at about 500 rifles (*O. R.*, 46, pt. 1, pp. 1162, 1168–69), but the subsequent haul of prisoners showed it must have exceeded 800 or 900.

[49] This was because the Southside, now the Norfolk and Western Railroad, crossed to the North of the Appomattox at High Bridge and recrossed to the south bank at Farmville.

[50] Apparently, when he wrote his memoirs, General Longstreet had forgotten the exact terms of Lee's orders of 4:30 A.M., April 6. At that hour, movement to the north side of the Appomattox was permissive but not mandatory. The defeat at Sayler's Creek changed this, but at the time Rosser got his orders, the battle on the creek had not been fought. It is for this reason that "might," not "would," is used in the text.

[51] Latrobe to Rosser, Apr. 6, 1865—*Latrobe MSS*. It is possible that Rosser arrived earlier than would be indicated by Longstreet, 612.

[52] *Longstreet*, 612.                    [53] *O. R.*, 46, pt. 1, p. 1169.

the Confederates.[54] Taken by surprise, Rosser's mounted men took shelter in a wood, formed there, dashed out and overpowered the Union troopers.[55] The infantry then offered little resistance and soon surrendered en masse.[56] Total prisoners numbered about 780.[57] Casualties included the death of General Read and the mortal wounding of Col. Francis Washburn, who led the Federal cavalry. Confederate losses were not light. The desperate front-line leadership shown by so many officers after the Battle of the Wilderness opened, cost in this Battle of High Bridge the lives of three Confederates of distinction—Brig. Gen. James Dearing,[58] Col. Reuben B. Boston of the Fifth Virginia Cavalry and Maj. James W. Thomson of the horse artillery, who charged with the cavalry. His guns were not on the field.[59] Maj. James Breathed, also of the horse artillery, barely escaped death in a hilt-to-hilt encounter.[60] Rosser was wounded once more, but was too busy to pay heed to his injured arm. He dispatched word to Longstreet that he had "captured everything except a few cav[alry] that escaped by swimming the river." [61] When Rosser rode back to Rice to give Longstreet the details, he was riding a fine black animal and was carrying a different sword. With enthusiasm he commented: "It was a gallant fight. This is Read's horse and this is his sabre. Both beauties, aren't they?" [62]

The fighting spirit of the cavalry was matched by the Second Corps in courageous defense. Virtually all the way from Amelia Springs to Sayler's Creek, fourteen miles,[63] Gordon's men had been under attack by Humphrey's II Corps. At intervals, Gordon halted behind any natural barrier that could be strengthened with fence rails or earth, and there he held off the hard-pushing Union line till the wagons gained a mile or two. His artillery was employed again and again—effectively, his adversary admitted [64]—to cover the retreat. After Gordon turned from Ewell's route and followed the wagon trains by the road nearest the river, he soon

54 *Ibid.*    55 *F. M. Myers,* 376–78, 380.
56 *O. R.,* 46, pt. 1, pp. 1162, 1215, 1220, 1302.
57 *Ibid.,* 1302.
58 For the circumstances of his death, a short time after he was shot, see *F. M. Myers,* loc. cit. He was the last general officer of the Army of Northern Virginia killed in action.
59 *O. R.,* 46, pt. 1, pp. 1302–03.    60 *F. M. Myers,* 377–78.
61 Rosser to Longstreet, MS, Apr. 7, [6] 1865—*Latrobe MSS.* In spite of the date of the original dispatch, internal evidence shows that it was written on the 6th.
62 *Owen,* 377.    63 *O. R.,* 46, pt. 1, p. 682.
64 *Ibid.*

found himself at a difficult crossing of Sayler's Creek. Pursuing Federals were almost upon him. The column, said Gordon, "struck my command while we were endeavoring to push the ponderous wagon trains through the bog, out of which the starved teams were unable to drag them." He explained: "Many of these wagons, loaded with ammunition, mired so deep in the mud that they had to be abandoned. It was necessary to charge and force back the Union lines in order to rescue my men . . ." [65]

By 5 o'clock, Gordon was so desperately pressed that he feared he would lose all of the wagons if he did not get help, but he was mindful, as usual, of the calls on the commanding General. In the midst of all the wild clang of battle, Gordon wrote a tactful note that displayed perfectly his courage, his candor and his consideration of his chief. He did not ask for help; he said only: "So far I have been able to protect [the wagons], but without assistance can scarcely hope to do so much longer." [66] The cavalry of W. H. F. Lee, which boldly had covered Gordon's retreat, had been withdrawn. Gordon fought with no troops except his own. One assault he repulsed. After Ewell's troops were captured, Gordon's right was attacked from the South while his front was under heavy pressure and his left was being threatened. His line broke in much confusion, but, West of the creek, Gordon rallied the survivors.[67] Although his loss on that Flodden Field of the Confederacy was about 1700, his had been a gallant fight.

The reason Gordon received no help on Sayler's Creek was the tragic one: the Army had no reserves. While Ewell and Anderson had been fighting their hopeless battle at the upper crossing and Gordon at the lower, Longstreet had remained at Rice. He had no serious action,[68] but as he was covering the roads that led to the Appomattox Bridges, he felt that he should not move Field or Wilcox, who were in the front line. Wilcox's Division was so small that it needed Heth in immediate support. Mahone's Division thus had been the only one available for service elsewhere. After the disaster to Anderson and Ewell, the Division of Mahone had been moved by the commanding General to a hill west of the scene of the surrender.

[65] *Gordon*, 429–30.          [66] *Lee MSS.*
[67] Gordon's MS Report—*Lee MSS*; O. R., 46, pt. 1, p. 1266.
[68] *Longstreet*, 612.

There, in the late afternoon, occurred an incident that Mahone himself described: ". . . the disaster which had overtaken our army was in full view . . . hurrying teamsters with their teams and dangling traces (no wagons), retreating infantry without guns, many without hats, a harmless mob, with the massive columns of the enemy moving orderly on. At this spectacle General Lee straightened himself in his saddle, and, looking more the soldier than ever, exclaimed, as if talking to himself: 'My God! has the army dissolved?' As quickly as I could control my voice I replied, 'No, General, here are troops ready to do their duty'; when, in a mellowed voice, he replied, 'Yes, General, there are some true men left. Will you please keep those people back?' As I was placing my Division in position to 'keep those people back,' the retiring herd just referred to had crowded around General Lee while he sat on his horse with a Confederate battleflag in his hand. I rode up and requested him to give me the flag, which he did." [69] With the flag and his own trusted men, Mahone drew a line behind which the fugitives rallied.

Night scarcely brought relief. In other battles, more men had been killed and wounded, but in no engagement had so large a part of the Army of Northern Virginia been destroyed. The day's casualties, which were between 7000 and 8000, represented probably one-third of the men of all arms that had left Amelia and Jetersville the previous day. Worst of all, time had been lost, the time bought by the agonizing night march of the 5th–6th. The Union infantry now were on the heels of the Confederates. Sheridan had been on the flank all day. If he got ahead of the Army. . . .

[69] Mahone in *Longstreet*, 614–15.

# CHAPTER XXXVI

## The Army Sees a Red Western Sky

WHATEVER THE dreadful possibilities of the morrow, Headquarters on the night of April 6 had to collect the scattered fragments of broken commands [1] and had to formulate plans for withdrawing them to a place of safety. Anderson, Pickett and Bushrod Johnson were somewhere in the woods. The few survivors of their commands, plus Henry A. Wise's Brigade, could be placed under Gordon. He and Longstreet now headed the two Corps that remained. They could count six Divisions, but four of these were wrecked. Field's and Mahone's alone were strong enough to make an all-day fight against an adversary who still had close to 100,000 men ready for combat.[2] As for routes, manifestly the Army could not strike immediately South via Prince Edward Court House. It must put the Appomattox between it and the enemy and after that must describe a wider arc toward the Roanoke or, if need be, westward toward the mountains.

To get the Army across the river, "Billy" Mahone's experience as a railroad construction engineer prompted a suggestion that was adopted and elaborated at field headquarters to this effect: Longstreet, with Heth and Wilcox, should continue on the road to Farmville; Mahone's Division, Gordon and the men who had escaped Anderson's and Pickett's defeat should cross the Appomattox under "High Bridge" and should rejoin at Farmville.[3] When all the troops were on the north bank of the river, the bridges could be burned. In this way the lost day might be recovered. The Army of Northern Virginia might get one march ahead of the pursuers.

After darkness the march began. The night was chill—snow fell the next day at Burkeville [4]—and was maddening to men who

[1] Cf. *O. R.*, 46, pt. 1, p. 1266.　　　[2] For the details, see 4 *R. E. Lee*, 93.
[3] Mahone's account (*Longstreet*, 615) indicated that he suggested only the movement of his Division and of Longstreet's Corps, and that Lee did not then direct either the reconcentration at Farmville or the use by Gordon of the crossing under "High Bridge." These additions to the plan doubtless were made later in the night.
[4] *Eppa Hunton*, 124.

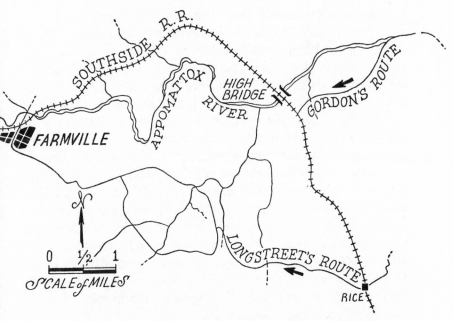

Sketch of the Crossings of the Appomattox River in the Vicinity of Farmville. The wagon bridge at Farmville appears immediately West of the railroad bridge. After Michler's Map of 1867

scarcely could drag their legs. Disorganized troops and hundreds of men separated from commands wandered hopelessly along and crowded the road.[5] Many who had endured all the hardships of the march from Petersburg lost heart that night and lay down by the road to die or to await helplessly the arrival of an enemy who, if he imprisoned, at least did not starve soldiers.[6] The hardiest and most resolute kept on. Besides a sense of duty, they had firm assurance—and no guesswork as at Amelia—that rations were awaiting them at Farmville. Commissary General St. John had seen Lee at Amelia Springs and had hurried on to the railroad to be sure the cars from Lynchburg with bacon and meal were ready when the troops arrived. If manhood could survive that torturous, interminable night, the remnant of the Army would not starve![7]

Marching conditions varied somewhat on the two routes. Longstreet's men had the worse of it on a crowded road deep in mud.[8] In the advance via the wagon road under High Bridge, General

[5] *Alexander*, 597.                           [6] Cf. *F. M. Myers*, 388–89.
[7] See St. Johns's MS Report in *Lee MSS*.     [8] *Owen*, 377.

Wise kept his Brigade together. During the night or perhaps later, the dejected Bushrod Johnson found some of his men and joined them, though he apparently made no attempt to exercise command. Gordon soon had the survivors of the Second Corps marching in their regular order by Brigades. Though some of these Brigades were smaller than a feeble regiment should have been, they did not throw off their discipline. At last—the night seemed a month—they crossed the Appomattox on the wagon bridge and pushed on toward the town where rations were awaiting them.

Mahone covered the retirement of the Second Corps. The engineers assigned to burn the bridges awaited his order to do so and, when they received none, they sent to find him. He at once authorized the firing of a span of the High Bridge and the destruction of the wagon bridge. The engineers set the lofty structure aflame but they could not get the wagon crossing vigorously afire before the enemy was upon them. Whether Mahone forgot to give the orders earlier or assumed the engineers would act when he marched off, it is impossible to say.[9]

From the bridge with Gordon moved Wise's Brigade and what was left of Wallace's. These troops and their chief bivouacked late in the night North of the Appomattox and, the next morning, April 7, proceeded toward Farmville. General Wise had lost all his horses and most of his extra clothing at Sayler's Creek, and he marched afoot. Around his shoulders a coarse gray blanket was held together by a wire pin. Even this protection was the gift of some unknown soldier who during the night had covered the sleeping General. The oddity of Wise's dress was aggravated by his color. He had performed his toilet in a mud puddle and had the red clay in streaks over his face as if it had been the war paint of a Comanche.

Plain speech and a picturesque political career had made Wise a privileged character in the Army. He had never hesitated to speak his mind to his superiors. Once he had insisted that Lee

---

[9] See Col. T. M. R. Talcott, engineer officer in charge, 32 *S.H.S.P.*, 71. The Federal accounts will be found in *O. R.*, 46, pt. 1, pp. 652, 683, 713. Four spans of the High Bridge were burned; the others were saved by the efforts of Federal pioneers under Col. Thomas L. Livermore. See his *Days and Events*, 449 ff. After the war, when General Mahone had become unpopular through a change of political faith, there were hints that he had failed to burn the High Bridge because he was head of the railroad that owned it. This was untrue. Mahone did not become President of the Southside Railroad till Dec. 7, 1865 (N. M. Blake, *William Mahone of Virginia*, 73).

hear him read a long, long memorandum.[10] Now, when Wise saw Lee on a little eminence where the weary commander was trying to rally stragglers, he made straight for the place. Lee gave him a good morning and asked the condition of Wise's command. "Ready for dress parade," the quick-witted Brigadier answered stoutly, and, with no further introduction, he swore: "General Lee, these men shall not move another inch unless they have something more to eat than parched corn taken from starving mules!"

"They deserve something to eat, sir," Lee answered, and he directed Wise to move to a nearby hill where rations from the cars at Farmville would be issued. Then Lee ordered Wise to take charge of the stragglers and lost soldiers who were wandering about. Wise was quick to protest that he had no horses and could not assume command; but inwardly he was pleased for a reason distinctly personal: He had seen behind Lee his own division commander, Bushrod Johnson, who normally would have been assigned this duty. When Lee repeated the order, Wise answered: "I will, sir, or die atrying, but I must first understand it." He proceeded: "It is not the men who are deserting the ranks, but the officers who are deserting the men who are disorganizing your Army. Do you mean to say, General Lee, that I must take command of all men of all ranks?"

"Do your duty, sir," Lee said. Wise was certain that Lee turned away, at the word, to suppress a smile. If Wise was correct, it was one of the last smiles of the Confederacy.[11]

The men of Wise's command and of Gordon's Corps received two days' rations, which they undertook to cook in such skillets and frying pans as had survived the long retreat. Longstreet's men, who were arriving in Farmville from Rice, could draw their rations, move to the north bank of the river, and prepare them. A few hours might then be allowed for rest, because, to repeat, with the bridges destroyed, the Appomattox would be impassable temporarily for the Federal infantry. The Union cavalry would be able to ford the stream, but they could be engaged and held. With good fortune, what was left of Lee's Army might march toward

10 *Heth's MS Memoirs*, 166–67.
11 Wise's early account of this familiar incident was in a speech of 1870 approximately (25 *S.H.S.P.*, 1 ff). The colloquy quoted is in *ibid.*, 18–19. This report of the conversation is probably much more nearly literatim than the more theatrical versions printed subsequently.

Lynchburg and try, once again, to move toward a junction with the waiting troops of "Joe" Johnston.

This hope was reviving dimly as fires crackled and bacon fried, but soon there was an alarm: The enemy was advancing! Federal troops who had reached the wagon crossing at High Bridge had extinguished the fire and had continued the pursuit with little delay. Mahone had not succeeded in pushing them back. Instead of enjoying a rest, the disheartened Confederates must make the north side of the river a battleground. Those troops who had finished their cooking could eat and fight. Others must leave their fires and throw away their dough, or take with them what they could snatch. Some thousands of men in the rear Brigades, shuffling pitifully into Farmville, found the issue of rations halted and the trains gone.[12] The best for which commanding General and commissaries could hope in that miserable hour was that the cars might be run up toward Lynchburg and stopped again at some convenient point on the Southside track that paralleled the road along which the Army must renew its retreat.

The start of this heartbreaking new retreat was full of anguish and excitement. "Old Pete" Longstreet kept his head and felt afterward that he had saved the commanding General from yielding to panic.[13] When Lee tried to lead a counter-attack, a North Carolina Brigade[14] cried out in the spirit of the Wilderness of 1864, "No, no, but if you will retire, we will do the work!"[15]

For the first few miles from Farmville, the road ran northward. Near Cumberland Church, about three and a half miles above the town,[16] the line of the Confederate retreat crossed that of the Federal advance from High Bridge. Mahone's Division accordingly was posted at the road junction, where it was able to throw up a few light fieldworks before the arrival of the Federals. When they came, they threatened a heavy attack. Mahone had to fight to keep them at a distance. Gordon, meanwhile, marched through the woods by the flank to cover the wagons against attack by the Federal cavalry. Fitz Lee's troopers, who from exhaustion were scarcely able to keep their saddles any longer, met and repulsed one cav-

---

[12] 4 R. E. Lee, 100, where the detailed references are given.
[13] Longstreet, 616.
[14] Lewis's of Early's Division of the Second Corps.
[15] 3 N. C. Regts., 283–84.
[16] This was via the coal pits and Hobson's. The direct route to Hobson's was shorter but worse.

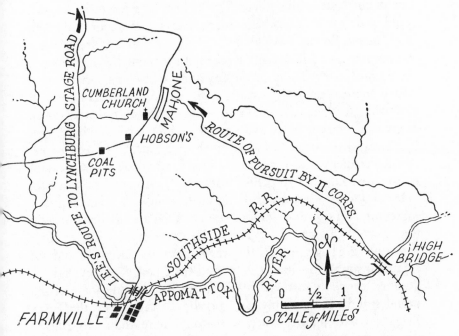

Terrain North of Farmville, to illustrate how the advance of Humphreys's II Corps by the wagon crossing at High Bridge necessitated on Apr. 7, 1865, a renewal of the retreat of the Army of Northern Virginia—after Michler's Map of 1867

alry attack on the trains and, in doing so, captured no less a person than its brigade commander, Bvt. Brig. Gen. J. Irvin Gregg.[17] This episode was encouraging, but it showed that the danger to the Army remained essentially the same as that of the 6th: The enemy would press hard from the rear [18] while his cavalry tried to strike from the South the left flank of the Confederates in their retreat to the West. Presumably, too, Federal infantry in large numbers were marching South of Lee's Army and parallel to it. If those strong blue columns of infantry, or even the cavalry, outmarched the Southerners, the only line of escape would be to the North, the direction opposite that of the desired movement to unite with Johnston.

This was plain to every informed officer and to all intelligent enlisted men who kept their sense of direction and the mastery of their benumbed minds. Some other soldiers still could not or

17 O. R., 46, pt. 1, pp. 1109, 1142, 1303; Owen, 378.
18 This was the advance of the II Corps, for which see O. R., 46, pt. 1, pp. 683–84.

would not believe that their Army, their long-invincible Army, could be defeated. They believed, as always in the hour of danger, that "Marse Robert" would find a way out. In hundreds of instances, strength failed many whose faith remained. The scenes of the night of the 5th and of the day and night of the 6th were repeated more poignantly because most of those who had kept up since the 4th were of stout fibre. They hated to quit the ranks. Many true men contrived to drag along with the column by throwing away their arms.[19] In the hope of a ride, hundreds of exhausted soldiers stayed with the wagons and added to the woes of half-maddened, half-stupefied teamsters.[20] An artillerist wrote: "Horses and mules dead or dying in the mud. . . . The constant marching and fighting without sleep or food are rapidly thinning the ranks of this grand old army. Men who have stood by their flags since the beginning of the war fall out of their ranks and are captured, simply because it is beyond their power of physical endurance to go any farther." [21] This happened among some of the proudest units of the Army. In a brush with the enemy, the Texas Brigade could put into action scarcely more than 130 rifles,[22] though many other veterans had the fibre to pick themselves up and to rejoin their command during the night.[23] One of the Brigades of Early's Division,[24] when called to support the Washington Artillery in repulsing Gregg, mustered about 200 men.[25]

The wreck of the Army, in a word, was of every shade of dejection and of persistent hope. A few preserved the sense of humor that always had been an amazing quality of Lee's men. One famished, ragged North Carolinian was wandering along a rail fence in the hope of surprising a chicken when a squad of well-fed, warmly clothed Union troops descended on him.

"Surrender, surrender," they yelled, "we've got you!"

"Yes," said Johnny Reb, as he dropped his gun, "you've got me, and the hell of a git you got!"

For those who escaped the fate of this realist, there was first a long, long wait in rear of Mahone's position. Then began an agonizing tramp to New Store, about twenty miles from Farm-

[19] F. M. Myers, 388-89.
[20] Cf. Lee in O. R., 46, pt. 1, p. 1266.
[21] Owen, 379.
[22] E. M. Boykin, The Falling Flag, 39.
[23] Cf. O. R., 46, pt. 1, p. 1277.
[24] The Division was under Brig. Gen. James A. Walker (O. R., 46, pt. 1, f. 1270).
[25] Owen, 378.

ville. Regimental officers were told that when New Store was reached, the men were to be allowed to rest till 1 A.M. of the 8th. Gordon was to be moved forward to be the advance of the next day; Longstreet's Corps would become rearguard.[26] With nothing more encouraging than this in prospect, most of the officers and men were too benumbed and confused in mind to do more than continue their torturing march. Their seniors were excited by two developments. During the late afternoon of the 7th, efforts had been made by the Federals to pass a flag of truce, but the fire had been too hot. About 9 P.M., another flag was presented opposite Mahone's lines and was received. A Federal officer handed to Capt. H. H. Perry of Sorrel's [27] Brigade, a letter addressed to General Lee.[28] It was hurried immediately to field headquarters, which were close to the rear.[29] The fact of the receipt of this letter and of the prompt dispatch of an answer became known to many officers during the night. Some of them correctly guessed what the letters concerned. Longstreet, but probably no one else, was shown the communication received from the Federal lines. He received it from Lee's hands, read it and returned it with two words of comment—"Not yet." [30]

The other development of that woeful, waning 7th of April was without any precedent and technically was contrary to stern terms of Army Regulations. During the day,[31] several of the general officers talked of the plight of the army and of the black alternatives it faced: it could disperse and attempt to reassemble and reorganize or it could abandon all trains and cut its way out. To scatter through the countryside would be to subject the whole region to foraging and plunder by uncontrolled detachments that might never be brought together again. If the second alternative were adopted and the trains were abandoned, the army's ammuni-

26 See the references in 4 R. E. Lee, 106 ff. Most of these are from the unpublished reports of the Appomattox Campaign.

27 Formerly Wright's.

28 The authoritative version, that of Captain, later Judge Perry, is in Sorrel, 297 ff and in 20 S.H.S.P., 56 ff. A second-hand account, substantially the same, appears in 16 C. V., 282–83. The narrative of Alexander (op. cit., 599) probably confused the details of the passing of the flags.

29 For their probable location, see 4 R. E. Lee, 103 n. 62.

30 Longstreet, 619.

31 From Pendleton, 401–02, the inference is that the conversations occurred during the forenoon, and probably while the infantry were waiting West of Cumberland Church, but the language is confused. There is no assurance that Pendleton himself was authority for this particular statement.

tion soon would be exhausted. There remained, then, no humane, practical alternative to the one thing no soldier had wished to consider or to mention—immediate surrender. In that conviction, the officers felt that General Lee should be told that his Generals believed the struggle hopeless and thought themselves unjustified in permitting more blood to be shed. Lee must be informed, also, that a desire to spare him the entire burden of decision prompted them to make their statement.[32] General Pendleton was suggested as the person to lay the opinion of the officers before Lee. At an early stage of the informal exchanges, John B. Gordon, who had not shared the first conversation,[33] suggested to Pendleton that Longstreet be informed before the matter was presented to Lee.[34]

No opportunity of consulting Longstreet was offered Pendleton before the march was resumed on the 8th. Then, for some hours, it seemed that the humiliating suggestion of surrender might be avoided. The morale and the outlook of the Army improved during a calm forenoon of quiet and of encouraging sunshine. A few of the cavalry had found their wagons and, having eaten vastly and at leisure, had found renewal of spirit also.[35] In other commands, there were few rations and fewer utensils for cooking them.[36] As the men marched westward, they manifestly were much jaded[37] but they were less despairing. The enemy was not troubling them; their march was unimpeded. Even the news of the capture of Ewell's command, heard for the first time by some of the troops, did not shake the stout hearts. Many of the men began to predict they would reach Lynchburg. "Once there," they thought, their "safety seemed to be almost perfectly secured."[38]

Headquarters, needless to say, anticipated a harder struggle than the average soldier seemed on the 8th to expect. Supplies had been ordered to Appomattox Station, 25 miles west of Farmville on the Southside Railroad. These must be secured before the enemy got them. Half dead though the troops were, they must be kept in the road.

Another unpleasant duty had to be discharged. "Dick" Ander-

[32] Gordon, 433; Pendleton, 402.    [33] Gordon, 433.
[34] Pendleton, 402. This explanation seems to be the only one that reconciles Gordon's statement that he did not attend the conference and Pendleton's recital of the circumstances in which he was asked by Gordon to speak to Longstreet. In Sunset of the Confederacy, 143–44, General Morris Schaff thought there might be an unhappy question of veracity between Pendleton on one side and Gordon and Longstreet on the other.
[35] E. M. Boykin, op. cit., 45.    [36] Grimes, 113.
[37] Ibid.    [38] Caldwell, 233.

son, George Pickett and Bushrod Johnson still were with the Army, but they did not have commands that fitted their rank. To assign them to head other troops would entail the displacement of officers who had done their full duty and had not suffered defeat. On the other hand, to call on the three Generals to remain with the Army and to have no part in its battles was a humiliation. They accordingly were relieved and were authorized to return home. If there was any implication in these orders that the three men had been culpable and not merely unfortunate in the loss of their troops —Pickett at Five Forks and the others at Sayler's Creek—their comrades-in-arms never knew it. Pickett nursed resentments for this treatment of him, or for what had happened at Gettysburg.[39] "Dick" Anderson remained to the end the loyal lieutenant and in his final report voiced no protest. Johnson filed his report, also, and publicly said nothing. Disposal of his troops was simple. Wise's Brigade and the men collected from the other units of Johnson's Division were assigned to Grimes's Division of Gordon's Corps.[40] No fragment of infantry now remained outside the two Corps in the determined hands of Longstreet and of Gordon. Both these men still were withstanding the strains of the agonizing week; both remained clear-headed.

During the forenoon, Longstreet showed his old fighting spirit. Pendleton reached First Corps field headquarters, sought out the Lieutenant General, told him of the conferences of the previous day, and asked if Longstreet would lay before General Lee the conclusion of his officers. Instantly "Old Pete" reminded Pendleton of the article of war which provided the death penalty for proposing surrender. "If General Lee doesn't know when to surrender until I tell him," stormed Longstreet, "he will never know!"[41] In a short while, Pendleton later wrote, Longstreet cooled down and "preferred that himself be represented with the rest."[42] Longstreet's own narrative would indicate that he remained inflexible and did not know until long afterward that Pendleton went to see the commanding General.[43]

[39] See 4 R. E. Lee, 445–46.
[40] Grimes, 117; O. R., 46, pt. 1, p. 1291.
[41] Longstreet, 620.
[42] Pendleton, 402.
[43] Longstreet, 620: "It seems that General Pendleton went to General Lee and made the report." Alexander, who was with Pendleton later in the day, quoted Longstreet as saying "his duty was to help hold up Lee's hands, not to beat them down; that his Corps could still whip twice its number and as long as that was the case he would never be the one to suggest a surrender" (op. cit., 600).

The artillerist found Lee resting on the ground beneath a large pine tree. Without a word, Lee permitted Pendleton, doubtless at some length, to state what had happened. Then, firmly and probably with some sharpness, Lee answered that he still had too many brave men to think of surrendering.[44] Lee's manner did not encourage argument or reiteration. Pendleton quickly left. "From his report of the conversation," Alexander said of Pendleton, "he had met a decided snub, and was plainly embarrassed in telling of it." [45]

As the day wore hungrily on, nothing occurred on the line of advance of the two Corps. Longstreet subsequently wrote: "The enemy left us to a quiet day's march . . . nothing disturbing the rearguard, and our left flank being but little annoyed . . ." [46] The excitement was in the ranks of the cavalry, most of whom covered the rear of the First Corps.

If the commander of the mounted forces had been negligent at Five Forks, he was atoning now. Two miles behind Longstreet's troops, Fitz Lee was watching and was calculating. He had no fight to wage at the moment because he was pursued by infantry alone. That fact was itself suspicious. It led him to conclude that Sheridan's Divisions had left the rear and were moving parallel to the Southern infantry, in order to cut off supplies at Appomattox Station or to get across the Confederate line of advance. By 1 P.M., Fitz decided that he, too, should leave the rear and go to the front of the column. In his firm, flowing hand, on half a sheet of paper, split lengthwise, he asked the commanding General if he should not do this.[47] Two hours later Fitz learned that the Federal cavalry were moving up the Southside Railroad, twenty miles East of Appomattox, and he determined to advance his whole force, other than a rearguard for the First Corps.[48] Sheridan must be met quickly, because he marched fast; and he must be met with every gun and every sabre the Confederates could command.

To the West, in the late afternoon, when Gordon's van approached Appomattox Court House, a halt was called. Near the front was riding General Pendleton, who probably had heard of the proximity of the surplus batteries that Lindsay Walker had

[44] For the disputed language of Lee, see 4 *R. E. Lee*, 109–10 and particularly n. 15.
[45] *Alexander*, 600–01.                          [46] *Longstreet*, 619–20.
[47] Fitz Lee to R. E. Lee, MS, 1 P.M., Apr. 8, 1865—*Lee MSS.*
[48] Fitz Lee to R. E. Lee, MS, 3 P.M., Apr. 8, 1865—*Lee MSS.*

been directed to move from Amelia ahead of the Army. While the Second Corps arranged its bivouac, Pendleton went forward to seek the artillerists and the ordnance. Two miles on the road from the Court House to Appomattox Station, he found the batteries, which had been parked for the night. Federal cavalrymen soon found them, also, and, while Pendleton was there, made a surprise attack. This was beaten off, with no great difficulty, by two companies of artillerists who were serving as infantry. In the time thus saved, Walker was able to get some of his guns into action and, with these, to repulse the enemy. Pendleton then left to report to Army Headquarters. En route he narrowly escaped capture by Federal horsemen who roared confidently along the road to Appomattox Court House.

The experience was not a happy one. Pendleton was proud of Walker's defense and of course grateful for his own deliverance, but he was fearful lest Walker, unsupported by infantry, would be overwhelmed.[49] About 9 P.M., there was sound of artillery fire from the direction of Walker's camp, and then suddenly, complete silence. Pendleton correctly interpreted this to mean that Walker and his guns were doomed and might already have been captured.[50]

The abrupt cessation of the cannonade was not the sole omen of disaster. Another was in the heavens. From the elevated ground of an open field, where some of the troops were bivouacked, a wide sweep of sky could be observed. It had dimmed slowly after the sun set at 6:22, because the moon, almost full, was mounting the heavens.[51] When the last glint of the sun had faded, there was silvered darkness, but it was not long unchallenged. To the East there was redness near the earth. From the South came the same reflections, dim but unmistakable. Westward, too—hearts stood still at the sight!—the light of kindled campfires slowly spread. Only to the North was the darkness unrelieved by fiery notice that the enemy was waiting and almost had surrounded the Army.[52]

While the skies proclaimed this red warning, Longstreet, Gor-

49 Pendleton in *O. R.*, 46, pt. 1, p. 1282.
50 *Ibid.* The attack on Walker was made by Custer, who, in his final assault, captured twenty-four guns. Incredibly, Custer reported (*O. R.*, 46, pt. 1, p. 1132) that the "train was guarded by about two Divisions of infantry, in addition to over thirty pieces of artillery."
51 E. M. Boykin, *op. cit.*, 49.                    52 *MS Memoirs of W. B. Freeman.*

don and Fitz Lee were conferring with the commanding General. A few horses, blankets, and odds and ends of equipment represented all that was left of Army headquarters. Lying by a fire, the two younger men heard that an exchange of letters with General Grant had been in progress since the previous evening.[53] The letter passed by flag of truce through Mahone's lines, the letter which Longstreet had read and had handed back to Lee with the comment "not yet," had been a call by Grant for the surrender of the Army of Northern Virginia in order to stop the needless effusion of blood. Lee had replied that he did not take Grant's view of the hopelessness of further resistance, but reciprocated the desire to stop the flow of blood and therefore asked what terms Grant would offer. In a second letter, dated the 8th,[54] Grant replied: "Peace being my great desire, there is but one condition I would insist upon, namely, that the officers and men surrendered shall be disqualified for taking up arms against the government of the United States until properly exchanged." Lee had made this letter the occasion of a proposal to meet Grant, not to negotiate surrender of the Army of Northern Virginia, but to consider how Grant's proposal "may affect the C.S. forces under my command and to tend to the restoration of peace."[55] Lee, in other words, had rejected a demand for the surrender of his Army and had returned to the type of negotiation that had failed after the correspondence between Longstreet and Ord.[56]

To this second letter from Lee, no answer had been received. In the light of this and in the face of the known military situation, Gordon and Fitz Lee and Longstreet were asked what they thought the Army should do on the 9th. Discussion ranged from the tactics of another battle to the future of the Southern people,[57] but the decision was unequivocal and unanimous in behalf, substantially, of the second plan rejected the previous day at the informal conference of officers: One more effort must be made to break through toward Lynchburg and then to turn southward. The artillery must be reduced to two battalions. Only the ammunition wagons were to accompany the Army. Remaining guns and trains should be headed for Lynchburg. Fitz Lee would open the attack, sup-

[53] Gordon, 435.
[54] For the reception of the flag, see 8 C. V., 258.
[55] The official text of these letters is in Grant's report (O. R., 46, pt. 1, pp. 56–57).
[56] See supra, p. 643.　　　　　[57] Gordon, 435.

ported by the Second Corps, and then he and Gordon would wheel to the left to cover the passage of the vehicles. Longstreet would close behind the trains and would hold the position. If this succeeded, the Army would fight on.[58] In the event of failure, the end would have come. This alternative was faced with candor and courage,[59] but Fitz Lee made one request: He would like to be notified, before a surrender, in order that he and his men might leave the field and go to North Carolina to unite with Johnston,[60] provided this could be done honorably and without compromising the General-in-chief. The request was granted; the conference ended. At 1 A.M. on the morrow, the 9th of April, the movement would begin. The old Army would shake off its pursuers or perish on the field.

[58] *O. R.,* 46, pt. 1, p. 1267; *Gordon,* 436.
[59] *Gordon,* 435–36.          [60] *O. R.,* 46, pt. 1, p. 1304.

# CHAPTER XXXVII

## Appomattox: Exeunt Omnes

About the hour set for the beginning of the movement to cut a way through the enemy's lines, General Pendleton reached Army headquarters. He reported not only the attack on Walker's parked artillery but also the sound of railroad trains in the direction of Appomattox Station.[1] Fitz Lee was informed of this, after he left headquarters, and was told to ascertain the strength of the Federals in front and on the flank. If necessary, he could delay the advance until daylight.[2] Fitz waited, though Gordon's ghost of the Second Corps moved up in the darkness to approximately the ground from which it was to attack. At daybreak, Palm Sunday, half a mile West of the Court House, on the road to Lynchburg, Gordon boldly spread his men in line of battle. They numbered no more than 1600[3] muskets of the 7500 that had been in the soldiers' hands as recently as the 1st of March.[4] On the right of Gordon's troops were the cavalry—"Rooney" Lee next the infantry, then Tom Rosser and then Tom Munford.[5] Fitz Lee was determined but he was not hopeful. He believed, as all Confederate cavalry commanders did, that his men could whip any mounted troops the Federals could bring against him. As an experienced soldier he knew that with his 2400 men he could not break through strong Federal infantry. That was one reason he had made reservation the previous night. Privately he arranged with Gordon that if the Second Corps encountered infantry in its front, Gordon was to signal. Then Fitz would lead his cavalry off the field before a truce was declared.[6]

As soon as it was light enough to see westward across the fields to the crossroads ahead,[7] Federal earthworks were discernible.

[1] O. R., 46, pt. 1, p. 1282. This information probably supplemented that mentioned in R. E. Lee, 117 n. 2.

[2] O. R., 46, pt. 1, p. 1266.  [3] O. R., 46, pt. 1, p. 1303.

[4] Ibid., 389.  [5] Ibid., 1303.

[6] Ibid., 1304.

[7] That is, at the junction of the Lynchburg and Bent Creek Roads.

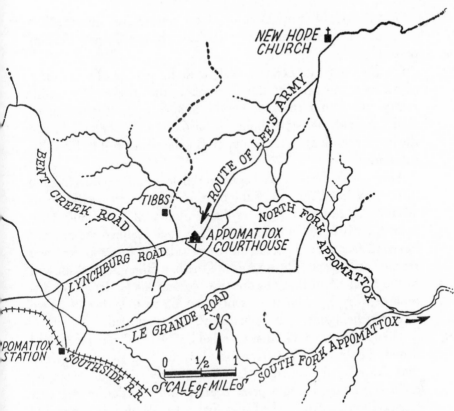

Sketch of the Vicinity of Appomattox Court House—after Michler's Map of 1867

They were new and not heavy, such works, in short, as any soldiers might have thrown up during the night. Neither Fitz Lee nor Gordon could tell, at the distance and in the dim light, whether the men occasionally visible behind the field fortifications were dismounted troopers or the familiar blue infantry. After careful scrutiny with his field glasses, Gordon was satisfied that the Federals were cavalry and were Fitz Lee's prey. Young Lee was convinced that the Unionists were infantry and therefore meat for Gordon. The two tired officers argued so long that Bryan Grimes, with all the zeal of a new Major General, broke in. Somebody, he said, must attack and at once. If this were done immediately, he believed the enemy could be driven from the crossroads. "I will undertake it." Grimes volunteered.

"Well,' answered Gordon, "drive them off!"

"I can't do it with my Division alone, but require assistance."

"You can take the other two Divisions of the Corps," Gordon replied.[8]

On this basis, Fitz Lee was ready to do his part, but he and most of his men still believed the bluecoats at the crossroads were infantry and would mow down the attackers. A cavalryman of Beale's Brigade probably spoke for the Corps when he said, before the bugle sounded: "Old Company E will call the roll in Hell this morning."[9]

At 5 o'clock the advance began in echelon on the right. In spite of the physical condition of the men, it was a smart, well-ordered advance that would have evoked "Stonewall" Jackson's terse "Good, good!" The quaver of the "rebel yell" saluted the dawn.[10] Forward went the line. At the crossroads, the breastworks were reached and swept. The uniform of the first fallen Federal showed to the relief of all that Gordon was correct: Defenders were dismounted cavalry who were sent hurrying to their horses. Two fine new fieldguns, with their teams, were captured.

Then, as directed, Gordon wheeled by the left flank and formed a new line of battle that faced southward. The Lynchburg road was cleared and covered, as Lee had directed. When the wagon train was ready, it could pass. Scarcely was Gordon in this new position than word reached him that Federals were in a wood to his right and rear—and Federal infantry at that, beyond all doubt infantry.[11] Action swiftly followed report. Within an hour, these Union troops vigorously attacked Fitz Lee and soon drove him back on Gordon's flank. More distant Union regiments emerged from the wood, in rear of the right of the Confederate infantry, and slipped to the East as if they intended to get between Gordon and Longstreet. Soon, too, Federal cavalry began to demonstrate against the left of Gordon's line. All this the enemy did smoothly and confidently and to the dismay of Gordon. Where he had hoped to encounter only cavalry and to drive them from

---

[8] *Grimes*, 114–15.     [9] *MS Diary of J. Armfield Franklin*, Apr. 9, 1865.
[10] Walter A. Montgomery in 5 *N. C. Regts.*, 260; also separately printed.
[11] Gordon's MS report—*Lee MSS*. *Cf.* Ord in *O. R.*, 46, pt. 1, p. 1162: "I marched my men from daylight on the 8th until 10 A.M. on the 9th of April, except three hours, and deployed my two Corps [Two Divisions of the XXIV and one of the XXV] across the head of the valley just as Lee's advance was pushing out of it, for, in spite of Sheridan's attempts to hold them, our cavalry were falling back in confusion before Lee's infantry. We were barely in time."

his front, he had Federal infantry to the West of him, the threat of infantry deployment to the East, and cavalry to the Southeast.[12]

The situation had grown desperate within three hours after the fight had opened. Gordon used his sharpshooters skillfully, and with his artillery he added greatly to the fire-power of his thin line of battle,[13] but against such odds as he saw on three sides, he realized that the fight was hopeless. If Gordon admitted that, even to himself, his plight was almost past redemption, because in a black hour at Sharpsburg and in the madness of the Bloody Angle, his had been the voice of unshakable confidence.

Now, about 8 o'clock, Col. Charles Venable of the staff of the commanding General rode up to ask how the contest was progressing. Never in his military career had Gordon been compelled to give such an answer as his honor demanded: "Tell General Lee I have fought my Corps to a frazzle, and I fear I can do nothing unless I am heavily supported by Longstreet's Corps." [14]

As Venable carried this message to Headquarters, and Gordon stubbornly renewed his fight, Longstreet was closing the rear. He had been informed by the few cavalrymen at his command that the Federals were beginning their advance from their bivouac.[15] "Old Pete" accordingly had to prepare to fight in front or in rear. His advance had to be cautious because he did not have full understanding, as yet, of what was happening ahead.[16]

Soon a courier brought Longstreet a message: The commanding General wished to see him at the front. Longstreet took several members of his staff with him, left Charles Field to guard the rear, and hurried toward the Court House. By the roadside, near a dying fire of fence rails, Longstreet presently saw Lee, Mahone and a number of other officers. Longstreet observed, as he drew

---

[12] Gordon's MS report—*Lee MSS.* There is, unfortunately, no accurate sketch of troop positions or of the order of battle at Appomattox. For a poor best, see Schaff, *op. cit.,* 220.

[13] *Gordon,* 437; his MS Report, *loc. cit.* There is no information concerning Fitz Lee's movements at this stage of the battle, though his report indicated (*O. R.,* 46, pt. 1, p. 1303) that he was in action until Gordon's later withdrawal.

[14] This is Gordon's republication of Venable's early account (*Gordon,* 438). In a much later version, Gordon quoted himself as saying, more rhetorically: "Tell General Lee that my command has been fought to a frazzle, and unless Longstreet can unite in the movement, or prevent those forces from coming upon my rear, I cannot long go forward."

[15] This force consisted of Humphreys's II Corps, which was followed by Wright's VI Corps. Humphreys started forward at 8 A.M. (*O. R.,* 46, pt. 1, p. 684); Wright moved at 5 (*ibid.,* 908) and soon overtook the II Corps.

[16] Cf. *Alexander,* 603.

rein, that Lee had dressed most carefully, as if for a grand review, and wore sword, sash and gold spurs. He looked vigorous, Longstreet thought. At closer range it was manifest that the commanding General was profoundly depressed.

As always, Lee's greeting was courteous but his preliminaries were brief: Venable, he said, had returned and had brought the news that Gordon was halted and was under heavy attack by infantry and cavalry. The Second Corps could not break through. The Army's subsistence stores doubtless had been lost on the railroad, which must be in the hands of the enemy. Gordon had asked help from the First Corps, but Longstreet, said Lee, doubtless would have his hands full in dealing with Meade, who was pressing the rearguard. It did not seem possible for the Army to get along: what did Longstreet think? At such a time, Longstreet never wasted words. He asked whether the sacrifice of the Army could in any way help the Southern cause elsewhere.

"I think not," Lee answered.

"Then your situation speaks for itself."

At that answer, Lee looked unhappily aside and called to "Little Billy" Mahone, who was shaking in the chill air, out of earshot and beyond the reach of such feeble heat as the dying fire offered. Mahone came forward on Lee's summons and explained quickly that he was shivering because he was cold, not because he was afraid. Longstreet heard Lee begin to Mahone such a résumé of the situation as he had himself received; but as messages from the First Corps came at the moment, Longstreet fixed his attention on them and not on the exchange between his chief and Mahone. When Longstreet was free to join in the conversation again, Mahone was questioning Lee about the condition of the Army. In a few minutes, Mahone told Lee he thought the Army should surrender and then he turned to "Old Pete." Did not Longstreet agree? The corps commander had to say he did.[17] Lee spoke to several others and to Porter Alexander, in particular, at some length.[18] Then Longstreet saw his commander mount and ride to the rear to meet General Grant in accordance with Lee's request of the previous evening, April 8, for an interview on general terms of peace.

[17] *Longstreet*, 624–25.
[18] *Alexander*, 603–05; summarized in 4 *R. E. Lee*, 122–23.

The prospect of having a conference between commanding officers occur in rear of his lines was disturbing to Longstreet. Nothing had been said about authorizing a truce. All the indications were that the Federals in the rear were preparing to attack: they should be assailed before they were reinforced. Besides, Gordon needed help at a time when pressure on the rear of the First Corps might be heavy. In this dilemma, Longstreet must continue to strengthen the rear, opposite the threatening Federals. When this was done, he should send Porter Alexander forward with such troops and guns as could be spared, and should post them on good ground in rear of Gordon.[19]

Field's veterans continued to fell trees and to dig dirt in ignorance of the fact that their surrender might be under negotiation. Longstreet told no one. He could hear, probably, the sound of Gordon's battle and he could tell that the Second Corps was not gaining ground. Perhaps the first definite report he had, to supplement what Lee had told him, came when a cavalry staff officer hurried from the front: Fitz Lee, said the young man, had found a route by which the Army could escape.[20] "Old Pete" waited only long enough to be sure he understood the message aright. Then he called lustily for a swift courier. There was none, but Col. John Haskell had at hand a thoroughbred mare, famous in the Army for her speed and beauty. Longstreet gave the message to Haskell and told the Colonel to overtake General Lee even if it cost the horse. Off hurried Haskell along the road Lee had followed.[21] Longstreet waited. Outwardly he was composed. Inwardly, his fighting blood boiled. If there was a way out, as Fitz Lee said, he would take it in the event Lee could not get honorable terms. "I know my Corps will follow me," he said, "and I know we can get through, though we may have a hard time."[22] Before many min-

19 *Longstreet*, 625–26.
20 *J. C. Haskell's MS Rems.*, 121. Colonel Haskell wrote that Fitz Lee "had broken the enemy's line and we could get through"; but the chronology of the artillerist is confused for the events of the day and almost certainly is in error on this point. Longstreet stated (*op. cit.*, 626) that "a break had been found through which we could force passage."
21 *Longstreet*, 626; *J. C. Haskell's MS Rems.*, 121. Colonel Haskell wrote that Longstreet called him and told him he must "catch General Lee if it was possible before [the General] got to Grant." In Longstreet's narrative he represents Haskell as volunteering to carry the message.
22 Haskell, *op. cit.*, 121. Colonel Haskell, here again, probably forgot the exact place of this remark in the sequence of events, but there is no reason to question the substantial accuracy of the quotation.

utes passed, another messenger from the commander of the cavalry rode up: General Fitz Lee regretted to report that he was mistaken; the route he had found at the front was not one by which the Army could escape.[23] This intelligence, of course, had to be forwarded immediately to General Lee. For this purpose, Col. John Fairfax was available and, as always, was at the service of his commander.

Again there was a wait, a long wait, at Longstreet's headquarters. After Field's men had completed their field works, part of the First Corps started forward to form the support line for Gordon. As Longstreet saw it, everything else depended now on whether the commanding General had received at the hands of General Grant terms that could be accepted. If they were terms of degradation, then the Army could do what "Jeb" Stuart said he had planned to do that June day when he thought he might be trapped on the bank of the swollen Chickahominy: The Army could "die game." [24]

At length Haskell returned on his winded mare. He had met Fairfax on the road and knew of Fitz Lee's second message. In fact, Haskell reported, the commanding General had not credited the first message. "Fitz," the General had said to Haskell, "has fooled himself." Haskell went on to explain that there had been some misunderstanding about the proposed meeting with General Grant. The Federal commander was not where Lee had expected to find him. All communication was being conducted through the ranking officer of the Federals in rear of the First Corps. Lee was still between the lines, Haskell said, and had this message for Longstreet: In hurrying to the rear the commanding General had forgotten to notify Gordon that a truce would be asked. Would Longstreet inform Gordon of the situation so that the Army would not be fighting in front while observing a truce in rear? In all other respects, while Lee was between the lines, Longstreet was to

[23] Colonel Haskell understood that Fitz Lee reported he had not broken through, as he had first thought, and had "only gone through an advance line of cavalry." All the other authorities cited in 4 R. E. Lee, 127–28, remembered the facts as stated in the text. In the absence of any reference in Fitz Lee's published report to his movements at this hour, doubt must remain, but it is difficult to see where he could have attacked and found the situation ascribed to him. It seems more reasonable to assume that he first thought he could escape by the trail that ran northward from the Tibbs House. No other known route was open then. Positive, final statement does not seem possible.

[24] See Vol. I, p. 302.

use his own judgment.[25] Longstreet listened, said little and called in a moment for a staff officer to ride to Gordon with Lee's message.[26]

Gordon's few men were still fighting, "fighting furiously in nearly every direction," to use their commander's words,[27] when Longstreet's messenger arrived at the front. Immediately Gordon directed Col. Green Peyton to ride out between the lines with a flag of truce and to tell General Ord, who was believed to be in command, that "General Gordon has received notice from General Lee of a flag of truce, stopping the battle."

Peyton, swallowing his grief, went off at once but returned quickly to report—it was a proud fact of history—that the Second Corps had no flag of truce.

"Well," said Gordon, "take your handkerchief and tie that on a stick, and go!"

Peyton felt his pockets: "General, I have no handkerchief."

"Then tear your shirt, sir, and tie that to a stick."

"General," said the staff officer, "I have on a flannel shirt, and I see you have; I don't believe there is a white shirt in the Army."

"Get something, sir; get something and go!" [28]

Colonel Peyton said no more. He rode off. To the left, in front, and on the right, the battle roared. Sixteen hundred men were slowly being exterminated though they and their artillery still were offering a volume of fire that made the enemy proceed with caution. John Gordon listened and observed, gave the best orders he could to aid the fight, and awaited the result of his flag of truce. When Peyton returned he had with him a Union officer whose long, tawny hair fell almost to his shoulders. Gordon noted the length of the hair and the slenderness and grace of the rider, who was handling a poor horse superbly. Another Confederate observed a little later that the Union officer was "dressed in a blue sack with the largest shoulder straps of a Major General I ever

25 *Longstreet*, 626–27; *J. C. Haskell's MS Rems.*, 122–23. These two narratives, though apparently in minor conflict, can be reconciled by assuming that Haskell brought back both messages.

26 Longstreet (*op. cit.*, 627) said with substantial accuracy that the officer was "Captain Sims, of the Third Corps staff, serving at my headquarters since the fall of A. P. Hill." In *J. C. Haskell's MS Rems.*, 123, he was mentioned as "Major Gibbes." Alexander (*op. cit.*, 607) spoke of him as "Major Sims." He doubtless was Capt. R. M. Simms, A. A. A. G., (15 *S.H.S.P.*, 69).

27 *Gordon*, 438.          28 *Gordon*, 438–39.

saw . . . with a gorgeous red scarf and in it a gold pin near two inches in length and breadth and in big letters 'George A. Custer, Major General.' " [29]

The officer galloped up to Gordon, saluted with his sabre and announced: "I am General Custer and bear a message to you from General Sheridan. The General desires me to present you his compliments, and to demand the immediate and unconditional surrender of all the troops under your command."

Gordon's reply was polite but instant: "You will please, General, return my compliments to General Sheridan and say to him that I shall not surrender my command."

"He directs me to say, General, if there is any hesitation about your surrender, that he has you surrounded and can annihilate your command in an hour."

Gordon was not to be shaken by threats. He was, he answered, probably as well aware of his situation as General Sheridan was. Nothing, said Gordon, did he have to add to the simple message that General Lee had asked a truce. If General Sheridan continued the fighting in the face of the flag of truce, the responsibility for the resultant bloodshed would be Sheridan's, not Gordon's.

Custer was puzzled. Presently he asked to be conducted to General Longstreet. The request was unusual but so was the situation. Gordon assented and sent Custer off under the escort of Maj. Robert Hunter. With these two, probably, rode Longstreet's staff officer.[30] Almost immediately another flag of truce was advanced toward Gordon's line. Under it on a tremendous horse, was a small man instantly identified as Maj. Gen. Phil Sheridan. He was approximately of Gordon's age, 33, and almost as thin. On him was the flush of victory. In manner and in spirit he was a conqueror. His "mounted escort," said Gordon afterward, was "almost as large as one of Fitz Lee's regiments." [31] So shining a target did Sheridan present that Gordon had twice to restrain one of his sharpshooters, a feebleminded fellow, from firing on the Union commander. "Let him stay on his own side," the sharpshooter insisted when Gordon caught the gun aimed at Sheridan.

[29] *J. C. Haskell's MS Rems.*, 122.
[30] *Gordon*, 438–39. To assume that Longstreet's officer returned with Custer and Hunter is the only way of reconciling Gordon's statement with Longstreet's (*op. cit.*, 627).
[31] *Ibid.*, 628.

Gordon rode out to meet his adversary. Sheridan was as anxious as Custer had been to receive the surrender of the Army, but he was met with the same assurances. Shown the message from Lee to Gordon, the Federal suggested that firing cease on both sides and that the two forces withdraw to agreed positions while they waited for a report of the outcome of the conference. Orders were dispatched immediately. Firing quickly ceased. The two Generals dismounted.

"We have met before, I believe," Sheridan began brusquely, "at Winchester and at Cedar Creek in the Valley."

"I was there."

"I had the pleasure," Sheridan pursued, "of receiving some artillery from your government, consigned to me through your commander, General Early."

Gordon read in Sheridan's tone a certain exultation, and he could not refrain from answering: "That is true, and I have this morning received from your government artillery consigned to me through General Sheridan."

The Union commander had not heard of that loss; he questioned and he doubted, but he was diverted from argument by a burst of musketry on the Confederate left. Sheridan sprang up. "What does that mean, sir?" he demanded fiercely.

"It's my fault, General," Gordon answered. "I had forgotten that Brigade. But let me stop the firing first and then I will explain."

Gordon looked, as he spoke, for a staff officer but found none. Seeing the Confederate's plight, Sheridan offered the service of one of his officers. Gordon accepted and sent the order by a Federal Captain, the last order for a unit of the Second Corps to cease fire. With the Captain, to accredit and to protect him, rode a muddy, ragged Confederate private. Most appropriately this man had belonged to the Stonewall Brigade.[32]

By the time Gordon and Sheridan suspended hostilities, Custer and his Confederate escort had reached the place on the roadside where Longstreet was awaiting Lee's return from the rear.[33] The

[32] *Gordon,* 441.
[33] There are four accounts of this exchange—Longstreet's, Alexander's, J. C. Haskell's and Adjutant W. M. Owen's. The last of these is the earliest in date and may have contemporary notes as its basis, but it does not quite satisfy one as the account of an eye witness. Alexander stated (*op. cit.,* 607–08) that Longstreet's rebuff of Custer was far more severe than was indicated in Longstreet's book, and Alexander referred to his own article

Federal—he was only 25—walked up to Longstreet[34] and called out in a voice audible to all in attendance on the General: "I have come to demand your instant surrender. We are in position to crush you, and unless you surrender at once, we will destroy you."

Longstreet blazed: "By what authority do you come in our lines? General Lee is in communication with General Grant. We certainly will not recognize any subordinate."

"Oh," answered Custer, "Sheridan and I are independent of Grant today, and we will destroy you if you don't surrender at once."

This was the spark to explode the wrath of Longstreet: "I suppose you know no better and have violated the decencies of military procedure because you know no better, but it will not save you if you do so again. Now, go and act as you and Sheridan choose and I will teach you a lesson you won't forget! Now go!" —and he raised both hand and voice.

Custer said no more, but when he got beyond the range of Longstreet's voice, he asked for a guard to take him back to his own lines. His mount, as it happened, was badly blown as well as of poor stock. He looked at his animal and then with surprise at some of those brought from home by Southern officers and tended with utmost care even on the retreat. One of Col. John Haskell's horses, in particular, caught the eye of the young Federal. He would like to have that mount, he said. Haskell replied promptly that the horse was not for sale or plunder. Already the South Carolinian, scrutinizing Custer, had observed a familiar pair of handsome spurs on the Union officer's boots. Was Frank Huger alive? Haskell asked, and explained that he identified the artillerist's spurs. Custer flushed visibly and explained that he was wearing them to take care of them for Huger whom he had known at West Point.[35]

---

in the *Century Magazine*, April, 1903—the correct year was 1902—for full details. They do not differ materially from those in Alexander's later narrative. The present text is, consequently, something of a composite of Alexander and Haskell, both of whom were young men, apt to remember the details of so sensational an affair.

[34] "Swaggered" is Haskell's verb (*op. cit.*, 123).

[35] Huger (*Cullum* No. 1877) was graduated thirty-first in the class of 1860; Custer (*Cullum* No. 1966) was thirty-fourth in the class of 1861. Haskell (*op. cit.*, 125) noted that the spurs were very handsome, Mexican and gold mounted. They had been General Santa Anna's and had been given to Gen. Benjamin Huger, father of Col. Frank Huger. "Years after," Haskell wrote, "Colonel Huger told me that he had never been able to get [the spurs] from Custer, who insisted on continuing to take care of them until his death" (*Ibid.*, 125)

Little more was said. Custer, with his guard, left Longstreet and returned to his own lines, where the truce arranged by Gordon and Sheridan continued. The Second Corps had withdrawn behind the north fork of the Appomattox. Before the truce had been arranged, Gordon had given the agreed signal to Fitz Lee. That officer, Rosser, and Munford and the greater part of their cavalry had ridden off to escape surrender and to renew the campaign, as they hoped, with Johnston.[36]

After Custer's departure, Longstreet must have inspected the flanks of his line. When he went forward again, after a time, he learned that Lee had passed through the line of battle Alexander had drawn by his order as a support line for the Second Corps. Longstreet rode on and soon came upon the commanding General on the edge of a little orchard. Lee was under an apple tree and was stretched out on a pile of fence rails that Porter Alexander had placed there and had covered with blankets.[37] Nearby were members of the headquarters staff and their horses. Around the group was thrown a detachment of the First Engineers.[38]

Lee explained anxiously that he had gone to the rear to meet Grant and, instead of finding him there, had received at the hands of a staff officer a letter in which—precisely as at the time of the correspondence through General Ord—the head of the Federal Armies had said that he had no authority to treat for peace. The proposed meeting, Grant's letter stated, could do no good. Grant had ended with an expression of hope that no more blood would be shed. Lee then had been compelled to ask for a meeting in accordance with Grant's previous offer of terms of surrender. As Grant was not within some miles of the place where Lee was waiting, a question had arisen whether anyone had authority, pending the receipt of new instructions from the Union commander, to halt an attack that previously had been ordered. To prevent this attack, a truce had been requested by Lee and, after some delay, had been granted by General Meade, who had reached that part of the line. At Meade's suggestion, Lee had written another letter to Grant and had dispatched it from the line near Appomattox Court House. Lee now was waiting for an answer. Not many minutes before Longstreet's arrival, a Federal staff offi-

36 Fitz Lee in *O. R.*, 46, pt. 1, p. 1303.
37 *Alexander*, 609.
38 32 *S.H.S.P.*, 72.

cer had been escorted to the apple tree under flag of truce and had been assumed to be Grant's representative, but he had proved to be from Sheridan. That officer had some doubt of his authority to declare a truce and asked permission to send his chief of staff through the Confederate lines, by the shortest route, to consult General Meade.[39]

All this was explained briefly to Longstreet. It ended with an admission by Lee that he was afraid Grant's refusal to meet him was due to a knowledge that the plight of the Confederate Army was worse and that more severe terms could be imposed. Lee did not say so, but his dread was that his men would be marched off to Federal prisons. Longstreet answered that he knew the Federal General-in-chief well enough to feel sure Grant would give such terms as, in reversed circumstances, the Federal commander would demand.

In his effort to reassure his chief, Longstreet saw that he was not succeeding and he did not press his point. Lee was disposed to silence. They sat together, with few words passing, till noon and a quarter after. Then arrived under flag of truce another Union officer with a Confederate escort. Longstreet looked at the Federal, guessed his mission and turned again to Lee. "General," he said, "unless he offers us honorable terms, come back and let us fight it out!" [40] As Longstreet watched Lee prepare to leave for the interview with Grant, it seemed to "Old Pete" that the prospect of a fight had braced Lee.[41]

By the time Lee rode forward with the Federal officer,[42] the duration of the truce and the reported passage of so many white flags had spread doubt and wild rumor through the ranks. As Bryan Grimes had carried back his troops to their position behind the Appomattox, he had inquired where he should form line of battle. "Anywhere you please," Gordon answered. That seemed so strange to the young Carolinian that he asked what Gordon meant. Sadly the Georgian answered that the Army would be surrendered. The hot-tempered division commander almost leaped at Gordon's throat: Why was he not given notice, so that he could take his troops with him and march to join "Joe" Johnston? He would tell

[39] The details and the text of the various notes will be found in 4 R. E. Lee, 124–31.
[40] Alexander, 609.     [41] Longstreet, 628.
[42] He was Col. Orville E. Babcock, aide-de-camp to General Grant.

his men, Grimes wrathfully said, so that those who wished to escape with him could do so. He galloped off to spread the news, but was overtaken by Gordon and was told he must not disgrace himself by violating a flag of truce. For a few seconds Grimes hesitated, and then decided he would say nothing to his Division about the prospect of surrender.[45]

Some of Alexander's gunners had heard the rumor, also, and had become clamorous: "We don't want to surrender any ammunition! We've been saving ammunition all this war! Hope we were not saving it for a surrender!" [44] Their officers made no reply, though several knew already what the truce forecast. When the Washington Artillery had reached the line Alexander had drawn, Adjutant W. Miller Owen had asked for instructions. "Turn into the field on the right," said Alexander, "and park your guns." He paused and in a low tone he added: "We are going to surrender today!" Adjutant Owen recorded: "We had been thinking it might come to that, sooner or later; but when the shock came it was terrible. And was this to be the end of all our marching and fighting for the past four years? I could not keep back the tears that came to my eyes." [45]

It had been 12:30, approximately, when Lee left the apple tree and rode forward under flag of truce. Three long hours passed, and more. Then there was a mutter along the road that led to the Confederate lines from Appomattox Court House. The men at a distance heard the beginning of a cheer, but it was stifled. A commotion on the road was discernible. Those inquisitive soldiers who still had strength enough for the exertion ran to the highway. They saw a sight that startled some and made others blanch, and halted still others as if by a sudden, shouted command. General Lee was riding along the road. Behind him were a Lieutenant Colonel and a Sergeant. Lee was flawlessly dressed. Traveller was perfectly caparisoned. On any other day, even a glimpse of him on a battlefield in that martial garb would have sent the rebel yell running through the ranks as it had at the Chancellor House that May noon in 1863. Now . . . it was different. Dignity and loftiness remained on his countenance but anguish was deeply cut in the angles of his mouth. He, supreme master of his emotions, was battling with tears. Late-comers caught the end of a disjointed

[43] Grimes, 118-19.          [44] Alexander, 604.          [45] Owen, 382.

answer to pleading inquiries from the men—"will all be paroled
and go to your homes till exchanged."

Each soldier seemed to have the same question in his throat:
"General, are we surrendered, are we surrendered?" His face
gave the answer but they followed him and thronged him and
tried to touch him. This man at his side wept unabashed;
starving soldiers seemed to feel more acutely his distress than their
own; sensitive boys choked as they sought to comfort him; the
defiant shouted that if he said the word they would "go after 'em
again."

They pressed about him till he reached the apple tree; they
ringed the little orchard as closely as the guarding engineers permitted. Later, when he and his staff rode from the apple tree to
his headquarters about a mile in rear, many of the men still clung
to the little cavalcade. At his tent in the woods, all who could do so
grasped his hand and made their soldierly avowals and then
slowly went away to rage, to ponder, to weep or to lie feebly down
and to pray for food and rest. "Blow, Gabriel, blow," shouted one
agonized North Carolinian, as he threw his musket from him.
"My God, let him blow, I am ready to die!" [46] Another cried: "Is it
true, is it true that General Lee has surrendered?" When his officer
had to admit it, he broke out: "My God, that I should have lived
to see this! Caldwell, I did not think I should live till this day. I
hoped I should die before this day!" [47] On the Charlottesville road,
when a cavalryman heard the news, he lifted his clenched fist
above his head: "If General Lee has had to surrender his Army,
there is not a just God in Heaven!" [48]

These were the extremes. Most of the surrendered troops were
bewildered. "A feeling of collapse, mental and physical, succeeded
for some hours. Very little was said by men or officers. They sat,
or lay on the ground in reflective mood, overcome by a flood of
sad recollections. Few were to be seen away from their camps, and
no life was there; in fact . . . there were more Union troops to
be seen on the road and in the fields within our line than Confederates." [49] When the dazed men recovered sufficiently to talk,

---

[46] *Grimes*, 119. References to the incidents of Lee's ride from the McLean House will
be found in 4 *R. E. Lee*, 144 ff.
[47] *Caldwell*, 237.
[48] L. W. Hopkins, *From Bull Run to Appomattox*, 194.
[49] Walter A. Montgomery in 5 *N. C. Regts.*, 262.

there was questioning, wonder, complaint, regret and lament, but almost all the soldiers tried "to console themselves with the thought that they had discharged their duty, and therefore that they bore no share of the national disgrace." [50]

During the late afternoon, commissary wagons entered the Confederate camps from the Union lines. Nothing except bread was issued to some commands that evening [51] and to some, meat only,[52] but whatever the food, it was devoured ravenously and gratefully. While this relief from the worst pangs of hunger eased somewhat the emotions of the men, the pain of defeat and the humiliation of surrender scarcely were lessened. Bitter feelings deepened in the shadows of the spring afternoon. At length, as one officer phrased it, "the sun went down, and with it all the hopes of a people who, with prayers, and tears and blood, had striven to uphold that falling flag." [53]

The next day brought rain, more food,[54] and the refreshment that came from the first long, untroubled night of sleep that some of the troops had been allowed since April 3. For the men, there was nothing to do except to hope for more rations, to plan the journey home and to wait for the issuance of paroles, which they were told they would receive and must retain. Officers had much work in preparing and in checking rolls. Marching and fighting had been so nearly ceaseless for a week that nobody knew who was present, who had straggled, or who had lost his rifle.[55] The corrected rolls had now to be made in duplicate, one copy for the victors, the other for the Confederates.[56] All the officers of corps and divisional rank and all the chiefs of general staff bureaux were directed promptly to prepare reports of the operations from Petersburg to the surrender.[57] In addition, every officer who was worthy of his insignia had to counsel perplexed men and, in some instances, to inquire of higher authority how the soldiers' difficulties might be relieved.

To three of Lee's lieutenants was assigned the task of arranging with a like number of Federals the details of the surrender. For this purpose, Lee designated Longstreet, Gordon and Pendleton.

[50] Caldwell, 237.
[52] Caldwell, 242.
[54] Montgomery, loc. cit.
[56] O. R., 46, pt. 1, pp. 57–58.
[57] Mrs. G. E. Pickett, Pickett and His Men, 393.

[51] Montgomery, loc. cit.
[53] E. M. Boykin, The Falling Flag, 61.
[55] Cf. O. R., 46, pt. 3, p. 706.

The Federal commissioners were Maj. Gen. John Gibbon, commanding the XXIV Corps, Bvt. Maj. Gen. Charles Griffin, who had succeeded Warren at the head of the V Corps, and Bvt. Maj. Gen. Wesley Merritt, second to Sheridan in the cavalry.

For the use of these commissioners, a room was assigned at Appomattox Court House in the McLean home, where the surrender had been completed. On the 10th, as Longstreet was going to this room, he had to pass one which Grant was using as headquarters. At the sound of Longstreet's boots, Grant looked up, recognized an old friend and spoke cordially. To both of them, in their personal relations, the war was over.[58]

In much the same spirit, the commissioners arranged readily for the formal surrender of arms, for the transfer of public property and horses and for the departure of the Confederates under their own commanders. Necessary transportation was to be assigned officers for their baggage. When the journey had been completed, these vehicles were to be turned over to the nearest United States quartermasters.

There was initial uncertainty concerning the men to be embraced in the surrender of the Army. Gordon, in something of a speech, said the Federals had been so generous that he felt he must give the most liberal interpretation to the question. Longstreet then suggested that the surrender cover all troops within twenty miles of Appomattox. This was adopted immediately and unanimously as a reasonable basis.[59] In the end, the surrender was made applicable to all forces operating with the Army when negotiations began on the 8th. The only exceptions were artillery units more than twenty miles from Appomattox on the 9th and those cavalrymen who "actually made their escape previous to the surrender."

Another clause provided that "couriers and mounted men of the artillery and cavalry, whose horses are their own private property, will be allowed to retain them." [60] At the meeting in the McLean House, after Grant had drafted the terms of surrender, Lee had pointed out that many of the horses in the Army belonged to individuals. The Federal commander did not know that this practice was followed in the Confederate forces and he had not felt that he should modify the formal terms; but he had said that

[58] *Longstreet*, 630.          [59] Gibbon in *Century Magazine*, April 1902, p. 941.
[60] *O. R.*, 46, pt. 3, pp. 685–86.

where any of Lee's men claimed animals, he would instruct his officers to let the men "take the animals home to work their little farms." [61] With Grant's approval this unofficial promise was incorporated in the convention.[62] The Federal commander went beyond that. By a separate order of April 10, he directed that all officers and men included in the surrender who had to go through Federal lines to reach their homes would "be allowed to do so, and to pass free on all government transports and military railroads." [63]

Announcement of these terms was the first step in the effective reconstruction of the Union. Said Cannoneer Ned Moore, so often quoted in these pages: "We had felt it as not improbable that, after an ordeal of mortifying exposure for the gratification of the military, we would be paraded through Northern cities for the benefit of jeering crowds. So, when we learned that we should be paroled, and go to our homes unmolested, the relief was unbounded. . . . The favorable and entirely unexpected terms of surrender wonderfully restored our souls. . . ." [64] This testimony a South Carolinian elaborated: "I am forced to admit that the Federal officers and troops conducted themselves with singular propriety throughout this time. We could hear, within their lines, an occasional cheer and the music of bands; but they did not approach us, or even give any indication of malicious triumph from the distance. A few of the general officers came into our lines, at different times, either on official errands or to visit their acquaintances among us; but they came without parade, and departed without uncourteous reference to our misfortune. Affiliation was out of the question; we were content with civility." [65]

How few survivors there were to respect this civility, the new muster-rolls tragically displayed. The four Corps had been directed, first and last, by six Lieutenant Generals. Longstreet alone remained with the troops. Forty-seven men had fought under Lee as Major Generals. Thirteen had started the retreat from Petersburg. Seven were left now in command of troops. Only one of these had a commission that dated back to May, 1863. Lee's Brigadiers had reached a total of 146. When "cease firing" was ordered, twenty-two of these men stood with the infantry. Not more than

61 See the detailed conversation in 4 R. E. Lee, 139.
62 O. R., 46, pt. 3, pp. 685–86.          63 Ibid., 687.
64 E. A. Moore, 290.                      65 Caldwell, 242.

eighty-five Colonels of that arm could be counted now; full organization called for upwards of 200. Organized, armed foot soldiers were reduced to 7892. Cavalrymen had numbered perhaps 2100 prior to the escape. Of all ranks and all branches of the armed service, equipped and weaponless, sick and able to fight, present or captured after the 8th of April, the lists were to show 28,231.[66]

Completion of the rolls that disclosed these facts in the ruin of a great Army occupied the time of many officers on the 10th and the 11th. Paroles for individuals were delayed because they had to be printed in Lynchburg.[67] By agreement the evidence that a Confederate was a paroled prisoner of war was the possession of one of these strips of paper, which bore date of April 10. Each parole was to be signed, not by the Provost Marshals of the victorious Army, but by a man's own commander or his commander's staff officer.[68]

Formal surrender of the artillery was put first, because the horses of the batteries were dying for lack of feed. The sad transfer of guns and animals, and the parole of the cannoneers were under the eyes of the independent Division of Maj. Gen. John W. Turner, XXIV Corps, Army of the James.[69] Remaining cavalrymen of "Rooney" Lee's Division laid down their swords that same day before Ranald MacKenzie's troops, and then rode sadly off.[70] Word was passed through the camps that the next morning the infantry were to go through the same last humiliation, that of surrendering arms, cartridge boxes and flags. The Confederate commissioners had pleaded hard for permission to place the arms, required accoutrements and standards on the ground in the camps; but to this General Grant would not consent, generous though he had been in every other particular. The surrender would be simple: it had to be actual, not symbolic.[71] Maj. Gen. Joseph J. Bartlett's 1st Division of the V Corps had been moved out at noon on the 11th to relieve Turner and to prepare for the reception of the arms.[72] The particular honor of receiving the surrender was awarded by Maj. Gen. Charles Griffin of the V Corps to Brig.

[66] The details epitomized here will be found in Appendix V.
[67] MS Memoirs of W. B. Freeman.          [68] O. R., 46, pt. 3, pp. 709–10.
[69] O. R., 46, pt. 3, p. 706; Joshua L. Chamberlain, The Passing of the Armies (cited hereafter as Chamberlain), 257.
[70] Chamberlain, loc. cit.          [71] Chamberlain, 248.
[72] O. R., 46, pt. 3, p. 706.

Gen. Joshua L. Chamberlain, who had much distinguished himself in the action of March 29. In spite of two wounds received that day, Chamberlain had fought admirably. His, too, had been the advance Brigade of the V Corps in the final attack on Gordon at Appomattox.[73] Grant, Meade and Sheridan had left Appomattox: they did not make the Southerners' defeat a triumph for themselves.

The morning of the 12th, the last day of the Army's life, was chill and gray but without the rain that had fallen almost continuously since the surrender.[74] At sunrise, the Confederates began to stir in their bivouacs. The column soon was formed on the high ground to the North of the little river. General officers mounted; the regimental commanders took their stations; each man had his musket. The Stars and Bars were at their proper place midway of some regiments, but a few flag staffs were without standards. The men had torn the bunting to bits or else had entrusted the banner to some soldier who had folded it and had hidden it under his jacket.[75]

To escort the flags and to time the march, there were no bands. Most of the instruments that had not been stored before the retreat had been lost on the road.[76] Without a beat of drum and in the silence of their black depression, the men started down the hill. Some were neat, in spite of rain and spring mud. Most of the veterans were in tatters and unabashed. Their concern seemed to be only for their mud-caked blankets, their oilcloths and their overcoats. Any other day, the musket would have been their first care.

At the front of the Second Corps, which headed the column, rode John B. Gordon. His was the same, erect soldierly figure, but now his chin was on his breast, his eyes were downcast.[77] Scarcely a career in the whole Army had been more remarkable than his—from inexperienced Captain to Major General and corps commander. If the final order of march had been arranged to honor those who had fought hardest and with highest distinction

73 See General Griffin's recommendation that Chamberlain be promoted, O. R., 46, pt. 3, pp. 730–31.
74 Caldwell, 242; Chamberlain, 258.     75 Gordon, 445–46.
76 The Fourth North Carolina retained its band (22 C. V., 260), as perhaps a few other units did; but none of these musicians is mentioned in accounts of the formal surrender.
77 Chamberlain in 32 S.H.S.P., 362. This account gave some details not in Chamberlain.

during the last year of the war, Gordon rightly would have been put first.[78]

Doubtless by Gordon's choice, first place fittingly was given the Stonewall Brigade which, in its earliest days, "Old Jack" had acclaimed proudly the "First." [79] Its 210 officers and men [80] marched deliberately and without faltering across the little river and up toward the village. Behind the men of Manassas moved the other Brigades of Gordon's Division. Shadows they were, but they represented most of the regiments of Jackson's old Division—Lawton's fine Georgians, "Dick" Taylor's famous fighters of Middletown and Winchester, nearly all the other troops from Louisiana. Once the units represented in that Division would have sufficed to form almost a Corps. Thirty-two regiments they were, the equivalent of eight Brigades. Now each of the regiments occupied so little of the muddy road that they created a dramatic illusion. Their flags appeared to be massed. A bloody bond of brotherhood encompassed them. Federals who saw them coming to the Court House had to look a second time to be sure what it was they beheld: "The regimental battleflags crowded so thick by thinning out of men, that the whole column seemed crowned with red." [81]

Gordon's men were obeying in their last march the endlessly repeated command of "Old Jack," the command heard on the way to Front Royal, and in Thoroughfare Gap, and along the forest road that led through the Wilderness to Hooker's flank—"Close up, men, close up!" As they closed now, they saw ahead of them, in line on the left and on the right of the road, two full Federal Brigades.[82] At the right of the line, the color guard carried the Stars and Stripes and the flag of the 1st Division of the V Corps.[83] Under the colors was a little group of officers. The central figure was General Chamberlain. Without a gesture of triumph or any of the suffusion of pride, he was watching the column as it came nearer. Confederates whose eyes were not on

[78] 32 S.H.S.P., 361.                    [79] Douglas, 16.
[80] The Second Virginia had seventy-two; the Fourth Virginia had forty-five; the Fifth Virginia had fifty-four; the Twenty-seventh Virginia had twenty-one; the Thirty-third Virginia had eighteen. These totals are reached by adding to the regimental paroles in 15 S.H.S.P., 88–93, the miscellaneous officers and men listed in ibid., 84–85.
[81] Chamberlain, 259–60.
[82] Chamberlain, 259. The lines extended from the river to the Court House.
[83] A red Maltese cross on a white field. See the sketches in O. R. Atlas, Plate CLXXV.

the road saw him and perhaps heard him speak a word to a man by his side. A bugle rang out above the shuffle of muddy feet. Instantly, regiment by regiment, as smartly as if on dress parade, the Union troops shifted from order arms to carry arms, the marching salute.[84] Gordon heard the familiar sound of the shift and, half startled, looked up. His figure stiffened; he turned his horse to General Chamberlain; he brought down his sword in salute and, wheeling again to his own column, gave the command to carry arms. Salute answered salute. Said General Chamberlain afterward: "On our part not a sound of trumpet more, nor roll of drum; not a cheer nor word nor whisper of vain-glorying . . . but an awed silence rather, and breath-holding, as if it were the passing of the dead." [85]

The column moved on until the head of it reached the Federal left. There it halted and faced to the South. Officers dressed the line and took their post. Gordon and his few Generals rode to the rear of the troops. At a word from officers, bayonets were fixed. A heavy pause ensued. Then, in low voice, the last command was given to "Jackson's foot cavalry." The men stepped forward four paces across the road and stacked their arms. Off came the cartridge boxes. In a moment these were hanging from the muskets.[86] The color sergeants folded the regimental flags and laid them, too, on the stack.[87] Silence held. "We did not even look into each others' faces." [88] They turned; they came back into the road, they marched ahead past the Court House. It was over.

As fast as the Divisions could—for waiting was torture—they moved up the road and repeated the ceremony. After Gordon came Rodes's old Division of Early's.[89] In the Division of Grimes, formerly of Rodes, the Brigade of Battle had been Rodes's at Seven Pines and at Sharpsburg. Grimes's Brigade had been Junius Daniels's. As every veteran knew, Cox's Brigade, formerly Dodson Ramseur's, included the famous First Carolina, the "Bethel Regi-

---

84 *Ibid.*, 261.          85 *Chamberlain*, 261.
86 *Owen*, 390; 14 *C. V.*, 179.
87 Chamberlain said the flags were laid on the ground, but Montgomery, *loc. cit.*, doubtless was correct in stating that the flags were placed on the stacks. That was "regulation."
88 5 *N. C. Regs.*, 264.
89 Chamberlain is authority for saying the Second Corps led and Anderson's followed. The Third came next and the First brought up the rear. Beyond this, nothing is known of the order of march. Mention here of smaller units must not be regarded as fixing their specific place in the column.

ment" that had shared the opening battle of the war in Virginia.[90] It counted now seventy-one present.[91] Twelve of its officers and men had fought at Big Bethel.[92] Remembrance of the dead had been apt to make men break down in the silence of the surrender, but the tension of the Carolinians was eased by an irrepressible member of the Fourth North Carolina. Audibly, as he placed his musket in the stack he spoke his farewell: "Sit there, Betsy: you've made many of them bite the dust!" [93] Behind the men who heard this, marched Phil Cooke's Brigade which had as its most renowned unit the Twelfth Georgia that had won its place in the Army's admiration by its conduct at Front Royal and at Cedar Mountain.[94] The Twelfth now numbered sixty men.[95] Some of them may have stood by Capt. W. F. Brown when he looked across Cedar Run and said to Jubal Early, "General, my ammunition is nearly out; don't you think we had better charge them?" [96] Brown was dead. So were the most distinguished commanders of every one of the Brigades of the Division.

Early's Division included the men who had been Garland's. With them marched Lewis's Brigade which in turn had been Trimble's and Hoke's and Godwin's. The Brigade of James A. Walker had a few of "Dick" Ewell's men of 1861. Pegram's Brigade originally had been Elzey's and then Early's. A hundred names, a thousand memories the passing of the Second Corps recalled! Gordon was mindful of them all and, after the last of his men had passed beyond the Federal line, he addressed them with overflowing eloquence and reminded them of their achievements, of their honor, of the richness of the Southern soil, and of their responsibility for the future of their land.[97]

While Gordon was speaking and many of his soldiers were weeping, Anderson's men were repeating the sad ceremony of surrender. Most of these were units that had not come to Virginia till the spring of 1864; but they included Wise's Brigade, a part of which had been with Rodes in his famous battle of May 30, 1862. Bushrod Johnson's Division, moreover, had borne much of the

---

[90] See Vol. I, p. 17.
[91] 15 S.H.S.P., 252–53, 260–61.
[92] 1 N. C. Regts., 122.
[93] 1 N. C. Regts., 276.
[94] See Vol. I, p. 416 and Vol. II, pp. 37–38.
[95] 15 S.H.S.P., 251–52.
[96] See Vol. II, p. 38 and J. A. Early, *Jackson's Campaign against Pope in August 1862,* p. 15.
[97] *Gordon,* 449.

sternest, bitterest day-by-day fighting in the hideous, red trenches of Petersburg.

Behind Johnson's Division moved to the village street the remnants of the Third Corps, which was under the immediate command of that gallant, ill-fortuned, generous gentleman Harry Heth. He wore a new uniform of gray [98] and looked every inch the soldier. The men he now surrendered to Chamberlain included all the Tennesseans who in many battles far from home always had acquitted themselves with honor, though seldom recruited and beset often by the unhappy knowledge that their families were within the Union lines. Gettysburg veterans Heth surrendered, also, and, in John R. Cooke's gaunt Brigade, the 118 survivors of the illustrious Twenty-seventh North Carolina which, with the great old Third Arkansas, had stopped the Federal attack on the centre at Sharpsburg.[99]

Wilcox's Division was as close to Heth's in the last hour as it had been in the Wilderness that May night of 1864 when, it now was plain, the Army was at the beginning of the end. The division commander, hero of Banks's Ford and Salem Church, wore a long, thick overcoat under which, if a friend of the "old Army" had not given him relief, he would have had only a shirt and his underclothes.[100] Cadmus's own famous Brigade of Alabamians was behind him, in Mahone's Division, but every one of Wilcox's Brigades that now laid down its arms was renowned—Thomas's had fought through nearly the whole of the war; Lane's had been Branch's till Sharpsburg, McGowan's had been Gregg's, and Scales's, Pender's. In short, this fragment of a Division, 2681 men, armed and unarmed, included four of the Brigades of A. P. Hill's famous old "Light" Division. Hill himself and four of the old Brigadiers, Branch, Gregg, Pender and Perrin, had been killed.

Whether Mahone's Division marched with the Third Corps or with the First on that Via Dolorosa, it had at its head, in its last hour, the soldier who shared with Gordon and with Hampton the highest distinction of the final year of war. Frail as Mahone looked, on his horse, while his men stacked their arms, he had

98 Maj. Gen. John Gibbon in *Century Magazine*, April, 1902, p. 939.
99 Fifteen men of the Twenty-seventh North Carolina are listed in 15 *S.H.S.P.*, 274–76, separately from those in *ibid.*, 278–79. In the *Cooke MSS* is an address to Cooke, Apr. 10, 1865, by the field officers of his Brigade. It is a remarkabe tribute to his leadership.
100 Gibbon, *op. cit.*, 939.

met with boldness one of the supreme tests of a great soldier: he had grown with his duties. Scarcely with an exception, each of his battles had been better than the one that preceded it. He could be proud of the troops that laid down their flags. Forney's Brigade had been Cadmus Wilcox's pride; Weisiger's had been led for more than two years by Mahone himself. Nat Harris had raised most notably the standard of Posey's Brigade, which once had been Featherstone's. The wounded Moxley Sorrel's Brigade had been "Rans" Wright's which at Malvern Hill had held on, along with Mahone's men, close to the Crew House. Survivors had not forgotten that Mahone's men had been "Dick" Anderson's that smoky day at Chancellorsville, when the Division had side-slipped to the left and then had swept northward through the Wilderness to the Plank Road. Well the Division had fought under Anderson, but never better than under Mahone. It was capable of giving battle until arms were stacked.

Last, now, the great old First Corps! [101] Of Kershaw's Division, which had been McLaws's, only 805 surrendered that day or later.[102] Their comrades were on the way to prison—the men who had fought at Fredericksburg under Tom Cobb, and Barksdale's Mississippians who had waged the battle of the pontoons, and McLaws's own fine Georgians. Pickett's men numbered 1031, of whom seventeen belonged to the First Virginia,[103] a regiment with a history that ran back to the French and Indian War. Most of the soldiers of Pickett's Division had lost their arms at Five Forks, or on the retreat or at Sayler's Creek. Those who formally laid down their weapons were merely "a little group," [104] perhaps 60,[105] but all the bloody grief of Gettysburg was typified by them— Pickett's exhortation, "Don't forget today that you are from Old Virginia," Armistead in the smoke with his hat on the point of his sabre, Garnett wrapped in his overcoat, Cemetery Ridge red with Southern banners and with Southern blood.

Field's Division was among the last to march between those

---

[101] Chamberlain (op. cit., 263) spoke of Longstreet as present; but if Chamberlain was correct in saying that the surrender occupied the whole of the 12th, it is difficult to see how Longstreet could have been as far on the road to Richmond as he was that evening. See 4 R. E. Lee, 159.

[102] O. R., 46, pt. 1, p. 1277.

[103] 15 S.H.S.P., 86. The total of Pickett's Division included men who surrendered in the rear after April 8. This was the case with all the commands.

[104] Chamberlain, 265.

[105] Pickett's MS Report—Lee MSS.

silent blue lines. Except for "Tige" Anderson, it had none of the Brigades of its earliest days, when part of it had been Whiting's and part David Jones's. The Division's most renowned commander, John B. Hood, had left in the autumn of '63 and had himself suffered in body and in spirit as miserably as had any of his old veterans of Gaines' Mill, of Second Manassas, of Sharpsburg or of the Wilderness. Evander Law had been transferred. Robert Toombs had resigned. John Gregg was dead. In the ranks still were some of "Rock" Benning's men who had stood opposite Burnside's Bridge on Antietam Creek that September afternoon in 1862 till A. P. Hill had arrived with the "Light" Division. Of the Texas Brigade itself, perhaps the most renowned of all, 476 officers and men marched up the road,[106] and stacked the rifles that had been heard in all the Army's great battles except Chancellorsville. For absence from that action, they had made atonement at Chickamauga and in Tennessee. Their name, their deeds, with which the old Third Arkansas was associated, already had become a part of the tradition of their State. Defeat, at the end of their military career, could not dim their record. "I rely upon [the Texans] in all tight places," Lee had said.[107]

The rearguard had surrendered the last cartridge, the last remnant of a bullet-torn flag. On the morrow, April 13, Chamberlain's men would go through the abandoned camps and would pick up 400 or 500 stands of arms that had been thrown away by soldiers who would not march out and surrender.[108] For the waning day, there was such converse, friendly or bitter, as might be exchanged by lingering "paroled prisoners of war." A few ranted and threatened; a few others were openly appreciative of the consideration shown them. "General," said a leader to Chamberlain, "this is deeply humiliating; but I console myself with the thought that the whole country will rejoice at this day's business."[109] One officer of high rank assured the Federal commander: "I went into that cause, and I meant it. We had our choice of weapons and of ground and we have lost. Now that is my flag and I will prove myself as worthy of it as any of you."[110] All such pledges were the exception. Most of the Confederates were humiliated by their

---

106 See the paroles in 15 *S.H.S.P.*, 160 ff.
107 2 *R. E. Lee*, 418.
108 *O. R.*, 46, pt. 3, p. 731. Cf. *ibid.*, 734.
109 *Chamberlain*. 266.    110 *Ibid.*

final defeat and still were half dazed from their long, hungry retreat. Such thought as they were able to fashion, when they started away, was of burned homes and fenceless farms, of a planting season without teams, or of a hungry urban family and no wages with which to feed wife and children.[111] With bitter thought, honest exhortation was joined: "Go home, boys," said Bryan Grimes to Rodes's veterans, "and act like men, as you always have done during the war."[112] Most precious of all were the words of Lee in his farewell order: "I need not tell the brave survivors of so many hard fought battles, who have remained steadfast to the last, that I have consented to this result from no distrust of them; but feeling that valor and devotion could accomplish nothing that could compensate for the loss that must have attended the continuance of the contest, I determined to avoid the useless sacrifice of those whose past services have endeared them to their countrymen. . . . You will take with you the satisfaction that proceeds from the consciousness of duty faithfully performed; and I earnestly pray that a Merciful God will extend to you His blessing and protection. With an unceasing admiration of your constancy and devotion to your Country, and a grateful remembrance of your kind and generous consideration for myself, I bid you all an affectionate farewell."[113] For that first day after the surrender, and for many another day, long and weary roads were theirs, and strange and sometimes winding; but the words of their leader they kept fresh in their hearts: "Consciousness of duty faithfully performed"—that was the consolation which became their reward, their pride, their bequest.

[111] For an outline of the careers of some of Lee's Lieutenants after 1865, see Appendix V.

[112] 1 N. C. Regts., 279.

[113] This is the text as it appears in Lee's MS Letter Book. In Marshall, 276–77, is one of the early drafts of the order, in the autograph of Marshall, signed by Lee. The only differences in the two texts are those of punctuation. Many later variants have been published. For the preparation of the order, see 4 R. E. Lee, 149–50, 154–55.

**THE END**

# APPENDICES

# APPENDIX I

## Reconnaissance on the Confederate Right, July 2, 1863.

by

Frederick Tilberg, Park Historian, and
J. Walter Coleman, Superintendent
Gettysburg National Military Park

Confederate reconnaissance toward the Union left on the second day at Gettysburg was seriously hindered by the ridge along which the Emmitsburg road runs. If Confederate officers had attempted to use the ridge in the general vicinity of the Codori buildings, they would have offered a conspicuous target for pickets and cannoneers as they would have been perilously close to the Union line. In the absence of comment by either army on such an attempt, we feel that the evidence is heavily against it. A scout, viewing the scene from a tree either in McMillan or Spangler Woods, could have observed troops no farther south than Sickles' right flank which rested in the low ground northwest of the G. Weikert house. Col. McAllister of the 11th New Jersey, Sickles' Corps, mentions fog that morning,[1] a condition that would have prevailed in the low ground in Sickles' area if anywhere. This was a possible deterrent to effective observation, particularly in the early morning, but does not preclude a reconnaissance.

A better view could have been obtained from the Emmitsburg road farther south, in the area from the Klingel (J. Smith) house to the Peach Orchard. This would have been restricted somewhat by the Trostle thicket north of the Trostle farm buildings, then lower and thinner than at present,[2] and by the woods south and east of the Trostle house. However, the presence of Sickles' Corps would have been disclosed to a trained observer if he could have reached the Emmitsburg road in that vicinity.

Buford's Cavalry, according to that officer's report,[3] had pickets extending from the Plum Run Valley to Fairfield on the night of July 1–2 and, beyond all reasonable doubt, they were on the road which runs

[1] O. R., 27, pt. 1, p. 552.
[2] O. R., 27, pt. 2, p. 618. See also survey map of the battlefield of Gettysburg, made under the direction of Maj. Gen. G. K. Warren, 1868–69.
[3] O. R., 27, pt. 1, pp. 927–28. See also Bachelder's troop position map, morning of July 2, for Buford's place of bivouac.

from Taneytown road, past Little Round Top and the Peach Orchard, to Fairfield. Pendleton mentions having encountered two Federal Cavalrymen on the ravine road (Willoughby Run) in the Confederate right rear in the early morning of July 2. Berdan's Sharpshooters also covered the Peach Orchard height, at least after 7:30 A.M. when they moved well beyond.[4] Reports of the 3rd Maine Regiment supporting Berdan indicate an advance "at early morn."[5] When Wilcox moved southward to the Spangler Woods vicinity before noon on the 2nd, he found pickets west of the Emmitsburg road,[6] and we believe that they would have been posted at least as far west as that road by daybreak.

Confederate reports consistently mention an enemy "in plain view" on somewhat higher ground than that of their own position,[7] an indication that they were writing of Cemetery Ridge north of the Copse of Trees. There is no mention of a left flank partially concealed or on low ground.

For these reasons we believe that Federal skirmishers had prevented a Confederate reconnaissance on the morning of July 2 from the only effective vantage point, namely, the Emmitsburg road.

[4] O. R., 27, pt. 1, p. 515.
[6] O. R., 27, pt. 2, p. 617.
[5] O. R., 27, pt. 1, p. 507.
[7] O. R., 27, pt. 2, pp. 614, 631, 650.

# APPENDIX II

THIS appendix has been prepared with the most substantial assistance from Runyon Colie of Newark, N. J., Harry W. Howerter, Jr., of Jersey City, N. J., and Dr. J. Walter Coleman, Superintendent, and Dr. Frederick Tilberg, of the Gettysburg National Military Park; but these gentlemen must not be held responsible for the conclusions. All parenthetical references are to pages in *O. R., 27,* pt. 1.

The end of the action of July 1 found on Cemetery Hill and to the South of it the I and XI Corps. Although badly battered, these two Corps still had fight in them. Reports of those units of the II Corps that took over part of the position of the I Corps on the 2nd of July show that the left of Robinson's 2nd Division of the I Corps, with its flanking artillery, extended almost to the "little grove of trees" (456, 478–79).

Maj. Gen. Winfield S. Hancock reached Gettysburg about 3 P.M. on the 1st, assumed command, and exercised it until "between 5 and 6 o'clock" (368), when he had completed essential first measures of security and felt that he could transfer command to his senior, Maj. Gen. Henry W. Slocum, who had arrived shortly after he had.

Before Hancock started back to report to Meade at Taneytown, Federal reinforcements began to arrive at Gettysburg. Brig. Gen. Alpheus S. Williams's 1st Division of the XII Corps, coming up from Two Taverns, was placed on the Federal right (368, 758), which is not involved in this discussion.

Following Williams's Division arrived Brig. Gen. John W. Geary's 2nd Division of the XII Corps, which Hancock placed on the "high ground to the right of and near Round Top Mountain" (368). Geary employed two Brigades only, the third having been detached (825), and he had on the whole of his front about 3200 men (833). Because of the various commanders' confusion of Little Round Top with Round Top proper, it is difficult to say whether Geary placed troops on both these eminences or the lower of them only. A reference by Brig. Gen. George S. Greene (855) shows that men were placed on Little Round Top, but Col. Charles S. Candy's reference to the occupation of "a high range of hills" (836) may be construed to apply to both the Round Tops. In any event, the 5th Ohio and the 147th Pennsylvania (*ibid.*)—about 600 muskets—occupied one or both the heights on the night of July 1-2. This is of importance only for the bearing it might have on the dramatic fact that Capt. S. R. Johnston found no troops on Round Top when he made his reconnaissance on the morning of July 2.

About 5:30 P.M. on the 1st (366, 482), shortly after Hancock relinquished command, Maj. Gen. David B. Birney's 1st Division of the III Corps approached Gettysburg from Emmitsburg (482). As it was that day, the Division consisted of two Brigades only (159-60). The Third, that of Col. P. R. deTrobriand, had been left, with a battery, at Emmitsburg (482). Birney went into bivouac on the right of Geary and probably on the low ground North of Little Round Top near the farm buildings of G. Weikert.

Humphreys's Division of the III Corps, less Burling's Brigade and a battery, reached the vicinity of Gettysburg during the night and at 1 A.M. on the 2nd (531) bivouacked "about 1 mile from Gettysburg and eastward of the Emmitsburg Road" (ibid.). There is every reason to assume, though there is no definite proof, that Humphreys was immediately on the right of Birney. How far Humphreys's own right extended to the North during the night it is impossible to say and, for present purposes, is not of prime importance.

Hancock's II Corps marched from Taneytown on the 1st of July and at an unspecified hour bivouacked, probably alongside the road, about three miles from Gettysburg (369), or about two and a half miles from the position taken the next morning (442). By 4 A.M., the first units of this Corps were moving to Cemetery Ridge (464), but at least four hours were required to get the Corps into position. This lapse of time probably was caused by the fact that Geary was moving from the extreme left to the right during the early morning of the 2nd and had to cross, at some point, the road on which Hancock was advancing. Part of Hancock's Corps may have been slow in taking position because, in the second place, it may have undertaken early the relief of the 2nd Division of the I Corps, which was on the left of the XI Corps and was facing to the left (261). Robinson, whose line, as stated, ran from the northern end of Ziegler's Grove almost to the "little clump of trees," spoke of being relieved by the II Corps on the afternoon of the 2nd (290), but one of the subsidiary reports of the Division mentioned relief by the II Corps "early this morning" of July 2 (302). Apparently, then, the transfer of Robinson's line to Hancock was in progress throughout the morning and into the early afternoon (290, 293, 305, 308). Hancock's report (369) reads as if, from the time of his arrival, he established his line on the right of the XI Corps. He said that the II Corps reached the field "about 7 A.M." and "soon" took position (Ibid.).

As indicated already, Geary moved from the extreme left on the morning of the 2nd. The first troops of the Division quit their position about 4 A.M. (868), the last about 6 o'clock (840). Apparently the Round Tops were abandoned about 5 A.M. (839). Birney's Division of Sickles's III Corps at 7 A.M. extended its left and "rested it" on Little Round Top. If Birney's own map is correct (486), he had no troops directly on Little Round Top. His picket line was on the Emmitsburg Road (482).

North of Birney, to repeat, was Humphreys. Next on the right came the three Divisions of the II Corps, which was to take over the front of the I Corps as far up Cemetery Ridge as the northern end of Ziegler's Grove. Hancock thus had a final front of 5400 feet from Ziegler's Grove to the G. Weikert house. Sickles's front was about 3600 feet. The total, then, was 3000 yards.

In advance of the Union left were two Brigades of Brig. Gen. John Buford's 1st Cavalry Division. The reserve Brigade of this Division was absent, en route to Emmitsburg (943). Buford's report and those of his subordinates (928, 939) show that on the night of July 1–2, the Union cavalry pickets were spread from the Plum Run Valley to Fairfield. It is the belief of Drs. Coleman and Tilberg, as stated in Appendix I, that Buford's men, in the early morning of July 2, were "on the road which runs from Taneytown road, past Little Round Top and the Peach Orchard, to Fairfield." According to Buford (928), he was relieved by the III Corps but the hour is uncertain. Col. G. J. Fiebeger (*Campaign of Gettysburg,* 101) was of opinion that Buford did not leave the vicinity of Gettysburg until noon.

Hancock, as of June 30, had 13,056 officers and men present for duty (151). Sickles, as of the same date, had 12,630 (151). The total of the two Corps thus was 25,686. From these figures are to be deducted Col. P. R. deTrobriand's (482) and Col. George C. Burling's (531) absent Brigades. Birney said deTrobriand reached him at 9 A.M. (482) but deTrobriand put the time an hour later (519). Assumed strength of these two Brigades was approximately one-third the total of Birney, who had presumably half of Sickles's aggregate. The deduction, then, is roughly 2000. Sickles's major force, say 10,600, and certainly half of Hancock's, 13,056, or about 6500 men, were available for action, with ample artillery, by 9 A.M. This made a body of troops of slightly more than 17,000. In addition, Robinson has to be counted on the sector here included. He was preparing to move out, but, of course, he could have shared in efforts to repulse an attack. His command was small, probably not in excess of 1200 men (*cf.* 290–91). In round numbers, then, as of 9 A.M., the Federals had between Ziegler's Grove and Little Round Top, both inclusive, approximately 18,200 men, or six per yard of front.

These are minimum figures. It is entirely possible that, in the event of action at 9 A.M., Hancock could have thrown into action the remaining half of his Corps. That would have made the total force in excess of 24,000, or eight men per yard of front. If, in addition, Buford be counted as still in advance of the Federal left, and Burling as arriving at 9, the Union left might have included as many as 27,000 men of all arms, or nine men per yard.

The hour of 9 has been given for this summary because that was the earliest time at which Longstreet could have put Hood and McLaws into action against even that part of Cemetery Ridge immediately opposite the point at which the two Divisions reported. This assumes other artillery support than that of the First Corps, because part of Longstreet's own guns did not arrive until 9 A.M. As of that hour, the conclusion is clear: If Lee had known the extreme weakness of Robinson's Division before the arrival of Hancock's men, an attack at dawn between Ziegler's Grove and the "little clump of trees" might have been successful, in spite of the Federal artillery; but by no process other than actual divination could Lee have known that particular stretch of line was vulnerable. Whatever may be thought of that possibility, the traditional picture of an unoccupied ridge, waiting seizure while Longstreet loitered, is entirely false. Cemetery Ridge on the 2nd of July, all the way from Cemetery Hill to Little Round Top, was adequately defended from the earliest moment, 9 A.M., at which the Confederates could have launched a strong attack.

# APPENDIX III

CAUSE OF DEATH OF MAJ. GEN. J. E. B. STUART

by

i. RIDGEWAY TRIMBLE, M.D., Lt. Col., Chief of Surgical Service,
118th General Hospital, U. S. A.

ON MAY 11, 1864, Maj. Gen. J. E. B. Stuart was struck about 4:30 P.M. in the side, presumably the right side, by a bullet from a cavalry pistol at no more than 10 or 15 yards; and in a few minutes he was lifted from his horse, placed in a seated position on the ground, lifted to another horse, again put on the ground, and then he was stretched out on a litter in an ambulance. It is significant that the velocity of the missile was not sufficient to knock him off his horse. The U. S. Army cavalry pistol at this time had a .44 caliber, a bullet weight of about 180 grains, with a muzzle velocity of about 700 feet per second.[1]

About half-an-hour after Stuart was hit, he was turned on his side by Surgeon Fontaine, who made a superficial examination and said that Stuart was close to "complete prostration." This "prostration" was obviously shock, whose onset was so rapid that it must have been due to hemorrhage. The force of the blow itself was not sufficient to produce the degree of shock obviously present. The effect of the drink of whiskey taken by Stuart is not recorded. If the bullet had penetrated the stomach, the whiskey on leaking through the hole into the general abdominal cavity should have caused an increase of his pain, and probably vomiting.

After these incidents, the General was carried, with much suffering, about seven miles over bad roads and city streets in a horse-drawn ambulance. Here for the first time pain is mentioned. Since no bones were broken the pain must have been due to peritonitis caused by the leakage of contents from a hole or holes in the intestine or the stomach into the peritoneal cavity. Hemorrhage alone would not have caused the severe pain which recurred in increasing spasms during the next day.

Death occurred at 7:38 P.M., May 12, approximately 27 hours after the wound. Peritonitis alone resulting from perforations in the stomach or intestine as mentioned above would in all probability not have

---

[1] For this information, acknowledgment is made most gratefully to Lt. Col. Calvin Goddard, Chief of the Historical Section of the Ordnance Department.

caused death to this young, vigorous man within 27 hours. Hemorrhage must have been present in addition to peritonitis.

The immediate cause of death was described as "mortification of the stomach induced by the flow of blood from the kidneys and intestines into the cavity of the stomach." By mortification of the stomach is meant what we should call peritonitis. It may have been to some extent induced by the irritative effect on the sensitive lining of the peritoneal cavity by blood coming from an injured kidney, or from some torn blood vessels supplying the intestine. The severe spasms of pain almost surely were caused by the escaping fecal contents from some perforation in the intestine.

An unconfirmed statement was to the effect that Stuart was snot through the liver. This may have been where the bullet ultimately lodged, but the liver is almost completely surrounded by the ribs, and it seems probable that the shot entered below the rib margin because there is no history of his coughing up blood. The sole reason for believing the bullet might have lodged in the liver is the fact that the pistol was fired by a man on the ground. This would have given an upward course to the bullet. Almost surely the "complete prostration" noted within one-half hour of the injury was due to shock caused by hemorrhage. The best presumption is that the bullet entered the right flank below the ribs, passed into the peritoneal cavity and probably perforated the intestine in one or more places and severed blood vessels of the mesentery supplying the intestine. A wound in the stomach itself is unlikely since he did not vomit and since the drinking of whiskey did not cause the severe pain which would be caused by the escape of gastric contents through a hole in the stomach into the peritoneal cavity. The bullet then became lodged in the muscles of the back or in the liver or right kidney.

In addition to the shock caused by loss of blood Stuart undoubtedly suffered with peritonitis due to perforation of his intestine as evidenced by his increasing paroxysms of abdominal pain. His rapid progress toward a fatal outcome leads one to suspect that the large bowel with its high content of bacteria was perforated, probably the ascending colon, making the peritonitis more severe than if the small intestine alone were perforated. As noted before, hemorrhage must have played a part as well as peritonitis since he would in all probability not have succumbed to peritonitis alone in a period of 27 hours. He died unquestionably from the combination of hemorrhage and peritonitis.

According to the Register of Sick and Wounded in the present U. S. Army Medical Department's Records of Morbidity and Mortality, such a wound must be described under the classification, "Wound, gunshot, penetrating or perforating, caliber of missile, location of entrance and exit, course of bullet, how, when, and where occurred."

We should, therefore, in present day terminology, describe his injury as "wound, gunshot, penetrating, .44 cal. bullet from U. S. Army cavalry pistol, point of entrance right flank just below costal margin, no point of exit, apparent course of bullet through ascending colon, mesentery of intestine, into liver, incurred when shot while on horseback at range of 15 yards by a dismounted enemy trooper, 11 May, 1864, during a withdrawal by the enemy."

# APPENDIX IV

(This Appendix is epitomized in a paragraph, Chapter XXXVII, p. 743)

EXCEPT for the men whose endurance outshone every strain, command had been eclipsed during the black hours of retreat. From the confused mass of the struggling, staggering, ever-marching Army, only Lee, Longstreet, Gordon, Mahone, Field, Fitz Lee, "Rooney" Lee and those of like vigor stood out. At Appomattox, others emerged again. Their emotions were as varied as those of the men. Nearly all the cavalry officers, except those of a part of W. H. F. Lee's command, had escaped with their regiments before the truce was arranged. Others had planned to slip through the enveloping lines and had hoped to reach Johnston's Army, but they had delayed too long or had desisted, as had Porter Alexander [1] and Bryan Grimes,[2] at the instance of their seniors. Of the three Lieutenant Generals, Longstreet, Ewell and "Dick" Anderson, who had commanded on the Richmond-Petersburg line— only "Old Pete" was with Lee on the 9th of April. Ewell, it will be remembered, had been captured at Sayler's Creek.[3] Anderson had left the Army, by permission, and had eluded the Federals.[4] During Lee's whole experience prior to his appointment as General-in-chief he had counted among his juniors six Lieutenant Generals—Longstreet, Jackson, Ewell, Powell Hill, R. H. Anderson and Early.[5] Of these, two were dead, one was a prisoner of war, two had been relieved of command.

Thirteen Major Generals had begun the retreat. One of them, John B. Gordon, was commanding a Corps. Three of the remaining twelve were cavalrymen—Fitz Lee, W. H. F. Lee and Tom Rosser. On the 10th of April, nine remained with the Army, but two of the nine, Pickett and Bushrod Johnson, did not have charge of troops. Custis Lee and Joseph Kershaw had been captured on the 6th. The six who were at the head of their troops, in divisional command at the last hour, were Charles W. Field, Bryan Grimes, Harry Heth, William Mahone,

---

[1] *Alexander*, 605–06.  
[3] See *supra*, p. 707.  
[2] *Grimes*, 119.  
[4] *Irvine Walker*, 212.  
[5] Excluded are Holmes, D. H. Hill, Hood, Taylor and Hampton, because all these received their promotion after they left the Army of Northern Virginia.

Cadmus Wilcox and W. H. F. Lee. Somewhere in the region of the surrender, presumably determined to reach "Joe" Johnston, were Fitz Lee and Tom Rosser.[6] Of the six who prepared to face the final surrender—not forgetting the acting corps commander Gordon—the senior was Harry Heth. His commission dated only from May, 1863.[7] Besides him, the only Major Generals at Appomattox who had held that rank for as long as a year were Wilcox[8] and Charles W. Field.[9] From Lee's assumption of command, June 1, 1862, to the last day at Appomattox, forty-seven men had served under him at the rank of Major General.[10] Nine of these forty-seven had been promoted,[11] but of these nine, Jackson and Powell Hill had been killed at higher rank. Five others had fallen in action or had died of wounds—Dorsey Pender, "Jeb" Stuart, Robert Rodes, Dodson Ramseur and Chase Whiting.[12] One Major General, David R. Jones, had died of natural causes.[13] As noted, two had been relieved,[14] two had been prompted to escape the final surrender and twenty-one, through the years, had been transferred, captured, invalided or named to civil office. Seven of forty-seven left— the grind of attrition had been hard!

When the Army began the final campaign, March 29, it had forty-one infantry Brigades and a stout Naval Battalion, together with eight cavalry Brigades. The last table of organization[15] showed twenty-five of these infantry and six of the cavalry Brigades under officers of appropriate rank. All the others, eighteen in the aggregate, had participated in the final operations under Colonels or, in one instance, under a Major.[16] After the fighting ended at Appomattox, twenty-two of the

---

6 W. H. F. Lee's name does not appear among those of officers paroled at Appomattax, and that of Fitz Lee does; but the report of the commander of the cavalry Corps (O. R., 46, pt. 1, p. 1304) showed the situation as given in the text. The prime list of officers and men surrendered at Appomattox is in *Paroles of the Army of Northern Virginia . . .*, 15 S.H.S.P. (1887). Although that list is remarkably accurate, considering all the circumstances of publication, the omission of a senior officer's name does not necessarily mean that he was not present at Appomattox. For example, neither General Lee nor any of his personal staff is listed, because they were paroled separately.

7 *Wright*, 33.                              8 Aug. 3, 1863 (*Wright*, 35).
9 Feb. 12, 1864 (*Wright*, 37).
10 Not included, because they were promoted after transfer, or were transferred immediately after promotion, are Richard Taylor, J. G. Walker, Howell Cobb, and Ambrose R. Wright. Excluded, also, is Jeremy F. Gilmer, whose brilliant service scarcely could be said to have involved field duty with Lee.
11 T. H. Holmes, James Longstreet, T. J. Jackson, R. S. Ewell, A. P. Hill, R. H. Anderson, J. B. Hood, J. A. Early and Wade Hampton. In addition, it will be remembered, D. H. Hill had received temporary promotion but had reverted to his rank of Major General.
12 John Pegram had been in divisional command when killed but, as noted on p. 629, he had not been given formal commission at that rank.
13 See Vol. II, p. 269.                      14 Pickett and Bushrod Johnson.
15 O. R., 46, pt. 1, p. 1267 ff.
16 This was Walker's, formerly Pegram's Brigade of Early's Division of the Second Corps. The last commander of this Brigade w.. Maj. Henry Kyd Douglas, who has been quoted scores of times in these pages.

infantry Brigades still had Brigadier Generals in command. In addition, two Brigadiers of cavalry, one of Engineers and three of artillery were listed.

The final roll of honor showed the following infantry officers of that rank present for surrender and parole: George H. Steuart, G. T. ("Tige") Anderson, H. L. Benning, John Bratton, W. F. Perry, James A. Walker,[17] C. A. Evans,[18] W. R. Cox, John R. Cooke, J. R. Davis, William McComb, William McRae, W. H. Forney, N. H. Harris, D. A. Weisiger, James H. Lane, Samuel McGowan, E. L. Thomas, W. H. Wallace, Y. M. Moody, Mat. W. Ransom, and Henry A. Wise.[19] The Brigadier of Engineers was the able W. H. Stevens. Artillerists were W. N. Pendleton, E. Porter Alexander and A. L. Long. The cavalrymen were R. L. T. Beale and W. P. Roberts. Approximately half of these general officers were familiar from long duty, but almost a fifth of them—Forney, Wm. Comb, Moody, Perry and Roberts—had been appointed to take the place of sick or fallen officers within less than two months of the surrender.

Still more of the tragedy of the attrition of command was in the absence of so many of the most distinguished of the Brigadiers. First and last, Lee had commanded in the Army of Northern Virginia approximately 146 men of that rank.[20] Thirty-three of these had been promoted, thirty-one had been transferred to other duty. One had died. Six had resigned. Five had escaped before the surrender. Eight had been captured during the last fortnight. The largest number was the saddest: thirty-five had been killed.[21] Of those who had accepted transfer or had resigned, four had been dissatisfied over their failure to receive promotion. One had left the Army under charges of cowardice in 1863. Incompetence, unmanageable temper or intemperance had accounted for the transfer, retirement or resignation of fifteen. Long imprisonment had been the fate of two. Not less than thirteen—among them some of the best Brigadiers—were physically incapacitated or were on limited duty at the time of the last campaign.

Parole lists showed worse losses in the lower commissioned ranks, relatively, than in the high command. In the entire Army, ninety-four men, more or less, were all who were listed on paroles as Colonels.[22]

---

[17] Commanding Early's Division.          [18] Commanding Gordon's Division.
[19] The arrangement of names is by Corps and Divisions.
[20] These figures exclude those who had received promotion to the rank of Major General before Lee assumed command, June 1, 1862. Excluded, also, are those commanded by Lee in Western Virginia and in the Carolinas but never directly connected with the Army of Northern Virginia.
[21] This list is based on *Wright* and may not be correct to the last digit, though *Wright* proves quite accurate on check, except for postwar dates.
[22] The count is from the index of 15 *S.H.S.P.*, which lists several Lieutenant Colonels as Colonels.

At least four of these were on military courts or in other staff positions. Three or more were artillerists. Not more than eighty-five Colonels of infantry were with troops. Some of these were acting as brigade commanders. As there were slightly more than 200 regiments of infantry [23] in the Army, on the opening of the campaign, scarcely more than 42 per cent of the infantry regiments were under Colonels.[24]

Enlisted strength had been weakened at every stage of the retreat. General Lee reported: "On the morning of the 9th . . . there were 7892 organized infantry with arms, with an average of seventy-five rounds of ammunition per man. The artillery, though reduced to sixty-three pieces, with ninety-three rounds of ammunition, was sufficient . . . I have no accurate report of the cavalry, but believe it did not exceed 2100 effective men." [25] On these figures, the fairest, most manly comment was that of Meade: "We had at least 50,000 around [Lee], so that nothing but madness would have justified further resistance." [26] Meade might have added that the Union troops within easy marching distance were equally numerous. Lee had no support and many stragglers.

Concerning those not in the ranks Gordon testified later: "There were present three times [as] many enrolled Confederates; but two-third of them were so enfeebled by hunger, so wasted by sickness, and so footsore from constant marching that it was difficult for them to keep up with the army." [27] Some of these were past all effort. They followed the column or the wagon train in the hope that they might find food. Others insisted on marching even if they were too feeble to carry weapons. Tradition has it that when Gordon formed his last line of battle, one man took his place in the ranks with both arms so wounded that he could not carry a gun. "What are you doing here?" an officer demanded. "You can't fight." The soldier answered: "I know I can't but I can still yell." [28]

When all the wounded, all the sick, all the exhausted men and all the stragglers were counted, and when Fitz Lee and the greater part of the escaped cavalry had come into the Federal lines and had surrendered, the totals of paroles were as follows:

[23] A total of 197 regiments were listed outside Custis Lee's and Stapleton Crutchfield's command, the exact composition of which is in doubt. Included in the total of 197 are all regiments that were regarded as separate organizations. Where two regiments had been consolidated, they are here counted as one. "Legions" are reckoned as regiments. Battalions are not included.

[24] No effort is made to determine the percentage of the twenty-eight cavalry regiments that had Colonels, because few of these, outside Beale's Brigade, surrendered as units at Appomattox. In that Brigade there were no Colonels at that time. See 15 S.H.S.P., 10 ff.

[25] O. R., 46, pt. 1, pp. 1266–67.

[26] 2 Meade, 270.                    [27] Gordon, 443.

[28] This was a favorite story of John P. McGuire, of blessed memory, long-time principal of McGuire's School, Richmond.

| Organization | Officers | Enlisted Men | Aggregate |
|---|---|---|---|
| General Headquarters ...... | 69 | 212 | 281 |
| Infantry ................... | 2235 | 20,114 | 22,349 |
| Cavalry ................... | 134 | 1425 | 1559 |
| Artillery ................. | 184 | 2392 | 2576 |
| Miscellaneous Troops ....... | 159 | 1307 | 1466 |
| Grand Total ............. | 2781 | 25,450 | 28,231 [29] |

Of the 22,239 infantry, Field's Division accounted for 4953 [30] and Mahone's for 3537.[31] If Wilcox's 2681 [32] were added to these, the total of 11,171 in three Divisions would be almost precisely half the infantry. Much praise was given Mahone and Field, particularly Field, for this showing,[33] which was wholly to the credit of officers and men; but it should be stated again that the two Divisions had been the advance of the Army and had not been entangled with the trains or engaged heavily with the enemy at any stage of the final operations. The smallest infantry commands were the survivors of Ewell's surrender—a bare 294.[34] Pickett had 1031, though most of them were without arms. Of Kershaw's command, 805 escaped the disaster at Sayler's Creek. Grimes had 1899, Walker, in Early's Division, only 1226. Gordon's Division, under Evans, counted 1768 officers and men. Heth listed 1527. Anderson's command mustered 2277 at the end.[35] The strength of the Corps was: First, 6805; Second, 5036; Third, 7937; Anderson's 2277. In this the surprise was that the Third was stronger than the First. All the cavalry units were mere fragments.[36] The artillery both of the First and the Second Corps still was in fighting order, except for the horses. Part of the Third Corps artillery had been regarded as "surplus" and, it will be remembered, had been sent from Amelia ahead of the Army. Stronger batteries of that Corps had been assigned to the First.[37]

[29] O. R., 46, pt. 1, p. 1279.
[30] Ibid., 1277.
[31] Ibid., 1278.
[32] Ibid.
[33] Cf. Companions in Arms, 522.
[34] O. R., 46, pt. 1, p. 1278.
[35] Ibid., 1277-78.
[36] Ibid., 1278-79.
[37] See supra, p. 692 ff. McIntosh's and Poague's Battalions had been among those transferred to the First Corps.

# APPENDIX V

## The Careers of Lee's Lieutenants after Appomattox

FOR THE conduct of the men who had fought under him, Gen. R. E. Lee after the war set an example of hard work, of reconciliation, of silence in partisan disputes, and of patience during the years when nearly all prominent Confederates were disfranchised. "The war being over . . ." he said, "and the questions at issue . . . having been decided, I believe it to be the duty of every one to unite in the restoration of the country, and the reestablishment of peace and harmony."[1] Some of his old soldiers thought he went too far in seeking pardon at the hands of President Johnson. Most of his lieutenants took his exhortation as their order. A few embraced extremes of reunion that he shunned.[2]

Longstreet left Appomattox in bitterness of spirit. For months, he confessed, he had felt the Southern cause was hopeless. The next time he fought he would be sure it was necessary.[3] With little difficulty he reached Louisiania and soon established a promising business in New Orleans, but he espoused the Republican cause when most of the white men who belonged to that party in the South were scallywags and carpetbaggers. Ostracized, he turned to his former enemies for employment. They afforded it. Almost to the end of his long life in 1904, he held one Federal appointment after another. It was because of his Republican affiliation and his none-too-choice use of weapons in historical controversy that he received at the hands of some of his former military associates far less than justice as a soldier.

"Dick" Ewell, after his release from prison, went to his wife's fine farm near Spring Hill, Maury County, Tennessee, and took no part in public life, though he maintained a friendly correspondence with old comrades. His end came in 1872.

D. Harvey Hill was newspaper and magazine editor and then college president in a life of large usefulness. He died in 1889.

---

[1] 4 R. E. Lee, 484.
[2] The paragraphs that follow on the careers of the general officers of the Army of Northern Virginia are not based on any original research. Except in a few instances where supplementary material is available, most of the references are from D. A. B. or from C. M. H. Treatment of the corps commanders is by seniority and of division chiefs by the Corps with which they last were connected.
[3] 4 R. E. Lee, 159.

"Dick" Anderson had a hard, pathetic fight that reduced him at one period virtually to the work of a day laborer. For a time he was a clerk in the office of the South Carolina Railway Company. He never had any position after the war more lucrative than that of phosphate agent for the State.[4]

Jubal A. Early suffered a brief but severe illness after he was relieved of command. When he had sufficiently recovered to ride a horse, he started southward, in the disguise of a farmer, to join Kirby Smith in Texas. As the forces in the Trans-Mississippi Department surrendered before "Jube" reached them, he proceeded to Mexico in a resolve, as he put it, to be "a voluntary exile rather than submit to the rule of our enemies."[5] From Mexico he went to Cuba and thence to Canada. In 1869 he returned to Virginia and established himself in Lynchburg to practice law. Later he shared with General Beauregard at a handsome salary the somewhat dubious honor of presiding over the Louisiana Lottery. As he had the leisure, means and inclination, he became the champion of Lee and of the Army of Northern Virginia against all critics. In the *Papers* of the Southern Historical Society, of which he was president, he had a dignified medium for the circulation of his views. During the Gettysburg controversy,[6] long-smouldering ill-feeling between him and Longstreet burst into flame. The exchange added nothing to the reputation of either man, but as Early was a more skilled controversialist than Longstreet, the Virginian had the verdict of most of the veterans. Unmarried, snarling and stooped, respected as a soldier but never widely popular as a man, "Jube" lived to be 77 and died in 1894.

Wade Hampton for the ten years following the war managed those of his farms to which he was able to hold after the crash of his fortune in 1865. From this quiet labor he was called to lead the fight against the forces of corruption that had seized control of his native State. His energetic courage and his wisdom accomplished the overthrow of a dark cabal without the horror of an often-threatened civil war. Twice Governor, he was named to the United States Senate where he served for two terms. Then he was defeated in the political uprising under Benjamin R. Tillman. The death of Hampton occurred in 1902.

John B. Gordon had a somewhat similar career. After some years of successful law practice, he devoted his efforts to assuring Georgia's readmission to the Union. This won him a seat in the United States

---

[4] Governor Stimson was quoted in the *Columbia Daily Record* of June 29, 1879, as saying this was the best position he had at his disposal when he sought to relieve the distress of Anderson. See also *Charleston News and Courier,* Oct. 8, 1891.
[5] *Memoir of the Last Year of the War,* 130.
[6] See D. S. Freeman, *The South to Posterity,* 76 ff.

Senate. A term as Governor was followed by re-election to the Senate. His lectures were popular, his effort to promote reconciliation was sincere. Perhaps his supreme satisfaction was that of serving for fourteen years as Commander-in-chief of the United Confederate Veterans. That honorable, unremunerated post was his when he died in 1904. The entire South mourned him.

Fitz Lee, like Gordon, never received the rank of Lieutenant General, but as the last chief of the cavalry Corps he was conspicuous for the long remainder of his days. For twenty years he farmed somewhat precariously in Northern Virginia. Then his art as a speaker, his geniality and his great name carried him into politics. Elected Governor of Virginia in 1885, he administered the office with much of his old dash and cheer; but in 1890 he suffered a humiliating defeat for the United States Senate at the hands of a man who enjoyed the support of railroad interests and of machine politicians. After another five years of difficulty, Fitz Lee was named Consul General to Cuba and was in that position on the outbreak of the war with Spain. He received commission as United States Major General of Volunteers, but saw no combat duty in the brief campaign of 1898. His career ended in 1905.

The Major Generals who commanded Divisions in the final battles of the Army of Northern Virginia fared after the war substantially as did their corps chiefs.

George E. Pickett established himself in Norfolk, Virginia, as an insurance agent. Although his earnings were meagre, he declined at Grant's hands the office of United States Marshal for Virginia because he thought acceptance might be regarded as disloyalty to his people. He was 50 years of age when he died in 1875.

Charles W. Field engaged in business, served as Inspector General of the Egyptian Army, held the office of doorkeeper of the Federal House of Representatives for a brief period and continued subsequently in government employ until his end in 1892.

Joseph B. Kershaw, the remaining division commander of the First Corps, spent several months in prison after capture at Sayler's Creek. When released he returned to South Carolina, took up his law practice, entered politics and in 1877 received election to the circuit court of the State. This position he held until declining health forced his retirement in 1893. He died the next year.

Of the Second Corps division chiefs, the only one who ranked as a Major General at Appomattox was Bryan Grimes. He rode home to his plantation, resumed farming and took no part in politics. In 1880 he was assassinated by a man who had some private grievance.

All three of the Third Corps division commanders were at Appomattox; all had different fates. Mahone organized a railroad system which he hoped to extend to the Mississippi and perhaps to the Pacific. Prospering, he became a politician, launched a plan to "readjust" the debt of Virginia and, in the end, joined the Republicans. He had a term in the United States Senate as his reward, but he suffered defeat in a canvass for Governor and in a later campaign to return to the Senate. Before his death in 1895, he had lost the greater part of the fortune he had accumulated.

Harry Heth had inherited mining and agricultural lands near Richmond, but in the economic débâcle he lost everything and, like many ex-Confederates, entered the insurance business. Subsequently he undertook engineering work for the Federal government and shared in the appointments President Cleveland bestowed generously on Southern officers. Heth always felt that he was blamed for the loss of Gettysburg and for that reason, as well as because of his financial difficulties, he had much unhappiness. In spite of his feeling to the contrary, he enjoyed widespread and affectionate esteem. He was much lamented when he died in 1899.

To a certain point, Cadmus Wilcox had misfortunes similar to those of his comrade Heth; but Wilcox, a bachelor, had a sister-in-law, widow of his brother John,[7] who felt as much concern for him as he had a sense of responsibility for her and her children. Although he emigrated to Mexico after the collapse of the Confederacy, he soon returned to the United States and went to live in Washington. For two decades he had varying fortune there. Then he was named by President Cleveland as chief of the railway division of the General Land Office, a position he held until his death in 1890. He had offers of commission in the service of Egypt and of Korea, but he preferred to remain in America where he could supervise the education of his niece and nephew and enjoy their company and that of their able mother. Long residence, gracious manners and consistent friendliness made him one of the most popular of the numerous Confederates in Washington.

G. W. Custis Lee never realized fully the promise of his brilliant early years. In 1871, after holding a professorship at the Virginia Military Institute, he succeeded his father as President of Washington College, which then was renamed Washington and Lee University. This position Custis Lee held until 1897, but he seemed to some of his friends to be hampered by a desire to do everything precisely as his father had done it. His demise was in 1913.

Bushrod Johnson, the sole Major General of "Dick" Anderson's small Corps, returned to his profession, that of educator, and held the pos

[7] See supra, p. 630.

of Chancellor of the University of Nashville. Unfortunately, this hopeful enterprise failed in 1874. Johnson then retired in ill health and broken spirits to a farm in Illinois, where he died in 1880, aged 63.

To turn to the cavalry Major Generals who served at Appomattox, William Henry Fitzhugh Lee—the "Rooney" or W. H. F. Lee of these pages—had inherited from his grandfather Custis an excellent farm. Young Lee returned to it, cultivated it successfully and served as President of the Virginia State Agricultural Society. Although he had none of the arts of the professional politician, he was elected to the Federal House of Representatives and was in his third term when he died in 1891.

Thomas L. Rosser went West after the war, supervised railroad construction, invested wisely in real estate, rose to be chief engineer of the Canadian Pacific and at length retired to be a gentleman farmer near Charlottesville, Virginia. Political insurgency put him at odds with some of his old friends. His feud with Thomas T. Munford continued to his death in 1910; but, all in all, he was one of the most successful of the Confederate Generals who followed a business or professional career.

Besides these corps commanders and Major Generals who surrendered at Sayler's Creek or Appomattox, twenty-seven Brigadiers were present at the end. Five or six Brigadier Generals had been captured on the 6th of April with Ewell, Kershaw and Custis Lee.[8] William G. Lewis was captured, badly wounded, on the 7th.[9]

In addition, there were elsewhere in the South, at the time of the surrender at Appomattox, sixteen officers who had served as Major Generals under Lee and then had performed different duty. Approximately sixty-three other men who had been Brigadiers under Lee were not at the surrender or among the officers made prisoner April 6–8. Some of the sixty-three had been sent to other posts, a few had resigned, others were absent on account of capture, wounds or illness. The appended list of officers, not separately mentioned in the preceding paragraphs, may be incomplete and probably is not altogether accurate but it suggests, at least, the diversity of occupations followed by Lee's lieutenants.[10]

[8] Five were: M. D. Corse and Eppa Hunton of Pickett's Division; Dudley M. DuBose and James P. Simms of Kershaw's Division, and S. M. Barton of Ewell's Richmond command. It is probable that P. T. Moore, commanding a Brigade of local defense troops, was the sixth, but no record of his capture has been found. Kershaw, it will be remembered, had been occupying part of the defenses North of James River and had retreated with Ewell. That was the reason he was caught while Field escaped with trifling losses.
[9] O. R., 46, pt. 1, pp. 674–75.
[10] All the officers on this list remained at the rank of Brigadier Generals while with Lee unless "Major General" appears before the name.

E. Porter Alexander: College professor, railroad executive, planter; highly successful.

G. T. Anderson: Freight agent; chief of police, Atlanta, Ga.

J R. Anderson: Wealthy manufacturer of iron and steel products.

L. S. Baker: Farmer, insurance agent, railroad agent.

Rufus Barringer: Lawyer, farmer.

S. M. Barton: Unspecified private business.

Cullen A. Battle: Lawyer, newspaper editor.[11]

R. L. T. Beale: Farmer, congressman.

H. L. Benning: Lawyer.

A. G. Blanchard: Surveyor and civil engineer.

John Bratton: Farmer, politician, lieutenant of Wade Hampton.

Maj. Gen. J. C. Breckinridge: Lawyer, railroad president.

Goode Bryan: Unspecified private business.

Maj. Gen. M. Calbraith Butler: United States Senator, lawyer, Major General of Volunteers, Spanish-American War.

R. H. Chilton: Unspecified private business.

T. L. Clingman: Unspecified private business.

Howell Cobb: [12] Lawyer; died 1868.

A. H. Colquitt: Governor of Georgia, U. S. senator, political leader in Georgia for a generation.

R. E. Colston: Writer, lecturer, clerk in War Department, inmate Soldiers' Home.

James Conner: Lawyer; attorney general of South Carolina.

Philip Cook: Farmer, lawyer, Georgia secretary of state, congressman.

John R. Cooke: Merchant; prominent in veteran activities.

M. D. Corse: Banker; blind for a number of years.

W. R. Cox: Lawyer, railroad president, judge, congressman, secretary of the U. S. Senate.

J. R. Davis: Lawyer.

T. F. Drayton: Farmer, insurance agent, president S. C. Immigration Society.

D. M. DuBose: Lawyer, congressman.

John Echols: Lawyer, bank president.

Stephen Elliott, Jr.: Died 1866.

Maj. Gen. Arnold Elzey: Farmer; died 1870.

C. A. Evans: Clergyman, historical editor, educator.

N. G. Evans: School teacher; died 1868.

W. S. Featherston: Lawyer, State legislator, judge.

---

[11] Often mentioned as a Major General but not listed in the *Journal C. S. Congress* as nominated or confirmed at that rank.

[12] Major General after leaving the Army of Northern Virginia.

Joseph Finegan: Lawyer.

W. H. Forney: Lawyer.

Maj. Gen. S. G. French: Unspecified private business.

B. D. Fry: Cotton manufacturer; cotton factor.

M. W. Gary: Lawyer; State senator.

Johnson Hagood: State comptroller; Governor of South Carolina.

N. H. Harris: A variety of large business enterprises.

H. T. Hays: Unspecified private business.

Maj. Gen. R. F. Hoke: Mine owner.

Maj. Gen. John B. Hood: [13] Cotton factor and commission merchant.

Maj. Gen. Benjamin Huger: Farmer.

B. G. Humphreys: Governor; farmer.

Eppa Hunton: Lawyer, U. S. senator.

J. D. Imboden: Unspecified private business.

Alfred Iverson: Orange grower.

W. L. Jackson: Lawyer; judge.

B. T. Johnson: State senator; active in veteran organizations; unspecified private business.

Maj. Gen. Edward Johnson: Farmer; died 1873.

R. D. Johnston: Lawyer.

J. R. Jones: Unspecified private business.

Maj. Gen. Samuel Jones: Farmer; U. S. War Department employee.

James L. Kemper: [14] Farmer, lawyer, Governor of Virginia.

W. W. Kirkland: Unspecified private business.

J. H. Lane: College professor.

E. M. Law: [15] Railroad employment, educator.

A. R. Lawton: Lawyer, State legislator, president American Bar Association; minister to Austria.

E. G. Lee: Unspecified private business; died 1870.

W. G. Lewis: State engineer, railroad chief engineer.

R. D. Lilley: Unspecified private business.

Maj. Gen. L. L. Lomax: Farmer, college president, historical editor.

A. L. Long: Engineer, postmaster, author; blind in his later years.

Maj. Gen. W. W. Loring: Commander of the Egyptian Army; unspecified private business.

John McCausland: Farmer.

William McComb: Farmer; unspecified private business.

[13] Lieutenant General and temporary General after leaving the Army of Northern Virginia.

[14] Promoted Major General after retirement from the Army of Northern Virginia on account of physical disability.

[15] Often styled Major General in post bellum writings but not nominated at that rank to the Confederate Senate.

S. McGowan: Lawyer; active in politics; judge.

Maj. Gen. Lafayette McLaws: Insurance agent, collector internal revenue, postmaster, port warden.

William McRae: Unspecified private business.

Maj. Gen. J. B. Magruder: Major General under Emperor Maximilian in Mexico; died 1871.

J. G. Martin: Student of law at 46 years of age; practicing attorney.

Y. M. Moody: Died 1866.

P. T. Moore: Insurance agent.

T. T. Munford: Farmer; various business enterprises.

F. T. Nicholls: Lawyer, twice governor of Louisiana; chief justice State supreme court.

W. H. F. Payne: Lawyer.

W. N. Pendleton: Clergymen; rector of "General Lee's Church," Lexington, Va.

E. A. Perry: Lawyer; Governor of Florida.

W. F. Perry: Farmer, educator.

R. A. Pryor: Lawyer, judge.

G. J. Rains: Unspecified private business; clerk U. S. Quartermasters Department.

M. W. Ransom: Lawyer; United States senator; minister to Mexico.

Maj. Gen. Robert Ransom: Express agent, city marshal, farmer, engineer.

R. S. Ripley: Unspecified private business; resided abroad for several years.

W. P. Roberts: State legislator, auditor of North Carolina.

Beverly H. Robertson: Insurance agent.

Jerome B. Robertson: Unspecified private business; by profession, a physician.

A. M. Scales: Lawyer, Governor of North Carolina, bank president.

James P. Simms: Lawyer, State legislator.

Maj. Gen. G. W. Smith: Manager of iron works, insurance commissioner, unspecified private business.

Maj. Gen. M. L. Smith: Died 1866.

G. M. Sorrel: Merchant, steamship agent.

G. H. Steuart: Farmer.

W. H. Stevens: Railroad construction engineer and superintendent in Mexico: died 1867.

W. B. Taliaferro: Farmer, State legislator.

William Terry: Lawyer, congressman.

W. R. Terry: State legislator, superintendent of penitentiary and, later. of Soldiers Home.

E. L. Thomas: Farmer, Federal employee.

Robert Toombs: Lawyer; active in politics.

Thomas F. Toon: Railroad employee, State legislator, teacher, State superintendent of public instruction.

Maj. Gen. I. R. Trimble: Unspecified private business.

J. C. Vaughn: Merchant, farmer.

J. G. Walker:[16] Unspecified private business; U. S. consul.

H. H. Walker: Unspecified private business.

James A. Walker: Lieutenant Governor of Virginia, congressman.

R. L. Walker: Farmer, construction engineer.

W. S. Walker: Unspecified private business.

W. H. Wallace: Farmer, lawyer, State legislator; judge.

D. A. Weisiger: Unspecified private business.

G. C. Wharton: Unspecified private business.

W. C. Wickham: Railroad executive, State legislator.

H. A. Wise: Lawyer.

W. T. Wofford: Farmer; active in public affairs.

A. R. Wright:[17] Newspaper editor.

Zebulon York: Unspecified private business.

Maj. Gen. P. M. B. Young: Congressman; U. S. consul and minister.

These lieutenants of Lee pursued so many vocations after the war that it is difficult to classify them precisely. In the appended table the effort has been made to give the principal post bellum activity of the individuals for the longest periods of time, and to note those men who might be said to have had more than one major vocation.

Banking: M. D. Corse, John Echols—2.

Business, not otherwise specified: S. M. Barton, Goode Bryan, R. H. Chilton, T. L. Clingman, S. G. French, N. H. Harris, H. T. Hays, J. D. Imboden, Bradley T. Johnson, J. R. Jones, W. W. Kirkland, E. G. Lee, R. D. Lilley, William McComb, William McRae, G. B. Rains, R. S. Ripley, J. B. Robertson, I. R. Trimble, H. H. Walker, W. S. Walker, D. A. Weisiger, G. C. Wharton, Zebulon York—24.[18]

Clergymen: C. A. Evans, W. N. Pendleton—2.

Died before resumption of career: Stephen Elliott, Jr., Y. M. Moody, M. L. Smith—3.

Editors: C. A. Battle, A. R. Wright—2.

[16] Transferred to Trans-Mississippi on promotion, Nov. 8, 1862, to rank of Major General.

[17] Major General after transfer from the Army of Northern Virginia.

[18] In a few of these instances, professions, instead of business, may have occupied the former Generals. Some farmers may be included. As far as can be ascertained, not more than one-fourth of these officers appear to have prospered.

Educators: N. G. Evans, D. H. Hill, B. R. Johnson, J. H. Lane, E. M. Law, G. W. C. Lee, R. E. Lee, L. L. Lomax, W. F. Perry, T. F. Toon —10.

Engineer, civil and construction: A. G. Blanchard, T. L. Rosser, R. L. Walker—3.

Farmers: Rufus Barringer, John Bratton, Arnold Elzey, R. S. Ewell, Benjamin Huger, B. G. Humphreys, Alfred Iverson, Edward Johnson, Samuel Jones, J. L. Kemper, Fitz Lee, W. H. F. Lee, John McCausland, T. T. Munford, G. H. Steuart, W. B. Talliaferro, W. T. Wofford—17.[19]

Governors of States: A. H. Colquitt,[20] Johnson Hagood,[21] John B. Gordon,[22] Wade Hampton,[23] B. G. Humphreys,[24] J. L. Kemper,[25] Fitz Lee,[26] F. T. Nicholls,[27] twice Governor; E. A. Perry,[28] A. M. Scales[29] —10.

Insurance: T. F. Drayton, P. T. Moore, George F. Pickett, B. H. Robertson—4.

Judges: W. R. Cox, W. S. Featherston, W. L. Jackson, J. B. Kershaw, Samuel McGowan, F. T. Nicholls, R. A. Pryor, W. H. Wallace—8.

Lawyers: H. L. Benning, Howell Cobb, James Conner, J. R. Davis, Joseph Finegan, W. H. Forney, M. W. Gary, Eppa Hunton, R. D. Johnston, A. R. Lawton, J. G. Martin, E. A. Perry, W. H. F. Payne, A. M. Scales, J. P. Simms, William Terry, Robert Toombs, Henry A. Wise—18.

Lottery Supervision: J. A. Early—1.

Manufacturers: J. R. Anderson, B. D. Fry, G. W. Smith—3.

Merchants: J. R. Cooke, J. B. Hood, G. M. Sorrel, J. C. Vaughn—4.[30]

Mine Operators: R. F. Hoke—1.

Public officials and employees, other than governors and legislators: G. T. Anderson, R. H. Anderson, Phil Cook, Johnson Hagood, Harry Heth, A. L. Long, James Longstreet, Lafayette McLaws, Robert Ransom, W. P. Roberts, W. R. Terry, E. L. Thomas, J. G. Walker, C. M. Wilcox, P. M. B. Young—15.

Railroad agents: L. S. Baker—1.

Railroad executives: E. P. Alexander, J. C. Breckinridge, W. G. Lewis, William Mahone, W. H. Stevens, W. C. Wickham—6.

United States House of Representatives: R. L. T. Beale, D. M.

[19] Many of these men had other business or political positions.
[20] Counted as U. S. Senator.
[21] Counted as public official.
[22] Counted as U. S. Senator.
[23] Counted as U. S. Senator.
[24] Counted as farmer.
[25] Counted as farmer.
[26] Counted as farmer.
[27] Counted as judge.
[28] Counted as lawyer.
[29] Counted as lawyer.
[30] It is probable that numbers of those listed under Business were engaged in merchandising.

Dubose, W. H. F. Lee,[31] William Terry, [32] J. A. Walker, P. M. B. Young—6.[33]

United States Senators: M. C. Butler, A. H. Colquitt, John B. Gordon, Wade Hampton, Eppa Hunton,[34] William Mahone,[35] M. W. Ransom—7.

Soldiers in foreign service: R. F. Colston, C. W. Field, W. W. Loring, J. B. Magruder—4.

Counted twice: 15.

From the lower commissioned ranks rose many of the public men and the industrial leaders of the South. After the readmission of the States to the Union, a man scarcely could aspire to office unless he had been in the Army or the Navy. The Confederate tradition was for fifty years the strongest influence, political and social, in the South.

# APPENDIX VI

### RANGES OF CERTAIN FIELD WEAPONS, 1861-65

"FIRE TABLES" of service field weapons of the War between the States are few. The most familiar are those published by the Federal government in 1863 with the subtitle: "Ranges of Guns, Howitzers and mortars Used in the Service of the United States." Some of the figures given below are based on that publication, but all specified distances are subject to the reservation that the range of artillery of Confederate manufacture seldom was as long or as accurate as that of weapons made at Federal arsenals. Cannon imported by the Confederacy often were superior in range to anything the United States army could bring to bear against them. These Armstrong or Whitworth guns were few in number and seldom were supplied with adequate ammunition of good quality.

*Smooth-bore 6 and 12 pounder cannon:* Of little use at ranges in excess of 1000 yards, except for deliberate defensive fire at 1200 to 1400 yards. Most effective at 600 to 700 yards.

*Ten-pounder Parrott and 3-inch rifle:* Ranges computed to 6200 yards with solid shot, but of small practical value at ranges beyond 1 mile. Spherical case shot could be used as far as 2350 yards; shell could not be employed with accuracy at more than 1800 yards.

---

31 Counted as farmer.                    32 Counted as lawyer.
33 Counted as public official. Several other Generals were elected for a single term or, when elected, could not take their seats under the Reconstruction Acts.
34 Counted as lawyer.                    35 Counted as a railroad executive.

*Twenty-pounder Parrott:* Solid-shot ranges considered useful to 4400 yards; shell of 18¾ pounds employed as far as 4500 yards but not effectively; case shot of 19½ recommended to ranges of 950 yards. In general, while powerful in the bombardment of fixed positions, the twenty-pounder Parrott was not much more useful in mobile combat than the 10-pounder Parrott or 3-inch rifle.

*Twelve-pounder bronze rifled gun:* This favorite weapon of the Confederates, styled the "Napoleon gun," could be used at 1800 yards but was most effective at 1200 yards.

Concerning the range of small arms, Maj. B. R. Lewis of the Ordnance Department, U. S. A., supplies the following information:

"Records of firing with smooth-bore muskets indicate that the practical range was from 100 to 150 yards. In a general action they were effective at 300 yards, and useless beyond 400. At 100 yards, the vertical variation was 4 feet, 8 inches and the horizontal greater. Aimed fire had little chance of hitting the target beyond 150 yards.

"The caliber .58 rifled-musket was quite accurate. Records indicate the following sizes of groups: 100 yards—4 inch, 200 yards—9 inch, 500 yards—27 inch. At 1,000 yards, the mean vertical deviation was 47.8 inches and the horizontal 29.1 inches. The caliber .577 Enfield rifle gave 30-inch groups at 500 yards. It was sighted to 800 yards, while the British rifled-musket, caliber .70 was sighted to 1,000 yards.

"Most of the Civil War carbines were sighted to 300 yards and were effective to 150 yards.

"The following tabulation shows penetration of various arms in white pine—one inch was considered disabling:

| Arm | Penetration | | | Weights grains Initial | | |
|---|---|---|---|---|---|---|
|  | 200yd | 600yd | 1000yd | Powder | Ball | Velocity |
| Rifled-Musket, cal. 58, M1855 | 11 | 6.33 | 3.25 | 60 | 510 | 914 |
| Harpers Ferry Rifle, M1841 | 9.33 | 5.66 | 3.0 | 70 | 510 | —— |
| Rifled-Musket, cal. 69, M1822 & '40 | 10.5 | 6.33 | 3.5 | 60 | 730 | 963 |
| Sharps Carbine | 7.27 |  |  | 60 |  |  |
| Burnside Carbine | 6.15 |  |  | 55 |  |  |

"Penetration by a round ball from a smooth-bore musket, cal. 69, was recorded against white oak, not against pine board. A ball of 412 grains fired from such a musket with 110 grains of powder would have an initial velocity of 1500 feet. The ball would penetrate half-an-inch of white pine at 30 feet. This accordingly was given as the distance from which a disabling wound could be delivered with the smooth-bore musket.

"Belgian Musket, cal. 69 (same general characteristics as S. B. Musket)."

## APPENDIX VII

UNIFORMS AND INSIGNIA OF RANK IN THE CONFEDERATE ARMY[1]

*On the uniform collar:*

GENERAL OFFICERS: A gold wreath in which were three gold stars. The central star was 1¼ inches in diameter; the other two were ¾ inch each.

COLONELS: Three gold stars, each of which was 1¼ inches in diameter.

LIEUTENANT COLONELS: Two stars of the same material and dimensions.

MAJORS: One star similar to those of other field officers.

CAPTAINS: Three horizontal bars, usually of gold. The uppermost bar was 3 inches in length; the others conformed to the curve of the collar and were slightly shorter. Each bar was ½ inch in width.

FIRST LIEUTENANTS: Two bars as above.

SECOND LIEUTENANTS: One similar bar.

*On the sleeve:* Around the sleeve of the cuff of the uniform coat and up the outside of the sleeve to the bend of the elbow an ornament in gold braid known in the service as a "Hungarian Knot." The braid was ⅛ inch in width. One strand was prescribed for Lieutenants, two for Captains, three for field officers, four for Generals.

*On the trousers:* For general officers, two stripes of gold lace on the outer seam, each stripe ⅝ inch wide; the stripes ⅛ inch apart. All other officers wore in the same place on the trousers a stripe of cloth 1¾ inches in width. This was of the color of the arm of the service to which the individual belonged.

*Buttons:* For general officers, two vertical rows of buttons on a double-breasted tunic; each row consisted of eight buttons placed in pairs; the distance between the rows 4 inches at the top and 3 inches at the bottom of the coat, which was of a length to reach midway between hip and knee. All officers below the rank of General wore two rows of seven coat buttons, spaced at equal distances on a similar tunic. Sketches of the various styles of buttons prescribed by regulations will be found in *O. R. Atlas*, Plate CLXXII.

*Head Dress:* Elaborate provision was made in army regulations for dress chapeaux, pompons, etc., which never became available. Examples are figures in the plate of the *O. R. Atlas* mentioned

[1] As prescribed by the Regulations of June 6, 1861; IV *O. R.*, 1, 369.

*supra.* Officers usually wore soft hats with wide brims. The men in the ranks wore anything they could get. By supplementary regulations of January 24, 1862, IV *O. R.,* 1, 879, a French kepi was authorized. It had four vertical gold braids for general officers, three for field officers, two for Captains and one for Lieutenants. Caps of many sorts were used, but the kepi seldom was seen.

*In general:* Tunics, overcoats and "fatigue jackets" were of "cadet gray," sometimes called "Charlottesville gray" after the name of the city in which the most popular cloth for uniforms was made. Trousers were of dark blue for general officers and of light blue for all other soldiers. Facings of the different branches of the service were: Adjutant General's, Quartermaster General's, Commissary General's and Engineer Departments, buff; Medical Department, black; artillery, red; cavalry, yellow; infantry, light blue. There was no uniformity of color to these facings. Nor was "Confederate gray" always or even usually "cadet gray." The hue of homespun garments, dyed with butternut, became familiar in later years of the war.

*Particularly to be noted:* There were no distinctions of uniform among general officers. The uniform of the Brigadier was similar to that of the General of full rank.

# SHORT-TITLE INDEX

(Cumulative for all volumes. As the short titles of manuscript sources are believed to be self-explanatory, they are not included here.)

*Alexander.* E. P. ALEXANDER. Military Memoirs of a Confederate.

*Allan's Army.* WILLIAM ALLAN. The Army of Northern Virginia in 1862.

*Allan, William.* WILLIAM ALLAN. History of the Campaign of Gen. T. J. (Stonewall) Jackson in the Shenandoah Valley of Virginia.

*Annals.* [A. K. McCLURE, ed.] Annals of the War . . .

*Avirett.* J. B. AVIRETT. The Memoirs of General Turner Ashby and his Compeers.

*Beale.* R. L. T. BEALE. History of the Ninth Virginia Cavalry.

*Beale, G. W.* G. W. BEALE. A Lieutenant of Cavalry in Lee's Army.

*Beauregard.* P. G. T. BEAUREGARD. Commentary on the Campaign and Battle of Manassas.

*Bigelow.* JOHN BIGELOW, JR. The Campaign of Chancellorsville.

*B. & L.* Battles and Leaders of the Civil War.

*Brent.* J. L. BRENT. Memoirs of the War Between the States.

*Brock, Miss.* "A Richmond Lady" [Sally Brock]. Richmond During the War.

*Brooks.* U. R. BROOKS. Butler and His Cavalry in the War of Secession 1861–1865.

*Caldwell.* J. F. J. CALDWELL. A History of a Brigade of South Carolinians Known First as "Gregg's" . . .

*Casler.* JOHN O. CASLER. Four Years in the Stonewall Brigade.

*Chamberlaine, W. W.* W. W. CHAMBERLAINE. Memoirs of the Civil War.

*Chamberlayne, Ham.* C. G. CHAMBERLAYNE, ed. Ham Chamberlayne—Virginian.

*Chesnut, Mrs.* MARY BOYKIN CHESNUT. A Diary from Dixie.

*Christian's Richmond.* W. A. CHRISTIAN. Richmond, Her Past and Present.

*C. M. H.* CLEMENT A. EVANS, ed. Confederate Military History.

*Com. Con. War.* Report of the Committee [of the U. S. Congress] on the Conduct of the War.

*Companions in Arms.* "A Distinguished Southern Journalist" [E. A. POLLARD]. The Early Life, Campaigns, and Public Services of Robert E. Lee, with a Record of the Campaigns and Heroic Deeds of his Companions in Arms.

*Conner.* MARY C. MOFFETT, ed. Letters of General James Conner.

*Cooke's Jackson.* J. E. COOKE. Stonewall Jackson, a Military Biography (edition of 1866).

*Cullum.* G. W. CULLUM. Biographical Register of Officers and Graduates of the U. S. Military Academy.

*C. V.* Confederate Veteran.

*D. A. B.* Dictionary of American Biography.

*Dabney.* R. L. DABNEY. Life and Campaigns of Lieut.-Gen. Thomas J. Jackson.

*Daly, Mrs.* LOUISE HASKELL DALY. Alexander Cheves Haskell.

*Dame.* WILLIAM MEADE DAME. From the Rapidan to Richmond.

*Davis.* JEFFERSON DAVIS. The Rise and Fall of the Confederate Government.

*De Leon.* T. C. DE LEON. Four Years in Rebel Capitals.

*De Leon B. B. B.* T. C. DE LEON. Belles, Beaux and Brains of the 60's.

*Dickert.* D. AUGUST DICKERT. History of Kershaw's Brigade.

*Douglas.* HENRY KYD DOUGLAS. I Rode with Stonewall.

*Dunaway.* W. F. DUNAWAY. Reminiscences of a Rebel.

*Early.* JUBAL A. EARLY. Autobiographical Sketch and Narrative of the War Between the States.

*English Combatant, An.* "An English Combatant" [Anon.]. Battlefields of the South.

*Fremantle.* ARTHUR LYON FREMANTLE. Three Months in the Confederate States.

*French.* S. G. FRENCH. Two Wars.

*Gilmor.* HARRY GILMOR. Four Years in the Saddle.

*Gordon, Armistead.* ARMISTEAD C. GORDON. Memories and Memorials of William Gordon McCabe.

*Grimes.* PULASKI COWPER, compiler. Extracts of Letters of Maj. Gen. Bryan Grimes to His Wife.

*Hagood.* JOHNSON HAGOOD. Memoirs of the War of Secession.

*Hamlin's Ewell.* P. G. HAMLIN, ed. The Making of a Soldier; Letters of Gen. R. S. Ewell.

*Harris, N. H.* W. M. HARRIS, compiler. Movements of the Confederate Army in Virginia and the Part Taken Therein by the Nineteenth Mississippi Regiment. From the Diary of Gen. Nat. H. Harris.

*Harrison, Walter.* WALTER HARRISON. Pickett's Men.

*Heitman.* FRANCIS B. HEITMAN. Historical Register and Dictionary of the United States Army.

*Henderson.* G. F. R. HENDERSON. Stonewall Jackson and the American Civil War.

*Hood.* J. B. HOOD. Advance and Retreat.

*Howard, McHenry.* McHENRY HOWARD. Recollections of a Maryland Confederate Soldier.

*Humphreys.* A. A. HUMPHREYS. The Virginia Campaign of 1864 and 1865.

*Hunton.* EPPA HUNTON. Autobiography.

*Jackson, Mrs.* MARY ANNA JACKSON. Memoirs of Stonewall Jackson.

*Jacobs.* M. JACOBS. Notes on the Invasion of Maryland, Pennsylvania and the Battle of Gettysburg.

*Johnston, R. M.* R. M. JOHNSTON. Bull Run, Its Strategy and Tactics.

*Johnston's Narrative.* J. E. JOHNSTON. Narrative of Military Operations.

*Journal C. S. Congress.* Journal of the Congress of the Confederate States of America, 1861–1865 (Washington ed., 1904–05).

*Laurel Brigade.* W. N. McDONALD. A History of the Laurel Brigade.

*Lee, R. E.* D. S. FREEMAN. R. E. Lee.

*Lee, R. E., Jr.* R. E. LEE, JR. Recollections and Letters of General Robert E. Lee.

*Lee's Dispatches.* D. S. FREEMAN, ed. Lee's Dispatches.

*Long.* A. L. LONG. Memoirs of Robert E. Lee.

*Longstreet.* JAMES LONGSTREET. From Manassas to Appomattox.

*Marshall.* FREDERICK MAURICE, ed. An Aide-de-Camp of Lee . . . The Papers of Col. Charles Marshall.

*McCabe.* J. D. McCABE, JR. Life and Campaigns of General Robert E. Lee.

*McClellan, H. B.* H. B. McCLELLAN. The Life and Campaigns of . . . J. E. B. Stuart.

*McDonald, Mrs.* HUNTER McDONALD, ed. Mrs. Cornelia McDonald. A Diary with Reminiscences of the War and Refugee Life in the Shenandoah Valley.

*McGuire.* HUNTER McGUIRE. [Two articles in] H. H. McGuire and Geo. L. Christian. The Confederate Cause and Conduct in the War Between the States.

*McKim.* RANDOLPH H. McKIM. A Soldier's Recollections.

*Meade.* GEORGE MEADE. Life and Letters of George Gordon Meade.

*M. H. S. M.* Papers of the Military Historical Society of Massachusetts.

*Mil. An. La.* NAPIER BARTLETT. Military Record of Louisiana . . . New Orleans, 1875.

*Moore, E. A.* E. A. MOORE. The Story of a Cannoneer Under Stonewall Jackson.

*Moore's Rebellion Record.* FRANK MOORE, ed. The Rebellion Record.

*Mosby, Stuart's Cavalry.* J. S. MOSBY. Stuart's Cavalry in the Gettysburg Campaign.

*Myers, F. M.* F. M. MYERS. The Comanches, A History of White's Battalion, Virginia Cavalry.

*N. C. Regts.* WALTER CLARK, ed. Histories of the Several Regiments and Battalions from North Carolina in the Great War, 1861–65.

*Neese.* G. M. NEESE. Three Years in the Confederate Horse Artillery.

*N. O. R.* Official Records of the Union and Confederate Navies in the War of the Rebellion.

*Oates.* W. C. OATES. The War Between the Union and the Confederacy.

*Old Bald Head.* P. G. HAMLIN. Old Bald Head (Gen. R. S. Ewell).

*O. R.* Official Records of the Union and Confederate Armies.

*Owen.* W. M. OWEN. In Camp and Battle with the Washington Artillery of New Orleans.

*Paxton.* P. G. P[AXTON], ed. Elisha Franklin Paxton Memoir and Memorials.

*Pendleton.* SUSAN P. LEE. Memoirs of William Nelson Pendleton.

*Polley.* J. B. POLLEY. Hood's Texas Brigade.

*Reiterschlacht.* HEROS VON BORCKE and JUSTUS SCHEIBERT. Die grosse Reiterschlacht bei Brandy Station.

*Roman.* ALFRED ROMAN. The Military Operations of General Beauregard.

*Ross.* FITZGERALD ROSS. Cities and Camps of the Confederate States.

*Rowland.* DUNBAR ROWLAND, ed. Jefferson Davis, Constitutionalist, His Letters, Papers and Speeches.

*R. W. C. D.*  J. B. JONES.  A Rebel War Clerk's Diary.

*S. H. S. P.*  Southern Historical Society Papers.

*Sorrel.*  G. MOXLEY SORREL.  Recollections of a Confederate Staff Officer.

*Southern Generals.*  Anon [W. P. SNOW].  Southern Generals.

*Smith, G. W.*  G. W. SMITH.  Confederate War Papers.

*Smith, J. P.*  Address.  J. P. SMITH.  Stonewall Jackson in Winter Quarters at Moss Neck ("From a Winchester Paper"—Hotchkiss MSS).

*Stiles.*  ROBERT STILES.  Four Years under Marse Robert.

*Stovall.*  PLEASANT A. STOVALL.  Robert Toombs.

*Talcott.*  T. M. R. TALCOTT.  General Lee's Strategy at the Battle of Chancellorsville in 34 S. H. S. P., 1 ff.

*Taylor, R.*  RICHARD TAYLOR.  Destruction and Reconstruction.

*Taylor's Four Years.*  W. H. TAYLOR.  Four Years with General Lee.

*Thomas.*  HENRY W. THOMAS.  History of the Doles-Cook Brigade . . .

*Thomason.*  J. W. THOMASON.  "Jeb" Stuart.

*Toombs, etc., Letters.*  ULRICH B. PHILLIPS, ed.  The Correspondence of Robert Toombs, Alexander H. Stephens and Howell Cobb.

*von Borcke.*  HEROS VON BORCKE.  Memoirs of the Confederate War for Independence.

*Walker, Irvine.*  IRVINE WALKER.  General Richard H. Anderson.

*Warren.*  Proceedings . . . of the Court of Inquiry . . . in the Case of Gouverneur K. Warren.

*Wearing of the Gray.*  J. E. COOKE.  Wearing of the Gray.

*Wells.*  EDWARD L. WELLS.  Hampton and His Cavalry in '64.

*Wingfield.*  H. W. WINGFIELD.  Diary of (Bul. Va. State Lib., July, 1927).

*Wise.*  J. C. WISE.  The Long Arm of Lee.

*Withers.*  R. E. WITHERS.  Autobiography of an Octogenarian.

*Worsham.*  J. H. WORSHAM.  One of Jackson's Foot Cavalry.

*Wright.*  MARCUS J. WRIGHT.  General Officers of the Confederate Army.

*Wright, Mrs.*  MRS. D. GIRAUD WRIGHT.  A Southern Girl in 1861 . . .

# ACKNOWLEDGMENTS

In THIS book as in all others from the same pen, the first acknowledgment must be to Inez Goddin Freeman, who so ordered life at Westbourne that time could be found from a crowded newspaper career for detailed research and undisturbed composition.

With unfailing kindness, John Stewart Bryan facilitated in myriad ways a work that most properly is dedicated to him.

Miss Henrietta Beverley Crump handled all correspondence, kept most of the files, and either transcribed the text and verified the footnotes or directed those who did so. She was assisted chiefly by Mrs. Dinah G. Wolfe and by Mrs. Floretta S. Watts, who made many helpful comments on their own account and pointed out various errors.

A particular obligation is due a company of gentlemen who, varying from journey to journey, visited most of the less familiar battlefields of Virginia and from diversified knowledge, military and engineering, settled many difficult questions of terrain. Included were Claude R. Davenport, Maj. Gen. G. H. Jamerson, U. S. A. ret., J. Ambler Johnston, Archibald G. Robertson and Henry Taylor. Besides sharing in all these enterprises, Mr. Johnston made the special study of the navigation of the Pamunkey River, mentioned in Vol. I, p. 206, n. 14.

During the early years of the investigation G. Mallory Freeman acted as research assistant in preparing the initial bibliography, in compiling notes and in copying from newspapers and manuscript records. His work was distinguished for accuracy and fine understanding.

To many libraries and archives a debt is due. Most frequently consulted was the Virginia State Library, over which presides Dr. Wilmer L. Hall with scholarly zeal. The Confederate Memorial Institute placed the Lee, the Jackson and the Hotchkiss Papers freely at the writer's disposal. In the same spirit the Confederate Museum of Richmond, through its House Regent, Miss India Thomas, made its treasures available. Nothing could have been more generous than the co-operation of the Alderman Library of the University of Virginia and, in particular, of Dr. Francis L. Berkeley. The Library of Congress loaned many books. Dr. St. George L. Sioussat, Chief of the Manuscripts Division, and H. S. Parsons, Chief of the Periodical Division, arranged for many things that obviated long visits to Washington. The North Carolina Department of Archives and History, through its secretary, Dr. Christopher Crittenden, answered promptly and with sound judgment all inquiries made of it. Like kindness was shown by Miss Charlotte Capers of the similar department of Mississippi, which loaned a copy of the rare Harris "Diary." On many occasions Dr. J. De R. Hamilton of the University of North Carolina made available his matchless knowledge of the Southern manuscript collections at Chapel Hill for which he primarily is responsible. Dr. Wayne S. Yenawine, Acting Director of libraries of the University of Georgia, generously loaned the writer a duplicate file of the *Illustrated London News* for the war period. Dr. H. J. Eckenrode and Col. Bryan Conrad of the Division of History and Archaeology of the Virginia Conservation Commission were invaluable consultants on many subjects. The staff of the Army War College gave frequent and invaluable assistance.

The subjoined acknowledgments are alphabetically arranged. Where no address is given, the generous individual resides in Richmond, Virginia.

Dr. William Allan of Charlotte, N. C., furnished invaluable matter from the collection of his father, Col. William Allan.

General James A. Anderson, Virginia Highway Commissioner, helped often in correcting maps and in establishing place names.

Alexander W. Armour of Princeton, N. J., gave several photostats and copies of early Lee papers and related documents.

President Stringfellow Barr of St. John's College shared generously in the futile search for the papers of Franklin Stringfellow.

Miss Lucy Brown Beale of Hague, Va., promptly settled a perplexing question regarding the time and place of the surrender of Brig. Gen. R. L. T. Beale.

M. S. Bennett of Warrenton, Va., assisted notably in the attempt to establish the location of Stuart's bivouac near Auburn Mills, October 13–14, 1863.

Mrs. Pelham Blackford and her sons, with characteristic kindness, permitted the largest use of Col. W. W. Blackford's MS Memoirs, which should be published.

Maj. Randolph F. Blackford, Chaplain U. S. A., Atlanta, Georgia, loaned his fine collection of Blackford Papers, which include information on a number of obscure phases of the war.

Mrs. C. E. Bolling, former President of the United Daughters of the Confederacy, was an informed and unfailing advisor.

Dr. Julian Boyd, Librarian of Princeton, provided with no small pains a photostat of a rare issue of the *Philadelphia Weekly Times.*

Col. and Mrs. Campbell Brown of Nashville, Tenn., loaned the MS

Memoirs of Col. Campbell Brown and his collection of records of Lt. Gen. R. S. Ewell's command.

Mrs. Pelham D. Brown of Tuscaloosa, Ala., procured with fine judg-ment much information on Maj. Gen. R. E. Rodes, on the "Warrior Guards" and on Alabama troops in general.

Rev. G. McL. Brydon, Historiographer of the Diocese of Virginia, supplied facts not elsewhere procurable, concerning the names and loca-tions of wartime churches.

Mrs. Pauline Wilcox Burke of Washington loaned all the Cadmus Wilcox Papers and much supplementary material of large interest.

W. A. Buck, Jr., of Lynchburg, Va., gave a finely mimeographed copy of the Diary of Lucy R. Buck, quoted in Vol. I, pp. 378–79.

Mrs. Berkeley D. Calfee of Culpeper, Va., most kindly undertook the identification of the Miller House on the battlefield of Brandy Station.

Robert Hill Carter most courteously placed at the writer's disposal his interesting collection of Confederate manuscripts.

Spencer L. Carter answered carefully many questions regarding his distinguished father, Col. Thomas H. Carter.

Mrs. Carol Simpson Chappell, Waterford, Conn., supplied material for the footnote on the fate of "Jeb" Stuart's spurs.

Mrs. Ellen H. Christian of Deerfield, Va., joined with her aunt, Mrs. George Holmes of Charleston, S. C., in placing the invaluable Hotchkiss Papers where they could be consulted readily.

Miss Betty Cocke, University, Va., again loaned the large and valu-able collection of Cocke Papers.

Dr. J. Walter Coleman, Superintendent of the Gettysburg National Military Park, proved a tireless consultant and, with Dr. Frederick Tilberg, generously supplied Appendix I of the third volume of this work.

Runyon Colie of Newark, N. J., rendered a service past reckoning in pointing out that in *R. E. Lee* the strength of the Federal left at Gettys-burg, July 2, 1863, had been disregarded. To this service Mr. Coli later added many others.

Mrs. Myrtle Cooper-Schwarz, of Williamsburg, Va., graciously loaned the papers of Brig. Gen. Robert S. Garnett.

Mrs. Mildred H. Core of Washington, D. C., gave much material on Brig. Gen. N. H. Harris, who deserves separate study.

Col. William Couper of the Virginia Military Institute corrected sev-eral errors in early volumes, prevented some in the third volume and, as always, gave generously of his incomparable store of information on V. M. I. and its graduates.

Col. T. Cruger Cuyler of Wayside, Jones County, Georgia, was prodigal in the loan of material from his interesting collection.

Col. Edwin Cox, U. S. A., donated the material collected by his father, the late Judge E. P. Cox, on the career of Maj. John Pelham.

Mrs. Louise Haskell Daly of Cambridge, Mass., gave a copy of the rare and beautifully printed biography of her father, Col. Alexander C. Haskell.

Dr. Henry Decker loaned the letters of the Decker brothers.

J. C. Derieux of Columbia, South Carolina, courteously copied for the writer an extract from an important letter by Wade Hampton.

John T. Draper drew the maps with intelligent care and fine draftsmanship.

William D. Duke was, as always, an invaluable authority on all that concerned the R. F. & P. Railroad.

Dr. Ellsworth Eliot, Jr., of New York loaned a careful transcript of part of the diary of Maj. Osmun Latrobe.

The late John Gary Evans, former Governor of South Carolina, loaned the papers of Brig. Gen. N. G. Evans and supplied much valuable information concerning Brig. Gen. M. W. Gary.

Mrs. Eugenia Tennant Fairfax gave copies of two unpublished letters of General Lee, renewed her loan of the papers of Col. John W. Fairfax, and also loaned Colonel Fairfax's copy of Gen. A. L. Long's *Memoirs of General Lee,* in which there is a valuable MS note by Colonel Fairfax.

The late Mrs. Vivian Fleming of Fredericksburg, Va., advised on Fredericksburg names and supplied a note on Brig. Gen. Daniel Ruggles.

Rev. Vincent C. Franks of St. Paul's Protestant Episcopal Church kindly searched the parish register and established the date of the marriage of Gen. John Pegram.

Dr. Allen W. Freeman of Baltimore, Md., assisted in the identification of Maryland sites, in proofreading and in valuable counsel of every sort.

Lt. Col. Calvin Goddard, Chief of the Historical Section of the Ordnance Department, Washington, D. C., was a patient and unfailing consultant on disputed questions of ordnance.

Miss Lucille Gregg, through Mrs. J. B. McFarland of Houston, Tex., gave data on Brig. Gen. John Gregg.

Lt. Col. Percy G. Hamlin, U. S. Medical Corps, of Williamsburg, Va., gave access to papers of Lt. Gen. R. S. Ewell and rendered other gracious services.

Ralph Happel, Historical Aide of the Fredericksburg and Spotsyl vania Court House Battlefield Memorial National Military Park, most carefully checked the various parts of the "Bloody Angle" of Spotsylvania Court House. He also supplied material on the site and frontage of the McCoull House.

Mrs. Preston H. Haskell, Jr., of Birmingham, Ala., gave a copy of the unpublished memoirs of Col. J. C. Haskell.

Harry Hayden, Wilmington, N. C., collected material on Maj. Gen. W. H. C. Whiting.

Samuel Hendrickson of Shepherdstown, W. Va., rendered a score of kindnesses in as many ways, and particularly with reference to the spurs "Jeb" Stuart left Mrs. Lilly Lee.

Mrs. Anne McClellan Holloway, who made the H. B. McClellan Papers accessible, most generously added several other interesting documents from the family collection.

Mrs. George Holmes of Charleston, S. C., with her niece, Mrs. Ellen H. Christian, rendered the invaluable service of sending to Richmond the great store of Maj. Jed. Hotchkiss' Papers.

Mrs. Pearce Horne of Washington, D. C., supplied a copy of a letter from "Jeb" Stuart to her grandfather, Maj. Henry Hill.

Harry W. Howerter, Jr., Jersey City, N. J., was most helpful in the restudy of the Federal left at Gettysburg, July 2, 1863.

Edward A. Hummel rendered many services in his capacity as Superintendent of the Fredericksburg and Spotsylvania Court House Battlefield Memorial National Military Park.

Rev. Wythe Leigh Kinsolving supplied careful notes on the Corbin family, from which he is sprung, and on the Moss Neck estate.

Mrs. Walter Lamar of Macon, Ga., former President of the United Daughters of the Confederacy, facilitated correspondence with the divisional historians.

Mrs. Brockenbrough Lamb loaned some of the Munford MSS and gave information concerning others.

Mrs. S. Elizabeth Latané gave a transcript of the diary of Capt. Robert G. Haile.

Miss Mary Randolph Lathrop answered an inquiry concerning her grandfather, Brig. Gen. P. T. Moore.

F. C. Latrobe of Baltimore, Md., through Rev. William Clayton Torrence, of the Virginia Historical Society, loaned part of the diary of Maj. Osmun Latrobe.

Mrs. Elsie Singmaster Lewars of Gettysburg, Penn., who has written so admirably of that battle and of Pennsylvania life, has been a generous and unfailing consultant on a diversity of questions about the Pennsylvania campaign of 1863. It is a pleasure to record that in her generosity and interest she has found the correct answer to every question put to her.

Douglas G. Lovell of Garrison P.O., Md., through R. E. L. Russell of Baltimore, Md., generously loaned the D. H. Gordon Papers which include some Pleasants letters.

Miss Cassie Moncure Lyne of Atlantic City, N. J., most graciously shared the many memoirs of her distinguished line and, in particular, of her uncle, Maj. Thomas Jefferson Moncure, engineer of McLaws's Division, First Corps.

Mrs. J. B. McFarland, Houston, Texas, supplied valuable material on Brig. Gen. John Gregg.

Parker S. Maddux of San Francisco, Calif., for the loan of the diaries of Mrs. G. B. Simmons, the wife of his maternal great uncle.

William E. Mansfield of Atlanta, Ga., sent a welcome pamphlet.

Mrs. Emlyn H. Marsteller of Manassas, Va., rendered the very large service of making available the unpublished memoirs of Gen. Harry Heth.

Burton Marye of the Virginia Highway Commission instituted many inquiries on place names and the identification of old roads and sites.

C. G. Milham of Williamsburg, Va., painstakingly answered, from his large store of knowledge, various questions concerning John Pelham.

Mrs. Mary Conner Moffett of Charleston, S. C., loaned a copy of the excessively rare *Letters of General James Conner, C. S. A.*

Maj. J. A. G. Montague of Ware Neck, Va., assisted in questions that related to Gen. W. B. Taliaferro.

W. A. Montgomery, University, Va., thoughtfully sent a reprint of his father's recollections of Appomattox as published originally in 5 *N. C. Regts.*

Lionel B. Moses of Chicago, Ill., had a careful copy made of the MS Memoirs of his grandfather, Maj. Raphael Moses, and presented it most graciously.

Robert B. Munford, Jr., gave fully of his unrivaled knowledge of Richmond names and history.

W. Tayloe Murphy aided in inquiries regarding the career of Gen. R. L. T. Beale in 1865.

W. C. Noland generally assisted in procuring permission to quote the Berkeley Papers.

O. F. Northington, Jr., Superintendent of the Petersburg, Va., National Military Park, supplied original information on the Federal defenses around Fort Stedman.

Bradford Noyes of Rochester, N. Y., gave an interesting letter of the Battle of Fredericksburg.

Miss Mary Page of Saratoga, Clarke Co., Va., supplied information on the movements of Col. Thomas H. Carter.

William C. Pender of Norfolk, Va., on his own account and in behalf of the family, was generous in collecting and in making available the Pender MSS and all the family's valuable material on that officer.

The late Mrs. Lucy Chandler Pendleton of Ashland, Va., with the assistance of her daughters, Mrs. Mary Pendleton Carter and Mrs. Elizabeth Pendleton Cox, answered questions concerning the death of "Stonewall" Jackson on her father's plantation at Guiney's Station.

Mr. and Mrs. Frank Powers carefully answered inquiries regarding Miss Mattie Ould.

Mrs. Julia Christian Preston, Washington, D. C., gave prompt and accurate information on the family connections of her grandmother, Mrs. T. J. Jackson.

Miss Louise Price loaned the diary and the interesting letters of Maj. Channing Price.

V. B. Ramseur of New York City supplied the picture of Maj. Gen. S. Dodson Ramseur used in Volume III and loaned various interesting relics of the General.

Mrs. Robert Ransom supplied a sketch of her husband, Maj. Gen. Robert Ransom, Jr. This was entrusted to the writer through her son, E. M. Ransom.

President Frank Robertson Reade of the Georgia State Woman's College, Valdosta, gave full access to the MS Memoirs of his grandfather, Lt. Frank Robertson, assistant engineer on the staff of "Jeb" Stuart.

Mrs. Henry C. Riely afforded some appreciated introductions.

The late Thomas L. Rosser, Jr., of Charlottesville, Va., and his daughter, Miss Barbara Rosser, loaned the interesting Rosser MSS.

Mrs. John W. Rothert, Jr., permitted examination of the interesting diary of O. O. Mull, 1863–64.

R. E. L. Russell of Baltimore, Md., as always was most helpful in advising on the maps of Lee's campaigns and on the various troop positions.

State Senator John W. Rust of Fairfax, Va., obligingly identified various sites on the Occoquan.

Mrs. John L. Sneed of Ashland, Va., aided materially in settling an important phase of the Gettysburg controversy by giving full access to the papers of her father, Col. S. R. Johnston, who made the reconnaissance of the Federal left on the morning of July 2.

Paul W. Schenck of Greensboro, N. C., patriotically sent a full transcript of the war letters of Maj. Gen. S. Dodson Ramseur.

Edward D. Smith, Jr., of Washington and South Carolina loaned a valuable letter of Capt. William Farley.

Branch Spalding, University, Va., while with the National Park Service, was a valued consultant on many things.

Alfred Whital Stern of Chicago, Ill., gave permission to quote from an unusual war letter.

Lt. Col. M. H. Sterne of Birmingham, Ala., was untiring in collecting material on commanding officers of Alabama troops.

William C. Storrick of Gettysburg, Penn., was generous in contributing from his vast knowledge of the battlefields that surround the city.

Gen. C. P. Summerall of The Citadel, Charleston, S. C., loaned a rare and valuably annotated work from the library of that fine school.

Major Thomas Suter, Jr., U. S. A., loaned freely from his fine collection of Confederate pamphlets, and also gave a transcript of the diary of J. Armfield Franklin.

R. E. Trice, Jr., of Louisa, Va., gave much help in the identification of sites connected with the Battle of Trevilian.

Charles Talbott loaned many Munford MSS and clarified several questions by means of his large knowledge of that collection.

George K. Taylor, Jr., of Amelia, Va., generously identified the sites of General Lee's headquarters in that vicinity.

Dr. Frederick Tilberg joined with Dr. J. Walter Coleman in preparing Appendix I and in advising on technical matters that concerned Gettysburg reconnaissance and troop positions.

Rev. William Clayton Torrence, Secretary of the Virginia Historical Society, added in many ways to a debt long accumulated.

Mrs. Emma Gray Trigg thoughtfully supplied a copy of a memoir by Mrs. Robert Randolph Carter of Shirley.

Lt. Col. I. Ridgeway Trimble, Medical Corps, U. S. A., sent with characteristic generosity a full transcript of the papers of Maj. Gen. I. R. Trimble and, in addition, prepared Appendix III, on the cause of death of Gen. J. E. B. Stuart.

M. R. Turner, as always, helped with the identification of sites, routes, etc., on the retreat to Appomattox.

Mrs. Douglas VanderHoof kindly supplied some of the later papers of Harry Heth.

A. Reid Venable gave a copy of a most valuable letter by his father, Maj. A. Reid Venable, on the wounding of "Jeb" Stuart.

Mrs. Edward Waller, Jr., opened freely the papers of Col. W. R. Aylett.

Alexander W. Weddell gave a photostat of an interesting letter of Gen. R. E. Lee.

Mrs. Virginia White of Gates Mills, Ohio, loaned all the R. H. Anderson Papers then at her disposal and most generously sought and found others.

Dr. B. Ran. Wellford explained various matters relating to the Wellford family and Catharine Furnace, supplied books from his notable Confederate collection, and advised on many bibliographical questions.

Raymond S. Wilkins, Boston, Mass., in circumstances of unusual kindness, supplied copies of Confederate autograph letters.

A. R. Wright of Atlanta, Ga., supplied the interesting MS account of Gettysburg written by his grandfather of the same distinguished name.

# SELECT CRITICAL BIBLIOGRAPHY

# SELECT CRITICAL BIBLIOGRAPHY

## GENERAL PREFATORY NOTE

THIS select critical bibliography undertakes to list in succinct form the more important manuscripts and printed works that relate to the command of the Army of Northern Virginia. All items that specifically concern Gen. R. E. Lee are excluded, because they appear at length in 4 *R. E. Lee*, 547 ff. Where secondary authorities are quoted once or twice only in the text, it had not been thought well to burden the bibliography with them. Nor are newspapers included. Those used in this work are substantially the same as those mentioned in 4 *R. E. Lee*, 567–69. The rule followed as respects them was to consult, for the entire period of the war, all available Richmond daily publications and the critical *Charleston Mercury*. Newspapers of other cities were searched for events occurring in the territory served by these journals.

In addition to the items here, some hundreds of minor bibliographical references and several thousand unused biographical and topical references were accumulated during the course of the inquiry. For the convenience of possible students, the cards containing this material have been deposited in the Confederate Memorial Institute, Richmond, Virginia.

This bibliography may be consulted by persons inexperienced in research who are desirous of investigating the career of some Confederate officer. As the references here are a minute fraction of those in existence, the shortest procedure is to look first at the *Dictionary of American Biography* (New York, 1928–37, 20 vols., Supplement One, 1944). If the individual is treated in that work, the bibliography at the end of the article will afford an excellent starting point. In the case of a Confederate General not included in *D. A. B.*, a sketch of him almost certainly appears in that volume of the *Confederate Military History* that relates to his State. In addition, if his name appears anywhere in the *Official Records of the Union and Confederate Armies*, he will be listed in the General Index, serial volume No. 130. The ante bellum military assignment of all Confederates who were graduated at West Point will be found in G. W. Cullum, *Biographical Register of the Officers and Graduates of the U. S. Military Academy . . .*, cited many times in these pages as *Cullum*. To be consulted, also, are Francis B. Heitman's *Historical Register* and the U. S. War Department *List of Field Officers . . . in the Confederate States Army* and the similar *List of Staff Officers*. These works are described more fully in Section II of this bibliography. Needless to say, where the date of death is known, newspaper obituaries usually are most helpful. Often, too, sketches of surprising excellence and detail will be found in collected biographical works of different States.

The arrangement of appended entries is as follows: First are cited the Manuscript Sources. Section Two covers printed items grouped as Collected

Source Materials and Biographies, General Reference Works and Important Serial Publications other than Newspapers. In Section Three will be found the Biographies and Personal Narratives. Section Four is devoted to Histories of Particular Commands and Accounts of Battles and Campaigns.

## SECTION ONE

### MANUSCRIPT SOURCES

ALEXANDER, E. P. Miscellaneous papers. Chiefly souvenirs; Library of Congress.

ALLAN, WILLIAM. Miscellaneous papers. Include memoranda of several post bellum interviews with Gen. R. E. Lee. Property of Dr. William Allan, Charlotte, N. C.

ANDERSON, RICHARD H. Draft reports, letters and souvenirs. Collection consists of only a few score papers but includes some unpublished letters and orders; the property of Mrs. Virginia White, Gates Mills, Ohio.

AYLETT, W. R. Miscellaneous papers. Cover the activities of a Colonel who for many months commanded a Brigade. The correspondence belongs to Mrs. Edward Waller, Jr., Richmond, Va.

BERKELEY, W. N. Wartime letters to his family. Chiefly personal, but include some items of importance; owned by Francis L. Berkeley, Jr., and deposited at the University of Virginia.

BLACKFORD FAMILY OF VIRGINIA. War letters of sons of Mr. and Mrs. William M. Blackford of Lynchburg, Va. Unusual letters by five exceptional men: Lt. Col. William W. Blackford, First Engineers, *q.v.*; Capt. Charles Minor Blackford, Second Virginia Cavalry; Lieut. Benj. Lewis Blackford, Corps of Engineers; Lieut. Launcelot Minor Blackford, Adjutant Twenty-fourth Virginia; Lt. Col. Eugene Blackford, Fifth Alabama. Transcript owned by Maj. Randolph F. Blackford, Finney Gen. Hospital, Thomasville, Ga.

BLACKFORD, W. W. MS memoirs, entitled Reminiscences of the War, 1861–1865. The most important of known unpublished MSS on cavalry operations. In the possession of Mrs. Pelham Blackford and sons, Richmond, Va.

BOSWELL, J. K. Official records as Topographical Engineer, Second Corps. These evidently are the papers found in his effects after he was killed at Chancellorsville. With the Hotchkiss Papers, *q.v.*

BROWN, CAMPBELL. Post bellum MS memoirs of the war, chiefly while on staff of Gen. R. S. Ewell. Incomplete but interesting; belong to Col. Campbell Brown, Nashville, Tenn.

BROWN, J. THOMPSON. Official records as chief of artillery battalion, Second Corps. In the Confederate Museum, Richmond, Va.

BUCK, LUCY R. Mimeo. diary of girl who lived near Front Royal, Va. Contains a few items of interest; received from W. A. Buck, Lynchburg, Va.

CARTER, ROBERT HILL and CARTER, BURR NOLAND. Miscellaneous papers. Included are those of John Spear Smith, *q.v.* Robert Hill Carter resides in Richmond, Va., and Dr. Burr Noland Carter in Cincinnati, Ohio.

CARTER, MRS. ROBERT RANDOLPH. Memoirs written after the war. By the mistress of Shirley, Charles City Co., Va. The memoirs are now at Shirley.

CHILTON, R. H. Wartime letters and official records. Included are some historic dispatches preserved by General Chilton as souvenirs; Confederate Museum, Richmond, Va.

COCKE, PHILIP ST. GEO. Battle reports and correspondence of 1861, with some biographical matter. Property of Miss Betty Cocke, University, Va.

COLSTON, R. E. Miscellaneous papers. A large collection, principally post bellum; has been acquired by the University of North Carolina.

COOKE, JOHN ESTEN. Wartime Journals. Irregularly kept and, circumstances considered, of small interest. They were described by J. B. Hubbell in *Journal of Southern History,* Vol. VII, No. 4; November, 1941.

COOKE, JOHN R. Wartime letters and official records. Apparently these were preserved by General Cooke because they had particular historical interest. Owners: P. St. George Cooke and brothers, Richmond, Va.

DABNEY, R. L. Miscellaneous post bellum papers. Some have large historical interest; with the Hotchkiss Papers, *q.v.*

DECKER, WALKER J. and MARSHALL E. Wartime letters. Written by two members of the Ninth Virginia Cavalry. The Decker brothers lived in the Wilderness and often served as couriers for senior officers. M. E. Decker's letters are chiefly of interest because of his immense hatred of war. The letters are in the custody of Dr. Henry Decker, Richmond, Va.

EARLY, JUBAL A. Official Correspondence and records. Most of those of war date are in *O. R.*; originals in the Library of Congress.

EVANS, N. G. Papers. A large collection with many documents and clippings but few letters. Owned by the heirs of Ex. Gov. John Gary Evans, of South Carolina. This collection includes material on Brig. Gen. M. W. Gary.

EWELL, R. S. Headquarters papers. With the Campbell Brown memoirs, *q.v.* Most of these papers appear in *O. R.* Property of Col. Campbell Brown, Nashville, Tenn. Other papers, correspondence and official records, including some letters of kinspeople, are in the Library of Congress. See also Brown, Campbell, *supra.*

FAIRFAX, JOHN W. Letters and memorabilia. Few but interesting; property of Mrs. Eugenia Tennant Fairfax, Richmond, Va.

FRANKLIN, J. ARMFIELD. Diary Oct. 30, 1864—Apr. 29, 1865. Contains numerous references to drunkenness among C. S. troops around Petersburg; good account of battle at Namozine Creek Apr. 1, 1865 and of final fighting at Appomattox. Transcript owned by Maj. Thomas Suter, Washington, D. C.

GARNETT, RICHARD B. Court martial papers. Documents collected for his defense on charges preferred by "Stonewall" Jackson after the Battle of Kernstown; Confederate Museum, Richmond, Va.

GARNETT, ROBERT S. Correspondence and narratives relating to his military service and death. Property of Mrs. Myrtle Cooper-Schwarz, Williamsburg, Va.

GARY, M. W. See Evans, N. G.

GORDON, D. H. War letters. Concern chiefly life in Fredericksburg, Va., with some family material. Owner: Douglas G. Lovell, Garrison P. O., Md.

GURNEY, HUBERT A. A Study of the McCoull House and Farm, Battlefield of Spotsylvania Court House. September, 1939; in the library of that military park.

HAILE, R. G. Diary, June 1862. By a Captain in Field's Brigade. Owner: Miss S. Elizabeth Latané, Richmond, Va.

HAMPTON, WADE. Papers and letters. In family possession; biography being written by James C. Derieux, Columbia, S. C.

HARMAN, J. S. Wartime letters. Copies of letters by Jackson's Quartermaster; amusingly critical of Jackson; with the Hotchkiss Papers, *q.v.*

HARRIS, N. H. Miscellaneous papers of war and post war date. Owner: Mrs. Mildred H. Core, Washington, D. C.

HASKELL, JOHN CHEVES. Memoirs written after the war. Not uniformly accurate, because of failing memory, but wholly charming. A copy was given by Mrs. Preston H. Haskell, Jr., to D. S. Freeman, by whom it was deposited in the Confederate Memorial Institute, Richmond, Va.

HETH, HARRY. Miscellaneous papers and a memoir written after the war. Full of interest, though some of Heth's favorite stories were appropriated and printed by others. Owned by Mrs. Emlyn H. Marsteller, Manassas, Va.

HILL, D. H. Official correspondence and records. Nearly all printed in *O. R.* Originals in files of the North Carolina Department of Archives and History; a full set of photostats in Virginia State Library.

HOTCHKISS, JED. Papers. Large and invaluable collection of diaries, war letters, maps and post bellum clippings, letters and pamphlets. Covers the period from 1861 to about 1896. Concerned particularly with "Stonewall" Jackson and the Second Corps, A. N. Va. These papers belong to Mrs. George Holmes, Charleston, S. C., and Mrs. Ellen H. Christian, Deerfield, Va., and are on loan to the Confederate Memorial Institute, Richmond, Va.

JACKSON, T. J. Official correspondence and records. Include ante bellum notes on books and sundry religious exercises. MSS of war date appear to be those found in Jackson's desk after his death; photostats represent other wartime correspondence, the originals of which it has been impossible to trace. Owned by the Confederate Memorial Institute, Richmond, Va. In the Hotchkiss Papers of the same Institute are abstracts of Jackson's lost Order Books and Letter Books. Jackson's Order Book while commanding at Harpers Ferry in 1861 is in the Confederate Museum, Richmond, Va. Sundry MSS are in the collection of the Virginia Military Institute, Lexington, Va.

JOHNSTON, JOSEPH E. Official and personal correspondence. These surviving papers and much material collected by R. W. Hughes, one of Johnston's biographers, were bequeathed by him to the College of William and Mary, Williamsburg, Va.

JOHNSTON, S. R. Wartime papers and post bellum correspondence. Include Johnston's letters regarding the reconnaissance on the Confederate right, July 2, 1863, at Gettysburg. The papers are the property of Mrs. John L. Sneed of Ashland, Va.

LATROBE, OSMUN. Wartime diary. Part owned by Dr. Ellsworth Eliot, Jr., another part by F. C. Latrobe, Baltimore, Md. A transcript of Mr.

Latrobe's section of the diary is in the collection of the Virginia Historical Society.

LEE, R. E.  Papers, official and personal. See 4 *R. E. Lee*, 547 ff. General Lee's Letter Books, Order Books and Papers of the Appomattox campaign, cited in this work as *R. E. Lee MSS*, have been deposited in the Confederate Memorial Institute, Richmond, Va.

LONG, A. L.  Wartime memoirs. Sketchy; written soon after his appointment as Chief of Artillery, Second Corps. Owned by the heirs of Armistead L. Long, Lynchburg, Va.

LONGSTREET, JAMES.  Letter Book, Feb. 1–Apr. 1, 1865. Copied almost in its entirety for *O. R.*; the original given by Mrs. Eugenia Tennant Fairfax to D. S. Freeman and by him deposited in the Confederate Memorial Institute.

McCLELLAN, H. B.  Miscellaneous papers of war and post war date. Include material on "Jeb" Stuart. Given by Mrs. Anne McClellan Holloway to the Confederate Memorial Institute, Richmond, Va.

McGUIRE, HUNTER H.  Miscellaneous papers of the Medical Director of the Second Corps. Included are various medical records of the Corps and many post bellum papers of importance. The principal collection is in the Confederate Museum, Richmond, Va. Other items and some duplicates are in the Confederate Memorial Institute of the same city.

MAGRUDER, JOHN B.  Official records. Few in number and not of large importance. In the Confederate Museum, Richmond, Va.

MOSES, RAPHAEL.  Memoirs written after the war, probably on the basis of wartime notes. By Longstreet's chief commissary. Most diverting, though brief; owned by Lionel B. Moses of Chicago.

MUNFORD, T. T.  Papers. This large collection, including much controversial post war correspondence, has been acquired by Duke University.

PELHAM, JOHN.  Various post bellum family memoirs. Collected by Judge E. P. Cox and given by his son, Col. Edwin Cox, to D. S. Freeman, Richmond, Va.

PENDER, W. DORSEY.  Wartime letters to his wife. A full and at times interesting collection, with which some useful miscellaneous matter is included. Owner: W. C. Pender, Norfolk, Va., as trustee for the family.

PENDLETON, W. N.  Official records. His Order Book and his Letter Book are in the Confederate Museum, Richmond, Va., but they contain nothing of importance that does not appear in *O. R.*

PLEASANTS, CAPT. JAMES.  Wartime letters to his sister, Mrs. D. H. Gordon. Some of interest. With the D. H. Gordon letters, *q.v.*

RAMSEUR, S. DODSON.  Wartime letters. A large, fine series of letters to his wife for the entire period of the war. Owned by Paul W. Schenck, Greensboro, N. C.

RANSOM, ROBERT.  Miscellaneous post bellum papers. Chiefly memorabilia; owned by his widow; for whom her son, E. M. Ransom, of Atlanta, Ga., has acted.

ROBERTSON, FRANK.  Memoirs written after the war. By the assistant engineer of the Cavalry Corps. Informative. Owner: Pres. Frank Robertson Reade, Georgia State Woman's College, Valdosta, Ga.

ROSSER, THOMAS L.  Wartime family and official letters. Not a large collection, but valuable, especially for Rosser's relations with Stuart. Much post bellum material included; the whole owned by Miss Barbara Rosser, Charlottesville, Va.

SMITH, JOHN SPEAR. Diary and family papers. Records of a distinguished Baltimorean. Included his diary and that of his son Louis. They are part of the R. H. and B. N. Carter collection, *q.v.*

TRIMBLE, I. R. Miscellaneous wartime papers. A small but interesting collection. Throws much light on the methods employed to gain promotion. Owned by Lt. Col. I. Ridgeway Trimble, Baltimore, Md.

TALIAFERRO, W. B. Official papers. Of wide diversity and worth study as an example of the documents, etc., that accumulated at divisional headquarters. In the Confederate Museum, Richmond, Va.

TAYLOR, WALTER H. Wartime letters and post bellum papers. These manuscripts of Gen. R. E. Lee's able A. A. G. are described fully in 4 *R. E. Lee*, 552. Owner: W. H. Taylor III, Norfolk, Va.

# SECTION TWO

COLLECTED SOURCE MATERIAL AND BIOGRAPHIES, GEN-
ERAL REFERENCE WORKS AND IMPORTANT SERIAL PUBLI-
CATIONS OTHER THAN NEWSPAPERS.

(Arranged by authors or editors, except for serial publications, which are entered by title.)

Annals of the War, Written by Leading Participants North and South . . . Philadelphia, 1879. Reprints from articles in the *Philadelphia Weekly Times*, which published many other narratives as good as these. A file of the paper is in the Library of Princeton University.

[ANON.]. The War and its Heroes . . . Richmond, Va., 1864. Issued by Ayers & Wade, this "First Series" consisted of seventeen sketches which, presumably, had appeared in the *Southern Illustrated News*, published by the same firm.

Battles and Leaders of the Civil War . . . New York, [1887–88]. 4 vols. These narratives of participants are invaluable though marred some-times by the partisanship of the authors and the aggressiveness of the editors.

BENNETT, WILLIAM W. A Narrative of the Great Revival which Prevailed in the Southern Armies . . . ; Philadelphia, 1877. See also Jones, J. William.

BRADFORD, GAMALIEL. Confederate Portraits; Boston, 1917. Among the sub-jects are Joseph E. Johnston, Longstreet, J. E. B. Stuart and Robert Toombs.

CANDLER, ALLEN D., comp. The Confederate Records of the State of Geor-gia; Atlanta, 1909–11, 6 vols.

CLARK, WALTER, ed. Histories of the Several Regiments and Battalions from North Carolina in the Great War 1861–65; Written by Members of the Respective Commands . . . Raleigh and Goldsboro, N. C., 1901. While the articles vary much in historical value, this probably ranks next after *O. R., S. H. S. P.,* and *B. & L.* in value to the student of the Army of Northern Virginia.

CONFEDERATE, A [pseudonym]. The Grayjackets . . . Philadelphia, 1867. Anecdotes; illumine many a dull chapter of formal history.

CONFEDERATE STATES OF AMERICA, CONGRESS. Journal of the Congress of the Confederate States of America, 1861–1865; Washington, 1904–5, 7 vols. (Sen. Doc. No. 234, 2nd sess., 58th Cong.). Essential in the study of command because it contains all nominations and confirmations of Con-federate officers. Adequately indexed.

CONFEDERATE VETERAN; Nashville, Tenn. 1893–1932, 40 vols. Includes many personal narratives but these often are subject to some question of fail-ing memory or lack of access to source material.

Cooke, John E. Wearing of the Gray . . . Being Personal Portraits, Scenes and Adventures of the War . . . New York, 1867. Invaluable on "Jeb" Stuart, Wade Hampton and other cavalry commanders.

Couper, William. One Hundred Years at V. M. I. . . . Richmond, 1939, 4 vols. A thorough, full-length history of the Virginia Military Institute, with quotations from many documents.

Cullum, Geo. W. Biographical Register of the Officers and Graduates of the U. S. Military Academy . . . from its Establishment, in 1802, to 1890 . . . Boston, 1891. 4 vols. Indispensable on the ante bellum assignments of Confederate officers who were graduates of the United States Military Academy.

[De Fontaine, F. G.] Marginalia, or Gleanings from an Army Note-book, by Personne, Army Correspondent of the Charleston Courier . . . Columbia, S. C., 1864. Anecdotes and war correspondence by a man of some ability.

Eliot, Ellsworth, Jr. West Point in The Confederacy; New York, 1941. Service records of all known graduates.

Evans, Clement A., ed. Confederate Military History, Atlanta, Ga., 1899, 12 vols. and a supplement, vol. 13. Particularly valuable for the sketches of general officers. See the introduction to this bibliography.

Freeman, D. S., ed. A Calendar of Confederate Papers . . . Richmond, 1908. Covers the earlier collections of the Confederate Museum, Richmond, to which some notable additions have been made.

Freeman, D. S., ed. Lee's Dispatches . . . New York, 1915. The confidential correspondence of Lee with Davis, unavailable to the editors of the *Official Records*.

Freeman, D. S. The South to Posterity. An Introduction to the Writing of Confederate History; New York, 1939.

Heitman, Francis B. Historical Register and Dictionary of the United States Army . . . Washington, 1903. 2 vols. Contains names of all known officers of the United States Army to 1903 and the dates of their service.

Hendrick, Burton J. Statesmen of the Lost Cause. Jefferson Davis and His Cabinet; Boston, 1939. Chiefly on the cabinet and the diplomacy. Of especial interest concerning Benjamin, Gov. Joseph E. Brown of Georgia and Gov. Zebulon B. Vance of North Carolina.

Henry, Robert S. The Story of the Confederacy; Indianapolis, 1931. An excellent general view of the war.

Hill, D. H. A History of North Carolina in the War Between the States . . . Raleigh, N. C., 1926, 2 vols. Extends to Sharpsburg only. Written by a son of Lt. Gen. D. H. Hill, it contains many bibliographical notes of interest.

Jones, J. William. Christ in the Camp or Religion in Lee's Army . . . Richmond, 1887. Somewhat unrelated chapters concerning the "great revival." See also, Bennett, W. W.

La Bree, Benjamin, ed. Camp Fires of the Confederacy . . . Louisville, 1899. A Miscellany.

The Land We Love, a monthly magazine devoted to literature, military history, and agriculture. May 1866–March 1869, Charlotte, N. C. D. H. Hill, editor.

LONN, ELLA. Desertion during the Civil War; New York, 1928. Scholarly and discerning.

LONN, ELLA. Foreigners in the Confederacy; Chapel Hill, N. C., 1940. With a notable bibliography.

MAURICE, SIR FREDERICK. Statesmen and Soldiers of the Civil War. A Study of the Conduct of War; Boston, 1926. Informative, detached view of Davis's relations with Joseph E. Johnston and with R. E. Lee.

MILITARY HISTORICAL SOCIETY OF MASSACHUSETTS. Papers . . . Boston, 1895–1913, 13 vols. Sound and, in the main, detached.

MOORE, ALBERT BURTON. Conscription and Conflict in the Confederacy . . . New York, 1924. Brief but scholarly. The only study of its kind.

MOORE, FRANK, ed. The Rebellion Record . . . New York, 1862–1871, 12 vols. Along with much worthless newspaper correspondence, this contains some valuable documents.

[NORTH CAROLINA, UNIV. OF] Guide to the Manuscripts in the Southern Historical Collection of the University of North Carolina . . . Chapel Hill, N. C., 1941. Well arranged and amply indexed guide to a large and growing collection.

OUR LIVING AND OUR DEAD . . . Raleigh, N. C., 1874–1876; 3 vols. and one no. of vol. 4. Contains several narratives of value.

[POLLARD, E. A.]. The Early Life, Campaigns, and Public Services of Robert E. Lee, with a Record of the Campaigns and Heroic Deeds of His Companions in Arms . . . by a Distinguished Southern Journalist . . . New York, 1870. First published in 1867 as Lee and His Lieutenants, but not exclusively a biography of Lee. Of small value except as it shows the high contemporary reputation of some officers now almost forgotten. D. H. Hill made an attack on Pollard in 5 Land We Love, 281 ff. He charged Pollard with plagiarism.

RAMSDELL, CHARLES W. The Confederate Government and the Railroads (American Historical Review, vol. 22, no. 4, July, 1917).

RAMSDELL, CHARLES W. General Robert E. Lee's Horse Supply, 1862–1865. (American Historical Review, vol. 35, no. 4, July, 1930.)

RANDALL, JAMES G. The Newspaper Problem in its Bearing upon Military Secrecy during the Civil War (American Historical Review, vol. 23, no. 2, January, 1918).

RICHARDSON, JAMES D., ed. A Compilation of the Messages and Papers of the Confederacy . . . Nashville, Tenn., 1906; 2 vols.

ROPES, JOHN C. The Story of the Civil War . . . New York, 1894–1913. 3 parts in 4 vols., completed by W. R. Livermore. One of the best and most nearly detached.

SNOW, WILLIAM PARKER. Southern Generals, Who They Are, and What They Have Done . . . New York, 1865. Published anonymously. Reissued in 1867 as Lee and His Generals and credited to Snow. Outdated and inaccurate.

SOUTHERN HISTORICAL SOCIETY PAPERS; Richmond, Va., 1876–1944; 49 vols. An author-and-title index through vol. 38, compiled by Mrs. Kate Pleasants Minor, was issued as the July–October, 1913 number of the Virginia State Library Bulletin.

U. S. Congress. Joint Committee on the Conduct of the War. Reports . . . Washington, 1863–66. 8 vols. Three volumes appeared in 1863, three in 1865 and two in 1866 as a "Supplemental Report."

U. S. War Department. List of Field Officers, Regiments, and Battalions in the Confederate State Army, 1861–1865. [Washington, n.d.] A vade mecum.

U. S. War Department. List of Staff Officers of the Confederate States Army; 1861–65; Washington, 1891. Not complete but contains thousands of names, invaluable for identifications.

U. S. War Department. The War of the Rebellion: A Compilation of the Official Records of the Union and Confederate Armies; Washington, 1880–1901, 70 vols. in 128. Some missing papers will be found in Freeman, D. S., ed. Lee's Dispatches, q.v.

Walker, Charles D. Memorial, Virginia Military Institute. Biographical Sketches of the Graduates and Élèves of . . . who fell in the War between the States; Philadelphia, 1875. Many sketches of men not treated in detail elsewhere.

Wiley, B. I. The Life of Johnny Reb . . . Indianapolis, Ind., 1943. Although this valuable study relates, in the main, to soldiers of the Army of Tennessee, it contains much of high interest on the Army of Northern Virginia.

Wise, Jennings C. The Long Arm of Lee . . . Lynchburg, Va., 1915, 2 vols. The artillery of the Army of Northern Virginia is here analyzed. Sketches and photographs of the corps and battalion artillery commanders are excellent.

Wise, Jennings C. The Military History of the Virginia Military Institute from 1839 to 1865; Lynchburg, Va., 1915. Much useful detail on V. M. I. men in the Army of Northern Virginia. See also Couper, William and Walker, Charles D.

Wright, Marcus J. General Officers of the Confederate Army, Officers of the Executive Departments of the Confederate States, Members of the Confederate Congress by States; New York, 1911. Not indexed, but a guide to all commissions of general officers. Inaccurate in post bellum references.

# SECTION THREE

## BIOGRAPHIES AND PERSONAL NARRATIVES

(Arranged by author, with cross reference to subjects of biographies or sketches.)

ALEXANDER, E. P. Military Memoirs of a Confederate . . . New York, 1907. Inaccurate in some small details but altogether the best critique of the operations of the Army of Northern Virginia. For other narratives by Alexander (most of them rewritten and incorporated in this work) see 1 *S. H. S. P.*, 61–76; 3 *ibid.*, 357–68; 4 *ibid.*, 97–111; 9 *ibid.*, 512–18; 10 *ibid.*, 32–45, 382–92, 445–64; 11 *ibid.*, 98–113; 3 *B. & L.*, 745–50.

ALLAN, ELIZABETH RANDOLPH PRESTON. A March Past. Reminiscences of . . . Edited by her Daughter, Janet Allan Bryan; Richmond, 1938. Memoirs of the wife of Col. William Allan, Chief Ordnance Officer, Second Corps.

ANDERSON, RICHARD H. See Bratton, John; Walker, C. Irvine.

ANDREWS, SNOWDEN. See Smith, Tunstall, ed.

ARMISTEAD, LEWIS A. See Poindexter, James E.

ARNOLD, THOMAS J. Early Life and Letters of General Thomas J. Jackson . . . New York [1916].

ASHBY, THOMAS A. Life of Turner Ashby . . . New York, 1914.

ASHBY, TURNER. See, also, Ashby, Thomas; Avirett, James B.; Thomas, Clarence.

AVERY, ALPHONSO CALHOUN. Life and Character of Gen. D. H. Hill; 21 *S. H. S. P.*, 110–50.

AVIRETT, JAMES B. The Memoirs of General Turner Ashby and his Compeers; Baltimore, 1867. Includes several brief memoirs by other writers. Avirett was Chaplain of Ashby's Cavalry.

BASSO, HAMILTON. Beauregard, the Great Creole; New York, 1933.

BEALE, G. W. A Lieutenant of Cavalry in Lee's Army; Boston, 1918. By the son of the commander of the Ninth Virginia Cavalry.

BEATY, JOHN O. John Esten Cooke, Virginian; New York, 1922. Contains information on "Jeb" Stuart and on the military career of Cooke, a novelist and historical writer who served on the staff of Stuart.

BEAUREGARD, P. G. T. See Basso, Hamilton; Roman, Alfred.

BENNETT, P. T. General Junius Daniel; 18 *S. H. S. P.*, 340–49.

BLACKFORD, MRS. SUSAN LEE (COLSTON). Memories of Life in and out of the Army in Virginia during the War between the States . . . Lynchburg, Va., 1894–96, 2 vols. These remarkable family letters include a part only of the Blackford Papers.
See Manuscript Sources, *supra*.

BLAKE, NELSON MOREHOUSE. William Mahone of Virginia, Soldier and Political Insurgent; Richmond, 1935. Contains a long note on a controversy of 1871 between Early and Mahone.

[Booth, Geo. W.]. Personal Reminiscences of a Maryland Soldier in the War Between the States, 1861–1865 . . . Baltimore, 1898. Captain Booth belonged to the First Maryland. His narrative is interesting, in particular, for the Valley Campaign of 1862.

Borcke, Heros von. Memoirs of the Confederate War for Independence . . . London, 1866, 2 vols. An over-dramatic narrative in which the author is distinctly the hero; useful for the correct interpretation of many incidents in the history of Stuart's cavalry.

Bragg, Braxton. See Seitz, Don.

Bratton, John. Tribute to Gen. "Dick" Anderson. 13 S. H. S. P., 419–20.

Brent, Joseph L. Memoirs of the War Between the States; [New Orleans, 1940]. Contains the only detailed account by a third person of John B. Magruder's behavior during the Seven Days.

Brooks, U. R. Hampton and Butler. 23 S. H. S. P., 25–37.

Brown, Philip F. Reminiscences of the War of 1861–1865 . . . Richmond, 1917. Some useful detail on Malvern Hill and Crampton Gap.

Butler, M. C. Address . . . on the Life, Character and Services of General Wade Hampton; Washington, 1903.

Butler, M. C. Biography of Wade Hampton [with selections from his writings]; Library of Southern Literature, Atlanta, Ga., 1923, v. 5, 2061–71.

Campbell, John A. Reminiscences and Documents Relating to the Civil War During the Year 1865; Baltimore, 1887. Mr. Justice Campbell's account of his efforts to restore peace and public order.

Casler, John O. Four Years in the Stonewall Brigade . . . Guthrie, Okla., 1893. Casler was a man of limited education who was a member of the Thirty-third Virginia, Stonewall Brigade. His amusing and realistic narrative is an antidote for the excessive idealism of much that has been written about the Army of Northern Virginia. There can be no true portrayal of the private soldier of that Army unless Casler is consulted.

Chamberlaine, William W. Memoirs of the Civil War . . . Washington, 1912. Exceptionally intelligent personal narrative.

Chamberlayne, C. G., ed. Ham Chamberlayne—Virginian . . . Richmond, Va., 1933. Invaluable on the artillery of Lee's Army. The author was attached to the Third Corps and was a young gentleman of much candor.

Chesnut, Mary Boykin [Mrs. James]. A Diary from Dixie . . . New York, 1905. The accepted standard work on Southern society during the war, but marred by confusion and transposition of incidents.

Clay, Mrs. Clement C. A Belle of the Fifties; New York, 1904. Chiefly of value for its exhibit of the social "atmosphere" of the Richmond government.

Claiborne, J. H. Seventy-five Years in Old Virginia; Washington, 1904. Contains some useful material on the retreat to Appomattox.

Cobb, T. R. R. Extracts from letters 1861–1862; 28 S. H. S. P., 280–301.

Conner, James. See Moffett, Mary C.

Conrad, Thomas Nelson. The Rebel Scout . . . Washington, 1904. By a cavalry scout who several times visited Washington.

Cook, Roy Bird. The Family and Early Life of Stonewall Jackson . . . Richmond, 1924. Much material not elsewhere available.

Cooke, Giles B. Just Before and After Lee Surrendered to Grant . . . n.p., 1922. Reprinted in two editions from the *Houston* (Texas) *Chronicle,* Oct. 8, 1922.

[Cooke, J. E.] The Life of Stonewall Jackson . . . by a Virginian . . . Richmond, 1863. Much expanded in later editions. That of 1876 is the definitive one.

Cooke, John Esten. See Beaty, John O.

Corbin, Richard W. Letters of a Confederate Officer to His Family in Europe during the Last Year of the War of Secession . . . New York, 1913. Unfortunately rare, this book includes the candid letters of a member of Maj. Gen. C. W. Field's staff, who described interesting details of operations North of the James subsequent to June, 1864.

Cowles, Wm. H. H. The Life and Services of Gen. James B. Gordon; Raleigh, 1887.

Cox, William Ruffin. Major General Stephen D. Ramseur; 18 *S. H. S. P.*, 217–60; published separately, Raleigh, 1891.
Also in Peele, W. J., Lives of Distinguished North Carolinians. 1898.

Cox, William Ruffin. Address on the Life and Services of Gen. James H. Lane, Army Northern Virginia; Richmond, Va., 1908.

Dabney, Robert Lewis. See Johnston, T. Cary.

Daly, Louise Haskell. Alexander Cheves Haskell. The Portrait of a Man; Norwood, Mass., 1934. Privately printed. Contains some of the wartime letters and the later memoirs of an officer of Maxcy Gregg's staff, subsequently Colonel of the Seventh South Carolina Cavalry.

Dame, William Meade. From the Rapidan to Richmond and the Spotsylvania Campaign . . . Baltimore, 1920. The author, subsequently a distinguished minister, was a member of the First Company of the Richmond Howitzers Battalion.

Daniel, John Warwick. Character of Stonewall Jackson; Lynchburg, Va., 1868.

Daniel, Junius. See Bennett, P. T.

Davis, Jefferson. Dunbar Rowland, ed. Jefferson Davis, Constitutionalist, His Letters, Papers and Speeches . . . Jackson, Miss., 1923, 10 vols.

Davis, Jefferson. The Rise and Fall of the Confederate Government . . . New York, 1881, 2 vols. Not nearly so accurate in detail as President Davis thought it was. His memory played curious tricks on him. Much that one would like to know, Mr. Davis scarcely mentioned.

Davis, Jefferson. Life and Reminiscences of, by Distinguished Men of his Time . . . Baltimore, 1890. [Anon, introduction by John W. Daniel.] Contains numerous sketches, recollections, etc.

Davis, Jefferson. See, also, Davis, Varina Howell; Dodd, W. E.; Dunbar, Rowland, ed.; Eckenrode, H. J.; Gordon, Armistead Churchill; Jones, J. William; McElroy, Robert.

[Davis, Varina Howell] Jefferson Davis . . . A Memoir by His Wife; New York, 1890, 2 vols. The most persuasive view of Davis.

Dabney, R. L. Life and Campaigns of Lieut.-Gen. Thomas J. Jackson . . . New York, 1866. As Jackson's Chief of Staff for a time in 1862,

Dabney had good opportunities of observing the Valley Campaign and the Seven Days.

DAWSON, FRANCIS W. Reminiscences of Confederate Service . . . Charleston, 1882. By an Englishman who served on Longstreet's staff and later made a place for himself in Charleston, S. C. A candid view of Longstreet and his entourage.

DE LEON, T. C. Belles and Beaux and Brains of the 60's . . . New York, 1909.

DE LEON, T. C. Four Years in Rebel Capitals . . . Mobile, Ala., 1890. These are familiar, chatty books, often inaccurate but crowded with facts not printed elsewhere.

DODD, W. E. Jefferson Davis; New York, 1907. An excellent brief biography.

DOUGLAS, HENRY KYD. I Rode With Stonewall . . . Chapel Hill, N. C., 1940. By one of Jackson's aides. Charming recollections, admirably written, but inaccurate in many small details.

DUNAWAY, WAYLAND F. Reminiscences of a Rebel . . . New York, 1913. The author, later a distinguished minister, was a Captain of the Fortieth Virginia, Field's (Brockenbrough's) Brigade, A. P. Hill's Division.

DUNCAN, BINGHAM, ed. Letters of General J. E. B. Stuart to His Wife, 1861; Atlanta, Ga., 1943. Previously unpublished; full of interest.

DUNLOP, W. S. Lee's Sharpshooters . . . Little Rock, Ark., 1899. Covers, principally, the operations from Spotsylvania Court House to Appomattox.

DRAKE, JAMES VAULX. Life of General Robert Hatton; Nashville, Tenn., 1867. Hatton was killed at Seven Pines. His letters are typical of hundreds.

EARLY, JUBAL A. A Memoir of the Last Year of the War for Independence in the Confederate States of America . . . Lynchburg, Va., 1867.

EARLY, JUBAL A. Autobiographical Sketch and Narrative of the War Between the States; with notes by R. H. Early . . . Philadelphia, 1912. With a few significant changes, this long narrative incorporates the whole of the preceding item. Early's contributions to S. H. S. P. were numerous.

ECKENRODE, H. J. Jefferson Davis, President of the South; New York, 1923. "An effort to apply anthropological science to American history."

ECKENRODE, H. J. and CONRAD, BRYAN. James Longstreet, Lee's War Horse . . . Chapel Hill, N. C., 1936. The fullest study of Longstreet.

EGGLESTON, GEORGE CARY. A Rebel's Recollections . . . New York, 1875. Much diverting incident along with a young soldier's impression of the men "higher up."

ELLIOTT, STEPHEN, JR. See Hamilton, John A.; Trescott, William Henry.

EWELL, RICHARD S. See Hamlin, Percy Gatling.

FLEMING, FRANCIS P. Memoir of Capt. C. Seton Fleming of the Second Florida Infantry, C. S. A. . . . Jacksonville, Fla., 1884. The regiment of Captain Fleming belonged to Finegan's Brigade. Included are some letters on operations of the summer of 1864.

FRENCH, SAMUEL G. Two Wars: An Autobiography; Nashville, Tenn., 1901. Useful on Longstreet's Suffolk campaign of 1863.

FLETCHER, W. A. Rebel Private, Front and Rear . . . Beaumont, Texas, 1908. By a member of Hood's Texas Brigade.

GILL, JOHN. Reminiscences of Four Years as a Private Soldier in the Confederate Army . . . Baltimore, 1904. Service with the First Maryland on the part of a young soldier who subsequently attained to distinction in Baltimore. He was one of Jackson's couriers during the Seven Days.

GILMOR, HARRY. Four Years in the Saddle; New York, 1866. By a cavalry officer who served often on detached duty in Northern Virginia.

GORDON, ARMISTEAD C[HURCHILL]. Jefferson Davis; New York, 1918. A brief but sound biography.

GORDON, ARMISTEAD CHURCHILL. Memories and Memorials of William Gordon McCabe; Richmond, 1925. 2 vols. Includes reminiscences of the Adjutant of Pegram's Battalion, a close friend of Col. W. J. Pegram.

GORDON, JAMES B. See Cowles, Wm. H. H.

GORDON, JOHN B. Reminiscences of the Civil War . . . New York, 1903. Altogether charming but subject to the critique that always must be applied to oft-told stories committed to print late in life.

GRAHAM, HENRY TUCKER. An Old Manse; Richmond, 1916. A charming sketch of the manse in Winchester, Va., where "Stonewall" Jackson and his wife resided in the winter of 1861–62.

GRAHAM, JAMES A. The James A. Graham Papers; edited by H. M. Wagstaff . . . Chapel Hill, N. C., 1928. Chiefly reflections on army life and home in the letters of a young North Carolinian who belonged to the Twenty-seventh North Carolina.

GRIMES, BRYAN. Extracts of Letters of . . . to His Wife. Written while in Active Service in the Army of Northern Virginia . . . Compiled by Pulaski Cowper . . . Raleigh, 1883. In part fragmentary. Some of the notes were never developed. In spite of these limitations, valuable, in particular on Appomattox.

GRIMES, BRYAN. See London, H. A.

HAGOOD, JOHNSON. Memoirs of the War of Secession from the Original Manuscripts of . . . Columbia, S. C., 1910. Careful narrative of operations of a fighting unit of Hoke's Division.

HAMILTON, JOHN A. Stephen Elliott; 9 S. H. S. P., 476–79.

HAMLIN, PERCY GATLING, ed. The Making of a Soldier; Letters of General R. S. Ewell; Richmond, Va., 1935.

HAMLIN, PERCY GATLING. Old Bald Head (General R. S. Ewell), The Portrait of a Soldier . . . Strasburg, Va., 1940. Contains some material not found elsewhere.

HAMPTON, WADE. See Brooks, U. R.; Butler, M. C.

HARRIS, W. M., compiler. Movements of the Confederate Army in Virginia and the Part Taken Therein by the Nineteenth Mississippi Regiment. From the Diary of Gen. Nat. H. Harris . . . Duncansby, Miss., 1901. A brief narrative presumably based on but not quoting the diary of General Harris.

HARRISON, MRS. BURTON. Recollections Grave and Gay . . . Richmond, 1911. Pictures of wartime Richmond by a girl of high station.

HASKELL, ALEXANDER CHEVES. See Daly, Louise Haskell.

HATTON, ROBERT. See Drake, James Vaulx.

HENDERSON, G. F. R. Stonewall Jackson and the American Civil War; London, New York, 1898, 2 vols. A great narrative—one of the books every student of the war will find worth while. Henderson always was interesting, though a hero-worshiper.

HILL, AMBROSE POWELL. See Walker, James A. For details of Hill's death and burial, see articles in 11 *S. H. S. P.*, 564–69; 12 *ibid.*, 183–87; 19 *ibid.*, 183–86; 20 *ibid.*, 349–51; 27 *ibid.*, 26–38. *Ibid.* vol. 20 is devoted largely to A. P. Hill. A biography of Hill by W. J. Robertson appeared serially in the magazine section of the *Richmond* (Va.) *Times-Dispatch*, Oct. 14–Nov. 11, 1934. It deserves separate publication.

HILL, DANIEL HARVEY. See Avery, Alphonso Calhoun.

HOOD, JOHN B. Advance and Retreat . . . New Orleans, 1880. This autobiography of a great combat officer is unfortunately brief on operations in Virginia. Hood as a man of society is portrayed charmingly by Mrs. Mary Boykin Chesnut, *q.v.*

HOPKINS, LUTHER W. From Bull Run to Appomattox, a Boy's View . . Baltimore, 1908; 2nd edition, 1911. By a member of the Sixth Virginia Cavalry, W. E. Jones's Brigade.

HOWARD, McHENRY. Recollections of a Maryland Soldier and Staff Officer . . . Baltimore, 1914. With Winder, Trimble, Steuart and Edward Johnson. One of the most important personal narratives of Second Corps operations.

HUDSON, JOSHUA H. Sketches and Reminiscences . . . Columbia, S. C., 1904. By the Lieutenant Colonel of the Twenty-sixth South Carolina, Wallace's Brigade. Helpful on the last phase at Petersburg.

HUGHES, ROBERT M. General [Joseph E.] Johnston; New York, 1893. Adheres closely to Johnston's *Narrative* but is the standard work.

HUNTER, ALEXANDER. John Reb and Billy Yank . . . Washington, 1905. A long work of incidents, anecdotes and memorabilia.

HUNTON, EPPA. Autobiography; Richmond, Va., 1933. By one of Pickett's later Brigadiers. Privately printed.

JACKSON, EDGAR ALLAN. Letters of . . . n.p., n.d. Cover experiences to Chancellorsville, where he was killed. He belonged to the First North Carolina. The letters are admirably edited.

JACKSON, MARY ANNA. Memoirs of Stonewall Jackson . . . Louisville, Ky., 1895. By his widow. Contains many intimate letters not found elsewhere.

JACKSON, THOMAS JONATHAN. See Arnold Thomas J.; Cook, Roy Bird; Daniel, John Warwick; Douglas, Henry Kyd; Henderson, G. F. R.; Jackson, Mary Anna; McGuire, Hunter H.; Wayland, John W.

JENKINS, MICAH. See Thomas, John F.

JOHNSON, BRADLEY T. A Memoir of the Life and Public Service of Joseph E. Johnston . . . Baltimore, 1891.

JOHNSTON, DAVID E. The Story of a Confederate Boy in the Civil War . . . [Portland, Ore., 1914], 2nd edition. By a youthful, and most intelligent member of the Seventh Virginia, Kemper's Brigade, Pickett's Division, First Corps.

JOHNSTON, JOSEPH E. Narrative of Military Operations during the late War between the States . . . New York, 1872. Indispensable for operations through May, 1862, but reserved and disappointing.

JOHNSTON, JOSEPH E. See, also, Hughes, Robert M.; Johnson, Bradley T.

JOHNSTON, T. CARY. Robert Lewis Dabney; Richmond, 1903. Gives the brief military career of "Stonewall" Jackson's temporary Chief of Staff.

JONES, B. W. Under the Stars and Bars. A History of the Surry Light Artil·lery . . . Richmond, 1909. Good letters. Relate chiefly to operations around Petersburg.

JONES, J. B. A Rebel War Clerk's Diary . . . Philadelphia, 1866, 2 vols. The "classic" on Richmond during the war but glossed occasionally by the insertion of after-judgments. The critique to be applied in using this work (R.W.C.D.) is to remember that Jones was not the military prophet he sometimes represented himself to be. A reprint of 1935 unfortunately included many notes that lacked accuracy.

JONES, J. WILLIAM. The Davis Memorial Volume; or Our Dead President, Jefferson Davis, and the World's Tribute to His Memory . . . Richmond, 1890. Much better than its title.

LANE, JAMES H. See Cox, William Ruffin.

LETCHER, GREENLEE D. General Elisha Franklin Paxton. Lexington (Virginia) Gazette, Feb. 2, 9, 1944.

LEWIS, JOHN H. Recollections from 1860 to 1865 . . . Washington, 1895. By a lieutenant in the Ninth Virginia, Armistead's Brigade, Pickett's Division, First Corps. A book of singular accuracy regarding Pickett's charge. See D. S. Freeman, The South to Posterity, 182.

LEWIS, RICHARD. Camp Life of a Confederate Boy of Bratton's Brigade . . . Charleston, S. C., 1883. Bratton's Brigade had been Micah Jenkins's.

LONDON, H. A. Memorial Address on the Life and Services of Bryan Grimes . . . Raleigh, 1886.

LONGSTREET, HELEN (DORTSCH). Lee and Longstreet at High Tide; Gettysburg in the Light of the Official Records; Gainesville, Ga., 1905.

LONGSTREET, JAMES. From Manassas to Appomattox, Memoirs of the Civil War in America . . . Philadelphia, 1896. This is General Longstreet's inclusive narrative. It was written, with literary assistance, late in life, and without consulting his earlier contributions to Annals and to B. & L. Because of inaccuracies, the book is even more unjust to the wartime Longstreet than to any of those he criticized. See Washington Post, June 11, 1893; 4 S.H.S.P., 4; 5 ibid, 273–74; New Orleans Republican, Feb. 27, 1870; Philadelphia Weekly Times, Feb. 23, 1878; 39 S.H.S.P., 104.

LONGSTREET, JAMES. See, also, Eckenrode, H. J. and Conrad, Bryan (coauthors).

McCABE, WILLIAM GORDON. [Sketch of William Johnson Pegram] in Pegram Battalion Association Annual Reunion . . . Richmond, Va., May 21, 1886 . . . Richmond, 1886.

McCABE, WILLIAM GORDON. See Gordon, Armistead Churchill.

McCARTHY, CARLTON. Detailed Minutiae of Soldier Life . . . Richmond, 1882. Exactly described by its odd title. Includes much that is unique.

McCLELLAN, H. B. The Life and Campaigns of Maj.-Gen. J. E. B. Stuart . . . Richmond, Va., 1885. By Stuart's A.A.G. This remains the standard work and, if supplemented by J. E. Cooke and ton Borcke, gives a full, fair picture. McClellan's address, the next item, is more sharply etched.

McCLELLAN, H. B. The Life, Character and Campaigns of Major-Gen. J. E. B. Stuart. Address . . . Before the Virginia Division of the Army of Northern Va. . . . Richmond, 1880.

McDONALD, CORNELIA. A Diary with Reminiscences of the War and Refugee Life in the Shenandoah Valley 1860–1865; Annotated and Supplemented by Hunter McDonald; Nashville, 1934. [Copyright, 1935] A unique record of suffering in the Shenandoah Valley.

McELROY, ROBERT. Jefferson Davis—the Unreal and the Real; New York, 1937, 2 vols. The fullest biography.

McGUIRE, HUNTER [H] Stonewall Jackson. An address . . . at the Dedication of Jackson Memorial Hall . . . [Richmond, 1907]. By the Medical Director of the Second Corps.

McGUIRE, JUDITH W. [MRS. JOHN P.] Diary of a Southern Refugee . . . Richmond, 1889, 3rd edition. Next to Jones's Diary, the most familiar account of Richmond during the war. Has the virtue of unglossed day-by-day entries.

McKIM, RANDOLPH H. A Soldier's Recollections . . . New York, 1910. The author was on the staff of "Maryland" Steuart. Especially useful on the operations of the Confederate left at Gettysburg.

MAHONE, WILLIAM. See Blake, Nelson Morehouse.

MALONE, BARTLETT Y. Diary of . . . edited by W. W. Pierson, Jr. . . . Chapel Hill, N. C., 1919. A member of the Sixth North Carolina Infantry (Hoke's Brigade, Early's Division, Second Corps), Malone was especially interested in the weather. He might be termed the unofficial meteorologist of the Army of Northern Virginia.

MARSHALL, CHARLES. An Aide-de-Camp of Lee, Being the Papers of Colonel Charles Marshall . . . Edited by Major General Sir Frederick Maurice . . . [Boston, 1927]. Although incomplete as a military memoir, this contains much useful material.

MERCER, PHILIP. The life of the Gallant [John] Pelham; Macon, Ga., 1929. Contains a few letters.

MOFFETT, MARY C., ED. Letters of General James Conner, C.S.A.; [Columbia, S. C., 1933] Candid letters to his mother; of particular value on affairs of second corps headquarters under Ewell. Privately printed and excessively rare.

MIXSON, FRANK M. Reminiscences of a Private . . . Columbia, S. C., 1910. Fine narrative by a member of the First South Carolina of Jenkins's, later Bratton's Brigade, Field's Division, First Corps. Useful on operations North of the James in the autumn of 1864.

MONCURE, E. C. Reminiscences of the Civil War . . . n.p., [1914?] Relates to the march from Spotsylvania to the North Anna, May, 1864; republished (W. W. Scott, ed.) in Virginia State Library Bulletin, July, 1927.

MONTGOMERY, WALTER A. Life and Character of Major-General W. D. Pender . . . n.p., [1894?]

MOORE, EDWARD A. The Story of a Cannoneer under Stonewall Jackson . . . New York, 1907. This narrative by a member of the Rockbridge Artilıery is one of the best accounts of the war from the standpoint of a private soldier.

MORGAN, W. H. Personal Reminiscences of the War of 1861–65 . . . Lynchburg, Va., 1911. The author was a member of the Eleventh Virginia, Kemper's Brigade, Pickett's Division, First Corps.

MOSBY, JOHN S. Memoirs of [edited by Charles W. Russell]; Boston, 1917.

MOSBY, JOHN S. War Reminiscences . . . Boston, 1887. A major item in the large literature of Mosby's command.

NEESE, GEORGE M. Three Years in the Confederate Horse Artillery; Washington, 1911. By a member of Chew's Battery, Stuart Horse Artillery. Neese evidently kept a diary, but his narrative must have been elaborated greatly after the war. It is difficult, as stated in the text, to distinguish the contemporary from the later entries.

NISBET, JAMES COOPER. Four Years on the Firing Line. Chattanooga, Tenn., 1914.

NOLL, ARTHUR HOWARD. General Kirby Smith . . . Sewanee, Tenn., 1907. Contains little on the activities of Smith in Virginia.

OATES, WILLIAM C. The War between the Union and the Confederacy . . . with a History of the 15th Alabama Regiment . . . Washington, 1905. Colonel, later Brig. Gen. Oates, belonged to Law's Brigade.

O'FERRALL, CHARLES T. Forty Years of Active Service . . . Washington, 1904. Memoirs of a Valley Cavalryman.

PAXTON, ELISHA FRANKLIN. Memoir and Memorials . . . Composed of his Letters from Camp and Field . . . Collected and Arranged by his son, John Gallatin Paxton; Washington, 1907. The letters, strongly religious in tone, contain some useful references to the controversies and the battles of the Second Corps.

PAXTON, ELISHA FRANKLIN. See, also, Letcher, Greenlee D.

PECK, R. H. Reminiscences of a Confederate Soldier . . . Fincastle, Va., n.d. By a member of the Second Virginia Cavalry.

PEGRAM, WILLIAM JOHNSON. See McCabe, William Gordon.

PELHAM, JOHN. See Mercer, Philip.

PHILLIPS, U. B., ED. The Correspondence of Robert Toombs, Alexander H. Stephens and Howell Cobb . . . Washington, 1913. For present purposes, chiefly of value for Robert Toombs's fiery letters.

PICKETT, GEORGE E. Soldier of the South . . . Pickett's War Letters to his Wife . . . Boston, 1928. Mrs. Pickett edited several editions of letters.

POINDEXTER, JAMES E. Address on the Life and Services of General Lewis A. Armistead . . . [Richmond, 1909?] The author was a Captain of the Thirty-eighth Virginia, Armistead's Brigade, Pickett's Division.

POLK, J. M. Memories of the Lost Cause and Ten Years in South America . . . Austin, Tex., 1907.

POLK, W. M. Leonidas Polk: Bishop and General; New York, 1893, 2 vols. Of use, in this study, for Polk's relation to the "round robin" and the other controversies of Longstreet and of D. H. Hill with Bragg.

POLLEY, J. B. A Soldier's Letters to Charming Nellie . . . New York, 1908. The author belonged to Hood's Texas Brigade. His letters are apt to prove less interesting than his account of the Brigade, q.v. One is likely to find the letters a bit too finished to suggest the full authenticity of the battle front.

POTTS, FRANK. The Death of the Confederacy . . . edited by D. S. Freeman; Richmond, 1928. Published originally in the *Palmetto Leaf*, Cedar Springs, S. C., Dec. 25, 1926, Jan. 1 and 8, 1927. Concerns the evacuation of Richmond and the surrender at Appomattox.

PRYOR, MRS. ROGER A. Reminiscences of Peace and War; New York, 1904. She was the wife of General Pryor. For part of the war she lived near Petersburg.

PRYOR, MRS. ROGER A. My Day; Reminiscences of a Long Life; New York, 1909.

RAMSEUR, STEPHEN DODSON. See Cox, William Ruffin.

ROBSON, JOHN S. How a One-Legged Rebel Lives: Reminiscences of the Civil War . . .; Charlottesville, Va., 1891. By a member of the Fifty-second Virginia.

ROMAN, ALFRED. The Military Operations of General Beauregard . . . New York, 1884, 2 vols. Almost an autobiography of Beauregard. Quotes or reprints many important papers.

ROYALL, WILLIAM L. Some Reminiscences . . . Washington, 1909. Contains a narrative by Col. W. H. Palmer, A. P. Hill's Chief of Staff, on the Battle of the Wilderness.

SEITZ, DON. Braxton Bragg, General of the Confederacy; Columbia, S. C., 1924. Based primarily on the official reports and correspondence.

SHOTWELL, RANDOLPH A. The Papers of . . . Edited by J. G. de R. Hamilton . . . Raleigh, 1929. Much military gossip, most of which is second hand.

SLAUGHTER, PHILIP. A Sketch of the Life of Randolph Fairfax . . . Third Edition; Baltimore, 1878.

SORREL, G. MOXLEY. Recollections of a Confederate Staff Officer; New York, 1917, 2nd ed. A famous and delightful memoir by Longstreet's Chief of Staff.

SMITH, E. KIRBY. See Noll, Arthur H.

SMITH, TUNSTALL, ED. Richmond Snowden Andrews . . . A Memoir; Baltimore, 1910. Concerns the belligerent chief of Andrews's Battalion, Second Corps artillery.

STEWART, WILLIAM H. A Pair of Blankets . . . New York, 1911. An awkwardly arranged but useful memoir by the Lieutenant Colonel of the Sixty-first Infantry, Mahone's (Weisiger's) Brigade, Anderson's (Mahone's) Division, Third Corps.

STILES, ROBERT. Four Years Under Marse Robert; Washington, 1903. By an officer of wide acquaintance and intellectual connections. Full of anecdote and interest. Especially useful on Northside operations of 1864–65 and on Sayler's Creek.

STONEBRAKER, JOSEPH R. A Rebel of '61 . . . New York, 1899.

STRINGFELLOW, FRANK. War Reminiscences, n.p., n.d. An undated pamphlet which includes personal letters from Jefferson Davis, R. E. Lee, and J. E. B. Stuart; cited as a source in *D. A. B.*, but in reality merely an advertisement of his post bellum lectures.

STUART, J. E. B. See Duncan, Bingham, ed.; McClellan, H. B.; Thomason, John W., Jr.

TAYLOR, RICHARD. Destruction and Reconstruction: Personal Experiences of the Late War; New York, 1879. Probably the most captivating of

Confederate memoirs. Taylor's treatment of Jackson's Valley Campaign helped to fix the pattern of all subsequent narrative as late as Henderson.

THOMAS, CLARENCE. General Turner Ashby . . . Winchester, Va., 1907.

THOMAS, JOHN F. Career and Character of General Micah Jenkins, C. S. A.; n.p., n.d.

THOMASON, JOHN W., JR. Jeb Stuart; New York, 1930. A sprightly recasting of McClellan, von Borcke, et al.

TONEY, MARCUS B. The Privations of a Private . . . Nashville, Tenn., 1905. An amusing narrative.

TOOMBS, ROBERT. See Phillips, U. B., ed.

TRESCOTT, WILLIAM HENRY. General Stephen Elliott. Address . . . Columbia, S. C., 1926. Delivered Sept. 8, 1866.

WALKER, C. IRVINE. The Life of Lieutenant-General Richard Heron Anderson . . . Charleston, S. C., 1917. Inadequate because of the loss of most of Anderson's personal letters.

WALKER, JAMES A. Address at the unveiling of the Statue of Gen. A. P. Hill, Richmond, Va., May 30, 1892 in 20 S.H.S.P., 370–86.

WAYLAND, JOHN W. Stonewall Jackson's Way: Route, Method, Achievement; Staunton, Va., 1940. Includes photographs, old and new, of most of the scenes associated with Jackson's military career.

WELCH, SPENCER G. A Confederate Surgeon's Letters to his Wife . . . Washington, 1911. The author was surgeon of the Thirteenth South Carolina, Gregg's, later McGowan's Brigade. Welch's letters are one of the most important sources on army health and morale.

WEST, JOHN C. A Texan in Search of a Fight . . . Waco, Texas, 1901. Written by a member of the Fourth Texas, Hood's Brigade.

WINGFIELD, H. W. Diary of . . . ed. by W. W. Scott, Virginia State Library Bulletin, July, 1927.

WISE, BARTON H. The Life of Henry A. Wise of Virginia; New York, 1899. H. A. Wise was one of the earliest and most picturesque of Confederate Brigadiers. During the operations around Petersburg, he commanded a Brigade in Bushrod Johnson's Division.

WITHERS, ROBERT E. Autobiography of an Octogenarian . . . Roanoke, Va., 1907. Colonel Withers was disabled at Gaines' Mill while commanding the Eighteenth Virginia, Pickett's Brigade, Longstreet's Division.

WOOD, JAMES H. The War . . . Cumberland, Md., 1910. By a captain in the Thirty-seventh Virginia, an old regiment of Jackson's Third Brigade which subsequently became Steuart's, of Edward Johnson's Division, Second Corps.

WORSHAM, JOHN H. One of Jackson's Foot Cavalry . . . New York, 1912. Among the best of personal narratives; written with much care and a sound memory; by a member of the Twenty-first Virginia, of Jackson's Second Brigade, later John M. Jones's Brigade, Edward Johnson's Division, Second Corps.

WRIGHT, MRS. D. GIRAUD. A Southern Girl in '61 . . . New York, 1905. Contains some useful material on Wade Hampton and on Hood's Texas Brigade.

# SECTION FOUR

## HISTORIES OF PARTICULAR COMMANDS AND ACCOUNTS OF BATTLES AND CAMPAIGNS

### (Arranged by Authors)

ALLAN, WILLIAM. Jackson's Valley Campaign. Address . . . before the Virginia Division of the Army of Northern Virginia . . . Richmond, 1878. This apparently was the first of the several forms of Allan's study of The Valley Campaign of 1862.

ALLAN, WILLIAM. The Army of Northern Virginia in 1862 . . . Cambridge, 1892. An early standard authority. Particularly good for its maps.

ALLAN, WILLIAM. History of the Campaign of Gen. T. J. (Stonewall) Jackson in the Shenandoah Valley of Virginia . . . Philadelphia, 1880. Several other editions. The most readily accessible is that in 43 S.H.S.P.

BARTLETT, NAPIER. Military Record of Louisiana; including Biographical and Historical Papers relating to the Military Organizations of the State; A Soldier's Story of the Late War . . . New Orleans, 1875. Rare. Contains much useful material. Sometimes listed as Military Annals of Louisiana.

BAYLOR, GEORGE. Bull Run to Bull Run . . . Richmond, 1900. In substance a history of Co. B., Twelfth Virginia Cavalry, which, in its great day, was Col. A. W. Harman's regiment of Jones's Brigade.

BEALE, R. L. T. History of the Ninth Virginia Cavalry . . . Richmond, 1899. Brief but valuable. The regiment was part of "Rooney" Lee's Brigade.

BEAUREGARD, P. G. T. A Commentary on the Campaign and Battle of Manassas . . . New York and London, 1891.

BERNARD, GEORGE S., ED. War Talks of Confederate Veterans . . . Petersburg, Va., 1892. With special reference to the Battle of the Crater.

BIGELOW, JOHN, JR. The Campaign of Chancellorsville . . . New Haven, 1910. The fullest narrative; many detailed maps.

BLACKFORD, CHARLES M., JR. Annals of the Lynchburg Home Guard . . . Lynchburg, Va., 1891.

BORCKE, HEROS VON AND SCHEIBERT, JUSTUS. Die grosse Reiterschlacht bei Brandy Station . . . Berlin, 1893. The most comprehensive narrative of Brandy Station.

BOYKIN, E. M. The Falling Flag: Evacuation of Richmond, Retreat and Surrender at Appomattox . . . New York, 1874. Concerns chiefly the cavalry brigade of Mart Gary.

BROCK, MISS SALLY [MRS. RICHARD PUTNAM]. Richmond During the War . . . New York, 1867. A familiar post bellum narrative. It is more often read than quoted and is a work from which one finds difficulty in extracting many specific facts.

BROOKS, U. R. Butler and His Cavalry in the War of Secession . . . Columbia, S. C., 1909. Loosely done but all there is.

BROWN, CAMPBELL. Ewell's Division [written in 1862]; 10 *S.H.S.P.*, 255–61.

[BROWN, CAMPBELL] The First Manassas. Correspondence between Generals R. S. Ewell and G. T. Beauregard . . . Nashville, 1885. Concerns alleged delay of Ewell. Appears also in 13 *S.H.S.P.*, 41–47.

BROWN, MAUD MORROW. The University Grays Company A Eleventh Mississippi Regiment . . . Richmond [1940]. Contains some useful letters of soldiers. The regiment belonged to Davis's Brigade at Gettysburg.

G., J. C. Lee's Last Campaign . . . Raleigh, 1866. Concerns the preliminaries of the withdrawal from Petersburg and gives some details of the retreat of Appomattox.

CALDWELL, J. F. J. The History of a Brigade of South Carolinians Known First as "Gregg's" and subsequently as "McGowan's Brigade" . . . Philadelphia, 1866. Altogether the best history of a Brigade in Lee's Army. A wise, well-written book, which should be republished.

CARDWELL, D. Gen. Hampton's Cattle Raid; 22 *S.H.S.P.*, 147–56.

CHAMBERLAIN, JOSHUA L. Passing of the Armies . . . New York, 1915. Quoted often on the surrender of the Army of Northern Virginia, which surrender Chamberlain received.

CHAMBERLAYNE, E. H., JR. War History and Roll of the Richmond Fayette Artillery, 38th Virginia Battalion Artillery, Confederate States Army, 1861–1865; Richmond, 1883.

[CUSSONS, JOHN.] The Passage of Thoroughfare Gap and the Assembling of Lee's Army for the Second Battle of Manassas, by a Confederate Scout . . . York, Penn., 1906.

DANIEL, FREDERICK S. Richmond Howitzers in the War . . . Richmond, 1891. T. J. Macon and Carlton McCarthy, *q.v.*, also wrote of this command. See, also, McKim, R. H.

DAVIS, NICHOLAS A. The Campaign from Texas to Maryland . . . Richmond, 1863. Contemporary account of the operations of the Fourth Texas through the Battle of Fredericksburg. Excessively rare.

DICKERT, D. AUGUSTUS. History of Kershaw's Brigade . . . Newberry, S. C., 1899. This account of a famous Brigade of McLaws's Division, First Corps, expands many incidents scarcely mentioned in reports.

BARKSDALE, WILLIAM. Barksdale's Brigade; 32 *S.H.S.P.*, 250–70; 36 *ibid.*, 17–25.

EARLY, JUBAL A. Jackson's Campaign against Pope in August, 1862. An Address . . . before the First Annual Meeting of the Association of the Maryland Line \ . . . [Baltimore? 1883?]

ENGLISH COMBATANT, AN. Battlefields of the South, From Bull Run to Fredericksburg . . . [Dedication signed T. E. C.] . . . New York, 1864, 1 vol. edition; London, 1863, 2 vol. edition. Of small value.

FIELD, CHARLES W. Campaign of 1864 and 1865; 14 *S.H.S.P.*, 542–63.

FIGG, ROYAL W. Where Men Only Dare to Go . . . Richmond, 1885. History of the Parker Battery of Richmond, a famous command of boys in their 'teens.

FONDEREN, C. A. A Brief History of the Military Career of Carpenter's Battery . . . New Market, Va., 1911. This unit was originally the

"Alleghany Roughs." Co. A., Twenty-seventh Virginia, Stonewall Brigade.

FREMANTLE, LT. COL. A. J. L. Three Months in the Southern States, April-June, 1863; New York, 1864. The observations of a British regular who was at Gettysburg.

GOLDSBOROUGH, W. W. The Maryland Line in the Confederate States Army; Baltimore, 1869. Although badly arranged, this is a useful and, in the main, an accurate book.

GRIMSLEY, DANIEL A. Battles in Culpeper County, Virginia, 1861–1865, and Other Articles. Culpeper, Va., 1900. Some unique topographical data.

HACKLEY, WOODFORD B. The Little Fork Rangers . . . Richmond, 1927. The command belonged to the Fourth Virginia Cavalry, Williams C. Wickham's old regiment, Fitz Lee's Brigade.

HARRISON, GEORGE F. Ewell at First Manassas; 14 S.H.S.P., 356–59.

HARRISON, WALTER. Pickett's Men . . . New York, 1870. A brief history of the division. Includes most of the text of Pickett's last report.

HAY, THOMAS ROBSON. Hood's Tennessee Campaign . . . New York, 1929. The standard work.

HAYDON, F. STANSBURY. Aeronautics in the Union and Confederate Armies with a Survey of Military Aeronautics Prior to 1861; Baltimore, 1941. Publication interrupted by the author's military service. This authoritative account covers the first year of hostilities with some references to later events

[HENDERSON, G. F. R.] The Science of War . . . London, 1905. Includes a study of the Wilderness Campaign.

HENDERSON, G F. R. The Campaign of Fredericksburg Nov.-Dec., 1862 . . . by a line officer . . . London, 1886. The best study of Fredericksburg; the book that brought Henderson his opportunity.

HERBERT, ARTHUR. Sketches and Incidents of Movements of the Seventeenth Virginia Infantry . . . n.p., n.d. The regiment belonged to Corse's Brigade, Pickett's Division, First Corps.

HILL, D. H. The Lost Dispatch; 13 S.H.S.P., 420–23.

HOKE, JACOB. The Great Invasion of 1863; Dayton, Ohio, 1887. A Pennsylvania view.

HORN, STANLEY F. The Army of Tennessee, A Military History . . . Indianapolis [1941]. Most useful for Joseph E. Johnston and John B. Hood.

HOTCHKISS, JED AND ALLAN, WILLIAM. The Battlefields of Virginia. Chancellorsville . . . New York, 1867. Notable for its maps.

HOWARD, WILEY C. Sketch of Cobb Legion Cavalry . . . [Atlanta? 1901?]

HURST, M. B. History of the Fourteenth . . . Alabama Volunteers . . . Richmond, 1863. The regiment was part of Pryor's and then of Wilcox's Brigade.

IRBY, RICHARD. Historical Sketch of the Nottoway Grays, Afterwards Co. G., Eighteenth Virginia Regiment . . . Richmond, 1878. This rare sketch deals with a unit of Garnett's Brigade, Pickett's Division, First Corps.

IZLAR, WILLIAM V. A Sketch of the War Record of the Edisto Rifles . . . Columbia, S. C., 1914. The unit belonged to Hagood's Brigade, which was ordered to Virginia in May, 1864, and was embodied in Hoke's Division.

JACOBS, M. Notes on the Invasion of Maryland and Pennsylvania, and the Battle of Gettysburg . . . Gettysburg, Penn. (after 1888, though first edition carried copyright of 1863).

JOHNSTON, R. M. Bull Run, Its Strategy and Tactics; Boston, 1913. The best study but, on close use, not altogether satisfactory.

JONES, J. WILLIAM, COMPILER. Army of Northern Virginia Memorial Volume . . . Richmond, 1880. A valuable collection of important addresses before the Virginia Division of the Army of Northern Virginia Association. Some are listed separately here.

JONES, SAMUEL. The Siege of Charleston . . . New York, 1911. Principally valuable for the unconscious disclosure of the man himself.

LANE, J. H. History of Lane's North Carolina Brigade. In S.H.S.P. as follows: v. 7, pp. 513–22; v. 8, pp. 1–8, 67–76, 97–104, 145–54, 193–202, 241–48, 396–403, 489–96; v. 9, pp. 29, 71, 124, 145, 241, 353, 489; v. 10, pp. 57, 206, 241.

LAW, E. M. Lookout Valley; 8 S.H.S.P., pp. 500–506.

LAW, E. M. The Fight for Richmond in 1862 (Southern Bivouac, vol. 2, nos. 11 and 12, 1887). With particular reference to the Battle of Gaines' Mill.

LEE, FITZ. Chancellorsville. Address . . . before the Virginia Division of the Army of Northern Virginia . . . Richmond, 1879. An indispensable narrative of Jackson's march to Hooker's right.

LOEHR, CHARLES T. War History of the Old First Virginia Infantry Regiment . . . Richmond, 1884. The "Old First" was part of Kemper's Brigade, Pickett's Division, First Corps.

McCARTHY, CARLTON, ED. Contributions to a History of the Richmond Howitzer Battalion; Richmond, 1883–86. 4 pamphlets. Includes the diary of William S. White.

McCRADY, EDWARD. Gregg's Brigade of South Carolinians in the Second Battle of Manassas; 13 S.H.S.P., 1–40. A famous narrative.

McDANIEL, J. J. Diary of Battles, Marches, and Incidents of the Seventh S. C. Regiment . . . n.p., 1862. Brief sketch of a regiment of Kershaw's Brigade.

McDONALD, WILLIAM N. A History of the Laurel Brigade . . . edited by Bushrod C. Washington; [Baltimore, 1907]. This traces the history of the development of the Brigade from the Seventh Virginia Cavalry.

McGUIRE, HUNTER AND CHRISTIAN, GEO. L. The Confederate Cause and Conduct . . . Richmond, Va., 1907. Second edition. Includes Dr. McGuire's account of the wounding, illness and death of "Stonewall" Jackson.

McINTOSH, DAVID GREGG. The Campaign of Chancellorsville; Richmond, 1915. This is a discerning postwar article by the commander of a famous artillery battalion.

MACON, T. J. Reminiscences of the First Company of Richmond Howitzers; Richmond, n.d.

MARSHALL, CHARLES. Appomattox. An Address Delivered before the Society of the Army and Navy of the Confederate States in the State of

Maryland on Jan. 19, 1894 . . . Baltimore, 1894. Most of this was embodied in Marshall's An Aide de Camp of Lee, q.v.

MAURY, RICHARD L. The Battle of Williamsburg . . . Richmond, 1880. One of the few narratives of this battle. Not entirely clear.

MOSBY, JOHN S. Stuart's Cavalry in the Gettysburg Campaign; New York, 1908. Controversial.

MYERS, FRANK M. The Comanches: A History of White's Battalion, Virginia Cavalry, Laurel Brig., Hampton Div., . . . Baltimore, 1871. A realistic and amusing story of a unit of the Ashby-Jones-Rosser Brigade. In spirit, this is the cavalry counterpart of J. O. Casler, q.v.

OWEN, WILLIAM M. In Camp and Battle with the Washington Artillery of New Orleans; Boston, 1885. A standard authority. Includes some documents not found elsewhere.

[PAGE, R. C. M.]. Sketch of Page's Battery, or Morris Artillery, 2d Corps, Army of Northern Virginia; New York, 1885. By "One of the Company," but almost certainly Doctor Page.

PARK, ROBERT EMORY. Sketch of the Twelfth Alabama Infantry of Battle's Brigade . . . Richmond, 1906. A reprint from 33 S.H.S.P.

POLLEY, J. B. Hood's Texas Brigade . . . New York, 1910. An informative work on a Brigade that was, perhaps, the most renowned unit of the Army of Northern Virginia.

PORTER, FITZ JOHN (defendant) Proceedings and Report of the Board of Army Officers . . . in the case of Fitz John Porter . . . Washington, 1879. Two editions. That in two volumes (Congressional Series No. 1871, 1872) contains the important maps. The contested issue was that of Porter's handling of his troops at Second Manassas. He was made scapegoat for Pope.

ROBERTSON, LEIGH. The South Before and at the Battle of the Wilderness . . . Richmond, 1878.

ROSS, FITZGERALD. A Visit to the Cities and Camps of the Confederate States . . . Edinburgh and London . . . 1865. Reprinted from Blackwood's Magazine. Useful, in particular, for Gettysburg. Quite readable. The author was an Austrian professional soldier.

SCALES, ALFRED M. The Battle of Fredericksburg . . . Washington, 1884.

SCHEIBERT, JUSTUS. Der Bürgerkrieg in den Nordamerikanischen Staaten; Militärisch beleuchtet für den deutschen Offizier . . . Berlin, 1874. One of the few contemporary studies of command and of the service of supply. Available in French and in English translations.

SHAVER, LEWELLYN A. History of the Sixtieth Alabama Regiment . . . Montgomery, 1867. Exceptionally accurate. The regiment at Appomattox was part of Moody's Brigade.

SHOEMAKER, JOHN J. Shoemaker's Battery; Memphis, Tenn., n.d. This battery belonged to the Stuart Horse Artillery.

SLOAN, JOHN A. Reminiscences of the Guilford Grays . . . Washington, 1883. Subsequently, this unit was Co. B., Twenty-seventh North Carolina, John R. Cooke's own regiment and the keystone of his later Brigade.

SMITH, GUSTAVUS W. Confederate War Papers; Fairfax Court House, New Orleans, Seven Pines, Richmond, and North Carolina . . . New York, 1884.

SMITH, GUSTAVUS W. The Battle of Seven Pines . . . New York, 1891.
These two works, the second partly duplicating the first, are Smith's
defense.

STEELE, JAMES COLUMBUS. Sketches of the Civil War, especially of Companies A, C, and H . . . and the 4th N. C. Regimental Band. States-
ville, N. C., 1921. The regiment belonged to Ramseur's Brigade. This
is one of the few narratives by a Confederate bandman.

STRIBLING, ROBERT M. Gettysburg Campaign and Campaigns of 1864 and
1865 in Virginia; Petersburg, Va., 1905. Contains scarcely anything
personal to the author, who commanded artillery attached to various
units and, at the end, to R. H. Anderson's Corps.

THOMAS, HENRY W. History of the Doles-Cook Brigade . . . Atlanta, 1903.
Contains much useful information regarding a famous Brigade of
Rodes's Division, Second Corps.

TURNER, EDWARD RAYMOND. The New Market Campaign May, 1864; Richmond, 1912. Quite full. Contains various survivors' statements.

U. S. WAR DEPARTMENT. Proceedings, Findings, and Opinions of the Court
of Inquiry . . in the case of Gouverneur K. Warren . . . Washington, 1883, 3 vols. Sheridan alleged that Warren failed him at Five
Forks. Several Confederates testified for Warren.

VENABLE, C. S. The Campaign from the Wilderness to Petersburg. Address
. . . Before the Virginia Division of the Army of Northern Virginia
. . . Richmond, 1879. Reprinted 14 S.H.S.P. One of the best accounts
of this campaign, though brief.

WARDER, T. B. AND CATLETT, JAMES M. Battle of Young's Branch . . .
Richmond, 1862.

WARE, W. H. The Battle of Kelley's Ford, fought March 17, 1863. Newport
News, Va., n.d. Inaccurate in some details.

WELLS, EDWARD L. [Wade] Hampton and His Cavalry in '64; Richmond,
1899. Helpful but far from adequate.

WHITE, E. V. History of the Battle of Ball's Bluff . . . Leesburg, Va.
[1902?] Contains a detailed map.

WISE, GEORGE. History of the Seventeenth Virginia Infantry . . . Baltimore, 1870. Of Corse's Brigade, Pickett's Division, First Corps. See,
also, Herbert, Arthur.

YOUNG, C. P. A History of the Crenshaw Battery, of Pegram's Battalion;
Richmond, 1904. Printed also in 31 S.H.S.P., 275-96.

# INDEX

FOR VOLUMES III AND IV

# INDEX

Unless otherwise indicated or generally familiar, all place or county names in this index are for Virginia, which in 1861 included the present State of West Virginia. The rank credited to officers is the highest, regular, volunteer, provisional or brevet, held in either Union or Confederate service, at any time during the War Between the States. In the case of men who held commission in the United States Army or Navy before secession and subsequently served as officers of the Confederacy, the Confederate rank only is given. All references to "Regiments" are to infantry commands, entered under the names of the several States. Cavalry commands are separately entered under the State names.

195; promoted to be Maj. Gen., 209–12; rivalry between him and Fitz Lee, 210–1; his new officers, 215; his Division protects the right in advance on Bristoe Station, 239 and n.; his wound still keeps him from action with Stuart, 248; his men under Stuart, 249, 252, 261, 278–9, 413; praises Rosser, 278; his Division alone left to confront Meade, 278; at Parker's Store, 279; keeps three Brigades when most Divisions are reduced to two, 411; silent rival of Fitz Lee, he is not advanced to take the place of Stuart, 436 and n., 517, 523; his help to Ewell near the Ny River, 440; supplies a Brigade for reconnaissance on the Pamunkey River, 499; reports Sheridan's activities there, 516; with Fitz Lee he sets off against Sheridan, 516–23, 528; fights off the enemy in his rear, 521–2 and n.; compared with Stuart, 522–3, 556; praises cooperation of Fitz Lee, 523 and n.; brilliant action at Samaria Church, 540, 549, 551; his name acquires new lustre, 550–2; skill as commander, 568; is given command of cavalry, 575; his "cattle raid," 590 and n., 593; opposes new Federal advance, 591–4 and n.; brilliant action at Burgess' Mill, 615; tragedy of his sons, 616 and n.; opposed to Grant, 622; goes to South Carolina, 639, 642; his great ability, xx, 639, 749; he is missed, 656; his praise of Munford, 667 n.; his promotion to rank of Lieut. Gen., 764 n., 765 n.; brilliant career as Governor and Senator after the war, 770, 778–9; his character, xxiv. See also xiv, xvi, 216 n., 316, 639 n.

Hampton, Wade, Jr., 616
Hancock, Md., 48, 208, 328
Hancock, Maj. Gen. Winfield Scott, U.S.A., 61 and n., 127 n., 170, 172, 176 n., 191 n., 351 n., 355 n., 359–60 and n., 388–9, 392–3 and n., 396, 404 n., 409, 437, 439, 441, 531 n., 532, 757–60
Hanover Co., 337 n.
Hanover Junction, 416–7, 454
Hanover, Pa., 65, 67, 69 and n., 71, 97, 99, 104, 136
Hanover Railroad, Gettysburg and, 96
Hanover Road, 94 n., 129 n.
Happel, Ralph, 409 n.
Hardee, Lieut. Gen. William J., C.S.A., 230 and n., 325, 638–9, 641–2
Hardy Co., Va., 328 and n., 572
Hare House, 531 n.
Harman, Col. Asher W., C.S.A., 9, 11, 17, 196 n.
Harman, Maj. John A., C.S.A., 29, 167

Harpers Ferry, 21, 23–5, 559 and n., 574
Harris, Col. D. B., C.S.A., 478
Harris, Brig. Gen. Nathaniel H., C.S.A., 280, 406–7, 448–9, 515 n., 589, 682, 750, 766, 775, 777
Harris, W. M., 246 n.
Harrisburg, Pa., 28–9, 31, 33–5, 36 n., 65, 68, 77, 137
Harrison, Confederate spy, 48–9 and n., 226–7 and n.
Harrison, Fort, 590–4, 615
Harrison House, 397–8, 409 n.
Harrison, Lt. Col. Walter, C.S.A., 136 n., 146 n., 657 n., 706 n.
Harrisonburg, 267, 595–6
Hart, Capt. James F., C.S.A., 9–10, 17
Hartranft, Maj. Gen. J. F., U.S.A., 653 n.
Harvie, E. J., 667 n.
Haskell, Col. Alexander C., C.S.A., 342 n., 381, 383, 686
Haskell, Fort, 650
Haskell, Col. John C., C.S.A., 193 and n., 361 n., 381 n., 543 n., 553, 731–2 and n., 733 n., 735 n., 736 and n.
Hatcher's Run, 615 n., 616 n., 627 n., 655, 657, 661–2, 664, 666–7, 669, 671, 675, 684
Hawkes, Maj. Wells J., C.S.A., 29
Haw's Shop, 424 n., 500, 520, 550
Haxall's Landing, 482
Hay Market, 61, 260, 262 n.
Hays, Brig. Gen. Alexander, U.S.A., 246 n.
Hays, Maj. Gen. Harry T., C.S.A., 22–3, 89, 94 n., 99, 129, 132–40, 177, 205 and n., 265–8, 270, 369 n., 391, 393, 512–3, 526, 558, 775, 777
Hazard, Brig. Gen. John G., U.S.A., 154 n.
Hazel Grove, 78
Hazel River, 7, 17 n.
Heckman, Brig. Gen. Charles A., U.S.A., 459 and n.
Heidlersburg, Pa., 35–6, 82
Henagan, Col. John W., C.S.A. (mistakenly mentioned as Col. Kennedy), 382 n., 581
Hendricks, Sam H., 429 n.
Henry, Col. Guy V., U.S.A., 348 n.
Henry, Patrick, xvii
Henry, Robert S., 238 n.
Herbert, Lieut. Col. J. R., C.S.A., 21, 270 n.
Heth, Maj. Gen. Harry, C.S.A., xxiv, 73–4, 77–82, 86–8, 90, 145–6, 150, 157–8, 160, 167 and n., 181–2 and n., 184–7 and n., 190 and n., 192, 193 n., 195 n., 198, 200, 241–6 and n., 340, 346, 351–6, 358–9, 388, 390, 392, 398, 403, 406, 442–3, 456, 588, 615, 624, 630 and n., 657–8, 672–3, 675–8, 680, 688–90, 692, 699, 710, 712, 749, 764–5, 768, 772, 778